BUSINESS PLANNING

MATERIALS

ON THE

PLANNING OF CORPORATE
TRANSACTIONS

TEMPORARY SECOND EDITION, 1984

including

The Revised Business Planning Problems

and

The Model Business Corporation Act

By

DAVID R. HERWITZ

Professor of Law, Harvard University

Mineola, New York
THE FOUNDATION PRESS, INC.
1984

5th Reprint—1990

PREFACE

Ordinarily, the preface to the second edition of a casebook provides the opportunity for both taking stock of substantive changes in the field during the intervening period and reflecting on the experience in using the materials in the classroom. There is a special call for observations along these lines when the time between editions is as distressingly long as in this case. Nevertheless, the invitation will have to go unaccepted for the moment, and instead await the appearance of the permanent second edition; time simply has run out, if these materials are to be available for the fall of 1984. That also accounts for the absence of any revision in Section 5 of Chapter 5, dealing with the carryover of tax attributes in combination transactions; I was reluctant to omit that material entirely, although even with the elimination of old Problem No. II I have not managed to reach Section 5 for years, and I gather from discussions with other teachers using the book that my experience is not unique.

Anyone who has followed the development of new material in the Supplement (as it grew from under two hundred pages to over five hundred) is well aware of how significant the changes and growth in the law in these areas have been. The students here have increasingly chafed at the need to go back and forth between the Supplement and the casebook; while I rather liked the fact that such efforts more closely parallel the work of a lawyer in this field than proceeding lockstep through a casebook, no doubt the integration of the two was overdue. In addition, it was high time to switch to the current version (and section numbering) of the Model Act; indeed, even that version may soon be dated, in view of the comprehensive new revision of the Act that is already in draft form.

To close these brief comments on an upbeat note, I continue to be enthusiastic about the problem approach in the business planning area, and it has worked fairly well over the twenty-five years we have been at it here.

In the current climate of more attention to lawyering
skills, the emphasis on weighing alternatives and reaching an informed judgment in the problem-solving context
seems clearly in step. Moreover, the students appear to
find the approach engaging (although I might add that
I have long since ceased either to rely on volunteers
or call on people cold, in favor of appointing panels
of three or four students in advance of each class,
to assure a reasonable level of class discussion.)

I am very grateful to Meg Jacobs, a 1984 graduate
of Harvard Law School, for valuable research and editor-
ial assistance.

June, 1984   David R. Herwitz

CHAPTER 1. -- Continued
Section

---

* Section 5 is taken from the prior edition without
    revision.
                                    *

TABLE OF CASES
(Principal cases underlined)

BUSINESS PLANNING

Chapter 1

ORGANIZATION OF A CLOSE CORPORATION

SECTION 1. ENTERPRISE VALUATION

A. INTRODUCTION

Often the organization of a new corporation involves the incorporation of a going business, previously carried on in either the proprietorship or partnership form. In such cases a common first step is to value the existing enterprise, in order to determine the amount of the consideration which the corporation is receiving in exchange for its stock, and to prepare its opening books of account. In addition, if the incorporation transaction involves bringing in new parties valuation of the existing business will be needed to arrive at a proper allocation of the interests in the new corporation among the various participants.

A recent publication of the Small Business Administration provides an excellent introduction to the subject of valuing a business.

GOULD & CODDINGTON, HOW DO YOU KNOW WHAT YOUR BUSINESS IS WORTH?

SBA Management Aid No. 166, 1964.

Corporations whose stocks are actively traded on the major exchanges are valued continuously by the investing public. But how do owner-managers of small closely held companies determine how much their business is worth when they, for instance, seek outside financing?

Or how do you value a business for situations such as those involving estate and gift taxes? And what about the value of a company which you may purchase in order to strengthen your own business?

NO SET FORMULA FOR VALUATION

Various methods can be used for computing a company's worth, but no set formula exists. Keep in mind that the buyer, or investor, wants an answer to one question: What percent of return can I get on my investment? Or said another way: What is the value of the future earning power of this company?

The best way to answer that question is by using the capitalized earnings method for evaluating the worth of a company. But first, look at two other commonly used methods: (1) asset valuation, and (2) market valuation.

Asset Valuation

Companies are often evaluated by their assets as reflected in book value, reproduction value, and liquidation value. However, assets are significant only as they enable a company to manufacture and sell products, or services, that will generate profits.

Book value. Sometimes a company's book value does not hold up in the market place. One company, for example, sold for $300,000 even though its net worth or book value was $600,000. The reason: a large part of the assets was tied up in specialized equipment and slow-moving inventory, sales volume was down, and the company's net income after taxes was only $30,000. The purchasers decided that the company to them was worth only 10 times earnings, or $300,000.

Another disadvantage of valuing a company on its net worth is that book value can be high because of retained earnings over a long period of time. The company can still be a poor investment because its current earnings are down and prospects for increased future earnings are dim.

Reproduction value. Many small businessmen value their companies in terms of reproduction value—the current cost of reproducing the assets of the business. They reason like this: The cost of duplicating my business will be higher than what is shown on my balance sheet because many items have been depreciated. Also inflation has increased the prices of certain pieces of machinery.

A disadvantage of reproduction value is that it tends to set a high asking price on a business. Often a man can start a new one with less capital than it takes to buy a company on its reproduction value.

Liquidation value is the amount that would be available to the common stockholders in the event that a small business is liquidated. In liquidation, time is often a factor; outside pressures demand action; and the business is sold at a sacrifice. However, this method has some use in placing a floor under the value of a company—determining the minimum asking price.

Market Value

Quoted prices on stock exchanges constitute market value of common stock. Usually such prices in a broad and active market can be considered the current value of a company. But even so a company is sometimes merged or sold at quite a different value from the current value of its marketable common stocks.

Market value can be subjected for example, to short-term swings caused by rumors, opinions, and other factors. The fickleness of over-the-counter stock prices tends to be even greater than that of the major stock exchanges. For example, the announcement of potential contracts often raises the over-the-counter value of the stock of an electronics company out of proportion to its real value.

Where thin, limited markets exist, differences between the current value and market price of a company's stock are apt to be great. For example, a company with 300,000 shares outstanding might sell at 5 to 10 times earnings and under book value per share because demand for the stock is slight. The industry is highly competitive, the company's sales are down, and profits have been declining. At the same time, another company with 300,000 shares outstanding—but with strong earnings and growth prospects—might sell at 30 to 50 times earnings and many times book value.

CAPITALIZED EARNINGS VALUE

Whether you buy or sell a small company you need to know about the company's ability to earn profits—especially future profits. The capitalized earning approach considers a business as a living, changing organism which uses its assets to produce the greatest possible return on investment.

Two steps are used in capitalizing earnings. First, you find a company's true earning power, based on both its past experience and future probabilities. Second, you capitalize these earnings at a rate which is realistic for the risks involved.

Finding a Company's Earnings

A company's *past earnings* record gives a buyer, or investor, an indication of what he might reasonably expect in the future. He learns about this record from past income statements. Looking at them for a 5-year period helps him to see trends.

The buyer should make adjustments to the income statement for: (1) nonrecurring items that a buyer should not expect to encounter in the future, (2) unusually large bad debts, (3) inventory write-offs, (4) excessive salaries, (5) low salaries that might have to be raised in order to get qualified assistants, and (6) nonbusiness ventures.

The kind of accounting procedure used can also have a direct effect on reported earnings. For example, one company may charge the cost of tools and dies as expense items in the year in which they were bought. Another may amortize the cost of such equipment over a period of years and thereby increase earnings.

When a potential buyer adjusts for nonrecurring items and for varying accounting practices, he is trying to judge what future earnings might be under his ownership. His return on investment has to come from possible *future earnings*.

Therefore, the buyer needs income statement projections based on what he thinks he can do with the company. Often an independent study of the company's prospects for sales helps to give a sound basis for earnings projections.

Even though selling may be your last thought at this point, it is a good idea to look ahead. Make sure that your accounting system records the information necessary for making realistic earnings projections. Thus you can base your negotiations on facts should you ever decide to sell. Also, don't buy, or sell, without having an independent audit of the company's books.

Finally, from the 5-year period, you have to pick one annual earnings figure as the true *earning power* of the business. If the company has a proven record, current earnings can often be used. In well-established companies, *proven past profits* and *projected income* for the current year usually go together to make the true earnings figure. However, when a company is fairly new but with good potential, future earnings estimates are weighed heavily.

What Capitalization Rate Should Be Used?

The rate at which you capitalize a company's average earning power depends on the risks involved. The higher the risk of generating projected earnings—and thus creating a return on the buyer's investment—the lower the capitalization rate.

Suppose, for example, that the earning power of two companies is the same—$100,000. Suppose further that Company A has a proven record of profits and a very substantial annual earnings growth rate. With highly favorable prospects for the future. Company A might be capitalized at 20 times earnings for a value of $2 million. At the start, the investor would get 5 percent return on investment, and the proven growth of earnings would increase his possibility for a greater return in the future.

However, keep in mind that valuation is also subjective—what the buyer thinks the business is worth to him. Some may be willing to pay a much lower multiple of earnings for a closely held company even though the present owners have built an outstanding record for growth and prospects appear favorable.

On the other hand, Company B is relatively small and in a highly competitive industry. The company is growing but has not established itself. A buyer would need a high percentage return—20 percent or more—on investment. If he needed 20 percent, earnings could be capitalized at 5 times for a value of $500,000.

External Influences

When determining the proper capitalization rate, or price-earnings multiple, external influences have to be weighed. Some of them are:

(1) Economy. What effect will the state of business and the regional and national economic outlook have on the company?

(2) Industry. Do industry factors—such as competitive structure, cyclical, seasonal and Governmental influences, and industry glamour—make the company attractive to investors? Unattractive?

(3) Company position. How does the company compare with its competitors in size, growth, margins, order backlog, suppliers, patents, and freight advantages?

(4) Financial strength. How do the company's balance sheets and income statement ratios compare with competitors and with credit statistics for the industry as a whole? A debt-free company, of course, can borrow capital for expansion and diversification.

(5) Management. Is the company's management strong? Does its past performance indicate that it can maintain and increase profits in the future?

(6) Character of investment. In a closely held company—one person or a small group owning more than half the stock—the price-earnings multiple will be lower because of the nonmarketability of the investment.

Factors Which The Buyer Injects

In addition to these external influences, the price-earnings multiple is often determined by factors which the buyer, or investor, may throw into the situation. Some examples are:

(1) Buyer's price-earnings multiple. If an investing company can buy a company at a price-earnings multiple below its own, its stockholder's position is not diluted. For example, if a buying company's stock is selling at 15 times earnings, it can afford to issue stock with a value up to—but not more than—15 times earnings for an acquisition. However, if the buying company pays more than 15 times earnings, its stockholders will earn less per share on the combined earnings.

(2) Competitive investments. When buying for investment, the return on the purchase price of a company must compare favorably with other things—such as stocks, bonds, real estate, or savings deposits—for which the buyer could spend his money.

(3) Job money. Companies are often sold to buyers who want to take over active management, and such a buyer may be willing to pay a little more.

(4) Buyer's needs. Another company might pay a higher price than an individual buyer in order to fill needs such as management, products, brands, patents, franchises, or licensing agreements.

(5) Method of payment. Tax factors have to be considered. Acquisitions effected through merger, sale of stock, or sale of assets for either cash or stock depend on tax factors involved with the corporation's assets and net worth as well as each stockholder's personal position.

(6) Minority stockholders. The value of a minority ownership position in a closely held company is not as great as a majority stockholder because of the additional risks associated with lack of control.

(7) Cash flow. Cash flow—net profits after taxes plus non-cash charges, such as depreciation, depletion, and amortization, has become an important factor in valuation. The cash generated from operations can be used for capital expenditures, reduction of debt, payment of dividends, and expansion. So a company may be sold at a very high multiple of earnings yet at a reasonable ratio to cash flow. This cash "payout" often determines the ultimate value of a business and is becoming increasingly important.

APPLICATION OF METHODS

When determining how much your company is worth, keep in mind that its marketable value may vary according to what you are planning to do.

If you set a value in order to get *public financing*, bear in mind that a public underwriting of securities should be priced so that the investment will be attractive in comparison with stocks of other companies in your industry. Such pricing should also give the stock room to rise after the issue has been floated.

The situation is somewhat different if you seek *private financing*. When buying non-marketable securities, an investor needs a higher return. Usually private venture capital sources seek investments which will double in value and be marketable within 3 years.

In a *private sale* to one individual, he buys on what he thinks he can earn from the company. If he plans to operate the company himself, he may pay more for the intangible benefits of having managerial responsibilities.

Above all, in buying or selling, keep in mind that value varies with individuals. The worth of a going company is largely a subjective matter—what a person thinks the business is worth to him. But even so, the capitalized earnings approach embodies facts which can be used to arrive at a realistic value.

———

Here is a more recent piece on valuation:

B. Current Valuation Methods

Seven ways to value your business

7 The Business Owner (No. 10, Oct. 1983) 4-6

Valuation methods

1. Fixed price
2. Tangible book value
3. Adjusted tangible book value
4. Multiple of earnings
5. Discounted future earnings
6. Liquidation value
7. Replacement value

Business owners frequently face the need to set a value on their businesses. And, as you know, it's not an easy task. The problem is compounded because there are many different ways to value a closely held business, with no simple answer that covers every business. Furthermore, the motives and goals of business owners differ greatly.

The first step in setting a value is to identify the purpose of the valuation. Example:

   • Do you want a *high* valuation because you're selling your business or raising equity capital for expansion?
   • Do you want a *low* valuation because you're gifting the stock in your business to your children or valuing it for estate tax purposes?

Here is a review of the seven principal methods of valuation.

Fixed price

If there are two or more owners, they can set an initial value themselves; i.e., what they think the stock is worth. This is a common method used in buy-sell agreements (stock repurchases) between stockholders. The value can be the reported book value per share, a certain multiple of earnings, or any of the six other values discussed in this article.

Example: Your company is owned equally by you and another individual. You each have 50,000 shares of common stock (a total of 100,000 shares outstanding). Your company's net income is $100,000 and its balance sheet looks like this: Let's compute some values.

Assets	$1,000,000
Liabilities	$ 600,000
Net book value	400,000
	$1,000,000

Book value per share = $4.00
Earnings per share = $1.00

If we assume a price-earnings multiple of ten, the value of each share of stock is $10. You and your partner can arbitrarily decide to place a 50% weight on your book value per share and 50% on your multiple of earnings value. Based on these two assumptions, the *weighted value per share* would be computed as follows:

Method	Value	Weight	Weighted value
Book value	$ 4	50%	$2
Multiple of earnings	$10	50	5
		100%	$7

Buy-sell value: Both of you can decide that $7 per share is the per-share value for the purchase of the other's stock on death—purchased by either of you (cross-purchase agreement) or by your company (stock-redemption agreement).

Advisory: Keep in mind that a buy-sell agreement should be revised yearly to allow for changes in the value per share. To accomplish this, provide some formula in the initial agreement, such as the increase or decrease in the company's book value per share (see below).

2 | Tangible book value

This is set by the company's last balance sheet. It's the book value (net worth) of the business—total assets less total liabilities adjusted for any intangible assets such as goodwill and deferred financing costs. Some companies simply use the book value as reported by their accountant.

Example: If your book value is $400,000 and there are $50,000 of intangibles, the net value is $350,000. Assuming there are 100,000 shares outstanding, the tangible book value per share is $3.50.

Adjusted tangible book value

This method uses the prior *tangible book value* approach, but it adjusts for certain assets, which have values in excess of their reported book value. The principal items that should be adjusted are: inventory, bad-debt reserves, and plant and equipment.

The upward or downward adjustments reflect the excess of the *fair market value* of each asset above the value reported on the company's balance sheet.

Example: A company has the following assets, which are worth more than their reported net book value of $520,000:

	Reported net book value	Fair market value
Inventory	$100,000	$130,000
Land and plant	350,000	500,000
Equipment	70,000	120,000
	$520,000	$750,000
Excess value		$230,000

If the total net book value is $400,000, the adjusted book value is $630,000 ($230,000 excess plus $400,000). If there are $50,000 of intangibles, the *adjusted tangible book value* is $580,000.

Multiple of earnings

Net income for the last year is determined and then capitalized using a price-earnings multiple. A 15% capitalization rate is often used, which is equivalent to a price-earnings multiple of 6.7 (1 divided by 0.15). If a business has an excellent growth rate, a low capitalization rate should be used, say, 5% (a multiple of 20).

In contrast, if the business is stable, a higher capitalization rate of 10% is used (a multiple of 10). Whichever capitalization rate and multiple you use, the resulting value is then divided by the total number of shares outstanding to get a value per share.

Example: If last year's net income was $100,000, the value of the business would be $800,000 (using a price-earnings multiple of 8, which is a capitalization rate of 12.5%). If there are 100,000 shares of common stock outstanding, then the value per share is $8.

Alternatively, some valuation analysts simply compute the average price-earnings multiples of comparable public companies and then apply this multiple to the company's earnings.

▪ Discounted future earnings

The real value of any on-going business is its future earning power. Accordingly, this approach, more than any other, determines the true value of a business.

The discounted earnings method projects future earnings over a five- or ten-year period and then calculates their *present value* using a certain discount or present value rate (e.g., 15%). The total of each year's projected earnings is the company's value. The basic principle underlying this method is that a dollar earned in the future is worth less than a dollar earned today. Thus, it is not only the amount of projected income (or net cash flow) that a company is expected to generate that determines its value but also the *timing* of that income.

Example: You may be projecting an increase in earnings from $100,000 today to $500,000 in five years. In placing a value on the total earnings for the five years, you must take the present value of *each year's projected earnings.* With a discount rate of 15%, the present value of $500,000 of earnings received five years from today is only $248,500 (fifth-year present value factor of 0.497 times $500,000). A calculator or present value tables found in most financial books will easily compute the present value of each year's projected earnings.

▪ Liquidation value

Unlike all other methods, this approach assumes that the business ceases operation, sells all assets, and pays all liabilities. The net liquidation value (after payment of all liabilities) is distributed to the company's owners in proportion to their percentage stock position in the business.

This approach gives the absolute bottom value for a business, below which it would be better to liquidate the business rather than sell it.

Example: Here is a simple way to determine your liquidation value. The percent allocations are approximate. You'll have to determine the range of percentages with your accountant or appraiser.

Assets	Percent on liquidation	Reported book value	Value
Cash	100%	$ 30,000	$ 30,000
Accounts receivable	90	250,000	225,000
Inventories	50	250,000	125,000

Land and			
building	100	350,000	350,000
Equipment	60	70,000	42,000
Deferred finan-			
cing costs	-0-	10,000	-0-
Other assets	10	40,000	4,000
		$1,000,000	$776,000

Less: Liabilities		(600,000)
Net liquidation value		$176,000

The above percentages are approximate and principally depend on: (1) the length of time to sale (the longer you can wait, the better) and (2) the saleability of the assets.

Illustrations: Note the equipment percentage of 60 cents on the dollar. If your equipment were specialized, in-house built items, you may realize much less (say, 30 cents). The same is true for leasehold improvements and the mix of your inventory (raw material is more saleable than work-in-process). Also, your land and building, if purchased or built many years ago, may have a fair market value and liquidation value greatly in excess of their reported book value.

Replacement value

Since many assets are undervalued, many valuation experts will determine the value of each asset as if it had to be replaced. Because of inflation and the annual depreciation of capital assets, the replacement value can be substantially greater than the reported book value.

This valuation approach can be used when determining a value for your business for sale to a larger company which wants to get into your line of business. In this case, your assets can be worth substantially more than your accountant's reported book value.

Use of appraiser: In many instances, a valuation cannot be agreed on by the owners, buyers, and sellers of stock. If this is the case, the stock's value can be determined by an *independent* appraiser or a panel of appraisers. Before selecting an appraiser, check his references and review valuation reports that he prepared for other companies.

Weighted value: In many cases, the appraiser will determine a final value by using a combination of the

methods discussed in this article after applying a
"weight" to each method, e.g., 25% to tangible book
value, 50% to multiple of earnings value, and 25% to
discounted future earnings value.

NOTE

Until fairly recently, asset valuation played a dominant role in the valuation of a small business. One of the
leading financial texts, Graham, Dodd & Cottle, Security
Analysis (4th ed. 1962) 553, expressly contrasted public and
private enterprises in this respect, stating that "net worth
is a primary factor of value in most privately owned businesses", and adding the explanation that "the private owner
has no clear-cut measure of the value of his business other
than that shown on his balance sheet". However, these
authors somewhat overstated the matter: even without any
resort to capitalization of earnings, valuation of a business
is not governed entirely by the balance sheet figures, since
accounting statements are primarily based upon cost and do
not purport to reflect the current value of assets. Hence,
when the objective is valuation of the enterprise, it is
appropriate to take account of evidence that some of the
assets have a higher (or lower) value than the figures
listed on the books. An example of this approach appears as
the third valuation method in the foregoing article from The
Business Owner.

There is also the question of what effect, if any,
should be given to intangible assets, particularly goodwill,
which typically do not appear on the balance sheet at all
(except perhaps in the case of intangibles purchased from
others). Occasionally, goodwill may be among the company's
most valuable assets, but this is particularly rare in the
case of small enterprises. In addition, there does not
appear to be any way of valuing self-developed intangibles
like goodwill, except by way of some variant of capitalization of earnings (which is hardly surprising, in view of the
fact that the typical commercial significance of goodwill is
the company's ability to earn a larger profit than might
otherwise have been expected -- so-called "super-profit");
since the primary role of the adjusted asset value approach
is to avoid (or at least serve as a check on) capitalization
of earnings, it would not make sense to inject this technique
into the asset valuation process. However, this does mean
that for an enterprise with any material amount of goodwill
or the like, the common practice of ignoring intangibles in
determining the asset value can lead to an undervaluation of
the enterprise; capitalization of earnings might well produce
a higher figure, since in focusing upon earnings it necessarily
takes account of the contribution of goodwill to enterprise value

In any event, there is now much greater acceptance of
the notion that, for a small business as well as a large
one, earning power is likely to provide the most meaningful
guide to value, as the foregoing SBA publication recognized
years ago. On the tax side, too, the IRS has been on record
since 1959 in favor of primary emphasis on earnings in
valuing a closely-held company, at least when it is primarily
engaged in selling products or services to the public. Rev.
Rul. 59-60, 1959-1 Cum. Bull. 237.

C. Valuation of a Large Enterprise

However, it is still true that most of the judicial
learning about enterprise valuation in general, and capitalization of earnings in particular, comes in the context of
valuing large enterprises, particularly in connection with
statutory proceedings for the appraisal of the stock of
minority stockholders who dissent to a proposed merger or
other type of fundamental reorganization of their corporation. Here is a particularly thoughtful recent example:

IN RE VALUATION OF COMMON STOCK OF

LIBBY, MCNEILL & LIBBY*

Supreme Judicial Court of Maine, 1979. 406 A.2d 54.

McKUSICK, C.J.

*   *   *

In this proceeding, the Superior Court (Cumberland
County) had the task of determining the "fair value" as of
February 17, 1976, of the common stock of Libby, McNeill &
Libby (hereafter "Libby"), a former Maine corporation,
engaging primarily in production of canned foods. Libby,
McNeill & Libby, Inc. (hereafter "petitioner"), the Delaware
successor by merger to the Maine corporation, sought this

_____

*[Ed. note] Portions of the text and some of the foot-
notes omitted.

determination in order to establish the magnitude of its liability to former Libby shareholders who dissented from the merger authorized by all necessary votes on February 18, 1976. The Superior Court valued the Libby stock at $8.55 per share. On appeal, petitioner maintains that the Superior Court justice should have accepted the recommendation of the court-appointed appraiser, who valued the stock at $6.00 per share. . . . The dissenting shareholders cross-appeal, claiming that the Superior Court's valuation of $8.55 per share is too low . . . .

. . . On reviewing the record made before the appraiser, we conclude that the Superior Court should have accepted the appraiser's recommendation that a fair value of $6.00 per share be set for the Libby stock. Accordingly, we sustain petitioner's appeal and deny the shareholders' cross-appeal.

I. Facts of the Case

Pursuant to the procedure for a "short form merger" . . . Libby was in early 1976 merged into a Delaware corporation, Universal Food Specialties (hereafter "UFS"), a wholly owned subsidiary of Nestle Alimentana S.A., a Swiss company (hereafter "Nestle").

The corporate relationship between Nestle and Libby dates from 1960. In that year Nestle and its affiliates began buying Libby shares. In 1963 Nestle increased its holdings to 9% of all outstanding common stock. By 1967 Nestle owned 36% of the Libby stock and had become Libby's principal shareholder.

*   *   *

By 1974 Nestle had increased its holdings to over 60%. Then, in 1975, Nestle decided to eliminate all minority shareholders and to turn Libby into a wholly owned subsidiary. Nestle transferred ownership of all its Libby shares to the wholly owned Nestle subsidiary UFS, and on May 29, 1975, UFS made public its tender offer to acquire all remaining shares of Libby common stock. By its tender offer UFS clearly apprised the public that if it received enough Libby stock to raise its holdings to more than 90%, UFS intended to effect a "short form merger" of Libby with UFS. UFS offered to pay $8.125 per share, a price 65% above the stock market price of $4.88 per share on the New York Stock Exchange at which Libby stock traded on May 23, 1975, the last day prior to announcement of the UFS tender offer.[1] More than three quarters of all available shares of Libby common stock were sold to UFS in response to its tender offer, thus giving UFS an aggregate holding of more than 90% of Libby common stock.

On February 18, 1976, Libby's board of directors approved the plan for a short form merger of Libby and UFS pursuant to [the Maine Statute]. . . . From among those who had rejected the UFS offer of $8.125 per share, 110 shareholders owning 66,140 shares of Libby stock filed written demands for payment of the fair value of their shares and otherwise perfected their right to participate in this valuation proceeding. . . .

On May 7, 1976, petitioner commenced this Superior Court proceeding to determine the "fair value" of the Libby common stock as of February 17, 1976, "the day prior to the date on which the vote . . . of the directors . . . was taken approving the [merger], excluding any appreciation or depreciation of shares in anticipation of such corporate

---

[1]The fact that tender offers frequently, if not usually, involve a premium in excess of current market price is established both by the evidence introduced before the appraiser in the case at bar and by reported court decisions, see, e.g., Gibbons v. Schenley Industries, Inc., 339 A.2d 460, 468 (Del. Ch. 1975). The investment banker advising the Nestle affiliate in its tender offer for Libby stock recommended the premium in order to overcome stockholder inertia. He testified: "Typically, when a common stock is so widely dispersed not only is it difficult to reach all the shareholders, but many small shareholders are indifferent to tender offers because the process of tendering shares is complicated and it is not worth their while to fill out the necessary papers."

Dissenting shareholders who refused the tender offer and instead insisted on a judicial determination of fair value are not entitled to receive the tender offer premium. In other words, the $8.125 premerger tender offer price does not establish any floor under the amount the court may fix as the value of the Libby stock in the appraisal proceeding. Id. That is not to say, however, that the tender offer price might not have some evidentiary significance, at least if no explanation were presented for the tender offer's including a premium. . . .

action." . . . the Superior Court appointed to serve as appraiser a retired justice of the Supreme Judicial Court, with statutory authority "to receive evidence and recommend a decision on the question of fair value." The appraiser held hearings for four days late in April 1977, receiving expert testimony on behalf of both petitioner and the dissenting shareholders. He submitted his report on December 27, 1977, which he supplemented on January 16, 1978.

The appraiser determined that three components should be considered in determining "fair value": stock market price, investment value, and net asset value. After assigning dollar-per-share values to those components, the appraiser weighted the factors to reach a composite "fair value" per share. The Superior Court justice accepted the appraiser's recommended values for each of those three components. However, the justice rejected the relative weightings assigned by the appraiser to those components, and thus rejected the appraiser's recommendation for the per share value of the Libby stock. The table below sets forth the differing approaches and results of the appraiser and the Superior Court:

		Weightings	
Components		Appraiser	Superior Court
Stock Market Price ($ 4.88)		40% ($1.95)	10% ($0.49)
Investment Value ($ 2.52)		40% ($1.01)	45% ($1.12)
Asset Value ($15.41)		20% ($3.08)	45% ($6.94)
Total ("Fair Value")		$6.04	$8.55

Noting that expert opinions based on alternative valuation methods placed the value of the Libby stock in the range of $5.00 to $6.50 per share, the appraiser recommended that the Superior Court round off the "computation" of the composite value and find a fair value of $6.00 per share for the Libby common stock.

In assigning weights to the components of value, the appraiser and the Superior Court relied upon different conceptions of the meaning of "fair value." We now address ourselves to the issue of the proper definition of that statutory term.

II. The Judicial Determination of "Fair Value"

Nowhere does the Maine Business Corporation Ace define the "fair value" which it in section 909(1) directs that dissenting shareholders should be paid. . . . Among other jurisdictions with valuation statutes similar to our own, we do find, however, a consensus that the component elements to be relied upon in determining "fair value" are stock market price, investment value, and net asset value.

While it is generally agreed that the process of stock appraisal involves consideration of all three of those elements of value, "[t]he weight to be given to these factors depends upon the circumstances of each individual case. . . ." In a given case, one element may be particularly unreliable, thus necessitating greater reliance on one or both of the other elements. The weighting of these interdependent elements of fair value is more akin to an artistic composition than to a scientific process. . . .

If the public stock market functioned as a perfect market, where all actors relied upon complete and accurate information, then courts would need to look only to the stock market price, and the valuation of dissenters' shares would be greatly simplified. Unfortunately, a perfect market is only a theoretical and abstract ideal, and in the real world the stock market is to varying degrees less than a perfect indicator of the value of a corporate concern. Thus, consideration of the net asset value and of the investment value of a corporation provides a check against myopic reliance on the sole criterion of stock market price.

All three components of "fair value" may not influence the result in every valuation proceeding, yet all three should be considered. "Compelling the consideration of all of them, including those which may turn out to be unreliable in a particular case, has the salutary effect of assuring more complete justification . . . of the conclusion . . . reach[ed]." Endicott Johnson Corp. v. Bade, 37 N.Y.2d 585, 588, 338 N.E.2d 614, 616 (1975). In the case at bar all three elements of fair value suffered from particular weaknesses that cautioned against excessive reliance on any one factor. Although the appropriate valuation date was February 17, 1976, the last available stock market price unaffected by the announcement of the intended Nestle/Libby merger was the market price of nearly nine months earlier; i.e., that of May 23, 1975. The investment value factor also had weaknesses as a measure of fair value, given the

highly subjective nature of the determination of a capitalization ratio and the erratic history of Libby earnings.
The use of book value as the surrogate for net asset value
made reliance on the net asset value element especially
suspect.

The appraiser, faced with these shortcomings of all
three elements, was required to make the best of what he had
to do with. Relying on the expert testimony available to
him, it was the appraiser's job to assess the relative
deficiencies of the three elements and to arrive at a weighting
scheme which, in his judgment, would best reflect the "fair
value" of the dissenters' shares. He determined that stock
market price and investment value as indicators of fair
value were roughly equal in reliability and significance,
and that roughly half as much emphasis ought to be placed
upon net asset value. Accordingly, the appraiser assigned
weights of 40%, 40%, and 20% to stock market price, investment value, and net asset value, respectively. As we shall
explain, we believe that in arriving at his recommendation
the appraiser exercised sound judgment, well supported by
the factual record and by relevant principles of law.

Both the appraiser and the Superior Court considered
all three elements of fair value and engaged in the process
of giving relative weights to them. However, the Superior
Court departed from the weighting recommendations of the
appraiser, because of the court's belief that the fact the
minority shareholders were unwilling sellers, forced to part
with their shares in the course of the statutory merger,
should be given special consideration. . . .

The Superior Court's "view[ing] the [merger] in terms
of the respective losses and benefits to the parties to the
actual transaction" does violence to the statutory mandate . . .
that the value of the dissenters' shares shall be value
without relation to the proposed merger. We cannot read any
other way the statutory provision that the fair value of the
shares shall be determined as of the day before the merger
vote was taken and furthermore shall "exclud[e] any appreciation or depreciation of shares in anticipation of such
corporate action." The dissenting shareholders are entitled
to receive the full fair value of their shares, but that
value must be determined independently of the merger transaction that gave the dissenting shareholders the statutory
right to be bought out and their corporation the statutory
duty to pay them off. The appraisal proceeding is not at
all concerned with the losses to the particular dissenting

shareholders or with the benefits derived by the <u>particular</u>
acquiring corporation in the merger, except as those losses
and benefits would be reflected in the price that would be
bargained out in a completely free market between <u>any</u> willing
buyer and <u>any</u> willing seller in absence of the merger.

Although we must set aside the Superior Court's judgment
based as it was upon an erroneous view of the meaning of
"fair value," we do not find it necessary to remand this
case for further proceedings in the Superior Court. Where,
as here, the trial court's decision is rendered entirely
upon the basis of written evidence, an appellate court can
read and evaluate the record as well as can the trial justice.
Furthermore, under the circumstances of this case, the Law
Court can best perform its lawgiving responsibility for the
guidance of counsel, appraisers, and Superior Court justices
in future dissenting shareholder cases, by actually applying
to this written record the proper rules as we see them. We
proceed, then, to place ourselves in the position of the
Superior Court, and to make for it a determination of the
"fair value" of the dissenting shareholders' stock.

In setting the fair value of the Libby stock, the
recommendation of the appraiser, elaborated by his reasoned
report, serves the court both as a starting point and as a
useful guide. The appraiser lived with this case for several
months and at the four-day hearing held to receive financial
data and expert opinion he served as the eyes and ears of
the court. Of course, the court is not bound by either the
findings of fact or the conclusions of law made by the
appraiser. The statute provides that "[t]he <u>court</u> shall . . .
fix the fair value of the shares." (Emphasis added) On the
other hand, the statute authorizes the appointment of an
appraiser "to receive evidence <u>and</u> [to] recommend a decision
on the question of fair value." (Emphasis added) Had the
legislature intended to limit the role of the appraiser to
that of merely "receiving evidence," it would not have also
empowered the appraiser to "recommend a decision" on the
ultimate question of value. While the final determination
of fair value remains always the responsibility of the
Superior Court, the question the court addresses is, Should
the appraiser's "recommend[ation of] a decision on the
question of fair value" be accepted? In seeking an answer
to that question, the court carefully examines the appraiser's
analysis of the record and the applicable law by which he
arrived at his recommended decision.

In the case at bar, the question before the Superior Court--and now before this court in lieu of remand--is, Should the court accept the appraiser's recommendation that it decide that the fair value of Libby stock on the pertinent valuation date was $6.00 per share? Specifically, the question for the court is whether the appraiser, on this record, was correct (i) in fixing the dollar amount of the three individual components of fair value, namely, stock market price, investment value, and net asset value, and (ii) in ascribing weight to those components of 40%, 40%, and 20%, respectively. We now turn to a consideration whether the appraiser correctly weighed the constituent elements of fair value. We will return later, in connection with consideration of the dissenting shareholders' cross-appeal, to the appraiser's determination of the individual elements.

III. Weighting the Components of Fair Value

A. Stock Market Price

Where the evidence reveals the existence of a free and open market, characterized by a substantial volume of transactions that makes the market a fair reflection of the judgment of the investing public, a court may justifiably assign a greater weight to stock market price than to net asset value or investment value. . . .

In the case at bar the appraiser recommended assigning stock market price a weight of 40%. The dissenting shareholders argue that the market for Libby common stock was, in the time period immediately preceding the tender offer, too "thin" to be a reliable indicator of fair value and, therefore, that the appraiser should have assigned less weight to the stock market price component of fair value. A "thin" market is characterized by a low volume of public trading. Courts have reduced the weighting assigned to stock market price in cases where evidence of a "thin" market is present. . . In the record of the present case, however, we see no such evidence as to invalidate the appraiser's 40% weighting.

On the contrary, the record convincingly demonstrates that the stock market price of May 23, 1975, was determined by a substantial market of willing buyers and willing sellers. Libby was a public company, and ownership of its common stock was widely dispersed. Prior to the tender offer, 3.768 million shares were held by persons other than Nestle, constituting a sizeable public "float" available for trading. Moreover, those shares were widely distributed among some 15,700 shareholders of record.

Trading activity in Libby stock was relatively brisk. The stock was listed on the New York Stock Exchange (NYSE), the Midwest Stock Exchange, and the Pacific Stock Exchange. In the year preceding the tender offer, more than one million Libby shares (excluding shares purchased by Nestle and its affiliates) changed hands. During the first quarter of 1975, Libby's average daily trading volume was 2,700 shares, well in excess of the daily trading volume in other cases where stock market price has been given primary emphasis in the determination of fair value. . . .

The dissenters also contend that Nestle's position as a majority shareholder prior to the date of the tender offer should have induced the appraiser to give less weight to the stock market price component. We recognize that an acquiring parent corporation which occupies the position of a majority shareholder may be able to control "the timing of the decision to merge based on the parent's anticipation of a substantial increase in the subsidiary's earnings." A majority share-holder may have access to information affecting future prospects of the subsidiary corporation that is not available to the general public, and that is not yet "reflected in the market price of the subsidiary's stock. . . ." Thus the acquiring corporation may be "in a position to induce appraisal at a time when the outsiders seeking the appraisal have little or no capacity to ascertain . . . the likelihood that the enterprise is currently worth more than its past record suggests." . . . Nestle's ownership of 61% of all Libby shares prior to its announcement of its tender offer and impending merger on May 27, 1975, was of course well known to the expert witnesses and the appraiser. We find nothing in this record to justify making a further reduction of the already reduced weight of 40% accorded to stock market price by the appraiser on the basis of expert testimony.

In summary, whatever weaknesses inhere in stock market price as an indicator of the fair value of Libby stock, we conclude that the appraiser's recommendation of a weight of 40% for this component reflects careful consideration of all relevant circumstances. He reduced stock market price to a minority position among the component factors, and considering the weaknesses that impair reliability of "investment value" and "net asset value" in the case at bar, the appraiser in our judgment was none too high in his assessment of a relative weight of 40% for stock market price. We accept his recommendation.

B.   Investment Value

The determination of investment value represents an estimate of the corporation's earning capacity. Investment value is fixed in a two-step process. First, based on the corporation's recent earnings history, an average annual earnings figure is calculated. In arriving at this figure, one must select a period of years of sufficient length to assure an adequate data base. Here the expert offered by petitioner chose to survey earnings over the most recent five year period, 1971-1975. In addition to the selection of the applicable time frame, the determination of average annual earnings requires the exercise of subjective judgment in excluding from consideration those gains and losses that are viewed as "extraordinary" (i.e., gains or losses stemming from transactions not expected to recur).

The second step in the process of calculating investment value is to select a capitalization ratio, or earnings multiplier. The product of the capitalization ratio and the average annual earnings figure yields the investment value of the corporation under examination.

The earnings record of Libby had undergone some fluctuation in the years preceding the Nestle tender offer. Petitioner's expert witness compiled the following figures representing its earnings per share:

Year Ending June 30	Earnings (loss) per share	
	Excluding Extraordinary Items	Including Extraordinary Items
1966	$ 0.87	$ 0.94
1967	0.70	0.74
1968	1.19	1.19
1969	(0.11)	(1.85)
1970	(1.26)	(1.01)
1971	0.04	1.47
1972	(0.19)	(0.07)
1973	0.45	(0.90)
1974	1.08	1.38
1975	1.00	1.00

In computing the average annual earnings per share,
petitioner's expert concluded he should give more weight to
the recent years of 1973, 1974, and 1975 than to the earlier
years of 1971 and 1972 because increased capital expenditures
during the early 1970s accomplished a significant upgrading
of Libby's operating facilities and made the earnings record
of the later years a better predictor of future earnings.
By assigning a weight of 2/13 to each of the years 1971 and
1972 and a weight of 3/13 to each of the more recent three
years, that expert computed an average annual earnings for
that five year period of $0.56 per share.[13]

Petitioner's expert then examined the capitalization
ratio of companies comparable to Libby in order to determine
an appropriate earnings multiplier. Finding Del Monte,
Green Giant, and Stokely-Van Camp to be comparable companies
based on their participation with Libby in the national
market for canned fruits and vegetables, petitioner's expert
made an extensive study of the sales, profit margins, inventory turns, capital spending history, and dividends records
of each of those three companies and contrasted those data
with comparable data on Libby. He found capitalization
ratios of 6.0, 6.6, and 5.5 for Del Monte, Green Giant, and
Stokely-Van Camp, respectively. From the fact that Libby
had lagged well behind all three of its competitors in all
the areas investigated, the expert concluded that Libby
should be assigned a capitalization ratio of 4.5. Applying
this multiplier to Libby's average annual earnings of 56
cents per share, he determined that the investment value of
the dissenting shareholders' stock was $2.52 per share. The
appraiser concluded that petitioner's expert exercised "fair
and rational judgment" in his computation of investment
value. We agree.

The expert witness presented by the dissenting shareholders gave his opinion that Libby's earnings record was so
erratic that no weight whatever should be assigned to investment value as a component of fair value. Indisputably, the
erratic nature of Libby's earnings detracts from the relative

---

[13]This weighting procedure accords with recommended
valuation practice. "[I]f the most recent years are
deemed to be of greater significance than earlier years,
the average is weighted in favor of the later years."
8 Cavitch, Business Organizations § 169.07 [3] (1979).

weight that should be accorded investment value computed on
the basis of averaging widely fluctuating annual earnings.
On the other hand, the erratic nature of Libby's earnings is
apparently a fact of life of its business, depressing the
intrinsic value of its shares, and if that fact is appropriately recognized in a reduced capitalization ratio, it
should properly have an impact on the fair value determination. The mere fact that Libby's earnings record has been
erratic is no reason for denying investment value any part
at all in the determination of fair value. It is merely
another factor to consider in assessing the relative reliability of the three tests of stock value.

On this record the appraiser had ample support in
according a 40% weight to investment value. Conceptually,
investment value is a central component of fair value. "The
assets of a company are of value chiefly because of their
earning capacity . . . ." 8 Cavitch, supra, § 169.07[3].
Here Libby had a history of returning a profit in each of
the three years immediately preceding the tender offer and
in seven of the preceding ten years. We accept the appraiser's
recommendation that investment value be assigned a weight of
40% in this case.

C.   Net Asset Value

Generally net asset value should not be heavily weighted
in stock valuation unless the valuation being made is for
liquidation purposes. Where the acquired business will be
continued as a going concern, the value of the corporate
assets bears little or no relation to the value of the stock
of the corporation. A recent decision of a Delaware court
noted:

> "There is good reason for not taking the
> asset-value factor seriously. The average market
> price of a common stock over the years depends
> chiefly on the earning power and the dividend
> payments. These, in turn, usually do not bear any
> close or reasonably consistent relation to the
> asset value. . . . Investors and speculators have
> found that the asset value is typically no guide
> at all to earning-power value or average market
> price. Hence they have gradually come to give the
> asset-value factor practically no weight." Gibbons
> v. Schenley Industries, Inc., 339 A.2d 460, 473
> (Del. Ch. 1975), quoting from Graham, Dodd, Cottle
> & Tatham, Securities Analysis 217 (4th ed. 1962).

To have its maximum persuasiveness in finding the "fair value" of Libby stock, net asset value should have been determined by a current appraisal of all the corporation's property, tangible and intangible. No such asset appraisal was made in the case at bar--by either petitioner or the dissenting shareholders. As a substitute for net asset value, both sides relied on net book value determined from Libby's audited balance sheet. The net value of corporate assets reported on the balance sheet in accordance with accounting convention represents principally historical cost less book depreciation. Book value of property would be equal or even close to its actual current value only by sheer coincidence. "There is nearly complete agreement that book value does not accurately represent the fair value of corporate assets." Note, "Valuation of Dissenters' Stock," 79 Harv. L. Rev. 1453, 1457 (1966). As Judge Learned Hand stated over fifty years ago:

> "The suggestion that the book value of the shares is any measure of their actual value is clearly fallacious. It presupposes, first, that book values can be realized on liquidation, which is practically never the case; and second, that liquidation values are a measure of present values. Every one knows that the value of shares in a commercial or manufacturing company depends chiefly on what they will earn, on which balance sheets throw very little light." Borg v. International Silver Co., 11 F.2d 147, 152 (2d Cir. 1925).

In the opinion of petitioner's expert, net asset value should receive a weight of 20%, only half the weight accorded each of the other two factors. The dissenting shareholders' expert, however, contended that net asset value should be the sole criterion for determining "fair value"; that is, should receive a weight of 100%. Recognizing that net asset value was "the weak link in the chain of appraisal factors" and that there were dangers inherent in the use of book value as a valuation tool, the appraiser agreed with petitioner's expert. We believe the court should accept the appraiser's recommendation. The shareholders' expert placed exclusive weight on net asset value because of his belief that stock market price and investment value were unreliable indicators of "fair value" in this case. We have already indicated, however, that in our view stock market price and investment value, although here subject to deficiencies as indicators of fair value, were properly assigned weights of 40% each. In view of the obvious imprecision of using book

value as a measure of asset value and also in view of the
fact that net asset value, even if accurately appraised, is
in the words of Judge Hand in <u>Borg v. International Silver Co.</u>,
<u>supra</u> at 152, little indication of "what people will pay for
the shares," the weighting of 20% recommended by the appraiser
is, if anything, on the high side.

D.   Conclusion

In summary, we accept in the case at bar the appraiser's
recommended weight assignments of 40% to stock market price,
40% to investment value, and 20% to net asset value, considering the way in which each of those elements of fair
value was here determined. The relative weight to be given
to those three elements depends much upon the facts of the
individual case, including the relative confidence that the
weighing tribunal has in the accuracy of those three subsidiary determinations themselves. On all the facts of this
case we can find no reason for not following the recommendation of the appraiser.

IV.   Cross-Appeal Issues

On their cross-appeal the dissenting shareholders
raised issues affecting the valuation of component elements
of fair value. They maintain that the Superior Court justice erred in accepting the appraiser's recommended per-share
values assigned to the component elements and that each
element has been undervalued.

First, the dissenting shareholders challenge the determination of stock market price. They contend that the
figure of $4.88 per share, taken from the closing price of
Libby stock on the New York Stock Exchange on May 23, 1975,
fails to take into account the change in general market
prices that occurred between that date and February 17,
1976, when the Libby board of directors voted to approve
the Nestle/Libby merger. They argue that the Superior Court
should have undertaken to construct hypothetically what the
"true" market price of Libby stock would have been on the
New York Stock Exchange on February 17, 1976, if no tender
offer announcement had every been made. They urge the court
to assume that Libby stock would have shared the fortunes of
the stock of Libby's food packing competitors. We find the
assumption that Libby stock would have enjoyed a price
increase similar to that enjoyed by its competitors' stock
during that nine month period a speculative exercise at

best. Furthermore, evidence in the record indicates that Libby stock did not regularly participate in general market upswings. And, finally, Libby's earnings during the nine months following the tender offer declined sharply, a fact which in the absence of the tender offer at a higher price would have tended to depress the Libby stock price.

In cases where limited transactions in stock make determination of a stock market price difficult, courts have approved the construction of a hypothetical market price based on expert testimony. . . . Here, however, there is no occasion for resorting to hypotheticals. The Libby stock price on May 23, 1975, was approximately the same as for several months preceding the tender offer announcement. It provides a solid basis for the stock market price component of fair value. To depart from that established figure in this case on the basis of supposition would reduce the reliability of that element in the ultimate weighting.

Second, the dissenting shareholders allege that the Superior Court erred in accepting the appraiser's recommended figure for investment value. They contend that the appraiser should not have accepted the judgment of petitioner's expert witness who testified that the exclusion of certain "extraordinary" gains derived from Libby's sale of fixed assets and from a change in the inventory accounting method used by Libby was in accord with accepted accounting practices.

In calculating average annual earnings, one excludes "extraordinary" transactions, or those transactions which are unrelated to normal business operations.[15] But the

---

[15]One Court has succinctly distinguished between the exclusion of "extraordinary items", a proper valuation practice, and the exclusion of unusually good or bad years, an improper practice:

"[E]xtraordinary transactions, which are not related to normal business operations, are customarily excluded from earnings in an appraisal action. See Adams v. R.C. Williams & Co., Inc., [39 Del. Ch. 61, 158 A.2d 797 (1960)] in which the court distinguished between the act of excluding unusual and extraordinary transactions and the inappropriate action of the appraiser in that case in

dissenters contend that the sale of fixed capital assets was a regular corporate practice and that Libby made capital gains from sales of fixed assets in 15 out of the 20 years preceding the Nestle tender offer. Petitioner's expert, however, responded that it was unlikely that such sales would continue to be a source of income in future years and that sales of such fixed assets were properly viewed as a temporary management strategy for disposing of obsolete facilities while replacing them with more modern and technologically more efficient plants. The appraiser and the Superior Court accepted the testimony of petitioner's expert as persuasive. We see no reason to do otherwise. Similarly, the exclusion of the income derived from the change in inventory accounting was entirely proper, since the change brought about a realization of "income" that will not be repeated in the future and that is not indicative of the future earnings potential of the enterprise.

Third, the shareholders claim that net asset value has been understated because the appraiser and the Superior Court failed to take into account the value of Libby's trademark and management organization. The shareholders' expert argued that $10 per share should be added to Libby's net book value in order to reflect the value of those two intangibles.

No one would disagree with the abstract proposition that the assets to be valued in determining the net asset value component should include intangibles to the extent they have value separate from tangible assets. There are, however, several bases for justifying the refusal by both the appraiser and the Superior Court to add $10 per share to the $15.41 per share net book value of Libby common Stock. First and foremost, there is little in the shareholders' appraisal of those intangibles at $10 per share to commend it as an accurate appraisal or as a significant factor in the intrinsic worth of the Libby stock. The expert conceded that he fixed the $10 per share value on those intangibles

---

(footnote continued)

> restricting the number of years for averaging earnings to the two years immediately preceding the merger solely on the ground that the company had substantial savings in such years." Gibbons v. Schenley Industries, Inc., 339 A.2d 460, 469 (Del. Ch. 1975).

through an "extremely subjective" process. He based his valuation of the trademark on "public acceptance of the name Libby and a buying of five hundred million dollars of their product a year." Thus, he recognized that the value of the trademark was already reflected in sales, and thus also in earnings. The other components of fair value--stock market price and investment value--reflect and indeed measure the extent to which assets, including intangibles, in fact contribute to the corporation's earning capacity and intrinsic worth. In view of the fact that the stock market says the Libby stock is worth only $4.88 per share and also the fact that analysis of actual Libby earnings indicates an earnings potential or investment value of only $2.52 per share, it is difficult to conceive that the Libby trademark and corporate organization have any value that is not more than adequately covered by the $15.41 per share assigned to "net asset value."

Furthermore, the crude inexactitude of using book value as the equivalent of asset value works against adding something more onto that already uncertain base. One could as well assume that book value covers the current value of all assets, including intangibles (whether or not carried on the balance sheet), as to assume that it is equal to current appraised value of merely tangible assets. In the application of such a grossly imprecise measure, a fully depreciated physical asset (reflected at zero in net book value) is hard to distinguish from an intangible asset that is carried on the balance sheet at zero or at only a nominal figure.

In any event, for good and sufficient reasons discussed in Part III(C) of the opinion, net asset value is entitled to minor weight in determining fair value. The appraiser was in our opinion overgenerous, if anything, in assigning a 20% weight to the net asset value figure of $15.41. This record utterly fails to show that the end result of the appraiser's determination of the three constituent elements and application of a 40-40-20 weighing (namely, a computed "fair value" of $6.04) does not adequately reflect any value of the Libby trademark and corporate organization.

Fourth and finally, the dissenting shareholders maintain that the appraiser and the Superior Court erred in refusing to accept the testimony of their expert witness that the book value of Libby's assets should be adjusted upwards, by means of a technique known as "price level accounting." By that technique the historical cost of previously acquired assets is indexed upward to account for the effects of inflation. Not only is there an absence of judicial precedent to support the claim that price level accounting can properly be utilized in a stock appraisal proceeding, but a generally accepted treatise on accounting practices specifically cautions against the use of such techniques for appraisal purposes. Deloitte, Haskins & Sells, Accounting Practices 876 (1978). There is no reason in logic to support the contention that the particular mix of property owned by Libby appreciated or depreciated in step with changes in general average price levels.

V.   Conclusion

In summary we reject each of the cross-appeal claims raised by the dissenting shareholders concerning the proper determination of stock market price, investment value, and net asset value. Having previously decided that the appraiser' recommendations as to the 40-40-20 weighting of those factors should be accepted, we conclude that the appraiser's ultimate recommendation as to the fair value of the dissenters' stock should also be accepted. Other evidence in the record tending to prove a value of the Libby stock of less than $6.00 justified the appraiser's rounding off the computed "fair value" of $6.04. Accordingly, we direct the entry of a judgment fixing $6.00 per share as the fair value of the Libby common stock on February 17, 1976.

*   *   *

D.   NOTE ON CAPITALIZATION OF EARNINGS

1.   The Earnings to be Capitalized

In applying the capitalization of earnings formula, the first question is how to compute the earnings to be capital-ized. In theory, the answer is clear enough: the value of an enterprise depends upon the future earnings it will generate, and the past earnings are quite beside the point, except as an index to the likely future earnings. Indeed, the capitalization formula, under which the multiplier is the reciprocal of the capitalization rate, represents a summation of all future earnings, discounted to present value at the assumed capitalization rate. Hence, the earnings figure to be capitalized should be the best estimate of the average future annual earning power of the enterprise from here to eternity.

Obviously, however, even an attempt to estimate earnings for a few years into the future is a highly speculative exercise. Therefore, the practice has developed of relying primarily upon recent past earnings as a guide to future earning power. For established companies, like Libby, the tendency is to go back at least five years, in order to get a balanced picture of the ups and downs of the business. In fact, this has become virtually a rule of law in the dissenting shareholder appraisal cases. See e.g., In re Watt & Shand 304 A. 2d 694, 699-700 (Sup. Ct. Pa. 1973) (involving an appraisal of the shares of dissenting minority shareholders of a close corporation engaged in operating department stores):

> The lower court used but a single year (the year ended January 1969) to obtain the average earnings of Watt & Shand. In our judgment this was error, but since neither party complains of the action, we will not review it.
>
> However, we do point out that in this kind of proceeding "[i]t is best to average earnings over several years to avoid undue emphasis on one exceptionally good or bad recent year." Note, Valuation of Dissenter's Stock under Appraisal Statutes, 79 Harv.L.Rev. 1453, 1464 (1966). The purpose of any average is to balance off extraordinary profits against extraordinary losses, in order that a hypothetical figure of what might be considered the ordinary profit or inherent earning capacity of the business may become discernible.[10]

10. In his treatise, Financial Policy of Corporations (5th ed. 1953), Prof. Dewing notes that a period of five years is frequently used, although he goes on to explain at p. 376 that:

"There is no mystical significance in taking a ten- or five- or three-year average of earnings to get a more accurate picture of the fundamental earning capacity of the business than is given by the earnings of a single year; and there is no reason why one period should be used for all businesses. It must, however, to use the words of a legal decision, be broad enough to '. . . cover a sufficient period to show the settled condition of things.'"

See also Volume 1, Bonbright, Valuation of Property, p. 253 (1st ed. 1937), where the author states:

"There is still an agreement among writers that a capitalization of average earnings over a period of 3 to 5 years (occasionally 10 to 15 years) is preferable, in most cases, to a capitalization of the earnings of any single year."

While our research disclosed no cases on point in this jurisdiction, the Delaware Chancery Court has held it error to use only the two years prior to appraisal. Adams v. R. C. Williams & Co., 39 Del.Ch. 61, 158 A.2d 797 (1960), preferring to average at least the five previous years. In Sporborg v. City Specialty Stores, 35 Del.Ch. 560, 123 A.2d 121 (1957), the appraiser considered only the fiscal year immediately preceding the effective date of the merger in arriving at the earnings value to be capitalized. The court found this to be error, saying: "True, the upward trend of this Corporation in the last fiscal year may suggest the likelihood that future earnings may be even greater than those of preceding years. But this does not justify the use of only a single year's earnings." 123 A.2d at 125. Again the five-year period was insisted upon.

This insistence upon going back a number of past years is especially troublesome when the enterprise has been enjoying a steady rise in earnings. In such a case, the average of past years may not be very good evidence of the prospective future earnings: a better measure might well be obtained by looking at only the most recent year (or two), or perhaps even by projecting the increasing earnings trend a few years into the future. However, the litigated cases provide no support at all for future projections of this kind, and instead confine themselves to some average of the past years' figures (but with some disposition to take account of a rising earnings trend in selecting the multiplier). E.g., Frances I. duPont & Co. v. Universal City Studios, Inc., 312 A.2d 344 (Del. Ch. 1973), aff'd, 334 A.2d 216 (Del. Sup. Ct. 1975), involving appraisal of the shares of stockholders of a motion picture company dissenting to a merger in early 1966. The Chancellor approved the appraiser's use of the average of earnings per share for the most recent five years, 1961-1965, which amounted to 5.77 per share, although those earnings showed a steady rise through that period, being $3.32, $4.96, $6.22, $6.32 and $8.02 respectively. The dissenting stockholders urged that the most recent earnings (1965) of $8.02 per share should have been used in the capitalization formula, arguing that averaging past earnings is appropriate only when the earnings history has been erratic, and offering the testimony of a securities analyst that the standard financial practice is to capitalize present earnings. However, the Chancellor stated flatly that under Delaware law capitalization must be based upon historical earnings, not prospective earnings, and that the most recent five-year period was the most representative and reasonable period of time over which to compute the average.

The stockholders also contended that at least the earlier years were not representative of the company's earning power as of the merger in 1966 because it was not until well into the five-year period that the company had begun to lease its film library to the television networks, which had made a marked contribution to the growth in earnings (and promised even more significant increases in the immediate future). The Chancellor conceded that the new television arrangement had contributed substantially to the company's earnings and represented a relatively permanent new market. However, he saw this as simply a change in the nature of the company's market, and not in the fundamental nature of its business. As the Chancellor put it, with or without the television market the company's "earning experience over the long term remains subject to the variables in its managerial

and artistic talent, the ability and ingenuity of its competitors and the uncertainties of public tastes in enter-
tainemnt."

The Chancellor observed that the rising trend in earnings
was not only no reason for abandoning the traditional averaging
approach but also provided no basis for eliminating any of
the five years as unusual, adding that the "trend has significance in the choice of the multiplier." He regarded the
company's earnings over the five-year period as representative of the company's experience in the broad context of its
business of producing feature length films, whether for the
theatre market or for television, or both, pointing out that
an important purpose of averaging over five years is to
balance extraordinary profits or losses which might distort
the earnings data if a period of only one or two years was
used.

Businessmen are more likely to give much greater, if
not exclusive, weight to the most recent earnings, so long
as the most recent year is not marked by any significant
distortions. That is especially true of relatively young
companies which may still be in the process of getting
established. But even at the opposite end of the spectrum,
in the stock market, price-earnings ratios are usually addressed in terms of the earnings for the most recent year
(or perhaps even the most recent quarter). And for a company with a strong growth pattern, using the most recent
year's earnings could constitute a sensible compromise
between an average of past years' results and a projection
of earnings growth into the future.

Whatever the past period looked to, it is of course
necessary to take account of any changes in the nature of
the enterprise which would make the past experience not
truly representative of the future. For example, in Perlman
v. Feldmann, 154 F. Supp. 436 (D. Conn. 1957), on remand for
valuation of the enterprise after the Second Circuit's
condemnation of the principal stockholder's sale of control,
the court used the earnings for just two months of the most
recent year before the valuation date ("annualized", by
multiplying six times), because only then had certain new
manufacturing facilities come on line and begun to contribute to operating results. Compare Allen H. Dahme Associates,
Inc. v. U.S., 436 F.2d 486 (Ct. Cl. 1971), where a business
in existence for only one year was valued on the basis of
just the last five months' earnings, because the earlier
period was a start-up and hence not representative of the

future. This general principle has been recognized by the
Supreme Court, in Protective Committee for Independent
Stockholders of TMT Trailer Ferry, Inc. v. Anderson, 390
U.S. 414, 452-3 (1968) (reversing a determination of value
in a reorganization proceeding because of the trial court's
refusal to consider evidence of the company's future prospects):

"If it is shown that the record of past earnings is
not a reliable criterion of future performance, the
court must form an estimate of future performance by
inquiring into all forseeable factors which may affect
future prospects. In forming this estimate, 'mathematical certitude' is neither expected nor required.

". . .It should have been clear to the trial court
that the circumstances brought out at the two hearings
showed that the past earnings record was not a reliable
criterion of future performance, and that sound evaluation of the company as a going concern required examination of the future prospects of the company. The court
was not dealing with an established company in a static
market, nor was it being asked to value the company's
future prospects by hypothesizing unforseeable changes
in operations or market structure. It was evident that
certain specific and predictable alterations would have
to be made in the equipment and operations of the company in order to meet forseeable alterations in the
market. The trial court shut its eyes to these important
developments and in so doing ignored a cardinal principal
of proper evaluation."

2.   Determination of the Capitalization Rate (Multiplier)

The following excerpt from Bonbright, the Valuation of
Property, Vol. I, 259-264 (1935), though it is now some
fifty years old and refers illustratively to interest rates
that have not been seen in decades, is still unsurpassed as
an introduction to the process and the problems associated
with capitalization of earnings:

The Application of the Capitalized-earnings Method: The Rate of Capitalization.

In the words of Arthur S. Dewing, "perhaps the most difficult,
and so far as results are concerned the most important point in any
theory of value based on earning power, is the rate at which earnings
shall be capitalized."

No wonder that the problem is difficult; for the relationship between the value of an enterprise and its reported or estimated net earnings is so indirect that it has never been adequately analyzed as a matter of abstract theory, to say nothing of being reduced to valid mathematical expression in any concrete case. The assumptions underlying the capitalization of the reported net earnings of a corporation at, say, 10 per cent, are quite different from those underlying the capitalization of a perpetuity at 4 per cent—different in nature and not merely in the use of a higher rate as an offset to the higher risk factor.

It is important, first, to distinguish between two different methods of valuation, both of which involve a choice of a rate of capitalization. Sometimes the earnings to be capitalized are the annual *realized* earnings, either for a single year or for a longer period in the past. Sometimes, however, the rate of capitalization is applied to the appraiser's forecast of *future* earnings. Since the latter procedure is the simpler one from the standpoint of theory, it will be discussed first.

Capitalization of Estimated Future Earnings.

The simplest problem of capitalizing estimated future net earnings arises only in those rare situations where these earnings may be expected to remain stable, year by year, during a specific term of years, or during that indefinitely long period of time which, for appraisal purposes, is the rough equivalent of eternity. Here the prospective flow of earnings is usually valued as one would value an annuity certain or a perpetuity.

But even here, the risk factor is usually much greater than in the case of an annuity—so much so, that its proper treatment becomes critical. In the absence of statistical data such as those embodied in life-insurance mortality tables, whereby the risk of nonreceipt of the anticipated earnings may be expressed mathematically, it has been customary vaguely to allow for the risk factor by the choice of a rate of capitalization higher than the rates fixed by the market place on highgrade bonds. The current yield on these bonds has been taken to approximate the rate of interest on a "riskless investment." If this rate is 4 per cent, the prospective annual earnings of an enterprise with an indefinitely long life expectancy may be capitalized, say, at 10 per cent, or at some higher or lower rate depending on the appraiser's judgment of the riskiness of the business. The differential between the chosen rate of capitalization and the rate of yield on relatively secure bonds is supposed to represent an allowance, not merely for the "actuarial" or "mathematical" risk factor, but also for the "psychological" risk factor. Ordinarily, investors are supposed to demand a premium for successful risk taking; and under this assumption, the rate of capitalization is fixed at a higher amount than would be justified by probability tables, were such tables available.

This attempt by appraisal experts simultaneously to allow for the interest factor and the risk factor by a single, high rate of capitalization, raises actuarial questions that have been given surprisingly little attention by writers in finance. It subjects the risk-factor allowance to a process of compounding, the validity of which may be seriously questioned. To illustrate the point by an artificially simple example, let us assume an enterprise with anticipated stable and continuous net earnings of $100,000 per year. Assume that, if these earnings could be anticipated with that confidence which is the psychological equivalent of certainty, a 4 per cent rate of capitalization would be indicated. But assume, further, that there are nine chances in favor of the exact realization of these anticipated earnings as against one chance in favor of the nonrealization of any net earnings whatsoever. On actuarial principles, and disregarding the "psychological" risk factor, the enterprise should then be valued as a 90 per cent chance of receiving a perpetual income of $100,000 per year and hence as the equivalent of a certainty of receiving $90,000 per year. A 4 per cent capitalization of $90,000 per year would give $2,250,000 as the present value of the enterprise.

This same valuation would be reached by the traditional method only if the appraiser were to capitalize the anticipated net income ($100,000) at 4.44+ per cent. But such a rate would hardly be hit upon except by accident, since it could not be rationally constructed save by going through the mathematical process just indicated. It would seem that the only practical defense of the prevalent practice, whereby both the interest factor and the risk factor are allowed for in a single rate of compound discount, lies in the appraiser's inability to make a more direct estimate of the risk of nonachievement of his prophesied earning power. But such a defense is tantamount to an admission that enterprise valuation, so far from being based on scientific principles, is little more than guesswork, which indeed it is in the present stage of the art of appraisal.

Still assuming that the enterprise whose value must be estimated will have fairly stable annual earnings, so that its probable earning power can be expressed by a single figure (say, $100,000 per year), we have now to take into account the fact that almost never can the appraiser assume that his estimated future earnings will either turn out to be approximately right, or else will be belied by a record of zero earnings. The much greater likelihood is a record of earnings materially higher or lower than the estimates. How may the appraiser take into account this range of expectancies?

If it were possible separately to calculate the likelihood of alternative income ranges, the present value of the enterprise might still be determined on actuarial principles. But the lack of any statistical basis for such calculations has led appraisers to fall back upon the concept of a "most probable" annual income, which they capitalize at a rate supposed to take account of the likelihood of deviations. One might suppose that, after estimating most probable annual net earnings, the appraiser would assume that the chances of a more favorable record would roughly balance the chances of a less favorable record. On this assumption, the estimated earnings might be capitalized at a rate similar to the yields of secure bonds, save for a possible allowance for the psychological risk factor. In practice, however, even the more cautious appraisers often indulge in considerable optimism in their estimates of future earnings, with the result that they do not feel justified in regarding the hope of greater success as even a mathematical offset to the fear of less success. But the art of enterprise valuation has not yet reached the point where nice issues of this nature are discussed in the individual appraisal reports or in the general literature of finance.

We have now to note a further complication in the process of capitalizing anticipated earnings. With most enterprises—those of the decadent type no less than those of the expanding type—any assumption that the future earnings will be stabilized at a fixed amount per year is absurd on its face. This fact would seem to preclude the capitalization of any single estimate of annual earnings and to require the separate discounting of a whole series of estimated earnings. With enterprises of a short life expectancy, such as single-mine ventures, the latter procedure is often adopted. But with enterprises of an indefinite life expectancy, much cruder methods of capitalization are resorted to. As a rule, a purely fictitious "typical" annual earning power is assumed. Where an upward trend is anticipated, the "typical earnings" are set higher than those expected for the next few years, but lower than those expected in the more distant future. Thus the appraiser converts an expected series of unequal earnings into the valuational equivalent of a perpetual annuity. The crudeness of this conversion is apparent.

Still another complication should be mentioned. With an expanding business, the anticipated increase in earnings cannot be credited entirely to the present capital investment. This increase will be attainable only if more funds are invested in the business. But the necessity of investing these funds is a factor adverse to the present value of the enterprise, and it must be allowed for if the appraiser includes the higher anticipated earning power in his estimate of capitalizable earnings.

The problem of making such an allowance could be treated scientifically only by a forecast of the further capital outlays required, year after year, as a means of realizing the estimated increased earning power. The present discounted adverse value of these future outlays could then be deducted from the positive value of the discounted anticipated earnings. But the difficulty of predicting the times and amounts of capital expansion has generally precluded such calculations. Instead, appraisers have made a vague allowance for the possibilities of business expansion by capitalizing at a lower rate than would otherwise be warranted the estimated earnings attainable under the present or immediately prospective capacity of the plant.

From what has been said it is apparent that the determination of a rate at which to capitalize the prospective earnings of a business is a hit-and-miss procedure. Its inaccuracies are generally conceded by the financial writers; but its wild crudeness has seldom been fully exposed even by the experts.

The Rate of Capitalization of Realized Earnings.

While new enterprises are usually appraised by a capitalization of *prophesied* earnings, enterprises with an established earnings record are perhaps more frequently appraised by a capitalization of reported realized earnings averaged over a period of years. We have already noted that *realized* earnings have no appraisal significance except as an index of future earning power. But many appraisers prefer to capitalize the realized earnings directly, even though they anticipate a measurable change in future earnings. They allow for any anticipated change by shifting their rate of capitalization rather than by recalculating the annual earnings. On theoretical grounds there is no good reason for this preference; for the difficulty of predicting the future earnings directly is no more serious than the difficulty of making an appropriate allowance in the rate of capitalization. But there seems to be an impression among investment analysts that, for psychological reasons, appraisers will play safer by taking indirect account of a prospective change in earnings, through a relatively slight shift in their capitalization rate, than by taking direct account of the same situation through an overt forecast of earnings trends. The present author is skeptical of this point of view; especially so since a slight change in the rate of capitalization corresponds to a very large change in the predicted earnings. There is the further danger that an adjustment of the capitalization rate rather than of the estimated annual earnings will give to the appraisal a specious appearance of reliability, because the reported earnings seem to be predicated on "actual facts" rather than on a mere prediction.

The Arthur S. Dewing referred to at the beginning of the foregoing excerpt is the author of the two volume treatise, Financial Policy of Corporations, which appeared in its fifth (and final) edition in 1953. Professor Dewing's work has been the source most frequently consulted by courts and commentators alike for guidance on the choice of an appropriate multiplier, especially his comprehensive effort to divide industrial businesses into separate categories of increasing riskiness and assign an appropriate capitalization rate (multiplier) to each one. Here is the relevant text from Volume I of the fifth edition, at 288-292, 390-391

If we assume that a statistical study has disclosed the earnings to be capitalized, the rate at which they shall be capitalized is by no means clear. Under our competitive system of economic values, the business is the instrument which creates the earnings, and the valuation of the business is the valuation of this instrument. It is true, too, under our competitive system, that the price which men will pay for this instrument will depend on the relative certainty with which these earnings can be counted upon to continue. In other words, the rate at which a business shall be capitalized, to obtain its value, will depend on the confidence the buyer may feel in the continuation of the earnings. This is the relative risk of the business itself. The greater the risk, the greater the doubt of continued earnings, the lower is the capitalized value of these earnings; and conversely, the lower the risk, the greater the value. Consequently, to proceed further with a study of the rate of capitalization, we must analyze the risk of the business as an instrument for producing earnings.

The risk of a business rests on one dominant factor and on numerous contributing factors of less moment. The dominant factor is the relative importance of management, one of the group of those intangible values into which we have attempted to divide organization. The factors of less moment are the influence of the alternation of business booms and depressions, the uncertainties of trade customs, of sources of supply of the materials of the business, of changes in tariff laws or patent laws, of changes in political theory bringing about new and restrictive legislation. There are other factors peculiar to individual types of enterprise, but these are included in the idea of management in the sense that they present problems which must be met and solved by the management if the business is to continue to be profitable.

In the long run the interest on the capital invested tends to become equal among different kinds of enterprises. That is, the mere rate of return on capital, without considering the risk incident to carrying it on, inclines to be the same for all businesses. Furthermore, in the long run, the larger return obtained in certain risky enterprises is counterbalanced by the greater frequency of losses, while the smaller return to stable businesses less frequently bears the burden of losses. A building may be used as part of the fixed capital of a risky business or as part of the fixed capital of a stable business. It is the same building in either case. Yet if the building is used as a storage warehouse, far less organization, particularly skill of management, is required than if the building is used for the manufacture of fancy dancing slippers. In the combination of capital and management, management is of much less relative importance in the former case than in the latter. In brief, the contribution of skill of management to success is greater in a risky than in a stable business. This difference is reflected, moreover, not only in the larger earnings which the risky business must produce in order to compensate for the greater losses, but also in the fact that, if the business is offered for sale, there are fewer men willing and qualified to buy it and to manage it successfully.

This difference as regards the relative importance of management affects directly the ratio at which net earnings in different kinds of business should be capitalized. For if management is of relatively greater importance to insure success in certain businesses than in others, a buyer will gauge his valuation in accordance with this phase of the business. He will pay comparatively little for the combination of fixed and current assets and past management, represented by the capitalized past earnings, in those businesses in which the importance of good management is so great a prerequisite to success that the future earnings can with difficulty be predicted from the past earnings. Or, stating the same idea differently, the greater the risk of the business, the smaller the ratio between past earnings and present value; and, conversely, the greater the stability of the business—and the less degree to which management is a prerequisite to success—the closer the connection between past earnings and present value. The relative importance of management gives us a key to the relative value of a business in terms of the record of past earnings.

Ratios for Capitalization of Net Earnings in Various Businesses. In the light of the relative importance of management—corresponding to the inherent risks of the business—it is possible to arrange businesses in the order of the ratios by which one may capitalize the past earnings. Those that are very stable, to which skill of management is least essential for success, are at one end of the series; those that are very risky and require unusually great skill of management are at the other end of the series. A gravity system water works is, in the writer's opinion, the easiest kind of business enterprise to administer. It requires much fixed capital but little skill. Even the aldermen of a city can manage the water works with not too destructive inefficiency. At the other end are businesses, like ladies' fancy millinery or drama production, which are so uncertain and risky that only a few people of rare ability are likely to succeed in them. The quantity of assets at the command of the managers of this latter kind is of relatively little importance in forecasting success, and if men of marked ability with highly specialized knowledge withdraw, this skeleton of assets remaining is of little value to other men. Between these two extremes lie the great majority of enterprises. Toward one end of the series would be grouped the large variety of local utilities protected by franchise from direct competition and from confiscatory rates by the Fourteenth Amendment. Toward the other end would be found the extra hazardous businesses involving keen foresight, personal attention to details, and marked power to coordinate all the parts of the enterprise.

The ratios of percentages at which the extremes of this series should be capitalized in order to translate earnings into value must depend on a variety of conditions. Businesses requiring only a small amount of capital will sell for a higher price, relatively, than those requiring a large amount, because there are a greater number of possible buyers; on the other hand, businesses that require large amounts of capital will appeal more strongly to investment bankers and will, therefore, have a readier access to investment funds. Businesses which are pleasant and give the owner a social standing will sell for more than businesses which are disagreeable to conduct or which carry social discredit. Seasonal and fluctuating types of enterprise have certain apparent disadvantages; so have those which require a highly specialized background of training and demand a fund of information available only to a few.

Perhaps the most difficult, and so far as results are concerned, the most important point in any theory of value based on earning power, is the rate at which earnings shall be capitalized. A comparatively large error in computing net earnings—by an over- or an underestimate of depreciation, for example—is not of as much importance in the final result as a comparatively small difference in the rate at which earnings shall be capitalized. Yet the determination of this rate is at best a matter of guesswork, but guesswork supported by the evidence of prices at which businesses of various kinds are being actually valued at any one time. This evidence from current experience with reference to the value of different enterprises can be culled not only from the prices at which enterprises are actually sold, but also from the valuation put upon them by bankers extending credit to them and by investors who are willing to buy their bonds and stocks. In other words, such guesswork is subject to the best kind of pragmatic test, namely the evidence of actual experience.

Summary Statement of Capitalization of Earnings. From these various methods of approach, it is possible to throw industrial businesses into diverse categories in accordance with which we can form some estimate of the value of a business by capitalizing its earnings. These categories could be described in the following manner:

1. Old established businesses, with large capital assets and excellent goodwill—10%, a value ten times the net earnings. Very few industrial enterprises would come within this category.

2. Businesses, well established, but requiring considerable managerial care. To this category would belong the great number of old, successful industrial businesses, large and small—12½%, a value eight times the net earnings.

3. Businesses, well established, but involving possible loss in consequence of shifts of general economic conditions. They are strong, well established businesses, but they produce a type of commodity which makes them vulnerable to depressions. They require considerable managerial ability, but little special

knowledge on the part of the executives—15%, a value approximately seven times the net earnings.

4. Businesses requiring average executive ability—and at the same time comparatively small capital investment. These businesses are highly competitive, but established good-will is of distinct importance. This class includes the rank and file of medium-sized, highly competitive industrial enterprises —20%, a value approximately five times the net earnings.

5. Small industrial businesses, highly competitive, and requiring a relatively small capital outlay. They are businesses which anyone, even with little capital, may enter—25%, a value approximately four times the net earnings.

6. Industrial businesses, large and small, which depend on the special, often unusual skill of one, or of a small group of managers. They involve only a small amount of capital; they are highly competitive and the mortality is high among those who enter the competitive struggle—50%, a value approximately twice the net earnings.

7. Personal service businesses. They require no capital, or at the most a desk, some envelopes and a few sheets of paper. The manager must have a special skill coupled with an intensive and thorough knowledge of his subjects. The earnings of the enterprise are the objective reflection of this skill; and he is not likely to be able to create "an organization" which can successfully "carry on" after he is gone. He can sell the business, including the reputation and the "plan of business," but he cannot sell himself, the only truly valuable part of the enterprise—100%, a value equal, approximately, to the earnings of a single year.

This summary of categories is not a classification in the sense of clearly defined and marked classes. There are innumerable intermediate stages. These seven categories are of the nature of nodal points in the organization of industry, according to the relation of earnings and value. There may be businesses so highly stabilized, so immune to the shocks of industrial depression and incompetent management, that they are worth more than ten times their annual earnings; there may be businesses so peculiar and individual that they are, in the hands of another, not worth even the earnings of a single year

While the Dewing capitalization table has been frequently referred to in the decided cases, a number of them
tend to treat it as somewhat dated. For example, the Watt &
Shand case, referred to in subsection A above, contained the
following comments in footnote 13, in support of the court's
conclusion that use of a multiplier of 10 was within the
range of reason:

13. Many courts still look to Dewing's treatise, The
     Financial Policy of Corporations, as a guide to
     the selection of a multiplier. Therein are de-
     scribed seven common types of businesses and
     suggested capitalization rates ranging from one to
     ten times earnings. Dewing assigns a value of ten
     times the net earnings to "old established busi-
     nesses with large capital assets and excellent
     good will" and adds "very few industrial enterprises
     would come within this category." [p. 390] A
     value of eight times net earnings (12½%) is assigned
     to "[b]usinesses, well established, but requiring
     considerable managerial care. To this category
     would belong the great number of old, successful
     industrial business - large and small." [p. 390]
     Dewing's work was last revised in 1953 and in
     certain situations may be dated, although we feel
     the ratio used instantly was appropriate and are
     fortified in this belief by the record testimony
     concerning the price earnings ratio of Strawbridge
     and Clothier, a somewhat comparable department
     store in Philadelphia.

In the Universal City Studios case, also cited in the
previous section, the Chancellor approved the use of a
multiplier of 16.1, which was the average price earnings
ratio of nine comparable publicly-held motion picture companies. In answer to the objection of the company that the
16.1 multiplier was too high, the Chancellor noted that
while many of the cases and treatises approve a multiplier
of around 10, "that is based largely on the economics and
pricing structure of an earlier day and, under the circumstances here present, the use of any such number would be

artificial." The Chancellor particularily stressed the
trend of the company's earnings, the predictability of
income from television in the next few years, and the reasonableness of looking to the average multiplier of other
companies in the business.

On appeal, the Delaware Supreme Court sustained the use
of the 16.1 multiplier. While acknowledging that Professor
Dewing's "works in the past have been accorded deferential
treatment in Delaware", the Court found unpersuasive his
view that a multiplier of 10 is the highest value that can
be assigned to a business. Rather the Court relied on an
earlier Delaware case, Swanton v. State Guaranty Corp.,
215 A. 2d 242, 246(Del. Ch. 1965), for the proposition that
"Professor Dewings's capitalization chart was not the 'be-all
and end-all', and it did not 'freeze the subject matter for
all time', especially since 'contemporary financial history'
reveals a 'need for flexibility'." The Court added in a
footnote that the "profound changes in interest rates, money
supply and the wage-price spiral since Professor Dewing's
pronouncement are self-evident".

In support of a high multiplier in this case, the
Supreme Court pointed to the company's steady increase in
earnings, and the virtually certain additional growth in the
immediate future due to the company's leasing of its films
to television. These were persuasive indications of "future
economic success and stability", which were "sufficient to
warrant a departure from Dewing's capitalization chart".
The Court also noted that the years 1964 and 1965 witnessed
a marked resurgence for the motion picture industry, after a
long period of slumping profits due to competition from
television. In addition, the standard stock market indices
in 1966 showed average price-earnings ratios of more than
17. These factors justified the use of the price earnings
ratio of 16.1 derived from the other companies in the motion
picture business.

3.   Capitalization of the Earnings of Small Enterprises

Applying capitalization of earnings to a small business
poses some special problems. For one thing, the entrepreneurs
of a small enterprise, particularly when it is not incorporated, often do not isolate compensation for their own services
from the rest of their entrepreneurial return. In such
cases it is necessary to determine and deduct the reasonable
worth of such services in arriving at the figure for estimated
future earnings to be capitalized, since the value of the

enterprise should be based upon its earning power in excess
of reasonable compensation for any services rendered.

Should income taxes be deducted in determining the
earnings to be capitalized? Normally, for a business already
in corporate form the corporate income taxes should be
deducted, whereas presumably in valuing a proprietorship or
a partnership no deduction is made for the income taxes
incurred by the individuals on the earnings of the business
(particularly since their respective tax brackets depend upon
their gain and losses from other sources). But suppose a
business in proprietorship or partnership form is being
valued in connection with a proposed transfer to a corporation. No doubt if the acquirer is a going corporation it
would take account of the prospective corporate income
taxes; but the question is harder when the transfer is to a
newly-organized corporation, for example, in conjunction
with a deal to bring new capital into the venture. Probably
for a growing enterprise it would be wise to take account of
estimated corporate taxes, since it may not be long before
incorporation would be dictated in any event, in order to
shield the earnings of the enterprise from the higher,
graduated tax rates applicable to individuals. But in any
event the value of an enterprise should not depend upon
whether it is in fact incorporated and hence subject to
corporate taxes. Therefore, in practice it seems likely
that a lower multiplier would be used to capitalize pre-tax
earnings than would be used with post-tax earnings, so that
the ultimate enterprise value would come out about the same
either way. This makes sense, since there is at least a
substantial chance of ultimately becoming subject to corporate
taxes, and so pre-tax earnings are less secure than post-tax
earnings.

Choosing the multiplier for a small enterprise also
poses some special difficulties. There is much less recorded
experience in valuing such businesses from which guidance
may be obtained (and of course very little likelihood of
finding any public companies which are sufficiently comparable
to make their price earnings ratios useful even as a starting
point in selecting an appropriate multiplier). As to the
Dewing chart, while it does purport to apply to small companies, as a practical matter the delineations among the
paragraphs in the lower ranges of the chart, numbers 4, 5
and 6, are not exactly clear-cut. There is also the question
of the extent to which the current financial climate calls
for an upswing in the Dewing multipliers in these lower
ranges. Schreier and Joy, Judicial Valuation of "Close"

Corporation Stock: <u>Alice in Wonderland</u> Revisited, 31 Okla.
L. Rev. 853, 858-860 (1978), cites the Dewing chart as
relevant, but offers only the abstract comment that a close
corporation's capitalization rate "is a function of both the
rates of return expected by the investment community for
various types of investments under current market conditions
and the amount of risk with which an investment in the
valued, closely held business is associated, when compared
with the risk underlying alternate investment opportunities".

An interesting recent effort to refine the process of
choosing the multiplier for closely held enterprises is set
out in Schilt, A Rational Approach to Capitalization Rates
for Discounting the Future Income Stream of a Closely Held
Company, The Financial Planner (January, 1982) 56. The
author starts with the premise that the capitalization rate
should be based upon the current risk-free rate of return
(for which he would look to long-term United States Treasury
Bonds), plus a premium for the risk associated with the
particular income stream. He notes that for a broad group
of publicly-traded stocks the compound annual rate of return
over the 53 years from 1925 through 1978 was approximately
9%, which represented a risk premium of almost 6% when
measured against treasury bonds over the same period.
Obviously, the risk adjustment for closely-held business
would be higher, usually much higher. The author offers the
following table (set out on the next page) of risk categories, somewhat paralleling the Dewing chart, with the
appropriate risk premium for each one (in a range of five
percentage points, to allow for some flexibility). These
premiums would be added to the interest rate on long-term
treasury bonds (which was approximately 14% in early 1982
when the article was published, but had declined to nearer
12% by the end of 1983), and the resulting capitalization
rates, according to the author, are designed to be applied
to pre-tax income, because of the wide variation in the
effective tax rates among companies. (Incidentally, the
author makes no reference to the point that in these inflationary times the interest rate on long-term securities
represents not only pure interest on a riskless investment
but also a premium to compensate for the possible impact of
inflation on a fixed rate of return and a long delay in the
repayment of the principal; inflation poses less of a risk
to business earnings, which tend to increase with a rising
price level.)

Risk Premiums for Discounting
Projected Income Streams

Category	Description	Premium
1.	Established businesses with a strong trade position, are well financed, have depth in management, whose past earnings have been stable and whose future is highly predictable.	6-10%
2.	Established businesses in a more competitive industry that are well financed, have depth in management, have stable past earnings and whose future is fairly predictable.	11-15%
3.	Businesses in a highly competitive industry .that require little capital to enter, no management depth, element of risk is high, although past record may be good.	16-20%
4.	Small businesses that depend upon the special skill of one or two people. Larger established businesses that are highly cyclical in nature. In both cases, future earnings may be expected to deviate widely from projections.	21-25%
5.	Small "one man" businesses of a personal services nature, where the transferability of the income stream is in question.	26-30%

For an example of capitalization of the earnings of a modest enterprise (which, however, contains some obvious errors in application), see the valuation set out in the findings of fact in the Turner case, at pages 107-108 in the Casebook.

E. MORE ON VALUATION: THE TULLY CASE

Estate of Tully v. United States, 78-1 USTC ¶13,228 (Ct. Cl. 1978), involves the valuation for estate tax purposes of 50% of the stock of T&D, a closely-held corporation which had been in the construction business for forty years and had become one of the largest in the New York City area.

Following the guidelines in a number of tax pronouncements, which expressly refer to the company's prospective earning power, its net worth, and its dividend-paying capacity as relevant factors in valuation, the parties' respective experts focused on capitalization of earnings, book value, and dividend potential, and the opinion illustrates a number of variations on these themes. (In addition, both the experts and the Court were influenced by the explicit instruction in IRC §2031(b) that in valuing non-traded stock consideration should be given to the value of the stock of listed corporations engaged in similar lines of business.)

In determining the earnings to be capitalized, the Court used a straight average of the five full most recent fiscal years prior to the decedent's death on March 7, 1964, which were as follows (rounded off):

Fiscal year ending Oct. 31	Net Income
1963	$709,000
1962	173,500
1961	177,000
1960	374,500
1959	324,000

The Court eschewed any extra weight for the more recent years because it viewed the erratic earnings pattern as due not to any unusual circumstances but rather simply the normal ups and downs of the heavy construction business. In addition no account was taken of the results of operations for the first four months of fiscal 1964, through February 29, 1964, which showed earnings of $128,000 for that period. The Court merely commented that even if those earnings were "annualized" (i.e., multiplying them by three), they would still be substantially less than the earnings for fiscal 1963.

As to the multiplier, in effect the Court accepted the approach used by both experts of looking to the price-earnings ratios of comparable publicly-traded companies, which averaged approximately 10.6 (but ultimately the value of T&D's stock was discounted to reflect the fact that it was not marketable).

With respect to book value, which the Court said "represents the underlying asset value of the stock", the starting point was concededly the assets minus liabilities, or stockholders' equity, shown on the corporation's balance sheet, and for this purpose the Court did use the most recent statement, for February 29, 1964, rather than the October 31,

1963 figures. The Court noted that the fair market value of
some of the corporation's assets, particularly its real
estate, was greater than the cost less depreciation shown on
the books, a common situation which according to the Court
"accounts in large part for the unreliability of book values".
Not surprisingly, the expert for the Government urged that
all unrealized appreciation should be taken into account,
while the taxpayer's expert took the opposite point of view,
on the ground that the current value of the assets was
already reflected in the earnings. The Court concluded that
any unrealized appreciation on operating assets should be
ignored because those assets were not going to be sold, but
that investment assets, such as real estate not used in the
business, should be taken into account at current value. To
translate this adjusted book value into a factor to be used
in the ultimate determination of fair market value, the
Court adopted the taxpayer's approach of multiplying it by
the average ratio of market value to book value for the
comparable public companies, which was 81.75%.

As to dividend-paying capacity, the Court observed that
the corporation had not paid any dividends throughout its
history and determined that it was not in position to pay
dividends as of the decedent's death, despite the large
amount of cash it had on hand; the ratio of current assets
to current liabilities had declined over the five-year
period and was down to 1.75 to 1, well below the 2.5 to 1
rule of thumb which appears in some of the accumulated
earnings tax cases. However, the Court thought that lack of
dividend-paying capacity was not very significant here
because historically T&D was geared toward using its earnings
to finance expansion, and looking to capital appreciation
for the stockholders' "reward".

Turning to the weighting of the three factors, the
Court noted that the taxpayer's expert had given 50% weight
to the capitalization of earnings, and 25% weight each to
book value and dividend-paying capacity (the latter measured
at zero). The Government's expert gave 50% weight to both
earnings and book value, and ignored dividend-paying capacity.
The Court decided that the dividend-paying factor (of zero)
should not be omitted entirely, and assigned it a weight of
10%. As to the other two factors, the Court concluded that
the taxpayer's expert was correct in giving earnings twice
the weight of book value, in view of the emphasis in Rev.
Rul. 59-60 on the importance of earnings in evaluating a
business which sells products or services (as distinguished
from an investment-type business). Accordingly, the Court

weighted the capitalization of earnings factor at 60% and adjusted book value at 30%, which resulted in a tentative value of $294.22 per share, as follows:

Capitalization of earnings factor of
$300.80 (average earnings per share for
1959-1963 of $29.38 times average
multiplier from comparable companies
of 10.6), weighted at 60% $180.50

Adjusted book value per share of
$463.67 on February 29, 1964, times
average ratio of market value to
book value from comparable companies
of 81.75%, weighted at 30% 113.72

Dividend-paying capacity of 0,
weighted at 10% 0

Total $294.22

The Court then addressed the question of a discount, to take account of the lack of marketability of this closely-held stock, and other related valuation factors. (Since the decedent's shares represented a 50% interest, neither an extra discount for minority position nor a premium for control was called for.) The death of one of the principals of the company obviously raised questions about the continued success of management, but the company's long history of profitability and its strong position in the construction industry provided a basis for optimism. There was also the fact that the owner of a 50% interest was in position to assure employment at attractive compensation levels for himself and members of his family (as had in fact occurred here). Taking account of the various factors of this kind presented, with particular emphasis on lack of marketability as a negative factor (as both experts had agreed), the Court applied a discount of 20%, resulting in a final valuation figure of $235.38 per share.

Would the outcome have been very different if the Court had taken a more simple, not to say simplistic, approach to value and relied solely upon capitalization of the company's most recent earnings? Assuming the results for the first third of fiscal 1964 were reasonably representative of that year as a whole (bearing in mind that the period November to February is normally not the most active for the construction industry in the Northeast), the $128,000 could be "annualized" by tripling it, to $384,000; averaging that

figure with the $709,000 shown by the company in the last
preceding full year, fiscal 1963, results in a figure for
earnings of $546,500. Using a nice round multiplier of 8
(based upon the 10.6 for comparable companies, but reduced
by, say, 25% to take account of the fact that the corporation's stock was not publicly traded) would result in an
enterprise value of $4,392,000. From this should be deducted
the $1,500,000 liquidation preference of the preferred stock
outstanding, which would leave $2,872,000 as the total value
of the common stock. (The Court had deducted the $1,500,000
for the preferred stock in computing the book value of the
common stock, but ignored the preferred stock's dividend
claim in determining the earnings available to the common
stock, on the ground that no dividends were in fact ever
paid on the preferred.) For the 12,500 shares of common
stock outstanding, then, the value per share would be just
under $230 per share, a figure within 3% of the result
reached by the Court.

This is not, however, to criticize the much more comprehensive and detailed approach taken by the Court, even if
questions may be raised with respect to its conclusions on
particular points. The "reasoned elaboration" of the final
result, including the attention paid to the approaches taken
by the respective experts, probably serves to make the
outcome more palatable to both parties; perhaps even more
important, it provides guidance to anyone faced with the
task of valuing stock in similar circumstances. In this
connection, it may be useful to take a harder look at the
Court's handling of book value and dividend-paying capacity,
both of which pose problems.

    1.   Book Value.

As noted earlier, the Court at one point says that book
value represents the "asset value" of the stock; later, in
explaining why substantially more weight should be given to
valuation based on earnings, the Court characterizes book
value as "essentially an approximation of liquidation value",
and hence entitled to less weight because liquidation would
be difficult if not ruinous for a construction business
which is constantly in the midst of long-term contracts
running for five years or more. But as is clear from the
Court's rejection of unrealized appreciation (except on
investment property), the book value of assets minus liabilities does not represent present values, which, as here, may
be significantly higher than the figure on the books (and
might, in other situations, be lower). Even less does book

value "approximate" liquidation value, which would almost
always be far lower. It was for these reasons that the
Court in the <u>Libby</u> case downgraded the significance of book
value.

If some measure of the assets does have a separate role
to play in the valuation of a going business, there is much
to be said for using the replacement cost of the assets,
since that could be an indication of what it would cost to
duplicate the business, and hence what somebody else might
be willing to pay to acquire it. (The high replacement cost
of productive facilities is often suggested as one of the
reasons for the large premiums being offered these days in
takeover bids.) Liquidation value, on the other hand,
represents an absolute minimum valuation which would not be
directly relevant except where dissolution of the enterprise
is projected. However, since in these inflationary times
book value usually lies somewhere between the replacement
cost of the assets and their realizable value upon liquidation, the book value figure may represent a sensible compromise between the two. There is also the practical advantage
that book value is readily available from the financial
statements of the corporation, whereas any effort to determine replacement cost or realizeable value is certain to
spark considerable controversy (except perhaps with respect
to assessing the current value of investment property, which
can often be objectively ascertained).

In any event, even if it makes sense to include book
value as a separate element in the valuation process, factoring it by the average ratio of market value to book value of
comparable public companies, as the Court in <u>Tully</u> did,
seems hard to justify. It is one thing to look to comparable
publicly companies (in the relatively rare cases where such
can be found) for guidance as to an appropriate multiplier
in capitalizing earnings (subject to a significant discount
at some stage in the process, to reflect the lack of marketability for closely-held stock); it is quite another to
assume some parallel relationship of book value to market
value. The ratio of market value to book value does not
have any clearly defined significance in the financial world
akin to that between value and earnings (except perhaps for
an implicit danger signal that the value is too high, if it
soars above, say, several times the book value).

Parenthetically, it might be observed that in most of
the litigated valuation cases the asset value factor,
however derived, has been higher than the product of capital-

izing earnings, and hence its inclusion has resulted in a
higher overall valuation. See Note, Dissenting Shareholder's
Appraisal Remedy, 30 Okl. L. Rev. 629, at 641 (1977), for a
chart detailing the amount and the weighting of the various
factors in a number of Delaware appraisal cases. And of
course this was the situation presented in the Tully case,
where the adjusted book value used as the asset factor was
more than 50% higher than the capitalization of earnings
figure. In such circumstances, instead of adjusting the
asset factor downward, on the basis of the ratio of market
value to book value for the comparable public companies, the
Court could have accomplished the same end result of reducing the impact of the adjusted book value by lowering the
weight assigned to that factor (on the ground that book
value is generally lower than market value in this industry).
Reducing the weight according to adjusted book value down
to, say, 15%, while giving 75% weight to capitalization of
earnings (and leaving the dividend-paying capacity of zero
weighted at 10%) would result in almost exactly the same
figure as the Court derived by its approach.

2.   Dividend-Paying Capacity

Perhaps the most debatable aspect of the Court's opinion
in Tully is the treatment of so-called "dividend-paying
capacity", an element injected no doubt in response to the
suggestion in some of the tax authorities that a company's
dividend record might be included as a factor in the valuation process (as has occurred on occasion in the dissenting
shareholders' appraisal cases). But of course a reluctance
to pay dividends is endemic among close corporations, so
such companies normally do not have any dividend track
record. Therefore, if any account is to be taken of this
element a surrogate of some sort must be used, such as
measuring the ability of the company to pay dividends.
Obviously, it will often be the case, as the Court found in
Tully, that the corporation is not in position to pay dividends, because of the need to utilize its internally-gener-
ated funds for working capital, expansion, etc., to avoid
resorting to borrowing, especially when interest rates are
high. (Indeed, a contrary finding could raise havoc for the
corporation under the accummulated earnings tax, as we shall
see later.) Hence, treating the inability to pay dividends
as a negative factor, as the Court in Tully did by "valuing"
dividend-paying capacity at zero and weighting it at 10%, is
really little different from applying a further discount to
the corporations's stock on account of its status as a close
corporation. If the Court had simply weighted the earnings

factor at twice as much as the adjusted book value factor, leaving dividend-paying capacity out entirely, and then applied a discount (for non-marketability of the stock and other related factors) of 25%, as the taxpayer's expert did, instead of 20%, which the Government's expert used, the final value figure would have been just about the same.

The Court does not indicate how it would have dealt with this factor if it had found that the corporation did have the capacity to pay dividends. Perhaps the Court would have determined how large an annual dividend the corporation could have paid and then used this "constructive dividend" to find a value for the dividend factor (to be weighted along with the earnings and book value factors in the overall valuation of the stock). For example, the Court might have looked to the average ratio of dividends to market value for the comparable publicly-traded construction companies, which it had noted was 5%, and multiplied the "constructive dividend" by 20 to determine the value of the dividend factor. Whatever figure that might have produced, and however much weight it might have been assigned, it is clear that a higher final value for the stock would have resulted.

For corporations which do pay regular dividends, there has been much debate about the role of the company's dividend record in valuing the enterprise. In the cases involving appraisal of dissenting shareholders' stock in public corporations, from which has come so much of the current learning on enterprise valuation, although there were some early suggestions that dividend payment should be taken into account as a separate factor, along with asset value, capitalization of earnings, and market value, the present tendency is to ignore dividends entirely, as the Court in Libby did. In another recent appraisal case, the Court explained the lack of attention to dividends this way [Piemonte v. New Boston Garden Corp, 377 Mass. 719, 728, 387 N.E.2d 1145, 1150 (1979)]:

"The judge did not have to consider the dividend record of Garden Arena, as the defendant urges. Dividends tend to reflect the same factors as earnings and, therefore, need not be valued separately. See Felder v. Anderson, Clayton & Co., 39 Del.Ch. 76, 88-89, 159 A.2d 278 (1960). And since dividend policy is usually reflected in market value, the use of market value as a factor in the valuation process permitted the low and sporadic dividend rate to be given some weight in the process. Beyond that, the value of the

plaintiffs' stock should not be depreciated because the
controlling interests often chose to declare low dividends or none at all."

On the other hand, some of the theoretical commentary
on enterprise valuation has suggested that the dividend
record, past and prospective, is the most important of all
factors in valuing publicly-traded stock -- indeed, that it
is really dividends rather than earnings which should be
capitalized to determine the value of stock. The argument
is that investors buy a company's potential dividends, not
its earnings, since dividends are the only observable return
that stockholders receive on their investment. This theory
does not imply that retained earnings are irrelevant, but
their relevance would be confined to the prospect of producing
higher dividends in the future. The expectation would be
that at least a portion of the earnings retained each year
would be invested in additional income-producing assets, so
that stockholders could look forward to a growing rather
than static stream of future dividends. Hence the capitalization rate to be applied to the current annual dividend
must be adjusted to take account of projected growth due to
the expected return on the reinvested earnings.

a. Adjusting Capitalization Rates for Growth

The way the theoreticians do this is to reduce the
capitalization rate that would otherwise have been appropriate
for the current dividend by the amount of the projected
growth rate, thereby increasing the multiplier. The growth
rate in the company's earnings due to reinvestment is equal
to the product of the company's internal rate of return on
its operating assets times the percentage of its earnings
which are reinvested in additional income-producing assets;
since it is assumed that the percentage of earnings paid out
as dividends remains constant, the same growth rate is
applicable to dividends. To see how the adjustment in the
capitalization rate for dividends works, suppose a company
earning $5.00 per share is paying an annual dividend of
$2.25 per share, for which an appropriate capitalization
rate without regard to growth would be 10%; $.75 is retained
each year for maintenance or replacement of existing capacity;
and $2.00 is invested annually in new income-producing
assets. That means that 40% of the company's earnings are
being retained for new investments; if the company's expected
internal rate of return was, say, 12½%, the growth rate
would be 5% (40% x 12.5%), which would be deducted from the
"normal" capitalization rate of 10% applicable to the company's
annual dividend, leading to a final capitalization rate for
the current dividend of 5%, or a multiplier of 20. The
resulting valuation would be $45 per share (which, it might

be noted, is the same figure that would be produced by
applying a multiplier of 9 to the total earnings per share
of $5).

Whatever may be said of this approach with respect to
public corporations, it obviously has little relevance in
the valuation of small, closely-held companies, where stockholders rarely expect or receive dividends. On the other
hand, the notion of adjusting the capitalization rate for
expected growth could also be applied in connection with a
straight-forward capitalization of earnings, to take account
of an estimated increase in the earnings stream. Thus if
the appropriate capitalization rate for the earnings of a
relatively risky closely-held company was 25% (a multiplier
of 4), but there was a solid basis for projecting growth in
earnings of, say, 10%, for the reasonably forseeable future,
the capitalization rate might be lowered to 15%, resulting
in a multiplier of 6 2/3. In practice, however, predicting
the growth rate for a small and risky business, especially
one of recent origin, is just too speculative to be indulged.
After all, a relatively new business might readily increase
its earnings as much as 50% or more in the early years, in
view of the small earnings base it is likely to be starting
from: that would not provide much of a foundation for
projecting the future growth rate of the enterprise. Instead,
the likely response to solid prospects for continued earnings
increases is simply to select a higher multiplier than would
otherwise be used, rather than attempting to inject a specific
adjustment formula into the already all too imprecise choice
of the multiplier which would be appropriate without regard
to growth.

Note on the Role of Long-Term Liabilities

One other special problem presented in applying the capitalization of earnings method to a small business relates to the handling
of long-term liabilities. In valuing a large enterprise, long-term debt,
particularly when it is represented by bonds held by the public, is
often treated as part of the ownership of the enterprise, along with
the equity, on the theory that the allocation between long-term debt
and equity is largely within the control of the parties and should
therefore not unduly affect the valuation of the enterprise. Under
this view of course the interest on the long-term debt is not deducted
in arriving at the "earnings" to be capitalized, and the resulting
enterprise value includes both the debt and equity components. The
value of the equity interest alone can then be determined by deducting the amount (or, if it is clearly substantially different, the value)
of the long-term debt from the total enterprise value figure.

Alternatively, it is possible to value the equity interest directly, by capitalizing just the post-interest income available for the equity. Under this approach it is common to use a somewhat higher capitalization rate (lower multiplier) than would be applied to pre-interest earnings, since the interest "comes off the top," so to speak, and represents the most secure, least risky portion of the total earnings stream.

To illustrate these two approaches, assume that a corporation has $500,000 of long-term debt, paying 12% interest, and an estimated earning power of $200,000 before interest. Under the first alternative, the value of the equity interest would be determined by choosing a multiplier for the earnings before interest, say 7, producing a figure of $1,400,000, from which would then be deducted the $500,000 debt to arrive at an equity value of $900,000. Under the second alternative, if the same multiplier of 7 was applied to the post-interest earnings of $140,000 available for equity (ignoring any tax effects), the result would be a value for the equity of almost $1,000,000. But if the multiplier applied to the earnings after interest is reduced to 6.5, perhaps reflecting the greater riskiness of the remaining earnings after the $60,000 for the debt comes "off the top", the value of the equity comes out at about the same $900,000 produced by the first alternative.

The role of long-term debt in the valuation of a small enterprise is a little more troublesome. For one thing, except for debt held by stockholders, which is often, as we shall see later, almost literally a form of equity, it is not very realistic to think of the long-term debt of a small business as akin to equity. Rather for the small enterprise long-term debt is more often than not just another way of meeting the shortage of working capital which tends to plague small businesses. Moreover, for a small enterprise, where the overall multiplier is not likely to be even as high as five, there is an enormous jump to the multiplier of 15 or more which is inherent in any normal interest rate on the debt. Accordingly, the first alternative above, under which the earnings before interest are capitalized and the face amount of the long-term debt is deducted, would tend to understate the value of the equity. It seems more sensible to use the second alternative, under which only the post-interest earnings available for the equity are capitalized, and to take account of the presence of any substantial amount of long-term debt in such cases by using a slightly lower multiplier than would otherwise be in order.

SECTION 2.   ALLOCATION OF MANAGERIAL CONTROL

A.   ALLOCATION OF DIRECTORSHIPS

Obviously, the matter of allocation of control over the affairs of the proposed business enterprise is of prime concern to the parties. There are of course three primary levels of control in the corporate hierarchy: (1) the stockholders, who elect the board of directors, and also have residual power over fundamental corporate changes such as an amendment of the certificate of incorporation or a merger; (2) the directors, to whom is committed general management of the business and affairs of the corporation; and (3) the officers, who in theory execute the policy determined by the directors, but in practice, particularly in a small business, often have wide latitude in determining the course of the operations of the business. Since the principal source of power to control the operations of the corporation resides in the board of directors, allocation of directorships is often the first order of business for each of the interested parties.

However, before pursuing this subject it should be recalled that under many of the modern corporation statutes the parties may throw tradition to the winds and opt not to have a board of directors at all, leaving the powers and duties of the directors to be performed by such person or persons as shall be provided in the articles. E.g., MBA §35. Under such a statute the management of the business could presumably be confided to one or more of the stockholders, or a designated officer, or perhaps even to some third person.

For corporations which follow the traditional path, under which the board represents the seat of power, each interested party can be expected to press for control of as many board positions as possible, and in any event at least one seat. The following constitutes a capsule review of the techniques most commonly used to achieve this objective.

1. Cumulative Voting

Under cumulative voting, each shareholder is entitled to cast as many votes as are equal to the number of his shares multiplied by the number of directors to be elected, and he may cast all of such votes for a single director or distribute them among the candidates as he sees fit. E. g., MBA §33. The formula for determining the number of the total voting shares of a corporation which are needed to elect one director may be expressed mathematically as $\dfrac{V}{n+1} + 1$ where V is the total number of voting shares of the corporation and n is the number of directors to be elected. Thus if, for example, there were four directors to be elected, it would take one-fifth (20%) of the stock plus one share to be sure of electing one of the directors.

Where cumulative voting is merely permitted rather than required, a shareholder relying on it to control a position on the board must make sure that he cannot be out-flanked by an amendment of the certificate of incorporation to eliminate cumulative voting. And even when cumulative voting is mandatory the value of the right may be impaired through such maneuvers as removal of a director, reduction in the number of directors, or classification of directors. Probably the best defense against these devices is a provision in the certificate prohibiting any such action if the votes cast against it would have been sufficient to elect a director under cumulative voting prior to the proposed change. Cf. MBA § 39.

Where cumulative voting is mandatory, the use of any other technique for the allocation of the voting control may be subject to challenge as inconsistent with cumulative voting. Indeed, where, as in some jurisdictions, cumulative voting is embodied in the state constitution, even a device expressly permitted in the corporation statute may be invalidated as inconsistent with the constitutional cumulative voting provision. Thus in Wolfson v. Avery, 6 Ill.2d 78, 126 N.E.2d 701 (1955), a longtime provision of the Illinois corporation statute similar to MBA §57 authorizing the division of directors into several classes with only one class being elected each year was held invalid on the ground that it impaired the right of cumulative voting guaranteed in the Illinois Constitution. On the other hand, in Janney v. Philadelphia Transportation Co., 387 Pa. 282, 128 A.2d 76 (1956), a similar contention was rejected on the ground that the Pennsylvania Constitutional provision requiring cumulative voting was intended simply to give a minority interest an opportunity to acquire representation on the board of directors, but did not purport to insure the maximum effectiveness of the exercise of that right. The court noted that the cumulative voting strength of a minority might be diluted by many techniques other than staggering the terms of directors, such as having a smaller board of directors, making the directors' terms of office longer than one year, or issuing non-voting stock, so that a decision holding classification of directors unconstitutional would presumably have required invalidating these well-recognized techniques also. It may be of some relevance that the provision in the Illinois Constitution requiring cumulative voting had also been construed to require that all stock be entitled to vote, whereas non-voting stock is permissible in Pennsylvania.

Where mandatory cumulative voting is provided by statute rather than in the constitution, other provisions of the corporation statute are of course of equal rank, and hence a provision inconsistent with cumulative voting need not necessarily yield. Thus in Humphrys v. The Winous Co., 165 Ohio St. 45, 133 N.E.2d 780 (1956), a corporation with three directors divided them into three classes as then permitted by the statute, so that only one director was elected each year. This meant that the plaintiff, who owned more than 40% of the voting stock, could not secure any representation on the board, despite the provision requiring cumulative voting in the Ohio corporation statute. Nevertheless, the Supreme Court of Ohio sustained the classification of the directors, holding that the cumulative voting provision did not nullify the classification provision. The court noted that in 1955 the legislature had amended the classification provision to require that each class consist of not less than three directors.

However, the result might be different if a technique was used for allocating voting control which was not only inconsistent with cumulative voting but also not expressly sanctioned by the corporation statute. This issue must be considered before any of the following other devices for allocation of voting control are used in a jurisdiction where cumulative voting is made mandatory by statute.

2. Classification of Shares

The devices of non-voting shares or several classes of shares are often used to achieve the allocation of directorships desired by the parties. Most corporation statutes, like MBA §15, permit the creation of several classes of stock, or one or more series of stock within a class, with such voting power, full, limited, or none, as may be provided in the certificate of incorporation. Under such a statute, it seems permissible to arrange for several different classes of common stock which are identical except for the fact that a specified number of the directors are to be elected by each class of shares. Thus if a corporation had three shareholders with unequal holdings of stock, representation for each of them on a three-man board of directors could be assured simply by dividing the stock into three classes and giving each class, regardless of the number of shares in the class, the right to elect one of the three directors. Dividends and liquidation rights would presumably be left on a share for share basis.

It should be noted that the allocation of voting power resulting from classification of shares could reach beyond the election of directors. Under statutes requiring certain types of transactions to be approved by "each class" of stock, such classification could result in giving a stockholder a veto power to which he would not be entitled under "straight" voting. This is much less of a problem under statutes like MBA § 60 which require a class vote only when the proposed transaction has some special impact on the particular class. In Shanken v. Lee Wolfman, Inc., 370 S.W.2d 197 (Tex.Civ.App.1963), each of a corporation's three stockholders owned a separate class of stock, the three classes being identical in all respects except that class

A had the right to elect three directors, and classes B and C one director each. There were 150 shares of stock authorized in each class, of which 100 had been issued to the respective stockholders. In connection with a contemplated acquisition of a related enterprise, the holders of classes A and B proposed that the authorized stock of each class be increased to 250 shares, but the plaintiff, who owned all of the class C stock, was able to block any increase in the authorized stock of his class under the Texas counterpart of MBA § 60(a). The other two stockholders then resolved simply to increase the aggregate number of the shares of classes A and B to 325 each. The plaintiff contended that he was also entitled to a class vote on this proposal, under a provision of the Texas statute (patterned on one originally included in the Model Act but dropped in the 1957 amendments) to the effect that "the holders of the outstanding shares of any class entitled to vote upon a proposed amendment by the provisions of the articles of incorporation shall be entitled to vote as a class thereon if the amendment . . . would change the shares of any class, whether with or without par value, into a different number of shares of the same class." *Held*, the proposed amendment did not *change* the original shares in classes A and B into a greater number of shares, but merely *added* 175 shares to each of such classes. The court also ruled that the proposed amendment did not "change the designations, preferences, limitations, or relative rights" of the plaintiff's class C stock within the meaning of the Texas counterpart of MBA §60 (e) because the *"quality and relative rights of the shares* in each class, as distinguished from the relative position of the classes in the capital structure, have remained identical."

As to the issue of whether classification can be squared with cumulative voting, consider the following:

OPINION OF THE ATTORNEY GENERAL OF MISSOURI

No. 238, 1964.

Your official opinion request of June 19, 1964, raises the following question relating to a corporation organized under the provisions of [the Missouri corporation statute].

> "May the Articles of Incorporation (or amendments) provide that each of two classes of voting stock shall elect one-half of the directors of a six-member board of directors, regardless of the number of voting shares in each class of stock?"

Article XI, Section 6 of the Missouri Constitution provides:

> "In all elections for directors or managers of any corporation, each shareholder shall have the right to cast as many votes in the aggregate as shall equal the number of shares held by him, multiplied by the number of directors or managers to be elected, and may cast the whole number of votes,

either in person or by proxy, for one candidate, or distribute such votes among two or more candidates; and such directors or managers shall not be elected in any other manner . . . ."

. . . The shareholders' right to "distribute such votes among two or more candidates" clearly means that each voting shareholder has a right to vote cumulatively for any or all directors to be elected and to have those votes counted.

The placing of limitations on the number of directors a class of stock may elect would completely ignore the number of votes within that class of stock and prevent the distribution of such votes as each shareholder desired. This is contrary to Article XI, Section 6 of the Constitution of Missouri, which clearly provides that shareholders may vote for all directors to be elected. In addition, the shareholders of a particular class might thereby be given voting power disproportionate to the number of votes to which such shareholders are entitled under the Constitution. On the other hand, the shareholders might be precluded from exercising their full voting power under the Constitution by not having their votes counted cumulatively towards the election of all directors. Under the Constitution shareholders entitled to vote do so as shareholders of the corporation and not as members of a particular class of stock. Therefore, we are of the opinion that Articles of Incorporation (or amendments) which would arbitrarily limit the voting rights of a particular class of voting stock to the election of one-half of the directors is inconsistent with the constitutional provision of cumulative voting. . . .

Just as classification may be utilized to allocate voting control while dividend and liquidation rights are left on a share for share basis, so it may be used to allocate dividends and liquidation rights while voting is left on a straight per share basis. Thus the certificate of incorporation might provide for three classes of stock, each entitled to a specified percentage of any dividend or liquidating distribution, for example, 50% for class A, 30% for class B, and 20% for class C, regardless of the number of shares in the class. Assuming that voting rights would be left on a per share basis, voting power would be the only matter affected by the number of shares in the respective classes, and hence the numbers could be fixed to achieve whatever voting allocation was desired.

Non-voting stock can also be used to make voting power disproportionate to total equity interest. For example, if three stockholders making unequal capital contributions wanted to have equal voting power, they could each take the same amount of voting stock, while satisfying any additional equity interest with non-voting stock which was identical as to dividends, liquidation rights and the like. However, it must be kept in mind that the use of non-voting stock also affects the allocation of voting power on matters other than election of directors, unless the statute permits shares which are non-voting only as to the election of directors and entitled to vote on all other matters.

3. Shareholder Voting Agreements

Another common device to fix the composition of the board of directors is an agreement by two or more shareholders to vote their shares as a unit. While such agreements may cover a wide range of matters upon which shareholders have the power to act, they most commonly relate to the election of directors. Here the agreement may specify that the shares are to be voted for particular named persons as directors; or it may provide simply that the shares are to be voted as a unit. In the latter case, the question arises as to how the shares are to be voted in the event of disagreement among the parties. Presumably, in the absence of some express provision covering disagreement, the shares cannot be voted at all if the parties can not agree.

In dealing with such agreements, often referred to as "pooling agreements", the courts have usually been confronted with two questions: (a) whether such agreements are contrary to public policy; and (b) if they are valid, how and against whom they may be enforced. Most of the cases involving such agreements have upheld their validity, at least where the agreement did not go beyond the legitimate sphere of shareholder activity and attempt to bind the discretion of directors as well. However, if the consideration for entering into a pooling agreement gives a private benefit to the shareholder, the pooling agreement may be invalidated. For example, in Palmbaum v. Magulsky, 217 Mass. 306, 104 N.E. 746 (1914), one of three shareholders agreed to cancel a debt owed to him by another shareholder if the latter would vote with him on the question of whether to sell all of the corporate assets. In a subsequent action on the debt, performance of this agreement was held to be no defense on the ground that the agreement "operated as a fraud" upon the third shareholder.

More difficulty has been encountered in determining the appropriate remedy for violation of such agreements. In Smith v. San Francisco & N. P. Ry. Co., 115 Cal. 584, 47 P. 582 (1897), an agreement between three shareholders that they would vote their shares in such manner as should be decided by a ballot among them was held to give the majority on such ballot an irrevocable proxy to vote the shares of the third member of the pool, regardless of the latter's objection. The three stockholders had purchased their stock in reliance upon an understanding that such an agreement would be made immediately after the purchase. But in Roberts v. Whitson, 188 S.W.2d 875 (Tex. Civ.App.1945), the court refused to enforce a pooling agreement between two shareholders which provided that the shares were to be voted jointly and that the decision of arbitrators would control in the event of a disagreement among the parties. In addition to holding that the provision for arbitration constituted an illegal separation of ownership and the power to vote, the court held that mere mutual promises were not sufficient consideration to make the pooling arrangement irrevocable.

The risk of relying on this kind of agreement is perhaps most strikingly illustrated by the now classic case of Ringling Bros.-Barnum & Bailey Combined Shows v. Ringling, 29 Del.Ch. 610, 53 A.2d 441 (Sup.Ct.Del.1947). There two of the three shareholders of the corporation, who owned slightly less than one-third of the stock each, executed an agreement which provided that they would vote their shares jointly and that in the event of any disagreement, they would submit the matter to a named arbitrator whose decision was to be binding upon the parties. After some years of maintaining control over the corporation's affairs by voting together, the parties fell out, and one of them sought to vote her own shares in violation of the directions of the arbitrator. The Chancellor upheld the agreement and found an implied proxy in the willing party to vote the shares of the unwilling party in accordance with the instructions of the arbitrator. On appeal, the Supreme Court also upheld the agreement but refused to find any implied proxy. Accordingly, the court confined relief to prohibiting the unwilling shareholder from voting her shares against the instructions of the arbitrator. The result of this decision was that the third shareholder, who controlled slightly more than one-third of the shares, assumed control of the corporation, the very circumstance which the voting agreement had been designed to prevent.

Another potential danger in a pooling agreement is illustrated by the contention in the Ringling case that the pooling agreement was invalid because it in effect constituted a voting trust which was invalid for failure to conform to the statutory requirements for such instruments. Although the Ringling court rejected this contention, it cannot be ignored, particularly under new corporation statutes like the Model Act which deal extensively with the requirements for a valid voting trust while making no reference whatever to pooling agreements. Moreover, subsequent to the Ringling case the Supreme Court of Delaware, in Abercrombie v. Davies, 36 Del.Ch. 371, 130 A.2d 338 (1957), held that a purported pooling agreement which was little different in practical effect from the one involved in Ringling, although it was admittedly somewhat more complicated and far-reaching, did constitute a voting trust and was therefore invalid for failure to comply with the statutory formalities.

Here again the modern corporation statutes have taken a hand. For example, MBA §34 responds to the foregoing difficulties by providing that shareholders' agreements for the voting of their shares shall be valid and enforceable in accordance with their terms, and shall not be subject to the provisions relating to voting trusts.

4. Other Arrangements

There are, of course, a variety of other possibilities for achieving the desired allocation of control in particular circumstances. A voting trust may be a useful technique in some situations, but the scope of this device is limited by statute in many jurisdictions, particularly as to the permissible duration which is normally confined to ten years. See MBA § 34.

Another useful device is the requirement of a higher than majority vote for shareholder action. E. g., MBA § 32. A shareholder unanimity agreement, under which no action can be taken by shareholders except by unanimous consent, is an extreme variation of this approach. However, in view of the normal presumption of majority rule in the absence of express statutory support, the validity of such a provision may be open to question. And even where such a provision is valid it would seem to be effective only to maintain the status quo, rather than as an independent means for securing a position on the board of directors. In other words, if the parties start with the desired allocation of directorships, a unanimity agreement among the stockholders would be effective to maintain that allocation; but in the event of changed circumstances, as for example the death of one of the directors, such a provision would not enable the interests formerly represented by the deceased director to elect his successor, but would only make it possible for them to block anyone they opposed.

Closely allied with the high vote requirement is the high quorum requirement. See MBA § 32. For example, requiring the presence of all of the shareholders for a quorum can be an indirect method for maintaining the status quo, since any shareholder can remain away from the meetings and thus eliminate any possibility of action prejudicial to his interests. Again, however, there is the question of whether such a quorum provision is valid in the absence of specific statutory support. In addition, there may be a question as to whether a shareholder may remain away from meetings for the sole purpose of preventing a quorum. Cf. Matter of Gearing, discussed at page 70 infra.

5. General Problems

Common to all of the foregoing devices for allocation of control is the question of the effect of a transfer of some or all of the stock of one of the parties, whether by sale, pledge, gift, or death. Of course this problem can be minimized by imposing restrictions upon the transfer of the stock, as is commonly done in close corporations. When a transfer does occur, the subsequent effect of the control arrangement may depend upon whether it is embodied in a corporate regulation, either a certificate of incorporation provision or a by-law, in which event it would presumably bind any transferee, or in a private shareholders' agreement, where it would probably not be binding upon a transferee unless he had notice of the agreement. So a certificate provision calling for cumulative voting (in a jurisdiction where cumulative voting is merely permissive) or for classification of shares would be no less binding upon a transferee than upon the original holder; but if the arrangement was incorporated in a shareholders' agreement a transferee might not be subject to the burdens, or entitled to the benefits, of the agreement.

There may be other distinctions between corporate regulations and outside agreements. Particularly because corporate regulations are likely to bind subsequent transferees of stock, such regulations may be held to a strict standard of compliance with the statutory "norm", whereas the parties to a voluntary shareholders' agreement may be free to waive or limit some of their statutory rights. Thus a particular allocation of voting power in a by-law or certificate of incorporation provision might be condemned as inconsistent with the statutory norm, although the same provision in a shareholders' agreement would be held valid and binding upon the parties to the agreement. The further consequence of this distinction is that when a by-law or certificate of incorporation provision is invalidated, the question may arise as to whether the invalid corporate regulation can be viewed as a contract among the shareholders who adopted it, and upheld to that extent. These problems are nicely illustrated in Sensabaugh v. Polson Plywood Company, 135 Mont. 562, 342 P.2d 1064 (1959), where, despite a provision in the Montana Constitution requiring cumulative voting, a committee of the corporation's directors (including the plaintiff) had proposed an amendment to the by-laws to eliminate cumulative voting in favor of "straight" voting for the election of directors, and the stockholders unanimously approved the amendment. A few years later the plaintiff and a few other stockholders sought to cumulate their votes, and upon being refused the plaintiff brought an action to invalidate the amended by-law as inconsistent with the constitutional provision. The court held unanimously that the constitutional provision prohibited the corporation from depriving the stockholders of the right of cumulative voting by any regulation or act on its part. And one member of the court took the view that a contract among the stockholders calling for "straight" voting would be equally void as inconsistent with the established public policy of the state. However, a majority of the court thought that the stockholders were free to contract with one another to limit or deny the right of cumulative voting even though the corporation could not do so. Therefore, the question was presented as to whether the invalid by-law could be enforced as a contract requiring "straight" voting among the stockholders who had adopted it. On this issue too the court divided, but a majority held that the by-law could not be enforced as a contract:

> "[There] must at all times be borne in mind the difference
> between stockholders' contracts between themselves without
> the realm of the corporate structure and those carried on or
> attempted within. Here we have the majority of the stock-
> holders, including plaintiff herein, in 1956 desiring to bind
> themselves from cumulative voting. If their purpose at that
> time was, as appears from the record, for the good of the cor-
> poration and themselves as stockholders, they could have
> easily entered into a valid contract between themselves to
> that end. . . . The Constitutional provision involved
> here was not designed as a restriction on the rights of stock-
> holders to make their contracts which violate no rule of the

common law, and which affect no rights, except their own. Here the stockholders did not do so without the realm of the corporate structure but carried it within, by amending the by-law. By such a method the majority attempted to bind all stockholders, including those not represented at the meeting when the by-law was amended."

6. Special Statutory Provisions

In recent years a number of corporation statutes have been amended expressly to validate shareholder voting agreements, and also to permit departures from the usual statutory norm that the corporation is to be managed by the board of directors, particularly for close corporations. In the Model Act, this development took the form of the addition, in 1968, of the last paragraph of section 35 the "except" clause at the end of the first sentence of section 35 and the second sentence of section 35 Delaware, on the other hand, in its 1967 revision, adopted an elaborate new subchapter relating to close corporations, consisting of sixteen sections of special provisions, including a definition of a close corporation (in terms of the stock being held of record by no more than thirty persons and being subject to one or more restrictions on transfer), validation of agreements restricting the discretion of directors, and permission to eliminate the board entirely and have the business managed by the shareholders. Somewhere between the Model Act and Delaware approaches is the following Rhode Island section, adopted in 1969 in connection with the revision of the Rhode Island corporation statute along otherwise essentially Model Act lines:

7-1.1-51. Special provisions relating to close corporations.—(a) Provisions of the articles of incorporation or by-laws of a corporation organized under this chapter, or provisions of an agreement relating to such a corporation, which would otherwise be invalid because they (i) restrict, or assign to one or more shareholders or other persons, any or all of the powers normally vested in the board of directors or provide that there shall be no board of directors, or (ii) grant the right to one or more stockholders to dissolve the corporation at will or on the occurrence of a specified contingency, or (iii) impose too great a restraint on the transfer of shares of the corporation, shall nevertheless be valid if such provisions have been approved by all the shareholders of the corporation and if the corporation's original or amended articles of incorporation contain a heading immediately after the name of the corporation stating that it is a close corporation pursuant to § 7-1.1-51. This subsection shall not be deemed to invalidate any provision in articles of incorporation, by-laws or agreements that would otherwise be valid. A provision authorized by clause (i) of this subsection may include a provision that there shall be no board of directors.

(b) The provisions of § 7-1.1-32 limiting the duration of a voting trust or shareholders' agreement to ten (10) years shall not be applicable to a close corporation that complies with subsection (a). If close corporation status is terminated pursuant to subsection (d), the effective term of voting trust or shareholders' agreement shall be ten (10) years from such termination or the term provided therein, whichever is shorter.

(c) The effect of any provision authorized by clause (i) of subsection (a) shall be to relieve the directors and to impose on the person or persons undertaking to exercise such responsibility the liability for managerial acts or omissions that would otherwise be imposed on directors to the extent that and so long as the discretion or powers of the board in its management of corporate affairs is controlled by any such provision. Action which is valid pursuant to clause (i) of subsection (a) will be deemed to be action by the board of directors for purposes of compliance with any provision of this chapter providing for action by the board of directors.

(d) The articles of incorporation shall be amended to terminate close corporation status pursuant to this section if:

(i) all of the shareholders, or such lesser number as may be specified in the articles of incorporation, the by-laws, or an agreement relating to the corporation, approve such termination; or

(ii) there are more than thirty (30) shareholders of record and any shareholder, after thirty (30) days' notice to the corporation of his intention to do so during which time such number is not reduced to thirty (30) or less, demands such termination; or

(iii) any person who acquires of record shares of the corporation without notice or knowledge of such close corporation status demands such termination, provided, that notice shall be conclusively presumed if certificates representing the shares so acquired state on their face, under the name of the corporation, that it is a close corporation pursuant to § 7–1.1–51.

If the directors and shareholders fail to effect such amendment promptly, the superior court shall have jurisdiction to enter whatever order is necessary to effect such amendment. Such termination shall not affect the validity of any provision relating to the corporation or its management which would be valid notwithstanding the provisions of this § 7–1.1–51.

B. ASSURING LONG-TERM EMPLOYMENT

Normally, it is contemplated that most if not all of the participants in a closely-held corporation will hold full-time positions with the company and will draw their basic livelihood from it. Hence, once the allocation of control at the board of directors level has been established, the parties are likely to turn their attention to assuring their respective roles as salaried officers or other employees of the corporation. A capsule review of the problems which may arise in accomplishing this seems in order at this point.

The appointment of corporate officers is normally a matter for the board of directors unless specifically reserved to the shareholders by the corporation statute. And the hiring of employees for the corporation, as well as fixing the compensation of corporate agents at whatever level, seems clearly within the mandate of the board of directors to "manage the business". Typically, at the outset of a venture this "statutory norm" presents no obstacle to fixing the original positions and compensation of the parties in accordance with their agreement. However, under many corporate statutes some officers must be reappointed each year. In addition, the board of directors often has the power to remove any officer or agent regardless of cause. E. g., MBA § 51. Hence, each party needs some assurance that the board will not change the status quo in the future.

Of course the hornbook general rule is that the discretion of the directors cannot be bound in advance. Nevertheless, at least in the close corporation area, some variation from this corporate norm is permitted. Thus today a contract among the shareholders of a closely-held corporation which includes provisions allocating positions and salaries among the participants will probably be effective to put the parties in those positions and keep them there, despite the fact that to this extent the future discretion of the directors has been curtailed.

An alternative to such a shareholders agreement, at least for positions which do not call for annual appointment, might be found in long-term employment contracts with the corporation. It is now clear that the board of directors has the power to execute an employment contract extending beyond its own term; and in the close corporation area it is likely that the duration of an employment contract, even one for the life of the employee, would not be a ground for invalidating it. However, such a contract might still be subject to the express or implied power of the corporation, acting through the board of directors, to terminate the employment regardless of cause. While such a removal would presumably give the employee a right to contract damages, cf. MBA § 51, this may not be sufficient protection to one who wants to continue to take an active role in the operations of the enterprise in which he has a substantial financial stake. A possible solution to this problem is suggested by the fact that a party who has control of at least one-half of the board of directors would seem to be entirely safe from this quarter, since he can prevent any affirmative action terminating his employment. Every employee who is also a director can obtain the same veto power over changes in his position or salary under a provision requiring a unanimous vote of the board of directors for any action affecting his employment arrangement.

Provisions requiring a higher than majority vote for action by the board of directors of a closely-held corporation have been receiving increasingly sympathetic treatment from the courts. In addition, many modern corporation statutes appear to expressly contemplate either a certificate of incorporation or by-law provision requiring a higher than majority vote by the directors. E. g., MBA § 39. And even in a jurisdiction where a requirement of a higher than majority vote for all action by directors might be invalid, such a requirement might be sustained if it were limited to a few particular matters within the board's competence.

At the board of director level, as at the shareholder level, the practical effect of a veto power may be achieved by setting a high quorum requirement for action by the directors. See MBA § 39. A provision requiring the presence of all the directors for a quorum would in effect give every director a veto power, since each could block any action by the board simply by staying away from the meeting. However, unless such a quorum provision can be combined with a rather strict requirement for notice of the business to be transacted at each director's meeting, any director seeking to block a matter would have to avoid every meeting, which would cut down the chances of getting the directors together to thrash out their differences. In addition, a recent New York decision, Matter of Gearing, 11 N.Y.2d 201, 182 N.E.2d 391 (1962), takes a dim view of such use of the quorum requirement, indicating that a director who stays away from directors' meetings in order to prevent the existence of a quorum may later be estopped from attacking action taken without the presence of a quorum.

C. ALLOCATION OF CONTROL OVER DESIGNATED AREAS OF OPERATION

Often the closely-held corporation constitutes a combination of quite different skills represented by the various participants. To what extent may a party be given complete control in the area of his special competence? In analyzing the following possible approaches to such an objective, be sure to consider also whether such an objective is a desirable one.

In view of the ultimate responsibility of the board of directors for "management of the business," it is generally assumed that any authority reposed in a corporate officer or other employee, whether that authority springs from a by-law, an employment contract, a resolution of the board of directors, or from the inherent powers of the particular corporate office involved, is subject to the supervision and control of the board of directors. To be sure, like any agent the corporate officer or employee may have power to bind the corporation well beyond his actual authority; but as between any officer or employee and the board of directors, the authority of the individual is subservient to the ultimate power of the board. Accordingly, even if a by-law expressly conferred very broad authority upon one of the officers, for example in a particular sphere of operations such as sales or production, the exercise of that authority would presumably still be subject to the ultimate control of the board. And it seems unlikely that anything short of a clear statutory mandate would be sufficient to authorize a departure from this normal corporate hierarchy—which is probably a complete answer to the possible implication the other way in the second paragraph of MBA § 50

Assuming that a by-law, however broadly phrased, would still leave the corporate officer or employee subservient to the will of the directors, what would be the effect of a deadlock among the directors which made it impossible to say what the board's will was? Surely a stalemate among the directors should not necessarily paralyze the operations of the business, and presumably each officer or employee would be empowered to continue to carry on his normal operations. But suppose, for example, the vice-president in charge of sales, operating under a very broad by-law authorization in that area, proposed to pursue some change in sales policy, and the board of directors was evenly divided on the matter. One view of the situation would be that once the board of directors has considered a matter within its competence, it has assumed "jurisdiction" of the matter, and a deadlock means that the matter failed to carry. On the other hand, it might be contended that if the proposed action is within the general authority delegated to the officer, he is authorized to act unless the board affirmatively denies him permission. Under this view, the deadlock of the directors would mean that permission had not been refused, and the officer would remain free to act.

Under the view that the officer's authority remains unimpaired in the face of a board of directors deadlock, any party can be given virtually complete control in a particular area by giving him very broad express authority, together with power to deadlock the board. And it would seem that the power to deadlock can be achieved for any party who is a director by requiring unanimity among the directors for any action on a matter relating to the particular area, so that in effect the person would have a veto power over any interference with his exercise of authority.

There is only scant authority on the question of the power of an officer to act in the face of a deadlocked board, and practically all of what there is comes from the same jurisdiction, New York, relates to the same corporate office, the presidency, and involves the same type of action, the instigation of litigation on behalf of the corporation. In Sterling Industries, Inc., v. Ball Bearing Pen Corp., 298 N.Y. 483, 84 N.E.2d 790 (1949), the plaintiff corporation was owned and controlled equally by two groups, one of which also owned the defendant company. After the plaintiff and defendant had entered into a contract, the plaintiff's president called a special meeting of its board of directors to consider the advisability of instituting suit against the defendant for an alleged breach of that contract. At the meeting, the directors were evenly divided and the president declared that the motion had failed to carry. Nevertheless, the president later caused the plaintiff to institute suit against the defendant. The court held that the suit should be dismissed as unauthorized, on the ground that any actual or implied authority of the president to commence the action was terminated when a majority of the board failed to sanction it. The court relied upon the "statutory norm" that the business of the corporation should be managed by the board of directors, and remitted the president to a stockholder's derivative action.

However, Paloma Frocks, Inc. v. Shamokin Sportswear Corp., 3 N.Y.2d 572, 147 N.E.2d 779 (1958), seems to suggest an important distinction. Here it was the defendant corporation which was owned and controlled by two groups, one of which also controlled the plaintiff corporation. The two corporations entered into a contract which included a provision for submitting any dispute to arbitration. After some performance under the contract, the president of the defendant served a demand on the plaintiff for arbitration under the contract. The plaintiff sought an injunction against the proposed arbitration on the ground that it had never been authorized by the defendant's directors. The president of the defendant conceded that the directors of the defendant had not acted, but contended that a meeting of the board would have been an idle gesture since the group interested in the plaintiff corporation would never have voted for the arbitration and the board would have been deadlocked. *Held*, reversing the lower court which had relied upon the Sterling Industries case, the president of the defendant was authorized to institute the arbitration proceeding. The Court of Appeals purported to distinguish the Sterling case on two grounds, the first being that in Sterling the president had asked the board's permission to bring the suit and had failed to obtain the consent of a majority, whereas in this case the board had never acted at all on the matter. Second, in the instant case the president of the defendant was merely carrying out an existing agreement that all disputes should be submitted to arbitration; although the board of directors presumably had the power to forbid a particular arbitration, they had not done so here.

The first ground of distinction in the Paloma Frocks case was carried to a perhaps drily logical extreme in West View Hills, Inc. v. Lizau Realty Corp., 6 N.Y.2d 344, 160 N.E.2d 622 (1959). There the plaintiff corporation was owned by three equal stockholders who were also its three directors. The same three men had also formerly been equal stockholders and the three directors of the defendant corporation, but shortly before the commencement of this action, the one who was the president of the plaintiff had sold his stock in the defendant to the other two and severed his connections with the defendant. Subsequently, the president of the plaintiff launched it on this suit against the defendant and the two other individuals on a claim that they had caused the plaintiff to perform valuable construction services for the defendant without any compensation. The defendants contended that the suit should be dismissed on the ground that the board of directors of the plaintiff had never authorized it. The Court of Appeals held that the president's authority to commence an action on behalf of the plaintiff corporation was not eliminated because a majority of the board of directors were in a position to withhold authorization. Once again the court distinguished the Sterling case on the ground that there the president's authority to bring suit was effectively terminated by the board's refusal to sanction it, whereas here the board of directors had never taken any action prohibiting the president's bringing of the suit. Two judges dissented, finding that the decision of the majority conflicted with the basic principle that the corporation was to be managed by the board of directors. The dissent contended that however relevant the absence of direct prohibition against the bringing of suit by the directors might be in a deadlock situation, it could hardly be decisive where the president knew that an actual majority of the board opposed the suit. In the view of the dissenting judges, the majority opinion amended the corporation statute to read that the corporation "shall be managed by its board of directors, except when one member of the board, who happens to be president, disagrees with the majority, in which case it shall be managed by the president." Incidentally, the court seemed to ignore the fact that the corporation in question was a Connecticut corporation, as appears in Zaubler v. West View Hills, Inc., 148 Conn. 540, 172 A.2d 604 (1961), where the president obtained an injunction against a withdrawal of the New York suit after he had been removed as president and a director of the corporation by the other two directors.

A similar control allocation might be achieved by making a broad delegation of the powers of the board in particular areas to executive committees, coupled with a provision for deadlocking the full board. Even assuming that such committees would have to consist of more than one director, the composition of each committee could be fixed to maximize the influence of particular persons in particular areas of operation.

Another technique for allocating control over specific areas of the business to particular persons might be the use of multiple corporations. For example, suppose the parties organizing an ordinary manufacturing enterprise want to allocate special control over sales matters to one of the parties and over production matters to another. If separate corporations for sales and production were organized, it would be possible, by the use of non-voting shares, classification, or other techniques discussed earlier, to give the designated persons control of the board of directors of the respective corporations. Under this approach, it would not be necessary to try to put an officer's authority beyond the control of the board of directors. Presumably, the allocation of financial interests in the two corporations among the parties would be identical, since otherwise there would be a real conflict between the two corporations in their mutual dealings, and the whole nature of the over-all enterprise would be drastically changed.

There are, however, some difficulties with this multiple corporation route. For one thing, giving a person control of the board of directors of one of the corporations goes well beyond the allocation of control over a particular sphere of operations such as sales or production. Such control would also encompass all the other areas within the competence of the board of directors, including the payment of dividends. In addition, any party other than the two persons to whom the control over the respective corporations would be allocated would not share in control at all under this approach, whereas with only one corporation there would be room for such a party to wield some influence. Of course such difficulties might be met by confining the power of the designated persons to the specified areas of operations, presumably by the use of veto powers and the like. Or perhaps the separate operating corporations could be made wholly-owned subsidiaries of a common parent, which would be governed by the parties' more general allocation of control. However, if resort to such devices becomes necessary query whether the multiple corporate set-up is worth undertaking, at least so far as allocation of control is concerned.

SECTION 3. ALLOCATION OF INTERESTS IN A NEW ENTERPRISE

A. NOTE ON THE CHARACTERISTICS OF VARIOUS TYPES OF STOCKS AND BONDS *

The various types of business units—sole proprietorships, partnerships, business trusts, corporations—all are distinctive modes of organizing business enterprise. *They are modes of allocating three elements of enterprise: (1) the risk of loss, (2) the power of control, and (3) the participation in the proceeds of the business activity.* In corporate enterprises it is the corporate "capital structure" through which this allocation of risk, control, and profit is effected. Capital structure refers to the aggregate of the "securities" issued by the corporation—the instruments, such as shares of stock and bonds, which represent relatively long term investment in the corporation. The distribution of risk, control, and profit is worked out through the fixing of the terms of the various classes of securities and their relative amounts in the capital structure.

The most important characteristics of corporate securities as forms of investment are their variations with regard to: (1) the right to an early claim on the income of the enterprise before other security holders receive any payments; (2) the right to the "residual" income, however large, after others have been paid promised amounts; and (3) the right to vote on personnel and policy in the corporation, and hence the power to control the corporation.

The arrangement of the capitalization section of the balance sheet illustrates the traditional classification of corporate securities based upon the distinction between debt securities and shares of stock (preferred or

---

* The following material is adapted, with permission, from unpublished materials prepared by Professor Wilbur G. Katz of the University of Wisconsin Law School.

common). For many purposes, however, a more significant distinction is that between "senior" securities, which have a prior and limited claim upon earnings, and securities with a residual interest in earnings. Securities in this second category are often called "equity" securities, a usage traceable to the term "equity of redemption" in connection with mortgaged property. In classifications based on this distinction, senior securities include both debt securities and the typical preferred stock; equity securities include not only common stock but also the "participating preferred stock" described below.

Before describing securities in detail, one point should be emphasized: that the rights of preferred shareholders and bondholders (and of common shareholders if there are several classes of them) are a matter of contract. For a draftsman, the security is whatever he chooses to make it. There are historically certain characteristics which are common to specific types of securities. Even they may vary with business conditions, for the primary consideration is what is most attractive to the market at the time. In a period of prosperity, for example (such as 1956–57), a conversion feature is often found in debentures as well as preferred stock.

The traditional forms of securities will therefore be first described, then some of the more frequent variations and hybrid categories.

Debt Securities

Typical debt securities (bonds, debentures, notes) are issued in bearer form, although provision is often made for registration in the owners' names. They carry no voting rights in the election of directors and are issued with a stated maturity date on which the principal or "face" amount is payable. Gradual reduction of the amount outstanding is often provided, either by serial maturities or by a *"sinking fund."* The latter is an arrangement under which specified amounts are periodically applied to the retirement of the securities. The sinking fund installments are sometimes fixed and unconditional; in other cases they are made partly or wholly contingent upon earnings.

Debt securities are typically *redeemable* at the option of the corporation, usually at the face amount plus a premium which declines as the maturity date approaches. The redemption privilege is important, for when interest rates decline it may become profitable to "refund," i. e., to replace the issue with another carrying a lower interest rate.

Typical debt securities carry an obligation to pay *fixed interest,* i. e., whether or not income has been earned. The interest obligation is usually represented by semi-annual "coupons" (small notes attached to the bonds) which are detached and surrendered in exchange for the semi-annual interest payments.

Debt securities are often issued pursuant to an *"indenture,"* an elaborate contract between the corporation and a trustee for the benefit of the holders of the securities. Indenture provisions are of great variety and have an important bearing upon the risk assumed by the security holder. The federal Trust Indenture Act of 1939 prescribes requirements for indentures and qualifications for indenture trustees.

Holders of debt securities are, of course, creditors and, as such, in the event of default their remedies include those of initiating proceedings for receivership, bankruptcy, or reorganization, although some of these remedies are often limited by provisions of the indenture. It is easy to overemphasize the formal rights of the various security holders. When a corporation becomes bankrupt and unable to meet its financial obligations, a compromise agreement is usually worked out whereby all classes of security holders make some sacrifice, scaling down their interests in order to keep the corporation in operation because it is worth more as a going concern.

Mortgage Bonds. In this type of debt security, the indenture constitutes a mortgage upon described property of the corporation, the indenture trustee being mortgagee for the benefit of the bondholders. Mortgage security theoretically makes available the usual remedies of mortgage foreclosure; but what is of greater practical importance, the mortgage establishes priorities which are respected in large measure in proceedings for corporate reorganization. Mortgage indentures typically contain elaborate covenants covering maintenance and insurance of mortgaged property, payment of taxes, etc., and defining events of default which may justify acceleration of the maturity of the bonds.

Another type of secured obligation is the collateral trust bond. Here the property standing as security consists of other securities pledged to the indenture trustee for the protection of the bondholders.

Debentures. This is the customary term for relatively long-term debt securities which have no mortgage or pledge of corporate property. These obligations rest upon the general credit of the corporation and upon the force of the various indenture covenants, such as prohibitions against incurring further indebtedness, the mortgaging of corporate property to other creditors, the payment of dividends, etc.

Shares of Stock

Stock certificates (unlike typical debt securities) are issued in the name of the holder and transfer is made on his written order and on surrender of the certificate. The relative rights of holders of various classes of stock are usually prescribed in the corporation's certificate of incorporation. Under some statutes, however, preferred stock may be issued in series the respective terms of which may be fixed by the board of directors.

Cumulative Preferred Stock. Holders of typical preferred shares are entitled to dividends at a specified rate per year in priority to dividend distributions on common shares. Typical preferred shares are non-participating in that their holders are limited to dividends at the rate specified regardless of the amount of earnings or of the dividends paid on common shares. Preferred dividends (unlike bond interest) are not payable unconditionally but only from earnings or other funds legally available under the statute governing dividends. Preferred dividends are typically *cumulative*, i. e., if dividends for any year are not paid currently they accumulate (whether earned or not) and must be paid before any dividends may be paid on common shares. Accumulations of preferred dividends are not technically a debt but merely a priority in future dividend distributions. Only when dividends have been declared are they listed among the liabilities on corporate balance sheets, although arrearages should be disclosed parenthetically or by footnote. No interest or additional dividends accrue on the accumulations however long they remain unpaid. As will be seen in a later chapter, directors have wide discretion as to the time of paying dividends and typical preferred shareholders have no remedies comparable to those of holders of debt securities when interest is in arrears.

Investment in typical preferred stock is a long-term investment; there is no "maturity" date on which the stock must be retired. On dissolution or other liquidation of the corporation, preferred stock often has a specified *liquidation preference,* usually an amount approximating the amount of the investment plus dividend arrearages. (Often the preference is slightly greater in the event of "voluntary dissolution" than "involuntary dissolution.") Typical preferred shares, like debt securities, are made redeemable at the option of the corporation and sometimes the charter provides for a sinking fund for the retirement of preferred stock.

Preferred stock frequently carries no ordinary *voting rights* in the election of directors, except in a state like Illinois where all classes of shares must have one vote per share. It is common, however, to provide for *contingent voting rights* when preferred dividends are in arrears. These provisions typically permit the preferred shareholders then to elect a specified number of directors, sometimes a majority of the board. In addition, corporate statutes usually give the preferred stock a class vote on certain fundamental matters such as merger or dissolution, as well as on other proposed changes which may adversely affect the interests of the preferred. And of course the scope of protection to the preferred by class vote may be expanded by appropriate provision in the certificate of incorporation.

Participating Preferred Stock. Among the special classes of stock, the most common are those which entitle the holder to an initial preferred dividend and also (after the junior stock has received its initial dividend) to participation in further distributions on a parity with the junior stock. These are "participating preferred shares" and are sometimes given other names, such as "Class A Common." Provisions applicable to such shares are not standardized, but the initial preferred dividend is now usually made cumulative. It is usual, also, for such shares to have an initial preference on liquidation with further participation after an initial distribution on junior shares.

Common Stock. Typical common stock is easily described since it represents the residual interest in corporate assets, earnings and control. Occasionally common stock is divided into two classes which are identical except that voting rights are in one class exclusively.

Warrants are essentially contracts, pursuant to which the corporation agrees to sell to the holder a certain number of shares at a specified price. They are frequently sold to the public along with an issue of bonds or stock, and are sometimes issued to investment bankers as a bonus, or in a reorganization to holders whose claims were not otherwise recognized.

Convertibles and Other Hybrid Securities

Both debentures and preferred shares are often made convertible at the option of the holder into common shares at a specified rate. The rate is typically such that at the outset the debenture or preferred share is worth more than the common shares into which it is convertible. The value of the conversion privilege lies in the possibility of appreciation of the common shares. Frequently the conversion rate is on a sliding scale with the holder entitled to fewer common shares as conversion is postponed. After the necessary appreciation of the common shares, the market fluctuations of the convertible security follow closely those of the corresponding common shares.

Convertible securities (like other debt securities and preferred shares) are typically made redeemable, but the conversion privilege continues after notice of redemption is given until the date fixed for actual redemption. Thus while an ordinary debenture or preferred share will not frequently reach a market level above its redemption price, this is not true of a convertible. Convertible securities require carefully drafted provisions against "dilution" of the conversion privilege through transactions such as splits of common shares and stock dividends. Under such provisions the number of common shares into which the security is convertible is increased proportionately in the event of such transactions.

As already noted, rights of preferred shareholders and bondholders are largely a matter of contract. It is therefore possible to create stock which approximates the characteristics of debt securities. The most common of these hybrid types is the "income bond" or debenture, a debt security on which interest is payable only to the extent covered by the corporate earnings. In addition, there are subordinated debentures, which are subordinated to other borrowings. None of these features is mutually exclusive and there is practically no limit to the variety of combinations which the draftsman may adopt.

Preferred share provisions sometimes make it mandatory that dividends be declared if earnings are available. Furthermore, preferred shares are sometimes issued with a maturity date on which they must be retired. Here the character of a debt security is approached, although such matured preferred shares do not rank as a debt if the corporation is insolvent.

Capital Structures

In considering capital structures there are at least two separate questions to consider: (1) What should be the relation between the basic equity interests and senior securities? (2) What type of senior securities should be issued?

The answer to the first question will vary widely in accordance with the circumstances of the company and the industry. The S.E.C., for example, has a working policy of 60–10–30; i. e., sixty percent funded debt, ten percent preferred stock, and thirty percent common stock, for public utilities subject to their jurisdiction. (22d Annual Report of the S.E.C. (1956), p. 159.) Earnings must be relatively steady and predictable (as in this industry) in order to justify such a heavy ratio of debt and preferred. On the other hand, if the concern were closely held, and the senior securities were held by the owners of the common, there would be little risk if the company were in default, and hence greater justification for "thin capitalization." Though by no means assured, this device may afford stockholders equal participation with outside creditors in the event of bankruptcy and the further possibility of tax advantages. These points will be considered later in this chapter.

In any event, whenever senior securities are to be issued to outsiders, consideration must be given to the types and amount of the corporation's other outstanding securities. The risk of the holder of a debt security is of course reduced by the existence of substantial junior investment. The assets and earning power provided by the junior investment constitute a safety factor, or cushion, for the holders of the senior securities. It is equally obvious that the risks and dividend prospects of a common shareholder are affected by the amount and character of outstanding senior securities.

. . .

B. NOTE ON SPECIAL PROBLEMS IN PLANNING SENIOR SECURITIES

The term "senior securities" encompasses all interests in the corporation having either an earnings or assets claim which is prior to that of the basic common stock equity. Obviously such senior claims may take the form of either debt or equity interests—indeed, as noted in Chapter I, the line between the two has become rather blurred, and at least in economic terms seems less significant than the line between basic equity on the one hand and any type of senior security on the other. Nevertheless, even the most modern corporation statutes give little evidence of any departure from the traditional distinction between debt as a representation of a creditor's claim and equity as the embodiment of a proprietary interest.

So far as the preparation of senior securities is concerned, any type of stock would be governed by MBA § 15 and its counterparts which give the parties very broad power to fix the terms of any stock issued by the corporation; and of course the terms of debt securities are almost exclusively a matter of private agreement between the parties. Accordingly, the preparation of senior securities is primarily a planning exercise, calling for a recognition of the likely problems, a judgment as to how they should be resolved (which may ultimately be determined by negotiations between the parties), and careful draftsmanship to assure that the intention of the parties is clearly expressed. The following material is designed to illustrate both a number of the classic senior security problems which the parties must resolve and the possible fate of careless drafting.*

---

1. ANNUAL RETURN ON SENIOR SECURITIES

---

a. DIVIDENDS ON PREFERRED STOCK

In the absence of special provisions, of course, the payment of dividends on any stock, preferred or common, is within the discretion of the directors. Hence a "preference" in dividends usually amounts in the first instance to no more than a right to be paid *first*, when and if any dividend payments are made.

A dividend preference may take a variety of forms, ranging all the way from a mere specified preferred dividend, "and no more", to a full right of participation with the common in any further distribution, presumably after the common have first received a dividend equal to the preferred's.

---

* Some of the material in this note is adapted, by permission, from Baker & Cary, Cases on Corporations (3d ed., unabridged 1959) 955–1009.

What happens when the terms of the preferred stock do not specify whether the preferred is limited to the specified dividend? The authorities are divided on whether to presume that preferred are entitled, in addition to any express priorities they may have, to all the rights of the common unless the contrary is expressly provided, see St. Louis Southwestern Railway Co. v. Loeb, 318 S.W.2d 246 (Mo.1958); Christ, Rights of Holders of Preferred Stock to Participate in the Distribution of Profits, 27 Mich.L.Rev. 731 (1929), or to assume that any specified priority in dividends for the preferred precludes any further participation unless it is specifically provided for, the view apparently preferred by most of the commentators. E. g., Tennant v. Epstein, 356 Ill. 26, 189 N.E. 864 (1934); see Stevens, Corporations (1949) 481, Ballantine, Corporations (1946) 506. An analogous question to be considered below is whether the mere existence of a liquidation preference gives rise to a presumption that the preferred is limited to that amount upon a liquidation.

Turning now to the specified preferred dividend itself, the primary question is the extent to which it is cumulative, that is, whether and to what extent unpaid back dividends on the preferred must be paid before any dividends are paid on the junior securities. The range of possibilities extends from the traditional non-cumulative provision, under which there are no rights of any kind in dividends not paid, to the classic cumulative clause, which calls for complete cumulation of unpaid dividends, even those not earned.

However, certain recognized variations of these polar positions tend to bring them closer together, and indeed may even make them virtually identical. Thus a cumulative preference might be regarded as calling for cumulation only as to dividends actually earned, a construction which has sometimes been adopted in liquidation preference cases, as will be discussed below. Such a provision would then be little different from the New Jersey version of non-cumulative preferred under its so-called "dividend credit rule", where it is held that in the absence of express provision to the contrary, a non-cumulative preferred dividend nevertheless cumulates for any year in which it is earned. E. g., Sanders v. Cuba Railroad Co., 21 N.J. 78, 120 A.2d 849 (1956). In that case the court analyzed the rule in the following terms:

> It may be acknowledged that New Jersey's dividend credit rule has not generally been accepted by the other states or in the federal courts. See Wabash Railway Co. v. Barclay, 280 U.S. 197 . . . . . In the recent case of Guttmann v. Illinois Central R. Co., 189 F.2d 927, 930 (2 Cir., 1951), . . . Judge Frank expressed the view that nothing in the terms of the ordinary non-cumulative preferred stock contract points to "a contingent or inchoate right to arrears of dividends" and that the contrary notion is an invention "stemming from considerations of fairness, from a policy of protecting investors in those securities." There seems to be little doubt that equitable factors did play a significant part in the development of New Jersey's doctrine. In the Wabash Railway case, supra, Justice Holmes stated that there was a common understanding that dividends which were passed (though there were profits from which they could have been declared) were forever gone insofar as non-cumulative preferred stock was concerned; but he referred to no support-

ing materials and there are those who have suggested a diametrically opposite understanding. See Lattin, Non-Cumulative Preferred Stock, 25 Ill.L.Rev. 148, 157 (1930).

This much is quite apparent—if the common stockholders, who generally control the corporation and will benefit most by the passing of the dividends on the preferred stock, may freely achieve that result without any dividend credit consequences, then the preferred stockholders will be substantially at the mercy of others who will be under temptation to act in their own self-interest. . . . While such conclusion may sometimes be compelled by the clear contractual arrangements between the parties there is no just reason why our courts should not avoid it whenever the contract is silent or is so general as to leave adequate room for its construction. In any event, New Jersey's doctrine has received wide approval in legal writings and there does not seem to be any present disposition in this court to reject it or limit its sweep in favor of the Supreme Court's approach in the Wabash Railway case.

As a further illustration of how close these two rules may come, it might be observed that in the Guttmann case, referred to in the foregoing excerpt from the Sanders opinion, the plaintiff was actually contending for only a rather limited version of the New Jersey dividend credit rule, which would have conditioned the application of the rule not only on the existence of earnings but also their availability for distribution, in the sense of not having been invested in fixed assets or the like; on the other hand, in the Sanders case, it was suggested that the New Jersey court should limit the operation of the dividend credit rule on just such a basis, with the court incidentally displaying little enthusiasm for the suggestion.

The New Jersey dividend credit rule is not the only doctrine which has developed to mitigate or avoid the rigors of the traditional non-cumulative view. For one thing, an ambiguous preferred stock instrument seems likely to be presumed to be cumulative. See Buxbaum, Preferred Stock—Law and Draftsmanship, 42 Cal.L.Rev. 243, 244 (1954). Moreover, assuming a clear non-cumulative provision, a court may be more likely to find that the dividend is "mandatory", that is, that the dividend must be paid for any year in which it is earned, than if the stock were cumulative. Id. at 254. Of course this "mandatory" issue is also one that should be clearly resolved in the drafting, whether or not the stock is non-cumulative.

b. INTEREST ON DEBT SECURITIES

Typically of course the annual interest on debt is payable in all events, at least once a year, without regard to the earnings of the enterprise or the discretion of the directors. However, there are so-called "income" bonds on which interest is payable only to the extent earned, which comes rather close to a mandatory preferred stock. In planning an income bond, questions may arise reminiscent of the distinction between cumulative and non-cumulative preferred: for example, is interest which is not earned, and hence not paid, in a prior year required to be paid in any subsequent year in which the net earnings exceed the interest due for that year?

2. RIGHTS ON LIQUIDATION

a. PREFERRED STOCK

Although preferences on liquidation are still in common use, their practical value is somewhat doubtful, at least in the case of involuntary liquidation. Typically such a liquidation is the fate of a failing enterprise, and at such a time there is rarely anything left over for stockholders, so that preferences among them are of little moment. The situation may be different in the case of a voluntary liquidation, of course—and this may be one reason why some preferred stock contracts differentiate between the two types of liquidation with regard to the existence and the amount of any preference. Where that is the case, any collateral reference to liquidation preferences, for example in a contractual limitation on reduction of capital, must clearly indicate which one is meant. This precaution was carefully observed in the Model Act, e. g., §§ 21, 46(d), 66 and 69, although it is not entirely clear just how or why the particular choices reflected there were made.

It should be noted that while stock may often have a liquidation preference but no dividend preference, a cumulative dividend preference should seemingly always be accompanied by a liquidation preference and that preference should include any unpaid dividends. Otherwise, the junior stockholders, who usually control the management, might be tempted to pass preferred dividends in contemplation of a liquidation and thus deprive preferred stockholders of their dividends.

Assuming a liquidation preference which does include unpaid cumulative dividends, in some such language as "par plus accrued dividends", the question has arisen whether this includes the unpaid dividends for years in which they were not earned. In Hay v. Hay, 38 Wash.2d 513, 230 P.2d 791 (1951), where the corporation being liquidated had never had any earnings, the court held (en banc, with four dissents) that the liquidation preference included the dividends for all prior years, against the objection that this resulted in part of the investment of the common stockholders being distributed to the preferred stockholders. The closeness of this question is further illustrated by Wouk v. Merin, 238 App.Div. 522, 128 N.Y.S.2d 727 (1st Dept. 1954), where the contrary result was reached, once again by a divided court.

A question previously alluded to is whether the existence of a specified liquidation preference exhausts the rights of the preferred on liquidation despite the absence of a specific provision to that effect. In Mohawk Carpet Mills, Inc. v. Delaware Rayon Corp., 35 Del.Ch. 51, 110 A.2d 305 (Del.Ch. 1954), the preferred stock had a specified non-cumulative dividend of 10%, an express right to participate equally with the common in any further dividends after the payment of a 10% dividend on the common, and a liquidation preference of "par value . . . before any payment in liquidation is made" to the common. In holding that the express liquidation preference was "clearly exhaustive", the court emphasized the absence of any express right to participate in liquidation beyond the specified liquidation preference, in contrast with the presence of such a participation provision in connection with dividends. The court did not comment on the fact that under its interpretation the common would have a great incentive to resist the payment of any dividends, at least once a liquidation was contemplated, since upon liquidation the common would get all the accumulated earnings while the preferred merely got back its par value.

b. DEBT SECURITIES

Of course all debt securities have an inherent priority over any form of equity interest. Among themselves, however, in the absence of some special provision all creditor's claims, including accrued but unpaid interest on interest-bearing debt (but not interest on defaulted interest), stand on the same footing.

The most common device for giving one class of creditors priority over another is a security interest, such as a mortgage on some specified property. While an analysis of mortgage bonds or other secured instruments is beyond the scope of these materials, it may be observed that security indentures are among the most complicated (and cumbersome) of legal instruments. Just to illustrate the types of problems which must be considered, the planner must decide whether a particular mortgage is to be "closed", meaning that no more securities may be issued under that lien, or "open-end", meaning there may be successive issues secured by the same lien. At the same time a decision must be reached on what is almost the converse question, i. e., whether to include an "after-acquired property" clause, under which property obtained by the borrower subsequent to the mortgage nevertheless becomes subject to the lien of the mortgage. Such clauses are particularly ticklish because courts tend to read them rather strictly, if indeed they uphold them at all as against intervening lienors —and caution may dictate the inclusion of a requirement that the corporation deliver supplemental mortgages on after-acquired property at stated intervals.

Another illustration of a special provision varying the normal priority of claims is a subordination clause, under which a particular class of creditors agrees to defer its claims to those of another class. Here too there are a host of issues on which some resolution must be reached and then clearly expressed, such as the time and amount of the subordination, and the classes it is intended to benefit.

---

3. VOTING RIGHTS

One of the clearest illustrations of the traditional distinction between debt and equity is in the area of voting rights. Under most corporation statutes, any type of stock, preferred or common, is normally presumed to be fully entitled to vote, although the modern permissive provisions like MBA § 15 do give the parties broad power to limit or deny the voting power of any class. Moreover, under some statutes even a class of stock which is given no right to vote by the certificate of incorporation nevertheless retains the right to vote on certain fundamental matters such as, for example, merger and consolidation. E. g., Del.Corp.Law § 251; contra, MBA §§ 59,73.

As to debt securities, on the other hand, only a few states, such as California and Delaware, have provisions expressly permitting such securities to have voting rights. In the absence of such express authority, there is considerable doubt as to the validity of a provision giving voting rights to debt securities. To be sure, a class of debt securities can obtain the virtual equivalent of a class vote on any matter by providing, as a term of the securities, that such matter requires the consent of a specified percentage of the holders of the debt securities. But a private contract may well not be effective to convey regular voting rights, i. e., for the election of directors; and a provision in the certificate of incorporation giving voting rights to debt securities seems likely to founder upon the fairly clear implication in sections like MBA § 15 that voting rights are an attribute of stock, notwithstanding the broad permission in such sections as MBA § 48(i) to include "any provision, not inconsistent with law, which the incorporators elect to set forth in the articles of incorporation for the regulation of the internal affairs of the corporation."

Coming back to the voting rights of preferred stock, it should be noted that even a right to vote on a share for share basis with the common may not constitute "equal" voting rights for the preferred, unless the required investment per share for the two classes is approximately the same. In other words, there is a considerable disparity in voting rights if the preferred stock gets one vote per share constituting an investment of $100, and the common stock gets one vote per share representing $5.

Today the most common practice is to give contingent voting rights to the preferred stockholders, usually in the form of a right to vote upon default in the payment of dividends for a specified period. The extent of the preferred's participation in voting under such circumstances may range anywhere from an exclusive right to elect all the directors, to a right merely to elect one. (For example, New York Stock Exchange Rule A–15 requires, as a condition to listing a preferred stock, that it have the right to elect at least two directors upon a default in six or more quarterly dividends.)

Such contingent voting provisions involve many complications and call for considerable care in drafting. One particularly troublesome problem relates to the circumstances under which a default is cured and the voting power of the preferred terminated. In Ellingwood v. Wolf's Head Oil Refining Co., Inc., 27 Del.Ch. 356, 38 A.2d 743 (Sup.Ct.1944), the contingent voting provision was as follows:

> If at any time the corporation shall be in default in respect to the declaration and payment of dividends in the amount of two years' dividends on the preferred stock, then the holders of a majority of the preferred shall have an election to exercise the sole right to vote for the election of directors and for all other purposes, to the exclusion of any such right on the part of the holders of the common stock, until the corporation shall have declared and paid for a period of a full year a 6% dividend on the preferred stock, when the right to vote for the election of directors, and for all other purposes, shall revert to the holders of the common stock

Prior to 1942 the corporation was in substantial default on its preferred stock, which had assumed the voting power. For 1942 the corporation declared and paid a full 6% on the preferred, but it was still more than two years in default, and the question was whether the right to vote had reverted to the common stock. A majority of the court held for the preferred on the ground that the two year default provision was controlling; the minority thought that the provision relating to payment of a full year's dividend governed, and entitled the common to a return of voting power until and unless the corporation subsequently defaulted for another two years.

Of course, once again the real villain here was poor draftsmanship. On the merits, however, it does seem that normally the preferred should retain the vote until the total default has been reduced below a specified minimum, lest the management be tempted to manipulate the dividend policy primarily for the purpose of restoring voting power to the common from time to time.

The importance of distinguishing between voting rights for preferred as a class and individual voting rights per share is well illustrated by State ex rel. Cullitan v. Campbell, 135 Ohio St. 238, 20 N.E.2d 366 (1939). There the question was the meaning of a charter provision which provided that upon default "the holders of preferred stock shall be entitled to the same voting power as the holders of the common stock". The preferred contended that the meaning of this provision was that as a class they should have the same voting power as that of the common as a class, which would in effect have given the preferred approximately 90 votes per share. The court rejected this contention and held that in the absence of language clearly indicating otherwise, the normal rule that each share, preferred or common, was entitled to one vote would be presumed to apply.

---

4. CONVERTIBILITY

---

a. IN GENERAL

FLEISCHER AND CARY, THE TAXATION OF CONVERTIBLE BONDS AND STOCK *

74 Harv.L.Rev. 473–476 (1961).

. . . Conversion is the act of exchanging one class of securities for another, the conversion right being created by written contract between the holder of the security and the company which issued it. Although there have occasionally been convertibility provisions authorizing an exchange of a security for a more senior issue,** or for stock of another com-

* Copyright ©, Harvard Law Review Association, 1961. Reprinted by permission. Portions of the text and all footnotes omitted.

** [Ed. note] Some modern statutes forbid any "uphill" conversion into more senior stock. E. g., MBA §15(e). And of course, a right to convert stock into any type of debt instrument in effect amounts to an option to compel repurchase of the stock, which today is generally regarded as invalid, at least as against creditors. See Ballantine, Corporations (1946) 513.

pany, conversion almost always involves a shift from a security with higher priority into common stock of the same concern. Another characteristic of convertible securities is that the holder typically has the right not only to acquire common stock but also to pay for it in full by turning in the security he presently owns.

In general, there seems to be three main reasons why publicly held corporations issue convertible bonds and convertible preferred stock. First and possibly most important is the desire by management to raise common capital indirectly. "[M]anagements many times view the convertible as a device permitting them to raise funds today at tomorrow's higher common stock prices." The conversion feature has been attractive among growth companies where current market prices of the common shares are regarded as substantially lower than long-range investment value. This may explain the frequent relationship between rising stockmarket prices and a relative increase in the use of convertible securities. To the extent that their recent popularity is attributable to the uninterrupted prosperity since the war, it might correspondingly decline in the event of unfavorable business conditions.

A further advantage of raising equity capital through convertibles is that the new funds will be contributing to income by the time the debentures are converted. In the interim, while the company is putting the new money effectively to work, the charge takes the form of interest—deductible for tax purposes—rather than a reduction in income per share. Thus the dilution of earnings which traditionally accompanies an equity issue is deferred until the firm is making more money.

Another reason for issuing convertible securities is the desire to improve market acceptance of a bond or preferred-stock contract. In the capital market, as with apparel, fashion often prescribes what is readily acceptable to the buyer. The "sweetening" effect of the conversion feature is especially apparent when it is included in subordinated debenture bonds or second-priority preferred stock. In this type of financing it may be useful as a means of keeping down the interest or dividend rate, or of relieving the borrower from a heavy sinking fund or some other burdensome provision.

In the case of many companies, especially those which are closely held, a convertibility provision has more than a mere sweetening function in raising initial capital. In the early stages of a firm's history, the investor may be unwilling to accept stock alone for his contribution and may insist upon the protection of a debt claim. At the same time, he is obviously not satisfied with a high interest rate as an adequate return for the risk involved. In this context the convertible serves dual objectives, and affords the investor a flexibility which new businesses are willing to provide in order to attract needed financing.

Finally, to the investor the convertible bond not only offers the self-evident advantage of a debt security, but is also more attractive from the standpoint of borrowing. Federal Reserve Regulation U restricts loans by banks for the purpose of purchasing or carrying stock but not debt. In 1959, therefore, although a buyer of common had to pay down ninety per cent of the purchase price, he might pay as little as ten per cent if he acquired a debenture convertible into the same number of shares. Investor acceptance has thus played a significant part in the resort of corporations today to convertible securities.

Historically, convertible securities are not a recent development in corporate finance. . . . Until recent times, however, convertibility was not one of the hallmarks of a high-grade corporate issue. Now the tide seems to have shifted. American Telephone and Telegraph Company has been a leader in the field, with an almost continuous policy of offering rights to convertible bonds to its shareholders. Since the war especially, many of the well-established growth companies have resorted to convertible financing—with distinct success.

. . . Currently, the SEC's statistical studies indicate that nearly ten per cent of all bonds and notes offered during the years 1956 to 1960 were convertible, and a recent survey concluded that roughly half the preferred stock offered to the public during 1959 and the first half of 1960 contained a conversion privilege. . . .

---

b. PROBLEMS OF CONVERTIBLE SECURITIES AND WARRANTS

Despite the above it is clear that convertible securities do not represent a panacea for all corporate financing problems. First of all, the two-fold nature of a convertible is inherently complicated and confusing, particularly for an unsophisticated investor. More important, the prospective dilution of the common stock by conversion often goes unnoticed until it actually occurs, to the possible detriment of those who have acquired common stock in the meantime. And finally, there is the danger that neither component of a convertible security will receive as much care in planning as it needs: for the prospect of conversion may make the senior aspects of the security loom less important, while the inherent deferral of the junior component tends to push that aspect into the background. In other words, the presence of the convertible feature may lead a prospective investor to let down his guard in examining the senior security elements of the instrument, while at the same time he is not paying close enough attention to the junior security features just because they are clothed at the outset in senior security form. Under these circumstances, of course, convertible securities could combine the worst of both the senior and junior financing worlds, rather than the best as is often claimed.

Some of the foregoing disadvantages of convertible securities might be lessened by switching to straight senior securities, to be accompanied by stock warrants, that is, options to buy stock at a specified price. Such a package can give the investor much the same combination of safety and speculative opportunity that a convertible offers, while making it easier to focus separately upon the two components of the package. Normally, the warrants are made transferable so that it is not necessary to actually make the investment called for by the warrant in order to realize upon any market rise. On the other hand, unless the warrants are perpetual, ultimately someone must make that investment, and therein lies one of the chief disadvantages of warrants—that is, the receipt of additional capital by the corporation upon the exercise of warrants is not in any way geared to or based upon the corporation's need for additional funds. As a matter of fact the relationship is quite likely to be inverse. Warrants are most often exercised when the corporation is prospering, at which time the corporation's capital needs can usually be met by other means without difficulty. On the other hand, when the corporation is faring badly and may well be in need of funds, the warrants are not likely to be exercised; worse yet, their existence will substantially impair the corporation's ability to finance with other junior capital.

Another objection to warrants is that they tend to end up in the hands of professionals, which means that the warrants have not really performed any sound investment function. For reasons like these, the SEC has generally taken a dim view of warrants and has opposed their use in reorganization situations falling within its jurisdiction. See Childs Company, 24 S.E.C. 85, 120–122 (1946).

Turning to the problems of planning convertible securities or warrants, one obvious requisite is that the company be in position to honor any conversions (or exercises of warrants) by maintaining sufficient authorized but unissued (or perhaps treasury) shares. Other important substantive issues include the amount of the conversion or exercise price, and the duration of the conversion or warrant privilege. Obviously, these factors are somewhat interrelated—for example, it is not uncommon to provide in the case of a long-term convertible or warrant that the conversion or exercise price shall increase with the passage of time. In any event, ultimately such factors of general financial import as price and term must be fixed in the light of all the relevant market factors, as well as the comparative bargaining power of the parties.

One of the most intricate of all problems relating to senior securities is the matter of protecting convertible securities or warrants against dilution. For example, when stock is split two for one, the holder of a security convertible into that stock presumably should be entitled to receive twice as many shares when he converts. Similar problems arise in the event of a stock dividend, recapitalization, or issuance of stock pursuant to employee stock options, or indeed whenever additional common stock is issued for a consideration less than the conversion or warrant price. Because protection against dilution under general legal principles is far from clear in these circumstances, today it is common to include express contractual provisions dealing with the matter. In view of the many situations which must be covered, and the intricacies of the relationships involved, these "anti-dilutions" provisions are among the most complicated in corporate finance. An excellent illustration of this is provided by the case of Merritt-Chapman & Scott Corp. v. New York Trust Co., 184 F.2d 954 (2d Cir. 1950), where even a very lengthy and detailed anti-dilution provision failed to make clear whether the effect of a stock dividend on outstanding warrants was to increase the number of shares which the warrant holder was entitled to receive for the specified price, or to leave the number of shares unchanged but reduce the exercise price proportionately.

It is also common to include a contractual provision protecting conversion and warrant rights against destruction or impairment by merger, consolidation, or the like. The format often used to protect convertibles in the event of merger is to provide that the convertible security is to become convertible into whatever interest would have been received in the merger if the convertibles had been converted prior thereto.

5. REDEMPTION 89

Many modern bond and preferred stock issues contain provisions permitting the corporation at its option to redeem, that is, to pay off and eliminate from the corporation's capital structure, all or part of the issue. Obviously, it is of great advantage to the issuing corporation to be able to get rid of an outstanding issue when it can be attractively replaced. For example, if the cost of money has declined since the original issue, the corporation can reduce its charges (or dividend requirements, in the case of preferred stock) by calling the outstanding issue and floating a new one at a lower yield. Or an outstanding issue, particularly of debt securities, may contain some onerous provisions such as restrictions on later financing, which could be eliminated by floating a new issue.

Of course, in view of the costs inherent in a refinancing, the advantages of the new issue must be reasonably significant in order to make a change worthwhile. Nevertheless, the ability to adjust the corporation's capital structure to varying economic conditions is considered an extremely important adjunct of fund raising. Accordingly, a corporation is normally willing to pay a premium for the right to exercise a redemption privilege. This is usually accomplished by setting the redemption, or "call", price at a figure somewhat in excess of the original issue price of the securities. Sometimes, particularly when the prospective lender has substantial bargaining power, as in the case of a large insurance company, the borrower may be required to forego the redemption privilege for some specified period after issue, if not entirely.

Since the redemption of outstanding debt securities constitutes the discharge of a liability, there are no limitations as to permissible sources for the funds. Redemption of preferred stock, on the other hand, does constitute a repurchase of its own stock by a corporation, which is normally permitted only out of surplus. But there is an important distinguishing feature of redeemable stock, in that the prospect of such repurchase is recognized and publicized from the very outset, which serves to forewarn third parties that this investment may not be a permanent one. Accordingly, under most corporation statutes redemption of redeemable stock constitutes an exception to the normal restrictions on repurchase and instead may be charged against the stated capital attributable to the shares being redeemed. E. g., MBA §§ 6, 66. However, if the redemption price includes a call premium, or accrued but unpaid dividends, these components may stand on a different footing and may have to be covered by surplus. E. g., Del.Corp.Law § 243; contra, MBA §§ 66, 67.

In the absence of provision to the contrary, the question whether and when to exercise the power to redeem would normally be a matter for the board of directors. Here is another point where difficulty can be caused by laying too great stress on the equity character of preferred stock, and not enough on its practical similarity to debt. In the case of straightforward debt securities, it would scarcely be suggested that in deciding whether to redeem the directors should take account of the interests of the holders of the debt securities. But when it comes to redeeming preferred stock, there is a danger that a need to consider the best interests of the preferred stock may be inferred from various abstract legal principles, such as that directors must act for the benefit of all the stockholders, and directors may not favor one class of stockholders over another. However, the fact is that the very purpose of including a redemption provision is to permit the junior stockholders to eject the redeemable seniors from the enterprise when it suits the convenience of the juniors. Viewed in this light, surely it should be no objection to a redemption that the directors own, or are controlled by the owners of, a majority of the junior shares, despite the contrary intimation in the classic case of Zahn v. Transamerica Corporation, 162 F.2d 36 (3d Cir. 1947).* On another branch of the same litigation, the Kentucky court, in Taylor v. Axton-Fisher Tobacco Company, 295 Ky. 226, 173 S.W.2d 377 (1943), seemed to show greater awareness that the redemption provision was primarily for the benefit of the junior stockholders, when it decided that a redemption call once made could not be altered or revoked by the directors against the will of the junior stockholders. Even there, however, the court seemed to concede that directors could originally exercise the redemption privilege by making it optional with the holders of the redeemable stock, which certainly seems like a doubtful construction of a provision designed for the benefit of the junior stockholders.

On the other hand, substantial holdings of the redeemable stock on the part of the directors would seem to create a significant conflict of interest with regard to exercise of the redemption privilege. Obviously, a redemption which is beneficial to the redeemable stock is likely to be a disservice to the junior securities, and vice versa. Thus it would appear that the court in Stieglitz v. Electrol, Inc., 60 N.Y.S.2d 490 (Sup.Ct.,Sp.T. 1945), gave too short shrift to the argument by a junior shareholder that a redemption authorized by a three to two vote of the directors should be enjoined because two of the three directors who voted in favor were holders of the redeemable stock. In denying relief the court seemed to rely simply on the general proposition that in the absence of fraud or the like, directors were not precluded from voting on questions involving stock just because they were stockholders; the court did not appear to even notice the special inter-class conflict involved.

A number of redemption problems call for special care in planning and drafting. One is the manner of selecting the stock to be redeemed when less than the entire class is called. In order to prevent possible discrimination within the class, it is common today to provide for redemption "pro rata", or "by lot", so as to insure equal treatment of members of the same class.

Another area of concern relates to the period during which the redemption privilege may be exercised, if it is not available immediately after the issuance of the stock and/or it does not run forever. An object lesson in careless drafting is provided by Thompson v. Fairleigh, 300 Ky. 144, 187 S.W.2d 812 (1945), where the charter provided that the preferred stock could be retired at a stipulated price "at the end of five years from

---

* The actual result in that case seems clearly sound, however, i. e., that since the redeemable stock was also convertible, the directors should have given the stockholders sufficient information to enable them to make a sound decision on whether to convert instead of surrendering their stock for redemption.

July 1, 1925". Twelve years later, when the preferred stock was worth much more than the redemption price, the corporation's effort to redeem the preferred failed. Relying upon the rule that "where one party is given the right of election he is bound to exercise it promptly and may not delay in order to speculate on future contingencies", the court decided that the right must be exercised within a reasonable time, and that twelve years was not reasonable.

In addition, some decision should be made and clearly spelled out as to the status of the holders of redeemable stock at various stages in the redemption process, with particular regard to such matters as the right to vote or receive dividends during the period between the call and the date fixed for surrender of the securities. Similarly, if the redeemable stock is also convertible, the precise relationship between the exercise of the redemption privilege and the option to convert should be clearly indicated.

6. SINKING FUNDS

An increasingly common alternative to a right of redemption is a provision for systematic retirement of outstanding bonds (and not infrequently preferred stock as well). This is often accomplished by creating a sinking fund, that is by setting aside a sum each year to be used to purchase, or "sink", the issue in question. (Serial bonds, i. e., debt with serial maturities, is a common alternative for periodically reducing an issue of debt securities, but of course this method is not available for preferred stock.) Sinking funds for bonds are typically paid over to a trustee, who may be the trustee under the bond indenture; for preferred stock, the funds are usually handled directly by the company. The funds are generally used to buy in the securities involved, usually in the open market, although the securities are normally made redeemable lest exclusive reliance on open market purchases drive the market price too high. * Sinking funds may thus achieve two purposes: first, to reduce the amount of the stock or bonds outstanding and thereby improve the position of the remainder of the issue; and second, to support the market for the issue.

The need for a sinking fund may vary with the industry involved. Where technological change occupies a significant role, affecting not only plant and equipment but also the line of products manufactured, the use of a sinking fund to periodically reduce the claim (or interest) of the senior security holders seems wise from both the point of view of the company and that of the investors. Similarly, if the company is engaged in mining or other exploitation of wasting assets, a sinking fund may afford essential protection by reducing the outstanding issue as the value of the property shrinks.

---

* Open market purchases of stock on which there are accrued but unpaid cumulative dividends may pose some special problems of fairness, since there could be a temptation to pass dividends in order to depress the market price of the stock, as well as to conserve the cash with which to make the acquisition. See generally, Buxbaum, Preferred Stock—Law and Draftsmanship, 42 Cal.L.Rev. 243, 267–268 (1954).

Among the questions posed in the preparation of a sinking fund provision is that of the appropriate accounting "source" of the funds, that is, the account to which they are to be charged. As a strictly legal matter, it would seem that any source eligible for reacquisition of the securities should be available for the sinking fund. Obviously, there would be no problem with regard to debt securities; for preferred stock, on the other hand, there would be the question of whether sinking funds would be limited to surplus, or could be "backed" by stated capital, as in the case of straight redemption. However, in practice sinking-fund contributions are often tied to annual net earnings, which of course introduces quite different, although equally troublesome, problems.

As to remedies for failure to perform a sinking fund agreement, in the case of debt securities it should surely constitute a default under the accompanying indenture, although the trustee might be slow to invoke foreclosure or other default remedies on this account alone. On the preferred stock side, a mandatory injunction would seem to be about the only suitable remedy, and presumably even an individual stockholder would have standing to maintain such an action.

7. CONTRACTUAL RESTRICTIONS

Senior security contracts often include special provisions restricting the conduct of the corporation in various areas. While theoretically the permissible scope of such contractual restrictions is virtually unlimited, in practice they tend to be designed principally to maintain adequate working capital and a cushion for senior securities. In other words, the emphasis is primarily on minimizing the flow of cash out of the corporation in the form of dividends, other distributions to junior stockholders, excessive salaries or the like.

BUXBAUM, PREFERRED STOCK—LAW AND DRAFTSMANSHIP *

42 Cal.L.Rev. 255–257 (1954).

The basic protection of shareholders against destruction of their proprietary interest is today provided by the financial restrictions found in nearly all articles. The statutory and decisional law concerning these provisions is nonexistent; for they are hyper-legal, offering protection beyond the law's minima. Only construction questions can arise here and generally careful draftsmanship has avoided even these.

Restrictions against dividends to junior stock fall into a few major categories. Some contracts require the existence of a certain amount of total assets, whether in the aggregate or per share. Others require the retention of a certain amount of working capital after the dividend is paid.

* Reprinted by permission of the California Law Review. Footnotes omitted.

A third group require a certain surplus position for payment of dividends, which will protect against stock dividends. They are all expressed negatively. A covenant to maintain set margins is a practical absurdity and would give shareholders the right to litigate over their company's financial status at a level far below the usual "breaking point" of equitable insolvency. The most common provision forbids a dividend declaration unless after the putative payment the aggregate dividend payments on all stock from, say, January 1, 1950 are still less than the sum of $X plus the consolidated net income earned since January 1, 1950 plus proceeds from the sale of junior stock since that date (or net proceeds, after cost of junior stock acquired in any way). The same equation is often expressed so that the consolidated net income (with or without the $X) is to exceed all payments on all stock plus the cost of all junior shares acquired (or usually, net cost after proceeds from the sale of junior shares).

Careless drafting may indirectly destroy the effect of the safeguard. If instead of "all payments to all stock" the phrase read merely "dividend distributions," sinking fund payments or nondividend distributions could be made without entering into the equation, thus destroying the provision's value. Or if the provision were that all payments should not exceed the sum of dated consolidated net income *plus proceeds from the sale of junior stock,* common stock could be refunded by an acquisition and reissue, bloating the amount legally available for junior dividends (by raising the limit which these dividends may not exceed) though the clause intends to count only net proceeds after cost of acquiring any junior stock. Though open to abuse, this latter aberration is still common.

Certain legitimate exceptions may of course be made in these clauses. Thus when the dividend restriction reads "all payments to all junior stock shall not exceed . . ." etc., it normally exempts refunding—the acquisition of junior shares out of proceeds from the sale of new junior shares. Otherwise these payments to acquire the old shares are "payments on junior stock" which reduce the permissible dividend payments. Further, dividends payable in junior stock are usually exempt from the restriction "all payments. . . ." However, if dated consolidated surplus, not net income, is used in the equation, payments may in effect be limited anyway—if the applicable state law requires capitalization of earned surplus upon the declaration of stock dividends.

A more direct provision implementing the Delaware type of statute requires that after the putative payment consolidated net current assets equal 150% of this and all prior stock's liquidation preferences. Several variations of this type of protection are used: after the dividend, consolidated net current assets are to remain above $X, or (rarely, since it is little used) above consolidated funded debt; or that consolidated net tangible assets remain 200% of consolidated fixed liabilities plus preferred stock (at par). Except for the size of the protection these are all of the same sort. Often the clause provides that assets are to equal a multiple of several items, which usually intends a multiple of the aggregate of these items. A sentence creating the latter in the disjunctive, as "assets to be two times fixed liabilities, plus preferred stock" is therefore, whether intended or not, an evasion of the supposed protection. A simple yet proper protection which does not run this risk is often found, expressed absolutely or relatively: after the putative payment capital and surplus shall remain

94

above $X; or that the year's total dividend and other distributions be no more than one-third of that year's net income. Unless the latter were construed as a general expression of dividend policy, requiring that so much be paid out, these are effective means of protecting the preferred's share in the corporate assets.

As to all these clauses, it is vital that all payments, distributions, acquisitions, etc., include those of subsidiaries; otherwise the provisions can be totally avoided. Also many of these clauses are based on the dollar ratio between certain items—net current assets, tangible assets, etc. —which are vague until defined. The definition is a contractual matter detailed in most articles. Thus defective definitions of these concepts might weaken the supposed protection. If the articles are silent as to meaning, the more or less standard accounting interpretations would govern in litigation. It is because the courts honor any contractual definition, no matter how unusual accounting-wise, that exact definition becomes important.

C. THE AUTHORIZATION AND ISSUANCE OF STOCK

Every corporation statute has some counterpart of MBA §§15, 16 and 48(d), (e), and (f), which give to the parties very broad powers to decide what amount and types of stock a corporation shall have authority to issue. Whatever the parties decide must be set out in the certificate of incorporation, thereby becoming a matter of public record and subject to change only by an amendment of the certificate, which universally requires the consent of the shareholders. See MBA § 58.

The number of shares actually issued does not appear in the certificate of incorporation, although many jurisdictions do require that a report covering each issuance of stock be filed and made a matter of public record. The actual issuance of shares, including the matter of to whom they are to be issued and for what consideration, is generally committed to the board of directors, except that in some jurisdictions, as under MBA § 18, the right to fix the consideration for no-par shares may be reserved to the shareholders. However, even apart from such a provision the directors do not have unlimited discretion over the issuance of stock. The corporation statute invariably imposes some restrictions as to the type of consideration for which shares may be issued, e. g., MBA § 19, as well as the usual requirement that par value shares be issued for no less than par (to avoid watered stock liability, as under MBA §25). In addition, the directors as fiduciaries would undoubtedly be subject to general equitable control if they attempted to issue shares unfairly—for example, to themselves or their nominees at an unduly low price, or for the purpose of affecting the balance of control over the corporation.

NOTE ON THE ISSUANCE OF STOCK FOR SERVICES

Among the most troublesome problems in connection with stock issues are those that relate to the issuance of stock for services. They are analyzed in the following article, along with a number of related corporate and tax issues involved in the organization of a close corporation.

HERWITZ, ALLOCATION OF STOCK BETWEEN SERVICES AND CAPITAL IN THE ORGANIZATION OF A CLOSE CORPORATION *

75 Harv.L.Rev. 1098 (1962).

1. First Business Setting—Organization of a Brand New Enterprise with Two Participants

It is a familiar rule under corporate law that stock may not be issued for future services. Various aspects of the federal tax laws may also serve to discourage such transactions. Despite this apparent disfavor, it is submitted that the issuance of stock primarily on account of future services is a desirable and even necessary element in many business situations, particularly those involving the organization of a close corporation. To take a fairly typical illustration, assume that S is a person who has little or no capital but does have special service skills, as for example in the design and production of ladies' belts. C is a person with substantial capital to invest in new enterprises, but his time is fully occupied in his own business affairs. C and S decide that a combination of C's capital and S's services could produce a profitable business operation. Certainly such a proposed enterprise would hold little attraction for S if he were expected to become a mere employee of the new organization. And S has good reason to insist upon some substantial proprietary interest. When viewed from the point of view of sound planning and practical business judgment, the ultimate profits of a small business based upon a combination of capital and services should be shared by those who contribute necessary service skills, rather than be allocated exclusively to the contributors of capital. The same is true of the power to control the operations of the new business. So if the new venture took the form of a partnership, S would expect the partnership agreement to give him a substantial share in the future profits of the business, as well as a considerable voice in the management of its affairs, regardless of the amount of capital which he could personally contribute to the enterprise.

If instead the parties chose to form a corporation, S would be no less eager to obtain a reasonable share of the future profits, as well as a right to participate in control. But under the corporate form, control and the right to profits inhere in the stock of the corporation, particularly the basic equity stock. Thus S could satisfy his desires only by obtaining a substantial portion of that stock. But if S could make no more than a nominal capital investment, most of his stock would be received essentially on account of his future service, and thus run head-on into the corporate and tax obstacles. The object of this paper is to demonstrate how sound planning may nevertheless accommodate the justifiable interests of the parties in such circumstances.

2. Future Services as Consideration for Stock

Typically the corporate bar against issuing stock for services has been based upon some provision of the corporation statute such as "no corporation shall issue shares of stock except for money, labor done or property." Since it was generally accepted that even without any statutory authority stock might be issued for consideration other than cash, such provisions appear to have been designed primarily to restrict the quality of consideration eligible for the issuance of stock. This was doubtless originally motivated primarily by concern for the interests of creditors, since the capital contributed by shareholders was expected to serve as a substitute for the personal liability of the owners of the business. And it was later recognized that stockholders too have interests to be protected against the issuance of stock for ephemeral or valueless consideration.

It is obvious that quite apart from any statute it would not be proper to issue stock for future services *in vacuo*, without either a promise to perform such services or some other consideration sufficient to support an ordinary contract. But as an original matter the question whether stock might properly be issued for a promise to perform future services under such a statute is not entirely free from doubt. Although such a promise cannot qualify as "labor done," it is less clear that a promise to perform future services could not constitute "property" within the meaning of the statute. Some of the early cases suggest that the term "property" should be narrowly construed, to the exclusion of intangible items, but today it is clear that intangible property can qualify as valid consideration for the issuance of stock so long as the required value is present. And the acquisition of the specialized, skilled services of a particular person may constitute an item of considerable value to a business enterprise.

The issuance of stock for promised future services might have been justified by analogy to the treatment of cash prepayments for similar purposes. There seems to be no reason why a corporation may not make a substantial advance payment of compensation to a prospective employee. At least under generally accepted accounting principles, such an advance payment would properly be recorded as an asset, reflecting the fact that the corporation had not yet received the benefit of the promised future services. The asset could then be amortized over the period for which the advance payment constituted additional compensation.

*   *   *

The traditional concern about future services as consideration for stock lies chiefly in the fact that such services can prove valuable to a business only as a going concern and are totally devoid of realizable value for creditors or stockholders in the event of a liquidation of the enterprise. While of course other intangible items, notably goodwill, may prove worthless upon the failure of an enterprise, promised future services are subject to the special objection that they have no realizable value from the outset.* Moreover, future services do not lend themselves readily to any objective standards for measuring the quantity of value involved. This difficulty is aggravated by the fact that such items are commonly transferred by the very people in control of the corporation, who thereby become judges of the

---

* See Scully v. Automobile Fin. Co., 11 Del.Ch. 355, 101 A. 908 (Ch.1917), where the court, in holding that a plan of doing business was not "property" for which stock could be issued although the corporation had prospered in the use of the plan, made the following observation, which might equally apply to promised future services: "The business idea was not salable or transferable, and had no commercial value, and was not property in any sense." Id. at 358, 101 A. at 909.

amount of their own contributions. And in any event it has been common experience that corporate promoters are more likely to be extravagant when making payments in stock than when laying out hard cash . . . . .

The traditional bar against issuing stock for future services cannot be avoided merely by using no-par stock. Despite the suggestion in some of the early cases that no-par stock could be issued even for nothing, there is no longer any doubt that there must be some consideration, and it must qualify under the statute dealing with the types of consideration for which stock may be issued. These statutes, unlike the ones dealing with the required quantity of consideration, refer simply to "stock" without any distinction between par and no-par and there seems little basis for constructing one. Certainly there is no less injury to other shareholders from an overly generous allocation of no-par stock to corporate insiders for future services than from a similar allotment of par value stock. And there is still substantial danger of overvaluation of the consideration received for no-par stock, despite the reduced pressure in that direction resulting from the absence of any required minimum amount per share: ultimately some dollar figure must be assigned to the capital stock issued and the consideration received therefor, if only because of the practical necessity of recording the corporation's financial position in dollar terms. Accordingly, whether or not a recipient of no-par stock for future services would be liable to creditors in the event of subsequent corporate insolvency, he would at least be subject to the threat of cancellation of his stock for failure to pay lawful consideration.

Whatever may have been the historical justification for the prohibition against issuing stock for future services, there seems to be reason to question the need for any continuing flat bar. Today creditors more often recognize that the true security for the payment of their claims lies in the prospective earnings of the debtor corporation; in any event, for accurate reflections of the real financial position of an enterprise they have become accustomed to rely more upon commercial credit reports and the like than on its ostensible capital. And the ever-increasing pressure toward full disclosure of financial transactions has reduced the danger to stockholders from overly generous allocations of stock for questionable consideration.

In any event, a flat bar against the issuance of stock for future services is particularly unwarranted in the case of the close corporation. Here all of the stockholders are ordinarily privy to the agreement for the distribution of stock, and the likelihood of some stockholders overreaching others with extravagant issues of stock for future services is practically nil. So far as creditors are concerned, while it is perhaps true that the smaller the enterprise the more attention that is paid to the stated asset values, a requirement of conservative valuation of promised future services, as well as full disclosure of the character of such a contribution in the corporation's financial statements, would seem sufficient to protect this group.

* * *

3. Alternatives to Issuance of Stock Expressly for Future Services

Actually, however, the rule forbidding the issuance of stock for future services amounts to little more than a trap for the unwary, in view of the ease with which it can be circumvented. One who is to receive stock primarily on account of future services or other doubtful consideration can validate his stock under the statute dealing with eligible consideration merely by contributing some modest amount of qualified property. The fact that other parties pay a substantially higher price for their shares is of no concern, for there is normally no requirement in the corporation statutes that stock be issued for the same consideration, even when it is issued at the same time. To be sure, an arbitrary sale of stock at different prices to different shareholders at the same time may be actionable. But where there are practical business reasons for such differences in prices and all the shareholders consent with full knowledge, there would seem to be no valid objection to this procedure.

Thus in our illustration, if S and C were to form a new corporation with authorized capital of 1,000 shares of no-par stock, to be divided evenly between them, a consideration of as little as $500 might be set for the shares to be issued to S, even though the consideration for the 500 shares to be issued to C was $50,000. So long as the assets and the paid-in capital on the corporation's financial statements were each carried at no more than $50,500 as a result of the transaction, there would seem to be no basis for attacking it either at the outset or upon the later behest of creditors.

As a practical matter, however, this approach does not normally provide a very satisfactory resolution of the problem. When stock is issued to S for a nominal consideration compared to that paid by C for his stock, there is in effect an immediate transfer by C to S of an undivided pro rata interest in the capital contributed by C. For example, S would be entitled from the outset to one-half of the income earned on C's capital even if it were deposited in a savings bank and S's services contributed in no way to that income. Moreover, upon a subsequent liquidation of the enterprise S would be entitled to one-half of the total net assets even though they represented primarily the capital contributed by C. Under these circumstances it is understandable that C would not be willing to allow S to obtain very much of the stock of the new corporation for his nominal consideration, with the result that S would receive a smaller interest in the future profits of the enterprise than he would want. In effect, S would have to accept a smaller share of the future profits than he desired because he would be receiving an interest in underlying asset value, which he did not particularly desire or need.

Prima facie, S would also end up with a correspondingly limited share of the control which resides in the holders of the stock. But the control pattern can be rearranged quite easily either by using nonvoting stock or by dividing the stock into two classes, each of which has the right to elect a specified number of directors. Alternatively the parties might resort to one of the many other available control devices, such as unanimity agreements, shareholders' pooling agreements, or cumulative voting, although the validity and effect of these devices are somewhat less clear.

*　*　*

4. Tax Aspects of the All Common Stock Structure

In addition to receiving less stock and hence a smaller share of future profits than he would like, S would be faced with the possibility of a substantial tax burden as a result of any stock which he does obtain for a price substantially less than that paid by C. Suppose that S receives twenty per cent of the stock of the corporation in exchange for $500, while C contributes $50,000 for the remaining eighty percent of the stock. It seems clear that at this point the value of the enterprise, and hence the value of all of its stock, would be equal to the total amount of the cash paid in. Thus S's twenty percent of the stock would be worth $10,100, although he would be paying only $500 for it. Normally, it is true, a purchase of property for less than its fair value does not constitute a taxable event. But quite the contrary obtains in the case of a bargain purchase by an employee from his employer; here it is generally held that such a transaction constitutes compensation income to the employee to the extent of the bargain. The fact that S had not formally taken up employment at the time of the bargain purchase would not seem sufficient to avoid the application of this rule in the instant situation, since such employment would be an integral part of the business plan. And any argument that S's bargain purchase actually constituted a gift of stock from C would doubtless fail, in view of the total absence of any donative intent in the picture. While the corporation would presumably get an offsetting deduction against income, this tax benefit could be substantially less than the tax burden on S, and in any event would not help to provide S with the funds necessary to pay the tax imposed upon him.

*　　*　　*

5. The Advantages of Senior Securities

In addition, S would still be receiving a senior return in the form of compensation for services as well as sharing in the entire return on C's capital regardless of the contribution made by S's services. To be sure, these factors can be taken into account in deciding upon the basis of allocation of the ultimate profits between S and C. But it is virtually impossible to find any objective criteria for computing the percentage of the future profits which S should yield in consideration of these immediate interests in C's capital contribution, particularly since estimation of the likely amount of total future profit at this stage can be little more than a guess.

It is submitted that the way to a sounder accommodation of the interests of the parties is opened by recognizing that C's capital, no less than S's services, is entitled to a senior return, representing reasonable compensation for its use in the enterprise, prior to the determination of the profits to be allocated between C and S. To put it another way, just as the profits in which C is to share on the basis of his stock interest should be determined only after a reasonable compensation for S's services, so the profits in which S is to share should be determined only after a reasonable return on C's capital. To be sure, determination of a fair return on C's capital may be even more difficult than arriving at fair compensation for S's services. No fixed return would adequately compensate C for the risk involved in putting up practically the entire capital for a new small business. That is precisely why C would demand and be entitled to a substantial share of the equity interest in the enterprise in addition to any senior return he might receive. But the fact that no fixed return on his capital contribution would alone adequately compensate C does not mean that no provision for a senior return on that capital should be made.

What is needed, then, is both a recognition of C's superior rights in the capital contributed by him, particularly in the event of a liquidation, and a senior return upon such capital before determination of the profits to be divided between S and C. These two requirements are the very essence of a senior security. Thus C might receive debt securities with their automatic asset preference and senior return, or preferred stock with a cumulative dividend and a liquidation preference, or some combination of the two, in the total amount of his capital contribution. The return on the senior securities, like S's compensation, would be left to the bargaining arena, but presumably it would be substantial, in recognition of the high degree of risk involved.

The important corollary of interposing senior securities representing C's capital contribution is that the common stock, while still retaining all of its control features, is nevertheless reduced to a basic equity security representing solely the prospective profits in excess of a reasonable return on the capital invested in the enterprise. In view of its extremely speculative character such stock would quite appropriately be issued for purely nominal consideration. Hence it becomes quite simple to allocate the stock between the parties in accordance with whatever bargain is reached as to the division of profits and control. Since the two parties would pay the same price per share for this stock, the question of disproportionate consideration would not even arise; and there would seem to be no basis for finding any compensation income to S for tax purposes since his stock would be worth no more than the amount he paid for it.

Of course this approach does not in itself resolve the difficult question of the basis upon which the common stock should be allocated between the parties. But it is submitted that this mode of analysis can help to bring more clearly into focus just what is being allocated, and why. Normally, the final decision will depend upon a variety of factors, and will of course vary widely from case to case. Absent any objective standards for appraising the relative contributions of capital and services in the particular business involved, the final allocation will probably be controlled largely by the relative bargaining positions of the parties.

*   *   *

7. Second Business Setting—Incorporation of a Going Enterprise with the Injection of Additional Services and Capital

How does this approach work out in the common but more complicated situation involving the incorporation of an already existing business? Assume that P is the proprietor of a going business which has been making steady progress since its inception a few years earlier. P has decided that the services of another skilled executive plus substantial additional capital must be obtained if the business is to achieve its maximum potential. He has approached S, who has been working for P for some time, during which S has demonstrated the important executive skills needed to supplement P's own talents. However, S has indicated that he would be interested in remaining with the venture over the long term only if he can obtain a substantial proprietary interest. P has also spoken with C, once again an outsider who has substantial capital to invest but whose time is fully occupied with his own business affairs.

Suppose that the three parties decide that the combination of P's existing business, the respective talents of P and S, and substantial capital from C could produce a highly successful enterprise. Obviously here also at the outset the question arises as to the appropriate allocation, among the three participants, of interests in the proposed new venture. While it might be ideal to divide the ultimate profits and control of the enterprise evenly among the three, in practice such an allocation is unlikely to be achieved. No matter what basis for allocating profits and control between capital and services is selected, it seems clear that P must end up with [a substantially larger interest than either S or C, since P would] be contributing as much in services as S, and at least as much capital, in the current value of his business, as C is likely to contribute in fresh money. Thus the parties would probably be aiming at an even division between P on the one hand, and C and S on the other.

Such an allocation of the interests, moreover, would facilitate a reasonable arrangement for division of control over the operations of the enterprise, in the form of a four-man board of directors, consisting of C, S, P, and P's nominee. Under this arrangement, P would have the power to block any action at the board of directors level, which is no less than his due as a fifty percent owner, whereas C and S would have such power only when acting in concert.

The first step in the bargaining process might well be to determine the current value of P's business, to be approximately matched by C's capital contribution. Assume . . . a figure of $60,000 as the current value of P's proprietorship, to be approximately matched in cash by C.

The next step in the negotiations would be to determine the appropriate basis for allocation of the ultimate profits of the enterprise among the three participants. In the first instance, this question would seem to be of little concern to P, since he should receive a fifty percent interest in profits regardless of the basis for allocating such profits between capital and services. As between C and S the situation is very much as it was in the simpler two-man situation dealt with earlier. Under the corporate form, in the absence of any senior securities, the issuance of any substantial portion of the single class of stock to S essentially on account of his future services not only would be inequitable to C but also would subject S to a substantial risk of compensation income.

8. Tax Aspects of the Incorporation of a Going Business—§ 351

In this kind of situation a further tax difficulty is presented which would directly involve P if, as is often the case, the current value of P's business exceeds the total tax basis of the constituent assets in his hands because of either increased asset values or a good earnings record. P would probably want to qualify the incorporation under § 351 of the Code in order to avoid the recognition of gain in the transaction. But such tax-free treatment will be lost if in the incorporation transaction more than twenty percent of the stock is issued for services, unless the recipient of such stock also contributes some significant amount of cash or other property for stock. Thus in the instant situation, assuming that S could make no more than a nominal investment of cash or other property, receipt by him of more than twenty per cent of the stock would disqualify the transaction under § 351, and P would be forced to recognize for tax purposes the unrealized appreciation in the value of his business.

It is no idle possibility that S would expect more than twenty per cent of the stock of the proposed new enterprise. For example, any allocation of ultimate profits to the contributors of services in excess of the forty per cent assumed earlier in connection with the two-party situation would entitle S to more than twenty percent of the stock for his contribution of one-half of the vital executive services. In addition, receipt of more than twenty per cent of the stock could practically guarantee S a directorship, as he would like. While stock classification or some type of voting agreement might assure S of a position on the board regardless of the amount of stock he holds, cumulative voting, required in many jurisdictions and permitted in most others, would provide an even surer method. With cumulative voting and a four-man board of directors, any stockholder owning at least one share more than twenty percent of the total voting stock can assure himself a position on the board. On the other hand, as we have seen, the issuance of just one share more than twenty percent of the voting stock of the corporation to one who is contributing essentially only services would prevent qualification of the transaction for tax-free treatment under § 351. . . .

9. The Impact of Senior Securities

. . . The question therefore becomes whether the use of senior securities can relieve the threat of nonqualification under § 351, as well as the danger of compensation income to S from his receipt of a substantial stock interest for nominal consideration. Assuming that C will contribute capital in an amount corresponding to the assumed $60,000 current value of P's business, P and C would receive equal amounts of senior securities with a preference in liquidation equal to their respective contributions and whatever senior return is agreed upon by the parties. . . .

[As to the division with respect to debt and preferred stock, pro rata allocation between C and P is an obvious alternative; but the case for validity of the debt would be greatly enhanced if only one of them had debt (say C, who is putting up hard-to-come-by new money), and all the preferred went to P (who is sewed into business anyway, and is getting the benefit of non-recognition of gain)]

10. The Effect of Senior Securities on Compensation Income

Once senior securities have been issued to take care of the major capital contributions by P and C, the common stock would again be reduced to a security representing simply the prospective profits of the enterprise. Such stock could therefore be issued at a nominal price to each of the three parties, in whatever proportion they have decided to allocate the future profits. Assume that fifty percent of the stock is issued to P for $500, twenty-nine percent to C for $290, and twenty-one percent to S for $210. Have we eliminated all risk of compensation income to S? To be sure, here, as in the earlier two-party situation, on a liquidation basis the common stock would be worth no more than what was paid for it, and on this basis there would appear to be no bargain purchase by S. But unlike the earlier situation this venture is not being started from scratch but rather is succeeding to an already existing profitable business. Accordingly it is not so clear that the stock should be valued solely on a liquidation basis. Perhaps it should also be appraised in the light of its right to share in future profits, the existence of which is no longer a matter of sheer speculation. • • •

[Certainly, there is every reason to expect the new enterprise to earn at least as much as was predicted for P's proprietorship (before the infusion of new capital), plus reasonable additional earnings on the money invested by C. Of course, the return on the senior securities must be deducted in order to compute the profits remaining for the common stock. Something in the order of 12% might be a commercially reasonable rate to use for the mix of preferred stock and debt here; although this is much below the market rate for this risky little business, P and C both have a significant equity "kicker" as well, and in any event the parties will not want to burden the new corporation with excessive fixed charges. Deducting the senior return may still leave relatively large earnings for the common stock, enough so that applying a reasonable multiplier will produce a value for S's stock well in excess of the $210 he pays for it. Any such excess would appear to represent a bargain purchase, taxable as compensation income.]

Such an analysis does seem to accord with the economic realities of the situation, for it is clear that the parties were intending to confer some substantial economic benefit on S on account of his future services. Surely the parties would not be willing to sell any additional common stock to outsiders at the same price even if it were non-voting stock with no share in control over the enterprise.

Some difficulty is presented by the fact that both P and C also obtained their stock at the same price per share. If S's stock was worth substantially more than the price paid, and hence constituted a bargain purchase, so did the stock of P and C. Of course P also might be receiving a bargain purchase on account of his promised future services. But there would still remain the question of why P should receive over twice as many shares as S at this bargain price when their service contributions were expected to be approximately equal, as well as why C should participate in the bargain purchase at all, since he is not expected to contribute any services. The answer might be that the substantial capital contributions of P and C entitle them to receive some common stock in addition to the senior securities, because the latter do not constitute full consideration for the capital contributed. • • • In effect, both P and C are permitted to obtain common stock at a bargain price because the amount purportedly paid for the senior securities is excessive.

Such an analysis again seems to comport with the economic realities of the situation. For as we saw in connection with the earlier two-party situation, it is precisely because the senior securities received by a contributor of capital do not fully compensate him for the risk involved that he is entitled to receive a substantial share in the ultimate profits of the enterprise represented by the common stock.

Nevertheless, establishment of a value for the common stock in excess of the price paid for it would be no easy task. For one thing, in the valuation of a business as small as the one involved here it is still common to rely a good deal more on asset value than on estimated earnings. And one of the important reasons for this is particularly relevant here: the future earnings of such a business often defy reasonable estimation, even when there is a previous earnings history. So in the instant situation, the expanded operations undoubtedly contemplated by the parties might as soon turn the previous profits into losses as increase them. Moreover, even if the hoped-for earnings are realized, there is little chance of any dividends on the common stock in the foreseeable future in view of the normal dependency of this type of business upon retained earnings for both current working capital and any projected expansion, to say nothing of the possible retirement of senior securities. And account must also be taken of the extremely limited market for the common stock of such an enterprise. So it is entirely possible that the parties could defeat any effort to revalue their stock and securities in order to cast the transaction in a mold different from the one expressly adopted by them.

Even if it could be demonstrated that S, and to some extent P, have received a bargain purchase of the common stock essentially on account of future services, there remains one further argument for avoiding the imposition of tax on such compensation at that time. As noted above, the interposition of senior securities ahead of the common stock reduces the latter to what in economic terms amounts primarily to a right to share in the future profits of the enterprise. The receipt of a mere right to participate in future profits, even by an employee from his employer, would not seem to constitute a taxable event. For example, when a young lawyer becomes a partner in an established law firm and hence entitled to some specified percentage of future partnership profits, surely he is not to be taxed upon the discounted value of those future profits; a rule to the contrary would certainly cast a considerable pallor over the now-joyous Christmas occasions on which such ascendency to partnership is typically celebrated. Perhaps the reason in the partnership situation is that the new partner must continue to work for the partnership in order to become entitled to his share of annual profits, and hence "earns" such amounts only as he performs the required services annually.* If so, the receipt of a common stock in a corporation would be analogous only if the employee were bound to resell the stock at his cost upon leaving the corporation's employ, in which event there might well be no compensation income on receipt of the stock anyway because its value would be limited to the resale price. But it seems also to be true that receipt by a cash basis taxpayer of an unsecured right to future payments, particularly where the amount of such payments is unascertainable, is not a taxable event. It is under this view that the analogy of the common stock in the instant situ-

* [Ed. note] But one who receives a partnership interest in both capital and profits as compensation for past services must include in income the fair market value of the interest upon its receipt. United States v. Frazell, 335 F.2d 487 (5th Cir. 1964), rehearing denied, 339 F.2d 885 (5th Cir. 1964).

ation to a mere right to future profits would have its maximum force. But the fact is that such stock constitutes a good deal more than mere evidence of a right to future profits, despite the interposition of senior securities. Rather the stock constitutes a traditional proprietary interest embodying rights in property and control, however limited, as well as in profits. Hence, if a bargain-purchase element can be isolated in the instant situation, it seems likely that a tax on compensation income would result.

11. The Effect of Senior Securities on Qualification under § 351

A showing that some of the parties obtained their stock at a substantial bargain price, and hence in large part on account of future services, could have important ramifications on the question of tax-free incorporation under § 351. For example, if it were determined that S's twenty-one percent stock interest was actually worth $5,500, it might well follow that he received only a proportionate amount of that stock for his $210 cash contribution, and the remainder on account of future services. In our assumed case, less than one-twentieth of S's total twenty-one percent of the stock could be attributed to the cash payment of $210. Thus S would have received more than twenty percent of the total stock of the new corporation for services, which could lead to disqualification of the transaction under § 351 if it were found that S's nominal cash contribution was designed primarily to qualify the incorporation for tax-free treatment.

12. The Effect of Senior Securities on Basis

The true value of the common stock would also be a critical element in the determination of the basis of the senior securities received by P and C. Under § 358, when a party to a tax-free incorporation under § 351 receives more than one class of stock or securities, the basis of each of the various classes is to be determined in accordance with their respective fair market values at the time received. Thus in the instant situation, P's total basis in the assets contributed by him to the corporation, including the $500 in cash paid for the common stock, would be allocated between his senior securities and common stock in accordance with the fair market value of each. Obviously, the Government would be anxious to maximize the value, and hence proportionate share of basis, allocated to the common stock, in order to reduce the basis of the senior securities, which are likely to be disposed of in a taxable transaction at an earlier date than the common stock.

A finding that the common stock was worth more than the amount purportedly paid for it would create a further complication whenever the senior securities accompanying such stock included debt obligations. For if it is established that the amount actually paid for the debt obligations was less than their face value, the difference would presumably constitute original issue discount. . . .

Despite the many potential difficulties observed in the foregoing, it is submitted that here, no less than in the two-party situation, utilization of senior securities can help the parties to reach a fair accommodation of their respective interests. . . . the most important advantage of using such senior securities can certainly be achieved in that the parties can thereby obtain a much clearer picture of just what is involved in the allocation of the interests in a new business and how their various interests can be most fairly accommodated.

Despite the fact that from the point of view of practical corporate financial management long-term debt securities have become increasingly regarded as merely an alternative type of investment in an enterprise, corporate law still distinguishes sharply between all types of creditors' claims on the one hand, and ownership or equity interests on the other. (Of course it is not always so easy to decide on which side of the line a particular hybrid security containing both debt and equity features may fall.) One illustration of this difference in treatment between the two is the fact that the Model Act, like most corporation statutes, does not have any counterpart of §§15 and 16 to expressly authorize the issuance of debt securities. Nevertheless, ample authority for the issuance of various kinds of debt obligations can be implied from the counterpart in practically every corporation statute of MBA § 4(h), which gives every corporation the general power to incur liabilities and to evidence such liabilities by notes, bonds, or the like.

The sharp distinction drawn between debt and equity, primarily in connection with priority in the assets of an insolvent enterprise, has been sorely tested in cases involving debt obligations owned by people who are also stockholders. It is of course clear that there is no fixed rule prohibiting a stockholder from also being a creditor of the corporation. But obviously such a dual role can play havoc with the fundamental doctrine that in the event of financial difficulty, the claims of creditors take precedence over the interests of stockholders. The problem is somewhat aggravated by the fact that in most of the cases the stockholder-creditors are in complete control of the corporation and can pretty much dictate the form in which to cast their investment in the corporation. Of course the presence of stockholder-owned debt may lead third parties to withhold credit from the corporation, or at least to require the stockholders to guarantee the corporation's debts, but prospective creditors often do not investigate sufficiently to learn the facts.

This question of the extent to which stockholders may set up part of their contributions as "loans" to the corporation may well be part of a broader inquiry as to the responsibility of the organizers of a corporation to provide it with a reasonable amount of capital for the business which it is to undertake. The imposition of such responsibility can easily be defended as an appropriate price to be paid for the limited liability which the shareholders enjoy. But the application of such a rule would require a difficult factual determination in each case as to what was a reasonable amount of capital.

The following cases represent recent judicial efforts to grapple with the corporate problems presented in the area of a stockholder debt and inadequate initial capitalization.

1. SUBORDINATION OF SHAREHOLDER DEBT

COSTELLO v. FAZIO

United States Court of Appeals, Ninth Circuit, 1958.
256 F.2d 903.*

[Fazio, Ambrose, and Leonard were partners in a plumbing supply business which they decided to incorporate. The capital accounts of the partners prior to incorporation were approximately $43,000 for Fazio, $6,000 for Ambrose, and $2,000 for Leonard. In contemplation of incorporation, Fazio and Ambrose reduced their capital accounts to $2,000 each, by obtaining promissory notes from the partnership in the amounts of approximately $41,000 and $4,000 respectively. At the close of its last fiscal year the partnership's current liabilities had exceeded the current assets, and the business had suffered a loss of $22,-000, on sales of approximately $390,000, compared to a profit of $40,-000 on sales of approximately $665,000 for the preceding year. The new corporation issued 200 shares of no-par common stock, with a stated capital of $10 per share, to each of the three partners, and assumed all the liabilities of the partnership, including the notes to Fazio and Ambrose. Two years later, after suffering continued losses, the corporation was in bankruptcy. Fazio and Ambrose filed claims on their notes as general creditors. The trustee in bankruptcy sought to subordinate their claims on the ground that they really represented a portion of the capital investment in the business. The referee held that the claims should be allowed, the district court affirmed, and the trustee appealed.]

HAMLEY, CIRCUIT JUDGE. . . . Clifford V. Heimbucher, a certified public accountant and management consultant, called by the trustee, expressed the view that, at the time of incorporation, capitalization was inadequate. He further stated that, in incorporating a business already in existence, where the approximate amount of permanent capital needed has been established by experience, normal procedure called for continuing such capital in the form of common or preferred stock.

Stating that only additional capital needed temporarily is normally set up as loans, Heimbucher testified that " . . . the amount of capital employed in the business was at all times substantially more than the $6,000 employed in the opening of the corporation." He also expressed the opinion that, at the time of incorporation, there was "very little hope [of financial success] in view of the fact that for the year immediately preceding the opening of the corporation, losses were running a little less than $2,000 a month. . . . "

* Portions of the opinion and all of
the footnotes omitted.

William B. Logan, a business analyst and consultant called by the trustee, expressed the view that $6,000 was inadequate capitalization for this company. John S. Curran, a business analyst, also called by the trustee, expressed the view that the corporation needed at least as much capital as the partnership required prior to the reduction of capital.

Robert H. Laborde, Jr., a certified public accountant, had handled the accounting problems of the partnership and corporation. He was called by the trustee as an adverse witness. . . . Laborde readily conceded that the transaction whereby Fazio and Ambrose obtained promissory notes from the partnership was for the purpose of transferring a capital account into a loan or debt account. He stated that this was done in contemplation of the formation of the corporation, and with knowledge that the partnership was losing money.

The prime reason for incorporating the business, according to Laborde, was to protect the personal interest of Fazio, who had made the greatest capital contribution to the business. In this connection, it was pointed out that the "liabilities on the business as a partnership were pretty heavy." There was apparently also a tax angle. Laborde testified that it was contemplated that the notes would be paid out of the profits of the business. He agreed that, if promissory notes had not been issued, the profits would have been distributed only as dividends, and that as such they would have been taxable.

* * *

In any event, when we speak of inadequacy of capital in regard to whether loans to shareholders shall be subordinated to claims of general creditors, we are not referring to working capital. We are referring to the amount of the investment of the shareholders in the corporation. This capital is usually referred to as legal capital, or stated capital in reference to restrictions on the declaration of dividends to stockholders. . . . The corporate accounts and the undisputed testimony of three accounting experts demonstrate that stated capital was wholly inadequate.

* * *

It does not require the confirmatory opinion of experts to determine from this data that the corporation was grossly undercapitalized. In the year immediately preceding incorporation, net sales aggregated $390,000. In order to handle such a turnover, the partners apparently found that capital in excess of $50,000 was necessary. They actually had $51,620.78 in the business at that time. Even then, the business was only "two jumps ahead of the wolf." A net loss of $22,000 was sustained in that year; there was only $66.66 in the bank; and there was an overdraft of $3,422.78.

Yet, despite this precarious financial condition, Fazio and Ambrose withdrew $45,620.78 of the partnership capital—more than eighty-eight per cent of the total capital. The $6,000 capital left in the business was only one-sixty-fifth of the last annual net sales. All this is revealed by the books of the company. . . .

* * *

We therefore hold that the factual conclusion of the referee, that the corporation was adequately capitalized at the time of its organization, is clearly erroneous.

The factual conclusion of the trial court, that the claimants, in withdrawing capital from the partnership in contemplation of incorporation, did not act for their own personal or private benefit and to the detriment of the corporation or of its stockholders and creditors, is based upon the same accounting data and expert testimony.

Laborde, testifying for the claimants, made it perfectly clear that the depletion of the capital account in favor of a debt account was for the purpose of equalizing the capital investments of the partners and to reduce tax liability when there were profits to distribute. It is therefore certain, contrary to the finding just noted, that, in withdrawing this capital, Fazio and Ambrose did act for their own personal and private benefit.

It is equally certain, from the undisputed facts, that in so doing they acted to the detriment of the corporation and its creditors. The best evidence of this is what happened to the business after incorporation, and what will happen to its creditors if the reduction in capital is allowed to stand. The likelihood that business failure would result from such undercapitalization should have been apparent to anyone who knew the company's financial and business history and who had access to its balance sheet and profit and loss statements. Three expert witnesses confirmed this view, and none expressed a contrary opinion.

Accordingly, we hold that the factual conclusion, that the claimants, in withdrawing capital, did not act for their own personal or private benefit and to the detriment of the corporation and creditors, is clearly erroneous.

Recasting the facts in the light of what is said above, the question which appellant presents is this:

Where, in connection with the incorporation of a partnership, and for their own personal and private benefit, two partners who are to become officers, directors, and controlling stockholders of the corporation, convert the bulk of their capital contributions into loans, taking promissory notes, thereby leaving the partnership and succeeding corporation grossly undercapitalized, to the detriment of the corporation and its creditors, should their claims against the estate of the subsequently bankrupted corporation be subordinated to the claims of the general unsecured creditors?

The question almost answers itself.

* * *

Appellees argue that more must be shown than mere undercapitalization if the claims are to be subordinated. Much more than mere undercapitalization was shown here. Persons serving in a fiduciary relationship to the corporation actually withdrew capital already committed to the business, in the face of recent adverse financial experience. They stripped the business of eighty-eight per cent of its stated capital at a time when it had a minus working capital and had suffered substantial business losses. This was done for personal gain, under circumstances which charge them with knowledge that the corporation and its creditors would be endangered. Taking advantage of their fiduciary position, they thus sought to gain equality of treatment with general creditors.

In [some prior] cases, there was fraud and mismanagement present in addition to undercapitalization. Appellees argue from this that fraud and mismanagement must always be present if claims are to be subordinated in a situation involving undercapitalization.

This is not the rule. The test to be applied . . . is whether the transaction can be justified "within the bounds of reason and fairness."　. . .

The fact that the withdrawal of capital occurred prior to incorporation is immaterial. This transaction occurred in contemplation of incorporation. The participants then occupied a fiduciary relationship to the partnership; and expected to become controlling stockholders, directors, and officers of the corporation. This plan was effectuated, and they were serving in those fiduciary capacities when the corporation assumed the liabilities of the partnership, including the notes here in question.

Nor is the fact that the business, after being stripped of necessary capital, was able to survive long enough to have a turnover of creditors a mitigating circumstance. The inequitable conduct of appellees consisted not in acting to the detriment of creditors then known, but in acting to the detriment of present or future creditors, whoever they may be. . . .

* * *

Reversed and remanded for further proceedings not inconsistent with this opinion.

In Obre v. Alban Tractor Co., 228 Md. 291, 179 A.2d 861 (1962), Obre and Nelson pooled certain equipment and cash for the purpose of forming a corporation to engage in the dirt-moving and road building business. Obre transferred equipment independently appraised at $63,874.86, plus $1,673.24 of cash, in exchange for $20,000 in par value of non-voting preferred stock, $10,000 in par value of voting common stock, and an unsecured five-year note for $35,548.10, with interest at 5%. Nelson's contribution was equipment valued at

$8,495.00 and cash of $1,505.00 for which he received $10,000 in par value voting common stock. The corporation experienced financial difficulty from the outset and was insolvent before the end of the second year. No interest was ever paid on Obre's note. The trial court rejected Obre's claim as a general creditor on the ground that the purported loan actually represented a contribution to risk capital, primarily because the corporation could not have carried on its operations without the equipment contributed by Obre.

The Court of Appeals reversed. The court assumed without deciding that even absent some element of fraud, mismanagement or estoppel, the claim of a principal shareholder might be subordinated if the corporation was undercapitalized, citing, among other cases, Costello v. Fazio. However, the court found no showing that $40,000 was inadequate capitalization for an enterprise of this size, "particularly in view of the careful planning that went into determining its capital structure". The parties had wanted their control of the corporation to be equal from the outset, and their ownership eventually to be equal, and the excess of Obre's contribution over the $30,000 in stock received by him was not treated as a capital investment "since this would have made the desired end of eventual equal ownership that much more difficult". The court also noted that the parties' memorandum agreement for the proposed capital structure expressly stated as to the permanent equity capital of $40,000 that "all parties consider [it] entirely adequate for the foreseeable needs of the corporation". The court continued as follows:

> In our view, appellees have failed to show that $40,000 was an unreasonable amount of capital upon which to predicate success in the corporate venture. No evidence was offered to reflect the financial status of the corporation other than its authorized capital stock and the fact that it encountered financial difficulties early in its operations and eventually foundered. This, in our view, failed to establish that the financial set-up of the corporation was a sham, or worked an injustice. . . . What may appear hazardous by hindsight may not have been unreasonable at the outset. It is not unusual in corporate financing to have approximately one-half of contributions put in as risk capital and the balance as loan capital. There can be no question but that, if a third party had advanced the money represented by Obre's note, he would validly be considered a creditor of the corporation.
>
> Our view in no way compromises the position of the corporate creditor. . . . It is obvious that the creditors in this case could have determined (if they actually did not do so) the financial status of the corporation by simply inspecting the stock issuance certificate filed with the State Tax Commission, or by requesting financial reports, or by ob-

taining credit ratings from the sources available. . . . In the instant case, the note to Obre was listed on the monthly financial reports of the corporation as a debt of the corporation. In addition, though interest was never actually paid, the fact that there was a provision for payment of interest on the note further establishes its character as a loan and not a risk capital investment. The fact that the note was taken at the time of incorporation is not significant in view of the failure to establish inadequate capitalization of the corporation.

In Arnold v. Phillips, 117 F.2d 497 (5th Cir. 1941), cert. den. 313 U.S. 583 (1941), Arnold organized a corporation to engage in the brewing business. The corporation had an authorized capital stock of $50,000, all of which Arnold purchased for cash. He then advanced to the company an additional $75,500 in order to enable it to complete the construction of a plant and to commence its operations. After initial success the business began to lose heavily, and Arnold advanced substantial additional sums. He obtained a mortgage on the plant securing both the original loan of $75,500 and the later advances. Upon bankruptcy liquidation, Arnold's claim upon his original loan of $75,-000 was rejected on the ground of inadequate capitalization, but his claim as a secured creditor for the later advances was sustained. The court said:

The two series of advances differ materially as respects their nature and purpose. Those made before the enterprise was launched were, as the district court found, really capital. Although the charter provided for no more capital than $50,-000, what it took to build the plant and equip it was a permanent investment, in its nature capital. There was no security asked or given. Arnold saw that he could not proceed with his enterprise unless he enlarged the capital. There can be little doubt that what he contributed to the plant was actually intended to be capital . . . a sort of interest-bearing redeemable stock . . ..

After two years of prosperity, with the original capital thus enlarged demonstrated to be sufficient, with a book surplus of nearly $100,000 after payment of large salaries and dividends in the form of interest, there arose a situation very different from that in the beginning. Adversity then occurring raised a problem not different from that which commonly faces a corporation having losses. It may borrow to meet its needs. Had this corporation borrowed of a bank upon the security of the plant, the debt would no doubt be valid. What would render it invalid when Arnold furnished the money? As to each of these later advances, it is testified without contradiction that it was made after consultation with Otto, the Secretary and Treasurer, and on the security of the deed of trust. The money went to relieve the needs of the business exactly as it would have done if a bank had advanced it. No other creditor was prejudiced or misled. There are no circumstances which discredit the testimony. They were truly loans and not new capital. . . .

We do not think a case is presented where the corporate entity ought to be disregarded as being a sham, a mere obstacle to justice, or instrument of fraud. It is not denied that a corporation owned by one man save for qualifying shares, is lawful in Texas. That it was created to shield the owner from liability beyond the capital set up by the charter does not show an unlawful or fraudulent intent, for that is a main purpose of every incorporation. It becomes an evidence of fraud only when the capital is unsubstantial and the risk of loss great, or the contributions to capital are greatly overvalued, and the like. It would be hard to say in this case that $50,000 was not a substantial capital, and impossible so to say after holding that the real capital was $125,500, though some was irregularly paid in.

---

2. IMPOSITION OF UNLIMITED LIABILITY UPON SHAREHOLDERS

The question of maximum concern to the parties in connection with substantial stockholder debt is whether a subsequent finding of "too much" debt and too little equity could lead a court to ignore the corporate entity altogether and subject the shareholders to unlimited personal liability. In a few cases, notably in California, the courts have imposed this extreme sanction in cases where the parties started a new enterprise in corporate form with nowhere near the capital needed to operate the business. Several of the California cases have referred approvingly to the following excerpt from Ballentine on Corporations 302-303 (Rev. ed. 1946):

"If a corporation is organized and carries on business without substantial capital in such a way that the corporation is likely to have no sufficient assets available to meet its debts, it is inequitable that shareholders should set up such a flimsy organization to escape personal liability. The attempt to do corporate business without providing any sufficient basis of financial responsibility to creditors is an abuse of the separate entity and will be ineffectual to exempt the shareholders from

corporate debts. It is coming to be recognized as
the policy of the law that shareholders should in
good faith put at the risk of the business unencumbered capital reasonably adequate for its prospective
liabilities. If the capital is illusory or trifling
compared with the business to be done and the risks
of loss, this is a ground for denying the separate
entity privilege."

However, the harsh remedy of looking through the corporation to reach the individual shareholders is not likely to be
imposed in cases where the charge of undercapitalization is
based upon excessive shareholder debt. Assuming the shareholders have not withdrawn any funds in purported repayment of
the debt, subordination is available, and that, as the court
in Arnold v. Phillips recognized, in effect turns the debt
retroactively into capital, which should be sufficient to overcome any claim of gross undercapitalization. Moreover, the
few cases in which limited liability has been lost have always involved some deficiency in the incorporation process
going beyond insufficient capital, such as not issuing the
stock in accordance with the permit obtained from the state
authorities, Temple v. Bodega Bay Fisheries, Inc., 4 Cal.
Rptr. 300, 180 Cal. App. 2d 279 (1960), or the total failure
to issue stock or raise any capital at all, Minton v. Cavaney,
15 Cal. Rptr. 641, 364 P.2d 473 (Sup. Ct. 1961) (where the unsuccessful defendant was the lawyer for the new corporation,
who seemed to have agreed to become a shareholder, director,
and officer as a convenience to his client). In addition,
some of the later cases have expressly ruled that lack of
adequate capital does not automatically lead to personal liability on the shareholders. E.g., Harris v. Curtis, 87 Cal.
Rptr. 614, 8 Cal. App. 3d 837 (1970)(undercapitalization does
not ipso facto result in ignoring the corporate entity).

TAX ASPECTS OF INCORPORATION

SECTION 1.   RECEIPT OF STOCK FOR SERVICES

   A.   Historical Developments

      As indicated at pages 99 and 103, supra, the
receipt of stock (or other property) by an employee
from his employer without paying full value will normally give rise to compensation income, in the amount
of the difference between the consideration paid by
the employee (if any) and the fair market value of the
stock.   Since 1969 this result has found expression in
§83 of the Code, which provides for reporting as income the bargain purchase spread on any property transferred "in connection with the performance of services".
Among the cases subject to this bargain-purchase rule,
both before and since the enactment of §83, is the
issuance of stock to a prospective employee upon the
original incorporation of an enterprise.   For example,
in Baltimore v. Commissioner, 17 T.C.M. 388 (1958), the
taxpayer, upon agreeing to serve as the manager of a
new corporation, received 20% of the stock for nothing,
while four other persons each contributed $10,000 for
a 20% interest.   In holding that the taxpayer had received income of $8,000, the court rejected the taxpay-
er's contention that the stock represented a gift, finding that it had been received in consideration for the
taxpayer's terminating his previous employment and
accepting the position of general manager with the new
enterprise.

      However, prior to 1969 the timing and the
amount of the compensation income in such cases depended
in large measure upon whether the stock when received
was subject to restrictions on transferability of one kind
or another.   Obviously, such restrictions could have an adverse effect on the value of the stock, and hence reduce the amount of compensation income received by the employee.   Moreover, some courts
had refused to tax the employee at all upon the receipt of stock subject to such restrictions (even when the restrictions were relatively
innocuous or short-lived, such as a prohibition against sale of the stock
for a year or a requirement that the stock be resold at cost if the employee terminated his employment within the year), on the ground
that the restrictions deprived the stock of an ascertainable market
value, without which the amount of the compensation income could
not be determined.   If this approach had been accompanied by a general acknowledgement that recognition of income was merely being
postponed, and that the tax would become due if and when the restrictions lapsed (as they usually did), this might have been a tolerable

method of treating these kinds of cases (though hard to administer); but when the Tax Court held that the lapse of the restrictions was not a taxable event, a gaping loophole had emerged, which called for strenuous countermeasures by the Government.

The initial response was by way of amendment to the Regulations, in 1959, to provide that when property received in part or in whole as compensation for services was subject to a restriction which significantly affected its value, no tax would be imposed upon receipt of the property; but when the restriction lapsed (or the property was disposed of), compensation income had to be recognized, in the amount of the difference between the value of the property *without the restriction* as of the time of receipt and the consideration paid, if any. Among the examples given of restrictions having a significant effect on value were (1) a requirement that under certain circumstances the employee resell the stock to the corporation at the price he or she paid for it, and (2) a provision giving the corporation a right of first refusal at book value before the employee could dispose of the stock during his employment. Since this result was achieved by cross-referencing the bargain purchase cases from the general provision in Reg. § 1.-62–5 to the section dealing with stock options, Reg. § 1.421–6, a brief detour to review the even more twisting tax path of stock options is called for.

Granting a stock option to an employee, that is, giving the employee a right to purchase stock at a fixed price for a specified period, has long been a common way of using corporate stock to reward valuable services. For a time, employee stock options often escaped all compensation income tax, both at the time of the grant and the time of exercise, on the ground that they were primarily intended to provide the employee with a proprietary interest in the business rather than additional compensation income; but in Commissioner v. LoBue, 351 U.S. 243 (1956), the Supreme Court held that employee stock options always result in compensation income, generally as of the time when the option is exercised (rather than at the earlier date of grant of the option), and in the amount of the excess of the value of the stock at the time of exercise over the option price paid by the employee. In other words, the grant of the option was looked at as in effect a nontaxable invitation to deal, with the later exercise of the option treated as a taxable bargain purchase of stock by the employee at that time.

It is to be noted that the grant of the option could well have been viewed as the compensatory event: the employee's receipt without consideration (other than his services) of a binding commitment entitling him to share in any subsequent appreciation in the value of the stock could be treated as a taxable payment of compensation in kind. Actually, this would be a more favorable approach for taxpayers, even though it would result in an earlier imposition of tax, since it would limit the amount of the compensation income to the value of the option at the date of the grant (less any price paid for the option, which almost never occurs in conjunction with employee stock options); any subsequent appreciation in the value of the stock would be taxed only when the stock acquired upon exercise of the option was sold, and then only at capital gains rates. But typically the option grant was conditioned upon further services by the employee, was not transferable, and was very difficult to value in any event, since it depended so heavily upon the future course of the value of the underlying stock. (Even when an option is immediately exercisable at a price below the present fair market value—for example, a right to buy stock selling at $10 per share for only $7 per share—so that it has a value at least equal to the current spread, and *a fortiori* when the option price is above the current market price, there is an element of value present (which is very difficult to compute) in the continuing right to purchase stock at a fixed price without having to make any investment or take any risk of loss until and unless the option is exercised.) Therefore, while the courts reserved the possibility that the grant of the option might be the taxable event, at least if the option was transferable and had a readily ascertainable value, in practice the Service generally prevailed in its view that the grant should be ignored and the exercise of the option treated as a bargain purchase, with the entire spread at the date of exercise included as compensation income.

However, in the business world employee stock options proved to be an idea whose time had come, and Congress responded on the tax side. Starting in 1950 (and until the Tax Reform Act of 1976) the Code provided, in §§ 421 et seq., that for employee stock options qualifying under the statutory conditions (which included, after some tightening up over the years, such requirements as approval of the plan by stockholders; prohibition on transfer of the options; an option price no less than market value at the date of grant; exercise of the option within five years of the grant (and within three months of termination of employment); and holding the stock acquired upon exercise for at least three years), there would be no tax on either the grant or the exercise of the options, and only a capital gains tax upon the ultimate sale of the stock acquired. The Tax Reform Act of 1976 repealed this favorable tax treatment for qualifying options (except for § 423, authorizing non-discriminatory employee stock-purchase plans, which must be open to virtually all employees), temporarily closing that chapter. However, the Economic Recovery Tax Act of 1981 revived qualified options under a new name, Incentive Stock Options, with largely the same requirements for qualification. Among the few differences, which mostly favor taxpayers, are a ten-year period for exercise, instead of the previous five years; a reduction in the required holding period for the stock received on exercise to only the greater of one year after exercise or two years after grant, instead of the prior three years from exercise; and a new limitation of $100,000 on the value of stock on which options can be granted in any one calendar year to one employee.

Options which do not meet the tests for the new incentive stock options are left to be treated according to the rules which have governed non-qualifying options all along. To examine these rules, we must return to the 1959 amendment to the regulations dealing with the treatment of receipt of restricted stock or other property as compensation. As noted above, that amendment was specifically geared to Reg. § 1.421–6, which was adopted at the same time to deal with the tax incidents of the receipt of a non-qualifying stock option and its later exercise. (It is interesting to note that this regulation was attached to § 421, apparently for lack of any better location, even though § 421 dealt only with options qualifying for the favorable tax treatment reviewed above, and made no reference to options not subject to its provisions.) Reg. § 1.421–6 adopted the long-standing Government view that by and large the receipt of a non-qualifying option was not a taxable event, but was rather merely a prelude to a later bargain purchase, which should be taxed as compensation when it occurs, i.e., when the option is exercised. Initially, Reg. § 1.421–6 had taken the view that employee stock options should always be taxed at exercise, not receipt; but the regulation was later amended to reflect a somewhat grudging acceptance of the proposition that if the option had a "readily ascertainable fair market value", its receipt might be the proper time to measure and tax the compensation involved. According to the regulation this test could be satisfied only if (1) the option was freely transferable, (2) it was exercisable in full immediately, (3) neither the option nor the stock was subject to any restriction or condition having a significant effect on value, and (4) the value of the option privilege (that is, the riskless call on the stock at a fixed price) was readily ascertainable; and in practice an employee stock option would not very often satisfy all of the first three of those conditions, let alone the last one (whether or not the option price was less than the current market value of the stock).

The fact that it was quite common for the stock acquired upon the exercise of a non-qualifying option to be subject to restrictions made it inviting for Reg. § 1.421–6 to go on and deal with the tax treatment of receipt of restricted stock in such circumstances; that in turn became a convenient cross-reference for the rules governing compensatory receipt of restricted property generally. As noted earlier, the rule laid down in Reg. § 1.421–6 for the taxation of restricted stock acquired upon exercise of a non-qualifying option (and made applicable by the cross-reference to all compensatory bargain purchases of restricted property) was that taxation was deferred until the restriction lapsed, at which time compensation, measured by the difference between the option price paid for the stock and its market value (without the restriction) at the time it was received, would be taxed. To illustrate, suppose that an employee received a non-qualifying option to purchase stock for $10 per share at a time when its market value was $8, and that by the time the option was exercised the stock was selling at $20 per share. Suppose also that the stock received by the employee upon exercise of the option was subject to a two-year restriction on transfer which reduced the value of the stock received to $18 per share. Under the pre-1959 practice (assuming no claim that receipt of the option was the taxable event), the employee would probably not have recognized income in the year of receipt of the stock (on the ground that the restriction had a significant effect on value), and then might well also have failed to report any income upon the lapse of the restriction, on the ground that lapse was not a taxable event, an argument accepted by the Tax Court on one occasion, Lehman v. Commissioner, 17 T.C. 652 (1951); alternatively, if the employee did recognize compensation income in the year of receipt of the stock, it would have been in the amount of only $8 per share. Under Reg. § 1.421–6, the employee would not recognize any income upon receipt of the stock, but upon the lapse of the restriction recognition of $10 of compensation income would be required (unless the market value of the stock had declined below $20 by that time, in which event the amount of income would be proportionately reduced). And, of course, by virtue of the cross-reference referred to, the same result would obtain if there was no option in the picture, and the employee was simply permitted to acquire directly, for $10 per share, stock with a market value of $20 per share but subject to a restriction which reduced its value upon receipt to $18.

Notice that Reg. § 1.421–6 did not eliminate all the advantages of using restricted stock or other property as compensation, since the employee's taxable income was limited to the spread in value at the time of receipt, but he was able to postpone the payment of tax until the lapse of the restriction, while still sharing in the benefit of any appreciation in the value of the stock (or other property) in the meantime. As a result, Congress decided to take a hand in 1969, with the addition of § 83 to the Code.

B. The Impact of § 83

Section 83 completely rewrote the tax rules which apply when restricted property is received, either for no consideration or in a bargain purchase, as compensation for services. The statute put an end to that tax bonanza under which a taxpayer could defer reporting any compensation income upon the receipt of restricted stock (or other property), and then either ignore the subsequent lapse of the restriction or merely recognize at that time the amount which would have been compensation income at the outset. Prior to the enactment of § 83 in 1969 the Treasury had already begun to move on this front on its own, by proposing new regulations under § 1.421–6 requiring the taxpayer, upon the lapse of a restriction on stock received for services, to include in compensation income the spread between the amount paid for the stock (if any) and the full market value of the stock at the date of the lapse. Section 83 adopts just that approach when the restriction on the stock constitutes a substantial risk of forfeiture, such as a condition that the stock be surrendered for whatever was paid for it (which might even be nothing), unless substantial services are performed by the employee in the future:

taxation is postponed until the risk of forfeiture lapses (as almost always happens, since a permanent risk of forfeiture would render the stock virtually worthless), or until the stock becomes transferable to someone else free of the risk of forfeiture, if that occurs earlier; but then the full market value of the stock as of that date, less any consideration paid, must be included as compensation income. This means that any appreciation on the stock in the interim will be included in ordinary income at that time, instead of not being taxed until sale of the stock, and then only at capital gains rates (or perhaps not being taxed at all if the stock is held until death). If the restriction does not amount to forfeitability, the compensation income is taxed at the date of receipt, on the basis of the fair market value of the stock upon receipt, determined without regard to any effect the restriction might have upon value (unless the restriction is one which by its terms will never lapse).

The statute makes these rules applicable to any transfer of property "in connection with the performance of services", so that not only employees but also independent contractors, underwriters and the like are covered; and the compensation income, whenever it is recognized, is taxed to the person who performed the services (referred to herein interchangeably as the "taxpayer" and the "employee"), regardless of who actually receives the stock (or owns it at the date of a later recognition of compensation income). As under prior law, the corporation is entitled to a deduction in the same amount taxed as income to the taxpayer, and in the year of the corporation which includes the end of the taxable year of the taxpayer in which the compensation income is recognized.

The Senate Finance Committee Report (Sen.Rep.No.91–552, 91st Cong., 1st Sess. 119, 120–124) contains the following explanation of the new provisions:

> *Explanation of provisions.*—Both the House bill and the committee amendments provide that a person who receives a beneficial interest in property, such as stock, by reason of his performance of services is to be taxed on the value of the property at the time of receipt unless his interest in the property is subject to a substantial risk of forfeiture. In this latter case, he is to be taxed on the value of the property at the time the risk of forfeiture is removed.

> If there is no substantial risk of forfeiture, the recipient of the beneficial interest is required to include in income at the time of the receipt of the property the excess of the fair market value of the property over the amount paid for it. For this purpose, the fair market value of the property is to be determined without regard to any restriction, except a restriction which by its terms

will never lapse. Agreeing with the House bill, the committee feels that restrictions which by their terms never lapse—for example, a requirement that an employee sell his stock back to the employer at book value or some other reasonable price if he terminates his employment—are not tax motivated and should be distinguished from restrictions designed to achieve deferral for tax saving purposes.

If, at the time the property is transferred to the person, his interest in the property is subject to a substantial risk of forfeiture, he is not to be required to include any amount in income with respect to the property until such time as his interest in the property either becomes transferable or no longer is subject to a substantial risk of forfeiture. A substantial risk of forfeiture will be considered to exist where the person's rights to the full enjoyment of the property are conditioned upon his future performance of substantial services. In other cases, the question of whether there is a substantial risk of forfeiture depends upon the facts and circumstances. An interest in property will be considered to be transferable only if the rights of a transferee are not subject to any substantial risk of forfeiture.

In the situation where a person is allowed to sell property only at a price determined under a formula, and this restriction by its terms will never lapse, the restriction is taken into account in valuing the property. In such a case, the restriction is an inherent limitation on the recipient's property rights, and his income should be determined accordingly. The bill provides that the formula price is to be deemed to be the fair market value of the property, unless established to the contrary by the Secretary or his delegate.

If a restriction on property which by its terms will never lapse is canceled, the owner of the property, in effect, is to include in income as compensation, for the taxable year in which the cancellation occurs, the net increase in value he realizes as a result of the cancellation. The bill provides that the amount included in income is to be the excess of the fair market value of the property (computed without regard to the restriction) at the time of cancellation over the sum of: (1) the fair market value of such property (computed by taking the restriction into account) immediately before the cancellation, and (2) the amount, if any, paid for the cancellation. This rule is not to apply, however, if the owner of the property can establish that the cancellation is not compensatory and that the person who would be entitled to a deduction if it were compensatory will not treat the transaction as compensatory.

The rules provided by the bill with respect to restricted property are not to apply to: * * * (3) the transfer of an option without a readily ascertainable fair market value; or (4) the transfer of property pursuant to the exercise of an option with a readily ascertainable fair market value at date of grant. . . .

The holding period for property subject to the restricted property rules prescribed by the bill is to begin at the first time the taxpayer's rights in the property are transferable or are not subject to a substantial risk of forfeiture, whichever occurs earlier (i. e., the time he is deemed to receive compensation).

* * *

Although the committee adopted the major provisions of the House bill relating to restricted stock, it made several minor modifications.

The House bill requires the recognition of income by an employee upon receipt even though his interest in the property is forfeitable if it is transferable. The committee believes that the employee should not be treated as realizing income merely because he can give his forfeitable interest to another person, if the other person is also subject to the forfeitability condition. The committee change provides that an interest in property is to be considered to be transferable only if a transferee would not be subject to the forfeitability conditions—for example, where the employee has a forfeitable interest in stock, but the fact of forfeitability is not indicated on the stock certificate, and a transferee would have no notice of it.

Under another modification made by the committee, where the employee gives forfeitable property to another person, he (and not the donee) would be taxable at the time the donee's rights become nonforfeitable. However, if an employee who has a forfeitable interest in property sells the property in an arm's length transaction, the employee will be treated as realizing income at that time.

To add flexibility, the committee adopted a provision allowing recipients of restricted property the option of treating it as compensation in the year it is received, even though it is nontransferable and subject to a substantial risk of forfeiture. If this election is made, the restricted property rules are not to apply, and later appreciation in the value of the property is not to be treated as compensation. However, if the property is later forfeited, no deduction is to be allowed with respect to the forfeiture. The employee must make this election not later than 30 days after the date of transfer (or the date of enactment of the bill, if later). The election may not be revoked except with the consent of the Secretary of the Treasury or his delegate.

* * *

The committee amendments provide that if restricted stock (or other property) is exchanged in a tax-free exchange for other stock (or property) subject to substantially the same restrictions, the exchange will not cause the holder of the stock to become taxable, and the stock received in the exchange will be treated as restricted property. The same principal applies where stock not subject to the restricted property provision because of the effective date is exchanged in a tax-free exchange. The stock received in the exchange is not to be treated as subject to the new restricted property rules if it is subject to substantially the same restrictions as the stock given up.

The committee provided rules for the employer's deduction for restricted property given to employees as compensation. The allowable deduction is the amount which the employee is required to recognize as income. The deduction is to be allowed in the employer's accounting period which includes the close of the taxable year in which the employee recognizes the income. Where restricted property is not subject to the new rules governing recognition of income, existing rules regarding the amount of the deduction will continue to apply.

* * *

In general, where a parent company's or a shareholder's stock is used to compensate employees under a restricted stock plan, the transfer of the stock by the parent company or shareholder is to be treated as a capital contribution to the company which is to be entitled to a deduction in accordance with the restricted property rules. The parent company or the shareholder merely is to reflect the contribution as an increase of the equity in the company which is entitled to the compensation deduction.

When property other than the employer company's own stock is given as compensation to an employee subject to a substantial restriction and the restrictions lapse at a later date, the company is required under existing law to recognize income in an amount by which the compensation deduction exceeds the company's basis in the property. Likewise, where the basis of the property exceeds the amount recognized as the compensation deduction, the employer can deduct this amount as a loss. The gain or loss would be reported in the employer's accounting period which includes the close of the taxable year in which the employee recognizes the compensation income. The committee intends no change in these rules of existing law.

The effect of § 83 is to deprive restricted stock of virtually all of its special advantages as a compensation technique. If the restricted stock is non-forfeitable, the taxpayer must report compensation income upon receipt, on the basis of the fair market value at that time (ignoring any restriction other than one which will never lapse); in such cases the taxpayer is no better off than if he had received cash, and he is probably worse off when the restriction is one which will lapse eventually but currently prevents any transfer, since the taxpayer not only receives no cash from which to defray the tax but also cannot use any of the stock to raise the necessary funds. If instead the stock is forfeitable, with the consequent recognition of income at the time when the restriction lapses, including any interim appreciation on the stock, the result is much the same as a deferred compensation arrangement (but of uncertain amount, since it depends upon the fair market value of the stock of the date of the lapse) and again the taxpayer receives no cash with which to pay the tax.

As to which of these two approaches will be applied to the taxpayer in any particular case, § 83 makes quite clear that it turns essentially on forfeitability, but is nowhere near as helpful in indicating the scope of that concept. The statute does, in § 83(c) (1), state that forfeitability is present when the "rights to full enjoyment" of the property are conditioned upon the future performance of substantial services by any individual, but the Senate Report indicates that this is not the exclusive test for forfeitability since it states that in other cases the question of whether there is a substantial risk of forfeiture depends on the facts and circumstances. But even under the statutory test the distinction between forfeitability and other types of restrictions may not be readily discernible. To illustrate, no doubt a requirement that the employee simply give back his stock if he terminates his employment within a specified period of years would be regarded as forfeitability; presumably, the result would be the same if the requirement was that he sell the stock back to the corporation for $1 per share, at least assuming that the value of the stock was significantly more than that. But what about a requirement that the employee sell the stock back for, say, book value? If book value may be expected to be well below actual market value, would this not interfere with the "rights to full enjoyment" of the property, within the meaning of § 83(c) (1)? Yet the Senate Report refers to "a requirement that an employee sell his stock back to his employer at book value or some other reasonable price if he terminates his employment" as an example of a restriction which never lapses and hence one that must be taken into account in valuing the property when received; the clear implication is that this is not an example of forfeitability, since otherwise valuation of the property when received would not be called for. Perhaps the critical point in the Senate Report is the reference to a "reasonable price", so that forfeitability would depend upon how far from market value the resale price was. But unless there is some significant difference between the resale price and market value, the resale requirement is hardly a restriction worth taking into account at all; indeed, the pre-1969 regulations specifically stated that a restriction requiring resale of stock to the employer at fair market value was not a restriction having a significant effect on value. On the other hand, if forfeitability is to turn on how large the difference between the resale price and fair market value is, a very troublesome uncertainty would be introduced into a statutory pattern that was supposed to bring a high degree of predictability. And the uncertainty would involve not only the question of how much of a difference is "too much", but also the matter of whether it is the difference at the outset that counts or rather the estimated difference which is likely to obtain in the future.

The regulations under § 83, which did not appear in final form until 1978, introduce the term "substantially vested", which does not appear in the statute, to describe the general category of property received for services which results in immediate compensation income, either because is it not subject to a substantial risk of forfeiture, or because, even though forfeitable, the stock can still be transferred to someone else free of the risk of forfeiture (the special meaning of "transferable" under § 83(c)(2)). This provides an apt occasion to point out that if immediate taxation of restricted stock is desired even though it is not substantially vested, in order to avoid the subsequent inclusion of interim appreciation on the stock in compensation income upon the lapse of the restriction, the preferable course may be to make the stock substantially vested by causing it to be "transferable", perhaps by following the suggestion in the Senate Finance Committee Report of not noting the restriction on the certificate. The advantage of this approach would be that the taxpayer would not have to resort to election under § 83(b) to get immediate taxation, and hence if the stock is ultimately forfeited the taxpayer would not be deprived of a deduction for the amount included in income, which is the price exacted for following the election procedure of § 83(b). As a practical matter, there seems little danger that this would actually enable the holder of the stock to escape from the forfeitability restriction, since a potential buyer, particularly of stock in a closely-held corporation, is likely to make sufficient inquiry to be put on notice of the existence of the restriction.

The final regulations under § 83 also focus the need for a preliminary inquiry as to whether there has been any "transfer" of property at all, before the question of deferral of tax because of forfeitability even arises. This issue is described as follows, in Nolan, Deferred

Compensation and Employee Options under the New Section 83 Regulations, 57 Taxes 790, 791 (1979):

"Taxable Event: The 'Transfer'; . . .

"The key factor in deferred compensation planning is establishing the time when the service provider, usually a key employee, will be taxed on benefits provided to him. The planning may seek to accelerate this time, so that future appreciation in value of the property rights will be accorded capital gain treatment on sale or will escape taxation upon death [because of the basis step-up]. Alternatively, the planning may seek to defer this time to reduce the true ordinary income burden. The income will be taxed only when there has been a *transfer* of property rights *and* there is either an absence or an expiration of any substantial risk of forfeiture.

"Under the Section 83 regulations, a transfer occurs when a person acquires a beneficial ownership interest in property, disregarding any restriction that is not a substantial risk of forfeiture and that will terminate in the future. The grant of an option is not a transfer unless the option has a readily ascertainable fair market value at the time of grant. A transfer of property to an employee in exchange for his obligation to pay its fair market value secured by the property itself, but as to which the employee has no personal liability, may, under the regulations, be treated like the grant of an option and thus may not constitute a transfer, depending on the circumstances. An example in the regulations indicates that, if the employee makes no principal payments on his obligation, the likelihood of his paying the purchase price is in doubt and no transfer of the property has occurred. The result may be that until the employee does make payments, and only to that proportionate extent, will the employee be treated as having acquired the property. This could require a complex determination—the transfer may be that portion of the fair market value of the property at the time any payment is made that the amount of such payment represents of the total payments to be made. The time and measure of his income will be its fair market value only as and when the transfer is deemed to occur, if at all. Appreciation in value prior to that time will be ordinary income; the employer will get no deduction prior to then.

"The regulations also provide that no transfer may have occurred where property is transferred under conditions that require its return upon the happening of an event that is certain to occur, such as the termination of employment. Circumstances indicating that a transfer would not be deemed to occur in such a case would be that the transferee, the employee, does not have the risk of a beneficial owner that the value of the property at the time of transfer will decline substantially. For example, if the employer sells an employee its own stock for $100 on condition that, upon the employee's termination of employment, the employee must sell the stock back to the employer for the greater of its fair market value at that time or $100, no transfer is deemed to have occurred. The employee has never been at risk that he would lose the $100 of property rights that he originally acquired because he will always receive back at least that $100 of value. The net effect of the transaction is that the employer has agreed to pay him a bonus in the future equal to the amount, if any, that the value of the stock increases above $100. Although the promise is funded by the stock held by the employee, the Section 83 regulations do not tax the employee until his termination of employment, and he then has ordinary income equal to the full amount, if any, by which the value of the stock paid by the employer at that time exceeds $100.

"The regulations indicate a transfer may not occur if the amount to be paid for the property in the future upon its surrender 'does not approach' its fair market value at that time. Thus, the sale of employer stock to an employee on condition that he sell it back on termination of employment for the excess of its book value at that time over its book value when it was first acquired is not a transfer. Similarly, such a transfer requiring it to be sold back for the amount of dividends that have been paid on the stock since it was acquired would not be a transfer.

"These rules and examples point up the importance in deferred compensation planning of knowing when a transfer will be deemed to occur under the Section 83 regulations so that future appreciation in value will be capital gain, not ordinary income."

* * *

Even though most of the benefits of restricted stock were eliminated by § 83, there may still be some advantages in arrangements involving restrictions which never lapse, particularly in situations where stock is expected to appreciate sharply, perhaps by virtue of a foreseeable public offering or the like, and the purpose of the arrangement is to make it possible for an employee to acquire substantially more stock than he could afford even at the current value. Suppose, for example, a corporation has 50,000 shares outstanding, with a current value of $10 per share, and because of prospects that the stock might be worth as much as $30 per share in the not too distant future the corporation wishes to make 5000 shares available to a key employee who has only limited outside resources. The shares might be issued to the employee subject to a perpetual restriction that prior to any sale or transfer of the shares the employee must offer them to the corporation at, say, $8 less than the current fair market value. Assuming that this does not constitute forfeitability under the statute, the stock would be included in the employee's income upon receipt; but since the stock is subject to a restriction which never lapses, the restriction would be taken into account in valuing the stock at the time of receipt. Whether this restriction would reduce the current fair value of this stock all the way down to $2 per share is not clear. Under § 83(d) (1) a perpetual restriction "which allows the transferee to sell such property only at a price determined under a formula" fixes the fair value at that price, unless the Government can sustain the burden of proving the contrary. Assuming that pegging the price at $8 less than fair market value represents a "formula", does a right of first refusal in the corporation constitute a restriction "which allows the transferee to sell such property only at" the formula price? Theoretically, the answer would seem to be "no", since if the corporation does not exercise its right of first refusal the employee would be free to sell to others at full value. But as a practical matter the corporation is quite likely to take advantage of such a bargain price, and its failure to do so would probably constitute a cancellation of the restriction, giving rise to ordinary income, as noted below (unless perhaps there is some legal restriction on the repurchase of stock). Moreover, this would seem to be the type of restriction contemplated by § 83(d) (1); indeed, one that literally conformed to the words of that provision and flatly prevented the employee in perpetuity from selling to anyone except at a formula price below market value would leave the employee in position to decide whom he wished to favor with this bargain purchase, which would in and of itself be an indirect form of value to the employee. In any event, even if a right of first refusal does not fix the value of the stock under § 83(d)(1), it would be likely to reduce the value to a figure close to the formula price; though the recipient of the stock is not required to sell and can therefore enjoy the full value of the other elements of the stock, the fact remains that at least in the case of a minority interest in a publicly-held stock, the price at which the stock can be sold is the dominant factor in valuation. Assuming a $2 value for the stock when received, and assuming further that the stock was issued for only nominal consideration, the employee would have to pay tax on compensation income of only approximately $10,000 as the price of being able to reap the rewards of appreciation at capital gains rates on 5,000 shares; without the restriction the same tax bite would be incurred upon the receipt of a mere 1000 shares.

One other aspect of perpetual restrictions worth noting is the fact that since the corporation will normally retain the power to cancel the restriction, the corporation will have a continuing power to provide the employee with a "bonus" at any time (or from time to time, since the restriction need not be cancelled on all the shares at the same time), in the amount of the difference between the fair market value of the stock with the restriction and without it. As might be expected, the statute, in § 83(d)(2), makes this "bonus" normally taxable as compensation income, in the year of cancellation; presumably, it is taxable to the person who performed the services, no matter who owns the stock (even though § 83(d)(2) does not expressly say so, and the Senate Report quoted above refers to including such gain from the cancellation of restrictions as compensation income to the "owner" of the stock), since § 83(h), which allows the employer a corresponding deduction for such "cancellation income" as well as for any other compensation income taxable under § 83, assumes, and indeed is literally conditioned upon, the inclusion of the compensation in the "income of the person who performed" the services. Thus, in straight tax terms cancellation of stock restrictions offers no particular advantage over a regular cash bonus, and it may be disadvantageous to the employee if he has no funds with which to pay the tax. But again as a practical matter the perpetual (at least until cancelled) stock restriction provides a useful pre-existing vehicle for additional compensation, which may afford the advantage of not reducing the company's net income for accounting purposes, unlike a direct issuance of stock as compensation; and by judicious timing the cancellation may be made to coincide with either lower tax brackets for the employee, or his sale of at least some of the stock so that he will thereby be in funds with which to pay the tax on the compensation income (as well as the capital gain tax on any appreciation on the stock since its receipt.) Moreover, the statute even affords the possibility that the cancellation "bonus" need not be included in income, if, as provided in § 83(d)(2)(A) and (B), the employee can establish that the cancellation was not compensatory (which will probably be very hard to do), and the corporation also agrees to the non-compensatory treatment by foregoing any compensation deduction for the amount involved.

While restricted property is the main objective of § 83, the statutory pattern actually applies by its terms to any transfer of property in connection with the performance of services. However, § 83(e) exempts from the operation of the section the transfer of an option without a readily ascertainable fair market value, thus preserving existing law under which the transfer of such an option is not a taxable event (and compensation income is taxed at the date of the exercise of the option, measured by the fair market value of the stock acquired at that time). Also exempt is a transfer of property pursuant to the exercise of an option which had a readily ascertainable fair market value at the date of the grant, since pursuant to prior law, and now by operation of § 83, such an option is taxed upon receipt at its fair market value, and the exercise of the option thereafter is not a taxable event.

The latest word on the taxation of stock options at the date when the options are granted appears in the Joint Committee's Summary of the Tax Reform Act of 1976 (at page 25), in conjunction with that Act's repeal of the special statutory rules favoring qualifying options (subsequently revived by the Economic Recovery Tax Act of 1981). The Summary, proceeding on the assumption that thereafter all options would be governed by the general rules applicable to non-qualifying options, noted that if an option had a "readily ascertainable fair market value" at the date of grant compensation income would be taxed at that time, but otherwise the compensation would be measured and taxed at the time of the option's exercise. The Summary continued with the following:

> It is intended that in applying these rules for the future, the Internal Revenue Service will make every reasonable effort to determine a fair market value for an option (i. e., in cases where similar property would be valued for estate tax purposes) where the employee irrevocably elects to have the option valued at the time it is granted (particularly in the case of an option granted for a new business venture). It is intended that the Service will promulgate regulations and rulings setting forth as specifically as possible the criteria which will be weighed in valuing an option which the employee elects to value at the time it is granted.
> * * *

No such promulgations have ever appeared; query if they ever will, now that the 1981 Act has reintroduced special, favorable tax treatment for options qualifying as Incentive Stock Options.

Two final, unrelated comments may be in order. First, since § 83(h) expressly provides that a deduction for the employer "shall be allowed" under § 162 in the amount included in the income of the taxpayer, it would appear that the usual "reasonable allowance" limitation of § 162(a) (1) is not applicable to this deduction; but query whether an amount arising out of a restricted stock arrangement will be taken into account in testing the overall reasonableness of the rest of the employee's compensation. Second, on the question as to how the death of the person who performed the services affects the taxation of restricted stock which has not yet been taxed because it was forfeitable, if the forfeitability continues in the hands of whoever receives the stock, the death of the employee should not result in the imposition of tax; a later termination of forfeitability will presumably result in income to the holder, taxable as income in respect of a decedent. Similarly, if the employee's death terminates forfeitability (or at least permits transfer free of the risk of forfeiture), according to Reg. § 1.83–1(d) the income realized is to be treated as income in respect of a decedent.

A.   Issuance of Stock for Property

The tax incidents to the corporation upon the issuance of its stock for money or other property can be simply stated: by virtue of §1032, no gain or loss is recognized, and it makes no difference whether the corporation is just being organized or has been in operation for some time, or whether it is treasury stock rather than authorized but unissued stock that is used. The corporation's basis in property acquired for its stock depends upon the tax treatment accorded to the transferor of property, which will be examined immediately below. (Stock issued in exchange for services, on the other hand, will usually give rise to a compensation deduction for the corporation, but the amount and the timing depends upon the taxation of the compensation income involved, which will be discussed separately later.)

With respect to the recipient of stock, obviously a simple purchase for cash does not ordinarily produce any tax consequences (unless it is a bargain purchase), and the basis in the stock would be the price paid, under the normal cost principle of §1012. When stock is acquired in exchange for property, prima facie the transaction constitutes a taxable exchange under §1002, calling for recognition of gain or loss by the transferor of property, in the amount determined under §1001. The basis of the stock received would again be its cost. In an exchange transaction, the "cost" of the property acquired is normally measured by the fair market value of the property given up; however, in an arm's length transaction the fair market value of the property received can be used instead, if it is more readily apparent, since the value of the two should be equal. Indeed, in the rare circumstance when the respective values of properties exchanged in a taxable transaction are not equal even though no gift or other special factor is present, the basis of the property received must be measured by its value rather than by the value of the property given up, so that the new cost basis of the property received will correspond to the figure used for the amount realized in computing gain (or loss). Philadelphia Park Amusement Co. v. United States, 126 F. Supp. 184 (Ct. Cl. 1954).

The Corporation's basis in the property received is determined under the normal cost rule, Reg. §1.1032-1(d), and would therefore be measured by the fair market value of the stock issued for it (or, as just noted, the fair market value of the property itself).

There are a number of exceptions to the general rule of §1002 requiring the recognition of gain or loss upon an exchange. One of the most important of these is §351, which provides for non-recognition in connection with certain transfers of property to a corporation in exchange for its stock or securities. Speaking generally, §351 precludes the recognition of gain or loss when the transferor or transferors of property receive only stock or securities of the corporation and thereafter they own enough to be "in control" of the corporation, which is defined in §368(c) to mean ownership of 80% of the total combined voting power of the corporation and 80% of all other classes of stock. For the purposes of §351, the term "stock" does not include either warrants or options, Reg. §1.351-1 (a)(1); but it does include a non-assignable, contractual right to receive additional stock contingent upon future earnings, so that both the right, and ultimately any stock, may be received tax-free. Hamrick v. Commissioner, 43 T.C. 21 (1964.) Since the term "securities" is used in conjunction with "stock", it obviously refers to debt instruments: more precise parameters will be considered below.

If, in a transaction which meets the control test of §351, a transferor of property receives not only non-recognition property, i.e., stock or securities of the corporation, but also "boot", i.e., money or other property, §351(a) no longer applies to prevent the recognition of gain. However, §351(b) comes into play to limit recognition of gain on the transaction to the amount of any money plus the fair market value of any other property received. A loss on the transaction would still go unrecognized.

Often, particularly in connection with the incorporation of a going proprietorship or partnership, property is transferred to a controlled corporation subject to liabilities, with the corporation either expressly assuming the liabilities or taking the property subject to them. Without more, relieving the transferor of liabilities, whether directly, by assuming them, or indirectly, by taking the property subject to them, would constitute other consideration moving to the transferor and hence boot under §351(b). But the practical effect of such a result would be to nullify one of the primary objectives of §351, which is to enable parties to incorporate a going business enterprise without invidious tax consequences. Accordingly, it is provided in §357 that the assumption of a transferor's liabilities will generally not be treated as boot (but as a corollary there will be a corresponding reduction in the transferor's basis in the stock or securities received from the corporation, under §358(d)). However, there are two exceptions in §357: subsection (b), which provides for boot treatment if the principal purpose for the corporation's assuming a liability (or taking property subject to a liability) is to avoid income tax, or in any event is not a bona fide business purpose; and subsection (c), which requires boot treatment, regardless of purpose, to the extent that the total of the liabilities "transferred" by a taxpayer exceeds the total basis of the property transferred by him to the corporation.

The principal purpose exception of §357(b) is designed to combat such situations as a taxpayer borrowing on property just before its transfer to a controlled corporation and retaining the proceeds while leaving the corporation to repay the loan. E.g., Drybrough v. Commissioner, 376 F.2d 350 (6th Cir. 1967). In addition, any effort to foist upon a controlled corporation purely personal obligations of the transferor, such as liability for his individual income taxes, would invite the application of §357(b). E.g., Campbell v. Wheeler, 342 F.2d 837 (5th Cir. 1965). But the Government has failed in efforts to apply §357(b) to cases where the controlled corporation assumes the purchase money obligation incurred by the transferor when he acquired the property he subsequently transfers to the corporation. Simpson v. Commissioner, 43 T.C. 900 (1965); Jewell v. United States, 330 F.2d 761 (9th Cir. 1964). In the latter case the court commented rather wryly on the twofold test in § 357(b) of whether the principal purpose was to avoid taxes, or in any event was not a bona fide business purpose: "We think that when, if ever, this combination of motives and action occurs, it will be noteworthy. It would require that the action be immune from both tax avoidance motive and business sense."

Section 357(c) can be best understood in the light of the basis provisions governing § 351 transactions. If a transferor receives only non-recognition property, under § 358 his basis in that property is the same as his basis in the property transferred. If the non-recognition property consists of both stock and securities, or more than one class of stock, the carryover basis is allocated among the various classes of stock and securities received in accordance with the fair market value of each. Reg. § 1.358–2(b)(2). When the transferor is required to recognize some gain because of the receipt of boot, his basis in the non-recognition property received is equal to his basis in the property transferred plus the amount of any gain recognized, less the amount of any money and the fair market value of any other boot received. Section 358(a)(1). His basis in the boot would be its fair market value. Section 358(a)(2). If the corporation assumes any liabilities in the transaction, or takes the property transferred subject to liabilities, then although the transferor does not have to recognize gain on that account, his basis in the non-recognition property is reduced by the amount of such liabilities. Section 358(d). To illustrate, if property with a basis of 100 and a present market value of 130 is transferred, subject to liabilities of 40, to a corporation in exchange for stock worth 80 and cash of 10, the transferor would actually have a gain of 30, but it would only be recognized to the extent of 10. His basis in the stock would be 60, computed as follows: 100 (basis of the property transferred) plus 10 (recognized gain) less 10 (cash received) less 40 (liabilities to which the property was subject).

Suppose that in the preceding illustration the current value of the property transferred to the corporation was 230, and the liabilities to which it was subject totalled 140. In that event, the application of § 358 would produce a minus basis for the non-recognition property received by the transferor (100 plus 10, less 10, less 140, or minus 40). Prior to the 1954 Code it was not clear whether a minus basis was permissible or whether instead transactions of this kind required the recognition of enough gain to bring the basis up to zero. In Easson v. Commissioner, 294 F.2d 653 (9th Cir. 1961), the court found no significant objection to a minus basis under the prior law and held that no additional gain had to be recognized. It is this situation with which § 357(c) of the 1954 Code deals, and that section now expressly requires a transferor to recognize gain in the amount by which the accompanying liabilities exceed the total basis of the property transferred. See generally, Cooper, Negative Basis, 75 Harv.L.Rev. 1352 (1962).

The corporation's basis in § 351 transactions is governed by § 362. Under that section the basis of the transferred property in the hands of the corporation is the same as it was in the hands of the transferor, increased by the amount of any gain recognized by the transferor. Thus in the preceding example where property with a basis of 100 and present value of 130 was transferred, subject to liabilities of 40, in exchange for stock worth 80 and cash of 10, the corporation's basis in the property acquired would be 110, the sum of 100 (the transferor's basis) plus 10 (gain recognized to the transferor). Notice that the liabilities play no part in the determination of the corporation's basis, whether or not they are assumed. Notice too that the operation of the basis provisions results in their being two potential gains, one to the corporation on the property and the other to the stockholder on his stock, where only one existed before.

For property transferred to the corporation in a § 351 transaction, § 1223(2) allows the corporation to tack the holding period of the transferor. Section 1223(1) allows the transferor to tack on to the holding period for his stock the holding period of the property transferred, if the property was either a capital asset or an asset eligible for capital gain treatment under § 1231. If, as would typically be true in the incorporation of a going business, the transferred assets include some that are eligible for capital gains treatment and others that are not, presumably the stock would be allocated between the two types of property in accordance with their fair market values, in order to determine how much of the stock would be entitled to a tacked holding period and how much would not.

Sometimes a taxpayer wants to *avoid* the non-recognition provisions of § 351, in which event, since the section is not elective, pains must be taken not to comply with the conditions of § 351. For example, the taxpayer may be seeking to recognize a loss on a transfer of assets which have depreciated in value. Or he may want recognition even if a gain is present, in order to obtain the concomitant "step-up" in the corporation's basis in the acquired property to the fair market value of the property, rather than carrying over the transferor's basis, as would be required if § 351 applied; if the gain to be recognized is subject only to the favorable capital gains rate, the taxpayer may be willing to incur that tax in order to give the corporation a stepped-up basis for depreciable assets which would decrease, through depreciation deductions, the corporation's ordinary income. However, before pursuing this course there are several factors that must be carefully weighed. First, the entire tax on the gain must be paid at the outset, whereas the corresponding depreciation deductions will be spread out over the useful life of the property. Second, the gain recognized by the transferor will not produce any corresponding tax benefit to the corporation to the extent such gain is allocable to non-depreciable assets like land and goodwill. Third, under § 1245 any gain on depreciable personal property will be taxed to the transferor as ordinary income rather than capital gain, to the extent of any depreciation previously taken. (A similar though much more limited threat is posed in the case of gain on depreciable real property by § 1250.)

Finally, there is the possibility of being subjected to §1239, which provides ordinary income treatment for any gain recognized on a sale or exchange of depreciable property between certain related parties, including one between a taxpayer and a corporation of which the taxpayer and his spouse own 80% or more in value of the outstanding stock (after application of the attribution of stock ownership rules of §318, other than family attribution beyond spouses). The purpose of §1239 is to foreclose the tax advantage referred to above of getting a higher basis for depreciation

purposes, deductible against ordinary income, at a cost of
only capital gain taxation to a related party (a benefit not
entirely eliminated by §§1245 and 1250, as for example in
the case of appreciated real estate on which only straight-
line depreciation has been taken). In the light of this
purpose, it seems that §1239 should apply to original incorporation as well as to transactions with an already existing
corporation. However, this result can be reached only by
applying §1239's 80% test after the transaction in question
(when that is the first issuance of stock); the statutory
language, on the other hand, makes no reference to "immediately after", as §368(c) does, and hence is just as consistent with requiring the 80% holding before the challenged
transfer. One case has expressly adopted the latter view,
ruling that §1239 did not apply when the taxpayer's holding
(in an already existing corporation) only went above the
required 80% in value as a result of the challenged transaction. Robishaw v. Commissioner, 616 F.2d 507 (Ct. Cl.
1980). Incidentally, although §1239 only deals with recognized gain, it can intersect with §351, if there is partial
recognition of gain by virtue of the presence of boot.

Notice that §1239's 80% test is directed to the value
of the outstanding stock, unlike the control test of §368(c),
which looks primarily to voting power (plus the number of
shares, so far as non-voting stock is concerned). This
difference will be examined in more detail below.

B. QUALIFICATION UNDER §351

1. Introduction

As noted, in order to qualify under §351 the one or
more persons who transfer property to a corporation must
"immediately after" be "in control" of the corporation,
within the meaning of §368(c). In the simple case of
incorporation of an existing proprietorship or partnership
the requisite stock ownership under §368(c) will normally be
readily satisfied, with the proprietor or partners transferring all of the property received by the new corporation and
ending up with all of its stock. However, occasionally some
of the stock may be issued at the outset to a non-transferor
of property perhaps as compensation for services to the
corporation; or stock received by a transferor of property
may be promptly assigned to a third person, maybe as a gift,
or pursuant to a prior commitment to the third party.
Situations of this kind can present serious problems under
the control test. There may also be difficulties with the
control requirement in connection with transfers to an
on-going corporation, as the following case demonstrates:

ESTATE OF KAMBORIAN v. COMMISSIONER

Court of Appeals, First Circuit, 1972.
469 F.2d 219.

ALDRICH, SENIOR JUDGE: Four individuals, hereinafter taxpayers, owned some 76% of the stock of X corporation, and two of them, as trustees for the wife of another, held 50,000 additional shares, or slightly in excess of 13%. Taxpayers individually owned all of the stock of Y corporation. For bona fide business reasons X corporation decided to acquire the Y stock in exchange for 22,871 X shares. The exchange was perfected pursuant to a formal agreement which included, with the wife's consent, the purchase of 418 X shares by the trust.[1] This resulted in increasing taxpayers' combined holdings in X to 77.3%; the trust's interest was reduced to just under 13%, notwithstanding its purchase. However, the combined holdings of taxpayers and the trust remained in excess of 80%, and taxpayers took the position that the transaction was, accordingly, to be viewed as a tax-free exchange. 1954 Int.Rev.Code, §§ 351, 368(c). The Commissioner disagreed, claiming that the "control" group, or the transaction, see post, was to be limited to taxpayers as the former owners of the Y stock. In refusing to include the trust's purchase the Commisioner relied, in part upon Regulation 1.351–1(a)(1)(ii).[*]

The Tax Court ruled in favor of the Commissioner, 56 T.C. No. 66 (1971), and taxpayers seek review. Basically, they make a frontal attack on the regulation urging us to hold it invalid as going beyond what they claim is a plain and positive statute.[2]

We start with the general proposition expressed in section 1002 of the Code,

> "Except as otherwise provided in this subtitle, on the sale or exchange of property the entire amount of the gain or loss, determined under section 1001, shall be recognized."

Section 351 provides,

> "TRANSFER TO CORPORATION CONTROLLED BY TRANSFEROR.
>
> "(a) *General Rule.*—No gain or loss shall be recognized if property is transferred to a corporation by one or more persons solely in exchange for stock or securities in such corporation and immediately after the exchange such person or persons are in control (as defined in section 368(c) of the corporation."

1. The trust paid $5,016, or $12 a share. On this basis the shares acquired by taxpayers were worth $274,452. The Tax Court found they were worth slightly more.

* [Ed. note] That Regulation provides that "stock or securities issued for property which is of relatively small value in comparison to the value of the stock and securities already owned (or to be received for services) by the person who transferred such property, shall not be treated as having been issued in return for property if the primary purpose of the transfer is to qualify under this section the exchanges of property by other persons transferring property". For the guideline used by the IRS in applying this provision, see Subsection 3.07 of Rev. Proc. 77–37, p. 205 infra.

2. Alternatively, taxpayers argue that even if the regulation is valid, the Tax Court erred in applying it to their transaction. This claim is patently erroneous. After a review of the record it is clear that the Tax Court's findings were not only reasonably supported, but manifestly correct.

"Control" is defined in section 368(c) as the possession of 80% of the stock of the transferee corporation.

Taxpayers' brief contains a wistful aside that there is involved a large tax and only a small discrepancy. We are not moved, legally or emotionaily, by this fact. But in order to avoid any overfall therefrom, we will imagine another case that would have to be decided against the government if taxpayers are correct and all arranged transactions, regardless of their purpose or their connection with one another, are to be viewed as a single exchange. Let us suppose that P owns 10% and S 90% of the stock of W, and P owns all of the stock of Z. If P transfers his Z stock to W for further W shares, ending up with a 30% interest, it is obviously not a tax-free exchange. But if P induces S to buy, contemporaneously, one share of W stock for cash the present petitioners would say that P and S are to be considered jointly as exchanging property, and since together they owned over 80% of the transferee corporation, P may claim the statutory exception.

Our analysis does not lead to such a result. By the term "property [that] is transferred," the statute contemplates a single transaction, even though, as it goes on to recognize, there may be a number of transferors or participants. What is a transaction must be determined in the light of the statutory purpose, lest taxpayers be allowed to frustrate that purpose by manipulation of clearly taxable exchanges. . . . We stated that purpose long ago in speaking of the predecessor of section 351, which contains no presently material variance.

> "It is the purpose of Section 112(b)(5) to save the taxpayer from an immediate recognition of a gain, or to intermit the claim of a loss, in certain transactions where gain or loss may have accrued in a constitutional sense, but where in a popular and economic sense there has been a mere change in the form of ownership and the taxpayer has not really 'cashed in' on the theoretical gain, or closed out a losing venture."

Portland Oil Co. v. Commissioner, 1 Cir., 1940, 109 F.2d 479, 488, cert. denied 310 U.S. 650, 60 S.Ct. 1100, 84 L.Ed. 1416.

Thus in our hypothetical, considering P alone, there was not a "mere change in the form of ownership." Before the transaction P "owned" Z corporation, since he owned 100% of its stock. After the transaction his ownership of Z was reduced to 30% because he held only a 30% interest in W, the transferee corporation. In keeping with "economic sense" a taxpayer may be allowed a certain amount of slack. This has been ruled to be 20%; and had P ended with an 80% interest in W, and thus of Z, his ownership of the latter would not be thought to be materially changed. 1954 Int.Rev.Code § 368(c). But where P does not own that 80% it can be permissible to consider transfers by other owners only if those transfers were, in economic terms, sufficiently related to P's to make all of the transfers parts of a single transaction.

It is possible that a valid association may exist even when different types of property are transferred to the transferee corporation by different transferors. Thus in Halliburton v. Commissioner, 9 Cir., 1935, 78 F.2d 265, funds contributed by other parties were found to be as necessary to the overall purpose of the transaction as was the exchange by the litigating taxpayers. In our P and S case, however, there is no economic connection, and hence no basis for regarding the two transfers as parts of one transaction, and hence of considering P and S as a unit in terms of control. If a taxpayer were able, so simply, to effect a concatenation and say that the statute applied to him, the statute would be meaningless.

The instant case presents no better claim of a connection in an economic sense. The four shareholders of Y decided it would be advantageous to merge Y with X. Finding themselves short of the requirements for tax-free treatment, they persuaded a shareholder of X, who was a complete stranger to Y, to make a token purchase of X shares. Other than the fact that the trust's participation was incorporated into the acquisition agreement, there was no relation between the exchange of Y shares and this very minor purchase. The trust transferred no Y shares. The cash it contributed to X—$5,000 for 418 shares of a corporation with nearly 400,000 shares outstanding—could have had no significant impact on X's ability to conduct its business. The trustees' desire to help the Y stockholders avoid taxes, warrantably found by the Tax Court to have been the primary motive for the trust's purchase,[3] cannot be used to make a single transaction out of otherwise unrelated transfers.

Without going into every ramification of the Regulation, in this case it appropriately and fairly fits our interpretation of the statute. Taxpayers' criticisms of the Tax Court's opinion in this regard are not readily persuasive. However, if, in some fashion, taxpayers could remove the Regulation from consideration or application altogether, it would avail them nothing.

3. The court's use of "primary motive" was to coincide with the language of the Regulation. On the basis of its findings it seems apparent that it was the sole motive. The only effect we can see from the point of view of the trust was to reduce its income.

2. Composition of the Control Group - "Property" under §351

Since the control test looks to how much of the stock of the corporation is owned by the persons who transferred property to the corporation in the transaction under consideration, it is necessary to identify who the transferors of property are, and that requires a determination of what constitutes "property" for this purpose. The two most significant items about which there might be some question are cash, which, as the Kamborian case indicates, is included, and services, which are expressly ruled out by §351(d)(1). The primary purpose in excluding services seems to have been to make sure that §351 could not enable a recipient of stock for services to escape the recognition of compensation income, a goal with which there can be little quarrel. However, the approach taken also prevents stock issued to someone who has only contributed services from being included in the control group for the purpose of testing control under §351. Thus, if upon the incorporation of a business more than 20 percent of the stock is issued to one who contributes only services, the control test cannot be satisfied. This seems like an unnecessary obstacle to the issuance of stock for services, particularly since the burden of non-qualification under §351 falls upon the party (or parties) who transferred property to the corporation, and does not affect the contributor of services (who is taxed on compensation income in any event).

From the point of view of a transferor of property, the role of §351 is presumably to distinguish between a mere recasting of the form of his investment, and a transaction which amounts to a change of the investment, akin to an ordinary sale or exchange. It is hard to see any reason of policy why the issuance of more than 20% of the stock to one who is only rendering services to the corporation should ipso facto mean that the transfer of property by others is more like a sale than a mere change of form. Actually, a transfer of property to a corporation in exchange for stock more nearly resembles a sale when a substantial amount of the stock is issued to others for cash than when it is issued for services. However, the law is otherwise: hence, if a sole proprietor transfers his business to a newly-organized corporation for, say, 50% of the stock, §351 is satisfied if the rest of the stock is issued to another for cash, but not if the rest of the stock is issued to someone else for services.

It is submitted that stock issued for services to the corporation should be includible in testing for the requisite 80% control under §351, although of course this should not preclude the recognition of compensation income on account of stock received for services. As a matter of fact, this is just the treatment accorded when stock is issued for services to one who has also transferred property to the corporation: the stock issued for services is counted in the control group, Reg. §1.351-1(a)(2), but nevertheless constitutes taxable income to the recipient (as the cross reference in §351(f)(4) confirms). There seems no reason why the same approach could not be taken with respect to stock received for services by one who does not contribute any property.

Under the present system, then, it makes quite a difference whether one who receives stock for services is also a transferor of property; if he is, all of his stock counts in applying the control test, whereas if not, none of his stock is included. This puts too much strain on these provisions, since, literally, anyone can become a transferor of property merely by paying a few dollars for the shares received (or perhaps just a "peppercorn" or two). And the fact is that some payment will almost always be present, even when the stock is being issued essentially for expected future services to the corporation, because most corporation statutes forbid the issuance of stock solely for future services and hence the recipient of the stock will make at least a nominal contribution of cash or other property in order to comply with corporate law. If this were enough to bring all of the stock received by the service-provider into the control count, the services exclusion would be a dead letter (which might be desirable, as noted above, but should probably await legislative action).

A similar issue arises with respect to transfers of property to an existing corporation, where, too, all of the stock owned by the transferors of property counts in applying the control test, regardless of whether such stock was received in connection with the current transfer or was previously owned. But this kind of transaction raises a more substantial policy issue under §351. If, for example, one who already owns at least 80% of the stock of a corporation transfers property to it in exchange for more stock, that is really just a change in the form of ownership of the property, and non-recognition of gain or loss is entirely fitting; the same is true if the pre-existing 80% interest is owned by several persons, and they all participate in the current transfer of property. On the other hand, suppose instead that one who owns only, say, 30% of the outstanding stock transfers property for additional stock which raises his percentage interest to, say 40%, or even 70%, and none of the other stockholders participate in the transaction: in that case, the current transfer is not so clearly just a change in the form of ownership of the property transferred, but may be more akin to a sale or exchange, and under the policy of §351 it would fall on the taxable side of the line. However, once again, taking the language of §351 literally the rest of the outstanding stock could be brought into the control count as long as the holders transfer some cash or property for additional shares. Here such a result would do some violence to the policy underlying §351, unlike the case of a nominal transfer of property by one who is essentially receiving stock for services, where, as suggested earlier, there seems no reason not to count the stock received for services even without the embroidery of a nominal transfer of property.

Of course this is the issue presented in the Kamborian case. It can be no surprise that the Service has sought to deal with the issue of nominal transfers of property, by way of the regulation under §351 discussed in Kamborian (and set out in the editor's note to the opinion). The "relatively small value" test of the regulation has been objectively quantified in ¶3.07 of Rev. Proc. 77-37, in terms of whether the value of the property transferred is equal to at least 10% of the value of the stock already owned, or received for services. Nevertheless, there may still be some measurement problems in the services cases, especially when

in form the stock is issued for consideration, but there is alleged to have been a bargain purchase, and hence the stock must be valued to determine how much was issued for the purchase price and how much was in reality transferred for services.

Conversely, the "primary purpose" test, while necessarily subjective, may offer more promise in the services context than in the already-owned cases like Kamborian, because of the variety of business, corporate, and tax factors that are usually intertwined in deciding who gets how much stock, particularly upon initial incorporation.

Another important factor in the services case is the possibility that one alleged to be receiving stock solely for for services is actually contributing some type of secret process, formula, or technical "know-how" which amounts to property under §351. Rev. Rul. 64-56, 1964-1 Cum. Bull. 133, holds that such items can qualify, whether or not patentable; and the fact that there is an accompanying agreement to provide services does not preclude a finding that "property" was transferred (although if the services are not merely ancillary to the property transfer, a reasonable allocation between the two must be made, for the purpose of focusing and taxing the amount of the stock which represents compensation income).

The question of whether a property interest has been transferred is particularly troublesome when the alleged transferor is also to become a long-term employee of the corporation. If this prospective employee's future services are closely related to the operations in which the putative intangible property, such as a secret process, will be used, obviously the line between a mere promise of future services and a claimed transfer of property could be exceedingly fine. But as long as the benefits to be derived from the intangible do not depend exclusively upon the

services of the particular transferor, property treatment is
at least a possibility.

On the other hand, the fact that the taxpayer has completed
his efforts on behalf of the corporation by the time he receives
his stock provides no assurance that what he has transferred will
be viewed as property. Stock issued for legal services performed
in organizing the corporation is a good example. Another
illustration is James v. Commissioner, 53 T.C. 63 (1969), where
the taxpayer and Talbot agreed to develop a real estate project
together, Talbot contributing the land, the taxpayer arranging
for the needed FHA commitment and the financing for the
project. After the taxpayer had completed the arrangements, the
land and the financing commitments were transferred to a corporation, and the stock was divided equally between Talbot and
the taxpayer. The court rejected the taxpayer's contention

> that he had transferred property to the corporation, in the
> form of contract rights, to which §351 applied; rather the
> stock was received for services, and hence represented
> compensation taxable as ordinary income. In addition, since
> Talbot was left as the only transferor of property, and he
> received less than 80% of the stock, the control test was
> not satisfied, with the result that §351 did not apply to
> his transfer and gain had to be recognized.

3. "Immediately After" under §351

Under §351 the control test is to be applied "immediately after" the transfer(s) of property to the corporation.
Taken literally, this sounds as though the requisite computation of the total stock outstanding and the amount owned
by the transferors of property must be made as of a particular point in time, right after the transfer(s) in question.
But in practice the time at which the test should be applied
can not be so precisely pinpointed. There may be subsequent
changes in the total stock outstanding, or the amount owned
by the transferors of property, and if such changes were
already committed at the time of the transaction in question,
or perhaps if simply planned though not legally binding,
they might well be taken into account in applying the control
test. For example, a series of relatively contemporaneous
but not simultaneous transfers of property to the corporation
raises a question as to after which transfer the control
computation should be made. Even more significant is the
issue of what view to take when one of the transferors of
property to the corporation shortly thereafter disposes of
some of the stock he received, in a transaction which was at
least clearly in prospect from the outset, if not actually
committed.

With respect to seriatim transfers of property to the
corporation, Reg. §1.351-1(a)(1) provides that "the phrase
'immediately after the exchange' does not necessarily require
simultaneous exchanges . . ., but comprehends a situation
where the rights of the parties have been previously defined
and the execution of the agreement proceeds with an expedi-
tion consistent with orderly procedure". Pursuant to that
regulation, Rev. Rul. 78-294, 1978-2 Cum. Bull. 141, held

that §351 was satisfied when property was transferred to a newly-created corporation in exchange for all of its stock, followed shortly by a planned public offering of stock by the corporation for cash. At first blush this result might be regarded as obvious: on the one hand, the original transferors of property were clearly in control before the public offering; on the other hand, if that offering is taken into account then the cash paid by the buyers of that stock represents property transferred to the corporation, and the stock they received counts in applying the control test, so that again the transferors of property would own 100% of the stock. And it does seem sensible to conclude that if the subsequent issuance of stock for cash is sufficiently related to the original transfers of property to be taken into account in measuring the total stock outstanding, those later transfers of cash deserve to be fully integrated with the initial transfers of property, making those who buy the subsequent issue from the corporation includible in the transferor group for purposes of the control test. But remember that if the public offering takes the form of a "firm underwriting", under which the underwriter buys the stock from the corporation and resells it to the public, the public shareholders would not have transferred anything to the corporation; hence, if more than 20% of the total stock is re-sold to the public, qualification under §351 must depend upon either not taking account of the public offering, or finding, as Rev. Rul. 78-294 did, that there is enough uncertainty as to how much of the stock will be sold by the underwriter, and when, to treat the stock as owned, for purposes of the control test, by the underwriter (who was concededly a transferor to the corporation).

In other situations involving a contemplated disposition of stock by the transferors of property which will deprive them of the requisite 80% control, the test has often been stated in terms of whether there was a plan to part with control at the time of the property transfers in question. A binding commitment is not essential to defeat §351; it is enough that the original transfer(s) of property and the subsequent disposition of some of the stock received were mutually interdependent transactions, such that "the legal relations created by one transaction would have been fruitless without a completion of the series". Culligan Water Conditioning of Tri-Cities, Inc. v. United States, 567 F.2d 867, 869, note 2 (9th Cir. 1978). (Under this test, incidentally, Rev. Rul. 78-294, supra, could easily have gone the other way.)

Here is a homely example of a planned disposition of stock by the transferors of property:

D'ANGELO ASSOCIATES, INC. v. COMMISSIONER

United States Tax Court, 1978.
70 T.C. 121.

WILBUR, J. * * *

This controversy has its origin in events occurring during June 1960. Petitioner was organized on June 21, 1960. Shortly thereafter, initial capital in the amount of $15,000 in cash was transferred to petitioner by Dr. D'Angelo, and petitioner issued 60 shares of common stock, 10 shares to Mrs. D'Angelo and 10 shares each in the names of the five D'Angelo children. On June 30, 1960, Dr. and Mrs. D'Angelo, in a transaction formally designated a sale, transferred various property to petitioner, including the building and equipment whose basis is now at issue. In exchange for this property, the D'Angelos received $15,000 in cash; the assumption by petitioner of a liability of the D'Angelos, secured by a mortgage on property transferred to petitioner; and a 6 percent interest bearing demand note payable to Dr. D'Angelo in the amount of $96,727.85. Thereafter, in claiming depreciation, petitioner treated the transfer as a sale.

We must determine the proper basis for depreciation of the rental property (building and equipment) transferred to petitioner. This issue depends on whether or not section 351 applies to the transfer of this property to the petitioner. Section 351 applies when property is conveyed to a corporation solely in exchange for stock or securities, and immediately after the exchange, the transferors control the corporation. If section 351 is applicable, petitioner must depreciate the transferred assets using the transferors' basis. See section 362(a)(1). If section 351 is inapplicable, and the transfer of assets to petitioner was, as petitioner contends, a sale, depreciation would be based on the purchase price of those assets, a figure concededly greater than the transferors' adjusted basis. Petitioner would accordingly realize larger depreciation deductions. See sections 167(g), 1011, and 1012.

Respondent contends that the transfer of the rental property to petitioner was pursuant to a nontaxable exchange under section 351(a). He argues that the transfer of cash for stock and the exchange of the rental property for cash and notes were contemporaneous events that were in substance integral parts of a single transaction. Respondent contends that the notes were securities, and finds the requisite control by viewing the purchase of the stock and the exchange of the property for securities as one transaction followed by a gift of stock to the children.

Petitioner, on the other hand, contends that section 351 is inapplicable to the transfer for several reasons. Petitioner asserts that the transfer of the rental property was a transaction separate from the contributions of cash and should be characterized as a taxable sale. Petitioner argues that Dr. and Mrs. D'Angelo never owned more than 10 of the 60 shares outstanding in petitioner (the 50 shares constituting "control" being issued to non-transferors prior to the sale), and that the note received by Dr. D'Angelo was not "stock or securities" within the meaning of section 351. * * *

For the following reasons, we agree with respondent.

a. *Sale or Exchange:* It is well established that the economic substance of a transaction must govern for tax purposes rather than the time sequence or form in which the transaction is cast. Gregory v. Helvering, 293 U.S. 465 (1935). Where a series of closely related steps are taken pursuant to a plan to achieve an intended result, the transaction must be viewed as an integrated whole for tax purposes. See Redwing Carriers, Inc. v. Tomlinson, 399 F.2d 652, 658 (5th Cir. 1968); Atlee v. Commissioner, 67 T.C. 395 (1976).

Petitioner has failed to convince is that a sale took place. The events significant to the creation of petitioner occurred almost simultaneously. The formation of petitioner, the transfer of $15,000 cash to petitioner for the issuance of 60 shares of stock, and the transfer of the rental property to petitioner for the return of the $15,000 in cash and the notes all occurred within an interval of less than 10 days. See section 1.351-1(a)(1), Income Tax Regs. The evidence demonstrates that these steps were integral parts of a plan designed by Dr. D'Angelo to transfer the assets used primarily in his dental practice from individual to corporate ownership.

Any reason for petitioner's existence would have vanished absent the transfer of the rental property in accordance with the overall plan. It is also clear that the unsecured "demand" notes were originally intended and subsequently treated as indefinite obligations to be satisfied when and if the vicissitudes of the rental business (consisting essentially of income from the property transferred) permitted.[5] We believe this record demonstrates a continuing interest by Dr. D'Angelo in the transferred rental property consistent with the policy underlying the nonrecognition provisions of section 351 and unlike that contemplated by a sale. See Portland Oil Co. v. Commissioner, 109 F.2d 479, 488 (1st Cir. 1940), cert. denied 310 U.S. 650 (1940); Bittker & Eustice, Federal Income Taxation of Corporations and Shareholders, par. 3.01, p. 3-4 (3d ed. 1971).

Sequential protocol is of marginal relevance in determining whether contemporaneous events should be viewed as a single integrated transaction or as independent transactions. Rather, the boundaries are defined by including events contemplated for the success of the business plans from which they emanate. Commissioner v. Court Holding Co., 324 U.S. 331 (1945); United States v. Cumberland Public Service Co., 338 U.S. 451 (1950). In this light it is clear that the success of the corporate undertaking motivated both the transfer of cash for stock and the transfer of the rental property for the corporate obligation. As we noted in Nye v. Commissioner, 50 T.C. 203, 212 (1968):

> [T]hey gave no reason why the transaction was divided into two parts, the transfer of cash for stock and the purported sale of the business assets for the note. Such evidence might have confirmed that the form in which the transaction was cast was consistent with its true nature. * ° ° Lack of such evidence is worthy of note because it fails to negate the inference to be drawn from other facts indicating that the two parts of the transaction were inseparably related. ° ° * In the absence of evidence of a business reason for dividing the transaction, we conclude that a separate sale has not been shown. [Citations omitted]

5. No interest or principal payments were made for a period of 10 years, see infra. Whether a transaction constitutes a sale or exchange, the characterization of an obligation as a stock or security, and the determination of control under sec. 351 are often discussed as separate factors. Given the complexity of many cases arising under sec. 351, and the varying importance and novelty of each factor in a particular case, this may simplify presentation. Nevertheless, the factors are usually interrelated and overlap. Even in those cases that decide a prior finding of a sale dispenses with the necessity of characterizing obligations as notes or securities, the criteria that would have been applied to characterizing the obligations have already been carefully evaluated in deciding the transaction was a sale. See Curry v. Commissioner, 43 T.C. 667, 696 (1965) and the cases there cited. In many instances, though possibly not all, this may eliminate the concern that analysis of the words "transferred ° ° ° solely in exchange for stock or securities" (the words of sec. 351) is overlooked in the focus on a "sale" (a word not occurring in sec. 351.) See Note, "Section 351 Transfers to Controlled Corporations: ' The Forgotten Term—Securities'," 114 U.Pa.L.Rev. 314 (1965).

145

b. *Control:* We view the events before us as equivalent to the formation and capitalization of the corporation, followed by a gift to the D'Angelo children of the controlling interest when Dr. and Mrs. D'Angelo caused petitioner to directly issue the 50 shares to the children. At the end of the series of transactions on June 30, 1960, all of the assets remaining in the corporation were contributed by Dr. and Mrs. D'Angelo, including the $15,000 in cash.[6] This cash was in the possession of Dr. and Mrs. D'Angelo both before and after the transfers with the petitioner merely issuing stock directly to Mrs. D'Angelo and in the names of the children. The D'Angelo children did not purchase the stock issued in their names, but were simply the beneficiaries of a gift from their parents.[7]

The loss of control of petitioner resulting from the gift of stock does not preclude the application of section 351(a), which requires that the transferors be in control of the transferee corporation "immediately after the exchange." This requirement is satisfied where, as here, the transferors transfer by gift the stock they were entitled to receive in exchange for the property they transferred to the corporation, regardless of whether such disposition was planned before or after acquiring control. See Wilgard Realty Co. v. Commissioner, 127 F.2d 514, 516 (2d Cir. 1942) . . . . .
The issuance of the stock by petitioner to the D'Angelo children is the direct consequence of "the absolute right" of Dr. and Mrs. D'Angelo to designate who would receive all of the stock. Stanton v. United States, supra, at 17; Wilgard Realty Co. v. Commissioner, supra, at 516. Since it is possession of this power which is essential under section 351 for control, it follows that the transferors herein, Dr. and Mrs. D'Angelo were in control of petitioner immediately after the exchange. . . .

Petitioner nevertheless argues that since the stock was issued directly to Mrs. D'Angelo and the children, Dr. D'Angelo never held any stock in the corporation. We recognize that the *Wilgard* decision

6. In all likelihood, the $15,000 in cash remained in the corporation, and was evidenced by the $15,000 demand note payable to Dr. D'Angelo issued by petitioner on June 30, 1960, the same day the $96,727.85 note was issued. Under this assumption the consideration received from petitioner corresponds with the stated "sales" price; if the cash was distributed as well as the $15,000 note, there is an unexplained $15,000 discrepancy. Accordingly, we find that no adjustment in the adjusted basis of the rental property is needed on account of the $15,000 cash. Additionally, since the $15,000 note is a security for the same reasons we find the $96,727.85 note a security (see infra), no adjustment in basis would be required.
If in fact, the $15,000 was returned to the D'Angelos along with the $15,000 demand note, the same result would be required, since the consideration for the transfer of the rental property would be the $15,000 note (along with the stock and other notes), rather than the contemporaneous return of the same $15,000 contributed a few days earlier.

We also note that petitioner does not contend that the assumption of liability for the mortgage by petitioner should be treated as money received by the transferors by reason of sec. 357(b).

7. As noted earlier, the stock was issued to Dr. D'Angelo as trustee for the children pursuant to the New York State Uniform Gift to Minors Act. Respondent does not argue that the transferors retained control because the trust was illusory or because of the powers Dr. D'Angelo exercised as trustee. In view of respondent's position, we assume for purposes of this case that the trustee acted independently and solely on behalf of the best interests of the beneficiaries, although there is considerable evidence to the contrary. We therefore do not base our decision to any extent on the circumstance that Dr. D'Angelo as trustee acted on behalf of the children; the result would be precisely the same if the children had reached majority when the stock was issued and received title to the stock in their own names.

146

was predicated on the transferor's freedom of action *after* he acquired the stock, and that Fahs v. Florida Machine & Foundry Co., 168 F.2d 957 (5th Cir. 1948) may be read to support petitioner's viewpoint. See also Heberlein Patent Corporation v. United States, 105 F.2d 965 (2d Cir. 1939). Additionally, in Mojonnier & Sons, Inc. v. Commissioner, 12 T.C. 837 (1949), in distinguishing *Wilgard*, this Court stated:

> In the instant proceeding, however, the stock, exclusive of the 1,490 shares issued to Mojonnier and his wife, was not issued to the transferors and then conveyed by them to members of their family, but was issued directly to the members of the family in accordance with the plan and offer of F. E. Mojonnier. Thus, the transferors were never the owners or holders of a sufficient amount of stock to place them in "control" of the corporation within the meaning of section 112(j). Cf. Heberlein Patent Corporation v. United States, supra. [Id. at 850]

Nevertheless, the decisions in both *Wilgard* and *Stanton* were clearly predicated on the power of the transferor to designate who will receive the stock rather than the precise moment that the power was exercised. These cases do not turn on whether the tune Dr. D'Angelo called was written in two/four time, but on his power to call the tune. And it is on this score that both Florida Machine & Foundry Co. and Mojonnier & Sons, Inc., are distinguishable from *Wilgard, Stanton*, and the facts before us.[8] • • •

c. *Note or Security:*

We must now determine whether the $96,727.85 demand note constitutes "stock or securities" within the meaning of section 351(a). To dispose of this issue, it is sufficient to determine that the demand note is a security of petitioner.[9] We conclude that that note is a security.

It is well settled that promissory notes may qualify as securities for purposes of section 351. •. • •

---

8. If immediately prior to forming the corporation, five-sixths of the rental properties was given to the children and transferred to the corporation in return for the controlling interest (along with their parents' remaining one-sixth interest) petitioner's basis would be the basis of Dr. and Mrs. D'Angelo. Similarly, if the transfers were made directly to the corporation by Dr. and Mrs. D'Angelo in return for stock and the stock then given to the children, petitioner does not seriously contend section 351 would be inapplicable. That this transaction has been squeezed into the seemingly non-existent time interval between these two situations surely cannot produce a different result. Cf. sec. 1.351–1(b)(1), Income Tax Regs., and S.Rept.No.1622, to accompany H.R. 8300 (Pub.L.No.591), 83d Cong., 2d Sess. 264, 265 (1954), which, although not addressing the control problem directly, at least suggest the result we reach. Additionally, the prior precedents, by making the power to designate the distributee of the stock dispositive, avoid potential abuses in-

herent in options that would otherwise be available to taxpayers. Bittker & Eustice, Federal Income Taxation of Corporations and Shareholders, par. 3.01, p. 3–4 (3d ed. 1971). Culligan Water Conditioning of Tri-Cities, Inc. v. United States, 567 F.2d 867 (9th Cir. 1978).

9. Actually, it is sufficient to determine that the note constitutes "stock or securities", without determining precisely which. See Campbell v. Carter Foundation Production Co., 322 F.2d 827 (5th Cir. 1963).

At trial, respondent's counsel indicated in his opening statement that the note should also be characterized as equity rather than a debt security. While respondent submits that the indicia of equity are manifestly satisfied, he maintains that the evidence adduced at trial renders unnecessary a determination that the note is equity. Therefore, the issue as presented and argued on brief by the parties is whether the note was a security for purposes of sec. 351.

The basic approach for determining whether such debt instruments qualify as "securities" as that term is used in section 351 is that adopted by this Court in Camp Wolters Enterprises, Inc., v. Commissioner, 22 T.C. 737 (1954), aff'd. 230 F.2d 555 (5th Cir. 1956), cert. denied 352 U.S. 826'(1956):

> The test as to whether notes are securities is not a mechanical determination of the time period of the note. Though time is an important factor, the controlling consideration is an overall evaluation of the nature of the debt, degree of participation and continuing interest in the business, the extent of propriety interest compared with the similarity of the note to a cash payment, the purpose of the advances, etc. It is not necessary for the debt obligation to be the equivalent of stock since section [351(a)] specifically includes both "stock" and "securities." [Id. at 22 T.C. 751]

Thus, securities are investment instruments which give the holder a continuing participation in the affairs of the debtor corporation. They are to be contrasted with short-term notes which are essentially the equivalent of cash and represent the termination of the holder's interest in the property transferred to the corporation.

An overall evaluation of the $96,727.85 note given to Dr. D'Angelo shows that it was a security within the meaning of section 351. The note did not evidence an isolated transaction of purchase and sale subsequent to and separate from the formation and capitalization of petitioner. Rather, the note was an integral part of the corporate birth, and represented one form of Dr. D'Angelo's continuing interest in the rental property transferred to petitioner. See Camp Wolters Enterprises, Inc. v. Commissioner, supra. Moreover, the properties for which the note was issued constituted a permanent contribution of assets virtually indispensable to petitioner; such property did not represent short-term advances to be used by petitioner for temporary or current corporate needs. . . .

In no sense was the note the equivalent of cash. See Pinellas Ice Co. v. Commissioner, 287 U.S. 462 (1933). It gave Dr. D'Angelo a continuing investment in the property he transferred to petitioner. At the time the note was issued, the petitioner did not have sufficient liquid assets to retire it. Its repayment at any time proximate to the issuance date could have been accomplished only through the sale of the assets transferred to petitioner, and such a sale would have extinguished the purpose for which petitioner was created. As a practical matter, payment of the note was intended to be derived from the rental earnings of the property transferred, a process that would take many years. Furthermore, any expectation of repayment of the $96,-727.85 obligation would realistically be subsequent to the satisfaction of the substantial liability assumed by petitioner upon transfer of the rental property to it, a liability which encumbered the income producing assets.

Petitioner maintains that the $96,727.85 note was not, and is not, a security. It asserts that an unsecured demand note by its very nature cannot constitute a security but is "an instrument of true indebtedness." Petitioner's reliance on the form of the note and the absence of a maturity date is misplaced, and reflects a fundamental misunderstanding of the term "securities" as it is used in section 351.

It is generally true that short-term notes do not constitute securities within the meaning of section 351.

· · · However, a short-term note, and demand notes, will be considered securities in circumstances where the stated maturity is either unrealistic, see Aqualane Shores, Inc. v. Commissioner, 269 F.2d 116 (5th Cir. 1959), affg. 30 T.C. 519 (1958); or is ignored by the parties, see United States v. Mills, 399 F.2d 944 (5th Cir. 1968).

In the instant case, there is no evidence to support the possibility of payment of the note on demand at any future time foreseeable at the date of its issuance. No payments of principal or interest were made for over 10 years, and those that were eventually made were accomplished in an unusual manner. As of trial, some 16 years after the date of issuance, only about 50 percent of the principal amount of the note had been credited as paid, and interest payments with one exception have not been made. These facts merely serve to reinforce our conclusion that the note represented a continuing interest of Dr. D'Angelo in the rental property, as contemplated by the *Camp Wolters* approach.

Petitioner attempts to excuse the dilatory payment of the note with the argument that it was prohibited from making payments by the terms of the S.B.A. loan authorization. We are not persuaded that this moratorium on payments of principal and interest is sufficient reason to overcome the evidence indicating that payment of the note was not contemplated until many years after its issue. First, petitioner made no payments of principal or interest for at least 2 years after issuance of the note and prior to any negotiations for the S.B.A. loan authorization, and for another year thereafter before any credit was actually extended. Second, it was Dr. D'Angelo who ultimately approved the moratorium on payments, in order to assist him in obtaining the S.B.A. guaranteed financing to benefit his trade or business. Finally, it is apparent from the payment history of petitioner with respect to this note, beginning in 1971, that petitioner was at no time in the 16 years after issuance of the note inclined to or capable of liquidating the debt. Such circumstances are simply not consistent with the alleged short-term character of the note.

In sum, the facts demonstrate that Dr. D'Angelo, as holder of the $96,727.85 demand note, had a continuing interest in the rental property. We conclude that the note was a security, and that section 351(a) therefore applies to the transfers of rental property as contended by the respondent.

a. NOTE ON LOSS OF CONTROL BY TRANSFERORS OF PROPERTY

The D'Angelo case seems on sound ground in holding that stock issued to non-transferors of property may nevertheless be counted in the control group in some circumstances. As the court concluded, what matters is whether the transferor of property has the power to designate who will receive the stock; if so, it should make no difference whether the transferor of property goes through the formality of first receiving the stock, as in the case of Wilgard Realty Co. v.

Commissioner, cited in D'Angelo, and then making a gift to
others. Nor is this principle limited to cases involving
gifts of stock. For example, in O'Connor v. Commissioner,
16 T.C.M. 213 (1957), the taxpayer organized a corporation
to exploit certain of his patents, which were transferred to
the corporation for 51,000 shares of its stock. No stock
was immediately issued, but shortly thereafter the taxpayer
caused 11,000 of the 51,000 shares to be issued to certain
persons who had previously advanced money to help him finance the work on the patents. Although this left the taxpayer with less than 80% of the corporation's stock, the
court held that the control test was satisfied. Since there
was no evidence that the taxpayer's creditors had obtained
any interest in either the patents or the stock to be issued
in exchange for them, the taxpayer had complete control over
the 51,000 shares of stock, regardless of whether the stock
was actually issed to him. He was thus free to deal with
the stock as he wished, and the fact that he arranged for
some of his stock to be issued to others designated by him
did not affect the control which he had "immediately after"
the exchange.

At the opposite end of the spectrum, stock which a
transferor of property is obligated to convey to a third
party is not includible in the control count (and again it
is irrelevant whether or not the stock is first issued to
the transferor of property). Hence, if upon the incorporation of a proprietorship outsiders receive more than 20% of
the stock pursuant to a binding obligation of the proprietor,
the control test is not satisfied. That was the situation
in Mojonnier & Sons, Inc. v. Commissioner, cited in D'Angelo,
where a father had promised his sons and a foreman that if
they continued to work in his business they would receive
some stock when he incorporated the business a few years
later. Upon the later incorporation, stock was issued
directly to the sons and the foreman, and the father received less than 80% of the total. Held, at the behest of
the corporate taxpayer which was seeking a stepped-up basis,
the predecessor of §351 did not apply because of the absence
of control. The Commissioner's argument that the father had
in effect received all the stock and then made gifts to the
others was rejected, on the ground that the transfers of
stock were not gifts but were rewards for past services
pursuant to the prior commitment.

Fahs v. Florida Machine & Foundry Co., also cited in
D'Angelo, presented a similar fact pattern. There a father
and son entered into an agreement under which if the son
continued to work in his father's business he was eventually
to receive a one-half interest in it. Some three years
later the father organized the taxpayer corporation and
conveyed to it all of the assets of his business, receiving
in exchange just over 50% of the stock, with the rest of the
stock going to the son. Once more it was the taxpayer
corporation which was arguing against qualification under
§351, in order to obtain a stepped-up basis for the property,

and again the Court held the control test was not satisfied
because of the prior commitment that the stock go to one who
was not a transferor of property.

However, there were two additional issues in the Fahs
case which deserve attention. First, the Court held that
the taxpayer corporation was not estopped from claiming that
§351 did not apply (in order to get a stepped-up basis in
the property), even though the father had not reported gain
on the transaction in the year of incorporation (and that
year was now barred by the statute of limitations). Second,
and more immediately in point here, the Commissioner argued
that as a result of the father's commitment to transfer a
share of the business to his son if he continued his services, as of the time of incorporation the son had at least
an equitable interest in the business, making him a joint
transferor of property with his father when the enterprise
was transferred to the new corporation. This contention was
curtly dismissed by the Court as "not borne out by the
evidence". However, that response scarcely did justice to
the argument, the thrust of which was that as a matter of law
a binding promise to transfer stock upon the incorporation
of a business results in the promisee having an interest in
the enterprise in the meantime which is cognizable in equity.
Under this view, no specific evidence of the creation of
such an interest would be needed; it would be presumed to
exist unless the parties were shown to have otherwise agreed.
Of course there might be an unwelcome collateral tax consequence, in the form of compensation income upon the creation
of the equitable interest (rather than awaiting incorporation
and the actual receipt of stock), although perhaps such an
equitable interest could be viewed as too difficult to
value, as well as too ephemeral in nature, to call for
recognition as compensation income, especially by a cash-
basis taxpayer. (Notice that these factors would not necessarily prevent such an equitable interest from being treated
as "property" for §351 purposes.)

In any event, the parties obviously could eliminate any
uncertainty and specifically provide in their deal for the
creation of an equitable interest. Thus in Roberts Co. Inc.
v. Commissioner, 5 T.C. 1 (1945), attorneys undertook to
establish the rights of their clients in certain land, in
consideration of a contingent fee entitling them to a specified percentage of those rights; the Court held that the
attorneys had obtained a property interest which qualified
them as part of the transferor group when the property was
conveyed to a corporation. This points up the fact that
§351 is pretty much an elective provision in these situations, since the applicability of the section turns entirely
upon whether or not an interest in the property to be transferred to the corporation is assigned to the outsider before
incorporation, although there may be little if any independent legal significance in this choice. To illustrate
further, consider the case of May Broadcasting Co. v. United
States, 200 F.2d 852 (8th Cir. 1953), where a corporation

which owned a radio station in addition to other enterprises
agreed to make a one-fourth interest in the station available to
a third party. In pursuance of this agreement, the radio station
was transferred to the newly-organized taxpayer in exchange for
all of its stock. After a nine month delay due to the necessity
of obtaining FCC approval of the transaction, one-fourth of the
stock of the taxpayer was sold to the third party in accordance
with the previous agreement. The Court held, for the taxpayer,
that the transaction did not qualify as a tax-free incorporation
because the ultimate loss of control was pursuant to a contract
existing at the time of incorporation. Yet it seems clear that
if the transaction in the May Broadcasting Co. case had taken
the form of a sale to the third party of an individed one-quarter
interest in the station, prior to incorporation, followed by a
joint transfer of the station to the new corporation in exchange
for three-quarters and one-quarter of its stock respectively,
§351 would have been satisfied (and the corporation would have
had a stepped-up basis in one-quarter of its assets to boot).
Similarly, if the owner of the radio station had transferred the
property to the new corporation for three quarters of its authorized stock, while the third party transferred cash for the
remaining one-quarter of the stock, the transaction would have
qualified under §351 (although in that event the price paid by
the third party would be in the new corporation instead of in
the pocket of the former owner of the radio station). Query
whether the form actually adopted in May Broadcasting differs
enough from these alternatives to warrant the difference in tax
treatment.

Suppose that upon incorporation there is a binding commitment
that the corporation issue more than 20% of its stock to a third
party when he has completed certain services to be performed for
the corporation. In Kaczmarek v. Commissioner, 21 T.C.M. 691
(1962), the taxpayer formed a corporation for the purpose of
developing a piece of real estate he owned. The taxpayer received 75% of the new corporation's authorized stock, and agreed
with his lawyers that they would receive the remaining 25% when
they had completed certain legal work relating to rezoning the
property, preparing certain leases, and the like. More than a
year later the taxpayer and his lawyers had a falling out, which
the taxpayer settled by paying cash to the lawyers in exchange
for their rights to acquire stock. Held, the control test was
satisfied. The court concluded that the proposed issuance of
stock to the lawyers was not an interdependent step in the
incorporation transaction, particularly in view of the fact that
they never did complete the services or actually receive the
stock.

4.   Computation of Control

When there is only a single class of stock outstanding,
which would necessarily be voting stock, computation of control
under §368(c) parallels the number of shares precisely: that
is, in order to have 80% of the total voting power, the transferors must obtain 80% of the number of shares outstanding. On
the other hand, a straight number count may not be determinative

under the value test used in §1239 (and employed in conjunction
with the total combined voting power test in a number of Code
provisions, such as §1563, which limits the number of under-46%
tax brackets available to corporations in an affiliated group).
The reason is that the control associated with a large majority
of shares may give them a greater value than the minority shares,
so that something less than 80% in number of a single class of
stock outstanding might represent 80% or more in value. This
issue has been litigated in several cases arising under the
pre-1976 version of §1239, which required ownership of more than
80% of the value of the corporation's stock. In United States
v. Parker, 367 F.2d 402 (5th Cir. 1967), where the taxpayer
owned exactly 80% of the one class of shares outstanding, the
Court held that the minority shareholder's 20% of the stock was
worth something less per share than the taxpayer's 80%, because
the minority interest had no say in control and was also subject
to certain restrictions on transfer; in the circumstances, this
was enough to conclude that the taxpayer owned more than 80% of
the value of the stock, thereby invoking that earlier statutory
test. And Dahlgren v. United States, 553 F.2d 434 (5th Cir.
1977), in which the taxpayer owned 79.975% of the stock while
the remaining stock was held equally by two stockholders, held
it was error for the trial court not to give the Government's
requested charge that a controlling block of stock inherently
has a greater per share value than shares outside the block.

On the other hand, in Trotz v. Commissioner, 26 T.C.M. 632
(1967), where the taxpayer owned 79% of the corporation's shares,
the Court held that the majority shares did not have a value
greater than their proportionate number; in the Court's view,
since the small construction business there involved had no
going concern value separate from the personal skill of the
taxpayer, a prospective purchaser would only be interested in
the underlying assets, and there would be no basis for any
control premium. The Court focused entirely on sales value of
the stock, ignoring the operating control currently enjoyed by
the taxpayer; in addition, no weight was given to the fact that
the minority shareholder's 21% interest was pledged to secure a
loan from the taxpayer, so that in effect it could be purchased
by the taxpayer for book value at any time. In a somewhat
similar vein, Robishaw v. United States, 616 F.2d 507 (Ct. Cl.
1980), found that 79.64% in number of shares did not amount to
more than 80% in value (prior to the transfer of property challenged under §1239, which, according to the Court, was when the
value test was to be applied), because the corporation had not
yet become an operating enterprise and hence it had only a
liquidating value, which would have been shared between the
shareholders in exact proportion to their respective number of
shares.

When there is more than one class of stock outstanding,
application of the value test of §1239 will normally require
valuation of each class, in order to determine whether the
taxpayer owns at least 80% of the total value of all the stock
outstanding. But sometimes a relative valuation will be sufficient to provide the answer: for example, if a taxpayer owns

50% of the common stock and 100% of the preferred stock, it is easy to demonstrate that the overall 80% test will be satisfied if the value of all the preferred stock is at least one and one-half times the value of all the common.

There is more of a problem with the application of the §368(c) control test when the corporation has several classes of stock outstanding. Section 368(c) distinguishes between voting stock and non-voting stock, lumping all of the former together for the purpose of measuring the "total combined voting power", while subjecting non-voting stock to a separate test based upon the number of shares. However, it is not clear whether several classes of non-voting stock should be looked at separately or together in determining whether the control group has the requisite "80 percent of the total number"; the position of the Service is that the control test requires 80% of each class. Rev. Rul. 59-259, 1959-2 Cum. Bull. 115.

As to what constitutes voting stock for the purpose of computing "total combined voting power", it is generally assumed that voting power looks to a current right to participate in the election of directors. Thus, merely having the power to vote on particular kinds of transactions, whether as a class or otherwise, would not count; neither would a contingent right to vote for directors, such as upon a failure to pay preferred dividends, unless the right has become operative.

While it is clear that all stock which is presently entitled to vote for directors must be treated together in determining "total combined voting power", the statute affords no guide as to how to treat two or more classes which have different powers in the election of directors. In the common case of stock divided into several classes with each one having the power to elect a specified number of directors, the approach has been to weight each class in accordance with the percentage of the board of directors which the class is entitled to elect. I.T. 3896, 1948-1 Cum. Bull. 72. In that ruling a parent corporation owned all of its subsidiary's common stock, which was entitled to elect six of the seven directors, and 55.5% of the preferred stock, which was entitled to elect one director; and the question was whether the parent owned "stock possessing at least 95 per centum of the voting power of all classes" within the meaning of §141(d) of the 1939 Code. According to the Ruling, six-sevenths, or 85.71%, of the total voting power should be attributed to the common stock, and one-seventh, or 14.29%, to the preferred stock. Since the parent owned 100% of the common stock, it was regarded as owning the entire 85.71% of voting power attributable to that stock; as to the 14.29% of voting power attributable to the preferred, the Ruling treated the parent as owning 7.93% by virtue of its 55.5% ownership of the preferred. Therefore, the total voting power owned by the parent was 85.71% plus 7.93%, a total of 93.64%, which fell short of the necessary 95%. Rev. Rul. 63-234, 1963-2 Cum. Bull. 148, assumes without discussion that the approach of I.T. 3896 would be followed in the control test of §368(c).

I.T. 3896 was declared obsolete in Rev. Rul. 68-100, 1968-1 Cum. Bull 572, but only because the voting power test for filing consolidated returns had long since been reduced to 80%. The I.T. 3896 method of computing voting power was used in applying the present 80% test for consolidation in Rev. Rul. 69-126, 1969-1 Cum. Bull. 218.

Rev. Rul. 76-223, 1976-1 Cum. Bull. 103, confirms the "bundling" of voting power under the control test of §368(c), ruling that where a corporation had outstanding 81 shares of voting common and 19 shares of voting preferred, the preferred and common each having one vote per share, the acquisition of all of the common satisfied the control test.

There is more question as to whether and how such voting arrangements as pooling agreements and voting trusts would affect the computation of control. In Commissioner v. National Bellas Hess, Inc., 220 F.2d 415 (8th Cir. 1955), the Court stated that "control relates to equitable ownership", in holding that the deposit of stock in a voting trust did not affect the computation of control. But this case was decided under an earlier counterpart of §368(c) which defined control in terms of "ownership of at least 80 per centum of the voting stock" instead of the present "ownership of stock <u>possessing</u> at least 80 percent of the total combined voting power". (Emphasis supplied) Perhaps in determining how much voting power is "possessed" by certain stock, as the statute now seems to require, account must be taken of any existing voting trust or other agreement. Thus if a voting agreement gives a particular stockholder more power in the election of directors than the number of his shares would otherwise afford, the application of a weighting formula analogous to I.T. 3896 might be called for. Compare Reg. §1.563-1(a)(6), which provides that in measuring the voting power of stock for purposes of a control test much like that of §368(c) the terms of the stock as set out in the certificate of incorporation provide the starting point, but account will be taken of voting agreements which vary the formal voting rights possessed by the stock.

It seems clear that §368(c) does not require control to be allocated among the transferors of property in proportion to their respective interests in the property transferred. E.g., Holstein v. Commissioner, 23 T.C. 923 (1955) (control test satisfied where in effect A transferred property worth $16,710 for 210 shares of common stock and 16,500 shares of non-voting preferred, while B transferred $210 in cash for 210 shares of common). Nor is there any requirement that every transferor of property receive some voting stock. Thus if in a case like <u>Holstein</u>, supra, A had received only non-voting preferred and B had received all the voting common, §351 would still have been satisfied. Burr Oaks Corp. v. Commissioner, 43 T.C. 635 (1965).

5. Contributions to Capital

When a shareholder contributes property to a corporation and receives no shares of stock in return, presumably the transaction constitutes a contribution to capital, and there is no occasion for recognizing either gain or loss. But even if a constructive "exchange" could be found because of the increase in value in the existing shares, § 351 would usually be applicable to provide non-recognition treatment. The transferor would add his basis in the contributed property to his basis in his stock, and the corporation under § 362(a)(2) would take the transferor's basis in the property.

When property is transferred as a contribution to capital by persons other than shareholders, as when a community organization makes property available to a corporation to induce it to locate in the area, § 362(c), added to the Code in 1954, makes the basis of the property to the corporation zero.

----

6. Some Tax Accounting Aspects of §351 Transactions

The question has arisen whether the non-recognition of §351 may be overridden in some cases by such classic tax principles as the assignment of income doctrine or the tax benefit rule. An example of the former is the transfer of "earned" but unpaid receivables to a new corporation by a cash-basis taxpayer. For a time it seemed to be the view of the Service that the transfer of such items constituted a realization of income by the transferor, rather than a "gain on the transfer of property" shielded by §351; but Kniffen v. Commissioner, 39 T.C. 553 (1962), held that §351 did apply to prevent recognition of income to the transferor in such circumstances, and the Service acquiesced in the result.

An illustration of the tax benefit rule was the early insistence by the Service that when an accrual basis taxpayer transferred its accounts receivable to a new corporation, the reserve for bad debts had to be "restored" to income, on the ground that there was no longer any possibility of the transferor incurring the losses for which the reserve was created. However, the Supreme Court rejected this view in the Nash case, discussed in the following ruling:

REVENUE RULING 78–280

1978–30 Int.Rev.Bull. 7.

Advice has been requested as to the effect of the decision of the Supreme Court of the United States in Nash v. United States, 398 U.S. 1 (1970), 1970–1 C.B. 72, in the situation described below.

A, an individual, transferred property used in a sole proprietorship, including accounts receivable, to a newly formed corporation solely in exchange for all of the stock of such corporation in a transaction in which no gain or loss is recognized pursuant to section 351 (a) of the Internal Revenue Code of 1954. A had accounts receivable with a face amount of $100x$ dollars and a reserve for bad debts of $5x$ dollars. Prior to the transfer, A used the accrual method of accounting under section 446(c) in the business and has previously deducted additions to a reserve for bad debts with respect to such accounts pursuant to section 166(c). All additions to the reserve for bad debts in prior years resulted in tax benefits. The value of the stock received for the accounts receivable was $95x$ dollars.

The principal question presented is the extent to which the amount of the transferor's reserve for bad debts is includible in the transferor's gross income. Related questions concern the transferor's and the transferee's basis in the transferred accounts receivable and the treatment of these accounts receivable by a transferee using the reserve method of treating bad debts under section 166(c) . . . .

In the *Nash* case, the taxpayers were partners in a partnership using the accrual method of accounting and the reserve method of treating bad debts under section 166(c) of the Code. The reserve for bad debts was deemed reasonable. The assets of the partnership, including the accounts receivable, were transferred solely in exchange for corporate stock in a transaction qualifying under the nonrecognition of gain or loss provisions of section 351. The value of the stock received in exchange for the accounts receivable was equal to the net value of the accounts transferred, that is, the face amount of the accounts receivable previously included in income less the amount of the reserve for bad debts.

The Court held that although the need for the reserve ended with the transfer, this did not result in a recovery within the meaning of the tax benefit cases. That is, there was no recovery of an item that had produced an income tax benefit in a prior year and therefore nothing had to be added to income in the year of the transfer.

In essence, the decision in *Nash* holds that because there is no double benefit if the consideration received in exchange for the transfer of accounts receivable by a taxpayer using the accrual method of accounting is equal to the net value of the accounts receivable (the face amount of the accounts receivable previously included in income less the reserve for bad debts), there is no recovery within the meaning of the tax benefit cases. . . .

Accordingly, A has no recovery within the meaning of the tax benefit rule.

The *Nash* case did not involve the determination of the transferor's basis in the accounts receivable for the purpose of applying sections 358(a)(1) and 362(a) of the Code.

. . .

In the case of a taxpayer on an accrual method of accounting using the specific charge-off method of treating bad debts, the basis of an account receivable is reduced by the amount of a specific charge-off claimed with respect thereto. . . . A similar approach is appropriate in the case of an accrual basis taxpayer using the reserve method of treating bad debts. In the aggregate, such a taxpayer's bad debt reserve reduces the basis of the accounts receivable to which it relates.

Furthermore, in the present situation, because the transferor has already deducted additions to the bad debt reserve with respect to the accounts receivable and because under *Nash* the amount of the bad debt reserve is not includible in income at the time of transfer, it is necessary to prevent the transferee from also taking a deduction with respect to the accounts receivable. The reduction of their aggregate basis by the amount of the bad debt reserve prevents this double deduction. . . .

Accordingly, in the situation described above, for the purposes of applying sections 358(a)(1) and 362(a) of the Code, the basis of the transferor in the transferred accounts receivable is $95x$ dollars, their net value.

If the transferee corporation uses the reserve method of treating bad debts under section 166(c) of the Code, it must establish a bad debt reserve with respect to the transferred accounts receivable equal to the difference between their face amount ($100x$ dollars) and their basis as determined under section 362(a) ($95x$ dollars). The establishment of this reserve is not considered an addition to a bad debt reserve and thus the initial amount in the reserve ($5x$ dollars) cannot be deducted. The collection of these accounts receivable will not require the inclusion in income of the excess of collections over $95x$ dollars, and the inability to collect an amount equal to $95x$ dollars will not entitle the taxpayer to specific charge-offs. Rather, these transactions will be reflected in the taxpayer's determination of a reasonable reserve for bad debts in future periods.

· · ·

The Revenue Act of 1978 resolved a serious problem which had arisen under § 351 for cash basis taxpayers incorporating a going business, due to the provision in § 357(c) for recognizing gain to the extent that the liabilities assumed (or to which the property transferred is subject) exceed the basis of the property transferred. For an accrual-basis taxpayer § 357(c) usually poses little threat, because a typical going business is likely to have cash plus receivables in excess of its current liabilities, and inventory plus fixed assets in excess of longer-term obligations. On the other hand, a business on the cash basis will normally not have any inventory (indeed, if it does, the accrual method would be required, per Reg. § 1.446–1(b)(2)(i)), and its receivables would have a zero basis (since they will not yet have been included in income); hence, the liabilities will often exceed the basis of the assets transferred. As a result, cash-basis taxpayers sought to exclude obligations arising in the ordinary course of business (which had not yet been deducted, under the cash-basis method) from the scope of "liabilities" subject to § 357(c), in order to prevent the recognition of gain in these circumstances; while some courts proved quite sympathetic, conflicting rationales were advanced, and other decisions rejected the argument entirely, leaving the whole area in a state of uncertainty. The 1978 Act excludes from the liabilities counted under § 357(c) any obligation whose payment would have given rise to a deduction by the transferor (provided the incurring of the liability did not create or increase the basis of any property). Similarly, such obligations will not be treated as liabilities under § 358(d), and hence will not have any effect on the basis of the stock or securities received upon a transfer of property to a corporation under § 351.

The Senate Finance Committee Report makes it clear that this provision does not affect the definition of liabilities for any other section of the Code, including § 357(a) and (b). The Report also states that the amendment is not intended to have any effect on the corporation's tax accounting for the excluded liabilities. Presumably this means that the corporation may deduct the payment of such liabilities to the same extent as the transferor could have; although there are no cases squarely in point, a dictum in Bongiovanni v. Commissioner, 470 F.2d 921, 925 (2d Cir. 1972), supports this result, and it appears that the Service has been granting private rulings to this effect, suitably circumscribed. On the income side of this coin, by the way, Hempt Bros., Inc. v. U. S., 490 F.2d 1172 (3d Cir. 1974), contains a careful review of the proper treatment of accounts receivable transferred by cash-basis partners, with the interesting and perhaps significant twist that since the partnership had inventories, as evidenced by the fact that some of its accounts receivable arose from the sale of inventory in the ordinary course of business, it should not have been using the cash basis, (and the new corporation was not permitted to use the cash basis): the court concluded that § 351 applied to prevent the recognition of gain upon the transfer of accounts receivable in these circumstances, and held that the corporation was taxable upon receipt of payment of the accounts receivable.

7. NOTE ON RULINGS GUIDELINES

REVENUE PROCEDURE 77-37
1977-2 Cum.Bull. 568.

Section 1. Purpose
.01 The purpose of this Revenue Procedure is to . . . [set] forth certain operating rules of the Internal Revenue Service pertaining to issuing ruling letters and in determining whether it should decline to issue ruling letters.

. . . .

Sec. 2. Background

.01 When requested by taxpayers or their authorized representatives, the Reorganization Branch of the Corporation Tax Division issues ruling letters as to the tax consequences of corporate reorganizations, liquidations, stock dividends and redemptions; transfers to and distributions of stock or securities of controlled corporations; . . . .
The Reorganization Branch also determines whether distributions, redemptions, exchanges or transfers referred to in sections 306(b)(4), 355(a)(1)(D)(ii), 367, 1492, and 1494 of the Internal Revenue Code of 1954 are in pursuance of a plan having as one of its principal purposes the avoidance of Federal income taxes and answers questions under section 1244 relating to small business stock. In addition, the Reorganization Branch issues ruling letters concerning transactions involving collapsible corporations under section 341 and special limitations on net operating loss carryovers under section 382.

.02 The Reorganization Branch has developed certain operating rules for determining whether a ruling will be issued in certain types of cases and the conclusions which will be expressed in such rulings.

.03 These operating rules are being published solely to provide assistance to taxpayers and their representatives in preparing ruling requests. These operating rules do not define, as a matter of law, the lower limits of "continuity of interest" or "substantially all of the properties"; nor do they define any other terms used in the Internal Revenue Code, Income Tax Regulations and prior Revenue Procedures discussed below.

.04 A requested ruling involving a question covered in Sec. 3 of this Revenue Procedure will ordinarily be issued if the applicable operating rule or rules set forth in Sec. 3 of this Revenue Procedure are complied with and if all other pertinent provisions of the Internal Revenue Code, Income Tax Regulations, Revenue Procedures and Revenue Rulings are satisfied.

Sec. 3. Operating Rules for Issuing Ruling Letters

.01 The "substantially all" requirement of sections 354(b)(1)(A), 368(a)(1)(C), 368(a)(2)(B)(i), 368(a)(2)(D), and 368(a)(2)(E)(i) of the Code is satisfied if there is a transfer (and in the case of a surviving corporation under section 368(a)(2)(E)(i), the retention) of assets representing at least 90 percent of the fair market value of the net assets and at least 70 percent of the fair market value of the gross assets held by the corporation immediately prior to the transfer. All payments to dissenters and all redemptions and distributions (except for regular, normal distributions) made by the corporation immediately preceding the transfer and which are part of the plan of reorganization will be considered as assets held by the corporation immediately prior to the transfer.

.02 The "continuity of interest" requirement of section 1.368–1 (b) of the Income Tax Regulations is satisfied if there is continuing interest through stock ownership in the acquiring or transferee corporation (or a corporation in "control" thereof within the meaning of section 368(c) of the Code) on the part of the former shareholders of the acquired or transferor corporation which is equal in value, as of the effective date of the reorganization, to at least 50 percent of the value of all of the formerly outstanding stock of the acquired or transferor corporation as of the same date. It is not necessary that each shareholder of the acquired or transferor corporation receive in the exchange stock of the acquiring or transferee corporation, or a corporation in "control" thereof, which is equal in value to at least 50 percent of the value of his former stock interest in the acquired or transferor corporation, so long as one or more of the shareholders of the acquired or transferor corporation have a continuing interest through stock ownership in the acquiring or transferee corporation (or a corporation in "control" thereof) which is, in the aggregate, equal in value to at least 50 percent of the value of all of the formerly outstanding stock of the acquired or transferor corporation. Sales, redemptions, and other dispositions of stock occurring prior or subsequent to the exchange which are part of the plan of reorganization will be considered in determining whether there is a 50 percent continuing interest through stock ownership as of the effective date of the reorganization.

.03 In reorganizations under sections 368(a)(1)(A), 368(a)(1) (B), and 368(a)(1)(C) of the Code where the requisite stock or property has been acquired, it is not necessary that all of the stock of the acquiring corporation or a corporation in "control" thereof, which is to be issued in exchange therefor, be issued immediately provided (1) that all of the stock will be issued within five years from the date of the transfer of assets in the case of reorganizations under sections 368(a)(1)(A) and 368(a)(1)(C), or within five years from the date of the initial distribution in the case of reorganization under section 368(a)(1)(B); (2) there is a valid business reason for not issuing all of the stock immediately, such as the difficulty in determining the value of one or both of the corporations involved in the reorganization; (3) the maximum number of shares which may be issued in the exchange is stated; (4) at least fifty percent of the maximum number of shares of each class of stock which may be issued is issued in the initial distribution; (5) the agreement evidencing the right to receive stock in the future prohibits assignment (except by operation of law) or, in the alternative, if the agreement does not prohibit assignments, the right must not be evidenced by negotiable certificates of any kind and must not be readily marketable; and (6) such right can give rise to the receipt of only additional stock of the acquiring corporation or a corporation in "control" thereof, as the case may be. Stock issued as compensation, royalties or any other consideration other than in exchange for stock or assets will not be considered to have been received in the exchange. Until the final distribution of the total number of shares of stock to be issued in the exchange is made, the interim basis of the stock of the acquiring corporation received in the exchange by the shareholders of the acquired corporation (not including that portion of each share representing interest) will be determined, pursuant to section 358(a), as though the maximum number of shares to be issued (not including that portion of each share representing interest) had been received by the shareholders.

.04 The "substantially all of its assets" requirement of section 355(b)(2)(A) of the Code is satisfied if at least 90 percent of the fair market value of the gross assets of the corporation (assets undiminished by liabilities) consists of stock and securities of controlled corporations which are engaged in the active conduct of a trade or business as defined in section 355(b)(2).

.05 In determining stock ownership to be attributed to a trust or from a trust under the rules of sections 318(a)(2)(B)(i) and 318(a)(3)(B)(i) of the Code in those cases where a surviving spouse is entitled to all the income for life from the trust and also holds a power of appointment over the corpus of the trust, and in default of the exercise of the power the property held by the trust is to pass to the children of the surviving spouse, attribution will be computed as if the surviving spouse has exercised the power in favor of his or her children, so that they will be considered beneficiaries in the absence of evidence that the power has been differently exercised.

.06 In reorganizations under sections 368(a)(1)(A), 368(a)(1)(B), and 368(a)(1)(C) of the Code where the requisite stock or property has been acquired, a portion of the stock of the acquiring corporation, or a corporation in "control" thereof, that is issued in the exchange may be placed in escrow by the exchanging shareholders, or may otherwise be made subject to a condition pursuant to the agreement or plan of reorganization, for possible return to the acquiring corporation under specified conditions provided (1) there is a valid business reason for establishing the arrangement; (2) the stock subject to such arrangement appears as issued and outstanding on the balance sheet of the acquiring corporation and such stock is, in fact, legally outstanding under applicable state law; (3) all dividends paid on such stock will be distributed currently to the exchanging shareholders; (4) all voting rights of such stock (if any) are exercisable by or on behalf of the shareholders or their authorized agent; (5) no shares of such stock are subject to restrictions requiring their return to the issuing corporation because of death, failure to continue employment or similar restrictions; (6) all such stock is released from the arrangement within 5 years from the date of consummation of the reorganization (except where there is a bona fide dispute as to whom the stock should be released to); and (7) at least 50 percent of the number of shares of each class of stock issued initially to the shareholders (exclusive of shares of stock to be issued at a later date as described in .03 above) is not subject to the arrangement.

.07 When a person transfers property to a corporation in exchange for stock or securities of such corporation and the primary purpose of the transfer is to qualify under section 351 of the Code the exchanges of property by other persons transferring property, the property transferred will not be considered to be of relatively small value, within the meaning of section 1.351–1(a)(1)(ii) of the regulations, if the fair market value of the property transferred is equal to, or in excess of, 10 percent of the fair market value of the stock and securities already owned (or to be received for services) by such person.

* * *

Sec. 5. Rulings Under Section 306(b)(4) of the Code

.01 A ruling will usually be issued under section 306(b)(4) of the Code to the effect that a distribution of "section 306 stock" (other than a distribution under section 305, or, in the case of any recapitalization under section 368(a)(1)(E), a distribution which has the effect of a pro rata stock dividend, that is, a distribution under section 305) and the disposition or redemption of the "section 306 stock" is not pursuant to a plan of tax avoidance if the stock of the issuing corporation is widely held and

(a) the "section 306 stock" is not by its terms redeemable for at least five years from the date of issuance; and

(b) it is represented that there will be no redemption of the "section 306 stock," by tender or otherwise, within the five-year period.

.02 A ruling will usually be issued under section 306(b)(4) of the Code to the effect that a distribution of "section 306 stock" (other than a distribution under section 305, or, in the case of any recapitalization under section 368(a)(1)(E), a distribution which has the effect of a pro rata stock dividend, that is, a distribution under section 305) and the disposition of the "section 306 stock," other than by redemption and other than in anticipation of a redemption, is not pursuant to a plan of tax avoidance if the stock of the issuing corporation is widely held and

(a) the "section 306 stock" is by its terms redeemable within five years from the date of issuance, or

(b) the "section 306 stock" is not redeemable within five years from the date of issuance but the issuing corporation will not represent that there will be no redemption (as a result of a change in the terms of the stock, an invitation for tenders or otherwise) within five years from the date of issuance.

The creation of a debt obligation in exchange for money constitutes a simple borrowing transaction, which is not taxable to either the borrower or the lender. This is true whether the debt is evidenced by a formal instrument, such as a note or bond, or is merely represented by an open account indebtedness on the corporation's books. The lender's basis in the debt is the amount he advanced in exchange for it, at least at the outset. (However, as we shall see later, if the face amount of the debt is different from the amount of money received by the borrower, there will be original issue discount or premium, which must be accounted for as an adjustment of the interest rate and will affect the basis.)

When property is acquired in exchange for debt, the transaction amounts to a purchase on credit, which is likewise generally not a taxable event for the purchaser. On the other hand, as to the transferor of the property the transaction, whether viewed as a sale on credit or an exchange of one type of property for another (i.e. a claim against the transferee), would be normally taxable. The basis of both parties would be determined under the normal cost rule. (No original issue discount arises in connection with the issuance of debt for property, but §483 may apply to produce imputed interest in the transaction.)

However, as the D'Angelo case indicates, when it is to a corporation that property is transferred in exchange for debt obligations, §351 may come into play to prevent recognition of gain or loss to the transferor, if the obligations constitute "securities". (The suggestion in D'Angelo that debt obligations might actually represent "stock" stems from the possibility that in some circumstances stockholder-owned debt may be characterized as equity for tax purposes, a subject that will be considered at length later.) D'Angelo also confirms that not every debt obligation qualifies as a "security". While the term is not defined in the Code, in general it has been assumed to require a written, perhaps even relatively formal, instrument with a reasonably long duration. As D'Angelo intimates, the notion is that when short-term obligations are received the transaction comes so close to a sale for cash that gain should be recognized. Hence it may be incautious to expect security classification for obligations with a duration much less than five years. Compare Rev. Rul. 56-303, 1956-2 Cum. Bull. 193 (notes of under four years' duration held not securities) with Penfield v. Davis, 105 F. Supp. 292 (N.D. Ala. 1952), aff'd 205 F.2d 798 (5th Cir. 1953) (five year debentures redeemable at a premium prior to maturity held securities).

Nevertheless, the formal term of the obligations is not necessarily determinative, as the D'Angelo case illustrates in dramatic fashion by according "security" status to notes payable on demand (which is about as short-term as one can get). The reasoning in D'Angelo was that what was in form a demand note

was in fact the functional equivalent of a term loan of significant duration (if not, indeed, an equity interest), since there
was no prospect or expectation of repayment of the principal in
the foreseeable future. Compare Prentis v. United States,
273 F. Supp. 460 (S.D.N.Y. 1967), which held that a six-months
note qualified as a security (even though the case was on remand
from a Court of Appeals decision, sub. nom. Turner Construction
Co. v. United States, 364 F.2d 525 (2d Cir. 1966), holding that
six months is just too short for security classification, except
in very special circumstances); the District Court viewed the
note as really representing merely a transitory stage to the
issuance of preferred stock, with which the note was discharged
about seven months after it was issued.

When debt obligations which do not qualify as securities·
are received in a transaction to which §351 otherwise applies,
the obligations are treated as "other property" under §351(b),
with the result that gain (but not loss) is recognized to the
extent of the fair market value of the obligations. As a corollary, under §362(a) the carryover basis of the property received
by the corporation in exchange for the debt obligations is
increased by the amount of the gain recognized by the transferor,
and the latter's basis in the obligations is their fair market
value.

TURNER v. COMMISSIONER*

United States Tax Court, 1961. 20 T.C.M. 468.
Affirmed, 303 F.2d 94 (4th Cir. 1962)

Memorandum Findings of Fact and Opinion

TIETJENS, JUDGE: The Commissioner determined a deficiency in
petitioners' income tax for 1957 in the amount of $11,670.36. The
issues presented are (1) whether there was a recognized gain upon the
incorporation of a sole proprietorship; . . . .

Findings of Fact

Some of the facts have been stipulated and are incorporated herein by reference.

Petitioners are husband and wife and reside in Martinsville,
Virginia. For the calendar year 1957 they filed a joint income tax
return with the director of internal revenue for the district of Virginia.

Rufus F. Turner, hereinafter referred to as petitioner, as a sole
proprietor, had engaged in the operation of a fresh produce wholesale grocery business for 36 years in Martinsville under the name of
Cash Produce Company. Also associated with the business were petitioner's wife, Marguerite H. Turner, who had been employed for 26
years as a bookkeeper, and James R. Ingram, petitioner's son-in-law,
who had been employed for 7 years and was petitioner's principal
assistant.

On November 14, 1956, petitioner incorporated the sole proprietorship under the name of Cash Produce Company, Inc., hereinafter re-

ferred to as Cash Produce. The corporation transacted no business until January 1, 1957. A stock statement was filed with the Virginia State Corporation Commission on December 6, 1956, advising it of a plan to issue 135 shares of common stock for $6,750 in cash. Also in December 1956, petitioner conferred with his attorney and his certified public accountant with respect to the manner in which to accomplish the proposed transfer of the proprietorship assets to the new corporation. At that time the accountant made the following computation of the proprietorship goodwill:

Net earnings (before income taxes)—

1952	$ 29,887.34
1953	18,468.80
1954	19,536.61
1955	24,830.86
1956	21,535.87
Total	$114,259.48
Less income taxes—25% average	28,564.87

Total net earnings	$ 85,694.61	
5 year average	$ 17,138.92	
Net earnings capitalized at 10%		$171,389.20
Less net invested capital at 12–31–56		
excluding goodwill (75,534.48 + 21,535.87)		97,070.35
Goodwill at date of incorporation		$ 74,318.85
Rounding off	$ 74,300.00	

On January 1, 1957, with the exception of real estate and certain other fixed assets, all of the assets of the sole proprietorship together with certain liabilities were transferred to Cash Produce in exchange for 1,365 shares of common stock. These assets had a cost basis of $49,593.46. A summary of the balance sheet of the proprietorship as of December 31, 1956 was as follows:

Current Assets		$ 47,077.44
Fixed Assets	$ 91,455.07	
Less Depreciation	$ 36,490.09	54,964.98
Other Asset		230.10
TOTAL ASSETS		$102,272.52
Current Liabilities		$ 5,202.17
R. F. Turner, Capital:		
Balance 1-1-56	$116,013.78	
Earnings for year 1956	21,535.87	
	$137,549.65	
Drawings for 1956	40,479.30	97,070.35
TOTAL LIABILITIES		$102,272.52

* * *

A financial statement for Cash Produce as of January 1, 1957 was prepared by the accountant on January 19, 1957, and transmitted to the Produce Reporter Company, Wheaton, Illinois which publishes a credit rating reference book of produce firms.   The following is the balance sheet from that financial statement:

CURRENT ASSETS		
Cash	$ 9,092.61	
Accounts receivable—customers	12,339.46	
Merchandise inventory—at the lower of cost (determined by the first-in-first-out method) or market	25,645.37	$ 47,077.44
FIXED ASSETS		
Store fixtures, furniture, equipment and vehicles— at cost	$25,002.29	
Less accumulated depreciation	17,514.20	7,488.09
INTANGIBLE ASSETS		
Good Will	$74,300.00	
Incorporation expense	230.10	74,530.10
TOTAL ASSETS		$129,095.63

CURRENT LIABILITIES			
Accounts payable:			
Trade	$2,312.01		
Other	625.02	$ 2,937.03	
Accrued liabilities:			
Salaries and wages	$2,024.58		
Taxes (other than taxes on income	240.56	2,265.14	$ 5,202.17
NONCURRENT LIABILITY			
Note payable to officer—unsecured and without interest			$ 48,893.46
CAPITAL			
Common stock—authorized, 3,000 shares of $50 par value; issued and outstanding, 135 shares		$ 6,750.00	
Subscriptions to common stock, 1,365 shares		68,250.00	75,000.00
TOTAL LIABILITIES			$129,095.63

Thereafter petitioner received the following reply from the Produce Reporter Company in regard to the financial statement submitted:

The statement of Cash Produce Company, Inc., does present several problems from a rating standpoint.

The item of "good will" is very correctly listed as an "intangible asset", it is the type asset which is eliminated from credit consideration in arriving at Blue Book financial ratings.

When your good will and incorporation expenses of $74,530.10 are eliminated from your statement, that January 1, 1957 Corporation financial statement then shows a net worth of less than $500.

We believe we have a feel of what your accountant and tax attornies [sic] have attempted to accomplish in handling your incorporation on a basis which provides for a corporation note payable "to officer" of $48,893.46. Such an arrangement does, however, deplete completely the corporation's financial responsibility for credit rating purposes.

Your accountant can, of course, advise you on the advisability of issuing corporate stock for that indebtedness to officers.

Frankly, Mr. Turner, we hesitate very much to recommend a subordination agreement covering the notes payable to officers and do so only as a last resort.

In the event your accountants or attornies [sic] would want to prepare a subordination agreement which would clearly set forth that no payments are to be made on indebtedness to officers as long as there are any trade obligations and indicate clearly that you will notify Produce Reporter Company prior to the time any payment is made on that indebtedness, then such a subordination agreement could be accepted.

It is the type exception, however, which is "loaded" with possibilities of misunderstanding for the future.

* * *

In response to this letter petitioner wrote the following:

As principal stockholder, president and manager of Cash Produce Co., Inc. the undersigned will continue to honor credit extension with the same integrity and ability as in the past, and to personally guarantee payment of the corporations debts in the same manner as prior to incorporation.

Though you suggest in your letter that a subordination agreement as to the corporations debt to me is "loaded" with possibilities of misunderstanding, you may accept this letter over my signature below as such an agreement, to the effect that any trade obligations will most certainly be paid before any liquidation of this debt. Any drawings I made from the corporation above the minimal salary allowance provided for me will be charged against my annual profit-sharing. Furthermore, your letter ignored the fact that the note payable to officer of $48,893.46 was created by the charge for goodwill, and that the goodwill was a capitalization at 10% of the average net profits of the past five years. . . .

Nevertheless, to eliminate goodwill from credit consideration as you state, should also require elimination of the debt which it created, leaving a remaining net worth of

Herwitz–Bus.Planning Tem. 2nd Ed.—7

$49,363.36. To the latter should be added, if not more, by the subordination described above, the value of the business real estate which I retained in my own right in the amount of $47,476.89, giving a total net worth for credit purposes (excluding other personal assets) in the amount of $96,840.-25, exclusive of goodwill.

* * *

As evidence of the $48,893.46 designated on the balance sheet submitted to the Produce Reporter Company as "NONCURRENT LIABILITY, Note Payable to officer—unsecured and without interest", the accountant prepared the following instrument which was executed sometime between January and November 1957:

Notice of Indebtedness

January 1, 1957

For value received, We, Cash Produce Co., Inc., do hereby promise to pay to Mr Rufus F. Turner, his heirs or assigns, the amount of Forty-eight thousand, eight hundred, ninety-three dollars and forty-six cents, ($48,893.46) without interest, payable at the office of the corporation on or after February 1, 1958; also the corporation is not to furnish security of any type for this indebtedness. It is also agreed that the payee may draw funds from the corporation at any time upon the pledge of this note as security, said drawings to be deducted from the amount of this liability prior to settlement.

Accepted and agreed to the above this date January 1, 1957.

(S) Rufus F. Turner   Cash Produce Co., Inc.
_____
        Payee

                        (S) Rufus F. Turner
                    _____
                            Registered
                              Agent
                            President

This instrument was not adopted or ratified by any formal resolution of the stockholders or the board of directors of Cash Produce.

A meeting of the board of directors of Cash Produce was held on February 25, 1957. Relevant parts of the minutes of that meeting are as follows:

WHEREAS, Rufus F. Turner, sole proprietor and owner, trading and doing business previously as the Cash Produce Company, Martinsville, Virginia, has the below mentioned personal property assets of $129,095.63, and said Rufus F. Turner, owner and sole proprietor, being subject to liabilities of $54,095.63, he having previously purchased for cash 135 shares at $50.00 per share for $6,750.00 cash; therefore, total liabilities outstanding by purchase of said stock being the sum of $60,845.63, and the difference between said assets and liabilities being net assets and net worth of $68,250.00, and he has offered to sell the personal assets of said Cash Product [sic] Company for the below sum, subject to said liabilities, with the remaining value in net assets and worth of $68,250.00 to the Cash Produce Company, Incorporated payable in common stock of the corporation, representing the difference between the assets subject to said liabilities.

WHEREAS the said Rufus F. Turner, owner, has offered to transfer the said current, fixed and intangible personal property assets of said Cash Produce Company with the assumption of said liabilities to the Cash Produce Company, Incorporated, in exchange for $68,250.00 to be paid in 1365 shares of the capital stock of the corporation of the par value of $50.00 each, and it is necessary for this Board of Directors to determine the value of such property in current money of the United States of America, as well as to accept or reject the said offer:

NOW, THEREFORE, BE IT RESOLVED:

First, that this Board, in the exercise of its best skill and judgment, fixes and determines the value of the said property in current money of the United States in accordance with the Financial Statement of Cash Produce Company, . . . a copy of which is hereby attached and incorporated [14] . . . .

Second, that the said offer of the said Rufus F. Turner, owner, trading as the Cash Produce Company, Martinsville, Virginia, be, and the same hereby is, accepted, in the sale of the above valued assets of $129,095.63, subject to the liabilities of $54,095.63, to the Cash Produce Company, Incorporated, and that 1365 shares of the Common stock of the par value of $50.00 each in the total sum of $68,250.00 of said Corporation be issued, (in addition the amount $6,750.00 has previously been issued to him by said Corporation for cash) and the remaining amount of $68,250.00 now be issued to Rufus F. Turner by said Corporation, to cover the actual net worth and net assets as shown in the First Resolution above.

A fiscal year ending July 31 was adopted by Cash Produce. Petitioner's wife, as bookkeeper, incorrectly credited the $48,893.46 to "Accounts Payable" and subsequently certain drawings of petition-

14. [Ed. note] Identical to the one set out above.

er were debited to this account with the result that the financial statement of Cash Produce for its fiscal year disclosed notes payable as $42,090.29. This error was corrected in January 1958 when the accountant audited petitioner's drawing account in preparation of the joint income tax return.

On November 15, 1957, the accountant left the firm by which he had been employed and shortly thereafter opened his own office in Martinsville. On January 1, 1958, petitioner and Cash Produce became the accountant's clients. On or about January 8, 1958, the accountant's immediate supervisor of his former firm telephoned him and also advised petitioner by letter that the incorporation of Cash Produce was, in the supervisor's opinion, taxable rather than tax free.

On January 14, 1958, a debenture bond in the amount of $48,893.-46 issued by Cash Produce to petitioner was filed with the Virginia State Corporation Commission. Although this debenture bond was dated January 1, 1957, it was prepared by Cash Produce's attorney from a form supplied by the accountant a few days prior to the filing. Pertinent provisions of this debenture bond are as follows:

> Cash Produce Company, Incorporated, a Corporation organized and existing under the laws of the State of Virginia, (hereinafter called the "Corporation"), for value received, hereby promises to pay to Rufus F. Turner, or order, his heirs or assigns, the total sum of $48,893.46, bearing interest at three per cent (3%) per annum, and being payable as follows: $5,000.00 on January 1, 1962, and $5,000.00 on the first day of each year thereafter until the total sum of $48,-893.46 herein owed is paid unto the said Rufus F. Turner, or order, his heirs or assigns, together with 3% interest per annum and with the first payment of interest being due and payable on said sum on January 1, 1958 and on the first day of each year thereafter.

> The issue of the within corporate debenture is made and executed pursuant to the articles of incorporation of the said Corporation and in pursuance of a resolution of said Corporation passed on the 1st day of January, 1957 and said debenture herein being debenture No. 1.

> * * *

> This debenture is of an authorized issue debenture due as hereinabove set forth of the Corporation (hereinafter called debenture) of the aggregate principal amount of Forty-Eight Thousand Eight Hundred Ninety-Three Dollars and Forty-Six Cents ($48,893.46), duly authorized by resolution of the Board of Directors of the Corporation adopted January 1, 1957.

The liability reflected in the debenture bond was recorded on the books of Cash Produce by the accountant as a "Long Term Liability" with the explanation "Indenture due Rufus F. Turner from transfer of assets at date of incorporation." Although entered on the books in January 1958 it was dated January 1, 1957.

* * *

The Commissioner explained in the statement accompanying the statutory notice of deficiency:

It is held that you realized a gain of $74,300.00, recognized as a long-term capital gain to the extent of $48,893.46 (taxable at 50%), which represents the fair market value of non-interest bearing note received as part payment in the transfer of your net equity in assets to the Cash Produce Company, Incorporated. Therefore, taxable income has been increased in the amount of $24,446.73.

* * *

Opinion

. . . In contesting the Commissioner's determination the petitioner argues (1) that the incorporation was entirely tax free as the "Notice of Indebtedness" was not a legal instrument, but only a memorandum prepared for petitioner's personal satisfaction until a debenture bond was issued and that the petitioner's receipt of such debenture bond on January 14, 1958 was an integral and concluding step in the plan of incorporation; (2) that the notice of indebtedness does not constitute "other property" within the concept of section 351; (3) that even if the notice of indebtedness is "other property" it had no fair market value; (4) that if it is "other property" and in addition had a fair market value, nevertheless no gain was realized upon the receipt of the stock and "other property" because the value of the property received was not in excess of the net adjusted cost basis of the tangible assets transferred; and (5) that the notice of indebtedness represented an equity interest equivalent to stock.

[The court first held that the "Notice of Indebtedness" constituted an enforceable note rather than a mere memorandum having no legal significance, and that the issuance of the note had been duly authorized by the board of directors of the corporation.]

The next approach taken by petitioner is that the notice of indebtedness does not constitute "other property" within the meaning of section 351(b). This contention is not predicated upon an agreement that the notice of indebtedness was a security under section 351 (a), but rather that the notice of indebtedness was received by petitioner only as evidence of an existing obligation and not in payment of an obligation. We agree with petitioner that the notice of indebtedness is written evidence of an existing enforceable obligation. However, we do not agree that this is not "other property" within the purview of section 351(b). Petitioner cites *Jay A. Williams*, 28 T.C. 1000 (1957), and extracts from context our statement that "A note received only as security, or as an evidence of indebtedness, and not as payment, may not be regarded as income". In *Williams* we dealt with the question of whether a note received in payment of services was income to the recipient. We held the note was not income as it was established to our satisfaction that the note was not received in payment of the outstanding debt due the taxpayer for the performance of services and that "a simple change in the form of indebtedness from an account payable to a note payable is insufficient to cause the realization of income by the creditor".

It is obvious that petitioner by this contention has completely misconceived the import of the note in this case. The question presented here is not whether the receipt of the note resulted in ordinary income under section 61(a) . . . . but whether gain was recognizable on the incorporation as a result of the receipt of the note under section 351. Our afore-going conclusion was that the notice of indebtedness was an enforceable note and the cases have uniformly held that a note of such duration does not comply with the statutory concept of a security. . . . Inasmuch as it does not qualify as a security under section 351(a), it is "other property" under section 351(b). Rev.Rul. 56–303, 1956–2 C.B. 193.

Petitioner continues, that even if the notice of indebtedness is "other property" it had no fair market value. He says that it is apparent from the financial condition of the corporation and the testimony of the parties concerned that there was no immediate intention or ability to pay the obligation. The evidence does not disclose an inability on the part of the corporation to pay the note. Although there was evidence regarding the value of the note it was focused primarily on the aspect of its value as collateral security for a loan. There is a question as to whether it could be discounted; however, it should be kept in mind that, as previously indicated, this note was not an ordinary note whose value would increase as the maturity date approached, but was *sui generis*, as its provision that "the [petitioner] may draw funds from the corporation at any time upon the pledge of [the] note as security, said drawings to be deducted from the amount of [the] liability prior to settlement" made it in effect a drawing account. As we see it, the fair market value of the note was at all times its stated value as petitioner at any time could have withdrawn such amounts, the only barrier to such withdrawals being the voluntary, self-imposed subordination agreement which could have been rescinded at any time by petitioner. We do not think that the evidence introduced establishes that the amount determined by Commissioner to be the fair market value is arbitrary or unreasonable.

Petitioner in another phase of his assault upon Commissioner's determination argues that if we should find that the note has a fair market value nevertheless petitioner realized no gain on the transfer for the reason that the value of the stock and "other property" received was not in excess of the net adjusted cost basis of the tangible assets transferred. Simply stated, petitioner contends that the $74,300 which was ascribed to goodwill at the time of the incorporation was incorrect and that no goodwill existed or was transferred, or, if any was transferred, its value was negligible. The Commissioner says that the sole proprietorship possessed transferable goodwill with a value of $74,300. This presents a paradox as petitioner now attempts to retreat from his original position by relying on [authorities] in which the Commissioner challenged the transfer of goodwill. Conversely, the Commissioner here does not challenge, but acquiesces in the original amount designated by petitioner as goodwill. In addition to the aforementioned case and ruling, petitioner also calls attention to the testimony of a representative of Produce Reporter Company who stated that goodwill had no value in arriving at a rating for a produce business. A query from the Court revealed that this rating was from the standpoint of a creditor rather than a possible purchaser and that all assets were viewed in regard to their basis at liquidation in order to ascertain their worth to creditors in the event of such liquidation. This sheds little light upon the problem.

We are convinced that the corporation acquired something more in value at the incorporation of the sole proprietorship than the tangible assets transferred, which was goodwill, and petitioner has not shown the Commissioner's determination of the amount of this goodwill to be erroneous. . . . It follows that the Commissioner's determination must be sustained. .

Even if debt obligations do qualify as "securities", non-recognition under §351 depends upon satisfaction of the control test, just as when stock is received; however, the problem is different in the case of debt obligations since they play no part in that test, which is based on ownership of voting power and other stock by the transferors of property. See subsection 1 below. When §351 does apply, under §362(a) the corporation takes the property received in exchange for the securities at its basis in the hands of the transferor, and under §358 the transferor carries over his basis in the property to the securities received. (If the transferor receives both stock and securities, the carryover basis is allocated between the two in proportion to their respective fair market values. Reg. §1.358-2(b)(2).)

1. The Impact of Securities on the Control Test

How does the §368(c) control test operate with respect to transfers of property to a corporation in exchange for securities, in the light of the fact that debt obligations normally have no role in the computation of the necessary 80% control? Obviously, if the recipient of the securities either already owns enough stock, or receives enough in the transaction in which the debt was received, to be in control of the corporation himself, §351 is satisfied, and no gain or loss is recognized upon receipt of the securities. The same is true if the recipient of the securities is part of the group which owns, or obtains, sufficient stock to satisfy the control test. But a question arises when the recipient of securities does not also receive (or already own) any significant amount of stock, even if he is part of a transferor group that ends up in control of the corporation. Although there is nothing in the words of §351 that calls for a distinction between stock and securities in this regard, the Service has ruled that pursuant to the underlying policy of §351 the statute does not apply to one who only receives securities (and does not already own any stock), Rev. Rul. 73-472, 1973-2 Cum. Bull. 114; the theory is that the transferor of property has undergone more than a mere change in the form of ownership, since he is only a creditor of the corporation, and has no proprietary interest in the enterprise. (As to how much stock the recipient of securities must receive (or already own) to make §351 applicable, the obvious analogy is to Reg. §1.351-1(a)(1)(ii), and the guideline set out in Section 3.07 of Rev. Proc. 77-37, dealing with how much stock must be received for property by one who also receives substantial stock for services, in order to make the latter eligible for inclusion in the control count.)

Here is an interesting twist on the relationship between "securities" and the control test:

REVENUE RULING 79-70
79-1 Cum. Bull. 144.

ISSUE

Is the control requirement of section 351(a) of the Internal Revenue Code of 1954, which provides for nonrecognition of gain or loss on transfers of property to a controlled corporation, satisfied where part of the stock of the controlled corporation received by a transferor in exchange for property is sold to another person who transferred property to the corporation in exchange for securities?

FACTS

Corporation X transferred property to a newly organized corporation, Newco, in exchange for all of Newco's stock (a single class of voting common stock). Pursuant to a prearranged binding agreement between X and corporation Y, X sold 40 percent of its Newco stock for its fair market value to Y, and Y purchased securities for cash from Newco. Newco would not have been formed if Y had not agreed to purchase securities for cash from Newco and part of the Newco stock from X.

LAW AND ANALYSIS

The specific sections of the Code that are applicable are section 351(a), which provides that no gain or loss will be recognized if property is transferred to a corporation by one or more persons solely in exchange for stock or securities in such corporation and immediately after the exchange such person or persons are in control of the corporation, and section 368(c) which defines control for purposes of section 351(a) to mean the ownership of stock possessing at least 80 percent of the total combined voting power of all classes of stock entitled to vote.

Since the sale of Newco stock by X to Y was an integral part of the incorporation and pursuant to a binding agreement entered into prior to the exchange, the control requirement of section 351(a) of the Code is determined after the sale. See [authorities holding] that the control requirement of section 351(a) is not satisfied where, pursuant to a binding agreement entered into prior to the transfer of property to the corporation, a transferor loses control of a corporation by a sale of some of the stock received . . . to a third party, who does not transfer property to the corporation in the transaction. After the sale was completed in the instant case, 60 percent of the Newco stock was owned by X and 40 percent of the stock was owned by Y. However, since Y was not a "transferor" of property to Newco with respect to Newco stock, Y's ownership of the Newco stock purchased from X cannot be counted in determining whether the control requirement of section 351(a) was met. The fact that Y transferred cash to Newco in exchange for securities as part of the transaction does not make Y a transferor for purposes of the control requirement of section 351(a). See Rev. Rul. 73-472, 1973-2 C. B. 114, and Rev. Rul. 73-473, 1973-2 C. B. 115, which hold that a person who receives only securities from a corporation in exchange for property, and who is not a shareholder prior to the exchange, is not a "transferor" for purposes of satisfying the section 351 control requirement.

HOLDING

Since X only owned 60 percent of the Newco stock "immediately after the exchange" within the meaning of section 351(a) of the Code, the 80 percent control requirement of section 351(a) was not satisfied. Gain or loss to X will be determined and recognized under section 1001.

2.   Sale versus Exchange under §351

As the D'Angelo case illustrates, a taxpayer desirous of avoiding §351 with respect to a transfer of property for securities may try to divorce that transaction from any transfers for stock, and then argue that the transfer for debt was a separate sale transaction not subject to §351. The short answer to such a contention is that §351 by its terms applies to transfers of property for securities as well as for stock (at least whenever

the recipient of securities also owns more than a nominal amount
of stock), and there does not appear to be any basis for a
different treatment because the transaction is characterized as
a sale. Nevertheless, some cases have held that a transaction
cast in the form of a separate sale is not covered by §351.
E.g., Shannon v. Commissioner, 29 T.C. 702 (1958), where the
Court held that once the transaction was found to be a sale, "it
follows for the same reasons that it was not an exchange within
the meaning of" §351, and therefore it was not necessary to
determine whether the installment obligation received might be
deemed a security "if the transaction were other than a sale".

The D'Angelo opinion did not dismiss the possibility of a
distinction for "sale" transactions, but found it inapplicable
to a case where the transfer for debt was an integral part of
the overall transaction. This tracks a familiar issue under
§351: as we saw earlier, if a transferor of property to a
corporation assigns some of the stock received to a non-transferor, that stock will be out of the control computation if the
assignment was committed at the outset (or at least was an
interdependent element in the total transaction). But there is
an important difference here, in that, unlike the assignee of
stock, the recipient of the debt obligations is himself a transferor of property to the corporation. Hence, even if that
transaction could be viewed as separate and independent, if the
obligations constitute "securities" and the recipient already
owns a significant amount of stock there seems no reason why
§351 should not apply, as noted above. And when the recipient
of the securities neither already already owns any stock nor
receives any along with the debt, then §351 does not apply
anyway, according to Rev. Rul. 73-472, supra, even if the
transfer of property for debt is fully integrated with transfers
for stock.

Accordingly, as footnote 5 to the D'Angelo opinion intimates,
the primary question in these situations should perhaps be
whether the debt obligations qualify as securities. Incidentally,
it is when the obligations are not securities that the integration
issue may be most relevant. When non-security obligations are
received outside of any §351 transaction, the transaction is
simply accounted for as a sale on credit. On the other hand, if
the taxpayer's receipt of non-security debt is integrated with a
transfer by him of property for stock under §351, then the debt
would constitute boot under §351(b); in that event, recognition
of gain is not confined to the property exchanged for debt, but
includes the total gain on the overall transaction, although
recognition is limited to the extent of the fair market value of
the boot.

Any planning in conjunction with the receipt of debt obligations from a corporation in exchange for property is made all
the more hazardous by the fact that one of the topics on which
the Service will "ordinarily" not issue a ruling is the tax
effect of a transfer to a corporation where part of the consideration received by the transferor consists of debt obligations and the term of the debt is less than ten years. Rev.
Proc. 82-22, Section 4.019, 1982-2 Cum. Bull. 469, 472. Query
whether this represents a veiled hint as to the minimum duration
necessary for "security" classification.

As under corporation law, so under the tax laws a sharp distinction is drawn between debt and equity—and again, the comparison substantially favors debt. Without attempting to make a complete catalogue of the differences in tax treatment between debt and stock, the following review of the more important differences should serve to illustrate the range of issues which underlies any choice between the two.

1. DIFFERENCES AT THE CORPORATE LEVEL

Perhaps the best-known tax consideration bearing on the choice between debt and equity is the fact that the annual return on debt in the form of interest is deductible by the corporation, while dividends on stock (with the exception of certain public utility preferred stocks) are not. Also deductible as interest is any original issue discount arising upon the issuance of the debt, as will be discussed in detail below.

Upon the repayment of a debt obligation, a corporation may have income from cancellation of indebtedness if the debt is settled at less than face, or a loss may result from retirement at a premium. Apart from such factors, however, neither income nor earnings and profits are affected by the repayment of debt. As to stock, redemption for cash is not normally a taxable event for the corporation, but a distribution of appreciated property in redemption of stock may give rise to recognition of gain. §311. In either event, a reduction in earnings and profits may result, §312.

One other factor worth noting here is that the accumulation of corporate earnings to repay bona fide debt will generally not run afoul of the accumulated earnings tax, but accumulation to redeem stock may incur serious risk under that tax, as we shall see later.

2. DIFFERENCES TO THE HOLDER -- ANNUAL RETURN
AND GAIN UPON DISPOSITION

The most important difference between stock and debt from the holder's point of view is that the taxability of dividends as ordinary income depends upon whether they are covered by earnings and profits, whereas interest on debt constitutes income to the recipient in any event. Moreover, for an individual recipient dividends are subject to a $100 exclusion, §116, while corporations get an 85% intercorporate dividend deduction (or even 100%, for an affiliated corporation), §243; in both cases, interest is fully taxable.

With regard to gain on a sale or exchange, both debt obligations (in whatever form, except for accounts receivable arising in the ordinary course of business) and stock would normally qualify as capital assets, so that gain would be capital if the holding period was satisfied.

One of the most important differences between stock and debt arises in connection with the treatment of payments made in retirement or redemption. As to debt obligations, the receipt of payment is a return of capital to the extent of the holder's basis in the obligation. Moreoever, for corporate debt evidenced by a written instrument (but not if the maker is an individual), §1232(a) treats payments in redemption as if they were received upon a sale or exchange of the instrument, so that gain will normally be capital (except to the extent of any original issue discount). Distributions in redemption of stock, however, can give rise to ordinary income taxation as a dividend under §302, a subject which will be considered at length later.

3. DIFFERENCES TO THE HOLDER -- TREATMENT OF INVESTMENT LOSS

a. Losses on Debt

In the case of sale or exchange of a debt obligation (which, as just noted, includes the retirement of a written corporate obligation), whether the loss is ordinary or capital will depend upon the character of the obligation in the hands of the taxpayer. The treatment of loss upon worthlessness of a debt is a good deal more complicated. If the debt obligation is evidenced by a written instrument which is either registered or in coupon form, it falls within the special definition of "security" in §165(g)(2)(C), and any loss upon worthlessness is treated as if it arose from a sale or exchange of the obligation on the last day of the taxable year. If the obligation is not covered by §165(g)(2)(C), the treatment of loss due to worthlessness is

governed by §166, dealing with bad debts. When such debt is
held by a corporation, any loss due to worthlessness will be
ordinary. But losses of an individual are subject to the
distinction drawn in §166 between business and non-business
bad debts, with loss on the latter limited under §166(d) to
short-term capital loss treatment regardless of the holding
period involved.

NOTE ON BUSINESS BAD DEBTS

i. Is the Taxpayer Engaged in Business?

Stockholders who also make advances to their corporation
(not evidenced by §165(g)(2)(C) "securities") have often
sought business bad debt treat ent for losses suffered on
their advances when the enterprise fails. In many of the
cases it was found that the creditor-shareholder was not
himself in business, but rather was merely an investor
looking to the fruits of the corporation's business for a
return on his investment. However, for a time some taxpayers
who were involved in a number of ventures succeeded with the
argument that their pattern of investments in and advances
to several enterprise amounted to a business separate and
distinct from the businesses carried on by the corporations
themselves. But in Whipple v. Commissioner, 373 U.S. 193
(1963), the Supreme Court rejected this approach in holding
that involvement with several corporations did not change a
taxpayer's status from investment to business; the so-called
"promoter" category was limited to cases where the taxpayer
could establish "a regular course of promoting corporations
for a fee or commission . . . or for a profit on their
sale," which might well mean that any gain realized would be
taxed as ordinary income, but in any event would exclude
most stockholder-creditors from qualifying.

However, the Supreme Court determined that the taxpayer's
ownership and leasing of the premises occupied by the corporate debtor did represent a business, and remanded for
consideration of whether the loan in question was incurred
in the taxpayer's "business" of being a landlord. In principle, it is not apparent why a taxpayer who rents a single
piece of property to a corporation is carrying on a business,
while the taxpayer who lends funds, even to several corporations, is not. Although lending money is normally a more
passive activity than leasing property, the distinction
between the two is at most a matter of degree, and may even
disappear entirely in the case of a "net lease" where the

lessee assumes all responsibility for the property and the lessor simply collects rent. To be sure, continuous activity in the leasing of property can constitute a business by any standard; indeed, equipment leasing is a substantial industry. But the same is true of money lending, and the question remains why so much more should be required to establish a money-lending business than a leasing business. The practical impact of such a distinction may be that any well-advised taxpayer who decides to incorporate a business will retain some of the operating assets in his own hands and lease them to the corporation -- a practice which might have some other significant tax advantages as well, as we shall see shortly.

In a footnote the Supreme Court also referred with apparent approval to the case of Dorminey v. Commissioner, 26 T.C. 940 (1956), where the taxpayer was involved in the wholesale produce business, both as a sole proprietor and through several wholly-owned corporations. He customarily made advances to a number of different enterprises which were either customers or suppliers of his produce business. The taxpayer controlled some of the concerns to which he made advances, while in others he had no financial interest at all. The advances in question had been made to a corporation which the taxpayer had organized to engage in the business of importing bananas, because of his difficulty in obtaining a steady supply of bananas for his produce business. The new corporation ran into financial difficulties and was forced to borrow from the taxpayer as well as outsiders. By the time of the ultimate failure of the new corporation, the taxpayer had advanced almost $16,000. The Tax Court held that these advances had been made to assure a supply of bananas for the taxpayer's sole proprietorship, and accordingly allowed business bad-debt treatment. But it is troublesome to note that in deciding Dorminey the Tax Court seemed to rely primarily upon "promoter" cases, including two which were expressly disapproved in Whipple.

ii.   Relation of the Debt to a Conceded Business

Even if the taxpayer can show that he is in a business of his own, as distinguished from one carried on by the debtor corporation, he is not out of the woods -- he must still show the necessary degree of relationship between his personal business and the debt in question to qualify for business bad-debt treatment. For example, since employment

constitutes a trade or business, a loan by an employee to
his employer designed to maintain his job could constitute a
business debt. But if, as is so often the case in such
situations, the employee-taxpayer is also a substantial
shareholder of the employer, the question arises whether the
real genesis of the loan was the taxpayer's shareholder
status rather than his position as an employee. And the
Supreme Court has made it all the harder for the taxpayer to
prevail in circumstances of this kind, by holding that the
relationship to the taxpayer's business must be the dominant
motivation for the loan (instead of being merely a significant
motive, as a number of courts had held). United States v.
Generes, 405 U.S. 93 (1972). Not many employee-shareholders
will be able to demonstrate that in making loans to their
close corporations they were primarily motivated by their
positions as employees rather than their interests as shareholders.

How about the lawyer who makes a loan to a corporate
client in which he also has an equity interest? In Garlove
v. Commissioner, 24 T.C.M. 1049 (1965), the court allowed
business bad-debt treatment to a lawyer for an advance to a
corporation in which he was a minority stockholder, director,
and inactive officer. The court found that the lawyer had
made the loan in order to help support a good client, as
well as to accommodate the two principal stockholders of the
corporation, who were also regular clients. The court
regarded it as unreasonable to infer that the taxpayer would
have advanced $15,000 just to protect his investment in the
corporation, which amounted to only $7,000.

iii. Loss on Shareholder Guaranty of Corporate Debt

In Putnam v. Commissioner, 352 U.S. 82 (1956), the
Supreme Court concluded that when the guarantor of a debt is
required to pay it, by subrogation he steps into the shoes
of the original creditor, and if he can not recover from the
debtor his loss is one from worthlessness of a debt. Hence,
the business vs. non-business bad debt dichotomy is applicable
in determining whether an ordinary loss is available. Some
courts have reached the same result even where there is no
right of subrogation under state law, seizing on the language
in Putnam that there "is no real or economic difference
between the loss of an investment made in the form of a
direct loan to a corporation and one made indirectly in the
form of a guaranteed bank loan." 352 U.S. at 92-93. E.g.,
Horne v. Commissioner, 523 F. 2d 1363 (9th Cir. 1975).

b. Losses on Stock

In general, any loss on stock, whether incurred upon a sale or exchange, a redemption, or worthlessness, will be capital loss, long-term or short-term depending upon the holding period. There is, however, one very important exception: § 1244 provides ordinary loss treatment for up to $50,000 of loss ($100,000 on a joint return) on stock which satisfies the requirements of that section. Faithful to its purpose of encouraging investment of risk capital in modest enterprises, § 1244 applies only to common stock, which was acquired directly from the corporation; in addition, at the time of the issuance of the stock for which § 1244 qualification is sought, the corporation must not be over a specified size, as measured by the requirement that the sum of (1) the consideration to be received for the stock in question plus (2) the amount of money or other property (measured at its basis to the corporation upon receipt) previously received by the corporation in exchange for stock, as a contribution to capital, or as paid-in surplus, must not exceed $1,000,000. In effect this means that a new corporation can have a maximum of $1,000,000 of § 1244 stock, while for an already existing corporation the allowable amount is reduced by any previous investments of capital in the corporation (whether or not they qualified under § 1244). If a proposed issuance of stock would take the corporation beyond this limit, whatever amount of stock can be issued within the $1,000,000 limitation is permitted to qualify, and the corporation may designate which of the new shares constitute the § 1244 stock.

Section 1244 stock can only be issued for money or other property, which excludes services; by special statutory definition, stock and securities are also excluded, meaning, among other things, that stock issued upon the conversion of a security can not qualify. There is also one condition that can not be tested until the date of the loss on the stock: the corporation must not, for a period up to five years prior to the loss on the stock, have derived as much as 50% of its gross receipts from inactive sources such as dividends, rents and royalties (unless its total deductions exceeded its gross income).

In 1978 the requirements for qualification under § 1244 were considerably eased by virtue of the elimination of (1) the need for the stock to be issued pursuant to a "plan", which had provoked considerable litigation, and (2) a complex prohibition against overlapping offerings of stock. That still leaves some problems with the "common stock" requirement. Presumably, any express preference either in dividends or upon liquidation would be a disqualification. However, particularly in connection with liquidation rights, there may be arrangements which are arguably preferential in substance, though not in form. For example, suppose that X acquires half of the common stock of a corporation for $90,000, while Y, who is expected to provide important services to the venture, is to receive the other half of the stock for $10,000. In order to take account of this substantial difference in the amount of capital invested, the parties might arrange for the creation of two classes of stock which would be identical except that upon liquidation the first $100,000 of assets would be allocated between the two classes in the ratio of 9 to 1; any excess over $100,000 would be distributed on a share for share basis. Or the parties might achieve the same effect by giving one class nine times as many shares as the other (accompanied by an appropriate allocation of voting power by classes rather than on the basis of the number of shares), and then providing that upon liquidation the first $100,000 is to be distributed on a share for share basis, with any excess divided equally between the two classes. Would the class with the greater liquidation benefits qualify as "common stock" under § 1244?

The combination of getting an ordinary loss deduction under § 1244 if the stock goes down while being eligible for capital gain treatment when the stock goes up makes a mighty attractive package, especially when the stock has a public market, or prospects of one in the not too distant future, so that if the enterprise does prosper the stockholders can actually sell the stock and realize the profit. But in the case of a close corporation, where the stockholders do not contemplate sale in the foreseeable future and might have trouble finding a buyer if they wanted to, a more likely means of enjoying the fruits of the company's prosperity without prohibitive tax cost is for the stockholders to put some of their investment in the form of debt (and of course this also gives the corporation a deduction for any annual return paid to the stockholders by way of interest on their debt). On the other hand, to the extent of any debt he takes the taxpayer will have to forego the chance of ordinary loss treatment, since that is rarely available for loss on the debt, so § 1244 provides a counterweight to the usual impetus for the shareholders of a close corporation to put as much of their investment in the form of debt as possible.

In the circumstances, the stockholders are pretty much put to a choice, since the more of their investment they allocate to their common stock, in order to increase its basis (which is what determines the amount of a loss for § 1244 purposes if the enterprise goes sour), the less is available to augment the basis of their debt and hence the amount which can later be withdrawn tax-free from the corporation if it prospers. Faced with a choice between the two, the typical close corporation entrepreneur seems likely to choose the tax advantage associated with success of the enterprise over one dependent upon failure. Note that preferred stock does not offer either of these tax advantages, which may create pressure for a capital structure consisting of only common and debt, but at the cost of not being able to reduce the value of the common stock to merely a right to future profits, with a consequent decline in planning flexibility.

182

Would it be possible for stockholders to have their cake and eat it too, by taking some debt at the outset, and then, if the business portents become unfavorable, exchanging the debt for common stock to qualify under § 1244? At first blush such a transaction might seem financially unwise, since it would mean that the former debt-holder would no longer be able to participate in the proceeds of an insolvency liquidation. But if, as is so often the case, the amount available for distribution to general creditors upon insolvency would be rather small anyway, then the combination of the liquidation proceeds plus a capital loss for the unpaid balance might well not be worth as much as an ordinary loss on the full amount, which § 1244 would facilitate. To be sure, such a clear-cut tax motivation could make the transaction suspect; but after all, it is not unusual for stockholders to attempt to resuscitate their company by subordinating their claims against it, or even putting in fresh capital. In any event, an effort to switch from debt to § 1244 stock will clearly not succeed if the debt obligation constitutes a "security", since as noted above § 1244 does not apply to stock issued in exchange for securities (or other stock, either), thereby injecting the uncertain scope of the term "securities" into this area.

However, suppose that the taxpayer has a debt claim which is not a security (for example, a demand note, although compare the *D'Angelo* case, supra, page 142. For one thing, keep in mind that receipt of such debt would constitute boot, if the taxpayer was a transferor of property under § 351. But more to the immediate point, qualification under § 1244 will fail if the purported debt is reclassified as equity for tax purposes, since then the putative § 1244 stock will have been issued for "stock". That is a particular danger in the circumstances here assumed, as indicated by the warning in Hollenbeck v. Commissioner, 50 T.C. 740 (1968), aff'd 422 F.2d 2 (9th Cir. 1970), that debt which was valid when issued may have become so unlikely to be repaid in the face of looming failure for the enterprise that reclassification as equity would be called for. Alternatively, the court of appeals in Hollenbeck noted that the purpose of § 1244 was to encourage the flow of capital to small business concerns, and that this purpose was in no way served by the transaction there since the decision to terminate operations had already been made by the time of the exchange of the debt for stock.

Even if all these hurdles could be overcome, note that the transfer of debt which is not a security to the corporation in exchange for stock would not be tax-free under § 351 (or § 354 either), even if the rest of the section's requirements were met, as a result of the addition of § 351(b)(2) by the Bankruptcy Tax Act of 1980. Hence the taxpayer would have to recognize gain or loss on the exchange transaction—presumably loss, since the taxpayer's basis in the debt is likely to be well above its value at that point, and at least equally above the value of the stock received in the exchange. That loss would of course be capital, and the taxpayer would get a (cost) basis in the stock equal to its value, which would be the limit of the ordinary loss deduction under § 1244.

E. LIMITATIONS ON STOCKHOLDER–OWNED DEBT

SLAPPEY DRIVE INDUSTRIAL PARK INC. v. UNITED STATES *

United States Court of Appeals, Fifth Circuit, 1977.
561 F.2d 572.

GOLDBERG, CIRCUIT JUDGE. This tax refund suit involves seven closely held real estate development corporations that Spencer C. Walden, Jr. organized and manages. The first issue, the one most extensively debated by the parties, is whether certain purported debts that the corporations owed their shareholders should be treated for tax purposes as contributions to capital. . . . The district court . . . resolved each issue in the government's favor. We affirm.

I. Facts

Spencer C. Walden, Jr. is a successful real estate developer in Albany, Georgia, a city of some 100,000 located less than 50 miles southeast of Plains. Acting primarily through the partnership of Walden & Kirkland, Walden has developed numerous residential subdivisions and various commercial properties. This case concerns a subset of his activities.

Among the properties Walden has developed are several tracts originally owned by his father-in-law, J. T. Haley, and Haley's descendants. With Walden directing organizational efforts, members of the Haley family formed six corporations over a fifteen year period. Those corporations were Pecan Haven, Inc. (Pecan Haven), Lake Park, Inc. (Lake Park), Sherwood Acres, Inc. (Sherwood), Lake Park Additions, Inc. (Additions), Forest Estates, Inc. (Forest Estates) and Slappey Drive Industrial Park, Inc. (Slappey). Each of these is a party to this case. The other corporate party is Cairo Developers, Inc. (Cairo Developers), which Walden formed in conjunction with two individuals not members of the J. T. Haley family.

Walden was the moving force behind each of these corporations. He was president of each enterprise, and his partnership, Walden & Kirkland, handled their development work. All but Slappey were to develop residential subdivisions; Slappey's project was an industrial park.

On this appeal the government . . . contends that purported debts that each corporation owed its shareholders should receive equi-

---

* Portions of the text and most of the
footnotes omitted.

ty treatment. The debts arose from eight transfers of land (ostensibly credit sales) and three transfers of money (ostensibly loans) that the shareholders made to the corporations. We develop the facts relevant to these contentions by discussing the corporations in the order of their incorporation,[2] referring to the contested transfers by alphabetical labels.

Pecan Haven. Pecan Haven was formed in June 1947. The shareholders were Walden (1 share), his wife Cornelia Haley Walden (59 shares) and her twin sister Loretta Haley (60 shares). They paid $12,000 for their shares. Pecan Haven developed several tracts obtained from Loretta and Cornelia and later developed a tract purchased from their father J. T. Haley.

Transfer A occurred July 26, 1960. Spencer Walden transferred 69.435 acres to the corporation in exchange for its $65,000 five-year 3% installment notes. Appellants assert that the corporation's book net worth at that time was $83,000 and that its "true" net worth, taking into account the appreciated value of its real estate holdings, was $476,000. The corporation failed to make timely payments of principal or interest, and $20,000 remains outstanding.

Lake Park. J. T. Haley's three children—Joel T. Haley, Jr., Cornelia and Loretta—organized Lake Park in November 1950 intending to develop lands they held jointly. They took equal shares of the corporation's stock, for which they paid a total of $28,000. The corporate books reflected the contributions as $9,000 paid-in capital and $19,000 paid-in surplus. The corporation immediately acquired land from its shareholders that it developed.

Transfer B occurred September 7, 1954. The shareholders transferred 100 acres to the corporation in exchange for $10,000 cash and a $40,000 demand note bearing 4% interest. Appellants contend that at the time of the transfer the corporation's net worth was $50,000

2. This appeal actually involves twelve separate refund suits, one brought by each of the seven corporations and five brought individually by shareholding members of the Haley family. The individual suits turn on the propriety of the Commissioner's classification as equity of the contested transfers to the corporations, raising no issues not present in one of the corporate suits. The tax years in question are those ending in 1961 through 1965, though some of the actions involve fewer years. The taxes contested in these suits total about $350,000 plus interest, and the amount of tax liability affected in these and other years will presumably run much higher.

Because the facts are crucial in cases of this type, we set them forth in plentiful detail. Our discussion may rank with any drug on the market as a cure for insomnia, though we trust that our version of "the Waldens" will prove more lively than a current Thursday night television series. [Ed. note: Some of the facts omitted.]

and that its "true" net worth was $78,000. Lake Park made irregular principal payments and retired the note in 1959. The corporation did not pay interest as provided in the note, making only a single $2,500 interest payment in 1956.

Sherwood. The Lake Park shareholders—Joel, Cornelia and Loretta—formed Sherwood in September 1954. Each took one-third of the new corporation's stock, for which they paid a total of $21,000. The next day they made transfer C, conveying to the corporation 48 acres in which each owned a one-third undivided interest. In exchange the corporation paid $6,000 cash and an $18,000 demand note bearing 4% interest. The corporation made irregular principal payments and a single interest payment, retiring the debt in 1960.

By the time of the second contested Sherwood transaction, Joel had died, leaving to his wife Katherine and his two children equal portions of his stock and the remaining property owned in conjunction with the other shareholders. This new lineup of shareholders made transfer D in January 1960. In exchange for 126.48 acres, the corporation issued five-year 3% notes to each shareholder totalling $189,720.02. Appellants assert that at that time the corporation had a book net worth of $62,000 and a "true" net worth of $206,000. Sherwood made irregular principal and interest payments, and a $32,000 balance remains outstanding.

Transfer E occurred in December 1964 when Sherwood's shareholders conveyed an additional 84.252 acres to the corporation. In exchange they received five-year 5% notes totalling $126,000. Appellants contend that the corporation had a $117,000 book net worth and a $240,000 "true" net worth. In September 1965 the corporation retired the notes held by Katherine and her two children. The corporation has made no payments on the notes held by Loretta and Cornelia. The corporation made an interest payment to Katherine and her children in 1965 and made annual interest payments to Loretta and Cornelia from 1967 through 1971.

* * *

Slappey. On July 7, 1962, Cornelia Haley Walden organized Slappey, paying $9,000 for all its issued stock. On July 9 she transferred the stock in equal segments to her three children. The next day Cornelia made transfer K, conveying 80.78 acres to the corporation in exchange for $6,366.50 cash and an eight-year 4% note for $75,000. Slappey planned to develop the land for industrial and commercial establishments. The corporation made irregular principal and interest payments, failing to pay the debt on its due date.

Transfer L occurred May 27, 1963. Each of the three shareholders advanced the corporation $5,000 in exchange for one-year 6% notes. Slappey has made no payments of principal or interest on these notes.

Overview. We may assume, as appellants contend, that in each ostensible sale of property to a corporation the price reflected the fair market value.[11] Nonetheless, the recurring pattern in regard to all the loans has been the corporations' failure to adhere to the announced repayment schedules. Although the corporations did make some principal and interest payments, in not a single case did the payments conform to the terms included in the notes. In addition, Spencer Walden's deposition testimony makes clear that the creditor-shareholders viewed their situation not at all as normal creditors would. The shareholders entered no objections to the passing of payment dates and requested payments only when the corporations had "plenty of cash." In explaining the willingness to tolerate delinquencies even when interest was not being paid, Walden candidly stated that the individuals were more concerned with their status as shareholders than in their status as creditors.

II. Debt-Equity

The tax code provides widely disparate treatment of debt and equity. In regard to a typical transfer at issue here, involving an individual's transfer of property to his corporation in exchange for the instrument in question, the classification as debt or equity may affect the taxation of the original transaction, the resulting bases and hence the taxation of subsequent transfers, and the taxation of payments the corporation makes to the shareholder with respect to the instrument. In the case at bar debt classification would greatly benefit the taxpayers.

Unfortunately, the great disparity in the tax treatment of debt and equity does not derive from a clear distinction between those concepts. The problem is particularly acute in the case of close corporations, because the participants often have broad latitude to cast their contributions in whatever form they choose. Taxpayers have often sought debt's advantageous tax treatment for transactions that in substance more closely resembled the kind of arrangement Congress envisioned when it enacted the equity provisions. . . . Thus

11. We note also that the ostensible lenders took no security interests in the transferred property or otherwise and that, with a single exception . . . the debts at issue were not subordinated to other corporate obligations.

the labels that parties attach to their transactions provide no guarantee of the appropriate tax treatment. . . .

Articulating the essential difference between the two types of arrangement that Congress treated so differently is no easy task. Generally, shareholders place their money "at the risk of the business" while lenders seek a more reliable return. . . . That statement of course glosses over a good many considerations with which even the most inexperienced investor is abundantly familiar. A purchaser of General Motors stock may bear much less risk than a bona fide lender to a small corporation. . . .

Nevertheless, the "risk of the business" formulation has provided a shorthand description that courts have repeatedly invoked. Contributors of capital undertake the risk because of the potential return, in the form of profits and enhanced value, on their underlying investment. Lenders, on the other hand, undertake a degree of risk because of the expectancy of timely repayment with interest. Because a lender unrelated to the corporation stands to earn only a fixed amount of interest, he usually is unwilling to bear a substantial risk of corporate failure or to commit his funds for a prolonged period. A person ordinarily would not advance funds likely to be repaid only if the venture is successful without demanding the potential enhanced return associated with an equity investment. . . .

These considerations provide only imperfect guidance when the the usual situation encountered in debt-equity cases. It is well established that shareholders may loan money to their corporations and achieve corresponding tax treatment. . . . When making such loans they could hardly be expected to ignore their shareholder status; their motivations will not match those of potential lenders who have no underlying equity interest. The "risk of the business" standard, though, continues to provide a backdrop for our analysis. While we should not expect a creditor-shareholder to evidence motivations and behavior conforming perfectly to those of a mere creditor, neither should we abandon the effort to determine whether the challenged transaction is in substance a contribution to capital masquerading as debt.

Rather than attempt to measure concrete cases against an abstract formulation of the overriding test, we have identified numerous observable criteria that help place a given transaction on one side of the line or the other. We have always recognized, however, that the various factors are not equally significant. "The object of the inquiry is not to count factors, but to evaluate them." . . . Each case turns on its own facts; differing circumstances may bring different factors to the fore. . . .

With that preliminary caveat, we note the factors that prior cases have identified:

(1) the names given to the certificates evidencing the indebtedness;

(2) the presence or absence of a fixed maturity date;

(3) the source of payments;

(4) the right to enforce payment of principal and interest;

(5) participation in management flowing as a result;

(6) the status of the contribution in relation to regular corporate creditors;

(7) the intent of the parties;

(8) "thin" or adequate capitalization;

(9) identity of interest between creditor and stockholder;

(10) source of interest payments;

(11) the ability of the corporation to obtain loans from outside lending institutions;

(12) the extent to which the advance was used to acquire capital assets; and

(13) the failure of the debtor to repay on the due date or to seek a postponement.

Estate of Mixon v. United States, 464 F.2d 394, 402 (5th Cir. 1972).[16] As indicated above, these factors are but tools for discerning whether a transaction more closely resembles the type arrangement for which Congress provided debt or equity treatment.[17]

In the case at bar the most telling of the *Mixon* factors is the corporate debtors' consistent failure to repay the debts on the due

16. The list is not exhaustive; our cases undoubtedly mention considerations that have yet to take a number. Congress has recently authorized the Secretary to promulgate regulations setting forth appropriate factors. See I.R.C. § 385. For the time being, however, we must rely on our own pronouncements.

17. The issue is primarily one of law. We must uphold the district court's findings of basic facts unless clearly erroneous, but the ultimate characterization of the transactions as debt or equity receives no such protection. . . .

dates or to seek postponements. More generally, that failure and the corresponding absence of timely interest payments combine with Walden's testimony regarding the parties' view of their relationships to make clear that these transactions were in substance not at all the type arrangements for which debt treatment is appropriate.

The individuals' failure to insist upon timely repayment or satisfactory renegotiation indicates that the compensation they sought went beyond the announced interest rate, for an investor would not ordinarily undertake such a risk for so limited a return. . . . The failure to insist that the corporations pay the interest that the agreements provided underscores the inference; "a true lender is concerned with interest." . . . When a corporate contributor seeks no interest, it becomes abundantly clear that the compensation he seeks is that of an equity interest: a share of the profits or an increase in the value of his shareholdings. . . .

Walden's testimony confirms these conclusions. He acknowledged that the individuals sought payments of principal or interest only when the corporations had "plenty of cash" and that the investors did so because they were more concerned with their status as shareholders than as creditors. That statement of how the individuals viewed their situation corresponds almost perfectly to the classic equity situation. A corporation normally declares dividends only when it has "plenty of cash." Shareholders ordinarily acquiesce in such dividend policies because their primary concern is the health and long-term success of the enterprise. Walden's statement indicates that the individuals here possessed precisely those motivations and that they believed it appropriate for the corporations to decide when to make payments on the same basis that corporations customarily make dividend decisions. . . . The taxpayers' pattern of conduct belies any intention to structure their affairs as parties to a debt transaction ordinarily would. In the circumstances here, these factors indicate that all the transactions should be characterized for tax purposes as equity arrangements.

In reaching this conclusion we have not ignored the other factors our cases have identified. Appellants place particular reliance on the intent of the parties. Here, appellants contend, the form in which the parties cast the transactions conclusively demonstrates their intent to create a debt relationship. In relying so heavily on this factor, however, appellants misconceive its import. The question is not whether the parties intended to call their transaction "debt" and thus to achieve advantageous tax treatment; that a person wants to pay

190

less tax rather than more provides little basis for discerning how much tax Congress decided he should pay. Instead, the relevant inquiry is the actual manner, not the form, in which the parties intended to structure their relationship. If the intended structuring accords with the type arrangement that qualifies for taxation as debt, that intent supports a finding of debt. Here, however, the parties intended to structure their relationship in a manner placing funds at the prolonged risk of the businesses; they intended decisions whether to make payments on the advances to be based on the criteria usually associated with dividend decisions. To the extent that intent is relevant, it favors equity classification.

Another *Mixon* factor to which appellants look for support is the extent to which the advance was used to acquire capital assets. They argue that here the corporations used none of the advances for that purpose. Instead, appellants note, the corporations used the contributions primarily for land, which constitutes the inventory of these real estate development firms. Whatever force this factor might have in other settings, appellants here can garner little support from it. Most of these advances, while perhaps not used for capital assets, nonetheless served "to finance initial operations." . . . Providing the bulk of the necessary first assets without which a corporation could not begin functioning is as traditional a usage of capital contributions as is purchasing "capital assets."

Another factor from *Mixon* that sometimes proves most instructive is the identity of interest between creditor and stockholder. Courts and commentators have often discussed this criterion under the rubric "proportionality." When each shareholder owns the same proportion of the company's stock as he does of the ostensible shareholder debt, the parties' framing of the transaction contributes little to the analysis. . . . In that situation the owners' decision regarding how much of their contribution to cast as equity and how much as debt does not affect the distribution of control over the company. Non-tax considerations may play little role in the choice, and reviewing courts accordingly must scrutinize carefully the resulting transaction. When, on the other hand, an individual holds different percentages of the corporation's stock and shareholder debt, the casting of debt in that form ordinarily will affect substantial nontax interests. There is thus reason to believe that the parties' debt characterization has substance as well as form.[19]

19. Even when a corporation incurs bona fide debt, of course, the opportunity to advance the funds and earn the corresponding return provides both tax and other advantages to the shareholder. Individual shareholders may therefore insist upon receiving their share of such advantages. Thus "proportionality" justifies courts in applying careful examination of the transactions but is not necessarily inconsistent with a finding of bona fide debt.

Appellants argue in the case at bar that many of the challenged transfers exhibited imperfect proportionality and that some displayed none at all.[20] While that argument would carry weight in the usual case, it has little force here. The disproportional holdings all occurred among close relatives. Although we do not treat the various shareholding members of the J. T. Haley family as an indivisible unit, neither do we treat them as unrelated individuals. For all that appears in this record, relations among the various family members were completely harmonious. Because shareholding family members were thus less likely to attribute major significance to departures from strict equality in their positions, the instances of disproportionate debt and equity holdings provide a much weaker inference than they ordinarily would that the ostensible debt was in fact what it purported to be.

Finally, appellants strenuously urge that the level of the corporations' capitalization does not undermine their position. We have not, however, based our decision on the inadequacy of the corporate capitalization. While some of the purported loans were made to corporations with woefully inadequate capital, others were not. In some cases, as the taxpayers note, capitalization was adequate.[22] These facts

20. Transfers B, C, H and L exhibited perfect proportionality; each shareholder took the same percentage of shareholder debt as he or she held of the corporation's stock. Transfers D and E originally showed complete proportionality but became somewhat disproportional when the corporations made principal payments in different amounts to the different shareholders. Transfer F was not completely proportional; Katherine's children made loans but held no shares. Treating Katherine and her children as a unit, however, transfer F exhibited perfect proportionality. Similarly, transfer K evidenced no proportionality but was totally proportional treating Cornelia and her children as a unit. Transfer J was only roughly proportional. While different shareholders (or their businesses) made advances at different times, each of the three equal shareholders put up roughly one-third of the funds when considered in conjunction with their other loans to the corporation. Transfer G was not proportional; a one-third shareholder made the entire advance. Transfer A was completely disproportional; Spencer made the loan but held no stock.

22. Taxpayers urge that these businesses involved little risk and there-

fore needed little capital. The apparent failure of Forest Estates, however, belies their assertion. The ventures incurred development expenses running into six figures and required as much as two or three years to begin receiving any revenues by selling lots. These considerations demonstrate the inadequacy of, for example, the initial capitalizations of . . . $9,000 for Slappey, and $21,000 for Sherwood. Thus the capitalization factor favors the government with respect to transfers made to those corporations upon their formation.

In regard to transfers made at later times, however, we agree with appellants that net worth, not initial capitalization, provides the relevant data. . . . At the time of transfer E Sherwood's net worth was $117,000. That figure would become much greater if we were to take into account the appreciated value of Sherwood's real estate holdings or if we added the amounts of the earlier purported debts (originating from transfers C and D) that we reclassify as equity. We need not decide the propriety of these steps, for we agree with appellants that in any event Sherwood's capitalization at the time of transfer E was adequate.

strengthen our conclusion as to some transactions, weaken it for others. They do not, however, suffice to change the conclusion we have derived from the parties' pattern of conduct and from Walden's testimony.[23]

Because the parties to the transactions in question intended to conduct and did conduct their affairs in a manner that the tax code labels equity rather than debt, taxation of the transactions as equity is appropriate. Contrary to appellants' assertions, in reaching that result we do not disapprove their decisions concerning how to organize the corporations, and we do not substitute our business judgment for theirs. We merely announce the tax consequences that attach to their decisions. While appellants are correct that they were free to decide without our supervision how much of the corporate financing to derive from loans and how much from capital contributions, they were not free to decide for themselves what tax consequences would attach to their conduct.

* * *

23. The *Mixon* factors not discussed in text carry little weight in this case. The source of principal and interest payments and the questionable availability of similar loans from outside lenders provide slight support to the government. That most of the obligations possessed fixed maturity dates would favor appellants had they not consistently ignored those dates. Similarly, the individuals' legal right to enforce payment does not aid appellants in light of the apparent understanding, as manifested in observable behavior, that they would not enforce those rights. The lenders already controlled corporate management; that they derived no more control as a result of the ostensible loans does not cut against the equity classification. . . . Finally, that appellants did not subordinate their loans to other corporate obligations, *see* note 11 *supra*, provides slight support for appellants but does not undermine the conclusion we have drawn from the more significant indicia discussed in text.

NOTE ON LIMITATIONS ON SHAREHOLDER DEBT

As the <u>Slappey Drive</u> case indicates, the substantial tax advantages enjoyed by debt has put considerable strain on the line between debt and equity when both are held by the shareholders of a close corporation. In such cases the shareholders are in position to allocate their contributions between the two without the constraint that leads to limitations on the amount of debt in arms-length dealings with outsiders: the fear that too much debt, with its fixed schedule for payment of interest and principal, could lead to involuntary termination of the enterprise if the business falls upon hard times. Debt held by shareholders obviously does not pose this threat, since the shareholders do not have to stand on the letter of their rights as creditors. That of course is one of the reasons for subordination of shareholder debt in insolvency proceedings. The problem is even more demanding on the tax side, since so often it is the potential tax advantages of debt that lead to casting

some of the shareholders' contributions in the form of loans
to the corporation. Of course this does not mean that no
debt held by shareholders can be valid for tax purposes.
But it does call for carefully scrutinizing purported debt
claims in the hands of stockholders, and the courts have
struggled to develop guidelines for determining when the
debt is valid.

As indicated in footnote 16 to the Slappey Drive opinion,
Congress finally took a hand in this area, with the enactment
of §385 authorizing the promulgation of regulatory guidelines
for determining when purported debt should be treated as
equity, and suggesting a list of factors to be taken into
account. For convenience those factors are set out here:

> (1) Whether there is a written unconditional
> promise to pay on demand or on a specified date a sum
> certain in money in return for an adequate consideration
> in money or money's worth, and to pay a fixed rate of
> interest;

> (2) Whether there is subordination to or preference
> over any indebtedness of the corporation;

> (3) The ratio of debt to equity of the corporation;

> (4) Whether there is convertibility into the stock
> of the corporation; and

> (5) The relationship between holdings of stock in
> the corporation and holdings of the [debt] in question.

Since §385 was adopted in 1969, it was not exactly "recent"
in 1977 when Slappey Drive was decided; three more years
would go by before the appearance of any regulations, which
have still not gone into effect (as will be described below).
In the meantime, the courts have pretty much ignored the
statute and its checklist of factors; as in Slappey Drive,
they have continued to decide this issue on a case by case
basis.

a.   The Terms of the Debt Instrument

As the Slappey Drive opinion stresses, one of the
factors most adverse to recognition of debt is a failure on

the part of the shareholder-creditor to enforce the obligation in accordance with its terms (the very flexibility which keeps shareholder debt from representing the same threat to the corporation that liabilities to outsiders do). In a number of the early cases taxpayers had sought to forestall this danger by using "hybrid" instruments, which omitted some of the burdensome features of debts, for example, by replacing a fixed schedule for interest payments with a provision making interest payable only if earned. As suggested by the first four Mixon factors set out in Slappey Drive, the use of such a "hybrid" instrument is likely to be no less a negative element than the failure of the parties to abide by whatever the terms of the instrument are. The same warning is sounded by the first factor in the §385 checklist; in addition, the reference to subordination and convertibility (the second and fourth factors) strengthen the implication that any departure from straightforward, traditional debt instruments is likely to cause problems. Hence these days most parties use instruments that meticulously include all (and only) the formal requisites for debt, and try scrupulously to comply with those terms in order to avoid the fate of the taxpayers in Slappey Drive.

b. Adequate Capitalization and the Debt-Equity Ratio

Many of the earlier cases were also marked by special attention to the comparative amounts of stockholder debt and equity, looking at both the absolute size of the total equity contribution and the ratio thereto of the amount of stockholder debt. The Slappey Drive opinion refers to the first of these two, in its factor number 8, but found it inconclusive there. As to the second, the debt-equity ratio (assuming a reasonably adequate equity base is present), there was for a time a tendency to apply a rule of thumb, such as the 4-1 debt-equity ratio which happened to exist in a Supreme Court decision finding valid debt. However, the effort to distill a meaningful objective standard was never very successful, and this factor seems to have faded in importance, except when the ratio is grossly high; it was not even mentioned in Slappey Drive. On the other hand, the factor is specifically included in the §385 checklist, which means that it could be in for a resurgence if regulations under §385 do ultimately come into play.

As recognized in <u>Slappey Drive</u>, it is hardest to sustain
the validity of debt when the shareholders hold debt in the
same proportion as their stock. In those cases there are
virtually no restraints on how much of their total contribution the shareholders will put in the form of debt, since
all the shareholders preserve the same relationship to the
corporation. In addition, when the holdings are proportional
there is no difference between payments of interest (or
principal) on the purported debt and dividends on the stock,
except for the tax treatment. Hence such cases have always
received close judicial scrutiny, and it should be no surprise
that proportionality is one of the factors included in the
§385 checklist. However, the court in <u>Slappy Drive</u> provides
a thoughtful counterbalance with the observation in footnote 19
that proportionality should not be fatal since even without
any tax considerations shareholders might well opt for proportionate holdings of debt, in order to get their pro rata
share of the non-tax advantage of debt, i.e., parity with
outside creditors in the event the corporation fails.

Needless to say, something less than perfect proportionality may nevertheless give rise to an adverse inference.
Like most of the authorities, <u>Slappey Drive</u> did not attempt
to reduce this to a precise mathematical calculation (especially in the light of the family relationships involved).
However, in the latest version of the regulations under §385
before they were shelved there is a formula for testing
proportionality which is at least instructive and could
influence courts in the future. The test is based upon the
so-called "overlap factor", which is defined as the lesser
of a person's percentage of the class of debt instruments
under inquiry and his percentage of the stock of the corporation: if the sum of the overlap factors for all the shareholders is greater than 50%, proportionality is established.
The example given is that of a corporation with one class of
stock and a class of debt instruments which are owned by
four unrelated shareholders as follows:

	A	B	C	D
Stock	40%	10%	50%	0%
Debt Instruments	20%	60%	10%	10%

The respective overlap factors for the four shareholders are
20% for A, 10% for B, 10% for C, and 0% for D, a total of
40%, so the holdings are not proportionate. If a corporation
has more than one class of stock, the regulation provides
that the computation should generally take into account only
stock that "participates in corporate growth or has other
characteristics which would reduce the incentive of holders
of such [stock] to establish or enforce arm's length terms
on [debt] issued to such holders."

Under this proposed test it is clear that proportionality may be found even though one or more substantial shareholders has no debt at all. In effect the same result has
been reached in several cases without the aid of a mathematical
formulation, with the courts refusing to draw a favorable
inference from the lack of proportionality because of the
particular circumstances involved. Thus, in Reed v. Commissioner, 242 F.2d 334 (2d Cir. 1957), the majority shareholder,
owning 165 shares, advanced $130,000 over several years,
while the minority stockholder, owning 135 shares, made no
advances. Apparently only some $300 was paid in for the
stock. In denying debt classification for the advances by
the majority stockholder the court said:

> "It is true that the advances made by the
> taxpayer were not proportionate to his stockhold-
> ings--a condition which, if present, often affords
> cumulative support for a finding that the advances
> constituted contributions of risk capital. But
> here the amounts paid in for capital stock were so
> small as to be purely nominal and the taxpayer's
> contribution in cash was balanced by highly skilled
> services contributed by other stockholders. In
> such a case, neither reason nor authority requires
> that for purposes of federal tax law advances by a
> stockholder shall constitute risk capital only if
> contributed in proportion to existing stockholdings."

Similarly, in Broadway Drive-In Theater v. United States,
220 F. Supp. 707 (E.D.Mo. 1963), the court paid no heed to
the fact that one of the four principal stockholders made no
advances to the corporation, commenting that he "was in the
position of contributing managerial services as he was
president and had previous experience in operating drive-in
theaters."

Moreover, in general the courts have not viewed the absence of proportionality as in and of itself sufficient to sustain challenged debt. In The Colony, Inc. v. Commissioner, 26 T.C. 30 (1956), other issues in 244 F.2d 75 (6th Cir. 1957), 357 U.S. 28 (1958), the court remarked that the disproportionate holdings of stock and debt were entitled to "no greater weight than if petitioner had issued disproportionate amounts of common and preferred stock." In Diamond Brothers Co. v. Commissioner, 322 F.2d 725 (3d Cir. 1963), substantial advances made by the holder of 50% of the corporation's stock were denied debt treatment, even though the other stockholders had not made any advances, because of the finding that the parties intended the advances to be repaid only if the corporation prospered and the funds were put at the risk of the corporation's business.

Nevertheless, a lack of proportionality can be a significant factor in the taxpayers' favor, because it does reintroduce some internal restraint on the amount of shareholder-owned debt in the picture. For example, any shareholder who for whatever reason will have little or no debt has a strong incentive to try to minimize the amount of debt his fellow shareholders receive for their additional contributions, and to persuade them to take, say, preferred stock instead. From the vantage point of a shareholder with no debt, while debt owned by other shareholders is not as threatening as debt held by outsiders, there is an obvious potential conflict between shareholders who hold debt and those who do not, which would be largely avoided by using preferred stock instead of debt. However, the restraint on the amount of shareholder debt from this quarter may be more theoretical than real: shareholders who are making additional contributions to the corporation are usually in control of the situation, if only for that reason alone, and the other shareholders may have little or no power to insist upon limiting the amount of debt; no doubt this was the situation in cases like Reed, supra, which downplayed the significance of the lack of pro rata debt holdings for stockholders who were contributing mostly services rather than capital for their stock.

d. The Risk Factor

The Slappey Drive opinion places a good deal of emphasis on the concept that the dividing line between debt and equity is whether the contribution was put "at the risk of

the business." This risk factor stems from the proposition
that traditionally a debt claim is expected to be more
secure than equity, which is of course why the return on
debt has traditionally been lower than on equity. It is a
reasonable corollary that the riskier the investment, the
more it takes on the character of a capital contribution
rather than a loan, whatever the form in which it may be
cast.

The risk factor perhaps reached its zenith in Gilbert
v. Commissioner, 248 F.2d 399 (2d Cir. 1957), on remand,
17 T.C.M. 29 (1958), aff'd, 262 F.2d 512 (2d Cir. 1959).
There two families each owned fifty percent of the stock of
a corporation with a total paid in capital of approximately
$80,000. The corporation required additional funds to
conduct its operation, and the two families made substantial
advances from time to time, evidenced by promissory notes at
a modest rate of interest. The ratio of debt to equity was
never excessive. Some of the notes were repaid, and the
amount of the advances by the parties varied from time to
time, but a rough proportionality was maintained between the
two families. The enterprise was not successful, no interest was ever paid on the notes, and the corporation ultimately failed. The issue was whether the advances represented
debt or equity for the purpose of determining the tax treatment of the loss. The Tax Court held that the advances by
the principal taxpayer were really contributions of risk
capital and did not give rise to bona fide debts. The Court
of Appeals remanded, on the ground that the Tax Court had
not made clear enough the reasons for its conclusion. In
the primary opinion, Judge Medina took the position that the
critical issue under the tax law was whether there was a
reasonable expectation of repayment regardless of the success
of the venture, or whether instead the advances were actually
placed at the risk of the business--in other words, the
degree of risk involved. Judge Medina urged that the risk
factor was really at bottom in the other factors which had
been stressed in previous decisions. Thus, inadequate
original capitalization makes any subsequent advance extremely
risky; an agreement to keep loans proportional to stockholdings suggests a lack of confidence that the loans will be
repaid; and the question of whether outsiders would be
willing to make such advances plainly turns upon the degree
of risk involved. Judge Medina also ruled that neither the
taxpayer's intention that the advances should be loans, on
the one hand, nor his motive to minimize taxes, on the
other, should be regarded as crucial.

Judge Learned Hand dissented, taking the view that the majority's approach still left the proper test undefined, because it did not state the facts that should be determinative. For him, the critical question was whether the taxpayer had entered into a transaction which did not appreciably affect his beneficial interests except to reduce his taxes, in which event the transaction should be disregarded for tax purposes. Accordingly, he proposed the following statement of the applicable test, under which the taxpayer would have the burden of proving that he qualified:

> "When the petitioners decided to make their advances in the form of debts, rather than of capital advances, did they suppose that the difference would appreciably affect their beneficial interests in the venture, other than tax-wise?"

More recently, the Court of Appeals for the Third Circuit has stressed the importance of the riskiness of the investment in determining whether it should be viewed as debt or equity. Scriptomatic, Inc. v. United States, 555 F.2d 364 (3d Cir. 1977). After citing an earlier case to the effect that the ultimate question in "whether the investment, analyzed in terms of its economic reality, constitutes risk capital entirely subject to the fortunes of the corporate venture or represents a strict debtor-creditor relationship," the court restated the issue as "whether the transaction would have taken the same form had it been between the corporation and an outside lender--whether, in sum 'the shareholder's advance is far more speculative than what an outsider would make'." The court went on to stress the importance of determining whether an outsider would have purchased an instrument on the terms available to the shareholder, and concluded with the following observation: "The crucial issue is the economic reality of the marketplace: what the market would accept as debt is debt."

Emphasis on the risk factor could have an unfortunate by-product, if it were used to reject debt treatment for advances made by shareholders to a seriously-troubled enterprise, in a last-ditch effort to resuscitate the business. Obviously, any advances under such conditions would be very risky, and it is highly doubtful that any outsider would extend credit in those circumstances. Nevertheless, there is a strong case to be made for sustaining such advances as

bona-fide debt. The injection of fresh money into a failing
enterprise may offer the only realistic chance of getting
the enterprise back on its feet. But the existing shareholders, who are realistically the only possible source of
new funds, may understandably shrink from "throwing good
money after bad," unless they have a chance at parity with
other creditors to the extent of these eleventh-hour advances.
Encouraging such efforts by the shareholders is clearly in
the best interests of the outside creditors, as was recognized in Rowan v. United States, 219 F.2d 51 (5th Cir.
1955), where the court downplayed the significance of the
debt-equity ratio, warning against any rule which would
discourage a stockholder from advancing "money to strengthen
the faltering steps of his corporation (which, of course,
may be greatly to the benefit of the other creditors)."

Incidentally, there is some basis for optimism that in
these circumstances the objective of obtaining a parity with
other creditors can be achieved. In Arnold v. Phillips,
pages 112-113,   supra, while the initial loans by
the controlling shareholder were subordinated, the later
advances to meet corporate needs resulting from operating
losses were not. And the presence of such a clear non-tax
motive may make it easier to find valid debt for tax purposes
in situations of this kind.

It should be noted that the §385 checklist of relevant
factors does not refer as such to the riskiness of the
advance, or economic reality in general; but that may stem
from the fact that the quest there was to develop objective
guidelines, and trying to measure riskiness would not be
likely to advance that goal.

    e.   <u>Debt in Conjunction with Incorporation of a Going
Business</u>

There could be a special problem if upon the incorporation of a going business its former owner (or owners) receives
some debt, since obviously all of the assets are already at
work in the enterprise and hence could be seen as being "at
the risk of the business." Costello v. Fazio, pages
107-110,   supra, suggested as much, in the non-tax,
subordination context, although that decision might be
confined to extreme cases, like the attempt there to put
almost 90% of the partnership capital into the form of debt
of the new corporation. In any event, on the tax side,

except for a couple of district court opinions this argument
has not made much headway.   In Brake & Electric Sales Corp.
v. United States, 185 F. Supp. 1 (D. Mass. 1960), aff'd.,
287 F.2d 426 (1st Cir. 1961), a sole proprietor organized a
new corporation to take over his business, and contributed
$20,000 cash for all of the new corporation's stock.   The
proprietor then transferred to the corporation all of the
assets of the proprietorship (except for some real estate,
which was subsequently leased to the corporation) in exchange
for a note for $90,000 (plus the assumption of the proprietor-
ship's liabilities).   In holding that the interest paid on
the note was not deductible, because the note actually
represented an additional capital investment, the District
Court stated:

> "The $90,000 transaction represented the
> transfer to the corporation of substantially all
> of the assets shown on the books of the individual
> proprietorship, except for cash and the real
> estate.   They were assets essential to the conduct
> of the business and . . . it could not have been
> carried on without them.   A transfer of this
> character seems rather to be a permanent invest-
> ment in the risk of the business rather than the
> temporary loan which the parties represented it to
> be."

However, in affirming the Court of Appeals took pains to
point out that no single factor was determinative of the
result.   The fact that the property exchanged for the debt
obligation consisted of essential operating assets of the
predecessor proprietorship drew only the comment that "the
nature of the assets and their importance to the operation
of the business would not be very strong evidence of intent
to make a risk-capital investment in every case but they are
some evidence to be taken together with the other circumstances of the case."

In Charter Wire, Inc. v. United States, 309 F.2d 878
(7th Cir. 1962), involving a situation much like Brake &
Electric, the trial court had stressed the fact that the
purported debt was issued in exchange for all of the partnership's operating assets "without which the business could
not be carried on," but the Court of Appeals merely referred
to this element as "another factor that may be used to weigh

the balance." And Daytona Marine Supply Co. v. United
States, 61-2 USTC para. 9523 (S.D.Fla. 1961), expressly
rejected the Government's attack on debt created upon the
incorporation of a going enterprise:

"The government in this case appears in
reality to be contending for a new or novel rule
of law to the effect that no bona fide indebtedness for Federal tax purposes can be created where
the organizers of a new corporation cause operating
assets to be transferred to it as a part of its
initial capitalization in return for the issuance
of bonds and stock. The Court knows of no such
rule of law and no direct authority in support
thereof has been cited by Counsel for the Defendant.
I do not think it appropriate to enunciate such a
rule in this case."

Assuming no absolute bar to injecting some debt when a
going concern is incorporated, the validity of such debt
presumably should be judged by the same standards applicable
in other situations. Here the test of whether outside
creditors might have made similar advances is particularly
instructive. For a modest-size enterprise, this test poses
a considerable obstacle to any long-term debt, since it
would be rare indeed for an outside creditor (other than
perhaps the Small Business Administration operating pursuant
to a specific statutory mandate) to make a loan to a small
business for any extended period. On the other hand, small
enterprises often do have considerable short-term debt,
quite apart from the open trade liabilities account to
suppliers which are always present. For example, machinery
and equipment can often be purchased on the basis of a
deferred payment obligation running over a period of a few
years (but generally secured by a mortgage on the property).
Sometimes additional working capital can be obtained on a
term basis by factoring accounts receivable. Hence receipt
by the shareholders of a reasonable amount of short-term
debt, perhaps similarly secured, upon the incorporation of a
going business might well pass the "outside creditor" test.

The case for recognition of such debt may be strengthened by actually casting the transfer of particular assets
in the form of a "sale" to the corporation on a deferred
payment basis evidenced by the debt obligation received, as

discussed on page 2.2-46, supra, instead of just having a package deal under which all the assets of the business are exchanged for stock and debt obligations of the corporation (plus assumption of accompanying liabilities). However, it would be wise to confine the "sale" approach to the type of assets which would be most likely to be sold to the corporation by an outsider in similar circumstances. In some of the cases involving challenged debt created upon incorporation of a going business the court has given considerable weight to the type of property for which the debt obligations were issued. Compare Rowan v, United States, page 200, supra, (stressing the fact that the advances were for "working capital (not, it will be noted, purchase of capital assets)" in sustaining debt treatment), with Moughon v. Commissioner, 22 T.C.M. 94 (1963) (rejecting debt classification for bonds issued in exchange primarily for goodwill and other intangibles which were "permanent assets of the corporation" and "were placed at risk of the corporate business").

f. The §385 Regulations

As noted earlier, it was not until 1980, some eleven years after the enactment of §385, that proposed regulations first appeared. As might have been expected, they involved a number of guidelines aimed at providing "safe harbors" which would assure recognition of debt for tax purposes. Not surprisingly, one of the key factors was payment of interest and principal when due. Another was absence of proportionality (as measured by the overlap factor, discussed above); but proportionately-held debt could still pass muster, provided it met certain additional tests, such as a reasonable interest rate in the light of such objective criteria as the prime rate or the yield on U.S. treasury obligations, and, in some circumstances, a debt-equity ratio no greater than 3 to 1. Needless to say, the proposed regulations drew a great deal of comment, much of it critical; after significant changes final regulations were adopted in December, 1980, scheduled to take effect on April 30, 1981. However, in the interim extensive additional criticism led to putting the regulations on hold, to permit a thorough reconsideration. As a result, new proposed regulations were promulgated in January, 1982, which initially carried an effective date of June 30, 1982, subsequently postponed to the later of January 1, 1983, or ninety days after adoption of the amended regulations in final form. Later in 1983 the Service withdrew the regulations entirely, putting them in a kind of "limbo" for the time being, and it is far from clear that they will ever emerge.

g. Substitutes for Stockholder Advances

One obvious alternative to advances by stockholders is outside borrowing by the corporation. Presumably the corporation could deduct the interest paid to outsiders, and although the stockholders would not be receiving that interest they should be able to earn a corresponding amount by investing somewhere else the funds not advanced to the corporation. More important, by not putting those funds into the corporation in the first place the stockholders would spare themselves the problems involved in trying to get the money out later without onerous tax consequences. However, the plain fact is that in many close corporation situations the shareholders are the only realistic source of additional funds; the corporation is simply not able to borrow any significant amount of money from outsiders, at least absent a personal guaranty of the indebtedness by the stockholders. Hence the inquiry shifts to how stockholder-guaranteed debt should be viewed--and, at least in theory, there is no reason why resorting to outsider debt guaranteed by the shareholders should enable the parties to escape the limitations on stockholder-held debt. Moore and Sorlien, Adventures in Subchapter S and Section 1244, 14 Tax L.Rev. 453, 493, note 108 (1959), put it this way:

> "If a bank is the creditor, an additional step must be taken by the Commissioner, as the corporation will point out that the interest has been paid to a bank and ask how in the world the Commissioner can deny that deduction. The answer would have to be that the shareholder, by endorsing the note, has placed himself in a dual position--creditor of the corporation and debtor to the bank. In effect, then, the interest is paid to the shareholder, who in turn pays it to the bank. If the capitalization were thin, the analysis would be that the 'interest' paid by the corporation was a dividend to the shareholder, who receives an equivalent deduction for interest paid the bank. Thus, the bank pays tax on the interest, the shareholder is even, and the corporation loses its interest deduction."

The Government has made this kind of contention in a few cases, with mixed results. In Murphy Logging Co. v. United States, 378 F.2d 222 (9th Cir. 1967), the two partners in a logging business organized a new corporation with $1500 in cash; the corporation then bought the business for some $238,000, using the proceeds of a bank loan guaranteed by the shareholders. The District Court adopted the view of the Commissioner that the shareholders had transferred their business to the corporation as a capital contribution under §351, while in effect borrowing the money from the bank themselves, so that purported interest payments on the guaranteed debt were really constructive dividends to the shareholders and deductible payments of interest by them to the bank. The Court of Appeals reversed, holding that the loan was to the corporation and the interest payments were deductible, largely on the ground that the debt-equity ratio was not excessive after taking account of intangible assets like managerial skill and business reputation obtained from the shareholders, along with the $1500 in cash.

On the other hand, in Plantation Patterns, Inc. v. Commissioner, 462 F.2d 712 (5th Cir. 1972), where a corporation capitalized with $5,000 purchased a business by issuing notes which were guaranteed by the controlling shareholder (and largely subordinated to other creditors), the court treated the transaction as a loan to the shareholder and a contribution by him to the corporation. The debt-equity ratio was more than 100 to 1, the court refusing to give any weight in determining the equity to the intangible financial skills of the shareholder.

For another look at shareholder-guaranteed debt, in a rather special context (and an ideal bridge to the subject of S Corporations), read the Blum case set out immediately after the following paragraph.

A more attractive alternative to creating stockholder debt upon the organization of a new corporation may lie in having one or more of the stockholders retain some of the operating assets and lease them to the corporation. The corporation would deduct the rental payments, which would presumably amount to approximately as much as the interest on any debt which might have been created plus the depreciation deduction the corporation would have enjoyed if it had owned the assets. And the stockholder would in effect receive tax-free repayments of principal by virtue of being able to deduct depreciation on the assets from the rental payments. However, here too there is the danger that the Service and the courts will refuse to be bound by the form of the transaction. There is no reason why stockholders should be more free to lease operating assets to a corporation than to "lend" them by way of an exchange for debt obligations, and the same policy which enables a court to treat an alleged debt obligation as additional capital may prove sufficient to justify similar treatment for an alleged lease.

BLUM v. COMMISSIONER *

United States Tax Court, 1972.
59 T.C. 436, No. 41.

OPINION

FAY, JUDGE: Respondent determined a deficiency in petitioner's income tax for the taxable year 1968 in the amount of $8,039.49. A certain concession having been made, the sole issue remaining for decision is the amount of corporate net operating losses deductible by petitioner under section 1374.

All of the facts have been stipulated. The stipulation of facts and exhibits attached thereto are incorporated herein by this reference and are adopted as our findings.

Peter E. Blum (petitioner) was a resident of Atlanta, Georgia, at the time of the filing of the petition herein. Petitioner filed his Federal income tax return for the taxable year 1968 with the Southeast Service Center, Chamblee, Georgia.

Peachtree Ltd., Inc. (hereinafter referred to as the corporation) was incorporated under the laws of the State of Georgia on December 29, 1966, for the stated purpose of "raising and racing horses."

On July 29, 1967, the corporation filed an election under section 1372 to be treated as a small business corporation. Fifty shares of $100 par value common stock were authorized and were issued by the corporation to petitioner for $5,000 on July 15, 1967. Petitioner has, at all times, been the sole stockholder, president, and treasurer. The corporation filed a Federal income tax return for the period ended November 30, 1967, showing a net operating loss of $3,719.12. On

* Footnotes by the Court omitted.

his 1967 Federal income tax return petitioner deducted the loss of $3,719.12 from the corporation.

During the corporation's taxable years 1967 and 1968 petitioner made loans totalling $3,150 to the corporation. These loans were evidenced by the corporation's 6 percent demand notes and were completely repaid during the corporation's fiscal year ended November 30, 1968. In March of 1968 the corporation borrowed a total of $5,-000 from the First National Bank of Atlanta on 7½ percent, 90-day notes. These loans were renewed for 90-day periods and remained outstanding on November 30, 1968.

During the period beginning on March 18, 1968, and ending November 25, 1968, the corporation borrowed money from the Citizens & Southern National Bank of Atlanta on eight notes. Payment of all notes referred to in this paragraph was guaranteed by petitioner and was secured by collateral consisting of petitioner's 200 shares of common stock of Communications Satellite Corporation and 100 shares of common stock of Kerr McGee Corporation. The collateral during the taxable year 1968 had at all times a fair market value in excess of the total indebtedness of $16,500 evidenced by the notes which remained outstanding at November 30, 1968.

During most of the time in which these loans were negotiated the corporation's unaudited balance sheets disclose that liabilities exceeded assets, and from March 31, 1968, through November 30, 1968, there was a deficit balance in the stockholder's equity account.

As of November 30, 1968, the corporation had liabilities to banks in the amount of $21,500 and did not have any indebtedness to petitioner.

The corporation filed a Federal income tax return for the fiscal year ended November 30, 1968, showing a net operating loss of $12,-766. On his 1968 Federal income tax return petitioner deducted a loss from the corporation of $14,214. Respondent in his notice of deficiency increased petitioner's taxable income to reflect the allowance of this deduction only to the extent of $1,281, which was petitioner's adjusted basis in the capital stock.

The corporation, with the consent of its sole shareholder, the petitioner, elected under section 1372 not to be subject to the taxes imposed by chapter 1 of the Code. In its fiscal year ending November 30, 1968, the corporation realized a net operating loss of $12,766. Section 1374(a) provides, as a general rule, that a net operating loss of an electing small business corporation for any taxable year shall be allowed as a deduction from the gross income of the shareholders of such corporation. Section 1374(c) limits the extent to which an individual shareholder can reflect the corporation's losses. Specifically, a shareholder's deductible portion of the net operating loss may not exceed the sum of his adjusted basis in his stock in the electing corporation and the adjusted basis of any indebtedness of the corporation to the stockholder. At issue in the present case is the precise amount of petitioner's adjusted basis in the stock or the indebtedness of the corporation to petitioner. Petitioner originally had an equity investment in the corporation of $5,000. The basis of this investment was reduced to $1,281 when petitioner deducted $3,719.12 on his 1967 Federal income tax return. This reflected the corporation's loss for its taxable year of 1967. It is respondent's contention that for the year 1968 petitioner is limited to a deduction of $1,281, his remaining basis in the stock of the corporation for any losses incurred by the corporation.

Petitioner challenges respondent's position with two alternative theories. His claim is that loans guaranteed by him which were made to the corporation by third parties were either indebtedness of the corporation to him or in substance loans to him by the third parties, followed by his capital contribution to the corporation. Petitioner in reliance on these theories contends that the basis in his stock or indebtedness must be increased and he is therefore entitled to additional loss deductions under section 1374.

Petitioner's first contention, that guaranteed notes represent corporate indebtedness to the guarantor, has been raised and correctly rejected by this Court on numerous occasions. See for example . . . Milton T. Raynor, 50 T.C. 762 (1968). As was noted in those cases, the fact that shareholders may be liable on indebtedness of a corporation to a third party does not mean that this indebtedness is "indebtedness of the corporation to the shareholder" within the meaning of section 1374(c)(2)(B).

> No form of indirect borrowing, be it guaranty, surety, accommodation, comaking or otherwise, gives rise to indebtedness from the corporation to the shareholders until and unless the shareholders pay part or all of the obligation. Prior to that crucial act, "liability" may exist, but not debt to the shareholders. * * * [Milton T. Raynor, supra at 770–771]

In the absence of a showing that the debt in question runs "directly to the shareholder" we must reject petitioner's first contention. See Ruth M. Prashker, 59 T.C. 172 (1972).

Petitioner's second contention represents a new twist in a taxpayer's attempt to reap the benefits of guaranteed loans to a subchapter S corporation for purposes of the limitations imposed by section 1374(c)(2). Petitioner contends that the loans were indirect capital contributions which were in fact loans by the bank to petitioner followed by an increased capital contribution on his part, and as such the adjusted basis of his stock in the corporation must be increased to the extent of the guaranteed loans. Petitioner's only argument in this regard is that his corporation was thinly capitalized and according to an unaudited balance sheet was in fact insolvent at the time of the loans. Petitioner contends that there are numerous cases which hold that guaranteed loans to a corporation in such straits are in substance equity investments.

It is true that the respondent on numerous occasions has attempted to apply the "substance over form" doctrine and recharacterize guaranteed loans as equity investments. See Murphy Logging Co. v. United States, 378 F.2d 222 . . ., and Plantation Patterns, Inc. v. Commissioner, 462 F.2d 712 (C.A.5, 1972), ...

It is also true that at least on one occasion this Court has permitted the taxpayer to successfully challenge the form of his own choosing and claim that guaranteed loans were in substance an equity contribution by the taxpayer. See J. A. Maurer, 30 T.C. 1273 (1958).

The question of whether advances made by a stockholder to a corporation constitute debts or contributions to capital usually arises in cases where the respondent has disallowed deductions claimed on account of the accrual or payment of alleged interest. Petitioner has not cited and we have not found any cases in which the debt-equity determination was resorted to for purposes of increasing a shareholder's loss basis in a subchapter S corporation. However, regardless of the context in which a debt-equity determination arises, we can see no distinction in principle between the case before us and the numerous cases in the area which serve as judicial guideposts. See J. A. Maurer, supra at 1289.

As we stated in Santa Anita Consolidated, Inc., supra at 550, "Whether such debt [guaranteed debt] is to be treated as an indirect capital contribution must be resolved by an investigation of the facts in light of traditional debt-equity principles." In the present fully stipulated case, after applying many of those traditional principles, we find that petitioner simply has not carried his burden of proof and has not convinced this Court that the guaranteed loans should properly be characterized as equity investments.

In determining whether a debt in form is to be considered an equity interest for tax purposes, no single factor is controlling and each case must be decided upon its own peculiar facts, with the taxpayer bearing the burden of proof. Thin capitalization is only one of many factors indicative of an equity investment, Rowan v. United States, 219 F.2d 51 (C.A.5, 1955), and often not one of prime importance. Certainly a corporation's purported insolvency at the time of a loan is evidence that the lender may be relying on the guarantor for repayment. However, an unexplained guaranteed loan to an insolvent corporation does not require a finding that the loan was in fact made to the guarantor and not his corporation. One factor which stands out in the case at bar is that there is absolutely no evidence to refute the fact that the bank expected repayment of its loan from the corporation and not the petitioner. To find that petitioner made a capital contribution of the guaranteed loans we must find that the bank in substance loaned the sums to petitioner, not the corporation, and that petitioner then proceeded to advance such funds to the corporation. See Murphy Logging Co., supra at 224; and Santa Anita Consolidated, Inc., supra at 550. Based on the evidence presented we cannot make such a finding.

There were potentially innumerable witnesses who could have better informed this Court about the circumstances and expectations surrounding these loans (i. e., bank employees, petitioner, etc.). The absence of their testimony is unexplained.

The burden of proof [is] upon petitioners and we cannot assume that the testimony of a critical absentee witness would have been favorable . . .. Indeed the normal inference is that it would have been unfavorable. . . .

There are numerous other factors which support a finding of corporate indebtedness to the lending institutions and are therefore contradictory to petitioner's argument. The loan instruments evidenced an unconditional obligation to pay a fixed sum on a fixed maturity date. The debts bore a fixed rate of interest payable unconditionally. The debt was unsubordinated and carried no voting right. In J. Paul Smyers, supra, we held that all of these factors helped to support a finding that guaranteed debt was indeed a debt and not an equity interest.

Petitioner's reliance on J. A. Maurer and Plantation Patterns is misplaced. Both of those cases are distinguishable on their facts. In those cases guaranteed debts clearly were in substance equity investments and properly recharacterized by the courts as such.

Decision will be entered under Rule 50.

F.   S CORPORATIONS

Sections 1371 et seq. of the Code, which permitted closely-
held corporations to elect to be taxed somewhat in the manner of
a partnership, were completely rewritten by the Subchapter S
Revision Act of 1982, Pub. L. 97-354, which dropped the historic
term "Subchapter S corporation" dropped in favor of simply "S
corporation" (with all other incorporated enterprises hereafter
to be known as "C corporations"). The new Act brings the treatment of an S corporation even more closely into line with the
taxation of a partnership: Whereas the prior law more or less
simply allocated the corporation's net income among the stockholders, the new Act treats an S corporation as a conduit, like
a partnership, with each item of income, loss, deduction or
credit of the corporation for the year passed through to the
shareholders, on a pro rata, per day basis, and all of the items
retaining their original character, i.e., capital gain, charitable contribution, etc., when reported on the returns of the
shareholders. As under prior law, shareholders can only deduct
their pro rata share of losses up to the amount of their basis
in the stock of the corporation, plus any debt obligations they
may own, but the new Act allows a carryforward of any excess
loss, which may be used when some basis has been restored. A
stockholder's basis is increased by corporate income taxable to
him, and reduced by corporate losses, as well as any distributions he receives from the corporation on his stock (or on the
principal of any debt).

The rules relating to distributions by S corporations have
also been revised and simplified. For a corporation which has
had S status from the outset, any distribution will be treated
as a nontaxable return of capital to the extent of the shareholder's basis in his stock (which of course is decreased by the
amount of such distribution). Distributions received in excess
of a stockholder's basis in his stock will be taxable as capital
gain. If a corporation has a non-S period in its history in
which it accumulated earnings and profits, any distributions
will still first be treated as coming from accumulated income
taxed to the shareholders under S after 1982, and only when that
is exhausted will the distribution be viewed as out of the
earlier earnings and profits and hence taxed as dividend income.
If appreciated property is distributed (other than in complete
liquidation), it will be treated as a taxable disposition by the
S corporation, and the shareholders' basis in the property
received will be its fair market value.

Paralleling prior law, which had already deprived Subchapter
S corporations of the favorable corporate treatment of pension
and profit-sharing plans, the new Act eliminates the deductibility of a number of other corporate fringe benefits, such as
premiums on group term life insurance or amounts paid for certain health plans, with respect to employee-shareholders who own
more than 2% of the S corporation's stock (after application of
attribution of stock ownership rules).

Qualification as an S corporation. The new Act raises the maximum number of shareholders an S corporation may have from twenty-five to thirty-five (counting a husband and wife as only one, even if they own their stock separately), but the stock-holder group is still limited to individuals, estates, or certain types of trusts (primarily, trusts whose income is taxable to the grantor, and voting trusts, with each beneficial owner viewed as a separate stockholder in applying the limit of thirty-five).

The other principal requirement for eligibility is that the corporation not have more than one class of stock. However, the new Act adds a liberalizing feature in providing that classes of stock which are identical except for differences in voting rights will not be treated as two classes of stock. Also resolved was the nagging question under prior law of whether stockholder-owned debt viewed as equity for tax purposes should be treated as a disqualifying second class of stock: the new Act rules out such treatment for "straight debt", i.e., a written, unconditional promise to pay, on a fixed date (or on demand), a specified amount, provided the interest is not contingent on profits and the obligation is not convertible into stock. However, this safe harbor with respect to S corporation eligibility does not mean that such instruments will necessarily be regarded as debt for all other tax purposes, and it is contemplated that regula-tions will be issued to coordinate the general tax treatment with the S corporation rules.

Unlike §1244, the S corporation provisions do not set any maximum amount of assets. The prior limitation on how much passive income, such as dividends and interest, an S corporation could receive has been eliminated for corporations which either have had S status throughout their existence, or never accumu-lated any earnings and profits while a C corporation; for all other corporations, this limitation has been relaxed, with the allowable amount raised from 20% to 25% of gross receipts, and a corporate tax on excess passive income substituted for loss of S corporation qualification (except in cases where the violation continues for three years).

Election and Termination. While there has been no change in the requirement that S corporation status must be affirmatively elected, by unanimous consent of the shareholders, either during the prior taxable year or in the first 2 1/2 months of the year in which it is to take effect, the rules for ending S status were substantially altered by the new Act. With respect to voluntary revocation of the election, only a majority vote is now required, instead of the former unanimity, and the revoca-tion may specify a prospective effective date; absent such a specification, a revocation is effective at the beginning of the tax year if made within the first 2 1/2 months of the year, otherwise at the beginning of the following year. Of course termination of S status will also result from the corporation

ceasing to satisfy the definition of a small business corporation, for example, by issuing a second class of stock, exceeding
the limit of 35 stockholders, or having an ineligible stockholder (such as a corporation or a partnership); hence the
parties may seek to minimize this risk by imposing appropriate
restrictions on the transfer of stock. However, under the new
Act involuntary termination takes effect on the date cessation
as a small business corporation occurs, instead of being retro-
active to the beginning of that tax year, which will curtail the
use of involuntary termination as a substitute for voluntary
revocation. The new Act also eliminated the troublesome requirement that any new shareholders consent to the S election in
order to keep it in force.

Advisability of Being an S Corporation. Obviously, the question
of whether to elect to be taxed as an S corporation depends upon
the particular circumstances. For example, the stockholders of
a corporation anticipating operating losses would normally want
S treatment, to take advantage of the net operating loss pass-
through, which allows each shareholder to use his proportionate
share of the loss in his individual return (subject to the
important qualification that the amount of such loss a shareholder
can utilize is limited to his total basis in his stock (and debt)
of the corporation). So far as profitable companies are concerned,
in the relatively rare case of a close corporation which distributes
most of its taxable income to its stockholders in the form of
dividends, the elimination of tax at the corporate level for S
corporations should prove distinctly advantageous. At the
opposite end of the spectrum, if an enterprise has little taxable
income, particularly if that is because the stockholders in
effect draw out most of the "profits" by way of compensation, it
could nevertheless find S status desirable, as a way of avoiding
disputes about the reasonableness of the salaries of stockholder-
employees (or maybe the validity of stockholder debt).

However, in what is perhaps the most common type of case,
where the corporation must accumulate a substantial portion of
its profits to meet its business needs, the desirability of S
treatment is basically a matter of tax arithmetic, and at least
at lower levels of corporate income the arithmetic seems adverse
to S. The current corporate tax rate is 15% on the first $25,000
of corporate taxable income, 18% on the next $25,000, 30% on the
next $25,000, 40% on the next $25,000, and 46% on the excess
over $100,000. (That means the tax on the first $50,000 of
taxable income is $8,250, some $2,250 less than the $10,500 it
would have been under the 1977 rates, which in turn had been
reduced in 1975 from $17,500 on the first $50,000 of taxable
income; for the first $100,000 of taxable income, the current
rates represent a total reduction in taxes of $8,750 from the
1977 rates.) Hence the present corporate rates on the first
$100,000 of net income are quite favorable, and will often be
lower than the individual tax rates on the stockholders, especially if they have some outside income (including by way of
compensation from the corporation) to be added to the income
passed through from the S corporation in determining the tax
brackets of the stockholders. Whether or not the corporation
makes additional distributions to the stockholders to help them
defray their extra taxes (on the income passed through to them),
as a group the corporation and the stockholders end up with less
funds than if no S election had been made (quite apart from the
extra legal and accounting fees that S status may entail). In
addition, to the extent that there are substantial variations in
the tax brackets of the stockholders, the burden of being taxed
on their pro rata shares of the corporation's income will fall

unevenly, which coula produce some friction in the ranks of the stockholders. Thus at corporate income levels up to $100,000 the parties will normally be better off if the earnings which the business needs to retain are taxed to the corporation in normal fashion, rather than being taxed to the shareholders. Indeed, shielding business income from the higher individual tax rates is one of the common reasons for incorporating a small enterprise in the first place. (On the other hand, for corporate income in excess of $100,000 the 46% tax rate is not much less than the 50% maximum rate on individuals, which makes S treatment much more inviting.)

Note that the foregoing arithmetic does not take account of the fact that the taxation of an S corporation's income to the stockholders is accompanied by an increase in the stockholders' basis in their stock, which would diminish or eliminate capital gain taxes upon a subsequent sale of the stock. However, this will probably not be a very important factor in deciding whether to make an S election, at least in the typical case where the stockholders are in for the long haul, since there is unlikely to be a sale for quite a while in any event, and when the stock is held until the stockholder dies any interim basis adjustments will be rendered moot by the jacked-up basis at death.

The issues may be somewhat different when the question is whether the availability of S treatment should lead an existing partnership or proprietorship to incorporate. S status does enable the parties to obtain whatever non-tax advantages may inhere in operating as a corporation, without incurring any additional tax. But remember that most of the tax advantages of being a corporation are gone, now that the 1982 Act has ruled out fringe benefits like group life insurance or health plans for S corporations so far as employees who own more than 2% of the stock are concerned (joining the earlier loss of eligibility for the favorable corporate pension and profit-sharing provisions). In addition, there is the cost of incorporating, plus the increased expense and reduced flexibility which may accompany operating as a corporation. Obviously, the ultimate balance will vary with the circumstances of each case.

G.   MULTIPLE CORPORATIONS

The above-mentioned reduction in the corporate tax rates applicable to the various segments of the first $100,000 of corporate income makes it all the more tempting to try to split up a profitable enterprise among several corporations and thereby qualify more of the income for the lower rates. However, since 1964 IRC §§ 1561–1563 have treated any "controlled group of corporations", as there defined, in effect as if it were one corporation so far as the benefit of lower taxes on the first portion of a company's income is concerned; and the 1978 Act continues this pattern by confining any such controlled group to only one of each of the four $25,000 brackets which are taxed at less than the maximum 46% rate. These brackets will be divided equally among the members of the group unless they consent to some other plan of apportionment. Section 1563 defines a controlled group of corporations to include (1) parent-subsidiary groups, meaning a chain of corporations connected with a common parent corporation through ownership of 80% of the stock (measured by either voting power or value), and (2) brother-sister controlled groups, meaning any two or more corporations as to which five or fewer individuals (or trusts or estates) own at least 80% of the stock, in voting power or in value, of each corporation, and their identical percentage ownership in the several corporations (which in effect means taking into account for each stockholder only the smallest of his percentage interests in the corporations) amounts to more than 50%. For example, if, say, A, B and C own 50%, 25% and 25% respectively of the stock of X Corp., while their holdings in Y Corp. are 30%, 50%, and 20% respectively, then the identical ownership in the two corporations is 30% for A, 25% for B, and 20% for C, which totals 75% and therefore readily satisfies the requirement of more than 50% identical ownership.

The Supreme Court recently resolved an issue which had arisen in the application of the stock ownership tests with respect to a stockholder who did not own any stock in one of the corporations sought to be included in a brother-sister group. To illustrate, suppose again that the stockholding percentages of X Corp. are 50% for A, 25% for B, and 25% for C, but that the stock of Y Corp. is owned 40% by A, 40% by B, and 20% by D (with none owned by C). The identical stock ownership requirement would still be satisfied, since A's 40% and B's 25% add up to 65%. The question was whether C's stock in X could be counted in applying the 80% test to that corporation, even though he did not own any stock in Y, and the Supreme Court said no, with the result that X and Y would not be a controlled brother-sister group. United States v. Vogel Fertilizer Co., 455 U.S. 16 , 102 S.Ct. 821, 70 L.Ed.2d 792 (1982).

When a controlled group of corporations does exist, it should be kept in mind that the lower tax brackets on the first $100,000 of corporate income do not have to be apportioned equally among the corporations, and a different allocation will often be advantageous. For example, if X and Y constitute a controlled brother-sister group, in the absence of a special arrangement each corporation would be entitled to have the first $12,500 of income taxed at 15%, the next $12,500 taxed at 18%, and so forth. But if X's taxable income was only $30,000, while Y's was $70,000, they would not enjoy the full benefit of the lower tax brackets, since Y would have $20,000 taxed at 46% while X would have only $5,000 available to be taxed at the 30% rate and none to be taxed at 40%. In such a case, the two corporations should consent to a different apportionment of the lower tax brackets, perhaps allocating the first and second $25,000 brackets equally between the two corporations, but only $5,000 of the third $25,000 bracket and none of the fourth $25,000 bracket to X; then no portion of these favorable brackets would be wasted on X, and Y would have the benefit of $20,000 taxed at 30% and $25,000 taxed at 40%, with none of its income subjected to the 46% rate.

*

Chapter 3

DIVIDENDS AND OTHER CORPORATE DISTRIBUTIONS

Introduction

From the very beginning, state corporation statutes have imposed limitations on dividends and other distributions to stockholders. These limitations were generally framed, directly or indirectly, in terms of the par value of the stock issued to stockholders, which was assumed to be a measure of the minimum original investment by the stockholders in the enterprise. The theory was that this amount, often referred to as "legal capital", ought not to be voluntarily returned to the stockholders because creditors of the corporation, who could look only to the corporate assets and not to the individual liability of the stockholders, should be able to rely upon such legal capital as a safety margin for the payment of their claims.

As the material in the next few sections of this chapter illustrates, much of the historic development in the area of corporate finance has been directed to the interpretation and application of this "legal capital" concept. For example, the primary issue in the classic "watered stock" cases was whether the issuance of stock of a specified par value did in fact constitute a representation that an amount equal thereto had been invested by the stockholders. In the dividend cases, the central issue has usually involved some aspect of the "measuring rod" function of legal capital, in connection with a limitation of dividends to the excess of net assets over legal capital. And of course the reduction-of-capital cases raise the question of how and when this "legal capital" measuring rod can be reduced.

SECTION 1. LIQUIDATION PREFERENCES AND STATED CAPITAL

Today, most modern corporation statutes provide specifically as to how legal capital, now commonly called "stated capital", is to be determined under various circumstances. E. g., MBA §21. The effect of such statutes is to give the parties very broad power to fix the stated capital figure, either by setting the par value, in the case of par stock, or, as to no-par stock, by allocating a portion of the consideration received to capital surplus. However, the statutes often impose some limitations with regard to the stated capital attributable to stock having a liquidation preference. Thus MBA § 21 limits the amount which may be allocated to capital surplus in the case of no-par preferred stock with a liquidation preference to the excess, if any, of the consideration received for such stock over the liquidation preference. In the same vein, § 69 imposes restrictions upon the reduction of the stated capital attributable to no-par stock whenever the corporation has any stock with a liquidation preference outstanding.

These provisions in the Model Act dealing expressly with certain aspects of the relationship between the liquidation preference of no-par stock and the stated capital attributable to such stock suggest some other questions about that relationship which the Act does not expressly resolve. Thus it might be asked whether the Act impliedly forbids the issuance of no-par stock with a liquidation preference for a consideration less than the amount of the preference. A less extreme possibility is that the Act by implication requires that the stated capital attributable to such stock be fixed at not less than the amount of the liquidation preference, regardless of the amount of consideration for which the stock was issued. If either of these limitations are to be found, obviously it must be by inference from the express provisions in the Act, such as §§ 21, 46(d) and 69; and before drawing such inferences it would be important to compare the objectives and beneficiaries of such proposed implied limitations with the objectives and beneficiaries of the express provisions. There is also the question of where low-par stock with a substantial gap between par value and liquidation preference stands in the light of a provision like MBA § 21 which deals expressly only with no-par stock so far as allocation to capital surplus is concerned. The following materials may shed some light on these various issues:

KATZ, ACCOUNTING PROBLEMS IN CORPORATE DISTRIBUTIONS *

89 U. of Pa.L.Rev. 776–778 (1941).

One problem in accounting for preferred shares furnishes another illustration of the influence of accounting requirements in the reform of corporate practices. This is the problem of preferred shares with a par or stated value less than the amount of the preference on involuntary liquidation. This type of preferred shares has been referred to by Commissioner Healy as "that excrescence, that abomination which charter-mongering states — corporation 'Reno's' . . ., have put upon us . . . in their 'liberalization' of corporation

---

*   Reprinted by permission of the University of Pennsylvania Law Review. Most of the footnotes omitted.

laws." Commissioner Healy gave as an example shares sold for $50, having a par value of $40, and entitled to an annual dividend of $3 and to a $50 preference on liquidation. In such a case, the shares are almost invariably carried on the balance sheet at the par value of $40 with the $10 additional consideration shown as capital surplus.

A more extreme case was presented by the financing of Dodge Brothers, Inc., in 1925. Here preference shares without par value were set up on the balance sheet at $1 per share despite a liquidation preference of $105 per share and a $7 annual dividend rate. It was with respect to this balance sheet that Professor Ripley used the terms "prestidigitation", "acrobatics", and "accounting monstrosity".

The SEC now requires that a spot-light be focused upon such acrobatics. The following information with respect to preferred shares must be set forth in balance sheets or in explanatory notes:

> "Preferences on involuntary liquidation, if other than the par or stated value, shall be shown. When the excess involved is significant there shall be shown (i) the difference between the aggregate preference on involuntary liquidation and the aggregate par or stated value; (ii) a statement that this difference, plus any arrears in dividends, exceeds the sum of the par or stated value of the junior capital shares and the surplus, if such is the case; and (iii) a statement as to the existence, or absence, of any restrictions upon surplus growing out of the fact that upon involuntary liquidation the preference of the preferred shares exceeds its par or stated value."

In recent security issues, the statement made in most prospectuses, pursuant to the requirement of clause (iii), is that "there are no restrictions upon surplus growing out of the fact that upon involuntary liquidation the preference of the preferred shares exceeds its par or stated value." The chief accountant of the Commission has suggested that the requirement of a statement of such restrictions on surplus arose "out of the feeling that, if surplus had been contributed by the preferred shareholders,* a court of equity might enjoin dividends, at least to common shareholders, which reduced such surplus below an amount necessary to satisfy the liquidating value of the preferred shares . . . ." It is possible, however, that restrictions on surplus might exist in other situations; it is possible that a dividend on common shares might be enjoined in any case where the difference between the aggregate liquidation preferences and the aggregate stated value of the preferred shares exceeds the total stated value of the common shares. . . .

---

* In some states part of the consideration received for preferred shares may be set up as paid-in surplus only if the amount allocated to stated capital is equal to the aggregate liquidation preference. . . .

COMMONWEALTH & SOUTHERN CORPORATION, 13 S.E.C. 84 (1943), involved a Delaware corporation subject to the jurisdiction of the Commission as a registered public utility holding company. Since the corporation had shown a profit for the current year, the management wanted to pay a dividend on the preferred stock, but they were concerned about the possible impact of the substantial diminution in the value of the company's investments in its various subsidiaries. The management was prepared to rely upon the "nimble dividend" provision of Del.Corp.Law § 170, which permits dividends out of current net profits even if the corporation has an overall deficit unless "the capital of the corporation . . . shall have been diminished by depreciation in the value of its property, or by losses, or otherwise, to an amount less than the aggregate amount of the capital represented by the issued and outstanding stock of all classes having a preference upon the distribution of assets." However, the management was concerned that some dissident stockholder might contend that the diminution in the value of the assets of the corporation had reached so far that this proviso was in operation. Accordingly, the company sought the permission of the Commission to reduce the capital of its 1,500,000 shares of preferred stock from $100 a share to $10 a share, basing its request upon advice of counsel that any question as to the legality of the dividends under Delaware law would be avoided by such a reduction. No change was proposed in the cumulative dividend rate of $6 per share, the redemption price of $110, or the liquidation preference of $100 per share plus accrued dividends (which at that time amounted to about $25 per share). The company was prepared to restrict the resulting capital surplus of $135,000,000 so that it could not be used for the payment of dividends on, or repurchase of, common stock. It was also agreed that no use would be made of the capital surplus which would reduce it to an amount less than $90 per share of preferred stock, and that there would be no change in these restrictions without the approval of 60% of the preferred stock.

In denying the company's application for approval of the proposed reduction, the Commission expressed doubt that the reduction would validate the proposed dividend. After pointing out that the phrase "capital represented by" the preferred stock in the Delaware statute had not been construed by the Delaware courts, the Commission continued as follows:

> Counsel employed by the company testified before us that in his opinion the phrase means the stated or par value of the preferred. The legislative history of the Section affords support to this view.* The argument for the other view

---

* [Ed. note] The legislative history of Del. § 170 is rather more forceful than might be inferred from this mild comment. Prior to its amendment in 1929 the quoted proviso was in terms of "the aggregate amount to which the holders of . . . stock of all classes having a preference upon the

runs as follows. The stock has a liquidating preference of $100, a redemption value of $110, and a dividend rate of $6 per share. The indications are that it actually contributed capital to the corporation at the rate of $100 per share. It is unrealistic to say that the question whether the capital represented by this stock is impaired should be judged on the basis of $10 per share. Is the capital represented by these shares $100 or $10? The least significant of all the figures mentioned is the $10. It has no relation to the liquidation value, the redemption value, the dividend rate, or the capital contributed—it represents nothing but a lawyer's inventiveness. If the real purpose of the Delaware statute is to protect the preferred capital, actually contributed, from being dissipated in the form of dividends, the construction given the statute by the counsel called by the management will accomplish the directly opposite result.

The Commission disapproved its earlier opinion in United Corporation, 11 S.E.C. 67 (1942), where a Delaware holding company was permitted to reduce the stated value of its no-par preference stock from $50 to $5 per share, while the assets preference of the redemption price remained at $50.

———

HILLS, MODEL CORPORATION ACT*

48 Harv.L.Rev. 1355–1356, 1363–1364 (1935).

26. Shares having a distribution preference . . . including shares with and without par value, [should be] . . . treated alike and covered by the same provision. Existing statutes treat shares with par value separately from shares without par value, but there is no real basis for a difference, since shares without par value may or may not have a preference to assets comparable with a par value.
. . .

. . . Shares without par value which have a distribution preference should not be issued for a consideration less than the highest amount of distribution preference thereof. The majority of existing statutes allow the board of directors to issue shares without par value for an unlimited amount of consideration, greater or less than their preference to assets in the event of liquidation or dissolution. That privilege has been abused to the detriment of equity shares and shares having junior preferences by the issuance of shares for less than their

distribution of assets would be entitled upon such distribution". Comparison of that language with the present wording makes it clear that the draftsman recognized the possibility of a difference between the stated capital attributable to preferred stock and

its liquidation preference, and wanted to be sure that the former rather than the latter controlled.

* Copyright (c), Harvard Law Review Association, 1935. Reprinted by permission. Hills' Model Act is not related in any way to the MBA.

distribution preference. Some recent corporation laws place a minimum limit on the amount of consideration which must be credited to stated capital, but none assure the attainment of a consideration equal to the minimum of stated capital to be derived therefrom. . . . A provision requiring receipt of consideration of a value not less than the highest amount of distribution preference cannot be fairly criticized. . . .

* * *

27. Shares subject to redemption may be redeemed from stated capital. It follows that the amount of consideration received on the issuance of redeemable shares, and the amount thereof credited to stated capital, must be not less than the highest redemption price. It is not uncommon to have different redemption prices for the same shares graduated according to successive periods of time. The highest price at any time payable should be the minimum amount of consideration, unless the policy of paying a fair premium for exercising the privilege of redemption is to be recognized as a reasonable business objective, ...

* * *

46. Precedent decrees the capitalization of surplus upon the payment of a share dividend from shares previously unissued. The writer has not followed that precedent with respect to shares without a distribution preference. Under existing corporation laws, the payment of shares having a par value increases stated capital by the aggregate par value of the shares issued, but the payment of shares without par value increases stated capital by an undetermined amount to be fixed by a variety of methods. The writer has again classified all shares as shares with or without a distribution preference. Shares with a distribution preference should be capitalized in an amount not less than their preference, but shares without a distribution preference need not be capitalized unless the board of directors so determines.

* * *

Shares having a distribution preference and shares subject to redemption (with or without par value) should be capitalized at the highest amount to which they may become entitled as they forthwith acquire a preference or an opportunity to be redeemed out of stated capital. On the other hand, there is no sound reason for requiring the capitalization of surplus on the payment of a dividend of shares not entitled to a distribution preference and not subject to redemption. Such shares, whether paid to shareholders of the same or a different class, represent a further subdivision of net assets in excess of all preferences. If paid to shareholders of the same class, as in the great majority of cases, a dividend of such shares is no more than a subdivision of issued shares and the equity represented thereby. The board of directors has authority at any time to transfer all or a part of surplus to stated capital and can do so in conjunction with a share dividend if it so elects.

OPINION NO. 473 OF THE ATTORNEY GENERAL
OF ILLINOIS

1933 A.G.O. 618.

Hon. Edward J. Hughes, Secretary of State:

Dear Sir:

I have your letter of August 29, 1933, enclosing letter from De-Frees, Buckingham, Jones & Hoffman of Chicago, Illinois, in which you desire my opinion as to the construction of Sections 17, 19 and 60 of the Business Corporation Act, particularly as to whether the above sections considered as a whole establish the fact that it was the intent of the Legislature to establish as a principle the public policy in this state that the retirement and redemption price of stock having a preferential right cannot exceed the stated capital, or if the Legislature intended that this principle should apply only to decreases made in stated capital after the corporation had commenced functioning under its charter, and not to provisions made at the time of the organization of the corporation in the first instance; the particular question involved in the instant case being whether or not shares of no par value preferred stock may be issued in an amount less than the involuntary liquidating price of such shares.

These questions require a consideration of Sections 17, 19 and 60 of the Business Corporation Act, the pertinent provisions of said Sections being as follows:

"Sec. 17. Shares without par value may be issued for such consideration as may be fixed from time to time by the board of directors unless the articles of incorporation reserve to the shareholders the right to fix the consideration."

"Sec. 19. **Determination of amount of stated capital.** A corporation may determine that only a part of the consideration for which its shares may be issued, from time to time, shall be stated capital *provided* that in the event of any such determination:

* * *

"(b) If the shares issued shall consist wholly of shares without par value, all of which shares have a preferential right in the assets of the corporation in the event of its involuntary liquidation, then the stated capital represented by such shares shall be not less than the aggregate preferential amount payable upon such shares in the event of involuntary liquidation.

"(c) If the shares issued consist wholly of shares without par value, and none of such shares has a preferential right in the assets of the corporation in the event of its involuntary liquidation, then the stated capital represented by such shares shall be the total consideration received therefor less such part thereof as may be allocated to paid-in surplus. . . ."

* * *

"Sec. 60. **Regulations governing reductions of stated capital and distribution of assets.** No reduction of stated capital shall be made which would reduce the stated capital represented by shares without par value having a preferential right in the assets of the corporation in the event of involuntary liquidation to an amount less than the aggregate preferential amount provided from time to time to be payable upon such shares in the event of such involuntary liquidation.

"Paid-in surplus, whether created by reduction of stated capital or otherwise, may be distributed in cash or in kind to the shareholders entitled thereto, subject to the following additional restrictions and in the following manner:

"(a) No such distribution shall be made to any class of shareholders unless all cumulative dividends accrued on preferred or special classes of shares entitled to preferential dividends shall have been fully paid.

"(b) No such distribution shall be made to any class of shareholders which will reduce the remaining net assets below the aggregate preferential amount payable in event of voluntary liquidation to the holders of shares having preferential rights to the assets of the corporation in the event of liquidation."

I understand that a specific case has arisen in which it is desirable that a new corporation be formed to take over certain bonded indebtedness of an existing corporation and that the general creditors are willing to accept preferred stock in lieu of their claims, provided that in case of any voluntary or involuntary liquidation of the new corporation, such creditors shall receive the face amount of their present claims; that it is impossible to issue preferred no-par stock for the full amount of the claims of the general creditors, as the stated capital of the corporation would then exceed the value of the property of the corporation.

It was the evident intention of the Legislature, as indicated by the express language of Section 60, to provide that the rights of shares having preferential rights in the assets of the corporation be protected in the event of liquidation, before any amount be paid to the stockholders not enjoying such preferential rights. This protection was expressly extended such preferential stock in paragraph (b) of said Section, which prohibits the payment of dividends out of paid-in surplus to the detriment of such preferred stock.

Section 19 provides that the corporation *may* determine that only a part of the consideration for which its shares may be issued shall be stated capital, *provided that in the event of any such determination,* if the shares consist wholly of shares without par value having preferential right in the assets of the corporation, in the event of involuntary liquidation, then the stated capital represented by such shares shall be not less than the aggregate preferential amount payable upon such shares in such event.

It was the apparent intention of the Legislature that the use of the word "may" does not make it mandatory upon the corporation to make any allocation to paid-in surplus; and this construction is further borne out by the proviso "provided that in the event of any such determination" that such shares (in such event) shall be in an amount not less than the aggregate preferential amount payable on the same in the event of such involuntary liquidation.

It is my opinion that the corporation is not required to make such allocation (to paid-in surplus) and that in default of such affirmative action in making such allocation to paid-in surplus, the entire consideration received in whatever amount it may be, remains and is stated capital and the requirement of paragraph b of Section 19 applies only in the event that the corporation determines that only a part of the consideration for which its shares are issued be stated capital;

. . . .

The provisions of all the sections considered indicate that it was the intention of the Legislature to protect the holders of stock enjoying preferential rights in the assets of the corporation in the event of involuntary liquidation, from any diminution of value of their stock by reducing the stated capital represented by their shares to an amount less than the involuntary liquidating value.

It also was the evident intention of the Legislature to limit the redemption of stated capital after the corporation had commenced functioning under its charter to an amount which would not jeopardize the rights of stock having the preferential right. This provision is intended to protect such class of stock in cases where the corporation already in existence and having greater assets than the involuntary liquidating value of its no par value preferred stock might otherwise attempt to reduce the aggregate stated capital represented by such shares below the involuntary liquidating value of the same and thus reduce the assets relied upon for the protection of such shares in the event of such liquidation. This procedure is prevented on account of the fact that stock in the hands of the public, entitled to preferred rights, may be adversely affected by diminishing its value by action of the board of directors. In the instant case, the rights of the preferred stockholders are expressly protected, both by contract and by provisions in the certificates issued, by providing therein that in the event of involuntary liquidation, such stock be accorded the preference, in order and amount to which it is entitled relative to the common stock not entitled to such preferential rights and, accordingly, I can see no objection to the plan suggested.*

---

* In Opinion No. 727, 1934 A.G.O. 397, the question presented to the Attorney General of Illinois was whether, for the purpose of computing franchise taxes based on "stated capital", § 19 (b) of the Illinois Act constituted a definition of stated capital attributable to no-par shares with a liquidation preference which controlled the general definition in § 2(k) [the counterpart of MBA § 2(j)]. The Attorney General ruled that § 2(k) governed, stating that § 19(b) "was not intended as a definition of the term 'Stated Capital'; but was meant as a protection to the holders of shares without par value who purchased the same upon the assumption that it had a definite involuntary liquidation price, which they were entitled to believe would be held for their protection without depletion."

SECTION 2. THE FUND AVAILABLE FOR DIVIDENDS

A. In General

1. From Kummert, The Financial Provisions of the New
Washington Business Corporation Act,* 41 Wash. L. Rev. 207,
235-238 (1966):

The prime characteristic of corporations is a limitation
of shareholder liability for corporate debts to the amount
of the shareholder's original investment. Although this
characteristic pre-dated the American Revolution, the law at
that time provided no safeguards for the corporation's
creditors beyond those that were provided for the protection
of creditors of individuals. Corporations at this time were
accustomed to issue shares for any amount of consideration
that they pleased. No distinction was made between capital
and surplus with the result that dividends were repeatedly
paid out of capital. Creditors of corporations were seriously
disadvantaged under these rules because of their inability
to call for new capital contributions in the event that the
capital remaining after distributions to shareholders was
not sufficient to cover corporate debts. Protection for
corporate creditors was first generally announced in the
celebrated case of Wood v. Dummer [30 Fed. Cas. 435 (C.C.D.Me.,
1824)] where Judge Story stated:

> [T]he capital stock of banks is to be deemed a pledge
> or a trust fund for the payment of the debts contracted
> by the bank. The public, as well as the legislature,
> has always supposed this to be a fund appropriated for
> such purposes. . . . The charter relieves [the share-
> holders] from personal responsibility, and substitutes
> the capital stock in its stead. Credit is universally
> given to this fund by the public, as the only means of
> repayment. During the existence of the corporation, it
> is the sole property of the corporation, and can be
> applied only according to its charter, that is, a fund
> for a payment of its debts. . . .

---

*Footnotes omitted. The new Washington statute, referred
to in the excerpts which follow as the "New Act", is
virtually identical to the Model Business Corporation
Act; references to the prior Washington statute are
included merely for the sake of completeness.

Shorn of its trust fund connotations, this language establishes the concept of legal, or stated, capital which lies at the heart of the provisions in both the old and new acts regulating corporate finance. Those provisions may be arbitrarily divided into rules regulating the obligation of the shareholder to pay for shares obtained from the corporation and rules regulating the distribution of corporate assets to the shareholders.

The thought that creditors relied upon the amount of "capital stock" in a corporation in advancing credit made it imperative to assure that the aggregate par value of shares outstanding was a true indicator of the actual value of the consideration received therefor. Hence, shareholders were early required by statute, and are still required by both acts, to pay the amount of the par value of shares in full with a type of consideration that can be valued with reasonable accuracy. If a shareholder received shares without paying the required consideration, he has for many years been potentially liable for the amount of the shortage in the event of the corporation's insolvency under various common law theories relating to watered stock.

Creditors were protected against withdrawal of assets by shareholders as early as 1825 by general corporation statutes which gave them a remedy against directors where a particular distribution to shareholders would reduce the net assets of the corporation (total assets less total liabilities) to an amount less than the amount of "capital stock." This formula, restated in terms of a surplus test (i.e., the excess of net assets over state capital), was used by the old act. A surplus test may have afforded creditors sufficient protection before no-par stock was authorized, since most of the surplus probably then arose from earnings rather than from amounts of capital contributed by shareholders in excess of the required stated capital. But with the advent of no-par shares and the availability of corporate power to determine what portion of the consideration received for no-par shares should be transferred to stated capital and what portion should be transferred to surplus, protection of creditors and senior shareholders required a re-examination of the breadth of the fund available for distribution to shareholders. The New Act, in recognition of these interests, has distinguished between surplus arising from earnings and other types of surplus ("capital surplus"), and has made earned surplus the primary source for dividend payments. Capital surplus under the New Act is treated more like stated capital than like earned surplus and is less readily available for distribution to shareholders.

Although American corporation laws generally work to maintain in the corporation net assets equal to the amount of legal capital, most modern statutes recognize that, in addition to creditors, preferred and common shareholders, employees, and the public have an interest in the size of the fund available for distribution. Hence, they allow certain distributions of assets to shareholders in further-ance of the interests of one of these other interested groups even though the assets remaining after the distribu-tion will not meet the legal capital test. Both acts permit distributions of assets to shareholders in wasting-asset corporations from depletion reserves. The New Act (but not the old) permits dividends to be paid from current earnings despite the fact that the net assets after the dividend is paid will not be equal to the amount of the stated capital. In addition, most modern corporation statutes permit the amount of the legal capital--the creditors' "cushion"--to be reduced in various circumstances where it is thought that the creditors' interest is protected by sufficient notice. Both acts permit the redemption of preferred stock with a corresponding reduction of the amount of stated capital. Both acts also permit the stated capital to be reduced with varying consequences: . . . the the New Act provides that any surplus arising from a reduction of capital will be capital surplus and hence distributable only on further action by the shareholders.

Because of their similarity on the one hand to divi-dends and on the other to reductions of capital, modern statutes regulate the circumstances under which share re-purchases may be made. . . . The New Act restricts repur-chases except to the extent of earned surplus (or capital surplus if authorized by article provision or shareholder vote) but makes an exception for several types of share repurchases which may be made from stated capital.

2. From Note, The 1980 Amendments to the Model Business Corporation Act: A Positive Alternative to the New York Statutory Approach,* 47 Albany L. Rev. 1019, 1025-1029 (1963):

B. Creditor Protection

As discussed, the intention behind the traditional statutory scheme of rigid rules based on stated capital,

---

*Footnotes omitted.

capital surplus, and earned surplus is to provide a cushion
for the protection of creditors. Not only do these statutory restrictions fail to provide such protection, but . . .
they may even mislead creditors to the extent that creditors
are led to believe they do provide some protection. The
inability of the statutes to protect creditors is evidenced
by the restrictive covenants generally found in loan agreements and indentures, the contracts which set forth the
terms of a debt issue. These covenants typically limit the
payment of dividends and restrict other activities of the
corporation by standards much stricter than those found in
corporate dividend statutes. The terms of indenture covenants are negotiated between the corporation and an underwriter or trustee, representing the interests of the ultimate creditors, and thus reflect a more realistic view of
what creditors desire for their protection.

The inadequacies of current dividend statutes are
further revealed by the content of restrictive covenants.
Unlike the statutes, the covenants are not concerned with
the static concepts of stated capital and surplus, which
reflect the past history of the company. Rather, the covenants are based on future earnings and liquidity. A creditor
must rely on the future prospects of a company, mainly its
earnings potential, to generate cash necessary for payments
of interest and sinking funds. The earnings potential of a
corporation depends upon a multitude of factors, many of
which are not quantifiable. Indenture covenants cover the
tangible factors which are relevant to earnings potential.
Typical indenture provisions restrict distributions of
assets in relation to future earnings, require the maintenance of a certain level of liquidity [often based upon some
required minimum amount of net tangible assets, determined
in accordance with generally accepted accounting principles],
and limit further issuance of debt thus limiting the lever-
aged risk of the corporation. A breach of any covenant
constitutes a default, an event neither party desires.

It is thus apparent that a creditor's focus is not on
the sufficiency of assets remaining upon liquidation of the
corporation for the settlement of his claim, but rather on
the corporation's prospects for remaining a viable, on-going
concern. To this extent, statutes requiring that a given
amount of assets be maintained to satisfy claims upon liquidation are inappropriate and unnecessarily restrictive.

Herwitz-Bus.Planning Tem. 2nd Ed.—9

B.   UNREALIZED APPRECIATION AS A SOURCE OF DIVIDENDS

1.   RANDALL v. BAILEY

The starting point for any consideration of the propriety of dividends from revaluation surplus is the classic case of Randall v. Bailey, 288 N.Y. 280, 43 N.E.2d 43 (1942). In that case, the corporation had written up its shipping terminal facilities to the amount at which the land and buildings were assessed for local property taxes, and dividends had been paid on the basis of the resulting appreciation of more than seven million dollars. In an action by the trustee in bankruptcy to hold directors liable for such dividends, the question presented was succinctly stated by the Court of Appeals as follows: "May unrealized appreciation in value of fixed assets held for use in carrying on a corporate enterprise be taken into consideration by directors in determining whether a corporate surplus exists from which cash dividends may be paid to stockholders?" The applicable statute, which governed the payment of dividends in New York from 1923 to September 1, 1963, (the effective date of the new Business Corporation Law) was § 58 of the Stock Corporation Law:

> No stock corporation shall declare or pay any dividend which shall impair its capital or capital stock, nor while its capital or capital stock is impaired, nor shall any such corporation declare or pay any dividend or make any distribution of assets to any of its stockholders, whether upon a reduction of the number of its shares or of its capital or capital stock, unless the value of its assets remaining after the payment of such dividend, or after such distribution of assets, as the case may be, shall be at least equal to the aggregate amount of its debts and liabilities including capital or capital stock as the case may be.

In holding for the defendants, the trial court first observed that if "the part of the statute containing the words 'unless the value of its assets' etc. is to be read as relating back to the beginning of the section, the lack of merit in plaintiff's contention is apparent." However, the court concluded that "the structure of the statute is such as to make that reading grammatically impossible", which meant that the regular recurring dividends here involved were governed solely by the "capital impairment" test imposed by the first portion of the statute.

The plaintiff pitched his argument primarily on the theme that only realized gains could be taken into account for dividend purposes (notwithstanding the fact that he was contending at the same time that unrealized diminution in the value of assets, here investments in subsidiaries, *did* have to be taken into account). In rejecting this construction of the statute, the trial court concluded that although such an argument might have had force under the "surplus profits" language used in earlier New York statutes, the complete abandonment of that language in favor of the "capital impairment" limitation in § 58 indicated an effort to abolish any limitation based on realization. The test now, said the court, is "whether or not the value of the assets exceeds the debts and the liability to stockholders," for which purpose "all assets must be taken at their actual value." The court then continued as follows:

> I see no cause for alarm over the fact that this view requires directors to make a determination of the value of the assets at each dividend declaration. On the contrary, I think that is exactly what the law always had contemplated that directors should do. That does not mean that the books themselves necessarily must be altered by write-ups or write-downs at each dividend period, or that formal appraisals must be obtained from professional appraisers or even made by the directors themselves. That is obviously impossible in the case of corporations of any considerable size. But it is not impossible nor unfeasible for directors to consider whether the cost of assets continues over a long period of years to reflect their fair value, and the law does require that directors should really direct in the very important matter of really determining at each dividend declaration whether or not the value of the assets is such as to justify a dividend, rather than do what one director here testified that he did, viz. "accept the company's figures." The directors are the ones who should determine the figures by carefully considering values, and it was for the very purpose of compelling them to perform that duty that the statute imposes upon them a personal responsibility for declaring and paying dividends when the value of the assets is not sufficient to justify them. What directors must do is to exercise an informed judgment of their own, and the amount of information which they should obtain, and the sources from which they should obtain it, will of course depend upon the circumstances of each particular case. [23 N.Y.S.2d at 184.]

The decision of the trial court was affirmed by the Court of Appeals, which, however, differed in its construction of the statute and concluded that both portions of the statute applied to all dividends. On the basis of this construction, (as well as the legislative abandonment of the "surplus profits" language, and a state dividend tax decision to be noted below) the court approved the view that § 58 looked to the current value of assets. However, curiously enough the court then ended its opinion by importing the concept of "surplus" into the picture, although that term is nowhere used in § 58:

> The Legislature having declared that dividends may be paid when there is no impairment of capital or capital stock caused thereby and when the value of the corporate assets remaining after the payment of such dividends is at least equal to the aggregate amount of its debts and liabilities including capital or capital stock as the case may be, Stock Corporation Law, § 58, in other words from its surplus, our inquiry turns to the question whether surplus may consist of increases resulting from a revaluation of fixed assets. Surplus has been well defined as follows in Edwards v. Douglas, 269 U.S. 204, 46 S.Ct. 85, 70 L.Ed. 235, Brandeis, J.: "The word 'surplus' is a term commonly employed in corporate finance and accounting to designate an account on corporate books. . . . The surplus account represents the net assets of a corporation in excess of all liabilities including its capital stock. This surplus may be 'paid-in-surplus,' as where the stock is issued at a price above par; it may be 'earned surplus,' as where it was derived wholly from undistributed profits; or it may, among other things, represent the increase in valuation of land or other assets made upon a revaluation of the company's fixed property. See LaBelle Iron Works v. United States, 256 U.S. 377, 385, 41 S.Ct. 528, 65 L.Ed. 998."

---

2.   ANALYSIS OF RANDALL v. BAILEY

Since the basic themes involved have implications which go well beyond the particulars of New York § 58, it is worth analyzing the views taken of that statute by the two New York courts. At the outset, it must be observed that the trial court's construction of § 58 seems rather inconsistent with the court's conclusion that the two parts of the statute were directed to different types of dividends. If the legislature took the trouble to separate out the two types of dividends, and then to phrase the respective tests in quite different language, (i. e., "impair capital" as against "value of assets"), it hardly makes sense to conclude that the two tests meant the same thing.

Moreover, there was reason to expect that the legislature would want to single out for special treatment dividends resulting from a reduction of capital, which would seem to be the subject of the second portion of the statute. A reduction of capital calls for special attention to the interests of creditors because the "safety-margin" for their claims, which is what stated capital represents, is being reduced. In such quasi-liquidation situations, the legislature might well require that the *value* of assets be up to snuff before any distribution to stockholders is made, while being content to rely on an accounting cost basis for ordinary dividends.   See Reduction of Capital, Section 3 infra.

Turning to the Court of Appeals, it did not have to deal with the foregoing issue once it decided that both portions of the statute were applicable to the dividends involved.   However, the court failed to provide any real answer to the trial court's view that this reading was "grammatically impossible".   Certainly the court's reliance on the fact 'that both portions of the statute expressly applied to "any dividend" is not very persuasive, particularly since that phrase is followed by the modifying "whether upon" clause in the second portion of the statute, and the real question at issue was the significance of that clause.

A more important question is whether a finding that both portions of § 58 applied to all dividends was as adverse to the plaintiff's case as the court and the parties seemed to think.   Apparently it was accepted that because of the plaintiff's emphasis on the realization test, it was imperative for him to avoid the "value of its assets" language in the statute.   But this overlooked the fact that the "value" language does not purport to create an affirmative source of dividends.   Rather, both portions of the statute are phrased in negative terms, and each constitutes a *prohibition*, not a permission.   In other words, the effect of finding both portions of the statute applicable to a dividend is simply that there are then two hurdles which must be overcome before a dividend is in the clear; but such a finding can scarcely expand the power to pay dividends.

Furthermore, if there are two hurdles to clear, presumably they must be different.   Since the second part of the statute is clearly addressed to a minimum required value of assets, the only meaning left for the first portion of the statute is a required minimum of assets computed on the basis of cost less depreciation in accordance with generally accepted accounting principles.   The result of this construction would be that the corporation could not pay a dividend unless *both* the value and the adjusted cost basis of its net assets exceeded stated capital.   In short, unrealized appreciation would not provide any affirmative source of dividends; but any diminution in value of assets would have to be taken into account.   And this of course was the very interpretation which the plaintiff was urging in this case.

Recognition of the possible force of this line of argument may well be what led the Court of Appeals to translate the statutory test under § 58 into "surplus" terms at the end of its opinion.   Indeed, the first sentence of the concluding paragraph in the opinion actually states the two portions of § 58 in negative terms, and in the conjunctive.   So the court was perhaps seeking to replace those two negatives with a single affirmative fund, to lay a basis for reading-in permission to use revaluation surplus.

Turning to a different issue, it should be observed that the courts which decided Randall v. Bailey may have been influenced by the fact that as of the date of the challenged dividends liability under the New York statute was not limited to negligence, willfulness or bad faith. That is, directors were virtually insurers of the propriety of a dividend, and a finding that the statute had been violated would presumably have resulted in liability on the directors no matter how ambiguous the statute or how careful the directors. See Quintal v. Greenstein, 142 Misc. 854, 256 N.Y.S. 462 (Sup.Ct.1932), aff'd without opin., 236 App.Div. 719, 257 N.Y.S. 1034 (1st Dept. 1932) (in an action charging directors with improper dividends, *held*, "defenses of good faith and due care, however worded, are insufficient in law.") In other jurisdictions, courts have sometimes read into ambiguous or silent statutes a requirement that at least negligence on the part of the directors be shown before holding them liable. See Baker & Cary, Cases and Materials on Corporations (3d ed.1959) 1355–1359. In 1939, in conformity to a general statutory trend toward limiting the liability of directors to cases of willful or negligent conduct, New York § 58 was amended to give the directors an affirmative defense if they could show that they had "reasonable grounds to believe and did believe, that such dividends or distribution would not impair the capital of such corporation."

Notwithstanding the citation by both courts in Randall v. Bailey of New York authority which allegedly required, or at least supported, the decision, it is fair to say that there was no compelling authority one way or the other, either within or without New York. Actually, the only cited New York cases where unrealized appreciation on corporate assets was even present were cases like People ex rel. Wedgewood Realty Co. v. Lynch, 262 N.Y. 202, 186 N.E. 673, 262 N.Y. 644, 188 N.E. 102 (1933), a state dividend tax case which the Court of Appeals referred to as "decisive"; and of course cases involving the tax treatment of distributions to stockholders do not necessarily turn on the validity of the distributions under corporate law.

Probably the best known prior authority outside New York was a dictum in Kingston v. Home Life Insurance Company, 11 Del.Ch. 258, 272, 101 A. 898, 904 (Ch. 1917), affirmed without note of this point, 11 Del.Ch. 428, 104 A. 25 (Sup.Ct.1918), to the effect that an estimated increase in the value of a company's office building did not provide a source for the payment of dividends. However, in stating that such unrealized appreciation, "however accurately the increase be estimated, is not a net profit arising from the business of the company", the Chancellor did not do full justice to the Delaware statute, which as of that date permitted a corporation to pay dividends "out of surplus or net profits arising from its business." Unless "surplus" and "net profits arising from its business" were synonymous, they represented two separate funds;[*] and since they were phrased in affirmative terms, unlike New York § 58, either one was sufficient to support a dividend. Hence it was incumbent upon the court to inquire whether unrealized appreciation might constitute "surplus" within the meaning of the statute, even if it did not qualify as "net profits arising." Since the Kingston decision the Delaware statute has been substantially rewritten, and now permits a corporation to pay dividends "out of its net assets in excess of its capital", or if the corporation has a deficit, to pay so-called "nimble dividends," that is, out of net profits for the current or preceding fiscal year. Del.Corp.Law § 170(a). The question of dividends out of revaluation surplus has not arisen in Delaware since the revision of the statute. Morris v. Standard Gas & Electric Co., 31 Del.Ch. 20, 63 A. 2d 577 (Ch.1949), which is often cited as permitting dividends out of unrealized appreciation, see e. g., Note, Cash Dividends Payable from Unrealized Appreciation on Fixed Assets—A Reconsideration of Randall v. Bailey, 20 U. of Pitt.L.Rev. 632, 638 (1959), actually does no more than determine that the proviso to § 170, prohibiting nimble dividends if the net assets of the corporation "have been diminished by depreciation in the value of its property" to an amount less than the stated capital attributable to stock with a liquidation preference, had not been touched off by the *decline* in asset values which had taken place. Notice the analogy between a proviso which makes the special privilege of nimble dividends turn on value of assets, and the suggested construction of New York § 58 making the special privilege of paying dividends pursuant to a reduction of capital turn on value of assets.

[*] See Goodnow v. American Writing Paper Co., 73 N.J.Eq. 692, 69 A. 1014 (Ct.Er. and App.1908), where the court expressed the view that under the New Jersey statute of 1896, permitting a corporation to pay dividends "from the surplus or net profits arising from its business . . .", there was "room to contend that the words 'net profits' were intended to be synonymous with the word 'surplus';" but under the 1904 amendment, which added a comma after "surplus" and made the language read "from its surplus, or from the net profits arising from the business . . .", the court thought that "this contention is no longer possible; . . . [t]he evident intention of the change is to point out two funds from which dividends may be made." Query, however, how much doubt there really was as to the two-fund nature of the 1896 statute. It had succeeded an earlier version phrased in terms of "from the surplus profits arising from the business", and the insertion of the words "or net" certainly seems designed to create two funds. See Kehl, Corporate Dividends (1941) 59–60. Moreover, the Goodnow court virtually ignored the phrase "arising from its business", which presumably only modified "net profits", and not "surplus". Interestingly enough, the "arising" phrase was dropped from the Delaware statute a month before the Kingston decision, a fact not noted by the Chancellor despite the fact that the dividend issue was essentially a prayer for an injunction against future improprieties.

3. THE ROLE OF ACCOUNTING

The trial court in Randall v. Bailey paid no attention to accounting practice with regard to unrealized appreciation in deciding whether such appreciation constituted a source of dividends under the New York statute. Rather the court's view was that "the question is not one of sound economics, or of what is sound business judgment, or financial policy or proper accounting practice, or even what the law ought to be. . . . The problem is one of statutory construction." Of course this view overlooks the fact that the words of a dividend statute are typically terms of accounting art, not legal art, and their meaning comes primarily from the accounting background from which they spring. Even the phrase "impair capital" used in New York's § 58, while perhaps less familiar in accounting than "net assets", "net profits", or "surplus", is nonetheless an obvious reference to a balance sheet computation, which takes us immediately into the accounting domain. Since it can hardly be assumed that the legislature was wholly unaware of the accounting significance of the accounting terms which it used, the traditional first step in statutory construction—the quest for legislative intention—must at least start with the accounting background. In other words, the initial inquiry under § 58 might well have been the extent to which unrealized appreciation on fixed assets is normally recognized on the corporate books for accounting purposes.

This is not to say that the proper construction of the dividend statute as to unrealized appreciation, or any other issue for that matter, should be entirely controlled by accounting views or practice. There is as much danger in giving too great weight to accounting implications as in giving too little. Unless the accounting significance of a term is so clear that no other meaning could rationally be attributed to the legislature—and such complete freedom from ambiguity is as rare in accounting as in the law—the accounting implications simply represent one factor to be taken into account. Like any other inferences which may be drawn from the language used in the statute, they may have to yield to contrary implications flowing from the statutory purpose. Thus the difference between the policy underlying dividend regulation, to accommodate fairly the interest of creditors as well as the interests of shareholders *inter se,* and the primary purpose of financial accounting, to disclose meaningfully the financial condition of an enterprise, might well lead to different views on unrealized appreciation. But certainly as a first step in interpreting the statute it is essential to know whether accounting encourages, simply permits, or actually condemns the recognition of unrealized appreciation in financial statements.

The Court of Appeals in Randall v. Bailey seemed to move in this direction of looking to accounting for guidance: after importing the term "surplus" into the test under § 58, the court cited the accounting definition of surplus, as set forth in an opinion by Mr. Justice Brandeis, to show that it included unrealized appreciation on the company's property. See page 232 supra. Unfortunately, this venture into "accounting" background was led somewhat astray by the court's adoption of Justice Brandeis' citation of the LaBelle case as an authority apparently recognizing revaluation surplus. Actually, the Supreme Court in LaBelle seemed to take a rather dim view of recognizing unrealized appreciation on fixed assets. In holding that an excess profits tax could constitutionally fail to give the taxpayer any credit for unrealized appreciation in the value of its assets, the Court said:

> The principal line of demarcation—that based upon actual costs, excluding estimated appreciation—finds reasonable support upon grounds of both theory and practice, in addition to the important consideration of convenience in administration, already adverted to. There is a logical incongruity in entering upon the books of a corporation as the capital value of property acquired for permanent employment in its business and still retained for that purpose, a sum corresponding not to its cost but to what probably might be realized by sale in the market. It is not merely that the market value has not been realized or tested by sale made, but that sale cannot be made without abandoning the very purpose for which the property is held, involving a withdrawal from business so far as that particular property is concerned. Whether in a given case property should be carried in the capital account at market value rather than at cost may be a matter of judgment, depending upon special circumstances and the local law. But certainly Congress, in seeking a general rule, reasonably might adopt the cost basis, resting upon experience rather than anticipation.

In any event, if the accounting view of unrealized appreciation is to be taken into account, it should be obtained from accounting, rather than legal, authorities. And the accounting view for many years has been four-square against any revaluation of fixed assets: Accounting Principles Board Opinion No. 6, ¶17, states flatly that "property, plant and equipment should not be written up by an entity to reflect appraisal, market or current values which are above cost to the entity" The prohibition against recognizing unrealized appreciation on current assets is even more stringent, coupled as it is with the requirement that decreases in value be reflected, pursuant to the lower of cost or market doctrine.

Of late there has been more pressure to depart from strict historical-cost accounting, to take account of the impact of inflation on the value of the dollar, as well as the current cost of replacing assets now in use. In FASB No. 33, the Financial Accounting Standards Board, the authoritative accounting standards-setter presently, required the very large public enterprises to include supplementary schedules showing financial data restated to reflect both current replacement costs and price level changes, but at least for the moment historical cost continues to hold sway in the primary statements.

4. Some Practical Consequences of Revaluation

Allowing dividends to be paid on the basis of unrealized appreciation has had some important practical consequences, especially in the real estate field. For example, it means that a corporation which owns rental property can in effect ignore depreciation on such assets so long as the value of the properties does not decline (and in this long period of steady inflation the value of real property has often gone up rather than down); as a result, such a corporation can pay out its annual "cash flow" as a dividend, without any reduction for depreciation expense.

A somewhat similar use of revaluation was involved in the so-called "windfall profits" cases of an earlier day, in order to validate large distributions to shareholders prior to the realization of any earnings by the corporation. Those cases usually started with a substantial over-estimation of the expected cost of a new construction project, for the purpose of getting an FHA-insured construction mortgage for an amount in excess of the actual cost. Once the project was completed, it was revalued to a figure at least equal to the amount actually borrowed (which was quite often by then a fair appraisal of the value of the property, on the basis of occupancy and other factors) ; and the excess mortgage proceeds were then distributed to the stockholders, free of any dividend tax since the corporation typically had little or no earnings and profits at the time of the distribution. The Government tried strenuously to plug this loophole by establishing that any distribution to stockholders was taxable as a dividend so long as it did not "impair capital" under corporate law, but the courts refused to depart from the traditional view that cash distributions to stockholders are taxable only to the extent of earnings and profits, which are not augmented by unrealized appreciation. Commissioner v. Gross, 236 F.2d 612 (2d Cir. 1956).

The 1954 Code closed this loophole, at least as to the proceeds of loans insured by government agencies like the FHA, by providing that any corporation which makes a distribution to its stockholders, at a time when it has such a loan in an amount in excess of the basis of the property securing the loan, shall have its earnings and profits increased by the amount of such excess.

The use of revaluation to validate the distribution of the "windfall profits" under corporate law did not pass without adverse comment. In Loftus v. Mason, 240 F.2d 428 (4th Cir.1957), the circumstances were much like those in Gross except that the certificate of incorporation limited dividends to "net earnings of the corporation", and the FHA claimed that the distribution of the excess mortgage proceeds was a violation of that provision. The court held that the distribution clearly violated the certificate limitation, so that it was unnecessary to discuss the general question of the effect of a "reappraisal of corporate property" upon the payment of dividends. However, the court apparently could not resist adding the observation that "in application of sound accounting principles dividends may ordinarily be declared only out of actual earnings or profits and not upon a theoretical estimate of an unrealized appreciation in value of assets", citing the Kingston and LaBelle cases, with a "cf." for Randall v. Bailey.

5. Revaluation in New York Since Randall v. Bailey

In Marx v. Bragalini, 6 N.Y.2d 322, 160 N.E.2d 611 (1959), the court confronted the question whether under the state income tax statute, patterned after the federal, the earnings and profits needed to make a dividend taxable to the shareholders could be augmented by unrealized appreciation. The court reached the same negative conclusion as the federal authorities, but the opinion contains some observations about unrealized appreciation which seem to undercut the decision in Randall v. Bailey, although that case was not discussed in any detail:

> The exclusion of unrealized appreciation from "earnings and profits" as a source of taxable dividends is soundly and wisely based, for to make the determination of the corporation's "earnings and profits" at the time of each corporate distribution depend upon a revaluation of all the corporate assets would create serious administrative difficulties. There is probably no problem in the administration of the tax laws which is fraught with more uncertainty, is more time-consuming and expensive, or leads to less satisfactory results than the problem of the valuation of property. Nothing short of a clear legislative mandate would persuade us to decide that it is necessary to have a current valuation of all corporate assets, wherever located, for the purpose of determining the taxability of corporate distributions.

This attitude toward valuation is in particularly marked contrast to the view of the trial judge in Randall v. Bailey, who saw "no cause for alarm over the fact that this view requires directors to make a determination of the value of the assets at each dividend declaration."

The most recent chapter in the revaluation story in New York has been written by the legislature, with the enactment of the new Business Corporation Law as of September 1, 1963. That act completely recasts the dividend and other financial provisions in terms much like those used in the Model Act, with the definitions of "surplus", "net assets", and "capital surplus" modelled closely upon the Model Act provisions. The same is true of "earned surplus", except that the New York version expressly excludes "unrealized appreciation of assets" from the definition. However, the basic permission to pay dividends under N.Y.B.C.L. § 510(b) differs from that of the Model Act, since it merely limits dividends to "surplus only, so that the net assets of the corporation remaining . . . shall at least equal the amount of its stated capital. . . ." Hence the distinction between earned surplus and other types of surplus becomes relevant only for the purpose of the statutory requirement that notice be sent to the stockholders of the source of any dividends which do not come from earned surplus. N.Y.B.C.L. § 510(c).

While the statute does not expressly provide that unrealized appreciation may be included in capital surplus (where it would be available for regular dividends, subject to the notice requirement), that seems a fair inference from the express exclusion of unrealized appreciation from earned surplus. And confirmation of this view is provided by the following statement in the Explanatory Memorandum on Business Corporation Law of the Joint Legislative Committee: "There is no basic change in the present law that permits dividends to be paid out of any surplus, including unrealized appreciation of assets." New York Legislative Document No. 12, Appendix C, 62 (1961). On the other hand, it is to be noted that nowhere does the new statute refer to the "value of assets", a phrase which loomed large in the decision by the Court of Appeals in Randall v. Bailey. Moreover, this was intentional, as evidenced by the following comment appearing in the Revisers' Notes and Comments relating to the definition of "net assets": "The expression 'value of assets' has been avoided . . . to eliminate any construction that would require appraisal of assets rather than reliance on ordinary accounting figures for computations of surplus." In view of the possibility of conflicting inferences from these various sources, it may be too early to consign Randall v. Bailey and its New York progeny to the history books.

---

6. Unrealized Appreciation in Other Jurisdictions

Although the commentators at the time were quite critical of the decision in Randall v. Bailey, most of the handfull

of authorities in other jurisdictions since that case have
reached the same result. Some of those cases have involved
challenged repurchases of stock by the corporation, rather
than dividends, but as we shall see later the statutory
tests are pretty much the same. Thus, Mountain State~Steel
Foundries, Inc. v. Commissioner, 284 F.2d 737 (4th Cir.
1960), set out at page 322, infra, presented the question of
whether the corporate taxpayer could deduct interest paid on
debt obligations incurred in the repurchase of its own
stock, and that was assumed to turn on the validity of the
repurchase transaction. The court held that the governing
statute, which provided that no corporation should "use its
funds or property for the purchase of its own shares . . .
when such use would cause any impairment of . . . capital",
did not require "a blind acceptance of book values as real",
but rather looked to the realistic current value of assets.
Randall v. Bailey was cited with apparent approval. Similarly,
in Baxter v. Lancer Industries, Inc., 213 F. Supp. 92 (E.D.N.Y.
1963), on the issue of the existence of sufficient surplus
for the repurchase of stock, the court said: "What little
authority there is suggests that actual values, albeit
conservatively applied, rather than book values, are determinative".

On the other hand, in Woodrow v. Lee, 73 N.M.425,
389 P.2d 196 (1963), the court held that a statute confining
dividends to "surplus or net profits arising from the business"
precluded relying on unrealized appreciation; Randall v.
Bailey was viewed as turning principally on the specific
language of the New York statute and its prior history.

The English cases have divided on this question.
Westburn Sugar Refineries Ltd. v. Inland Revenue, 1960 S.L.T.
297 (Scot. Ct. of Sess.), ruled against dividends out of
unrealized appreciation, pointing to the general practice of
accountants, and warning against "dangerously premature
distribution of the funds of a company which a change in
economic or trading conditions might prove to be disasterous
after a few years". A dissent would have made an exception
for unrealized appreciation on depreciable assets to the
extent that depreciation taken to date had reduced accumulated
earnings. But Dimbula Valley (Ceylon) Tea Co. Ltd. v.
Laurie, [1961] 2 W.L.R.253 (Ch.), expressly declined to
follow the lead of the Westburn Sugar decision; instead the
court took the view that unrealized appreciation on fixed
assets represented a capital surplus from which dividends
could be paid, noting that the company would still "be left
with assets of sufficient value to meet the commitments
shown on the liability side of the balance-sheet, including
paid-up share capital". The court added that such a course
of action might not be wise, but refused to find it illegal.

7. Revaluation under the Model Act

Read the comments to MBA §§2, 45 and 48. These comments were added in the second edition of the Model Corporation Act Annotated, published in 1971, and hence are more in the nature of interpretation than legislative history. The comments also came well after the publication of the following three articles, which analyze the status of revaluation under the Model Act. The prior version of MBA §48 described in the editor's note following the comment to that section is the same as the §43 referred to expressly in the first two of the articles, and discussed without citation in the third.

a. Seward, Earned Surplus -- Its Meaning and Use in the Model Business Corporation Act, 38 Va. L. Rev. 440 (1952), tackles the revaluation inquiry by first looking to the definitional provisions, and seems to find more support there for revaluation than may be immediately apparent:

> The accounting definitions in the Model Act do not fix a particular time as of which they shall be applied and they do not state what standards of value are to be utilized. . . . "Net assets," the key term of the definition, is defined to mean "the amount by which the total assets of a corporation, excluding treasury shares, exceed the total debts of the corporation." The test is a current one, and while a standard of values is not prescribed, the book values clearly are not determinative. Consequently a decrease in values will reduce surplus, and an increase in values will augment it. Realization of the gain or loss by sale or other disposition is not prerequisite to its effect upon surplus. . . .

> The fact that the test of value is a current one does not require frequent revaluations of assets on the corporate books. The book values may be relied upon unless there is good reason to believe them to be incorrect. [citing §43 (the predecessor of §48)]

Mr. Seward, who was a member, and later chairman, of the ABA committee responsible for preparing the Model Act, then goes on to argue that revaluation augments earned surplus, on the ground that unrealized diminutions in value must be recognized and charged against earned surplus (a doubtful proposition, except in the case of very substantial, long-term declines, for which no authority is advanced), so unrealized gain should be credited to the same account.

b. Hackney, The Financial Provisions of the Model
Business Corporation Act, 70 Harv. L. Rev. 1377 (1957), the
classic commentary on the subject, looks principally to the
silence of the Model Act and the construction of the predecessor of §48 for his conclusion that revaluation is permis-
sable:

> The Model Act contains no express prohibition
> against using unrealized appreciation or revalua-
> tion surplus in computing surplus, as contained in
> so many of the statutes in the last thirty years.
> It is thus arguable that under the Model Act
> unrealized appreciation may be written up on the
> books and surplus can be created therefrom. The
> Model Act definition of earned surplus does not
> use the word "value," but the third paragraph in
> section 43 would seem to accomplish the same thing
> since it provides in effect that the board in good
> faith may, in determining the amount available for
> dividends, consider the assets to be of their book value.

> George C. Seward . . . argues that unrealized
> appreciation in asset values is available under
> the Model Act as earned surplus. . . . Neverthe-
> less, in view of the virtual unanimity on the
> subject among accountants, the bar, and the
> reported cases, . . . it seems unlikely that any
> court would allow a write-up of fixed assets to
> create an earned surplus available for dividends,
> unless it felt compelled to do so by a specific
> statutory provision . . . . Some courts might
> well hesitate on a policy basis even to allow the
> creation of capital surplus by revaluation,
> because of the permissible uses of capital surplus
> under the Model Act. . . . Nevertheless, as
> previously shown, the Model Act would seem to
> allow a writeup of assets, the resulting surplus
> being construed as part of capital surplus under
> section 2(m).

c. Gibson, Surplus, So What? -- The Model Act Modernized, 17 Bus. Law. 476 (1962), takes a very firm view that
revaluation is clearly contemplated, relying particularly
upon the predecessor of MBA §48:

> [Since "surplus" has a] vital role in corpor-
> ate policy, the average prudent director may well
> inquire what surplus is. The Model Act reassuring-
> ly informs him that it is the "excess" of net
> assets over stated capital.

> But how do net assets exceed stated capital?
> In length, breadth, or thickness? None of these

244

standards would satisfy the creditor, who is the
person primarily to be protected, or even the
stockholder, who is the person secondarily to be
protected. Value is obviously the governing
standard, though the Act refrains with studied
care from any reference to that standard except in
saying that a director shall not be personally
liable for dividend distributions if believing in
good faith that the assets have a "value" at least
equal to the amount stated on the books. But one
reference is enough. Value of fixed assets is
thus the eventual and governing test of surplus
and hence of permissible dividends under the Model Act.

However, Mr. Gibson, Mr. Seward's successor as chairman
of the ABA Committee on Corporate Laws and chiefly responsible for the thoughtful 1962 amendments to the Model Act,
then goes on to decry this view on the ground that a value
approach presupposes a liquidity of assets which simply does
not exist in the modern industrial corporation. He recommends that instead the test for dividends should be based
upon earnings, either accumulated or current, for which he
assumes a change in the Model Act would be required. Of
course a change was necessary to authorize "nimble dividends," that is, dividends out of current earnings despite
the existence of an overall deficit, as is now permitted by
alternative §45(a), added in 1965. But so far as limiting
dividends to accumulated earnings is concerned, it may well
be argued that this is the very test embodied in the term
"earned surplus" under the Model Act; and the strong case
against using values as a basis for dividends might better
have been addressed to construing the Model Act than to
amending it.

Where value of assets is significant for dividend purposes, how
is it to be measured? Among the possible approaches are appraised
value (for each asset or class of assets); secondhand replacement
cost, where such a market exists; reproduction cost new less depreciation (presumably based on engineering "observation" rather than
straight-line or other accounting depreciation); or overall enterprise
valuation, based upon capitalization of projected earning power. The
authorities offer little guidance on the issue.

Actually the method of valuation proposed could well be a critical
factor on the question of whether to permit dividends on the basis of
revaluation. For example, if liquidation value, i. e., immediate realizable value, were the criterion, there might be little objection to regarding any excess of that conservative measure of value over book
value as available for dividends. Conversely, however, reproduction
cost, though doubtless highly significant in measuring the amount of
invested capital for the purposes of computing the ratio of earnings
to invested capital, affords little basis for paying dividends, particularly if the earnings potential of the assets is such that no one
would actually reproduce them.

C. STOCK DIVIDENDS

1. IN GENERAL

A distribution by a corporation of its own stock to its stockholders without consideration has always been a troublesome item in corporate finance. Although often termed a stock "dividend", such a distribution is in fact almost the antithesis of a dividend in cash: not only does the corporation not part with any of its assets, but also the distribution of stock is normally accompanied by a "capitalization" of surplus, i. e., a transfer of surplus to stated capital, which actually reduces the corporation's legal power to pay cash dividends. At least from the point of view of the recipient, then, a typical dividend of common on common (which is the case assumed throughout unless otherwise noted) amounts simply to a division of the same "pie" into a larger number of small slices. Accordingly, it has generally been agreed that a stock dividend does not constitute income to the recipient. ARB No. 43, Ch. 7B; May, Stock Dividends and Concepts of Income, 96 J. Accountancy 427 (1953); cf. Eisner v. Macomber, 252 U.S. 189, 40 S.Ct. 189, 64 L.Ed. 521 (1920) (stock dividend not income for tax purposes). But see Wilcox, Accounting for Stock Dividends: A Dissent from Current Recommended Practice, 96 J. Accountancy 176 (1953).

There has been much less uniformity as to the proper manner of reflecting a distribution of stock on the corporation's books. See generally, Manne, Accounting For Share Issues Under Modern Corporation Laws, 54 Nw.U.L.Rev. 285, 317–327 (1959). Of course there is no dispute that to the extent of an increase in the stated capital of the corporation, which always accompanies a distribution of par stock, an amount equal thereto must be transferred from some surplus account to stated capital in order to "back" the new stock and preclude its being watered. This requirement is embodied in practically every state statute. E. g., MBA § 45(d) (1). As to the question of how much surplus, if any, to transfer to stated capital in the case of no-par shares, that is normally left to the discretion of the directors. E. g., MBA §45(d) (2). But agreement ends on the question of whether this requirement is enough. The AICPA has attempted to set up standards for determining the circumstances under which something more may be required, at least for accounting purposes:

STOCK DIVIDENDS AND STOCK SPLIT–UPS

Accounting Research Bulletin No. 43, Ch. 7B (1953).

1. The term *stock dividend* as used in this chapter refers to an issuance by a corporation of its own common shares to its common

shareholders without consideration and under conditions indicating that such action is prompted mainly by a desire to give the recipient shareholders some ostensibly separate evidence of a part of their respective interests in accumulated corporate earnings without distribution of cash or other property which the board of directors deems necessary or desirable to retain in the business.

2.   The term *stock split-up* as used in this chapter refers to an issuance by a corporation of its own common shares to its common shareholders without consideration and under conditions indicating that such action is prompted mainly by a desire to increase the number of outstanding shares for the purpose of effecting a reduction in their unit market price and, thereby, of obtaining wider distribution and improved marketability of the shares.

3.   This chapter is not concerned with the accounting for a distribution or issuance to shareholders of (a) shares of another corporation theretofore held as an investment, or (b) shares of a different class, or (c) rights to subscribe for additional shares or (d) shares of the same class in cases where each shareholder is given an election to receive cash or shares.

* * *

Stock Dividends

10.   .   .   .   [A] stock dividend does not, in fact, give rise to any change whatsoever in either the corporation's assets or its respective shareholders' proportionate interests therein.   However, it cannot fail to be recognized that, merely as a consequence of the expressed purpose of the transaction and its characterization as a *dividend* in related notices to shareholders and the public at large, many recipients of stock dividends look upon them as distributions of corporate earnings and usually in an amount equivalent to the fair value of the additional shares received.   Furthermore, it is to be presumed that such views of recipients are materially strengthened in those instances, which are by far the most numerous, where the issuances are so small in comparison with the shares previously outstanding that they do not have any apparent effect upon the share market price and, consequently, the market value of the shares previously held remains substantially unchanged.   The committee therefore believes that where these circumstances exist the corporation should in the public interest account for the transaction by transferring from earned surplus to the category of permanent capitalization (represented by the capital stock and capital surplus accounts) an amount equal to the fair value of the additional shares issued.   Unless this is done, the amount of earnings which the shareholder may believe to have been distributed to him will be left, except to the extent otherwise dictated by legal requirements, in earned surplus subject to possible further similar stock issuances or cash distributions.

11. Where the number of additional shares issued as a stock dividend is so great that it has, or may reasonably be expected to have, the effect of materially reducing the share market value, the committee believes that the implications and possible constructions discussed in the preceding paragraph are not likely to exist and that the transaction clearly partakes of the nature of a stock split-up as defined in paragraph 2. Consequently, the committee considers that under such circumstances there is no need to capitalize earned surplus, other than to the extent occasioned by legal requirements. It recommends, however, that in such instances every effort be made to avoid the use of the word *dividend* in related corporate resolutions, notices, and announcements and that, in those cases where because of legal requirements this cannot be done, the transaction be described, for example, as a *split-up effected in the form of a dividend.*

* * *

13. Obviously, the point at which the relative size of the additional shares issued becomes large enough to materially influence the unit market price of the stock will vary with individual companies and under differing market conditions and, hence, no single percentage can be laid down as a standard for determining when capitalization of earned surplus in excess of legal requirements is called for and when it is not. However, on the basis of a review of market action in the case of shares of a number of companies having relatively recent stock distributions, it would appear that there would be few instances involving the issuance of additional shares of less than, say, 20% or 25% of the number previously outstanding where the effect would not be such as to call for the procedure referred to in paragraph 10.

---

2.   STOCK DIVIDENDS—A FURTHER ANALYSIS

Much of the difficulty in this area has stemmed from the failure to recognize that although a distribution of stock and a transfer from surplus to stated capital are often combined in a stock dividend, the two are not necessarily related. Quite the contrary, each can occur wholly independent of the other; and presumably they achieve different objectives. Thus it is not necessary to issue additional shares in order to capitalize surplus — the directors may at any time transfer any type of surplus to capital. MBA §§ 2(j), 21, 70. On the other hand, it is not so easy to say what is accomplished by such capitalization. While it does pro tanto reduce the power of the directors to pay dividends, capitalization is hardly necessary for this purpose since the directors could simply decline to pay dividends anyway. And while capitalization may serve as notice to shareholders that the directors have decided to reduce the amount of dividends which the corporation could pay, this seems of importance only on the doubtful assumption that shareholders regard a corporation's entire surplus as being actually available for dividends. Perhaps the best that can be said for such capitalization of surplus is that it reflects a judgment by management that the amount involved must be permanently committed to the enterprise.

It is also perfectly possible to issue additional shares pro rata to existing shareholders without any capitalization of surplus. For example, existing par shares may be replaced with twice as many shares having one-half the par value, constituting a "split-up" in the true sense of the word. And in the case of no-par shares, there would seem to be no obstacle to issuing additional shares without capitalizing any surplus, in the absence of an express statutory requirement.*

However, at least in theory there would seem to be little point to such a stock distribution. The result should simply be a decline in the per share market value proportionate to the increase in the number of shares, with the total value of all the stock outstanding remaining the same. After all, the value of the enterprise has not changed — nor have the respective interests of the shareholders, although such interests are now represented by a greater number of shares. And it should make no difference whether the distribution of stock is accompanied by a transfer from surplus to stated capital. Such an intra-proprietorship-account transfer, whether or not in conjunction with a distribution of stock, does not affect either net assets or earning power and so should have no impact on value.

Nevertheless, the fact is that in practice the stock market, which really determines the economic impact of a stock dividend (of a publicly-held company), has its own way of operating. Even in the case of

---

* Query whether MBA § 4 5(d)(2) is intended to require capitalization of at least some surplus in conjunction with a no-par stock dividend. See Hackney, The Financial Provisions of the Model Business Corporation Act, 70 Harv.L.Rev. 1357, 1386, note 136 (1957):

. . . A corporation may have a stated capital of a round figure which it dislikes to disturb; it would prefer to pay a stock dividend and merely shift some earned surplus (equal to the market value of the shares) to capital surplus. A stock split of no-par shares may be accomplished by charter amendment, Model Act § 5 8(i), without the capitalization of any surplus. Interpreting § 4 5(d) so as not to require the capitalization of any surplus on the issuance of no-par shares allows the board of directors to accomplish the same thing without amendment. The Model Act does not seem to contemplate a per-share stated capital or stated value for no-par shares, similar to per-share par value, which can only be changed by the shareholders; the articles of incorporation must state merely the total authorized number of shares and the par value of each or that they are without par value. See Model Act § 5 4(d).

Hackney's observations are certainly sound, but they do not seem to take any account of the contrary implication in the language of § 4 5(d)(2). However, the question may well be academic as a practical matter, for it would appear that whatever number of new no-par shares is desired can be issued by the board of directors without any capitalization of surplus simply by treating the transaction as a "split-up" under the last paragraph of § 4 5.

a large stock distribution, where, as Chapter 7B of ARB No. 43 points out, the market will necessarily be affected, the decrease in market price may not be proportionate to the increase in the number of shares. There are some important "market" factors which come into play here. First, since many stockholders are more attracted to lower-priced stocks, and would simply rather buy 100 shares at $50 than 50 shares at $100, lowering the market price of stock may in and of itself increase the demand for it. Thus a 2 for 1 stock distribution on a stock selling at say, 90, might well result in an ultimate market price significantly above 30.

Secondly, a stock distribution often heralds an increase in total cash dividends. For example, a company about to increase its cash dividend by 20% might accomplish the same thing by declaring a 20% stock dividend and then maintaining the same per share dividend rate. (Some managements favor this method of increasing dividends because it may attract less attention from interested observers such as labor unions and the like.) Of course the larger the size of the stock distribution, the smaller the likelihood of a pro rata increase in dividends; but even 2 for 1 and 3 for 1 distributions have frequently been accompanied by at least some overall dividend increase.

Finally, there is that most peculiarly "market" phenomenon of all — that is, that in a long-term bull market of the type we have been experiencing for quite some time, announcement of a proposed stock distribution is likely to boost the market price of a stock *ipso facto*, without regard to such underlying economic factors as the likelihood of a more attractive price range or an increase in dividends.* Indeed, particularly among the so-called "glamour" issues, a kind of reverse psychology has developed in connection with the relationship of stock dividends to cash dividends; stock distributions may be hailed as an indication that cash dividends will not be paid because the earnings are being plowed back in the business, which in turn is regarded as a badge of that much-sought-after category, the "growth" company.

However, it is to be noted that Chapter 7B does not suggest that any account be taken of the overall increase in the value of stockholders' holdings which so often accompanies a large-size distribution of stock. Yet the accounting for a small-size stock distribution seems to be based entirely, although not expressly, upon this increase-in-value phenomenon. For when Chapter 7B speaks of a distribution small enough not to "have any apparent effect upon the share market price", it is not to be taken literally. Any distribution of additional shares reduces the market value per share. What happens is that, just as in the

---

* Some earlier studies seem to indicate that in the case of a substantial stock distribution, the market run-up is likely to disappear unless some increase in cash dividends is forthcoming. And of course an increase in cash dividends would independently support a price rise, without the need of any distribution of stock. See Barker, Effective Stock Splits, 34 Harv.Bus.Rev. (Jan.–Feb., 1956) 101; Barker, Stock Splits in A Bull Market, 35 Harv.Bus.Rev. (May–June, 1957) 72.

case of a large-size distribution, the prospect of the distribution causes a run-up in the market, and that increase is enough to offset the decline in price resulting from the distribution itself, because the relatively small distribution produces only a small decline.

Why should the increase in value accompanying a relatively small stock distribution be treated so differently from the increase which occurs in the case of large-scale distribution? The price rise associated with stock dividends does not appear to be any more permanent — as in the case of larger distributions, the increase in market price is likely to last only where the distribution of stock is accompanied by an increase in cash dividends.* However, there is something special about an increase in value which is exactly equal to the old market price per share times the number of dividend shares received, so that the market price of the stock is not changed by the distribution of stock. For it is under these circumstances that a stockholder can sell his dividend shares without reducing the total market value of his investment in the company (although of course such a sale would reduce his percentage interest in the enterprise). And it is this phenomenon that leads some shareholders to view a stock dividend as equivalent to a distribution of earnings in the amount of the fair market value of the dividend stock, which in turn is largely responsible for the recommendation that an equivalent amount of earned surplus be capitalized.

However, quite apart from its inconsistency with the treatment of split-ups, this approach creates some problems. Since a stock dividend does not in fact constitute income to the recipient, as the first portion of Chapter 7B, omitted from the above excerpts, specifically concludes, why, as a dissent to Chapter 7B asks, should the corporation's accounting be "based upon the assumption that the stockholder may think otherwise"? To put it a little differently, regardless of whether shareholders regard a stock dividend as a distribution of earnings, the fact is that most corporation statutes require no more than the minimal stated capital "backing".** Of course it is not uncommon for an accounting rule to go beyond the corresponding legal rule; the disclosure function of accounting is not limited merely to portraying a corporation's legal position. However, here the accounting rule goes well beyond mere disclosure. In fact its avowed aim is to change the corporation's legal position by reducing its earned surplus and accordingly its capacity to pay dividends, which seems like a rather doubtful role for accounting to attempt to play.

Curiously, Chapter 7B does not appear to mention what is perhaps the strongest argument for capitalizing earned surplus to the extent of

---

* See Barker, Evaluation of Stock Dividends, 36 Harv.Bus.Rev. (July-Aug., 1958) 99.

** However, some statutes, like the Model Act, do expressly contemplate the possibility of capitalizing more than the bare legal minimum. For example, notice the phrase "at least", added to MBA § 45(d)(1) in 1957. See generally, Sprouse, Accounting Principles and Corporation Statutes, 35 Acc.Rev. 246 (1960).

the fair market value of the dividend shares, i. e., that the transaction should be viewed as if it were a cash dividend followed by an issuance of new stock for cash. Such a transaction would of course ultimately result in a transfer of earned surplus equal to the fair market value of the dividend stock to stated capital and/or capital surplus. However, both a cash dividend and a new issue of stock would have independent legal consequences, such as federal income taxes on the former, which make it awkward to adopt such a constructive view of a stock dividend.

The case against requiring capitalization of earned surplus to the extent of an amount equal to fair market value of a stock dividend is put this way by Paton and Paton, in their excellent analysis of the relationship between stock distributions and capitalization of earnings: *

The market-price formula has no logical basis. The possibility of capitalizing earnings rests on the conception of a stockholders' equity consisting of two main sections: (1) capital and (2) retained earnings. The act of capitalization consists of a formal transfer from the second compartment to the first. The market value per share at any time represents the current appraisal in the financial market of the *entire* equity per share, including both capital and retained earnings. Accordingly there is no rhyme or reason in a proposal to use the market value of *both* sections as a unit of measure in effecting a transfer from *one* section to the other. Without much doubt the sponsoring of this type of formula results in part from a misconception as to the nature of the capitalization process, when accomplished through the issue of additional shares. Continued use of the term stock "dividend" has created a persistent impression, not unnaturally, that something of "value" is transferred to the shareholder by the act of multiplying the number of units he holds.

The preferable accounting procedure, accordingly, is to determine the number of shares needed to capitalize a given amount of retained earnings by using as a divisor the *capital* book value per share (either par or stated value or, more logically, average amount received per share from stockholders). . . . **

In the light of the foregoing analysis, what is the impact of a distribution of stock "out of capital surplus", as is authorized by many

---

* Paton and Paton, Corporation Accounts and Statements (1955) 125. Reprinted by permission of the publisher, The MacMillan Company.

** It is not clear why the authors reach the view that the amount to be capitalized on a stock dividend is the average amount received on shares of that class from the stockholders. The logic of their analysis seems to call for no capitalization at all, except as compelled by legal requirements. Such a proposal, i. e., that no capitalization of surplus be required (except when the dividend stock either is redeemable or has a liquidation preference), was made in Hills. Model Corporation Act, 48 Harv.L.Rev. 1334. 1363-4, note 46, set out at pages 221-222, supra.

statutes either directly, or, as in the Model Act, indirectly, by not confining stock dividends to earned surplus? To an accountant, such a transaction may well be regarded as a "weird performance, and one having no relation whatever to the capitalization of earnings." * Since accountants regard capital surplus as much more akin to capital than to surplus, capitalization of capital surplus, that is, a transfer of capital surplus to stated capital, is looked at somewhat askance. However, the fact remains that under corporation statutes capital surplus, although often not as available for distribution as earned surplus, is invariably less restricted than stated capital, which means that a transfer from capital surplus to stated capital is not without significance.

Nevertheless, authorization to declare stock dividends out of capital surplus can create problems. The theory often advanced is that since no distribution of assets is involved, whatever reasons there may be for confining property dividends to earned surplus do not apply to stock dividends. But such reasoning assumes that a distribution of stock is to be judged, at least in the first instance, by the standards applicable to dividends of property, whereas we have seen that a stock dividend is really just a combination of a stock split-up and a capitalization of surplus. This difference in view is more than just theoretical. For example, under a statute like MBA § 45(d), the question may arise as to whether the necessary backing for a stock dividend may be "charged" against capital surplus even though some earned surplus exists. If a stock dividend is viewed as a type of "distribution" out of surplus, the question would presumably be decided in the light of the express requirement in both § 67 and the last paragraph of § 46 that earned surplus must first be exhausted in the circumstances involved in those sections (although it is far from clear which way those express provisions cut in cases not covered by those sections). On the other hand, if it is recognized that a stock dividend simply combines a stock split with a capitalization of surplus, there is no reason for any particular priority since capital surplus is fully as eligible for capitalization as earned surplus.

There are, however, some cases where the limitations on property dividends might be thought more clearly applicable to stock dividends. For example, if a dividend in redeemable preferred was charged to capital surplus, and thereafter was redeemed out of capital, as is permitted under most statutes, the ultimate impact of the transaction would be little different from a cash dividend out of capital surplus. And of course if the amount transferred to stated capital upon the stock dividend was less than the redemption price, to that extent the transaction is no different from a dividend out of stated capital. (However, it must be observed that the prospect of indirectly paying a dividend out of stated capital is much less earth-shaking than it might once have been, because of the present ease with which stated

---

* See Paton and Paton, Corporation Accounts and Statements (1955) 124.

capital can be transformed into capital surplus by a reduction of capital. See Reduction of Capital, Section 3, infra.)

A similar problem may be presented when a dividend is declared in stock having a liquidation preference. As was suggested in Section 1, supra, when such stock is issued for consideration, the question arises whether the stated capital attributable to such stock should have to be set at not less than the liquidation preference. If an affirmative answer is given there, then when stock having a liquidation preference is distributed as a dividend, the amount of surplus transferred to stated capital should similarly be at least equal to the liquidation preference of the stock.

As a matter of fact, since dividends in preferred stock are normally declared on common, these problems are really part of the larger question of how to treat a dividend in one class of stock distributed to the holders of another class. Such distributions really constitute recapitalizations which affect the relative rights of the shareholders, at least if there was already more than one class of stock outstanding. Here there would seem to be considerable force in analogizing the transaction to a cash dividend followed by a purchase of the new stock at fair market value, which argues for a capitalization of earned surplus to the extent of the fair market value of the dividend stock. See Manne, op. cit. supra page 245, at 326–327. In any event, this is a far cry from a mere split-up, and indeed may well be too fundamental a matter to be left entirely to the directors. MBA § 45(e) provides some protection here by prohibiting a dividend in shares of another class without the approval of a majority of the outstanding shares of that class. However, this provision does not appear to cover a case where two classes of stock are outstanding and a stock dividend is declared in a third class which was not previously outstanding but does affect the relative interests of the other two classes.

---

3. STOCK DIVIDENDS OUT OF REVALUATION SURPLUS

Occasionally corporate statutes which expressly forbid cash or property dividends based upon unrealized appreciation have nevertheless allowed stock dividends from that source. This dichotomy represents a legislative recognition of the important differences between these two types of distribution.

Under a statute like the Model Act, which does not expressly refer to unrealized appreciation, but does allow stock dividends out of any type of surplus, the question is whether unrealized appreciation can be a source of any type of surplus. This in turn means that the real issue is whether the Act contemplates recognition of unrealized appreciation at all, since if it does, the appreciation quite clearly must feed some type of surplus.

Of course, the wisdom of permitting stock dividends out of revaluation surplus is a quite different issue, but it may be a relevant one, at least where the statute is ambiguous. As we have seen, there may be doubt about the wisdom of authorizing stock dividends "out of" any type of capital surplus; but presumably, exactly the same result can often be accomplished by combining a transfer of capital surplus to stated capital with a stock split-up. And as to whether unrealized appreciation should be included in capital surplus, the fact that capital surplus can be used to back stock dividends would seem to be a less important objection than some of the other uses to which capital surplus can be put, such as a partial liquidation under §46, or a repurchase of stock under § 6.

SECTION 3.   REDUCTION OF CAPITAL

A.   HISTORICAL BACKGROUND

As we have seen, the traditional role of stated capital has been that of a measuring rod, to be applied to net assets in order to determine how large a dividend could be paid "out of surplus," or "without impairing capital." Accordingly, it may come as a surprise to see how easily this stated capital measuring rod can be reduced. Actually, authorization to reduce capital has been included in corporation statutes from the very beginning, although under somewhat different circumstances. The original purpose of capital reduction under the general incorporation statutes * may perhaps best be inferred from the early rule that upon a reduction of stated capital, the corporation was required to distribute assets to the shareholders in the amount of the reduction. E.g., Seeley v. New York National Exchange Bank, 8 Daley 400 (N.Y.C.P. 1878), aff'd, 78 N.Y. 608 (1879). The implication of this rule is that reduction of stated capital was designed to enable a corporation which had more assets than it could usefully or

---

* Probably the earliest occasions for reduction of stated capital stemmed from the requirement that a corporation organized pursuant to a special act could not commence business or enforce individual subscriptions until the entire authorized capital had been subscribed. The theory seems to have been that the authorized capital was the amount regarded as necessary to launch · the enterprise successfully, and therefore no shareholder should be held to his subscription if that amount of capital had not been raised. But the rule proved to be a substantial impediment to incorporation, and it became common to provide for reduction of the authorized capital, presumably down to the amount which had in fact been raised. By the time of the general incorporation statutes, the requirement that a corporation's entire authorized capital be subscribed had disappeared.

profitably employ in its business — perhaps because the enterprise had never assumed its full proportions, or because of a desire to retrench — to return those excess assets to the shareholders despite the absence of a sufficient surplus. Obviously, if the reason for reducing capital was the existence of excess assets which the corporation could no longer usefully employ, it followed that those assets should be returned to the stockholders.

However, it was soon recognized that if a corporation's capital was already impaired at the time of the reduction, whether by losses, diminution in the value of property, or otherwise, the amount of assets to be distributed to the stockholders should be reduced by the amount of the impairment, so that the corporation would be left with assets equal to the capital as reduced, and the impairment would be eliminated. E. g., Jerome v. Cogswell, 204 U.S. 1, 27 S.Ct. 241 (1907). This link between capital impairment and reduction of stated capital paved the way for the development of what is today the most common use of reduction of stated capital — to eliminate an existing impairment of capital. See para. C(1) infra. And there appears to be no longer even a vestige of the requirement that a reduction of stated capital result in a distribution to stockholders. E.g., Jay Ronald Co., Inc. v. Marshall Mortgage Corp., 291 N.Y. 227, 52 N.E.2d 108 (1943).

B. MECHANICS OF A REDUCTION

As for the mechanics of carrying out a reduction of capital, the original view, developed when there was only par stock, and stated capital was thought to be tied directly to par times the number of shares outstanding, was that capital reduction should be tied to a reduction of either the par value per share or the number of shares outstanding. Since the par value of authorized stock was fixed in the certificate of incorporation, while the number of shares outstanding was not, reduction of par required an amendment to the certificate, whereas a change in the number of shares outstanding did not. All that the latter required was an acquisition of some of its shares by the corporation, which might be accomplished by a pro rata surrender of stock by all of the shareholders, and a cancellation of the shares reacquired. Unfortunately, this led some people to think that a reduction of capital was effected by any acquisition of stock, including a repurchase.*

---

* This confusion greatly hampered the development of the law relating to repurchase of stock, until it was finally recognized, often under the impetus of a change in a corporation statute, that a repurchase of stock really constituted a combination of an acquisition of stock plus a distribution of as-

Such a view overlooked the fact that reduction of the stated capital measuring rod could be effected only in accordance with specific statutory authorization. That is, neither reduction of par value nor reduction in the number of par shares outstanding could in and of itself effect a valid reduction of capital; conversely, a reduction of capital pursuant to statutory formalities might be accomplished without either one of those two steps. Thus in the case of no-par stock, which does not call for any required minimum amount of stated capital, neither a change in the stated capital per share nor a change in the number of shares outstanding is required to produce a reduction of capital. And today the same may be true even where only par stock is present, if stated capital is greater than par times the number of shares outstanding because of a previous transfer from some type of surplus to stated capital.

In the light of the foregoing, consider the approaches to reduction of capital reflected in the following authorities, as well as the Model Act pattern embodied in §§58–60 and 68–70.

STATE EX REL. RADIO CORP. OF AMERICA v. BENSON

Superior Court of Delaware, 1924.
32 Del. (2 W.W.Harr.) 576, 128 A. 107.

PENNEWILL, C. J., delivering the opinion of the court:

The plaintiff filed in this court a petition praying for the issuance of a peremptory writ of mandamus to the defendant directed, commanding him to forthwith file in the office of the Secretary of State a certain certificate evidencing and embodying a proposed amendment to its Certificate of Incorporation.

The defendant refused to accept and file said certificate because the proposed amendment was adopted in compliance with Section 26 of the general incorporation law of the State (Rev. Code 1915, Sec. 1940) when, in his opinion, to legally accomplish the purpose sought, it should have been adopted in compliance with Section 28 of said law (Section 1942) and because the filing of such a certificate would be contrary to the established practice in the office of the Secretary of State.

sets, and that such a transaction could not be safely governed by the reduction of capital provisions alone. See Section 8 infra.

The total authorized capital stock of the plaintiff corporation, at the time of the adoption of the proposed amendment, was five million shares of preferred stock of the par value of five dollars a share, amounting in the aggregate to twenty-five million dollars, and seven million five hundred thousand shares of common stock without nominal or par value.

Of the authorized stock there had been issued three million, eight hundred and ninety thousand, two hundred and seventy-six shares of preferred stock, and five million, seven hundred and eleven thousand, three hundred and two shares of common stock having no par value. By the amendment it is proposed that the total authorized capital stock of the corporation shall be five hundred thousand shares of "A" preferred stock of the par value of fifty dollars per share, amounting in the aggregate to twenty-five million dollars; and one million, five hundred thousand shares of "A" common stock, without nominal or par value.

It is further provided in the amendment that the entire voting power of the corporation shall be lodged in the holders of the preferred stock and the holders of the common stock without nominal or par value, and that the holders of the "A" preferred stock are to have ten votes for each full share thereof, or one vote for each one-tenth share thereof, represented by fractional certificates of said "A" preferred stock; holders of "A" common stock are to have five votes for each full share thereof, and one vote for each one-fifth share thereof, represented by fractional certificates of "A" common stock.

The parts of Sections 26 and 28 of the general incorporation laws material to the issue here involved are as follows:

> Section 26.　[Now § 242.]　"Any corporation of this State, . . . may, from time to time, when and as desired, amend its charter of incorporation . . . by increasing or decreasing its authorized capital stock; or by changing the number and par value of the shares of its capital stock;" etc.

> Section 28.　[Now § 244.]　"Any corporation organized under this chapter may reduce its capital stock at any time by a vote of, or by the written consent of stockholders representing two-thirds of its capital stock," etc. ". . . No such reduction, however, shall be made in the stock of any corporation until all its debts which are not otherwise fully secured shall have been paid and discharged. . . . The decrease of capital stock issued may be effected by retiring or reducing any class of the stock, or by drawing the necessary number of shares by lot for retirement, or by the surrender of every shareholder of his shares, and the issue to him in lieu thereof of a decreased number of shares, or by

the purchase at not above par of certain shares for retirement, or by retiring shares owned by the corporation or by reducing the par value of shares."

To amend a certificate of incorporation under section 26, a majority vote of the stockholders is required.

The Secretary of State has the right, and it is his duty, to refuse to file an amendment to a certificate of incorporation that is sought to be made under a section of the law that does not authorize the proposed amendment, but if the thing sought to be done might be legally done under the amendment offered, the Secretary has no right to refuse to file it because he thinks the corporation may do something thereunder which could only be legally done under a different section of the law.

If the purpose of the corporation, in securing the desired amendment, was to decrease the number of the shares of its capital stock, without reducing the capital represented by the stock, a procedure under section 26 would seem to be appropriate and permissible, because the section provides that a corporation may amend its charter by decreasing its authorized capital stock or by changing the number and par value of the shares of its capital stock.

The State admits that the amendment is good so far as it relates to the reduction in the number of shares, and the increase in the par value of preferred stock, because, after the provisions of the amendment are carried into effect, the capital, as distinguished from shares, would be the same, and the financial interests of creditors and stockholders would not be affected. But it is insisted that the amendment is not good as to the no par stock.

The question is whether section 26, under which the amendment was adopted, authorized a decrease in the number of the shares of no par stock issued, as well as authorized and unissued? We think it does because shares of no par stock represent aliquot or proportionate parts of the capital, and when decreased in the same proportion, they represent the same aliquot or proportionate parts of the capital.

It being possible for the corporation, under section 26, to issue the shares of no par stock as proposed in the amendment, we will assume that it will be done in the manner in which it can be legally done, so that only the shares will be reduced and the capital remain unchanged.

If the decrease in the number of shares is to be made in a way that would diminish the capital it represents, as by the disbursement of a portion of capital assets among stockholders, the procedure to amend must be as provided in section 28.

When the two sections are read together and carefully considered, it seems clear that section 26 was designed primarily for the convenience of the corporation, and section 28 for the protection of the creditors and stockholders of the corporation.

It is a well-known fact that corporations sometimes desire to greatly reduce the number of the shares of their capital stock for business reasons only, and no creditor can be injured thereby if the capital of the corporation is not decreased. But it is otherwise if not only the shares, but the capital they represent is reduced. And manifestly that is the reason for the requirement in section 28, that no reduction shall be made in the capital stock of a corporation until all its debts are paid. It means that the capital of the corporation, which is the creditors' security, shall not be impaired. It will be observed that the procedure provided in section 28 for reducing capital stock is very different, and much more strict and exacting, than that provided in section 26 for decreasing capital stock and changing the number and par value of its shares; and the only reasonable explanation is, that if the corporation wants to reduce its capital stock in some way that will diminish its capital and thereby impair the creditors' security, the strict requirements of section 28 must be met. But if the purpose is simply to change the number of shares for the convenience of the corporation, without diminishing the capital, then the easier procedure of section 26 may be followed.

Whether section 26 or section 28 applies in a particular case depends, not upon the character of the stock to be decreased, whether with or without par value, but upon the manner and effect of the proposed reduction.

The test by which the application of section 26 or section 28 may be determined, is whether the security of creditors or stockholders will be in any wise impaired by the proposed amendment. If the capital which the stock in question represents would not be reduced, the amendment may be under section 26, otherwise it must be under section 28.

Such construction of the law, we think, makes the two sections harmonious, and should remove any confusion or uncertainty that may exist respecting the proper application of the law to any proposed amendment for reducing the capital stock, or changing the number and par value of the shares of the capital stock of a corporation.

The conclusion of the Court is, that it being possible for the plaintiff corporation to issue the new no par stock under section 26, the amendment proffered to the Secretary of State should have been accepted and filed. If the corporation should attempt, under the amendment, to reduce its capital stock in such a way as to diminish its capital, which could be legally done only under section 28, the act would be not only unauthorized, but unlawful.

For the reason stated, the motion of the defendant to discharge the rule and dismiss the petition is refused.

OPINION NO. 766 OF THE ATTORNEY GENERAL
OF ILLINOIS

1935 A.G.O. 85.

Hon. Edward J. Hughes, Secretary of State:

Dear Sir:

I have your letter of April 18, 1935 enclosing therewith Articles of Amendment to the Articles of Incorporation of The Aridor Company, in which you ask whether or not a resolution passed by the stockholders amending the Articles of Incorporation as provided in Section 52 of the Business Corporation Act so as to change the number of authorized shares to be issued or the par value thereof, has the effect of decreasing the stated capital, unless there is passed at the same meeting of stockholders, a resolution specifically decreasing the stated capital.

You advise that it has been insisted that the reduction in par value or the number of shares to be issued, does not carry with it as a corollary thereto, the determination of the amount of stated capital in its reduced amount; in other words, the question is, should the resulting effect upon stated capital be spelled out in the amendment resolution, when the reduction is made in connection with an amendment reducing the par value of shares?

The pertinent portions of Section 52 [counterpart of MBA § 53] are as follows:

"Sec. 52. **Right to Amend Articles of Incorporation.** A corporation may amend its articles of incorporation, from time to time, in any and as many respects as may be desired, *provided* that its articles of incorporation as amended contain only such provisions as might be lawfully contained in original articles of incorporation if made at the time of making such amendment, and, if a change in shares or an exchange or reclassification of shares is to be made, such provisions as may be necessary to effect such change, exchange, or reclassification as may be desired and as is permitted by this Act.

"In particular, and without limitation upon such general power of amendment, a corporation may amend its articles of incorporation, from time to time, so as: .   .   .

"(e) To increase or decrease the par value of the authorized shares of any class having a par value, whether issued or unissued.

"(f) To exchange, classify, reclassify, or cancel all or any part of its shares, whether issued or unissued."

Section 55 sets out the method of reporting the action of the stockholders' meeting to the Secretary of State, as follows:

"Sec. 55. **Articles of Amendment.** The articles of amendment shall . . . set forth:

"(a) The name of the corporation.

"(b) The amendment so adopted.

* * *

"(e) If such amendment provides for an exchange, reclassification, or cancellation of issued shares, or a reduction of the number of authorized shares of any class below the number of issued shares of that class, then a statement of the manner in which the same shall be effected.

"(f) If such amendment effects a change in the amount of stated capital or the amount of paid-in surplus, or both, then a statement of the manner in which the same is effected and a statement, expressed in dollars, of the amount of stated capital and the amount of paid-in surplus as changed by such amendment.

"If issued shares without par value are changed into the same or a different number of shares having par value, the aggregate par value of the shares into which the shares without par value are changed shall not exceed the sum of (1) the amount of stated capital represented by such shares without par value, and (2) the amount of surplus, if any, transferred to stated capital on account of such change, and (3) any additional consideration paid for such shares with par value and allocated to stated capital."

It will be noted that subsection (f), above, provides for the setting out of the amendment adopted, *in haec verba*, which, if it involves a reduction in par value of the value of the shares, will conclusively show the change in the capital structure.

Subsection (f) provides for the setting out of the rearranged capital structure, involving a statement, expressed in dollars, of the amount of stated capital and paid-in surplus, as changed.

Sections 52 and 55 must be read together. Section 55(f) is designed to report the consequences of the amendment. If the change in capital structure, reflected in dollars, were to be inserted in subsection (b), there would be no purpose in (f).

Section 2(k) defines "stated capital" applicable to par value shares at any particular time as, "the sum of the par value of all shares then issued having a par value." Therefore, the amount of the stated capital applicable to par value shares must be determined at all times by multiplying the number of the outstanding shares having a par value, by the par value of such shares.

Sections 19 and 60 provide for the restatement of stated capital and paid-in surplus, to be made by the board of directors. The amendment requires such restatement or reallocation, but the result of such restatement is not a proper part of the amendment.

If the amendment affected shares without par value, the resulting changes in stated capital and paid-in surplus should properly be made a part of the amendment resolution, in order that it be complete and not misleading. However, this is not necessary in the case of changes in par value shares, as the result involves a mere matter of computation in such case. In fact, the resolution of amendment adopted by the stockholders fixing the amount of the stated capital at any sum not in accordance with the par value and number of shares would be ineffective, and a resolution fixing the amount of stated capital at the identical sum determined as provided by the Act, would be surplusage and unnecessary.

It is my opinion that the change made by the amendment in the amount of the stated capital and paid-in surplus of the corporation is correctly set forth in Article Sixth of the Articles of Amendment, as required by Section 55(f) of the Act and that the resolution adopted by the stockholders need not set forth the change in the amount of the stated capital and paid-in surplus effected by such amendment.

C. IMPACT OF A REDUCTION OF CAPITAL

1. UPON CREDITORS

The earlier capital reduction statutes clearly recognized that the rights of creditors might be imperiled by a reduction of the safety margin represented by stated capital; accordingly, authority to reduce capital was normally conditioned upon some requirement like the payment of all debts not otherwise fully secured, as in the Delaware statute involved in the Benson case. The modern tendency, however, has been to forego any protection to creditors in connection with capital reduction. Thus, today both in Delaware and under the Model Act it is not even necessary to inform creditors of a reduction of capital, much less to seek their approval. Instead, creditors are left to seek the aid of a court of equity in case of a capital reduction which unfairly prejudices their interest.

Actually, however, it is not the reduction of stated capital itself which can adversely affect creditors; the danger lies in the possible distribution or other use of the reduction surplus thereby created. Thus the real question is the uses to which reduction surplus can be put. Generally speaking, reduction surplus is just another type of capital surplus, as MBA § 70 expressly provides. That means that under some statutes, such as Delaware's "out of its net assets in excess of its capital", reduction surplus is as eligible for dividend distributions as earned surplus. And even when the use of capital surplus is more restricted, as under the Model Act, the effect of any distribution that is made is in essence to return to the shareholders a portion of the safety margin upon which creditors were supposed to have been entitled to rely.

Is there any basis for inferring special limitations on the distribution of reduction surplus? For example, the view might be adopted that because of the special risk to creditors entailed in a reduction of capital, the amount of reduction surplus available for distribution to stockholders should be determined only after taking account of any decline in the value of assets, whether or not recognition of such decline in value would have been required under normal circumstances.* Some judicial support for this approach may be derived from Benas v. Title Guaranty Trust Co., 216 Mo.App. 53, 267 S.W. 28 (St.L.Ct.App.1924), involving a corporation which reduced its capital by $1,500,000 and declared a dividend in property worth $1,150,000. The corporation's books showed net assets in excess of capital as reduced of substantially more than the amount of the dividend; but on the basis of the actual value of its assets the corporation had had a deficit of almost $700,000 prior to the reduction of capital and accordingly had a surplus of only $800,000 after it. The court held, against the objection of minority stockholders, that the board of directors had not only the power but the duty to rescind the $1,150,000 dividend because it would have violated the prohibition against impairment of capital. However, it is not clear that in requiring recognition of the current value of the corporation's property the court intended to announce a special rule for cases involving reduction of capital. Since the court scarcely mentioned the reduction of capital, Benas may well simply represent a decision in accord with Randall v. Bailey that in all circumstances it is the actual value rather than book value of property which determines the amount of surplus available for dividends.

When the purpose for which reduction surplus is created is the elimination of a deficit rather than a distribution to shareholders, the threat to creditors is less immediate; but it is just as real, since future earnings will be freed for distribution instead of having to be retained to make up the deficit. As to whether and when reduction surplus can be used for this purpose, here again the first question might be whether capital surplus generally can be used to eliminate a deficit and thereby provide a "fresh start" for the corporation. Of course in jurisdictions like Delaware where capital surplus seems to be just as free for distribution as earned surplus, this question is largely academic because in any event the net balance of the sur-

* Note that this is the very result produced by the trial court's construction of New York § 58 in Randall v. Bailey, under which the second portion of the statute, expressly calling for valuation of assets, was confined to capital reduction situations. See page 232 supra.

plus accounts is available for dividends. But where the primary source of dividends is earned surplus (or any other fund based upon accumulated profits), it becomes important to decide to what extent a deficit in that account can be written off against capital surplus.

As is so often true in corporate finance, considerable guidance may be obtained by looking to the accounting approach on this problem. There, the first question is whether this problem can be side-stepped entirely by charging a particular loss directly against capital surplus in the first instance, thereby avoiding the creation of a deficit in earned surplus. Obviously, this can not be done in the case of normal operating losses which are automatically closed to earned surplus. But in the past it was sometimes done as to special non-recurring losses, or diminutions in the value of property. To forestall this practice, the following Rule No. 2 was adopted by the AICPA in 1934:

> Capital surplus, however created, should not be used to relieve the income account of the current or future years of charges which would otherwise fall to be made thereagainst. This rule might be subject to the exception that where, upon reorganization, a reorganized company would be relieved of charges which would be required to be made against income if the existing corporation were continued, it might be regarded as permissible to accomplish the same result without reorganization provided the facts were as fully revealed to and the action as formally approved by the shareholders as in reorganization.*

Chapter 7(A) of ARB No. 43 states that adjustments of the kind described in the exception in the Rule constitute a "quasi-reorganization", and goes on to prescribe the requirements for such a transaction in the following terms:

> 3. If a corporation elects to restate its assets, capital stock, and surplus through a readjustment and thus avail itself of permission to relieve its future income account or earned surplus account of charges which would otherwise be made thereagainst, it should make a clear report to its shareholders of the restatements proposed to be made, and obtain their formal consent. It should present a fair balance sheet as at the date of the readjustment, in which the adjustment of carrying amounts is reasonably complete, in order that there may be no continuation of the circumstances which justify charges to capital surplus.

---

* While Rule No. 2 refers expressly only to relieving the *income account* of proper charges, by common consent the Rule is regarded as equally forbidding the use of capital surplus to relieve *earned surplus* of proper charges against it (such as items which by-pass the income statement). See Baker and Cary, Cases on Corporations (3d ed., unabridged 1959) 1303.

4. A write-down of assets below amounts which are likely to be realized thereafter, though it may result in conservatism in the balance sheet at the readjustment date, may also result in overstatement of earnings or of earned surplus when the assets are subsequently realized. Therefore, in general, assets should be carried forward as of the date of readjustment at fair and not unduly conservative amounts, determined with due regard for the accounting to be employed by the company thereafter. . . .

6. When the amounts to be written off in a readjustment have been determined, they should be charged first against earned surplus to the full extent of such surplus; any balance may then be charged against capital surplus.

* * *

10. After such a readjustment earned surplus previously accumulated cannot properly be carried forward under that title. A new earned surplus account should be established, dated to show that it runs from the effective date of the readjustment, and this dating should be disclosed in financial statements until such time as the effective date is no longer deemed to possess any special significance. *

It may be noted that the accounting view of a quasi-reorganization provides some additional support for the idea that a reduction of capital is a good time to recognize any diminution in the value of the corporation's property. The accounting approach clearly calls for a complete shakedown of asset values to current levels, at least whenever reduction surplus is to be used to eliminate a deficit in earned surplus.

Conversely, however, as paragraph 4 of Chapter 7A indicates it is also important to guard against writing assets down to figures below current values in the course of a quasi-reorganization. There might be some temptation to do that in a case where there is ample stated capital to absorb such a reduction and the company is not looking to end up with a net balance in reduction surplus available for distribution. The objective would be to lower the depreciation charges in future years, thus increasing net income and hence the balance in earned surplus from and after the quasi-reorganization. This would of course be a clear violation of Rule No. 2. See generally, Comment, Writing Down Fixed Assets and Stated Capital, 44 Yale L.J. 1025 (1935).

There have only been a few cases in this area. In the most recent one, Hamilton Mfg. Co. v. United States, 214 F.2d 644 (7th Cir. 1954), the court seemed somewhat hostile to the idea of using capital surplus to wipe out an operating deficit and thereby obtain a fresh

---

* The SEC takes much the same view of a quasi-reorganization. See Rappa-port, SEC Accounting Practice and Procedure (2d ed. 1963) 3.28–3.30.

start on "net profits", the statutory source of dividends. However, the impact of the case is sharply limited by the fact that actually the corporation involved had not sought to effect a quasi-reorganization; at most the issue was somewhat obliquely presented (in connection with a special tax laid on undistributed earnings) as to whether such a transaction could have served to free current earnings for dividends under state law. Two earlier cases, Haskell Mfg. Co. v. United States, 91 F.Supp. 26 (D.R.I.1950), and Lich v. United States Rubber Co., 39 F.Supp. 675 (D.N.J.1941), aff'd without opin., 123 F.2d 145 (3d Cir.1941), neither of which was cited in the Hamilton case, seemed to take a more favorable view of quasi-reorganization.

In many jurisdictions the statute specifically authorizes the use of capital surplus to write off a deficit in earned surplus. E.g., MBA § 70. Query the extent to which these statutes incorporate the standards imposed on quasi-reorganization by the accounting authorities. Perhaps the most important question in this connection is whether earned surplus must always be exhausted before capital surplus is resorted to, as the accounting authorities require. Under MBA § 70 this question is specifically answered in the affirmative. On the other hand, under Illinois § 60A, which provides that a "corporation may, by resolution of its board of directors, reduce its paid-in surplus by charging against its paid-in surplus (1) all or any part of any deficit arising from operating or other losses or from diminution in value of its assets . . .", the Attorney General of Illinois ruled that paid-in surplus could be used to write off a loss due to diminution in the value of assets, despite the existence of earned surplus which might have been used. Opinion No. 682, 1934 A.G.O. 273. Doubt about the soundness of this ruling has been expressed in 1 Ill.Bus.Corp.Act Ann. (2d ed.1947) 268:

> This opinion involves a construction of the words "any deficit arising from operating or other losses or from diminution in value of its assets" as including a net loss of any period regardless of the amount of accumulated profits of prior periods. The soundness of this opinion may be questioned, since the words quoted above might be interpreted to involve the recognition of the existence of a "deficit" only when losses or shrinkage in value of assets have eliminated any earned surplus.

---

2. IMPACT OF A REDUCTION UPON PREFERRED STOCKHOLDERS

The impact of a reduction of common capital upon the holders of preferred stock with a liquidation preference is quite analogous to the effect of any capital reduction on creditors, since the stated capital attributable to the common serves as a cushion for the liquidation preference in much the same way that all capital serves as a safety margin for the claims of creditors. As with creditors, preferred stockholders are normally assumed to have contracted in the light of the express permission to reduce capital contained in the statute; and accordingly, something more than the mere existence of a liquidation preference is needed before a contractual restriction on reducing capital will be inferred. However, reduction of capital could touch off the provision in practically every state corporation statute which gives a class vote, or sometimes even a right to require the corporation to purchase the stock at its appraised value, in the event of an amendment to the certificate of incorporation which is prejudicial to the interests of the class. To illustrate, in Matter of Kinney, 279 N.Y. 423, 18 N.E.2d 645 (1939), the court held that a certificate amendment reducing the stated capital attributable to common stock by 90%, as a result of changing the common from no-par stock with a stated value of $10 per share to par stock with a par value of $1, fell within a New York statute which entitled preferred stockholders to receive the appraised value of their shares in the event of an amendment altering a "preferential right". Said the court:

> We are thus brought to a consideration of the provision of the amended certificate which reduced the stated capital of the corporation . . . the resulting reduction in the stated capital, totaling $1,440,000, being thereby transferred to surplus. Prior to such transfer, the eight-dollar cumulative preferred stock was in a position to benefit from the earning power of such capital, and in the event of liquidation or dissolution such capital would be available for distribution to such stockholders, subject only to diminution by losses in business operations. It could not have been used for dividends or for the purchase of any shares of stock. When this sum of $1,440,000, amounting to about one-third of the capital of the corporation, was transferred from capital to surplus, the eight-dollar cumulative preferred stock lost its right to rely upon this portion of capital. The capital structure was so altered that it was placed within the power of the corporation to deprive forever the preferred stockholders of their preferential rights in regard to this portion of the capital structure. In brief this $1,440,000 was in itself a security of approximately twenty-eight dollars for each share of the old preferred stock and has now by this amendment of the certificate of incorporation become a surplus that may no longer support such stock.

Although most state statutes provide only a class vote instead of an appraisal remedy to stockholders whose preferential rights are adversely affected, the Kinney decision would appear to be equally pertinent on that issue. Thus under the Model Act a certificate amendment reducing common capital by reducing the par value of outstanding shares might well be thought to "change the . . . preferences" of preferred stock with a liquidation preference within the meaning of § 60(e), which provides for a class vote in such circumstances. However, there is a difficulty here which seems to have been entirely overlooked in the Kinney case. Under most corporation statutes, including both the New York statute and the Model Act, a class vote or other special class right is conditioned upon a *certificate amendment* which adversely affects the class. That puts reduction of capital into a somewhat anomalous position, because in many cases reduction of capital can be accomplished without any amendment of the certificate. E.g., MBA § 69. In such cases it is clear that any remedy conditioned upon amendment of the certificate is not available, despite the fact that the impact on the preferred is exactly the same as if the reduction of capital had involved an amendment of the certificate. And since the rights of preferred stock in connection with reduction of capital should presumably be the same whether there is an amendment of the certificate or not, perhaps this suggests that, despite the Kinney decision, capital reduction pursuant to a certificate amendment should be held not to touch off a provision like MBA § 60.*

Suppose the proposal is to reduce the stated capital attributable to the preferred. Of course no change in the contractual terms of the preferred stock without fair compensation could be imposed upon an unwilling preferred stockholder; for example, a compulsory pro rata reduction in the number of the preferred shares, which of course would effectively reduce the total annual dividend of the preferred, and the total liquidation preference, would not be sustained. See Kennedy v. Carolina Public Service Co., 262 F. 803 (N.D.Ga.1920). But it is possible to reduce the stated capital attributable to preferred stock without purporting to affect any of the other terms of preferred. See Commonwealth & Southern Corp., page 220, supra. In that event, there would be a good deal less reason for concern on the part of the preferred, since their interest depends upon their contractual terms, and not the amount of capital attributable to the preferred. Accordingly, there may be doubt about the wisdom of the requirement in Page v. Whittenton Mfg. Co., 211 Mass. 424, 428, 97 N.E. 1006, 1007 (1912), to the effect that in the absence of statute common capital must "be first resorted to to the point of extinction before the preferred stock can be compelled to contribute" to a reduc-

---

* In Delaware this problem is even more acute. Presumably in order to confirm the decision in the Benson case, supra, that any reduction of capital must be carried out under § 244 of the Delaware law, and not § 242 relating to certificate amendments, § 242 was changed to expressly require that any amendment of a certificate effecting a change in issued shares "shall set forth that the capital of the corporation will not be reduced under or by reason of the amendment". In the face of that language, it seems clear that even if capital is reduced in conjunction with a certificate amendment, the reduction of capital can not be the basis for a class vote under the provision in § 242 authorizing such a vote in the case of a *certificate amendment* which "would alter or change the preferences" of the class.

tion of capital. In any event, such a rule is self-defeating, since normally no reduction of the capital attributable to any class can be effected without the support of the common's voting power, and the common are certainly not going to vote their own "suicide."

It follows, then, that it is the total stated capital remaining after a reduction of capital which is of primary significance, and not the particular amounts allocated to the various classes. Further confirmation of this view under the Model Act may be found in the fact that the provision in § 69 prohibiting reduction of capital below the liquidation preferences of preferred stock relates to total stated capital rather than preferred capital alone. There are, however, some difficulties with this latter provision which might be noted here. First, there is no counterpart limitation applicable to a reduction of capital pursuant to certificate amendment under § 58, which introduces another unfortunate distinction between par and no-par stock in the area of the relationship between stated capital and liquidation preferences. In addition, the measure of the limitation on reduction of capital in § 69 seems inconsistent with the provisions of § 21 relating to stated capital upon original issue. On the one hand, the § 69 limitation is more strict, since there is no prohibition against starting out with stated capital upon original issue less than liquidation preferences; on the other hand, the § 69 limitation is more lenient than the provision for allocation of consideration in § 21 which looks solely to preferred stated capital rather than total stated capital as in § 69.

Finally, query how desirable an absolute restriction against reducing stated capital below the total liquidation preferences is. As a practical matter, it may simply mean that if the preferred should be willing to permit a deeper cut, they would have to accept a cut in their liquidation preference as well.

Despite what has been said, however, it does make some difference whether it is the preferred capital rather than the common which is reduced. First, the preferred are more likely to get a class vote upon a reduction of preferred capital, e. g. Brill v. Blakeley, 308 N.Y. 951, 127 N.E.2d 96 (1955), particularly if, as has typically been true, the preferred is par stock and hence subject to statutes like MBA § 60 (b) which provide such a vote to any class whose par is changed. In such a case, incidentally, the preferred ought to be very wary of approving a reduction in preferred capital while any substantial amount of common capital remains, for the very reason that the latter may be subject to further reduction without any approval by the preferred.

---

3. RESPECTIVE RIGHTS OF PREFERRED AND COMMON IN REDUCTION SURPLUS

The other possible area of difference between reduction of preferred capital and reduction of common relates to the distribution of any net reduction surplus which may result. Once more this is part of the broader question of the extent to which there are limitations on the distribution generally of various types of capital surplus.

In the absence of statute, there seems little doubt that paid-in surplus on junior shares is not restricted to distribution to preferred; and the same would appear to be true as to capital surplus created by reduction of capital. Although in the reduction case there is some force in the argument for a freeze on dividends to the junior stockholders until the impairment of the senior "cushion" resulting from the reduction of common capital has been restored, it seems unlikely that such a freeze could be implied merely from the inter-class contract between the preferred and the common.

It is much easier to imply equitable limitations on the use of capital surplus stemming from the preferred, whether upon original issue or pursuant to a reduction of capital. Presumably, any prohibition would apply to not only direct distribution of such capital surplus to the junior stock, but also such indirect benefits to the juniors as charging preferred dividends to that capital surplus despite the existence of earned surplus (or some other capital surplus), thus preserving the latter for dividends to the junior. Cf. MBA § 46 (last paragraph).

Nevertheless, there are some difficulties with this analysis, particularly under a modern statute like the Model Act which appears to have taken some account of these inter-class conflicts but is completely silent on this item. Note, for example, that § 46 (d), which specifically limits distributions of capital surplus in terms of preferred liquidation preferences, neither expresses nor invites any further distinction based upon the original source of the capital surplus.[26] Hence the result may be that even as to capital surplus contributed by the preferred, they obtain no special rights except such as are expressly provided in the preferred share contract embodied in the certificate of incorporation.

SECTION 4. TAX ASPECTS OF
CORPORATE DIVIDENDS

A. CORPORATE DISTRIBUTIONS IN GENERAL

The starting point for the income tax treatment of corporate distributions to shareholders is § 301, which covers, generally speaking, all distributions by a corporation to its shareholders in their capacity as shareholders except (1) distributions of stock of the corporation, or rights to such stock, and (2) distributions in redemption of stock under certain circumstances, including partial and complete liquidation. As to those distributions which are covered, § 301 distinguishes between corporate distributions which are *dividends in the tax sense*, within the meaning of § 316, and those which are not. Taxable dividends must be included in gross income under §§ 301(c)(1) and 61(a)(7), while distributions which are not dividends in the tax sense are applied against the basis of the stock under § 301(c)(2), with any excess treated as a gain from the sale or exchange of property under § 301(c)(3)(A).

The definition of a dividend in the tax sense in § 316(a) is based primarily upon the concept of corporate "earnings and profits": any distribution to a shareholder is a dividend if it is (1) out of earnings and profits accumulated after February 28, 1913,* or (2) out of the earnings and profits of the current year (*computed as of the close of the year*, regardless of when the distribution was made) whether or not there are any accumulated earnings and profits. Section 316(a) eliminates most tracing requirements by specifying that whenever there are any earnings and profits, a distribution is deemed to be out of the earnings and profits rather than from any other source—and from the most recent earnings and profits. Moreover, in many situations it is clear that the distribution is covered by one of the two sources of earnings and profits, in which event it is not necessary to

* This limitation based upon the date of the enactment of the 1913 Income Tax Act represents a legislative policy decision rather than a constitutional requirement, Lynch v. Hornby, 247 U. S. 339, 38 S.Ct. 543, 62 L.Ed. 1149 (1918), and is no longer of much practical significance anyway.

determine the exact amount of either one. However, in some cases the precise dollar amount of at least one of the two sources does become crucial, in which event the question of how to compute earnings and profits must be resolved. See topic B, infra.

Taxable dividends received by individuals (including trusts and estates) are subject to an exclusion of the first $100 of dividends received. A husband and wife are each entitled to a $100 exclusion, but such exclusion may only be applied against dividends received by the particular spouse or on jointly owned stock. As to corporations receiving taxable dividends, § 243 provides a deduction in the amount of 85% of any dividends received—in other words, only 15% of intercorporate dividends are included in taxable income. In addition, members of an "affiliated group" of corporations which file separate returns may elect to obtain a 100% dividends received deduction (subject to certain terms and conditions, including the limitation of the affiliated group to one surtax exemption and one minimum accumulated earnings credit).

As already indicated, there are some types of distributions which are not subject to § 301, but are governed by some other specific Code provision. See § 301(f). For example, the effect of § 302 is to except distributions in redemption of stock from § 301. But this exception only applies if the redemption distribution is not essentially equivalent to a dividend, which makes the whole matter somewhat circular. A redemption distribution which is not equivalent to a dividend is treated as *in exchange* for the stock, which brings the capital gain or loss provisions into play. Similarly § 331 excepts distributions in a complete or partial liquidation of a corporation, where again the distribution is treated as in exchange for the stock. The definitions of complete and partial liquidations, while having nontax antecedents, are tax words of art, and are both extremely important and quite complex. In addition, the definition of partial liquidation in § 346 is also in terms of a distribution not essentially equivalent to a dividend, thus being as circular as the redemption definition.

Distributions of a corporation's own stock, or rights to such stock, are governed by §§ 305, 306 and 307, which expressly make such distributions nontaxable. However, as will be seen later, under certain circumstances the stockholder may have ordinary income rather than capital gain when he disposes of the dividend stock.

These non-dividend corporate distributions are among the most troublesome transactions in the tax law, since they are right on the borderline between capital gain and ordinary income. If corporate earnings are distributed to stockholders, ordinary taxable dividends will result. If instead the corporation retains its earnings there are no tax incidents to the stockholders, even though the value of their stock is likely to rise; and upon a subsequent sale of the stock, the gain due to the accumulated earnings will simply be a part of the total gain on the transaction, which will normally be taxed at capital gains rather than ordinary income rates. What the stockholders would most like is to obtain some of the corporate earnings at capital gains rates without having to give up their stock interest, as they have to do in the case of a sale; and it is here that such borderline transactions as stock redemptions, partial liquidations and stock dividends occur.

In addition to this basic pattern there are two polar factors which are operative in this area. On the one hand, § 1014(a) provides that upon the death of a stockholder his stock gets a new basis equal to its value at that time, which means that if stock is held until death and then sold the earnings accumulated up to the date of death will not even have produced a capital gain tax. On the other hand, § 531, to be discussed in detail later, imposes a special additional tax on any corporation which accumulates its earnings for the purpose of avoiding income tax to stockholders, and the threat of this tax may constitute powerful pressure toward the distribution of taxable dividends.

B. COMPUTATION OF EARNINGS AND PROFITS

Despite the fact that the whole dividend structure is bottomed on the "earnings and profits" concept, that term is nowhere defined in the Code. While § 312 does describe the effect of certain transactions, such as redemptions and corporate divisions, on earnings and profits, it does not give any comprehensive picture of how earnings and profits are to be determined.

It is clear that earnings and profits for the year are not the same as taxable income—the increase in corporate earned surplus would be a more accurate, though still far from exact, measure of earnings and profits. Thus Reg. § 1.312–6, which helps to fill some of the void here, expressly provides for the inclusion in earnings and profits of exempt income, which would include such items as tax-exempt interest and life insurance proceeds. Similarly, certain special deductions allowed in the determination of net income, such as for dividends received, are not deductible in determining earnings and profits. And depletion must be based on cost, rather than the percentage method permitted in computing taxable income. On the other hand, many items not permitted as deductions in computing taxable income, such as federal income taxes, excess charitable contributions, and unreasonable compensation, are deductible in determining earnings and profits.

On matters of timing, earnings and profits follow taxable income much more closely. Thus Reg. § 1.312–6 provides that the same method of accounting used in determining taxable income should be used in determining earnings and profits. Similarly, gains and losses are recognized for earnings and profits purposes at the same time they are recognized as taxable income, thus importing the whole tax-free exchange pattern into the earnings and profits area. This same notion has been applied, without any express support in the regulations, to postpone reflecting in earnings and profits a gain from cancellation of indebtedness which had not yet been recognized in the determination of taxable income. Bangor & Aroostook Ry. Co. v. Commissioner, 193 F.2d 827 (1st Cir. 1951).

See generally, Rudick, "Dividends" and "Earnings or Profits" Under the Income Tax Law: Corporate Non-Liquidating Distributions, 89 U.Pa.L.Rev. 865 (1941); Albrecht, "Dividends" and "Earnings or Profits," 7 Tax L.Rev. 157 (1952); Bittker, Federal Income Taxation of Corporations and Shareholders (1959) 141–149.

C. DISGUISED DIVIDENDS

It is clear that a distribution may be a dividend for tax purposes although it is not a formal dividend under state law, and even though it is not pro rata among the stockholders. Some cases involve a payment to a stockholder which purports to be something other than a dividend, i. e., interest, rent, or compensation. In these circumstances characterization of the payment as a dividend will normally not affect the shareholder (except perhaps for the dividend exclusion) because the payment represents ordinary income to him anyway, and the real issue is the deductibility of the payment by the corporation. In other situations, the disguised dividend may take the form of a benefit obtained by the shareholder as a result of corporate action— for example, a "bargain" sale or lease by the corporation to a stockholder. Lying somewhere between these two situations is one of the most troublesome types of case, the loan to a controlling stockholder, which as a practical matter gives the stockholder the benefit of corporate funds to the same extent as a dividend.

D. DIVIDENDS IN KIND

1. **Effect upon the Corporation.** When a corporation distributes property rather than cash as a dividend to its stockholders, there are a number of problems which test the tax relationship between a cor-

poration and its stockholders. One of the most important early questions was whether a corporation which distributed property that had appreciated in value as a dividend was required to include the unrealized appreciation in its income. Although the case of General Utilities & Operating Co. v. Helvering, 296 U.S. 200, 56 S.Ct. 185, 80 L.Ed. 154 (1935), is widely regarded as having answered this question in the negative, actually the Court did not pass on that question, because it had not been raised in the lower courts. Rather the Court simply affirmed the finding of the trial court that the corporation had not declared a dividend in a specified dollar amount and then satisfied the dividend obligation by distributing property (a case in which concededly the spread between the dollar amount of the dividend and the basis of the property distributed would have been taxable to the corporation). In any event, the 1954 Code confirmed the.view usually attributed to General Utilities by providing in § 311, at least so far as dividends are concerned, "no gain or loss shall be recognized to a corporation on the distribution, with respect to its stock, of . . . property."

However, § 311 does not eliminate all the problems in this area. For example, where, as in the General Utilities case itself, the property distributed to the stockholders is promptly sold to a third party, in accordance with arrangements previously made by the corporation, it is at least open to argument that the corporation rather than the stockholders really made the sale. (It was on this basis that the Court of Appeals had decided for the Government in General Utilities; but this argument too had not been raised in the trial court, and accordingly the Supreme Court refused to consider it.) Moreover, the Senate Finance Committee Report, S.Rep.No.1622, 83rd Cong., 2d Sess. (1954) 247, expressly seeks to preserve some flexibility in this area:

> Your committee does not intend, however, . . . to alter existing law in the case of distributions of property, which has appreciated or depreciated in value, where such distributions are made to persons other than shareholders or are made to shareholders in a capacity other than that of a shareholder. . . . [In addition] your committee does not intend to change existing law with respect to attribution of income of shareholders to their corporation as exemplified for example in the case of Commissioner v. First State Bank of Stratford (168 F.2d 1004 [5th Cir. 1948]).

In the Bank of Stratford case referred to in the Committee Report a bank had charged off certain notes as worthless prior to 1942, thereby obtaining a tax benefit. When it appeared in 1942 that substantial payments would be made on the notes, the bank declared the notes as a dividend in kind and transferred them to the stockholders. The Commissioner successfully included in the bank's income for 1942 the amounts collected by the stockholders during that year on the notes. In holding that the dividend in kind in effect represented an anticipatory assignment of income, since the notes when collected would have been income to the bank, the court said:

> Like Banquo's ghost, the question that will not down is this: May a bank detach interest coupons from negotiable bonds owned by it, assign the coupons to its shareholders as a dividend in kind, and avoid the payment of income tax on the interest subsequently collected by the assignee of the coupons? In other words, by means of a dividend in kind, may a corporation avoid income taxes by doing exactly what was done (without success) by an individual by means of a gift in Helvering v. Horst, 311 U.S. 112, 61 S.Ct. 144? If so, a corporation need not ever again pay an income tax on interest derived from coupons detached from negotiable bonds.
> . . .
>
> The avoidance of taxes may be perfectly legitimate, but it cannot be done by the anticipatory assignment of notes representing income, as a dividend in kind, and the subsequent collection of said notes by the assignees. The respondent is a banking corporation, organized and operated for profit. The acquisition of profits for its shareholders was the purpose of its creation. The collection of interest on loans was a principal source of its income. The payment of dividends to its shareholders was the enjoyment of its income. A body corporate can be said to enjoy its income in no other way. Like the "life-rendering pelican" it feeds its shareholders upon dividends. Whether they are in the form of notes or money is immaterial if the dividend is out of earnings, or consists of property purchased from earnings or which is regarded as earnings for accounting purposes. The respondent exercised its power to procure payment of its income to another, which was "the enjoyment, and hence the realization," of its income.
>
> The distinction between General Utilities v. Helvering, supra, and this case lies in the difference in the character of the respective properties distributed as dividends in kind; one represented a capital asset, the other represents income. In the former, the fruit was on the trees; in the latter, the tree itself represents fruit of prior years that was not taxed. The distinction is the same as would have existed in the Horst case if the father had given his son the bond with the unearned-interest coupons attached.

A somewhat similar case is First National Bank of St. Elmo, Illinois v. United States, 194 F.2d 389 (7th Cir. 1952), where a bank, after litigation over oil royalties on land held by it, reached a settlement under which it would receive previously impounded royalties in return for the surrender of certain claims, and thereupon transferred its rights to its stockholders as a dividend in kind. The impounded royalties later paid to the stockholders were held taxable income to the bank.

A classic illustration of the tax avoidance possibilities in this area appears in Rudco Oil & Gas Co. v. United States, 113 Ct.Cl. 206, 82 F.Supp. 746 (1949), in which a family corporation, having determined that its cash position justified a dividend of approximately $60,000, conveyed its interests in oil and gas leases to its shareholders to be held by them until the lessees had paid that sum. By the end of the year over $59,000 had been paid, and the shareholders reconveyed the interests to the corporation. The court held that the amount received by the stockholders was taxable to the corporation (as well as a dividend to the shareholders), since the conveyance was merely "the assignment of future income . . . . , a transaction without purpose or intended consequences except in relation to income tax liability."

Does the rationale of the foregoing cases reach the situation where a corporation distributes its inventory as a dividend in kind to its stockholders who thereafter sell it to a third party? In United States v. Lynch, 192 F.2d 718 (9th Cir. 1951), a corporation in the business of growing and marketing apples declared a dividend in kind to its three stockholders of 22,000 boxes of apples. The stockholders then agreed with the corporation that it should sell the apples for their account. Although the corporation was liquidated two months later, the court found that the dividend was not intended to be a liquidation distribution. In taxing the net profit from the sale of the apples to the corporation, the court said:

> The dividend in question was not the kind of a distribution contemplated by [the predecessor of § 316(a)], and must be ignored for tax purposes. Distribution of corporate inventory with the expectation of immediate sale by the shareholders pointedly suggests a transaction outside the range of normal commercially-motivated and justifiable corporate activity, yet we have here a stronger case, because the sale was to be made by utilizing the corporation's facilities in the ordinary course of its business; the shareholders did not engage in a separate and independent business in which the apples were to be used. The shareholders, under the circumstances of this case, cannot avoid payment of the price Congress has decreed must be paid for use of the corporate entity.

Accord, A.B.C.D. Lands, Inc. v. Commissioner, 41 T.C. 840 (1964). In Louisiana Irrigation and Mill Co. v. Commissioner, 14 T.C.M. 1252 (1955), the Tax Court refused to find income to the corporation upon a distribution of appreciated inventory to its stockholders. However, it should be noted that in this case the Commissioner had predicated the realization of income by the corporation exclusively upon the fact that appreciated inventory was distributed to the stockholders — he did not rely at all upon later sale of that inventory by the stockholders, despite the fact that the corporation had made arrangements to facilitate such sale by the stockholders. Hence the court found the Lynch and Stratford cases inapplicable because they involved attribution to the corporation of income received by the stockholders. And as to the corporate realization of income simply as a result of distributing property to stockholders, the court cited General Utilities and held that no different result was called for merely because it was inventory that was distributed. Accord, Rev.Rul. 57–490, 1957–2 Cum.Bull. 231. See generally, Comment, The Imputed Sale and Anticipatory Assignment of Income Doctrines: Their Effect on IRC §§ 311 & 336, 15 Buffalo L.Rev. 154 (1965).

2. **Tax Incidents to the Shareholders.** *Prima facie*, a dividend in kind should be treated just as though it were a dividend in cash in an amount equal to the fair market value of the property distributed. However, the earnings and profits limitation on taxable dividends produces some complications where the dividend in kind involves appreciated property. If the corporation's earnings and profits exceed the basis of the property distributed, but are less than its fair market value, is the full market value nevertheless taxable as a dividend? Commissioner v. Hirshon Trust, 213 F.2d 523 (2d Cir. 1954), and Commissioner v. Godley, 213 F.2d 529 (3d Cir. 1954), both answered that question in the affirmative under the pre-1954 law. It seems to have been conceded that under the General Utilities rule the unrealized appreciation on the distributed property did not increase earnings and profits, just as it did not increase taxable income. However, both courts concluded that since in the case of a dividend in kind the statute called for a reduction in earnings and profits only in the amount of the corporation's basis in the property, and not its fair market value, the entire distribution was "out of earnings and profits", and therefore constituted a dividend in the tax sense. Once the whole distribution constituted a taxable dividend, it was subject to the ordinary rule that a dividend in kind is taxable to the stockholders at its fair market value. *

As an original matter, the status of the Hirshon-Godley rule under the 1954 Code was not entirely clear. The express retention in § 312 (a) of the rule limiting the charge against earnings and profits in the case of a dividend in kind to the basis of the property certainly left room for importing the Hirshon-Godley rule. However, there were some implications the other way, not only in the committee reports, see S.Rep.No.1622, 83rd Cong., 2d Sess. (1954) 248, but also in the

---

* Subsequently, the Commissioner sought to interpret Hirshon and Godley as holding that any corporate distribution constitutes a dividend in the tax sense so long as it does not impair capital, in order to tax a cash distribution which exceeded earnings and profits but was not "out of capital" in corporate terms; but the court refused to so far abandon the earnings and profits concept. Commissioner v. Gross, 236 F.2d 612 (2d Cir. 1956).

statute itself, such as §§ 312(b) and (g) which expressly provide for increasing earnings and profits in connection with a limited number of specified appreciated property situations. In any event, Reg. § 1.316–1(a)(2) expressly rejects Hirshon-Godley by restricting the amount of any dividend for tax purposes to the amount of the corporation's earnings and profits. And this result is further confirmed by the fact that the Hirshon-Godley rule was retroactively overruled as respects pre-1954 years, except for situations which after 1954 would fall under §§ 312(b) or (g). Public Law 629, 84th Cong., 2d Sess. (1956).

When a corporate shareholder receives appreciated property, § 301 (b)(1)(B) restricts the amount of the dividend to the basis of the property distributed, and § 301(d)(2) in turn carries over that basis to the recipient corporation. These provisions are designed to prevent the transferee-corporation from obtaining a stepped-up basis equal to market value while incurring a tax cost of only the relatively modest intercorporate dividend tax.

SECTION 5.   TAX ASPECTS OF STOCK DIVIDENDS

A.   HISTORICAL BACKGROUND

A brief view of the tortuous history of stock dividends under the tax law may help to set the 1954 Code provisions in perspective. An appropriate starting point is Towne v. Eisner, 245 U.S. 418, 38 S.Ct. 158, 62 L.Ed. 372 (1918), holding that under the 1913 Act, which was silent about stock dividends, a dividend of common on common was not intended to be taxed. The 1916 act expressly made stock dividends taxable, but Eisner v. Macomber, 252 U.S. 189, 40 S.Ct. 189, 64 L.Ed. 521 (1920), held that a dividend of common on common was not taxable as income under the Sixteenth Amendment.

From 1921–1935 successive revenue acts expressly exempted stock dividends from tax; but this only served to shift the constitutional issue to the basis arena. Thus in Koshland v. Helvering, 298 U.S. 441, 56 S.Ct. 767, 80 L.Ed. 1268, 105 A.L.R. 756 (1936), a taxpayer who owned non-voting, cumulative preferred received a dividend in voting common, after which her preferred was redeemed. The Commissioner applied the regulation calling for an allocation of basis to stock received tax-free as a stock dividend, thus increasing the amount of the gain realized upon the redemption of the preferred. However, the Court agreed with the taxpayer that a dividend of common on preferred was constitutionally taxable as "income", despite Eisner v.

Macomber, because it changed the proportionate interests of the stock-holders, so that the allocation-of-basis regulation did not apply. Similarly, in Helvering v. Gowran, 302 U.S. 238, 58 S.Ct. 154, 82 L.Ed. 224 (1937), the Court held that a dividend of preferred on common, where some preferred was already outstanding, was outside the Macomber rule because it changed the proportionate interests of the stockholders, which meant that no part of the taxpayer's basis in the common stock was allocable to the dividend preferred.

From 1936 to 1953, the statutory rule provided that a stock dividend "shall not be treated as a dividend to the extent that it does not constitute income to the shareholders within the meaning of the Sixteenth Amendment." Under this statute the Treasury sought to overthrow Eisner v. Macomber, but failed when the Supreme Court held, in a series of three cases decided in 1943, that the statute codified the rule of that case. The Court reaffirmed the proportionate interest test and held that dividends of common on common, Helvering v. Griffiths, 318 U.S. 371, 63 S.Ct. 636, 87 L.Ed. 843 (1943), preferred on common where only common was outstanding, Strassburger v. Commissioner, 318 U.S. 604, 63 S.Ct. 791, 87 L.Ed. 1029, 144 A.L.R. 1335 (1943), and non-voting common on voting and non-voting common, Helvering v. Sprouse, 318 U.S. 604, 63 S.Ct. 791, 87 L.Ed. 1029, 144 A.L.R. 1335 (1943), were all non-taxable under the statute because they did not change the proportionate interests of the stockholders.

In the foregoing cases, no special point was made of the purpose for the stock dividend, or any prospective later use for sale, gift or otherwise. The net effect, therefore, seemed to be that it was possible to "bail out" substantial amounts of accumulated corporate profits by issuing a non-taxable stock dividend, say of preferred on common, and then selling the preferred to a third party, at merely a capital gains tax cost. The common stockholders would still have the basic equity interest (presumably including voting power) represented by the common; and in any event a redeemable feature would make it possible to get rid of the preferred stock if and when that should prove to be desirable. In 1947 the Treasury Department, recognizing the seriousness of this preferred stock bail-out problem, sought to meet the situation by refusing to issue rulings favorable to such an arrangement. Because of the very high stakes involved — a dividend tax on the proceeds of a bail-out would leave very little for the stockholders — most lawyers would not risk a bail-out transaction, and the Treasury succeeded in keeping these transactions to a minimum. See generally, Darrell, Recent Developments in Nontaxable Reorganizations and Stock Dividends, 61 Harv.L.Rev. 958 (1948).

However, in 1953, almost on the eve of the 1954 revision, this stalemate ended when the Court of Appeals for the Sixth Circuit reversed the Tax Court and granted capital gains treatment to a classic bail-out transaction effected in 1946. Chamberlin v. Commissioner, 207 F.2d 462 (6th Cir. 1953). The case involved a preferred stock dividend by a prosperous close corporation which had previously arranged with an insurance company to purchase the preferred from the stockholders and had in fact tailored the terms of the preferred to meet the specifications of the insurance company. The Commissioner contended that the preferred stock dividend was taxable; but the court concluded that under the Supreme Court cases the dividend of preferred on common was non-taxable and neither the purpose to sell the dividend stock nor the actual sale changed that result.

Obviously, the result in Chamberlin made the bail-out area a matter of high priority in the 1954 revision. The following is an excellent analysis of the problem and some of the possible methods of dealing with it, directed toward the American Law Institute Federal Tax Statute proposal, which in material terms was much like the treatment ultimately adopted in the 1954 Code.

COHEN, SURREY, TARLEAU AND WARREN, A TECHNICAL REVISION OF THE FEDERAL INCOME TAX TREATMENT * OF CORPORATE DISTRIBUTIONS TO STOCKHOLDERS

52 Col.L.Rev. 9–14 (1952).

2. **Common Stock Dividend on Common Stock.** One possible course of revision, frequently urged, is that all stock dividends be made taxable as ordinary income. The shareholder is receiving an item which, it may be assumed, represents accumulated corporate profits, and it is therefore urged that the time of receipt is an appropriate point at which to impose the tax. The shareholder's basic investment is represented in his original shares and any reckoning of gain or loss on the investment, as distinguished from interim receipts of corporate profits as dividend income, can await the disposition of the original shares. This all-out approach meets its first obstacle, however, in the case of a common stock dividend issued on identical common stock. It can here be contended that mere receipt of additional pieces of identical paper hardly warrants a policy decision to impose a tax on their value. Furthermore, corporate reasons for this kind of stock dividend, such as the easier marketability of lower-value stock, a wider distribution of stock, or a lower dividend rate, are usually not such as to lead to shareholder taxation.[36] More important, for policy purposes can issuance of a stock dividend be sufficiently distinguished from a split-up of stock? The corporate reasons which lead to the choice between dividend and split-up do not seem relevant to the decision to tax

*. Reprinted by permission of the Columbia Law Review. Most of the footnotes omitted.

36. Where the stock dividend is an annual affair, replacing *pro tanto* a regular cash dividend, the argument for taxability is stronger. The text deals principally with those stock dividends which represent a significant change in the capital structure. Since establishment of a dividing line between the two is impractical, the treatment of the annual stock dividend must follow that accorded to the stock dividends discussed in the text.

in the one case and not in the other. If the capitalization of earnings is relied on as a basis of distinction between stock dividends and split-ups, would it not become necessary under such a policy to impose a tax on the shareholder when there is a capitalization of earnings without any distribution of stock? Moreover, a decision to tax the stock dividend probably would lead to all split-ups and no stock dividends.

Finally, the ordinary income-capital gain issue is not really present. True, if not taxed on receipt the stockholder can later sell his stock dividend and obtain capital gain treatment for the increase in value of his investment resulting from the capitalized corporate earnings. But under accepted principles he can achieve the same result by selling a part of his original stock if no stock dividend has been distributed. Since in both cases he is altering his basic position with respect to voting power and participation in earnings and assets, the stock-dividend-and-sale transaction is more akin to a sale of stock than to receipt of a cash dividend. In short, any statutory revision should leave untaxed a dividend of common stock identical with the common stock on which it is distributed. Such an "identical pieces of paper" standard would not be difficult to apply.

3. **Preferred Stock Dividends.** The next area involves the receipt of a dividend in stock that is different from the stock on which it is distributed. Consider the distribution of a preferred stock dividend on common stock, with no other stock outstanding. Here the arguments leading to non-taxation of a dividend in identical stock are not applicable. There is no problem of distinguishing between alternative corporate courses of conduct, as in the split-up case. Further, a definite ordinary income-capital gain issue is present. Suppose the shareholder sells the preferred stock dividend. How should the cash so obtained be taxed? He still has his voting control and his residual interest in earnings and assets. The cash represents capitalized corporate earnings and is in reality a cash return on the investment which he retains. If he is accorded capital gain treatment he can in effect convert ordinary income into capital gain. While in the sale case cash has not left the corporation, earnings have been capitalized in the preferred stock issue and the shareholder does have cash in his hands. Is the situation appreciably different from a distribution of cash to the shareholder, taxable as ordinary income, followed by an issue of preferred stock in exchange for cash? Once the preferred is redeemed, is the result materially different from a distribution of a cash dividend without any preferred stock in the picture? Or, suppose the shareholder later sells the preferred stock, not to an outside buyer, but to the corporation itself. Here also is the net result significantly different from a simple cash distribution?

It has been urged that these considerations point to treating as a taxable dividend a distribution of preferred stock on common stock when only common stock was previously outstanding. If we followed this course, we would end with a revision under which all stock dividends would be taxable upon receipt except for the "identical pieces of paper" common stock dividend on common stock already discussed. The rule would be fairly simple, and would eliminate improper capital gain advantage in the stock dividend area.

It would probably eliminate preferred stock dividends too. The high individual income tax rates would make such distributions far too expensive in most cases. Whether this result is desirable depends in part on whether there are business or family uses of the preferred stock dividend mechanism which are entitled to recognition in the determination of tax policy. But before we consider this question, we should note that the main argument for taxability is premised on the consequences of a sale by the shareholder, whether to other persons or to the corporation itself by way of redemption. Suppose, however, that the shareholder does not sell his dividend stock, but instead retains it or disposes of it in another fashion. If the danger is that the profit from a sale may be treated as capital gain, then a tax imposed at the time of receipt of the dividend stock may be quite wide of the mark if there exist future desirable courses of conduct other than sale. Stated differently, it can be argued that mere receipt of the preferred stock dividend is not an appropriate occasion for imposing the tax. The shareholder has two pieces of paper in place of one, but he possesses no greater interest than he had before, other than the power now to move on to a tax advantage through a sale. Until he so moves, is the potentiality enough to warrant treating the receipt of the dividend as the occasion for taxing the shareholder on the profits of the corporation? It must not be overlooked that the dividend is not in cash and, while a non-cash receipt may obviously be income, in such a situation it is necessary to consider whether it is proper policy to impose on a non-cash receipt a tax that must be paid in cash. We thus should consider whether there are sound business or family needs served by the preferred stock dividend.

It is urged that these needs exist in several family and business arrangements which occur rather frequently. Suppose a father owns all the common stock of a family corporation. He desires on retirement or death to leave the ownership to his children, but in so doing would like to have his sons run the business while his daughters obtain a more secure interest without participating in management. A preferred stock dividend would solve his problem, since he could then leave the common stock to the sons and the preferred stock to the daughters. Such a rearrangement of family ownership does not appear to give the family an unfair tax advantage. Yet a tax on the father's receipt of the dividend, urged because he might gain an advantage through sale of the dividend, would prevent issuance of the preferred stock and consummation of the arrangement, although it did not involve a sale of the preferred stock. To take another example, the sole shareholder may desire to transfer the active management and an equity interest to junior executives. In order both to reduce the price of the common stock so as to enable them to purchase it and to obtain an investment interest for himself, he has the corporation distribute a preferred stock dividend. He then retains the preferred stock and sells the common stock to the junior executives.

These two situations indicate that a preferred stock dividend has uses which are not dependent on a sale of the preferred stock. There may be other such desirable arrangements, or at least other arrangements which the tax laws need not discourage. Most of these would involve a closely-held or family corporation, though on occasion a widely-held company does declare a preferred stock dividend. While the latter type of corporation probably would not experience any serious disadvantage if the tax law in effect prevented preferred stock dividends, planning for the closely-held family corporation would be handicapped in some situations, perhaps seriously. If possible, therefore, a revision should seek not to impede distribution of preferred stock dividends, while at the same time preventing the occurrence of undesirable tax consequences on a sale of the preferred stock. These two objectives can be satisfied by not taxing the preferred stock dividend at the time of receipt, but taxing as ordinary income the amount obtained on a sale if the common stock shareholder does in fact sell the preferred stock. Action by the shareholder involving neither a sale nor a redemption by the corporation would thus permit him to stay clear of ordinary income consequences.[40]   . . .

B.   CURRENT LAW—RECEIPT OF STOCK DIVIDENDS

The 1969 Act substantially rewrote § 305 to greatly expand the taxability of stock dividends; in terms somewhat reminescent of the pre-1954 law, the new provisions aimed principally at cases of disproportionate distributions among stockholders, as, for example, when some stockholders receive stock and others receive cash or other property, or some receive preferred stock while others receive common stock. Pursuant to an extremely complex set of transitional rules, the disproportionate distribution rules of § 305(b)(2) will in many cases be inapplicable until 1991 with regard to distributions

---

40. The existence of preferred stock in the hands of others does not alter these conclusions. The reasons developed in the text for not taxing the preferred stock dividend on its receipt are unaffected by the fact that preferred stock is already outstanding.

on stock outstanding on January 10, 1969 (the date on which the Treasury had promulgated new regulations under § 305 which had somewhat presaged the path ultimately taken by the 1969 legislation), or April 22, 1969, in cases to which those 1969 regulations would not have applied.

The 1969 changes in the law were explained in the accompanying Senate Report (Sen.Rep.No.91–552, 91st Cong., 1st Sess. 150–154) as follows:

L. STOCK DIVIDENDS

(Sec. 421 of the bill and secs. 301 and 305 of the code)

Present law.—In its simplest form, a stock dividend is commonly thought of as a mere readjustment of the stockholder's interest, and not as income. For example, if a corporation with only common stock outstanding issues more common stock as a dividend, no basic change is made in the position of the corporation and its stockholders. No corporate assets are paid out, and the distribution merely gives each stockholder more pieces of paper to represent the same interest in the corporation.

On the other hand, stock dividends may also be used in a way that alters the interests of the stockholders. For example, if a corporation with only common stock outstanding declares a dividend payable at the election of each stockholder, either in additional common stock or in cash, the stockholder who receives a stock dividend is in the same position as if he received a taxable cash dividend and purchased additional stock with the proceeds. His interest in the corporation is increased relative to the interests of stockholders who took dividends in cash.

Present law (sec. 305(a)) provides that if a corporation pays a dividend to its shareholders in its own stock (or in rights to acquire its stock), the shareholders are not required to include the value of the dividend in income. There are two exceptions to this general rule. First, stock dividends paid in discharge of preference dividends for the current or immediately preceding taxable year are taxable. Second, a stock dividend is taxable if any shareholder may elect to receive his dividend in cash or other property instead of stock.

These provisions were enacted as part of the Internal Revenue Code of 1954. Before 1954 the taxability of stock dividends was determined under the "proportionate interest test," which developed out of a series of Supreme Court cases, beginning with Eisner v. Macomber, 252 U.S. 189 (1920). In these cases the Court held, in general, that a stock dividend was taxable if it increased any shareholder's proportionate interest in the corporation. The lower courts often had difficulty in applying the test as formulated in these cases, particularly where unusual corporate capital structures were involved.

Soon after the proportionate interest test was eliminated in the 1954 Code, corporations began to develop methods by which shareholders could, in effect, be given a choice between receiving cash dividends or increasing their proportionate interests in the corporation in much the same way as if they had received cash dividends and reinvested them in the corporation. The earliest of these methods involves dividing the common stock of the corporation into two classes, A and B. The two classes share equally in earnings and profits and in assets on liquidation. The only difference is that the class A stock pays only stock dividends and class B stock pays only cash dividends. The market value of the stock dividends paid on the class A stock is equated annually to the cash dividends paid on the class B stock. Class A stock may be converted into class B stock at any time. The stockholders can choose, either when the classes are established, when they purchase new stock, or through the convertibility option whether to own class A stock or class B stock.

In 1956, the Treasury Department issued proposed regulations which treated such arrangements as taxable (under sec. 305(b)(2)) as distributions subject to an election by the stockholder to receive cash instead of stock. In recent years, however, increasingly complex and sophisticated variations of this basic arrangement have been created. In some of these arrangements, the proportionate interest of one class of shareholders is increased even though no actual distribution of stock is made. This effect may be achieved, for example, by paying cash dividends on common stock and increasing by a corresponding amount the ratio at which convertible preferred stock or convertible debentures may be converted into common stock. Another method of achieving this result is a systematic periodic redemption plan, under which a small percentage, such as 5 percent, of each shareholder's stock may be redeemed annually at his election. Shareholders who do not choose to have their stock redeemed automatically increase their proportionate interest in the corporation.

On January 10, 1969, the Internal Revenue Service issued final regulations (T.D. 6990) under which a number of methods of achieving the effect of a cash dividend to some shareholders and a corresponding increase in the proportionate interest of other shareholders are brought under the exceptions in section 305(b), with the result that shareholders who receive increases in proportionate interest are treated as receiving taxable distributions.

General reasons for change.—The final regulations issued on January 10, 1969, do not cover all of the arrangements by which cash dividends can be paid to some shareholders and other shareholders can be given corresponding increases in proportionate interest. For example, the periodic redemption plan described above is not covered by the regulations, and the committee believes it is not covered by the present statutory language (of sec. 305(b) (2)).

Methods have also been devised to give preferred stockholders the equivalent of dividends on preferred stock which are not taxable as such under present law. For example, a corporation may issue preferred stock for $100 per share which pays no dividends, but which may be redeemed in 20 years for $200. The effect is the same as if the corporation distributed preferred stock equal to 5 percent of the original stock each year during the 20-year period in lieu of cash dividends. The committee believes that dividends paid on preferred stock should be taxed whether they are received in cash or in another form, such as stock, rights to receive stock, or rights to receive an increased amount on redemption. Moreover, the committee believes that dividends on preferred stock should be taxed to the recipients whether they are attributable to the current or immediately preceding taxable year or to earlier taxable years.

Explanation of provisions.—The bill continues (in sec. 305(b) (1)) the provision of present law that a stock dividend is taxable if it is payable at the election of any shareholder in property instead of stock.

The bill provides (in sec. 305(b) (2)) that if there is a distribution or series of distributions of stock which has the result of the receipt of cash or other property by some shareholders and an increase in the proportionate interests of other shareholders in the assets or earnings and profits of the corporation, the shareholders receiving stock are to be taxable (under sec. 301).

For example, if a corporation has two classes of common stock, one paying regular cash dividends and the other paying corresponding stock dividends (whether in common or preferred stock), the stock dividends are to be taxable.

On the other hand, if a corporation has a single class of common stock and a class of preferred stock which pays cash dividends and is not convertible, and it distributes a pro rata common stock dividend with respect to its common stock, the stock distribution is not taxable because the distribution does not have the result of increasing the proportionate interests of any of the stockholders.

In determining whether there is a disproportionate distribution, any security convertible into stock or any right to acquire stock is to be treated as outstanding stock. For example, if a corporation has common stock and convertible debentures outstanding, and it pays interest on the convertible debentures and stock dividends on the common stock, there is a disproportionate distribution, and the stock dividends are to be taxable (under section 301). In addition, in determining whether there is a disproportionate distribution with respect to a shareholder, each class of stock is to be considered separately.

The committee has added two provisions to the House bill (secs. 305(b) (3) and (4)) which carry out more explicitly the intention of the House with regard to distributions of common and preferred stock on common stock, and stock distributions on preferred stock. The first of these provides that if a distribution or series of distributions has the result of the receipt of preferred stock by some common shareholders and the receipt of common stock by other common shareholders, all of the shareholders are taxable (under sec. 301) on the receipt of the stock.

The second of the provisions added by the committee (sec. 305 (b) (4)) provides that distributions of stock with respect to preferred stock are taxable (under sec. 301). This provision applies to all distributions on preferred stock except increases in the conversion ratio of convertible preferred stock made solely to take account of stock dividends or stock splits with respect to the stock into which the convertible stock is convertible.

The bill provides (in section 305(b) (5)) that a distribution of convertible preferred stock is taxable (under sec. 301) unless it is established to the satisfaction of the Secretary or his delegate that it will not have the result of a disproportionate distribution described above. For example, if a corporation makes a pro rata distribution on its common stock of preferred stock convertible into common stock at a price slightly higher than the market price of the common stock on the date of distribution, and the period during which the stock must be converted is 4 months, it is likely that a distribution would have the result of a disproportionate distribution. Those stockholders who wish to increase their interests in the corporation would convert their stock into common stock at the end of the 4-month period, and those stockholders who wish to receive cash would sell their stock or have it redeemed. On the other hand, if the stock were convertible for a period of 20 years from the date of issuance, there would be a likelihood that substantially all of the stock would be converted into common stock, and there would be no change in the proportionate interest of the common shareholders.

The bill provides (in sec. 305(c)) that under regulations prescribed by the Secretary or his delegate, a change in conversion ratio, a change in redemption price, a difference between redemption price and issue price, a redemption treated as a section 301 distribution, or any transaction (including a recapitalization) having a similar effect on the interest of any shareholder is to be treated as a distribution with respect to each shareholder whose proportionate interest is thereby increased. The purpose of this provision is to give the Secretary authority to deal with transactions that have the effect of distributions, but in which stock is not actually distributed.

The proportionate interest of a shareholder can be increased not only by the payment of a stock dividend not paid to other shareholders, but by such methods as increasing the ratio at which his stock, convertible securities, or rights to stock may be converted into other stock, by decreasing the ratio at which other stock, convertible securities, or rights to stock can be converted into stock of the class he owns, or by the periodic redemption of stock owned by other shareholders. It is not clear under present law to what extent increases of this kind would be considered distributions of stock or rights to stock. In order to eliminate uncertainty, the committee has authorized the Secretary or his delegate to prescribe regulations governing the extent to which such transactions shall be treated as taxable distributions.

For example, if a corporation has a single class of common stock which pays no dividends and a class of preferred stock which pays regular cash dividends, and which is convertible into the common stock at a conversion ratio that decreases each year to adjust for the payment of the cash dividends on the preferred stock, it is anticipated that the regulations will provide in appropriate circumstances that the holders of the common stock will be treated as receiving stock in a disproportionate distribution (under sec. 305(b) (2)).

It is anticipated that the regulations will establish rules for determining when and to what extent the automatic increase in proportionate interest accruing to stockholders as a result of redemptions under a periodic redemption plan are to be treated as taxable distributions. A periodic redemption plan may exist, for example, where a corporation agrees to redeem a small percentage of each common shareholder's stock annually at the election of the shareholder. The shareholders whose stock is redeemed receive cash, and the shareholders whose stock is not redeemed receive an automatic increase in their proportionate interests. However, the committee does not intend that this regulatory authority is to be used to bring isolated redemptions of stock under the disproportionate distribution rule (of sec. 305(b) (2)). For example, a 30 percent stockholder would not be treated as receiving a constructive dividend because a 70 percent stockholder causes a corporation to redeem 15 percent of its stock from him.

The provision giving the Secretary authority to treat certain transactions as distributions (sec. 305(c)) also applies to distributions on preferred stock. For example, assume that a corporation issues preferred stock convertible into its common stock, and that the preferred stock pays no cash dividends, but the ratio at which it may be converted into common stock increases annually by a specified percentage. It is anticipated that the regulations will provide that the change in conversion ratio in such a case constitutes a taxable distribution of a right to acquire stock. Similarly, a corporation may issue preferred stock which pays no cash dividends, but which may be redeemed after a specified period of time at a price higher than the issue price. It is anticipated that, unless the increase is a reasonable call premium, it will be treated under the regulations as constructively received by the stockholder over the period during which the preferred stock cannot be called for redemption.

It is anticipated that the regulations will provide that if preferred stockholders are given stock in a recapitalization, or an increase in proportionate interest by means of a constructive distribution, as payment of current dividends or dividend arrearages, sec. 305(b) (4) is to apply whether or not the recapitalization or other transaction is an isolated transaction. Thus, if in a recapitalization preferred stockholders are given additional preferred stock in satisfaction of several years dividend arrearages, the distribution of the additional stock will be taxable (under sec. 301).

* * *

Effective date.—This amendment is to apply to distributions (or deemed distributions) made or considered as made after January 10, 1969, in taxable years ending after that date.

The amendment is not to apply to a distribution (or deemed distribution) made before January 1, 1991, with respect to stock outstanding on January 10, 1969, or issued pursuant to a contract binding on January 10, 1969, on the distributing corporation. A contract is considered binding on the distributing corporation on January 10, 1969, if it is binding on the management of the distributing corporation on that date, even though necessary stockholder approval is obtained later.

* * *

Under the House bill, shareholders of corporations to which the transitional rule applies would be taxable on stock dividends paid on stock issues after January 10, 1969, even if the new stock was issued as a dividend on stock to which the transitional rule applies. Under the committee amendments, the transitional rule also applies to additional stock, whether sold or distributed as stock dividends, if the new stock is of the class of stock having the largest fair market value of all the classes of stock subject to the transitional rule. (This would normally be common stock of the corporation.) It also applies to stock received as dividends on stock to which the transitional rule applies.

Under the committee amendments, the transitional rule ceases to apply if at any time after October 8, 1969, the corporation issues any stock (other than in a distribution with respect to stock of the same class) which is not—

(a) nonconvertible preferred stock;

(b) additional stock of the class of stock having the largest fair market value of the classes of stock subject to the transitional rule;

(c) preferred stock convertible into the class of stock referred to in (b), if it has full antidilution protection.

* * *

Here is an example of §305(c) in action, followed by an important ruling on the valuation of preferred stock received in a recapitalization:

REVENUE RULING 83-119
1983-33 Int. Rev. Bull. 6.

ISSUE

In a recapitalization where a corporation issues preferred stock that must be redeemed on the holder's death at the price in excess of one hundred and ten percent of the issue price, is the amount of the excess redemption premium treated, by reason of section 305(c) of the Internal Revenue Code, as a distribution with respect to preferred stock within the meaning of section 305(b)(4)? If so, when is this distribution deemed to be received?

FACTS

A domestic corporation, X, had outstanding 100 shares of common stock. A owned 80 shares of the X common stock and B, A's child, owned the other 20 shares. A was actively engaged in X's business as its president, and B was a key employee. A retired from the business and resigned as a director, officer, and employee of X with no intention to take part in the future activities of X. Pur-

suant to a plan of recapitalization for the purpose of transferring control and ownership of the common stock to B in conjunction with A's retirement, a single class of nonvoting, dividend paying preferred stock (as defined in section 1.305-5(a) of the Income Tax Regulations) was authorized. There are no redemption provisions with regard to the preferred stock, except that on the death of a shareholder of the preferred stock, X is required to redeem the preferred stock from the shareholder's estate or beneficiaries at its par value of 1,000x dollars per share. On January 1, 1981, A had a life expectancy of 24 years determined by using the actuarial tables provided in section 1.72-9 of the regulations. On January 1, 1981, A exchanged 80 shares of common stock for 80 shares of preferred stock. Following this exchange, A held all of the preferred stock, and B held all of the common stock that X then had outstanding.

On the date of the exchange the X common stock surrendered had a fair market value of $1,000x dollars per share, and the X preferred stock had a par value of $1,000$x dollars per share. The one-for-one exchange ratio resulted because the par value of the preferred stock was presumed to represent its fair market value. However, the fair market value of the preferred stock was only 600x dollars per share. See Rev. Rul. 83-118, page 5, this Bulletin, for factors taken into account in valuing common and preferred stock. Thus, A surrendered X common stock with a fair market value of 80,000x dollars (80 × 1,000x dollars) in exchange for X preferred stock with a fair market value of 48,000x dollars (80 × 600x dollars).

The exchange of all of A's X common stock for X preferred stock is a recapitalization within the meaning of section 368(a)(1)(E) of the Code. Under section 354, no gain or loss will be recognized to A with regard to the receipt of the preferred stock to the extent of its 48,000x dollars fair market value. However, the 32,000x dollars excess in the fair market value of the X common stock surrendered by A as compared to the fair market value of the preferred stock A received will be treated as having been used to make a gift, pay compensation, satisfy obligations of any kind, or for whatever purposes the facts indicate. Section 356(f) of the Code and Rev. Rul. 74-269, 1974-1 C.B. 87.

LAW AND ANALYSIS

Section 305(a) of the Code provides generally that gross income does not include the amount of any distribution of the stock of a corporation made by such corporation to its shareholders with respect to its stock, except as otherwise provided in section 305(b) or (c).

Section 305(b)(4) of the Code provides, in part, that section 305(a) will not apply to a distribution by a corporation of its stock, and the distribution will be treated as a distribu-

tion of property to which section 301 applies, if the distribution is with respect to preferred stock.

Section 305(c) of the Code provides, in part, that the Secretary shall prescribe regulations under which a difference between issue price and redemption price will be treated as a distribution with respect to any shareholder whose proportionate interest in the earnings and profits or assets of the corporation is increased by the transaction. Section 1.305-7(a) of the regulations provides, under the authority of section 305(c), that an unreasonable redemption premium on preferred stock will be treated in accordance with section 1.305-5.

Section 1.305-5(b)(1) of the regulations provides that if a corporation issues preferred stock which may be redeemed after a specific period of time at a price higher than the issue price, the difference will be considered under the authority of section 305(c) of the Code to be distribution of additional stock on preferred stock (section 305(b)(4)) constructively received by the shareholder over the period of time during which the preferred stock cannot be called for redemption. However, section 1.305-5(b)(2) states that section 1.305-5(b)(1) will not apply to the extent that the difference between issue price and redemption price is a reasonable redemption premium, and that a redemption premium will be considered reasonable if it is in the nature of a penalty for the premature redemption of the preferred stock and if such premium does not exceed the amount the corporation would be required to pay for the right to make such premature redemption under market conditions existing at the time of issuance. Section 1.305(b)(2) also states that a redemption premium not in excess of 10 percent of the issue price on stock which is not redeemable for five years from the date of issuance shall be considered reasonable.

Section 1.305-7(a) of the regulations provides, in part, that a change in conversion ratio, a change in redemption price, a difference between redemption price and issue price, a redemption which is treated as a distribution to which section 301 applies, or any transaction (including a recapitalization) having a similar effect on the interest of any shareholder will be treated as a distribution to which sections 305(b) and 301 apply if (1) the proportionate interest of any shareholder in the earnings and profits or assets of the corporation deemed to have made such distribution is increased by such transaction, and (2) such distribution has the result described in paragraph (2), (3), (4), or (5) of section 305(b).

Section 1.305-3(e), Example (12), of the regulations illustrates a situation where section 305 does not apply to exchanges of stock in a recapitalization that is a "single and isolated transaction". However, section 1.305-7(c)(1) of the regulations provides that a recapitalization, whether or not an isolated transaction, will be deemed to result in a distribution to which section 305(c) of the Code and section 1.305-7 of the regulations apply, if, among other things, it is pursuant to a plan to periodically increase a shareholder's proportionate interest in the assets or earnings and profits of the corporation.

One element which is necessary to taxability under sections 305(b) and (c) is that there must be a distribution. Regarding this requirement, section 305(b) deals with actual distributions, and section 305(c) deems certain transactions which are not actual distributions to be distributions for section 305 purposes. Certain recapitalizations, even if isolated, are treated as distributions under regulations section 1.305-7(c). That is, an actual exchange of stock, even

though clearly isolated, can be treated as a distribution if the exchange is pursuant to a larger plan to periodically increase a shareholder's proportionate interest. Section 1.305-5(c) of the regulations provides, "For rules for applying sections 305(b)(4) and 305(c) to recapitalizations, see section 1.305-7(c)". This means that section 1.305-7(c) of the regulations is the rule used to impose section 305(b)(4) and (c) of the Code on an exchange of stock which qualifies as a recapitalization. However, it does not mean that section 1.305-7(c) must be found to be applicable to a transaction in order for any deemed distribution which may result from the transaction to be subject to section 305(b)(4) and (c) and the regulations thereunder.

Although an exchange of stock in an isolated recapitalization would not in itself result in section 305(b) and (c) applicability, the terms of the preferred stock used in the exchange may result in this applicability. The difference between issue price and redemption price (section 1.305-7(a) of the regulations) and the fact that the stock cannot be called for redemption for a specific period of time (section 1.305-5(b) of the regulations) are the factors which combine to produce a deemed distribution. The imposition of tax results from the deemed distribution of additional preferred stock over the period the stock cannot be called or presented for redemption.

Section 1.305-5(d), Example (7), of the regulations describes the proper treatment of preferred stock issued pro rata to the holders of a corporation's common stock. The fair market value of the preferred stock immediately after its issuance was $50x$ dollars. The preferred stock is redeemable at the end of five years for

105x dollars per share. There is no evidence that a call premium in excess of 5x dollars per share is reasonable. The 50x dollars excess of the call premium (55x dollars) minus the deemed reasonable premium (5x dollars) is considered to be a distribution of additional stock on preferred stock to which sections 305(b)(4) and 301 of the Code apply. This 50x dollar excess is considered to be distributed to the shareholders ratably over the five year period.

In the present situation, X common stock was exchanged by A for X preferred stock. Since the exchange was not part of a plan to periodically increase a shareholder's proportionate interest, the recapitalization itself did not result in a deemed distribution. However, the preferred stock will be redeemed by X on the death of a shareholder at a price of 1,000x dollars per share. Since the preferred stock had a fair market value of 600x dollars per share on the date of issuance, the preferred stock has a redemption premium of 400x dollars per share. There is no evidence that a call premium in excess of 60x dollars was reasonable. Because (1) the X stock is closely held, (2) no public offerings are planned, (3) the X stock is held by members of a family group within the meaning of section 318(a), and (4) the stock is not readily marketable, it is presumed that, at the time of the exchange, the shareholders intended that A would not transfer the preferred stock, and, therefore, redemption would occur upon A's death. Although the exact duration of A's life is not yet known, A's life is "a specified period of time" within the meaning of section 1.305-5(b)(1) of the regulations. Because A has a life expectancy of 24 years, the 400x dollar redemption premium on the X preferred stock has substantially the same effect as a 400x dollar redemption premium payable at the end of a fixed term of 24 years.

HOLDING

The recapitalization in which X issues X preferred stock that must be redeemed on the shareholder's death at a price (1,000x dollars) which exceeds the issue price (600x dollars) results in the recipient, A, being deemed to receive a distribution of additional stock with respect to preferred stock, within the meaning of section 305(b)(4) of the Code, by reason of section 305(c), in the amount of 340x dollars (400x dollars less a deemed reasonable redemption premium of 60x dollars) on each share of preferred stock. This amount will be constructively received ratably (14.16x dollars per share per year) over A's life expectancy of 24 years, and will be treated as a distribution to which section 301 applies. If A should die earlier, any part of the 340x dollars per share not yet constructively received by A would be deemed received at the time of A's death.

REVENUE RULING 8 3–120
1983–33 Int. Rev. Bull. 8.

SECTION 1. PURPOSE

The purpose of this Revenue Ruling is to amplify Rev. Rul. 59-60, 1959-1 C.B. 237, by specifying additional factors to be considered in valuing common and preferred stock of a closely held corporation for gift tax and other purposes in a recapitalization of closely held businesses. This type of valuation problem frequently arises with respect to estate planning transactions wherein an individual receives preferred stock with a stated par value equal to all or a large portion of the fair market value of the individual's former stock interest in a corporation. The individual also receives common stock which is then transferred, usually as a gift, to a relative.

Sec. 2. BACKGROUND

.01 One of the frequent objectives of the type of transaction mentioned above is the transfer of the potential appreciation of an individual's stock interest in a corporation to relatives at a nominal or small gift tax cost. Achievement of this objective requires preferred stock having a fair market value equal to a large part of the fair market value of the individual's former stock interest and common stock having a nominal or small fair market value. The approach and factors described in this Revenue Ruling are directed toward ascertaining the true fair market value of the common and preferred stock and will usually result in the determination of a substantial fair market value for the common stock and a fair market value for the preferred stock which is substantially less than its par value.

.02 The type of transaction referred to above can arise in many different contexts. Some examples are:

(a) *A* owns 100% of the common stock (the only outstanding stock) of *Z* Corporation which has a fair market value of 10,500x. In a recapitalization described in section 368(a)(1)(E), *A* receives preferred stock with a par value of 10,000x and new common stock, which *A* then transfers to *A*'s son *B*.

(b) *A* owns some of the stock of *Z* Corporation (or the stock of several corporations) the fair market value of which stock is 10,500x. *A* transfers this stock to a new corporation *X* in exchange for preferred stock of *X* corporation with a par value of 10,000x and common stock of *X* corporation, which *A* then transfers to *A*'s son *B*.

(c) *A* owns 80 shares and his son *B* owns 20 shares of the common stock (the only stock outstanding) of *Z* Corporation. In a recapital-

ization described in section 368(a)(1)(E). *A* exchanges his 80 shares of common stock for 80 shares of new preferred stock of *Z* Corporation with a par value of 10,000x. *A*'s common stock had a fair market value of 10,000x.

SEC. 3. GENERAL APPROACH TO VALUATION

Under section 25.2512-2(f)(2) of the Gift Tax Regulations, the fair market value of stock in a closely held corporation depends upon numerous factors, including the corporation's net worth, its prospective earning power, and its capacity to pay dividends. In addition, other relevant factors must be taken into account. *See* Rev. Rul. 59-60. The weight to be accorded any evidentiary factor depends on the circumstances of each case. *See* section 25.2512-2(f) of the Gift Tax Regulations.

SEC. 4. APPROACH TO VALUATION—PREFERRED STOCK

.01 In general the most important factors to be considered in determining the value of preferred stock are its yield, dividend coverage and protection of its liquidation preference.

.02 Whether the yield of the preferred stock supports a valuation of the stock at par value depends in part on the adequacy of the dividend rate. The adequacy of the dividend rate should be determined by comparing its dividend rate with the dividend rate of high-grade publicly traded preferred stock. A lower yield than that of high-grade preferred stock indicates a preferred stock value of less than par. If the rate of interest charged by independent creditors to the corporation on loans is higher than the rate such independent creditors charge their most credit worthy borrowers, then the yield on the preferred stock should be correspondingly higher than the yield on high quality preferred stock. A yield which is not correspondingly higher reduces the value of the preferred stock. In addition, whether the preferred stock has a fixed dividend rate and is non-participating influences the value of the preferred stock. A publicly traded preferred stock for a company having a similar business and similar assets with similar liquidation preferences, voting rights and other similar terms would be the ideal comparable for determining yield required in arms length transactions for closely held stock. Such ideal comparables will frequently not exist. In such circumstances, the most comparable publicly-traded issues should be selected for comparison and appropriate adjustments made for differing factors.

.03 The actual dividend rate on a preferred stock can be assumed to be its stated rate if the issuing corporation will be able to pay its stated dividends in a timely manner and will, in fact, pay such dividends. The risk that the corporation may be unable to timely pay the stated dividends on the preferred stock can be measured by the coverage of such stated dividends by the corporation's earnings. Coverage of the dividend is measured by the ratio of the sum of pre-tax and pre-interest earnings to the sum of the total interest to be paid and the pre-tax earnings needed to pay the after-tax dividends. *Standard & Poor's Ratings Guide*, 58 (1979). Inadequate coverage exists where a decline in corporate profits would be likely to jeopardize the corporation's ability to pay dividends on the preferred stock. The ratio for the preferred stock in question should be compared with the ratios for high quality preferred stock to determine whether the preferred stock has adequate coverage. Prior earnings history is important in this determination. Inadequate coverage indicates that the value of preferred stock is lower than its par value. Moreover, the absence of a provision that preferred dividends are cumulative raises substantial questions concerning whether the stated dividend rate will, in fact, be paid. Accordingly, preferred stock with noncumulative dividend features will normally have a value substantially lower than a cumulative preferred stock with the same yield, liquidation preference and dividend coverage.

.04 Whether the issuing corporation will be able to pay the full liquidation preference at liquidation must be taken into account in determining fair market value. This risk can be measured by the protection afforded by the corporation's net assets. Such protection can be measured by the ratio of the excess of the current market value of the corporation's assets over its liabilities to the aggregate liquidation preference. The protection ratio should be compared with the ratios for high quality preferred stock to determine adequacy of coverage. Inadequate asset protection exists where any unforeseen business reverses would be likely to jeopardize the corporation's ability to pay the full liquidation preference to the holders of the preferred stock.

.05 Another factor to be considered in valuing the preferred stock is whether it has voting rights and, if so, whether the preferred stock has voting control. See, however, Section 5.02 below.

.06 Peculiar covenants or provisions of the preferred stock of a type not ordinarily found in publicly traded preferred stock should be carefully evaluated to determine the effects of such covenants on the value of the preferred stock. In general, if covenants would inhibit the marketability of the stock or the power of the holder to enforce dividend or liquidation rights, such provisions will reduce the value of the preferred stock by comparison to the value of preferred stock not containing such convenants or provisions.

.07 Whether the preferred stock contains a redemption privilege is another factor to be considered in determining the value of the preferred stock. The value of a redemption privilege triggered by death of the preferred shareholder will not exceed the present value of the redemption premium payable at the preferred shareholder's death (i.e., the present value of the excess of the redemption price over the fair market value of the preferred stock upon its issuance). The value of the redemption privilege should be reduced to reflect any risk that the corporation may not possess sufficient assets to redeem its preferred stock at the stated redemption price. See .03 above.

SEC. 5. APPROACH TO VALUATION—COMMON STOCK

.01 If the preferred stock has a fixed rate of dividend and is nonparticipating, the common stock has the exclusive right to the benefits of future appreciation of the value of the corporation. This right is valuable and usually warrants a determination that the common stock has substantial value. The actual value of this right depends upon the corporation's past growth experience, the economic condition of the industry in which the corporation operates, and general economic conditions. The factor to be used in capitalizing the corpora-

tion's prospective earnings must be determined after an analysis of numerous factors concerning the corporation and the economy as a whole. *See* Rev. Rul. 59-60, at page 243. In addition, after-tax earnings of the corporation at the time the preferred stock is issued in excess of the stated dividends on the preferred stock will increase the value of the common stock. Furthermore, a corporate policy of reinvesting earnings will also increase the value of the common stock.

.02 A factor to be considered in determining the value of the common stock is whether the preferred stock also has voting rights. Voting rights of the preferred stock, especially if the preferred stock has voting control, could under certain circumstances increase the value of the preferred stock and reduce the value of the common stock. This factor may be reduced in significance where the rights of common stockholders as a class are protected under state law from actions by another class of shareholders, *see Singer v. Magnavox Co.*, 380 A.2d 969 (Del. 1977), particularly where the common shareholders, as a class, are given the power to disapprove a proposal to allow preferred stock to be converted into common stock. See ABA-ALI Model Bus. Corp. Act, Section 60 (1969).

C. CURRENT LAW—DISPOSITION OF DIVIDEND STOCK

1. THE OPERATION OF § 306

Section 306 represents the 1954 legislative response to the preferred stock dividend bail-out problem. The purpose and effect of this complex statutory pattern is described in the following excerpts from the Senate Finance Committee Report:

298

SENATE FINANCE COMMITTEE REPORT

S.Rep. No. 1622, 83d Cong., 2d Sess. 46, 242–245 (1945).

Your committee has also acted to close a possible loophole of existing law known as the "preferred stock bail-out". . . . Your committee's approach to this problem imposes a tax on the recipient of the dividend stock at the time of its sale. This dividend stock would be called "section 306 stock" and any stock received as a dividend would be section 306 stock to the extent of its allocable share of corporate earnings at the time of issuance, except common stock issued with respect to common stock.

The tax imposed at the time of the sale of the stock is at ordinary income rates to the extent of its allocable share of earnings and profits of the corporation at the time the stock dividend was declared. Any amount received for the section 306 stock which exceeds the earnings and profits attributable to it will be taxed as capital gain. If, instead of selling the section 306 stock, the shareholder redeems it, the proceeds received will be taxed as a dividend to the extent of corporate earnings at the time of redemption. . . . [C]ertain exceptions to this basic rule of ordinary income treatment with respect to dispositions of section 306 are provided. . . .

If the section 306 stock is sold the amount realized is treated as gain from the sale of property which is not a capital asset to the extent of the stock's ratable share of earnings and profits of the issuing corporation at the time of its distribution. Thus, assume that a shareholder owns 1,000 shares of the common stock of a corporation and that they are the only shares of its stock outstanding. Assume also that the shareholder acquires 1,000 shares of preferred stock with a fair market value for each share of $100 issued to him as a dividend on his common stock at a time when the corporation has $100,000 in accumulated earnings. There is no tax to the shareholder at the time of receipt of the stock but it is characterized as section 306 stock. If it is sold for $100,000 the shareholder will be taxed on the entire sale proceeds at the rates applicable to ordinary income.

The determination of the section 306 stock's ratable share of earnings at the time of its distribution is to be made in accordance with its fair market value at such time. It should also be noted that it would be immaterial that $100,000 were distributed to the stockholder as a dividend on his common stock subsequent to the distribution of the stock dividend. The stock dividend is nevertheless section 306 stock because of the corporate earnings in existence at the time of its distribution. A shareholder may, in such a case, only dispose of his section 306 stock through redemption by the issuing corporation and thereby avoid its inherent ordinary income characteristics. See discussion of paragraph (2) of subsection (a), below.

Subparagraph (B) of paragraph (1) provides that if the amount received from the sale of section 306 stock exceeds the amount treated as ordinary income, such excess shall, to the extent of gain, be accorded capital-gain treatment. Thus, if in the preceding example the stock had been sold for $110,000 (instead of $100,000) the $10,000 would be taxed at the rates applicable to capital gain.* Subparagraph (C) of paragraph (1) provides that in no event is any loss to be allowed with respect to the sale of section 306 stock.

Paragraph (2) of subsection (a) provides that if the section 306 stock is redeemed, the amount realized is to be treated as a distribution of property to which section 301 applies. Thus, if the section 306 stock was distributed at a time when there was an amount of corporate earnings attributable to it equal to its full fair market value at that time, but if there are no corporate earnings, accumulated or current, at the time of redemption, the amount received on redemption of section 306 stock would be treated under section 301 as a return of capital. No loss would be allowed in such a case under section 301.

It should be noted that where section 306 stock is redeemed the rules of section 302(a) and (b), relating to cases where amounts received in redemption of stock will be taxed at capital gain rates, are not applicable. Section 306 operates independently of section 302 and contains its own rules concerning instances where your committee does not consider it appropriate to tax proceeds received with respect to section 306 stock at the rates applicable to ordinary income.

* * *

Paragraph (4) of subsection (b) excepts from the general rule of subsection (a) those transactions not in avoidance of this section where it is established to the satisfaction of the Secretary that the transaction was not in pursuance of a plan having as one of its principal purposes the avoidance of Federal income tax. Subparagraph (A) of this paragraph applies to cases where the distribution itself, coupled with the disposition or redemption was not in pursuance of such a plan. This subparagraph is intended to apply to the case of dividends and isolated dispositions of section 306 stock by minority shareholders who do not in the aggregate have control of the distributing corporation. In such a case it would seem to your committee to be inappropriate to impute to such shareholders an intention to remove corporate earnings at the tax rates applicable only to capital gains.

Subparagraph (B) of subsection (b) (4) applies to a case where the shareholder has made a prior or simultaneous disposition (or redemption) of the underlying stock with respect to which the section 306 stock was issued. Thus if a shareholder received a distribution

---

* [Ed. note] This example seems to be in error since an appropriate portion of the shareholder's basis in the common stock should be allocated to the preferred stock and then offset against the $10,000.

of 100 shares of section 306 stock on his holdings of 100 shares of voting common stock in a corporation and sells his voting common stock before he disposes of his section 306 stock, the subsequent disposition of his section 306 stock would not ordinarily be considered a tax avoidance disposition since he has previously parted with the stock which allows him to participate in the ownership of the business. However, variations of the above example may give rise to tax avoidance possibilities which are not within the exception of subparagraph (B). Thus if a corporation has only one class of common stock outstanding and it issues stock under circumstances that characterize it as section 306 stock, a subsequent issue of a different class of common having greater voting rights than the original common will not permit a simultaneous disposition of the section 306 stock together with the original common to escape the rules of subsection (a) of section 306.

Section 306(c) sets forth the definition of section 306 stock. . . . [Section 306(c) (1) (C)] would remove from the category of section 306 stock, stock owned by a decedent at death since such stock takes a new basis under section 1014.

Paragraph (2) of subsection (c) excepts from the definition of section 306 stock any stock no part of the distribution of which would have been a dividend at the time of distribution if money had been distributed in lieu of the stock. Thus, preferred stock received at the time of original incorporation would not be section 306 stock. Also, stock issued at the time an existing corporation had no earnings and profits would not be section 306 stock.

Subsection (d) provides that stock rights shall be treated as stock for purposes of this section and if stock is acquired through the exercise of stock rights, such stock shall be treated as section 306 stock to the extent the rights themselves had the character of section 306 stock at the time of distribution.

---

2. SOME CURRENT § 306. ISSUES

One important question under §306 is whether in determining the amount taxable as ordinary income in the case of a sale of §306 stock the amount of earnings and profits are to be measured on the date of the distribution of the §306 stock or at the end of the year in which the distribution occurred. Most of the commentators seem to assume the former--and there are some implications that way in the regulations. Cf. Reg. § 1.306-3(a). On the other hand, the constructive cash dividend test in §306(a)(1)(A)(ii) would seem to import the general rule of §316, under which earnings and profits for the current year are measured at year-end. This view finds support in Example 1 in Reg. § 1.306-1(b)(2), which refers to the earnings and profits of a calendar year corporation on December 31 although the distribution of §306 stock occurred on December 15.

However, a 1978 change in the regulations under section 306 may have been designed to resolve this question. Prior to the change Reg. § 1.306-3(a) restated the exception to the definition of "section 306 stock" under section 306(c)(2) in terms of a proviso that "the distributing corporation has earnings and profits at the time of the distribution" of the stock, thus emphasizing the language of the caption to the statutory provision rather than the words of the statute itself. The 1978 amendment changed the wording of this regulation (and Reg. § 1.306-3(b) dealing with stock rights as well) to make qualification as "section 306 stock" turn on whether "a distribution of money by the distributing corporation in lieu of such stock would have been a dividend in whole or in part", thereby more precisely tracking the language of the statute. T.D. 7556, 78-9 CCH ¶6818, which promulgated this amendment to the regulations, does not contain any explanation for the change. However, the shift in language seems to have the consequence, and hence perhaps the objective, of making it clear that the test for section 306 stock looks to whether the corporation has any earnings and profits by the end of the year (just as in the case of a cash dividend), and not whether there are earnings and profits at the time of the distribution of the stock. This in turn would support the view that in determining the amount of ordinary income resulting under section 306(a) from a sale or other disposition of section 306 stock, what counts is the amount of the earnings and profits at the end of the year in which the stock was distributed, not the amount at the date of the distribution.

The observation in the Senate Finance Committee Report that the "taint" of section 306 stock is removed by the death of the holder, because of the step-up in basis under section 1014, is a bit cryptic: in the hands of the new taxpayer (the decedent's estate or other successor), the stock obviously does not meet either of the first two definitional requirements of section 306(c)(1), i.e., received as a stock dividend or in a reorganization; and the third possibility, a carryover basis from other section 306 stock, is precluded by the new basis at death. The flirtation in the late 1970's with a carryover basis at death raised a significant threat that death would not free stock from the reach of section 306 (and led to the addition of section 306(b)(5) to make sure that section 303, which provides capital gain for redemptions from estates in certain circumstances, would take precedence over section 306 if there was a conflict); but the traditional stepped-up basis at death seems now to be back in place for good.

Prior to the Tax Reform Act of 1969 it was possible to sidestep the "taint" on §306 stock by contributing the stock to a charitable organization. However, that loophole was eliminated by the amendment to §170(e)(1)(A) to provide that the deduction for a charitable contribution of property is reduced by the amount of ordinary income the taxpayer would have recognized if the contributed property had been sold for its fair market value.

Notice that although a sale of §306 stock may result in ordinary income, it is not "dividend" income. Accordingly, such provisions as the $100 dividend exclusion for individuals and the dividends-received deduction for corporations do not apply; and the earnings and profits of the corporation at the time of the sale are neither relevant to, nor reduced by, the taxation of ordinary income to the stockholders. On the other hand, redemption of §306 stock is subject to the dividend rules. Query whether there is anything in the policy of §306 which calls for this difference in treatment.

Section 306(c)(1)(A) turns on the interpretation of the term "common stock," but there is no general definition supplied by the Code or regulations. Common stock which is convertible into other than common stock is not "common stock," Reg. §1.306-3(f); and neither is stock redeemable at the option of the corporation at a price in excess of its book value. Rev. Rul. 57-132, 1957-1 Cum. Bull. 115. In addition, any preference possessed by a class of stock would presumably make it "other than common stock." But non-voting common stock qualifies, as the following ruling confirms (while providing some general illumination on the basic concept of "bailout" which underlies §306):

REVENUE RULING 76–387

1976–2 Cum.Bull. 96.

Advice has been requested whether, under the circumstances set forth below, the class A nonvoting common stock is "common stock" for purposes of section 306(c)(1)(B) of the Internal Revenue Code of 1954.

Corporation X had outstanding class A nonvoting common stock, class B voting common stock, and nonvoting preferred stock. The preferred stock was limited and preferred as to dividends, had no dividends in arrears, had a fixed liquidation preference, and was "section 306 stock" within the meaning of section 306(c) of the Code. Neither the class A nor the class B stock was limited or preferred with respect to dividends or distributions in liquidation and neither had a preference over the other in any respect. The only difference between the two classes of common stock was that the class B stock had voting rights while the class A stock did not. Neither the class A stock nor the class B stock was by its terms redeemable.

X desired to simplify its corporate structure by eliminating the preferred stock. Pursuant to a plan of recapitalization, the holders of the preferred stock exchanged such stock solely for shares of class A stock of equal value. The transaction qualified as a reorganization (recapitalization) under section 368(a)(1)(E) of the Code and no gain or loss was recognized to the exchanging shareholders pursuant to section 354. There was no intent to redeem the class A stock when the exchange was made.

Section 306(c)(1)(B) of the Code provides, in part, that "section 306 stock" is any stock, except common stock, that is received by a shareholder in exchange for other "section 306 stock" in pursuance of a plan of reorganization under section 368 with respect to the receipt of which gain or loss to the shareholder was to any extent not recognized. Therefore, if the class A stock in the instant case is "common stock," it is not "section 306 stock" within the meaning of section 306(c)(1)(B). Neither the Code nor the Income Tax Regulations define "common stock" for purposes of section 306.

In determining whether newly issued stock is "common stock" for purposes of section 306 of the Code, the bailout abuse Congress sought to preclude by enactment of that section provides guidance. See S.Rep.No.1622, 83d Cong.2d Sess. 46 (1954). See also Chamberlin v. Commissioner, 207 F.2d 462 (6th Cir. 1953), cert. denied, 347 U.S. 918 (1954). A bailout occurs if the stockholders can dispose of their stock in question without a loss of voting control and interest in the unrestricted equitable growth of the corporation.

While the class A nonvoting common stock in the instant case can be disposed of without a loss of voting control in X, it cannot be disposed of without the shareholder parting irretrievably with an interest in the unrestricted equitable growth of X represented by such stock.

Accordingly, the class A nonvoting common stock in the instant case is "common stock" for purposes of section 306(c)(1)(B) . . . . .

The Tax Equity and Financial Responsibility Act of 1982 made two important changes in the reach of §306. Most important, subsection 306(c)(4) was added to §306 to make the attribution rules of §318 applicable in determining whether preferred stock received in a recapitalization or other tax-free reorganization was substantially the same as the receipt of a stock dividend and hence subject to the §306 taint. In addition, the tax avoidance device of transferring stock of a controlled corporation to a newly-organized holding company in exchange for its common and preferred, with the preferred escaping §306 treatment because the new holding company does not have earnings and profits, was blocked by the addition of §306(c)(3) which in effect attributes earnings and profits of the original corporation to the holding company. See page 423, supra.

Section 306(b)(4), excepting from the operation of §306 any transaction which does not have a principal purpose of avoiding tax, may be of little help in the planning context. The regulations content themselves with merely repeating some of the examples given in the Senate Finance Committee Report. More important, the question of whether §306(b)(4) applies to a particular transaction is one of the "areas in which rulings will not ordinarily be issued" by the Service, according to Section 4.01(13) of Rev. Proc. 84-22, 1984-13 I.R.B. 18, 23. However, this provision was the subject of one of the few decided cases to date of §306 (which involves rather special facts, but does contain a clear implication that it may not be absolutely necessary to present a request for relief under §306(b)(4) to the Service before relying on that provision).

FIREOVED v. UNITED STATES *

United States Court of Appeals, Third Circuit, 1972.

462 F.2d 1281.

ADAMS, CIRCUIT JUDGE: This appeal calls into question the application of section 306 of the Internal Revenue Code of 1954 . . .. In particular we are asked to decide whether the transaction here in question had "as one of its principal purposes the avoidance of Federal income tax," [and] whether a prior sale of a portion of the underlying common stock immunized a like proportion of the section 306 stock from treatment as a noncapital asset, ...

* Portion of opinion relating to another
  issue, and most of the Court's footnotes omitted.

I. Factual Background

On November 24, 1948, Fireoved and Company, Inc. was incorporated for the purpose of printing and selling business forms. At their first meeting, the incorporators elected Eugene Fireoved, his wife, Marie, the plaintiffs, and a nephew, Robert L. Fireoved, as directors of the corporation. Subsequently, the directors elected Eugene Fireoved as President and Treasurer and Marie Fireoved as Secretary. The corporation had authorized capital stock of 500 shares of $100 par value non-voting, non-cumulative preferred stock and 100 shares of $1 par value voting common stock. On December 31, 1948, in consideration for $100 cash, the corporation issued Eugene Fireoved 100 shares of common stock; for $500 cash, it issued him five shares of preferred stock; and in payment for automotive equipment and furniture and fixtures, valued at $6,000, it issued him an additional 60 shares of preferred stock.

In 1954, when Mr. Fireoved learned that his nephew, Robert, was planning to leave the business, he began discussions with Karl Edelmayer and Kenneth Craver concerning the possibility of combining his business with their partnership, Girard Business Forms, that had been printing and selling business forms for some time prior to 1954. Messrs. Fireoved, Edelmayer and Craver agreed that voting control of the new enterprise should be divided equally among the three of them. Because Mr. Fireoved's contribution to capital would be approximately $60,000 whereas the partnership could contribute only $30,000, it was decided that preferred stock should be issued to Mr. Fireoved to compensate for the disparity. In furtherance of this plan, the directors and shareholders of Fireoved and Company, in late 1954 and early 1955, held several meetings at which the following corporate changes were accomplished: The name of the company was changed to Girard Business Forms; the authorized common stock was increased from 100 to 300 shares and the authorized preferred stock was increased to 1,000 shares; Mr. Fireoved exchanged his 100 shares of common and 65 shares of preferred stock for equal amounts of the new stock; an agreement of purchase was authorized by which the company would buy all the assets of the Edelmayer-Craver partnership in return for 200 shares of common and 298 shares of preferred stock; and Mr. Fireoved was issued 535 shares of the new preferred stock as a dividend on his 100 shares of common stock, thereby bringing his total holding of preferred stock to 600 shares to indicate his $60,000 capital contribution compared to the $29,800 contributed by the former partnership.

As the business progressed, Mr. Edelmayer demanded more control of the company. In response, Mr. Fireoved and Mr. Craver each sold 24 shares of common stock in the corporation to him on February 28, 1958.

On April 30, 1959, the company redeemed 451 of Mr. Fireoved's 600 shares of preferred stock at $105 per share, resulting in net proceeds to him of $47,355. The gain from this transaction was reported by Mr. and Mrs. Fireoved on their joint return for the year 1959 as a long term capital gain. Subsequently, the Commissioner of Internal Revenue (Commissioner) assessed a deficiency against the Fireoveds of $15,337.13 based on the Commissioner's view that the gain from the redemption of the 451 shares of preferred stock should have been reported as ordinary income and the tax paid at that rate based on section 306. Mr. and Mrs. Fireoved paid the assessment on March 14, 1963, but on March 10, 1965, filed a claim for a refund with the Commissioner.

After the Commissioner disallowed the refund claim on March 8, 1966, the Fireoveds instituted the present action against the United States on August 4, 1967 seeking a refund of the $15,337.13 plus interest on the ground that the transaction came within an exception to section 306, and that they were therefore entitled to report the income as a long term capital gain. The case was tried to the court without a jury on stipulated facts. It is from the district court's determination, on October 29, 1970, that $8,885.50 should be refunded to the taxpayers that both parties appeal.

II. Background of Section 306

Because we are the first court of appeals asked to decide questions of law pursuant to section 306, it is appropriate that we first examine the circumstances that led to the inclusion in 1954 of this section in the Code.

* * *

A temporarily successful plan for converting ordinary income to long term capital gain is described by the facts of Chamberlain v. C. I. R., 207 F.2d 462 (6th Cir. 1953). * * *

The legislative reaction to the *Chamberlain* decision was almost immediate, resulting in the addition of section 306 to the 1954 Code, in order to prevent shareholders from obtaining the tax advantage of such bail-outs when such shareholders retain their ownership interests in the company.

* * *

Based on the history of section 306 and its plain meaning evidenced by the provisions, it is not disputed that the 535 shares of preferred stock issued to Mr. Fireoved as a stock dividend in 1954 were section 306 stock. Additionally, it is clear that in 1959, when the company redeemed 451 shares of Mr. Fireoved's preferred stock, the general provisions of section 306—aside from the exceptions—would require that any gain realized by Mr. Fireoved be taxed at ordinary income rates rather than long term capital gain rates, because the company had earnings at that time of $48,235—more than the $47,-355 required to redeem the stock at $105 per share.

Thus, the questions to be decided on this appeal are (1) whether certain of the exceptions to section 306 apply to permit the Fireoveds' reporting their gain as a long term capital gain, * * *.

III. Was the distribution of the stock dividend "in pursuance of a plan having as one of its principal purposes avoidance of Federal income tax?"

Mr. Fireoved asserts that the entire transaction should fall within the exception established by section 306(b)(4)(A), which provides: "If it is established to the satisfaction of the Secretary or his delegate * * * that the distribution, and the disposition or redemption * * * was not in pursuance of a plan having as one of its principal purposes the avoidance of Federal income tax," then the general rule of section 306(a) will not apply.

As a threshold point on this issue, the Government maintains that because Mr. Fireoved never attempted to obtain a ruling from the "Secretary or his delegate" the redemption should be covered by section 306(a), and the district court should not have reached the question whether the exception applied to Mr. Fireoved. Mr. Fireoved urges that the district court had the power to consider the matter *de novo*, even without a request by the taxpayer to the Secretary or his delegate. Because the ultimate result we reach would not be altered by whichever of these two courses we choose, we do not resolve this potentially complex procedural problem.

The district court, based on the assumption that it had the power to decide the question, found that although one of the purposes involved in the issuance of the preferred stock dividend may have been business related, another principal purpose was the avoidance of Federal income tax.

Mr. Fireoved's analysis of the facts presented in the stipulations would reach the conclusion that the *sole* purpose of the stock dividend was business related. He relies heavily on that portion of the stipulation which describes why the decision was made to combine his business with the Edelmayer-Craver partnership: "The partnership could provide the additional manpower which the expected departure of Robert L. Fireoved from the Corporation would require. Additionally, the partnership needed additional working capital which the Corporation had and could provide." Based primarily on the latter sentence, Mr. Fireoved asserts that the district court had no choice but to find that the transaction was business related and that it therefore had no avoidance incentive.

In making this argument, however, Mr. Fireoved overlooks the plain import of the language of section 306(b)(4). Whether the section requires the decision to be made by the Secretary or the district court, it is clear that "one of [the] principal purposes" of the stock dividend was not [sic] for "the avoidance of Federal income tax." The stipulation demonstrates no more than that the reorganized company required more capital than could be supplied by the partnership alone. The stipulation is completely in harmony with the following fact situation: After the partnership was combined with the corporation, the business required the $30,000 contributed by the partnership and all of the $60,000 Mr. Fireoved had in the corporation. Mr. Fireoved decided to take the stock dividend rather than to distribute the cash to himself as a dividend, and then to make a loan to the corporation of the necessary money because if he took the cash, he would subject himself to taxation at ordinary income rates. Therefore "one of the principal purposes" of the stock dividend would be for "the avoidance of Federal income tax."

In a situation such as the one presented in this case, where the facts necessary to determine the motives for the issuance of a stock dividend are peculiarly within the control of the taxpayer, it is reasonable to require the taxpayer to come forward with the facts that would relieve him of his liability. Here the stipulation was equivocal in determining the purpose of the dividend and is quite compatible with the thought that "one of the principal purposes" was motivated by "tax avoidance." We hold then that the district court did not err in refusing to apply the exception created by section 306(b)(4)(A).

IV. Did the prior sale by Mr. Fireoved of 24% of his underlying common stock immunize such portion of the section 306 stock he redeemed in 1959?

The district court construed section 306(b)(4)(B) to mean that any time a taxpayer in Mr. Fireoved's position sells any portion of his underlying common stock and later sells or redeems his section 306 stock, an equivalent proportion of the section 306 stock redeemed will not be subject to the provisions of section 306(a). The Government has appealed from this portion of the district court's order and urges that we reverse it, based on the history and purpose of section 306 and the particular facts here.

The stipulations indicate that, "On February 28, 1958, Fireoved and Craver each sold 24 shares of common stock in the corporation to Edelmayer," and that appropriate stock certificates were issued. From this fact, Mr. Fireoved reasons that his sale of 24 of his 100 shares of common stock was undertaken solely for the business purpose of satisfying Mr. Edelmayer's desire for more control of the corporation, and therefore he should be given the benefit of section 306 (b)(4)(B). In addition, Mr. Fireoved urges that the disposition of his section 306 stock was related to a business purpose because he used part of the proceeds to pay off a $20,000 loan that the company had made to him.

Mr. Fireoved has the same burden here of showing a lack of tax avoidance purpose that he had in section III supra. It is clear from the limited facts set forth in the stipulations that he has not established that the disposition of 24% of the 535 shares of the section 306 preferred stock he owned "was not in pursuance of a plan having as one of its principal purposes the avoidance of federal income tax." [12] More important, however, is that an examination of the relevant legislative history indicates that Congress did not intend to give capital gains treatment to a portion of the preferred stock redeemed on the facts presented here.

It is apparent from the reaction evinced by Congress to the *Chamberlain* case, supra, that by enacting section 306 Congress was particularly concerned with the tax advantages available to persons who controlled corporations and who could, without sacrificing their control, convert ordinary income to long term capital gains by the device of the preferred stock bail-out. The illustration given in the Senate Report which accompanied section 306(b)(4)(B) is helpful in determining the sort of transactions meant to be exempted by section 306(a):

> Thus if a shareholder received a distribution of 100 shares of section 306 stock in a corporation and sells his voting common stock before he disposes of his section 306 stock, the subsequent disposition of his section 306 stock would not ordinarily be considered a tax avoidance disposition *since he has previously parted with the stock which allows him to participate in the ownership of the business.* However, variations of the above example may give rise to tax avoidance possibilities which are not within the exception of subparagraph (B). Thus if a corporation has only one class of common stock outstanding and it issues stock under circumstances that characterize it as section 306 stock, a subsequent issue of a different class of common having greater voting

12. Consistent with Mr. Fireoved's sale of 24 shares of common stock in 1958 could have been his knowledge that one year later he would be selling his section 306 stock and a desire on his part to avoid taxation at ordinary income rates. As noted later in the opinion, the sale of just 24 shares was enough so that he retained effective control—in the form of veto power—over the corporation. Moreover, the fact that Mr. Fireoved needed $20,000 of the proceeds to pay off a loan to the corporation would not meet his burden. The proceeds of the redemption totaled $47,355. Thus, although $20,000 of the redemption may not have been to avoid taxes, we can ascribe no purpose other than tax avoidance to the receipt of the additional $27,355. Therefore, since one of the principal purposes of the redemption of 451 shares of preferred stock was "the avoidance of Federal income tax," Mr. Fireoved may not take advantage of § 306(b)(4)(B) for any part of the redemption.

rights than the original common will not permit a simultaneous disposition of the section 306 stock together with the original common to escape the rules of subsection (a) of section 306. S.Rep.No.1622, 83d Cong., 2d Sess., 1954 U.S.C.C.A.News 4621, 4881 (emphasis added).

Thus, it is reasonable to assume that Congress realized the general lack of a tax avoidance purpose when a person sells *all* of his control in a corporation and then either simultaneously or subsequently disposes of his section 306 stock. However, when *only a portion* of the underlying common stock is sold, and the taxpayer retains essentially all the control he had previously, it would be unrealistic to conclude that Congress meant to give that taxpayer the advantage of section 306(b)(4)(B) when he ultimately sells his section 306 stock.[13] *Cf.* Davis v. Commissioner, 397 U.S. 301 (1970).

After Mr. Fireoved's corporation had been combined with the Edelmayer-Craver partnership, significant changes to the by-laws were made. The by-laws provided that corporate action could be taken only with the unanimous consent of all the directors. In addition, the by-laws provided that they could be amended either by a vote of 76% of the outstanding common shares or a unanimous vote of the directors. When the businesses were combined in late 1954, each of the directors held ⅓ of the voting stock, thereby necessitating a unanimous vote for amendment to the by-laws. After Messrs. Fireoved and Craver each sold 24 shares of common stock to Mr. Edelmayer, Mr. Fireoved held 25⅓% of the common (voting) stock, Mr. Craver 25⅓% and Mr. Edelmayer 49⅓%. It is crucial to note that the by-laws provided for a unanimous vote for corporate action, and after the common stock transfer, the by-laws were capable of amendment only by a unanimous vote because no two shareholders could vote more than 74⅔% of the common stock and 76% of the common stock was necessary for amendment. Thus, although Mr. Fireoved did sell a portion of his voting stock prior to his disposition of the section 306 stock, he retained as much control in the corporation following the sale of his common stock as he had prior to the sale. Under these circumstances it is not consonant with the history of the legislation to conclude that Congress intended such a sale of underlying common stock to exempt the proceeds of the disposition of section 306 stock from

13. Although this point was neither briefed nor argued, it might be contended, based on an analogous provision of the Code, § 1239, that § 306 should look strictly to a change in ownership rather than actual control of the corporation. When dealing with questions arising under § 1239, courts have considered only changes in the percentage of ownership without regard to whether control of the corporation has shifted. See, e. g. United States v. Parker, 376 F.2d 402 (5th Cir. 1967); Trotz v. Commissioner, 361 F.2d 927 (10th Cir. 1966). However, the legislative intent embodied in § 306 is so different from that of § 1239, that, based on the facts presented here, control is the relevant inquiry under § 306.

treatment as ordinary income. Accordingly, the district court erred when it held that *any* of the preferred shares Mr. Fireoved redeemed were not subject to section 306(a) by virtue of section 306(b)(4) (B).[14]

* * *

14. It is important to note that our decision relates only to the facts of this case. We express no view on the situation in which less than all the voting shares are sold but enough are disposed of to relinquish effective control prior to or simultaneous with the sale of section 306 stock.

SECTION 6. RECAPITALIZATION UNDER CORPORATE LAW

While the term "recapitalization" may include practically any change in the capital structure of a going concern, it most often refers to a transaction involving a change in the rights of existing stockholders, either by alteration of the terms of outstanding stock or by the issuance of new securities in exchange for the old. Incidentally, the distinction between a *change* in existing stock and an *exchange* of new shares for the old ones is often far from clear. For example, what is the difference between a reduction in the par value of outstanding shares under MBA §58 (e) and the issuance of new shares with a lower par value in exchange for the old shares pursuant to §58 (f)—or between a "change" of par shares into no-par shares under §58 (h) and an "exchange" of new no-par shares for the old par shares under §58(f)—bearing in mind that as a practical matter a "change" transaction is quite likely to be accompanied by the issuance of new shares reflecting the changes effected. In the same vein, there would seem to be virtually no difference between a stock dividend of, say, one new share for each old share outstanding, and a recapitalization exchange of two new shares for each old share outstanding.

While there are a variety of purposes which may be served by recapitalization, by far the most common objective of the transactions which have come before the courts is the elimination of unpaid dividend arrearages on cumulative preferred stock. (Although of course such arrearages do not constitute a debt and hence do not represent any threat to the existence of the corporation, they do prevent the payment of dividends on common stock and therefore impede new common stock financing.) The following enlightening description of recapitalizations and the manner in which they are effected comes from the late Professor Dodd's classic article on the standards of fairness applicable to such recapitalizations:

DODD, FAIR AND EQUITABLE RECAPITALIZATIONS *

55 Harv.L.Rev. 780–789 (1942).

There are two situations in which the management of a business corporation is likely to attempt to revamp the capital structure so as substantially to modify present and future rights of existing security holders: (1) reorganizations of insolvent corporations, involving modification of the rights of creditors, including bondholders, and (2) recapitalization of solvent corporations, involving modification of the relative rights of classes of shareholders. . . .

* * *

Recapitalization differs radically from reorganization in that it involves only the rights of persons who, as shareholders, have in general no right to receive payment at any time prior to the liquidation of the enterprise. Liquidation cannot normally be accomplished without the assent of those who have voting control over the enterprise, which in most instances means the common shareholders. . . .

[With one minor exception] recapitalization, unlike reorganization, is never necessary for the purpose of relieving the corporation from legal demands which it is unable to meet. Although there are intimations to the contrary in some judicial opinions, it is unlikely that any corporation has been ruined as a result of its inability to modify claims to accrued dividends or to make any other readjustments in its capital structure.

* * *

The need for permitting corporations to modify their charters so as to adapt themselves to circumstances which were unforeseen when the enterprise was created is so obvious that modern corporation statutes invariably authorize the majority or some larger percentage of the shareholders to amend the charter in various ways, usually including the adoption of amendments which create new classes of shares and amendments which change the preference of an existing class of shares. In enacting such statutes, legislatures have sometimes attempted to safeguard the interests of a particular class by requiring the affirmative vote of a majority of the members of that class for the adoption of the amendment, and they have sometimes attempted to safeguard the interest of dissenters by giving them the right to receive the fair value of their shares in cash if they do not desire to continue with the enterprise in its amended form. But the prescribed method of amendment has been, almost universally, that of a shareholders' vote rather than that of judicial proceedings, which has always been characteristic of reorganizations. Corporation statutes which confer some particular power on a group within the corporation, whether shareholders or directors, do not ordinarily admonish the group in question that they are to exercise their powers only so as to produce results which are fair and equitable, and statutes which permit recapitalizations are no exception to the rule.

Attempts have been made to use these statutes to adopt two different types of amendments which reclassify shares in such a manner as to eliminate or modify accrued dividend rights. The first type of amendment affects such rights directly by providing for their elimination or modification, or for the substitution therefor of some other right, such as the right to receive additional preferred or common shares in lieu of accruals. The courts have on the whole been unwilling to construe the statutes as authorizing amendments of this type unless the statutory language is very explicit.

The other type of amendment is more complicated. A plan is proposed which includes the creation of prior preferred shares and the offer of such shares, sometimes with a bonus of common, to the holders of the existing preferred shares in return for the surrender of their claim to accruals. Those who decline retain their accruals but become subordinated to the holders of the new prior preferred shares and are subjected in some instances to certain other disadvantages. The courts, with some notable exceptions, have tended to uphold this type of amendment, often relying largely on language in the original charter which impliedly authorized the creation of prior preferred shares.

As the foregoing excerpt indicates, any recapitalization transaction may present a preliminary question as to whether the statute authorizes the use of the particular mechanics to achieve the particular objective. For example, it has been held that elimination of dividend arrearages on cumulative preferred stock can not be accomplished by amendment of the certificate under a statute permitting certificate amendment by "increasing or decreasing its authorized capital stock or reclassifying the same, by changing the number, par value, designations, preferences, or relative, participating, optional, or other special rights of the shares, or the qualifications, limitations, or restrictions of such rights, . . .". Keller v. Wilson & Co., Inc., 21 Del.Ch. 391, 190 A. 115 (Sup.Ct.1936); Consolidated Film Industries, Inc. v. Johnson, 22 Del.Ch. 407, 197 A. 489 (Sup.Ct.1937). On the other hand, the Delaware court did find authority to eliminate such arrearages under the merger statute, even in the course of a merger with a wholly-owned subsidiary. Federal United Corporation v. Havender, 24 Del.Ch. 318, 11 A.2d 331 (Sup. Ct.1940). Notice that the Model Act specifically authorizes a corporation to "cancel or otherwise affect" dividend arrearages by certificate amendment. MBA § 58 (k).

Where the recapitalization calls for an exchange of shares, there is a threshold question relating to the mechanics for carrying out the exchange. For example, Model Act §58 (f) authorizes an amendment of the articles of incorporation "to exchange . . . all or any part of its shares, whether issued or unissued"; and §60 (d) provides a class vote in the event that an amendment would "effect an exchange, or create a right of exchange, of all or any part of the shares of another class into the shares of such class". But it is far from clear just how an amendment to the articles can in and of itself "exchange" shares.* Nor is it easy to see why an amendment to the articles would be used to "create a right of exchange", unless that right constituted one of the continuing terms of that class of stock within the meaning of § 15.

This problem seems to have been recognized in Model Act §58 which provides, in cases where an exchange of shares is to be made, for inclusion of "such provisions as may be necessary to effect such . . . exchange". Even without such statutory assistance, in practice the parties have generally by-passed whatever theoretical difficulties there might be by utilizing the concept of a "plan of recapitalization", in which such classic amendment matters as the creation of new shares are joined with such non-amendment items as an exchange of shares. Thus in Shanik v. White Sewing Machine Corp., 25 Del.Ch. 371, 19 A.2d 831 (Sup.Ct.1941), where the court upheld a plan to get rid of preferred arrearages by offering a package consisting of one share of new prior preferred and 3 shares of new common stock for each old share of preferred, only the creation of the new prior preference stock (and the change of the old common stock into 2/5 of a share of new common stock) were included in the amendment of the certificate, although the overall "plan" adopted by the shareholders included the provision permitting each preferred stockholder to exchange his old preferred for the package of new preference stock and common. But see the involved arrangements in the Hartzell case, page 327 infra, apparently undertaken in order to avoid feared impediments to the proposed exchange transaction under the corporation statute.

---

* But see the amendment provision in Rio Grande Oil Co. v. Welsh, 101 F.2d 454 (9th Cir. 1939), which provided expressly, in connection with an exchange of five new no-par common shares for each old $25 par common share outstanding, that the holders of the old shares "shall surrender the same to the corporation for cancellation and shall receive and accept in place thereof certificates for shares of the new capital stock".

The following case illustrates a "recapitalization" transaction found not to be authorized by the governing statute:

BOWMAN v. ARMOUR & CO.

Supreme Court of Illinois, 1959.
17 Ill.2d 43, 160 N.E.2d 753.

HERSHEY, JUSTICE. This is an equity proceeding for a declaratory judgment seeking to determine the validity of a 1954 amendment to the articles of incorporation of the defendant, Armour and Company, an Illinois corporation. The plaintiffs-appellants here seek to have the amendment declared invalid and further seek a declaration that action taken pursuant to that amendment be declared ineffective.

The original plaintiffs, as well as the intervenors, are owners of cumulative convertible prior preferred stock of Armour and Company, hereinafter referred to as "Armour." The stock will, in this opinion, be referred to as the "prior stock." The plaintiffs assert that the 1954 plan of recapitalization contained in the amendment operates to deprive them of rights and privileges as holders of the prior stock contrary to constitutional inhibitions.

The case was heard below on an agreed statement of facts, documents, and testimony. The trial court, in a written opinion, found the issues for the defendants and held the recapitalization plan as embodied in the amendment to the articles of incorporation to be valid and further held that the applicable sections of the Business Corporation Act that were construed as the statutory basis for the authorization of the amendment were constitutional.

Constitutional questions having been presented below and decided, this court has jurisdiction on direct appeal.

In 1954, prior to the plan of recapitalization here under attack, the capital structure, debt and surplus of Armour and Company, in thousands of dollars, were:

Long-term debt	$124,699
Prior stock	50,000
Common stock	20,329
Capital and paid-in surplus	33,619
Earned surplus	134,079
	$362,726

The prior stock had, by the terms of the stock certificates and the articles of incorporation, these material features: It had a stated value of $100 per share. Cumulative dividends of $6 per year were to be paid when and if declared and each share was convertible for six shares of common stock and could, at the option of the company, be redeemed at a price of $115 per share plus accumulated dividends.

Each share of the prior stock had one vote in corporate matters and enjoyed certain preferences in the event of liquidation, whether voluntary or involuntary.

The plan of recapitalization proposed to amend the articles of incorporation by a vote of two thirds of the holders of each class of stock providing that the board of directors would be authorized to redeem the prior stock "at a price of $120.00 per share, payable in (i) debentures of like principal amount of the company, maturing November 1, 1984, bearing interest at the rate of 5% per annum cumulative from November 1, 1954, and to be subordinated to other *indebtedness* of the Company, and having such sinking fund provisions and other terms and conditions as the board of directors of the company may determine, (ii) one transferable warrant for the purchase of one share of common stock of the Company, at such price or prices and having such other terms and conditions as the board of directors of the company may determine, (iii) and no more."

The debentures were to mature in 30 years and the stated interest rate of 5 per cent was payable out of earnings. The redemption as authorized by the amendment would, upon the exercise of the power to redeem as contained in the amendment, be compulsory. The amendment was voted upon by the shareholders and adopted by a vote of more than two thirds of each class of outstanding stock, the shareholders voting by class.

Questions relating to the necessity of the recapitalization, the tax advantages to the corporation, the fairness of the plan, the financial consequences of its adoption on the prior stockholders and the infringement of "contractual" or "vested" rights, as well as constitutional rights, have been ably presented on the appeal of this case. However, in view of the fact that our interpretation of the applicable provisions of the Business Corporation Act is determinative of this appeal, it is unnecessary to consider the question of fairness or, in fact, to consider any question other than statutory interpretation and *laches*.

The charter or articles of incorporation of an Illinois corporation is a contract of a three-fold nature. It is operative as between the corporation and the State and it creates rights and duties as between the corporation and its shareholders, as well as between the shareholders themselves. . . . The express nature of the contract is not limited to the specific language found in the articles of incorporation but the contract in its entirety includes the statutory provisions in force when the charter is granted as though those statutory provisions were literally recited in the contract. . . . The holders of the prior stock thus held rights and privileges as expressed in the articles prior to the amendment subject at all times to variation, modification or change to the extent that the articles could be amended from time to time as authorized by the Business Corporation Act.

Section 52 of the Business Corporation Act   .   .   .   provides in part as follows:

"Right to amend articles of incorporation. A corporation may amend its articles of incorporation, from time to time, in any and as many respects as may be desired, provided that its articles of incorporation as amended contain only such provisions as might be lawfully contained in original articles of incorporation if made at the time of making such amendment, and, if a change in shares or an exchange or reclassification of shares is to be made, such provisions as may be necessary to effect such change, exchange, or reclassification as may be desired and as is permitted by this Act.

"In particular, and without limitation upon such general power of amendment, a corporation may amend its articles of incorporation, from time to time, so as:

. . .

"(g) To change the designation of all or any part of its shares, whether issued or unissued, and to change the preferences, qualifications, limitations, restrictions, and the special or relative rights in respect of all or any part of its shares, whether issued or unissued."

The authority for the amendment here in question must be found in the quoted portion of section 52 subject to the general limitation that the amendment, in order to be valid, must be by the affirmative vote of two thirds of the outstanding shares of each class of stock issued. (See sec. 53(c) and sec. 54, Business Corporation Act.) In this connection, it is established and uncontroverted that more than two thirds of each class voted for the amendment.

It is, of course, a fundamental rule of statutory construction that the grant of power contained in the Business Corporation Act, like any other grant of power, is to be strictly construed and the enumeration of the series of powers therein contained exclude other powers not fairly incidental to the powers expressly granted.   .   .   .

The grant of power to amend found in section 52 of the act and, specifically material to this case, the power found in subparagraph (g) is very broad. Amendments, however, must be limited to matters that would be permitted in the original articles, and section 14 of the Business Corporation Act relating to preferences in original articles clearly contemplates the issuance of shares redeemable at the option of the company at a price not exceeding the price fixed by the articles of incorporation.   .   .   .

*   *   *

The language of subparagraph (g) of section 52, authorizing amendment of articles of incorporation makes rights and privileges of preferred stock defeasible to the extent that amendments are authorized. The question here is not one of the existence of the power to amend nor is the question here one of the authority to divest certain rights and privileges. Rather, the question is whether this quoted language gives to Armour the right to amend to the extent that holders of the prior shares are required to surrender their ownership in said stock and accept in lieu thereof the earnings bonds as specified.

The amendment, whether it is viewed as effecting a purchase of the prior stock with bonds or as a compulsory redemption thereof, obviously contemplates that the fundamental relationship of stockholder as between the holders of the prior stock and Armour will be changed and the prior stockholders will become mere creditors of the company.

A share of stock in a corporation is a unit of interest in the corporation and it entitles the shareholder to an aliquot part of the property or its proceeds to the extent indicated. The interest of a shareholder entitles him to participate in the net profits in proportion to the number of his shares, to have a voice in the selection of the corporate officers and, upon dissolution or liquidation, to receive his portion of the property of the corporation that may remain after payment of its debts. A change in preferences, qualifications or relative rights may increase or decrease the right to participate in profits, the right to participate in distribution of the assets of the corporation on dissolution or liquidation, or other indicia of ownership manifest by the ownership of corporate stock. But the change here contemplated is more than that; it is a compulsory redemption or a purchase of the stock rather than a divestiture of certain rights and privileges.

The plan of recapitalization here is not a divestiture of rights or privileges or an increase or decrease in relative rights of shares but it is, as we have said, a compulsory redemption or purchase that results in a change of the status of the shareholder from that of a shareholder to that of a creditor. The ownership of some equity in the corporation is not modified or changed leaving some resulting ownership, but it is liquidated and a corporate owner prior to the amendment finds that subsequent to the amendment he is a creditor.

A corporation has no inherent right to redeem its preferred stock and can do so only if authorized by law. . . . Section 14 of our Business Corporation Act provides for the issuance of preferred shares and further provides that the same may be redeemed "at not exceeding the price fixed by the articles of incorporation. . . ." The articles of Armour expressly provided that the prior stock could be redeemed at a price of $115 per share plus accrued dividends.

This provision, in effect, was the grant of an option by the owners of the prior stock to Armour authorizing redemption on the stated terms. Notwithstanding this provision, it is the contention of the defendants in this case that the holders of the prior stock can be forced to permit the redemption on the basis of the issuance of earnings bonds.

It is the position of the plaintiffs that the only way the stock can be redeemed is by compliance with the provisions of the article and the payment in dollars of the sum therein provided. The plaintiffs assert that the word "price," as used in the statute, is definable only to mean money and not bonds or other evidences of debt.

It is a well established rule that in the absence of contrary statutory definition, words used in a statute are used in their popularly understood meaning. . . . The word "price" has a narrower meaning and is more restricted in scope than the word "consideration," and "price" has been defined as the amount of money given or received in exchange for anything. . . .

The word "price" is used in the redemption language of section 14 and is also found in section 15 of the Business Corporation Act with reference to the issuance of preferred or special shares in a series. It is there provided that there may be variations between series of stock as to price. Further, in section 18 of the Business Corporation Act, the word "price" is not found, and in that section it is obvious that when the legislature wished to broaden the meaning of the term it did not use the word "price" but used the word "consideration" and defined it to include many things—money, property, labor or services actually performed.

A consideration of these sections can lead us only to the conclusion that when the legislature makes reference to the payment of money it uses the word "price." When it is concerned with a broader definition it found adequate words to express its intention.

We have carefully considered the cases cited from other jurisdictions with reference to redemption or retirement of stock out of bonds and a fair statement of the reasoning there found may be found in section 5315 of Volume 11, Fletcher Cyclopedia of Corporations, stating the general rule to be that preferred shares convertible by the holder into bonds or credit obligations, call, in effect, for a purchase by the corporation of its own shares, and like provisions for compulsory redemption should be expressly prohibited. The case there discussed of Berger v. United States Steel Corp., 63 N.J.Eq. 809, 53 A. 68, relates to the redemption of preferred stock by the issuance of bonds therefor and was based upon a specific and peculiar statutory provision, and even in that case it is to be noted that rather strict limitations were imposed as a condition precedent to such redemption and it was required that the holder of the stock sought to be redeemed consent thereto.

It seems to us to be evident that the effect of the amendment here sought to be sustained was, in fact, a purchase with bonds by the Armour company of its own outstanding preferred stock without the consent of the owners of said stock. While the Business Corporation Act does, under certain circumstances, permit a corporation to purchase its own stock, it can do so only when the shareholder is willing to sell, and no amendment passed with the approval of a two-thirds vote of the shareholders can force him to sell.

Further, that section 52(g) should be construed as we have indicated is made more clear by referring to the express safeguards found in the Business Corporation Act applicable to merger. Section 61 expressly provides that on merger the shares of each merging corporation may be converted into shares or other securities or obligations of the corporation. Section 70 provides safeguards for shareholders who may dissent from the merger by permitting them to obtain the fair market value of their shares. To construe section 52 as to authorize the recapitalization plan here under consideration would mean that a minority shareholder would not have the protection on recapitalization that the legislature has provided on merger, even though the recapitalization plan could more drastically affect his interest than would a merger. It is obvious to us that the legislature did not intend to authorize a recapitalization program by amendment of the nature and to the extent of the one here involved but, rather, by the language of section 52(g) contemplated only changes in relative rights, privileges, restrictions or limitations. . . .

SECTION 7.   TAX ASPECTS OF RECAPITALIZATION

A.   IN GENERAL

As indicated in the corporate discussion, although a recapitalization generally involves some type of exchange of stock or securities between a corporation and its stockholders, rather than a "distribution" in the ordinary sense, many exchange transactions which constitute recapitalizations are virtually the same in ultimate effect as ordinary distribution transactions. For example, a recapitalization consisting of an exchange by common stockholders of all of their old common for proportionate amounts of new preferred and common would be practically the same as a stock dividend of new preferred on the old common. The same would be true if each holder of old common exchanged a pro rata portion of his common for new preferred; a change in the number of common shares owned by each stockholder is of no moment, so long as the proportionate interest of each in the basic equity remains the same.

Again, a pro rata distribution of debt securities to common stockholders would presumably constitute a dividend in kind and as such be includible in ordinary income. Should the transaction be treated differently if instead the shareholders exchange all of their old common for proportionate amounts of new debt securities and common, or if the shareholders exchange a pro rata portion of old common for debt securities?

The origins of special tax treatment for recapitalizations are rooted in the early recognition that certain types of corporate readjustments which left the interests of corporate investors in "corporate solution" did not constitute a sufficient change in the nature of the taxpayer's investment to warrant imposition of tax. Such transactions, described as "reorganizations", range all the way from the absorption of one existing corporation by another engaged in a completely different business to a mere change in the state of incorporation of a going concern; and from the outset, the definition of "reorganization" has included "recapitalization", as it does in § 368(a) (1) (E) today.

On the other hand, there has never been any definition of "recapitalization" in the statute, or in the regulations either. Perhaps the term when first used was regarded as having some fairly well-defined corporate significance, but in fact, as we saw earlier, that has really never been so; even today recapitalization is more of an informal concept than a well-defined term of corporate art. The present regulations, in lieu of any effort at comprehensive definition, simply provide five examples of exchange transactions which are classified as recapitalizations. And the nearest thing to a judicial definition is the description of a recapitalization in Helvering v. Southwest Consolidated Corp., 315 U.S. 194, 202, 62 S.Ct. 546, 551, 86 L.Ed. 789 (1942), as a "reshuffling of a capital structure within the framework of an existing corporation."

In any event, if a transaction does fall within the term "recapitalization" it thereby qualifies as a "reorganization" for tax purposes, which means that it becomes subject to the special "tax-free" reorganization pattern. The pivotal provision in this pattern is § 354 which excepts from the normal recognition of gain or loss under § 1002 certain transactions in which stock or securities are exchanged with a corporation solely for new stock or securities pursuant to a reorganization.* Section 354 is supplemented by § 356 which provides for partial non-recognition when such an exchange involves the receipt of some "boot", that is, property not permitted to be received tax-free. Section 356 also deals with the circumstances under which boot may be treated as a dividend, rather than as a payment in exchange for property which would be eligible for capital gain treat-

---

* It is to be noted that § 354 may overlap § 1036 as to exchanges involving merely new preferred for old preferred, or new common for old common. But where such an exchange occurs outside of a reorganization, as would presumably be true of any exchange among individual shareholders, tax-free treatment can only come from § 1036.

ment. (If only boot, i. e., no non-recognition property, is received, then even if the transaction does constitute a reorganization, the tax treatment of what is received must be determined under the other distribution sections, 301, 302, 331, and 346.) Section 358 prescribes the basis rules for exchanges governed by §§ 354 and 356.

Such recapitalization exchanges are also tax-free to the corporation, but no special provision to that effect is needed because from the corporation's point of view, these transactions simply represent a new issuance of stock or securities. Section 1032 precludes the imposition of any tax upon an issuance of stock by a corporation, including when the new stock is issued in exchange for old stock, Reg. § 1.1032–1(b); and under § 311 the same is true when it is new securities that are issued in exchange for the old stock. (The effect on the corporation of an exchange of new debt securities for old debt is less clear; if the principal amount of the new debt securities is smaller than the principal amount of the old debt securities, cancellation of indebtedness income under § 108 might be present.)

On the other hand, any transfers of property between two or more corporations, as occurs in the more complicated types of reorganization such as mergers or corporate divisions, do require some special provision to avoid being taxed. Section 361 performs this operation (supplemented by § 357); and the corollary basis rules applicable to such tax-free inter-corporate transfers of property are provided in § 362(b), in conjunction with § 358. However, since recapitalization involves only a single corporation, these sections do not come into play; accordingly, further analysis of them can await discussion of corporate combinations and separations later in these materials.

B. DISTRIBUTIONS HAVING THE EFFECT OF A DIVIDEND

As previously noted, when boot is distributed to stockholders in the course of a reorganization exchange, at a minimum there should be recognition of gain to the extent of the boot, and § 356(a) (1) so provides. But something more than partial recognition of gain is called for when such a transaction really amounts to the distribution of a dividend. Here § 356(a) (2) comes into play, subjecting to dividend tax any distribution of boot which "has the effect . . . of a dividend."

The classic case construing the "effect of a dividend" test is Commissioner v. Estate of Bedford, 325 U.S. 283, 65 S.Ct. 1157, 89 L.Ed. 1611 (1944), which involved a recapitalization of Abercrombie & Fitch. At the start of 1937 the company had a surplus deficit as the result of stock dividends charged against surplus in the late 1920's and losses incurred in the 1930's. In order to get into position to pay its current earnings as dividends, the company adopted a plan of recapitalization designed to eliminate its $100 par value cumulative preferred stock by exchanging for each three shares of such stock 3½ shares of new $75 par value preferred, 1½ shares of $1 par value common, and $45.24 in cash. For its 3,000 shares of old preferred stock, the taxpayer received 3500 shares of new preferred, 1500 shares of common, and $45,240 in cash, which had a total value exceeding the taxpayer's basis in the old preferred by almost $140,000. Admittedly, this gain was taxable to the extent of the cash received; but the Commissioner contended that the cash was taxable as a dividend under the predecessor of § 356(a) (2), and the Supreme Court agreed:

> Although Abercrombie & Fitch showed a book deficit in the surplus account because the earlier stock dividends had been charged against it, the parties agree that for corporate tax purposes at least earnings and profits exceeding the distributed cash had been earned at the time of the recapitalization. That cash therefore came out of earnings and profits and such a distribution would normally be considered a taxable dividend. . . . It has been ruled in a series of cases that where the stock of one corporation was exchanged for the stock of another and cash and then distributed, such distributions out of earnings and profits had the effect of a distribution of a taxable dividend under [the predecessor of § 356(a)(2)] . . . . The Tax Court has reached the same result, that is, has treated the distribution as a taxable dividend, in the case of the recapitalization of a single corporation. . . . We can not distinguish the two situations and find no implication in the statute restricting [it] to taxation as a dividend only in the case of an exchange of stock and assets of two corporations.

Taken literally, the Bedford case might mean that any distribution of boot to a shareholder pursuant to a reorganization should be taxed as a dividend to the extent of the shareholder's ratable share of earnings and profits. After all, the language of the opinion is rather sweeping; and the Court ominously ignored the fact that the taxpayer owned no common stock so that this was far from a "classic" dividend equivalence case. Moreover, such a broad construction would have the advantage of substituting an objective standard for the uncertainty which would otherwise be inherent in a provision like § 356(a)(2).

On the other hand, the Bedford result can be reconciled with a less extreme view of dividend equivalence despite the fact that the taxpayer owned only preferred stock. Indeed, since the dividends on the preferred stock in Bedford were in arrears, and the arrearages exceeded the amount of the cash received, <u>Bedford</u> comes close to being a "classic" dividend equivalence case after all. And, as pointed out in Darrell, The Scope of Commissioner v. Bedford Estate, 24 Taxes 266 (1946), in the absence of dividend arrearages preferred stockholders would not normally have any "ratable share of the undistributed earnings and profits of the corporation", which is the touchstone of §356(a)(2).

The IRS initially seemed to espouse the notion of "automatic dividend" treatment, since Example 1 in Reg. §1.356-1(c) assumes dividend treatment for cash received in a reorganization exchange without any analysis of the surrounding circumstances. But the Government itself successfully resisted the rule in another preferred stock case where the taxpayer was seeking dividend treatment in order to enjoy the benefit of a special deduction for dividends received on preferred stock under §247. Idaho Power Co. v. United States, 161 F. Supp. 807 (Ct. Cl. 1958). And in Rev. Rul. 74-515, 1974-2 Cum. Bull. 118 the Service abandoned the automatic dividend rule, in favor of examining all the facts and circumstances. The most important factor cutting against dividend treatment for boot is an accompanying significant reduction in the taxpayer's basic equity interest in the enterprise, which parallels the guidline applied in testing for dividend equivalence in cases of stock redemption (to be discussed in detail later in this chapter). E.g., Rev. Rul. 75-83, 1975-1 Cum. Bull. 112.

These are some important differences between dividend treatment under § 356(a)(2) and that imposed by the general provision of §301. One already mentioned is the restriction of the dividend under §356(a)(2) to the taxpayer's "ratable share" of earnings and profits, which has no counterpart under §301. Of even more importance is the limitation of the dividend treatment under §356(a)(2) to the amount of the gain on the exchange transaction. This seems hard to justify: the amount of the taxpayer's gain on the overall transaction is not a factor in other constructive dividend situations, such as redemption of stock, and no reason appears why it should be here. The presence of such qualifications in §356(a)(2) can only cause difficulty. On occasions the Service has tried to by-pass the gain limitation of §356(a) (2) by moving directly under §301. See Rev. Rul. 61-156, 1961-2 Cum. Bull. 62.

After some early resistance the Service has accepted §356(a)(2) "dividends" as eligible for the dividends-received deduction. Rev. Rul. 72-327, 1972-2 Cum. Bull. 197.

C. PREFERRED STOCK RECAPITALIZATIONS

---

1. RECAPITALIZATIONS EQUIVALENT TO A STOCK DIVIDEND

As previously noted, a recapitalization may amount in effect to a preferred stock dividend—for example, if common stockholders exchange all of their old common for new preferred and common, or exchange some of their old common for new preferred. It seems clear that such transactions should be treated the same for tax purposes as an express stock dividend; and this is accomplished by § 306(c) (1) (B) which applies the "section 306 stock" taint to preferred stock received in a reorganization where "the effect of the transaction was substantially the same as the receipt of a stock dividend." This test is quite analogous to the above-mentioned test of whether boot received in a reorganization will be treated as a dividend under § 356(a) (2); and the regulations, § 1.306-3(d), in a seeming overstatement of this analogy, restate the test for § 306 stock in terms of whether cash received in lieu of the stock in question would have been treated as a dividend under § 356(a) (2). Cf. Note, Exclusion from Section 306 Treatment in Unifying Reorganizations, 76 Harv.L.Rev. 1627 (1963).

The revenue rulings thus far appear to treat as § 306 stock any preferred received by a shareholder whose proportionate common stock interest remains substantially as large as before. E. g., Rev. Rul. 56–116, 1956–1 Cum.Bull. 164; Rev.Rul. 59–197, 1959–1 Cum. Bull. 77. Notice also that a recapitalization producing § 306 stock can occur even though there is no direct exchange of stock. Thus, in Rev. Rul. 56–654, 1956–2 Cum.Bull. 216, a corporation with outstanding common and preferred stock amended its charter to increase the liquidation preference of the preferred. According to the ruling, such a transaction constitutes an exchange of all the preferred and some of the common for new preferred, which means that the increase in value of the preferred stock is subject to the "section 306" taint.

In addition, today there is the spectre of a recapitalization giving rise to a taxable stock dividend under §305. Section 305(c) specifically contemplates that a recapitalization may have an effect on the interest of shareholders similar to a change in conversion ratio or a difference between redemption price and issue price, and hence call for treatment as a distribution with respect to each shareholder whose proportionate interest is thereby increased. See, e.g., Rev. Rul. 83-119, page 291 supra.

2. NON PRO RATA RECAPITALIZATIONS

Is it necessary to finding a recapitalization that all members of the same class of stockholders participate pro rata in the exchange transaction? This question arose in one of the earliest preferred stock recapitalization cases, Muchnic v. Commissioner, 29 B.T.A. 163 (1933). There the corporation involved had 20,000 shares of no-par common stock outstanding when its charter was amended in 1925 to authorize the issuance of 5,500 shares of 7% cumulative, redeemable preferred stock. The new preferred was offered to the common stockholders in exchange for common at the rate of six-tenths of a share of preferred for each share of common. Seven of the sixteen stockholders of the company accepted the offer, exchanging 9,166 shares of common for 5,499.6 shares of preferred. The taxpayer, who was a member of the controlling family group, and with his wife owned about 40% of the common, did not participate in this exchange. By 1929, all of the preferred had been redeemed, and all of the common stock acquired by the company in the exchange had been reissued by sale or stock dividend. In 1929, the company again gave the opportunity to its stockholders to exchange their common for the preferred upon the same basis as before. This time only the taxpayer and his wife accepted the offer, each of them turning in 2500 shares of common for 1500 shares of preferred.

The Commissioner sought to tax the gain on the 1929 exchanges but the Board held that the transaction constituted a recapitalization upon which no gain or loss should be recognized under the predecessor of § 354. The Board first rejected the Commissioner's contention that if any reorganization occurred, it was when the corporation amended its charter to authorize the issuance of preferred stock, rather than when such preferred stock was issued in exchange for common. The Board cited language in both corporate and tax authorities indicating that an exchange of preferred stock for common which effected a change in the capital structure of the corporation constituted a recapitalization (and hence a reorganization). The Board then concluded as follows:

> Respondent contends, however, that the instant exchanges fall short of effecting a recapitalization for the reason that not all of the stockholders participated. The answer to that is one of fact; two stockholders made the exchange offered by the company to all, and as a result the capitalization of the company was changed. Before the exchanges, it had outstanding 20,000 shares of common stock having a stated value of $500,000. After the exchanges, it had outstanding 15,000 shares of common stock having a stated value of $375,000 and 3,000 shares of preferred stock of a par value of $300,000; thus disclosing an increase

in its liability upon stock of $75,000. Moreover, there was a "readjustment of existing interests." New priorities as to the company's assets and earnings were assumed upon the issue of the preferred stock, which, together with the reduction in the common stock outstanding, effected a revision of the existing interests of the common stockholders. It cannot be denied that such readjustments affecting the capital of the company constitute a recapitalization.

Although the Commissioner's complaint about the non pro rata nature of the transaction in Muchnic received short shrift, the fact remains that such a non pro rata recapitalization is really essentially equivalent to a transaction consisting of a pro rata stock dividend followed by exchanges among the individual stockholders to reach whatever proportionate holdings of new and old stock are desired. The similarity between these two approaches is dramatically illustrated by the case of Hartzell v. Commissioner, 40 B. T. A. 492 (1939). There the petitioner was one of thirteen stockholders who owned all of the authorized capital stock of a corporation, consisting of 10,000 shares of $100 par value common stock. Six of the stockholders were over 60 years old, and they owned a total of 7,550 shares; the younger seven stockholders, including the petitioner, owned the remaining 2,450 shares. Of the older stockholders, one was president and one was treasurer; the younger stockholders included the general manager, the secretary, and the heads of each of the five departments of the business. All of the older stockholders had children, none of whom was identified with the affairs of the company. The younger stockholders were apprehensive that upon the death of the older stockholders their stockholdings might go to their children, with the result that voting control of the company would pass into the hands of people totally unfamiliar with its affairs.

After several discussions the two groups of stockholders agreed upon a plan to give the older stockholders preferred stock while the younger stockholders ended up with the common stock of the company. The attorney retained by the parties drafted an agreement calling for a pro rata distribution of both new preferred stock and new common to each stockholder, after which the younger stockholders were to transfer their preferred stock to the older stockholders in exchange for the latter's common stock. The stockholders objected to this circuitous approach, but the attorney explained that the initial pro rata distribution of the new preferred and common to each stockholder was merely a "detour" to comply with Ohio laws in filing the certificate of reorganization and that the subsequent exchange of preferred and common stock between the older and younger stockholders would produce the desired end result. The attorney also pointed out that the actual exchange of the stock among the stockholders could be avoided by having the company issue directly to each stockholder the amount of preferred or common stock he was supposed to end up with.

Pursuant to the agreement of the parties, the corporation's articles were amended to authorize the appropriate number of preferred and common shares. The agreement also provided that instead of actually issuing to each stockholder his pro rata portion of both preferred and common stock, the company would distribute directly to each stockholder the amount of preferred or common respectively which each was supposed ultimately to own, "thereby accomplishing the results agreed to by all the stockholders without the necessity of an actual exchange". Accordingly, the shareholders turned in all of their old stock, and the corporation issued all of the new preferred to the older stockholders, while all the new common was issued to the younger stockholders.

The petitioner reported no gain upon his receipt of the new common for his old common, treating it as an exchange made in pursuance of a plan of recapitalization under the predecessor of §368(a)(1)(E) and hence tax-free under the predecessor of §354. However, the Commissioner viewed the transaction as consisting of two separate and independent steps: a pro rata exchange of new preferred and common for old common, which he conceded did constitute a recapitalization; and a subsequent exchange among the shareholders in their individual capacities, which he contended was not part of the recapitalization, despite the fact that the corporation issued all of the preferred stock directly to the older stockholders and all of the common stock directly to the younger stockholders. Accordingly, the Commissioner determined that the exchanges among the shareholders were taxable under the predecessor of §1002.

The Tax Court found for the taxpayer, holding that the ultimate effect of the overall transaction was an exchange by some of the stockholders of all of their common stock for new preferred, which constituted a recapitalization under the Muchnic case, supra. The court disregarded the intermediate step of pro rata exchange of new preferred and common for old common, viewing it as merely a response to feared impediments under the Ohio corporate statute.

Since the Hartzell case, the authorities have been uniform in treating such non pro rata exchanges by some of the common stockholders of a corporation of all of their common stock for new preferred stock as tax-free recapitalizations. Perhaps the best known is Dean v. Commissioner,

10 T.C. 19 (1948), where all of the stock of a corporation
was owned by a family group, consisting of the active manager of the corporation, and his wife, sister and nieces.
The manager was persuaded the inactive women stockholders to
switch over to preferred stock, so that the common stock
could more readily be used to attract new executive talent,
and the danger of control passing to inexperienced shareholders would be eliminated. Accordingly, a plan was adopted under which all of the shareholders were permitted to
exchange each share of old common for one and ¼ shares of
new preferred, having a $5 cumulative dividend and a pref-
erence on liquidation. All of the inactive women stockholder
exchanged their old common stock for the new preferred,
while the manager kept his common. The company then limited the $5 preferred stock to the shares already issued,
and authorized a new $4 preferred stock to be issued for
sale to investors, plus additional common stock to be made
available to employees. The Tax Court held that the exchange
by the inactive stockholders of all of their old common for
new preferred constituted a tax-free recapitalization.

Having in mind that what is in form a recapitalization
may in substance amount to a stock dividend, is there any
danger that a recapitalization of the Dean-Hartzell type
could fall into the clutches of §305? That was feared in
1969 when §305 was substantially expanded, and in the
debates on the floor of the Senate it was specifically
indicated that such transactions were not intended to be
reached by the new §305. 115 Cong. Rec. 37902 (1969). The
Regulations adopt this view, stating that §305 does not apply
to "single and isolated" preferred stock recapitalizations.
Reg. §305-3(e), Ex. 12.

D. SECURITIES RECAPITALIZATIONS

The term "recapitalization" also embraces transactions involving exchanges of debt securities. Perhaps the most comprehensive
examination of this issue appears in Commissioner v. Neustadt's
Trust, 131 F.2d 528, 529 (2d Cir.1942), involving an exchange of outstanding 20-year, 6% debentures for a like amount of 10-year, 3¼%
convertible debentures of the corporation:

It is not disputed that the corporation's offer to its
old debenture holders constituted a plan of reorganization if
there was a "recapitalization." This term, which has been
in the tax law since 1921, has never been defined in the
Revenue Acts. Nor have the Treasury Regulations attempted any definition except by way of illustration. . . .
In Helvering v. Southwest Consolidated Corp., 315 U.S. 194,
202, 62 S.Ct. 546, 552, 86 L.Ed. 789, Mr. Justice Douglas

remarked that "recapitalization" contemplates a "reshuffling of a capital structure within the framework of an existing corporation." But this advances solution of the problem only by substituting the necessity of defining the phrase "a capital structure" instead of the word "recapitalization." The commissioner contends that only a change in authorized or outstanding capital stock of a corporation can properly be denominated a recapitalization or a reshuffling of the capital structure. He describes an exchange of old debentures for new debentures in the same corporation as a mere refinancing operation. In support of this view reference is made to definitions suggested by certain commentators. . . . But in common financial parlance the long term funded debt of a corporation is usually regarded as forming part of its capital structure. Instances of such usage may be found in Graham & Dodd, Security Analysis, 1934, p. 461; Kraft & Starkweather, Analysis of Industrial Securities, 1930, pp. 153, 154; Paul & Mertens, Law of Fed. Inc. Taxation, 1934, Vol. 2, p. 208; Fletcher, Cyclopedia on Corporations, 1938 Ed. Vol. 15, § 7215. The Security and Exchange Commission has required the funded debt of a corporation to be listed under the caption of "capital securities." The Interstate Commerce Commission treats funded debt as part of the corporate capital structure. . . . A court is justified in believing that when Congress employs in a tax law words having a well defined meaning in the business world, it used them with that meaning in the absence of clear evidence to the contrary. . . . There is no evidence to the contrary. On the other hand the purpose of the statutory nonrecognition of gain or loss from reorganization transactions, favors ascribing to the word "recapitalization" a broad rather than a restricted meaning. Such purpose, as indicated by the Congressional reports printed in the margin, was apparently twofold: To encourage legitimate reorganizations required to strengthen the financial condition of a corporation, and to prevent losses being established by bondholders, as well as stockholders, who have received the new securities without substantially changing their original investment. The transaction in the case at bar meets both of these tests. By changing the interest rate and date of maturity of its old bonds and adding a conversion option to the holders of the new, the corporation could strengthen its financial condition, while the bondholders would not substantially change their original investments by making the exchange. "Recapitalization" seems a most appropriate word to describe that type of reorganization and it is the very kind of transaction where Congress meant the recognition of gain or loss to be held in suspense until a more substantial change in the taxpayer's original investment should occur. We hold that the exchange of securities was made pursuant to a plan of "recapitalization."

Similarly, an exchange of new stock, preferred or common, for outstanding bonds constitutes a recapitalization. E.g., Commissioner v. Capento Securities Corporation, 140 F.2d 382 (1st Cir. 1944); Reg. § 1.368–2(e) (1).

More difficulty is presented by transactions involving the exchange of new debt securities for outstanding stock. For one thing, such a transaction really amounts to a repurchase of stock on credit, see Bowman v. Armour & Co., page 315 supra; and repurchase transactions have always been approached rather gingerly for tax as well as corporate purposes. More important, such transactions present a classic bail-out possibility—indeed, even more so than preferred stock exchanges because debt securities are more liquid than preferred stock and easier to sell (or redeem). Under the pre-1954 law this problem was particularly serious because there was then no counterpart of §§ 354(a)(2) and 356(d), and the literal language of the predecessor of § 354(a)(1) made the receipt of debt instruments in a reorganization tax-free so long as they qualified as "securities." However, the Supreme Court went far toward closing this loophole with its decision in Bazley v. Commissioner, 331 U.S. 737, 67 S.Ct. 1489, 91 L.Ed. 1782, 173 A.L.R. 905 (1947), involving an exchange of new no-par common and ten-year, callable debentures for old $100 par common. The Court held that a transaction which produced "for all practical purposes, the same result as a distribution of cash earnings of equivalent value, cannot obtain tax immunity because cast in the form of a recapitalization-reorganization. . . . A 'reorganization' which is merely a vehicle, however elaborate or elegant, for conveying earnings from accumulations to the stockholders is not a reorganization under [§ 368(a) (1)]."

On the other hand, non pro rata exchanges of new securities for outstanding stock have uniformly been held to qualify as recapitalizations eligible for tax-free treatment under the pre-1954 law. E.g., Hickok v. Commissioner, 32 T.C. 80 (1959) (rejecting the contention, *inter alia*, that an "upstream" exchange, i.e. of new debt for outstanding stock, did not constitute a recapitalization because it weakened rather than strengthened the corporation); Davis v. Penfield, 205 F.2d 798 (5th Cir.1953).

The solution of the 1954 Code is to treat as boot any excess in principal amount of securities received over securities surrendered, which of course means all securities received when none is surrendered. Generally speaking, under § 356 either gain will be recognized to the extent of the value of such excess securities or that amount will be taxed as a dividend. (If no non-recognition property is received, § 356 does not apply, and the transaction is left to be taxed under one of the other distribution provisions, §§ 301, 302, 331 or 346.)

SECTION 8.   REPURCHASE OF STOCK

A.   POWER TO PURCHASE

MOUNTAIN STATE STEEL FOUNDRIES, INC. v. COMMISSIONER *

United States Court of Appeals, Fourth Circuit, 1960.   284 F.2d 737.

HAYNSWORTH, CIRCUIT JUDGE.   Deficiencies of income tax for the fiscal years 1951–1954 were asserted against this corporate taxpayer upon (1) the disallowance of deductions for interest paid upon notes given in part payment of the purchase price of the stock of dissident stockholders upon the ground that the stock purchase agreement impaired the capital of the corporation and was invalid under state law, and (2) the assessment of the [accumulated earnings tax under the predecessor of §§ 531–537] upon the ground that by the redemption of the stock the corporation had been availed of for the purpose of avoiding surtaxes upon its remaining shareholders by accumulation of earnings.   In an unreviewed decision, the single judge of the Tax Court sustained the commissioner upon both questions.

Since we are of the opinion there was no income tax deficiency, we do not consider the Tax Court's computation of the [accumulated taxable income under the predecessor of § 535], a computation with which both parties find fault.

The transaction which gave birth to these problems was consummated in an effort to resolve difficulties arising out of the death of a partner in an antecedent partnership.   The story should start with the beginning.

Ben Miller and Harold F. Stratton, of Parkersburg, West Virginia, were the principal partners in a partnership engaged in manufacturing steel castings.   Miller died in 1945, and his widow and two daughters then became owners of his fifty per cent interest in the partnership, the other fifty per cent interest being owned by Stratton, his sister and two nephews.

On July 1, 1947, the business was incorporated.   Mountain State Steel Foundries, Inc., the taxpayer acquired all of the partnership assets in exchange for which it issued one thousand shares of its common stock, having a par value of $100 each, to the Millers and a like number of shares to the Strattons.   It assumed all of the partnership obligations.

---

*   Some   of   the   court's   footnotes omitted.

The Millers were not happy with the situation. Except that Mrs. Miller was a member of the Board of Directors, they took no active part in the conduct of the business, but felt the need of larger and more certain income than prospective dividends would provide. The business is said to have been subject to wide fluctuations in earnings. Additionally, the Strattons, who were active in the business and derived income from it through salaries, were interested in expanding and improving the business and its fixed assets and in utilizing a portion of current earnings in good years for that purpose.

This conflict in the interests of the stockholders led Mrs. Miller to demand that the business be sold. Stratton sought to find a purchaser for all of the stock or the corporate assets on a basis which would enable the stockholders to realize $1,700,000. Later, he reduced his asking price to $1,500,000. Some people were interested in the plant, but not at those prices.

In 1950, an accountant, who did work for the taxpayer and its stockholders, suggested to Mrs. Miller that the corporation might buy the Miller stock if she and her daughters would accept payment over a substantial number of years. Mrs. Miller thought well of the idea, and approached the Strattons about it. An agreement was then worked out for the corporation to purchase all of the Miller stock at a price of $450,000, payable $50,000 in cash and the balance, with interest at four per cent per annum, payable in level payments of $11,000 each six months until April 1, 1977 and of $5,000 each six months thereafter until April 1, 1994.[2]

The corporation has met its maturing obligations under these notes. The interest increment of its payments during its fiscal years 1951–1954, respectively, was $11,969.99, $15,757.00, $15,504.77 and $15,242.37. On its income tax returns for those years it deducted those amounts as interest paid.

The Commissioner disallowed these deductions on the theory that the purchase of the stock impaired the capital of the corporation in violation of § 3051 (31–1–39) of the West Virginia Code of 1955 and that, because of that statute, the obligations with respect to which the interest was paid were unenforceable and invalid. He further imposed the [accumulated earnings] tax on the theory that, since the Strattons might have bought the stock, had the Millers been willing to accept their personal obligations, and declared additional dividends to provide them with funds to meet their individual obligations, the corporate redemption of the Miller stock established, during each of the tax years, a use by the Strattons of the corporation for the avoidance of personal surtaxes by corporate accumulation of income.

2. Mrs. Miller received $30,000 of the cash payment and a note for $195,000, the principal and interest being payable at the rate of $6,000 each six months, or until April 1, 1977. Each daughter received $10,000 in cash and a note for $102,500, the principal and interest being payable at the rate of $2,500 each six months or until April 1, 1994. The taxpayer reserved the right to anticipate these payments after April 1, 1961.

After the Tax Court approved the Commissioner's theories on both aspects of the case, the taxpayer brought an action in the state court against the Millers seeking a declaratory judgment as to its obligations. This proceeding resulted in a decree of the Circuit Court of Wood County, West Virginia, in which it was held that the redemption of the stock did not impair the capital of the corporation within the meaning of § 3051 of the West Virginia Code and that the corporate notes were valid and enforceable. On the basis of this decree, the taxpayer sought leave to file a motion for further trial in the Tax Court. This was denied for lack of merit, apparently on the ground that the state court action was collusive or not really adversary. It does appear that the taxpayer's position in the state court action was that its officials believed the notes to be valid, binding obligations, but that no further payments would be made on them until the court determined and declared the rights and duties of the parties. Honestly, it hardly could have taken any other position.

[Part I *]

The Interest Deduction

By statute,[3] West Virginia has authorized a corporation organized under her laws, other than a banking institution, to purchase, hold and sell shares of its own capital stock. There is a proviso, however, that funds and property of the corporation may not be used to purchase its own shares if the use would impair the capital of the corporation.

The Tax Court was apparently of the opinion that the net worth of the corporation should have been reduced by the full amount of the purchase price as soon as the repurchase agreement was entered into and that the question of impairment should be determined by reference to book figures without regard to the real value of the assets. The Circuit Court for Wood County, West Virginia, on the other hand, held that the real value of the assets, which it found to be substantially more than the book figures, was crucial under the statute. The Commissioner finds the entries in the books so authoritarian that he conceded on argument that if the taxpayer had written up the value of its fixed assets on the basis of an appraisal in line with the testimony in this case and in the state court proceeding, there would have been no capital impairment. He does not question the disparity between real and book values; to him, it is the failure to

---

* [Ed. note] Division of the opinion into "Parts" is by the editor.

3. § 3051 of West Virginia Code of 1955. ". . . Every corporation organized under this chapter, or existing under the laws of this State, shall have the power to purchase, hold, sell and transfer shares of its own capital stock: Provided, that no such corporation shall use its funds or property for the purchase of its own shares of capital stock when such use would cause any impairment of the capital of the corporation; . . ."

have recorded the real value on the books which occasioned the asserted impairment of the capital.

We think a determination of the substantive rights of creditors, stockholders and the corporation, in the application of this statute, should not be so circumscribed by managerial decision to make or withhold particular entries on the books or by the accounting procedures followed by management, procedures which may, or may not, have been realistic or enlightened. Write ups by appraisal are frequently suspect. As a practice they are now usually frowned upon. The suggestion is startling that such a ministerial act, which alters the real situation not in the least, could enlarge corporate power to purchase its stock.

When the legislature spoke of impairment of capital, we think it had a more objective standard than a computation which is the product of years of financial history of an enterprise. If write ups by appraisal be subject to criticism in the world of corporate finance, a blind acceptance of book values as real is much more vulnerable. An overstatement of assets because of a failure to charge off obsolescent equipment should not enlarge the power of the corporation to buy its stock, nor should an understatement because of appreciation in values and the decline in the worth of money restrict it.

Corporate power to purchase its own stock has been frequently abused. Done by corporations conducting faltering businesses, it has been employed to create preferences to the detriment of creditors and of the other stockholders. It was to protect and preserve the margin of safety supplied by the real value of contributed capital that such statutes were enacted. That purpose is not served if the statute is applied in terms of unrealistic values, whether higher or lower than real values. At least until the highest court of West Virginia should otherwise decide, we think for our collateral purpose the statute should be construed as prohibiting the purchase of its own stock if the use of its funds for the purpose would deplete the realizable value of its assets to a point below the total of its liabilities and capital.

What little can be found in decided cases applying similar statutes suggests that actual values, rather than book figures, are critical to the inquiry. Though impressive argument may be made that unrealized gain should not be available justification for dividends, similar language in statutes restricting dividend distributions has been similarly construed.[6]

If we are to look to actual values in applying the statute, the spirit of the statute requires that they be conservatively determined. Opinion evidence of appreciation should be received with skepticism if insolvency ensues. Here, however, no one questions the fact that

6. Randall v. Bailey, . . . ; Morris v. Standard Gas & Electric Co., 31 Del.Ch. 20, 63 A.2d 577.

the real worth of the plant substantially exceeds its depreciated cost.[7] In subsequent years this small manufacturing enterprise has continued to prosper. Its subsequent earnings have been sufficient to maintain a good current position, meet the obligations to the Millers, pay for substantial plant additions and improvements and pay moderate dividends. Its subsequent history is one of prosperity, not of decline. No creditor has suffered loss or delay.

[Part II]

We think the Tax Court also misapplied the statute in declaring unenforceable an executory agreement without regard to the "use" of funds which the statute proscribes. Literally read, the statute prohibits use by a corporation of its funds to purchase its own stock if such use will impair the capital. It says nothing of executory agreements which create no rights enforceable in competition with the rights of creditors. Nor do we find anything in the purpose of the statute to protect creditors' rights which requires an extension of the literal language to executory agreements which have not, and in performance cannot, impair the preferred rights.

It is now well-established that the claims of former stockholders under such executory agreements are subordinate to the claims of other creditors existing at the time of performance.[8] When a corporation purchases a portion of its outstanding stock with an agreement to pay for it at a subsequent time, it may not perform its promise if the use of its funds in performance will impair its capital. This is true though earlier performance at the time of consummation of the executory agreement would have occasioned no impairment of the capital.

The promise, therefore, is conditional.[9] The corporation's promise is to pay provided at the time of payment it has sufficient surplus that disbursement of the funds will occasion no impairment of capital. In effect, the statute is read into the agreement. The mere existence of an executory promise to pay so conditioned that it may not be per-

---

7. For tax purposes, the corporation was required to use as its basis for its fixed assets the depreciated cost of its antecedent partnership. Starting with those figures, it showed on its balance sheet at the end of its fiscal year, 1950, a gross plant account of $543,235.46, a depreciation reserve of $345,355.59 and net book value of fixed assets of $197,879.87. It had approximately $150,000 of current assets to pay $20,000 of current liabilities. It had, according to the books, earned surplus of $132,527.53, which, added to the capital account of $200,000, gave it a net worth of $332,527.53. If, as the testimony indicates, its fixed assets had a realizable sales value of at least $1,000,000, its real net worth was more than $1,100,000.

8. See, among others, . . . In re Fecheimer Fishel Co., 2 Cir., 212 F. 357; . . . Richards v. Ernst Wiener Co., 207 N.Y. 59, 100 N.E. 592; . . .

9. This was the express holding in Topken, Loring & Schwartz, Inc. v. Schwartz, [noted at page 437, note 52, infra].

formed if performance will impair the capital, hardly may be said, itself, to have impaired the capital.[11]

In most of the cases which have dealt with the problem, the corporation, when it made the promise, had an apparent surplus sufficient to support it. In Christie v̇. Fifth Madison Corp.,[12] however, the corporation had no surplus when the promise was made. Since the promise was held to be conditioned by the statute, it was held to be a lawful obligation.

Whether the corporate surplus is more or less than the obligation conditionally undertaken, the application of the statute should be the same. In either case, existing creditors suffer no injury when the conditional promise is given. If creditors are prejudiced, it is performance in the use of corporate funds in violation of the statute which works the harm. Those creditors existing at the time of performance are the ones who need the protection of the statute, not those earlier creditors whose claims were unaffected by the executory promise.

What happened here is illustrative. When the agreement was executed in 1950, no creditor was injured. The corporation has prospered since then. With subsequent earnings, it has met its maturing obligations under this agreement, paid for plant additions and improvements and maintained a good cash position. The 1950 creditors' claims long ago were paid in full. If the corporation should suffer financial reverses, creditors of a future day may be exposed to prejudice by further performance of this agreement. For the benefit of those future creditors who may need the protection of the statute, the impact of the statute should be felt at the time of performance, to which its language is directed. In the meanwhile, when corporate use of corporate funds adversely affects no creditor, the statutory language need not be expanded to thwart the reasonable purposes of the corporation and of its present and former stockholders.

As we stated in connection with the other branch of this problem, we deal with the statute only collaterally. If the literal language of the statute is to be expanded to have the effect for which the Commissioner contends, it should be done by West Virginia's legislature or her courts. We find no justification for our interpreting the statute, for our purpose, to have so expanded and so technical an application.

The Commissioner seeks to support the holding of the Tax Court upon the additional ground that the transaction brought no new money

11. Perhaps the condition is more accurately expressed as being that performance should not occasion a violation of the statute. In liquidation, the claim of the promisee, deferred to the claims of all general creditors, would be preferred over the interests of the remaining stockholders. Until the claims of all other creditors are fully satisfied, however, the practical effect of the condition may be stated in the language of the statute.

12. 123 N.Y.S.2d 795 [noted at page 348. infra].

into the corporation. He relies upon cases dealing with hybrid securities where the courts have disregarded the labels attached by the parties to securities and to distributions to the security holders. In such cases the fact that no fresh money came into the corporate treasury when the securities were issued may be of importance. Here, however, the Commissioner does not contend that the Millers are not creditors, or that the notes should be treated as preferred stock. His basic contention is that they are creditors, holding notes, the issuance of which impaired the capital. Under the circumstances, the fact that issuance of the notes brought no new money into the till is irrelevant.

[Part III]

The Avoidance of Surtax upon Stockholders Through Accumulation of Earnings

The Tax Court upheld the imposition of the [accumulated earnings tax] because of the fact that an accountant suggested the purchase of the Miller stock by the corporation. It reasoned that he must have known that if the corporation had paid additional dividends to the Strattons in an amount equal to the disbursements to the Millers, the Strattons would have had larger surtax obligations. It was of the opinion the purchase of the Miller stock served no corporate purpose, and that the Strattons must have learned of the tax considerations from their accountant and must have acted as they did for the purpose of avoiding additional surtax on their personal income.

There was no finding that the Millers, who suggested the corporate purchase to the Strattons, would have been willing to accept the personal obligations of the Strattons or that the Strattons would have been willing to obligate themselves and their estates to make payments extending over a period of 44 years. There was no finding that in any year accumulated earnings were unreasonable or in excess of the needs of the business.[14] There was only the opinion that these disbursements served no legitimate corporate purpose and were arranged by the Strattons with a purpose of avoidance of surtaxes.

We disagree with the premise of the Tax Court that these disbursements served no corporate purpose.

The problem which confronted the widow and daughters of Ben Miller and the Strattons is one that frequently arises upon the death of one co-venturer in a relatively small business enterprise. Many of those enterprises are worth substantially more to those who are able and anxious to manage them, deriving livelihoods from salaries, than to passive investors who must look only to prospective dividends for a return upon their investment. The Miller stock clearly was worth much less as a continuing investment to Mrs. Miller than it would have been worth to Ben Miller had he survived and remained

---

14. See Young Motor Company Inc. v.
Commissioner, 1 Cir., 281 F.2d 488.

active in the management of the business. It was natural that she should demand that the business be sold or liquidated, and it would have been essentially unfair to have left her and her daughters indefinitely in a position in which they could expect relatively small and uncertain income from what everyone regarded, with reason, as a valuable property.

This sort of situation leads to demands for dividends out of consideration of the stockholders' personal financial need, perhaps without appropriate regard for the need of the corporation to make capital expenditures in order to maintain a competitive position. On the other hand, those stockholders active in the management of the business deriving salaries from it may be able to afford indulgence of an ambition to enlarge future earnings through still larger current capital expenditures, an indulgence which other stockholders may ill afford.

When the stockholders have such conflicting interests, the corporation and its future are necessarily affected. When the situation results in demands that the business be sold or liquidated, as it did here, the impact of the conflict upon the corporation is direct and immediate. That it is of concern to employees is illustrated by the brief *amicus curiae* of United Steelworkers, the bargaining agent of the taxpayer's employees, filed in support of the taxpayer's position. The resolution of such a conflict, so that the need of the corporation may govern managerial decision, is plainly a corporate purpose.

Many business men now anticipate such problems and provide solutions through agreements, and implementing devices, to take out the estate of a co-venturer, who dies, on a basis designed to be fair to the estate, to the enterprise and to the surviving co-venturers. It has been held that corporate disbursements to pay insurance premiums to provide a fund with which to purchase stock from the estate of the person whose life is insured do serve a corporate, business purpose. If disbursements to create a fund with which to purchase stock serve a corporate purpose, surely the disbursement of the created fund in purchasing the stock serves the same purpose.

For a long time there was controversy over the tax consequence to shareholders when a corporation made disproportionate distributions in partial redemption of its stock. Congress finally acted in this field. Among other things, it specifically provided that a partial redemption of the shares held by an estate would be treated as a sale, not as a distribution of earnings, if the amount of the distribution did not exceed the estate's liabilities for estate and inheritance taxes, interest and funeral and administration expenses. When Congress specifically provided favorable tax treatment for such transactions and sought to encourage them to facilitate the administration of estates, it hardly could have intended to penalize the corporation for doing the favored act.

We need not say that under no circumstances may a stock purchase be relevant to a question arising under [the accumulated earnings tax]. When it is done out of cash accumulations which reasonably may be thought excessive, such a purchase, along with other factors, may be considered appropriately in arriving at ultimate findings.[18] The fact of redemption, of itself, however, furnishes no basis for imposition of the [accumulated earnings] tax. In the circumstances in which they were made, the disbursements in payment for the stock, themselves, do not support a finding that they were withdrawn from excess funds accumulated from earnings beyond reasonable corporate need. Nor is the situation altered by the fact that the Strattons may have been aware that travel along another route would have cost something more in taxes. If they had a choice of routes, they were not required to choose the one which would be most costly to them in taxes.

Reversed.

18. See Pelton Steel Casting Co. v. Commissioner, 7 Cir., 251 F.2d 278.

NOTE ON ACCOUNTING FOR TREASURY SHARES

Before analyzing the installment repurchase issues involved in the foregoing case it may be useful to take a quick look at the handling of a simple cash repurchase. Like most of the modern statutes, MBA §6 subjects repurchases of stock to virtually the same limitations as are imposed on dividend distributions. That is certainly sensible: as indicated in the first two paragraphs after heading I on page 342 (which should be read at this point), from the vantage point of creditors, who are the primary beneficiaries of dividend restrictions, repurchase transactions are pretty much the same as dividends, since a corporation's acquisition of its own shares gives it nothing of value so far as creditors are concerned. Consequently, a direct charge to earned surplus (or capital surplus, as allowed in some circumstances) might have been required in connection with a repurchase of stock, just as is true in the case of a dividend. However, such an approach would ignore the feature of stock repurchase which is not shared by dividends -- that the repurchased shares (often referred to as "treasury stock") can be resold. Arguably, a resale of the repurchased shares (assume, for simplicity, at a price equal to the amount paid upon repurchase) should put the corporation back in the same position as it was before the repurchase. But that result is hard to reach if earned surplus is actually reduced upon the repurchase, because of the accepted accounting practice that a sale of shares by the issuer should not create earned surplus. Perhaps an exception could have been carved out for the resale of treasury stock, although it should be kept in mind that such a transaction is something of a fiction anyway, since the corporation could as well instead have simply issued new shares, to which the general accounting rule would clearly apply. In any event, the Model Act expressly opts for preserving the opportunity to restore earned surplus upon a resale of treasury stock, by providing that upon a repurchase earned surplus is merely restricted (so that it can not be "used" again to support another repurchase of stock, or a dividend), rather than being reduced. As a corollary, the cost of the treasury stock is held in a kind of suspense account (awaiting a decision as to whether that stock will be resold), by carrying it as a general deduction from the total of shareholders' equity on the right-hand side of the balance sheet, offsetting the decline in the assets equal to the purchase price paid. Then if the treasury stock is in fact resold the treasury stock deduction from shareholders' equity is eliminated, balancing the restoration of the assets due to receipt of the selling price, and the restriction on earned surplus is removed (subject to appropriate adjustments if the amount received upon resale is different from the repurchase price).

If instead the repurchased shares are cancelled, again the treasury stock deduction would be eliminated, but this time without any accompanying restoration of assets, so there is no escape from an actual reduction of surplus to reflect the original distribution of assets in payment of the repurchase price. The obvious approach would be to translate the original restriction on earned surplus into a permanent reduction, which is what would have occurred at the outset but for the suspense procedure of restricting earned surplus and carrying the cost of the treasury stock as a deduction from shareholders' equity. However, it is not clear that this is the result reached by the statute. Under MBA §68, a cancellation of the reacquired shares constitutes a reduction of capital, in the amount of the capital attributable to those shares, producing an equal amount of capital surplus, pursuant to §70. At the same time, under §6 the restriction on earned surplus is removed; but the statute does not say expressly that earned surplus is to be reduced. Hence, it is possible to reduce the capital surplus resulting from the cancellation, leaving the earned surplus intact (except to the extent of any excess of the purchase price of the treasury shares over the stated capital attributable to them, which would necessarily fall on earned surplus).

The comment to §6 states that the latter is "clearly" the proper outcome, but, with respect, that is far from obvious. Certainly the language of §6 itself does not require this construction. More important, as several commentators who reached the same view have lamented, under this approach it would be possible to use a small amount of earned surplus to keep buying in shares and cancelling them, without ever having to get the approval of shareholders which would be required if capital surplus were being relied on to "back" a repurchase of stock. It seems more sensible to assume that any particular amount of earned surplus can be used only once to support repurchase of shares (unless they are resold), a result achieved by requiring that the entire cost of cancelled shares be charged against earned surplus. Then it would be the capital surplus, produced by the reduction of capital stemming from the cancellation, which would be left after the transaction. Unless the corporation had additional earned surplus, any further repurchase of stock would be subject to the limitations on the use of capital surplus under §6.

NOTE ON INSTALLMENT REPURCHASE TRANSACTIONS

HERWITZ, INSTALLMENT REPURCHASE OF STOCK: SURPLUS LIMITATIONS

79 Harv.L.Rev. 303–326 (1965).

In effect, the Mountain State holding means that an installment repurchase transaction is to be treated as if the successive installments constituted a series of independent repurchase transactions, each of which is to be tested separately under the statute. Of course, the precise question presented for decision in the Mountain State case was whether the total face amount of the installment obligations has to meet the surplus test at the outset, and not whether each installment has to pass the test. But these two issues are obviously interdependent in that the statutory test must be applied at one of the two points, and therefore a decision that the statute need not be satisfied at the outset necessarily means that each installment must be tested independently. The purpose of this Comment is to explore these two alternatives in an effort to determine whether the installment-by-installment approach adopted in Mountain State is sound.

I. HISTORICAL BACKGROUND—THE INSOLVENCY CUTOFF

Perhaps the best starting point for this analysis is a brief historical survey of the treatment of repurchase transactions. While from the very beginning state corporation statutes have generally restricted dividends to surplus in order to preserve the capital invested in the enterprise as a safety margin for creditors, the same limitations were not originally applied to the repurchase of stock. Of course, it is now clearly recognized that there is no less an invasion of the safety margin for creditors when capital is returned to shareholders through a repurchase of their stock than when the return takes the form of a dividend. But most American courts, absent an express statute, refused to limit repurchases to surplus, contenting themselves instead with imposing such vague conditions as that there be "no prejudice to the rights of creditors." To be sure, there was early recognition that the repurchase of stock could not be treated as a reduction of legal capital unless there had also been compliance with the statutory formalities for a capital reduction transaction, so that a repurchase of stock did not affect the stated capital measuring rod used in determining how much surplus there was. But this rule was offset by treating the repurchased shares as an asset replacing the cash or other property exchanged for them, leaving net assets also unaffected by the transaction.

Today, of course, it is almost universally recognized that stock should not be viewed as an asset in the hands of the issuer. Once reacquired, such "treasury" stock is no different from authorized but unissued stock, which has never been accorded asset status. And insofar as creditors are concerned, they usually become worried about the makeup of the assets of a corporation as a source for payment of their claims only when they are not being paid in ordinary course, and at such times treasury stock is almost certain to be worthless.

In any event, it was generally assumed that under the majority "no prejudice" rule, once a corporation became insolvent repurchase of stock was no longer permissible. Probably repurchase by an insolvent corporation would be voidable as a fraudulent conveyance anyway, since payment would be in exchange for an "asset" demonstrably worthless. On the other hand, a repurchase completed while the corporation was still solvent was not invalidated by subsequent insolvency. . . .

Obviously, under the prevailing approach it was necessary to determine whether repurchase had preceded insolvency or vice versa — a question that in turn required a determination of not only the date of insolvency but also the date when the repurchase "occurred" for this purpose. This posed a special problem in cases in which payment of the redemption price was deferred: was the critical time when the repurchase agreement was executed, or the date on which the price was due? The nearest analogy seemed to be presented by the cases involving resale options, that is, options granted to stockholders (usually at the time they purchased their stock) to require a corporation to repurchase the stock at a specified price. Most of these cases involved attempts by stockholders to exercise their options after the corporation became insolvent, and in this situation the courts showed little hesitancy in holding that the exercise came too late. Exercise of a resale option does not differ from the execution of a new repurchase agreement, particularly from the point of view of creditors, who will rarely have had any notice of the option prior to its exercise. . . .

Thus the resale option cases were of little help in cases in which a solvent corporation executed a binding repurchase agreement, whether in pursuance of an option or otherwise, but became insolvent before completing payment of the redemption price. . . .

Nevertheless, most of the courts insisted on solvency at the date of payment. Once a corporation became insolvent, any payment on a repurchase obligation was regarded as "prejudicial" to the interests of other creditors, and the unpaid balance on the obligation was subordinated to their claims. An excellent illustration is the oft-cited case of Robinson v. Wangemann,[18] in which the court reversed the allowance of a claim against a bankrupt corporation based on a note given by the corporation for the purchase of some of its stock:

> Arthur Wangemann loaned no money to the corporation. The note he accepted for his stock did not change the character of the transaction nor did the renewals have that effect. A transaction by which a corporation acquires its own stock from a stockholder for a sum of money is not really a sale. The corporation does not acquire anything of value equivalent to the depletion of its assets, if the stock is held in the treasury, as in this case. It is simply a method of distributing a proportion of the assets to the stockholder. The assets of a corporation are the common pledge of its creditors, and stockholders are not entitled to receive any part of them unless creditors are paid in full. When such a transaction is had, regardless of the good faith of the parties, it is essential to its validity that there be sufficient [excess of assets over liabilities] . . . to retire the stock, without prejudice to creditors, at the time payment is made out of assets. In principle, the contract between Wangemann and the corporation was executory until the stock should be paid for in cash. It is immaterial that the corporation was solvent and had sufficient [excess of assets over liabilities] . . . to make payment when the agreement was entered into. It is necessary to a recovery that the corporation should be solvent and have sufficient [excess of assets over liabilities] . . . to prevent injury to creditors when the payment is actually made. This was an implied condition in the original note and the renewals accepted by Arthur Wangemann.

Decisions such as Robinson v. Wangemann were doubtless due at least in part to an increasing concern on the part of the courts that the "no prejudice" rule might be too liberal; and naturally there was particular resistance to letting former shareholders share in any guise with regular creditors in the assets of an insolvent enterprise. Moreover, at least when the selling stockholders were insiders, a delay between the execution of the repurchase agreement and the payment date might really amount to a hedge against financial disaster for the selling stockholders, since the insiders were in a position to rescind the repurchase if the fortunes of the corporation took a turn for the better. In addition, the analogy to a repurchase for cash followed by a loan of the redemption proceeds to the corporation was not very convincing, since more often than not the corporation was already in a precarious financial condition at the time of the repurchase transaction. Thus the corporation typically had neither the necessary cash nor the power to borrow it elsewhere, particularly for the purpose of repurchasing stock; and the idea that stockholders who had just sold out for cash would lend the money back to such a corporation was equally unrealistic.

There is also a special reason for applying the insolvency test to each installment when, as was usually the case, the equity insolvency test is involved. Under that test, with its emphasis on current liabilities, pre-

18. 75 F.2d 756 (5th Cir.1935).

sumably only so much of the repurchase obligation as is due currently (or within the relatively near future) is to be taken into account. As previously noted, if the total face amount of the obligation is not tested at the outset, then obviously each installment should be.

There were occasional chinks in the fairly solid wall of judicial opinion refusing to allow enforcement of a repurchase obligation on a parity with claims of general creditors after a corporation has become insolvent. Perhaps the most forceful statement of the contrary view appears in Wolff v. Heidritter Lumber Co.,[21] in which the court, after distinguishing the cases refusing to allow exercise of a resale option after insolvency, argued as follows:

> [If a purchase of stock] . . . would be valid if the money were then and there paid out of the corporate treasury, it is not perceived why the purchase would be invalidated if the company instead of giving its check in payment gave its note or its other obligation for deferred payment. The contract would be complete; the corporate assets necessary to pay debts would be no differently affected; the corporation's creditors would have no greater right to complain. The stockholder would become a creditor, an unpaid creditor instead of a paid vendor; but the debt due him, being valid then, would not become invalid by reason of the company subsequently becoming insolvent before the date of the debt's maturity. . . .

Plainly there is much to be said for this reasoning, at least when, as was true in the Wolff case, the corporation is prosperous enough at the time of the transaction to make the analogy to a cash repurchase and a loan of the proceeds not too farfetched. • • • Nevertheless, the Wolff approach garnered very few adherents over the years, and at this point the insolvency cutoff rule may well be regarded as a settled matter of public policy which is unlikely to be overturned absent an express statutory mandate.

II. Application of the Surplus Limitation

It is against this background that the question arose as to whether a statutory surplus test should be applied to the total of an installment repurchase obligation when executed or to each installment as paid. Obviously, there is at least a surface analogy between the surplus test and the insolvency test, which invites the easy assumption that the rule should be the same in the two cases, with the surplus test also applied on an installment-by-installment basis. Thus in Mountain State the court proceeded directly from the proposition that "the claims of former stockholders under such executory agreements are subordinate to the claims of other creditors existing at the time of performance" (for which it cited a number of authorities most of which involved the insolvency cutoff), to the proposition that "when a corporation purchases a portion of its outstanding stock with an agreement to pay for it at a subsequent time, it may not perform its promise if the use of its funds in performance will impair its capital," without any discussion of possible distinctions between the two situations.

21. 112 N.J.Eq. 34, 163 A. 140 (Ch.1932).

Similarly, in California, where repurchase is both generally confined to earned surplus and expressly conditioned upon solvency, the courts seem to have moved from an insolvency cutoff to a surplus cutoff without any real consideration of possible differences between the two situations. In the case of In re Mathews Constr. Co.,[26] the court rejected a claim on a repurchase obligation, stating: "An agreement by a corporation to repurchase stock, though valid at the time entered into, becomes invalid if,. at the time of payment, there is no surplus. . . . Bankruptcy having intervened, obviously there can be no surplus from which payment for repurchased stock may be made." . . .

In fact, there are some important differences between the insolvency and capital impairment situations which must be considered before concluding that the two should be treated alike. It is true that, as under the insolvency test, if the surplus test is not applied at the outset then each installment must be tested or else the statutory limitation would have no impact at all. But, unlike the insolvency test, the surplus test does not look only to current liabilities and thus there is no obstacle to applying the surplus test to the total face amount of an installment obligation at the outset. Moreover, the Mountain State opinion makes quite clear that its decision not to apply the surplus test at the outset is a consequence of its conclusion that each installment must pass the test, rather than the other way round. Therefore, it makes sense to examine the installment-by-installment rule on its own merits.

An appropriate starting point is the analogy, rejected in connection with the insolvency test, between an installment repurchase transaction and a repurchase for cash accompanied by a loan of the redemption proceeds back to the corporation. When the corporation has sufficient surplus to cover the total repurchase obligation at the outset, such a view of the transaction is no longer so unrealistic. . . .

Does fairness to creditors require a contrary view? While it was concern for the interest of creditors that led to installment-by-installment testing for insolvency, it is much harder to justify a flat bar against payments simply because surplus has declined since the execution of the agreement to an amount less than the next installment due. Payment of an installment that impairs capital is surely a far cry from putting former stockholders on a parity with creditors in the liquidation of an insolvent enterprise.

No doubt any distribution that impairs capital is a matter of some concern to creditors, and particularly so when it follows a period of losses, as may well have occurred if a surplus large enough to cover the total obligation at the outset is no longer sufficient to cover a particular installment. But in weighing this concern, it is important to keep in mind that nowadays the general ban on distributions that impair capital is often more apparent than real. Under modern statutes, stockholders commonly have the power to make what is in effect a distribution out of capital simply by reducing stated capital and then distributing the resulting capital surplus, measured by the amount of net assets in excess of the capital as

26. 120 F.Supp. 818 (S.D.Cal.1954).

reduced. It seems harsh to bar a corporation from continuing to honor a bona fide repurchase obligation in circumstances in which, absent such an obligation, the corporation could put itself in a position to make a voluntary distribution to stockholders. Indeed, in such circumstances perhaps the corporation should be obliged to take the necessary steps to reduce its capital in order that it can continue to make the agreed payments. Of course, thoughtful counsel could foresee this problem and plan for it in the repurchase agreement. But the important point is that such a problem would not even arise if the surplus test were applied only to the total obligation at the outset.

Another problem created by a surplus cutoff rule relates to the position of the selling stockholder if and when the bar is applied in midstream. Unlike the analogous problem under an insolvency cutoff, here the matter is of considerable practical importance, since a corporation may carry on indefinitely despite an impairment of capital. Accordingly, it is necessary to make sure that the selling stockholder does not end up in a kind of limbo, without the status of either creditor or stockholder.

. . . it would hardly be fair to the corporation (or perhaps more accurately, to the remaining stockholders) to provide that the selling stockholders may regain all of their stock at any time when there is a default prior to final payment, since such a rule could result in a windfall to the selling stockholders unless they were compelled to return all prior payments. These questions are a good deal easier to state than to answer. Doubtless here also astute counsel could plan for them in advance, although a solution fair to both sides is not immediately apparent.[40] But again the important point is that this whole chain of complications stems directly from a surplus cutoff rule, and could therefore be avoided by adopting the contrary view.

Another problem that must be faced when the surplus test is applied on an installment-by-installment basis is the relative position of the holder of a repurchase obligation vis-à-vis subsequent creditors with knowledge of the repurchase commitment. While the authorities have uniformly assumed that a creditor is not excluded from the protection of the statutory repurchase limitation merely because his claim arose after the repurchase transaction, some cases have indicated that if such creditors had specific knowledge of the repurchase commitment the opposite result might be reached. Distinctions based upon knowledge are always difficult to draw, particularly since they involve that even more slippery concept, notice; and nowhere is the difficulty better illustrated than in the context of ascertaining what information certain financial statements have disclosed, and deciding whether they were or should have been examined. . . .

40. One possibility might be to provide some mechanics whereby, during any extended default on a repurchase obligation, the former shareholders would regain voting control—or at least voting power equal to what they formerly had—though not the equity in the shares. This result might be achieved by such devices as contingent voting rights for the repurchase obligations (if state law permits), or a pledge of the repurchased shares to secure the obligations, with contingent voting rights for the pledgees, or a voting trust arrangement.

Application of the surplus test on an installment-by-installment basis also poses some knotty problems in accounting for a repurchase transaction. Although a repurchase of stock does not necessarily require a reduction of surplus, it does at least necessitate a restriction on surplus in the amount of the purchase price, in order to prevent the use of the same surplus for the payment of dividends or for other repurchases. Obviously, in the case of an installment repurchase transaction, there are the same questions as to when and how this surplus restriction should be applied as there are in applying the surplus test itself. Since the surplus restriction requirement is really a corollary of the surplus test, presumably the same schedule should be adopted for both purposes, so that if the surplus test is applied on an installment-by-installment basis, surplus need only be restricted to the extent of each installment as paid. But the result of this approach would be that even if the corporation had ample surplus to cover the total repurchase obligation at the outset, it would not be required to restrict that much surplus, and instead would be free to use it for dividends or other repurchases. Indeed, absent some contractual restriction, either express or implied, a former stockholder holding an installment repurchase obligation might be powerless to prevent the corporation from so dissipating its surplus as to render itself unable to make future installment payments when due.

* * *

There is also a serious problem as to how to deal with the interest payments that may be called for in connection with an installment repurchase obligation. In the only case that expressly involved the matter, Christie v. Fifth Madison Corp.,[48] it was assumed without discussion that under installment-by-installment testing the periodic interest payments as well as the principal payments were required to pass the surplus test. As a logical matter, the installment-by-installment approach, which sees the payment of cash as all-important, may make a reluctance to distinguish between interest payments and principal payments quite understandable, particularly since the interest rate and schedule of payments are so much within the control of the parties. Nevertheless, application of the surplus test to the interest payments is unsupportable if the interest has been deducted in computing the corporation's net income (as would typically be true), since it would mean that interest was really being taken into account twice in applying the surplus test.

This problem too would be largely avoided if the surplus test were applied to the total repurchase obligation at the outset rather than on an installment-by-installment basis. Once the total principal amount of the repurchase obligation had been validated under the surplus test at the outset, the repurchase obligation would be a binding, unconditional debt of the corporation, and the interest component of the subsequent individual installments would be treated no differently from interest on any other debt. To be sure, this approach might leave some room for maneuver by the parties by virtue of their control over the allocation between interest and principal. Thus a corporation contemplating a repurchase of stock for an amount in excess of its then available surplus, payable in installments at a specified in-

48. 123 N.Y.S.2d 795 (Sup.Ct.1953).

terest rate, might rewrite the transaction to reduce the principal amount to a figure covered by existing surplus while increasing the interest rate enough to make the annual installments approximately the same as before.

The foregoing analysis leads to the conclusion that application of the surplus test, to the total repurchase obligation at the outset is not only feasible but also avoids a number of difficult problems inherent in the installment-by-installment approach. Are there any critical disadvantages in applying the test at the outset? None has been suggested in any of the cases adopting the installment-by-installment approach, apart from the basic concern reflected in cases such as Mountain State that application of the surplus test at the outset would make it impossible to effect desirable repurchase transactions (particularly in close corporation situations) for lack of sufficient surplus at the time of the original agreement. But it is perfectly possible to uphold such transactions without insisting upon an installment-by-installment construction of the statute in those cases in which there is sufficient surplus at the start. There is nothing to prevent a corporation that does not have enough surplus at the time of the agreement to validate the total repurchase obligation from executing a concededly conditional repurchase agreement under which each installment would in fact constitute a separate repurchase transaction. In effect this arrangement would be equivalent to the installment-by-installment approach. In such cases, counsel would have to be on their guard to consider and plan against the various difficulties which that approach entails. But in those cases in which the surplus at the outset was sufficient, counsel would no longer have to be concerned about the amount of the corporation's surplus thereafter.

III. SOME OBSERVATIONS ON PLANNING

Naturally, counsel for shareholders reselling their stock to a corporation have sought to plan around the insolvency and surplus cutoff rules. Once again a tax case provides an excellent example. In United States v. General Geophysical Co.,[59] the taxpayer corporation and the family of its deceased founder agreed that the seventy-seven percent stock interest held by the latter would be redeemed for cash and notes. The corporation's earned surplus was sufficient to cover the total purchase price. However, counsel for the retiring stockholders advised against the proposal on the ground that, under Robinson v. Wangemann [supra], the repurchase notes would be subordinated to the claims of other creditors in the event the corporation became bankrupt. In an effort to avoid this risk the parties decided to have the corporation redeem the stock in exchange for cash and corporate properties having a market value equal to the principal amount of the previously proposed notes. A few hours after the transfer, the corporation repurchased the properties for notes in the same amount as had originally been agreed on for the repurchase of the stock, securing the notes by a mortgage covering those and other properties of the corporation. While there had been no prior formal agreement by the former stockholders to resell the properties to the corporation, this prospect had been discussed, and prior to the redemption transaction, documents for a resale had been prepared in case that course was followed.

---

[59]. 296 F.2d 86 (5th Cir.1961)

The tax issue was whether the corporation could use as its basis for depreciating the reacquired properties the price paid to the retiring stockholders, which was substantially in excess of the corporation's former basis in those properties. Since the corporation was not required to recognize any gain upon the transfer of the properties in redemption of its stock,* use of the higher basis would have represented a considerable tax windfall. The taxpayer pointed to the important nontax reason that had led to the transaction and persuaded the district court that the reacquisition of the properties should be recognized as a purchase giving rise to a new basis for tax purposes. However, the court of appeals reversed. It conceded that there had been a valid business purpose for the transaction, but observed that this only sufficed to preclude a summary finding that the arrangement constituted a mere subterfuge. The real question, said the court, was whether there had been a sufficient interruption in the ownership of the properties to produce a new basis. And it was concluded that there had not been a sufficient interruption, in view of the facts (1) that the corporation had made no physical delivery of any of the properties; (2) that it had parted with only bare legal title to the property and only for a few short hours; and (3) that while the retiring stockholders may have been legally free not to resell the properties to the corporation, it was a foregone conclusion that they would sell them to someone—the very reason for the original sale of their stock was that they no longer wished to own or manage these properties—and the taxpayer corporation was the logical purchaser since the properties constituted almost fifty per cent of its assets and were fully integrated into its operations.

The more important question in the present context is whether this transaction would have achieved its alleged primary purpose of avoiding the insolvency cutoff. It is hard to believe that it would have. For the same factors relied upon by the court of appeals in concluding that there was an insufficient interruption of ownership to justify a change in tax basis would seem to call equally for a decision that the nature of the transaction had not really changed from a repurchase of stock to a repurchase of property. Certainly from the point of view of creditors there is no basis for treating the transaction in General Geophysical differently from a straightforward installment repurchase of stock. And the courts, at least of late, have been no less quick in corporate cases than in tax cases to look through the form of a transaction to find its real substance.

---

*[Ed. Note] By virtue of IRC §311, which has since been amended, as discussed at pages 419-421, infra.

WILLIAMS v. NEVELOW

Supreme Court of Texas, 1974.
513 S.W.2d 535.

REAVLEY, JUSTICE. Highway Drilling Company, Inc., a Texas corporation, repurchased its own stock from Harvey D. Williams.

It gave a promissory note for the purchase price and executed a security agreement covering its personal property to assure payment of the note. At the time of the exchange of the promissory note for the stock, the corporation was solvent and had unrestricted earned surplus in excess of the amount of the note. After the corporation became insolvent, the holder of the note foreclosed upon certain personal property pursuant to the security agreement. The lower courts have set aside the foreclosure and sale in favor of the corporation's trustee in bankruptcy. 501 S.W.2d 942. We disagree; we uphold the stock repurchase, the security agreement, and the foreclosure.

On December 20, 1968 the Board of Directors of Highway Drilling, Inc. passed a unanimous resolution, which was thereafter confirmed and adopted by all shareholders, authorizing the purchase by the corporation of 1,164 shares of its own stock from Harvey D. Williams. Pursuant to this resolution and shareholder approval, the corporation issued to Harvey D. Williams a promissory note dated December 20, 1968, in the principal sum of $100,691.00 bearing 4% interest. The note was payable in 84 monthly installments beginning on February 15, 1969, of $335.64 each, covering interest only, followed by 36 monthly installments of $2,972.81 each. The note was secured by: (1) the equipment, tools, inventory and personal property of the corporation; (2) a pledge of the certificate evidencing ownership of the 1,164 shares; and (3) by two life insurance policies, each in the principal sum of $50,000.00, covering the life of Harvey D. Williams. The corporation executed a security agreement covering all the personal property owned by the corporation to secure payment of the note.

In October and November of 1969 the corporation was in default in payments due on the note, and news reached Williams that the corporation was in serious financial difficulty. He gave notice that a public sale would be held on December 29, 1969, pursuant to the terms of the security agreement, and certain property was purchased at the sale by Williams for the sum of $20,000.00. While there is some controversy as to the market value of the property acquired at the sale, there is no evidence that its value exceeded the amount owed to Williams by the corporation on the promissory note. Williams has made no claim for any deficiency in the bankruptcy proceeding.

The corporation filed a voluntary petition in bankruptcy in federal court in February of 1970, and thereafter Nathan Nevelow was appointed trustee in bankruptcy on March 17, 1970. Nevelow filed this suit on November 1, 1971 to set aside the foreclosure sale. In a trial before the court, judgment was rendered for Nevelow setting aside the sale. The trial court's pertinent findings of fact were: (1) that on December 30, 1968, the retained earnings of the corporation were $140,633.17; (2) that the claims of creditors represented by

Nevelow were incurred after December 23, 1968; and (3) that Harvey D. Williams in November 1969 had notice that the corporation did not have money to continue doing business, could not pay its creditors, could not make the installment payments due on the $100,691.00 note, and that the filing of a voluntary petition in bankruptcy was contemplated.

Prior to the adoption of modern business corporation statutes, courts were inclined to be suspicious, if they permitted the repurchase by a corporation of its own stock. Dodd, Purchase and Redemption By a Corporation of Its Own Shares: The Substantive Law, 89 U.Pa. L.Rev. 697 (1941). Texas courts upheld the authority of a solvent corporation to do so. San Antonio Hardware Co. v. Sanger, 151 S.W. 1104 (Tex.Civ.App.1912, writ ref'd). In those cases where the payment of the purchase price was deferred, or where a promissory note was given by the corporation for the stock, the majority rule was to require solvency not only at the time when the transaction was closed and the note was issued but also at the time of the payment of cash to discharge the corporate obligation. Robinson v. Wangemann, 75 F.2d 756 (5th Cir. 1935); Anno: Corporation—Acquisition of Owned Stock, 47 A.L.R.2d 758, 774 (1956). The court in Robinson v. Wangemann held that the claim of the holder of a note received for repurchased stock was subordinate to the claim of the other creditors for the reason that the transaction by which a corporation repurchased its stock was not really a sale but was a method of distributing a portion of the assets to the stockholder. So the court held:

> When such a transaction is had, regardless of the good faith of the parties, *it is essential to its validity* that there be sufficient surplus to retire the stock, without prejudice to creditors, at the time payment is made out of assets. 75 F.2d 757. (Emphasis added.)

This rule, designed to protect against prejudice to creditors, prevented the corporation from making a valid *transfer of any asset* for this purpose unless at the time of the transfer the solvency and the surplus of the corporation would not be impaired. The lower courts have both based the holding in favor of the trustee in this case on the rule of Robinson v. Wangemann. Assuming this to have been the rule in Texas prior to 1955, the passage of the Texas Business Corporation Act, V.A.T.S., in that year is inconsistent with the rationale and the holding of Robinson v. Wangemann. The pertinent part of Article 2.03 of that Act from 1955 to 1973 provided as follows:

> A. A corporation shall not purchase directly or indirectly any of its own shares unless such purchase is authorized by this Article and not prohibited by its articles of incorporation.

. . .

C. Upon resolution of its board of directors authorizing the purchase and upon compliance with any other requirements of its articles of incorporation, a corporation may purchase its own shares to the extent of unrestricted earned surplus available therefor if accrued cumulative preferential dividends and other current preferential dividends have been fully paid at the time of purchase.

. . .

E. To the extent that earned surplus, capital surplus or reduction surplus is used as the measure of the corporation's right to purchase its own shares, such surplus shall be restricted so long as such shares are held as treasury shares, and upon the disposition or cancellation of any such shares the restriction shall be removed pro tanto as to all of such restricted surplus not eliminated thereby.

F. In no case shall a corporation purchase its own shares when there is a reasonable ground for believing that the corporation is insolvent, or will be rendered insolvent by such purchase or when, after such purchase, the fair value of its total assets will be less than the total amount of its debts.

Bearing in mind that the statute does not purport to encompass equitable grounds for setting aside a transaction, the Corporation Act by the quoted language provides that the corporation may purchase its own shares to the extent of unrestricted earned surplus available *at the time of the purchase* (in the absence of unpaid preferential dividends or added restrictions in the articles of incorporation). The statute also provides that no purchase may be made when such purchase will render the corporation insolvent. Thus the validity of the transaction and the authority of the corporation to repurchase its shares are determined at the time of the purchase, and the statute places no restriction upon the transfer of cash or other assets at a subsequent date.

The "purchase" of the stock by Highway Drilling Company took place in December of 1968. A purchase is the voluntary transmission of property from one person to another in exchange for a valuable consideration. . . . No statute is known to use the term "purchase" to mean the act by which the buyer finally parts with tangible property and not to mean a consummated trade which may be the unconditional exchange of a promissory note for stock. . . .

A contrary construction of the time and meaning of "purchase" would be inconsistent with Article 2.03(E). The statute there provides, in part, that earned surplus used as the measure of the right of the corporation to purchase its own shares, need be maintained only until the purchased shares are disposed of by the corporation—whether or not its promissory note is then unpaid. If it were held that the corporation must have a surplus when the cash payment is made on the note, the effect would be to require as much as double the amount of the surplus as the price paid for the stock.

This case is determined by the statutory authority or power of the corporation to reacquire shares. If fraud or bad faith or conduct misleading to the creditors were shown, equitable ground for rescission of the purchase and the foreclosure would be established. 1 G. Hornstein, Corporation Law & Practice, § 495 (1959). Contentions have been made of this nature in the present case. They are based on provisions in the note of the corporation related to a note in the amount of $186,000.00 given by three directors of the corporation to the same Harvey Williams, for their purchase of 2,136 shares in the corporation. It was provided that the corporation's note could not be prepaid as to any part or portion of principal or interest until the other $186,000.00 promissory note had been fully paid and, in addition, that upon default of payment on the $186,000.00 note, the note of the corporation could be matured at the option of the holder. It is argued that these provisions had the effect of pledging the assets of the corporation as a security for the personal note as well as for the obligation of the corporation. That is not the case, since payment of the corporation's note would fully terminate any security interest affecting its property. These provisions do not impair the negotiability of the corporation's note. Section 3.105(a)(3) of the Texas Business and Commerce Code provides that a promise or order that is otherwise unconditional is not made conditional by the fact that the instrument "refers to a separate agreement for rights as to prepayment or acceleration." The record in this case raises no issue of bad faith and does not justify the contention that the stock repurchase transaction in itself had any effect upon the subsequent creditors or contributed in any manner to the bankruptcy of the corporation.

Some courts have retained the common law rule as to the effect of corporation repurchases despite the enactment of the Model Corporation Act or comparable statutory language. McConnell v. Estate of W. H. Butler Const. Co., 402 F.2d 362 (9th Cir. 1968); In re Peoples Loan & Investment Co., 316 F.Supp. 13 (W.D.Ark.1970). We read the statute to require a contrary result. *See* Palmer v. Justice, 322 F.Supp. 892 (N.D.Tex.), aff'd per curiam, 451 F.2d 371 (5th Cir. 1971); Tracy v. Perkins-Tracy Printing Co., 278 Minn. 159, 153 N.W.2d 241 (1967); . . .

We note that Sec. F of Art. 2.03 of the Texas Business Corporation Act was amended in 1973 to include the emphasized language below which was added by its draftsmen to the Model Business Corporation Act in 1957:

> F. In no case shall a corporation purchase *or make payment, directly or indirectly,* for its own shares when there is

reasonable ground for believing that the corporation is insolvent, or will be rendered insolvent by such purchase or *payment,* or when, after such purchase, *or payment,* the fair value of its total assets will be less than the total amount of its debts.

The addition of "payment" indicates some distinction between "payment" and "purchase." It does not necessarily follow that a different result would be reached in the present case if the amended language of the statute with reference to the solvency of the corporation were applicable. The issuance of a secured negotiable instrument could be considered "payment" for the repurchased stock. Hartmann and Wilson, supra, 26 Sw.L.J. 725, 735. A decision on this point is not necessary to the disposition of the present case. In view of the historical judicial prohibition against enforcement of otherwise unconditional promises of payment after the time of insolvency it would be well for the Legislature to settle the question expressly.

The judgments of the lower courts are reversed; judgment is here rendered that Nathan Nevelow, Trustee, be denied all recovery against Harvey D. Williams.

NOTE

As the court in Williams v. Nevlow indicated with respect to the Texas statute, the addition of the words "or payment" in the insolvency proviso in MBA §6 is rather telling on the question of how that provision should be construed. In the light of the history of this area, reviewed above, it seems highly likely that the draftsman wanted to be sure that the insolvency cut-off had been codified, and he evidently assumed, or at least feared, that the term "purchase" would only reach the execution of the original agreement, and not the actual payments that might come later. The express reference to "payment" certainly suggests that the insolvency test applies to any transfer by a corporation of cash or property in payment for the repurchase of stock, no matter when it occurs. Query whether other courts will follow the dictum in Williams v. Nevlow that transfer of a secured, negotiable promissory note could constitute "payment" within the meaning of this provision.

However, this construction of the statute has an important corollary with respect to the application of the surplus
test. Since the basic surplus restriction in the first
paragraph of MBA §6 was not changed in 1957 and continues to
refer only to "purchase", not "payment", there is a strong
implication that the surplus test applies in the first
instance only to the total repurchase obligation at the
outset, and if satisfied at that time would not come into
play later in connection with the subsequent payments. On
the other hand, if a repurchase agreement can not pass the
surplus test at the outset, then presumably it is not a
"purchase" at all at that point, within the meaning of the
statute, and hence each installment payment thereafter would
be viewed as a separate repurchase in the amount of the
installment (probably including any portion that purports to
be interest), which must satisfy the surplus limitation at
the time it is paid.

It is also worthy of note that the court in Williams v.
Nevlow did not appear to attach much importance to the fact
that the repurchase obligation there was secured by a mortgage
on most of the operating assets of the corporation. The
inference may be that the mortgage did not significantly
enhance the former shareholder's position (even though
virtually everything he received from the corporation came
by way of foreclosure of the mortgage), and that if the
insolvency cut-off had been applicable the existence of the
mortgage would not have saved him. That would be quite
understandable, since the very purpose of the insolvency
cut-off is to make sure that the creditors of an insolvent
enterprise come ahead of any stock interest, past or present,
and giving effect to a mortgage securing a repurchase obligation would not only defeat that objective but even give the
former shareholder a priority in the pledged assets.

Nevertheless, some courts have reached the opposite
conclusion, taking the view that while insolvency may cut
off the former shareholder's remaining claim on the repurchase obligation, it does not invalidate his mortgage. This
result might appear to leave the parties stymied, with the
former shareholder unable to enforce his claim, while the
representative of the creditors cannot avoid his mortgage;

but as a practical matter, the creditors' representative
will want to clear the mortgage, in the hope that the pledged
assets will produce an excess available for the other creditors, or perhaps to facilitate sale of the enterprise as a
going business, and hence the former shareholder is likely
to end up about as well off as he would under an ordinary
foreclosure of the mortgage. That was the outcome in National
Tile & Terazzo Co. v. Walsh, 537 F.2d 329 (9th Cir. 1976), a
particularly forceful case because it was decided with
reference to California law, which has long been very strict
in enforcing the insolvency cut-off (and a surplus cut-off
as well). The court noted that there were two lines of
authority dealing with what effect unenforceability of a
note should have on an accompanying mortgage: where the bar
to enforcement of the note was more or less procedural, as
when the statute of limitations has run, the mortgage normally
survives, whereas the existence of a substantive impediment
to enforceability which makes the note unenforceable from
the outset, such as fraud in the original execution, generally
invalidates the mortgage as well. Since the repurchase
obligation in this case was valid at the outset, being fully
covered by surplus at that point, and only became unenforceable
as a result of the subsequent insolvency, a majority of the
court concluded that it was closer to the statute of limitations type of case, and held that the mortgage remained
effective.

B. FIDUCIARY LIMITATIONS ON REPURCHASE OF STOCK

As indicated in the foregoing material, in the past
repurchase of its stock by a corporation was often a device
for favoring insiders by giving them more for their stock
than other stockholders could obtain. Under today's fiduciary standards such a transaction would obviously be
vulnerable to attack for unfairness.

Insiders can also be favored by corporate repurchases
from other stockholders, if the stock is obtained at unfairly low prices. The benefit to the insiders from this process is somewhat diluted compared to purchase by the insiders
personally, but this is offset by the fact that repurchase
by the corporation eliminates the need to commit any individual funds. However, it is now clear that insiders have

the same obligation to act fairly, including making appropriate disclosure, when they cause the corporation to repurchase stock as when they purchase it themselves.

A third situation in which corporate repurchase of stock may be used to benefit insiders is in connection with efforts to ward off a threatened loss of control. The wave of takeover bids in recent years has spawned a wide variety of defensive tactics by incumbents, which include corporate repurchase of stock from the public to prevent the hostile bidder from obtaining control, or purchasing the holdings of a potential insurgent (usually at a premium price) in order to eliminate the threat to control from that quarter. Indeed, the prospect of reselling to the corporation at a high price is sometimes the very objective of acquiring a block of stock, and the acquirer in such circumstances is labelled a "barracuda." On the issue of repurchase of stock to preserve control there has been a substantial run of litigation under Delaware law:

KORS v. CAREY

Court of Chancery of Delaware, 1960.
39 Del. Ch. 47, 158 A.2d 136

[Lehn & Fink Products Corporation was a manufacturer of cosmetics and household drugs listed on the New York Stock Exchange. In March of 1956, United Whelan, a national drug store chain which was a customer of Lehn & Fink, started buying the latter's stock and by March 1, 1957, its holdings totaled over 45,000 shares. The Lehn & Fink management became concerned about United's purchases and had a meeting with its president and largest stockholder, Charles Green. Green indicated that United's retail business policy was to try to make special deals with various manufacturers, a policy which Lehn & Fink had consistently resisted. While no demands of any kind were made by United at that meeting, it continued to acquire Lehn & Fink stock, and by the end of 1957 United held 60,200 shares, representing approximately 16% of the total outstanding.

The Lehn & Fink management was aware that Green had waged proxy fights against the managements of a number of different business enterprises, including his successful one for control of United in 1951. The Lehn & Fink management

decided that United Whelan should be eliminated as a stockholder, and late in 1957 Lehn & Fink authorized a broker to
attempt to purchase the stock held by United. United never
inquired as to the identity of the purchaser and never knew
that it was Lehn & Fink. United's stock was purchased in
February, 1958, for $28 per share, at which time the stock
was selling in small lots at about $25 1/2 per share.

The plaintiff, a minority stockholder of Lehn & Fink,
brought this action against the directors of the company on
the ground that Lehn & Fink's purchase of its own shares was
not made for a proper corporate purpose and involved both an
excessive price and excessive brokerage, legal, and other
costs. The market price of Lehn & Fink stock at the time of
the trial ranged from $45 to $48 per share.]

MARVEL, Vice Chancellor [after setting out the facts].*
The individual defendants have advanced a number of reasons
for their decision to acquire United Whelan's stock, including the unlikely one of a desire to have stock available for
the acquisition of desirable business assets notwithstanding
the existence of 600,000 authorized but unissued shares
which could be utilized for such a purpose. I conclude . . .
that the real basis for the decision to eliminate United as
a stockholder . . . is found in a fundamental divergence in
these two corporations' business policies. [The court then
reviewed the evidence showing that the Lehn & Fink directors
believed United Whelan did not measure up to Lehn & Fink
either in its finished product or in business principles,
and that for United to have a major voice in the affairs of
Lehn & Fink could not only be injurious to the latter's
reputation but might also lead to possible violations of the
Robinson-Patman Act by reason of United's insistence on
special promotional schemes; there was also concern that
Lehn & Fink's other chain store customers would be troubled
by the prospect of a competitor holding a large stake in one
of their suppliers.] In brief, a comparison of the over-all
business record of United Whelan . . . with that of Lehn &
Fink's demonstrated that the continuance of United Whelan as
a dominant force in Lehn & Fink posed a serious threat to
the welfare of the latter corporation and its stockholders.

Plaintiff, in answer to these contentions, derides the
motives of the individual defendants, pointing out that Lehn &

---

*Portions of the opinion and all footnotes omitted.

Fink's aging president and dominant management stockholder,
Edward Plaut, is concededly desirous of having his son
succeed him in office and that in greater or lesser degree
all of the Lehn & Fink directors have an interest in retaining management in office. Plaintiff argues that Lehn &
Fink's directors, on learning of United's continuing purchases of stock, became the victims of unreasoning panic,
imagining that the possible loss of a proxy fight would
somehow spell the end for Lehn & Fink, when actually the
only matters thereby placed in jeopardy were defendants'
selfish interests, plaintiff insisting that the purchase
complained of was made secretly and surreptitiously for the
improper purpose of retaining jobs and control of corporate
power. Plaintiff insists that under the circumstances
disclosed at trial any buying out of United Whelan's stock
should have been made by means of a spending of personal
rather than corporate funds by the individual defendants.

There is no doubt, however, about the right of a Delaware
corporation in a proper case to purchase, hold, sell and
transfer shares of its own capital stock provided the spending of its own funds in any such transaction does not cause
an impairment of its capital. . . . [And] it is established
in Delaware that directors may validly spend corporate funds
for the defense of corporate policy in a proxy fight. . . .

. . . plaintiff has failed to carry the burden of
proving any misconduct or abuse of discretion on the part of
the Lehn & Fink directors. While the actual decision to buy
out United Whelan was arrived at quickly late in January,
1958, the factors which went into the decision had been
carefully weighed and evaluated over the preceding months
during which various methods of coping with United's potential bid for control were under more or less constant discussion by board members not only inter sese but with professional experts such as members of the faculty of the
Harvard Business School and officials of Georgenson & Co.,
proxy solicitors. Without regard to the many bits of questionable evidentiary information which appear in the record,
there is no doubt in my mind but that the business methods
of Charles Green, which stress liquidity, the spending of
substantial sums for aggressive promotional schemes, and a
readiness to sacrifice an established mode of doing business
for quick profits, presented a threat of a possible future
business course which was entirely at odds with Lehn &
Fink's traditions. . . .

As to plaintiff's contentions that the Lehn & Fink directors were selfishly voting for the retention of their offices and the emoluments thereof, I conclude, having heard the testimony of the principals involved and considered their personal evaluation of the dilemma posed by the existence of a substantial block of their stock in the hands of United Whelan, that plaintiff has not succeeded in overcoming the presumption that directors form their judgment in good faith. . . . While it appears that the five active members of Lehn & Fink's management currently receive salaries ranging from sums in excess of $35,000 per annum to Mr. Edward Plaut's of slightly more than $100,000 per year, that consultant directors receive compensation ranging from $3,200 to $12,100 and that substantial legal fees have been paid to lawyer-directors, I find no evidence that a selfish desire to retain jobs on the part of the non-managerial Lehn & Fink directors was a factor in their decision. Furthermore, assuming the Edward Plaut, who had most at stake in preserving the status quo at Lehn & Fink, was strongly influenced by family considerations in reaching his decision, nonetheless I am not persuaded that he so dominated the board that its non-managerial members were unable to make their own decisions about the purchase under attack.

Finally, even assuming that the purpose of all the individual defendants was primarily a selfish desire to retain control and jobs through the device of negativing United Whelan's potentiality by a buying out, how has plaintiff been injured? United Whelan having by its sale patently waived its opportunity to seek control, plaintiff, who never exercised voting control alone or with any group or faction cannot . . . successfully claim any injury to the shareholders generally as a result of the transaction complained of. On the contrary, the record discloses a substantial increase in value on the part of Lehn & Fink's traded shares since February 1958. . . . While plaintiff vigorously contends that the buying out deprived the general body of stockholders of their right to make a choice between the type of management which they might have expected to receive from a board under the influence of Mr. Green as opposed to the incumbent board, . . . plaintiff has no possible basis for complaining about a so-called lost opportunity to vote for a Green sponsored management. To be sure the opportunity was lost, however, in losing the opportunity plaintiff and those in her class were deprived of no rights. . . .

BENNETT v. PROPP

Supreme Court of Delaware, 1962. 187 A.2d 405.

[Noma Lites, Inc. is a Delaware corporation engaged in the business of selling decorative lighting equipment. Its stock is listed on the American Stock Exchange. Sadacca owned about 11% of Noma's approximately 950,000 outstanding shares and was chairman of the board of directors. In late 1958 the Noma management learned that Textron was seeking to acquire the assets of American Screw Company, 20% of whose stock was owned by a Canadian subsidiary of Noma. To block Textron's efforts, the Canadian subsidiary bought enough additional American Screw stock to bring its holdings up to 51%. Shortly thereafter, on Saturday, November 22, Sadacca received word from Royal Little, the chairman of the board of Textron, that Textron was about to try to acquire more than 50% of Noma's stock. On the following Monday Sadacca started buying Noma stock in the market. After an unsatisfactory conference with Little on Tuesday, Sadacca resumed his purchases on Wednesday and his total purchases for the two days approximated 200,000 shares. The only other director of Noma who was even aware of Sadacca's activities was Ward, the president. During that period the price of Noma stock rose from 9 to 13, and the average price paid by Sadacca was $11.67. These purchases were made in Sadacca's own name, apparently because he was fearful of the possible effect upon the market of purchases in Noma's name. On Saturday, November 29, at a special meeting of the Noma board, Sadacca reviewed the prior events and indicated that he had purchased the stock for Noma's account. Without discussion of any other alternatives, such as Sadacca's personal assumption of the stock purchases, the board adopted a resolution approving and ratifying Sadacca's actions in purchasing stock "in behalf of the corporation". The board then considered the means for raising the more than $2,300,000 needed to finance this acquisition, and ultimately consummated a short-term loan from a factor, the terms of which included interest at one-thirtieth of one per cent per day, a pledge of the purchased stock and other collateral, and an assignment of accounts receivable.

The plaintiff, a minority stockholder, brought this action alleging that Sadacca, Ward and the other directors had caused Noma to waste its corporate assets in a purchase of unneeded Noma stock solely for the purpose of perpetuating Sadacca's control of Noma. The Vice Chancellor held that all the defendants (except one director who did not vote on the November 29 resolution) were liable to account to Noma for its damages, and the defendants appealed.]

SOUTHERLAND, Chief Justice [after reviewing the facts and the decision below].

First, [the defendants] urge that Sadacca's purchases, and the directors' ratification, were justified because Little's actions posed a serious threat to Noma's welfare. They rely on the Vice Chancellor's prior decision in Kors v. Carey, Del.Ch., 158 A.2d 136.

Second, they urge that the imminence of the deadline [for payment for the stock] confronted the directors with an emergency of a serious nature. If Noma failed to pay for the shares bought by Sadacca, the brokers would sell the shares to protect themselves and would seek to hold Noma responsible for any loss. Noma's credit would be adversely affected. The directors' decision to ratify was thus one made in the exercise of business judgment, and they may not be held liable. . . .

1. The Vice Chancellor rejected the directors' first contention, and we think that he was right. Sadacca's purchases were made to preserve the control of the corporation in himself and his fellow directors. His statement to his board in the November 29 meeting practically admitted as much; at all events we have no doubt about it. The use of corporate funds for such a purpose is improper.

* * *

An exception to the rule was recognized in Delaware in Kors v. Carey, ...

This decision does not help the directors here. Little's attempt to buy American Screw had already been defeated. His letter of November 21 to Sadacca posed no immediate threat. In our opinion, contrary to plaintiff's, it was a thinly-veiled attempt to induce Sadacca and his fellow stockholder-directors to sell out to Little. There was no immediate indication that Little would start to buy large amounts of stock in the market. The argument that Little was dangerous because of his record as a "liquidator" was answered by the Vice Chancellor. He found from the evidence that the attacks at the trial on Little were largely afterthoughts.

In any event, the directors made no finding of immediate threat. They were not even consulted.

The case of Martin v. American Potash & Chemical Corp., . . . also relied on, involved a reduction of capital. The statute applicable to that case permits the purchase of shares for retirement at private sale. The fact that the purchase was prompted by existing dissension in the board was held not to render it illegal.

The decision is obviously distinguishable on two grounds. First, a reduction of capital surrounded by the statutory safeguard of a notice and a stockholders meeting is quite different from the purchases of common stock made here under the general power conferred by § 160 of the corporation law, 8 Del.C. § 160. Second, the elimination of a dissentient faction for genuine business reasons, as in the Kors case, is quite a different thing from the purchase of stock for control purposes before any real threat to corporate policy has occurred. The Potash case is also of no help to defendants.

It is our opinion that Sadacca's sudden decision to buy 200,000 shares of stock in two or three days was not only an unauthorized act on behalf of Noma, but was unjustified on the facts.

We must bear in mind the inherent danger in the purchase of shares with corporate funds to remove a threat to corporate policy when a threat to control is involved. The directors are of necessity confronted with a conflict of interest, and an objective decision is difficult. See the comments on the instant case in 62 Col.L.Rev. 1096, 1100. Hence, in our opinion, the burden should be on the directors to justify such a purchase as one primarily in the corporate interest. See 70 Yale L.J. 308, 317. They sustained that burden in the Kors case; they have not done so here.

It is our opinion that so far as the directors' defense depends on the rule of the Kors case it must fail.

2. The alternative defense is that of a business decision made in a sudden emergency to protect the corporation from serious injury. The defendant's contention may be thus summarized:

At the meeting of November 29 most of the directors learned for the first time what Sadacca had done. They were suddenly and unexpectedly confronted with a situation which threatened financial embarrassment and possible disaster to Noma. The commitment must be met. The day was Saturday, the larger part must be met by Monday. Under the circumstances they did the best they could; they raised the money, ratified the transaction, and preserved Noma's credit. In their business judgment it was the only thing to do. In the exercise of that judgment the law protects them from liability. So runs the argument.

* * *

This defense impresses us as having merit. It will not do, as plaintiff argues, to say that the brokers had no case. It is reasonable to believe that they would certainly have sought to hold Noma; and who can say what the consequences might have been? Sadacca had confronted his directors with a *fait accompli,* as the Vice Chancellor put it. But the Vice Chancellor in effect held that the directors' emergency did not relieve them from the duty of exploring other methods of coping with the situation. In our view, the pressure of time excused them from such efforts. They may not have made the best decision; we cannot say. Perhaps a telephone call to the brokers might have given time for negotiation; on the other hand it might well have precipitated serious litigation Monday morning. Upon the whole, we think that the directors cannot be blamed for deciding to take up the stock in the interest of protecting the corporation from dangerous litigation.

* * *

But this conclusion does not, as defendants' counsel appear to assume, dispose of the case as to Sadacca or as to Ward. Their positions are different. They will be separately considered.

First, as to Sadacca. We are of opinion that the resolution ratifying Sadacca's acts was not effective to legalize the purchases. The directors were without power to ratify them, for they were illegal when made. . . . It follows that the resolution has legal validity only to the extent of authorizing the officers to take up the stock to save the corporation from financial difficulty. Under § 160 they had legal power to do it, and because of the special circumstances we think that the power was not abused. But Sadacca remains liable for his acts.

Second, as to Ward. We have already exonerated the directors who learned about the matter for the first time at the meeting, on the ground that they were confronted with the necessity for a sudden decision in an emergency. We have thus made an exception to the general rule that directors who use corporate funds to preserve control commit a wrong. This exception depends upon the two circumstances proved in this case: prior ignorance and immediate emergency. If either of these circumstances had been absent the directors approving and ratifying Sadacca's purchases would clearly have been jointly liable with him to the corporation.

Ward's prior knowledge of these purchases is sufficient to deprive him of the benefit of the exception. He was the president of the corporation. He had enough time before the following Monday to consult with his fellow officers and directors, to consult counsel, and to take steps to make some arrangements with the brokers beneficial to Noma. As president, he could surely have called a directors' meeting. He did nothing. Apparently he did not even inquire of Sadacca how many shares Sadacca had bought, how much had been paid for them, or how Sadacca expected to finance the purchases. One gets the impression from the record that he was entirely subservient to Sadacca.

We think that his knowledge of the purchases, his silence and failure to act, coupled with his vote on the resolution, constituted a course of conduct amounting to approval of and participation in Sadacca's wrongful acts. This is not to hold Ward guilty of negligence as counsel seem to think the Vice Chancellor did. It is to hold that his actions made him jointly and severally liable with Sadacca for the tort of using corporate funds to maintain control.

We are of opinion that, with the exception of Ward, the directors who voted for the resolution must be exonerated of wrong doing; and that Sadacca and Ward must be held liable for any damages proximately suffered by Noma as a result of Sadacca's unlawful acts.

. . . .

CHEFF v. MATHES

Supreme Court of Delaware, 1964.   199 A.2d 548.

[The Holland Furnace Company is a Delaware corporation engaged in the manufacture and sale of furnaces, air conditioners, and other home heating equipment. In 1957 Holland had outstanding approximately 883,500 shares of stock which were listed on the New York Stock Exchange. The company had seven directors: Cheff, who owned about 6,000 shares and was also the chief executive officer, at an annual compensation of $77,400; Mrs. Cheff, who was a daughter of a founder of the company and who owned, in addition to approximately 5,800 shares of Holland outright, almost 50% of Hazelbank United Interest, Inc., an investment vehicle for members of the Cheff-Landwehr family group which owned almost 165,000 shares of Holland stock; Landwehr, Mrs. Cheff's nephew, who owned about 24,000 shares of Holland personally, and approximately 9% of Hazelbank; Trenkamp, general counsel of the company who was not on an annual retainer but did receive substantial sums for legal services; and three "outside" directors who had joined the board at the request of Mr. Cheff: Ames, a partner in a Chicago investment firm; Boalt, an officer of a cosmetics concern; and Spatta, the president of a large manufacturer of earth-moving equipment. None of the directors except Cheff and Trenkamp received any compensation from Holland other than a director's fee of $200 per meeting.

Holland's method of operation from its inception was to sell its products directly to consumers through its own retail salesmen, without any intermediate dealers. This practice, which was unique in the furnace business, was regarded by the management as a vital factor in the company's success. Holland employed approximately 8,500 persons and maintained 400 branch sales offices located in 43 states. However, the business had not been prospering since the postwar period, with sales declining from over $41 million in 1948 to less than $32 million in 1956. In addition, the company's marketing methods had been made the subject of serious charges by the Federal Trade Commission. But in 1956 there was apparently some reorganization of the sales department, including the closing of certain unprofitable branch offices, which the management believed would arrest the decline in sales.

Beginning late in June, 1957, the trading activity in Holland stock increased substantially, rising from a previous monthly average between 10,000 and 25,000 shares to a figure of almost 40,000 shares for the last week in June. The price per share rose to $12, a high for the year. During that same week Mr. Cheff met with one Maremont, the president of Maremont Automotive Products, Inc., and chief executive officer of a number of other concerns, who inquired about the feasibility of a merger between Motor Products and Holland. However, Cheff indicated that because of difference in sales practices between the two companies a merger did not seem feasible, whereupon Maremont indicated that he had no further interest in Holland.

The high level of activity in Holland stock continued into July, and although at first they did not connect it with Mr. Maremont, the Holland officers learned later in July that Maremont had acquired some 55,000 shares of Holland stock. Accordingly, the Holland board decided to investigate Mr. Maremont and learned that he had "been a participant, or had attempted to be, in the liquidation of a number of companies." On August 23, 1957, at his request Maremont met with Mr. Cheff. Maremont indicated that he thought Holland's method of distribution was obsolete, and that "furnaces could be sold as he sold mufflers, through half a dozen salesmen in a wholesale way." Immediately after this meeting Cheff caused Holland to engage in active buying of its own stock and some 1900 shares had been purchased by August 29. On August 30, the Holland board adopted a resolution calling for a stock option plan and authorizing the president to purchase for the corporation up to 71,000 shares for such a plan at a price not to exceed $16.50 per share. Recent purchases by officers of 4900 shares of stock for the corporation were ratified, and a fund of some $500,000 for further purchases by the corporation was set up. In addition, Mrs. Cheff indicated that she was willing to invest an equal amount of her own funds to prevent a Maremont takeover, and authorized her brokers to purchase Holland stock for her individual account.

According to evidence subsequently introduced by the Holland officers, the appearance of Maremont on the scene created a good deal of unrest among the employees of Holland, with a number of employees in the field considering leaving because of their fear of the consequences of a Maremont acquisition. Several branch managers approached corporate officers for reassurances that Maremont would not be allowed to gain control. At the same time the company received a Dun and Bradstreet report which indicated that Maremont's practice was to achieve quick profits by sale or liquidation of companies acquired by him.

A New York broker was engaged to act as agent for Holland and for Mrs. Cheff personally in the purchase of Holland stock in equal proportions, and the broker was advised that as much as $1,500,000 of stock might be acquired, to be divided in equal thirds among Mrs. Cheff, Holland, and Hazelbank. In the meantime, Mr. Maremont had written to each Holland director on September 13, noting the decline in Holland's fortunes over the recent years and recommending that a broad engineering survey be made "for the benefit of all the stockholders." During September Holland and Mrs. Cheff each acquired approximately 23,000 shares, while Motor Products added 31,000 shares to its holdings, with the stock rising to more than $16 per share, its highest price in over two years. On September 25, by which time Holland had acquired some $380,000 worth of its stock, both Mrs. Cheff and Holland discontinued the purchases.

In early September Maremont had offered to sell his Holland holdings to the corporation for $14.00 per share but shortly thereafter he withdrew his offer. At the end of September he wrote to Mrs. Cheff's sister, a stockholder of Hazelbank, offering either to sell his Holland stock to Hazelbank and the Cheff family group, or to buy their stock. However, some of the Hazelbank stockholders were reluctant to acquire any more Holland stock, and Maremont's proposal was referred to the Hazelbank finance committee for further study. On October 14 Trenkamp met with Maremont and reached a tentative agreement that his 155,000 shares of Holland stock would be acquired for $14.40 per share, the closing price of the stock the previous day having been $11. At that point it was not clear who would purchase the stock and in what proportions, since Trenkamp was authorized to act for Holland, Hazelbank and Mrs. Cheff individually. On October 23, the Holland board met to consider the Maremont purchase, and the threat posed by Maremont was reviewed. The board was advised by Mrs. Cheff that either she or Hazelbank would take up any of the Maremont stock which Holland did not buy; the board was also informed that to finance the purchase of the entire Maremont block of stock Holland would have to borrow substantial sums.

The Holland directors, after reaching a consensus that purchase of the Maremont stock was the only alternative to a costly proxy fight, authorized the purchase by Holland of all of the Maremont stock. The directors concluded that the repurchase would sufficiently reduce the total dividend requirement to offset the interest on the borrowed funds, and that it would not be necessary to curtail the company's operations in any way.

In February, 1958, this minority shareholder's suit was commenced against the Holland directors, charging that the 1957 repurchase of stock by Holland had been for the purpose of perpetuating the control of the incumbent directors, and seeking, *inter alia*, to hold the directors liable for damages. The price of Holland stock had fallen back to about $10 per share after the purchase from Maremont; thereafter it reached a high of over $15 per share in early 1959 and then steadily decreased until it had fallen below $2 per share when the stock was delisted in 1964.

The Vice Chancellor found that the repurchase of stock had been made for the purpose of retaining corporate control and held Mr. Cheff, Mrs. Cheff, Landwehr and Trenkamp liable. He rejected the proffered reasons for the repurchase that the corporation wanted to have stock available for a proposed option plan or that the corporation was seeking to utilize its excess funds, since he found that the corporation already had ample treasury stock, and also had a new subsidiary in the finance business which could profitably utilize additional capital. However, the Vice Chancellor absolved the other directors of liability because they did not have an important stake in the affairs of Holland; in addition, he found that they did not understand, prior to the meeting on October 23 at which Holland's repurchase of Maremont's stock was authorized, that an alternative existed in the form of a purchase of some or all of that stock by Mrs. Cheff or Hazelbank. The defendants appealed.]

CAREY, JUSTICE [after setting out the facts].

Under the provisions of 8 Del.C. § 160, a corporation is granted statutory power to purchase and sell shares of its own stock. . . . The charge here is not one of violation of statute, but the allegation is that the true motives behind such purchases were improperly centered upon perpetuation of control. In an analogous field, courts have sustained the use of proxy funds to inform stockholders of management's views upon the policy questions inherent in an election to a board of directors, but have not sanctioned the use of corporate funds to advance the selfish desires of directors to perpetuate themselves in office. . . . Similarly, if the actions of the board were motivated by a sincere belief that the buying out of the dissident stockholder was necessary to maintain what the board believed to be proper business practices, the board will not be held liable for such decision, even though hindsight indicates the decision was not the wisest course. See Kors v. Carey, Del.Ch., 158 A.2d 136. On the other hand, if the board has acted solely or primarily because of the desire to perpetuate themselves in office, the use of corporate funds for such purposes is improper. See Bennett v. Propp, Del., 187 A.2d 405. . . .

Our first problem is the allocation of the burden of proof to show the presence or lack of good faith on the part of the board in authorizing the purchase of shares. Initially, the decision of the board of directors in authorizing a purchase was presumed to be in good faith and could be overturned only by a conclusive showing by plaintiffs of fraud or other misconduct. See Bankers Securities Corp. v. Kresge Department Stores, Inc., D.C., 54 F.Supp. 378. In Kors, cited supra, the court merely indicated that the directors are presumed to act in good faith and the burden of proof to show to the contrary falls upon the plaintiff. However, in Bennett v. Propp, supra, we stated:

> "We must bear in mind the inherent danger in the purchase of shares with corporate funds to remove a threat to corporate policy when a threat to control is involved. The directors are of necessity confronted with a conflict of interest, and an objective decision is difficult. . . . Hence, in our opinion, the burden should be on the directors to justify such a purchase as one primarily in the corporate interest." (187 A.2d 409, at page 409).

* * *

To say that the burden of proof is upon the defendants is not to indicate, however, that the directors have the same "self-dealing interest" as is present, for example, when a director sells property to the corporation. The only clear pecuniary interest shown on the record was held by Mr. Cheff, as an executive of the corporation, and Trenkamp, as its attorney. The mere fact that some of the other directors were substantial shareholders does not create a personal pecuniary interest in the decisions made by the board of directors, since all shareholders would presumably share the benefit flowing to the substantial shareholder. . . . Accordingly, these directors other than Trenkamp and Cheff, while called upon to justify their actions, will not be held to the same standard of proof required of those directors having personal and pecuniary interest in the transaction.

As noted above, the Vice Chancellor found that the stock option plan, mentioned in the minutes as a justification for the purchases, was not a motivating reason for the purchases. This finding we accept, since there is evidence to support it; in fact, Trenkamp admitted that the stock option plan was not the motivating reason. The minutes of October 23, 1957 dealing with the purchase from Maremont do not, in fact, mention the option plan as a reason for the purchase. While the minutes of the October 1, 1957 meeting only indicated the stock option plan as the motivating reason, the defendants are not bound by such statements and may supplement the minutes by oral testimony to show that the motivating reason was genuine fear of an acquisition by Maremont. See Bennett v. Propp, cited supra.

Plaintiffs urge that the sale price was unfair in view of the fact that the price was in excess of that prevailing on the open market. However, as conceded by all parties, a substantial block of stock will normally sell at a higher price than that prevailing on the open market, the increment being attributable to a "control premium". Plaintiffs argue that it is inappropriate to require the defendant corporation to pay a control premium, since control is meaningless to an acquisition by a corporation of its own shares. However, it is elementary that a holder of a substantial number of shares would expect to receive the control premium as part of his selling price, and if the corporation desired to obtain the stock, it is unreasonable to expect that the corporation could avoid paying what any other purchaser would be required to pay for the stock. In any event, the financial expert produced by defendant at trial indicated that the price paid was fair and there was no rebuttal. Ames, the financial man on the board, was strongly of the opinion that the purchase was a good deal for the corporation. The Vice Chancellor made no finding as to the fairness of the price other than to indicate the obvious fact that the market price was increasing as a result of open market purchases by Maremont, Mrs. Cheff and Holland.

The question then presented is whether or not defendants satisfied the burden of proof of showing reasonable grounds to believe a danger to corporate policy and effectiveness existed by the presence of the Maremont stock ownership. It is important to remember that the directors satisfy their burden by showing good faith and reasonable investigation; the directors will not be penalized for an honest mistake of judgment, if the judgment appeared reasonable at the time the decision was made. . . .

In holding that employee unrest could as well be attributed to a condition of Holland's business affairs as to the possibility of Maremont's intrusion, the Vice Chancellor must have had in mind one or both of two matters: (1) the pending proceedings before the Federal Trade Commission concerning certain sales practices of Holland; (2) the decrease in sales and profits during the preceding several years. Any other possible reason would be pure speculation. In the first place, the adverse decision of the F.T.C. was not announced until *after* the complained-of transaction. Secondly, the evidence clearly shows that the downward trend of sales and profits had reversed itself, presumably because of the reorganization which had then been completed. Thirdly, everyone who testified on the point said that the unrest was due to the possible threat presented by Maremont's purchases of stock. There was, in fact, no *testimony* whatever of any connection between the unrest and either the F.T.C. proceedings or the business picture.

The Vice Chancellor found that there was no substantial evidence of a liquidation posed by Maremont. This holding overlooks an important contention. The fear of the defendants, according to their testimony, was not limited to the possibility of liquidation; it included the alternate possibility of a material change in Holland's sales policies, which the board considered vital to its future success. The *unrebutted* testimony before the court indicated: '(1) Maremont had deceived Cheff as to his original intentions, since his open market purchases were contemporaneous with his disclaimer of interest in Holland; (2) Maremont had given Cheff some reason to believe that he intended to eliminate the retail sales force of Holland; (3) Maremont demanded a place on the board; (4) Maremont substantially increased his purchases after having been refused a place on the board; (5) the directors had good reason to believe that unrest among key employees had been engendered by the Maremont threat; (6) the board had received advice from Dun and Bradstreet indicating the past liquidation or quick sale activities of Motor Products; (7) the board had received professional advice from the firm of Merrill Lynch, Fenner & Beane, who recommended that the purchase from Motor Products be carried out; (8) the board had received competent advice that the corporation was over-capitalized; (9) Staal and Cheff had made informal personal investigations from contacts in the business and financial community and had reported to the board of the alleged poor reputation of Maremont. The board was within its rights in relying upon that investigation, since 8 Del.C. § 141(f) allows the directors to reasonably rely upon a report provided by corporate officers. . . .

Accordingly, we are of the opinion that the evidence presented in the court below leads inevitably to the conclusion that the board of directors, based upon direct investigation, receipt of professional advice, and personal observations of the contradictory action of Maremont and his explanation of corporate purpose, believed, with justification, that there was a reasonable threat to the continued existence of Holland, or at least existence in its present form, by the plan of Maremont to continue building up his stock holdings. We find no evidence in the record sufficient to justify a contrary conclusion. The opinion of the Vice Chancellor that employee unrest may have been engendered by other factors or that the board had no grounds to suspect Maremont is not supported in any manner by the evidence.

As noted above, the Vice Chancellor found that the purpose of the acquisition was the improper desire to maintain control, but, at the same time, he exonerated those individual directors whom he believed to be unaware of the possibility of using non-corporate funds to accomplish this purpose. Such a decision is inconsistent with his finding that the motive was improper, within the rule enunciated in Bennett. If the actions were in fact improper because of a desire to maintain control, then the presence or absence of a non-corporate alternative is irrelevant, as corporate funds may not be used to advance an improper purpose even if there is no non-corporate alternative available. Conversely, if the actions were proper because of a decision by the board made in good faith that the corporate interest was served thereby, they are not rendered improper by the fact that some individual directors were willing to advance personal funds if the corporation did not. It is conceivable that the Vice Chancellor considered this feature of the case to be of significance because of his apparent belief that any excess corporate funds should have been used to finance a subsidiary corporation. That action would not have solved the problem of Holland's overcapitalization. In any event, this question was a matter of business judgment, which furnishes no justification for holding the directors personally responsible in this case.

JOHNSON v. TRUEBLOOD*

United States Court of Appeals, Third Circuit, 1980.

629 F.2d 287.

SEITZ, Chief Judge.

The plaintiffs, Gilbert and Hervey John-son, appeal from a judgment for the de-fendants, majority shareholders and di-rectors of Penn Eastern Development Co., in this diversity suit charging the defend-ants with fraud and breach of fiduciary duty under Delaware law.

I.

The present controversy centers on the conduct of the affairs of Penn Eastern, incorporated in June 1968 as a real estate development company. The plaintiffs, Gil-bert and Hervey Johnson, owned a 47 per-cent interest in Penn Eastern. The defend-ants, Samuel and Arnold Trueblood and Harry Salwen, collectively owned the con-trolling 53 percent interest. At its incep-tion, a major asset of Penn Eastern was land known as the "Red Caboose" property owned by the Truebloods and a man named Louis Siana. This property was originally purchased for $48,000 and sold by the True-bloods and Siana to Penn Eastern in ex-change for $75,000 of its capital stock.[1]

Penn Eastern was the sole general part-ner in a limited partnership called The Vil-lage Center, Ltd. This partnership was formed for the development of a shopping center which was to be Penn Eastern's sole major asset. Penn Eastern, however, be-gan to develop severe cash flow problems in 1972. In November 1973, the Truebloods proposed acceptance of a loan to the corpo-ration by a Frank Pierce. The plaintiffs opposed this loan, urging that it was not beneficial and that they had the financial resources to loan Penn Eastern the requisite

capital. By its terms, however, the plain-tiffs' loan would have resulted in a shift in control of Penn Eastern from the True-bloods to the plaintiffs. By a 4–2 vote, the Penn Eastern Board of Directors,[2] rejected the plaintiffs' proposal and accepted the Pierce loan.

The Pierce loan failed to solve Penn East-ern's cash flow problems, and the corpora-tion ran into difficulties meeting the loan repayments. The defendants proposed an amendment to the Pierce loan agreement by which the Red Caboose property would be sold at absolute auction in May 1975. The plaintiffs opposed this action because the real estate market was depressed, and they feared Penn Eastern would sell one of its major assets at less than its full market value. The plaintiffs offered to tender the payments due on the Pierce loan to avoid auctioning off the Red Caboose property. This proposal was rejected and the property sold.

Penn Eastern's financial condition contin-ued to deteriorate when in November 1975, to shore up Penn Eastern's treasury, the defendants proposed a sale of twenty-one shares of Penn Eastern stock to Arnold Trueblood at the price of $750 per share. The plaintiffs counterproposed that Penn Eastern sell twenty shares of the stock to them at $1,000 per share. This would have resulted in a shift in corporate control to the plaintiffs, and it too was rejected and the sale to Arnold Trueblood approved. Despite the new infusion of capital arising out of the sale of stock, Penn Eastern's financial condition continued to deteriorate.

The plaintiffs filed the present sharehold-ers' derivative action in the district court alleging violation of the federal securities

---

*Portions of the opinion dealing with issues other than the alleged desire of the defendants to retain control omitted.

1. The Johnsons each paid $25,000 for their 25 shares in Penn Eastern. Samuel and Arnold Trueblood and Siana received 25 shares of Penn Eastern in exchange for their one-third interest in the Red Caboose property. Siana's 25 shares were repurchased by the corporation on August 21, 1978. Later purchases of stock by the Johnsons and Harry Salwen resulted in the 47 percent-53 percent split in ownership of Penn Eastern.

2. The Board of Directors was composed of the Truebloods, Salwen, the Johnsons, and Rolland Henderson, a nonshareholder director. The Truebloods, Salwen and Henderson voted in favor of the Pierce loan; the Johnsons against it.

laws and Delaware corporate law.[3] The complaint sought rescission of the sale of stock to Arnold Trueblood and damages on behalf of Penn Eastern. [A verdict was returned in favor of the defendants, and the plaintiffs appealed.]

*   *   *

III.

Next, the plaintiffs argue that the district court improperly charged the jury on their burden in overcoming the business judgment rule. That rule, which admittedly is part of the law of Delaware, provides that directors of a corporation are presumed to exercise their business judgment in the best interest of the corporation. The charge was as follows:

[T]he desire to retain control of a corporation in and of itself is an improper motive for decision of a director. Therefore, if you find by a preponderance of the evidence that the defendants acted solely or primarily because of a desire to retain control of Penn Eastern, then the presumption of the sound business judgment rule has been rebutted. However, I further instruct you that a director may properly decline to adopt a course of action which would result in a shift of control, so long as his actions can be attributed to a rational business purpose. In other words, so long as other rational business reasons support a director's decision, the mere fact that a business decision involves a retention of control does not constitute a showing of bad faith to rebut the business judgment rule. *That rule is rebutted only where a director's sole or primary purpose for adopting a course of action or refusing to adopt another is to retain control.* (emphasis supplied).

Instead of the emphasized language, the plaintiffs argue that they only needed to prove that control was "a" motive in the defendants' various actions to rebut the business judgment rule. We disagree for two reasons.

First, the purpose of the business judgment rule belies the plaintiffs' contention. It is frequently said that directors are fiduciaries. Although this statement is true in some senses, it is also obvious that if directors were held to the same standard as ordinary fiduciaries the corporation could not conduct business. For example, an ordinary fiduciary may not have the slightest conflict of interest in any transaction he undertakes on behalf of the trust. Yet by the very nature of corporate life a director has a certain amount of self-interest in everything he does. The very fact that the director wants to enhance corporate profits is in part attributable to his desire to keep shareholders satisfied so that they will not oust him.

The business judgment rule seeks to alleviate this problem by validating certain situations that otherwise would involve a conflict of interest for the ordinary fiduciary. The rule achieves this purpose by postulating that if actions are arguably taken for the benefit of the corporation, then the directors are presumed to have been exercising their sound business judgment rather than responding to any personal motivations.

Faced with the presumption raised by the rule, the question is what sort of showing the plaintiff must make to survive a motion for directed verdict. Because the rule presumes that business judgment was exercised, the plaintiff must make a showing from which a factfinder might infer that impermissible motives predominated in the making of the decision in question.

---

3. The complaint may be broken down into four basic charges:

    1. The Truebloods knowingly misrepresented to Gilbert Johnson the value of the Red Caboose property when it was sold to Penn Eastern in 1968 in exchange for Penn Eastern stock.

    2. The rejection of the Johnsons' proposed loan and acceptance of the Pierce loan was motivated by the defendants' determination to retain control over Penn Eastern regardless of the corporation's best interests and was accordingly a breach of fiduciary duty.

3. The rejection of the Johnsons' loan in favor of selling the Red Caboose property at absolute auction to meet the payments of the Pierce loan was in the disinterest of Penn Eastern and motivated by the defendants' desire to retain control over it.

    4. The rejection of Gilbert Johnson's offer to purchase twenty shares of Penn Eastern stock and acceptance of the Truebloods' loan proposal constituted breaches of fiduciary duty by the defendants.

The issues raised on appeal concern only the state law claims.

The plaintiffs' theory that "a" motive to control is sufficient to rebut the rule is inconsistent with this purpose. Because the rule is designed to validate certain transactions despite conflicts of interest, the plaintiffs' rule would negate that purpose, at least in many cases. As already noted, control is always arguably "a" motive in any action taken by a director. Hence plaintiffs could always make this showing and thereby undercut the purpose of the rule.

Second, the plaintiffs' argument is inconsistent with Delaware case law. Although scholars have argued about how much is required under Delaware law to rebut the business judgment rule, we need not resolve that debate. See E. Folk, The Delaware General Corporation Law 75–81 (1972); Arsht, *Fiduciary Responsibilities of Directors, Officers and Key Employees*, 4 Del.J.Corp.L. 652, 660 (1979). At a minimum, the Delaware cases require that the plaintiff must show some sort of bad faith on the part of the defendant. *See* Arsht, *supra.* We do not think that a showing of "a" motive to retain control, without more, constitutes bad faith in this context unless we are to ignore the realities of corporate life. Accordingly, unless the plaintiff can tender evidence from which a factfinder might conclude that the defendant's sole or primary motive was to retain control, the presumption of the rule remains.

The primary source of the "sole or primary motive" test used in the charge here is *Cheff v. Mathes*, 41 Del.Ch. 494, 199 A.2d 548 (1964). Although the case explicitly contains this language, see 199 A.2d at 554, the plaintiffs would dismiss *Cheff* as a momentary aberration in the law of Delaware. An examination of the relevant cases, however, reveals that the test was used both before and after *Cheff* by the Delaware courts.

For example, *Bennett v. Propp*, 41 Del.Ch. 14, 187 A.2d 405 (1962), relied on by *Cheff*, expressly characterized the defendant's actions as a "thinly veiled attempt" to retain control. 187 A.2d at 409. Indeed, a reading of the opinion as a whole reveals that the court felt that there was no reason other than control for the actions in question. We do not see how *Bennett's* failure to use the talismanic phrase "sole or primary motive" in any way renders it inconsistent with *Cheff*.

Cases after *Cheff* have shown no inclination to abandon the sole or primary motive test. In *Condec Corp. v. Lunkepheimer Co.*, 43 Del.Ch. 353, 230 A.2d 769 (1967), one of the cases relied on for this proposition, the vice chancellor made this express finding: "I have reached the conclusion that the *primary purpose* of the [actions in question] was to prevent control of Lunkenheimer from passing to Condec and to cause such control to pass into the hands of U.S. Industries." 230 A.2d at 775 (emphasis supplied). Other more recent cases have similarly spoken of "primary" motive in this regard. E. g., *Petty v. Pentech Papers, Inc.*, 347 A.2d 140, 143 (Del.Ch.1975). *Cf. Singer v. Magnavox Co.*, 380 A.2d 969, 980 (Del.1977) (stating that use of merger "solely" to eliminate minority violates majority's fiduciary duty).

[7] In short, we believe that under Delaware law, at a minimum the plaintiff must make a showing that the sole or primary motive of the defendant was to retain control. If he makes a showing sufficient to survive a directed verdict, the burden then shifts to the defendant to show that the transaction in question had a valid corporate business purpose. Because the charge fairly contains such a standard, we find no error.

*   *   *

V.

We have examined the remainder of the plaintiffs' contentions and find no reversible error. The judgment will be affirmed.

ROSENN, Circuit Judge, concurring and dissenting.

*   *   *

II.

A major issue in this case is whether the defendants acted in good faith in managing Penn Eastern's affairs or whether they acted for an improper purpose—namely, the desire to retain control over Penn Eastern when it was not in its best interest. If the defendants acted in good faith, the business judgment rule would insulate them from any losses as a result of their decisions.

The court instructed the jury as follows:
[T]he desire to retain control of a corporation in and of itself is an improper motive for decision of a director. There-

375

fore, if you find by a preponderance of the evidence that the defendants acted solely or primarily because of a desire to retain control of Penn Eastern, then the presumption of the sound business judgment rule has been rebutted. However, I further instruct you that a director may properly decline to adopt a course of action which would result in a shift of control, so long as his actions can be attributed to a rational business purpose. In other words, so long as other rational business reasons support a director's decision, the mere fact that a business decision involves the retention of control does not constitute a showing of bad faith to rebut the business judgment rule. *That rule is rebutted only where a director's sole or primary purpose for adopting a course of action or refusing to adopt another is to retain control.* (Emphasis added.)

The plaintiffs complain that the last sentence of the instruction incorrectly sets forth their burden of proof under Delaware law. They claim that to rebut the business judgment rule, they need not demonstrate that the defendants' "sole or primary" motive was the desire to retain control; only that control was a motive. I am persuaded that an examination of the relevant case law supports the plaintiffs' view that the district court's instruction was erroneous. I do not agree with the majority that plaintiffs' theory is inconsistent with Delaware case law.

I start with the case of *Bennett v. Propp*, 41 Del.Ch. 14, 187 A.2d 405 (1962), in which the plaintiffs-shareholders challenged the purchase of a large quantity of the corporation's stock on behalf of the corporation by its principal executive, allegedly to dissipate a take-over bid and to retain control over the corporation. The Supreme Court of Delaware invalidated the purchase, noting "the inherent danger in the purchase of shares with corporate funds to remove a threat to corporate policy." 187 A.2d at 409. Because the court recognized the corporate dangers when directors are confronted with a conflict of interest and the subtleties involved in their decisions under such circumstances, it imposed the burden on the directors of vindicating the transaction, stating: "The directors are of necessity confronted with a conflict of interest, and an objective decision is difficult. . . . Hence, in our opinion, the *burden should be on the directors* to justify such a purchase as one *primarily in the corporate interest.*"-*Id.* (emphasis added).

I read *Bennett* as holding that when a transaction involving control of a corporation raises a conflict of interest on the part of the board of directors, the burden is then thrust upon the defendants to go forward with proof establishing the fairness of the transaction. In other words, the business judgment presumption is dissipated once the plaintiffs show that an improper purpose—control—was a motive. This result is fully consistent with the purpose of the business judgment rule which is to insulate routine matters of corporate expertise from judicial scrutiny:

The theoretical justification for the business judgment rule is that courts should be reluctant to review the acts of directors in situations where the directors' expertise is likely to be greater than the court's; thus the rule may be viewed as a guide for judicial restraint. A strong implication follows that the courts should not apply the rule where the decisions of directors are influenced by forces tending to create conflicts of interest. In such contexts, there is a great danger that the directors will channel their expertise toward pursuit of personal advantage.

R. Gelfond & S. Sebastian, *Reevaluating the Duties of Target Management in a Hostile Tender Offer*, 60 B.U.L.Rev. 403, 435 (1980) (footnotes omitted).

Placing the burden of justifying the fairness of the transaction on the defendants, once control is implicated as a motive, appears to be confirmed in the case of *Cheff v. Mathes, supra,* which cites with approval the dispositive holding of *Bennett* concerning the burden of going forward with proof. *See* 199 A.2d at 554. The court in *Cheff,* however, citing *Bennett,* appears to have introduced an element of ambiguity when it stated: "[I]f the board has acted solely or primarily because of the desire to perpetuate themselves in office, the use of corporate funds for such purposes is improper." It is the court's mention of "sole" or "primary" purpose in *Cheff* which produced the problem in the instant case. This statement made in the court's discussion of *liability,* not the burden of proof, nonetheless cites *Bennett v. Propp, supra.* The district court and the majority read this language as placing an initial burden of proof on the plaintiffs to overcome the business judgment presumption. However, when it reached the question of the burden of proof to show the presence or lack of good faith on the part of the board of directors, the *Cheff* court fully and unequivocally reiterated the burden of proof rule it announced in *Bennett*, again stating that the burden is on the directors to justify the transaction "as one primarily in the corporate interest." *Cheff v. Mathes, supra*, 199 A.2d at 554. Nothing in *Bennett* or *Cheff* suggests that the plaintiff must first prove that the sole or primary purpose of the transaction was the directors' desire to retain control over the corporation.[6] Rather, the unequivocal thrust of *Bennett* is that once the record demonstrates that control is implicated in the transaction, a conflict of interest is *ipso facto* created. Once a conflict of interest is present, the burden of proof is shifted logically and pragmatically on the defendants "to justify [the transaction] as one primarily in the corporate interest." *Bennett, supra*, 187 A.2d at 409. Indeed, the "primary purpose" language of *Cheff* appears to be directed towards the defendant's burden in justifying the transaction, i. e., that the sole or primary purpose was not control.

The sole or primary purpose language of *Cheff* was not utilized in *Condec Corp. v. Lunkenheimer Co.*, 43 Del.Ch. 353, 230 A.2d 769, 776 (1967), where the court stated:

> Where, however, the objective sought in the issuance of stock is not merely the pursual of a business purpose but also to retain control, it has been held to be a mockery to suggest that the "control" effect of an agreement in litigation is merely incidental to its primary business objective.

This language supports *Bennett's* rule that the issue of control as a motive is so central

to the issue of business judgment that the burden is on the defendant to justify the soundness of the transaction as one primarily in the corporate interest.[7] Recent Delaware cases reveal a growing trend to impose stricter obligations on management to justify control-related transactions. *Cf. Singer v. Magnavox, Co.*, 380 A.2d 969 (Del. 1977) (freeze-out merger by majority shareholders subject to fairness test); *Sinclair Oil Corp. v. Levien*, 280 A.2d 717, 720 (Del. 1971) (instrinsic fairness test and not business judgment rule applies where parent corporation receives benefit to the exclusion and detriment of subsidiary); *Petty v. Penntech Papers, Inc.*, 347 A.2d 140, 143 (Del.Ch.1975) (a purchase of shares with corporate funds to remove a threat to management policy and control casts the burden on defendant directors to justify the purchase as "one primarily in the corporate interest and not their own").

Therefore, I believe that a standard requiring plaintiffs to show that control was the sole or primary purpose motivating the defendants' conduct imposes a burden on the plaintiffs not consistent with Delaware law. Unlike the majority, I believe that under Delaware law, once plaintiff has shown that the desire to retain control was a motive in the particular business decision under challenge, the burden is then on the defendant to move forward with evidence justifying the transaction as primarily in the corporation's best interest. Accordingly, I believe the district court erred in its charge to the jury and that the case should be remanded for new trial.

---

6. Indeed, I believe such a test would be exceedingly difficult to apply. For example, if the plaintiff could show that control dominated the corporate decision by 50% or more, would the business judgment presumption disappear; but if he shows only 49% control motive, the presumption remains? Further, we believe it would be difficult to determine exactly what subjective motive was involved since any decision may involve a multitude of considerations. Also, under the majority's reading of *Cheff*, it is unclear whose motive or purpose is involved: is it the entire board of directors, one director,

or a majority of the board?

7. Although the court in *Condec* found that control was the primary purpose of the transaction, *see* 230 A.2d at 775, nothing in the opinion suggests that plaintiffs must first prove control to be the sole or primary purpose before the business judgment presumption disappears. Indeed, the court in *Condec* refrained from placing the full burden on the defendants to justify the transaction because it was not established that the directors were acting in their own self-interest. *See id.* at 776–77.

NOTE ON REPURCHASE OF STOCK TO MAINTAIN CONTROL

1. Approval by Directors or Shareholders. Clearly, a decision to repurchase a substantial block of stock, whether
from a particular shareholder, such as a potential insurgent, or in a program of repurchases in the market, calls
for approval bv the board of directors. Assuming that none
of the directors, or other controlling insiders, are themselves the prospective sellers, such a repurchase would not
constitute a traditional "interested" transaction which
would bring into play the requirement for approval by disinterested directors. Nevertheless, the obvious self-
interest of the management in warding off a threat to its
position may put the inside directors in a position somewhat
analoguous to that of interested directors, making approval
of the transaction by the outside directors distinctly
advantageous. Whether such approval would provide whatever
freedom from attack is afforded by such statutes as MBA §41
is unclear, since at least literally only transactions
between the corporation and one or more of its directors,
directly or indirectly, are encompassed by these provisions.

As to whether to seek shareholder approval for such a
repurchase transaction, any advantage may be more psychological than legal. By analogy to the traditional interested director transactions, if there has been approval by a
sufficient number of disinterested (i.e., outside) directors,
ratification by the shareholders is not needed. Moreover,
if the repurchase is improper because no proper corporate
purpose is present, it would constitute a waste of corporate
assets, and anything less than unanimous shareholder approval
would be ineffective. (Again, the transaction would seem to
fall outside of §41, so that whatever insulation might be
provided by §41(b) would not be applicable.) Nevertheless,
approval by a disinterested majority of the shareholders
could well be useful in blunting possible shareholder criticism, as well as in putting the deal in a more sympathetic
posture if litigation ensues. (In the case of a listed
security such shareholder approval may actually be required
by the Exchange whenever the repurchase is from a substantial holder, as is likely to be the case in these circumstances.)

2. An Offer to Repurchase from Other Shareholders. A
related question is whether an offer to repurchase from all
other shareholders at the same price being paid to the
insurgent is either necessary or desirable. Such an offer

may well be even more likely to stifle shareholder complaints than shareholder ratification; but of course it only
takes one disgruntled shareholder to launch a derivative
suit. Moreover, if any substantial percentage of the remaining shareholders accepted the offer, the corporation would
probably not be able to finance the purchase of all the
shares tendered; hence the offer to shareholders other than
the insurgent would presumably have to reserve the right to
accept only a pro rata portion from each tendering shareholder, and that could cause more unrest among the stockholders than it cures.

As a general proposition, it seems to have been assumed
that a repurchase from some shareholders does not entitle
other shareholders to demand equal treatment. See e.g.,
Spiegel v. Beacon Participations, Inc., 297 Mass. 398, 431,
8 N.E.2d 895, 914 (1937) ("No provision of law required the
directors, in making these purchases of stock . . . to buy
them ratably from the stockholders"). This seems particularly apt in the case of buying out a potential insurgent,
since the purported goal of protecting existing business
policies against a threat posed by the insurgent would not
be advanced by repurchasing from other shareholders. The
fact that the insurgent is receiving a premium price may be
galling to the other shareholders, but it is well recognized
that a controlling (or otherwise significant) block of stock
will usually carry a premium, and as the Cheff court noted
the corporation must meet that "going rate" if it is to
obtain the stock in question. Moreover, if the repurchase
from the insurgent is indeed improper, because primarily
motivated by a desire to retain control, then paying out
additional corporate funds to repurchase stock from others
would not only provide no insulation against attack but
would in fact compound the waste of corporate assets involved.

These views find support in what appears to be the only
decided case on this point, Heine v. The Signal Companies,
Inc., 1976-77 CCH Fed. Sec. L. Rep. [Transfer Binder] ¶95,898
(S.D.N.Y. 1977). There the corporation, which had recently
sold one of its divisions for a large amount of cash, bought
out a substantial block of stock, amounting to 1,600,000
shares, from a group which disagreed with the management's
policies (and had, among other things, brought a suit attacking the recent sale of the division). Thereafter, as planned,
the corporation made a tender offer to purchase between
1,000,000 and 1,600,000 shares from the other shareholders

at the same price, reserving the right to pro-rate the
acceptances if the offer was oversubscribed. Some 6,400,000
shares were tendered, and the corporation purchased 1,000,000
shares pro rata. A class action was brought against the
corporation under both federal and state law complaining
that the tendering shareholders were entitled to have all of
their shares purchased. The court held for the defendant,
primarily on the ground that the gravamen of the complaint
was improper conduct by the directors, which called for a
derivative suit rather than an action against the corporation.
However, in the course of the opinion the court expressed
the view that there was a legitimate business purpose for
the purchase of stock from the dissident group, because of
its fundamental disagreement with the business policy of the
management, as exemplified, inter alia, by the suit over the
sale of the corporation's division. With respect to the
claim for equal treatment as such, the court said (in footnote 4):

"Without more, the claim of unequal treatment does not
state a cause of action under either state or federal law.
Neither federal nor Delaware law imposes on a corporation
any obligation to repurchase its outstanding shares on an
equal basis from all of its shareholders. . . . the Delaware
courts have upheld selective repurchase transactions like
the one challenged here in the absence of self-dealing on
the part of corporate officers or directors [citing the
Cheff and Kors cases]."

Later, the court added the following (at 91,316):

"If the directors acted wrongfully in using the corporation's money to buy its own shares from the [insurgent
group], the wrong would not be remediable by insisting
that the corporation buy a huge number of other shares
from a class of people who wanted to be let in on a similarly wrongful transaction. Nothing in the supposed
initial wrong could be cured by compounding it."

Of course, as already noted, a repurchase confined to
insiders, and designed to favor them, would probably be
condemned on equitable grounds; alternatively, outside
shareholders could probably succeed in compelling the same
treatment for their holdings. Indeed, the Massachusetts
court has purported to lay down a virtual rule of law that
in the close corporation setting a repurchase from the

controlling stockholders is invalid unless the same opportunity is made available to minority stockholders. Donahue
v. Rodd Electrotype Co., 367 Mass. 578, 328 N.E.2d 505
(1975). Since the decision was based primarily upon the
analogy of close corporations to partnerships, and the
significant fiduciary obligation that partners owe to one
another, the question of whether the holding should apply to
other corporations was expressly left for later decision in
an appropriate case. But the demarcation of a close corporation is far from clear, as is perhaps illustrated by an
earlier Pennsylvania decision, in which a strong dissenting
opinion somewhat anticipated the result in Donahue, although
the corporation was obviously more than a classic "incorporated partnership". Reifsnyder v. Pittsburgh Outdoor Advertising Co., 396 Pa. 320, 152 A.2d 894 (1959). There, the
plaintiff was a minority stockholder of the defendant corporation ("Pittsburgh"), owning 130 of the outstanding 15,000
shares. Some 9150 shares of Pittsburgh's stock was owned by
General Outdoor Advertising Company ("General"), which
elected all of the directors of Pittsburgh and operated it
as a subsidiary. In 1955 a consent decree entered in an
anti-trust proceeding required General to dispose of its
Pittsburgh stock at "not less than a fair market value."
There followed negotiations aimed at Pittsburgh's acquisition
of the 9150 shares held by General. The Pittsburgh board of
directors made a survey of its real estate and determined
that the reappraised book value of its stock was approximately $233 per share. The General officers originally
asked for $2,400,000 for General's stock, but finally agreed
to accept $2,150,000 ($232.38 per share). Pittsburgh had
planned to borrow $2,000,000 in order to finance the trans-
action, but was able to obtain only enough funds to purchase
7,750 of the shares held by General, so Pittsburgh's president offered to purchase the other 1400 shares personally at
the same price. At a special stockholders' meeting the
purchase and borrowing by Pittsburgh, as well as the purchase
by Pittsburgh's president, were approved. The plaintiff
cast the only negative votes, claiming that the price of
$232.88 per share was excessive. (He also complained of the
purchase by Pittsburgh's president, for the rather anomalous
reason that the price was too low, but when the 1400 shares
were offered to the plaintiff at the same price, he declined.)

In the plaintiff's derivative suit against the directors, the Chancellor found that the price per share "was
fair, reasonable and not excessive," and that "Pittsburgh's

officers and directors acted in good faith and with ordinary
prudence and skill." On appeal, the court held that the
action should be dismissed because an indispensible party,
General, had not been joined. However, a majority of the
court joined in an elaborate dictum approving the decision
of the Pittsburgh directors to purchase General stock "in
order to continue the present management and to prevent an
outsider or competitor from getting control of the company."
After noting that two independent appraisers had testified
that the purchase price was fair and reasonable, the court
added that "the wisdom of this purchase has been made apparent by the fact that since that time the corporation has
been very successful."

Two Justices took sharp issue with the majority with
regard to the transaction on the merits:

". . . whenever a corporation offers to purchase all of
the shares of the majority or all the shares of a controlling interest in a corporation, the corporation is
obligated to offer to acquire, at the same price, all the
shares of any dissenting shareholder or group of shareholders.

"Fair dealing, fiduciary responsibility, and the direct
obligation of loyalty owed to all the shareholders, would
dictate that a shareholder who did not want to go along
with this 'bale-out' of the majority should be given the
option of disposing of his shares on the same terms and on
the same conditions as the retiring majority. Otherwise,
the majority shareholders would have at their command a
ready purchaser (the corporation) for their holdings -- a
market that is denied to the minority. . . . In addition
to eliminating the element of unfairness that may or may
not exist when the majority "bales" itself out, the extension of the same offer of purchase to the minority would
eliminate the difficult proof problem of breach of fiduciary
duty or of anticipated future harm to the corporation, and
also would prevent disputes over what a proper sales price
for the stock would be. It might be argued that this
offer may force the dissolution of the corporation in some
cases. That is all the more reason why the majority
should not be permitted to liquidate its holdings through
the utilization of the corporate assets without also
extending the same opportunity of sale to the minority
shareholder. Here the majority stockholder has abandoned

its fiduciary responsibility to the minority and this
Court should not, even by way of dicta, countenance such
action."

3.   Corporate Financial Objectives for Repurchase. In
both the Kors and Cheff cases the defendants attempted to
justify the challenged repurchases on the basis of alleged
corporate need for the stock--in Kors for acquisition purposes, and in Cheff for a contemplated stock option plan.
In each case the court gave short shrift to the contention,
at least partly because the corporation already had ample
stock available, in the form of either unissued stock or
treasury stock (and of course could always have amended its
articles to authorize more shares anyway).

Nevertheless, there may be circumstances which would
justify repurchase of stock in connection with pending
options. At the outset, it should be observed that while a
new issue of stock may change the percentage interests of
existing stockholders, so long as the stock is issued for a
fair price the existing stockholders will not be adversely
affected, since their smaller percentage interests will be
offset by the fact that the total value of the corporation
has proportionately increased. When the new stock is issued
pursuant to stock options, while the option price actually
received by the corporation for the stock would normally be
less than its then current market value, presumably the
corporation has received other consideration (such as valuable services) for the rights being exercised, so that at
least in theory there should be no adverse "dilution."
However, if the corporation was not able to make profitable
use of the additional capital to be received upon the exercise of the options, then the existing stockholders might
well suffer a real dilution of their interests. Thus, if
the corporation were earning a certain percentage on its
invested capital, but could not earn as high a return on
additional capital, any issuance of additional stock would
result in a decrease in the earnings per share, and hence in
all likelihood a decline in the market price for the stock.
In such circumstances the corporation would not voluntarily
issue more stock; but of course it would have no choice if
outstanding options are exercised. Accordingly, the corporation might appropriately purchase its stock in the
market (especially if the stock was then attractively priced),
in order to avoid the "overcapitalization" expected to
result from the exercise of outstanding options. This would

constitute a reasonable exercise of business judgment, i.e., that repurchase of its own stock represents the best invest- ment the corporation can make with its available (or soon to be received) funds. There would be no violation of the rights of the selling shareholders, since presumably the corporation would be buying at current market prices from willing sellers, without taking advantage of any inside information or the like.

The use of corporate funds to repurchase stock could be equally justifiable even though the corporation has no plans to issue more stock, by way of stock options or otherwise, if the corporation is already overcapitalized, that is, it has on hand more liquid assets than it can profitably utilize. An argument much along these lines appears to have been made by the defendants in the Cheff case, i.e., that the corpora- tion was overcapitalized and thus had additional justifica- tion for the challenged repurchase. However, the Cheff case provides little guidance as to how effective such an argument may be, since neither court really reached that issue on the merits. The Vice Chancellor rejected the contention on the facts, finding that the corporation could have usefully employed additional funds in a finance business which had recently been set up as a wholly-owned subsidiary. For its part, the Supreme Court simply stated that such a use of its funds "would not have solved the problem of Holland's over- capitalization," without explaining why; but of course for the Supreme Court the overcapitalization issue had become moot in the light of its determination that the elimination of the insurgent was enough of a justification for the repurchase transaction.

In any event, it is quite possible that using corporate funds to repurchase stock may be beneficial to the remaining shareholders even if the corporation is not demonstrably overcapitalized (which is somewhat in the eye of the beholder anyway). If the price of the stock is low enough (whether in the market or pursuant to negotiated private deal), repurchase represents a kind of reverse dilution which increases the earnings and assets per share for the remain- ing shareholders. That in turn may lead to an increase in the market price for the remaining shares, which could be greater than the amount that would have been received per share if the total spent on the repurchase had instead been distributed as dividend pro rata to all the shareholders. In addition, there is the important tax aspect that realization of an increase in the market price per share would only be taxed at capital gains rates, whereas a pro rata dividend to all the shareholders wonld be subject to ordinary income taxation.

It is for this reason that public corporations often undertake a program of market repurchases, or perhaps a tender offer, when the market for their shares is low. Obviously, a corporation with ample cash resources is better positioned to make such a move, but if the price of the stock is attractive enough it may be worthwhile for the corporation to borrow the funds needed to finance a repurchase.

Can a corporate objective of this kind be combined with a desire to eliminate a potential insurgent, in order to strengthen the corporation's defense of business purpose for a challenged repurchase? An affirmative answer is suggested by the Heine case, cited in section 2, supra, where the court expressly found that the corporation's repurchase from the insurgent group "offered an advantageous use for the excess cash" acquired from the sale of one of its divisions, since it "would serve to increase the per share earnings and book value of each share of the common stock outstanding after the purchase." The possible interrelationship between improving the corporation's financial picture and combatting a potential takeover is also recognized in the following excerpt from Nathan and Sobel, Corporate Stock Repurchases in the Context of Unsolicited Takeover Bids, 35 Bus. Law. 1545 (1980):

"A common phenomenon in today's capital markets is stock repurchase programs by issuers, tvpically through a cash tender offer or an open market purchase program, but sometimes through negotiated purchases from holders of large blocks. . . . A variety of business reasons (such as, for example, favorable effects on earnings and, sometimes, book value per share, financial benefits of increased leverage particularly in an inflationary era, and reduction of aggregate dividend costs and shareholder servicing costs) are typically cited as justifying such stock repurchase and recapitalization programs. . . . An issuer stock repurchase program, however, is also often viewed as a preventive device intended to discourage third parties from making unsolicited acquisition offers or as a defensive technique in the face of an actual threatened or pending takeover proposal. This is not to say that there is always a distinct line between the implementation of a stock acquisition program for what one might characterize as garden variety business and financial reasons, as

opposed to preventive or defensive reasons. Indeed,
frequently there is a coalescence of such goals and motives."

4. Special Position of Non-Inside Directors. An attempt to impose
personal liability upon directors for allegedly improper corporate repurchases
raises the distinction between a director's duty of *loyalty* to his corporation
and his duty of *care*. Under the duty of loyalty, the director is required to
give primary, if not exclusive, consideration to the best interests of the
corporation, and in any case where the director favors his own interests over
those of the corporation he becomes a virtual insurer of any resulting loss.
On the other hand, under the duty of care, while the standard may be various-
give primary, if not exclusive, consideration to the best interests of the
corporation, and in any case where the director favors his own interests over
those of the corporation he becomes a virtual insurer of any resulting loss.
On the other hand, under the duty of care, while the standard may be various-
ly stated, the net effect is that the director is given wide latitude in the
exercise of his judgment on behalf of the corporation and will generally be
protected even for quite unwise conduct, so long as he was trying to advance
the best interests of the corporation.

This dichotomy between the duty of loyalty and the duty of care is
rather sharply illustrated in the decided repurchase cases themselves. Thus
in both the Kors and Cheff cases the defendant directors claimed a variety
of alleged corporate needs for stock as justifications for the challenged repurchase transactions. If any of these claimed reasons had been established
as the real purpose for the repurchase transactions in those cases, presumably the directors would have escaped liability even if they had been wrong
about the alleged corporate needs; for the posture of the matter would then
have been that the directors had been either foolish or stupid, but presumably
they would have been within the cloak of protection afforded by the business
judgment rule.

However, in both Kors and Cheff the court rejected the various justifications claimed by the defendants because it seemed clear that a different
purpose had in fact motivated the challenged transactions, namely the desire
to get rid of a potentially troublesome minority stockholder. Of course this
too can constitute a legitimate corporate reason for the repurchase transactions, so that the directors become entitled to the protection of the business
judgment rule even if their decision turns out to be unwise. However, the
special difficulty with this motive for repurchase, and the reason why directors are often reluctant to rely upon it alone, is that elimination of a troublesome minority stockholder may derive as much from the personal desire of
the controlling directors to retain their control as from a concern for the corporation's welfare. Ultimately, in the Kors case the court concluded that the
objective of the repurchase transactions did stem primarily from a concern
for the corporation's welfare; and, of course, there was no need to consider
whether the repurchase was prudent, in view of the special circumstance in
Kors that the price of the stock had gone up and the corporation had suffered
no damage. Conversely, however, in the Bennett case the court concluded
that the primary motive for the repurchase transactions was the desire of
the principal defendant to maintain his own controlling position. In the
light of that finding, it became equally unnecessary to decide whether the
decision to repurchase had been a sound one from the corporation's point

of view, but for a very different reason from that in Kors—in Bennett, since the decision was not in fact made "from the corporation's point of view," the defendant was charged with virtually absolute responsibility for the loss caused to the corporation.

Obviously, however, directors cannot be held to have acted in their own self-interest instead of for the best interests of the corporation unless it is established that in fact the directors had some personal stake in the transaction (or, at any rate, some reason to act in concert with those who did). This is simple enough so far as directors who are part of the management are concerned, in cases involving elimination of a troublesome minority stockholder group, since such directors are obviously anxious to maintain their executive positions, salaries and the like. But the situation is very different for those directors who do not receive any benefits from the corporation by way of substantial compensation or otherwise. Such directors can scarcely be accused of acting in their own self-interest, for they have no special interest to preserve or advance in the transaction. They may, of course, have been very careless, or stupid, or too servile to the wishes of the controlling group; and any one of these findings may be a basis for imposing liability. But the important point here is that such liability would be predicated upon a breach of the duty of care more than on a breach of the duty of loyalty; and, in that setting, the directors would be entitled to the protection afforded by the business judgment rule or the like.

This seems to have been the line taken by the Vice-Chancellor in the Cheff case when he dismissed the action as to those directors who had no personal stake in the transaction, while imposing liability on the inside group which had officerships, large stockholdings, or other personal interests at stake. Indeed, the Vice-Chancellor may have gone a little too far, since he did not appear to even consider the possible liability of the "disinterested" directors for breach of their duty of care. (Of course the disloyalty—negligence dichotomy became moot in the Cheff case when the Supreme Court reversed and absolved all the directors; and it is hard to know what to make of the Supreme Court's criticism of the Vice-Chancellor's distinction between interested and disinterested directors, because of the puzzling role of the fact that some of the shareholders had expressed a willingness to buy Maremont's stock on their own.) More attention was paid to this element in the Bennett decision where the court released the directors who had not participated in the original repurchase transaction only after finding that they had not violated their duty of care in "ratifying" the challenged stock repurchases.

Does this analysis square with the Supreme Court's insistence in the Bennett case that the president of the corporation, Ward, was held liable not for negligence but "for the tort of using corporate funds to maintain control"? That this "tort" is not absolute is clear from the court's release of the other directors from liability—so it would seem that either negligence or disloyalty is an essential ingredient. Yet it does not appear that the court was finding Ward guilty of disloyalty in the normal sense—for the court stressed "his silence and failure to act" in connection with Sadacca's purchases rather than any affirmative desire to preserve his own position. Perhaps the answer is that Ward was so subservient to Sadacca that his conduct transcended imprudence and even inattentiveness, and amounted to "disloyalty" in the sense of putting Sadacca's interests ahead of those of the corporation.

C. SOME SECURITIES LAW ASPECTS

1 . Securities Exchange Act of 1934, §§13(d) and (e):

(d) (1) Any person who, after acquiring directly or indirectly the beneficial ownership of any equity security of a class which is registered pursuant to section 12 of this title . . . , is directly or indirectly the beneficial owner of more than 5 per centum of such class shall, within ten days after such acquisition, send to the issuer of the security at its principal executive office, by registered or certified mail, send to each exchange where the security is traded, and file with the Commission, a statement containing such of the following information, as the Commission may by rules and regulations prescribe as necessary or appropriate in the public interest or for the protection of investors—

(A) the background and identity of all persons by whom or on whose behalf the purchases have been o· are to be effected;

(B) the source and amount of the funds or other consideration used or to be used in making the purchases, and if any part of the purchase price or proposed purchase price is represented or is to be represented by funds or other consideration borrowed or otherwise obtained for the purpose of acquiring, holding, or trading such security a description of the transaction and the names of the parties thereto, . . .;

(C) if the purpose of the purchases or prospective purchases is to acquire control of the business of the issuer of the securities, any plans or proposals which such persons may have to liquidate such issuer, to sell its assets to or merge it with any other persons, or to make any other major change in its business or corporate structure;

(D) the number of shares of such security which are beneficially owned, and the number of shares concerning which there is a right to acquire, directly or indirectly, by (i) such person, and (ii) by each associate of such person, giving the name and address of each such associate; and

(E) information as to any contracts, arrangements, or understandings with any person with respect to any securities of the issuer . . ..

* * *

(3) When two or more persons act as a partnership, limited partnership, syndicate, or other group for the purpose of acquiring, holding, or disposing of securities of an issuer, such syndicate or group shall be deemed a "person" for the purposes of this subsection.

* * *

(e) (1) It shall be unlawful for an issuer which has a class of equity securities registered pursuant to section 12 of this title, or which is a closed-end investment company registered under the Investment Company Act of 1940, to purchase any equity security issued by it if such purchase is in contravention of such rules and regulations as the Commission, in the public interest or for the protection of investors, may adopt (A) to define acts and practices which are fraudulent, deceptive, or manipulative, and (B) to prescribe means reasonably designed to prevent such acts and practices. Such rules and regulations may require such issuer to provide holders of equity securities of such class with such information relating to the reasons for such purchase, the source of funds, the number of shares to be purchased, the price to be paid for such securities, the method of purchase, and such additional information, as the Commission deems necessary or appropriate in the public interest or for the protection of investors, or which the Commission deems to be material to a determination whether such security should be sold.

---

2. Exchange Act Release No. 16112 (1979):*

SUMMARY: The Commission announces the adoption of a new rule and schedule relating to tender and exchange offers by certain issuers for their own securities. The rule defines certain fraudulent, deceptive and manipulative acts or practices in connection with such offers, and prescribes filing, disclosure, dissemination and other requirements as means reasonably designed to prevent such acts and practices.

* * *

IV. *Summary of Rule 13e-4*

A. *Rule 13e-4(a)*

Paragraph (a) of the Rule defines certain terms used throughout the Rule and Schedule. . . .

B. *Rule 13e-4(b)*

As proposed, the Rule defined certain fraudulent, deceptive or manipulative acts or practices intended to be prevented by other specific requirements of the Rule. . . . To obviate concern as to whether the Commission intended to introduce unfamiliar concepts of fraud, deceit and manipulation in this context, paragraph (b), as revised, defines fraudulent, deceptive or manipulative acts or practices in more general, traditional terms (as, for example in Rules 10b-5 and 13e-3 under the Act). . . .

---

* Portions of the text and footnotes omitted.

C. *Filing Requirements*

* * *

D. *Disclosure and Dissemination Requirements*

Rule 13e–4(d) sets forth specifically those terms of the tender offer which the issuer or affiliate is required to disclose to security holders in its offering materials. . . .

E. *Manner of Making the Tender Offer*

1. *Duration of the Tender Offer*

Rule 13e–4(f)(1) requires that an issuer tender offer remain open for at least fifteen business days from the date of commencement of the offer. The Commission believes that the fifteen business day period will provide holders of the securities for which the offer is made with a reasonable opportunity to consider an issuer tender offer, and to make an informed investment decision with respect to the tender offer.

2. *Subjects of the Tender Offer and Consideration*

As proposed, the Rule would have required that, except in the case of odd lot tender offers, persons subject to the Rule must extend the tender offer to all holders of the class of securities for which the offer is made. Several commentators suggested that, in a few limited contexts, an issuer may have valid business reasons for excluding certain security holders from its tender offer. The Commission has determined not to adopt the explicit requirement proposed at this time. The Commission has also determined not to adopt the provision of the Rule which, as proposed, would have required that issuers expressly offer the same consideration to all security holders to whom a tender offer subject to the Rule is made. However, in light of the Commission's continuing concerns with respect to tender offer practices generally, the Commission has directed the staff to consider in more detail, with a view toward the possibility of further rulemaking, the issues raised by an express requirement that all persons making tender offers must offer the same consideration to all holders of the security for which the tender offer is made.

3. *Withdrawal Rights*

. . . Security holders have the right to withdraw tendered securities at any time until the expiration of at least ten business days after the time the tender offer is commenced. This period of time is designed to give security holders who tender their securities soon after commencement of the offer an opportunity to reconsider their investment decision, and to protect such holders from being pressured into accepting the tender offer prior to the time all material facts relating to the tender offer are fully disclosed and disseminated.

In the event tendered securities have not been accepted for payment by the issuer, security holders have the right to withdraw their securities at any time after forty business days from the time the offer has commenced. This requirement of the Rule is intended to assure that security holders do not have their shares "locked in" for an unreasonable period of time. In addition, if tendered securities have not been accepted for payment, security holders must be afforded the right to withdraw their securities during the seven business days following the date a Schedule 14D–1 is filed with the Commission relating to a competing tender offer by a subsequent bidder or such tender offer is otherwise commenced. These additional withdrawal rights are intended to permit security holders to respond to a competing tender offer.

4. *Pro Rata Acceptance*

The requirements of the Rule relating to pro rata acceptance of tendered securities have been adopted substantially as proposed. Paragraph (f)(3) of the Rule requires that where a greater number of securities is tendered than the issuer will accept within at least ten business days of an offer, or within at least ten business days after notice of an increase in consideration is disseminated to security holders, the issuer or affiliate making the tender offer shall accept all such securities on a pro rata basis. The pro rata acceptance requirements of the Rule are based on the policy underlying Section 14(d)(6) of the Act, which was designed to allow all security holders an opportunity to participate in the offer. Moreover, as a means reasonably designed to prevent fraudulent or deceptive conduct, the pro rata acceptance requirements are intended to prevent an issuer from pressuring security holders, who might otherwise assume that all tendered securities will be accepted on a first come, first served basis, into making hasty, uninformed investment decisions. The ten day pro ration requirements are intended to establish minimum pro rata acceptance periods and do not address the acceptance procedure employed by an offeror beyond those minimum periods.

The Rule allows an offeror to permit security holders to tender their securities upon the condition that all, or a specified minimum number, or none of such securities be accepted. In recognition of the conflict between pro rationing and the elimination of odd lots, the Rule permits the offeror to accept odd lots in full prior to accepting other securities on a pro rata basis. . . .

5. *Increase in Consideration and Payment for Securities*

Paragraph (f)(4) of the Rule requires that, if the issuer or affiliate subject to the Rule increases the consideration offered after the tender offer is commenced, the issuer or affiliate must pay the increased consideration to all security holders whose tendered securities are accepted for payment. This requirement is patterned after an analogous provision contained in Section 14(d)(7) of the Act.

The so-called "best price" provision was designed "to assure fair treatment of those persons who tender their shares at the beginning of the tender period, and to assure equality of treatment among all shareholders who tender their shares." The Commission believes that the principle embodied in Section 14(d)(7) should be equally applicable in the context of an issuer tender offer. In addition, as a means reasonably designed to prevent fraudulent or deceptive conduct, Rule 13e–4(f)(4) is intended to prevent an issuer from misleading security holders with respect to the price it is willing to pay for the securities which are the subject of the tender offer.

Paragraph (f)(5) of the Rule requires that the person making the issuer tender offer must either pay the consideration offered, or return tendered securities, promptly after termination of the tender offer.

* * *

V. Disclosure Requirements—Schedule 13E–4
* * *

Item 4 of the Schedule requires disclosure of recent transactions in an issuer's securities by certain persons affiliated with the issuer. Several commentators suggested that, in light of the number of persons as to whom such information must be obtained, the two business day period provided in Instruction 2 of the Item would be inadequate for the gathering and filing of such information. Accordingly, the Commission has expanded this period to ten business days, which should be adequate to achieve the purpose of the provision, yet preserve the confidentiality of the tender offer. The Commission believes that the ten business day period obviates the need, suggested by certain commentators, to restrict the size of the class of persons with respect to whom such information must be filed. . . .

As published for comment, Item 5 of the Schedule would have required the disclosure of any contract, arrangement, understanding or relationship between the issuer and any person with respect to any securities of the issuer. The Commission agrees with the commentators that the requirement is unnecessarily broad, and, accordingly, Item 5 has been revised to provide for disclosure only of such contracts, arrangements, understandings or relationships which relate, directly or indirectly, to the tender offer.

As published for comment, Schedule 13E–4 did not contain an item specifically requiring disclosure of material financial information concerning the issuer. In the case of a registered exchange offer, of course, the Commission's registration forms under the Securities Act of 1933 require disclosure of a registrant's financial operations and conditions. To make it clear that there is a corresponding disclosure requirement for cash tender offers, the Commission has added to Schedule 13E–4 a specific item which requires disclosure of certain financial information, if material. In addition the person making the issuer tender offer may be required under Item 7(b) to disclose, if material, pro forma data with respect to the effect of the tender offer on, for example, the issuer's most recent balance sheet.

A. IMPACT ON THE WITHDRAWING STOCKHOLDERS

1. SECTION 302

UNITED STATES v. DAVIS *

Supreme Court of the United States, 1970.

70–1 USTC ¶ 9289.

MR. JUSTICE MARSHALL delivered the opinion of the Court: In 1945, taxpayer and E. B. Bradley organized a corporation. In exchange for property transferred to the new company, Bradley received 500 shares of common stock, and taxpayer and his wife similarly each received 250 such shares. Shortly thereafter, taxpayer made an additional contribution to the corporation, purchasing 1,000 shares of preferred stock at a par value of $25 per share.

The purpose of this latter transaction was to increase the company's working capital and thereby to qualify for a loan previously negotiated through the Reconstruction Finance Corporation. It was understood that the corporation would redeem the preferred stock when the RFC loan had been repaid. Although in the interim taxpayer bought Bradley's 500 shares and divided them between his son and daughter, the total capitalization of the company remained the same until 1963. That year, after the loan was fully repaid and in accordance with the original understanding, the company redeemed taxpayer's preferred stock.

In his 1963 personal income tax return taxpayer did not report the $25,000 received by him upon the redemption of his preferred stock as income. Rather, taxpayer considered the redemption as a sale of his preferred stock to the company—a capital gains transaction under § 302 of the Internal Revenue Code of 1954 resulting in no tax since taxpayer's basis in the stock equaled the amount he received for it. The Commissioner of Internal Revenue, however, did not approve this tax treatment. According to the Commissioner, the redemption of taxpayer's stock was essentially equivalent to a dividend and was thus taxable as ordinary income under §§ 301 and 316 of the Code. Taxpayer paid the resulting deficiency and brought this suit for a refund. The District Court ruled in his favor, 274 F.Supp. 466 (D.C. M.D.Tenn.1967), and on appeal the Court of Appeals affirmed, 408 F.2d 1139 (C.A.6th Cir.1969).

The Court of Appeals held that the $25,000 received by taxpayer was "not essentially equivalent to a dividend" within the meaning of that phrase in § 302(b) (1) of the Code because the redemption was the final step in a course of action that had a legitimate business (as opposed to tax avoidance) purpose. That holding represents only one of a variety of treatments accorded similar transactions under § 302 (b) (1) in the circuit courts of appeals.[2] We granted certiorari, 396 U.S. 815 (1969), in order to resolve this recurring tax question involving stock redemptions by closely held corporations. We reverse.

* Most of the Court's footnotes omitted.

I. The Internal Revenue Code of 1954 provides generally in §§ 301 and 316 for the tax treatment of distributions by a corporation to its shareholders; under those provisions, a distribution is includable in a taxpayer's gross income as a dividend out of earnings and profits to the extent such earnings exist. There are exceptions to the application of these general provisions, however, and among them are those found in § 302 involving certain distributions for redeemed stock. The basic question in this case is whether the $25,000 distribution by the corporation to taxpayer falls under that section—more specifically, whether its legitimate business motivation qualifies the distribution under § 302(b) (1) of the Code. Preliminarily, however, we must consider the relationship between § 302(b) (1) and the rules regarding the attribution of stock ownership found in § 318(a) of the Code.

Under subsection (a) of § 302, a distribution is treated as "payment in exchange for the stock," thus qualifying for capital gains rather than ordinary income treatment, if the conditions contained in any one of the four paragraphs of subsection (b) are met. In addition to paragraph (1)'s "not essentially equivalent to a dividend" test, capital gains treatment is available where (2) the taxpayer's voting strength is substantially diminished, (3) his interest in the company is completely terminated, or (4) certain railroad stock is redeemed. Paragraph (4) is not involved here, and taxpayer admits that paragraphs (2) and (3) do not apply. Moreover, taxpayer agrees that for the purposes of §§ 302(b) (2) and (3) the attribution rules of § 318(a) apply and he is considered to own the 750 outstanding shares of common stock held by his wife and children in addition to the 250 shares in his own name.

Taxpayer, however, argues that the attribution rules do not apply in considering whether a distribution is essentially equivalent to a dividend under § 302(b) (1). According to taxpayer, he should thus be considered to own only 25 percent of the corporation's common stock, and the distribution would then qualify under § 302(b) (1) since it was not pro rata or proportionate to his stock interest, the fundamental test of dividend equivalency. See Treas.Reg. 1.302–2(b). However, the plain language of the statute compels rejection of the argument. In subsection (c) of § 302, the attribution rules are made specifically applicable "in determining the ownership of stock for purposes of this section." Applying this language, both courts below held that § 318(a) applies to all of § 302, including § 302(b) (1)—a view in accord with the decisions of the other courts of appeals, a longstanding treasury regulation, and the opinion of the leading commentators.

Against this weight of authority, taxpayer argues that the result under paragraph (1) should be different because there is no explicit reference to stock ownership as there is in paragraphs (2) and (3)

2. Only the Second Circuit has unequivocally adopted the Commissioner's view and held irrelevant the motivation of the redemption. . . . The First Circuit, however, seems almost to have come to that conclusion, too.
. . .
The other courts of appeals that have passed on the question are apparently willing to give at least some weight under § 302(b) (1) to the business motivation of a distribution and redemption. . . . Even among those courts that consider business purpose, however, it is generally required that the business purpose be related not to the issuance of the stock, but to the redemption of it. . . .

394

Neither that fact, however, nor the purpose and history of § 302(b) (1) support taxpayer's argument. The attribution rules—designed to provide a clear answer to what would otherwise be a difficult tax question—formed part of the tax bill that was subsequently enacted as the 1954 Code. As is discussed further, infra, the bill as passed by the House of Representatives contained no provision comparable to § 302(b) (1). When that provision was added in the Senate, no purpose was evidenced to restrict the applicability of § 318(a). Rather, the attribution rules continued to be made specifically applicable to the entire section, and we believe that Congress intended that they be taken into account wherever ownership of stock was relevant.

Indeed, it was necessary that the attribution rules apply to § 302 (b) (1) unless they were to be effectively eliminated from consideration with regard to §§ 302(b) (2) and (3) also. For if a transaction failed to qualify under one of those sections solely because of the attribution rules, it would according to taxpayer's argument nonetheless qualify under § 302(b) (1). We cannot agree that Congress intended so to nullify its explicit directive. We conclude, therefore, that the attribution rules of § 318(a) do apply; and, for the purposes of deciding whether a distribution is "not essentially equivalent to a dividend" under § 302(b) (1), taxpayer must be deemed the owner of all 1,000 shares of the company's common stock.

II. After application of the stock ownership attribution rules, this case viewed most simply involves a sole stockholder who causes part of his shares to be redeemed by the corporation. We conclude that such a redemption is always "essentially equivalent to a dividend" within the meaning of that phrase in § 302(b) (1) and therefore do not reach the Government's alternative argument that in any event the distribution should not on the facts of this case qualify for capital gains treatment.[9]

The predecessor of § 302(b) (1) came into the tax law as § 201(d) of the Revenue Act of 1921, 42 Stat. 228–229:

> "A stock dividend shall not be subject to tax but if after the distribution of any such dividend the corporation proceeds to cancel or redeem its stock at such time and in such manner as to make the distribution and cancellation or redemption essentially equivalent to the distribution of a taxable dividend, the amount received in redemption or cancellation of the stock shall be treated as a taxable dividend . . . ."

Enacted in response to this court's decision that pro rata stock dividends do not constitute taxable income, Eisner v. Macomber, 252 U.S. 189 (1920), the provision had the obvious purpose of preventing a corporation from avoiding dividend tax treatment by distributing earnings to its shareholders in two transactions—a pro rata stock dividend followed by a pro rata redemption—that would have the same economic consequences as a simple dividend. Congress, however, soon recognized that even without a prior stock dividend essentially the same result could be effected whereby any corporation, "especially one which has only a few stockholders, might be able to make a distribution to its shareholders which would have the same effect as a taxable dividend." . . . In order to cover this situation, the

9. The Government argues that even if business purpose were relevant under § 302(b) (1), the business purpose present here related only to the original investment and not at all to the necessity for redemption. . . . Under either view, taxpayer does not lose his basis in the preferred stock. Under Treas.Reg. 1.302-2(c) that basis is applied to taxpayer's common stock.

law was amended to apply "(whether or not such stock was issued as a stock dividend)" whenever a distribution in redemption of stock was made "at such time and in such manner" that it was essentially equivalent to a taxable dividend. Revenue Act of 1926, § 201(g), 44 Stat. 11.

This provision of the 1926 Act was carried forward in each subsequent revenue act and finally became § 115(g) (1) of the Internal Revenue Code of 1939. Unfortunately, however, the policies encompassed within the general language of § 115(g) (1) and its predecessors were not clear, and there resulted much confusion in the tax law. At first, courts assumed that the provision was aimed at tax avoidance schemes and sought only to determine whether such a scheme existed. . . . Although later the emphasis changed and the focus was more on the effect of the distribution, many courts continued to find that distributions otherwise like a dividend were not "essentially equivalent" if, for example, they were motivated by a sufficiently strong nontax business purpose. See cases cited n. 2, supra. There was general disagreement, however, about what would qualify as such a purpose, and the result was a case-by-case determination with each case decided "on the basis of the particular facts of the transaction in question." . . .

. By the time of the general revision resulting in the Internal Revenue Code of 1954, the draftsmen were faced with what has aptly been described as "the morass created by the decisions." Ballenger v. United States, 301 F.2d 192, 196 (C.A. 4th Cir. 1962). In an effort to eliminate "the considerable confusion which exists in this area" and thereby to facilitate tax planning, H.R.Rep. No. 1337, 83d Cong., 2d Sess., at 35, the authors of the new Code sought to provide objective tests to govern the tax consequences of stock redemptions. Thus, the tax bill passed by the House of Representatives contained no "essentially equivalent" language. Rather, it provided for "safe harbors" where capital gains treatment would be accorded to corporate redemptions that met the conditions now found in §§ 302(b) (2) and (3) of the Code.

It was in the Senate Finance Committee's consideration of the tax bill that § 302(b) (1) was added, and Congress thereby provided that capital gains treatment should be available "if the redemption is not essentially equivalent to a dividend." Taxpayer argues that the purpose was to continue "existing law," and there is support in the legislative history that § 302(b) (1) reverted "in part" or "in general" to the "essentially equivalent" provision of § 115(g) (1) of the 1939 Code. According to the Government, even under the old law it would have been improper for the Court of Appeals to rely on "a business purpose for the redemption" and "an absence of the proscribed tax avoidance purpose to bail out dividends at favorable tax rates." . . . However, we need not decide that question, for we find from the history of the 1954 revisions and the purpose of § 302(b) (1) that Congress intended more than merely to re-enact the prior law.

In explaining the reason for adding the "substantially equivalent" test, the Senate Committee stated that the House provisions "appeared unnecessarily restrictive, particularly, in the case of redemptions of preferred stock which might be called by the corporation without the shareholder having any control over when the redemption may take place." S.Rep.No.1622, 83d Cong., 2d Sess., at 44. This explanation

396

gives no indication that the purpose behind the redemption should affect the result.[10] Rather, in its more detailed technical evaluation of § 302(b) (1), the Senate Committee reported as follows:

> "The test intended to be incorporated in the interpretation of paragraph (1) is in general that currently employed under section 115(g) (1) of the 1939 Code. Your committee further intends that in applying this test for the future that the inquiry will be devoted solely to the question of whether or not the transaction by its nature may properly be characterized as a sale of stock by the redeeming shareholder to the corporation. For this purpose the presence or absence of earnings and profits of the corporation is not material. Example: X, the sole shareholder of a corporation having no earnings or profits causes the corporation to redeem half of its stock. Paragraph (1) does not apply to such redemption notwithstanding the absence of earnings and profits." S.Rep.No.1622, supra, at 234.

The intended scope of § 302(b) (1) as revealed by this legislative history is certainly not free from doubt. However, we agree with

the Government that by making the sole inquiry relevant for the future the narrow one whether the redemption could be characterized as a sale, Congress was apparently rejecting past court decisions that had also considered factors indicating the presence or absence of a tax avoidance motive.[11] At least that is the implication of the example given. Congress clearly mandated that pro rata distributions be treated under the general rules laid down in §§ 301 and 316 rather than under § 302, and nothing suggests that there should be a different result if there were a "business purpose" for the redemption. Indeed, just the opposite inference must be drawn since there would not likely be a tax avoidance purpose in a situation where there were no earnings or profits. We conclude that the Court of Appeals was therefore wrong in looking for a business purpose and considering it in deciding whether the redemption was equivalent to a dividend. Rather, we agree with the Court of Appeals for the Second Circuit that: "the business purpose of a transaction is irrelevant in determining dividend equivalency" under § 302(b)(1). Hasbrook v. United States, 343 F.2d 811, 814 (1965).

Taxpayer strongly argues that to treat the redemption involved here as essentially equivalent to a dividend is to elevate form over substance. Thus, taxpayer argues, had he not bought Bradley's shares or had he made a subordinated loan to the company instead of buying preferred stock, he could have gotten back his $25,000 with favorable

---

10. See Bittker & Eustice, supra, n. 6, at 291: "It is not easy to give § 302 (b) (1) an expansive construction in view of this indication that its major function was the narrow one of immu..izing redemptions of minority holdings of preferred stock."

11. This rejection is confirmed by the Committee's acceptance of the House treatment of distributions involving corporate contractions—a factor present in many of the earlier "business purpose" redemptions. In describing its action, the Committee stated as follows:
"Your committee, as did the House bill, separates into their significant elements the kind of transactions now incoherently aggregated in the definition of a partial liquidation. Those distributions which may have capital-gain characteristics *because they are not made pro rata* among the various shareholders would be subjected, at the shareholder level, to the separate tests described in [§§ 301 to 318]. On the other hand, those distributions characterized by whr.; happens solely at the corporate level by reason of the assets distributed would be included as within the concept of a partial liquidation." S.Rep. No. 1622, supra, at 49. (Emphasis added.)

tax treatment. However, the difference between form and substance in the tax law is largely problematical, and taxpayer's complaints have little to do with whether a business purpose is relevant under § 302(b) (1). It was clearly proper for Congress to treat distributions generally as taxable dividends when made out of earnings and profits and then to prevent avoidance of that result without regard to motivation where the distribution is in exchange for redeemed stock.

We conclude that that is what Congress did when enacting § 302 (b) (1). If a corporation distributes property as a simple dividend, the effect is to transfer the property from the company to its shareholders without a change in the relative economic interests or rights of the stockholders. Where a redemption has that same effect, it cannot be said to have satisfied the "not essentially equivalent to a dividend" requirement of § 302(b) (1). Rather, to qualify for preferred treatment under that section, a redemption must result in a meaningful reduction of the shareholder's proportionate interest in the corporation. Clearly, taxpayer here, who (after application of the attribution rules) was the sole shareholder of the corporation both before and after the redemption, did not qualify under this test. The decision of the Court of Appeals must therefore be reversed and the case remanded to the District Court for dismissal of the complaint.

It is so ordered.

MR. JUSTICE DOUGLAS, with whom MR. JUSTICE BRENNAN concurs, dissenting: I agree with the District Court, 274 F.Supp. 466, and with the Court of Appeals, 408 F.2d 1139, that respondent's contribution of working capital in the amount of $25,000 in exchange for 100 shares of preferred stock with a par value of $25 was made in order for the corporation to obtain a loan from the RFC and that the preferred stock was to be redeemed when the loan was repaid. For the reasons stated by the two lower courts, this redemption was not "essentially equivalent to a dividend," for the bona fide business purpose of the redemption belies the payment of a dividend. As stated by the Court of Appeals:

> "Although closely-held corporations call for close scrutiny under the tax law, we will not, under the facts and circumstances of this case, allow mechanical attribution rules to transform a legitimate corporate transaction into a tax avoidance scheme." 408 F.2d, at 1144.

When the Court holds it was a dividend, it effectively cancels § 302(b)(1) from the Code. This result is not a matter of conjecture, for the Court says that in case of closely-held or one-man corporations a redemption of stock is "always" equivalent to a dividend. I would leave such revision to the Congress.

Note on §302

a. Introduction. As the Davis opinion indicates, the 1954 Code provided stock repurchase transactions with two principal "safe harbors" from dividend treatment (to be tested, however, only after applying the attribution of ownership rules of §318). The "substantially disproportionate" test in subsection (b)(2) requires a specified decrease in the taxpayer's percentage ownership of voting

398

stock (and of all common stock as well, whether voting or
non-voting); the complete termination of interest test of
subsection (b)(3) depends upon redemption of all of the
stock owned by the taxpayer, actually or by attribution
(subject to a possible out from the family attribution
rules, which will be reviewed below). However, even if
these tests are not met the taxpayer may still avoid dividend treatment under the general "not essentially equivalent
to a dividend" standard of §302(b)(1), by showing a meaningful reduction of his proportionate interest in the corporation, as required by the Davis case.

b. Substantially Disproportionate Redemption. Prior
to the 1954 Code, it was generally held that when a redemption substantially altered the taxpayer's voting strength,
dividend treatment was not justified. Section 302(b)(2)
sought to provide greater certainty in this area with its
mathematical "substantially disproportionate" test, satisfaction of which assures non-dividend treatment. The two
components of this test are, first, that the taxpayer's
percentage ownership of voting stock be reduced to less than
80% of his former percentage (with the same requirement as
to the taxpayer's percentage ownership of all common stock,
if some of the common stock is non-voting or there is some
voting preferred involved); and second, after the redemption
the taxpayer must own less than 50% of the total combined
voting power of the corporation's stock. Notice that although a qualifying redemption of voting stock can also
carry with it a simultaneous redemption of non-voting stock,
Reg. §1.302-3(a), a redemption of some of a taxpayer's
non-voting stock, whether preferred or common, cannot by
itself qualify under subsection (b)(2) and is left instead
to §302(b)(1).

Pursuant to §302(c)(1), the substantially disproportionate test must be judged in the light of the attribution
of ownership rules of §318, which provide an extensive
network of constructive ownership of stock. Thus stock may
be attributed between members of a family, between a trust
or estate and its beneficiaries, a partnership and its
partners, and a corporation and its controlling stockholders.
There may also be reattribution of stock--that is, stock
which is "owned" constructively by virtue of the attribution
rules may itself be attributed to someone else under the
rules. However, there are some limits on reattribution.
From the outset the statute precluded successive attribu-
tions under the family attribution rules; reattribution was
further narrowed in 1964 by elimination of "sidewise" reattribution, that is, attribution from a beneficiary to an
estate or trust for the purpose of reattributing the stock
to another beneficiary, or from a partner through the partnership to another partner, or the like. See §318(a)(5)(B)+(C).

Under §302(b)(2)(D), the proportionality of a particular
redemption distribution must be tested in the light of any
other contemplated redemptions which are part of a single
overall plan. Though not expressly covered by the statute,
the same may well be true of planned purchases of stock from
other stockholders by the taxpayer whose stock is redeemed;
indeed, if the taxpayer already has a firm right to purchase
additional stock, it should be attributed to the taxpayer in

making the substantially disproportionate computation, by virtue of the option attribution rule of §318(a)(5). On the other hand, sales of stock by the redeeming shareholder to unrelated third persons at the same time can presumably be combined with the redemption in order to satisfy the percentage requirements of §302(b)(2).

REVENUE RULING 75-447

1975-2 Cum. Bull. 113.

Advice has been requested as to the Federal income tax consequences, in the situations described below, of the redemption by a corporation of part of its stock.

Situation 1

Corporation *X* had outstanding 100 shares of voting common stock of which *A* and *B* each owned 50 shares. In order to bring *C* into the business with an equal stock interest, and pursuant to an integrated plan, *A* and *B* caused *X* to issue, at fair market value, 25 new shares of voting common stock to *C*. Immediately thereafter, as part of the same plan, *A* and *B* caused *X* to redeem 25 shares of *X* voting common stock from each of them. Neither *A*, *B*, nor *C* owned any stock of *X* indirectly under section 318 of the Internal Revenue Code of 1954.

Situation 2

Corporation *X* had outstanding 100 shares of voting common stock of which *A* and *B* each owned 50 shares. In order to bring *C* into the business with an equal stock interest, and pursuant to an integrated plan, *A* and *B* each sold 15 shares of *X* voting common stock to *C* at fair market value and then caused *X* to redeem five shares from both *A* and *B*. Neither *A*, *B*, nor *C* owned any stock of *X* indirectly under section 318 of the Code.

Section 302(b)(2) of the Code states that section 302(a), which provides for treating a redemption of stock as a distribution in part or full payment in exchange for the stock, will apply if the distribution is substantially disproportionate with respect to the shareholder. • • •

In *Zenz v. Quinlivan*, 213 F.2d 914 (6th Cir. 1954), a sole shareholder of a corporation, desiring to dispose of her entire interest therein, sold part of her stock to a competitor and shortly thereafter sold the remainder of her stock to the corporation for an amount of cash and property approximately equal to its earned surplus. The Government contended that the redemption was a dividend on the grounds that the result was the same as if the steps had been reversed, that is, as if the stock had been redeemed first and the sale of stock to the competitor had followed. The United States Court of Appeals rejected the Government's contention and held that the purchase of the stock by the corporation (when coupled with the sale of stock to the competitor) was not a dividend to the selling shareholder and that the proceeds should be treated as payment for the stock surrendered under the provisions of the Internal Revenue Code of 1939.

Rev. Rul. 55-745, 1955-2 C.B. 223, states that in situations similar to that in *Zenz*, the amount received by the shareholder from the corporation will be treated as received in payment for the stock surrendered under section 302(a) of the Code since the transaction when viewed as a whole results in the shareholder terminating his interest in the corporation within the meaning of section 302(b)(3).

In determining whether the "substantially disproportionate" provisions of section 302(b)(2) of the Code have been satisfied in *Situation 1* and in *Situation 2*, it is proper to rely upon the holding in *Zenz* that the sequence in which the events (that is, the redemption and sale) occur is irrelevant as long as both events are clearly part of an overall plan. Therefore, in situations where the redemption is accompanied by an issuance of new stock (as in *Situation 1*), or a sale of stock (as in *Situation 2*), and both steps (the sale, or issuance, of stock, as the case may be, and the redemption) are clearly part of an integrated plan to reduce a shareholder's interest, effect will be given only to the

400

overall result for purposes of section 302(b)(2) and the sequence in which the events occur will be disregarded.

Since the *Zenz* holding requires that effect be given only to the overall result and proscribes the fragmenting of the whole transaction into its component parts, the computation of the voting stock of the corporation owned by the shareholder *immediately before* the redemption for purposes of section 302(b)(2)(C)(ii) of the Code should be made before any part of the transaction occurs. Likewise, the computation of the voting stock of the corporation owned by the shareholder *immediately after* the redemption for purposes of section 302(b)(2)(C)(i) should be made after the whole transaction is consummated. Making the immediately before and the immediately after computations in this manner properly reflects the extent to which the shareholder involved in each situation actually reduces his stock holdings as a result of the whole transaction.

Therefore, for purposes of the computations required by section 302(b)(2)(C) of the Code, *A* and *B*, in *Situation 1*, will each be viewed as having owned 50 percent (50/100 shares) of *X* before the transaction and 33⅓ percent (25/75 shares) immediately thereafter. In *Situation 2, A* and *B* will each be viewed as having owned 50 percent (50/100 shares) of *X* before the transaction and 33⅓ percent (30/90 shares) immediately thereafter. Furthermore, in each situation, the result would be the same if the redemption had preceded the issuance, or sale, of stock.

Accordingly, in both *Situations 1* and *2*, the requirements of section 302(b)(2) of the Code are satisfied. Therefore, the amounts distributed to *A* and *B* in both situations are distributions in full payment in exchange for the stock redeemed pursuant to section 302(a).

------

c. Complete Termination of Interest. Since complete termination of a shareholder's interest is the polar example of a disproportionate redemption, if there were no difference between these two tests with respect to the application of the attribution of ownership rules §302(b)(3) would be confined to cases like redemption of non-voting preferred which can not satisfy the percentage reduction required under §302(b)(2). However, in applying the complete termination of interest test §302(c)(2) allows a waiver of the family attribution rules of §318(a)(1) under certain circumstances, which is not available under the substantially disproportionate test of §302(b)(2). This waiver procedure involves a number of intricate conditions (which were made even more complicated by a 1982 amendment, detailed below, with respect to redemptions from entities like estates or trusts). First, the distributee must end up with no interest in or position with the corporation, other than as a creditor (which poses the issue of whether purported "debt" is really debt, see Reg. §1.302-4(d)). Second, the distributee must not acquire any such interest in, or position with, the corporation within ten years after the date of the redemption distribution (exclusive of an acquisition of stock by bequest or inheritance). As a corollary of this second qualification, the distributee is required to file with his return an agreement that he will notify the Government of any such acquisition; and there is an accompanying extension of the statute of limitations for the assessment of any deficiency resulting from such an acquisition to at least one year beyond the date on which the distributee does give such notice. Third, the waiver of the family attribution rules is not available if the stock redeemed was acquired by the distributee within a prior 10-year period from a person whose stock would be attributable to the distributee (as where a wife-distributee had received the redeemed stock from her husband), or if a person whose stock would be attributable to the distributee acquired stock from the distributee during the 10-year period (as where it is the stock of the husband which is redeemed in the example just given). This third qualification is in turn subject to the limitation that it only applies if the transfer in question was tax-avoidance motivated.

Prior to 1982 there was a serious problem with respect to the reach of the waiver of family attribution under §302(c)(2). In Rev. Rul. 59-233, 1959-2 Cum. Bull. 106, the Service took the view that the waiver applied only to a family attribution which was the last link in the chain of attribution to the distributee, and not to an attribution under the family rules at some earlier point in the attribution chain. The ruling involved a redemption of the stock owned by a trust created under the will of a deceased mother for the benefit of her children. The father was the only other stockholder of the corporation, and by attribution of his stock to the children and then to the trust the latter constructively owned 100% of the stock. According to the ruling, since the family attribution (from the father to the children) was not the last link in the attribution chain, it could not be waived under §302(c) even though the trust met all of the other conditions of the statute. On the other hand, a redemption of the father's stock instead of the trust's would have been in the clear, since then the attribution chain would have been from trust to children to father, with the family attribution the last link in the chain; but in that case the father would have had to satisfy the conditions of §302(c), which of course in the circumstances he had no interest in doing.

Notice that if the children in Rev. Rul. 59-233 had owned any stock directly, there would have been no basis for qualifying under §302(b)(3), since that stock would have been attributed to the trust under the entity rules of §318(a)(3), and the statute contains no procedure for waiving those rules. Hence, the result of Rev. Rul. 59-233 was that an entity like a trust or an estate was simply not eligible for the waiver process of §302(c)(2). Rev. Rul. 72-472, 1972-2 Cum. Bull. 202.

With respect to waiver of family attribution earlier in the attribution chain, the Service was particularly concerned that the family member to whom attribution would be waived (e.g., the children in Rev. Rul. 59-233) might thereafter be able to acquire stock in the corporation with impunity, since the family member would not have undertaken the waiver process personally, and it was far from clear that his acquisition would be viewed as a "constructive" acquisition by the entity which would violate the latter's waiver agreement.

It took 14 years for this question of waiver by an entity to come before the courts, but when it did Rev. Rul. 59-233 did not fare well. In Crawford v. Commissioner, 59 T.C. 830 (1973), a wife owned one-sixth of the stock of a family corporation, and one-sixth was owned by the estate of her deceased husband, of which she was the beneficiary. The rest of the stock was owned by their two sons. Pursuant to a buy-sell agreement executed earlier between the corporation and the stockholders, all of the stock owned by the wife and the estate was redeemed, and both the wife and the estate filed §302(c)(2) waiver agreements. It was conceded that the redemption from the wife qualified under §302(b)(3), since her waiver agreement was effective to eliminate attribution from her children; but the Commissioner disallowed the estate's attempt to waive the family attribution rule, so the stock owned by the children was still attributable to the wife for the purpose of reattribution to the estate. However, the Court held that since the statute authorized waiver by the "distributee", and did not draw any distinction between individuals and entities in this regard, the estate's waiver was effective to eliminate family attribution no matter where it came in the attribution chain, and hence the redemption from the estate also qualified under §302(b)(3).

The Crawford case was followed in Rodgers P. Johnson Trust v. Commissioner, 71 T.C. 941 (1979), which involved the redemption of the stock of a close corporation owned by a testamentary trust created under the will of a father for the benefit of his son. Since the mother owned stock in the corporation, the trust had filed a waiver agreement (and, as a precautionary measure, so had the son, although he never owned any stock or held any position in the corporation). The Court held that the waiver agreement by the trust was valid, and hence the stock of the mother was not to be attributed to the son in testing for complete termination of the trust's interest under §302(b)(3).

Since in both Crawford and Johnson Trust the beneficiary of the entity to whom family attribution was sought to be eliminated had also filed a personal waiver agreement, there was no danger that the beneficiary would thereafter acquire stock in the corporation. However, in both cases the Tax Court specifically eschewed reliance on this factor, and held that the waiver agreement by the entity was sufficient. In Johnson Trust, the Court went on to suggest that a beneficiary's subsequent acquisition of stock could result in finding a violation of the entity's waiver agreement, quite apart from any waiver agreement the beneficiary might have filed personally, but the point was left open since it was not actually raised by the case.

Shortly thereafter, the Court of Appeals for the Fifth Circuit went well beyond both Johnson Trust and Crawford, holding that the estate attribution rules could be waived pursuant to §302(c)(2) (even though this conclusion seems to have no basis whatever in the statute, which makes reference only to waiver of the family attribution rules). Rickey v. United States, 592 F.2d 1251 (5th Cir. 1979). This was probably the catalyst for the 1982 amendment to §302(c)(2), which added subsection (C) to deal expressly with the waiver of attribution by entities. The new provision was actually inserted in conference, and according to the Conference Report, H.R. Rep. No. 97-760 (97th Cong., 2d sess.) 545, it was intended to overrule the Rickey decision (although it is not clear just what language in subsection (C) is supposed to accomplish this purpose). As to whether an entity like a trust or an estate can waive family attribution earlier in the attribution chain, subsection (C) expressly provides an affirmative answer, but only on condition that any family member to whom attribution is sought to be waived, in order to cut off reattribution to the entity, also complies personally with the waiver procedure. In addition, such family member must agree to be jointly and severally liable for any deficiency which may result from a prohibited subsequent acquisition of stock by either the entity or a family member who has filed the required waiver agreement. This could be quite harsh if there are several such family attributees, since one of them could be held liable for the tax deficiency resulting from acquisition of stock by another family attributee; but the Conference Report indicates that the Service will look first to the entity for satisfaction of the deficiency, then to the family attributee who acquired the stock, and only last to an innocent family attributee.

Notice that subsection (C) goes well beyond meeting the concern of the Service that the family member to whom attribution was waived might thereafter acquire stock without adverse tax implications. Imposing the waiver procedure personally on such family member not only bars him from acquiring any stock for the ten-year period but also requires the family member to sever all ties with the corporation, as an officer, director, or employee, which in some circumstances could prove more serious than the ban on stock acquisition.

    d. <u>Not Essentially Equivalent to a Dividend</u>. Under the Supreme Court's decision in <u>Davis</u>, a redemption can qualify as not essentially equivalent to a dividend only if it results "in a meaningful reduction of the shareholder's proportionate interest in the corporation". Unless §302(b)(1) is to be confined to cases which could not have qualified under §302(b)(2), such as a redemption of non-voting preferred, it must be contemplated that there will be some reductions in voting power or common stock interest significant enough to warrant non-dividend treatment even though falling short of the mathematical test under §302(b)(2). One obvious illustration would be a loss of control, and this has been confirmed by a number of rulings under §302(b)(1) since the <u>Davis</u> case. For example, in Rev. Rul. 75-502, 1975-2 Cum. Bull. 111, an estate held 250 shares of a corporation's single class of stock outstanding, and constructively owned

404

the 750 shares held by the sole beneficiary of the estate;
the remaining 750 shares were owned by an unrelated individual.
The corporation redeemed all of the estate's directly-owned
stock, reducing its percentage ownership from 57% before the
redemption to 50% after, which did not satisfy the disproportionate redemption test of §302(b)(2). The Ruling
finds a meaningful reduction in proportionate interest, and
hence qualification under §302(b)(1), because the redemption
not only reduced the estate's voting power and financial
stake in the corporation from 57% to 50% but also left the
remaining 50% interest in the hands of a single unrelated
shareholder. In a similar vein, Rev. Rul. 76-364, 1976-2
Cum. Bull. 91, held that a reduction from 27% to 22% was
sufficiently meaningful because the taxpayer lost his power
to control the corporation by simply acting in concert with
any one of the other three shareholders. Query whether in
measuring the effect of a redemption on control any account
should be taken of stock held by people who are allied with
the taxpayer but not connected through the attribution
rules: Rev. Rul. 77-218, 77-1 Cum. Bull. 81, seems to
suggest an affirmative answer since it makes reference to
such persons in the reasons for denying qualification under
§302(b)(1) (in the complicated context of redemption by a
related corporation under §304), but the critical element
may have been the fact that the distributee trust continued
to own more than 50% of the stock under the attribution
rules; the Ruling also alludes to the fact that one of the
co-trustees of distributee-trust managed and controlled the
corporation(s) involved.

On another level of control, it seems arguable that in
jurisdictions requiring a two-thirds majority vote by the
stockholders for approval of a "fundamental" transaction,
such as merger, or amendment of the articles, the reduction
of a controlling shareholder's percentage interest from
above to below 67% would qualify as meaningful because the
shareholder would no longer have the power to effect such
transactions on his own. A decline in percentage interest
to less than 33%, which would deprive the shareholder of
power to block a fundamental transaction, might be similarly
viewed. However, this position received less than a ringing
endorsement in Rev. Rul. 78-401, 1978-2 Cum. Bull. 127,
holding that a decline from 90% to 60% (which failed to
qualify under §302(b)(2) because the taxpayer continued to
own more than 50% of the stock) did not constitute a meaningful reduction in the circumstances, because there was no
fundamental transaction in the offing which would make the
loss of the two-thirds majority significant.

Although the Davis case left no doubt that the attribution rules apply in testing for dividend equivalence under
§ 302(b)(1), there has been a continuing question as to
whether Davis eliminated the so-called "family hostility"
doctrine, under which some courts had declined to give full
effect to the attribution rules under § 302(b)(1) in the face
of disputes which negated the normal commonality of interest
between related persons which the attribution rules assume.

METZGER TRUST v. COMMISSIONER*

U.S. Court of Appeals, Fifth Circuit, 1982. 693 F.2d 459.

PATRICK E. HIGGINBOTHAM, Circuit Judge:

We decide today a story driven by tensions as old as Genesis but told in the modern lexicon of the tax law. It is the story of David who built a business and left it in the charge of his eldest son Jacob to be shared with Jacob's two sisters Catherine and Cecelia, of their alienation and resulting quarrel with the tax collectors. In reviewing this decision of the Tax Court we are asked to determine the tax consequences of a reallocation of ownership of this family-owned business operated as a closely held corporation. In doing so we face three questions: (1) whether the attribution rules of I.R.C. § 318(a) must be applied despite family discord in determining whether a redemption meets the "not essentially equivalent to a dividend test" of § 302(b)(1); . . . .*

FACTS

The relevant facts are not in dispute and have been agreed to in a stipulation of record. Appellant David Metzger Trust was created by David Metzger in 1942 to benefit his wife as life income beneficiary and his three children, Jacob, Catherine, and Cecelia, as one-third remaindermen each. Jacob, the eldest son, was named trustee of the Trust. Four years later, David incorporated the family business as Metzger Dairies, Inc., the other appellant. The Trust became a shareholder of Metzger Dairies.

On David's death in 1953 Jacob Metzger assumed control of Metzger Dairies. Catherine and Cecelia were directors. In the years following the father's death the sibling quarrel grew in intensity. By the 1960's, open animosity developed among Jacob, Catherine, and Cecelia. Whatever the source of their alienation, a downturn in the success of the dairy only exacerbated the problem. Catherine and Cecelia became angry when the corporation stopped paying dividends. Catherine resented what she considered to be Jacob's interference in the management of Metzger Dairy of San Antonio, a corporation of which her son was president but whose stock was owned for the most part by the same parties who owned the stock of Metzger Dairies. Cecelia was annoyed at both Jacob and Catherine because both corporations failed to pay dividends.

---

*Portions of opinion omitted, including all discussion of waiver of entity attribution rules (which is now expressly precluded by the statute), and of the issue relating to deductibility of certain interest payments by the corporate taxpayer, plus most of the footnotes.

406

The argument among Jacob, Catherine, and Cecelia over these and other issues unrelated to the business of the corporations continued until 1972, when the acrimony reached the point that Jacob, Catherine, and Cecelia concluded that it was necessary to terminate their joint ownership of the corporations.

After lengthy negotiations all agreed that Jacob and his family would own Metzger Dairies, Catherine and her family would own Metzger Dairy of San Antonio, and Cecelia and her family would be cashed out. The plan was for Metzger Dairies to redeem all shares owned by Catherine, Cecelia, the trusts for Catherine and Cecelia, and the David Metzger Trust. It was necessary to include the David Metzger Trust in the redemption because Catherine and Cecelia were due to receive one-third of the Trust corpus on the death of David Metzger's widow.

Immediately before the redemption, the stock of Metzger Dairies was held as follows:

Stockholder	Shares
David Metzger Trust	420
Nora Metzger (David Metzger's widow)	420
Jacob Metzger	600
Trust for Jacob Metzger	120
Catherine	600
Trust for Catherine	120
Cecelia	600
Trust for Cecelia	120

The redemption occurred on January 22, 1973, leaving Metzger Dairies' stock as follows:

Stockholder	Shares
Jacob Metzger	600
Trust for Jacob Metzger	120
Trust for David Metzger, II (son of Jacob)	294
Trusts for Nan Metzger (daughter of Jacob)	207

407

The Commissioner concedes that the principal motivation for the redemption was not to receive undistributed earnings,1/ but to end a business relationship that was characterized by hatred and discord among Jacob, Catherine, and Cecelia. . . .2/

. . . The Tax Court upheld the deficiencies. After an agreed computation had been filed, it entered the judgment here appealed from.

THE TRUST'S APPEAL

(a) The Statutory Framework

*   *   *

Our specific analysis is channelled by the Code's structure: payments to shareholders from accumulated earnings will be treated as dividends unless the payment can be brought under an exception. That is, the controlling premise is that distributions by corporations to stockholders out of the taxable year's earnings or out of accumulated earnings are to be treated as dividends. I.R.C. § 316(a). Section 302 provides the exceptions. If the redemption is "not essentially equivalent to a dividend," § 302(b)(1), a "substantially disproportionate redemption of stock," § 302(b)(2), or a "termination of [the] shareholder's interest," § 302(b)(3), it will be treated as a distribution in exchange for the stock. At first glance, all three of these provisions are applicable to the Metzger transaction since the corporation purchased all the stock of Catherine, Cecelia, their trusts, and the David Metzger Trust, while at the same time made no payments to the other stockholders, namely Jacob Metzger and his trust. Yet the attribution rules of the Code pose immediate problems.

Attribution

*   *   *

[By virtue of the attribution] rules the Trust is the owner of the entire stock of Metzger Dairies both before and after the redemption.6/

---

1.   As of the time of redemption, Metzger Dairies had accumulated earnings of $1,815,060.77.

2.   The Commissioner assessed a deficiency of $292,977.47 against the Trust on the grounds that the $585,303.25 it received in redemption of the Metzger Dairies stock should have been reported as dividend income. . . .

6.   Before redemption the Trust was the constructive owner of Nora, Jacob, Catherine, and Cecelia's shares, because they were its beneficiaries. § 318(a)(3)(B).

408

The Code provides that, with one exception, these attribution rules "shall apply in determining the ownership of stock for purposes of" § 302. § 302(c)(1). . . . .

The Trust argues however (1) that family discord should "mitigate" against the applicability of the attribution rules, ...

(b) A Family Discord Exception to Attribution?

[1] The Trust argues that family discord may "mitigate" the application of the attribution rules in determining dividend equivalency, especially given the undisputed fact that the purpose of the redemption was not to distribute corporate earnings. From the stipulated fact that the purpose of redemption was to bring peace to a family quarrel, the Trust launches two attacks upon the attribution rules. First, it argues that because it is undisputed here that the family cannot function as an economic unit, the attribution rules, built as they are upon that premise, are inapplicable. Second, the Trust argues that even if the Trust by virtue of attribution is virtually the sole shareholder before and after, the redemption was nonetheless not essentially equivalent to a dividend. The argument continues that this follows from the undisputed purpose of the redemption. That is, the purpose not being to bail out corporate earnings, the central base for application of nonequivalency has been touched.

As will be seen the first argument fails because it is built upon the erroneous assumption that attribution is treated by the Code as a rebuttable presumption rather than a mandated view of familial relationships. The second argument fails because it denies full sway to the decision of the Supreme Court in United States v. Davis, 397 U.S. 301, 90 S.Ct. 1041, 25 L.Ed.2d 323 (1970). Indeed, Davis provides much of the answer to the first argument as well. For this reason we will address the arguments together, separating them only when necessary to context.

(Footnote continued)

Jacob, Catherine, and Cecelia were the constructive owners of the shares held by their individual trusts. § 318(a)(2)(B). Thus, the Trust constructively owned all of Metzger Dairies' stock.

After redemption the Trust remained constructive owner of all the stock because the shares held by the trusts for Jacob's children were attributable to the children, § 318(a)(2)(B), thence to Jacob, § 318(a)(1)(A), and finally to the Trust, § 318(a)(3)(B).

In <u>Davis</u> the Court held that the attribution rules of § 318(a) must be applied before determining dividend equivalency. The Court held that regardless of a purpose other than to distribute corporate earnings the after-attribution structure was such that the redemption was in the nature of a dividend. . .

In <u>Davis</u> the Court reasoned:

After application of the stock ownership attribution rules, this case viewed most simply involves a sole stockholder who causes part of his shares to be redeemed by the corporation. We conclude that such a redemption is always 'essentially equivalent to a dividend' within the meaning of that phrase in § 302(b)(1) . . .

Id. 397 U.S. at 307, 90 S.Ct. at 1045. <u>Davis</u> teaches that in applying the "essentially equivalent to a dividend" test after the attribution rules are applied, if the resulting structure has virtually the same incidents of ownership the corporate payments distribute earnings despite an indisputable contrary business purpose.

Treas. Reg. § 1.302-2(b)

Confronted by the Supreme Court's holding in <u>Davis</u>, the Trust argues that its position nevertheless is supported by Treas.Reg. § 1.302-2(b), language in <u>Davis</u> interpreting § 302(b)(1) as applying whenever there is a "meaningful reduction in the shareholder's proportionate interest," and the legislative history of § 302(b)(1).

Treas. Reg. § 1.302-2(b) provides:

The question whether a distribution in redemption of stock of a shareholder is not essentially equivalent to a dividend under section 302(b)(1) depends upon the facts and circumstances of each case. One of the facts to be considered in making this determination is the constructive stock ownership of such shareholder under section 318(a).

Pointing to this language the Trust argues that before and after structure is only one factor in the dividend equivalency inquiry. The argument continues that despite the circumstances that after attribution there was no shift in the incidents of control there was no dividend because indisputably the redemption was for another purpose.

Treas. Reg. § 1.302-2(b), however, contained the same language prior to the <u>Davis</u> decision. The regulation is ambiguous. It can be interpreted as the Trust would have it, namely that attribution is only a presumption. On the

410

other hand, it can be interpreted as saying that attribution rules must be given full effect, but are not necessarily decisive on the ultimate issue of dividend equivalency.

"Meaningful Reduction"

It is true, as the Trust points out, that some commentators and courts have indicated that Davis does not foreclose arguments for capital gains treatment based on family discord. Professors Bittker and Eustice have said, "The Davis decision . . . weakens, but does not eliminate, the 'family fight' argument in mitigation of § 318 attribution under § 302(b)(1) . . ." B. Bittker & J. Eustice, Federal Income Taxation of Corporations and Shareholders ¶9.24 n. 73 (4th ed. 1979). In Robin Haft Trust v. Commissioner, 510 F.2d 43 (1st Cir.1975), the First Circuit held that family discord might "negate the presumption" of the attribution rules that the taxpayer trusts exercised continuing control over the corporation after their actual holdings had been redeemed. Id. at 48. The trusts had been set up to benefit four children and were funded by shares of the corporation. The father of the children also owned a large percentage of the corporation's stock. While the father was going through divorce proceedings and was not even in contact with the children, the trusts' shares were redeemed as part of a program to terminate the involvement of the wife's family in the corporation. The IRS applied the attribution rules. Since the percentage of shares constructively owned by each of the trusts increased after the redemption, the IRS determined that the payment to the trusts was ordinary income. The Tax Court upheld the Commissioner. The First Circuit, however, directed the Tax Court "to reconsider taxpayers' claims in the light of the facts and circumstances of the case, including the existence of family discord tending to negate the presumption that taxpayers would exert continuing control over the corporation despite the redemption." Id. at 48.

For the most part, courts and commentators who urge that Davis leaves open the family discord question have emphasized that the Davis Court, despite its preference for objective tests, defined the "essentially equivalent to dividend" test in open-ended terms. "[T]o qualify for preferred treatment under [§ 302(b)(1)], a redemption must result in a meaningful reduction of the shareholder's proportionate interest in the corporation." 397 U.S. at 313, 90 S.Ct. at 1048. In Robin Haft Trust, the First Circuit concluded that "[t]his language certainly seems to permit, if it does not mandate, an examination of the facts and circumstances to determine the effect of the transaction transcending a mere mechanical application of the attribution rules." 510 F.2d at 48. Several commentators have similarly interpreted the "meaningful reduction" language.

411

These interpretations are not persuasive. The _Davis_
Court was referring to a meaningful reduction in the shareholder's interest _after_ application of the attribution
rules. It would be strange indeed if what the Court really
meant was that the attribution rules are to be applied
before determining dividend equivalency, but then in the
course of determining dividend equivalency their applicability could be reconsidered._12/_ If that were so, the attribution rules would hardly "provide a clear answer to what
would otherwise be a difficult tax question . . ." 397 U.S.
at 306, 90 S.Ct. at 1044._13/_

---

12.   As one commentator has noted, "On the one hand,
the provisions of section 302 apply the attribution
rules without mitigation. On the other hand, the
'essentially equivalent to a dividend' language of the
Code and the legislative history of section 302 require
a factual determination." Brogan, "The Interaction
Between Family Attribution Rules and Corporate Redemptions," 31 Case W.L.Rev. 304, 313 (1981). In this
commentator's view, the statute provides conflicting
guidance. Therefore, he argues that family disharmony
may mitigate application of the attribution rules. _Id._
at 313-319. We think this analysis is wrong. The two
statutory provisions can easily be reconciled if one
recognizes that, while the "factual determination"
required by § 302(b)(1) may take many factors into
account, it must accept the attribution rules as given.

We are more convinced by the following analysis:

> Although the _Davis_ Court did not call for a
> mechanical application of the attribution rules
> in so many words, it did observe that the rules
> were designed to 'provide a clear answer to what
> would otherwise be a difficult tax question.'
> This statement indicates the Court's desire to
> avoid having to analyze the hostility or amicabil-
> ity in the section 318 relationships in each case.
> Indeed, _Davis_ rejected the use of other subjective
> criteria, such as business purpose or tax-avoidance
> motives, in determining dividend equivalence under
> section 302(b)(1). It is doubtful that the Court
> would proscribe some subjective inquiries but at
> the same time approve ad hoc determinations of
> section 302(b)(1).

Postelwaite & Finneran, "Section 302(b)(1): The expanding
Minnow," 64 Va.L.Rev. 561, 592 (1978).

13.   The Commissioner argues that _Haft Trust_ is in any
event distinguishable because the attribution in the present case is not across unfriendly lines. Jacob Metzger was

412

* * *

We return to the first level of the Trust argument --
that attribution bottomed as it is on assumed family unity
ought not to be applied when the assumption is contrary to
stipulated fact. Nothing in the legislative history suggests
that the attribution rules are to be "mitigated" in special
cases. On the contrary, the Senate Report states that "the
rules for constructive ownership of stock section 318(a)
shall apply for purposes of this section generally." S.Rep.
No. 1622, 83d Cong., 2d Sess., reprinted in 1954 U.S. Cong.
& Ad. News 4621, 4872. Neither the language of the statute,
the Supreme Court's opinion in Davis, nor the legislative
history supports treating the attribution rules as rebuttable
presumptions as the Trust is seeking.

Under the Trust's approach the Commissioner and the
courts would be forced to highly case specific inquiries
into elusive fact patterns. The pattern, intensity, and
predicted duration of a family fight are difficult enough
for the solomonic justice of our domestic relations courts.
It is hardly the basis for a soundly administered tax policy.
The fixity of the attribution rules then in this sense is
not their weakness but their strength.

In summary, we believe that the Commissioner and Tax
Court were correct in refusing to take family discord into

(footnote continued)

the trustee of the David Metzger Trust; thus according
to the Commissioner attribution from him and his depen-
dents to the Trust did not raise an issue of family
hostility.

We are not convinced by this argument and prefer
not to rely on it. The proceeds of the redemption went
not to Jacob but to his sisters. Therefore, if the attribution rules are to be applied flexibly, ownership
of the shares held by the Trust should be attributed to
the sisters and not to Jacob. Either a flexible application of § 318(a) is appropriate or it is not. The IRS
cannot have it both ways.

It is arguable that this court approved Haft Trust
and the family hostility exception to the attribution
rules when it decided Rickey v. United States, 592 F.2d
1251 (5th Cir. 1979). In a footnote to its opinion,
this court rejected the contention that since Davis
family hostility could no longer be a relevant circumstance in determining dividend equivalency. "We do not
agree with that interpretation as Davis involved no
claim of family hostility," the court said. Id. at
1257 n. 6. We are free to disregard dictum and do so
here.

413

account in applying the attribution rules.16/ When a question is raised as to the dividend equivalency of a redemption, under § 302(b)(1) the correct approach is to apply the attribution rules <u>first</u>, then to determine whether there has been "a meaningful reduction of the shareholder's proportionate interest," without regard to whether the interest is actually or constructively held. What is "meaningful" then, to borrow a word, is essentially an inquiry into structure, a structure that applies statutorily dictated rules of economic unity.

* * *

---

e. <u>Partial Liquidation</u>. The safe harbor in §302(b)(4) for distributions to non-corporate shareholders "in partial liquidation", as defined in §302(e), was added to the statute in 1982. However, it was not a new provision, having previously appeared in more or less the same form (except for the exclusion of corporate shareholders) in §346 since 1954. It should help in understanding the role of partial liquidations in the statutory pattern, and the reasons for the 1982 change, to take a longer view of the legislative history.

Prior to the 1954 Code all stock redemptions were described as "partial liquidations", and since 1942 the statute had afforded such transactions exchange treatment, and hence capital gains taxation, unless the redemption was "essentially equivalent to the distribution of a taxable dividend." This was the pre-1954 statutory pattern reviewed by the Supreme Court in the <u>Davis</u> case, in trying to discern the meaning of the general "essentially equivalent" test preserved in §302(b)(1) of the 1954 Code. As noted in footnote 11 to the <u>Davis</u> opinion, in 1954 redemption transactions were divided into two separate categories, with different tests for determining when the distribution qualified for treatment as payment in exchange for the stock. Those guidelines looking to whether the distribution was sufficiently disproportionate among the shareholders were collected in §302, under the "Redemption" caption. The tests based on the impact of the distribution on the corporation itself (primarily, whether there was a significant contraction of the enterprise), were assigned to §346, under

---

16.   The Tax Court in its opinion below did suggest that in cases of non-pro-rata distribution family hostility "can be a relevant fact to be considered in determining whether the reduction in the shareholder's interest is meaningful so as to qualify the distribution as not essentially equivalent to a dividend under section 302(b)(1)." 76 T.C. 42, 62-63 (1981). That notion is inconsistent with our approach. Regardless, such a case was not presented below or here.

the heading "Partial Liquidation" (which also covered a series of distributions pursuant to a plan for complete liquidation of the corporation). Since §346 was indifferent to the effect of the transaction at the shareholder level, even a pro rata distribution could qualify under that provision (as continues to be true under present §302(e)(4)).

The definition of partial liquidation in §302(e) pretty much parallels the pre-1982 version of §346, and nothing in the legislative history of the 1982 Act suggests that any change in the substantive qualifications for such transactions was intended. Accordingly, the authorities dealing with what constitutes a partial liquidation under §346 continue to be relevant in connection with §302(e).

McCARTHY v. CONLEY *

United States Court of Appeals, Second Circuit, 1965. 341 F.2d 948.

BLUMENFELD, DISTRICT JUDGE. This is an appeal from a summary judgment adverse to the appellant in a suit for refund of income taxes paid to satisfy deficiency assessments for the years 1954, 1955 and 1956. The taxpayer, Mrs. Lora McCarthy, owned 1000 shares of the stock of The Andrew Radel Oyster Company, a family corporation, which she had acquired through inheritance. In December 1954, she sold her shares to the corporation which paid for them with liquid assets it had accumulated out of earnings and profits over a long period. It was the taxpayer's use of a claimed loss on this transaction to offset income for the years in question that the District Director disallowed.

The court below found that there was no genuine issue of fact which would rebut the District Director's determination that the payment made by the corporation for the purchase of her stock was not a distribution in partial liquidation and ruled that the loss deduction was properly disallowed under § 267 of the 1954 Code [which disallows losses on sales or exchanges between related persons except "in cases of distributions in corporate liquidations"]. We agree.

The issues before us have been narrowed somewhat. The government has conceded that the payment received by the taxpayer from the corporation escapes dividend tax treatment as a distribution under § 302(b)(3) of the 1954 Code. The taxpayer has conceded that since her two sisters and her two brothers owned the remaining 4000 outstanding shares of stock, the transaction out of which the claimed loss arose was between related taxpayers as defined in § 267(b) and that the recognition of any loss is governed by § 267 of the Internal Revenue Code of 1954.

[The court first ruled that although the exception in § 267 for "distributions in corporate liquidations" may have included all re-

---

* Portions of the text and most of the court's footnotes omitted.

demption transactions under the pre-1954 law (as well as complete liquidations), because under that law all redemptions were characterized as "partial liquidations" (see page 414, supra),the result of the 1954 Code's separation of "redemptions" in § 302 from "partial liquidations" in § 346 was to confine the § 267 exception to those redemption transactions which came within § 346.]

Appellant's second argument is that even if the § 267 exception is limited to partial liquidations as defined in § 346, that definition includes all distributions in redemption which are not essentially equivalent to a dividend. This argument differs from her previous one only in that she makes it with reference to the definition of partial liquidation now found in § 346 of the 1954 Code . . . . We were unable to expand the exception in § 267 to make room for distributions not essentially equivalent to a dividend without regard to the definition of "partial liquidation" in § 346. We are equally unable to hold that a distribution not essentially equivalent to a dividend standing alone is a "partial liquidation" within that definition.

It is true that §§ 302 and 346 both contain the phrase "not equivalent to a dividend." But a reading of all the legislative history reveals congressional purpose to effect a *separation* of the two main tests which had formerly been applied to distributions in redemption of stock. Thus, the fact that the distribution received by her was not essentially equivalent to a dividend under § 302 because it resulted in a complete termination of her interest has no relevance here. Section 346 is plainly designed to go further in its demands. This is made all too clear by the specification in § 346(c):

"The fact that, with respect to a shareholder, a distribution qualifies under section 302(a) . . . by reason of section 302(b) shall not be taken into account in determining whether the distribution, with respect to such shareholder, is also a distribution in partial liquidation of the corporation."

Taxpayer then takes another stand to argue that in any event contraction is not an absolutely essential element for a distribution to qualify under § 346. She relies upon the following portion of the Senate report as support for this contention:

"Subsection (a) [of § 346] is intended to provide a definition of partial liquidation which replaces that contained in section 115(i) of the 1939 Code. *Primarily,* this definition involves the concept of 'corporate contraction' as developed under existing law." (S.R.No.1622, 83d Cong. 2d Sess. 262, 3 U.S. Code Cong. & Adm.News 1954, p. 4899.) (Emphasis added)

Had Congress used the word "includes" in the § 346 definition of partial liquidation, we would be faced with 26 U.S.C. § 7701(b) of the 1954 Code: "The terms 'includes' and 'including' when used in a definition contained in this title shall not be deemed to exclude other things otherwise within the meaning of the term defined." But reading the Senate report in context, the word "primarily" is not misleading. It was not used to create a larger category of "partial liquidations," but to accent a predominant characteristic common to all which come within the statutory definition. It means that other requirements also have to be met, not a non-exclusivity allowing the use of all of the old pre-1954 tests. The requirements in § 346(a) (2) are not in the disjunctive. Thus, for a distribution to receive tax treatment as a partial liquidation, three requisites must be met: (1) It must not be essentially equivalent to a dividend; (2) It must be in redemption of part of the stock pursuant to a plan; and (3) It must occur within the taxable year.

However, it is urged that the term "partial liquidation" may include redemptions resulting from activities at the corporate level, or prompted by corporate needs, even though not involving a contraction. See Brodsky, Partial Liquidation: Definition of Partial Liquidation and Rules for Determining Termination of a Business, 15 Institute on Federal Taxation 539, 552 (1957). Examples suggested of such corporate needs are a corporation's desire to improve its credit rating or to make stock available to its employees. We find it unnecessary to pass upon this contention, for the only non-contraction purpose put forth by the taxpayer was a statement by her two brothers that they permitted the redemption to enable them alone to dissolve the corporation, *if they later so desired.* Under no theory could this be considered a corporate purpose. This was nothing other than a shareholder purpose, for it merely satisfied the wish of her brothers to gain control of the corporation to carry out their own ends.

The only question remaining is whether there was a "corporate contraction" pursuant to a "plan" under § 346. Both parties moved for summary judgment. The case was ripe for such disposition. It was not contended that there was a termination of a separate trade or business which would specifically qualify as a partial liquidation under § 346(b). Nor do we find any call for making a value judgment as to how much "corporate contraction" is necessary to constitute a partial liquidation under § 346(a). In determining that there was no genuine issue of fact as to whether there had been a partial liquidation, the court below properly took into account the concept of "corporate contraction" as developed under existing law by focusing attention on what took place at the corporate level. Nothing substantial was offered to challenge the District Director's determination that there was no immediately intended contraction of the corporation's business of producing, harvesting and selling oysters; a sale of certain oyster lands and facilities four years later, on the death of one of the two managing brothers, was properly deemed unrelated by the district judge. The purchase price of $128.50 per share was based on the then value of the *quick assets* of the firm other than inventory, less liabilities.[17]   Nor were any balance sheets or operating statements presented in opposition to the appellee's motion for summary judgment.

The transaction in question was clearly not a vertical liquidation which chopped off a part of the productive resources of the enterprise.   That portion of corporate capital remained intact.   It was a horizontal slice off the top of a nest egg of securities accumulated from past earnings and profits which did not in any degree impair the business activities of the enterprise as they had been carried on before.[18]

Nor, as held by the court below, did anything exist to indicate a "plan."

The judgment is affirmed.

NOTE ON §302(e)

i .   Corporate Contraction

The question left open in the McCarthy case as to how much "contraction" is required to qualify under §302(e) [formerly §346] continues to be troublesome. This much is clear: it is not necessary to meet the mechanical test now contained in §302(e)(2) and (3), since both the statute itself and the legislative history of the predecessor §346(b) confirm that these provisions are designed to create a kind of "safe harbor", akin to those under §302, so that capital gain treatment is assured if the test is satisfied but may be obtained even if it is not. A similar five year, separate business test is employed in connection with corporate divisions under §355, and the regulations thereunder provide some detailed examples of what constitutes sufficiently "separate" businesses.

As to what other types of contraction of an enterprise short of this safe harbor may nevertheless qualify under the general test of §302(e)(1), some guidance is afforded in the legislative history of former §346, Sen. Rep. No. 1122, 83d

17. Although in excess of the $100 par, this was substantially less than the fair market value of the shares at the time of the deaths of her father and her mother which was the basis she used to compute the loss. Cf. Twining v. Commissioner, 83 F.2d 954 (2d Cir.) . . .

18. Furthermore, the taxpayer did not deny that profits from the accumulated securities amounted to more than half a million dollars during the decade between 1950 and 1960. It was the proceeds of the sale of some of these securities that were used to effect the redemption, and while it is urged that they had been held as a contingency fund, the following passage from the Senate report on the Tax Code directly rejects that argument: "It is intended that a genuine contraction of the business as under present law will result in a partial liquidation. . . . However, a distribution of a reserve for expansion is not a partial liquidation." . . .

Cong., 2d Sess. (1954) 262, which expressly approved Imler v. Commissioner, 11 T.C. 836 (1948) as a case of "genuine contraction of the business." That case involved a closely-held corporation which owned a seven story building and several smaller buildings, and was engaged in retinning and soldering metals as well as renting its excess space. A fire destroyed the upper two floors of the seven story building in 1941. Because of the shortage of building materials, the corporation did not rebuild those two floors. Since its facilities were no longer adequate to store materials for the retinning and soldering activities, and the scarcity of materials had made those operations unprofitable anyway, the corporation discontinued them. It then distributed $15,000, which included the excess of the fire insurance proceeds over the repair costs, in a pro rata redemption of stock from its stockholders. *Held*, the redemption was not a dividend. The court stressed the bona fide contraction of business operations, the consequent reduction in needed capital, and the fact that except for the fire no distribution would have been made.

However, the question remains whether there must be a discontinuance of some specific line of activity, as in the Imler case, or whether simply reducing the scope of a single business can qualify. Rev. Rul. 60–322, 1960–2 Cum.Bull. 118, seems to require the former, at least where the source of the distribution is the profits earned by the enterprise in the past.

The latest word on the amount of contraction required for a partial liquidation is afforded by Rev. Proc. 84–22, 1984–13 I.R.B. 18, which provides in section 4 that one of the topics on which rulings or determination letters will ordinarily not be issued is "Whether a distribution will qualify as a distribution in partial liquidation under section 302(b)(4) and (e)(1)(A) (pre-TEFRA section 346 (a)(2)) of the Code unless it results in a 20 percent or greater reduction in (1) gross revenues, (2) net fair market value of assets, and (3) employees."

---

ii. Relation between Partial Liquidation and Other Redemptions

In general the treatment of the shareholder whose stock was repurchased was the same under §346 as §302, except with respect to computing the basis of the shares surrendered. While in a non-pro-rata transaction the basis of the actual shares surrendered should be controlling, a different rule is needed when a pro rata partial liquidation is involved, since then little else turns on how many shares the shareholders turn in (as long as everyone turns in the same percentage); accordingly, it is assumed that the ratio of the shares surrendered to the total shares is the same as the ratio of the assets distributed to the total value of the enterprise. Rev. Rul. 81-3, 1981-1 Cum. Bull. 125.

However, there was a very important difference between the two provisions with respect to recognition of gain by the corporation when the redemption distribution included appreciated property. Partial liquidations under §346 were treated the same as complete liquidations, meaning that pursuant to §336 no gain was recognized except with respect

to installment obligations (and, after 1982, lifo inventory).
Distributions qualifying under §302, on the other hand, like
dividends, were (and still are) subject to §311; while that
provision too originally provided generally that a corporation did not have to recognize gain upon a distribution of
appreciated property to shareholders, there were more exceptions, including one for lifo inventory, and also property
subject to a liability in excess of basis, as well as installment obligations. (Of course both §311 and §336 are
overridden by §§1245 and 1250 providing for recapture of
depreciation, and the same is true of investment credit
recapture.) The difference between §311 and §336 with
respect to recognition of gain by a corporation upon a
redemption distribution in kind was greatly expanded in
1969, by the addition of §311(d) which turned the statute
around and required the recognition of gain upon any redemption distribution of appreciated property, unless one of the
exceptions in §311(d) applied. The primary reason for the
change was to close the loophole under which public corporations, particularly insurance companies with investment
portfolios of appreciated marketable securities, were using
such property to redeem their own stock, thereby utilizing
the economic benefit of the appreciation in value without
having to pay any tax on it. One of the most important
exceptions in §311(d) under the 1969 amendment related to
complete termination of the interest (within the meaning of
§302(b)(3)) of a stockholder who had owned, for twelve
months or more, at least ten percent in value of the outstanding stock of the corporation.

Not surprisingly, the almost total freedom from recognition of gain enjoyed by partial liquidations also led to
some abuses. For example, if a corporation was interested
in disposing of a segment of its business, the prospective
buyer might acquire a block of the corporation's stock which
could then be redeemed in exchange for the desired segment;
as long as the disposition of the segment constituted a
sufficient contraction of the corporation's business, the
transaction qualified as a partial liquidation, and §336
would shield the corporation from recognition of gain. (To
be sure, such a transaction might be treated as in substance
a sale of assets by the corporation combined with a redemption for cash, cf. Rev. Rul. 80-221, 1980-2 Cum. Bull. 107,
but the judicial response was uncertain. Compare Idol v.
Commissioner, 38 T.C. 444 (1962), aff'm, 319 F.2d 647 (8th
Cir. 1963), with Standard Linen Service, Inc. v. Commissioner,
33 T.C. 1 (1959).) There was also a growing practice in
takeover situations for the acquiring corporation to cause
the acquired company to distribute selected appreciated
assets in a partial liquidation, allowing the acquiring
corporation to obtain a step-up of basis to fair market
value, at little or no tax cost to the acquired corporation
(particularly if consolidated tax returns were used).

Accordingly, the 1982 Act terminated the separate
treatment of partial liquidations in §346, moved these
transactions to §302(b)(4) (with the accompanying definition
of partial liquidation in §302(e)), and confined exchange
treatment in such transactions to non-corporate shareholders.
As a corollary of being shifted to §302, partial liquidations are now subject to §311 rather than §336 so far as
recognition of gain on property distributed in redemption is

concerned. At the same time, §311 was substantially revised, with some of the exceptions to recognition of gain upon redemption distributions in kind eliminated, and others narrowed: in particular, the exception for complete termination of the interest of a ten percent shareholder was not only tightened but also limited to transactions which qualify as a partial liquidation (as defined in §302(e)). Hence, a corporation which uses appreciated property to redeem all of the stock of even a longtime substantial stockholder will have to recognize gain unless the transaction also constitutes a partial liquidation, a change from the pre-1982 law which is not referred to, much less explained, in the legislative history.

One other aspect of the new statutory pattern deserves mention. Unlike the predecessor §346, §302(e) provides expressly that the question of whether a purported distribution in partial liquidation is essentially equivalent to a dividend is to be "determined at the corporate level rather than at the shareholder level". §302(e)(1)(A). While to some extent this merely confirms the prior understanding, as footnote 11 to the Davis case indicates, it may be significant that this qualification is not confined to contraction of the business. The much broader reference to the "corporate level" may invite an affirmative answer to the question left open in the McCarthy case, supra, as to whether a redemption distribution which does not involve sufficient "contraction" might nevertheless qualify as a partial liquidation if it meets some other type of corporate need. In that event, corporate business purpose, so firmly excluded from the other subsections of §302 by the Davis case, could find a new lease on life in partial liquidations under §302(b)(4). That might be entirely fitting; for whatever the force of the Supreme Court's analysis of the role of business purpose in pre-1982 §302, there was always some lingering doubt that Congress would have completely eliminated from the redemption scene a factor as well-established as business purpose without a word to that effect in the legislative history. Perhaps it would have been more sensible to find that in the 1954 split-off of partial liquidations from other redemptions, business purpose acccompanied partial liquidations into §346; and §302(e)(1)(A) could be seen as confirming that result some twenty-eight years later.

f. Service Ruling Policy. When the recemption transaction takes the form of an exchange for notes, planning is made more hazardous as a result of the reluctance of the Service to issue rulings with respect to redemptions in exchange for debt obligations in certain circumstances. Revenue Procedure 84-22, 1982-13 I.R.B. 13, includes the following, in Section 3, among the subjects on which rulings or determination letters will not be issued:

16. Whether section 302(b) of the Code applies when the consideration given in redemption by a corporation consists entirely or partly of its notes payable, and the shareholder's stock is held in escrow or as security for payment of the notes with the possibility that the stock may or will be returned to the shareholder in the future, upon the happening of specified defaults by the corporation.

17. Whether section 302(b) of the Code applies when the consideration given in redemption by a corporation in exchange for a shareholder's stock consists entirely or partly of the corporation's promise to pay an amount based on, or contingent on, future earnings of the corporation, when the promise to pay is contingent on working capital being maintained to a certain level, or any other similar contingency.

In addition, the Revenue Procedure includes in Section 4 as one of the topics on which rulings or determination letters ordinarily won't be issued (i.e., absent unique and compelling reasons to the contrary) the "tax effect of the redemption of stock for notes, when the payments on the notes are to be made over a period in excess of 15 years from the date of the issuance of such notes".

2. REDEMPTION TO PAY ESTATE TAXES

Section 303, first adopted in 1951, is designed to provide protection against the possibility of dividend treat-ment for redemptions of closely-held stock constituting a substantial portion of a decedent's estate, in an amount up to the total of the death taxes (both state and federal) and the funeral and administrative expenses allowable as estate tax deductions under section 2053. Making the treasury of a closely-held corporation available as a source of funds at the death of a principal shareholder can often materially ease the problem of meeting estate taxes. The reach of §303 was broadened in 1981 by reducing the required percentage of the estate which must be represented by the closely-held stock from 50% of the gross estate (less such allowable deductions as probate expenses, debts and losses, but not marital or charitable deductions) to 35%.

Section 303 was justified as follows in Sen. Rep. No. 2375, 81st Cong., 2d Sess. (1950) 54:

"It has been brought to the attention of your committee that the problem of financing the estate tax is acute in the case of estates consisting largely of shares in a family corporation. The market for such shares is usually very limited, and it is frequently difficult, if not impossible, to dispose of a minority interest. If, therefore, the estate tax cannot be financed through the sale of the other assets in the estate, the executors will be forced to dispose of the family business. In many cases the result will be the absorption of a family enterprise by larger competitors, thus tending to accentuate the degree of concentration of industry in this country."

Rev.Rul. 65–289, 1965–2 Cum.Bull. 86, holds that where stock was redeemed in exchange for an installment note having a fair market value equal to the face amount, there was a "distribution of property" within the meaning of § 303, "even though the note is not property of the corporation prior to delivery".

3. REDEMPTION THROUGH RELATED CORPORATIONS—§ 304

Section 304 is designed to prevent escape from the redemption-dividend rules by using related corporations to purchase stock. For example, suppose that the sole stockholder of Corporation A sells some of his A stock to Corporation B, a subsidiary of A. Under § 304, such a transaction is treated as a distribution from Corporation A. Or suppose that a stockholder owns all the stock of both A and B, and he sells some of his A stock to B. Here § 304 treats the transaction as a redemption of B stock and a contribution to its capital of A stock. (Under the attribution rules, this situation would also constructively involve a parent-subsidiary relationship, and hence might be treated the same as the first case.)

The conflict between §304 and §351 when a transaction falls within both sections was definitively resolved in 1982 by the addition of subsection 304(b)(3), which provides that §304 controls in cases of overlap. The following excerpt from the Conference Committee Report on the 1982 Act [TEFRA] describes the operation of §304(b)(3) (including its impact on §306, referred to on page 304 supra).

"[TEFRA] extends the anti-bailout rules of sections 304 and 306 of present law to the use of corporations, including holding companies, formed or availed of to avoid such rules. Such rules are made applicable to a transaction that, under present law, otherwise qualifies as a tax-free incorporation under section 351.

"Section 351 generally will not apply to transactions described in section 304. Thus, section 351, if otherwise applicable, will generally apply only to the extent such transaction consists of an exchange of stock for stock in the acquiring corporation. However, section 304 will not apply to debt incurred to acquire the stock of an operating company and assumed by a controlled corporation acquiring the stock since assumption of such debt is an alternative to a debt-financed direct acquisition by the acquiring company.

"Under [section 306(c)(3)], section 306 is made applicable to preferred stock acquired in a section 351 exchange if, had money in lieu of stock been received, its receipt would have been a dividend to any extent. [Thus] if the receipt of cash by the shareholder rather than stock would have caused section 304 as amended by the bill, rather than section 351, to apply to such receipt, some or all of the amount received might have been treated as a dividend. In such a case, the preferred stock acquired in the exchange will be section 306 stock.

"To the extent of any amount distributed (including any liability assumed or to which the stock is subject) in an exchange for stock to which section 304(a)(1) applies, the earnings and profits of the issuing corporation, to the extent thereof, will be deemed to be distributed to the acquiring company. This rule also applies in determining whether preferred stock acquired in a section 351 exchange is section 306 stock. . . .

B. IMPACT OF A REDEMPTION UPON THE REMAINING STOCKHOLDERS

REVENUE RULING 58-614

1958-2 Cum.Bull. 920.

The Internal Revenue Service will follow the decision [in Holsey v. Commissioner, 258 F.2d 865 (3d Cir.1958)], in cases involving similar facts and circumstances.

The decision holds that a remaining shareholder of a corporation does not receive a constructive dividend by way of enhancement in the value of his stock as a result of a purchase by the corporation of another shareholder's stock. In the future, the Service will not treat the purchase by a corporation of one shareholder's stock as a dividend to the remaining shareholders merely because their percentage interests in the corporation are increased. On the other hand, if the stock is in reality purchased by a remaining shareholder and paid for by the corporation, then, regardless of the form of the transaction, the payment will be considered a dividend to the shareholder who made the purchase. This position is in accord with the decisions of H. F. Wall v. Commissioner, 164 F.2d 462, Louis H. Zipp v. Commissioner [259 F.2d 119 (6th Cir.1958)], and similar court holdings.

In these transactions, if a shareholder surrenders stock to a corporation for less than its fair market value, such surrender may be a gift or compensation to the shareholders who remain interested in the corporation. Conversely, if a corporation pays more than fair market value for its stock, the payment may be compensation to the shareholder surrendering stock or may be a gift to him from the shareholders who remain interested in the corporation.

NOTE ON REV.RUL. 58-614

According to Rev.Rul. 58-614, the decision in the Holsey case left intact the Wall-Zipp line of cases to the effect that if the corporation pays for the stock of the withdrawing stockholder on behalf of the remaining stockholders, the latter will be treated as having received a dividend. To appreciate the significance of this assumption, it is necessary to analyze some of the varying factual patterns in this area. Let us start with the simple case of A and B each owning 50% of the stock of the corporation, with A wanting to withdraw from the enterprise by selling his stock for its fair market value of $100,000. Unless B is willing to have an outsider come into the enterprise, either he or the corporation must purchase A's stock. Obviously, if B simply uses his own private resources to purchase

A's stock, there will be no tax incidents to B; but he will have increased his investment in the corporation by $100,000. If B then wanted to draw upon the corporation's funds to replenish his private resources, he could cause the corporation to pay a dividend of $100,000 (assuming that the corporation's surplus position would make such a dividend lawful, and that its cash position would make the dividend feasible). But such a dividend would be fully taxable to B as such, assuming the presence of the necessary earnings and profits. It is into this mold — that is, purchase by the remaining stockholder followed by an ordinary dividend from the corporation to him — that the Commissioner would like to force transactions in this area whenever possible.

At the opposite end of the tax spectrum is the straight redemption by the corporation of A's stock. To be sure, some of the earlier cases suggested that even that transaction might constitute a constructive dividend to B because the redemption benefited him by increasing his percentage stock interest in the corporation (here to 100%). But of course, the short answer to such a contention is that while B does end up owning 100% of the corporation, the corporation is only half as large, having distributed half of its value to A in the redemption transaction. On the other hand, there is the disquieting thought that this is equally true when B purchases A's stock personally for $100,000 and then causes the corporation to distribute a dividend in that amount — there too B ends up as the sole owner of a corporation only half as large.

Actually, it would be rather harsh to treat the entire redemption distribution as a dividend to the remaining stockholder, just as it would be to regard the whole distribution as a dividend to the withdrawing stockholder (which today would be precluded in the case of a non pro rata redemption by § 302). Perhaps the Government would have achieved greater success in its effort to impose some dividend tax on non pro rata redemptions if it had sought to allocate the dividend treatment between the withdrawing and remaining stockholders. One way of accomplishing this would have been to view the redemption transaction as though it had consisted of a pro rata dividend to all stockholders to the extent of accumulated earnings and profits, followed by a purchase of the withdrawing stockholder's stock (now less valuable as a result of the distribution) by the remaining stockholders, using the proceeds of the dividend "received" by them. In other words, in the above situation the redemption distribution of $100,-000 would be taxed as dividend of $50,000 each to the two stockholders, and A would be treated as having sold his stock to B for $50,000. However, this approach seems never to have been advanced in any case, much less adopted; and it would now seem to be foreclosed in non pro rata redemption cases by § 302.

In any event, the Holsey case (plus the Commissioner's acquiescence) now preclude taxing the distribution in a straight-forward corporate redemption as a dividend to the remaining stockholders. Actually, the Holsey case is a particularly strong authority in this area, because the court decided for the taxpayer despite the fact that the option on the withdrawing stockholder's stock which the corporation acquired and exercised had originally been granted to the remaining stockholder. In other words, in Holsey the transaction had taken at least one modest step down the path of a purchase by the remaining stockholder, before emerging as a corporate redemption, which makes it at least a little easier to bring the case under the Wall-Zipp line treating the corporation's payments as made on behalf of the remaining stockholders. To appreciate the significance of this factor, let us consider some of the varying fact patterns in this area. Suppose first that in the above illustration B agreed to personally purchase the stock of A for $100,000 payable in installments; but thereafter B decided that the corporation should make the purchase and assigned the contract to the corporation. This is what happened in the Wall case, and the court held that subsequent payments by the corporation on the installment purchase contract assumed by it constituted dividends to the remaining stockholder. The court stressed the fact that the remaining stockholder was personally liable on the repurchase obligation, and remained so even after he had assigned it to the corporation. This led the court to say that when the corporation made the payments on the obligation, it "paid his indebtedness for Wall out of its surplus. It cannot be questioned that the payment of a taxpayer's indebtedness by a third party pursuant to an agreement between them is income to the taxpayer". Of course the soundness of this general principle is beyond dispute. However, it only applies where the taxpayer has given no consideration for the discharge of his indebtedness by the third party, whereas in Wall, as the taxpayer pointed out, he had assigned to the corporation the benefits of the stock purchase agreement (i. e., the right to receive the stock) which would seem to constitute ample consideration for the corporation's assumption of the corresponding indebtedness. But the court regarded the taxpayer's assignment to the corporation of his right to acquire the stock as little different from a sale by a sole stockholder of a portion of his stock to the corporation, which of course constitutes a classic dividend case.

This hardly did justice to the taxpayer's position. After all, the fact remains that the taxpayer's assignment to the corporation of his right to receive the stock was a complete answer to the discharge of indebtedness theory. Then as to the analogy to a redemption of stock from a sole stockholder, the important point is that the transaction in Wall was also virtually identical in ultimate effect to a direct corporate redemption from the withdrawing stockholder in the first place. Therefore, the real question was which of those two rather close analogies (with very different tax incidents) was to be followed. And this issue can not be resolved against the corporate redemption analogy merely by observing that where there is more than one alternative for achieving a desired result, "the method pursued is determinative for tax purposes without regard to the fact that different tax results would have attached if the alternative procedure had been followed." For it is equally true that the taxpayer in Wall did not actually acquire the stock personally and then have it redeemed by the corporation.

Perhaps what the court was trying to say in the Wall case is that once the transaction has started down the line of a purchase of the withdrawing stockholder's stock by the remaining stockholder, it is then too late to switch over to a corporate redemption and come within that safe harbor (as subsequently established by the Holsey case). If so, the soundness of this view is open to question, since it really amounts to a trap for the unwary, forever depriving a stockholder of the favorable tax treatment available for corporate redemption if he once starts down the stockholder-purchase route. Hence it should not be surprising that the force of the Wall case seems to be on the wane. Even in the recent cases which have purported to follow Wall, there has generally been some additional factor which led the court to impose a dividend tax on the remaining stockholder. Thus in the Zipp case, cited in Rev.Rul. 58–614 and decided just prior to Holsey, it appeared that the two taxpayers had acquired all of the stock of a corporation from their father without making any payment themselves, while he received almost $100,000 from the corporation. Here the analogy to a corporate redemption somewhat breaks down since the two taxpayers had to personally purchase at least some of their father's stock in order to become stockholders at all. To be sure, they could perhaps have purchased only a few shares each from their father, and then had the corporation redeem the rest of his stock, e. g., Zenz v. Quinlivan, 213 F.2d 914 (6th Cir. 1954); but here it might be fair to hold the taxpayers to what they actually did (or perhaps more accurately, what they failed to do).

In Deutsch v. Commissioner, 38 T.C. 118 (1962), the taxpayer had entered into an agreement to purchase all of the stock of a corporation from the widow of the deceased sole stockholder. The agreement called for the taxpayer to make a downpayment of $10,000 in exchange for 35 of the outstanding 350 shares, and to purchase, or cause the corporation to redeem, the remaining shares at the rate of 14 shares every three months for $4200. Except for the original downpayment, the corporation made all the payments, and the Tax Court held that they constituted dividends to the taxpayer. Here too it was a case of an outsider acquiring all of the outstanding stock of a corporation, rather than an existing stockholder becoming the sole stockholder by virtue of the withdrawal of the other stockholder; but unlike in Zipp the taxpayer clearly did purchase the first 35 shares personally. However, the court appears to have been influenced by the fact that the corporation was never a party to the agreement, and never adopted it. In addition, there was an unexplained provision in the agreement calling for the issuance of an additional 300 shares, apparently as a stock dividend, which does suggest that the taxpayer wanted to end up with a substantial number of shares no matter what procedure was followed, and hence does cut in favor of a stockholder-purchase view of the transaction.

In any event, the Tax Court has seemed to be much more willing of late to mitigate the rigors of the Wall decision, at least in cases like the above illustration where in effect one stockholder is withdrawing and the other is becoming the sole stockholder. Thus in Priester v. Commissioner, 38 T.C. 316 (1962), B bound himself to buy A's stock over a two year period but shortly thereafter realized he would have difficulty financing the purchase. Accordingly, B arranged with a third party to take over the contract, with the understanding that he could sell the stock to the corporation at a profit a short time thereafter. The Tax Court found no dividend to B upon the subsequent redemption, holding that the assignment of the contract to the third party was a bona fide transaction which could not be ignored, and that under Holsey the subsequent redemption of the stock from the third party produced no dividend to the remaining stockholder. See also Goss v. Commissioner, 22 T.C.M. 1219 (1963).

Assuming that these cases presage some relaxation of the Wall view, they also present some line-drawing problems of their own. For example, harking back to our earlier illustration, suppose that B has actually completed a cash purchase of A's stock when he realizes that a corporate redemption would have been better. Rather than risk an outright redemption at this point, B sells the stock acquired from A to a third party, from whom it is promptly redeemed as contemplated by the parties. Of course if B had been the sole stockholder for some time, such a device would hardly enable him to avoid dividend treatment upon a redemption of his stock. But where it involves stock just acquired from A, is it really any different from what was allowed in Priester?

But if this kind of transaction is to be sustained, what about a direct redemption from the remaining stockholder of stock just acquired from the withdrawing stockholder? Actually, such a redemption has occasionally escaped dividend treatment where it was found that the remaining stockholder really acquired the stock as the agent of the corporation. The leading case to this effect is Fox v. Harrison, 145 F.2d 521 (7th Cir. 1944), where it did appear that the parties had always intended that the corporation purchase all of the stock of the withdrawing stockholder, but since the corporation did not have sufficient surplus to purchase all of the stock, the remaining stockholder acquired a portion of it as a temporary measure, pending the corporation's ability to purchase it. However, the rule of Fox v. Harrison has proved a slender reed upon which to rely, and despite an effort to invoke it in practically every case following the Wall approach, e. g., Deutsch v. Commissioner, supra, the courts have only rarely been satisfied that the purchase by the remaining stockholder was on behalf of the corporation.

On the other hand, an even broader rule than that of Fox v. Harrison is suggested by the decision in McShain v. Commissioner, 22 T.C.M. 1611 (1963). There a contemplated corporate redemption of stock from the withdrawing stockholders was discarded in favor of a purchase by the remaining stockholder because the corporation did not have the necessary liquid funds to finance the acquisition. Subsequently the corporation redeemed most of that stock from the remaining stockholder at the same price. In holding that there was no dividend to the remaining stockholder, the court did not rest on the notion that he had bought as "agent" for the corporation; indeed, Fox v. Harrison was not even mentioned. Rather the court stressed the necessity of considering all the circumstances and added the following significant comment:

> There was no practical difference to [the remaining stockholder] between a corporate redemption of the shares of the retiring shareholders or a purchase by him of the stock of the retiring stockholders followed by a redemption from him of some of the shares purchased at the price he paid for them.

REVENUE RULING 69-608

1969-2 Cum. Bull. 42.

Advice has been requested as to the treatment for Federal income tax purposes of the redemption by a corporation of a retiring shareholder's stock where the remaining shareholder of the corporation has entered into a contract to purchase such stock.

Where the stock of a corporation is held by a small group of people, it is often considered necessary to the continuity of the corporation to have the individuals enter into agreements among themselves to provide for the disposition of the stock of the corporation in the event of the resignation, death, or incapacity of one of them. Such agreements are generally reciprocal among the shareholders and usually provide that on the resignation, death, or incapacity of one of the principal shareholders, the remaining shareholders will purchase his stock. Frequently such agreements are assigned to the corporation by the remaining shareholder and the corporation actually redeems its stock from the retiring shareholder.

Where a corporation redeems stock from a retiring shareholder, the fact that the corporation in purchasing the shares satisfies the continuing shareholder's executory contractual obligation to purchase the redeemed shares does not result in a distribution to the continuing shareholder provided that the continuing shareholder is not subject to an existing primary and unconditional obligation to perform the contract and that the corporation pays no more than fair market value for the stock redeemed.

On the other hand, if the continuing shareholder, at the time of the assignment to the corporation of his contract to purchase the retiring shareholder's stock, is subject to an unconditional obligation to purchase the retiring shareholder's stock, the satisfaction by the corporation of his obligation results in a constructive distribution to him. The constructive distribution is taxable as a distribution under section 301 of the Internal Revenue Code of 1954.

If the continuing shareholder assigns his stock purchase contract to the redeeming corporation prior to the time when he incurs a primary and unconditional obligation to pay for the shares of stock, no distribution to him will result. If, on the other hand, the assignment takes place after the time when the continuing shareholder is so obligated, a distribution to him will result. While a pre-existing obligation to perform in the future is a necessary element in establishing a distribution in this type of case, it is not until the obligor's duty to perform becomes unconditional that it can be said a primary and unconditional obligation arises.

The application of the above principles may be illustrated by the situations described below.

* * *

Situation 2

A and B are unrelated individuals who own all of the outstanding stock of corporation X. An agreement between them provides unconditionally that within ninety days of the death of either A or B, the survivor will purchase the decedent's stock of X from his estate. Following the death of B, A causes X to assume the contract and redeem the stock from B's estate.

The assignment of the contract to X followed by the redemption by X of the stock owned by B's estate will result in a constructive distribution to A because immediately on the death of B, A had a primary and unconditional obligation to perform the contract.

* * *

Situation 5

A and B owned all of the outstanding stock of X corporation. An agreement between A and B provided that upon the death of either, X will redeem all of the X stock owned by the decedent at the time of his death. In the event that X does not redeem the shares from the estate, the agreement provided that the surviving shareholder would purchase the unredeemed shares from the decedent's estate. B died and, in accordance with the agreement, X redeemed all of the shares owned by his estate.

In this case A was only secondarily liable under the agreement between A and B. Since A was not primarily obligated to purchase the X stock from the estate of B, he received no constructive distribution when X redeemed the stock.

* * *

Situation 7

A and B owned all of the outstanding stock of X corporation. An agreement between the shareholders provided that upon the death of either, the survivor would purchase the decedent's shares from his estate at a price provided in the agreement. Subsequently, the agreement was rescinded and a new agreement entered into which provided that upon the death of either A or B, X would redeem all of the decedent's shares of X stock from his estate.

The cancellation of the original contract between the parties in favor of the new contract did not result in a constructive distribution to either A or B. At the time X agreed to purchase the stock pursuant to the terms of the new agreement, neither A nor B had an unconditional obligation to purchase shares of X stock. The subsequent redemption of the stock from the estate of either pursuant to the terms of the new agreement will not constitute a constructive distribution to the surviving shareholder.

C. INSTALLMENT REPURCHASE TRANSACTIONS

WARREN JONES CO. v. COMMISSIONER
United States Court of Appeals, Ninth Circuit, 1975.
524 F.2d 788.

ELY, CIRCUIT JUDGE:

During its taxable year ending on October 31, 1968, the Warren Jones Company, a cash basis taxpayer, sold an apartment building for $153,000. In return, the taxpayer received a cash downpayment of $20,000 and the buyer's promise in a standard form real estate contract, to pay $133,000, plus interest, over the following fifteen years. The Tax Court held, with three judges dissenting, that the fair market value of the real estate contract did not constitute an "amount realized" by the taxpayer in the taxable year of sale under section 1001(b) of the Internal Revenue Code.[1] Warren Jones Co., 60 T.C. 663 (1973) (reviewed by the full Court). The Commissioner of Internal Revenue has appealed, and we reverse.

I. Background

On May 27, 1968, the taxpayer, a family-held corporation chartered by the State of Washington, entered into a real estate contract for the sale of one of its Seattle apartment buildings, the Wallingford Court Apartments, to Bernard and Jo Ann Storey for $153,000. When the sale closed on June 15, 1968, the Storeys paid $20,000 in cash and took possession of the apartments. The Storeys were then obligated by the contract to pay the taxpayer $1,000 per month, plus 8 percent interest on the declining balance, for a period of fifteen years. The balance due at the end of fifteen years is to be payable in a lump sum. The contract was the only evidence of the Storeys' indebtedness, since no notes or other such instruments passed between the parties. Upon receipt of the full purchase price, the taxpayer is obligated by the contract to deed the Wallingford Apartments to the Storeys.

The Tax Court found, as facts, that the transaction between the taxpayer and the Storeys was a completed sale in the taxable year ending on October 31, 1968, and that in that year, the Storeys were solvent obligors. The court also found that real estate contracts such as that between the taxpayer and the Storeys were regularly bought and sold in the Seattle area. The court concluded, from the testimony before it, that in the taxable year of sale, the taxpayer could have sold its contract, which had a face value of $133,000, to a savings and loan association or a similar institutional buyer for approximately $117,980. The court found, however, that in accordance with prevailing business practices, any potential buyer for the contract would likely have required the taxpayer to deposit $41,000 of the proceeds from the sale of the contract in a savings account, assigned to the buyer, for the purpose of securing the first $41,000 of the Storeys' payments. Consequently, the court found that in the taxable year of sale, the contract had a fair market value of only $76,980 (the contract's selling price minus the amount deposited in the assigned savings account.)

On the sale's closing date, the taxpayer had an adjusted basis of $61,913 in the Wallingford Apartments. In determining the amount it

---

1. Unless otherwise stated, all section references are to the Internal Revenue Code of 1954, 26 U.S.C. (1970). [Some of the later footnotes by the Court omitted.]

had realized from the sale, the taxpayer added only the $20,000 down-payment and the portion of the $4,000 in monthly payments it had received that was allocable to principal. Consequently, on its federal income tax return for the taxable year ending October 31, 1968, the taxpayer reported no gain from the apartment sale. The taxpayer's return explained that the corporation reported on the cash basis and that under the Tax Court's holding in Nina J. Ennis, 17 T.C. 465 (1951), it was not required to report gain on the sale until it had recovered its basis. The return also stated, however, that in the event the taxpayer was required to report gain in the taxable year of the sale, it elected to do so on the installment basis (I.R.C. § 453).

The Commissioner disagreed with the taxpayer's assertion that it had realized no gain on the sale, but he conceded that the sale qualified as an installment ... le. Consequently, the Commissioner recalculated the taxpayer's gain in accordance with section 453 and notified the taxpayer that it had recognized an additional $12,098 in long term capital gain. The taxpayer then petitioned the Tax Court for a redetermination of its liability.

Section 1001 provides, in pertinent part, as follows:

(a) COMPUTATION OF GAIN OR LOSS.—The gain from the sale or other disposition of property shall be the excess of the amount realized therefrom over the adjusted basis * * *.

(b) AMOUNT REALIZED.—The amount realized from the sale or other disposition of property shall be the sum of any money received plus the fair market value of the property (other than money) received.[2]

The question presented is whether section 1001(b) requires the taxpayer to include the fair market value of its real estate contract with the Storeys in determining the "amount realized" during the taxable year of the sale.

Holding that the fair market value of the contract was not includable in the amount realized from the sale, the Tax Court majority relied on the doctrine of "cash equivalency." Under that doctrine, the cash basis taxpayer must report income received in the form of property only if the property is the "equivalent of cash." . . .

The Tax Court majority adopted the following as its definition of the phrase, "equivalent of cash":

* * * if the promise to pay of a solvent obligor is unconditional and assignable, not subject to set-offs, and is of a kind that is frequently transferred to lenders or investors at a discount not substantially greater than the generally prevailing premium for the use of money, such promise is the equivalent of cash * * *.

Warren Jones Co., supra at 668–69, quoting, Cowden v. Commissioner, 289 F.2d 20, 24 (5th Cir. 1961). Applying the quoted definition, the Tax Court held that the taxpayer's contract, which had a face value of $133,000, was not the "equivalent of cash" since it had a fair market value of only $76,980. Had the taxpayer sold the contract, the discount from the face value, approximately 42 percent, would have been "substantially greater than the generally prevailing premium for the use of money."[4]

---

2. With certain exceptions not relevant here, section 1002 of the Code requires the full amount of gain determined under section 1001 to be recognized. . . .

4. The taxpayer's argument on appeal that to be a cash equivalent, a debt instrument must be negotiable is untenable. See, e. g., Heller Trust v. Comm'r, 382 F.2d 675, 681 (9th Cir. 1967); Cowden v. C. I. R., 289 F.2d 20, 24 (5th Cir. 1961).

The Tax Court observed that requiring the taxpayer to realize the fair market value of the contract in the year of the sale could subject the taxpayer to substantial hardships. The taxpayer would be taxed in the initial year on a substantial portion of its gain from the sale of the property, even though it had received, in cash, only a small fraction of the purchase price. To raise funds to pay its taxes, the taxpayer might be forced to sell the contract at the contract's fair market value, even though such a sale might not otherwise be necessary or advantageous. Most importantly in the Tax Court's view, if the taxpayer were required to realize the fair market value of the contract in the year of the sale, the sale transaction would be closed for tax purposes in that year; hence, the taxpayer's capital gain on the transaction would be permanently limited to the difference between its adjusted basis and the contract's fair market value plus the cash payments received in the year of sale. If the taxpayer did retain the contract, so as to collect its face value, the amounts received in excess of the contract's fair market value would constitute ordinary income. The Tax Court also noted that requiring the cash basis taxpayer to realize the fair market value of the real estate contract would tend to obscure the differences between the cash and accrual methods of reporting.

The Commissioner does not dispute the Tax Court's conclusion that the taxpayer's contract with the Storeys had a fair market value of $76,980, or any other of the court's findings of fact.[5] Rather, the Commissioner contends that since, as found by the Tax Court, the contract had a fair market value, section 1001(b) requires the taxpayer to include the amount of that fair market value in determining the amount realized.[6]

II. Statutory Analysis

The first statutory predecessor of section 1001(b) was section 202(b) of the Revenue Act of February 24, 1919, which stated:

When property is exchanged for other property, the property received in exchange shall for the purpose of determining gain or loss be treated as the equivalent of cash to the amount of its fair market value, if any * * *.

Ch. 18, § 202(b), 40 Stat. 1060. We have no doubt that under that statute, the taxpayer would have been required to include the fair market value of its real estate contract as an amount realized during the taxable year of sale.

Only three years later, however, in the Revenue Act of November 23, 1921, Congress replaced the language of the statute enacted in 1919 with the following:

5. Relying primarily on Bedell v. Comm'r, 30 F.2d 622 (2d Cir. 1929), the taxpayer disputes the Tax Court's finding that the sale of the Wallingford Apartments was a completed transaction in the taxable year ending October 31, 1968. The question whether a particular sale is completed is ordinarily a question of fact, Clodfelter v. Comm'r, 426 F.2d 1391 (9th Cir. 1970), and the disputed finding in the present case is most assuredly not clearly erroneous.

6. The Commissioner's theoretical approach to the result for which he contends is not altogether clear. He may be rejecting the doctrine of cash equivalency altogether, cf. Warren Jones Co., supra at 673-74 (Quealy, J., dissenting), or he may be contending that any property with a fair market value is the equivalent of cash in the amount of its fair market value. See Comment, The Doctrine of Cash Equivalency, supra n. 3, at 225-26; but see M. Levine, Real Estate Transactions, Tax Planning and Consequences § 731 (1973). Since as to a cash basis taxpayer, with which we are here concerned, both theories would achieve the same result, we need not distinguish between them. The taxpayer contends that the basic question before us is one of fact. We disagree. The question is essentially one of statutory construction and it therefore presents an issue of law.

On an exchange of property, real, personal or mixed, for any
other such property, no gain or loss shall be recognized unless the
property received in exchange has a readily realizable market
value * * *.

Ch. 136, § 202(c), 42 Stat. 230. The original statute had created "a
presumption in favor of taxation." H.R.Rep.No.350, 67th Cong., 1st
Sess. (1921), reproduced at 1939–1 Cum.Bull. (Part 2) 168, 175. In
the 1921 Act, Congress doubtless intended a policy more favorable to
the taxpayer. Interpreting the 1921 statute, the Treasury Regulations
provided that

[p]roperty has a readily realizable market value if it can be readily converted into an amount of cash or its equivalent substantially
equal to the fair value of the property.

Treas.Reg. 62, Art. 1564 (1922 ed.). The law established in 1921
appears to have been substantially in accord with the position taken in
this case by the Tax Court majority.

Notwithstanding the foregoing, in the Revenue Act of 1924, ch.
234, § 202(c), 43 Stat. 256, Congress again changed the law, replacing
the 1921 statute with the language that now appears in section 1001
(b) of the current Code. Of the 1921 statute, and its requirement of
a "readily realizable market value," the Senate Finance Committee
wrote in 1924:

The question whether, in a given case, the property received in
exchange has a readily realizable market value is a most difficult
one, and the rulings on this question in given cases have been far
from satisfactory. * * * The provision can not be applied with
accuracy or consistency.

S.Rep.No.398, 68th Cong., 1st Sess. (1924), ... Under the 1924
statute, "where income is realized in the form of property, the measure of the income is the fair market value of the property at the date
of its receipt." H.R.Rep.No.179, supra . . . .

There is no indication whatsoever that Congress intended to retain the "readily realizable market value" test from the 1921 statute as
an unstated element of the 1924 Act. Indeed, as noted above, Congress
sharply criticized that test. We cannot avoid the conclusion that in
1924 Congress intended to establish the more definite rule for which
the Commissioner here contends and that consequently, if the fair
market value of property received in an exchange can be ascertained,
that fair market value must be reported as an amount realized.

Congress clearly understood that the 1924 statute might subject
some taxpayers to the hardships discussed by the Tax Court majority.
In the Revenue Act of 1926, ch. 27, § 212(d), 44 Stat. 23, Congress
enacted the installment basis for reporting gain that is now reflected
in section 453 of the current Code. Under section 453, a taxpayer who
sells real property and receives payments in the year of sale totaling
less than 30 percent of the selling price may elect to report as taxable
income in any given year only

that proportion of the installment payments actually received in
that year which the gross profit, realized or to be realized when
payment is completed, bears to the total contract price.

26 U.S.C. § 453(a)(1).

By providing the installment basis, Congress intended " * * *
to relieve taxpayers who adopted it from having to pay an income tax
in the year of sale based on the full amount of anticipated profits
when in fact they had received in cash only a small portion of the sales
price." . . . For sales that qualify, the installment basis also eliminates the other potential disadvantages to which the Tax Court re-

ferred. Since taxation in the year of the sale is based on the value of
the payments actually received, the taxpayer should not be required
to sell his obligation in order to meet his tax liabilities. Furthermore,
the installment basis does not change the character of the gain received. If gain on an exchange would otherwise be capital, it remains
capital under section 453. Finally, the installment basis treats cash
and accrual basis taxpayers equally.

We view section 453 as persuasive evidence in support of the interpretation of section 1001(b) for which the Commissioner contends.
The installment basis is Congress's method of providing relief from
the rigors of section 1001(b). In its report on the Revenue Act of
1926, the Senate Finance Committee expressly noted that in sales or
exchanges not qualifying for the installment basis, "deferred-payment
contracts."

> * * * are to be regarded as the equivalent of cash if such obli-
> gations have a fair market value. In consequence, that portion
> of the initial payment and of the fair market value of such obli-
> gations which represents profit is to be returned as income as of
> the taxable year of the sale.

Sp.Rep.No.52, 69th Cong., 1st Sess. (1926), reproduced at 1939–1 Cum.
Bull. (Part 2) 332, 347.

On this appeal, however, the taxpayer has made another argument with respect to section 453. It contends that subsection (b)(3),
added to section 453 in 1969, may be read as Congress's definition of
the phrase "equivalent of cash." As noted above, the taxpayers who
sell property and receive "payments" in the year of sale that exceed
30 percent of the selling price may not report on the installment basis.
Under section 453(b)(2)(A)(ii), "evidences of indebtedness of the
purchaser" are not to be considered as "payments" in the year of sale
in determining whether the payments constitute 30 percent of the selling price. Section 453(b)(3), added by the Tax Reform Act of 1969,
provides that

> * * * a bond or other evidence of indebtedness which is payable
> on demand, or which is issued by a corporation or a government
> or a political subdivision thereof (A) with interest coupons at-
> tached or in registered form (other than one in registered form
> which the taxpayer establishes will not be readily tradable in an
> established securities market), or (B) in any other form designed
> to render such bond or other evidence of indebtedness readily trad-
> able in an established securities market, shall not be treated as
> an evidence of indebtedness of the purchaser.

In the taxpayer's view, property received in a sale or exchange should
not be considered the equivalent of cash under section 1001(b) unless
the property is of the types described in section 453(b)(3).[8]

Congress added section 453(b)(3) to the Code for the purpose of
excluding from the installment basis those taxpayers who sell property
and receive more than 30 percent of the selling price in the form of
highly liquid instruments of debt. Congress concluded that such taxpayers, like taxpayers receiving cash, would not suffer the hardships
that the installment basis was designed to alleviate. See H.R.Rep.No.
413, 91st Cong., 1st Sess. 107–08 (1969) . . . . We find no indi-

8. The argument upon which the taxpayer relies is fully developed in Comment, The Doctrine of Cash Equivalency, supra n. 3, at 233–38.

cation that Congress intended that section 453(b)(3) should be given a broader application. If we were to adopt the taxpayer's argument, we would substantially nullify section 453 with respect to cash basis taxpayers receiving deferred payment obligations other than those described in section 453(b)(3). Such taxpayers, not required to include the fair market value of their obligations in determining the amount realized under section 1001(b), would rarely, if ever, elect to report on the installment basis. In the light of the other legislative history of section 453, hitherto discussed, it is clear to us that Congress, in 1969, did not contemplate, or intend, such a result.

III. Case Law

The prior decisions of our own court support the conclusion we have reached. On several occasions, we have held that if the fair market value of a deferred payment obligation received in a sale or other exchange can be ascertained, that fair market value must be included as an amount realized under section 1001(b). Most recently, In re Steen, 509 F.2d 1398, 1404–05 (9th Cir. 1975), we held that the fair market value of an installment payment contract received in exchange for shares of stock was ascertainable and that, consequently, that fair market value was an amount realized in the year of the sale. In Heller Trust v. Commissioner, 382 F.2d 675, 681 (9th Cir. 1967), our court affirmed a Tax Court decision requiring a taxpayer to include the fair market value of real estate contracts as an amount realized in the year of a sale, even though the fair market value of the contracts there involved was only 50 percent of their face value. . . . [9]

There are, of course, "rare and extraordinary" situations in which it is impossible to ascertain the fair market value of a deferred payment obligation in the year of sale. See Treas.Reg. § 1.1001–1(a). The total amount payable under an obligation may be so speculative, or the right to receive any payments at all so contingent, that the fair market value of the obligation cannot be fixed. See Burnet v. Logan, 283 U.S. 404, 51 S.Ct. 550, 75 L.Ed. 1143 (1931); In re Steen, 509 F.2d 1398, 1403–04 (9th Cir. 1975) (right to payment depended on favorable judicial decision on novel question of state law); Westover v. Smith, 173 F.2d 90 (9th Cir. 1949). If an obligation is not marketable, it may be impossible to establish its fair market value. See Willhoit v. Commissioner, 308 F.2d 259 (9th Cir. 1962) (uncontradicted testimony that there was no market for high risk contracts); Phillips v. Frank, 295 F.2d 629 (9th Cir. 1961) (uncontradicted testimony that highly speculative contracts could not have been sold in the year

---

[9]. . . .
The Tax Court adopted as its definition of "cash equivalency" certain language from the opinion in Cowden v. Com'r, 289 F.2d 20 (5th Cir. 1961). In our view, the holding in *Cowden* does not conflict with the prior decisions of our court or with our present decision. In *Cowden*, the Fifth Circuit held that the Tax Court had overemphasized one of its findings of fact in reaching its decision and remanded the case for the Tax Court's reconsideration. The language adopted by the Tax Court appears within the context of the Fifth Circuit's discussion, in *Cowden*, of the taxpayer's contention that the deferred payment obligation he had received in exchange for an oil and gas lease could have no realizable value because it was not negotiable. In rejecting the taxpayer's contention, the *Cowden* court appears to have written the language adopted by the Tax Court principally as a description of the obligation involved in that case. See Dennis v. Comm'r, 473 F.2d 274, 285 (5th Cir. 1973), in which the Fifth Circuit, citing *Cowden*, states that when property received in a sale or exchange has a fair market value, that value constitutes an amount realized.

of sale). But see United States v. Davis, 370 U.S. 65, 71–74, 82 S.Ct.
1190, 8 L.Ed.2d 335 (1962) (wife's release of her marital rights in a
property settlement agreement held to have a fair market value equal
to the value of property that her husband transferred to her in exchange); Gersten v. Commissioner, [267 F.2d] at 197 ("It is not necessary to find any actual sales of like articles to establish a fair market value.")

The Tax Court found, as a fact, that the taxpayer's real estate
contract with the Storeys had a fair market value of $76,980 in the
taxable year of sale. Consequently, the taxpayer must include $76,980
in determining the amount realized under section 1001(b). As previously noted, however, the Commissioner has conceded that the taxpayer is eligible to report on the installment basis and has calculated
the taxpayer's deficiency accordingly.

The decision of the Tax Court is reversed, and on remand, the
Tax Court will enter judgment for the Commissioner.

Reversed and remanded, with directions.

NOTE ON DEFERRED PAYMENT TRANSACTIONS

1.   The Installment Method of Accounting - §453

Whatever view may be taken of the decision in Warren Jones
on the merits -- and we will be analyzing the case in detail
shortly -- it is clear that in the meantime Congress has affirmed
and strengthened the primacy accorded by the Court to the installment method of accounting as the means for avoiding immediate
full taxation of a deferred payment obligation received in
exchange for property. In 1980 Congress completely rewrote §453
of the Code, containing the installment accounting provisions,
and in effect made that section the starting point for dealing
with virtually any sale of property involving deferred payments.
Under that revision, §453 defines an installment sale as a
"disposition of property when at least one payment is to be
received after the close of the taxable year in which the disposition occurs", and provides that any such sale (other than one
made by a dealer who regularly sells personal property on the
installment plan, which is now covered by §453A, or a sale of
inventory) must be accounted for under the installment method
unless, pursuant to §453(d), the taxpayer affirmatively elects
out of that method on or before the due date of the return for
the year of the disposition.

This was a dramatic change in the reach of the installment
accounting provisions, since under prior law the method was
applicable only when a taxpayer affirmatively elected it. As a
corollary, the 1980 Act also eliminated most of the restrictions
and limitations that had previously circumscribed the use of the

installment method, such as the Service's insistence that there be at least two payments, the requirement in the prior law that the payments received in the year of disposition not exceed 30% of selling price, and the inability to use the method whenever contingent payments were involved.

The 1980 amendment did not change the basic mechanics of the installment method, under which the taxpayer recognizes a portion of each principal payment as gain, in an amount proportionate to the total expected gain on the transaction; as §453(c) puts it, "the income recognized for any taxable year from a disposition is that proportion of the payments received in that year which the gross profit . . . bears to the toal contract price". To illustrate, assume that a taxpayer sells property with a basis of $6,000 for $10,000, payable $4,000 down and $1,000 in each of the next six years (with appropriate interest): the gross profit of $4,000 represents 40% of the total contract price, so the amount of gain recognized in the first year would be $1,600 (40% X $4,000), with $400 (40% X $1,000) recognized in each of the following six years.

The revision also made no change in the effect given to the buyer's assumption of indebtedness of the seller. In general, whether or not the indebtedness assumed is specifically related to the property sold (as by way of a mortgage), neither the assumption nor the subsequent payments on the indebtedness by the buyer constitute "payments" received by the seller; but in turn the indebtedness is subtracted from the selling price in determining the "total contract price", although of course the indebtedness is still included in the computation of "selling price", and hence "gross profit" (which is equal to selling price less basis). Therefore, if in the above example the property was subject to a mortgage of $2,000, which the buyer assumed while paying only $2,000 in the first year (instead of $4,000), the selling price would still be $10,000, and the gross profit $4,000, but the total contract price would be only $8,000, so 50% of each payment received would be recognized as gain under the installment method. This was the rule under the prior regulation, §1.453-4(c), and it is carried forward in the temporary regulations issued under the 1980 statute. Reg. §15A.453-1(b)(2), (5) Ex. 2. There is, however, an exception if the indebtedness assumed exceeds the basis of the property transferred; any such excess does count as a payment received in the year of the disposition (and is included as part of the total contract price). It appears that there is also an exception for indebtedness of the taxpayer incurred incident to the disposition of the property, such as for legal fees. Reg. §15A.453-1(b)(2)(iv).

One of the important changes made by the 1980 amendment relates to the manner in which the installment method is applied when the consideration received upon a disposition includes both deferred payments and property which is eligible for non-recognition treatment under §356(a) (or constitutes "like kind" property under §1031). The approach now taken in such cases somewhat parallels the treatment of assumption of indebtedness, in that the fair market value of the non-recognition property is excluded in computing the total contract price, and the total gain to be recognized is allocated proportionately among the deferred payments of cash received.

Another important change was the extension of the install- ment method to cases involving a liquidating distribution of deferred payment obligations received by a corporation during the 12-month liquidation period under §337. The shareholders may allocate a proportionate share of their total gain to the installment obligation and use the installment method to report that amount of gain as the payments on the obligation are received.

One of the most significant departures from the pre-1980 law was the application of the installment method to cases where the selling price is subject to a contingency, which were there- tofore not eligible for installment accounting. The statute leaves to the regulations the task of providing specific rules for dealing with such transactions, pursuant to guidelines provided in the Committee Reports. Faithful to those guidelines, the temporary regulations provide that in any case where a maximum selling price can be determined, that is, assuming all contingencies, formulas, etc. operate in the taxpayer's favor (but ignoring incidental or remote contingencies), that figure is used to calculate total contract price and the gross profit ratio. If it is subsequently determined that a contingency will not be satisfied to some extent, thus reducing the maximum selling price, the taxpayer will report reduced income with respect to subsequent installments; if the taxpayer has already reported more income than the total recomputed gross profit, the excess may be deducted as a loss. Reg. §15A.453-1(c)(2).

In cases where the selling price is indefinite and no maximum selling price can be determined, but the obligation is payable over a fixed period of time, the basis of the property sold is recovered ratably over that period of time. If the payment received in any year is less than the allocable share of basis for that year, the unrecovered portion of the basis is carried forward to the next succeeding year, until the final payment year, at which time a loss will be allowed. Reg. §15A. 453-1(c)(3).

If the agreement specifies neither a maximum selling price nor a fixed period for the payments, it will be subject to careful scrutiny to determine whether it really represents a sale rather than an arrangement for the payment of rent, royalties, or the like. If a sale has indeed occurred, basis will be recovered ratably over a period of 15 years (unless the taxpayer can justify some other approach), subject to a similar proviso for postponing any recognition of loss until the final payment is received or the obligation has become worthless.

2.   The "Open Transaction" Method

Obviously, the desirability of accepting the option under §453(d) to elect out of the installment method depends upon the tax treatment to which the taxpayer would be remitted. That of course is the very issue on which the Warren Jones takes such a firm position in favor of immediate inclusion of the fair market value of the obligation in "amount realized" for the year of receipt. Nevertheless, the fact is that a considerable number of cases had allowed taxpayers who made isolated sales of non-inventory property on a deferred payment basis to report such transactions by the method condemned in Warren Jones, i.e., by treating the amount of cash received in the year of sale as a return of basis of the property sold, and recognizing gain only as and when the subsequent payments (of principal) on the install-ment obligation exceeded that basis. This well-established form of reporting is often referred to as the "open transaction" method (a term the Warren Jones opinion seems to have studiously avoided), which connotes the fact that a final tax balance is not struck at the time of the receipt of the deferred payment obligation, and instead the original transaction remains open, with all of the payments (apart from any portion representing express or imputed interest) treated as received in exchange for the property sold. The approach stems from the decision of the Supreme Court in the classic case of Burnet v. Logan, cited in Warren Jones, where the taxpayer acquired in a liquidating distribution the right to receive a fixed royalty per ton of ore taken from a certain mine, but without specification of either the total expected tonnage or the rate at which the ore would be mined. In such a case, the timing and amount of the prospective royalty payments are so speculative that any effort to value the right at the outset would be virtually guesswork, so it makes sense to allow the taxpayer simply to recognize the payments as received, first as return of basis until that has been fully recovered, and then as taxable gain. The type of gain is deter-mined by the character of the original sale or exchange, pursuant to the notion that the original transaction remain open: in other words, the payments (of principal) under the deferred obligation are treated just as they would have been if received at the outset.

Clearly, the open transaction approach is far more favorable for taxpayers than the immediate inclusion of the fair market value of the obligation upon receipt as an "amount realized" (which is often referred to as the "closed transaction" method). It is also better than the installment method, because the open transaction allows postponement of any recognition of gain until the taxpayer's basis in the property exchanged has been recovered, whereas the installment method requires recognition of some gain in each payment, starting with the downpayment, which comes right at the outset and is often the largest payment received in the transaction. (That explains why the taxpayer in Warren Jones was willing to litigate in an effort to use the open transaction method rather than the installment method.) In addition, it has to be said that, particularly if no report of the transaction is made in the year it occurs, by the time the payments of principal received exceed the taxpayer's basis in the property exchanged there is a greater risk that the transaction will be omitted entirely through inadvertence or otherwise.

As a result, taxpayers have long sought to extend the open transaction method, arguing that even for obligations far less uncertain than the one in Burnet v. Logan the fair market value could not be ascertained; the Service, in turn, has tried to limit the application of the open transaction approach by insisting that virtually every deferred payment obligation can and should be valued upon receipt, so that the original sale transaction can be "closed" and a final tax balance struck at that point. Thus the regulations under §1001 have long provided that "only in rare and extraordinary cases will property be considered to have no fair market value". Reg. §1.1001-1(a). (Taken literally, this might imply that the taxpayer must establish the absence of any value at all for the deferred payment obligation in order to avoid immediate recognition, but that could hardly be, since even the most speculative obligation has some value, as witness the one in Burnet v. Logan itself, which was clearly worth a great deal, even if it was not possible to say just how much.)

At an early stage, cash-basis taxpayers found another route to the benefits of open transaction treatment, based upon the principle that under the cash basis a taxpayer who is going to receive cash may normally wait until it is in hand before reporting income. A number of cases adopted the view that a cash-basis seller who obtains a simple contract promise to pay the rest of the purchase price is not required to value the obligation upon receipt and include it in income, but may instead merely report the cash as received, which results in the same tax treatment as the open transaction method. Thus in Johnston v. Commissioner, 14 T.C. 560 (1950), a cash-basis taxpayer sold stock in 1942 under a contract which called for one-half of the estimated purchase price to be paid in 1942 and the balance in 1943. The exact purchase price could not be determined until 1943, but was based upon a method of computation prescribed in the contract. The total amount ultimately received by the taxpayer resulted in a gain, which the Commissioner determined was taxable in 1943. The purchaser was financially capable of paying the full purchase price in 1942, and the taxpayer contended that the obligation to complete the purchase price should have been valued and included the "amount realized" under §1001 in 1942. However, the court concluded that the question of whether the value of a deferred payment obligation should be recognized as an amount realized upon receipt depended upon the taxpayer's method of accounting, and held that a mere "agreement to pay the balance of the purchase price in the future has no tax significance. .to [the] seller if he is using a cash system".

The Johnston case was followed in Ennis v. Commissioner, 17 T.C. 465 (1951), where the notion of "cash equivalency" discussed in Warren Jones was relied on as the test for determining when a deferred payment obligation received by a cash-basis taxpayer had to be valued and included in "amount realized" under §1001. According to the Ennis court, this test was not met where "the promise to pay was merely contractual [and] was not embodied in a note or other evidence of indebtedness possessing the element of negotiability and freely transferable". A dissent would have distinguished the Johnston case on the ground that there the total purchase price could not be determined at the time of the sale, whereas in Ennis the exact dollar price was fixed from the outset.

The effect of these cases was to move the open transaction test for cash-basis taxpayers from an inquiry as to whether the value of the obligation was ascertainable to whether the obligation was substantially "equivalent to cash". As to what constituted cash equivalence, the Johnston and Ennis cases provided some outside parameters: at one end of the spectrum, a simple contract promise, not embodied in a separate debt instrument, was not equivalent to cash, while at the other end, a negotiable promissory note of the kind that passes freely in commerce would qualify. This dichotomy has legitimate roots in the cash method of accounting. Even a cash-basis taxpayer must include in income upon receipt the present value of ordinary property like land or stock, just as §1001 contemplates, rather than wait until such property is turned into cash, which will represent a new and different taxable transaction. A deferred payment obligation is also property, but of a very special kind, in that it promises the receipt of cash without any additional transaction. Hence an obligation can fairly be viewed as merely evidence of the promise to pay cash in the future, allowing the cash-basis taxpayer to await receipt of the cash before being taxed on the transaction. On the other hand, the obligation might itself be regarded as the "payment" to the recipient, just as in the case of other types of property received, in which event inclusion of its value upon receipt would be in order. While there may not be a clear-cut line of demarcation between these two, ready transferability would obviously be a key element in treating an obligation just like any other property received.

Consistent with this view, it appeared for a time that negotiability of the obligation was the key to cash equivalence, but this view was rejected in the Cowden case, discussed in Warren Jones. After first observing that a negotiable note was not necessarily the equivalent of cash, because it "may have been issued by a maker of doubtful solvency or for other reasons such paper might be denied a ready acceptance in the marketplace", the Cowden court went on to hold that absence of negotiability was not a bar to cash equivalance, giving as an example the sort of non-negotiable obligation described in the quotation on Supplement page 357. Under this approach, cash equivalence can be found for even a simple contract promise, if it is "of a kind

that is frequently transferred to lenders and investors" at a
reasonable discount; the existence of a ready market in which
the recipient can easily turn the obligation into immediate cash
invites treating the obligation as itself payment, and thereto
taxable like any other property received, rather than merely as
evidence of a promise to pay cash in the future. Thus in a
number of cases involving so-called "land contracts", that is,
simple contracts providing for payment of the purchase price of
land in installments, secured by the land, the existence of a
ready market for such contracts led to a rejection of open-transaction treatment for cash-basis taxpayers in favor of immediate
recognition of the value of the contract as an "amount realized"
by the taxpayer. E.g., Phipps Industrial Land Trust v. Commissioner, 22 T.C.M. 1724 (1963). Little attention was paid to the
condition suggested in the Cowden opinion that the discount
reflected by the market price should not be "substantially
greater than the generally prevailing premium for the use of
money", as is dramatically illustrated by the Heller Trust case,
cited in Warren Jones, where the obligations were valued at only
50% of the face amount.

This emphasis on whether a ready market for the obligation
exists means that, as a practical matter, the cash equivalent
test for open transaction treatment may produce pretty much the
same results as the original ascertainability of value standard,
since whenever there is a market the value of the obligation can
be easily determined, whereas without a market the value may be
very hard to ascertain. The Warren Jones court implies as much,
with the observation in footnote 6 that as to the obligation
there involved, for which there was a market, it did not matter
whether the Commissioner contended that the special cash equivalency test should be completely rejected, or simply that by
virtue of the ready market the Warren Jones obligation satisfied
the test. But there could be a difference if effect is given to
the qualification in the Cowden case that even a marketable
obligation may not constitute the equivalent of cash if the
discount is "substantially greater than the generally prevailing
premium for the use of money". To appreciate the import of this
limitation, remember that a discount may simply represent an
adjustment in the effective interest yield, to bring it up to
what the market requires for the particular obligor in the
existing circumstances; when the difference between the value of
an obligation and its face amount evidences only a discount of
that kind, there is no reason why it should preclude a finding
of cash equivalence. But the situation is quite different if
the discount goes well beyond this level, since then the obligation is stamped as highly speculative, posing a significant risk
of default. Of course every interest rate takes some account of
the possibility of default, in combination with straight compensation for the use of money, but an unusually high interest rate,
as evidenced by a very large discount, indicates that the former
element was predominant. And when a substantial risk of non-payment is present, it seems quite harsh to require a cash-basis
taxpayer to recognize the value of an obligation upon receipt,

which is presumably the reason for the _Cowden_ court's resistance to finding cash equivalence for an obligation with a discount reflecting more than an increase in the interest rate to market levels for the use of money.

In any event, the Tax Court in _Warren Jones_ was apparently prepared to give new vitality to the _Cowden_ qualification, particularly because of concern that valuing an obligation at substantially less than face could transmute a substantial portion of the agreed purchase price from capital gain into ordinary income (a point which will be discussed further below). It was probably to forestall this development that the Court of Appeals undertook its comprehensive review of the issue, pointing _inter alia_ to the statutory history of §1001, the role of installment accounting, and the narrow reading of the _Cowden_ case referred to in footnote 9, in concluding that if the value of the obligation could be determined it must be included in income upon receipt, regardless of how large a discount might be present.

Actually, it seems unlikely that a ready market for a deferred payment obligation and a very large discount will be found in combination very often. A discount far in excess of any normal adjustment in the interest rate suggests a speculativeness that would ordinarily discourage trading in the instruments. To be sure, in _Warren Jones_ itself there was a finding of regular buying and selling of such obligations in the area, while at the same time the existence of a substantial discount was acknowledged. However, it seems plain that there were serious deficiencies in the computation of value in _Warren Jones_ which led to finding a discount of more than 40%. The actual sales value of the obligation involved in _Warren Jones_ was found to be around $115,000, reflecting a discount of only some 11.3%, and there was no justification for also deducting the entire $41,000 that would have been required to be deposited in an assigned savings account; the most that would be called for is some further discount reflecting a delay in free access to those funds (plus the small risk that the obligor would not pay the first $41,000 due on the obligation), which would not have made the total discount too large to be viewed as a "premium for the use of money", under the test applied by the Tax Court (in reliance on the quotation from the _Cowden_ case). Thus the _Warren Jones_ case is not really inconsistent with the proposition that a ready market will usually be accompanied by a discount somewhere in the order of a reasonable adjustment in the interest rate for the use of money; if the discount is in fact a good deal larger, a court may still confine _Warren Jones_ to its actual facts and apply the _Cowden_ qualification to allow open transaction treatment.

Where does the _Warren Jones_ case leave obligations which do not have a ready market, so that the present value (and the resulting discount) is difficult to ascertain? Despite the broad sweep of much of the opinion, which might have been viewed as a directive to the trier of fact to find a value as best it can in virtually every case, the court seems content simply to return to the ascertainability of value standard. Accordingly, exemption from valuation is conceded for cases like Burnet v. Logan, where value would be little more than a guess. However, the court also goes on to provide a very significant additional exception: "If an obligation is not marketable, it may be impossible to establish its fair market value." Although the court cites a couple of cases evidently designed to forestall any fixed rule of law that a market is essential to valuation, this seems to be a tacit recognition that valuation of an isolated obligation without the aid of market evidence may simply not be meaningful enough to be indulged in most cases. So, once again, it seems that the ascertainable value test is just about as dependent upon the existence of a market as the cash equivalence doctrine.

The Court of Appeals in Warren Jones also noted without comment the Tax Court's observation that requiring a cash-basis taxpayer to value an obligation upon receipt would blur the distinction between the cash and accrual methods of reporting. As an original proposition, it is far from clear how telling this point is: since §1001 makes no reference to the taxpayer's method of accounting, the implication may be that accounting method does not matter, in which event a special doctrine for cash-basis taxpayers, like cash equivalency, would be hard to justify. On the other hand, in a Ruling promulgated after Warren Jones, the Service itself has treated accounting method as overriding the valuation procedure set out in §1001, insisting that taxpayers on the accrual basis are required by that method to recognize the full face amount of any deferred payment obligation received in exchange for property (subject to adjustment for imputed interest, and perhaps a reasonable allowance for bad debts). Rev. Rul. 79-292, 1979-2 Cum. Bull. 287. The Ruling holds that recognizing merely the value of a deferred payment obligation, whether received in the ordinary course of business or upon a casual sale, "is inconsistent with the well-established principle that an accrual method taxpayer includes in income amounts which it has a right to receive"; since the transfer of property in exchange for the deferred payment obligation fixed the right to receive the full face amount, the accrual-basis taxpayer could not include just the fair market value of the obligation in income (which is referred to in the Ruling as the "cash method treatment specified in §1001").

Notice that as a result of Rev. Rul. 79-292, there is no danger that requiring cash-basis taxpayers to include the value of deferred payment obligations in income upon receipt will blur the distinction between the cash and accrual methods, as the Tax Court in Warren Jones feared. But more to the present point, if the valuation of deferred payment obligations seemingly called for by §1001 is overridden by the accrual method, the same could be true of the cash method, which would make a special test like cash equivalency for cash-basis taxpayers entirely in order. The Ruling's characterization of the fair market value approach specified in §1001 as the "cash method" was probably designed to undercut this line of argument. Another possible rationalization for the Ruling is that a promise to pay money in the future is not embraced by the term "property" as used in §1001, which would take such obligations outside the specific valuation-upon-receipt formulation in the statute and instead simply leave them subject to whatever treatment is called for by the cash or accrual method, as the case may be. Emphasis on the existence of a market in the case of cash-basis taxpayers would be consistent with this view, since a marketable obligation is treated like other property under the cash basis, and hence would be subject to valuation upon receipt pursuant under §1001. For a comprehensive analysis of Rev. Rul. 79-292, and its implications for the tax treatment of deferred payment obligations generally, see Meives, Revenue Ruling 79-292 and Deferred Reporting 36 U. of Miami L. Rev. 175 1982).

In the few cases that have arisen since Warren Jones, the Tax Court has been able to sidestep any conflict with the Court of Appeals for the Ninth Circuit by finding that it was not possible to ascertain the fair market value of the obligations in question. Thus in McShain v. Commissioner, 71 T.C. 998 (1979), a note secured by a second mortgage on a hotel leasehold was found not to have an ascertainable fair market value, in view of the facts that the cash flow projections made payment of the note quite speculative, the fifteen-year term of the note was substantially longer than normal for second-mortgage financing, and there was no real market for the note.

In Estate of Wiggins v. Commissioner, 72 T.C. 701 (1979), the court held that contracts for the sale of house lots, involving a down payment of only 5% of the sales price and monthly payments of only 1%, did not have an ascertainable fair market value. More than one-third of the contracts executed during the taxable years were voided for lack of payment. Although each contract was secured by the lot conveyed, the lots were subject to prior liens and other encumbrances. The court found that in these circumstances banks and other financial institutions would neither buy the contracts nor lend money against them, and private investors would not be interested in such contracts until they were "seasoned" by the payment of a substantial number of the monthly installments. In short, there was simply no present market for these instruments. The court acknowledged that the contracts were not valueless, but concluded that "it was impossible to determine with fair certainty the market value of the contracts . . . as of the date of sale under the traditional definition of fair market value".

In both of these cases the court observed that the absence of a readily ascertainable fair market value made it unnecessary to deal with the issues presented in Warren Jones. However, one of the court's arguments in Wiggins does seem to suggest that the Tax Court will continue to resist valuation of an obligation upon receipt when a deep discount is involved. After observing that "fair market value envisions a willing seller as well as a willing buyer", the court noted that the very business of the taxpayers was to sell lots on the stated basis, and there was no reason to think they would have been willing to dispose of these contracts for 60% of the unpaid face value (the figure at which the government expert had valued the contracts); hence the court doubted "that there would be a meeting of the minds on a sale". This approach could be used to reject valuation upon receipt whenever the result would be a substantial discount (unless perchance the taxpayer actually engages in sales of such obligations under similar circumstances).

3.   Impact of Amended §453 on the Open Transaction Method

The serious doubts raised by the Warren Jones case as to whether cash basis taxpayers have any special entitlement to use the open transaction method have been significantly increased since 1980 as a result of the amendment of §453 mentioned above. For one thing, there is language in the accompanying Committee Reports which suggests an intention to limit sharply the use of the open transaction method. The section of the Senate Finance Committee Report dealing with the topic of "Sales Subject to a Contingency", after describing the change allowing such sales to qualify for the installment method and then explaining how the statute would apply in such cases, concludes as follows (S.Rep.No. 96-1000, 96th Cong., 2d Sess. 24):

> "The creation of a statutory deferred payment option for all forms of deferred payment sales significantly expands the availability of installment reporting to include situations where it has not previously been permitted. By providing an expanded statutory installment reporting option, the Committee believes that in the future there should be little incentive to devise convoluted forms of deferred payment obligations to attempt to obtain deferred reporting. In any event, the effect of the new rules is to reduce substantially the justification for treating transactions as "open" and permitting the use of the cost-recovery method sanctioned by Burnet v. Logan, 283 U.S. 404 (1931). Accordingly, it is the Committee's intent that the cost-recovery method not be available in the case of sales for a fixed price (whether the seller's obligation is evidenced by a note, contractual promise, or otherwise), and that its use be limited to those rare and extraordinary cases involving sales for a contingent price where the fair market value of the purchaser's obligation cannot reasonably be ascertained."

Despite its location in the Report, it is not easy to confine the thrust of this excerpt to contingent payment cases of the Burnet v. Logan type. The specific reference to "sales for a fixed price" in the first clause of the last sentence clearly suggests otherwise, since a fixed price is virtually the antithesis of a classic Burnet v. Logan case. Moreover, the

parenthetical reference to the question of whether the obligation "is evidenced by a note, contractual promise, or otherwise"
seems clearly directed at eliminating the relevance of a factor
which had often been regarded as highly significant in the cash
basis cases. And the final clause seems a clear statement that
in no event should the open transaction method apply unless the
price is contingent.

On the other hand, there is nothing in the words of the new
statute itself which limits the applicability of the open transaction method, so this language in the Report may well be mostly
designed to endorse strongly the very narrow scope for the open
transaction method that cases like Warren Jones had already
found under §1001. Thus far, the commentators appear to have
assumed that the revision of §453 did not completelely eliminate
the right of a cash basis taxpayer to qualify for open transaction treatment for a fixed payment obligation. E.g., Emory and
Hjorth, An Analysis of Changes Made by the Installment Sales Act
of 1980--Part I, 54 J. Taxation 66 (Feb. 1981).

In any event, quite apart from the impact of this language
in the Report it is clear that the new statute imposes a serious
practical restraint upon the use of the open transaction method,
as a result of that requirement in §453(d) that the taxpayer
must affirmatively "elect out" of the installment method in
order to use any other method. First, merely as a matter of
inertia this will undoubtedly reduce resort to the open transaction method. More important, it will assure disclosure of the
transaction in the year of the sale, thereby effectively ending
the practice, condoned by some practitioners under the prior
law, of making no reference to the sale in the year of disposition on the ground that the open transaction was applicable and
payments had not yet exceeded the basis of the property sold.
Under this practice many a doubtful application of the open
transaction method never came to the Government's attention, at
least in time to permit effective response. Moreover, the
natural limitation on this approach--fear of being forced to
report on the closed transaction method if the use of the open
transaction was detected in time and successfully challenged--
was rendered largely inoperative when taxpayers who were denied
the right to use the open transaction method were then permitted
simply to shift to the installment method. Though there was a
well-established rule that the installment method could not be
elected once an inconsistent method had been used for the transaction, this was held not applicable when the method initally
chosen turned out to be invalid. E.g., Mamula v. Commissioner,
346 F.2d 1016 (9th Cir. 1965). Obviously, if the taxpayer could
always fall back on the reasonably favorable installment method,
there was little reason not to give the even more attractive
open transaction method a whirl.

The conditional election of the installment method in
Warren Jones (in case open transaction reporting was rejected)
was a variant of this practice, although at least under that

approach the existence of the transaction was disclosed at the
outset. As noted above, under the amended §453 the open transaction can not be used without disclosing the transaction in the
year it occurs, by virtue of the necessity of electing out of
the installment method under §453(d). And there does not seem
to be any possibility of making a conditional election or otherwise preserving a right to fall back on the installment method
in case the open transaction method should be subsequently ruled
invalid; §453(d)(3) provides flatly that an "election out" can
not be revoked without consent, which does not appear to leave
any room for mitigation just because a preferred alternative
method turns out to be unavailable. Hence the taxpayer who
tries for the open transaction and fails will be stuck with the
closed transaction approach, an in terrorem posture that seems
likely to result in a considerable decline in efforts to use the
open transaction method.

4.   The "Closed Transaction" Method

As noted earlier, inclusion of the fair market value of a
deferred payment obligation upon receipt in "amount realized"
under §1001 is often referred to as the "closed transaction"
method (although the Warren Jones opinion does not use the
term), connoting the fact that the original exchange transaction
is closed at that point and a final tax balance is struck, with
gain or loss measured by the difference between the basis of the
property surrendered and the sum of any cash plus the fair
market value of any property (including the obligation) received
in the exchange. To appreciate the concern of the Tax Court in
Warren Jones that the closed transaction approach might lead to
a transmutation of capital gain into ordinary income, it is
necessary to consider how the payments thereafter received on
the obligation are treated for tax purposes. One important
corollary of closing the original transaction is that the deferred
payment obligation takes a basis in the hands of the recipient
equal to the figure at which it was valued and included in
amount realized upon receipt. The other is that the subsequent
collection of the obligation constitutes a separate and distinct
transaction, on which there must be reckoning of gain or loss
measured by the difference between the total of the payments (of
principal) on the obligation and its new basis. E.g., Tombari
v. Commissioner, 299 F.2d 889 (9th Cir. 1962).

For this new transaction, there must also be an analysis de
novo of whether the gain or loss involved is capital, since the
nature of the original transaction is no longer relevant. The
problem that worried the Tax Court in Warren Jones stems from
the fact that, initially, collection of the payments due on an
obligation does not constitute a "sale or exchange" of the
obligation, as required for capital treatment under §1222.
Fairbanks v. United States, 306 U.S. 436 (1939). That deficiency has since been partially remedied by §1232(a)(1), which
extends capital treatment to the repayment of certain types of
corporate and governmental obligations, by treating the payments

in such cases as received "in exchange" for the obligation.
However, §1232(a)(1) does not apply to the obligations of individuals, which is why the taxpayer in Warren Jones stood to have
ordinary income on the difference between the figure at which
the obligation was valued for inclusion in "amount realized" and
the total proceeds ultimately collected).

Obviously, a taxpayer whose original transaction qualifies
for capital gain treatment would find the prospect of the closed
transaction approach all the more unwelcome if it is accompanied
by ordinary income treatment for gain upon repayment of the
obligation. Indeed, the taxpayer may face something of a dilemma
in such circumstances, when it comes to valuing the obligation
upon receipt pursuant to the closed transaction approach. A low
value for the obligation would have the advantage of minimizing
the taxpayer's capital gain at the outset, but the unwelcome
corollary would be a low basis for the obligation and hence a
larger amount of ordinary income upon receipt of the payments.
On the other hand, a high value for the obligation would increase
the immediate capital gain tax burden (without, of course,
producing any additional cash with which to pay the higher tax);
and if perchance the taxpayer should overshoot the mark and
value the obligation at more than the amount ultimately received,
he would presumably end up with only a capital loss (from a
non-business bad debt) of uncertain tax benefit. The Tax Court
in Warren Jones was obviously more moved by the plight of a
taxpayer in these circumstances than the Court of Appeals, which
was content to remit the taxpayer to the statutory relief provided by the legislature in the form of the installment method
of accounting. Of course this problem does not arise in the
case of a corporate or government obligation, on which gain
would be eligible for capital treatment under §1232(a)(1), since
then the taxpayer can safely try to value the obligation upon
receipt as low as possible, secure in the knowledge that the excess of the payments ultimately received over that value will
qualify as capital gain.

Whether the gain realized upon collection of an obligation
is ordinary or capital, there is also the question of when it
should be recognized. One possibility is to apply all of the
payments (of principal, that is, since interest, whether express
or imputed, is always treated separately) to recovery of the
basis of the obligation first, with no gain recognized until the
total receipts exceed the basis (similar to the way that under
the open transaction approach all payments are applied first
against the basis of the asset sold). However, most of the
cases appear to follow the other alternative, under which each
payment is allocated proportionately between return of basis and
taxable gain, e.g., Gilbert v. Commissioner, 6 T.C. 10 (1946);
the Tombari case, supra, assumed without discussion that this
was the proper course. The same approach is taken when an
installment obligation is purchased at a discount for cash in
the market, rather then received in exchange for property: the
discount is normally allocated on some rational basis among the

installments, and that portion of each installment payment must be recognized by the holder as gain (ordinary or capital, according to the circumstances). E.g., Darby Investment Corporation v. Commissioner, 315 F.2d 551 (6th Cir. 1963); Rev. Rul. 73-558, 1973-2 Cum. Bull. 298.

A major reason for this outcome lies in the analogy to accounting for express interest on an installment obligation, where it is standard practice to treat some portion of each installment as interest, and only the remainder of the installment as a payment of principal. When the discount from the face amount of an obligation to its value upon receipt represents simply an adjustment in interest to bring it up to the market rate for the use of money, there seems little reason why recognition of the indirect component of interest represented by the discount should not parallel the reporting of express interest. However, the situation is different when the obligation is highly speculative, resulting in a discount which is much greater than a mere adjustment of the interest rate because it reflects a substantial risk of default in payment of the obligation. In some cases of this kind, involving obligations purchased for cash, the uncertainty of repayment has led to permitting the taxpayer to recover his entire basis in the obligation before having to recognize any gain. E.g., Phillips v. Frank, 295 F.2d 629 (9th Cir. 1961). In Underhill v. Commissioner, 45 T.C. 489 (1966), the court held that the "ultimate test" for postponing recognition of the discount until after recovery of the basis of the obligation is whether the purchaser of the obligation "cannot be reasonably certain that he will recover his cost and a major portion of the discount". Among the factors listed by the court for making this determination were the general financial responsibility of the debtor, the extent of the security for the obligation, the marketability of the obligation, and the size of the discount.

In theory, obligations received in exchange for property should be equally subject to the Underhill test for when to recognize gain from a discount, but in practice the issue will probably rarely arise. That is because the elements of the test are the same as those which would determine whether an obligation received for property by a cash-basis taxpayer constitutes a cash equivalent. Accordingly, an obligation speculative enough to bring Underhill into play would presumably have been eligible for open transaction treatment on the original exchange, in which event the obligation would not have been valued upon receipt and no question of discount would arise.

5. A Further Look at Discount

The foregoing material suggests the wisdom of a more detailed analysis of the nature of "discount." Let us start with the simple case of a loan of $1000 for one year with interest at 8%. Obviously, when the creditor receives $1080 one year later, $1000 represents a repayment of principal and the additional $80 is interest, includible in ordinary income for tax purposes. If instead the creditor lends $1000 upon an obligation purporting simply to call for the payment of $1080 one year later, without interest, again the creditor would receive $80 more than he originally advanced, and the economic effect of the transaction is exactly the same as if there had been an express provision for interest at 8%. In the second case, no less than in the first, the extra $80 received by the creditor surely represents compensation for the use of the money by the debtor, and therefore constitutes interest.

Looking at such transactions from a different vantage point, no prospective creditor would advance as much as $1080 in exchange for a right merely to receive $1080 one year later, without any interest, since the creditor would insist upon some compensation for the use of whatever money he did advance. Speaking more generally, a deferred maturity obligation without interest cannot command a price as large as the face amount of the obligation. Instead, a prospective creditor would compute the amount which when augmented by interest thereon, at an appropriate rate for the period involved, would equal the face amount of the obligation. In other words, the creditor would attempt to determine the present value of such a deferred payment obligation without interest, by making allowance for the delay in getting the money back (plus the risk of possible non-payment). This is known as "discounting" the obligation to present value. The discounted present value of a deferred maturity obligation without interest may properly be regarded as the "real" principal sum involved in the obligation; and the difference between that present value and the face amount of the obligation (which really represents an interest component) is what is usually referred to as "discount". (Obviously, a discount may also be present even when the obligation expressly provides for interest, if the specified interest rate is lower than it should be for that particular obligation.)

When the appropriate interest rate for the obligation can be ascertained, the discounted present value of a deferred maturity obligation without interest can be determined from a so-called "discount" table, which gives the present discounted value of $1 payable after a specified number of years at a specified interest rate. That is, the table shows the various figures that will amount to $1 after varying numbers of years of delay, on the basis of varying interest rates. To determine the value of a right to receive $1080 after one year, assuming that 8% would be the appropriate interest rate for the transaction, one would start with the figure shown on the table as the present value of $1 payable at the end of one year with interest at 8%, which is .926, and then multiply by $1080. The resulting figure is, as should be expected, $1000.

Of course it is often difficult to ascertain the appropriate interest rate for a particular transaction with any precision since that depends upon such diverse factors as the financial strength of the particular debtor and the current

state of the money market. Even so, it may be possible to make
at least a rational estimate of the appropriate interest rate,
and that is obviously preferable to ignoring the discount entirely.
Moreover, in many cases the present value of an obligation may
be obtained from some independent evidence, such as the consideration given for the obligation in an arm's length transaction, or
the existence of a ready market for such obligations; in effect,
the "market" performs the operation of discounting the obligation
to present value. The fair market value of the obligation
constitutes the real principal sum involved, and the excess of
the face amount of the obligation over the fair market value
represents the discount, or interest component, in the transaction.

This concept of discount is no stranger to the tax law, and
over the years there have been numerous cases grappling with the
question of whether and when a discount should be focused and
taxed in the same manner as express interest. The matter is now
largely governed by statute. As to debt obligations issued for
cash, §1232(a)(2) ferrets out any "original issue discount"
(defined in §1232(b)(1) as "the difference between the issue
price and the stated redemption price at maturity") and subjects
it to ordinary income taxation. Prior to the adoption of these
provisions, a creditor who made a loan to a corporation on a
discount basis, i.e., calling for the repayment of a larger sum
instead of providing expressly for interest, stood a good chance
of avoiding any ordinary income on the transaction. The excess
of the amount received at maturity over the amount of the original
loan could qualify as gain from the sale or exchange of a capital
asset, pursuant to §1232(a)(1) which, as noted earlier, supplies
the needed "sale or exchange" treatment for receipt of payment
of a debt obligation when the obligor is a corporation (though
not when the obligor is an individual). Capital gain treatment
for what in effect constitutes interest income was costly to the
Government, especially since corporate debtors had long been
allowed to deduct discount against ordinary income, by way of
writing off the discount proportionately over the life of the
obligation. In any event, §1232(a)(2) has eliminated capital
gain treatment for the creditor in such circumstances, making it
clear that if, say, a taxpayer advanced $1000 for a debt instru-
ment calling for the payment of $1080 at the end of a year, the
$80 spread constitutes original issue discount under §1232(b)
and is taxed as ordinary income under §1232(a)(2).

Prior to the Tax Reform Act of 1969, a taxpayer could
postpone reporting original issue discount until the maturity of
the obligation (or its sale to a third party). The 1969 Act
required that a pro rata portion of any original issue discount
be reported by the holder each year (even if he was a cash-basis
taxpayer), which paralleled the annual amortization of the
discount allowed to the issuer of the obligation. The same rule
applied to any subsequent purchaser of the bond, subject to an
adjustment to take account of any reduction in the discount
reflected by the purchaser's cost.

The Tax Equity and Financial Responsibility Act of 1982 changed the rules to require that original issue discount be accounted for by both the issuer and the holder on a basis which corresponds more nearly to the actual economic accrual of interest than ratable allocation over the term of the obligation does. Under §1232A the original issue discount is recognized on an ascending scale, computed by assuming a fixed interest rate applied to a principal amount which starts out equal to the issue price and increases each year by the amount of the discount recognized to date. To take a polar illustration, suppose that on January 1, 1984, a $1000 bond payable at the end of five years without interest is issued to the holder for $681. Interest tables would be consulted to determine that the effective interest "yield" to maturity, that is, the interest rate which compounded annually for five years would raise $681 to $1,000, is 8%. Accordingly, 8% of $681, or $54.50, would be treated as the amount of the interest allocable to the first year of the bond, 1984, and that amount of the total discount would be recognized as interest income by the holder, and as interest expense by the issuer in 1984. For the second year, 1985, the principal amount of the obligation would be viewed as the sum of $681 and the $54.50 recognized as income, or $735.50; 8% of that amount, or $58.80, would be treated as the amount of the original issue discount to be included as interest income by the holder, and deducted as interest expense by the issuer, in 1985. For 1986, the amount of the original issue discount treated as interest by both the holder and the issuer would be $63.50 (8% x ($735.50 + $58.80)). For 1987 the interest would be $68.60, and for 1988, $74.10, making the cumulative total over the five years equal to the total original issue discount of $319 (except for rounding off adjustments).

These same rules are applicable to any original issue discount on obligations issued for cash which expressly provide for interest. They may also apply to express interest itself, if it is all payable at maturity, rather than annually or more often, e.g., a five-year obligation in the amount of $681, with express interest at 8% but all payable at maturity.

Needless to say, the term of an obligation does not normally coincide so neatly with the tax year of the holder and the issuer; for computation purposes, original issue discount is regarded as accruing on a daily basis. Thus if the above bond had been issued on July 1, 1984, the interest for the calendar year 1984 would be 184/365 x $54.50, or $27.45; for calendar year 1985, the interest would be 181/365 x $54.50 plus 184/365 x $58.80, or $56.70. Similar computations are called for when an obligation is transferred, in order to allocate the original issue discount between the transferor and the transferee (subject, as before, to a reduction in the amount of the transferee's interest income to take account of any decline in the discount reflected by the price he paid for the obligation).

454

Obviously, this approach to the allocation of original
issue discount requires some revision for installment obligation, since, as we shall be reviewing in some detail shortly,
the amount of principal outstanding declines with each payment.
Suffice it to say at this point that the Regulations in effect
treat each installment as a separate obligation, and provide a
formula for allocating the total discount among the several
installments (which in the case of level annual installments
works out to a kind of reverse sum of the years-digits method as
used in depreciation). Reg. §1.1232-3(b)(2)(iv)(f).

Under §6049 the issuer is required to file information
returns with respect to original issue discount income which is
taxable to the holders under §1232A (ignoring any adjustment in
the case of a transfer of the obligation), and the 1982 Act
reinforced this reporting requirement by mandating that thereafter obligations of a year's duration or more be registered,
unless they are not of a type offered to the public (or are
issued by an individual). The 1982 Act also made original issue
discount subject to the new rules for withholding tax on interest;
but since IRC §3455 limits the amount which can be withheld to
the cash received during the year, the withholding will actually
operate only in the year of redemption of the obligation.

It is important to note that original issue discount does
not arise with respect to obligations issued for property other
than cash, being expressly precluded by §1232(b)(2) (except
where the obligations, or the property exchanged for them, are
publicly traded). Hence, harking back for a moment to the
discussion above of the closed transaction method of accounting
for a deferred payment obligation received in exchange for
property, any discount which may result from valuing the obligation at less than face for inclusion in amount realized is not
subject to the rules governing original issue discount (and
hence, at least in the case of a corporate or government obligation, may qualify for capital gain treatment). However, obligations issued in exchange for property are subject to their own
special, limited form of discount accounting, pursuant to IRC
§483, which will be analyzed in detail below; under that provision, if a deferred payment obligation received in exchange for
property has too low an express interest rate, additional interest
will be imputed, somewhat paralleling the treatment of original
issue discount.

D. ACCOUNTING FOR INTEREST ON INSTALLMENT OBLIGATIONS

1. Express Interest

When an obligation is payable in installments, the question
arises as to how much of each installment represents interest.
So far as express interest is concerned, unless the parties have
otherwise agreed it seems logical to suppose that each installment
includes the interest due to that date. For a simple example of
an installment obligation, suppose that a creditor who makes a

loan of $1,000 for one year at 8% interest is not willing to
wait until the end of the year before receiving any repayment,
and instead insists upon getting back half of the loan at the
end of six months. It would make sense for the creditor to ask
that the interest for the first six months also be paid at that
time; then the other half of the principal, plus the additional
interest covering the second six months, would be payable at the
end of the year. Thus the transaction would take the form of a
two-installment obligation, the first installment composed of
$500 of principal plus $40 of interest, representing interest at
8% on $1000 for a half year, and the second installment composed
of the remaining $500 of principal plus $20 of interest, representing interest at 8% on $500 for half a year.

Obviously, there is no difficulty in isolating the interest
component in these two installments. However, it is worth
noting that the total interest of $60 is $20 less than in the
case where none of the principal is repaid until the end of the
year, because the debtor has had the use of only $500 for the
second six months, instead of the full $1000. As a corollary,
the second installment is smaller than the first even though the
amount of principal repayment is the same in both.

This kind of repayment schedule, with the interest accrued
to date added to each installment, can be used no matter how
long the term of the obligation, or how frequent the installments;
and of course if each installment includes the same amount of
principal, the total of each installment will decline, reflecting
a decline in the amount of interest for the period because of a
decrease in the amount of principal outstanding. However, the
parties often prefer, as a matter of administrative convenience,
to have the amount of each installment be the same; that is,
they want to use equal installments to discharge (or, as it is
often termed, "amortize") the principal and interest on the
obligation. Once again, resort to the appropriate interest
tables makes this entirely feasible. To see what is involved,
note that for any given principal sum and interest rate the
amount of each installment is dependent upon the number (and
timing) of the installments, and vice versa; in other words, if
the parties decide on the number of years for which installments
are to be paid (typically either annual or semi-annual), that
will fix the amount of each installment needed to amortize the
obligation, while if they start with the amount of each installment, that will determine the number of years for which installments are to be paid.

To illustrate, assume that the parties have decided to
amortize the simple obligation of $1000 at 8% interest by two
equal semi-annual installments, instead of the uneven payments
of $540 and $520. It should be obvious that the amount of the
two equal payments would not be $530, i.e. one-half of the total
principal and interest as computed above, since that schedule
would postpone the payment of $10 from the first installment to
the second without providing any compensation for the delay.

Just as the right to receive $10 immediately is worth more than the right to receive $10 at the end of six months, the difference being the value of interest on $10 for six months, so an obligation calling for the payment of $540 at the end of six months plus $520 at the end of a year is worth more than an obligation calling for the payment of $530 at the end of six months and $530 at the end of a year. However, the precise amount of the two equal semi-annual installments which will amortize the principal and interest on an obligation of $1000 at 8% can be readily obtained from one of the interest tables. The table gives the amount per year needed to amortize the principal and interest on an obligation of $1 at varying rates of interest and numbers of installments. Since the table normally assumes annual installments, an adjustment is necessary to apply it to a case of semi-annual installments. Based on the fact that the amount of interest on a given principal sum at a specified rate of interest for half a year is exactly the same as the amount of interest on the same principal sum at one-half the specified interest rate for a full year, the instant transaction can be viewed as an obligation of $1000 being amortized in two annual installments at 4% interest. Thus in order to find the amount of the two equal semi-annual installments which will amortize $1000 at 8% interest, we can simply take from the table the figure which will amortize $1 at 4% in two annual installments and multiply it by $1000. The resulting amount is $530.20.

Notice that the total of the two payments is $1060.40, which is 40 cents more than when the transaction took the form of paying $540 at the end of the first six months and $520 at the end of the second six months. That is due to the fact that with the equal installments the debtor has the use of an extra $9.80 for the second six months, on which the interest at an annual rate of 8% amounts to 40 cents.

When a schedule of equal installment payments is adopted, the question arises as to the amount of the interest component in each installment. It should not be assumed that the amount of interest included in the first installment is $30.20, one-half of the total interest in the transaction, since that would be inconsistent with the general premise noted earlier that each installment includes all interest accrued to date. Under this premise, the interest component in the first payment would be equal to the total interest to date of $40 (8% on $1000 for half a year); as a corollary, only $490.20 ($530.20 less $40) of the principal has been repaid at the end of the first six months, and the debtor still has the use of $509.80 of principal for the next six months. Hence the interest component of the installment paid at the end of the second six months should equal the interest on $509.80 at 8% for half a year, or $20.40. And these figures prove out, since the total of the two interest components equals $60.40, and the total of the two principal components equals $1000.

To see how this analysis applies to more complex, longer-term obligations, consider an obligation to pay $250,000 with interest at 8% in equal semi-annual installments for twenty years (a total of 40 payments). From the interest table we can determine the required amount for 40 annual, equal payments to amortize $250,000 plus interest at 4%. That figure is $12,630, and, as indicated above, it follows that 40 equal semi-annual payments of $12,630 would amortize $250,000 plus interest at 8%. The amount of interest in the first installment would be $10,000 (8% on $250,000 for half a year), and the remaining $2,630 would constitute repayment of principal. As a result, the principal outstanding for the second six months would be only $247,370 ($250,000 - $2,630), so the interest in the second $12,630 installment would be $9,895 (8% on $247,370 for half a year), and the remaining $2,735 would constitute repayment of principal. That in turn means that the principal outstanding for the third six-months period would be $244,635 ($247,370 - $2,735), so the interest component in the third $12,630 installment would be $9,785 (8% on $244,635 for half a year), and the principal component would be $2,845. This running calculation can be carried out for each of the remaining 37 installments.

Allocating interest among the periodic payments on an installment obligation in this way reflects the amount of interest which actually accrues each period as a matter of economics -- indeed, this approach is sometimes described as "economic accrual". It is also frequently referred to as the "declining-balance" method (a term perhaps more familiar in depreciation accounting), because the interest component declines in each successive installment, reflecting the decrease in the principal outstanding due to the fact that each installment includes some repayment of principal. One other label often used is the "constant interest" method, connoting the fact that it applies the same rate of interest (to a declining amount of principal) throughout the duration of the indebtedness. In this respect it parallels the method described above for reflecting original issue discount under §1232A (although of course §1232A produces increasing interest charges because there the constant interest rate is being applied to what is in effect a rising principal balance outstanding).

There are two other systems which can be used to allocate interest among the payments on an installment obligation, as long as the total amount of the interest on the obligation is known (which is usually the case, since it is simply the difference between the sum of all the installments and the face amount of the obligation). One is really just a rough-

hewn way of approximating the computation of interest on the
declining-balance (constant interest) basis, and it works
just like the sum of the years-digits depreciation method.
A homely example involving monthly installments, as on a
residential mortgage, will serve to illustrate. Suppose a
debtor agrees to repay a loan of $1,000, with interest at
12%, in twelve equal monthly installments, which according
to the interest tables would have to amount to $88.85 each.
Twelve payments of $88.85 add up to $1066.20, so it is
evident that the total interest on the transaction amounts
to $66.20 (substantially less than 12% on $1,000 for a year,
of course, since the full $1,000 of principal is outstanding
only for the first month, and by the last month the outstanding principal is less than $90). Under the sum of the
years-digits approach, all of the digits representing the
number of installments are added together, i.e., 1 + 2 + 3
and so forth, through 12, which totals to 78. The interest
in any installment is then determined by multiplying the
total interest on the obligation by a fraction of which the
denominator is the sum of the digits, here 78, and the
numerator is the number of the particular installment from
the end. Under this formula, the interest component in the
first installment would be 12/78 x $66.20 or $10.18; in the
second installment, the interest would be 11/78 x $66.20, or
$9.34; and in the third installment, 10/78 x $66.20, or
$8.49.

Of course these figures are not exactly the same as
those derived from a strict application of the economic
accrual declining-balance method: a precise running calculation shows that the interest component in the first $88.85
monthly installment is $10 (12% on $1,000 for one-twelfth of
a year), leaving $78.85 as repayment of principal; the
interest in the second installment would be $9.21 (12% on
$921.15 for one month), leaving $79.64 as repayment of
principal; for the third installment the interest would be
$8.40, and the repayment of principal $80.45. However, the
sum of the years-digits method does serve to allocate interest on a declining basis over the term of the loan.

Owing to its frequent use in allocating interest among
twelve monthly installments, where the sum of the digits
adds up to 78, this method is often referred to as the Rule
of 78's. However, the approach is workable no matter what
the number of the installments, so long as the total amount
of interest can be determined, and the installments are

evenly spaced. To illustrate, take the obligation above of
$250,000 with interest at 8%, to be amortized by 40 semi-
annual payments of $12,630, where the total interest can be
readily ascertained as the excess of $505,200 (the sum of 40
installments of $12,630 each) over the face amount of $250,000,
or $255,200. The sum of the digits from 1 to 40 is 820, so
the amount of interest in the first $12,630 installment
would be 40/820 x $255,200, or $12,400, leaving only $230 as
repayment of principal. In the second installment, the
interest component would be 39/820 x $255,200, or $12,090,
leaving $540 as repayment of princpal; and in the third
installment, the interest would be 38/820 x $255,200, or
$11,780, leaving $850 as repayment of principal.

Look back at the declining-balance schedule for the
first three installments of this obligation set out above,
and notice how much greater a disparity results under the
Rule of 78's than was the case with the foregoing twelve-
month obligation. Actually, the Rule of 78's always over-
states the amount of interest in the earliest installments,
with an offsetting understatement for the later installments,
but this departure from precise economic accrual is accentuated as the duration of the obligation lengthens and the
interest rate increases. Not surprisingly, the overstatement of interest in the early installments, and the consequent understatement of the amount of principal repaid, made
the Rule of 78's a favorite among lenders as the method for
computing the amount of principal still owing on an installment loan in case of a premature termination of the obligation. On the other side of the coin, borrowers found the
Rule of 78's very much to their liking for computing the
amount of interest deductible for tax purposes.

Another common system of reflecting interest (and
another analogy to depreciation accounting) is the "straight-
line" basis, under which the interest is allocated pro rata
among the installments: in the typical case of equal installments, each installment would be treated as including
the same amount of interest. Thus in the foregoing situation, where the total interest is known to be $225,200, each
of the 40 equal installments of $12,630 could be viewed as
including interest in the amount of 1/40 x $255,200, or
$6,380. While this method is even simpler administratively
than the Rule of 78's, it is also even more inconsistent
with the economic accrual of interest, substantially under-
stating the interest over the first half of the obligation's
life and overstating interest over the last half.

2. Discount

Thus far we have been considering obligations which expressly provide for interest. As we have seen, however, an obligation may include an interest factor even though none is expressed, in the form of a discount, and that is just as true of an install-ment obligation as it is for an instrument with a single maturity date. Thus, when a creditor receives an obligation which entitles him to $530.20 after six months, together with $530.20 after one year, without interest, that obligation is worth less $1060.40, and the amount of the difference, or discount, represents interest. In the absence of any independent measure of the fair market value of the obligation, its discounted present value might be judged by estimating the appropriate rate of interest for the obligation, and then using the applicable interest table to find the amount which would be amortized by two semi-annual install-ments of $530.20 at that interest rate. (This computation is just the converse of the one examined earlier, involving determin-ation of the size and number of installments which will amortize a given principal sum at a specified interest rate.) Assuming that 8% would be the appropriate interest rate for this transac-tion, the discounted present value of the obligation would of course be $1000. Therefore, such an obligation should be treated the same as if it were expressly a $1000 obligation at 8% being amortized in two semi-annual installments of $530.20.

The amount of the discount-interest included in each install-ment can be computed in the same fashion as for express interest, i.e., on a formal declining-balance basis, by the less formal Rule of 78's, or on the straight-line basis. The latter two methods are particularly inviting when the discount can be determined by independent evidence of the fair market value of the obligation. Thus, suppose that the value of the foregoing obligation consisting of two semi-annual payments of $530.20 could be determined from extrinsic market evidence to be $1000. Obviously, it would be possible to resort to the interest tables to find the interest rate at which a fixed principal sum of $1000 would be amortized by two semi-annual payments of $530.20 each (which would, of course, be 8%); and that rate could then be used to determine the interest component in each installment. However, if the amount of the discount can be determined without reference to the interest tables, then either the Rule of 78's method or the straight-line basis can be used to calculate the amount of interest in each installment, and the interest tables will not be needed at all.

The issues are no different when there are many install-ments, as in the case of our illustrative obligation involving the amortization of $250,000 at 8% interest with 40 semi-annual payments of $12,630 each. Suppose that instead of starting with a given principal sum and interest rate the parties had simply agreed upon an obligation calling for 40 semi-annual payments of $12,630, without interest. The present value of this obliga-tion, which of course would be far less than $505,200 (the sum of the total installments), might be determined by estimating an appropriate interest rate and then using the interest tables to compute the "real" principal of the obligation. If instead there were extrinsic market evidence indicating the present value of the obligation, resort to the interest tables would be unnecessary, and the excess of $505,200 over the present value, representing the discount-interest, could be accounted for by using either the Rule of 78's or the straight-line method.

Strictly speaking, it may not be technically accurate
to speak of "discount" in connection with an obligation of
this kind. According to Canellos and Kleinhard, The Miracle
of Compound Interest: Interest Deferral and Discount after
1982, 38 Tax L. Rev. 565, 572 (1983), which contains an
excellent review of the whole subject, a true discount
obligation is one on which the interest is not paid in full
periodically, and at least some accumulated interest is
included with the principal in one or more maturity payments
at the end; that would not include an ordinary installment
loan, where the periodic payments regularly exceed the
current interest on the debt (however measured), and that
excess amortizes the principal of the debt by maturity. The
authors also describe a discount obligation as one on which
the current cash flow is less than the yield on the debt,
whereas on an installment loan the current cash flow exceeds
the yield. However, the Service and the courts regularly
use the term "discount" with respect to any obligation on
which the "real" interest is greater than the express rate,
and we will continue to do so here.

3. Choice of Method for Reporting Interest

Until quite recently it seemed to be generally accepted
that any arrangement between the parties as to the allocation of interest among the payments on an installment obligation would be controlling for tax purposes. Thus, in Revenue
Ruling 72-100, 1972-1 Cum. Bull. 122, involving installment
obligations which provided that in case of prepayment the
amount of interest paid to date (and hence the remaining
principal due at that time) should be computed pursuant to
the Rule of 78's, it was held that both borrower and lender,
whether on the cash or accrual basis, should follow that
method in reporting the interest for tax purposes. As to
accrual-basis taxpayers, the ruling referred to two earlier
tax cases which allowed lenders to report interest income
pursuant to the understanding between the parties for allocation of interest in the event of prepayment (while rejecting
efforts by the Service to require immediate recognition of
the entire amount of interest on the obligation). E.g.,
Gunderson Bros. Engineering Corp. v. Commissioner, 42 T.C.
419 (1964) (Rule of 78's approved where it was the method
used for determining the amount of principal still due in
case of prepayment); Luhring Motor Co. v. Commissioner,
42 T.C. 732 (1964)(straight-line allocation operative in
connection with prepayments was accepted for tax purposes).

However, the ruling also noted that in James Bros. Coal Co. v. Commissioner, 41 T.C. 917 (1964), where there was no evidence that the parties had any understanding about allocation of interest, with respect to prepayment or otherwise, the Tax Court insisted on the straight-line method, and refused to allow a deduction on the basis of a formula similar to the Rule of 78's. Rev. Rul. 72-100 was content to simply distinguish that case from the present obligations, which expressly invoked the Rule of 78's in case of prepayment, and the ruling made no comment on the merits of what the result should be in the absence of an understanding between the parties. Subsequently, Revenue Ruling 79-228, 79-2 Cum. Bull. 200, approved the use of a declining-balance method by an accrual-basis lender, noting that Rev. Rul. 72-100 had accepted the Rule of 78's, a method "predicated on the theory that interest earned on a loan should decline over the loan period in proportion to diminution of the unpaid principal balance".

As to cash-basis taxpayers, Rev. Rul. 72-100 offered more guidance on the question of how interest should be allocated when there is no relevant understanding between the parties. Revenue Ruling 70-647, 1970-2 Cum. Bull. 38, was cited for the general principle that, unless the parties have a different understanding, partial payments on an indebtedness should be applied first to any accumulated interest, which certainly suggests some kind of declining-balance method, as opposed to straight-line allocation. Oddly, Rev. Rul. 72-100 then rests its approval of the use of the Rule of 78's upon this general principle, noting that there was no evidence that the parties did not intend it to apply; the fact that the Rule of 78's was included in the terms of the obligation with respect to prepayment was not relied on.

Rev. Rul. 72-100 concluded with the significant observation that "the right of the borrower to compute his interest deduction on a loan under the Rule of 78's method is not affected by the lender's use of a different method in reporting interest income on the loan"; it is not easy to see when or why a difference in treatment between the borrower and the lender would be justified.

In any event, in Revenue Ruling 83-84, 1983-23 I.R.B. 12, the Service revoked its prior approval of the Rule of 78's. The ruling involves a 30-year installment loan of

$100,000 at 12%, which required the borrower to make equal
annual payments of $12,414 and provided for the allocation
of interest amont the installments in accordance with the
Rule of 78's. On the economic accrual, declining-balance
basis the amount of interest in the first installment would
have been $12,000 (12% on the original principal of $100,000),
whereas the Rule of 78's called for interest of $17,575 in
the first installment (an amount substantially in excess of
the whole installment). The ruling states that the amount
of interest attributable to the use of money between payments
is determined by applying the constant "effective" rate of
interest on the loan to the outstanding balance of the loan
for that period. Thus economic accrual is the true cost of
borrowing for the period, and no deduction for interest in
excess of that amount will be allowed, whether the taxpayer
is on the cash or accrual basis of accounting. Rulings
72-100 and 79-228 were both expressly modified to the extent
they accept the Rule of 78's as a proper method of computing
and reporting interest. (However, as a matter of administrative convenience the Service announced in Revenue Procedure
83-40, 1983-23 I.R.B. 22, that the Rule of 78's may still be
used in connection with short-term consumer loans (no longer
than five years) which expressly provide for allocation of
interest in accordance with the Rule of 78's.)

The specific holding of the ruling is directed to the
deduction of interest by borrowers, doubtless because the
primary concern was the overstatement of interest under the
Rule of 78's in the early installments of a long-term obligation. However, the broad sweep of the language endorsing
the economic accrual declining-balance method as the proper
measure of the true cost of borrowing certainly suggests
serious doubts about use of the straight-line method for
allocating interest (by lenders, in computing and reporting
their interest income). At the same time, although the
ruling deals with a simple cash loan there seems no reason
why it should not also apply to installment obligations
received upon the sale of property.

4. Separate Obligations Approach

There is one other possible view which may be taken of an
installment obligation that does not expressly provide for
interest. Returning for a moment to the simple obligation
involving two semi-annual installments of $530.20, each install-
ment might be regarded as a separate obligation, rather than as
one of the elements of a single overall obligation. That is,
each installment could be treated as a separate deferred maturity
obligation issued at a discount. Such a view of the transaction

would result in a substantial change in the computation of the interest component in each installment. If the first $530.20 installment, payable at the end of six months, was regarded as a separate obligation, it would be analyzed in the same way as the single payment discount obligation of $1080 due at the end of one year dealt with above. In other words, that first $530.20 installment would be discounted to present value by determining from the tables the amount which, together with interest thereon for six months at the rate determined to be appropriate, would total $530.20. Still assuming that an annual rate of 8% would be appropriate, we would look to the tables to find the present value, on the basis of interest at 4%, of $530.20 payable after one period: the answer is $509.80, and the remaining $20.40 would constitute the discount, or interest component.

Analyzing the second installment of $530.20, payable at the end of the year, as a separate deferred maturity obligation issued at a discount, the question would be what amount plus interest thereon at 8% for one year would total $530.20. (Remember that we are assuming the interest is compounded semi-annually, that is, interest attributable to the first six months would itself be entitled to earn interest during the second six months; accordingly, the question may be more precisely framed in terms of what amount plus interest thereon at 8% for six months, plus interest on the sum of those two items for another six months at 8%, would total $530.20. So we look to the tables for the present value, on the basis of interest at 4%, of $530.20 payable after two periods: the answer is $490.20, and the remaining $40.00 would constitute the discount, or interest component in that second installment, viewed as a separate obligation.

Notice that when each installment is treated as a separate discount obligation (instead of as part of a single overall obligation), the interest component increases with each installment instead of declining. Hence, even though the total amount of the interest over the full term of the obligation would be the same under either approach, the difference in the amount of interest found in any particular installment could be very substantial. For example, applying the separate obligation approach to the first two installments of the illustrative indebtedness of $250,000 being amortized by 40 semi-annual payments of $12,630 each, the interest components would be $485 and $955 respectively, whereas on the declining balance method the interest components in those two installments amounted to $10,000 and $9,895.

It seems unlikely that this view of an installment obligation as a series of individual discount obligations would be accepted when, as would normally be the case, the parties in fact started with a single obligation for a given principal sum, at a specified interest rate, which was thereafter transformed into an installment obligation. But if the parties were simply to agree on a series of consecutive equal periodic installments, without any single overall principal sum, or specified interest rate, this approach could be adopted. More important, only this

separate obligation method would make it possible to calculate
an interest component in each installment in cases like Burnet
v. Logan, where neither the number nor the amount of the installments is fixed, and hence the total principal (and interest) in the transaction cannot be determined.

5. Discount Combined with Express Interest

We have already noted that a discount may be present even
though the obligation expressly provides for interest, if the
price for the obligation is less than the face amount, indicating that the specified interest rate is lower than the interest rate required by the market for that obligation. See,
e.g., Leavin v. Commissioner, 37 T.C. 766 (1962) (debentures
with a 2% interest rate issued for cash prices less than face).
Thus, an obligation for $1,000 payable one year from date with
interest at 8% would have a present value of less than $1,000 if
the market required a higher rate for the obligation, say, 10%.
In the absence of other evidence of the fair market value of the
obligation, the discounted present value, and hence the real
principal sum involved, could be determined by looking to the
tables for the present value, on the basis of interest at 10%,
of a right to receive $1,080 at the end of a year. That figure
would be $981.70; and the difference between that amount and
$1,000 would constitute a discount, and hence an additional
element of interest.

An installment obligation too can involve a discount even
though it carries an express interest rate. For example, take
the obligation consisting of two semi-annual payments of $530.20
designed to amortize a principal sum of $1,000 at an express
interest rate of 8% in two installments. If the appropriate
rate for this obligation was actually 10%, it would not command
a price of $1,000; the discounted present value of the obliga-
tion, and hence the real principal sum involved, would be determined by finding in the tables the amount which at 10% would be
amortized by two semi-annual payments of $530.20 each. The
figure would be $985.53. The transaction could then be treated
exactly as if it expressly consisted of a fixed principal sum of
$985.53 at 10% interest being amortized by semi-annual payments
of $530.20, with the interest component of each installment
payment being determined in exactly the manner outlined earlier.

This approach of combining the discount with the express
interest, and accounting for the total on a declining-balance
basis, is in theory equally applicable to installment obligations stretching over a number of years. However, in practice,
at least for tax purposes, the treatment of discount is regu-
lated by statute, as we have seen. Thus, to the extent the
discount is the product of a cash issuance price less than the
face amount of the obligation, the original issue discount
provisions of §1232 will apply (leaving the express interest on
the obligation to be reflected as usual, either on a declining-
balance basis or straight-line, as the case may be). When the

obligation is issued for property, we noted earlier that no
original issue discount under §1232 will arise, but additional
interest might be imputed under §483 (to be discussed shortly);
any such imputed interest would be taxed in the manner called
for by §483 (again leaving the express interest to be treated in
the usual fashion).

6. Section 483

It is now time to take a detailed look at §483, which
operates to impute interest on deferred payment obligations
received in exchange for property. As we have seen, §1232(a)(2),
which mandates ordinary income treatment for original issue
discount on a debt obligation, was amended in 1969 to preclude
its application to obligations issued for property in most
circumstances. Even before that amendment a number of cases had
held that original issue discount did not arise with respect to
a debt obligation issued in exchange for property. This provided
a considerable opportunity for tax avoidance: the owner of a
depreciable capital asset could sell it for a deferred payment
obligation without interest and treat the entire face amount as
the purchase price, with all the gain taxable at capital rates
(at least prior to §§ 1245 and 1250), while the buyer would
suffer no disadvantage from the absence of an interest deduction
because of the higher depreciation deductions resulting from
treating the full face amount of the obligation as the cost, and
hence the basis, of the property acquired. Accordingly, in 1964
§483 was adopted to make sure that a reasonable rate of interest
is recognized in all deferred payment sales of property for more
than $3,000 (except, with respect to the seller, when the gain,
if any, would be ordinary income). However, unlike §1232(a)(2),
§483 does not provide for an ad hoc determination of the amount
of interest in each transaction based on the issue price; instead,
the statute provides that the Secretary shall from time to time
fix an interest rate which will apply to all sales transactions
falling within the statute. Any deferred payment obligation
which does not carry a stated interest rate within 1% of the
rate specified by the Secretary is reconstructed for tax purposes
into an obligation at the specified rate. (The 1% leeway is
simply a de minimis rule to avoid the necessity of applying the
statute where the interest variation is minor.)

When §483 was first adopted, the rate specified by the
Secretary was 5%, compounded semi-annually, and the de minimis
rate was fixed at 4% simple interest. In 1975 the respective
rates were raised to 7%, compounded semi-annually, and 6% simple
interest. As of July 1, 1981 the rates were set at 10%, compounded semi-annually, and 9% simple interest.

The approach adopted under §483 to determine and account
for the imputed interest under the statute (referred to as
"unstated interest") is described as follows in the Report of
the House Ways and Means Committee, H. Rep. No. 749, 88th Cong.,
2d Sess. A84-A85 (1963):

Technical Explanation of the Bill

(a) <u>Amount constituting interest</u>. Section 483(a)
provides the general rule that part of each payment (under
a contract for the sale or exchange of property) to which
section 483 applies is to be treated as interest for all
purposes of the code. . . .

The amount to be treated as interest under section 483
is determined by multiplying each payment to which such
section applies by a fraction, (1) the numerator of which
is the "total unstated interest" under the contract and
(2) the denominator of which is the total of all the payments to which section 483 applies which are due under such
contract.

(b) <u>Total unstated interest</u>. Section 483(b) defines
"total unstated interest," with respect to a contract for
the sale or exchange of property, as an amount equal to the
excess of (1) the sum of the payments to which section 483
applies which are due under the contract, over (2) the sum
of the present values of such payments and the present
values of any interest payments due under the contract.
The present value of a payment is determined by discounting
such payment from the date the payment is due under the
contract back to the date of the sale or exchange. Thus,
the present value of a payment is the amount which, if left
at interest from the date of the sale or exchange to the
date the payment is due, would have increased to an amount
equal to such payment. The Secretary of the Treasury or
his delegate is to prescribe regulations which provide the
manner in which such present value is to be computed as
well as the rate of interest to be used. Such regulations
are to provide that payments are to be discounted on the
basis of 6-month brackets; and that the present value of
any interest payment which is due not more than 6 months
after the date of the sale or exchange is to be equal to
100 percent of such payment. Thus, a payment is to be
discounted from the nearest date which marks a 6-month
interval from the date of the sale or exchange. This will
make it unecessary to compute interest on a daily basis.

The computation and allocation of total unstated
interest with respect to a contract for the sale or exchange of property is illustrated by the following example:

<u>Example</u>. S sells Blackacre to P under a contract
which provides that P is to make payments in three equal
installments of $2,000 each, such installments being due 1,
2, and 3 years, respectively, from the date of the sale.
No interest is provided for in the contract. Assume that
the Secretary of the Treasury or his delegate has prescribed
by regulations that 5 percent per annum compounded semi-
annually is the rate of interest to be used. Section 483

applies to all three payments the sum of which is $6,000.
The present value of the installment due 1 year after the
sale is $1,903.63 ($2,000 discounted for 1 year after the
sale at 5 percent per annum compounded semiannually). The
present values of the other two installments are $1,811.90
($2,000 similarly discounted for 2 years) and $1,724.59
($2,000 similarly discounted for 3 years). The sum of the
present values of the three installments (the payments to
which sec. 483 applies) is $5,440.12 and therefore the
total unstated interest under the contract is $559.88
($6,000 minus $5,440.12). The part of each installment
treated as interest is $186.63, which is arrived at by
multiplying the amount of such installment ($2,000) by a
fraction, the numerator of which is $559.88 (total unstated
interest) and the denominator of which is $6,000 (total of
payments to which sec. 483 applies).

Notice that although the foregoing example in the Committee
Report seems to follow the separate obligations approach, described above, for the purpose of computing the total unstated
interest on an obligation, once the amount of unstated interest
has been determined it is allocated proportionately among the
installments, thereby following the straight-line method.
Moreover, in the common case where the deferred payment obligation consists of a given number of equal annual or semi-annual
payments, it is possible to determine more directly from one of
the standard interest tables what the present value of the total
obligation is at the interest rate specified by the Secretary
(that is, the principal sum which would be amortized by the
given installments if the obligation provided for interest,
compounded semi-annually, at the specified rate); the difference
between that present value, or "true principal", and the sum of
all the payments to be made constitutes the total unstated
interest (which is then allocated on the straight-line basis
among the installments). Thus for the Committee example the
table would tell us that the present value of $1 per year for 3
years at 5% interest is $2.72, and multiplying that figure by
the $2,000 per installment in the example produces the present
value of $5,440. (Tables of this kind, on the basis of the 10%
rate presently applicable, are included in the regulations.)

The same type of computation can be made when the obligation provides for some stated interest (at a rate lower than
the applicable de minimis rate of course, since otherwise §483
would not apply), except that the difference between the "true
principal" derived under §483 and the sum of all the payments
must be reduced by the total stated interest to produce the
amount of unstated interest. Notice that is such cases although
§483 mandates that the unstated interest be reported on a straight-
line basis, the stated interest may, and perhaps even should, be
reported on the declining-balance basis.

If at the time of the sale some or all of the payments are indefinite as to amount or timing, as, for example, if the payments depend upon future income derived from the property sold, §483 adopts the separate obligations approach both for computing the amount of unstated interest in each payment and for reporting purposes, which means that the unstated interest is accounted for on an ascending-balance basis.

It is important to keep in mind that §483 applies to any deferred payment obligation falling within the statute, regardless of what method is used for reporting the sale transaction itself. That is, whether the taxpayer follows the installment accounting method, qualifies for the open transaction approach, or is subject to closed transaction treatment, §483 must be applied first, and if there is any unstated interest under the statute the appropriate amount must be deducted from each installment and taxed as such. (Of course if there is express interest, that too must be stripped away from each installment, computed on either a declining-balance basis or straight-line, and taxed as interest.) Accordingly, the installment and open-transaction methods come into play only with respect to the remaining portion of each periodic payment after the elimination of all interest, express or unstated.

Similarly, under the closed transaction method the value of a deferred payment obligation upon receipt can not exceed the stated face amount less any unstated interest determined pursuant to §483, since that interest must be taxed as such under §483 rather than being included in measuring the gain realized in the sale transaction. A very different question is whether this "true principal" resulting from the application of §483 also represents a floor on the value of the obligation for closed transaction purposes. Certainly, §483 does not expressly preclude valuing an obligation below the restated principal in computing "amount realized"; and of course as a practical matter if the market requires a higher interest than §483's current 10% rate the obligation would be worth less than the "true principal" figure derived under §483. On the other hand, to value the obligation at less than this restated principal is in effect to produce additional discount, and it could be argued that since §1232 rules out original issue discount on obligations received in exchange for property (in most circumstances) no discount beyond the unstated interest produced by §483 is contemplated.

This issue was analyzed in detail in Caruth v. United States, 411 F. Supp. 604 (N.D.Tex. 1976):

Plaintiffs contend that the amount realized by them for tax purposes in the year of sale is the cash they received plus the present value of the non-interest-bearing notes as determined under section 483 of the Code. Defendant contends that the amount realized by Plaintiffs is the cash they received plus the fair market value of the notes determined without regard to the present value tables of section 483.

The issue presented is whether "present value" of non-interest-bearing notes calculated in accordance with section 483 is to be treated as a "fair market value" for purposes of determining "amount realized" under section 1001. If the amount realized is determined in accordance with the tables of section 483, there is no fact issue; if the amount realized is fair market value determined without regard to section 483, there is a fact issue. I have determined that "present value" calculated in accordance with section 483 is intended to determine "amount realized" under section 1001(b).

This issue has not been presented for judicial determination before. I therefore base my analysis on construction of the Code and the income tax regulations promulgated pursuant to the Code.

Section 483 provides for the imputation of interest on notes which bear no interest or a very low rate of interest. If payments are deferred into the future, section 483 requires that a portion of each such payment be treated as interest. This section was enacted as part of the Revenue Act of 1964 to prevent a seller from converting ordinary income into capital gain by lowering or abolishing interest and increasing the principal amount of the note. . . . The operation of section 483 is based on the discount of notes to a present value from their face amount by use of tables of present value promulgated by the Treasury Department. These tables appear in Income Tax Regs. section 1.483-1(g) and their use is mandatory.

Section 483(b) states that "the present value of a payment shall be determined . . . by discounting such payment at the rate, and in the manner, provided in regulations prescribed by the Secretary . . . ." Examples (1) through (4) of Reg. section 1.483-1(f)(5) treat the present value as determined under the section 483 tables as the amount realized for purposes of determining gain or loss. Those examples are predicated upon a contract providing for three payments of $2,000 each. No interest was provided in the contract. The example (1) then states:

> After applying section 483, total unstated interest is determined to be $559.88,* and the amount of each $2,000 payment which is treated as interest is determined to be $186.63. For the year 1963, A includes $1,440.12 [$5,440.12 ($6,000 value of B's obligation minus $559.88 total unstated interest) minus $4,000 adjusted basis] as long-term capital gain on the sale of the property.

*[Ed. note] Based upon the 5% imputed interest rate then applicable under §483.

Two points may be observed in this example. First,
even though B's obligation bore no interest, its value
[sic] was taken as face amount $6,000. Second, the amount
realized on the sale, $5,440.12, was determined by applying
the section 483 table to the face amount of the obligation
to arrive at a present value of $5,440.12. Present value
under section 483 was treated as the amount realized under
section 1001.

The only circumstances in which the regulations under
section 483 do not treat present value as the amount realized
is the limited case in which present value could not be
ascertained because there was no face amount to which the
discount tables could be applied. These examples appear in
Reg. section 1.483-1(e)(3). Examples (3) and (4) best show
this circumstance. The contract obligation had no fixed
face amount to which the present value tables could be
applied, so fair market value of the obligation was ascertained.

There is no example in the section 483 regulations in
which an obligation with a face amount was valued independently of the present value tables in those regulations.

The regulations under section 483 are "legislative" as
opposed to "interpretative" regulations because the Treasury
is specifically authorized and required to promulgate them.
They are, therefore, entitled to respect; and I do not find
them contrary to the statutory scheme or unreasonable and
arbitrary. The position urged by the defendant is contrary
to the Treasury regulations and cannot be sustained.

A construction of the two sections, which treats
present value under section 483 as . . . the amount realized
under section 1001(b), not only agrees with the examples of
the regulation, but also accords with the "old and familiar
rule that where, there is, in the same statute, a particular
enactment, and also a general one, which, in its most
comprehensive sense, would include what is embraced in the
former, the particular enactment must be operative, and the
general enactment must be taken to affect only such cases
within its general language as are not within the provisions
of the particular enactment." . . .

Finally, in those cases to which section 483 applies,
I believe that using present value determined under section 483
to determine "amount realized" under section 1001(b) is the
more practical and reasonable construction which effectively
integrates the two sections of the statute. Calculations
of present value and imputed interest under section 483 are
not used exclusively for section 483 purposes. In determining both selling price and total contract price under
the installment sale provisions of section 453, unstated

interest is excluded and only present value is considered as a part of selling price and total contract price. Income Tax Reg. section 1.453-1(b)(2).

I find Defendant's citation of Warren Jones Company v. Comm'r, 524 F.2d 788 (9th Cir. 1975) to be inappropriate. Section 483 of the Code was not involved in Warren Jones. The issue presented to the Court of Appeals was whether the sale should be treated as an "open" or a "closed" transaction. The Ninth Circuit simply held that the contract obligation involved, although not a "cash equivalent," was "other property" which had an ascertainable fair market value. Warren Jones only establishes what is clearly understood in the Fifth Circuit--that there is no open transaction if fair market value of the notes received can be ascertained . . . . The question of whether the transaction is open or closed is not presented here.

In light of the examples of Regulations section 1.483-1 (f)(5) which treat present value as amount realized and with regard to the other considerations above, I hold that present value for section 483 purposes should be considered to be the fair market value of the notes for purposes of determining the amount realized under section 1001(b).

Whatever may have been the situation in Caruth, today the restated principal produced by applying §483 will often be higher than the fair market value of the obligation, because the market rate of interest for the borrower is above the ten percent rate currently operative under §483. Valuing the obligation at that higher figure would mean a larger "amount realized", and, consequently, a greater amount of tax. Prima facie, then, it would seem that a taxpayer would want to avoid valuation pursuant to §483, in order to obtain a lower value for the obligation and thereby postpone some of the tax bill. But just the reverse would be true if the price of deferring tax on some of the gain is to subject that gain to higher tax rates in the not too distant future, and that is exactly what may happen here under some circumstances. To illustrate, assume that an installment obligation (which is not subject to §483) is required to be valued and included in the "amount realized" by a taxpayer (pursuant to the closed transaction approach), and the figure at which the obligation is valued is less than the principal amount; that difference will be taxed as the obligation is paid off, either pro rata in each installment, or after the taxpayer has recovered his basis (which of course is equal to the figure at which the obligation was valued). However, if the maker of the installment obligation is not a corporation (as was true in Caruth), so that §1232 is not available to supply the necessary "exchange" treatment for payments received on the obligation, the difference would be taxable at ordinary income rates, and even with the postponement that could be more expensive than additional tax at the outset, which would presumably have been at capital gains rates.

When §483 applies to an installment obligation, a new restated principal is derived, and of course the spread between this restated principal amount and the original face amount of the obligation is taxed as interest income by operation of §483. But if the obligation is valued for closed transaction purposes at a figure below the restated principal produced by §483, that difference can fall prey to this transmutation of what would have been additional capital gain at the outset into ordinary income later (either pro rata per installment, or after basis has been recovered). Hence in the case of a non-corporate installment obligation it is likely to be the taxpayer who is arguing for valuation of the obligation at an amount equal to the "true principal" derived under §483, with the Government pressing for a lower valuation consistent with the current market rate of interest, in order to reap a harvest of ordinary income later on.

Under the decision of the District Court in Caruth, it makes quite a difference whether an installment obligation being valued under the closed transaction method is subject to reconstruction under §483; if not, the obligation will surely be valued according to traditional valuation factors, the most important of which is the current market rate of interest, and will not have the floor on value provided by the Caruth case for obligations subject to §483. Notice, too, that this becomes in effect elective, since taxpayers can control whether an obligation will be subject to §483, simply by making the express interest rate less than the current de minimis test rate of 9% (1% below the operative rate of 10%). There seems little reason to suppose that Congress intended §483 to create collateral consequences of this kind.

The decision of the District Court in Caruth was reversed by the Court of Appeals for the Ninth Circuit, in an opinion which strongly suggests that §483 is not relevant in determining the fair market value of an installment obligation for the purpose of computing the "amount realized" under §1001(b). However, the actual holding of the court was that because the payment dates in the installment obligations under consideration were indefinite, it was not possible to determine a restated principal for the obligation at the outset under §483; hence valuation on the basis of traditional factors was the only feasible approach (and the unstated interest had to be determined separately for each installment, pursuant to subparagraph (e) of §483). Caruth v. United States, 566 F.2d 901 (5th Cir. 1978).

E. TAX INCIDENTS TO THE CORPORATION OF A REDEMPTION
DISTRIBUTION IN KIND

For a description of IRC §311 and a brief review of its tortuous history, see bottom of page 419 to top of page 421, supra.

F. DEDUCTIBILITY OF REDEMPTION EXPENSES

1. By the Corporation

REVENUE RULING 67-125

1967-17 I.R.B. 6.

Advice has been requested whether legal fees incurred by a corporation in securing advice on the Federal tax consequences of the following transactions before they are consummated can be deducted as ordinary and necessary business expenses under section 162 of the Internal Revenue Code of 1954: (1) A merger, (2) a stock split, and (3) a proposed distribution in redemption of outstanding stock under section 302 of the Code (which distribution would not qualify as a partial liquidation under section 346 of the Code).

The legal fees in this case were incurred in connection with the merger of one corporation into another, followed by a split of the stock of the surviving corporation. It was also proposed that the surviving corporation would distribute property acquired in the merger in redemption of a portion of its stock to meet certain anticipated conditions in connection with the future operations of the surviving corporation. Since these conditions did not materialize, the planned redemption was tentatively abandoned for the year of the merger and the stock split. However, no final decision has been made as to whether the redemption will be made or finally abandoned.

Section 162(a) of the Code allows as a deduction all the ordinary and necessary business expenses paid or incurred during the taxable year in carrying on a trade or business. Section 263 of the Code precludes a deduction for capital expenditures.

It is well established that expenditures incident to the alteration of the capital structure of a corporation are to be capitalized. . . . Thus, legal fees incurred for services performed in drafting a corporate merger agreement are to be capitalized as incident to the reorganization since the effect of a merger is to change the capital structure of the surviving corporation.

The basic question then in this case is whether the legal fees incurred for tax advice on the corporate activities involved are considered to be incident to the alteration of the corporation's capital structure or are ordinary and necessary business expenses.

The probable tax consequences resulting from various kinds of reorganizations or other changes in a corporation's capital structure are instrumental in determining the type of reorganization or other change in the capital structure of the corporation. Thus, legal fees for advice as to the tax significance of a particular type of reorganization are considered to be just as necessary in effecting a reorganization as those for the actual drafting of the reorganization agreement.

. . . .

The split of the stock of the surviving corporation and the proposed redemption of a portion of its stock operate to change the capital structure of the corporation for a period of indefinite duration. Thus, the legal fees incurred for tax advice on these transactions represent expenditures incident to the change of the capital structure of the surviving corporation. However, if the taxpayer can subsequently establish that it has made a final decision not to carry out the redemption, the costs attributable to the proposed redemption may be deducted in the taxable year in which such a decision was made. . . .

Accordingly, the legal fees incurred prior to the transaction in securing advice on the tax consequences of the merger, stock split, and proposed distribution in redemption represent capital expenditures incurred in connection with the change of the capital structure of the surviving corporation and are therefore not deductible as ordinary and necessary business expenses. However, in the event the proposed redemption of stock is subsequently abandoned, the capitalized fees attributable to such proposed redemption are deductible in the taxable year of abandonment.

WOODWARD v. COMMISSIONER OF INTERNAL REVENUE

Supreme Court of the United States, 1970.

397 U.S. 572, 90 S.Ct. 1302.

MR. JUSTICE MARSHALL delivered the opinion of the Court.*

This case . . . involve[s] the tax treatment of expenses incurred in certain appraisal litigation.

Taxpayers owned or controlled a majority of the common stock of the Telegraph-Herald, an Iowa publishing corporation. The Telegraph-Herald was incorporated in 1901, and its charter was extended for 20-year periods in 1921 and 1941. On June 9, 1960, taxpayers voted their controlling share of the stock of the corporation in favor of a perpetual extension of the charter. A minority stockholder voted against the extension. Iowa law requires "those [stockholders] voting for such renewal . . . [to] purchase at its real value the stock voted against such renewal." Iowa Code, § 491.25 (1966).

Taxpayers attempted to negotiate purchase of the dissenting stockholder's shares, but no agreement could be reached on the "real value" of those shares. Consequently, in 1962 taxpayers brought an action in state court to appraise the value of the minority stock interest. The trial court fixed a value, which was slightly reduced on appeal by the Iowa Supreme Court . . . . In July 1965, taxpayers purchased the minority stock interest at the price fixed by the court.

* Portions of the opinion and most of
the footnotes omitted.

During 1963, taxpayers paid attorneys', accountants', and appraisers' fees of over $25,000, for services rendered in connection with the appraisal litigation. On their 1963 federal income tax returns, taxpayers claimed deductions for these expenses, asserting that they were "ordinary and necessary expenses paid . . . for the management, conservation, or maintenance of property held for the production of income" deductible under § 212 of the Internal Revenue Code of 1954, 26 U.S.C. § 212. The Commissioner of Internal Revenue disallowed the deduction "because the fees represent capital expenditures incurred in connection with the acquisition of capital stock of a corporation." The Tax Court sustained the Commissioner's determination, with two dissenting opinions, 49 T.C. 377 (1968), and the Court of Appeals affirmed, 410 F.2d 313 (C.A.8th Cir. 1969). We granted certiorari . . . to resolve the conflict over the deductibility of the costs of appraisal proceedings . . . .. We affirm.

Since the inception of the present federal income tax in 1913, capital expenditures have not been deductible. See Internal Revenue Code of 1954, § 263. Such expenditures are added to the basis of the capital asset with respect to which they are incurred, and are taken into account for tax purposes either through depreciation or by reducing the capital gain (or increasing the loss) when the asset is sold. If an expense is capital, it cannot be deducted as "ordinary and necessary," either as a business expense under § 162 of the Code or as an expense of "management, conservation, or maintenance" under § 212.[3]

It has long been recognized, as a general matter, that costs incurred in the acquisition or disposition of a capital asset are to be treated as capital expenditures. The most familiar example of such treatment is the capitalization of brokerage fees for the sale or purchase of securities . . . . .

The regulations do not specify other sorts of acquisition costs, but rather provide generally that "[t]he cost of acquisition . . . of . . . property having a useful life substantially beyond the taxable year" is a capital expenditure. Treas.Reg. on Income Tax § 1.263(a)–2(a). Under this general provision, the courts have held that legal, brokerage, accounting, and similar costs incurred in the acquisition or disposition of such property are capital expenditures. . . . The law could hardly be otherwise, for such ancillary expenses incurred in acquiring or disposing of an asset are as much part of the cost of that asset as is the price paid for it.

More difficult questions arise with respect to another class of capital expenditures, those incurred in "defending or perfecting title to property." Treas.Reg. on Income Tax § 1.263(a)–2(c). In one

3. The two sections are in *pari materia* with respect to the capital-ordinary distinction, differing only in that § 212 allows deductions for the ordinary and necessary expenses of nonbusiness profitmaking activities. . . .

sense, any lawsuit brought against a taxpayer may affect his title to property—money or other assets subject to lien. The courts, not believing that Congress meant all litigation expenses to be capitalized, have created the rule that such expenses are capital in nature only where the taxpayer's "primary purpose" in incurring them is to defend or perfect title. . . . This test hardly draws a bright line . . . . .

Taxpayers urge that this "primary purpose" test, developed in the context of cases involving the costs of defending property, should be applied to costs incurred in acquiring or disposing of property as well. And if it is so applied, they argue, the costs here in question were properly deducted, since the legal proceedings in which they were incurred did not directly involve the question of title to the minority stock, which all agreed was to pass to taxpayers, but rather was concerned solely with the value of that stock.

We agree with the Tax Court and the Court of Appeals that the "primary purpose" test has no application here. That uncertain and difficult test may be the best that can be devised to determine the tax treatment of costs incurred in litigation that may affect a taxpayer's title to property more or less indirectly, and that thus calls for a judgment whether the taxpayer can fairly be said to be "defending or perfecting title." Such uncertainty is not called for in applying the regulation that makes the "cost of acquisition" of a capital asset a capital expense. In our view application of the latter regulation to litigation expenses involves the simpler inquiry whether the origin of the claim litigated is in the process of acquisition itself.

A test based upon the taxpayer's "purpose" in undertaking or defending a particular piece of litigation would encourage resort to formalisms and artificial distinctions. For instance, in this case there can be no doubt that legal, accounting, and appraisal costs incurred by taxpayers in *negotiating* a purchase of the minority stock would have been capital expenditures. . . . Yet the appraisal proceeding was no more than the substitute that state law provided for the process of negotiation as a means of fixing the price at which the stock was to be purchased. . . .

Further, a standard based on the origin of the claim litigated comports with this Court's recent ruling in United States v. Gilmore, 372 U.S. 39 (1963) . . . that the expense of defending a divorce suit was a nondeductible personal expense, even though the outcome of the divorce case would affect the taxpayer's property holdings, and might affect his business reputation. The Court . . . examined the origin and character of the claim against the taxpayer, and found that the claim arose out of the personal relationship of marriage.

The standard here pronounced may, like any standard, present borderline cases, in which it is difficult to determine whether the origin of particular litigation lies in the process of acquisition. This is not such a borderline case. Here state law required taxpayers to "purchase" the stock owned by the dissenter. In the absence of agreement on the price at which the purchase was to be made, litigation was required to fix the price. Where property is acquired by purchase, nothing is more clearly part of the process of acquisition than the establishment of a purchase price. Thus the expenses incurred in that litigation were properly treated as part of the cost of the stock that the taxpayers acquired.

Affirmed.

BILAR TOOL & DIE CORP. v. COMMISSIONER

United States Court of Appeals, Sixth Circuit, 1976.

530 F.2d 708.

EDWARDS, Circuit Judge.

This is a government appeal from a decision by a sharply divided Tax Court which allowed deduction of $4,000 in attorney fees as ordinary and necessary expenses. These fees resulted from legal work on a corporate division which split the Forway Tool & Die Company, Inc., into two equal parts. The taxpayer in this case, Bilar Tool & Die Corporation, as a result of a simple change of name, is the direct successor to the previous corporation. A new corporation was organized under the name of Four-Way Tool & Die, Inc.

The parties stipulated that the corporate division described above resulted from a dispute between two shareholders, Markoff and Sakuta, who had previously had equal ownership of the original corporation. They also stipulated that the agreed-on plan called for equal division of the financial and physical assets of the old corporation, as well as equal division of the liabilities. As a result, Markoff would own 100% of the stock of Bilar, and Sakuta 100% of the stock of the newly organized company, Four-Way. The plan contemplated what actually occurred, namely, that two corporations would continue in the same business in which the old corporation was engaged—but after the split, as competitors. The stipulation stated "the series of events evidenced by the above stipulated facts and joint exhibits constitute a single unified plan."

The stipulation also indicated that Bilar Tool & Die incurred legal and accounting fees in the sum of $11,500 "in connection with the plan." Taxpayer, however, did not see fit to introduce any specific evidence concerning those services, except as to the $4,000 of attorney fees. As to this an attorney testified that the $4,000 was a fee paid for devising and carrying out the unified plan referred to above.

He also testified that $400 of the $4,000 was directly attributable to expenses involved in the incorporation of the new corporation.

The majority of the Tax Court found that the $4,000 was an ordinary and necessary business expense under IRC § 162(a), 26 U.S.C. § 162(a) (1970). The Tax Court declined to allow deductibility as to the remaining $7,500 because of failure to prove that the expenses were ordinary and necessary. As to this issue, the taxpayer appeals.

The majority of the Tax Court found that the dominant aspect of the overall plan was a division of the business through a partial liquidation. It allowed deduction of the $4,000 of attorney fees as ordinary and necessary expenses under § 162(a) of the Code. In so doing it cited and relied on United States v. General Bancshares Corp., 388 F.2d 184 (8th Cir. 1968), and Transamerica Corp. v. United States, 392 F.2d 522 (9th Cir. 1968). The appellee adopts the Tax Court's view and urges us to do likewise.

On the other hand, the government contends that there was no liquidation at all, that this was simply a corporate reorganization where all the assets of the corporation were continued in business, albeit in divided form. Under this theory the expenses of reorganization are capital expenditures and nondeductible under IRC § 263 (a)(1), 26 U.S.C. § 263(a)(1) (1970).

The government also contends that the tax problem should be looked at from the point of view of the transaction taken as a whole and should not be viewed, as the majority of the Tax Court did, from the point of view solely of the Bilar half of the former corporation, which is the taxpayer here. In the government's view *Bancshares* and *Transamerica* were wrongly decided.

The majority opinion of the Tax Court found as a matter of fact that "[p]etitioner acquired nothing [through the total plan] that would be of any benefit to it in its future operations." The Tax Court also found "[s]o far as the corporate petitioner is concerned, there was no improvement or betterment of any capital asset it owned." We believe these findings are "clearly erroneous" . . . and that the decision of the Tax Court must be reversed.

The reasons for "the Plan of Reorganization" are set forth in the minutes of the meeting which adopted it:

4. On September 21, 1967, a special meeting of the Board of Directors of the Corporation was held and the following resolutions were made:

(a) That a disagreement had arisen in 1967 between the two shareholders of the Corporation which made it impossible for the Corporation to continue operations in its present corporate form,

(b) That the shareholders of the Corporation had agreed upon a division of the business whereby the assets of the Corporation would be divided and whereby approximately one-half (½) of the Corporation's total assets would be owned in a separate corporate form by Mr. Sakuta and the remaining assets would continue to be held by the Corporation which would be wholly owned by Mr. Markoff, and

(c) That a plan of corporate separation should be adopted.

The testimony of the president of the present taxpayer corporation vividly demonstrates just how important to the owners' investment in the old corporation the corporate reorganization plan for its division into two corporations actually was. At the Tax Court hearing Mr. Markoff testified:

MR. MOSHER: . . . Mr. Markoff, [the stipulation indicates] that there was a disagreement between you and Mr. Sakuta. Can you tell me what the nature of that disagreement was?

A   Yes, it was a disagreement about the working situation there at that time. The president of the corporation at that time, Joseph Sakuta and the foreman, had a big argument and it was either Joe Sakuta leaving the corporation or the foreman, Larry Caloia.

Q   Was Mr. Sakuta's son employed by the corporation at that time?

A   Yes, he was working for the corporation at that time.

Q   Was he an officer of the corporation?

A   No.

Q   Was there some dispute as to the amount of responsibility which Mr. Sakuta's son should have?

A   This was one of the big arguments of the corporation. It wasn't Joe Sakuta personally, but his wife and it got back to the corporation and it was always a turmoil there that the son should have more authority in the business, more responsibility and I would rather have, like I say, the fellow that I could depend on, Larry Caloia working in that category than his son Joey.

. . .

Q   Can you tell me what, in your mind, would have happened to the corporation if some agreement or some separation did not occur?

A   We would have had a real rough road to go and I think eventually would have went down the drain, as the way it was going there.

When a plan of reorganization of a corporation which is going "down the drain" produces two viable corporations by the equal division of the assets of the doomed (or threatened) corporation, we believe value has clearly been added to the capital structure of both the original corporation and the successor corporations. Such was the dominant purpose and result of the reorganization plan as this record clearly establishes. Under these facts the expenses of carrying out such a reorganization plan are nondeductible capital outlays. As stated in Mills Estate v. Commissioner, 206 F.2d 244, 246 (2d Cir. 1953):

> The part played in respect to the operation of the business is what counts in determining whether the necessary expense of obtaining it was an ordinary business expense . . . .

> This taxpayer, having decided to go out of the real estate operation part of its business and having turned its real estate into cash, underwent a recapitalization to give itself the capital structure it determined was best suited to carrying on that part of the business it was to continue. The services for which the attorneys were paid were all necessary steps to attain that end. What occurred was essentially a reorganization—a change in the corporate structure for the benefit of future operations—and the expenses of that sort of a corporate change are not deductible as ordinary and necessary expenses in carrying on a trade or business. . . . They are instead a part of the expenditure needed to give the corporation an intangible asset which we may call its altered corporate structure; and, as were the costs of its original organization, these expenditures were capital in nature.

Appellee taxpayer in this case relies principally, as did the Tax Court, on two bank cases, United States v. General Bancshares Corp., and Transamerica Corp. v. United States . . . . In these cases the banks concerned were required by the Bank Holding Company Act of 1956, 12 U.S.C. §§ 1841–49 (1970), to divest themselves of either their banking or nonbanking assets, and the courts concerned found no benefit to the taxpayers from the divestiture thus compelled. Such compelled divestiture of assets with no consequent enhancement of capital assets does not seem comparable to our instant facts.

Gravois Planing Mill Co. v. Commissioner, 299 F.2d 199 (8th Cir. 1962) is relied upon by the Tax Court majority and by the appellee in this case. Gravois, however, presented a quite different set of facts than those we deal with here. In Gravois the company's long-time president and 50% stockholder retired at the age of 67. This resulted in the company's purchase of the great majority of his stock by payment of all the cash the company could afford, transfer to the retiree (Beckemeier) of a corporation-owned insurance policy on his life, and the transfer to him of physical assets previously owned by the company. The latter (which included the plant) were then leased back to the company at a rental agreed upon for 10 years. The net result was that the three younger stockholders continued in business with greatly reduced capital assets. On these facts Justice Blackmun held for the Eighth Circuit in distinguishing *Mills Estate,* supra, "the dominant aspect of the *Gravois* transaction was the liquidation of the Beckemeier shares and not the recapitalization." Gravois Planing Mill Co. v. Commissioner, supra at 209. He also emphasized that "the basic problem with which they struggled was that of the disposition of the outstanding Beckemeier stock and was not one directed to change or any desired improvement in the form of the corporate structure." Id.

No such retirement and withdrawal of capital is involved in our instant case and there is both beneficial change and improvement shown in the instant plan. Additionally, although of less significance, it is interesting to note that the parties in *Gravois* referred to their plan as "liquidation" of the Beckemeier stock interest, whereas the parties in our present case termed their plan (accurately, we think) "Plan for Reorganization."

The plan we deal with must be looked at from the point of view of its totality. So regarded it is a typical reorganization, and as noted above, the minutes of both the Board of Directors' meeting and the Stockholders' meeting of the old corporation which adopted the unified plan characterized it as "The Plan of Reorganization." We are not able to find in the facts of this case any liquidation at all—partial or otherwise. This plan clearly fits the Reorganization [definition of Section 368(a)(1)(D), which provides:]

. . .

> (D) a transfer by a corporation of all or a part of its assets to another corporation if immediately after the transfer the transferor, or one or more of its shareholders (including persons who were shareholders immediately before the transfer), or any combination thereof, is in control of the corporation to which the assets are transferred; . . .

We recognize, of course, that this section does not pertain to corporation deductions, but we believe its definition is helpful nonetheless.

The controlling section is § 162:

SEC. 162. *Trade Or Business Expenses.*

> (a) *In General.*—There shall be allowed as a deduction all the ordinary and necessary expenses paid or incurred during the taxable year in carrying on any trade or business . . .

The attorney fees were expenditures for devising and carrying out the "unified plan." They were not "incurred . . . in carrying on any trade or business." They were not "ordinary or necessary expenses." They were of benefit to the whole of the original corporation because they served the purpose of terminating the dissension which threatened to wreck it. They were likewise of capital benefit to both successor corporations, since they were essential to making both possible. The $400 portion which was expended on incorporation of the new company is properly to be regarded as an expenditure for carrying out the total plan.

Thus, as we see the matter, the entire $4,000 was an expenditure to enhance capital which was calculated to benefit the taxpayer for much more than one year. . . .

On the basis of what has been said above, it goes without saying that we find no merit to taxpayers' appeal contending that the Tax Court should have allowed an additional $7,500 in deductions of expenses in connection with carrying out the corporate reorganization plan.

The decision of the Tax Court is reversed and the case is remanded for recomputation of the tax, with the entire $11,500 of claimed deductions disallowed.

NOTE

a. The "Partial Liquidation" Cases

The starting point for the analysis here is the rule stated in Rev. Rul. 67-125 and applied in the Bilar case: that expenses for the reorganization or recapitalization of a corporation must be capitalized, to be deducted (as a capital loss) only if and when the corporation is dissolved (just as was true of the expenses of organizing a corporation until the enactment in 1954 of §248 permitting organization expenses to be amortized over a period of five years or more). At the opposite end of the spectrum is the rule that a corporation may deduct its expenses of liquidating, which is usually justified on the ground either that such expenses do not relate to the creation or continuance of an asset, or that they represent the cost of accounting to the owners of the enterprise. As the Bilar case indicates, the opposing rules for liquidation and recapitalization collide in cases of partial liquidation (which under the 1939 Code, it will be recalled, included all stock redemptions), since such transactions may contain both liquidation elements, in that some of the stockholders retire from the enterprise and/or some of the corporation's activities are terminated, and recapitalization elements, in that the enterprise continues in altered form. Thus in Mills Estate, Inc. v. Commissioner, quoted from in the Bilar case, where the corporation had made a pro rata redemption distribution of the proceeds of sale of one of its business, the Tax Court commented as follows:

> "The expenditures involved herein have character-
> istics that partake of both lines of decisions. Peti-
> tioner's legal expenses were undoubtedly incurred in
> substantial part in order to amend its charter and
> reduce authorized capitalization, thereby providing for
> the acquisition and retirement of its stock followed by
> the issuance of new stock in reduced amount. This
> aspect of the transaction certainly brings this case
> within the [recapitalization] line of authority.
> However, the actual distribution of assets in partial
> liquidation was also a significant factor with respect
> to which the legal fees were paid, and it is difficult
> to perceive why the cost of a partial liquidation
> should be any the less an ordinary and necessary business
> expense than the cost of a complete liquidation."

Accordingly, the Tax Court allocated half of the legal fees and expenses to the recapitalization aspect of the transac-tion and half to the partial liquidation, and held the latter half deductible. This decision was reversed by the Court of Appeals, which took the view that all of the cor-porate steps amounted to "a single transaction" which "was essentially a reorganization," and therefore none of the expenses was deductible. The Court of Appeals also intimated some doubt about the rule permitting deduction of liquida-tion expenses, but in view of the outcome it did not have to pass on that question.

On the other hand, in the later Gravois case, discussed in Bilar, the Court of Appeals for the Eighth Circuit came down on the other side of the line, emphasizing the "liqui-dation" of the entire interest of the stockholder whose stock was redeemed. With respect to the recapitalization element, the Gravois court added the following observation:

> "Of course, the transaction involved a reduction in the
> corporation's stated capital and a continuance of the

corporate activity. And of course the amendment of the
articles was filed with the Secretary of State as
required by the Missouri statutes. These additional
facts, however, are necessary concomitants of this type
of partial liquidation. We regard them as constituting
only a secondary and not the dominant aspect of the
entire transaction."

In seeking to distinguish Gravois, the Bilar court
stated that here no "retirement and withdrawal of capital"
had occurred, and added that there did not appear to be "any
liquidation at all--partial or otherwise." But in reality
the effect of the transaction in Bilar was to withdraw
one-half of the assets of the original corporation, and the
distribution of those assets to the departing shareholder
liquidated his entire interest in that corporation. To be
sure, in Bilar the assets to be distributed were first
transferred to a new corporation (and presumably the expenses
incurred in organizing the new corporation would not be
deductible), with the new stock then distributed to the
departing shareholder (thereby qualifying as a reorganization
for tax purposes), whereas in Gravois the withdrawing shareholder received the assets directly. But under corporate
law the transaction in Bilar was a repurchase by the corporation
of its own stock in exchange for property, just as was true
in Gravois, and the business impact upon the distributing
corporation in the two cases was exactly the same. Had the
parties in Bilar omitted the new corporation and simply
distributed the assets directly (which would have precluded
qualification as a reorganization), the situation would have
been the same as Gravois; and it is hard to see why the
creation of the new corporation and distribution of its
stock should change the deductibility of the expenses of the
transaction (except perhaps for requiring capitalization of
the costs incurred in organizing the new corporation).

b.   The "Straight Redemption" Cases

Meanwhile, there had developed another, wholly separate
line of authorities which deny the corporation any deduction
for expenses incurred in a stock redemption without so much
as a reference to either "partial liquidation" or "recapitalization." This line of what might be termed "straight redemption"
cases viewed the repurchase of stock as simply the acquisition
of an asset by the corporation, and applied the normal rule

that expenses incurred in acquiring a capital asset must be added to the cost of the property rather than deducted currently. Curiously, no case in either line of authority has ever even acknowledged the existence of the other line.

The "straight redemption" line seems to stem from O.D. 852, 4 Cum.Bull. 286 (1921), where the Service ruled specifically that expenses incurred by a corporation in purchasing its own stock were not deductible, but were "to be considered part of the purchase price of the stock." In Commerce Photo-Print Corp. v. Commissioner, 6 T.C.M. 386 (1947), the court flatly denied a deduction by the corporate taxpayer of the legal expenses incurred in redeeming almost 50% of its outstanding stock, stating that fees relating to the acquisition of stock should be added to the cost of the stock; the court regarded it as immaterial on this issue that a primary objective of the transaction was to eliminate the friction between the two almost equal stockholders by buying out one of them. Accord, Southern Engineering and Metal Products Corp. v. Commissioner, 9 T.C.M.93 (1950) (legal fees expended by a corporation in redeeming all of the stock of one of the two equal stockholders were "not deductible as a business expense of petitioner corporation, but should have been treated as a capital expenditure, i.e., as part of the cost of the stock").

In 1961, less than a year before the Gravois decision, came two more "straight redemption" cases in which the court cursorily rejected the corporation's attempt to deduct legal expenses incurred in connection with the buy-out of some of its stockholders, without so much as a word about partial liquidation or recapitalization. In Atzingen-Whitehouse Dairy, Inc. v. Commissioner, 36 T.C.173 (1961), a corporate rift was resolved by having the corporate-taxpayer repurchase the stock of two of its three stockholders. In denying the corporation the right to deduct the $6,000 legal fee for that transaction, Judge Raum (who had written the opinion of the Tax Court in the Mills Estate case some years earlier) commented as follows:

"That payment is a capital expenditure which should have been treated as part of cost of the stock purchase. It is not deductible as an ordinary and necessary business expense. The fact that the purchase of the stock was motivated by a desire to eliminate friction between the [stockholders] is immaterial.

Certainly, the cost of the stock itself was a capital
expenditure rather than a deductible expense, and the
accompanying legal fee must be similary classified."

In somewhat similar circumstances, in Annabelle Candy
Co., Inc. v. Commissioner, 20 T.C.M. 873 (1961), reversed on
another issue, 314 F.2d 1 (9th Cir. 1962), Judge Raum cited
his own prior decision in Atzingen-Whitehouse for the proposition that the legal expenses incurred in a redemption
should be treated as part of the total capital expenditure.
However, the taxpayer in the Annabelle case argued that part
of the legal services had been directed toward avoiding dissolution of the corporation, with various plans having been
considered prior to the decision in favor of redemption, and
that legal fees attributable to reviewing these other plans
should be deductible. The court agreed that such fees might
well be deductible, and that an allocation between deductible
and non-deductible portions of the legal expense was possible,
but found no basis for it in this case since all of the
services described in the lawyers' bill related to the
redemption. The court added a caveat that since the same
lawyers represented both the corporation and the remaining
stockholders, any portion of the fee which was not applicable
to the ultimate corporate transaction (i.e., the redemption
here) would have called for careful scrutiny to make sure
that it was not incurred for the benefit of the remaining
stockholders personally rather than for the corporation.

c.   Evaluation of the Two Approaches

It is hard to fathom just how and why these two lines
of authority developed separately as they did. As we have
seen, unlike the 1954 Code the 1939 Code, under which most
of the cases in both lines arose, did not draw any distinction between redemption and partial liquidation--every
redemption was a partial liquidation and hence potentially
subject to the complete liquidation analogy. It is true
that the earlier partial liquidation cases involved pro rata
redemption transactions, while all of the "straight redemption"
cases have involved only non pro rata redemptions, usually
the complete termination of the interest of one or more
stockholders. However, this hardly explains the different
lines of authority, particularly since the Gravois case
itself involved the non pro rata redemption of all of the
stock of one stockholder.

It is to be noted that these "straight redemption" cases were no more sympathetic than Bilar to the argument that resolving friction among the shareholders should make the expenses incurred in the resulting redemption transaction deductible. In any event, even though neither Gravois nor Bilar even made reference to these "straight redemption" cases, they may have received a new lease on life under the Supreme Court's decision in the Woodward case, which puts such emphasis on the rule that expenses incurred in acquiring property must be capitalized. In this connection, it is interesting to note that in a companion case to Woodward, United States v. Hilton Hotels Corporation, 397 U.S. 580 (1970), the Court held that the surviving corporation in a merger could not deduct the expenses of an appraisal proceeding brought by dissenting shareholders of the acquired corporation who had exercised their statutory right to be bought out. Functionally, such a buy-out is very little different from an ordinary redemption of stock (and in fact is dealt with in the repurchase provision of some corporation statutes, e.g., MBA §6), but the Supreme Court made no reference to the redemption cases in holding that such expenses could not be deducted because, as in Woodward, they were associated with the acquisition of property.

In any event, there is a serious flaw in treating the repurchase of stock by a corporation as an acquisition of property which consequently prevents deduction of the related expenses. For it is clear that stock does not represent property in the hands of the corporation which issued it, even though it is property when held by anyone else. As we saw in section 8, supra, under modern corporation statutes treasury stock is not recognized as an asset, but instead is carried in a kind of suspense account, which appears as a general deduction from stockholders' equity on the right-hand side of the balance sheet. And from the tax point of view, while in theory a corporation may have a basis in repurchased stock equal to the amount paid for it, in practice that basis has no significance because §1032 precludes the recognition of gain or loss by a corporation upon any issuance of stock (including treasury stock); hence, capitalizing the expenses incurred in repurchasing stock would simply add them to this basis "limbo," which is a far cry from the usual tax significance of capitalizing expenses associated with the acquisition of property.

On the other hand, the partial liquidation-recapitalization dichotomy has not been very helpful as a guideline

for determining the deductibility of redemption expenses.
On the partial liquidation front, it must be noted that even
the starting point, allowing a corporation to deduct the
expenses of a complete liquidation, has been questioned, so
any extension is not very inviting. Moreover, there is
quite a distinction between partial and complete liquidation,
in that the latter totally eliminates the corporate vehicle,
and hence there is nothing left to which capitalized corporate
expenses could be attached, whereas that is not true in the
case of a partial liquidation. In addition, if taken literally
the term "partial liquidation" today would embrace only
repurchase transactions which involve contraction of the
enterprise, and yet these do not seem any more analogous to
complete liquidation than does, say, a redemption of all of
the stock of a shareholder which liquidates his entire
interest in the corporation. Ironically, this approach
would rule out the Gravois case, which did not involve any
reduction in the scope of the corporation's operations,
while including cases like Mills Estate, where there was
clearly a contraction of the enterprise. That this is no
idle possibility is evidenced by the parenthetical clause at
the end of the first paragraph in Rev. Rul. 67-125, which
implies that the result might be different for a redemption
which qualified as a partial liquidation under §346 (the
forerunner of present §302(b)(4)), i.e., where a corporate
contraction is involved.

However, attempting to pin a recapitalization label on
an ordinary redemption transaction is even more problematical, since any restructuring of the corporation in connection with a repurchase of stock is likely to be only collateral (as the Gravois opinion recognized). The exaggerated
significance attached to the recapitalization element in the
Mills Estate case was probably due to the fact that in
connection with the pro rata distribution there the corporation not only reduced its stated capital but also reclaimed
all of the original stock and issued new stock. In many
simple redemption cases, quite the reverse, the transaction
will not result in any change in the capital structure at
all, as where the repurchased stock is not cancelled and is
simply held as treasury stock.

d.   The Distribution Character of a Redemption

In any event, it may be time to drop the quest for
parallels to liquidation entirely, and instead accept as an
appropriate starting point that expenses incurred in connec-

tion with distributions to shareholders should be deductible.
Certainly the collateral costs associated with periodic
dividends of cash or property are assumed to be deductible,
and there is no reason why other distributions, whether pro
rata or not, which leave the corporation with fewer assets
should not be similarly treated. (Of course, if there is a
companion restructuring of the corporate vehicle, the portion
of the expense allocable thereto would not be deductible.)
This seems to have been the view taken in the General Bancshares
case (and followed in the Transamerica case), cited in
Bilar, where the corporate taxpayers were permitted to
deduct the expenses of distributing assets to shareholders
in connection with a court-ordered divestiture. The transactions were actually carried out by transferring the assets
to a new corporation in exchange for its stock, and then
distributing that stock to the taxpayers' stockholders,
thereby very much paralleling the Bilar facts (and similarly
achieving non-recognition treatment for the recipient stockholders). The dominant objective of the transactions was
the divestment of assets, which did not add anything of
value to the taxpayer or its corporate structure (even if
there were some related, collateral changes). That the
transactions qualified for reorganization treatment did not
matter, since it was the impact on the distributing corporation
which was controlling, and from that vantage point the
transfer to the shareholders had the same effect as a direct
distribution in kind, or a partial liquidation. The court
in General Bancshares expressly noted that none of the
expenses involved related to the organization of the new
corporation, which would not have been deductible; in addition,
deduction was disallowed for the cost incurred by the taxpayer
in changing its corporate name, which may have been occasioned
by the divestment plan but was not an integral part of it.

The court in the Bilar case purported to distinguish
General Bancshares and Transamerica by emphasizing that its
transaction was one of the defined statutory reorganizations,
and was also necessary to avoid the dissolution of the
enterprise. But the taxpayer corporations in the bank cases
presumably faced termination if they refused to comply with
the divestiture orders; and the divestments in those cases
qualified as tax-free reorganizations under a special legislative enactment. The real difference is that the bank
cases focused on the impact of the transaction on the distributing corporation, while the Bilar court insisted on
looking at the overall effect on all of the parties. Obviously, a simple redemption transaction will be readily
distinguishable from Bilar by virtue of the absence of any

statutory reorganization, and the predominant distribution
character should be sufficient to justify deduction of the
related expenses. But query, if the purpose of the redemption is, say, to eliminate a dissident stockholder who poses
a threat to the continued corporate existence: Bilar might
still be relied upon to require capitalization of the expenses
on the ground that there was a long-term benefit to all of
the parties.

---

2. Deduction by an Individual of Tax-Related Expenses--§212(3)

SHARPLES v. UNITED STATES

United States Court of Claims, 1976.   533 F.2d 550.

KUNZIG, JUDGE.

In this income tax refund suit plaintiff seeks a 1966 deduction
for legal expenses incurred while resisting a Venezuelan tax deficiency. The potential Venezuelan tax liability devolved on plaintiff as the
recipient of assets from a liquidated corporation that would have
incurred the tax. . . . We hold that plaintiff is entitled to deduct
the legal expenses under the provisions of subsection 212(3) of the
Internal Revenue Code of 1954.

As stipulated, Philip Sharples (plaintiff) was the majority shareholder of Sharples Oil Corp. (SOC), an entity organized under the
laws of Delaware, until its 1963–64 liquidation. In [1960 SOC in
effect sold certain Venezuelan property to a third party, in a transaction which all concerned treated] as a non-taxable sale under the
Venezuelan law.

In 1963–64, SOC . . . liquidated. Plaintiff received various
liquidating distributions as a transferee. Dissolution became final
in March 1964. Nearly seven months later, Venezuela issued a notice
to SOC of proposed tax deficiencies from the 1960 sale. Delaware
law would have imposed personal liability on the former SOC shareholders to pay the tax. However, plaintiff retained Venezuelan counsel to fight the Venezuelan tax deficiency.

Eventually these efforts were successful, and the tax avoided.
Plaintiff paid Venezuelan counsel $168,609.15. In his 1966 U. S. in-
come tax return, he deducted the legal expenses. The Internal Revenue Service (IRS) disallowed this deduction, treating the payments
as an additional capital contribution to SOC. The IRS assessed a
deficency which plaintiff paid. After the IRS rejected his subsequent
refund claim, plaintiff timely brought the present action.

Plaintiff justifies his 1966 deduction of the Venezuelan legal fees
as "ordinary and necessary expenses paid or incurred . . . in

connection with the determination, collection, or refund of any tax."
§ 212(3), Int.Rev.Code of 1954. Plaintiff buttresses this argument
by pointing to the income tax regulations. "[E]xpenses paid or incurred . . . for tax counsel . . . or in connection with any
proceedings involved in determining the extent of his tax liability
or in contesting his tax liability are deductible." Treas.Reg. § 1.212–1
(*l*).

Defendant resists plaintiff's use of the rather broad provisions
of subsection 212(3) and the regulations by urging application of
two exceptions to deductibility. Both exceptions involve variations
of what has been called the "origin of the claim" rule.[4] The first
exception arises in conjunction with subsection 212(3). It looks to
the origin of the tax claim in terms of the *person* liable for the tax.
A taxpayer receives a deduction for expenses incurred in contesting
his own tax, but cannot deduct expenses attributable to resisting a
tax imposed cn another. The Government argues that Sharples may
not use subsection 212(3) in the present action because the Venezuelan
tax was incurred by SOC, not plaintiff.

Until the instant case, the second exception has been applied to
deny only subsection *212(2)* and *162(a)* deductions.[5] This second
version of the "origin of the claim" rule looks to the *transaction* from
which the tax liability arose (initial transaction). As a general rule,
a taxpayer must subtract from the proceeds of a capital transaction
(*i. e.* capitalize) all expenses which arise, directly or indirectly, from
the capital transaction. Defendant would have us enlarge this second
exception in the present action to apply not only to subsection 212(2),
but also to 212(3). Under this rationale, defendant argues, we would
have to deny plaintiff's 1966 deduction because plaintiff incurred
the legal fees as a result of the SOC liquidation, a capital transaction.

The court rejects defendant's attempts to remove this case from
subsection 212(3) by use of the "origin of the claim" doctrine. We
hold that plaintiff may deduct the legal expenses under subsection
212(3).

4. The phrase "origin of the claim"
stems from the opinion of the Supreme
Court in *Woodward v. Commissioner*,
[Suppl. page 374, supra]. Construing
the decision in *United States v. Gilmore*, 372 U.S. 39 . . . (1963), the
Court noted that the proper test for
deductibility should focus on "the *origin* and character of the claim against
the taxpayer." . . . [Footnotes are
by the Court, but most have been
omitted.]

5. Subsection 162(a) governs the deductibility of *trade or business* expenses.

. . . Subsection 212(2) allows deductions for personal expenses incurred "for management, conservation,
or maintenance of *property held for
the production of income*." . . .
Subsection 212(3) controls deductions
for personal expenses paid in resolving
tax liabilities. . . . While the
three statutes are related in that they
all deal with deductions, they are unrelated in that each deals with a separate type of deductible expense.
Note that plaintiff relies only upon subsection 212(3) and *not* on subsections
212(2) and 162(a) in this refund suit.

I. Subsection 212(3):

We begin our analysis by examining the provisions of subsection 212(3). This statute provides:

> In the case of an individual; there shall be allowed as a deduction all the ordinary and necessary expenses paid or incurred during the taxable year . . . in connection with the determination, collection, or refund of any tax. [§ 212(3), Int.Rev. Code of 1954].

The legislative history of subsection 212(3) illustrates the breadth that Congress intended for this statute. *"Any expenses* incurred in contesting *any liability* collected as a tax or as a part of the tax will be deductible." H.Rep.No.1337, 83d Cong., 2d Sess. A 59 (1954) . . . .

Application of the clear language of subsection 212(3) would usually compel our holding for plaintiff, granting him the right to a deduction in the instant case for expenses incurred in fighting the Venezuelan tax. However, we must first deal with defendant's "origin of the claim" arguments in its attempt to override application of subsection 212(3).

II. Origin of the claim—person taxed:

In United States v. Davis, 370 U.S. 65 . . . (1962), a taxpayer paid his wife's legal expenses incurred pursuant to a divorce settlement. Part of such legal expense was directed toward his wife's tax treatment of property transferred during the divorce. The Supreme Court denied taxpayer's claim for a deduction, reasoning that subsection 212(3) only applied to the taxpayer's legal expenses and not expenses paid for the benefit of another.

> As to the deduction of the wife's [legal] fees, we read the statute, if applicable to this type of tax expense, to include only the expenses of the taxpayer himself and not those of his wife. Here the fees paid her attorney do not appear to be 'in connection with the determination, collection, or refund' of any tax of the taxpayer. [United States v. Davis, supra at 74 . . . .]

Later, in 1967, the Court of Claims further dealt with this subsection 212(3) exception. The court was faced with a case in which the taxpayer incurred legal expenses by resisting a tax liability of a corporation. Taxpayer's obligation to pay the debt was based on an indemnity agreement. The court held that the indemnity agreement did not make the corporation's legal expenses "those of the taxpayer" for purposes of subsection 212(3). Only if the taxpayer incurred the expense himself or by operation of law as a transferee could the expenses be deducted under subsection 212(3). Southern Arizona Bank and Trust Co. v. United States, 386 F.2d 1002 . . . .

In short, under the first "origin of the claim" exception the court must go beyond the statutory provisions of subsection 212(3) to determine the taxpayer's entitlement to a deduction. If the tax liability is personal to the taxpayer, either because it is his liability or because the liability is imposed on him by operation of law, subsection 212(3) applies. *Southern Arizona Bank*, supra. If, however, the tax obligation is that of another, subsection 212(3) is of no avail to the taxpayer.

Defendant would have the court find the instant tax liability to be that of SOC rather than plaintiff. The defendant is correct in its view that the original tax liability belonged to SOC. However, defendant ignores the fact that liability for the Venezuelan tax devolved upon plaintiff at the time of the liquidation by operation of Delaware law. Plaintiff's liability as created by Delaware law made him responsible for the debt within the test established by *Southern Arizona Bank*. The tax liability was personal to the taxpayer. Defendant's first argument is inapplicable to the present facts. Plaintiff is not precluded from gaining the benefit of subsection 212(3).

III. "Origin of the claim"—initial transaction:

Defendant further urges the court to enlarge the second "origin of the claim" exception in the instant case. In this second argument, defendant relies upon the rationale inherent in capitalization treatment of certain expenditures. Where expenses arise in connection with a capital transaction, the taxpayer must capitalize such expenses rather than deduct them from ordinary income. As stated above, defendant would have us enlarge this second exception to apply to subsection 212(3) as well as subsection 212(2). The liquidation of SOC was a capital transaction. Since the legal expenses arose in connection with a capital transaction reasons defendant, they should be capitalized by plaintiff rather than deducted under subsection 212(3).

We evaluate defendant's second argument in the context of the clear language of the statute, its legislative history, case law and policy considerations. Defendant's "initial transaction" version of the "origin of the claim" rule cannot be upheld in the present fact situation.

Again, we start with the clear wording of subsection 212(3). This provision grants a deduction for "expenses incurred" in conjunction with "any tax,"—certainly the clearest, most compelling reason to reject defendant's attempts to engraft an exception onto subsection 212(3). . . . Plaintiff is entitled to deduct the expenses incurred in fighting to Venezuelan tax under the clear wording of subsection 212(3). Defendant has not demonstrated that Congress intended to limit the statute by the "initial transaction" exception.

Further, defendant's own regulations underscore the breadth of subsection 212(3) and give no hint of any "initial transaction" exception. "Expenses paid . . . in conjunction with *any proceedings* involved in determining the extent of [taxpayer's] tax liability or *in contesting his tax liability* are deductible." Treas.Reg. § 1.212–1 (*l*) (emphasis added).

Congress, too, demonstrated its desire to have subsection 212(3) apply in a sweeping manner. "Any expenses incurred in contesting any liability collected as a tax or as part of the tax will be deductible." S.Rep.No.1622, *supra* at 218; . . . . Again, there is no indication of any intent that the "initial transaction" version of the "origin of the claim" rule override the clear meaning of subsection 212(3).

Despite the clear wording of subsection 212(3), the regulations and legislative history, defendant argues that the holdings in Arrowsmith v. Commissioner, 344 U.S. 6 . . . (1952), Woodward v. Commissioner, [supra, note 4] and United States v. Hilton Hotels Corp., 397 U.S. 580, . . . (1970) compel adoption of its "initial transaction" exception in the subsection 212(3) area. In *Arrowsmith*, the Supreme Court looked to the nature of the original transaction to deny business expense deductions claimed under the predecessor of subsection 162(a). Since the expenses in question arose from a capital transaction, reasoned the Court, expenses incident thereto should have been treated as capital items. This doctrine was later applied in both the subsection 162(a) and 212(2) contexts in *Woodward* and *Hilton Hotels*. Again, the nature of the original transaction was crucial to the determination. Where the original transaction was a capital transaction, expenses flowing therefrom had to be capitalized. Defendant contends that since the "initial transaction" exception overrides subsections 162(a) and 212(2) it should also override subsection 212(3).

The short answer to defendant's argument is that the statute, the regulations and the legislative history of subsection 212(3) provide *no different treatment* for expenses incurred in fighting a tax which arose from a capital transaction as opposed to expenses for contesting a tax which arose from a non-capital transaction.

Further, to the best of our knowledge no court has ever extended the *Arrowsmith* initial transaction rule to override subsection 212(3). Defendant has not directed our attention to any such case, and we have been unable to discover one. To the contrary, the cases to date dealing with subsection 212(3) seem without exception to have assumed that if the expense relates to a taxpayer's personal tax liability, the inquiry is complete and a subsection 212(3) deduction allowable. . . . Particularly notable along these lines is Collins v. Commissioner, 54 T.C. 1656 (1970). In *Collins*, the Tax Court allowed taxpayers a subsection 212(3) deduction for Certified Public Accountant (CPA) expenses incurred in tax planning despite the fact that much of the CPA's advice was directed to the purchase of an apartment building as an investment. Although the CPA expenses arose in a capital transaction, taxpayers were still allowed to use subsection 212(3). In short, defendant's argument that the *Arrowsmith* "initial transaction" rule overirdes subsection 212(2) [sic] does not find acceptance in case law.

In addition to principles of statutory construction and case law, policy considerations compel rejection of defendant's "initial transaction" exception to subsection 212(3). The philosophy inherent in subsection 212(3) seems to be based on the idea that taxpayers should be encouraged to assert their legal rights by contesting imposition of unjustified taxes. Defendant attempts to overcome this strong philosophy with the rationale that stems from the "origin of the claim" rule. This competing rationale rests on the belief that all expenses which stem from a capital transaction should rationally be "matched" or equated with all gains from the same capital transaction and the expenses should receive identical tax treatment as the gains. The "origin of the claim" reasoning is of some weight, but is not strong enough to overcome the subsection 212(3) philosophy. Given a choice between mere consistency of tax treatment embodied in the "origin of the claim" doctrine and encouraging taxpayers to assert their right to contest illegal taxes, we prefer the latter alternative.

Beyond the factors which compel us to reject defendant's personal liability and "initial transaction" exceptions, other overall policy considerations support our conclusion that plaintiff is entitled to a subsection 212(3) deduction for the legal expenses involved in the present action.

First, plaintiff's decision to contest the improper Venezuelan tax created a savings for defendant in non-tax areas. At a time when the United States balance of payments was unfavorable, plaintiff's resistance of the Venezuelan taxes prevented an even further imbalance. . . .

Second, defendant's negative attitude toward plaintiff's attempted deduction could have an additional negative impact on the Treasury. Had plaintiff paid the Venezuelan tax, he might have been entitled to a U. S. tax credit for his foreign tax payment, and the Government would have lost additional revenue. . . .

Third, acceptance of defendant's "origin of the claim" arguments would create a distinction without a logical difference in the instant case. Presumably, if plaintiff paid a tax attorney for advice as to whether or not to fight the Venezuelan tax from the point of view of planning its [sic] own tax affairs, such legal expenses would be deductible under subsection 212(3). Yet defendant would disallow the further legal expenses incurred in actually contesting the tax. We see no logical reason for treating either legal expense differently from the other. Again, we are led to reject defendant's attempt to engraft or broaden subsection 212(3) exceptions.

In summary, we are faced with a situation where taxpayer incurred legal expenses in 1966 pursuant to his resistance of a Venezuelan tax liability which would have devolved upon him as recipient of assets from a liquidated corporation, personally, by operation of Delaware law. The legal expenses were properly deductible from plaintiff's 1966 income under subsection 212(3) of the Internal Revenue Code of 1954. Neither the fact that plaintiff's corporation was initially liable for Venezuelan tax, nor the fact that the legal expenses arise in connection with a capital transaction precludes plaintiff's use of subsection 212(3). This conclusion emerges from Treasury Regulations, Congressional intent, case law, the philosophy inherent in subsection 212(3) and simply, *from the clear language of the statute.*

NOTE ON DEDUCTIBILITY OF EXPENSES FOR TAX ADVICE - §212(3)

Since the Sharples case dealt with expenses incurred in an actual tax litigation, the court did not have to confront the troublesome question of deductibility of expenses for tax advice and planning, which generally come well before any litigation (and, if successful, will eliminate the need for any contest over the tax incidents of the transactions). Before turning to that issue, however, it is worth noting that the Sharples opinion masks a fairly difficult problem of its own. In holding that §212(3) overrides the normal rule that expenses incurred in the acquisition of property must be capitalized, the Sharples court made no reference to the general requirement in §212, applicable to all the subdivisions of the statute, that the expenses be "ordinary and necessary." But it is this talismanic phrase upon which the Supreme Court relied in the Woodward case in ruling that capital expenses (i.e., expenses incurred in acquiring capital assets) could not be deducted under either §162 or §212(2). As the court put it (on page 3.10-3, supra): "If an expense is capital, it cannot be deducted as 'ordinary and necessary' either as a business expense. . . or as an expense of 'management, conservation, or maintenance' under §212." If the "ordinary and necessary" test rules out deduction for expenses incurred in acquiring property under §212(2), that would seem to be no less true under §212(3). The court in Sharples cited the Collins case as supporting tax deductibility under §212(3) for expenses relating to the acquisition of property; but Collins was decided in the same year as Woodward, and did not have the benefit of the Supreme

Court's emphasis on the capital nature of expenses incurred in acquiring property. In addition, the tax planning in Collins was largely directed to the taxpayer's desire to shelter a windfall gain he had enjoyed that year, rather than the actual acquisition of the property as such, and might therefore be outside the scope of the rule requiring capitalization.

In any event, the Collins case represents a useful bridge to the question of deductibility under §212(3) for expenses of advance tax planning, which the Tax Court seemed to allow without hesitation. Concededly, §212(3) was added to the Code to overcome the decision in Lykes v. United States, 343 U.S. 118 (1952), which held that legal fees paid to litigate the value of securities for gift tax purposes were not deductible under §212(1)or(2). Several pre-Collins cases grappled with the question of how far back of a tax contest §212(3) was designed to reach. Thus in Kaufmann v. United States, 227 F.Supp. 807 (D.C.W.D. Mo., 1963), the taxpayers were considering a proposal to exchange the stock of their highly successful close corporation for the shares of a listed company, and they retained an accounting firm to explore the tax consequences of the transaction, and to prepare a request for a ruling by the IRS that the transaction would qualify as a non-taxable reorganization. The IRS disallowed the deduction of the fee paid to the accounting firm, and the taxpayers sued for a refund. The Service contended that deductibility under §212(3) was confined to amounts expended in connection with a tax liability that had already arisen, i.e., from a transaction that had previously occurred, and did not apply to expenses incurred in determining the tax incidents in advance. The court found that §212(3) was not so limited (even though the legislative history of the provision repeatedly referred to expenses in connection with tax "contests"), and held that the cost of determining whether the transaction was tax-free (which was apparently an express condition of consummating the deal) fell with §212(3).

On the other hand, the court denied a deduction for the portion of the fee allocable to determination of what the taxpayers' basis in the new stock would be, on the the ground that while the tax basis represented useful information, and could have some future impact, its present computation was not "for the purpose of determining any tax." Query how sensible this distinction is, since the only significance of tax basis is its possible role in some future tax determination; on the other hand, unlike the reorganization, which had already been conditionally executed, the stock basis was not presently expected to be involved in a tax computation (and might never be, if the stock was held until death by the taxpayers, thereby receiving a new date-of-death basis).

A year later the Court of Claims, confirming an earlier ruling, held that §212(3) authorized deduction of the legal expenses incurred by a husband for advice and planning relating to the tax consequences of proposed alimony payments. Carpenter v. United States, 338 F.2d 366 (Ct.Cl.1964). The court said:

> In interpreting this subsection of the statute, Treasury Regulations §1.212-1(ℓ) does not restrict the deductibility of expenses for the employment of tax counsel to contest of a tax liability or preparation of tax returns for a single year. It provides, by way of illustration, four separate examples:
>
>> "expenses paid or incurred for the [sic] tax counsel or expenses paid or incurred in connection with the preparation of his tax return or in connection with proceedings involved in determining the extent of his tax liability or in contesting his tax liability." [Emphasis supplied.]
>
> There is nothing in the Regulation to suggest that these four illustrative examples of legal expenses deductible under Section 212(3) are exclusive as to its application. Subsection 1(g) of the same section of the Regulation provides for the deduction of fees paid for services of, among other things, "investment counsel." Obviously, a taxpayer does not employ investment counsel after he has made his investments, and he should not be restricted to deduction of expenses for tax counsel solely to discover the tax consequences of what has already transpired or a tax liability already accrued. One of the purposes of a taxpayer in obtaining tax counsel is to avoid tax contests, not to create them, and this also serves the interest of the Government in collecting taxes.

Judge Davis, in dissent, would have confined the deduction for tax advice under §212(3) to past or settled events,
thus excluding expenses for advance planning:

> The ultimate consequence of the [majority's view]
> is that individual taxpayers will be able automati-
> cally to deduct counsel fees paid for the general
> planning of their holdings and estates so as to
> minimize income, estate, or gift taxes in the
> years ahead, or for arranging marital or family
> affairs with the same end of tax-minimization in
> the future . . .. Hitherto, the large share of
> these costs which fall outside section 212(1) and
> (2) have been personal expenses, barred from
> deduction by Section 262 . . . .. I find nothing to
> intimate that Congress, in adding section 212(3),
> intended to overturn this accepted position by
> placing the expenses of trying to reduce one's
> future taxes in a different category from all the
> other personal expenses of living."

The question may since have been settled in favor of
deductibility for advance planning, by Revenue Ruling 72-545,
1972-2 Cum. Bull. 179. There the Service ruled that legal
fees incurred by the taxpayer for advice on the federal tax
consequences of a proposed property settlement agreement
with his wife incident to a divorce were deductible; and the
same was true for a taxpayer's cost of engaging tax counsel
to advise him on the federal income, gift, and estate tax
consequences of establishing a trust to make periodic support
payments to his wife after their divorce. The Ruling empha-
sizes the need to isolate the costs of tax counsel from the
other legal expenses, and finds that requirement satisfied
by either a careful allocation of the fee between tax and
non-tax matters, or the use of a law firm which limits its
practice to tax matters (which may give such firms something
of a competitive edge in these situations).

It should be noted that the ruling involved imminent
transactions, like the reorganization in the Kaufmann case,
supra; there may still be doubt about the status of advice
concerning a speculative, future tax matter, such as the
computation of the stock basis in Kaufmann. Somewhere
between these two poles lies the typical case of estate
planning, which, while certain to come into play sometime,
the taxpayer normally hopes will be long delayed. In Merians

v. Commissioner, 60 T.C. 187 (1973), the Government conceded that the portion of estate planning costs relating to tax considerations was deductible under §212(3) but insisted that the taxpayer had not adequately established how much that was. In this posture of the matter, a majority of the Tax Court was willing to follow the common practice of accepting a reasonable estimate of the deductible amount; however, a number of the judges expressed reservations about the Government's concession here (and in Rev. Rul. 72-545) that the expenses of advance tax planning were automatically deductible under §212(3), and so perhaps that question is still not finally resolved.

G. EFFECT OF A REDEMPTION ON EARNINGS AND PROFITS

ANDERSON v. COMMISSIONER *

United States Tax Court, 1976.

67 T.C. 522.

. . .

Issue 1

The legal issue we must first decide is what portion of a redemption distribution, described in section 302(a), is properly chargeable to earnings and profits pursuant to section 312(e) and (a). This issue is directly relevant to two separate factual situations, both involving CLT.

(a) *CLT common stock redemption.*—As of April 1, 1968, the beginning of its taxable year ended March 31, 1969, CLT had accumulated earnings and profits of $789,305 within the meaning of section 316(a)(1). During this year CLT had current earnings and profits of $758,568 before taking into account dividend distributions in the amount of $60,691 made to shareholders during the year and the redemption distribution described below. Immediately prior to the common stock redemption, CLT had outstanding the following shares of stock which possessed the indicated characteristics:

(i) 2,500 shares of $1 par value class A common stock ($2,-500) with paid-in capital of $16,704 attributable thereto.

* Portions of the opinion and many of the footnotes omitted.

(ii) 7,500 shares of $1 par value class B common stock ($7,-500) with paid-in capital of $50,110 attributable thereto.

(iii) 1,710 shares of $100 par value preferred stock ($171,-000) with no paid-in capital attributable thereto.

. . .

On December 15, 1968, CLT distributed $510,000 to one of its shareholders in redemption of 425 shares of class A common stock and 1,275 shares of class B common stock. CLT treated this distribution as one which came within the general rule of section 302(a) and thus applied the special rule provisions of section 312(e) in determining the resulting effect on its earnings and profits.[13] Respondent agrees that section 312(e) is the provision applicable in determining the effect of the distribution on CLT's earnings and profits, but the parties disagree on the manner in which this subsection operates.

Section 312(e) provides:

(e) *Special Rule for Partial Liquidations and Certain Redemptions.*—In the case of amounts distributed in partial liquidation (whether before, on, or after June 22, 1954) or in a redemption to which section 302(a) or 303 applies, the part of such distribution which is properly chargeable to capital account shall not be treated as a distribution of earnings and profits.

Neither the meaning of "capital account" nor the procedure for determining what part of a distribution is "properly chargeable" thereto is included in the Code or the regulations.

CLT applied section 312(e) as follows:

The 1,700 shares redeemed (425 class A shares and 1,275 class B shares) represented 17 percent of the outstanding common stock. CLT debited its corporate books accordingly:

Stated capital—class A common ..	$425	(17% of $2,500)
Stated capital—class B common ..	1,275	(17% of $7,500)
Paid-in capital	11,358	(17% of $66,814)
Retained earnings	496,941	
Total charge	510,000	(rounded)

For tax purposes, CLT accounted for the transaction in the same manner, i. e., CLT treated the term "capital account" as meaning total capital contributed by the shareholders with respect to the class(es) of stock redeemed. CLT determined that the proper charge to capital under section 312(e) was an amount equal to the percentage of the par

13. Section 312(a) provides that as a general rule on the distribution of property by a corporation with respect to its stock, the earnings and profits of the corporation shall be reduced by the amount of the money distributed. An exception to the general rule is contained in section 312(e) for cases where the distribution is in partial liquidation or qualifies as section 302(a) or section 303 redemptions.

able to capital account shall not be considered a distribution of earnings or profits . . . for the purpose of determining the taxability of subsequent distributions by the corporation.

Neither the definition of the term "capital account" nor the manner in which to make the "proper charge" thereto was contained in the Act of 1924. The legislative comments contained in the committee reports which accompanied this legislation were sparse. Both the House and Senate reports contained the same statement with respect to the provision which is now section 312(e):

No similar provision is contained in the existing law, although the provisions of the bill represent what is probably a correct construction of existing law and unquestionably what is in accord with business practice. [H.Rept.No.179, 68th Cong., 1st Sess. 11–12 (1924); S.Rept.No.398, 68th Cong., 1st Sess. 11–12 (1924).]

Upon examination of the "existing law" and the contemporary "business practice," the legislative comment proves to be less than enlightening. No more enlightening is the example contained in the "Statement of the Changes Made in the Revenue Act of 1921 by H.R. 6715 and the Reasons Therefor," 68th Cong., 1st Sess. 3 (Comm.Print 1924), to illustrate the effect of this section, which merely demonstrates that payment of par value in redemption of stock "constitutes a capital transaction and does not affect the earnings and profits of the corporation on hand for subsequent distribution."

The meaning of the term "capital account" was first alluded to in the case of *John B. Stewart*, 29 B.T.A. 809, 814 (1934), where it was assumed in the discussion that "capital account" meant the par value of the stock. *August Horrmann*, 34 B.T.A. 1178 (1936), was the first case to deal directly with the application of section 312(e) and the definition of capital account. The Court therein recognized a distinction between the accounting definition of capital and the term "capital account" as used in the Code and defined the statutory term as meaning "only paid-in capital." In doing so the Court reasoned:

We think that a proportional part of the paid-in capital must be considered as standing behind each of the shares outstanding at any particular time, so that on redemption of any of them a certain part of the redemption is properly chargeable against capital account. . . . [34 B.T.A. at 1186.]

Next, in *William D. P. Jarvis*, 43 B.T.A. 439, 444 (1941), we determined that a redemption of one-tenth of the outstanding stock required a proportionate charge to the capital account (as defined in *Horrmann*), and held the remainder of the distribution was to be charged to earnings and profits. On appeal, the Fourth Circuit affirmed. Helvering v. Jarvis, 123 F.2d 742 (4th Cir. 1941). The Fourth Circuit in the

value and paid-in surplus of the common stock which was equal
percentage of the outstanding common stock redeemed. In thi
17 percent of the common stock was redeemed and CLT charge
capital account in the amount of.$13,058.58; 17 percent of the c
contributed with respect to the common stock.

Petitioners contend that the above procedure used by CLT
in accordance with the interpretation given to section 312(e) by
Court in *William D. P. Jarvis,* 43 B.T.A. 439 (1941), as affirme
Helvering v. Jarvis, 123 F.2d 742 (4th Cir. 1941).

Respondent contends that the interpretation of section 312(e)
the formula for the application of that section contained in *Jarvi*
erroneous [14] and urges us to adopt his interpretation and for
which were enunciated in Rev.Rul. 70–531, 1970–2 C.B. 76. The h
of this controversy is the different meaning each party gives to
term "capital account." [15] Petitioner cites *Jarvis* for the propos
that under the facts of this case, the term "capital account" as
in section 312(e) includes only the par or stated value of the outst
ing common stock plus the paid-in capital attributable thereto.
spondent argues that the term "capital account" as used in section
(e) includes more than just the shareholders' contributed capital.
spondent contends that the account also contains the unrealized
preciation attributable to the assets owned by the distributor corp
tion, i. e., the excess of the fair market value of the corporate as
over the adjusted basis of those assets. The controversy under
cussion is not new but instead is one which has a long and interest
history and which we deem appropriate to discuss briefly and f
vital to our decision herein.

What is now section 312(e) first appeared in the Revenue Act
1924 as part of the last sentence of section 201(c) as follows:

In the case of amounts distributed in partial liquidatior
.   .   .   the part of such distribution which is properly char

---

14. Respondent does not address the
question of whether the method used
by CLT to compute the section 312
(e) charge to capital in fact comports
with the *Jarvis* rule (*William D. P.
Jarvis,* 43 B.T.A. 439 (1941), aff'd 123
F.2d 742 (4th Cir. 1941)). (See our
discussion on this point in n. 29, p. 543,
infra.)

15. Another factor contributing to the
difference in result is the respondent's
inclusion of the preferred stock into
the computation of the "proper charge"
to capital account, i. e., respondent argues that because of the right of the
preferred shareholders to participate

in dividends after payment of
4½-percent preferred dividends nec
sitates including the number of o
standing preferred shares into the
nominator with the outstanding co
mon shares to compute the percenta
of stock redeemed which is then us
to determine the proper charge to cap
tal. We discuss this proposal at p
542, 543, infra.

17. As defined by section 201(g) of th
Revenue Act of 1924, amounts paid i
partial liquidation included distribu
tions in redemption of part of the
corporation's stock.

course of its opinion noted an alternative argument made by the Commissioner that "the Board failed to take into account the *unrealized appreciation* of the corporation's assets. [Emphasis added.]" The court agreed with the Board and rejected this argument. Helvering v. Jarvis, supra at 746.

The Commissioner issued a nonacquiescence to the *Jarvis* decision at 1941–1 C.B. 16. A year later in 1942–2 C.B. 10, the Commissioner withdrew his nonacquiescence and substituted therefor an acquiescence.[19]

From the time of its enactment, section 201(c), *infra*, renumbered section 115(c) in the Revenue Act of 1928, remained virtually unchanged.

In 1954 the Internal Revenue Code underwent review which resulted in substantial amendments thereto and included among the changes was a comprehensive revision of subchapter C, "Corporate Distributions and Adjustments." As part of the revision to subchapter C the bill introduced by the House of Representatives (H.R. 8300) contained a new provision, section 310(c), which, in pertinent part, stated:

> (c) *Partial Liquidations, Corporate Separations, and Redemptions.*—. . . upon a redemption of stock . . . which is treated as a distribution in full or part payment for such stock under section 302(a), [a corporation's] earnings and profits shall be decreased by an amount which bears the same relation to the earnings and profits immediately prior to the transaction as the amount of money and the adjusted basis of the assets (plus the principal amount of securities, if any) distributed bears to the amount of money and the adjusted basis of the total assets immediately prior to such distribution. . . .

19. G.C.M. 23460, 1942–2 C.B. 190, contained an explanation of the Treasury's acquiescence: The memorandum was in response to a requested opinion as to whether the *Jarvis* opinion was in conflict with the Board of Tax Appeals' opinion in *Woodward Investment Co.*, 46 B.T.A. 648 (1942). (In *Woodward* the question presented was the proper amount of earnings and profits distributed in the first distribution of a complete liquidation of a corporation for purposes of determining the dividends-paid credit (see section 27(f), Revenue Act of 1936). We determined therein that the proper amount of earnings and profits distributed was determined as follows:

$$\text{Amount of distribution} \times \frac{\text{amount of earnings and profits}}{\text{amount of earnings and profits plus capital account}}$$

After discussing its interpretations of those opinions the Treasury concluded that they were not inconsistent but "merely reflect necessary differences in the application of a general principle to different types of situations" and thus acknowledged the withdrawal of the nonacquiescence in *Jarvis*.

In rejecting this proposed new rule the Senate Finance Committee responded:

> The House bill supplied an additional rule for the determination of the manner in which earnings and profits should be allocated when there was a . . . redemption. Your committee strikes this rule since it is believed that existing administrative practice, making these determinations as the facts of each case may indicate, has been successful in achieving correct results. [S.Rept. No.1622, 83d Cong., 2d Sess. 47 (1954).]

Section 312(e) of the 1954 Code was enacted in substantially the same language used in section 115(c) of the 1939 Code and section 201(c) of the 1924 Act. None of the amendments to the Code subsequent to 1954 have directly affected section 312(e).

In 1970 the Treasury adopted a change in the administrative practice respecting section 312(e) in Rev.Rul. 70–531, supra. In that ruling the Service considered a situation in which all of the stock of a corporation owned by one of two 50-percent shareholders was redeemed. The amount of the redemption distribution was such that application of the *Jarvis* formula resulted in the shareholder receiving a distribution in excess of the combined amounts of the paid-in capital as well as the earnings and profits. In light of this situation, the Service reexamined the holdings of *Jarvis*, *Woodward* and *F. & R. Lazarus & Co.* (a 1942 Tax Court decision which essentially affirmed the definition of capital account contained in *Jarvis*), which considered the term "capital account" to include only paid-in capital, and concluded that they were erroneous. Accordingly, the Service withdrew the prior acquiescence and proposed a new formula which purportedly yielded a result which was in accord with economic realities and also with the statute (section 312(e)). The Service stated that because of the implausible result reached under the *Jarvis* definition of capital account, said account must include, in addition to paid-in capital, all other similar attributes (i. e., those treated like capital in the sense that when distributed they are not taxed as dividends but instead are applied against and reduce the basis of the distributee's stock) such as unrealized appreciation (appraisal or valuation) surplus. The formula contained in the revenue ruling to determine the part of a redemption distribution which is "properly chargeable to capital account" is as follows: portion of paid-in capital ratably attributable to share redeemed + [(amount of the distribution) − [(portion of paid-in capital ratably attributable to share redeemed) + (portion of earnings and profits which is ratably attributable to share redeemed)]].

In 1972, in the case of *Herbert Enoch*, 57 T.C. 781 (1972), non-acquiesced on this issue 1974–1 C.B. 1, the propriety of respondent's ruling was first considered. In that Court-reviewed decision the applicability of Rev.Rul. 70-531 became an issue when we found that certain actions, taken subsequent to a section 302(a) redemption distribution, constituted a constructive dividend to the shareholder and thus necessitated a determination of the corporation's earnings and profits. The respondent had determined that the earlier stock redemption constituted a constructive dividend to the petitioner therein and accordingly reduced earnings and profits in full, pursuant to section 312(a); he did not make an alternative argument that Rev.Rul. 70-531 applied should we find said redemption qualified under section 302(a). In our decision in *Enoch* we computed the reduction to earnings and profits under section 312(e) resulting from the redemption pursuant to the *Jarvis* formula. We made reference to respondent's ruling and by way of footnote indicated our appreciation of the fact that we took a different course than he had charted in his ruling.

On brief in the case now before the Court, respondent asks us to reconsider our decision in *Enoch* not to adopt the approach contained in Rev.Rul. 70-531 as to the definition of "capital account" and the proper charge thereto under section 312(e).

Rather than engaging in a lengthy and, we believe, fruitless discussion of the relative merits and criticisms of the respective formulas for the application of section 312(e) espoused in *Jarvis* and Rev.Rul. 70-531, we shall briefly examine those formulas and discuss our reasons for rejecting respondent's request for us to promulgate a change of position.

Respondent's brief in this case is essentially an amplification of the justification given in Rev.Rul. 70-531 for conclusions contained therein. Respondent begins by restating the illustration given in that ruling wherein the amount of the cash redemption distribution exceeds both the capital account (as defined in *Jarvis*) and the earnings and profits account. Respondent, in an obvious allusion to the previously described legislative history (see p. 534, supra) concludes that this result makes little accounting or business sense. However unrealistic the hypothetical posed by respondent, his point is well taken. In a more realistic setting, we can imagine a situation in which a corporation has on hand cash, a portion of which represents some unrealized (taxwise) appreciation of assets and distributes some or all of that cash in an amount in excess of the redeemed shareholder's pro rata share of capital and earnings and profits. Under section 312(e) as interpreted by *Jarvis* the excess distribution will be charged to earnings and profits. This is the core of respondent's dissatisfaction with the *Jarvis* rule; a section 302(a) redemption which yields capital gains treatment to the redeemed shareholder and reduces more than a pro rata portion of earnings and profits for purposes of subsequent distributions to remaining shareholders. Nonetheless, respondent's

508

legal arguments in favor of including unrealized appreciation in the capital account, an argument specifically rejected in the *Jarvis* decision (see p. 535, supra), are unpersuasive.

In place of *Jarvis* the respondent would have us adopt the formula prescribed in Rev.Rul. 70–531, see p. 537, supra.

However, as has been pointed out elsewhere,[23] by means of simple algebra this formula breaks down into the following components: Proper charge to capital = amount distributed − [(shares redeemed ÷ total shares outstanding) × earnings and profits].

Consequently, under respondent's formula the redeemed shares' pro rata portion of earnings and profits is first determined and subtracted from the amount of the distribution and the remainder of the distribution is the "proper charge to capital account." We believe that this formula is contrary to the statutory language which requires computation of the charge to capital first *followed by* a charge of the balance of the distribution to earnings and profits. The result of adoption of respondent's formula would be to render meaningless the term "capital account" in the computation under section 312(e); [24] an effort which was made by the House of Representatives in its legislative proposal of 1954 and which was rejected by the Senate and full committee.[25] To adopt the respondent's formula in light of the foregoing would be too presumptuous to be countenanced, and we cannot and will not take such action.

To be sure, under some circumstances the formula pronounced in *Jarvis* presents some problems; however, the respondent acquiesced in *Jarvis* and by revenue ruling applied this rule for over 28 years.

23. See Reid, "To what extent will distributions in redemption of stock reduce earnings and profits?" 42 J. Taxation 29, 31 (1975).

24. The effect of using respondent's formula is to allocate all presumably unrealized appreciation (calculated by arithmetic rather than appraisal or valuation) to capital account. As indicated in some of the writings on this subject referred to elsewhere herein, this allocation can produce some bizarre results on subsequent distributions by the corporation. Here, respondent's computation states that CLT had earnings and profits totaling $1,282,599 at the time of the common stock redemption. Under the formula of Rev.Rul. 70–531, 1970–2 C.B. 76, only $185,977 of the $510,000 paid for the redeemed stock would be charged against earnings and profits, leaving a balance of $324,023 as "properly chargeable to capital account." However, CLT had only $247,814 in its capital account at that time, consisting of par value and paid-in capital attributable to all three classes of stock outstanding. If unrealized appreciation can be added to corporate accounts at all, it would seem more equitable to allocate the unrealized appreciation ratably between capital account and the earnings and profits account, although this, too, can produce seemingly unrealistic results at times.

25. We believe it noteworthy and indeed find it somewhat distressing that respondent, while devoting a substantial protion of his brief to an examination and interpretation of the legislative history surrounding section 312(e) both before and after 1954, makes no reference whatsoever to the congressional action taken in 1954 described above.

While there is generally no legal impediment to respondent's changing, his position in an attempt to correct a mistake of law . . . retroactively, we do not find that principle applicable here. The repeated congressional reenactment of section 312(e) without change, in the light of the Court's interpretation and application thereof in *Jarvis* and respondent's acquiescence therein, strongly suggests that Congress has accepted the *Jarvis* approach as the correct interpretation of section 312(e). . . .

In our examination of the writings on this subject we note that the authorities have criticized both the *Jarvis* approach and the respondent's approach in Rev.Rul. 70–531; with much of the criticism we are in agreement. However, we have found no suggested interpretation of the section consistent with the wording thereof which solves all of the possible problems which may arise upon its application. We believe that the problem encountered upon application of the *Jarvis* rule to the statute, as it currently exists, is a result of the timing of redemption distributions (i. e., a distribution before realization of gain from unrealized appreciation) and the lack of correlation between the tax effect on corporations and their shareholders as a result of corporate redemption distributions. (Under section 302(a) a shareholder's gain is taxed as capital gain without concern for the source of the distribution.)

The *Jarvis* rule is the result of an interpretation of congressional legislation which interpretation was subsequently explicitly adopted by Congress in 1954. Any change in said rule must now come from Congress.

SECTION 10. THE ACCUMULATED EARNINGS TAX

A. INTRODUCTION

For an initial look at the accumulated earnings tax, read the Central Motor Co. case, which starts on page 517 up to heading c on page 520. Several observations about the structure of this tax are in order at the outset. First, there is a threshold question as to whether the accumulated earnings tax is confined to close corporations, like the ones involved in Central Motor, or whether it could also apply to a publicly-held corporation. In Golconda Mining Corp. v. Commissioner, 507 F.2d 594 (9th Cir. 1974), the Court pointed to a longstanding practice of not applying the accumulated earnings tax to publicly-held corporations, which it viewed as having been approved by Congressional inaction over the years, and held that the taxpayer, with more than 2000 shareholders, was not subject to the tax. Although the opinion contains some sweeping language to the effect that the statute applies "to closely held corporations and these corporations alone", the Court also noted that the taxpayer's inside group owned at most seventeen percent of the stock, and concluded that "it is simply not the case that, as a matter of law, these persons . . . could exercise such 'control'over the corporation as to bring it within" the accumulated earnings tax provisions. In addition, the Court distinguished the two cases involving Trico Products Corp., the only publicly-held corporation to which the tax has apparently ever been applied, on the ground that more than fifty percent of that company's stock was controlled by a group of six insiders, of whom two were principal officers and the other four were apparently also active in management.

Second, keep in mind that, like the income tax, the accumulated earnings tax operates on an annual basis: each year must be looked at separately to determine whether earnings and profits were allowed to accumulate for the proscribed purpose of avoiding the tax on stockholders (and of course only years still open under the normal statute of limitations are subject to attack). However, it does not matter just how much earnings and profits are accumulated in the particular year (so long as the corporation's total accumulated earnings and profits have passed the minimum threshold of $250,000 set by §535(c)(2) for all but personal service companies); under the structure of the statute, assuming the proscribed purpose is present the accumulated earnings tax rate imposed by §531 is applied, not to the earnings and profits for the year, but rather to "accumulated taxable income" as defined in §535, which parallels taxable income for the year, subject to a number of adjustments. (Actually, the tax may even be applicable although no earnings and profits have been accumulated during the year in question, as, for example, when a redemption transaction eliminates all earnings and profits for the year; see footnote 15 to the Lamark Shipping Agency case, page 546-547, infra, and text thereat, which will be considered later.)

Hence the Central Motor opinion is not strictly correct in denominating an "unreasonable" accumulation as one of the elements of the tax: in theory, any accumulation can bring the statute into play, if the proscribed purpose is present. But as a practical matter the reasonableness of the accumulation does play a very significant role in the administration of the tax. That comes about because of the statutory response to the difficulty of dealing with the ultimate issue of the proscribed purpose. The purposes of a corporation depend upon the state of mind of those in control of it, and proving state of mind is always troublesome, since direct evidence is usually unavailable, making it necessary to rely on inferences from the surrounding circumstances. Thus it became desirable to attempt to relate the subjective question of the state of mind of those in control of the corporation to some more objective standard for judging conduct. Congress responded by injecting the subsidiary issue of reasonable needs of the business into the picture: §533(a) makes accumulation beyond the reasonable needs of the business "determinative of the purpose to avoid the income tax with respect to shareholders, unless the corporation by the preponderance of the evidence shall prove to the contrary".

To see how this works in practice, notice that the decision of the Supreme Court in the Ivan Allen Co. case, quoted from at the end of section I(b) of the Central Motor opinion, focuses on the amount of idle liquid assets that the corporation has accumulated, and how that compares with the forseeable needs of the enterprise requiring the expenditure of liquid funds. In other words, though

the statute is billed as an "accumulated earnings" tax, what matters
is not so much the amount of earnings accumulated (notwithstanding
the careless phraseology to that effect at one point in the Ivan
Allen Co. quotation) as it is the amount of the liquid assets the
company has on hand. This is quite consistent with the precise
language of §532, which speaks of a corporation "permitting [its]
earnings and profits to accumulate instead of being divided or
distributed", since it is normally only cash or cash equivalents
that are available for distribution to the shareholders. Accordingly, a company which is short of liquid assets, and even more so
one which has to borrow to meet its cash requirements, should have
nothing to fear from the accumulated earnings tax, even if the
company has accumulated all of its earnings since inception (and a
revenue agent is unlikely to give more than a passing glance to
such a company, so far as the accumulated earnings tax in concerned).
As the Court put it in Smoot Sand & Gravel Corp. v. Commissioner,
574 F.2d 495, 501 (1960), "to the extent the surplus has been
translated into plant expansion, increased receivables, enlarged
inventories, or other assets related to its business, the corporation may accumulate surplus with impunity". In such cases the
company is financing its business needs internally, and the cash
being generated by the company's earnings (as the normal result of
the production-sale-collection cycle) is simply not available for
distribution by way of dividends to the stockholders.

Conversely, if a company with significant earnings has built
up substantial liquid assets which are not being utilized in the
operation of the business, then absent some justification it may be
inferred that larger dividends could have been paid to the shareholders. Accordingly, the company would be a potential target for
the accumulated earnings tax with respect to its most recent taxable
year (and perhaps earlier years as well), and it would make no
difference how absolutely large the total accumulation of earnings
over the years had been (assuming the minimum threshold has been
passed); a fortiori, any further accumulation of earnings would
have to be justified in order to escape the tax. If, then, as of
the beginning of any particular year a company already has on hand
ample liquid funds to finance any contemplated business needs or
contingencies, it will be hard to justify the retention of the
funds derived from that year's earnings. This is what the Court in
Central Motor had in mind when it referred to "unreasonable accumulation" as one of the twin elements of the accumulated earnings
tax.

Incidentally, in determining the amount of a company's liquid
funds for the purpose of judging whether the accumulation exceeds
the forseeable needs of the enterprise, marketable securities
should be included, together with any other investments which are
not related to the business and can be readily converted into cash.
And under the decision of the Supreme Court in that Ivan Allen Co.
case referred to above, in this context it is the current market
value of such assets that counts, not the cost; in other words
unrealized appreciation is taken into account, but reduced by any
costs of disposition, like commissions, plus any gain taxes that
would be incurred upon a sale, since only the net figure is a
measure of the funds available from this source to meet the needs
of the enterprise.

The *Central Motor Co.* opinion contains some examples of business needs which the Regulations acknowledge will justify accumulating liquid funds instead of disbursing them as dividends. To that list must surely be added the repayment of corporate obligations, to banks or other lenders. Another example would be maintaining sufficient funds to meet a potential contingency, provided it is a realistic risk in the circumstances.

In determining the reasonable needs of its business, the taxpayer is not limited to the business which it has carried on to date, but may include the needs of any business which it has undertaken or is about to undertake, Reg. § 1.537–3; and the business may be one carried on through a subsidiary, as well as a directly-owned division of the taxpayer, provided the relationship with the subsidiary is such that its business in effect is operated by the taxpayer. While of course vague and unsubstantiated plans to undertake a new business will not suffice to ward off the accumulated earnings tax, just as is true of similar plans to expand an existing business, Reg. § 1.537–1(b), the taxpayer is entitled to some margin for flexibility. As the court put it in Electric Regulator Corp. v. Commissioner, 336 F.2d 339 (2d Cir. 1964):

> If the Treasury decides that the manufacture of "Regohm" is the "business", then it would forever consign petitioner to the manufacture of that product and view its needs accordingly. Courts, however, must not blind themselves to the realities in this age of rapid technological change. The product of today is frequently outmoded tomorrow. The results of research in the electronics, pharmaceutical and chemical fields alone justify this statement. Nor is it always possible for a company in advance to set aside a specific sum to achieve a specific goal. Comments made in the past to the effect that a definite plan actually followed through must be on the company's books and records before moneys assigned thereto become anticipated needs may have been appropriately qualified in particular cases.

As to plans which are sufficiently definite, is the taxpayer entitled to accumulate earnings equal to the total cost in advance? An affirmative answer seems generally to have been assumed, although there is an intimation the other way in Fenco, Inc. v. United States, 348 F.2d 456 (4th Cir. 1965), where the court suggested that the taxpayer's power to borrow for future expansion eliminated the need to accumulate earnings for that purpose.

Sometimes investment of liquid funds in apparently unrelated assets may actually amount to the operation of a second business. Thus in Sandy Estate Company v. Commissioner, 43 T.C. 361 (1964), a corporation whose principal business had been the operation of apartment properties persuaded the court that its very substantial investments in mortgage loans "were not simply isolated investments, unrelated to petitioner's business," but actually constituted the carrying on of a mortgage loan business for which accumulation of its funds was justified.

The most significant and recurring business need for liquid funds is the requirement inherent in every enterprise for cash to run the day-to-day operations of the business. Every going business must have substantial cash (or cash equivalents) on hand to meet its ongoing expenses for wages, salaries, inventory purchases and so forth. However, comparing the amount of a company's cash with its needs for these purposes is a very tricky proposition, because so much depends upon the rate at which such expenditures will be made, and also the rate at which the company's cash resources will be augmented by receipt of payment on its accounts receivable. What could appear to be a fairly large build-up of cash, say, at year-end (or any other point in time, for that matter), may well be due simply to the fact that the company has just received substantial payments on its receivables, or has not purchased any inventory for a while, or both. In other words, the amount of cash a company has on hand is continuously a function of how much it has recently received on its receivables and how much it has paid out of late to acquire more inventory (or defray other operating expenses). This inextricable linkage between cash on the one hand, and inventory plus accounts receivable on the other, is all the more awkward in the present context because although a build-up of cash may be suspect, inventory and accounts receivable are (except in rare circumstances) "busy" assets, at work in the operations of the business (as the quotation from the *Smoot* case above indicates). As a result, there seems to be no feasible way of judging the amount of the cash a company needs in its day-to-day operations separately from the amount of its inventory and accounts receivable. Accordingly, the present practice is to try to test the total amount of the company's net current assets, that is, the sum of cash (and cash equivalents), accounts receivable and inventory (and perhaps prepaid expenses as well, though they are usually small enough not to matter much), less current liabilities, a figure often referred to as "working capital".

In the earlier cases the courts attempted to formulate various rules of thumb for judging the amount of working capital a company needed, as a guide to testing whether its accumulation of liquid funds was excessive. For example, some courts suggested that a ratio of current assets to current liabilities in the neighborhood of 2½ to 1 or less was an indication that the build-up of liquid assets was not unreasonable (but it should be noted that such a ratio measurement is not very reliable, since it can be dramatically altered by the simple expedient of using some of the current asset to pay off an equivalent amount of liabilities).

Another rule of thumb was to the effect that an accumulation equal to one year's operating expenses (including the cost of goods sold, but not depreciation or income taxes) was reasonable. The basis for this rule was never fully explained, nor, indeed, was it entirely clear whether the rule was intended as a measure of allowable total working capital, or just the cash component (or perhaps the total accumulated earnings to date, as some cases suggested, although that hardly seems rational). However, from this slender reed came the approach now most in vogue for measuring the allowable amount of total working capital. The stage was initially set by cases which viewed this rule of thumb as too generous in many situations, as, for example, where there was a quick turnover of inventory and rapid collection of accounts receivable. Then in Bardahl Manufacturing Corp. v. Commissioner, 24 T.C.M. 1030 (1965), the court, after concluding that accumulation equal to a year's operating costs could not be justified in the light of the rate at which the company's inventory turned over and its accounts receivable were collected, refined the test to allow accumulation of working capital equal to the operating costs for a single operating cycle of the business. Such a cycle consists of the time required to go from cash to inventory (plus production time in the case of a manufacturer), from inventory to sale, and then from sale back to cash by virtue of collection of the receivable.

The computation of the operating cycle under the "Bardahl formula", as this approach has come to be known, is described as follows in the Internal Revenue Service Manual:

Bardahl Formula

(1) The Bardahl formula is a method of computation which determines whether the corporation may accumulate sufficient liquid assets as necessary working capital reserves to meet operating expenses for one normal business operating cycle. Under the Bardahl formula the operating cycle is computed as follows:

    (a) The cost of goods sold for the year is divided into the corporation's average inventory during the year and then multiplied by 365 to determine the number of days necessary to turn over the inventory.

    (b) The corporation's sales for the year are divided into the average balance of accounts receivable and then multiplied by 365 to determine the number of days necessary to collect accounts receivable.

(c) These two amounts are then added together to arrive at the total number of days in the operating cycle.

(2) The amount of working capital reserve which is required to carry the corporation through one operating cycle is determined by *multiplying*:

(a) The amount of the corporation's cost of goods sold plus its operating expenses for one year (excluding depreciation and Federal income taxes), *by*

(b) A fraction which has as the numerator the number of days in the operating cycle and a denominator of 365.

(3) The resulting figure is the amount of liquid assets necessary to meet the ordinary operating expenses for a complete operating cycle.

(4) To the amount computed as being necessary to meet the ordinary operating expenses for a complete operating cycle, as determined by the above method, is added the amount needed to meet specific and definite plans for expansion and any amounts necessary for anticipated extraordinary business expenses.

It should be noted that the same result can be achieved somewhat more simply by merely determining both the inventory turnover fraction and the accounts receivable collection fraction (without turning either one of them into a specified number of days), and then multiplying the total of cost of goods sold plus operating expenses for the year by the sum of those two fractions.

Of the many questions that have arisen in connection with the Bardahl computation, two deserve special mention. First, taxpayers have regularly urged, often successfully, that in computing the inventory turnover fraction the figure used as the numerator should be, not the average inventory during the year, but the peak inventory figure during the year (usually measured at some month-end, since those are the only figures the company is likely to have); obviously, this would produce a larger fraction and hence a greater amount of allowable working capital. Similarly, the numerator of the accounts receivable collection fraction might be the company's peak accounts receivable figure during the year, rather than the average figure. Perhaps the most sensible resolution of this issue appeared in the decision of the Tax Court in Kingsbury Investments, Inc. v. Commissioner, 28 T.C.M. 1082 (1969), where the court rejected both the average figures for inventory and accounts receivable, and the peak figures during the year for each of them, in favor of using the peak *sum* of the two; that is, the court used the figures for that month-end during the year when the sum of inventory and accounts receivable was highest.

Secondly, there is the question of whether the operating cycle, consisting of the sum of the inventory turnover fraction and the accounts receivable collection fraction, should be reduced by the average credit period extended to the company by its suppliers, presumably computed by dividing the company's average accounts payable during the year by the total cost of goods sold for the year. (The delay is paying operating expenses could also be taken into account, as it was in the *Kingsbury Investments* case, supra, by adding the company's average expenses payable to its average accounts payable, and then dividing that sum by the sum of the total operating expenses for the year (exclusive of depreciation and income taxes) and the cost of goods sold for the year.) This question of whether the operating cycle should be reduced to reflect a credit period is one of the principal issues in the Central Motor Co. case, and the remainder of that opinion should be read at this point.

Applying the *Bardahl* formula to the book figures for Cargill (including a reduction in the total operating cycle for the accounts payable cycle, but with no other refinements) yields the following:

$$\text{Inventory Cycle} = \frac{1{,}069}{7{,}237} = .15$$

$$\text{Accounts Receivable Cycle} = \frac{1{,}179}{12{,}305} = .10$$

$$\text{Less: Accounts Payable Cycle} = \frac{362}{7{,}237} = \underline{(.05)}$$

$$\text{Total Operating Cycle } .20$$

Cargill's total operating expenses last year consisted of cost of goods sold of $7,237,000, plus other expenses (exclusive of income taxes) of $3,536,000, which should be reduced by the depreciation expense for the year (here assumed to have been $46,000), producing an adjusted total of $10,727,000.

Hence, allowable working capital under the formula is computed as:

.20 × $10,727,000 = $2,145,000

The amount allowed under the *Bardahl* formula, together with any amount of liquid funds needed for special purposes, such as a planned expansion, is then compared with the company's actual working capital (presumably as of the end of the year) to see if there is an excessive accumulation. In computing working capital, both accounts payable and accrued expenses are deducted from the sum of current assets, regardless of whether either one of them is taken into account by way of a credit cycle under the *Bardahl* formula; liabilities to banks or other institutions, such as on short-term notes, can probably be treated either as a reduction of working capital or as a separate special need justifying accumulation of liquid funds.

CENTRAL MOTOR CO. v. UNITED STATES *

United States Court of Appeals, Tenth Circuit, 1978.

583 F.2d 470.

HOLLOWAY, CIRCUIT JUDGE.

These are consolidated actions brought pursuant to 28 U.S.C. § 1291 for refund of federal income taxes and accumulated earnings taxes for tax years ending in 1966, 1967 and 1968. The companies involved on this appeal are Central Motor Company (Central Motor), Central Credit Corporation (Central Credit), Cruces Credit Corporation (Cruces Credit), and Red Rock Investment Company (Red Rock). . . .

I

THE ACCUMULATED EARNINGS ISSUE

a. *The background of the taxpayer corporations*

The Internal Revenue Service in an audit of the appellants determined that each company was liable for accumulated earnings taxes for the three years in question under 26 U.S.C. §§ 531–537. The taxes assessed under § 531 were paid by the companies and individual refund actions were instituted. The cases were consolidated for trial on motion of the government on the accumulated earnings issue. A jury verdict was rendered in the form of answers to special interrogatories. Their effect was to deny any refund to the taxpayers except Red Rock for 1966. The jury's responses to the special interrogatories established: (1) that each taxpayer (except Red Rock for 1966) had permitted its earnings to accumulate beyond "reasonable present and future needs of the business" in each of the years in issue, (2) that tax avoidance with respect to individual shareholders was one of the purposes of such accumulations, and (3) that the amount of earnings and profits unreasonably accumulated for each year was the exact amount computed in the audit and assessed.

. . . The controlling individual behind the corporations was Mr. Clair Gurley. With respect to all the appellants, Mr. Gurley or his wife owned a substantial amount of the stock during the years in

---

* Portions of the opinion and many of the footnotes omitted.

question. Mr. Gurley served as president of each company. At trial Mr. Gurley testified that he made the final decision on matters affecting relationships between the companies and that he was the "controlling force" behind the companies. (R.A. II, 354). Briefly, the history of the corporations involved in this appeal is as follows:

Central Motor: This is a Ford dealership in Gallup, New Mexico, around which the activities of the other corporations revolved. Mr. Gurley acquired full ownership of Central Motor in 1935 and incorporated it in 1946. In 1957, Central Motor moved to a building and other property owned by Central Credit. Central Motor is a unique dealership because a large volume of its business involves sales of pickup trucks to Navajo and Zuni Indians. Mr. Gurley estimated that 65–70% of the sales were to Indians. During the period 1966–75, Central Motor experienced considerable expansion, both in the total volume of business and in the number of people employed. In this period, total sales rose from $2,915,000 to $10,-905,000, and the number of employees climbed from 47 to 95.

Following liquidation of Central Credit in 1969, the buildings occupied by Central Motor were sold to Mr. Gurley's son and son-in-law. Central Motor then purchased the building from them in 1974. At the time of trial Central Motor was in the process of constructing a new facility which was expected to be completed in a few months. The cost of $500,000–600,000 for the new facility was being financed by Mr. Gurley himself.

In fiscal 1975 Central Motor elected to take sub-chapter S tax status so that its income at the time of trial was being taxed directly to the shareholders (including Mr. Gurley).

Central Credit: Central Credit was incorporated by Mr. Gurley in January, 1956. The nature of its business was limited to ownership of the original land and buildings which were rented to Central Motor Company. During its existence, the only acquisition beyond the original Central Motor building was a body shop in 1961. Central Credit was liquidated in 1969 as a consequence of the audit by the IRS. (R.A. II, 363).

. . .

b. *The general principles governing liability under § 531 for accumulated earnings.*

Pursuant to Code § 532, the accumulated earnings tax of § 531 is imposed if a corporation was "formed or availed of for the purpose of avoiding the income tax with respect to its shareholders . . . by permitting [its] earnings and profits to accumulate instead of being divided or undistributed." Thus, there are two elements to the imposition of the tax: (1) intent to avoid shareholder taxes, and (2) unreasonable accumulation of earnings and profits.

The taxpayers here attack the findings of unreasonableness of their accumulations of earnings but not the jury's findings that there were tax avoidance motives.

The Supreme Court has recently stated the rationale for the imposition of the tax in Ivan Allen Company v. United States, 422 U.S. 617, 624–25, 95 S.Ct. 2501, 2504, 45 L.Ed.2d 435, as follows:

Because of the disparity between the corporate tax rates and the higher gradation of the rates on individuals, a corporation may be utilized to reduce significantly its shareholders' overall tax liability by accumulating earnings beyond the reasonable needs of the business. Without some method to force the distribution of unneeded corporate earnings, a controlling shareholder would be able to postpone the full impact of income taxes on his share of the corporation's earnings in excess of its needs . . .

In order to foreclose this possibility of using the corporation as a means of avoiding the income tax on dividends to the shareholders, every Revenue Act since the adoption of the Sixteenth Amendment in 1913 has imposed a tax upon unnecessary accumulations of corporate earnings effected for the purpose of insulating shareholders.

In ascertaining the reasonableness of accumulations of earnings, each business must be assessed in light of its own particular requirements. . . . Reasonableness of provisions made for business needs is necessarily for determination by those concerned with management of the business. . . . Whether a corporation has accumulated its earnings and profits beyond the reasonable needs of its business, including its reasonably anticipated needs, is a factual determination. . . . In a refund action the taxpayer must present evidence to overcome the presumptive correctness of the Commissioner's assessment. . . . This calls for "objective evidence" from the taxpayer as to the reasonableness of any accumulation made for the purpose of anticipated needs. . . .

Pursuant to Code § 533(a), a company may accumulate income for the reasonable needs of the business. Section 537(a)(1) provides that the reasonable needs of a business shall include its "reasonably anticipated needs."

Several Treasury regulations have been promulgated to serve as guidelines for evaluating the reasonableness of an accumulation. Reg. § 1.537–1(a) adopts the standard of a "prudent businessman" in determining the needs for accumulations. Reg. § 1.537–2(b) lists several grounds that are indicative of the fact that the "earnings and profits of a corporation are being accumulated for the reasonable needs of the business." These grounds include accumulations for expansion of the business, for working capital necessary for the business, and for investments or loans to suppliers or customers necessary to the business. Reg. § 1.537–2(c) states several factors tending to show that accumulations are unreasonable. These factors include: loans to an affiliated corporation whose business is not that of the taxpayer corporation,[6] investments in properties which are unrelated to the business of the taxpayer corporation, and retention of earnings to provide against unrealistic business hazards.

Beyond the general guidelines in the statutes and regulations the courts have pointed to numerous other factors tending to affect the reasonableness of an accumulation. These factors will be treated as we discuss the different taxpayer corporations involved in this appeal.

The basic guidelines are laid down in Ivan Allen Co. v. United States, supra, 422 U.S. at 626–28, 95 S.Ct. at 2506:

> The purport of the accumulated earnings tax structure established by §§ 531–537, therefore, is to determine the corporation's true economic condition before its liability for tax upon "accumulated taxable income" is determined. The tax, although a penalty and therefore to be strictly construed, Commissioner v. Acker, 361 U.S. 87, 91 (1959), is directed at economic reality.
>
> . . .
>
> . . . What is required, then, is a comparison of accumulated earnings and profits with "the reasonable needs of the business." Business *needs* are critical. And need, plainly, to use mathematical terminology, is a function of a corporation's liquidity, that is, the amount of idle current assets at its disposal. The question therefore, is not how much capital of all sorts, but how much in the way of quick or liquid assets, it is reasonable to keep on hand for the business.
>
> . . .

c.   *The Central Motor accumulated earnings case*

Central Motor's main contentions on this part of the case are (1) that the trial court erred as a matter of law in instructing the jury to consider the company's credit cycle on the accumulated earn-

---

6. Obviously, there are some cases in which a conflict will exist between Reg. § 1.537–2(b)(5) (permitting accumulations for investment or loans to suppliers or customers if necessary in order to maintain the business of the corporation) and Reg. § 1.537–2(c)(3) (loans to affiliated corporations, whose business is not that of the taxpayer, tend to reflect unreasonable accumulations). In such cases, the business of the taxpayer corporation and whether the affiliates are suppliers or customers of this business is the determinative factor.

ings issue; [8] and (2) that the evidence is insufficient to support the jury's verdict that Central Motor allowed its earnings and profits to be accumulated unreasonably. (Appellant Central Motor's Brief in Chief 8, 16–17). Central Motor asks that we reverse the judgment and allow all of its claims for refund in full, or alternatively, that we remand the earnings tax issue for trial separately from that of the other companies. (Id. at 48–49).

The parties are not in dispute over the basic approach to one phase of the accumulated earnings tax issue. That is the use of the operating cycle method developed in *Bardahl Manufacturing Corp.*, 24 T.C.M. 1030; . . . .. The Government presented its case on this basis and Central Motor says that the case law beginning with *Bardahl Manufacturing* "has developed an approximate method for determining working capital which bases the amount of necessary working capital on a taxpayer's business needs for one 'operating cycle.' " (Appellant Central Motor's Brief in Chief, 15; see id. at 17). Requirements for working capital (current assets less current liabilities, . . .), are determined by this operating cycle method in *Bardahl Manufacturing Corp.*, which the Tax Court there defined as follows (24 T.C.M. at 1034):

> Manufacturing's operating cycle, consisting of the period of time required to convert cash into raw materials, raw materials into an inventory of marketable Bardahl products, the inventory into sales and accounts receivable, and the period required to collect the outstanding accounts, averaged approximately 4.2 months during the 4 years here in question.

> Petitioner required working capital as of the end of each of the years in question at least in an amount sufficient to cover its reasonably anticipated costs of operation for a single operating cycle. Since its operating cycle during the period 1956 through 1959 averaged approximately 35 percent of a year, its working capital requirements for the continuation of its normal operations amounted to approximately 35 percent

---

8. In instructing the jury on the working capital question, the trial court stated (Orig. R. X, 451–52):

In considering the reasonable needs of a business, you may consider that the corporation may retain enough earnings and profits to meet its working capital requirements. That is, enough to cover its operating expenses during a business cycle. In considering what are the reasonable working capital requirements of the corporation, you should consider the nature of the business, its credit policies, the amount of inventories and rate of turnover, the amount of accounts receivable and the collection rate of those accounts and the extensions of credit to the corporation. Working capital is generally defined as the excess of current assets over current liabilities. Counsel for Central Motor objected to the reference to the credit extension matter. (Id. at 471).

of its reasonably anticipated (and steadily increasing) total annual operating costs and cost of goods sold as of the end of each of the years in issue.

The controversy here is not over use of this operating cycle method, but over the application of a refinement to it which was developed in *Bardahl International Corp.*, 25 T.C.M. 935. This refinement calls for the consideration of the period of time during which suppliers extend credit or permit deferral of payments. In *Bardahl International*, supra, 25 T.C.M. at 946, the Tax Court agreed with the Government that "consideration should be given, particularly under the circumstances existing here, to the length of time petitioner's accounts payable for the purchase of inventory remained unpaid; in other words the average period of credit extended petitioner by Manufacturing, its supplier." Applying this refinement to Central Motor the Government essentially argues for reducing the operating cycle from 40.15 days [9] by 30 days because suppliers extended credit for such a period. (See Government Exhibits 70–72, pp. 22–23). Central Motor says such a reduction is erroneous as a matter of law and is not supported by the evidence.

We must agree with the basic position of Central Motor that the evidence did not justify the drastic reduction in the allowance for working capital which resulted from the way the Government used the credit cycle factor. As noted, the Government's allowance for working capital was based on a reduction of the operating cycle of Central Motor from 40.15 days to 10.15 days. This in turn was based on what the revenue agent said was the "average credit period which has been extended by the suppliers. This was determined to be thirty days." (R.A. II, 490). From that premise, the Government argues that the available working capital was excessive and that the allowance for working capital should be reduced to about one quarter of the amount which the operating cycle method would otherwise have indicated. On the other hand, Central Motor says that during the years in question it needed more working capital

---

9. This is the 1966 calculation. In his calculations and testimony for that year and the others in question, the revenue agent considered only the inventory turnover (the time required for conversion of cash into raw materials through conversion of inventory into sales and accounts receivable), which he calculated as 40.15 days for 1966. From this he subtracted the 30-day credit cycle he relied on. He did not credit Central Motor with the time for the accounts receivable turnover (the time required for conversion of accounts receivable into cash). The latter turnover was calculated by Central Motor's accounting witness as 10.92 days for 1966. The revenue agent testified, however, that inclusion of the accounts receivable turnover in the cycle would not affect the final determination that § 531 applied. (R.A. II, 489–90).

It is the inclusion or exclusion of the 30-day credit cycle which is crucial, as the briefs of both sides recognize.

than was available. The conflicting figures in evidence were as follows:

FYE June 30	1966	1967	1968
(1) Central Motor's calculation on Working Capital Needs (Plaintiff's Ex. 86)	$ 336,766	$ 393,262	$ 467,381
(2) Government's calculation on Working Capital Needs (Plaintiff's Exs. 70, 71, 72 at 22, 28, 34)	86,350	77,110	153,239
(3) Available Working Capital (from Plaintiff's Exs. 70–72, pp. 23, 29 and 35).[12]	255,595.13	302,101.88	326,112.95

The Government contends that the credit cycle should be considered while Central Motor says that it should not. From the calculations just noted the Government concludes that there was an excess of working capital, while Central Motor concludes that there was a deficit of working capital. . . .

From [these] calculations the drastic effect of using the credit cycle as proposed by the Government is apparent. But most important, we feel, is the fact that this is done by mechanically reducing the operating cycle, as in 1966, from 40.15 days to 10.15 days on the sole basis of the determination by the revenue agent that this was "the average credit period extended by the suppliers." . . . Mr. Gurley testified that general suppliers were paid on a monthly or 30-day billing except for new automobiles which were paid for by cash paid on drafts. (R.A. II, 383).

The Government argues that the growing body of case law holds that any computation of working capital requirements must take into account the credit extended to a corporate taxpayer by its suppliers, citing *Bardahl International*, inter alia. (Brief for the Appellee, 32). It is true that several cases have applied the credit cycle refinement. But the Government's case here is not presented on a record like that

12. . . . The parties are in agreement that available working capital is defined by current assets minus current liabilities. The agent also treated an investment in land, which was not listed as a current asset on Central Motor's balance sheet, as an asset available to meet working capital needs because he believed that it was an investment unrelated to the business. (Plaintiff's Ex. 70–72, pp. 23, 29, 35). This property was valued on taxpayer's balance sheet at $62,346 in 1966 and 1967 and at $62,793 in 1968. The agent's treatment of this asset is not raised on appeal. Treatment of the land as an asset available to meet working capital needs still results in a working capital deficit if the 30-day credit extension is not considered.

in *Bardahl International.* There it was particularly stressed by the court that credit to the taxpayer corporation was extended by Bardahl Manufacturing; that Ole Bardahl was president and principal stockholder in both companies; and that in practice Bardahl International paid all other obligations first and then paid Bardahl Manufacturing "when it had the money to do so." 25 T.C.M. at 946. Moreover the average credit period in days extended specifically by Bardahl Manufacturing was determined, based on the turnover of accounts payable, for each year in question. Id. at 937. Obviously, the need for working capital was greatly diminished by the credit arrangements in such a case.

There is no such proof in our record—only the general 30-day reference to credit from suppliers, with no indication that Central Motor had any control over credit extended, or any assurance of it, and no evidence of the actual turnover of payables.[14] Working capital allowances based on the theory which the Government offers, without evidentiary support, might well mean that ". . . the Company would keep one step ahead of the sheriff if everything went right; they would result in prompt insolvency if anything went wrong." Schenuit Rubber Co. v. United States, 293 F.Supp. 280, 290 (D.Md.); . . .

The Government also relies on C. E. Hooper, Inc. v. United States, 539 F.2d 1276 (Ct.Cl.). There the credit cycle was considered in applying the operating cycle method for determining working capital requirements: However, the court pointed out the necessity of specific consideration of three classes of payables (interviewers' salaries, other salaries, and non-salary payables), of the percentage of total expenses within such class, and of the time within which each class of obligation was actually paid. Id. at 1282. Thus the actual impact of the credit cycle on the need for working capital was shown, which was not the case as to Central Motor.

We are persuaded that the evidence was insufficient to justify submission to the jury of the credit cycle theory and the Government's calculations of working capital based thereon. Those calculations called for a drastic reduction of the working capital allowance by about 75% from what the operating cycle method would otherwise show as justified. This reduction was based merely on evidence that a 30-day billing was used by "general suppliers." There were no de-

14. One formula suggested for the determination of the accounts payable cycle appears in Park & Gladson, Working Capital 30 (1963) and Ziegler, *The "New Accumulated Earnings Tax: A Summary of Recent Developments,"* 22 Tax L.Rev. (1966) 77, 98–99 as follows:

$$\frac{\text{Average accounts payable}}{\text{Materials purchased}} \times 365$$

See also *C. E. Hooper,* supra, 539 F.2d at 1282, where a payables cycle was determined for other categories of operating expenses.

tails as to the actual impact of credit extended such as the payables turnover reflecting actual use of credit in paying bills to particular categories of creditors, and no evidence as to Central Motor's control over any credit extensions or assurance of them, or the steady, availability of credit in actual practice.[15a] And we must remember we are dealing with a tax penalty statute which is to be strictly construed. See Ivan Allen Co. v. United States, supra, 422 U.S. at 627, 95 S.Ct. 2501.

Since the credit cycle theory had no basis in fact, we are convinced that the verdict against Central Motor on the earnings tax issue cannot stand. . . .[16] We do not hold that the credit cycle cannot be considered in determining the operating cycle and a reasonable working capital allowance, if evidence is present which justifies consideration of the credit cycle, as discussed earlier. On the remand we feel necessary, it will be open to the parties to develop a fuller factual record pertaining to the operating and credit cycle of the company. . . .

On the other hand, we do not agree with Central Motor that the record is such as to support judgment notwithstanding the verdict in its favor. We cannot say the evidence points all one way so as to be susceptible of no reasonable inference to sustain the Government's position. . . . For aside from the operating cycle and credit cycle issues with respect to working capital, there are other factors which are present to raise factual questions as to the reasonableness of the accumulations of earnings. There were substantial loans made by Central Motor to the other corporations controlled by Mr. Gurley, Central Credit, Red Rock and Cruces Credit, which may indicate unreasonable accumulations. See Reg. § 1.537–2(c)(3). (See e. g., Government Ex. HH, R.A. IV, 951). Central Motor makes a substantial argument that their business was "that of the taxpayer corporation,"

15a. In addition, the length of the taxpayer's credit cycle in *Bardahl International*, supra, 25 T.C.M. 935, and in *C. E. Hooper*, supra, 539 F.2d 1276, was shorter than its receivables cycle (the period necessary to collect accounts receivable). We do not decide whether the credit cycle can reduce working capital needs to the extent that it exceeds the receivables cycle because we do not know what the length of Central Motor's credit cycle would be if properly developed by the evidence. If this problem arises on the remand we feel necessary, the trial court should admit evidence as to whether deduction of the credit cycle in excess of the receivables cycle is justified.

16. We realize there are other theories, discussed below, on which the Government challenged the accumulations of Central Motor and that they arguably could support the verdicts. However, it may well be that the jury adopted the Government's credit cycle theory in reaching its verdicts, and since the computations and consideration of the credit cycle should not have been submitted to the jury by the instructions on this record (see Note 8, supra), and we cannot be sure they were not relied on by the jury, the verdicts cannot stand. . . .

so that under the regulation this is not a factor indicating unreasonable accumulations. However, clearly as to Central Credit whose business was limited to ownership and leasing of a building to Central Motor, it is arguable that its business was not that of the taxpayer. Treas.Reg. §§ 1.537–2(c)(3) and 1.537–3. . . . And Mr. Gurley's testimony did not identify the purpose of particular loans between Central Motor and the other companies. (R.A. II, 401–402).[17]

Furthermore in the years 1966, 1967 and 1968 Central Motor paid dividends, respectively, of only $5,334, $5,299 and $5,294 leaving earnings, after taxes and cash dividends, of $21,140.94, $24,707.11 and $30,088.59. It is arguable that these were relatively small dividends which, with other factors, tend to show unreasonable accumulations. . . .

Countervailing arguments are advanced by Central Motor to justify the retention of earnings. First, it says that the accumulations were needed for expansion of the business. However, despite general testimony by Mr. Gurley of a need for expansion in 1966–1968, and proof of a considerable amount of later acquisitions, . . . there was evidence that the expansion plans were indefinite and that there were no plans drawn at that time. It is arguable from the evidence that specific, definite and feasible plans were lacking, see Reg. § 1.537–1(b)(1), and that there was insufficient objective evidence that the taxpayer intended to carry out its spending program within a reasonable period of time. . . . Second, Central Motor argues that business hazards—strikes and self-insurance—required the accumulations made. While these factors are legitimate grounds for accumulations, again the evidence was such that we cannot say that a judgment n. o. v. is justified. Thus, none of the alternative grounds argued is sufficient to call for a judgment n. o. v. for Central Motor; these issues will remain open for the trial on remand and further evidence is not foreclosed. . . .

In sum, we feel that the verdicts and the judgment against Central Motor on the claim for refund of the accumulated earnings tax cannot stand because of the basic defect in the record on operating and credit cycle matters. We cannot agree with Central Motor, however, that it is entitled to judgment notwithstanding the verdicts. Accordingly, the judgment as to Central Motor denying its claim for refund of the accumulated earnings tax is set aside and the cause is remanded for a new trial on that claim.

. . .

17. Central Motor also argues that there were substantial loans from the other companies to Central Credit which offset the loans made by Central Motor. We do not feel that the record clearly established the offsetting effect of the loans, and a factual question did remain as to whether the loans were some indication of unreasonable accumulations.

e. *The Central Credit accumulated earnings case.*

. . .

. . . Central Credit claims error in the revenue agent's determination of liquid assets available to meet its working capital needs. The agent relied on figures stated in Central Credit's balance sheets filed with its tax returns and made no independent attempt to classify assets as long-term or short-term. Central Credit contends that approximately $200,000 of liabilities classified as non-current on the balance sheet, and also in the agent's calculations, should have been treated as current liabilities. Based on what it says should be a proper reclassification, Central Credit argues that there was not sufficient working capital available in any of these tax years to meet the working capital requirements allowed by the Government.

Despite the classifications on the balance sheet, Central Credit's accountant, Mr. Petranovich, testified that the loans were represented by demand notes payable on request and that such obligations should be regarded as current liabilities. (R.A. II, 465). The company's expert accounting witness, Mr. Rogoff, disagreed with the revenue agent's reliance on the balance sheet and said that it was improper accounting practice to classify such notes as noncurrent liabilities.

We do not feel that the testimony on accounting practices is controlling as a matter of law or that it compels the inference drawn by the taxpayer. . . .

. . . the taxpayer's balance sheets do serve as some evidence that it treated its assets and liabilities in a certain manner. Furthermore, such treatment was the consistent pattern followed by Central Credit over the years in question. In addition, the taxpayer's accountant, Mr. Petranovich, testified that some demand loans were carried over from year to year (R.A. II, 465–66), and the taxpayer did not establish the portion of such loans not carried over from year to year. The taxpayer's witness, Mr. Rogoff, did testify that even demand notes carried over from year to year should be treated as current liabilities (R.A. III, 571–72), but again the jury was not bound by his position on the proper treatment.

In Firstco, Inc. v. United States, 430 F.Supp. 1193 (S.D.Miss.), the court accepted a revenue agent's determination that the taxpayer could not justify accumulations on the basis of need to cover demand notes in similar circumstances. As in our case, the notes in *Firstco* bore interest, no demand for payment had been made, and "[f]rom time to time these notes were reduced, added to or renewed." Id. at 1197. The court looked beyond the label of the demand notes to the actual admitted facts that no demand had been made and that none was expected. Id. at 1202. . . .

Central Credit alternatively argues that if the Government was correct in treating the demand notes payable as noncurrent, then the comparable demand notes receivable by Central Credit from the related companies should also be treated as noncurrent assets. . . . In the circumstances of this case the jury was not bound so to find and could instead find that the taxpayer intended to treat the latter notes as it had treated them on its balance sheets. The evidence was sufficient to support the inference that Central Credit was in a position to demand payment on these receivables and to delay payment of its obligations to the related companies for some time. We find no error in connection with the Government's presentation on these matters and no compulsion from the evidence to rule in Central Credit's favor in disregard of the jury's verdicts.

Lastly, we are not persuaded in Central Credit's case that the evidence was insufficient to support the verdicts. We have noted the approach of the revenue agent in making allowances for working capital needs based on a year's operating expenses. The taxpayer presented no alternative computations. Moreover, there were sizeable loans to related companies, which loans substantially exceeded loans back to the taxpayer from those companies. See Reg. § 1.537–(2)(c) (3). In addition, no cash dividends were paid, while there were earnings after taxes of $19,054 in 1946, $21,444 in 1967 and $22,292 in 1968. (Government Exhibit Q, R.A. IV, 914).

In sum, we are satisfied that the record supports the verdicts and the judgment as to Central Credit, which we affirm.

. . .

---

1. NOTE ON THE BARDAHL FORMULA

Does the *Bardahl* formula lend itself to rational analysis? Let us start with a brief review of the steps involved. The starting point is a determination of the sum of (1) the cost of goods sold expense (CGS) for the year (presumably the most recent fiscal year, though in theory it should probably be the estimated amount for the following year) plus (2) the total operating expenses for the year, exclusive of depreciation (which requires no cash outlay), and income taxes (although recent cases are starting to include income taxes, perhaps because they are now on a pay-as-you go basis during the year). Then the so-called "operating cycle" (which represents a fraction of a year) is computed by adding (a) the inventory turnover fraction, determined by dividing inventory (at year end, or average month-end for the year, or maybe peak inventory during the year) by the cost of goods sold expense for the year (Inv/CGS), to (b) the accounts receivable turnover fraction, determined by dividing accounts receivable (again at year end, or average month-end, or maybe peak) by sales for the year (AR/Sales); under some authority, the sum of those two should then be reduced by deducting a current liabilities turnover fraction, which according to some views would be determined by dividing current liabilities (year-end or average) by the sum of the cost of goods sold expense for the year plus the operating expenses (Liab/CGS + Op Exp). The sum of the cost of goods sold and operating expenses for the year is then multiplied by the fraction computed in the preceding sentence.

This formula can be somewhat refined and reduced if it is expressed in quasi-mathematical symbols:

1. $\left(\dfrac{\text{Inv}}{\text{CGS}} + \dfrac{\text{AR}}{\text{Sales}} - \dfrac{\text{Liab}}{\text{CGS + Op Exp}} \right) \times \ (\text{CGS + Op Exp}) \ =$

2. $\dfrac{\text{Inv}}{\cancel{\text{CGS}}} \times \cancel{\text{CGS}} + \dfrac{\text{Inv}}{\text{CGS}} \times \text{Op Exp} + \dfrac{\text{AR}}{\text{Sales}} \times \ (\text{CGS + Op Exp})$

    $- \dfrac{\text{Liab}}{\cancel{\text{CGS + Op Exp}}} \times \cancel{(\text{CGS + Op Exp})} \ =$

3. $\text{Inv} - \text{Liab} + \dfrac{\text{Inv}}{\text{CGS}} \times \text{Op Exp} + \dfrac{\text{AR}}{\text{Sales}} \times \ (\text{CGS + Op Exp})$

A further refinement is possible by recalling that net income (NI) for a year is equal to Sales minus the sum of CGS plus Op Exp plus depreciation (Depr) and taxes. Thus, we can substitute for (CGS + Op Exp) in line 3 above its equivalent, (Sales − (NI + Depr + Tax), which gives us:

4. $\text{Inv} - \text{Liab} + \dfrac{\text{Inv}}{\text{CGS}} \times \text{Op Exp} + \dfrac{\text{AR}}{\cancel{\text{Sales}}} \times \cancel{\text{Sales}}$

    $- \dfrac{\text{AR}}{\text{Sales}} \times \ (\text{NI + Depr + Tax}) \ =$

5. $\text{Inv} + \text{AR} - \text{Liab} + \dfrac{\text{Inv}}{\text{CGS}} \times \text{Op Exp} - \dfrac{\text{AR}}{\text{Sales}} \ (\text{NI + Depr + Tax})$

Since the *Bardahl* formula is a measure of the allowable amount of working capital, i. e., Cash, Inv, and AR, less Liab, the formula as reduced in line 5 above results in providing a guide to the allowable amount of cash, since Inv, AR, and Liab are common to both actual working capital and the measure allowed by the formula, and can hence be eliminated. (The latter point is not strictly true, to the extent that peak figures for Inv, AR, and Liab are used in the formula; in that event the allowable cash is increased by the net difference between the peak figures and the year-end figures incorporated in the actual working capital being tested.) Cash, it seems, may be equal to the excess of the product of the inventory turnover fraction times operating expenses (in effect the amount of operating expenses for an inventory turnover cycle) over the product of the accounts receivable turnover cycle times the sum of net income, depreciation and taxes. This is not exactly a self-explanatory proposition.

Do we get any help by going back to line 3 above, before we made the substitution which produced line 4? The formula at that point was:

(Repeated)

3. $\text{Inv} - \text{Liab} + \dfrac{\text{Inv}}{\text{CGS}} \times \text{Op Exp} + \dfrac{\text{AR}}{\text{Sales}} \times (\text{CGS} + \text{Op Exp})$

which can be rewritten as

6. $\text{Inv} - \text{Liab} + \left(\dfrac{\text{Inv}}{\text{CGS}} + \dfrac{\text{AR}}{\text{Sales}}\right) \times \text{Op Exp} + \dfrac{\text{AR}}{\text{Sales}} \times \text{CGS}$

This seems to say that the formula will allow a corporation to have cash and receivables equal to the operating expenses for a full operating cycle (unreduced by the liability cycle) plus an amount equal to CGS times the account receivable cycle. Again, one may wonder whether this is a meaningful proposition.

C. THE PROCEDURAL SETTING

1. Burden of Proof -- In General

Although the reasonable business needs issue was intended to simplify the procedure involved in framing an accumulated earnings tax case, it did not turn out to be a panacea for all of the difficulties involved. Indeed, in its earliest form, §533(a) merely made accumulation beyond reasonable business needs "prima facie evidence" of the proscribed purpose, which seemed to add little to the presumption of correctness that normally attaches to any determination by the Commissioner. In 1938, in an obvious effort to strengthen the Government's hand in dealing with the elusive state of mind issue, the provision was cast in substantially its present language, except that the corporation could only disprove the proscribed purpose by a "clear" preponderance of the evidence. In this form, the statutory

presumption was more forceful than the normal presumption of
correctness resulting from a determination by the Commissioner,
since the statutory presumption could be overcome only by meeting
a more onerous burden of proof. However, in the 1954 Code the
word "clear" was dropped, as part of a general effort to lighten
the load for taxpayers defending against the tax; but this may
still leave the Government somewhat better off than with just
the general presumption of correctness, especially if the latter
is viewed as merely imposing a burden of going forward rather
than a full-fledged burden of proof.

In addition, the presumption of §535(a) is only a one-way
street: that is, no presumption against the existence of the
proscribed purpose arises from the fact that earnings were not
accumulated beyond the reasonable needs of the business.

Despite the rather chimerical role of the reasonable business needs issue in theory, in practice it has almost always
been the chief battleground of accumulated earnings tax cases,
and most of the cases have been won or lost on this factor.
Thus, taxpayers have rarely succeeded in disproving the existence of the proscribed purpose in the face of a showing of
accumulation beyond the reasonable needs of the business; conversely, a showing of reasonable business needs for a challenged
accumulation has generally resulted in a finding that the proscribed purpose was not present (and may even be conclusive in
favor of the taxpayer, under the current construction of the
credit for reasonable business needs in §535(c), to be discussed
shortly).

2. Section 534

In 1954, Congress was concerned about numerous complaints
with respect to the administration of the accumulated earnings
tax, ranging from the high costs incurred in such cases to
complaints that the Government was using the threat of this tax
to induce settlement of other issues. Accordingly, the 1954
Code sought to reduce the in terrorem impact of the accumulated
earnings tax, and one of the principal changes was the adoption
of the procedure contained in §534, permitting the taxpayer to
shift the burden of proof on the reasonable business needs issue
to the Commissioner (but only in cases tried in the Tax Court,
which explains why this provision was not involved in Central
Motor). The Senate Finance Committee Report, S.Rep. No. 1622,
83d Cong. 2d Sess. 70-71 (1954), contains the following explanation of §534:

At the present time if the Commissioner of Internal Revenue proposes a deficiency on the ground that
the taxpayer has accumulated earnings and profits in
excess of the reasonable needs of the business, the
taxpayer has the burden of proof as to the reasonableness of the accumulation. Moreover, if earnings and
profits are accumulated in excess of the reasonable

needs of the business, the accumulation is deemed to
be for the purposes of tax avoidance unless the taxpayer proves otherwise by the clear preponderance of
the evidence.

Your committee agrees with the House that this
imposition of the burden of proof on the taxpayer has
had several undesirable consequences. The poor record
of the Government in the litigated cases in this area
indicates that deficiencies have been asserted in many
cases which were not adequately screened or analyzed.
At the same time taxpayers were put to substantial
expense and effort in proving that the accumulation
was for the reasonable needs of the business. Moreover, the complaints of taxpayers that the tax is used
as a threat by revenue agents to induce settlement on
other issues appear to have a connection with the
burden of proof which the taxpayer is required to
assume. It also appears probable that many small
taxpayers may have yielded to a proposed deficiency
because of the expense and difficulty of litigating
their case under the present rules.

Under the House and your committee's bill, the
taxpayer may, upon receipt of notice of a proposed
deficiency with respect to the accumulated earnings
tax, file a statement of the grounds (together with
sufficient facts to indicate the basis for the statement) on which the taxpayer relies to establish the
reasonableness of the accumulation. If the taxpayer
submits such a statement within the proper time, the
burden of proof will be upon the Government as to
whether the accumulation is in excess of the reasonable needs of the business. If the taxpayer does not
file such a statement it must bear the burden of proof
as under existing law. In addition, if the taxpayer
presents grounds in its statement which are not supported by the facts in the statement, the burden of
proof with respect to these grounds must be borne by
the taxpayer. If the Secretary or his delegate fails
to give the taxpayer notification prior to the issuance of a notice of deficiency, then the Government
must bear the burden of proof even though the taxpayer
has filed no statement.

One of the first cases to deal with the impact of the new
burden-shifting procedure was Young Motor Co. v. Commissioner,
which before it was through had become a kind of classic on the
procedure in accumulated earning tax cases, and is surely un-
rivaled in the number of opinions produced: 32 T.C. 1336 (1959)
holding for the Government; reversed, 281 F.2d 488 (1st
Cir. 1960); decision on remand, 21 T.C.M. 711 (1962),
holding for the taxpayer; reversed, 316 F.2d 267 (1st
Cir. 1963); on remand, 23 T.C.M. 113 (1964), holding for
the Government; affirmed, 339 F.2d 481 (1st Cir. 1964).
(Young Motor actually arose under §102 of the 1939 Code,

the predecessor of §§531-537 of the 1954 Code, but §534 was in operation because it had been made applicable to all cases tried after 1955, unlike the credit for reasonable business needs in §535(c) to be discussed below.)

The taxpayer in <u>Young Motor</u> was an Oldsmobile agency, of which Young and his wife owned virtually all the stock, and Young was the principal operating officer. The taxpayer had been relatively successful, and its net income after taxes for the taxable years in question, 1950-1952, was $55,262, $37,402 and $16,374, respectively. The taxpayer had never paid any dividends, and Young drew no salary. The taxpayer occupied real estate owned by Young personally, and was charged rent approximating only actual maintenance costs. For a number of years the taxpayer had made substantial loans to Young and to enterprises in which he was interested, all but one without security, and all without interest until 1952. In addition, the taxpayer invested other funds in marketable securities which had no direct relationship to its business.

However, General Motors had reserved the right to require the taxpayer to substantially enlarge or improve its facilities or face cancellation of its franchise, which was terminable at will. From 1945 on General Motors continually pressed the taxpayer to enlarge its quarters, and finally in 1953 General Motors demanded that the taxpayer invest $500,000 in a new building. Upon the taxpayer's refusal its franchise was in fact cancelled, and the taxpayer was not able to obtain a franchise from a different manufacturer until 1956. Under the new franchise the taxpayer was required to maintain working capital of $400,000, and accordingly it recalled all of its loans to Young and his other enterprises.

The Commissioner asserted a deficiency for each of the three tax years, 1950-1952, and the taxpayer filed a statement designed to shift the burden of proof on reasonable business needs, in accordance with the procedure of §534. In holding for the Commissioner, the Tax Court said (32 T.C. at 1343-1345):

The burden of proving absence of the ultimate corporate activity prohibited by section 102 is concededly imposed upon petitioner. . . . Assuming in its favor that the evidentiary element of business need has not been rebutted by respondent because of the statement furnished by petitioner, see section 534, I.R.C. 1954, . . . that factor then merely becomes neutral.

An understandable confusion . . . exists between proof of "unreasonable accumulation" which, if present, is prima facie evidence of the prohibited purpose under section 102, I.R.C. 1939; and proof of absence of the condemned purpose, which does not follow automatically from affirmative proof of business need. There is nothing in section 102, either before or after the [new § 534 procedure], which makes the entire case turn on the unreasonableness of the accumulation as related to business needs. These are two separate questions. . . . Had there never been a reference in the Code to reasonable needs of the business, respondent's determination that a corporation's earnings were accumulated for the purposes described in section 102 would still be presumptively correct. If there is no proof by respondent of the unreasonableness of the accumulation as regards business needs and there is no other evidence, petitioner must still fail because the burden of proof of facts sufficient to show the error of respondent's determination is basically upon it as in all comparable proceedings. . . .

There can be no question that petitioner was availed of here to prevent imposition of the surtax upon its shareholders which would have occurred had the earnings been distributed. Our findings make it clear that many thousands of dollars would have been due from them as income taxes if the current earnings had been distributed. This, however, is no more than a preliminary requisite. The statute also calls for the existence of the inhibited purpose.

If this purpose exists it may be accompanied by other legitimate business objectives and still the statute will apply. . . . While it is always difficult to determine the state of a person's mind, and perhaps more especially that of a corporation, we think, on the present record, any corporate intent must be attributable purely to its guiding hand, Young, and that petitioner has failed to carry its burden of showing that one of the purposes of maintaining its relatively large corporate surplus was not to prevent the imposition of surtax upon Young and his wife by means of accumulating its earnings.

There is in fact no testimony anywhere in the record that this was not one of petitioner's purposes. Nor is there . . . any formal action of the board of directors stating a purpose of any kind for the accumulations. It is not unreasonable to assume that petitioner's controlling stockholder would expect and intend the corporate action to have its inevitable result of freeing the stockholder's income from tax by reason of the failure to distribute.

But in addition to the failure to rebut the presumption of correctness, there is affirmative evidence to support the determination. . . . No dividends have ever been paid by petitioner over its 20-odd-year history. Most of the accumulated surplus was loaned to the principal stockholder or his controlled but unrelated businesses. Nearly all the loans were without security, and all, as petitioner states in its brief, "were non interest bearing in the period in question." The stockholder not only permitted the dividends to accumulate but even failed to draw large amounts of salary. And although petitioner occupied property owned by the stockholder, there is evidence that the rent collected was unduly low in the years before us.

As noted earlier, the Court of Appeals reversed, holding that it was error for the Tax Court to virtually disregard the taxpayer's alleged business need (the impending requirement to greatly expand its facilities), just because that was only a subsidiary issue and not the determinative one in the case: "While the ultimate question here is not the reasonable needs of the business, the answer to that question may well be the single most important consideration in concluding whether taxpayer acted with a proper purpose in mind, or the proscribed one." 281 F.2d at 490-491.

The Court of Appeals also took the position that the statute applied only when the proscribed purpose was the primary or dominant motive for the accumulation. Several subsequent cases applied a more lenient standard for the Government, and the Supreme Court ultimately agreed, rejecting the "primary or dominant" test and holding that after a finding of accumulation beyond the reasonable needs of the business the taxpayer could rebut the presumption in section 533(a) only by establishing (by a preponderance of the evidence) that tax avoidance with respect to the shareholders was not "one of the purposes" for the accumulation. United States v. Donruss Co., 393 U.S. 297 (1969).

Incidentally, in view of the fact that the purposes of a corporation are determined by the motives of those in control of it, there are special problems when the shareholders, or directors, are divided on the matter of accumulation versus dividends. Compare Hedberg-Freidheim Contracting Co. v. Commissioner, 251 F.2d 839 (8th Cir. 1958) (tax imposed when one of two equal shareholders blocked dividends favored by the other), with Casey v. Commissioner, 267 F.2d 26 (2d Cir. 1959) (no tax where the two equal shareholders disagreed on whether further accumulations were needed to finance a contemplated project, and as a result of the deadlock dividends were not paid). In Atlantic Properties, Inc. v. Commissioner, 519 F.2d 1233 (1st Cir. 1975), the taxpayer had four equal shareholders, but its charter required an 80% vote of the stockholders for any corporate action. Three of the four shareholders favored paying dividends, but they were blocked by the fourth, who was motivated in part by tax considerations. The court held that the corporation was availed of for the proscribed purpose, even though a majority of the shareholders did not agree with that purpose.

One unanswered question under §534 is whether the Government can avoid the shift in the burden of proof on reasonable business needs by basing the notice of deficiency solely upon the existence of the proscribed purpose, leaving the reasonable business needs issue to be brought in, if at all, by the taxpayer as an affirmative defense, upon which it would bear the burden of proof. This might be a tempting path in any case, admittedly rare, where the Government has direct evidence of the proscribed purpose, such as incriminating corporate minutes,

or the testimony of a disgruntled former director.
Leaving to one side for a moment the impact of the
credit for reasonable business needs under §535(c) (to
which we turn in for a moment), the literal language of
§534(a) would seem to permit the Government to bypass the
reasonable business needs issue, since the statutory
condition for bringing the burden-shifting into play is
a deficiency notice "based in whole or in part
on the allegation that all or part of the earnings and profits
have been permitted to accumulate beyond the reasonable needs of
the business". But there are at least two indications the other
way. First, the Senate Finance Committee Report, supra, states
the condition for using the §534 burden-shifting procedure in
terms simply of a "proposed deficiency with respect to the
accumulated earnings tax", without any suggestion that an
allegation of accumulation beyond the reasonable needs of the
business is required. Second, §534 itself describes the
"preliminary notification" of subsection (b) in terms of
"informing the taxpayer that the proposed notice of deficiency
includes an amount with respect to the accumulated earnings
tax", again without any reference to an allegation that the
accumulation exceeded reasonable business needs.

3. The §535(c) Credit

The role of the reasonable business needs issue may have
been significantly altered by the introduction in 1954 of the
accumulated earnings credit (which is really not a traditional
"credit" at all, but rather a deduction in computing the
"accumulated taxable income" to which the accumulated earnings
tax applies). Section 535(c)(1)(A) provides for a reduction in
accumulated taxable income in "an amount equal to such part of
the earnings and profits for the taxable year as are retained
for the reasonable needs of the business" (less an adjustment
for capital gains). Like the tax itself, the accumulated earnings
credit is determined separately each year, on the basis of the
amount, if any, of earnings and profits which were accumulated
for the year in order to meet reasonable business needs; however,
the statute also allows every corporation (other than a holding
or investment company) to accumulate, without regard to business
needs, a total of $250,000 ($150,000 for a personal service
corporation) from its inception (not annually) before becoming
subject at all to the accumulated earnings tax, which is accomplished by the provision in §535(c)(2) for a minimum credit each
year equal to the excess, if any, of the threshold level of
$250,000 (or $150,000, as the case may be) over the corporation's total accumulated earnings and profits at the start of
the year.

It seems clear enough that the primary reason for intro-
ducing the accumulated earnings credit in the 1954 Code was to
eliminate the all-or-nothing character of the accumulated earnings tax which obtained prior to 1954, under which a finding of
any improper accumulation resulted in an imposition of the tax
on the entire amount of earnings and profits accumulated during
the year. See S. Rep. No. 1622, 83d Cong. 2d Sess. 72 (1954).
The penal character of this approach had resulted in some judicial reluctance to impose the tax, with a number of courts
straining to find no accumulation at all for the proscribed

purpose, and it was anticipated that by using the credit to
confine the tax to improper accumulations the statute would
prove a more effective and equitable policing device. A corollary
result of the credit is that where a corporation's accumulation
of earnings and profits for the year is all for the purpose of
meeting reasonable business needs, there will be no accumulated
taxable income, and hence no tax under §531 (subject to some
slippage because accumulated taxable income is not quite the
same as earnings and profits); but this was probably just a
coincidental by-product of the credit process, since such a
corporation would presumably have escaped the tax anyway, by
being able to show the absence of the proscribed purpose.

However, in practice the credit has turned out to have a
much more commanding role, with the courts according the credit
a controlling status which does away with any necessity for
inquiring into purpose. Under this view, if a corporation shows
sufficient reasonable business needs so that satisfaction of
them would absorb all of the accumulation for the year (plus any
prior accumulations not otherwise earmarked), then the credit
comes into play to eliminate all accumulated taxable income for
the year, and hence any tax, irrespective of the taxpayer's
actual motives for the accumulation. E.g., John P. Scripps
Newspapers v. Commissioner, 44 T.C. 453 (1965), where the Court,
after finding that there were reasonable business needs for the
taxpayer's accumulation, concluded this way:

> In view of the credit provided for in section 535(c)
> (1), it is unnecessary for us to consider whether or not
> petitioner was availed of for the proscribed purpose. We
> realize that the burden of proof as to this issue remains
> with petitioner. . . . However, even if petitioner were
> availed of for the proscribed purpose, it would still be
> entitled to a credit equal to the amount of earnings and
> profits for the taxable years which have been retained for
> the reasonable needs of the business. In this case the
> credit would be equal to the full amount of the retained
> earnings. Therefore, under section 535(a) the accumulated
> taxable income, on which the section 531 tax is imposed,
> would be zero.

Accord, Dielectric Materials Co. v. Commissioner, 57 T.C. 587
(1972).

This represents a dramatic shift in the statutory pattern
from the pre-1954 posture, under which it was uniformly assumed,
as in the Young Motor case, supra, that even if reasonable
business needs for the accumulations were shown the taxpayer
still had to establish the absence of the proscribed purpose in
order to prevail. See Fotocrafters, Inc. v. Commissioner,
19 T.C.M. 1401 (1960), where the Court expressly distinguished
between pre-1954 and post-1954 years with respect to the effect
of finding reasonable business needs, noting that for the former
the taxpayer also had to prove that the proscribed purpose was

not present, while assuming that for the latter the credit would automatically operate to wipe out accumulated taxable income and thereby eliminate any tax.

Despite the apparently uniform view of the authorities to date, it is submitted that this construction of the §535(c) credit is erroneous. As a matter of logic, there seems no reason why a taxpayer should receive a credit on account of the existence of reasonable needs for its business if in fact those needs were not the reason for the accumulation and the actual purpose was to avoid the tax on stockholders. Moreover, the silence of the legislative history is particularly noteworthy. It should be recalled that §533(a) only provides for a presumption in favor of the Government on the purpose issue (when accumulation beyond reasonable business needs is found); there is no counterpart presumption in favor of the taxpayer when it wins on the reasonable business needs issue. Accordingly, if there had been a change in the statute in 1954 merely to redress that balance, by granting to a taxpayer which establishes reasonable business needs for the accumulation a presumption on the purpose issue, some comment in the committee reports would certainly have been called for; yet the foregoing cases have construed the credit provision to go far beyond that and in effect to create an irrebuttable presumption on the purpose issue when reasonable business needs are shown to exist, despite the absence of a word of support in the legislative history. So far as the specific words of §535(c)(1) itself are concerned, query whether the current construction gives sufficient weight to the word "for" in the phrase "as are retained for the reasonable needs of the business". The word "for" is often used as shorthand for the phrase "for the purpose of", and by so interpreting it here the credit would be limited to cases where the reasonable needs were not only present but were also in fact the reason for the accumulation, just as was required under prior law.*

On the other hand, it may be that this potential dichotomy between whether any business needs existed and whether they motivated the company's accumulations may be more apparent than real. Remember that to constitute a business need justifying accumulations there must be a genuine intention on the part of

---

* Compare the following excerpt from the second opinion of the Tax Court in the Young Motor Company case, 21 T.C.M. at 714:

    We have found . . . that the accumulations were not "beyond the reasonable needs of the business". This is the statutory language. We have not found that the earnings were accumulated "for" the reasonable needs of the business, as petitioner requests us to do. That expression of causation, relevant as it might be to indicate an existing and possibly dominant purpose inconsistent with that proscribed by section 102, is one which, on this record, we can not conscientiously make.

those in control of the corporation to respond to the need, as distinguished from vague and unsubstanted plans. And at the other end of the spectrum, a real and definite plan, for example to expand operations by acquiring a new facility, would presumably qualify as a reasonable business need even though the people in control were not particularly enthusiastic about the project and would not be undertaking it but for the pressure from the accumulated earnings tax. But notice that, in the latter case the proscribed purpose could well be found to be at least one of the corporation's purposes for the accumulation, and under the Supreme Court's decision in Donruss, page 535 supra, that could be enough to subject the corporation to the tax. Of course, the Donruss formulation was addressed to a case in which the taxpayer had lost on the reasonable needs issue, and was therefore faced with trying to overcome the presumption of §533(a) that the proscribed purpose was present; it would not necessarily follow that the presence of the proscribed purpose as merely one of the motives is equally fatal in cases where the taxpayer has prevailed on the existence of reasonable business needs. In any event, under the current view of the role of the accumulated earnings credit, the latter question will not arise, since a showing of reasonable business needs for the accumulations during the year will prevent the imposition of any tax. Query the prospects for the reexamination of this proposition: it could be severely tested by a case in which a corporation, while able to justify its accumulations arithmetically under the Bardahl formula, is actually infected with the proscribed purpose.

With respect to the burden of proof under §535(c), it seems clear that the credit is an affirmative defense on which the taxpayer would bear the burden in the first instance. However, if the §534 burden-shifting procedure is successfully invoked, presumably the Commissioner would bear the burden of proof on reasonable business needs for all purposes, including the §535(c) credit. The report of the Conference Committee, H.Rep.No. 3543, 83d Cong., 2d Sess. 29 (1954), contains the following comment upon a Senate amendment inserting the words "all or any part of" before the words "the earnings and profits" in both §§534(a) and 534(c):

> The Senate amendment provides that the shift of the burden of proof under section 534 from the taxpayer to the Government applies not only in determining whether the earnings and profits of the corporation have been permitted to accumulate beyond the reasonable needs of the business, but also in determining the extent to which the earnings and profits of a corporation have accumulated during the taxable year beyond the reasonable needs of the business.

It is less clear what effect §535(c) may have, if any, on the operation of the burden-shifting mechanism. One possibility is that §535(c) makes it impossible for the Government to by-pass the reasonable business needs issue in its deficiency notice, because a failure to allow any §535(c) credit would be tantamount to a "determination" that there were no reasonable business needs. However, as an illustration of how interrelated these various issues are, the foregoing point would appear to be sound only if §535(c) is construed to be independent of any "purpose" issue.

D. ACCUMULATION OF EARNINGS IN CONNECTION WITH A REDEMPTION

MOUNTAIN STATE STEEL FOUNDRIES, INC. v. COMMISSIONER

74 Harv. L. Rev. 866, 900-908 (1961).

HERWITZ, STOCK REDEMPTIONS AND THE ACCUMULATED EARNINGS TAX *

74 Harv.L.Rev. 900-931 (1961).

1. Accumulation of Earnings Subsequent to a Redemption

. . . [In the Mountain State case] the accumulation occurred after the redemption, which was executed early in the first fiscal year for which the accumulated earnings tax was assessed. Thus, although accumulation of earnings was the method of financing the redemption transaction in Mountain State, the specific purpose for the accumulation was the payment of the corporate obligation previously incurred in the redemption.

Retirement of bona fide indebtedness seems clearly to constitute a reasonable need of the business. The regulations [§ 1.537-2(b) (3)] confirm this, but add the qualification that the indebtedness must be "created in connection with the trade or business." Of course, if the stock redemption is regarded as fulfilling a business need within the meaning of the statute, as the court of appeals seemed to imply

---

* Portions of the text and most of the footnotes omitted.

in the Mountain State case, this qualification would create no problem. But even if the stock redemption were not so regarded, the effect of this qualification might be in doubt. By way of analogy, suppose that a corporation borrows money for a purpose unrelated to its business operations, such as speculation in the stock market. Doubtless it is true that so long as repayment of this obligation could be financed by liquidating the unrelated assets, accumulation of earnings for such repayment could not be justified, since there would be no business need for the accumulation. The matter would stand no differently than an attempt to accumulate earnings for the very purpose of speculating in the market. But suppose that disaster befell the corporation's investments and they became worthless. Now the outstanding obligation is a direct claim against the corporation's business assets, and it is no longer so clear that accumulation of earnings to repay it should be regarded as beyond the reasonable needs of the business. A redemption transaction like that in Mountain State presents a similar situation. Since the redemption obligation constitutes a bona fide binding claim against the corporation, it can be argued that payment of that obligation is a reasonable need of the business for which accumulation of earnings would be justified.

Even if discharge of the redemption obligation were not considered a reasonable need of the business, the existence of that purpose might serve to rebut any presumption that the accumulation of earnings was designed to avoid the tax on shareholders. Discharge of that redemption obligation in accordance with its terms would be essential to the continued existence of the corporation. Quite commonly the redemption obligation would include provisions prohibiting or restricting the payment of dividends during the term of the obligation, as was apparently true in Mountain State; but even without such express restrictions, the financial drain of the redemption obligation is likely to have the practical effect of drastically curtailing, if not entirely precluding, the payment of dividends.

In any event, it should be recalled that a redemption in which the interest of one or more shareholders is entirely eliminated—the type involved in . . . Mountain State—may be regarded as akin to a liquidation transaction. That is, the redemption may be viewed as a substitute for a distribution in kind to the selling shareholders of their pro rata share of the corporation's net assets. For example, suppose that stockholders A and B each own fifty per cent of the stock of A-B Corporation which, it will be assumed for the purpose of making the illustration more graphic, carries on its business at two locations of the same size and capacity. If A wishes to sell out the business, and B prefers to continue operating it, an impasse would result since A would normally be unable to compel either a complete liquidation or a sale of all the assets. One obvious solution would be a "partial liquidation," under which A would surrender all of his stock in exchange for one of the plants and one-half of all the other assets in kind, assuming one-half of the liabilities; B would be left to operate the A-B Corporation on a drastically reduced scale. If thereafter A-B Corporation accumulated its earnings in order to expand to the more desirable scale of operations enjoyed prior to the redemption, there would seem to be no occasion for the imposition of the accumulated earnings tax. The regulations have long provided specifically that accumulation of earnings to provide for bona fide expansion will normally satisfy the reasonable-needs-of-the-business test. There seems to be no reason why the A-B Corporation should be denied the right to accumulate earnings for expansion because of the previous redemption transaction. Indeed, it could be argued that such a situation presents a particularly strong justification for accumulation of earnings, since the expansion would be aimed simply at restoring a previous level of operations, the feasibility and desirability of which had been demonstrated by actual experience.

The same result should obtain if shortly after the partial liquidation A-B Corporation borrowed funds to acquire a plant like the one distributed to A and thereafter accumulated its earnings to pay off the obligation incurred. Whether the purpose of the accumulation was characterized as retirement of bona fide indebtedness or expansion of the business, such an accumulation would seem to be justified under the regulations. Should the result be any different if A-B Corporation purchased from A the very assets distributed to him in the partial liquidation, reassuming the liabilities taken up by A, or if the corporation borrowed from A to finance the transaction by making the repurchase from him on credit? Again the repayment of the obligation incurred in expanding the business back to its original size should constitute a perfectly valid business reason for accumulating earnings. But the latter transaction is no different from a redemption of A's stock on credit for a price equal to the value of the net assets which A would have received through a partial-liquidation distribution in kind. The parties would be in exactly the same position as if they had adopted the more cumbersome and expensive procedure of a redemption in kind followed by a repurchase of the assets on credit. Viewing such a redemption transaction in this manner, an accumulation of earnings to discharge the obligation incurred in the redemption again seems justified as a business need. And this analysis would appear to be equally apt whether the redemption involved a minority of the outstanding stock, a majority, or exactly fifty per cent as in the Mountain State case. Hence, whatever may be the soundness of distinctions drawn among these situations in other types of cases, to be discussed later, such distinctions have no place in cases like Mountain State where the challenged accumulation occurs after the redemption transaction has been consummated.

* * *

On the basis of the foregoing, then, it is submitted that the accumulated earnings tax should not be imposed when earnings are accumulated for the purpose of discharging the obligation incurred in a previous good faith redemption of all of the stock of one or more shareholders. More difficulty is encountered when the redemption does not involve a complete termination of the interest of any of the shareholders, since the analogy based upon complete liquidation as to the selling shareholders fails. But a complete termination of interest is not required for favorable tax treatment of the redemption distribution. In addition, any obligation incurred in such a redemption is no less binding on the corporation. Therefore, when the redemption is not pro rata and effects a substantial change in ownership among the shareholders, of the kind contemplated by section 302(b)(2) of the 1954 Code, it might well be appropriate to permit the corporation to accumulate earnings to discharge a bona fide obligation so incurred.

2. Use of Previously Accumulated Earnings for Redemption

A harder question is presented when earnings are accumulated in advance of a redemption. If the accumulation is for the specific purpose of financing the redemption, there may well be no escape from the issue of whether and when a redemption itself may constitute a "reasonable need" within the meaning of the accumulated earnings tax statute. But the situation may be different when the corporation has accumulated its earnings for other business needs and then utilizes the accumulated earnings to redeem some of its stock. Here the Commissioner would be attacking the accumulation of earnings for the years prior to the redemption transaction still open under the statute of limitations, in the light of the actual use made of those earnings.

Of course where, despite the existence of other potential business needs, the real reason for the accumulation of earnings was to finance an expected redemption, the case should be treated as a conceded accumulation of earnings for the purpose of redeeming stock. But if in fact no redemption was even contemplated in the prior years, and the accumulation of earnings was for other purposes which did constitute reasonable needs of the business within the meaning of the statute, the subsequent decision to use the accumulated earnings to finance a redemption should not affect the justification for the accumulation in the prior years. The accumulated earnings tax, like the income tax generally, is applied on an annual basis. Each taxable year stands on its own footing, and the question whether earnings were accumulated beyond the reasonable needs of the business for any given year must be determined in the light of the factors and circumstances relevant to that year. This is further emphasized by section 535(c) (1) of the 1954 Code, which specifically provides for a credit for each taxable year in the amount of the earnings retained for the reasonable needs of the business during that year.

The regulations [§ 1.537–1(b) (2)] confirm this view with the provision that "subsequent events shall not be used for the purpose of showing that the retention of earnings or profits was unreasonable at the close of the taxable year if all the elements of reasonable anticipation are present at the close of such taxable year." This provision makes it clear that an accumulation of earnings in good faith for a reasonable business need during a particular year does not become subject to the special tax if later the purpose for which the earnings were accumulated has to be abandoned. Since there would obviously be no problem requiring special comment in the regulations if the original business objective was abandoned in the face of some other pressing business need, the thrust of the regulation quoted must be that it makes no difference why the original purpose was abandoned, nor indeed whether the previously accumulated earnings are presently needed for any business reason, although of course the issue of whether the corporation ever actually intended to consummate the original objective would remain. Hence, the abandonment of the original corporate purpose in favor of a redemption of all the stock of one or more stockholders should not affect the validity of the accumulation for the original purpose in the prior years, regardless of whether the redemption transaction is itself thought to constitute a reasonable need of the business. Indeed, this might well be a stronger case than one in which the original purpose is abandoned and no substitute is adopted, since the financial drain of a redemption would normally prevent the consummation of the original objective, and thus eliminate the need to explain why the original objective was abandoned.

---

3. Accumulation for the Purpose of Redeeming Stock

LAMARK SHIPPING AGENCY, INC. v. COMMISSIONER *

United States Tax Court, 1981. 42 T.C.M. 56.

OPINION

* * *

Petitioner timely submitted a statement pursuant to section 534 (c) in which it alleged that the earnings and profits for the taxable year ended September 30, 1976, were accumulated in order to protect

---

* Findings of fact, portions of the opinion, and many of the footnotes omitted

the corporation against the loss of major accounts, and not for the purpose of funding the stock redemptions which took place during that year. The statement further alleged that, should this Court determine that current earnings were actually accumulated for the latter purpose, the redemption of Victor Lamark's stock nevertheless served a reasonable business need for purposes of the accumulated earnings tax. No other grounds for the accumulation were contained in the statement. At a pre-trial hearing this Court ruled that the section 534(c) statement was sufficient to shift the burden of proof to respondent with respect to the grounds stated therein in accordance with section 534(a)(2). We note, however, that the burden of proof with respect to any additional grounds alleged by petitioner, as well as the ultimate question of whether the Corporation was availed of for the prohibited purpose, remains with petitioner. . . .

The parties in this case have confined their arguments to the familiar issues of whether the accumulation of earnings during the year was for the reasonable needs of the business and not for the purpose of avoiding income taxes. Nevertheless, the facts fairly present another, more fundamental legal issue which neither party has addressed: whether the distribution of all of petitioner's current earnings and profits in the redemption of its stock during the year bars the imposition of the penalty on the ground that no earnings were actually permitted to accumulate within the corporation.

The facts herein indicate that the portion of the redemption distributions allocable to earnings and profits greatly exceeded petitioner's earnings and profits for its fiscal year ended September 30, 1976. The amounts distributed in the redemptions were as follows:

Victor Lamark (1,769 shares)

Cash	$283,271.91	
Cash surrender value-life insurance policy	9,032.85	
Automobile (adjusted basis)	5,313.64	
		$297,618.40
Albert Lamark (25 shares)		
Cash		5,000.00
Rose Kozak (20 shares)		
Cash		4,000.00
Total		$306,618.40

Section 312(a) provides that amounts paid in connection with a redemption of stock are treated as distributions of earnings and profits to the extent they are not properly chargeable to the capital account under section 312(e). Further, section 316(a) provides that such distributions are to be charged first against the most recently accumulated earnings and profits. The facts indicate that each share of stock had a par value of $10. Consequently, of the total amount distributed in the redemptions, $18,140 ($10 per share × 1,814 shares redeemed) is properly chargeable to the capital account under section 312(e).[13] The balance of the distribution, or $288,478.40, is treated as a distribution out of current earnings and profits to the extent thereof under the provisions of sections 312(a) and 316(a). Thus, since petitioner's earnings and profits for its fiscal year ended September 30, 1976, amounted to only $111,197.17,[14] it can be argued that petitioner did not actually accumulate any earnings during the year and that the imposition of the accumulated earnings tax under such circumstances is inappropriate.

In GPD, Inc. v. Commissioner, 60 T.C. 480 (1973) (Court-reviewed), revd. and remanded, 508 F.2d 1076 (6th Cir. 1974), this Court decided this issue in favor of the taxpayer on similar facts and was reversed on appeal by the Sixth Circuit. Inasmuch as this case is appealable to the Third Circuit, we are not constrained to follow the Sixth Circuit's reversal, ... Therefore the matter is open for our reconsideration. However, because neither party has raised or briefed the merits of what has proved to be a fairly nettlesome legal issue, we think it inappropriate to undertake a reassessment of our position in GPD at this time.[15] Accordingly, we will decide this case solely on the basis of the arguments raised at trial and briefed by the parties.

We are confronted, then, with the question of whether the hypothetical accumulation of current earnings (resulting from a failure to

---

13. The proper charge to the capital account is generally held to be the pro rata portion of the contributed capital which is allocable to the redeemed shares, and this holds true even if the amount distributed in the redemption exceeds the book value of the shares because of unrealized appreciation in assets or goodwill which may be reflected in the redemption price. Anderson v. Commissioner, 67 T.C. 522 (1976), aff'd per curiam [78-2 USTC ¶ 9708] 583 F.2d 953 (7th Cir. 1978); Enoch v. Commissioner, 57 T.C. 781 (1972); Helvering v. Jarvis, 123 F.2d 742 (4th Cir. 1941); see also Rev.Rul. 79-376, 1979-2 C.B. 133.

14. We assume, since the parties have produced no evidence to the contrary, that petitioner's current earnings and profits for the year in issue were equal to its accumulated taxable income as computed in respondent's notice of deficiency. . . .

15. The resolution of this issue depends on how one interprets the relationship between several different Code provi-

sions. Section 532(a) provides that the accumulated earnings tax applies to any corporation formed or availed of for the purpose of avoiding income taxes with respect to its shareholders "*by permitting earnings and profits to accumulate* instead of being divided or distributed." (Emphasis added). Once this statutory requirement is satisfied, section 531 imposes the penalty on the corporation's accumulated taxable income as computed under section 535. Accumulated taxable income is essentially a measure of the corporation's current earnings and profits and is generally equal to taxable income after certain adjustments, less the dividends paid deduction and the accumulated earnings credit. The dividends paid deduction is defined in sections 561 through 565. The key provision insofar as the present issue is concerned is section 562(c), which provides that no distribution shall be eligible for the dividends paid deduction unless the distribution is pro rata. Under this rule a non-pro rata stock redemption does not qualify for the dividends paid deduction, and consequently does not distribute such amounts in the form of taxable dividends) exceeded petitioner's reasonable business needs during the year in issue. Normally this determination requires a comparison of the corporation's net liquid assets at year-end (generally current assets minus current liabilities) to its aggregate business needs. If net liquid assets are found to exceed business needs, a presumption is created that current earnings were accumulated with a tax avoidance motive. Section 533. Assuming the taxpayer is unable to rebut this presumption, the only issue left to be decided is the amount of the accumulated earnings credit.

In the present case, however, a substantial portion of petitioner's current and accumulated earnings and profits were distributed during the year, nearly all of it in the form of cash, in order to redeem the stock of several of its shareholders. Because the use of funds to redeem stock does not necessarily qualify as a reasonable business need, particularly where the facts suggest that the redemption is primarily a device to bail out earnings and profits at capital gain rates, the Corporation's net liquid assets at year-end ($28,231.41) [16] paint a

reduce accumulated taxable income (assuming, of course, that the redemption does not otherwise qualify as a reasonable business need eligible for the accumulated earnings credit provided under section 535(c)).

However, sections 312(a) and 316(a) provide that amounts paid in connection with a redemption of stock are treated as distributions out of current earnings and profits to the extent they are not properly chargeable to the capital account under section 312(e). Thus, under the statutory framework it is possible to have a stock redemption which consumes all of the current year's earnings and profits without effecting a corresponding reduction in the corporation's accumulated taxable income. Since section 532(a) arguably requires an *accumulation* of earnings and profits during the taxable year, the imposition of the accumulated earnings tax under these circumstances is subject to serious question.

In GPD, Inc. v. Commissioner, 60 T.C. 480 (1973), we relied on several of our prior decisions and held that the accumulated earnings tax could not be applied in a year in which, because of stock redemptions, no current earnings and profits were retained by the corporation. The Sixth Circuit, 508 F.2d 1076 (1974), relying in part on the opinion of the District Court in Ostendorf-Morris Co. v. United States, an un-

reported case (N.D. Ohio 1968, 26 AFTR 2d 70–5369, 70–2 USTC ¶ 9550), as well as on a lengthy analysis of the legislative history of the accumulated earnings tax provisions, concluded that the accumulated earnings tax could still be imposed under these circumstances, if the requisite tax avoidance motive were found to be present. Somewhat surprisingly, there have been no other reported cases dealing with this issue since the Sixth Circuit handed down its reversal in *GPD*. . . .

16. Neither party has requested findings of fact concerning petitioner's net liquid assets at the end of the year in issue. Because of the holding we reach in this case it is technically unnecessary for us to make a specific finding on this matter. For the sake of completeness, however, we have computed petitioner's net liquid assets as follows:

Liquid assets as of September 30, 1976

Cash	$19,529.76
Miscellaneous receivables	262.94
Loan receivable—Jay Lamark	9,411.65
Taxes payable	(972.94)
	$28,231.41

Loans to shareholders are generally included in liquid assets on the ground that a contrary rule would permit a

completely misleading picture of its ability to pay dividends during
the taxable year. By contrast, had the Corporation elected to invest
its idle cash in the acquisition of additional plant and equipment during the year, the year-end net liquid assets figure would be an appropriate measure of its dividend-paying capacity because the use to
which the excess funds were directed would unquestionably constitute
a reasonable business need. Thus, it becomes necessary to examine
the circumstances surrounding the redemptions to determine whether
they served a reasonable business purpose. If this question is answered in the negative, the assets distributed must be considered in
the same light as unrelated business investments or shareholder
loans; i.e., the amounts must be added back to the corporation's net
liquid assets and deemed available for the payment of dividends.[17]
See and compare Faber Cement Block Co., Inc. v. Commissioner, [50
T.C.] at 328–330 (unrelated business loans included in liquid assets);
Nemours Corp. v. Commissioner, 38 T.C. 585, 602–604 (1962), affd.
per curiam, 325 F.2d 559 (3rd Cir. 1963) (loans to shareholders included); Bremerton Sun Publishing Co. v. Commissioner, 44 T.C.
566, 587 (1965) (investment in stock of another company to insure
an adequate supply of material used in business not included);
. . ..

On brief respondent contends that the shift in burden of proof
ordered by this Court after consideration of petitioner's section
534(c) statement is ineffective with regard to the redemption issue,
since the statement specifically denied that earnings were accumulated for the purpose of redeeming stock. We note, however, that petitioner has not denied the fact of the redemptions; rather, petitioner
contends that it did not form an intention to redeem its stock until
just before the distributions took place. Until that time, it alleges,

corporation with excessive accumulations to lessen its exposure to the
penalty by temporarily diverting liquid
assets to its shareholders. . . .
In the instant case, however, most of
the funds loaned to Jay Lamark were
borrowed by the Corporation from the
Pittsburgh National Bank; in other
words, the Corporation acted merely
as a conduit in arranging a personal
bank loan for Jay Lamark to finance
his purchase of Victor Lamark's remaining share of stock. Thus, we
think the loan receivable from Jay
Lamark ($56,500) should be included
in liquid assets only to the extent it
exceeds the balance owed on the Pittsburgh National note ($47,088.35).
One other point deserves mention. Petitioner is a cash method taxpayer and
therefore the financial schedules do
not disclose any unbooked accounts

receivable or accounts payable at year-
end. Arguably these amounts (net of
estimated income taxes) should be included in the computation of net liquid
assets in order to arrive at a true
measure of petitioner's liquidity, even
though such amounts are not reflected
in the Corporation's accumulated taxable income. We will not address this
issue because there is insufficient evidence in the record to allow a determination of petitioner's accrual-based
liquid position at year-end.

17. While we think this treatment is
proper in the year in which the redemption takes place, it is doubtful
that the assets distributed should affect the computation of net liquid assets in subsequent years, since the
funds distributed are irretrievably lost
to the Corporation.

its sole purpose in accumulating earnings was to protect against the loss of accounts. Thus, petitioner insists that at no time did it actually *accumulate* earnings, on a day-to-day basis, with the purpose of avoiding income taxes by distributing earnings in a stock redemption. Petitioner's argument ignores the fact that all the events of the taxable year are relevant in determining whether earnings were accumulated with the proscribed purpose. . . .

Still, petitioner was careful to argue (and at some length) in its 534(c) statement that, assuming this Court found the redemption of Victor Lamark's stock to be relevant in determining the existence of the forbidden purpose, the redemption nevertheless served a reasonable business need of the Corporation. We see no reason to disregard this portion of petitioner's statement merely because it couched the redemption as an alternative, rather than a conjunctive, ground for the accumulation of corporate earnings. We hold, therefore, that respondent bears the burden of proof on the question of whether the redemption satisfied a reasonable business need.

Before addressing the arguments of the parties on this issue it is helpful first to restate the changes in stock ownership which took place during the year in issue. At the beginning of the year petitioner's stock was held as follows:

	Number of Shares Owned	Percent of Total Shares Outstanding
Victor Lamark	1,770	92.43%
Albert Lamark	25	1.31
Jay Lamark	100	5.22
Rose Kozak	20	1.04
Total	1,915	100.00%

The shares owned by Albert Lamark and Rose Kozak were redeemed on May 25, 1976 and June 1, 1976, respectively. On July 16, 1976, 1,769 shares of Victor Lamark's shares were redeemed, representing 94.6 percent of the 1,870 shares then outstanding. Victor sold his remaining share of stock to Jay Lamark for $60,000, thereby giving Jay sole ownership and control of the Corporation. In substance the redemption provided a vehicle through which the Corporation's retained earnings could be used to bootstrap the acquisition of the company by Jay, who apparently lacked sufficient personal assets to purchase all of Victor's stock directly. Because the assets distributed to Albert and Rose were insubstantial ($9,000) relative to the total distributed to Victor ($297,618.40), the remainder of our discussion will focus solely on the redemption of Victor's stock.[18]

18. We note that petitioner has made no argument that the redemption of the minority stock interests satisfied a reasonable business purpose.

Petitioner maintains that this redemption and the transfer in ownership which accompanied it were essential if the business was to continue to operate as a going concern. In support thereof petitioner contends the following:

(1) Victor and Jay anticipated serious financial difficulty in the face of the loss or impending loss of two of its major accounts, the Prudential-Grace and Moller lines, and thus they felt the Corporation could not afford to continue to pay the large salaries which the officers had been receiving.

(2) Dissension had arisen between Jay and Victor over whether to take on representation of a nonconference Russian line. The two also had disagreements over other policy matters, and at one point Jay gave serious consideration to leaving the Corporation.

(3) Because of his problems with Jay and his belief that the business was headed downhill, Victor decided it was time to cash in his investment, even though he was in good health and would have preferred to continue working with the company.

(4) Rather than liquidate the 50-year old family business and dismiss loyal employees, Victor chose to transfer control of the Corporation to Jay by selling one share of stock to him directly and causing the Corporation to redeem the remainder.

In short, petitioner argues that, because of the business reversals and the disagreements with Jay, Victor decided it was necessary to leave the company and allow Jay the opportunity to make a fresh start unencumbered by the burdensome salaries which Victor and Albert had been drawing. Since the only other alternative was liquidation, or so petitioner contends, the redemption necessarily satisfied a reasonable business purpose.

Respondent insists that the redemption was nothing more than a device employed by a majority stockholder to bail out current earnings and profits at capital gains rates, and therefore the purpose of the redemption was inherently personal. Further, respondent argues that current earnings could have been distributed in the form of dividends, without necessarily making it impossible for the planned redemption to occur. Finally, respondent argues that the alleged business purpose for the redemption, which depleted almost all of petitioner's accumulated cash reserves, is belied by petitioner's repeated averments of a desperate need to conserve working capital during the year in issue. Thus, respondent maintains this redemption cannot pass muster as a reasonable business need for purposes of the accumulated earnings tax.

The cases dealing with the reasonable needs issue in a redemption context are difficult to reconcile and can hardly be said to constitute a uniform body of law on the subject. No doubt this is due in large measure to the difficulties inherent in attempting to distinguish between corporate and shareholder purposes in a closely held corporate setting. In most cases the presence of a shareholder benefit is readily discernible because the redemption proceeds are invariably taxed to the departing shareholders at favorable capital gain rates. Since capital gain distributions are not the kind of distributions which the accumulated earnings tax was designed to promote,[19] the courts have been understandably reluctant to accord "reasonable need" characterization to earnings accumulated for the purpose of a redemption.

Nevertheless, the redemption of a dissenting minority or 50 percent shareholder has been found to serve a reasonable business purpose where the action appeared necessary to promote the harmonious transaction of corporate business or to prevent the sale of the minority stock to a hostile outsider. The case frequently cited for this proposition is Mountain State Steel Foundries Inc. v. Commissioner,
. . . ..
Other cases [embrace] the notion that the redemption of a non-controlling interest may serve a reasonable business need where a corporate purpose is evident . . ..

The leading case concerning the redemption of a majority stock interest is Pelton Steel Casting Co. v. Commissioner, 28 T.C. 153 (1957), affd. 251 F.2d 278 (7th Cir. 1958), cert. denied 356 U.S. 958 (1958). There two shareholders, one owning 60 percent of the corporation and the other owning 20 percent, decided to sell their stock but were unable to find a purchaser who could meet their price. A third shareholder, who owned the remaining 20 percent of the stock, had devoted most of his life to the business and was concerned that a sale of the majority interest to another corporation would interfere with his management of the business and possibly cause the loss of some key employees. Accordingly, he devised a plan whereby the corporation would redeem the shares for approximately $800,000, with $300,000 payable out of the corporation's liquid assets and the balance to be paid from the proceeds of a $500,000 loan. To insure the availability of the necessary cash the corporation declared no dividends for 1946. The redemption took place the following year. Subsequently the Commissioner determined an accumulated earnings tax deficiency for 1946 on the ground that the accumulation for the proposed redemption did not serve a reasonable business need, but instead indicated a purpose to avoid income taxes.

This Court sustained the Commissioner's determination and cited several factors as the basis for its decision. First, we observed that a dividend distribution would not necessarily have made it impossible

19. . . . We note, however, that Congress has seen fit to provide an exception for redemptions of stock which qualify under section 303. Section 537(a)(2) provides that earnings necessary to fund such redemptions will be deemed to have been accumulated for reasonable business needs, but only for the taxable year of the corporation in which the shareholder died or for any taxable year thereafter. See section 537(b)(1) and (4).

for the proposed redemption to occur, since the distribution presumably would have resulted in a corresponding reduction in the redemption price to be paid by the corporation. Second, we were unable to identify any reasonable corporate purpose served by the redemption. There was no evidence that the company was threatened with a sale of stock to an undesirable outsider. In fact, from a corporate standpoint the redemption may well have been counterproductive, since it caused a significant drain on the taxpayer's financial resources at a time when the taxpayer was alleging a need to accumulate earnings for additional working capital and plant improvements. Finally, in our view the fact that a majority stock interest was redeemed made it unlikely that the redemptions were motivated by anything other than a desire on the part of the redeeming shareholders to liquidate their interest at capital gain rates. Thus, we concluded that the redemption served no reasonable business purpose, but instead provided proof of the existence of the proscribed purpose.

We think the rationale of *Pelton Steel* applies with even greater force in the present case. Here nearly 95 percent of the outstanding stock of the Corporation, all of it belonging to a single shareholder, was redeemed in a transaction which consumed most of the Corporation's current and accumulated earnings and profits. The redemption proceeds were reported by Victor as long-term capital gain on his 1976 Federal income tax return. This personal tax benefit, coupled with Victor's undisputed control over corporate affairs before the redemption, raises, at the very least, a presumption that his personal objectives outweighed any alleged corporate purpose for the redemption.

The circumstances under which the redemption plan was conceived also suggest that personal considerations predominated in Victor's decision to leave the company. Victor was clearly worried about the future of the company in light of the loss of two major accounts, which collectively had accounted for 44 percent of the Corporation's gross revenues for the taxable year ended September 30, 1974. When asked at trial whether he considered simply retiring and assuming the role of a passive stockholder, he stated that it would have been unwise "to retain stock in a company if you know that their business is slipping." Petitioner's reply brief also states that "[Victor] had no confidence that the company would have had the continuing capacity to pay the dividends to give him a modicum of retirement security." Although we accept Victor's testimony that he left the business with great reluctance and would have preferred to continue on as an owner-employee, even though he was 72 years old, we nevertheless think his departure was spurred principally by a belief that the redemption and sale to Jay was the best financial avenue open to him. Considering that the company was, in Victor's words, "going down the drain," the deal with Jay presented a lucrative opportunity: in exchange for his stock Victor received from the Corporation cash and other assets worth $297,618.40, only $17,690 of which represented a return of capital ($10 par × 1,769 shares), and from Jay he received a $60,000 premium for the sale of his remaining share of stock. More importantly, all of the consideration he received was taxable as long-term capital gain. The income tax savings to Victor as a consequence of reporting the $283,271.91 cash payment from the Corporation alone as a capital gain distribution versus an ordinary income dividend amounted to $63,059.18. Thus, it appears to us that Victor, being aware of the Corporation's cash-rich position and believing that the economic tide had turned against the company, simply decided that the time was ripe to divest his ownership interest.

Petitioner concedes that, to a certain extent, Victor's decision to leave the company was in fact motivated by personal considerations, but at the same time petitioner contends that the redemption served a vital corporate purpose because the only other alternative was liquidation. Granted, it is entirely possible that this was the only other option Victor was willing to consider under the circumstances, and, indeed, we have found as a fact that at one point he considered and rejected this alternative. Nevertheless, this does not necessarily call for the conclusion that the distribution in redemption was essential from the standpoint of the Corporation. We note that petitioner has offered no rebuttal to respondent's contention that a dividend could have been declared during the year without frustrating the planned redemption. We found this to be a telling argument in *Pelton Steel*, and it is even more persuasive on these facts. Since Victor owned nearly 95 percent of the outstanding stock of the corporation immediately preceding the redemption, the benefit of any dividend distribution declared on the common shares would have inured almost entirely to him, with the holdover shareholder (Jay) deriving only a minor benefit. Likewise, the additional cash drain on the Corporation (relative to that caused by the redemption) would have been negligible. Furthermore, the distribution of earnings via a dividend would have reduced the book value of the Corporation and facilitated the forthcoming transfer of ownership to Jay in much the same manner as did the redemption. Thus, we are not convinced that the wholesale bailout of earnings and profits which accompanied the redemption was an unavoidable result of the desired shift in ownership.

Moreover, our doubts as to the validity of the alleged corporate purpose are compounded by the seemingly inconsistent positions which petitioner has taken during this litigation. The bulk of petitioner's argument on brief was aimed at establishing that the Corporation was near the brink of economic collapse during the taxable year in issue. Victor himself testified at trial that he thought the business was "going down the drain". The minutes of the board of directors' special meeting held on May 1, 1975 state that the loss of the Prudential-Grace line made it "necessary to preserve [the] cash balance for the survival of the company". Accordingly, petitioner has contended throughout these proceedings that its sole purpose in accumulating earnings prior to the redemption was to cushion the company against the shock of business reversals. Yet, despite the grim financial outlook portrayed by petitioner, the Corporation ultimately distributed virtually all of its liquid assets during the taxable year in the redemption of Victor Lamark's stock. As a result, the company found itself bereft of working capital and was forced to borrow $20,000 from the Pittsburgh National Bank to meet operating expenses immediately following the distribution. On brief petitioner conceded the effect of the redemption on its financial position, stating that "assuredly, it left the company staggering". Under these circumstances we find it paradoxical, to say the least, that on the one hand petitioner alleges a dire need to conserve working capital, while on the other hand contends that a redemption which stripped the company of its entire cash reserve somehow satisfied a reasonable business purpose. . . .

It is not our intention to suggest that the redemption of the stock of a majority shareholder can never be beneficial to a corporation. With regard to the present case, we are not prepared to say that the shift in ownership and control to Jay could not, in the long run, have a positive impact on the Corporation. By relieving the company of the salaries which Victor and Albert had been drawing, and by allowing Jay to exercise his unfettered judgment in the management of corporate affairs, the shift in ownership could conceivably have lifted the Corporation out of its alleged financial difficulties. The fact remains, however, that where a majority interest is redeemed in a capital gain distribution, the personal shareholder benefit inevitably permeates the entire transaction, and absent evidence of a bona fide and predominant corporate purpose, the distribution cannot qualify as a business need for purposes of the accumulated earnings tax. In this case petitioner has failed to rebut the unfavorable inferences which may be drawn from the evidence before us.

Accordingly, we find that respondent has met his burden of proof on this issue and hold that the redemption of Victor Lamark's stock did not serve a reasonable business need. Because the assets distributed in that redemption exceeded the Corporation's current earnings and profits, we conclude that all of the latter were accumulated beyond the reasonable needs of the business, thereby creating a presumption of a tax avoidance motive under section 533(a). That presumption stands unless petitioner proves otherwise by a preponderance of the evidence.

On this ultimate issue we find petitioner has failed to meet its burden of proof. Although throughout these proceedings Victor and Jay have vehemently denied that the Corporation ever accumulated earnings with the proscribed purpose, their testimony is unpersuasive. We reiterate the Supreme Court's view in United States v. Donruss Co. . . . that tax avoidance considerations need only contribute to the decision to accumulate to justify imposition of the tax. We refuse to believe that the redemption of Victor's stock was made in blissful ignorance of the favorable tax consequences which ensued. We also note that under the redemption agreement Victor would appear to be liable for at least a portion of any accumulated earnings taxes assessed for the taxable year in issue, and therefore he can hardly be called a disinterested party in this affair. Moreover, we note that from the date of its incorporation in 1966 until the end of the taxable year in issue the Corporation has paid only one dividend. That dividend totaled $8,000 and was paid during the taxable year ended September 30, 1974. A poor dividend history is a key factor to consider in evaluating a corporation's motives during a particular taxable year. . . . The failure to pay dividends in this case allowed Victor and the other redeeming shareholders to drain the Corporation of $288,478.40 in retained earnings, reducing its once-substantial cash hoard to almost nothing, while suffering only a capital gains tax in the process. Under these circumstances we find that the testimony elicited at trial is insufficient to overcome the presumption of tax avoidance created by section 533(a).

Accordingly, we hold that petitioner was availed of during the taxable year for the purpose of avoiding income taxes with respect to its shareholders by permitting earnings to accumulate instead of distributing them in the form of taxable dividends. Since petitioner has failed to prove that it was necessary to accumulate current year's earnings to meet its reasonable business needs, no accumulated earnings credit will be allowed to offset its accumulated taxable income.

To reflect the foregoing,

Decision will be entered for the respondent.

NOTE ON ACCUMULATIONS TO FINANCE A REDEMPTION

From Stock Redemptions and the Accumulated Earnings Tax, 74 Harv. L. Rev. 866, 908-931 (1961):

We come finally to the most troublesome kind of case in this area, one in which earnings are accumulated expressly in contemplation of a planned stock redemption. [That was the situation in the Pelton case (discussed in Lamark Shipping), where the court held that the contemplated redemption of a substantial majority of the outstanding stock not only failed as a reasonable business need but actually evidenced the presence of the proscribed purpose.] Are there circumstances where a planned redemption can qualify as a need of the business?

The treatment of this issue in the authorities, at least prior to the decision of the court of appeals in Mountain State, was not particularly enlightening. There is no specific reference to the question in the regulations, although the general reminder that the needs for which earnings are retained must be "directly connected with the needs of the corporation itself" is doubtless relevant. The two earliest cases involving the effect of a redemption transaction under the accumulated earnings tax, Gazette [121] and Dill,[122] indicated that redemption of a minority shareholder's stock to prevent it from falling into potentially unfriendly hands could constitute a reasonable business need. This view, while apparently not disapproved in Pelton, was nevertheless held inapplicable there on the ground that a majority of the outstanding stock, rather than a minority, was redeemed.

The basis of this distinction never clearly emerges from the Pelton opinion, perhaps because that court was not resting on the reasonable-business-needs issue anyway. As will be noted later, the premise that a minority redemption can constitute a reasonable business need may well be doubtful itself. But if the alleged distinction was meant to suggest that the redemption of a majority of the stock outstanding could not constitute as compelling a need "of the corporation itself" within the meaning of the regulations, it may be open to serious question. The alleged corporate business need which was thought in the earlier cases to underlie a redemption of a minority shareholder's stock was that of preventing the stock from falling into the hands of outsiders who might seek to change established lines of policy or otherwise create disharmony in the intracorporate family, with a consequent deleterious effect on operations. But the worst that can befall the corporation if the minority shareholder's stock is not redeemed is that he or his successor will prove a constant nuisance in the conduct of the corporation's affairs. Absent some special feature like a unanimity agreement among the shareholders or directors which gives the minority shareholder power disproportionate to his shareholdings, he cannot disturb the ultimate control of the majority.

Compare the potential for changes in corporate policy and rupture of the existing harmony among the stockholders if a majority of the stock changes hands. The new majority has the power to overhaul completely the corporation's business affairs. Moreover, upon the institution of new plans and programs, the psychological effect upon the holdover minority shareholders, particularly those who have been officers under the previous administration, offers far greater promise of discord than could arise from a mere transfer from one minority

121. Gazette Publishing Co. v. Self, 103 F.Supp. 779 (E.D.Ark.1952).

122. Dill Mfg. Co., 39 B.T.A. 1023 (1939).

shareholder to a new one. Thus, strictly from the point of view of the corporation as a separate entity, redemption of a majority of the stock to keep it from being transferred may be more vital than redemption of a minority interest.

* * *

Nevertheless, there is a basis for distinguishing between majority and minority redemptions. The question of the business needs of a corporation, though clearly more objective than the issue of the purpose for an accumulation of earnings, itself depends in large measure upon the decisions, or more generally the state of mind, of those in control of the corporation—normally the majority shareholders. But in the case of a contemplated redemption of the shares of the majority, the latter are no longer concerned with the needs of the corporation. Rather they are pursuing their personal desire to get out of the company. Hence, if the state of mind of those in control of the corporation is determinative, an accumulation of earnings to facilitate such a redemption may be regarded as actually motivated by the personal needs or desires of the shareholders rather than needs of the business.

On the other hand, it is true that so long as it is a redemption rather than a complete liquidation which is planned, some of the minority shareholders must be willing to carry on the corporation's business. It seems doubtful as a matter of corporate law today that the majority shareholders could compel a corporation to redeem their own shares, to the exclusion of the minority shareholders, unless the latter were willing. And it could be argued that since the effect of the very redemption transaction contemplated is to shift control of the corporation from the majority shareholders to the minority, the purpose to be attributed to the corporation in accumulating earnings for that objective should be that of the minority stockholders, who are anxious to carry on the enterprise. But the fact remains that, in the absence of special circumstances, minority shareholders do not have any legally protectible interest in maintaining particular corporate policies by preventing a transfer of the controlling shares or otherwise. Hence, though the question may be close, it would certainly be defensible to hold that a redemption of the controlling block of a corporation's stock does not amount to a business need of the corporation within the meaning of the statute.

* * *

However, the basic premise thus far—that a redemption of a noncontrolling block of stock does, or at least may, constitute a reasonable business need under the statute—is itself open to challenge. It has already been observed that a minority shareholder cannot normally present any legal obstacle to the carrying-out of the corporation's objectives as determined by the majority. And the practical danger which such a shareholder most often poses, particularly if he is neither an officer nor a director, is the threat to the untrammeled freedom of the majority shareholders in such matters as their own compensation, or dividend policy, which are primarily matters of individual rather than corporate concern. But even if the interest in preventing such conflict could rise to the level of a business need, developing a standard for handling this issue would be no mean task.

To illustrate, take the Gazette case, where the minority stockholder whose stock was redeemed was threatening to sell to particular outsiders whom the controlling shareholders had special reason for keeping out of the corporation. In the actual case the earnings had been accumulated for other reasons, so that the question of accumulation of earnings in contemplation of a redemption was not presented. But suppose that some years earlier the corporate managers had recognized the possibility that the minority shareholder might become dissatisfied and might consider the sale of his stock to an undesirable outsider. Adoption of a program to put the corporation in a position to redeem the stock of the minority shareholder, in case it might become necessary to prevent such a transfer, would seem to be reasonable enough. And the corporation would certainly be in a better position to prevent an undesirable transfer if it could offer to redeem the stock for cash, rather than on some long-term-credit basis. Accumulation of earnings in advance would offer a good deal more security than relying on the chance of being able to finance a cash redemption when necessary by borrowing.

But the question is whether this would be sufficient to establish a business need for accumulation of earnings. If not, would the added fact that the minority shareholder was already contemplating a sale of his stock change the result? Or would it be incumbent upon the corporation to show that there were some outsiders interested in getting into the company who would pose more than the usual threat of disharmony, and perhaps even that the minority shareholder was in negotiation with those particular outsiders?

Compare this kind of case with a situation where there are no particularly threatening outsiders but the existing minority shareholder has himself become obviously dissatisfied and threatens a rupture of the peace in the corporate family. In such a case, a sale by the minority shareholder to an outsider might distinctly improve the situation; but this is by no means certain, and in any event perhaps the minority shareholder has indicated no desire to sell. Would the desire to put the corporation in a position to make an attractive redemption offer to the minority shareholder if relations worsen amount to a business need justifying the accumulation of earnings?

It is true that under section 537 of the 1954 Code the reasonable-business-needs test has been extended to include "reasonably anticipated needs of the business." But this may well still constitute too blunt an instrument to be used successfully in distinguishing among the many various redemption situations, particularly since any redemption is at best a rather problematical business need. Consider the case of the minority shareholder who in perfect amicability indicates that he would like to withdraw from the corporation in the relatively near future, perhaps simultaneously with his contemplated retirement from an executive position. Suppose that the remaining shareholders are quite willing to have the corporation buy him out, if sufficient funds can be made available. Must the minority shareholder actually break the corporate peace or find an unattractive potential buyer for his shares before the corporation would be justified in accumulating its earnings to finance the proposed redemption?

* * *

In any event, the foregoing cases serve to illustrate the difficulty of attempting to apply a test based upon business needs to the redemption transactions of close corporations. Actually, any attempt to differentiate between corporate objectives and shareholder objectives in the area of close corporations is likely to prove futile. Such "incorporated partnerships," toward which the accumulated earnings tax is primarily directed, do not have any purposes or objectives completely independent of those of their stockholders. Moreover, a close corporation often represents far more than a mere incorporated venture to its proprietors. It may well constitute their life's work, and the foundation of their planning for the present and future security of their families. It is in this latter connection that redemption transactions particularly pursuant to stock-restriction agreements, so often play a key role. Such transactions are obviously inspired by the desires of the individual shareholder. And this is no less true of minority redemptions than of majority redemptions. In a minority redemption, the majority group, acting in its own self-interest, causes the corporation to redeem the stock of the minority shareholder who, likewise acting in his own self-interest, has decided to sell out.

It is true that the opinion of the court of appeals in the Mountain State case appears to have placed its stamp of approval upon the business-purpose analysis of redemption transactions under the accumulated earnings tax. As we have seen, the court was not confronted with the question of accumulation of earnings in advance of a contemplated stock redemption; but the court made clear its intention to include that kind of transaction under the business-purpose umbrella by referring with apparent approval to the decision in Emeloid Co. v. Commissioner. . . .

It would probably be unwise, however, to rely too far on the broad implications of the opinion in Mountain State. First of all, that court had no reason to, and therefore did not, consider the potential wholesale accumulation of earnings in advance of a contemplated redemption which those implications might justify. Moreover, in stressing the importance of resolving the conflict between the two equal groups of stockholders in Mountain State, the court emphasized the importance to the corporation of avoiding the alternatives of sale or complete liquidation of the enterprise which might otherwise have been necessary. But the court failed to consider whether the shareholders whose stock was redeemed could in fact have compelled either of those alternatives. If they could not, as may have been true under the West Virginia statute applicable in the Mountain State situation and would certainly be true in many other jurisdictions, then, as suggested above, the necessity for redemption of that stock from the corporation's point of view is a good deal less clear. And in any event, certainly the selling shareholders, who owned a full one-half interest in the corporation, were not concerned with the needs or purposes of the corporation in their demands to be bought out.

* * *

However, the necessary corollary of this approach is that in redemption cases the court must deal directly with the highly subjective issue of the proscribed purpose. . . .

In [that] event, the important question in these cases is whether the redemption transaction itself provides a basis for inferring the proscribed purpose. To this question the court of appeals in Mountain State gave a clear negative answer, remarking that the "fact of redemption, of itself, . . . furnishes no basis for imposition of the § 102 tax." However, this dictum only opens up the issue; it does not conclude it, particularly since that case did not involve the question of accumulation of earnings in advance of and in contemplation of a redemption.

Here the view expressed earlier, that a redemption of all the stock of the shareholder is akin to a complete liquidation as to that shareholder, may be relevant. In the normal case, when earnings are accumulated to finance a redemption, the selling shareholders will receive their share of the earnings so accumulated as a part of the redemption price. That is because the value of the stock interest to be redeemed will generally increase as the earnings are accumulated; only rarely would a price be set for a future redemption which did not provide for adjustments to take account of profits or losses in the interim. But in effect this means that, from the point of view of the selling shareholders, the situation is just about the same as accumulation of earnings in contemplation of liquidation. Certainly accumulation of earnings in order to distribute them in complete liquidation at capital-gains rates could serve no business need; rather it would go very far to demonstrate the existence of the proscribed purpose to avoid the tax on shareholders. Thus it could well be found that the principal purpose of the selling shareholders in the accumulation of earnings for the redemption of their stock is to avoid surtaxes. . .

* * *

[However,] any earnings accumulated after a final agreement on price is reached would redound entirely to the benefit of the holdover shareholder. As a practical matter, if the transaction is actually consummated within the same fiscal year, presumably no question of a dividend would even arise. It should make no difference that the delay happens to carry beyond the end of the current fiscal year, when under normal circumstances a dividend might be in order. A dividend would not ordinarily be paid prior to the redemption out of earnings accrued subsequent to the agreement on redemption price, since the selling shareholders would not be entitled to share in those earnings. If such a dividend were paid, the holdover shareholder would of course expect the selling shareholders to apply their proceeds against the redemption price. But it seems just as clear that the selling shareholders would not agree to any such procedure. Since the redemption price was determined without including any increment on account of current earnings, there is no reason why they should accept as partial payment of that price a dividend out of those earnings, taxable at surtax rate. Thus in this kind of situation it cannot fairly be said that a dividend out of current earnings would lead to a proportionate reduction in the redemption price. Moreover, there is no analogy there to the case of accumulation of earnings to be distributed in liquidation at capital gains rates, since the selling shareholders do not share in the current earnings being accumulated. Hence there is no basis for imputing to either group of shareholders the proscribed purpose to avoid the dividend tax and, accordingly, no basis for attributing that purpose to the corporation.

As a matter of fact, this kind of situation is very much like an accumulation of earnings subsequent to a redemption for the purpose of discharging the obligation incurred, where of course it is clear that the earnings are accumulated solely for the benefit of the holdover shareholder. Treating these two cases differently would put an undue premium on the time of execution of the redemption transaction, a factor which bears no relation to the critical question of the purpose for the accumulation of earnings. It is submitted that the consistent and proper result is reached by regarding the recommendation made earlier in connection with earnings accumulated subsequent to a redemption as merely an illustration of a broader principle: There is no basis for inferring the existence of the proscribed purpose to avoid the tax on shareholders when the challenged accumulation of earnings is for the benefit of the shareholders whose stock is not to be redeemed and who therefore do not stand to obtain those earnings in a redemption transaction at capital gains rates.

* * *

It is arguable that in every case, even one involving the redemption of a small minority interest, the purpose of the selling shareholders to obtain their share of accumulated earnings at capital gains rates should be imputed to the corporation, thus at least paving the way for imposition of the tax on the portion of the accumulated earnings distributed to the selling shareholders. But any advantages of such a rule seem almost certain to be more than offset by the complicated problems of allocating and tracing earnings that would be involved. Moreover, it would be more consistent with general corporate principles to retain the rule that the purpose to be attributed to the corporation is that of the shareholders in control of it. Under that rule, it would follow that whenever earnings are accumulated to finance a redemption of the stock of the shareholders in control of the corporation, and the redemption price reflects the selling shareholders' proportionate share of the earnings so accumulated, it would be proper to infer the existence of the proscribed purpose and hence to impose the tax.

If there is any doubt whether the accumulated earnings augmented the purchase price, . . . the taxpayer would bear the burden of proof on that issue in accordance with its normal burden of disproving a determination by the Commissioner that the proscribed purpose was present. In cases where only a minority interest is redeemed, and the majority shareholders intend to carry on the business of the corporation, it would not be permissible to infer the proscribed purpose merely from the fact of redemption. So far as a redemption of exactly fifty per cent of the stock is concerned, . . . the business motive of the holdover shareholders would be regarded as predominant, and the proscribed purpose would not be inferred.

However, it should be added that, following the recommendation made earlier, a minority redemption would be simply neutral on the reasonable-business-needs issue; in the absence of special circumstances, such a redemption would give rise to neither a section 535(c) credit in favor of the taxpayer nor a section 533 presumption in favor of the Government. And of course it would still be possible in such a case to infer from other circumstances, in accordance with the general principles operative in the accumulated earnings tax area, that the dominant motive for the accumulation of earnings was in fact the proscribed purpose to avoid the tax on shareholders. This might be of particular importance in cases involving a long-term accumulation of earnings in contemplation of a stock redemption, perhaps pursuant to a stock-restriction agreement.

----

4. Statutory Implications

By virtue of an amendment in 1969, §537 provides that the term "reasonable needs of the business" includes, for any year in which a stockholder dies or thereafter, the amount needed (or reasonably anticipated to be needed) to redeem stock included in the gross estate of the stockholder, up to the maximum amount which can qualify under §303. The reason for this provision was explained in the

Senate Report (S.Rep. No. 91–552, 91st Cong., 1st Sess. 280) as follows:

> *General reasons for change.*—Where there is a redemption of
> a large block of stock from a shareholder (whether or not to pay
> death taxes) the question arises as to whether the money accumulated to pay for the stock redeemed was accumulated for the
> reasonable needs of the corporation's business. If it was not so
> accumulated, the corporation becomes subject to the accumulated
> earnings tax (sec. 531).
>
> * * *
>
> The Internal Revenue Service sometimes has taken the position that any large redemption of stock indicates that the corporation had funds available for noncorporate purposes and therefore this is evidence that earnings were accumulated beyond the
> reasonable needs of the business. The courts have decided this
> issue in favor of the Service in a number of cases.
>
> The committee believes that amounts accumulated in the year
> of the death and later years to redeem stock in a redemption to
> pay death taxes (sec. 303), as well as amounts accumulated to redeem stock which constitutes an excess business holding in the
> hands of a foundation should not be considered unreasonable accumulations. To consider them as such would substantially interfere with the purpose of these two redemption provisions.

In view of the favorable attitude displayed by the
court in the Mountain State case toward accumulation of
earnings to finance a redemption covered by §303, there
is reason to wonder whether new legislation on this subject
was needed. But several cases after Mountain State had
cast doubt on whether such a redemption constituted a
"business" need of the corporation, rather than merely a
personal need of a shareholder, e.g., Young Rubber Corporation v. Commissioner, 21 TCM 1593 (1962), aff'd per
curiam, 331 F.2d 12 (2d Cir.1964); accordingly, Congress
decided to create an express safe harbor for at least post-
death accumulations for this purpose.

However, singling out any particular type of redemption accumulations -- here, post-death accumulations for
redemptions qualifying under §303 (and certain redemptions
from foundations) -- for favorable treatment leaves hanging
the proper treatment of redemption accumulations which
are not covered by the new provision, such as pre-death
accumulations for §303 redemptions, or any accumulation
for any other type of redemption transaction. Section 537
does not include any general provision against adverse in-

ferences in situations not covered by the statute; and this silence may be particularly troublesome, in the light of subsection 537(b) (4), captioned "No Inference as to Prior Taxable Years", which provides in essence that the applicability of § 531 to accumulations in years prior to the death of a stockholder shall be determined without regard to the fact that redemption distributions subject to § 303 are subsequently made. The primary purpose of this subsection is obviously to reject the position ascribed to the Service in the above-quoted Senate Report, i. e., that the availability of substantial funds to finance a redemption indicates that the corporation had accumulated funds beyond reasonable business needs in earlier years (a position which, by the way, was seemingly already inconsistent with existing law to the effect that the propriety of accumulations for any given year is to be tested in the light of the circumstances as of that year, with the fact that the accumulated funds are subsequently used for some other purpose, be it redemption or otherwise, viewed as irrelevant; see casebook pages 543–544). Note that subsection 537(b)(4) creates at least one negative implication as serious as the one it seeks to preclude; the express prohibition against drawing unfavorable inferences as to prior years from a current redemption covered by § 303 could be treated as an invitation to draw unfavorable inferences as to prior years when other redemption transactions occur currently. But more important is the question whether the presence of this rather narrowly-drawn anti-inference subsection can serve as a general invitation to draw adverse inferences as to all redemption situations which are not covered by the statute. In this connection, note that it is possible to read the subsection as also precluding adverse inferences with regard to pre-death accumulations for § 303 redemptions. However the words of the subsection are scarcely apt to accomplish this purpose; and in any event, such a construction would surely heighten the possibility of adverse inferences as to all other accumulations for redemption transactions not covered by the statute.

Chapter 4

CORPORATE LIQUIDATIONS

SECTION 1. LIQUIDATION, DISSOLUTION, AND SALE OF ASSETS

A. INTRODUCTION

Although the term "liquidation" is widely used, it is rarely defined in the corporate statutes, unlike the term "dissolution" which clearly refers to the final termination of corporate existence. E.g., MBA §§ 82–96 An excellent statement of the relationship between liquidation and dissolution appears in Lattin, Corporations (1959) 550:

> "Dissolution" . . . means the termination of the legal existence of the corporation so that the unit may no longer carry on under its former franchises, for it has none with which to function. Liquidation or winding up involves the process of collecting the assets, paying the creditors, and distributing whatever is left, after liquidation expenses, to the shareholders in accordance with their contracts and, if there are no special contracts, then pro rata according to their shareholding interest.

Typically, liquidation and dissolution will be preceded by a sale of substantially all of the corporation's assets, in order to facilitate distribution to the shareholders (unless of course a distribution in kind is desired). However, a sale of all or substantially all of a corporation's assets is not always a prelude to a liquidation—that is, it is perfectly possible to have a sale of all the assets of a corporation without going on to distribute the proceeds to the stockholders in liquidation. Thus a sale of all of the assets of a corporation does not *ipso facto* constitute a "liquidation" within the meaning of, say, a charter provision governing the liquidation preference of preferred stock. E.g., Levin v. Pittsburgh United Corp., 330 Pa. 457, 199 A. 332 (1938) ("The inevitable legal result of a sale of corporate assets is not necessarily dissolution to be followed by complete liquidation. . . . The remaining stockholders in a corporation may . . . embark again upon the same business or, by amending its charter, proceed into new enterprises.") ; Treves v. Menzies, 37 Del.Ch. 330, 142 A.2d 520 (Ch. 1958) (sale of substantially all of the assets of a corporation for cash did not constitute a "liquidation, dissolution, or winding-up" of the corporation entitling the preferred stockholders to receive their liquidation preference).

Similarly, a vote to sell all of a corporation's assets does not itself provide any authority to liquidate the corporation and distribute the proceeds. In Opelka v. Quincy Memorial Bridge Co., 335 Ill.App. 402, 82 N.E.2d 184 (1948), the corporation, which owned a toll bridge, had outstanding 4000 shares of $100 par cumulative preferred stock with a liquidation preference of par plus accrued dividends, and 10,-000 shares of no par common. In 1945, when the unpaid arrearages on the preferred stock amounted to $104.99 per share, the shareholders approved a plan calling for the sale of all of the corporation's assets and the distribution of the proceeds at the rate of $150.00 per share to preferred stockholders and $5 per share to common stockholders. The transaction was attacked by certain preferred stockholders on the ground, *inter alia*, that it violated the preferred stock liquidation preference. The defendants argued that the transaction was justified by the specific authority to sell all the assets of a corporation provided in § 72 of the Illinois Corporation Act (virtually identical to MBA § 79). The court held that the transaction was invalid:

> It is noted that this section provides for the sale of corporate assets other than in the regular course of business, but does not prescribe the method of distributing the consideration received. In fact, . . . [the counterpart of MBA § 79(c) indicates] that the corporation is to receive the sale price: . . . It logically follows that the consideration received by the corporation should be held for or distributed to the stockholders in accordance with their preferential rights as fixed by the charter and stock certificates. It seems to be the rule that approval of the sale of corporate assets does not extend to approval of a scheme of distribution of the sale price in conflict with the terms of the shareholders' contract as embodied in the charter, stock certificates, and the Corporation Act. In the case of Geiger v. American Seeding Machine Company, 124 Ohio St. 222, 177 N.E. 594, 79 A.L.R. 614, . . . [the Syllabus states that] "the sale of the entire assets of a corporation and the distribution of the proceeds of such sale among stockholders are separate matters between separate parties and based upon separate considerations; stockholders of different classes cannot be compelled to give their consent to one as a condition to their concurrence in the other."

> . . . Although this question apparently has not been passed upon by the courts of this state, the same distinction is recognized by the draftsmen of the Act in their authoritative commentary appearing in the Illinois Business

Corporation Act Annotated, wherein, with reference to Section 72, the following appears:

> "No provision, however, is contained in the Act permitting submission of a plan for the distribution among the various groups of shareholders of the shares received as consideration for the sale. *In the absence of unanimous consent, it would seem that the distribution of the consideration received can normally be effected only by following the procedure for voluntary distribution.*"

Defendants . . . [argue] that the reality of the situation confronting the Bridge Company called for some inducement to be offered common stockholders to secure their favorable vote for the plan. Inferentially, this suggests a new principle in law, i.e., that which would otherwise be illegal in corporate affairs may be validated by the exigency of a given situation. This revolutionary innovation cannot be adopted, as to do so would jeopardize the rights of the holders of preferred stock of all Illinois corporations, and, for all practical purposes, destroy the market for preferred stock in the future. If this policy is to be adopted, it becomes a matter for the legislature and not the courts. . . .

B. THE REQUIREMENT OF STOCKHOLDER APPROVAL FOR A SALE OF ASSETS

---

1. IN GENERAL

While liquidation and dissolution invariably require the affirmative vote of the stockholders, there is often a good deal more question as to whether the approval of stockholders is necessary for a sale of assets by the corporation.

SIEGEL, WHEN CORPORATIONS DIVIDE: A STATUTORY AND FINANCIAL ANALYSIS*

79 Harv.L.Rev. 534, 537–544 (1966).

A. Sale of Assets

It was generally held at common law that sale of all the assets of a corporation could be undertaken, except in rare circumstances, only upon unanimous vote of the shareholders, although a small body

* Copyright (c) Harvard Law Review Association, 1966. Reprinted by permission. Most of the footnotes omitted. [Current MBA section numbers have been substituted in brackets.]

of law and informed commentary argued that only a majority vote was necessary. Today, every state, with the sole exception of Arizona, has included in its corporation law a provision governing the sale of assets. A majority of these provisions specifically recognize stock of the purchasing corporation as acceptable consideration for the sale; and most others allow the terms of sale to be set by the board of directors, thus presumably permitting stock to be received as consideration. In some states, however, a minority stockholder may not be forced to accept the stock of the purchasing corporation as consideration for the sale.

Sections [78 & 79] of the Model Business Corporation Act are typical sale-of-assets provisions:

*   *   *

Whether the sale-of-assets component of a corporate division falls within [§79] turns on two issues: (1) Is there a sale of "all or substantially all" of the assets? (2) Is the sale in "the usual and regular course" of the business of the corporation?

    1. "All or substantially all."—Few cases have raised squarely the issue of what size or character of sale is covered by sale-of-assets statutes. The meaning of "all or substantially all" as used in the Model Act and a majority of state statutes remains unclear. Some guidance may be drawn from decisions under other statutes, which speak of sales of "all of its property and assets," "its property . . . or any part thereof,[22]" "any of its property . . . essential to the conduct of its corporate business and purposes," and several other formulations. . . . It seems clear that the size of a sale alone will not be determinative of whether the sale falls within the statute requiring shareholder approval. In all cases, the courts have engaged in a close examination of the facts surrounding the sale. The sale in In the Matter of Timmis * of the calendar department of a printing company, together with the goodwill thereof, was held to be effectively "going out of business *pro tanto*," even though the assets of the division sold represented only one-thirteenth of the total assets of the corporation. In requiring stockholder approval, the court emphasized that the corporation was by virtue of the sale indefinitely barred from reentering the calendar business and that this amounted to a permanent contraction of the nature of the business. Such reasoning applied with equal force to the sale by a corporation of its newspaper plant, although the plant did not constitute its entire business. By contrast, the sale by a drugstore chain of one of its stores was held not substantially to contract either the size or the character of the corporate business.

---

22. E. g., the New York statute dis-   *[Ed. note] See note 22, supra.
cussed in In the Matter of Timmis,
200 N.Y. 177, 93 N.E. 522 (1910).
 .   .   .

In Klopot v. Northrup,[30] a corset manufacturer sold its surgical corset department, and dissenting stockholders failed in their attempt to bring the sale within the statute. The court noted that the surgical department was new and experimental, and that it did not constitute such an integral part of the assets as to be essential to the corporate operations. Although factual distinctions clarify some of the decisions, differences in the statutory terms have often been determinative. In the Klopot case, some further explanation was necessary to demonstrate why a transaction strikingly similar to that in Timmis led to an opposite result. The Klopot court rested the distinction on the statutes involved:

> Our statute is not like that of New York, which authorizes a corporation, with the consent of two-thirds of its stock, to sell its property, rights, privileges and franchises "or any interest therein or any part thereof" . . . nor like the similar provision of the Maine statute . . . which applied to the sale of the franchises, entire property or any of the property of a corporation "essential to the conduct of its corporate businesses or purposes;" . . . nor even like the Ohio statute . . . which applied to the sale of "all or substantially all" the assets.

The Connecticut statute in Klopot was indeed different; at the time of that decision it applied to sales by a corporation of "all its property and assets, including its good will and franchises." While it may be argued that the "all assets" language of the statute was intended to exclude any sales of less than all assets, the Klopot court itself recognized the possibility that sales of essential assets, or of assets without which business could not be conducted, might fall within the statute. An Illinois court, faced with a similar statute, has held that "all" means "all or substantially all." But even with this modification, it is clear that the statute in Klopot was less inclusive than the enactment in Timmis and that this distinction was decisive.

These decisions suggest that while sales of all assets or essential assets will fall within the ambit of virtually all statutes, whatever their wording, determining whether sale of a corporate division [by a corporation owning two divisions] . . . would be held within the statute will depend on the particular facts and the statute involved. At one extreme, when language is presumptively directed at all sales, as was the New York statute, the Timmis result seems proper. At the other, when a statute appears limited to sales of "all" or "essential" assets, the reasoning of Klopot may be expected to prevail. Although the meaning of the "all or substantially all" test of the Model Business Corporation Act has not been authoritatively resolved, it seems closer in import to the "all assets" criterion. Had the drafters desired the Timmis result, they could have made

30. 131 Conn. 14, 37 A.2d 700 (1944).

tne test "all or a substantial part." It seems likely that the words "substantially all" were inserted not to expand the class of sales covered, but rather to prevent avoidance of the statute by retention of some minimal residue of the original assets.*   . . .

*[Ed. note] Compare the following views as to the meaning of "substantially all of the assets" of a corporation, in the context of the requirement in I.R.C. § 354(b) that to qualify as a D reorganization one corporation must acquire "substantially all of the assets" of the other. In Moffatt v. Commissioner, 42 T.C. 558 (1964), the court said:

We note preliminarily that "[the] term 'substantially all' is a relative term, dependent on the facts of any given situation". . . . "Whether the properties transferred constitute 'substantially all' is a matter to be determined from the facts and circumstances in each case rather than by the application of any particular percentage". . . . Moreover, in considering the "facts and circumstances" in any given case, it is a matter of importance to take into account the liabilities of the enterprise, so that the retention of what might be a large amount of assets in other situations would be of very little consequence if such assets were held back by the transferor in order to pay off its liabilities. . . .

* * *

Petitioners' position revolves largely around percentages of balance sheet assets of the old company . . . . Their contention is fatally defective because (a) they fail to take into account the important asset of the business that did not appear on the balance sheet at all . . . .

(a) . . . It is of the utmost importance to remember that the consulting engineering business is basically a service business. . . . As we have found, the most valuable asset of such business is its staff of trained personnel and the past performance and qualifications of its employees. . . . This was an asset of enormous importance . . . ; yet, it nowhere appears on the balance sheet, and was not taken into account in any way by petitioners in evaluating what was transferred . . . .

In James Armour, Inc. v. Commissioner, 43 T.C. 295 (1964), the court said:

In the instant case Armour, Inc. immediately prior to the transactions in question had assets of a fair market value of about $1,230,000. Among these assets the principal item in the conduct of the business was the construction equipment which had a value of $620,774.98 which was transferred to Excavating [a new corporation]. Also among the assets transferred were furniture and fixtures and automobiles of a value of $7,802.84. Thus, total assets of a value of $628,577.82 were transferred directly by Armour, Inc. to Excavating. [The court then noted that although real property with a value of approximately $180,000 was transferred to the stockholders of Armour, Inc., it was promptly leased to Excavating.] The remaining assets, consisting of cash and accounts receivable of approximately $425,000, were not acquired by Excavating. Thus, it will be seen that as a result of the transactions, Excavating either acquired title to, or the use of, all the assets essential to the conduct of the business enterprise. It seems clear that the assets which it did not acquire, namely, cash and accounts receivable, were not necessary to the conduct of the enterprise. If such unneeded assets had been distributed to the petitioners prior to the transfer of the essential assets to Excavating there clearly would be no question that substantially all of Armour, Inc.'s assets were acquired by Excavating. . . . The date of distribution is not decisive in such a situation as is here presented.

2. "Usual and regular course of business."—The Model Act and the statutes based on it require shareholder approval only for sales outside of the usual and regular course of business. Many statutes limit only the size of the sale and do not have this additional test. The statutes in both Klopot and Timmis were so drafted, but in Timmis the New York court judicially adopted the additional criterion: "Notwithstanding the broad language of [the sale of assets statute] . . . it is obvious that it was not addressed to ordinary sales by a corporation, nor even to those extraordinary in size but still in the regular line of its business . . .." Since the New York statute in Timmis covered the sale of corporate property "or any interest therein or any part thereof," the result of the decision was that any sale, however small, fell within the statute if it was outside the usual and regular course of business of the corporation. Under the Timmis rule, however, the sale of significant assets—as, for example, an entire store—would fall outside the statute if by virtue of its usual nature it were found to be within the ordinary course of business. The Model Act requires stockholder approval in fewer cases than does the Timmis rule, since the sales covered must be both outside the usual and regular course of business and dispositions of all or substantially all the assets of the corporation. However, since the Model Act's "all or substantially all" test remains open to varying interpretation, it is not unlikely that the nature of the sale—whether it is in the ordinary course of business—will be the major factor in determining whether the sale requires stockholder approval.

The courts have experienced some difficulty in defining a corporation's usual course of business: [as the court said in the Timmis case,] "The sale before us was not made in the ordinary course of the business of the corporation, for it was not organized to sell calendar departments, or any department that would involve going out of business *pro tanto*." Obviously the usual corporation is not organized to dispose of part of its business. Yet sales of major assets such as buildings or machinery in connection with replenishment programs are ordinarily within the powers specified or implied in the certificate of incorporation, although they may not be everyday occurrences. Corporate management would be hamstrung if every such transaction had to be submitted to a vote of shareholders. . . . Where is the line drawn? Sales of substantial assets by real estate corporations or by corporations organized to liquidate a business have been held within their usual course of business. Generally, a charter provision allowing sales of all assets without shareholder approval will also be held to render such sales usual. Absent such a charter provision, however, is there any ordinary business objective of the cor-

Accordingly, we conclude that substantially all of the assets of Armour, Inc., were acquired by Excavating . . . .

poration that might justify a disposition such as the sale of a . . . corporate division?

Several New York decisions have upheld dispositions of assets without stockholder approval when undertaken as part of a relocation plan, as when sale of one plant is followed by purchase of another. These cases have two significant facts in common: in none was goodwill sold, and in none was a new corporation organized. It has already been noted that disposition of goodwill might in itself bring a sale within the statute. Support for this conclusion is found in the Model Act: [§ 78] does not include dispositions of good will as part of the sales in the usual course of business, while [§ 79] does include such dispositions in sales outside of the usual course of business. Exclusion of goodwill from the sale will not assure that the sale may be consummated without shareholder approval, since [sect. 79] covers disposition "with or without the good will." Nevertheless, failure to sell the goodwill will be relevant to a decision that the sale is not out of the ordinary course of business.

The fact that a new corporation was not organized also influenced the decisions in the relocation cases. Yet one commentator has suggested that even when the relocation involves a change in the corporate entity (as by formation of a corporation in another state followed by transfer of assets in return for stock thereof), "such a transaction is within the literal language of those statutes . . . [governing] sale of assets, but hardly within their spirit." . . .

STILES v. ALUMINUM PRODUCTS CO.

Appellate Court of Illinois, First District, 1949.
338 Ill.App. 48, 86 N.E.2d 887.

FEINBERG, PRESIDING JUSTICE. Plaintiffs brought their action under Section 73 of the Business Corporation Act, [the counterpart of MBA §§ 80 and 81] to recover the reasonable value of 1240 shares of stock of the defendant company, owned by plaintiffs. . . .

There is practically no dispute as to the facts. It appears from the evidence that defendant was an Illinois corporation incorporated in 1911 and engaged in the manufacture and sale of aluminum and stainless steel cooking utensils, and also in the fabrication of aluminum and other metals. The charter was amended in 1935, giving it power to deal in real estate and securities. After the charter was amended, a subsidiary company known as General Homes Corporation, was organized, which erected some 30 apartments on real estate adjacent to the plants of the corporation, and appears to have been a housing project for the convenience of defendant's employees. The acquisition of the shares of the General Homes Corporation and a few shares of bank stock was the only exercise of the additional powers of the corporation prior to the sale of its assets in question. During the year 1945, negotiations were entered into for the sale of defendant's manufacturing plants, tangible property inventory, business and good will, to the Reynolds Metals Company, a Delaware Corporation. A contract of sale dated December 7, 1945, between defendant and the Reynolds Company was entered into, by which all of its manufacturing plants (four in number), its tools, dies, machinery, equipment, office furniture, trucks, inventory, good will and patents were sold to the Reynolds Company for $1,406,570. It did not sell its stock in General Homes Corporation, nor some stock in the LaGrange Trust and Savings Bank, money in bank, accounts receivable and some marketable securities and a 1942 Oldsmobile sedan. It was stipulated that the value of the assets not sold was $760,622.69. After the contract of sale was entered into, the directors sent out a notice, under Section 72 of the Business Corporation Act, for a stockholders' meeting to authorize the sale. Plaintiffs were substantial stockholders in the defendant company, and at the meeting did not vote in favor of the sale and followed the [appraisal] procedure prescribed by Section 73. . . .

No question is here raised that defendant did not conform to the statute in the matter of the notice and the holding of the meeting of the stockholders or the procedure necessary to effect a sale, nor is there any question raised here that plaintiffs did not comply with the procedure prescribed by said Section 73.

The only question, as we view it, presented upon this appeal is whether the sale in question was one of "substantially all of the assets" of the defendant company, not made in the usual and regular course of its business, within the meaning of Section 72 of said act. Plaintiffs' theory is that the mere exclusion from the sale of a second-hand automobile, some shares of stock in a subsidiary building company, accounts receivable, money in bank, and some marketable securities, does not take it out of the operation of the statute governing the sale of the "substantially all of the assets" of the company.

The primary object of the company was the manufacture of aluminum and stainless steel cooking utensils and the fabrication of aluminum and other metals. It owned four tracts of real estate, each improved with buildings, having an aggregate of 128,000 square feet, in which it carried on its manufacturing business. It had a vast stock of raw material and finished products, valuable patents, licenses, copyrights and good will, all resulting from the years of successful operation of its business, and all included in the sale in question. To hold out from the sale the choses in action described and an old automobile, and thus seek to prevent the sale from being "substantially all of the assets" of the company, within the meaning of the statute, is in our judgment an effort to circumvent the statute and defeat the rights of a dissenting stockholder under Section 73 of the act. . . .
[T]he present statute, while intending to liberalize the power of di-

rectors and stockholders to sell all or "substantially all of the assets" other than in the regular course of business, as provided in said act, . . . also intended to protect the minority stockholder who does not vote in favor of such a sale. It affords to him the remedy of recovering the reasonable value of his stock, whatever that may be as of the time of the sale. It will not permit resort to subterfuge, in a sale of assets, to defeat the rights of a dissenting stockholder.

We think upon the showing made that the sale in question was one of "substantially all of the assets" of the corporation within the meaning of the statute, and that plaintiffs are entitled to bring their action. . . .

KATZ v. BREGMAN

Court of Chancery, Delaware, 1981.
431 A.2d 1274.

MARVEL, CHANCELLOR:

The complaint herein seeks the entry of an order preliminarily enjoining the proposed sale of the Canadian assets of Plant Industries, Inc. to Vulcan Industrial Packaging, Ltd., the plaintiff Hyman Katz allegedly being the owner of approximately 170,000 shares of common stock of the defendant Plant Industries, Inc., on whose behalf he has brought this action, suing not only for his own benefit as a stockholder but for the alleged benefit of all other record owners of common stock of the defendant Plant Industries, Inc. . . . Significantly, at common law, a sale of all or substantially all of the assets of a corporation required the unanimous vote of the stockholders, Folk, The Delaware General Corporation Law, p. 400.

The complaint alleges that during the last six months of 1980, the board of directors of Plant Industries, Inc., under the guidance of the individual defendant Robert B. Bregman, the present chief executive officer of such corporation, embarked on a course of action which resulted in the disposal of several unprofitable subsidiaries of the corporate defendant located in the United States, namely Louisiana Foliage Inc., a horticultural business, Sunaid Food Products, Inc., a Florida packaging business, and Plant Industries (Texas), Inc., a business concerned with the manufacture of woven synthetic cloth. As a result of these sales Plant Industries, Inc. by the end of 1980 had disposed of a significant part of its unprofitable assets.

According to the complaint, Mr. Bregman thereupon proceeded on a course of action designed to dispose of a subsidiary of the corporate defendant known as Plant National (Quebec) Ltd., a business which constitutes Plant Industries, Inc.'s entire business operation in

Canada and has allegedly constituted Plant's only income producing facility during the past four years. The professed principal purpose of such proposed sale is to raise needed cash and thus improve Plant's balance sheets. And while interest in purchasing the corporate defendant's Canadian plant was thereafter evinced not only by Vulcan Industrial Packaging, Ltd. but also by Universal Drum Reconditioning Co., which latter corporation originally undertook to match or approximate and recently to top Vulcan's bid, a formal contract was entered into between Plant Industries, Inc. and Vulcan on April 2, 1981 for the purchase and sale of Plant National (Quebec) despite the constantly increasing bids for the same property being made by Universal. One reason advanced by Plant's management for declining to negotiate with Universal is that a firm undertaking having been entered into with Vulcan that [sic] the board of directors of Plant may not legally or ethically negotiate with Universal. But see Thomas v. Kempner, C.A. 4138, March 22, 1973.

In seeking injunctive relief, as prayed for, plaintiff relies on two principles, one that found in 8 Del.C. § 271 to the effect that a decision of a Delaware corporation to sell " * * * all or substantially all of its property and assets * * * " requires not only the approval of such corporation's board of directors but also a resolution adopted by a majority of the outstanding stockholders of the corporation entitled to vote thereon at a meeting duly called upon at least twenty days' notice.

Support for the other principle relied on by plaintiff for the relief sought, namely an alleged breach of fiduciary duty on the part of the board of directors of Plant Industries, Inc. is allegedly found in such board's studied refusal to consider a potentially higher bid for the assets in question which is being advanced by Universal, Thomas v. Kempner, supra.

Turning to the possible application of 8 Del.C. § 271 to the proposed sale of substantial corporate assets of National to Vulcan, it is stated in Gimbel v. Signal Companies, Inc., Del.Ch., 316 A.2d 599 (1974) as follows:

> "If the sale is of assets quantitatively vital to the operation of the corporation and is out of the ordinary and substantially affects the existence and purpose of the corporation then it is beyond the power of the Board of Directors."

According to Plant's 1980 10K form, it appears that at the end of 1980, Plant's Canadian operations represented 51% of Plant's remaining assets. Defendants also concede that National represents 44.9% of Plant's sales' revenues and 52.4% of its pre-tax net operating income. Furthermore, such report by Plant discloses, in rough figures, that while National made a profit in 1978 of $2,900,000, the profit from the United States businesses in that year was only $770,000. In 1979, the Canadian business profit was $3,500,000 while the loss of the United States businesses was $344,000. Furthermore, in 1980, while the Canadian business profit was $5,300,000, the corporate loss in the United States was $4,500,000. And while these figures may be somewhat distorted by the allocation of overhead expenses and taxes, they are significant. In any event, defendants concede that " * * * National accounted for 34.9% of Plant's pre-tax income in 1976, 36.9% in 1977, 42% in 1978, 51% in 1979 and 52.4% in 1980."

While in the case of Philadelphia National Bank v. B. S. F. Co., Del.Ch., 199 A.2d 557 (1969), rev'd on other grounds, Del.Supr., 204 A.2d 746 (1964), the question of whether or not there had been a proposed sale of substantially all corporate assets was tested by provisions of an indenture agreement covering subordinated debentures, the result was the same as if the provisions of 8 Del.C. § 271 had been applicable, the trial Court stating:

> "While no pertinent Pennsylvania case is cited, the critical factor in determining the character of a sale of assets is generally considered not the amount of property sold but whether the sale is in fact an unusual transaction or one made in the regular course of business of the seller * * * ".

Furthermore, in the case of Wingate v. Bercut (C.A.9) 146 F.2d 725 (1945), in which the Court declined to apply the provisions of 8 Del.C. § 271, it was noted that the transfer of shares of stock there involved, being a dealing in securities, constituted an ordinary business transaction.

In the case at bar, I am first of all satisfied that historically the principal business of Plant Industries, Inc. has not been to buy and sell industrial facilities but rather to manufacture steel drums for use in bulk shipping as well as for the storage of petroleum products, chemicals, food, paint, adhesives and cleaning agents, a business which has been profitably performed by National of Quebec. Furthermore, the proposal, after the sale of National, to embark on the manufacture of plastic drums represents a radical departure from Plant's historically successful line of business, namely steel drums. I therefore conclude that the proposed sale of Plant's Canadian operations, which constitute over 51% of Plant's total assets and in which are generated approximately 45% of Plant's 1980 net sales, would, if consummated, constitute a sale of substantially all of Plant's assets. By way of contrast, the proposed sale of Signal Oil in Gimbel v. Signal Companies, Inc., supra, represented only about 26% of the total assets of Signal Companies, Inc. And while Signal Oil represented 41% of Signal Companies, Inc. total net worth, it generated only about 15% of Signal Companies, Inc. revenue and earnings.

I conclude that because the proposed sale of Plant National (Quebec) Ltd. would, if consummated, constitute a sale of substantially all of the assets of Plant Industries, Inc., as presently constituted, that an injunction should issue preventing the consummation of such sale at least until it has been approved by a majority of the outstanding stockholders of Plant Industries, Inc., entitled to vote at a meeting duly called on at least twenty days' notice. Compare Robinson v. Pittsburg Oil Refining Company, Del.Ch., 126 A. 46 (1933).

In light of this conclusion it will be unnecessary to consider whether or not the sale here under attack, as proposed to be made, is for such an inadequate consideration, viewed in light of the competing bid of Universal, as to constitute a breach of trust on the part of the directors of Plant Industries, Inc., Robinson v. Pittsburg Oil Refining Company, supra.

Being persuaded for the reasons stated that plaintiff has demonstrated a reasonable probability of ultimate success on final hearing in the absence of stockholder approval of the proposed sale of the corporate assets here in issue to Vulcan, a preliminary injunction against the consummation of such transaction, at least until stockholder approval is obtained, will be granted. . . .

---

2. SALE OF ASSETS PURSUANT TO A DISSOLUTION

Does a sale of substantially all of a corporation's assets pursuant to a dissolution of the corporation still require a vote of the stockholders under a sale-of-assets statute like MBA § 79? Often it will not make much difference as a practical matter, since the dissolution will have to be approved by the stockholders, and normally there would be little difficulty in getting their approval for the sale of assets at the same time. However, as we have seen, dissolution is not the same as a sale of assets, and in some circumstances there might be stockholders who would vote for dissolution but not for a sale of assets—for example, if they preferred to receive a distribution in kind. In In re Mayellen Apartments, Inc., 134 Cal.App.2d 298, 285 P.2d 943 (2d Dist. 1955), the court held that once dissolution had been voted, it was no longer necessary to get the stockholders' approval for sale of all the assets because the statutory provisions dealing with dissolution expressly gave the directors power "to sell . . . or otherwise dispose of all or any part of the assets of the corporation, upon such terms and conditions and for such considerations as such board deems reasonable or expedient".

The Model Act provisions relating to this issue are rather puzzling, and if nothing else they further illustrate how complex the interrelationship between sale of assets and dissolution can be. Section 87(b) somewhat parallels the statute referred to in the Mayellen case, but there are some differences that could be important. First, the "wind-up" powers are conferred upon the corporation, rather than directly upon the board of directors, which may be designed to leave open the question of who acts for the corporation. Second, § 87(b) does not expressly authorize any "sale" of assets, much less the sale

of substantially all of them. There is also the question of what inference should be drawn from the fact that §80 (b), which provides
appraisal remedies for stockholders who dissent from a sale of assets
in certain circumstances, was amended in 1962 to expressly include "a
sale in dissolution". That the amendment was thought necessary at
all, and that no corresponding amendment was made in §79
itself, certainly suggest that dissolution sales are not
covered by §79*; but perhaps the draftsman assumed §79 coverage and merely wanted to make it clear that the fact of
dissolution did not ipso facto eliminate the right to appraisal. By the way, if a sale in dissolution is not subject
to §79, it is hard to see how a right to dissent from it can
be very meaningful. In other words, if a sale of all the
assets pursuant to a dissolution under §84 does not require
action by the stockholders under §79, there will not be any
occasion for the stockholders to dissent to the sale; on the
other hand, a dissent at the time of the vote on dissolution
may be premature, since there may not yet have been any decision on whether the assets are to be sold. Perhaps the
practical answer is that the stockholders should refuse to
approve a dissolution unless it is accompanied by a "plan"
which indicates whether the assets will be sold or distributed in kind. (In this connection, was it just a slip of
the draftsman's pen to refer in §80(b) to a "sale" in dissolution, but not an "exchange"?)

There is another puzzling aspect of §80(b) which relates to the interaction between a sale of assets and liquidation or dissolution. In view of the fact that a sale of
assets does not in and of itself involve or authorize the
distribution of the proceeds to stockholders, what is the
import of the exception to appraisal rights in §80(b) for
cases where the sale of substantially all of the assets is
"for cash on terms requiring that all or substantially all
of the net proceeds of sale be distributed to the shareholders in accordance with their respective interests within one year after the date of sale"? Even if the term "net
proceeds of sale" in this exception is read literally
(rather than as though it said "net assets", which would
seem more in keeping with the apparent purpose of the provision to isolate those cases where the stockholders will

---

* Compare New York Business Corporation Law § 1005(a)(3)(A), which expressly precludes the application of
the sale-of-assets statute to sales in
dissolution, but does require the approval of a majority of the voting
stock (as compared with the ⅔ requirement under the regular sale of
assets provision) for a sale in dissolution of substantially all of the corporation's remaining assets where the
consideration is in whole or in part
the stock or securities of the buyer.

receive their entire interest in cash fairly promptly),
it is hard to see how the required assurance of distribution to the stockholders could normally be given without a prior resolution to dissolve the corporation (except perhaps by reducing stated capital to a low figure
and relying upon distributions from capital surplus as
well as earned surplus); conversely, if the corporation had
substantial liabilities which were not assumed, literal
compliance would not be feasible, even with a vote to
dissolve, since a substantial portion of the "net proceeds
of sale" would have to be used to pay off the liabilities.
In any event, if as a practical matter a dissolution is going
to be needed to qualify under the exception in §80(b), it
would have been better to include dissolution as an express
condition. Compare New York Business Corporation Law §910,
where the proviso limiting shareholders' appraisal rights
in connection with the sale of substantially all of the
assets is expressly predicated on the shareholders' approval
being "conditioned upon the dissolution of the corporation
and the distribution of substantially all its net assets to
the shareholders in accordance with their respective interests within one year after the date of such transaction".

C. RIGHTS OF CREDITORS UPON A SALE OF ASSETS, LIQUIDATION OR DISSOLUTION

DARCY v. BROOKLYN & N. Y. FERRY CO.

Court of Appeals of New York, 1909.
196 N.Y. 99, 89 N.E. 461.

WILLARD BARTLETT, J.   On November 15, 1900, the plaintiff
duly recovered a judgment against the Brooklyn & New York Ferry
Company upon a cause of action which had accrued on the 2d day of
July, 1897.   The execution upon this judgment was returned unsatisfied.   The plaintiff found himself unable to enforce it because the defendant corporation on the 22d of August, 1898, had through its board
of directors assumed to sell, assign, and transfer the entire corporate
property to another corporation known as the Brooklyn Ferry Company of New York for $6,000,000.   The present suit was instituted on
the theory that the directors had violated their duties in making the
transfer in the manner in which they made it and hence could be compelled to satisfy the plaintiff's claim.   The consideration for the transfer did not pass from the purchasing corporation to the Brooklyn &
New York Ferry Company or its directors, but was turned over directly to the stockholders of the selling corporation and distributed
among them.   The Brooklyn & New York Ferry Company thereupon
immediately ceased doing business, having thus parted with all its
franchises, although no proceedings were ever taken to effect a dissolution of the corporation according to law.   No notice of the transfer was given to creditors nor was any property retained by the directors with which to meet the plaintiff's claim or any other indebtedness which might legally be established against the corporation.   At
the time of the transfer, however, the purchasing corporation did
agree to assume all the then existing debts and liabilities of the selling
corporation.   This agreement was the sole provision made by the directors for the payment of the creditors of the corporation which they
represented.

The narrative of the transaction leaves no doubt that what the
directors of the Brooklyn & New York Ferry Company sought to bring
about was a voluntary dissolution of the corporation and the distribution of its assets without taking the steps to that end which are prescribed by law.   Notwithstanding their failure to proceed under the
statute, they contend that a creditor of a corporation has no standing
to compel them to pay a claim of which they were ignorant at the
time of the transfer of the corporate property, in the absence of
proof of actual fraud on their part.   It is true that there is no allegation or finding of fraud; but there is evidence that the officers of
the company had knowledge of the injury to the plaintiff which was
the basis of his claim.   The liability of the directors is predicated, not

on the ground that their action in making the transfer was fraudulent, but upon the proposition that it is a violation of duty on the part of the directors of a corporation to divest it of all its property without affording a reasonable opportunity to its creditors to present and enforce their claims before the transfer shall become effective. This is the proposition involved in the judgment in this case which we are asked to reverse. We think it is sound in law, and should be upheld.

There is express statutory authority for the maintenance of an action by a creditor of a corporation against its directors to compel them to pay the value of any property which they have transferred to others by a violation of their duties. . . . The assets of a corporation constitute a trust fund for the payment of its debts. . . . A creditor cannot be deprived of his equitable lien thereon by an agreement between the corporation and a transferee of the property that the latter shall assume and pay all the corporate debts. The consent of the creditor to accept the substituted debtor is essential to make such an agreement valid as against him. Hence the fact that the Brooklyn Ferry Company of New York agreed with the Brooklyn & New York Ferry Company to assume all the debts of the latter did not justify the directors of the selling corporation in disposing of its assets without making some other provision for the payment of its creditors. The plaintiff was left in the position of the creditor so aptly described . . . [thusly]: "When he demands payment of his claim, he is referred to the empty shell which is all that is left of the live corporation whose tangible assets constituted a trust fund for the payment of his claim at the time of its creation." It is not necessary to determine precisely what the directors of a corporation must do in order to protect themselves against liability when they undertake to divest it of all its property and practically dissolve it without taking the proceedings for a voluntary dissolution which are prescribed by law. For the purposes of the present case, it is enough to say that they were bound to give some notice to creditors of the proposed transfer, and they gave none whatever. We think that their failure to do so was "a violation of their duties" under subdivision 2 of section 1781 of the Code of Civil Procedure, and rendered them liable to the plaintiff for the amount of the claim which he established against the corporation as having accrued before the transfer. The motives which induced the omission are immaterial. The entire assets could not lawfully be set over by the selling corporation to the purchasing corporation until some sort of opportunity had been given to the creditors of the latter to present and enforce their claims. The neglect to afford this opportunity is what constituted a violation of the directors' duties, and it matters not that they may have supposed they were not required to do any more than they did for the protection of creditors. . . . Their omission to make adequate provision for the protection of the creditors was proof of their dereliction and good faith constitutes no defense. Indeed, business men have little cause for complaint when, as in this case, they find themselves in trouble because they have attempted to accomplish privately what the law contemplates shall only be accomplished publicly, namely, the voluntary dissolution of a corporation. The judgment enforces a sound lesson in business morals and should be affirmed, with costs.

NOTE ON THE RIGHTS OF CREDITORS

a. **Liability of the Transferee of Substantially All of a Corporation's Assets.** Obviously, a transferee of a corporation's assets who, as in the Darcy case, assumes the transferor's liabilities is liable for the debts assumed. However, in some circumstances a transferee may find itself saddled with debts of the transferor which it never agreed to assume. The following is a brief analysis of this subject which should also provide some useful background for considering the liability of the transferor's directors in such circumstances, as illustrated by the Darcy case.

NOTE, RIGHTS OF CREDITORS AGAINST A SUCCESSOR CORPORATION*

44 Harv.L.Rev. 260 (1930).

It is common for a corporation to transfer all or nearly all of its assets to another corporation. This device may represent an honest revision of fiscal policy, or it may be adopted with a desire to escape embarrassing debts. But regardless of the motive behind these transfers, they are of vital interest to creditors, for it is out of the *quid pro quo* received in return that the debtor must meet its obligations. This consideration may consist of cash, stock in the new corporation, a promise of cash, or an assumption of the obligations of the old corporation. From a creditor's standpoint, any of these, if in fact an adequate return, probably constitutes value. Any one of them, however, may be objectionable if it hinders the creditor in procuring satisfaction of a judgment. Cash and stock are easily concealed and readily taken out of the jurisdiction; and the transferee's promise to pay money may be enforced only by an additional equitable or statutory proceeding. This is equally true of an assumption of liability, except where third party beneficiaries are allowed to sue. But even in such jurisdictions the creditor may be technically justified in regarding the conveyance as a hindrance, for he can not be compelled to accept a substitute debtor, and satisfaction of a judgment against the old debtor entails additional proceedings.

Even though the consideration paid, however, is found to be free from these objections, unsatisfied creditors may justly complain if it does not reach the old corporation. Since the transfer involves the bulk of the corporate assets,[12] the purchaser must be taken to know that the creditors,

---

* Copyright (c), Harvard Law Review Association, 1930. Reprinted by permission. All footnotes omitted except note 12, which has been supplemented by the editor.

12. Bulk transfers of assets are always viewed with circumspection by the courts. . . . The same considerations have caused the enactment of [so-called "Bulk Sales Acts", requir-

whose existence he should assume, have an interest in the consideration as the source of future satisfaction of their claims. No stockholder is entitled to the corporate assets or their product when any creditor can not be paid. Consequently the creditors may attack the transaction to the extent that the consideration is paid to the stockholders.

Where the transaction is improper, the obvious remedy of the creditors of the old corporation is to treat the transfer as a fraudulent conveyance, and after procuring judgment against the debtor, either to levy execution on, or to bring a bill in equity against, the property or its product. But many courts have not confined the creditors to this traditional remedy and have permitted the original suit to be brought directly against the transferee, subjecting it to a personal liability limited to the value of the assets transferred; and some courts, going still further, impose on the transferee all the obligations of the transferor.

Theories have not been wanting to explain these results. Some courts find an implied promise by the new corporation to pay the debts of the old to the extent of the value of the assets transferred. . . .

[Some cases rest] liability on the ground that there is a *de facto* merger or consolidation. This is fair enough when the old stockholders receive the consideration for the transfer. But if the old corporation itself receives the remuneration and is thereby kept alive, there seems to be nothing in the nature of merger or consolidation.

Finally, the transferee may be held liable because it is merely the old corporation under the mask of the new entity. This seems justifiable if the stockholders of both corporations are the same. But there are objections to this theory. . . . [I]t would seem desirable, if the new corporation has paid value, to free it of its predecessor's obligations despite the identity of the stockholders. Thus there is no liability where the stockholders of the new corporation have acquired their stock for a consideration entirely distinct from their interest in the old corporation. But when the new stock represents in whole or in part an exchange for the old shares, liability is imposed. To this extent the stockholders have received part of the consideration to which the creditors are entitled. In other words, the test of liability is that of a fraudulent conveyance, although the personal judgment is a remedy which goes beyond the law of fraudulent conveyances.

b. **Liability of the Directors of the Transferor.** The basis upon which the directors were held liable in the Darcy case is not entirely clear. The court purported to rest primarily upon the fact that all of the corporation's assets were transferred to a third party without any notice to the creditors, in violation of what was apparently an early version of a Bulk Sales Act. See f.n.12 on prior page. But at least today the directors of the transferor normally are not personally liable for failure to comply with a Bulk Sales Act — the only sanction is that the transferee of the assets takes them subject to the claims of the transferor's creditors.

ing notice to creditors of any bulk transfer of inventory, regardless of the disposition made of the proceeds. E. g., U.C.C. Article 6; see generally Coogan, Hogan and Vagts, Secured Transactions Under the U.C.C. (1964) Ch. 22.]

However, the court in the Darcy case was obviously influenced by the fact that the transfer of the assets was accompanied by an informal liquidation of the corporation, with the consideration received for the assets passing directly to the stockholders. Had the corporation received and retained it, that consideration would have been available to the corporation's creditors for the satisfaction of their claims. Obviously, directors may not distribute all of a corporation's assets to its stockholders without first providing for the claims of creditors. Indeed, absent some special authorization such a liquidating distribution would constitute the clearest kind of illegal dividend, for which directors would of course be liable. But even where such a liquidating distribution is authorized, as in the case of a formal dissolution of the corporation, the directors are no less charged with the responsibility of taking care of the claims of creditors. E. g., MBA §§ 87 (b), 48(c). And as further protection to the creditors upon a dissolution, the statutes often require notice to them. E. g., MBA §87 (a).

However, this does not necessarily mean that all liabilities must be paid off in cash before the corporation is liquidated. MBA § 87(b) is typical of the corporation statutes in requiring only that "adequate provision" for the creditors be made. Like most of the statutes the Model Act does not afford any guidance as to what constitutes such "adequate provision". Since the most common, practical substitute for payment of the liabilities in cash is to have them assumed by a responsible third party, it is particularly important to know whether this kind of arrangement constitutes "adequate provision" for creditors. The directors in the Darcy apparently thought that it did, but the court rather vehemently disagreed. However, it is not clear that there was any express statutory "adequate provision" test operative in the Darcy case; and in addition the court's reasoning on this issue is rather unsatisfactory since the "adequate provision" test seems to have been confused with the requirements for a full-fledged novation based upon the consent of the creditors.*

---

* Assuming that the transferee's assumption of liabilities did not constitute "adequate provision", could it have been regarded as producing an asset in the hands of the transferor corporation, i. e., a claim (against the transferee) by the transferor as promisee of a contract for the benefit of a third party (the creditors)? If so, such an asset would obviously not have been distributed to the transferor's stockholders but rather would still be on hand for the benefit of creditors, and perhaps this would be sufficient to forestall liability upon the directors. The Tax Court has rejected this asset notion in a case imposing transferee tax liability upon the stockholders of a corporation which transferred all of its assets in exchange for stock of the buyer and an assumption of liabilities, and then dissolved, distributing all of the stock received to its stockholders. Kimmes v. Commissioner, 22 T.C.M. 232 (1963). The court commented that "such an assumption is not an asset which can be levied upon and hence does not relieve stockholders of a transferor corporation of transferee liability arising out of the receipt of assets of the transferor corporation". See also Coca-Cola Bottling Co. of Tucson, Inc. v. Commissioner, 334 F.2d 875 (9th Cir.1964), where transferee tax liability was imposed upon the transferee-corporation which had purchased the stock of the transferor corporation and then dissolved it to obtain its assets. In addition to holding that the agreement by one of the stockholders of the transferor to indemnify both the transferor and the transferee against any liabilities of the transferor did not amount to an assumption of the liabilities of the transferor or otherwise constitute adequate provision for its creditors, the

In any event, today, more than 70 years after the Darcy decision, the cases as well as the statutes provide little guidance as to just what type of "provision" for the creditors will be regarded as legally "adequate", and in particular whether the assumption of liabilities by a responsible third party will suffice. One of the few efforts to crystallize the meaning of "adequate provision" in this context appears in the California statute, and since courts in other jurisdictions may well look to the pattern adopted there for aid in construing their own silent statutes, the California statute is worth examining here. Section 2004 of the Corporations Code requires the directors to determine "that all the known debts and liabilities of a corporation in the process of winding up have been paid or adequately provided for". Section 2005, entitled "Provision for payment of debts and liabilities," provides as follows:

> The payment of a debt or liability, whether the whereabouts of the creditor is known or unknown, has been adequately provided for if the payment has been provided for by either of the following means:
>
> (a) Payment thereof has been assumed or guaranteed in good faith by one or more financially responsible corporations or other persons or by the United States government or any agency thereof, and the provision (including the financial responsibility of such corporations or other persons) was determined in good faith and with reasonable care by the board to be adequate at the time of any distribution of the assets by the board . . . .
>
> (b) The amount of the debt or liability has been deposited [with an appropriate depositary].
>
> This section does not prescribe exclusive means of making adequate provision for debts and liabilities.

(footnote continued)

court held that if the indemnity agreement constituted an asset in the hands of the transferor it was transferred to the transferee upon the liquidation of the transferor.

SECTION 2. TAX ASPECTS OF CORPORATE LIQUIDATIONS

A. NON–RECOGNITION OF GAIN UNDER §337

NOTE, TAX-FREE SALES IN LIQUIDATION
UNDER SECTION 337 °

76 Harv.L.Rev. 780 (1963).

Prior to the enactment of the Internal Revenue Code of 1954, the taxation of corporations and shareholders during the process of liquidation was governed by three well-established principles embodied in the existing tax law: first, the distribution of a liquidating corporation's assets was not a taxable event for the corporation; * second, such a distribution of assets was a taxable event for the shareholders as if they had exchanged their stock; ** finally, any conversion of as-

---

° Copyright (c) Harvard Law Review Association, 1963. Reprinted by permission. Most of the footnotes omitted.

*[Ed. note] This rule is now embodied in IRC § 336. There is of course the possibility that in some circumstances income realized by the stockholders upon property received by them in liquidation will be attributed to the corporation, on the theory, *inter alia*, that the income was really earned by the corporation, see generally Kilbourn, Post-Liquidation Problems, Corporate and Individual, 23 N.Y.U. Fed.Tax Inst. 701 (1965), just as sometimes occurs when property, particularly inventory, is distributed as an ordinary dividend to stockholders and then sold by them. See pages 277–278 supra. However, there seems to be substantially more resistance to the application of this doctrine when there has been a complete liquidation than when the distribution takes the form of an ordinary dividend. See e. g., United States v. Horschel, 205 F.2d 646 (9th Cir.1953), stressing the

difference in this connection between a distribution in complete liquidation and a dividend by a company continuing in business.

**[Ed. note] This rule is now embodied in § 331. An exception to full recognition of gain under § 331 is available under the "one month liquidation" procedure of § 333, which provides for non-recognition of gain, and a corresponding carryover of the stockholders' basis in their stock to the corporate assets received, subject to two important provisos: (1) gain will be recognized (and taxed as ordinary income) to the extent of each shareholder's pro rata share of the corporation's accumulated earnings and profits; and (2) generally speaking, any additional gain will be recognized to the extent of any cash or securities received by the stockholder. Normally, an election under § 333 will be beneficial only for a closely held corporation with substantially appreciated assets but little accumulated earnings, as often occurs in the real estate field. See generally McGaffey, The Deferral of Gain in One-Month Liquidations, 19 Tax L.Rev. 327 (1964).

sets into cash resulted in recognition of gain or loss. To avoid double incidence of taxation upon liquidation, the corporation had to distribute its assets in kind, since a sale followed by distribution of the proceeds might result in a tax to the corporation upon the sale and a tax to the shareholders upon distribution. But in cases where shareholders were numerous, distribution in kind could cause difficulty in the disposition of a business. Problems accompanied both the parceling of assets among the shareholders and the distribution of indivisible assets to them as tenants-in-common.

The difficulties of avoiding corporate taxation by distributions in kind were increased by Commissioner v. Court Holding Co., where a closely held corporation had entered into an oral contract for the sale of its assets and had received part payment. On the day fixed for reducing the contract to writing the shareholders realized that the contemplated sale involved a substantial corporate tax and instead had the corporation declare a liquidating dividend of its property, following which they sold the property on substantially the same terms as in the prior contract. On these facts the Tax Court upheld the imposition of corporate income tax concluding that the sale had been made by the corporation notwithstanding the belated transfer to its shareholders; the Supreme Court affirmed. Considering the same issue in United States v. Cumberland Pub. Serv. Co. the Court explained that the question whether the corporation or the shareholders sold the assets was one of fact, to be determined by the trial court "upon consideration of the entire transaction." The two cases placed shareholders in an unfortunate dilemma. The Court's failure to lay down a more definite standard made it dangerous to plan a sale before liquidation, since shareholders could never be sure of the exact circumstances which would cause a sale to be attributed to the corporation. The danger was particularly acute in closely held corporations because of the ambiguity as to whether the negotiator was acting as a corporate officer or as a representative of the shareholders. On the other hand, if the property was distributed in kind without prior negotiation, the shareholders ran a double risk: if unable to find a buyer, the shareholders might be unable to raise the cash necessary to pay the capital gains tax incurred on the distribution; and, in the absence of prior sale, the Treasury might place an excessive valuation on the property for determining the capital gains tax due. The further danger that uninformed taxpayers would allow the corporation to negotiate the sale before obtaining competent legal advice added weight to Congress' conclusion that the two decisions "represent merely a trap for the unwary."

The legislative response to these uncertainties could have taken several forms. Congress might have provided criteria for determining conclusively which sales were attributable to the corporation and which to the shareholders; it might have attributed to the corporation all sales by shareholders within a certain period of time after a liquidating distribution; or it might have required the corporation to recognize gain on all distributions to its shareholders. Instead Congress provided that under certain conditions a corporation was free to sell its assets and distribute the proceeds without incurring a corporate tax. Although the committee reports indicate that the primary purpose of the section was to correct the formalistic problems presented by the Court Holding and Cumberland cases, the provisions in fact go much further: transactions clearly taxable to the corporation under prior law became tax-free under section 337. The draftsmen intended this solution "to provide a definitive rule" which would "eliminate . . . uncertainties." But the volume of recent cases and the inconsistencies in judicial interpretation indicate that, while the statute has resolved some difficulties, it has created others. This Note will explore the intended function of section 337 and the difficulties of determining the precise scope of its application. In part I certain technical prerequisites to the section's operation are discussed; part II delimits the area within the section's protection; and part III analyzes the interplay between section 337 and other relevant sections of the Code.

I. Prerequisites to Protection

A. *Date of Adoption of a Plan*

Under section 337 it is necessary to determine the date when a plan of liquidation is adopted, since the section operates only if the liquidation is completed within a fixed period afterward and protects only sales made following such adoption. The Code nowhere defines a "plan of complete liquidation" nor indicates how one is adopted although the term appears in several sections. As a matter of corporate law, however, voluntary liquidation can occur only with the approval of the shareholders.[18] Hence, passage of a shareholder resolution ordinarily would seem to be the event which marks the adoption of a plan of liquidation. The applicable regulation states that while the date of adoption of a plan of liquidation is "ordinarily" the date of the shareholder resolution, this date is conclusive only if the corporation has previously sold substantially all its property or if the corporation sells no substantial part of its assets prior thereto. In all other cases, i. e., where substantial sales are made both before and after the resolution date, the date of adoption is to be determined from all the facts and circumstances.[19] The Treasury's purpose in establishing these two quite different tests was to provide corporations a sure way to achieve either nonrecognition of a net gain on the disposition of all assets, or recognition of net loss, while thwarting attempts to obtain a double benefit through nonrecognition of gain on appreciated property

18. See [MBA §84] (1960), which is typical of the provisions of many state statutes.

19. Treas.Reg. § 1.337–2(b) (1955).

coupled with recognition of loss on property of diminished value. If a shareholder resolution were treated as conclusive of the date of adoption, the latter result could be achieved by straddling the resolution date — selling all loss property before and all gain property after its adoption.

If the resolution date is as a general rule determinative of the date on which a plan of liquidation was adopted, three significant questions arise. First, should the many small corporations whose major decisions are made without corporate formalities be denied the benefit of section 337? Second, should section 337's protection not be available in cases where involuntary disposition of the assets, through condemnation or destruction, makes it impossible for the shareholders to adopt a plan before the conversion occurs? Third, is the Treasury warranted in its attempt to prevent doubling of the benefit of section 337 through sales which straddle the resolution? The courts have not as yet succeeded in formulating clear answers to these questions.

Compelling circumstances for a finding that a plan of liquidation was adopted prior to the passage of a shareholder resolution exist where shareholders who control a block of stock sufficiently large to enable them to authorize liquidation can be shown to have agreed earlier to liquidate. Such a question is likely to arise where a closely held, informally operated corporation begins to sell its properties without making a formal resolution. Powell's Pontiac-Cadillac, Inc. v. Gross [21] involved the liquidation of an automobile dealership the sole shareholders of which were its president, his wife and son. Although the corporation had sold all its assets and distributed the proceeds many months before the passage of a formal resolution, the court found that a plan of liquidation was adopted immediately prior to the signing of the contract of sale. The business was sold because its president wished to retire on account of his wife's ill health; hence there was little likelihood that the corporation would continue to operate thereafter. In such a case it is easy to conclude that an actual, though informal, plan of liquidation existed already at the time of the sale. The danger of such speculation is, of course, that the intention may not yet have been formed; continued operation may then have been contemplated. Thus, the chief issue for resolution is whether the undesirability of importing a subjective test based on the elusive factor of intent into a taxing statute must require a corporation which wishes to obtain its benefits to follow a highly formal method of making that intention clear. Congress' refusal to define a plan of liquidation in formal terms may indicate that it did not wish to prevent the courts from making a judgment on that question on the facts of each particular case, as they had done in other contexts.[22] Probably it is

21. 60–1 U.S.Tax Cas. ¶ 9317 (D.N.J. 1960).

22. . . . It is of some significance that the House version of the 1954

Code defined the plan of liquidation in terms of either a shareholder or board of directors resolution to distribute all the company's property and

desirable to permit such corporations to assume the burden of proving the prior informal adoption of a plan for liquidation and to succeed if they sustain their burden of proof. Such factors as the evidence of intent disclosed in the corporate records, the degree of informality habitually practiced in reaching major decisions, the opportunity which existed for formal action, the length of the period in which substantial sales were made, the quantity and character of the property sold, and the size of the corporation, are obviously relevant on this issue. From the history of taxpayers' attempts thus far, it is likely that the courts will not permit abuse of the opportunity.[23]

Where the power to liquidate is not in the hands of the board of directors because they do not control the necessary proportion of stock, it is difficult to see how liquidation can be assured until the shareholders approve. Consequently, the corporation cannot, strictly speaking, adopt a plan of liquidation before obtaining that approval—ordinarily in the form of a resolution. Except in special circumstances,[24] therefore, a voluntary sale made by a corporation whose directors do not possess voting control should not qualify for nonrecognition unless it is made after the resolution. This result should not be considered harsh; the requirements for qualification under the statute are easily complied with in the great majority of cases and should be respected. However, where the property is transferred involuntarily, notably in a condemnation proceeding, the corporation may be unable to control the time of the transfer, and may not act quickly enough to complete the formal process of authorizing liquidation before the "sale" takes place. Although the corporate law problems in finding a plan of liquidation before the shareholders have agreed on this course are as great in cases of involuntary condemnations as they are in cases of normal sales, there would seem to be greater justification for such an interpretation where the formal requirements are not as easily met. The purpose of the plan requirement is prob-

---

retire all its stock. See H.R. 8300, 83d Cong., 2d Sess., § 336(c) (1954). No comparable provision appears in the Code as enacted.

23. The Powell's case is the only example of a successful taxpayer contention that a plan had been informally adopted, where the sale was voluntarily negotiated. In Whitson v. Rockwood, 190 F.Supp. 478 (D.N.D.1960), the court agreed that the facts and circumstances of a sale should be examined, but found that the evidence did not show an actual plan of liquidation at the time of the sale. [Ed. note. In Rev.Rul. 65–235, 1965–2 Cum. Bull. 88, the Service announced that it will no longer insist upon a formal shareholder's resolution and vote for the adoption of a plan of liquidation

in cases involving close corporations where more than the statutory percentage of stockholders had agreed at an informal meeting that the corporation sell all of its assets and distribute the proceeds.]

24. If it can be shown that, in addition to the directors, certain nondirector shareholders knew of and approved the board's plan at the time of sale, and their total votes were sufficient to authorize liquidation, the plan might be considered adopted at that time. Similarly, it would be reasonable to include the shares held by the wives of directors in figuring the proportion, although this would create problems when other close relatives or associates are sought to be included in the directors' total.

ably to prevent a corporation from escaping taxation on gain realized from sales made prior to a bona fide decision to liquidate. Without such a requirement all sales of property during the last twelve months of the corporation's life might be tax exempt, a benefit going far beyond what might have been accomplished through liquidating distributions to the shareholders. The danger of such abuse is not great where substantially all the property is taken involuntarily, since the shareholders have no choice but to liquidate or use the funds to acquire replacement property. Consequently, the purpose of the requirement would not be impaired if the gain so realized on condemnations qualified for section 337 protection. The requirement of a plan might be satisfied, in such a case, by a board of directors' resolution prior to condemnation recommending liquidation to the shareholders, provided they approve within a reasonable time afterward.

* * *

In view of the Tax Court's willingness to find a plan of liquidation in the circumstances preceding the shareholder resolution in [condemnation cases], one might expect decisions sympathetic to the Treasury's attempt to thwart straddle sales by finding an earlier adoption of a plan in the facts and circumstances. If permitted, such straddles would enable a corporation seriously to distort its tax position, not only for the year of liquidation but for preceding years as well through use of the loss carryback provisions of the Code. Furthermore, since many of the assets sold in the final period of operation normally will be section 1231 assets, these losses will offset ordinary income. Even though it was the general purpose of Congress to favor liquidating corporations, it is doubtful that so great a tax benefit was intended at so small a cost. The Commissioner's attempt to disallow recognition of straddle losses therefore would seem to deserve judicial support.

Nevertheless, the taxpayers have prevailed in both cases to date involving an apparent straddle maneuver. In Virginia Ice & Freezing Co.,[39] the first case under section 337, the corporation's board of directors approved the sale at a loss of two of its several plants on the same day that it resolved to hold a meeting ten days later to consider liquidation. At the second meeting, the board passed a resolution recommending liquidation to the twenty-six shareholders, a course which the shareholders unanimously approved at a special meeting shortly thereafter. Within twelve months the other properties were sold at a gain. The Treasury refused to allow recognition of the loss on the two plants, contending that the circumstances showed that a plan had been adopted before the sale was made. This determination was reversed by the Tax Court, which reasoned that there could be no assurance of liquidation until the shareholders approved, regardless

39. 30 T.C. 1251 (1958).

of the facts that their vote proved unanimous and that all actions of
the board had been unanimously approved for several years. Virginia
Ice might be explained on the ground that the directors did not control a majority of the stock, and hence could not assure adoption of the
corporate plan. But the recent case of City Bank of Washington,[40]
where the court relied on Virginia Ice, is not susceptible of this interpretation. Here a purchaser agreed to buy both the assets and the
outstanding shares of the taxpayer, City Bank, under a contract which
expressly provided for the taxpayer's liquidation. Three days before
the shareholder meeting, at a time when the purchaser had already
acquired nearly eighty per cent of the outstanding stock, City Bank
sold some treasury notes at a loss for which it claimed a deduction.
Despite a specific finding that liquidation was intended long before
this date, the Tax Court allowed the loss, reasoning that a "general
intention to liquidate" is not the same thing as a plan of liquidation.
It emphasized that a contrary result would produce uncertainty inconsistent with the statute's purpose to establish a clear and unam-
biguous rule.

If it is concluded that the Tax Court's reliance on the resolution
date in City Bank unduly favors the taxpayer, and that in other circumstances taxpayers should be permitted to establish early adoption
of plans, the question arises whether it is proper to interpret the statute's simple requirement of "adoption of a plan" as determined in
some instances by the adoption of a shareholder resolution and in other circumstances by a different test. Logically the question whether
and when a plan was adopted should be answered by the same criteria
whether it is the Commissioner or the taxpayer who seeks to make the
point, and whether or not the taxpayer's sales straddle the resolution
date. However, it is doubtful whether it would serve any statutory
purpose to allow the Treasury to attack the taxpayer's contention
that the shareholder resolution marked the date of adoption of a plan
in the cases where the taxpayer sold all its property either before or
after the date of resolution without attempting to straddle. In such
cases the taxpayer is merely attempting to comply with the formalities
of a largely elective section in order to obtain either nonrecognition
of net gain or recognition of net loss; either result is clearly contemplated under the statute. In view of the statute's purpose of providing substantial certainty as an aid in planning liquidation, the regulations seem justified to the extent that they bind the Treasury to
accept the resolution date for such cases.

* * *

II. SCOPE OF PROTECTION

A. *Statutory Language*

Assuming that a plan of liquidation has been properly adopted
and that sales and distributions have been made as required by section 337(a), there arises the question what types of transactions are
protected. The section states that "no gain or loss shall be recognized
. . . from the sale or exchange . . . of property . . .,"

40. 38 T.C. [713 (1962)].

but subsection 337(b) adds that " 'property' does not include" inventory or goods held for sale in the ordinary course of business (except when sold in bulk), or certain installment obligations. The regulation dealing with section 337 interprets the term "property" as including all assets owned by the corporation except those specifically excluded by the subsection, and in a recent series of cases the Tax Court seems to have taken a somewhat similar approach. However, the legislative history suggests that the statute's protection should be more narrowly restricted. Significantly, the Treasury, in apparent disregard of its own regulation, has persuaded the courts that the section's protection does not extend to gain from the sale of certain assets falling outside the express exceptions when that gain is, in effect, of an ordinary-income type. It is questionable whether the term "property" as used in the statute should be construed as broadly as the regulations seem to suggest.

As passed by the House of Representatives the section denied its protection to "any sale . . . in the ordinary course of business", and although the final bill replaced this broad exception with the present enumeration, the report of the Senate Finance Committee summarized the scope of the section by stating: "It is intended that, during the 12 month period, sales in the ordinary course of business shall result in ordinary gain to the corporation as if the corporation were not in the process of liquidating." Thus recorded indications of congressional intent suggest a purpose of preventing corporations from using section 337 to avoid paying a tax on sales or exchanges which represent income from the normal operation of the business. Furthermore, since the enumerated exceptions do not exclude receivables or rights to income, construing property as broadly as the regulations seem to suggest would allow nonrecognition on the sale of receivables arising from the prior sale of excluded types of property, such as inventory, and thus allow a cash basis corporation easily to bring all gain within the statute's protection.

* * *

B. *Assignment of Income*

Can a liquidating corporation use section 337 to escape taxation during its final year of operation through the sale of assets representing ordinary income which has not yet been reported? The Treasury initially stated its position in a ruling concerning a cash basis corporation in liquidation which had sold receivables along with the interest earned on them, but not yet collected.[61] The question was whether that portion of the sales price representing interest receivable was protected. The ruling first stated that section 337 applies to "all assets except those specifically excluded" by subsection (b), but then concluded that the section is intended to

61. Rev.Rul. 59–120, 1959–1 Cum.Bull. 74.

protect only "unrealized appreciation of business property." This conclusion can be defended, but it cannot follow from the stated premise, for many types of assets which represent ordinary income rather than appreciation are not included within the specific terms of the exceptions.[62] The ruling goes on to reason that the sale of the interest is not protected by section 337 because it does not represent appreciation in value, but is actually an assignment of a claim for ordinary income.

* * *

62. Such as interest receivable, dividends receivable, or accounts receivable arising from the sale of inventory.

1. **Requirement of a Complete Liquidation.** A series of revenue rulings have provided some practical guidance with respect to the requirement of § 337 that all of the corporation's assets (apart from those retained to meet claims) must be distributed in complete liquidation within one year. In Rev.Rul. 63–245, 1963–2 Cum.Bull. 144, a corporation adopted a plan of complete liquidation and within twelve months thereafter wound up its affairs, sold its assets, and distributed the proceeds among its stockholders. However, the corporation had a claim for refund of taxes which could not readily be either sold or divided among its stockholders, and accordingly, pursuant to the plan of liquidation, the claim was transferred to an independent trustee for the benefit of the stockholders. Under applicable local law such a trustee was authorized to receive a liquidating distribution for the benefit of stockholders, and to pay it over to the stockholders when it was reduced to cash. The ruling holds that although § 337 is not satisfied if the corporation retains any assets for distribution to stockholders, in the case of an asset which is not reasonably susceptible to sale or distribution it is sufficient for § 337 purposes if the corporation divests itself of the asset within the specified twelve-month period in a manner equivalent to a distribution of the asset to stockholders. The ruling adds that the person chosen to receive the refund claim for the benefit of the stockholders should be someone selected by the stockholders (or by a court), but indicates that this requirement is satisfied if the person is named in the plan of complete liquidation which is approved by the stockholders.

Rev.Rul. 65–257, 1965–46 I.R.B. 28, approves a similar method of dealing with the claims of stockholders who dissent from a sale of all the corporation's assets in connection with a complete liquidation. In the situation posed by the ruling, it appeared that the requisite judicial review of the appraiser's valuation of the dissenting stockholders' stock could not be obtained within the 12-month period specified in § 337. Accordingly, the corporation transferred to an independent escrowee the amount at which the stock had been valued by the appraiser (together with the statutory interest due thereon), prior to the termination of the 12-month period. The escrow agreement provided that the escrowee would pay to the dissenting stockholders the amounts finally determined to be due them, with any remaining proceeds to be distributed pro rata to the nondissenting stockholders. In the event of a deficiency in the escrow funds, the principal nondissenting stockholders were to pay whatever additional amounts might be needed. The ruling states that since the plan approved by the stockholders authorized the officers to take all appropriate steps necessary to effect a complete liquidation, and the transfer to an escrowee was such a step, it would be treated as though it were a transfer to an escrowee selected by the shareholders. Accordingly, the transfer to the escrowee constituted a distribution to the stockholders which completed the distribution of all the corporation's assets within the 12-month period specified by § 337.

---

2. Completing the Distribution Within 12 Months

VERN REALTY, INC. v. COMMISSIONER *

United States Tax Court, 1972. 58 T.C. 1006.

Aff'd, 73-1 U.S.T.C. ¶ 9455 (1st Cir.).

FEATHERSTON, JUDGE: Respondent determined a deficiency of $9,396.77 in petitioner's Federal income tax for its taxable year ending June 30, 1968. The only issue presented for decision is whether, within the meaning of section 337(a), all of the assets of petitioner, less assets retained to meet claims, were distributed within 12 months after the adoption of a plan of complete liquidation.

Findings of Fact

Vern Realty, Inc. (hereinafter referred to as petitioner), is a liquidated Rhode Island corporation which formerly had its principal office at 812 Industrial Bank Building, Providence, Rhode Island. Petitioner filed its Federal income tax return for the taxable year July 1, 1967, through June 30, 1968, with the director, internal revenue service center, Andover, Massachusetts.

Petitioner was organized under the laws of Rhode Island on July 8, 1959, to engage in the trade or business of renting real estate. Throughout the period of petitioner's business activity, it reported its income on a cash basis, using a fiscal year ending June 30. Its accounting records consisted solely of a checkbook in which were recorded the receipts of rent and the disbursements of expenses. During this period, Ronald H. Nani (hereinafter referred to as Nani) was the president and treasurer of petitioner.

At all relevant times, petitioner's individual shareholders filed their Federal income tax returns on the cash basis method of accounting.

Petitioner's initial capitalization of $6,700 was paid in by Nani and Verna J. Nani (hereinafter referred to as Verna). In return, they each received 200 shares of petitioner's no-par value common stock. This represented all of petitioner's outstanding stock.

On July 15, 1959, petitioner purchased an office building (hereinafter referred to as the office building) located at 1039 Reservoir Avenue, Cranston, Rhode Island, at a cost of $31,500. On the date of purchase, there were two tenants in the building. Subsequently, one tenant took over the rental of the entire building.

On August 20, 1963, Verna contributed 100 of her shares of petitioner's no-par value common stock to petitioner and these shares

* Some of the court's citations and footnotes omitted.

were retired. On the same date, she made a gift of 50 shares of petitioner's no-par value common stock to each of her children, Rhonda S. Nani and Douglas R. Nani. Also, on that date, Nani made identical gifts to the two children. The result was that thereafter Nani, Rhonda S. Nani, and Douglas R. Nani each owned one-third of petitioner's outstanding stock.

Petitioner, on December 27, 1967, purchased an apartment building (hereinafter referred to as the apartment building) located at 1049 Reservoir Avenue, Cranston, Rhode Island, at a cost of $17,000. The building was purchased for possible use in expanding petitioner's office building. Petitioner never rented this building. The apartment building and the office building represent all the property petitioner owned, with the exception of a small amount of cash in its checking account.

On February 15, 1968, at a special meeting of petitioner's shareholders, a plan [3] was adopted for the complete liquidation of petitioner which would meet the requirements of section 337. The desire to liquidate petitioner was prompted by the presence of a prospective buyer who wished to acquire petitioner's office building. On March 14, 1968, the information return which section 6043 directs corporations to file within 30 days after the adoption of a resolution or plan of dissolution, or complete or partial liquidation, was forwarded by petitioner to the district director of internal revenue, Providence, Rhode Island.

On March 15, 1968, petitioner sold the office building for a gross sales price of $66,500 and realized gain of $37,610.13 on the sale. The net proceeds of $38,000 were placed in petitioner's checking account. On April 5, 1968, petitioner opened a savings account in its name at the Citizens Savings Bank, Providence, Rhode Island, and the proceeds from the sale were transferred to that account. Due to Nani's position as the principal officer of the corporation, he was the only person authorized to draw on the savings account in petitioner's behalf.

Petitioner's checking account in the Citizens Trust Company, Providence, Rhode Island, was closed by Nani on February 12, 1969, and by that date its expenses had been paid. By February 15, 1969, 12 months after the date of the adoption of the plan of liquidation, all of petitioner's business activity ceased. Its assets consisted of the apartment building and $39,442.89 on deposit in its savings account, while its liabilities were a $10,551.85 mortgage on the apartment building and a $5,505.11 debt owed to Nani.

In satsifaction of the debt to Nani, petitioner transferred the apartment building, subject to the mortgage, to him by warranty deed on March 10, 1969. Nani sold the building on July 23, 1969, for a gross sales price of $17,000.

---

3. According to the minutes of that meeting, the plan provided that "all of the Company's assets (less assets retained to meet claims) will be distributed to the Company's stockholders in complete cancellation of its stock within the 12-month period beginning on the date of the adoption of said Plan of Complete Liquidation."

Nani did not close petitioner's savings account until March 13, 1969. At that time, the money was redeposited in the Citizens Savings Bank, Providence, Rhode Island, in three equal savings accounts for the shareholders.

In its income tax return for the period July 1, 1967, to June 30, 1968, petitioner included a notation regarding the sale of its office building but stated the transaction was not taxable because of the provisions of section 337. The balance sheets attached to that return showed that petitioner had cash on hand in the amount of $2,845.76 at the beginning of the fiscal year and $40,035.86 at the end of the fiscal year. Consequently, the balance sheets attached to petitioner's return for the period July 1, 1968, to March 12, 1969, showed that petitioner had cash on hand at the beginning of that period in the amount of $40,035.86.

In his notice of deficiency, respondent determined that petitioner had failed to comply with the provisions of section 337(a) in that it did not distribute all its assets in complete liquidation, less assets retained to meet reasonable claims, within the 12-month period after the adoption of the plan of complete liquidation.

Opinion

Section 337(a) lays down the general rule that no gain or loss is recognized to a corporation on the sale or exchange of its "property" if (1) it adopts a plan of complete liquidation on or after June 22, 1954, and (2) within the 12-month period following the adoption of the plan, "all" of the assets of the corporation, except "assets retained to meet claims," are "distributed in complete liquidation." The application of this general rule to particular facts can often be complicated by the numerous other requirements set forth in the section and various other lurking problems. The only issue presented in this case, however, is whether petitioner distributed all of its assets, except assets retained to meet claims, within the prescribed 12-month period. We are compelled to conclude that it did not.

The Congressional objective in enacting section 337 was "to provide a definitive rule which will eliminate the * * * uncertainties" flowing from the application of United States v. Cumberland Pub. Serv. Co., 338 U.S. 451 (1950), and Commissioner v. Court Holding Co., 324 U.S. 331 (1945). . . . Significantly, the section provides for the nonrecognition of losses, as well as gains, if the liquidation falls within its terms. . . . The section is elective in the sense that a taxpayer may plan and execute its liquidation in such a way as to fall within or without the rules of the section. However, if the transaction fits the fact situation described by the Code, the provision must be applied. Thus, an interpretation of the section which is unduly lenient as to one taxpayer may be unduly harsh as to another. Such an interpretation may cause the section to be complicated by unnecessary uncertainty and thus become a "trap for the unwary." This result would frustrate the Congressional quest for certainty reflected by the enactment of the section. . . .

In the present case, there is no dispute as to when the plan of liquidation was adopted. The parties have stipulated that the shareholders of petitioner, on February 15, 1968, "adopted a plan of complete liquidation of petitioner under Section 337 of the Internal Revenue Code of 1954." Thus, to avoid a tax on the gain derived from the sale of its office building, petitioner was required to show that all of its assets, except assets required to pay claims, were distributed within 12 months of that date.

When the plan of liquidation was adopted, petitioner owned the office building, an apartment building which it had never rented, and a small amount of cash in a checking account. During the following year, nothing transpired with respect to the apartment building. It was still owned by petitioner at the end of the 12-month period. In March and April 1968, petitioner sold its office building and deposited the net proceeds of the sale in a savings account carried in petitioner's name. The funds were not withdrawn from this account and paid over to the shareholders until March 13, 1969, almost 13 months after the plan of liquidation was adopted.

The apartment building had a value of $17,000 and this sum approximated the unpaid mortgage on the building plus petitioner's debt to Nani. Nani testified that he tried to sell the apartment building but decided that, if he was unable to sell it, he "would deed it over to * * * [his] name, subject to the mortgage, so that the excess of the value would be enough to satisfy my outstanding obligation from the corporation." However, this was not done until March 10, 1969, more than 12 months after the plan of liquidation was adopted.

Petitioner claims that it was not required to distribute the apartment building or its proceeds on the theory that it was reserved to pay the mortgage against it and the debt to Nani. However, notwithstanding the informalities which usually characterize the management of the affairs of a small closely held corporation, we are not satisfied that the apartment building was in fact reserved to pay petitioner's debts. Section 1.337–1, Income Tax Regs., provides that "Any assets retained after the expiration of the 12-month period for the payment of claims (including unascertained or contingent liabilities or expenses) must be specifically set apart for that purpose." Petitioner did not fulfill this requirement because nothing was done specifically to set apart the apartment building within the 12-month period for the payment of claims. We are not convinced that petitioner's failure to sell the apartment building, deed it to Nani in satisfaction of his claim, or otherwise set it apart in some way within the 12-month period is not explained by the same neglect which characterized his failure to cause the corporation to dispose of the proceeds of the sale of the office building.[6]

However, we do not rest our decision on petitioner's retention of the apartment building alone. More serious was the failure to distribute the office building sale proceeds. Nani, the sole shareholder, is a practicing accountant, and he knew of the 12-month requirement, evidently having handled other liquidations for his clients. Implicitly he admitted in his testimony that he did not cause the distribution of these funds within the 12-month period, explaining that "It was merely an error on my part in marking my calendar on the wrong date of that form, picking up March 14 rather than February 15, which made me twenty some days late in calendaring my notice." Section 337, unfortunately for petitioner, has no escape clause to permit disregard of the statutorily prescribed period for effectuating a distribution on such grounds.

The evidence is clear that petitioner did not regard the office building proceeds as having been distributed within the 12-month period. Such proceeds were deposited in a bank account maintained in the name of the corporation. No steps were taken to transfer them to the shareholders until after the 12-month period had expired. As noted in our Findings, the balance sheet attached to petitioner's income tax return for the fiscal year ending June 30, 1968 (signed March 13, 1969), reflects an increase in cash on hand from $2,-845.76 to $40,035.86 during the year, together with a corresponding decrease in its assets consisting of buildings and other fixed depreciable assets. This increase in cash reflected the receipts from the office building sale. Similarly, the balance sheet attached to petitioner's income tax return for the period July 1, 1968, to March 12, 1969, reflects cash on hand at the beginning of that period in the amount of $40,035.86. Thus, petitioner treated the deposit in the savings account as its asset, not as cash which it had distributed to its shareholders.

It is undoubtedly true that a corporation's transfer of assets, effective as between it and its transferee, would qualify as a distribution within the meaning of section 337. Bird Management, Inc., 48 T.C. 586, 593 (1967). However, these funds were deposited in the savings account on April 5, 1968, and nothing is shown to have happened to them within the statutory 12-month period. Nani testified that he did not distribute these funds immediately because he

---

6. Nani testified as to his reasons for not causing petitioner to distribute the cash, as follows:

I am a public accountant. January is the worst month of the year for us. I just was so busy I never got around to doing it. I usually mark these things a week or two before they are due. I negligently waited until the last minute to do it and I did not have the time to do it in January which, as I answered earlier, was the worst month of the year of practitioners.

thought there were "tax advantages" to the shareholders in deferring the receipt of these payments from 1968 to 1969. No explanation has been offered as to how the funds could have been distributed by petitioner during the 12-month period without their having been received by the shareholders for the purposes of computing their income tax liabilities.

We hold petitioner failed to distribute the funds within the 12-month period and that such failure is fatal to its claim to the benefits of section 337. If the petitioner had sustained a loss on the sale of the office building and, after the adoption of a plan of liquidation, had decided to avoid section 337 by delaying the distributions beyond the 12-month period, we cannot perceive how it would have acted differently.

Both parties have extensively briefed an argument by petitioner that the office building sale proceeds were constructively received by the shareholders within the 12-month period and, therefore, must be regarded as distributed by petitioner. The doctrine of constructive receipt may be concisely stated: "Income although not actually reduced to a taxpayer's possession is constructively received by him in the taxable year during which it is credited to his account, set apart for him, or otherwise made available so that he may draw upon it at any time, or so that he could have drawn upon it during the taxable year if notice of intention to withdraw had been given." Sec. 1.451–2(a), Income Tax Regs.

We are not satisfied that the doctrine of constructive receipt as applied to the shareholders provides the correct criterion for determining whether a corporation has "distributed" its assets for the purposes of section 337. That section is directed entirely to action by the corporation. The accompanying Congressional report explicitly states that "It is intended that all of the property except property retained to meet claims must be distributed by the corporation." S.Rept. No. 1622, to accompany H.R. 8300 (Pub.L. 591), 83d Cong., 2d Sess., p. 259 (1954).

We find nothing in the language or legislative history of the section which suggests that assets have been distributed by the corporation if they have been "made available" to the shareholders so that they may "draw upon" the funds at any time Sec. 1.451–2(a), Income Tax Regs. Indeed, the implication of the regulations interpreting section 337(a) is that this is not enough to constitute a distribution. Thus, for shareholders who cannot be located, section 1.337–2(b), Income Tax Regs., contemplates that their funds will be transferred to "a State official, trustee, or other person authorized by law to receive distributions for the benefit of such shareholders."

. . . Moreover, in a variety of situations the courts have recognized that there is no necessary correlation between the constructive receipt and the constructive payment of funds. . . . We have found no case applying the constructive receipt doctrine under section 337(a).

* * *

In any event, we do not think the funds derived from the office building sale were constructively received by petitioner's shareholders within the 12-month period. The mere adoption of a resolution to completely liquidate a corporation does not vest in the shareholders a right to the liquidating distributions that is sufficient to invoke the doctrine of constructive receipt. This is true even though the funds in the hands of the corporation are controlled by individuals as corporate officers who are also shareholders. . . . There must be some action manifesting an intention on the part of those individuals to take the property as their own. . . .

The issue as to whether Nani manifested an intention to take the office building proceeds for himself and his children is factual. We do not think he did. We have pointed out that he testified that he delayed the distribution so that the gain would be taxed in 1969 rather than 1968; thus, he did not intend to take the funds in 1968. He confirmed that the funds continued to belong to the corporation by showing them as assets in the balance sheets attached to the corporation's last two returns; both returns were signed after the expiration of the crucial 12-month period. He testified that he failed to make the distribution in January 1969 due to "neglect" and that he failed to do so in February due to the error in marking his calendar. We do not think the closing of the corporation's checking account on February 12, 1969, shows any intent to distribute the funds in the savings account. In sum, we find no evidence manifesting an intention on Nani's part to take the funds until the corporation's savings account was closed, after the 12-month period had expired. . . .

Petitioner argues that the February 15, 1968, corporate resolution providing for the distribution of the corporate assets within the prescribed period was self-executing and effected a distribution without further formal corporate action. As authority for this principle, petitioner cites [cases, but those] cases are distinguishable on their facts.[7]

7. In three of the cases there was an actual corporate transfer either to the shareholders or to a person who received the property for the shareholders. Some of the cases involved a mere delay in the issuance of stock certificates or voting trust certificates where the rights of the shareholders existed before the receipt of the certificates. Although petitioner claims that its savings account "like the stock interest in John E. Byrne, supra, may be beneficially owned by a person lacking certificates or other written evidence of ownership," we find no support in the record to justify such a conclusion in this case. The savings account at all pertinent times was in petitioner's

To support its contention that a distribution occurred within the 12-month period, petitioner also refers us to Gensinger v. Commissioner, 208 F.2d 576 (C.A.9, 1953), affirming in part and reversing in part 18 T.C. 122 (1952), for the principle that the timing of a liquidating distribution to a shareholder of a closely held corporation depends on what was actually intended. The argument is that the shareholder resolution of February 15, 1968, evidenced this intent and is thus sufficient to warrant a finding that a distribution occurred within the 12-month period. The court in that case observed (supra at 582):

> Where both the power to distribute property and the sole equitable right to it are held by a single person, who is both "distributor" and "distributee", and the only person with any interest in the matter, we see no reason why any more should be required to prove a "distribution" than that the person intended to presently take the property as his own and that his intention was manifested in some manner.[4] [Footnote omitted.]

This analysis does not apply in the instant case for two reasons. First, the court in the above statement was referring to a period after a shareholder had become a trustee in dissolution under local law. The court expressly rejected (supra at 579) the argument that this principle applies where, as in the instant case, the corporation has done nothing except adopt a resolution to distribute its assets within a stated period. The second reason is that, as discussed above, there was no objective manifestation on the part of petitioner's shareholders of an intention to take these funds as their own within the 12-month period.

We hold that petitioner did not comply with the requirements of section of section 337(a) and is, therefore, taxable on the disputed gain.

Decision will be entered for the respondent.

name, and, as discussed in the text, there was no showing that petitioner attempted to distribute the ownership of the account during the 12-month period.

3. Recognition of Income Despite the Application
of §337 (or §336)

BYRNE, THE TAX BENEFIT RULE AS APPLIED TO CORPORATE LIQUIDATIONS AND CONTRIBUTIONS TO CAPITAL: RECENT DEVELOPMENTS *

56 Notre Dame Law. 215–228 (1980).

* * *

II. Corporate Liquidations and the Tax Benefit Rule

Under Code sections 336 and 337, a liquidating corporation generally does not recognize gain or loss if it either sells its assets or distributes them to its shareholders. Section 336 provides that, except for the disposition of LIFO inventory and certain installment obligations under section 453, a corporation recognizes no gain or loss on the distribution of property in partial or complete liquidation. Section 336 was enacted as part of the 1954 Code and merely reflects the prior common law that a corporation cannot be deemed to realize a gain or loss on the mere distribution of an asset.

Section 337 provides that if a corporation distributes all of its assets less assets retained to meet claims, in complete liquidation within twelve months following adoption of a plan of complete liquidation, the corporation shall recognize no gain or loss from the sale or exchange of its property within that twelve month period. Section 337(b) excludes from the definition of "property," and thus from the nonrecognition rule, sales of inventory other than bulk transfers and certain installment obligations. Like section 336, section 337(f) contains an exception for LIFO inventory.** Unlike section 336, section 337 in no way reflected prior law. Before 1954, a corporation holding appreciated assets could liquidate in two ways. The corporation could sell its assets to a third party, distribute the proceeds to its shareholders, and be taxed on the gain realized from the sale. Alternatively, it could distribute the assets to the shareholders and escape taxation. However, depending on the formalities employed, a subsequent sale of distributed assets by shareholders could be attributed back to the corporation and the corporation would not escape taxation. Section 337 was enacted to avoid these formalistic distinctions and eliminate uncertainty.

* Volume 56 Notre Dame Lawyer, Issue 2 (December 1980). Reprinted with permission. © by the Notre Dame Lawyer, University of Notre Dame.

** [Ed. note] Section 337(f) was added by the Crude Oil Windfall Profit Tax Act of 1980, to require that in the case of inventory carried on lifo even a bulk sale requires the selling corporation to recognize as ordinary income the "lifo recapture amount", essentially the difference between the lifo basis of the inventory and what the basis would have been under lifo. A counterpart amendment to § 336 requires recognition of the "lifo recapture amount" when lifo inventory is distributed in kind to stockholders upon a partial or complete liquidation. § 336(b).

Thus, since 1954, there is generally only one taxable event involved in a distributing of liquidation assets. A corporation will generally escape tax on the appreciation of its distributed liquidation assets under either section 336 or section 337. However, the shareholders will generally be taxed on the difference between their basis in the stock and either the cash or the fair market value of the assets distributed to them in liquidation.

Despite the literal applicability of the nonrecognition rules of sections 336 or 337 to a transaction, in two general areas courts have forced corporations to recognize income in the course of liquidation under broad principles outside those sections. The first general area involves the distribution or sale by a corporation of rights to income. In such situations the courts have utilized two weapons in forcing recognition of income: the judicially created anticipatory assignment of income doctrine, and the authority granted the Commissioner under section 446(b) to change a taxpayer's accounting method when the existing method does not clearly reflect income.

The second general area involves application of the tax benefit rule. . . .

In addition to these broad overriding principles compelling recognition, code sections 1245 and 1250 employ the tax benefit rule to override sections 336 and 337 in the case of depreciation deductions. Prior to the enactment of sections 1245 and 1250, net gains from sales of depreciable business property were generally afforded capital gains treatment pursuant to section 1231, and no gain was recognized on the liquidating distribution or preliquidation sales of such property pursuant to sections 336 and 337. Sections 1245 and 1250 apply to all dispositions of depreciable property and generally override all other Code provisions, including such nonrecognition provisions as sections 336 and 337. In dispositions of personal property and certain types of real property, section 1245 recaptures as ordinary income all previously taken depreciation deductions up to gain realized. In dispositions of most types of real property, section 1250 effects a recapture generally only to the extent of excess over straight line depreciation.

In order to understand the application of the broad, judicially created tax benefit rule as it applies to section 336 and 337 transactions, it is first necessary to understand the development of the rule in two major areas of controversy: (1) the preliquidation sale of expensed assets, and (2) the preliquidation sale [or transfer upon incorporation] of accounts receivable with an unused bad debt reserve.

A. *Preliquidation Sales of Expensed Property*

Assets such as materials and supplies not held for sale to customers and having only a short useful life may be expensed under section 162. The taxpayer may thus recover the assets' full cost as a deduction in the taxable year of purchase even though their useful life may extend into the next taxable year. On the other hand, assets with a longer useful life should be capitalized and their cost recovered by way of section 167 depreciation deductions over a period of years corresponding to the assets' useful life.

A corporation which is about to liquidate may have on hand assets whose full cost has been expensed in a prior taxable year but whose useful life has not yet ended. Since the cost of these assets has been fully recovered their basis will be zero. But since the assets have not yet been fully consumed, they will retain some market value. These assets do not come within any of section 337's specific exceptions to nonrecognition and, since they are not depreciable assets, they are not subject to the recapture rules of sections 1245 and 1250 which specifically override section 337. Beginning in 1969 a series of cases considered whether, under the general, judicially created tax benefit rule, some portion of the previously taken expense deductions should be recaptured as income in the year of the preliquidation sale of expensed zero basis assets retaining some market value.

* * *

The government [has generally prevailed. Most recently,] in Estate of Munter v. Commissioner,[43] the full Tax Court, with no dissenters, held the tax benefit rule applicable to expensed items in liquidation sales under section 337. *Munter* involved the preliquidation sale of rental items which had been expensed either in the year of sale or in the two years preceding the sale. Section 337 permitted nonrecognition of gain from the sale. The Tax Court ruled that the receipt by the corporation of the additional tax benefit lacked legislative support and was inconsistent with the general intent of Congress in enacting revenue laws. The court considered the tax benefit rule applicable to both deductions taken in the year of sale and deductions taken in prior years.

These cases firmly establish the applicability of the tax benefit rule to preliquidation sales of expensed assets. Although there is some uncertainty as to whether it is more proper to apply the tax benefit rule or section 446(b) to sales of assets expensed in the year of sale, the result to the taxpayer is the same under both principles —the economic benefit of the deduction is lost. These cases highlight the overriding role of the tax benefit rule: preventing distortions of income arising from the taxpayer's use of a particular method of accounting.

B. Bad Debt Reserve

Section 166(c) permits an accrual method taxpayer to deduct a reasonable reserve for bad debts instead of deducting specific bad debts. The amount of bad debt reserve is derived by estimating the losses which reasonably can be expected to result from the worthlessness of debts outstanding at the close of the taxable year. Under the

43. 63 T.C. 663 (1975).

reserve method, specific debts upon becoming worthless are charged against the reserve and reduce its credit balance. If the reserve's end of year credit balance cannot cover reasonably expected losses attributable to debts outstanding at the end of the year, an appropriate addition is made to the reserve. Such an addition is deductible.

In a series of cases prior to 1970, . . . [the question arose whether upon a sale under section 337 or a liquidating distribution in kind the balance in the corporation's bad debt reserve had to be "restored" to income, pursuant to the tax benefit rule. A similar question was raised in connection with the transfer of a going business to a corporation under section 351, and the Supreme Court answered no. Read Rev.Rul. 78–280, page 153 supra.]

In Citizens Acceptance Corp. v. United States,[62] the district court considered the tax benefit rule's applicability to bad debt reserves in section 337 liquidations in light of the Supreme Court's holding in *Nash*. The court observed that many pre-*Nash* decisions had held that a corporation recognized the entire amount of its bad debt reserve upon liquidation pursuant to section 337. The court considered *Nash* as overruling those decisions, since the considerations governing section 351 also govern section 337. Accordingly, the court held that a bad debt reserve could be recaptured only to the extent the amount received for the accounts receivable in the preliquidation sale exceeded the receivables' net value. Although the Third Circuit reversed on factual grounds,[65] it impliedly accepted the district court's reasoning that under *Nash* the bad debt reserve could be recaptured only to the extent that the consideration received exceeded the net value of the receivables. In Revenue Ruling 78–279,[67] the Internal Revenue Service accepted the district court's application of *Nash* to section 337 liquidations. [See second ed. note on page 613.]

In view of *Nash* and the subsequent developments in the section 337 area, the law is well settled as to preliquidation sales of accounts receivable where unused bad debt reserves exist. However, *Nash* does raise the question whether a taxpayer must have a "recovery" or "economic benefit" for the tax benefit rule to apply. This question is crucial in determining the applicability of the tax benefit rule to liquidating distributions in kind.

62. 320 F.Supp. 798 (D.Del.1970), rev'd on other grounds, 462 F.2d 751 (3d Cir. 1972).

65. 462 F.2d at 755–56. The Third Circuit reversed on the factual question of the extent to which the amount realized on the sale exceeded the net value of the receivables. But see Home Sav. & Loan Ass'n v. United States, 514 F.2d 1199 (9th Cir.), cert. denied 423 U.S. 1015 (1975).

67. Rev.Rul. 78–279, 1978–2 C.B. 135. The Service stated:
The burden is on the taxpayer to show that the amount received in excess of the net value of the accounts receivable is not a recovery of a tax benefit but rather attributable to economic factors such as appreciation in value of interest bearing accounts receivable resulting from changes in prevailing interest rates.
Id. at 136.

HILLSBORO NATIONAL BANK v. COMMISSIONER

UNITED STATES v. BLISS DAIRY, INC.

Supreme Court of the United States, 1983

103 Sup. Ct. 1134.

Justice O'CONNOR delivered the opinion of the Court.

These consolidated cases present the question of the applicability of the tax benefit rule to two corporate tax situations: the repayment to the shareholders of taxes for which they were liable but that were originally paid by the corporation; and the distribution of expensed assets in a corporate liquidation. We conclude that, unless a nonrecognition provision of the Internal Revenue Code prevents it, the tax benefit rule ordinarily applies to require the inclusion of income when events occur that are fundamentally inconsistent with an earlier deduction. Our examination of the provisions granting the deductions and governing the liquidation in these cases lead us to hold that the rule requires the recognition of income in the case of the liquidation but not in the case of the tax refund.*

*   *   *

In No. 81-930, <u>United States v. Bliss Dairy, Inc.</u>, the respondent, Bliss Dairy, Inc., was a closely held corporation engaged in the business of operating a dairy. As a cash basis taxpayer, in the taxable year ending June 30, 1973, it deducted upon purchase the full cost of the cattle feed purchased for use in its operations, as permitted by § 162 of the Internal Revenue Code, 26 U.S.C. § 162. A substantial portion of the feed was still on hand at the end of the taxable year. On July 2, 1973, two days into the next taxable year, Bliss adopted a plan of liquidation, and, during the month of July, it distributed its assets, including the remaining cattle feed, to the shareholders. Relying on § 336, which shields the corporation from the recognition of gain on the distribution of property to its shareholders on liquidation, Bliss reported no income on the transaction. The shareholders continued to operate the dairy business in noncorporate form. They filed an election under § 333 to limit the gain recognized by them on the liquidation, and they therefore calculated their basis in the assets received in the distribution as provided in § 334(c). Under that provision, their basis in the assets was their basis in their stock in the liqui-

---

* [Ed. Note] Portions of the opinion, including all of the discussion of the Hillsboro National Bank case involving the tax refund, and most of the footnotes, omitted.

dated corporation, decreased by the amount of money received, and increased by the amount of gain recognized on the transaction. They then allocated that total basis over the assets, as provided in the regulations, Treas. Reg. § 1.334-2, 26 CFR § 1.334-2 (1982), presumably taking a basis greater than zero in the feed, although the amount of the shareholders' basis is not in the record. They in turn deducted their basis in the feed as an expense of doing business under § 162. On audit, the Commissioner challenged the corporation's treatment of the transaction, asserting that Bliss should have taken into income the value of the grain distributed to the shareholders. He therefore increased Bliss's income by $60,000. Bliss paid the resulting assessment and sued for a refund in the district court for the District of Arizona, where it was stipulated that the grain had a value of $56,565, see Pretrial Order at 3. Relying on Commissioner v. South Lake Farms, Inc., 324 F.2d 837 (CA9 1963), the district court rendered a judgment in favor of Bliss. While recognizing authority to the contrary, Tennessee-Carolina Transportation, Inc. v. Commissioner, 582 F.2d 378 (CA6 1978), cert. denied, 440 U.S. 909, 99 S.Ct. 1219, 59 L.Ed.2d 457 (1979), the Court of Appeals saw South Lake Farms as controlling and affirmed. 645 F.2d 19 (CA9 1981) (per curiam).

II

The Government in each case relies solely on the tax benefit rule -- a judicially developed principle that allays some of the inflexibilities of the annual accounting system. . . .

The taxpayers and the Government in these cases propose different formulations of the tax benefit rule. The taxpayers contend that the rule requires the inclusion of amounts recovered in later years, and they do not view the events in these cases as "recoveries." The Government, on the other hand, urges that the tax benefit rule requires the inclusion of amounts previously deducted if later events are inconsistent with the deductions; it insists that no "recovery" is necessary to the application of the rule. Further, it asserts that the events in these cases are inconsistent with the deductions taken by the taxpayers. We are not in complete agreement with either view.

[1,2] An examination of the purpose and accepted applications of the tax benefit rule reveals that a "recovery" will not always be necessary to invoke the tax benefit rule. The purpose of the rule is not simply to tax "recoveries." On the contrary, it is to approximate the results produced by a tax system based on transactional rather than annual accounting. . . . It has long been accepted that a taxpayer using accrual accounting who accrues and deducts an expense in a tax year before it becomes payable and who for some reason eventually does not have to pay the liability must then take into income the amount of the expense earlier deducted. . . .

The bookkeeping entry cancelling the liability, though it increases the balance sheet net worth of the taxpayer, does not fit within any ordinary definition of "recovery." Thus, the taxpayers' formulation of the rule neither serves the purposes of the rule nor accurately reflects the cases that establish the rule. Further, the taxpayers' proposal would introduce an undesirable formalism into the application of the tax benefit rule. Lower courts have been able to stretch the definition of "recovery" to include a great variety of events. For instance, in cases of corporate liquidations, courts have viewed the corporation's receipt of its own stock as a "recovery," reasoning that, even though the instant that the corporation receives the stock it becomes worthless, the stock has value as it is turned over to the corporation, and that ephemeral value represents a recovery for the corporation. See, e.g., Tennessee-Carolina Transportation, Inc. v. Commissioner, 582 F.2d 378, 382 (CA6 1978), cert. denied, 440 U.S. 909, 99 S.Ct. 1219, 59 L.Ed.2d 457 (1979) (alternative holding). Or, payment to another party may be imputed to the taxpayer, giving rise to a recovery. See First Trust and Savings Bank v. United States, 614 F.2d 1142, 1146 (CA7 1980) (alternative holding). Imposition of a requirement that there be a recovery would, in many cases, simply require the Government to cast its argument in different and unnatural terminology, without adding anything to the analysis.

*   *   *

When the later event takes place in the context of a non-recognition provision of the Code, there will be an inherent tension between the tax benefit rule and the nonrecognition provision. . . . We cannot resolve that tension with a blanket rule that the tax benefit rule will always prevail. Instead, we must focus on the particular provisions of the Code at issue in any case.

*   *   *

Our approach today is consistent with our decision in Nash v. United States, 398 U.S. 1, 90 S.Ct. 1550, 26 L.Ed.2d 1 (1970). There, we rejected the Government's argument that the tax benefit rule required a taxpayer who incorporated a partnership under § 351 to include in income the amount of the bad debt reserve of the partnership. The Government's theory was that, although § 351 provides that there will be no gain or loss on the transfer of assets to a controlled corporation in such a situation, the partnership had taken bad debt deductions to create the reserve, see § 166(c), and when the partnership terminated, it no longer needed the bad debt reserve. We noted that the receivables were transferred to the corporation along with the bad debt reserve. Id., at 5 and n.5, 90 S.Ct., at 1552 and n.5. Not only was there no "recovery," id., at 4, 90 S.Ct., at 1552, but there was no inconsistent event of any kind. That

the fair market value of the receivables was equal to the face
amount less the bad debt reserve, id., at 4, reflected that the
reserve, and the deductions that constituted it, were still an
accurate estimate of the debts that would ultimately prove
uncollectible, and the deduction was therefore completely consistent with the later transfer of the receivables to the incorporated business. . . .

[6] In the cases currently before us, then, we must undertake an examination of the particular provisions of the Code
that govern these transactions to determine whether the deductions taken by the taxpayers were actually inconsistent with
later events and whether specific nonrecognition provisions
prevail over the principle of the tax benefit rule.

*   *   *

IV

. . . Bliss took a deduction under § 162(a), so we must
begin by examining that provision. Section 162(a) permits a
deduction for the "ordinary and necessary expenses" of carrying
on a trade or business. The deduction is predicated on the
consumption of the asset in the trade or business. . . . In
general, if the taxpayer converts the expensed asset to some
other, non-business use, that action is inconsistent with his
earlier deduction, and the tax benefit rule would require inclusion in income of the amount of the unwarranted deduction.
Thus, if a corporation turns expensed assets to the analog of
personal consumption, as Bliss did here -- distribution to
shareholders -- it would seem that it should take into income
the amount of the earlier deduction.[32]

---

32. Justice STEVENS' dissent takes issue with this conclusion, character-
     izing the situation as identical to that in Nash, which he explains as
     a case in which we held that, although "a business asset matching a
     prior deduction . . . would not be used up . . . until it had passed to
     a different taxpayer," the transfer did not require the recognition of
     income. Post, at 1160. What is misleading in this description is its
     failure to recognize that in Nash the prior deduction was reflected in
     the asset transferred because of the contra-asset account: uncollec-
     tible accounts. That contra-asset diminished the asset, see generally
     W. Meigs, A. Mosich, C. Johnson and T. Keller, Intermediate Accounting
     140-141 (3d ed. 1974), and was inseparable from it. Therefore, the
     transfer of the notes did not establish that they were worth their face
     value, and there was no inconsistent event.

         In Bliss, the taxpayer took a deduction for an expense and credited
     the asset account. Unlike the debit to the expense account in Nash,
     the debit to the expense account did not reflect any economic decrease
     in the value of the asset. When the taxpayers transferred the asset,
     it became clear that the economic decrease would not take place in the
     hands of Bliss -- and possibly never would occur.

(footnote continued)

[12] That conclusion, however, does not resolve this case, for the distribution by Bliss to its shareholders is governed by a provision of the Code that specifically shields the taxpayer from recognition of gain -- § 336. We must therefore proceed to inquire whether this is the sort of gain that goes unrecognized under § 336. Our examination of the background of § 336 and its place within the framework of tax law convinces us that it does not prevent the application of the tax benefit rule.

Section 336 was enacted as part of the 1954 Code. It codified the doctrine of General Utilities Co. v. Helvering, 296 U.S. 200, 206, 56 S.Ct. 185, 187, 80 L.Ed. 154 (1935), that a corporation does not recognize gain on the distribution of appreciated property to its shareholders. . . . [The legislative] background indicates that the real concern of the provision is to prevent recognition of market appreciation that has not been realized by an arm's-length transfer to an unrelated party rather than to shield all types of income that might arise from the disposition of an asset.

Despite the breadth of the nonrecognition language in § 336, the rule of nonrecognition clearly is not without exception. For instance, § 336 does not bar the recapture under §§ 1245 and 1250 of excessive depreciation taken on distributed assets. . . . Even in the absence of countervailing statutory provisions, courts have never read the command of nonrecognition in § 336 as absolute. The "assignment of income" doctrine has always applied to distributions in liquidation. . . . That judicial doctrine prevents taxpayers from avoiding taxation by shifting income from the person or entity that earns it to someone who pays taxes at a lower rate. Since income recognized by the corporation is subject to the corporate tax and is again taxed at the individual level upon distribution to the shareholder, shifting of income from a corporation to a shareholder can be particularly attractive: it eliminates one level of taxation. Responding to that incentive, corporations have attempted to distribute to shareholders fully performed contracts or accounts receivable and then to invoke § 336 to avoid taxation on the income. In spite of the language of nonrecognition, the courts have applied the assignment of income doctrine and required the

----

(footnote continued)

To see the difference more clearly, consider the views of a third party contemplating purchasing the asset on hand in Nash and one contemplating purchasing the asset on hand in Bliss. In Nash, the purchaser would be willing to pay only the face amount of the receivables less the amount in the contra-asset account -- the amount earlier deducted by the taxpayer -- because that is all the purchaser could expect to realize on them. In other words, the deduction reflected a real decrease in the value of the asset. In Bliss, on the other hand, the purchaser would be happy to pay the value of the grain, undiminished by the expense deducted by the taxpayer. The deduction and the asset remain separable, and the taxpayer can transfer one without netting out the other.

corporation to recognize the income. Section 336, then, clearly does not shield the taxpayer from recognition of all income on the distribution.

[13] Next, we look to a companion provision -- § 337, which governs sales of assets followed by distribution of the proceeds in liquidation. It uses essentially the same broad language to shield the corporation from the recognition of gain on the sale of the assets. The similarity in language alone would make the construction of § 337 relevant in interpreting § 336. In addition, the function of the two provisions reveals that they should be construed in tandem. Section 337 was enacted in response to the distinction created by United States v. Cumberland Public Service Co., 338 U.S. 451, 70 S.Ct. 280, 94 L.Ed. 251 (1950), and Commissioner v. Court Holding, 324 U.S. 331, 65 S.Ct. 707, 89 L.Ed. 981 (1945). Under those cases, a corporation that liquidated by distributing appreciated assets to its shareholders recognized no income, as now provided in § 336, even though its shareholders might sell the assets shortly after the distribution. See Cumberland. If the corporation sold the assets, though, it would recognize income on the sale, and a sale by the shareholders after distribution in kind might be attributed to the corporation. See Court Holding. To eliminate the necessarily formalistic distinctions and the uncertainties created by Court Holding and Cumberland, Congress enacted § 337, permitting the corporation to adopt a plan of liquidation, sell its assets without recognizing gain or loss at the corporate level, and distribute the proceeds to the shareholders. The very purpose of § 337 was to create the same consequences as § 336. . . .

There are some specific differences between the two provisions, largely aimed at governing the period during which the liquidating corporation sells its assets, a problem that does not arise when the corporation distributes its assets to its shareholders. For instance, § 337 does not shield the income produced by the sale of inventory in the ordinary course of business; that income will be taxed at the corporate level before distribution of the proceeds to the shareholders. See § 337(b). These differences indicate that Congress did not intend to allow corporations to escape taxation on business income earned while carrying on business in the corporate form; what it did intend to shield was market appreciation.

[14, 15] The question whether § 337 protects the corporation from recognizing income because of unwarranted deductions has arisen frequently, and the rule is now well established that the tax benefit rule overrides the nonrecognition provision. . . .

[16] Thus, the legislative history of § 336, the application of other general rules of tax law, and the construction of the identical language in § 337 all indicate that § 336 does not permit a liquidating corporation to avoid the tax benefit rule. Consequently, we reverse the judgment of the Court of Appeals and hold that, on liquidation, Bliss must include in income the amount of the unwarranted deduction.

V

Bliss paid the assessment on an increase of $60,000 in its taxable income. In the District Court, the parties stipulated that the value of the grain was $56,565, but the record does not show what the original cost of the grain was or what portion of it remained at the time of liquidation. The proper increase in taxable income is the portion of the cost of the grain attributable to the amount on hand at the time of liquidation. In **Bliss**, then, we remand for a determination of that amount. . . .

[Justices Stevens, Marshall and Blackmun dissented from the decision with respect to Bliss Dairy, Inc.]

[Ed note] Compare Rev. Proc. 84-22, 1984·13 I.R.B. 18, which includes the following in section 3.01 (21), as one of the subjects on which rulings or determination letters will not be issued:

> Upon distribution of property in kind by a corporation to its shareholders, in complete liquidation under section 331 of the Code (when under the facts a sale of the property by the corporation would not qualify under section 337), in partial liquidation under [§302(b)(4) and(e)], or in redemption of stock under section 302(a), followed by a sale of the property, whether the sale can be deemed to have been made by the corporation under the doctrine of Commissioner v. Court Holding Company, ...

[Ed. note] Notice that if there were no nonrecognition provision in the picture, it would not particularly matter if the reserve was required to be restored to income even when the price received for the accounts receivable was only equal to net book value--for there would be an offsetting loss on the accounts receivable equal to the difference between the face amount (their tax basis) and the price received; and since accounts receivable arising in the ordinary course of business do not constitute capital assets, §1221(4), the loss would be ordinary and would counterbalance the restoration of the reserve to ordinary income. However, when the sale of the accounts receivable is subject to a nonrecognition provision, such as §337, the loss on the accounts is prevented from being recognized, and hence any restoration of the reserve represents net additional taxable income.

HINES v. UNITED STATES *

Court of Appeal, Fifth Circuit, 1973.
477 F.2d 1063.

GOLDBERG, J. This is an appeal from the denial of a claim by taxpayer, Harry H. Hines, Jr., for a recovery of income taxes and interest assessed and paid for the years 1966 and 1967.

Although this appeal involves only taxpayer's personal income tax liability, the controlling question is one of corporate taxation. Whether the proceeds from the sale of property that had been distributed to taxpayer by a family-owned corporation were properly imputed to the distributing corporation when that corporation (1) did not negotiate the sale prior to the distribution and (2) did not participate in the sale after the distribution. . . .

Taxpayer was a director and secretary of Peeler Realty Company, Inc. . . .

Peeler Realty is a family-owned corporation, incorporated in 1950 by taxpayer, taxpayer's grandmother, Mrs. Ethel Peeler, and taxpayer's grandfather, S. J. Peeler, a successful businessman who for many years operated a large lumber business in Kosciusko. In the course of conducting that business, S. J. Peeler acquired a large amount of cut-over timberland located in Attala and adjoining counties in Mississippi, most of which he obtained at tax sales in the late 1930's for amounts ranging from fifty to seventy-five cents per acre.

At the first meeting of the incorporators and subscribers of Peeler Realty, on November 6, 1950, S. J. Peeler transferred some 27,500 acres of timberland and numerous low-cost rental houses situated in Kosciusko to Peeler Realty for 3,998 shares of the corporation's 4000 shares of authorized capital stock. Immediately thereafter, he began transferring his shares to his wife, children, and grandchildren by way of gifts. By August 25, 1965, shortly before the period here in issue, he had divested himself of all of his stock interest in the corporation.

The business operations of Peeler Realty consisted almost entirely of holding the timberland conveyed to it by S. J. Peeler and renting out the low-cost houses. Although the corporation would occasionally sell small tracts of land or easements over the land and would sometimes market small quantities of timber, the corporate in-

---

* Portions of the opinion and footnotes
by the Court omitted.

come was derived primarily from rents collected on the low-cost houses.

Between 1954 and 1967, the corporation showed a profit in only four years; the losses during the other years were attributed primarily to the fact that the rental income was insufficient to pay the annual operating expenses and the ad valorem taxes on the timberland. The corporation's surplus account showed a deficit balance of $45,950.97 on October 31, 1966, the end of its fiscal year, and the deficit increased to $46,334.21 on October 31, 1967.

In the mid 1960's, the pulpwood industry in Attala County began to grow. The Georgia-Pacific Corporation had already purchased timberlands in the area and was eager to purchase other timberland to support its Mississippi mill operations. Moreover, during this period, the International Paper Company and the St. Regis Paper Company each built a pulpwood mill in Mississippi.

In November, 1964, following a "timber cruise," the Georgia-Pacific Corporation made a written offer to pay a cash price of $57 per acre for Peeler Realty's timberland. As an alternative inducement designed to accommodate Peeler Realty's desire to reduce the tax incidence of a sale of its timberland—Georgia-Pacific Corporation offered to pay a purchase price of $50 per acre in Georgia-Pacific stock, in the hopes of effecting a tax-free exchange. When these offers were rejected, Georgia-Pacific Corporation agreed to pay from $60 to $63 per acre for the timberland.

Some of the shareholders of the company were eager to sell the land to obtain cash, which they needed for various personal reasons. A minority of the shareholders representing 930 shares, did not wish to sell. Taxpayer was willing to sell for the right price, but he did not think the Georgia-Pacific offer was sufficient.

Other large paper mills and lumber dealers were also interested in acquiring Peeler Realty's timberland. In the latter part of 1965, taxpayer discussed a possible sale with International Paper Company, Weyerhaeuser Company, St. Regis Paper Company, and Attala Lumber Company. International Paper Company and St. Regis Paper Company made "cruises" of the timberlands after the corporation indicated it was interested in selling the land. Peeler Realty did not, however, enter into any solid negotiations with either of these firms.

Eventually, it was decided that the one firm offer from Georgia-Pacific was not acceptable because it was not high enough. On December 27, 1965, the shareholders and directors of Peeler Realty conducted a meeting to discuss the corporation's financial condition.

At this meeting, Robert W. Hartford (a lawyer and certified public accountant who had served S. J. Peeler for years and who had been elected chairman of the board of Peeler Realty on August 27, 1965) outlined the financial condition of the corporation and set forth the alternative courses of action available. Mr. Hartford advised the meeting that if things continued as they were going, the corporation would soon be bankrupt. He discussed the pros and cons of liquidation and of separating the heavily-taxed land from the corporation.

The majority of the shareholders wanted to sell the timberlands, and taxpayer, who was the informal spokesman for most of the shareholders, was fully aware of the tax consequences that would follow if the sale were made by the corporation. The tax basis of the property was quite low not exceeding $40,000, and the selling price clearly would be in excess of the 1.5 million dollars which had already been offered by Georgia-Pacific and rejected as insufficient. Furthermore, taxpayer and Hartford were aware that a corporate sale would result in the payment of a capital gains tax by the corporation followed by the imposition of an additional tax on the individual shareholders after distribution.

Liquidation and dissolution, a method provided by the Internal Revenue Code to avoid double taxation, was not thought feasible because the corporation could not be terminated because S. J. Peeler's will left certain real property to the corporation and he had become mentally incompetent to change his will.

On January 18, 1966, the directors held a special meeting and decided to recommend to the shareholders that the corporation's timberland be distributed to the shareholders as tenants in common, with the interest of each to be determined by his or her pro rata interest in the corporate stock. The shareholders authorized the withdrawal and a law firm was engaged to prepare the conveyance, prior to which it was necessary to do substantial searching of the land records of the counties in which the land was located.

The deed was executed by the directors on March 30, 1966, divesting Peeler Realty of title to the timberlands and leaving as its only asset the low-cost houses producing rental income. Once the deed was executed and recorded, the attorneys were authorized to make a title search of each tract and perform any work determined to be necessary in order to cure defects in the title and make the lands marketable.

The shareholders also executed a power of attorney giving taxpayer, Hartford, and Mrs. Ethel Peeler authority to handle the land and to sell it if they decided that a sale should be made. The power invested in the attorneys-in-fact by the document was very extensive, granting them an almost unlimited power to dispose of the property.

In October of 1966, as soon as the attorneys had completed their title search and the attorneys-in-fact had received assurances of the availability of title insurance, the attorneys-in-fact sent "Sales Guidelines" to International Paper Company, Georgia-Pacific Corporation, St. Regis Paper Company, and Attala Lumber Company, inviting them to submit sealed bids for the purchase of the land. The "Sales Guidelines" contained the conditions and terms of the sale and the method and manner of bidding on the land.

The bids were opened in the office of Peeler Realty on November 14, 1966, and on December 15, 1966, International Paper Company's bid was accepted and the land was sold and conveyed to it on December 15, 1966 for $2,533,580.50.

The money received from the sale of the timberlands, less expenses of the sale amounting to $99,831.27, was paid to the tenants in common, the shareholders of Peeler Realty. Taxpayer reported his pro rata portion of the proceeds from the sale of his interest in the timberland and claimed long-term capital gains status. Peeler Realty did not report the proceeds of the sale by its shareholders on its corporate income tax, nor did it treat them as additions to its earned surplus on the corporation's books.

The Commissioner concluded that the gain on the sales of the land should be imputed to Peeler Realty because the distribution lacked a normal and justifiable commercial motivation and was made for the principal purpose of avoiding tax.

By imputing the proceeds of the sales to the corporation, the Commissioner determined that Peeler Realty had current earnings and profits out of which to pay a dividend, see 26 U.S.C. § 316, and that therefore the distribution to the shareholders constituted a regular dividend to the extent of the current earnings and profits and the balance constituted a return of capital to the extent of the shareholder's basis in the Peeler Realty stock, with any excess being eligible for capital gains treatment. See 26 U.S.C. § 301. . . .

After filing for refund without success, he instituted this suit in the District Court. Relying on United States v. Cumberland Pub. Serv. Co., 1950, 338 U.S. 451, and on Sections 336 and 346 of the Internal Revenue Code, taxpayer argued that the gain from the sale of the property was improperly imputed to Peeler Realty because (1) Peeler Realty had not negotiated the sale of the timberlands and (2) bcause the distribution of the timberland was a liquidating dividend under Section 346. The Government responded that the proceeds from the sale of property distributed by a going concern in anticipation of a sale by the shareholders and with no valid business purpose other than tax avoidance are properly imputed to the distributing corporation. The principal authorities relied on by the Commissioner were Commissioner v. Court Holding Co., 1945, 324 U.S. 331; Commissioner v. Transport Trad. & Term. Corp., 2 Cir. 1949, 176 F.2d 570; and United States v. Lynch, 9 Cir. 1951, 192 F.2d 718.

The District Court found that: (1) Peeler Realty had not negotiated the sale of its timberland to anyone prior to transferring it to the shareholders and after the transfer, the stockholders were not obligated to sell the land to any particular purchaser and in fact they arranged their own sale with no participation by the corporation; (2) the distribution was not a liquidating distribution under Section 336 or Section 346 of the Internal Revenue Code; and (3) the primary or principal purpose for the distribution of the land was to avoid the double tax that would have arisen had the corporation sold the land and then distributed the proceeds.

The District Court realized that the factual situation in the case at hand differed from that in the cases relied upon by the Government in that in all of those cases the corporation to which income was attributed had participated in the sale transaction from which the income arose. The court reasoned, however, that those cases nevertheless justified an imputation of the income from the sale of the timberlands to Peeler Realty, and an order was entered denying taxpayer's claim for a refund. . . .

The controlling question on this appeal is whether the gains from the sale of the timberlands could properly be imputed to Peeler Realty when the District Court explicitly found that Peeler Realty had not participated in the transaction in which the timberlands were sold. The starting point of our analysis is the Internal Revenue Code itself. Under Section 311 of the Code, as enacted at the time [of] the transaction we here review, gain was ordinarily not realized by a corporation that distributed property to its shareholders. Section 311 was not, however, intended to alter the law regarding the imputation of gain to a distributing corporation from a sale of distributed property by the corporation's shareholders when the corporation actually participates in the transaction in which the distributed property is sold.

Our consideration of the propriety of applying the imputed income rule to Peeler Realty must begin with an analysis of Commissioner v. Court Holding Co., supra, the principal Supreme Court pronunciation in this area. In Court Holding, negotiations were entered into by a corporation with a particular purchaser for the sale by the corporation of its only asset, an apartment house. These negotiations culminated in an oral agreement by the corporation to sell the property. Subsequently, the corporation learned of the double tax that would arise if the corporation first sold the property and then distributed the proceeds of the sale to its stockholders.

The corporation therefore refused to sell the property, and instead, distributed the property to its shareholders who in turn sold the property to the same purchaser with whom the corporation had negotiated on the same terms as the corporation had negotiated. The Tax Court found that the sale was really made by the corporation in performance of the prior agreement and attributed the gain to the corporation.

The Fifth Circuit reversed, disagreeing with the Tax Court's fact-finding, but the Supreme Court reversed the Fifth Circuit, holding that the finding of the Tax Court that the sale was in reality made by the corporation must be accepted if supported by evidence. . . .

The Supreme Court's next consideration of the imputed income rule came in United States v. Cumberland Pub. Serv. Co., supra. In that case a corporation desired to go out of business, but its shareholders' offer to sell their stock to a competitor was rejected. The competitor countered with an offer to buy the corporation's equipment; however, the corporation turned down this offer in order to avoid paying a heavy capital gains tax.

The shareholders of the corporation then offered to acquire the equipment from the corporation and sell it to the competitor themselves, thereby avoiding capital gains treatment for the corporation. That offer was accepted and the plan was consummated. The Commissioner attributed the gain from the sale to the corporation, but the Court of Claims refused to impute the gain, finding as a fact that the sale had been made by the shareholders, not the corporation. The court reasoned that the sale was made by the shareholders because although the transaction was for tax avoidance purposes, the corporation at no time intended to sell the equipment and the liquidation and dissolution genuinely ended the corporation's activities and existence. In affirming the Court of Claims, the Supreme Court placed great emphasis on the fact that the corporation had in fact been liquidated, but the Court also emphasized the importance of the ultimate finding of the lower court that the sale in question was made by the shareholders rather than by the corporation itself.

A reading of Court Holding and Cumberland establishes that the proceeds of the sale of property distributed by a corporation to its shareholders should be imputed to the corporation only if the sale was in fact made by the corporation, not by the shareholders. In the instant case the District Court imputed to Peeler Realty the proceeds of a sale by its shareholders without finding that Peeler Realty had in fact made the sale.

Moreover, the District Court found that Peeler Realty had neither negotiated the sale prior to distribution nor participated in the sale after distribution. The Government argues that imputation was nonetheless proper because subsequent case law indicates that the imputed income rule must apply even where there are no pre-distribution sales negotiations, if the transfer was made (1) by an ongoing concern (2) in anticipation of a sale by the shareholders, and (3) with no valid business purpose aside from motives of tax avoidance. We cannot agree.

Our reading of the applicable case law in this area convinces us that the District Court erred. We hold that the sine qua non of the imputed income rule is a finding that the corporation actively participated in the transaction that produced the income to be imputed. Only if the corporation in fact participated in the sale transaction, by negotiation, prior agreement, post-distribution activities, or participated in any other significant manner, could the corporation be charged with earning the income sought to be taxed. Any other result would unfairly charge the corporation with tax liability for a transaction in which it had no involvement or control.

We are aided in reaching this conclusion by the Tax Court's reasoning in Waltham Netoco Theatres, Inc. v. Commissioner, 1968, 49 T.C. 399, aff'd, 1 Cir. 1968, 401 F.2d 333. In Waltham, after finding that a corporation had negotiated a sale prior to distributing property to its shareholders, the Tax Court imputed the proceeds of a sale by the corporation's shareholders to the distributing corporation. The court specifically rejected the Government's argument, raised again in the case before us, that "the protection of Cumberland may not be available to nonliquidating distributions in kind by an ongoing corporation and that the corporation may be held taxable simply on the ground that there was a tax motivated preconceived plan." Id., 49 T.C. at 405. . . . In affirming Waltham, the First Circuit accepted the rationale of the Tax Court and noted that nonimputation under Cumberland would be available to the nonliquidating corporation only "if the sale were the result of independent and active negotiations with [the purchaser] . . . ." Waltham Netoco Theatres, Inc. v. Commissioner, 1 Cir. 1968, 401 F.2d 333, 335. . . .

The cases relied on by the Government also support the position we reach. In each of these cases, which we list in the margin, the court specifically found that the taxpayer to whom income was imputed had participated in the sale made by other parties either through prior negotiations, prior agreements, or post-distribution assistance in the sale.

Although there is dicta in Commissioner v. Transport Trad. & Term. Corp., supra, that indicates the Second Circuit might accept the Government's argument, that case itself does not support imputation in the case at hand because its holding was based upon a finding that the sale from which income was imputed had already been negotiated by a controlling parent corporation prior to distribution by the taxpayer and that the subsequent sale was but a step in a sales transaction that had been finalized prior to distribution. Similarly, United States v. Lynch, supra, contains language that the Ninth Circuit was influenced by the Government's imputation theory, but we read the court's holding in that case as being based primarily on the fact that the selling shareholders utilized the distributing corporation's sales facilities and received favored treatment from the distributing corporation. We therefore conclude that Lynch is not compelling authority for imputing income to Peeler Realty, for the District Court found that Peeler Realty did not participate in the sale by its shareholders either before or after the distribution.

Only A.B.C.D. Lands, Inc. v. Commissioner, supra, actually supports the Government's position, for the Tax Court in that case held that regardless of corporate participation it would impute income to a distributing corporation because the distribution was made by an ongoing corporation for tax avoidance purposes with an expectation of immediate sale by the shareholders. Although we agree with the result reached in that case, we do so only because there were ample factual findings by the Tax Court to support a finding that the sale was in fact participated in by the distributing corporation, and we expressly disavow the imputation theory espoused in that case.

Although there does appear to be a monumental loophole in Section 301 of the Internal Revenue Code, which allows deficit corporations to distribute appreciated property without having the distribution taxed as ordinary income to the distributee, we do not think it proper to attempt to plug that loophole by conjuring up visions of corporate sales where no corporate activities justify such images. The tax loophole in this situation is not based upon imputation or non-imputation of corporate sales, but the aperture exists because distributions of appreciated property by a deficit corporation are not deemed distributions in the nature of dividends. We are not nearly so certain as the Internal Revenue Service, which administers the Code, that absent imputation the passage is marked "no trespassing" into the domains of ordinary income taxation under the facts of this case, but the Government takes a different position. Under the law and regulation, who are we to say nay, though as pathfinders we may have reached a different result.

Court Holding has not been judicially elasticized to the degree that the Government argues and its tentacles have to a large extent been amputated. Moreover, we do not believe that it is our function to play loop the loop for the Government because of some result oriented tax theory. In light of the fact that Peeler Realty had never actively negotiated with International Paper Company, the ultimate purchaser, and in light of the fact that the sale of the timberlands was conducted by competitive bidding, without Peeler Realty negotiating with the final purchaser, we do not find the District Court's fact finding that Peeler Realty did not participate in the sale of the timberlands clearly erroneous. We therefore hold that it was error to impute the proceeds of the sale of the timberlands to Peeler Realty and that the District Court's denial of taxpayer's claim for a refund must be reversed, for, absent imputation, Peeler Realty had no earned surplus from which an ordinary income-producing dividend could be paid.

Certainly, the fact finding of a legally auspicated tax avoidance motive does not inject taxability into the transaction. . . . Furthermore, we do not think that this taxpayer has been treated to a windfall. Taxpayer would not have been taxed at ordinary income rates had Peeler Realty liquidated, and although Peeler Realty did not in fact liquidate, it came close to liquidating, retaining only passive income-producing property, and it would have liquidated entirely had it not been for the unfortunate circumstance of S. J. Peeler's irrevocaable will. In a circumstance such as this, where the Code would not tax a liquidating corporation even if the corporation negotiated the sale, we do not think that the Code or the case law justifies imputing taxable income to a corporation that did not participate in the sale of the distributed property and that was only prevented from obtaining the safe harbor of liquidation by the quirk of an irrevocable bequest.

* * *

Chapter 5

CORPORATE COMBINATIONS

Introduction

The combination of two or more corporations into a single unified enterprise constitutes one of the most complicated of all corporate transactions. Part of the difficulty in this area stems from the fact that a variety of techniques are available for achieving a combination; accordingly, some analysis of these different methods at the outset is essential. While the term "merger" has often been used to describe all types of combination transactions, strictly speaking "merger" refers to the statutory proceeding under which an existing corporation absorbs one or more other corporations, thereby succeeding to all of their assets, franchises and powers, and becoming liable for all of their debts, and the stockholders of the merged (i. e. disappearing) corporation or corporations receive stock or securities of the surviving corporation in exchange for their previous holdings. Obviously, so far-reaching a procedure as this rests entirely upon express statutory authorization, such as MBA §§ 71–70.; and so does that close counterpart of merger, "consolidation," which is in essence nothing more than the merger of all of the existing corporations into a brand-new corporation, specially organized for the purpose. E. g., MBA § 72.

However, these express statutory techniques do not represent the only ways in which to achieve a combination. One obvious alternative for combining two corporations is for one of them to sell all of its assets to the other in exchange for the latter's stock. If the company which acquires the assets also assumes the selling company's liabilities, and the selling company distributes the stock it received to its stockholder in exchange for its own stock in a complete liquidation, the parties would end up in the same position as under a statutory merger.

Another method for amalgamating two corporations is for the acquiring corporation to acquire all (or substantially all) of the stock of the other corporation from the latter's stockholders, in exchange for stock of the acquiring corporation, thus turning all (or substantially all) of the stockholders of the acquired corporation into stockholders of the acquiring corporation. To be sure, this exchange of stock technique does not combine the two businesses under a single corporate roof as in a merger or asset acquisition. But there is little practical difference from the acquiring corporation's point of view between operating the acquired corporation's business directly as an outright-owned division and operating it through a controlled (if not wholly-owned) subsidiary; and in any event, the acquiring corporation would normally have the power to liquidate the subsidiary and thus reach the same end-point as under the other techniques.

SECTION 1. MECHANICS OF CORPORATE COMBINATIONS

A. IN GENERAL

Obviously, these different combination techniques vary quite widely in the corporate mechanics involved. (There may also be some important tax differences, as we will see later, although each of these combination techniques is included in the definition of "reorganization" for tax purposes.) The following represents one of the most thoughtful analyses of the non-tax aspects of these combination techniques, using the definitions applicable to tax-free-reorganizations under the Code as the point of departure:

DARRELL, THE USE OF REORGANIZATION TECHNIQUES IN CORPORATE ACQUISITIONS *

70 Harv.L.Rev. 1183–1206 (1957).

The subject to which the ensuing discussion is primarily addressed relates to the practical uses of the so-called tax-free-reorganization provisions of the Internal Revenue Code of 1954 in effecting corporate acquisitions of the stock or assets of existing corporations not already controlled by the acquiring corporation. While this topic is limited in scope, it encompasses an area of considerable practical importance. This is notably true in times which have witnessed the increasing popularity of business combinations.

It has been said on the basis of factual studies that the decision to effect a corporate acquisition is usually influenced more by business than by tax considerations, but that tax considerations usually do play an important role in the selection of the method by which an acquisition is carried out. Proposed corporate acquisitions considered desirable from a purely business standpoint have been known to succeed or to fail primarily because of tax and similar considerations. It is the purpose here to give primary attention to some of the principal factors, both tax and nontax, which bear upon the choice between taxable or

* Copyright ©, Harvard Law Review Association, 1957. Reprinted by permission. Portions of the text and most of the footnotes omitted.

tax-free acquisitions and, if the latter is chosen, upon the selection of the statutory tool most suitable for use in a given situation.

[To qualify for tax-free treatment, a combination transaction must fall within one of the definitions of "reorganization" contained in clauses (A), (B), and (C) of § 368(a) (1), which, speaking generally provide as follows:]

Type (A)—"statutory merger or consolidation." This definition refers to a merger or consolidation effected under the statutory provisions of the applicable local corporation laws.

Type (B)—"the acquisition by one corporation, in exchange solely for all or a part of its voting stock, of stock of another corporation if, immediately after the acquisition, the acquiring corporation has control of such other corporation (whether or not such acquiring corporation had control immediately before the acquisition)." "Control" for this purpose "means the ownership of stock possessing at least 80 percent of the total combined voting power of all classes of stock entitled to vote and at least 80 percent of the total number of shares of all other classes of stock of the corporation."

Type (C)—"the acquisition by one corporation, in exchange solely for all or a part of its voting stock (or in exchange solely for all or a part of the voting stock of a corporation which is in control of the acquiring corporation), of substantially all of the properties of another corporation, but in determining whether the exchange is solely for stock the assumption by the acquiring corporation of a liability of the other, or the fact that property acquired is subject to a liability, shall be disregarded." The basic requirements of this definition are therefore that the acquisition must be solely for voting stock of the acquiring corporation and that substantially all of the properties of the other corporation must be acquired.

* * *

In considering a proposed corporate acquisition, one must be familiar with the glosses the courts have put not only upon the tax statute but also upon state corporation statutes. Indeed, the lawyer should do more; he should try to anticipate what, if any, further glosses may be added in the future. In other words, as with any other legal problem, a proposed corporate acquisition must be considered in lawyer-like fashion in all its facets, with full awareness of the risks that might be encountered under laws which are not static, if the proposed transaction appears to contain elements running counter to any general legal or equitable principle.

In working out an agreement for a contemplated corporate acquisition, the parties concerned must iron out their conflicting interests through negotiation, and this frequently entails considerable give and take. When reference is made in the following discussion to the desire of any particular party, the purpose is simply to provide a convenient introduction to a particular problem and by no means to suggest that such party has sufficient leverage to accomplish the desired end.

It will be necessary on occasion to paint with a broad brush. There are qualifications and refinements to almost any proposition, and this is especially true in the field of corporate reorganizations. In the interest of a better understanding of a difficult and complicated subject, technical refinements have in some respects been sacrificed, and what is said should be considered with this in mind. Without further preliminary discussion, we may now turn to a consideration of some of the principal factors, both nontax and tax, which bear upon the desirability of accomplishing a contemplated corporate acquisition through use of the tax-free-reorganization provisions and upon the choice of reorganization techniques. The factors to be discussed are by no means all-inclusive; other will doubtlessly come to mind. Those mentioned are thought to be the ones that are most commonly present.

I. FACTORS OTHER THAN FEDERAL INCOME TAXES

Antitrust Laws.— One of the foremost problems in connection with corporate acquisitions, once the business decision is made that an acquisition is desirable, is the problem of legality under the antitrust laws. Attention to these problems has recently been accentuated by the current activities in this field of the Department of Justice, the Federal Trade Commission, and congressional committees. As shown by the report of the Attorney General's Committee, the application of the antitrust laws is in a developing state and is by no means clear. The most painstaking and exhaustive factual and economic studies are usually required to determine the propriety of contemplated acquisitions; and, in the end, rarely is the answer wholly certain.

However, we are here concerned with the solution only of related problems. In the first place, there is no longer any general distinction for antitrust purposes between asset acquisition and stock acquisition in the elimination of competition or the creation of a monopoly. But in view of the Department of Justice's recent practice of seeking to enjoin proposed business combinations before they become effective, the time that would be required to complete the prospective reorganization may be an important factor in the choice of reorganization procedure when some antitrust risk is involved but the proposed combination is not a *cause celebre* and management upon the advice of counsel is prepared to go ahead without clearing with the Department. The greater the time required to complete the reorganization, the longer the opportunity to enjoin remains open.

Another antitrust problem to be considered in selecting the type of reorganization is the question whether the acquired business is to be kept segregated from the acquiring corporation's business either as a precaution or pursuant to the terms of a court order. . . .

* * *

Stockholders' Approval and Appraisal Rights.— Upon a statutory merger or consolidation, state statutes customarily require formal approval of the agreement of merger or consolidation by the stockholders of all constituent corporations. This usually means the holding of formal stockholders' meetings for this purpose and securing the prescribed favorable vote of the stockholders entitled to vote. Proxy-solicitation expenses, the preparing and filing of proxy statements, and other acts in compliance with applicable rules of the SEC and of any stock exchange on which the stock is listed may thus become necessary. Moreover, state merger-and-consolidation statutes usually give to dissenting stockholders of any of the constituent corporations the right to demand and receive in cash the appraised value of their shares. Though the merger or consolidation may be conditioned on there being no greater than a limited percentage of such dissenters, the dual problem of stockholders' approval and appraisal rights has sometimes proven troublesome.

Upon an acquisition involving the transfer of substantially all corporate assets, whether in a taxable transaction or a type (C) reorganization, approval by a substantial majority of the transferor corporations' stockholders is normally required. Formal approval by the acquiring corporation's stockholders is generally not required unless insufficient authorized stock is available to be issued for the assets, in which event authorization of the additional stock by the acquiring corporation's stockholders may be necessary.[44] State statutes often give appraisal rights to the transferor's dissenting stockholders but usually not to stockholders of the transferee.

Upon a stock acquisition, . . . no formal stockholders' approval is usually necessary,* unless the stock to be acquired is owned by a corporation and approval of its stockholders is necessary to authorize the transfer, or unless approval by the acquiring corporation's stockholders is necessary to authorize the additional stock to be issued in the exchange. And there is normally no problem of stockholders' appraisal rights. In the case of a corporation having securities listed on the New York Stock Exchange, however, stockholders' approval will be required if directors, officers, or substantial stockholders have an interest in the acquired corporation or the stock to be issued represents an increase in outstanding shares of twenty percent or more.

Accordingly, upon consideration of these problems only, though a cash purchase might have some advantages from the standpoint of appraisal rights, as between the three types of reorganization the type

---

44. If the stock of the acquiring corporation is or is to be listed on any stock exchange, the rules of the particular exchange with respect to such matters as proxies and stockholders' meetings must of course be observed. For example, the New York Stock Exchange requires that approval of the acquiring corporation's stockholders be obtained when the new shares represent an increase in outstanding shares of 20% or more. [See note 15, page 644, infra.]

*[Ed. note] But see MBA §72A, added in 1976.

(B) reorganization would normally rank first, the type (C) second, and the type (A) third.

Stockholders' Pre-emptive Rights.— Stockholders' pre-emptive rights are not involved in an acquisition when treasury stock is issued or, normally, in connection with the issuance of new stock in a statutory merger or consolidation. At common law, stock could be issued for an adequate consideration consisting of property other than money without violating stockholders' pre-emptive rights. But some corporate charters and possibly some state laws may modify the common-law rules so that such rights would be involved in connection with the creation and issuance of stock in an asset or stock acquisition whether or not in a tax-free reorganization. This factor, however, is usually not of great significance in corporate acquisitions.

Dilution of Stockholders' Equity.— The problem of equity dilution appears in practice to be very real and to bear very distinctly not only upon the type of reorganization to be used but indeed upon whether a tax-free-reorganization plan should be adopted at all.

The management of an acquiring corporation will normally be reluctant to recommend the creation and issuance of additional common stock to acquire the stock or assets of another corporation if the effect would be to reduce the prospective earnings per share of its own common stock, and may feel the same if the effect would be to reduce the book value or equity of such stock. In such cases the acquiring corporation's management may favor a taxable acquisition or, if the tax-free-reorganization approach is desired for other reasons, may cast about for some method within that area of alleviating this problem. Under the 1954 Code any kind of stock may be issued in a type (A) reorganization; but only voting stock — though it may be of any class or classes — may be issued in an asset or stock acquisition qualifying as a type (C) or type (B) reorganization. In the past, a limited preferred stock, voting or nonvoting according to the requirements, has frequently been used in such cases. Indeed, a special type of acquisition stock is sometimes devised, such as a voting preferred stock convertible into common stock at a value in excess of the current market price for the common. When this latter device is used, the objective of the acquiring corporation is usually the ultimate disposal of the common issued upon conversion of the preferred at more than market value at the time the preferred is issued for the assets. However, under the 1954 Code the issuance in a tax-free reorganization of any stock other than common stock in exchange for common stock, particularly of a closely held corporation, has distinctly less appeal than formerly, because the new stock so issued would normally be section 306 stock. The problem of stock dilution is accordingly now more difficult to solve within the framework of a tax-free reorganization.

* * *

Continuing Minority Interests in the Acquired Corporation.—
Opinions may differ as to the advisability of having a corporate subsidiary with minority common stockholders. But ordinarily the existence of such minority interests is strongly disfavored by corporate
management because it contains the seeds of potential dispute. Accordingly, the management of an acquiring corporation usually desires
to avoid the possibility of any such continuing minority.

This, of course, would be automatically accomplished by a statutory merger or consolidation or an asset acquisition, whether taxable
or tax free, for the vote of the required percentage of stockholders in
favor of merger or consolidation or in favor of transfer of assets com-
mits all stockholders of the corporation to be acquired, leaving to dissenters their cash appraisal rights. The acquiring corporation would
then have nothing further to do with the stockholders of the acquired
corporation. This result cannot, however, be ensured by a stock acquisition, whether or not pursuant to a tax-free reorganization, unless
all the stockholders of the acquired corporation voluntarily agree to
exchange or sell their stock.[57]

**Creation of a Substantial Minority Voting Block in the Acquiring
Corporation.—** The problem of creation of too powerful a minority
voting block in the acquiring corporation is often serious in the eyes
of the acquiring corporation's stockholders or its management. This
problem arises, for example, when the stock of the corporation to be
acquired is in the hands of a family or closely related group and the
corporation to be acquired is of such size that, if its stockholders receive ordinary common stock of the acquiring corporation, their stock,
voted as a block, might be sufficiently powerful to give them effective
voting control or at least a veto power. When it is desired to issue
stock in an acquisition which qualifies as a tax-free reorganization, the
following are among the possibilities that might be considered in this
situation.

A nonvoting preferred stock or a nonvoting common stock of the
acquiring corporation could be used if permitted by the governing
state law, provided the acquisition is effected by statutory merger or
consolidation. But if such preferred stock would be section 306 stock,
it may not be acceptable. Moreover, there might be stock-exchange objections to the issuance of a nonvoting common stock if the stock is to
be listed on a national stock exchange. . . .

Ordinary voting common stock might be issued, but the stock
placed in a voting trust having acceptable voting trustees, with voting-
trust certificates being given to the stockholders of the acquired corporation. This apparently can be done in any of the three types of tax-

---

57. But even in such a case it may
sometimes be possible to eliminate the
minority by a subsequent merger or
other reorganization [particularly under the so-called "short-form" merger
statutes which provide a simplified
procedure for merger of an at least
90% owned subsidiary. See pages
679–682, 'infra.

free reorganization under discussion inasmuch as, under the existing administrative view, pure voting trusts are in effect looked through for tax purposes and the voting-stock requirements of the reorganization sections are deemed satisfied if the underlying stock is voting stock regardless of who actually exercises the vote. However, one disadvantage of a voting-trust arrangement is that under state law such a trust is ordinarily not valid for more than ten years, and the voting-block problem would therefore be only deferred and not solved.

. . .

It might be possible under state law to reduce the potential minority voting block by having the acquiring corporation create two classes of voting stock, each with one vote per share but with the shares of one class having a par value and relative worth many times greater per share than the shares of the other class. Use of the former as the acquisition stock would give the shareholders of the acquired corporation only a fraction of the voting power they would have if there were only one class of voting stock, except when a class vote is required. Perhaps the same result might be accomplished in some states by giving each class the same par or stated value per share, with one class receiving a greater vote per share than the other. This would seem acceptable from a tax-free-reorganization standpoint, since both classes would appear to be voting stock. But if either class had preferential rights as to dividends or assets it probably would be treated as "other than common stock" for purposes of section 306, regardless of what it might be called under state corporation law. Obstacles to having two classes of common stock are more likely to be encountered in connection with state corporate law, corporate-policy considerations, and rules of regulatory bodies or security exchanges.

Nonassignable or Burdensome Contracts and Franchises, Labor Unions, Deferred-Compensation Plans, Etc.—Sometimes the corporation that is to be acquired possesses valuable franchises, leases, or contracts which are not assignable without consent. In such cases a statutory merger or consolidation or, if consent to assignment would even then be required, a stock acquisition has an advantage over an asset acquisition in that the need to obtain consent to assignment is eliminated. Moreover, if assets are to be acquired, the task of attending to all the details involved in the transfer, such as the preparation and execution of deeds, would be simplified if the acquisition were by a statutory merger or consolidation. Again, state bulk-sales laws either would be of no concern or would not apply to an acquisition by statutory merger or consolidation, since the surviving or successor corporation automatically becomes responsible for all liabilities and a statutory merger or consolidation is not generally regarded as involving a sale. But a transfer in exchange for stock, in a type (C) reorganization or otherwise, probably does fall within the "sale" language of the bulk-sales statutes.

On the other hand, existing loan indentures or other agreements may contain restrictions upon a merger or consolidation or transfer of assets. If one or more mortgages are involved, after-acquired-property clauses therein might cause difficulty if a statutory merger or consolidation or asset acquisition were attempted. Undesirable leases or contracts including burdensome patent-license agreements may constitute an obstacle to a statutory merger or consolidation or a stock acquisition. Labor-union problems—the consequences, for example, of bringing a union or a different union into the picture — may present an obstacle to a statutory merger or consolidation or an asset acquisition but not to a stock acquisition. Problems of reconciling and meshing deferred-compensation plans of the corporations (including pension, profit-sharing, and stock-option plans as well as individual employment contracts and bonus policies) may present similar obstacles. Finally, the corporate charter of the corporation to be acquired may itself be important to preserve, as in the case of a banking corporation; or the preservation of the organization and its customers or even of an existing stock-exchange listing may make it desirable that the corporation to be acquired be technically the acquiring or surviving corporation or that its stock be acquired.

State and Local Taxation.— Not infrequently an asset acquisition, unlike a stock acquisition, will give rise not only to state or local excise taxes in connection with the transaction but will also involve some duplication of state or local franchise, business, and property taxes, including sales, use, transfer, or license taxes, and fees applicable to real estate, personal property, motor vehicles, and the like. Sometimes some of these extra taxes can be avoided entirely when the transfer is effected by operation of law through statutory merger or consolidation, and some of the duplication may be eliminated by timing the transfer so that it will occur at the end of the state fiscal or corporate tax year. The provisions of federal and state unemployment-insurance-tax laws relating to the period of employment required for employee coverage may, in combination with the federal credit provisions, involve extra taxes unless the acquisition is carefully timed so as to occur either at the end of the year or, if during the year, after the number of months of employment required for employee coverage has elapsed.

Known, Unknown, and Contingent Liabilities.— Freedom from responsibility for liabilities of the transferor or acquired corporation is frequently an important consideration in the eyes of the management of an acquiring corporation. When this is so, a simple clean-cut purchase of the desired property, leaving the transferor corporation with all responsibility for its own liabilities, has strong appeal. If, on the other hand, the acquisition is solely or largely for stock in a tax-free reorganization, problems may arise, depending upon the particular facts, as to the extent to which the acquiring corporation can escape from responsibility for the transferor or acquired corporation's actual and potential liabilities.

Upon a statutory merger or consolidation, the surviving corporation becomes liable for all obligations of the constituent corporations, whether or not known and disclosed and even though purely contingent at the time of merger or consolidation.* Some protection against contingent and unknown liabilities of a constituent corporation may nevertheless be obtained by providing in the agreement of merger or consolidation for withholding for a specified period of time part of the stock to be issued to the constituent corporation's stockholders, the stock so withheld to be sold at market or to be cancelled at a prescribed value to offset any such liabilities that arise within the specified period. If desired, certificates of contingent interest may be issued to represent the interests of the constituent corporation's stockholders in the stock so withheld. This procedure, however, should be approached with caution and with an awareness of the uncertainties of the tax consequences. . . .

A stock acquisition, whether or not in a type (B) reorganization, also involves the problem of unknown, undisclosed, and contingent liabilities, though the acquiring corporation in that case does not itself become responsible for them. Here, again, the acquiring corporation may be able to protect itself against over-payment for the stock acquired by insisting upon a suitable guarantee or escrow arrangement pending determination of such liabilities.

An asset acquisition, whether in a taxable purchase or in a type (C) reorganization, though usually accompanied by an express assumption of at least some of the transferor corporation's liabilities, has the distinct advantage over the other two procedures of enabling the acquiring corporation to obtain substantially all the assets of the other corporation without becoming responsible for any liabilities not specifically assumed by it under the agreement. But there would nevertheless remain in the case of a type (C) reorganization the problem of possible transferee liability.

Transferee Liability.— When management of the acquiring corporation is fearful of unknown contingent liabilities and cannot get or is not prepared to rely solely on the warranties of the principal stockholders of the corporation to be acquired, the question of potential transferee liability may become important. Though this sub-

* [Ed. note] E. g., MBA §76(e). These statutes usually go on to provide, as §76(e) does, that "neither the rights of creditors nor any liens . . . shall be impaired" by the merger. It seems generally to be assumed that these statutes require a showing of something akin to an "impairment of contract". Thus a creditor cannot block a proposed combination merely because "the quick asset condition of the consolidated company will, in relation to its liabilities, render it less desirable as a debtor from the viewpoint of current financial soundness than the constituent debtor". Cole v. National Cash Credit Ass'n, 18 Del.Ch. 47, 156 A. 183 (Ch.1931).

ject may be thought to relate primarily to federal income-tax problems, it is included here because of its potentially broader application.

In a type (A) reorganization by statutory merger or consolidation, the surviving corporation automatically, as a matter of corporate law, becomes responsible for all of the acquired corporation's liabilities, including its tax liabilities, whether it expressly assumes these liabilities or not. In a type (B) stock-for-stock reorganization there is no problem of transferee liability since the exchange of stock does not involve a transfer of the acquired corporation's assets.* If the acquired corporation is subsequently liquidated and the assets are distributed to the acquiring corporation as a stockholder, the acquiring corporation will be liable as a transferee under the same circumstances as any other stockholder.

In a type (C) reorganization the problem of transferee liability arises when there is no express assumption of liabilities by the acquiring corporation.[65] When an acquiring corporation purchases substantially all the assets of another corporation for cash in an arm's length transaction without assuming the latter's tax liabilities, it does not ordinarily become subject to transferee liability for such taxes. When, instead of paying cash, the acquiring corporation takes over such assets in exchange solely for stock, its freedom from liability as a transferee is uncertain. If the transaction is regarded as a *de facto* merger, if the acquiring corporation is merely a continuance of the debtor corporation, or if an intention to defraud can be found, there will probably be transferee liability on the part of the acquiring corporation. On the other hand, under the corporation law of some states the acquiring corporation does not become liable for the debts of the transferor corporation merely because the consideration to the transferor corporation is the stock of the receiving corporation. Should the acquiring corporation issue its stock directly to the transferor's stockholders, thus by-passing the transferor corporation as permitted in a type (C) reorganization, the risk of transferee liability on the part of the acquiring corporation becomes greater since, by deliberately by-passing the transferor, the transferee helped make it impossible for the transferor to pay.

On the question of transferee liability of the stockholders of the transferor corporation, the decisions indicate that, whether the transferor corporation actually receives the acquiring corporation's stock for its assets and then distributes it among its stockholders or whether upon acquisition of the assets the acquiring corporation's stock is issued by it directly to the transferor corporation's stockholders, the stockholders of the transferor corporation are liable

---

* [Ed. note] See Architectural Building Products, Inc. v. Cupples Products Corp., 221 F.Supp. 154 (E.D.Wis.1963).

65. Even when there is an express assumption of liabilities, problems of interpretation may arise. . . .

as between themselves and the Government as transferees for any unpaid income taxes of the transferor corporation even though the transferee corporation expressly assumed such liabilities. It has recently been held, however, that the transferor corporation's former stockholders are not so liable when the acquiring corporation acquired the stock of the transferor corporation in exchange for stock of the acquiring corporation and thereafter completely liquidated the transferor corporation. This decision seems sound if the distinction intended to be drawn is between a stock acquisition in a type (B) reorganization followed by complete liquidation of the acquired corporation and an asset acquisition in a type (C) reorganization followed by complete liquidation of the transferor corporation.

* * *

B. CHOICE OF COMBINATION TECHNIQUE

As Mr. Darrell indicates in his article, the differences in corporate mechanics among the various combination techniques may provide the basis for selection of one method over another. Consider the right of appraisal for dissenting shareholders: while practically every corporation statute affords this remedy to the stockholders of both corporations in connection with a statutory merger, a number of statutes do not provide appraisal in connection with an assets acquisition, and no statute requires it when a voluntary exchange of stock technique is employed. Obviously, a management anxious to avoid appraisal proceedings will veer away from the merger technique. However, the fact that the ultimate objective of the other two combination methods is the same as in a merger has led to contentions that although a particular transaction took the form of an asset or stock acquisition, it was really in substance a merger and hence subject to the rules governing such transactions. This is known as the "de facto merger" doctrine.

In his article on de facto mergers in 49 Va. L. Rev. 1261 (1963), Professor Folk comments as follows on the role of appraisal rights:

First, appraisal rights may severely impair the ready cash of the corporation, especially when it is seeking to step up business performance through an amalgamation. Indeed, if the dissenters own a large number of shares, they may block the transaction altogether,[74] although historically the remedy was designed to allow

---

74. In Farris v. Glen Alden Corp., 393 Pa. 427, 431 n. 5, 143 A.2d 25, 28 n. 5 (1958), it was conceded that if appraisal rights had to be met, "the re- sultant drain of cash would prevent Glen Alden from carrying out the agreement." . . .

corporate combinations to be carried out. Second, the recognition of appraisal rights results in somewhat arbitrarily carving out a group of transactions—usually mergers—for special treatment, since appraisal rights do not apply in other situations where the shareholder is realistically "hurt" or his investment changed just as much. Apart from the infinite variety of directors' business decisions which can affect a shareholder's interest adversely, there are a number of "fundamental corporate changes" which generate no appraisal right, such as corporate purchases of assets for stock, sales of stock for cash which in turn is used to purchase assets, amendments of the articles of incorporation, dissolution with distributions in kind, and sales of controlling blocks of shares. If the theory of the appraisal remedy is to aid the injured shareholder, appraisal rights should be available in many instances other than mergers, particularly if a shareholder injury is defined as a change in the nature of his investment or in his relationship to the corporation and the other shareholders.

RATH v. RATH PACKING CO.*

Supreme Court of Iowa, 1965.
257 Iowa 1277, 136 N.W.2d 410.

GARFIELD, CHIEF JUSTICE. The question presented is whether an Iowa corporation may carry out an agreement with another corporation, designated "Plan and Agreement of Reorganization," which amounts to a merger in fact of the two without approval of holders of two thirds of its outstanding shares, as provided by [the Iowa statute]. The question is one of first impression in Iowa. We must disagree with the trial court's holding this may be done.

Plaintiffs, minority shareholders of Rath, brought this action in equity to enjoin carrying out the agreement on the ground, so far as necessary to consider, it provides for a merger in fact with Needham Packing Co., which requires approval of two thirds of the holders of outstanding Rath shares and that was not obtained. The trial court adjudicated law points under rule 105, Rules of Civil Procedure, in favor of defendants Rath and its officers, and entered judgment of dismissal on the pleadings. It held approval of the plan by holders of a majority of Rath shares was sufficient. Plaintiffs appeal.

Plaintiffs own more than 6000 shares of Rath Packing Co., an Iowa corporation with its principal plant in Waterloo, Iowa, existing under Code 1962, chapter 496A, I.C.A. (Iowa Business Corporation Act). Rath has 993,185 shares outstanding held by about 4000 owners. It is engaged in meat packing and processing, mostly pork and allied products. Its yearly sales for the last five years were from

* Portions of the opinion omitted.

about $267,000,000 to $296,000,000. Its balance sheet as of January 2, 1965, showed assets of about $56,500,000, current liabilities of about $20,600,000, and long-term debt of about $7,000,000.

Needham Packing Co. is a corporation organized in 1960 under Delaware law with its principal plant in Sioux City, Iowa. Its total shares outstanding, including debentures and warrants convertible into stock, are 787,907, held by about 1000 owners. Both Rath and Needham stock is traded on the American Stock Exchange. Needham is also engaged in meat packing, mostly beef. Its annual sales were from about $80,000,000 to $103,000,000. Its balance sheet as of December 26, 1964, showed assets of $10,300,000, current liabilities of $2,262,000, and long-term debt of $3,100,000.

Pursuant to authority of Rath's board prior to April 2, 1965, it entered into the questioned agreement with Needham, designated "Plan and Agreement of Reorganization," under which Rath agreed to: (1) amend its articles to double the number of shares of its common stock, create a new class of preferred shares and change its name to Rath-Needham Corporation; (2) issue to Needham 5.5 shares of Rath common and two shares of its 80-cent preferred stock for each five shares of Needham stock in exchange for all Needham's assets, properties, business, name and good will, except a fund not exceeding $175,000 to pay expenses in carrying out the agreement and effecting Needham's dissolution and distribution of the new Rath-Needham stock to its shareholders, any balance remaining after 120 days to be paid over to Rath; (3) assume all Needham's debts and liabilities; and (4) elect two Needham officers and directors to its board.

Under the plan Needham agreed to: (1) transfer all its assets to Rath; (2) cease using its name; (3) distribute the new Rath-Needham shares to its stockholders, liquidate and dissolve; and (4) turn over to Rath its corporate and business records.

If the plan were carried out, assuming the new preferred shares were converted into common, the thousand Needham shareholders would have about 54 per cent of the outstanding common shares of Rath-Needham and the four thousand Rath shareholders would have about 46 per cent.

Under the plan the book value of each share of Rath common stock, as of January 2, 1965, would be reduced from $27.99 to $15.93, a reduction of about 44 per cent. Each share of Needham common would be increased in book value, as of December 26, 1964, from $6.61 to $23.90, assuming conversion of the new Rath-Needham preferred.

In the event of liquidation of Rath-Needham, Needham shareholders would be preferred to Rath's under the plan, by having a prior claim to the assets of Rath-Needham to an amount slightly in excess of the book value of all Needham shares. Needham shareholders are also preferred over Rath's under the plan in distribution of income by the right of the former to receive preferred dividends of 80 cents a share—about five per cent of Needham's book value. Shortly prior to the time terms of the plan were made public Rath and Needham shares sold on the American Exchange for about the same price. Almost immediately thereafter the price of Needham shares increased and Rath's decreased so the former sold for 50 per cent more than the latter.

At a meeting of Rath shareholders on April 26, 1965, 60.1 per cent of its outstanding shares, 77 per cent of those voted, were voted in favor of these two proposals: (1) to amend the articles to authorize a class of 80 c preferred stock and increase the authorized common from 1,500,000 shares ($10 par) to 3,000,000 shares (no par); and (2) upon acquisition by Rath of the assets, properties, business and good will of Needham to change Rath's name to Rath-Needham Corporation and elect as its directors Lloyd and James Needham. Holders of 177,000 shares voted against these proposals and 218,000 shares were not voted. The plan was not approved by the shareholders except as above stated.

Rath officers vigorously solicited proxies for the meeting by personal travel, telephone and through a professional proxy soliciting agency. This action was commenced five days prior to the meeting and four days thereafter a supplement and amendment to the petition were filed.

I. [The court first summarized the merger provisions of the Iowa corporation law (chapter 496A of the Iowa Code) which are patterned after MBA §§ 65–70, 73 and 74.]

The above sections are those on which plaintiffs rely. They contend these statutes specifically provide for effecting a merger and the same result cannot legally be attained at least without approval of the holders of two thirds of the shares and according to dissenters "appraisal rights"—i. e., the right to receive the fair value of their stock by compliance with the specified procedure.

Defendants contend and the trial court held compliance with the above sections was not required and defendants could legally proceed under other sections of chapter 496A which merely authorize amendments to articles of incorporation and issuance of stock. [The court then summarized the Iowa provisions dealing with amendment of the certificate, patterned after MBA §§ 53 and 54 (except that only a majority vote of the stock entitled to vote is required), and the provisions dealing with the issuance of stock, patterned after MBA §§ 17 and 18.]

II. The principal point of law defendants asked to have adjudicated . . . is that the provisions of chapter 496A last referred to are legally independent of, and of equal dignity with, those relating to mergers and the validity of the action taken by defendants is not dependent upon compliance with the merger sections under which the same result might be attained. The trial court accepted this view.

It is clear the view just expressed emanates from the opinion in Hariton v. Arco Electronics, Inc., Del., 188 A.2d 123, the only precedent called to our attention which sustains the decision appealed from. Virtually the only basis for the conclusion Hariton reaches is the statement of the law point these defendants raised. The opinion contains little discussion and cites no authority that supports the decision.

We can agree all provisions of our chapter 496A are of equal dignity. But we cannot agree any provisions of the act are legally independent of others if this means that in arriving at the correct interpretation thereof and the legislative intent expressed therein we are not to consider the entire act and, so far as possible, construe its various provisions in the light of their relation to the whole act. . .

We may also observe that the trial court "concluded the 'safeguards' written into the codes of most states, including Iowa and Delaware, with respect to rights of dissenting shareholders in connection with mergers are based on outmoded concepts of economic realities, particularly in the case of an enterprise such as Rath which is regularly traded on the American Exchange and has a diversified stock ownership with over 4000 shareholders. The court cites especially in this regard articles of Professor Manning, 72 Yale Law Journal 223, and Professor Folk, 49 Virginia Law Review 1261."

If the soundness of this view were admitted, the statutory safeguards should of course be removed by legislative, not judicial action. Our 1959 legislature evidently had a purpose in enacting what we may call the merger sections of chapter 496A as well as those relating to amending articles and issuing stock. We have frequently pointed out it is not the province of courts to pass upon the policy, wisdom or advisability of a statute. . . .

III.   The "Plan and Agreement of Reorganization" clearly provides for what amounts to a merger of Rath and Needham under any definition of merger we know.

[The court then quoted a number of definitions of merger in the authorities, including the following.] " . . . a merger signifies the absorption of one corporation by another, which retains its name and corporate identity with the added capital, franchises and powers of a merged corporation." 15 Fletcher Cyc. Corporations, 1961 Revised Volume, section 7041, page 6. . . .

If, as we hold, this agreement provides for what amounts to a merger of Rath and Needham, calling it a Plan and Agreement of Reorganization does not change its essential character. . . .

IV.   The power of a corporation to merge must be derived from the law of the state which created it. There must be some plain enactment authorizing the merger, for legislative authority is just as essential to a merger as to creation of the corporation in the first instance. . . . Legislative authority for a merger will not be implied but must be clearly, distinctly and expressly conferred. . . .

* * *

The merger sections of chapter 496A clearly and expressly confer the necessary power to merge. . . . Nothing in the sections dealing with amending articles and issuing stock purports to authorize a merger. They make no reference to merger. The most that may fairly be claimed is that they impliedly confer the required power to merge. But this is insufficient.

V. In seeking the scope and effect of the two sets of sections relied upon at least one fundamental rule of statutory construction is applicable. As stated, the merger sections specifically provide for a particular thing—mergers. The sections authorizing amendment of articles and issuance of stock apply to all amendments and stock issues, whether or not amending the articles or issuing stock is part of a merger, as they may or may not be. As applied to mergers, the sections on which plaintiffs rely are specific provisions, those on which defendants rely are not. . . .

"It is an old and familiar principle . . . that where there is in the same statute a specific provision, and also a general one which in its most comprehensive sense would include matters embraced in the former, the particular provision must control, and the general provision must be taken to effect only such cases within its general language as are not within the provisions of the particular provision. . . ."

* * *

A closely related rule, many times applied by us, is that where a general statute, if standing alone, would include the same matter as a special statute and thus conflict with it, the latter will prevail and the former must give way. The special provision will be considered an exception to or qualification of the general one. . . .

It is apparent that if the sections pertaining to amending articles and issuing stock are construed to authorize a merger by a majority vote of shareholders they conflict with the sections specifically dealing with the one matter of mergers which require a two-thirds vote of shareholders. The two sets of sections may be harmonized by holding, as we do, that the merger sections govern the matter of merger and must be regarded as an exception to the sections dealing with amending articles and issuing stock, which may or may not be involved in a merger.

The construction we give these sections is in accord with the cardinal rule that, if reasonably possible, effect will be given to every part of a statute. . . .

The merger sections make it clear the legislature intended to require a two-thirds vote of shareholders and accord so-called appraisal rights to dissenters in case of a merger. It is unreasonable to ascribe to the same legislature an intent to provide in the same act a method of evading the required two-thirds vote and the grant of such appraisal rights. The practical effect of the decision appealed from is to render the requirements of a two-thirds vote and appraisal rights meaningless in virtually all mergers. It is scarcely an exaggeration to say the decision amounts to judicial repeal of the merger sections in most instances of merger.

It is obvious, as defendants' counsel frankly stated in oral argument, that corporate management would naturally choose a method which requires only majority approval of shareholders and does not grant dissenters the right to be paid the fair value of their stock. The legislature could hardly have intended to vest in corporate management the option to comply with the requirements just referred to or to proceed without such compliance, a choice that would invariably be exercised in favor of the easier method. . . .

VI. 15 Fletcher, Cyc. Corporations, 1961 Revised Volume section 7165.5, page 307, contains this: "However, where a particular corporate combination is in legal effect a merger or a consolidation, even though the transaction may be otherwise labeled by the parties, the courts treat the transaction as a de facto merger or consolidation so as to confer upon dissenting stockholders the right to receive cash payment for their shares." Decisions from several jurisdictions are cited in support. Only Heilbrunn v. Sun Chemical Corp., 37 Del.Ch. 552, 146 A.2d 757, Affd. 38 Del.Ch. 321, 150 A.2d 755, 758, is cited as contra.

Basis of the Heilbrunn decision is the court's declared failure to see how any injury was inflicted on shareholders of a corporation that purchased the assets of another. No opinion was expressed as to whether shareholders of the selling corporation could obtain equitable relief. The Delaware court first decided that question in Hariton v. Arco Electronics, supra, Del., 188 A.2d 123.

We think the precedents which support the statement quoted from Fletcher are sound. Aside from Applestein v. United Board and Carton Corp., supra, 60 N.J.Super. 333, 159 A.2d 146, Affd. 33 N.J. 72, 161 A.2d 474, the case most frequently cited in support of such view is Farris v. Glen Alden Corp., 393 Pa. 427, 143 A.2d 25, 28. . . . .

VII. The trial court thought that while no Iowa case is directly in point, the policy of Iowa law is in accord with its decision, [citing several Iowa cases]. We find no conflict between the conclusion we reach and these precedents. Each of them may be distinguished on the ground the transaction there involved did not amount to a merger nor obligate any corporation to dissolve. This is also true of the three cases from other jurisdictions and Orzeck v. Englehart, Del., 195 A.2d 375, cited by defendants.

* * *

IX. We hold entry of judgment of dismissal on the pleadings was error, that defendants should be enjoined from carrying out the "Plan and Agreement of Reorganization" until such time, if ever, as it is approved by the holders of at least two thirds of the outstanding shares of Rath and in the event of such approval plaintiffs, if they dissent to such plan and follow the [appropriate procedure], shall be entitled to be paid the fair value of their shares in Rath. For decree in harmony with this opinion the cause is—Reversed and remanded.

NOTE

Since Mr. Darrell wrote, there have been some important legislative developments in the combination area, which are thoughtfully analyzed in the following excellent review of the current status of shareholder rights in acquisition transactions:

SCHULMAN AND SCHENK, SHAREHOLDERS' VOTING AND APPRAISAL RIGHTS IN CORPORATE ACQUISITION TRANSACTIONS*

38 Bus. Law. 1529 (1983).

INTRODUCTION

This article examines the availability of shareholder rights in a wide variety of transactions in which one corporation acquires another. It focuses on two significant shareholder rights—the right to vote upon the transaction and the right to dissent to it in order to obtain payment for shares from the corporation. This latter right commonly is referred to as appraisal, although some statutes use the term "dissenters' rights." The terms will be used interchangeably here. The subject is interesting and complex because corporate statutes frequently appear to vary these rights among transactions that have substantially equivalent effects upon shareholders. Unwilling to concede that form is conclusive, shareholders may claim that they are entitled to greater rights than those apparently available under the chosen acquisition format. This article considers when, if ever, such claims have merit.

STATUTORY PATTERNS

Essentially, acquisitions fall into three general categories—merger, purchase of assets, and purchase of shares. There are variations on these three basic techniques and, at times, the transactions become quite complex. This section describes a variety of acquisition transactions and tracks the statutory treatment of shareholder rights in each. The purpose is to highlight those situations in

---

*Reprinted by permission. Most of the footnotes omitted.

which the structure of the acquisition—its form—plays a critical role in the availability of shareholder rights.

The effect of form on shareholder rights is illustrated by provisions in the Model Business Corporation Act (Model Act). (Although the American Bar Association's Committee on Corporate Laws has tentatively adopted a revised Model Act, none of the proposed changes in the relevant acquisition provisions affect the shareholder rights problems we consider.) In a merger, a statutory procedure by which the merged corporation disappears and all of its assets and liabilities pass by operation of law to the surviving party, the general rule is simple. Shareholders of both merger constituents obtain voting and dissenters' rights. However, if the survivor's shareholders' proportionate investment interest is not substantially diluted in the merger—i.e., the survivor does not issue in the merger more than twenty percent of its previously outstanding shares—these shareholders may be denied voting and dissenters' rights. In these small-scale mergers, the drafters of the Model Act concluded that the acquiring corporation should be able to conduct the transaction without approval by its shareholders and certainly without giving them the right to opt out of the venture by exercising the right to dissent.[7]

At this point, one might infer that the policy of the Model Act is to afford rights to the shareholders of parties constituent to an acquisition, except when the shareholders do not face a significant alteration of investment. However, the logical pattern in the merger provisions frequently appears to yield to pure formalism. To simplify the discussion, we will separate the rights of an acquiror's shareholders from those of an acquired's shareholders, considering the former first.

Merger is not the only form of acquisition that may have a significant effect upon an acquiror's shareholders. For example, Corporation A may acquire the net assets of Corporation T in exchange for thirty percent of its previously outstanding shares. A may also acquire T, through a voluntary share exchange, by offering to purchase all the T shares from T's shareholders in exchange for the same thirty percent of A shares. In both cases, the acquisition produces a significant dilution in the proportionate equity interest of the shareholders holding shares of A before the acquisition. Had A paid this same consideration as a merger survivor, the Model Act would provide rights for its shareholders. Yet in either of the purchase transactions described above, A's shareholders apparently are denied rights. The Model Act is stonily silent regarding voting or appraisal rights for the shareholders of a corporation conducting an asset purchase or voluntary share exchange. Thus, as far as acquiror shareholders' rights are concerned, the statute appears to invite management to avoid rights by adopting a nonmerger form of acquisition.

7. Conard, *Amendments of Model Business Corporation Act Affecting Dissenters' Rights (Sections 73, 74, 80 and 81)*, 33 Bus. Law. 2587, 2595 (1978).

A second exception to the grant of shareholder rights in mergers occurs in a short-form merger, that is, one between a parent and a 90% or more owned subsidiary. Model Business Corp. Act §§ 75, 80(a)(1), (c) (1982); . . .. Because the parent's shareholders are not significantly affected by the merger, they are denied both voting and dissenters' rights. The minority shareholders, if any, of the subsidiary have dissenters' rights, but are denied voting rights since they obviously could not block the merger.

Even if Corporation A prefers to conduct the acquisition as a merger and issues thirty percent of its shares as the merger consideration, A's management may be able to circumscribe rights for its shareholders. This rights-limiting technique is the triangular or three-party merger. In this type of acquisition, a corporation intending to acquire another by merger does so not directly by merging the target into itself (a two-party merger), but indirectly through a subsidiary.

Until 1969 the Model Act may not have authorized the triangular merger as an acquisition technique. Prior to that time, like most corporate statutes, the Act apparently authorized as merger consideration only shares, securities, or obligations of the surviving party, thereby sanctioning only two-party mergers in which the survivor supplied such consideration. In 1969, the Model Act adopted broadened merger consideration provisions.[11] Beginning at about that time, similar changes in the merger consideration provisions were enacted in the great majority of jurisdictions. These amended provisions not only authorize the use of cash or other property as merger consideration, but also explicitly sanction the use of shares or securities of *any* corporation, thus permitting three-party mergers in which a subsidiary uses its parent's shares as the merger consideration. In these transactions, the subsidiary is funded with its parent's shares (P shares) and merges with the target in either a forward or reverse triangular merger. In a forward triangle the target merges into the subsidiary and the target shares are converted into the P shares held by the subsidiary. When the transaction is consummated, the subsidiary, which remains wholly owned by the parent, now possesses the assets and is responsible for the liabilities of the target. A reverse triangle is used when business or tax considerations demand that the target remain in existence. The transaction is more complex than the forward triangle. Basically, the subsidiary merges into the target and the plan of merger requires that the target's shareholders convert their shares into the P shares held by the subsidiary. The parent's share ownership in the subsidiary is converted into newly issued shares of the target. After completion of the transaction, the target is the nominal survivor to the merger with its assets and liabilities intact, but realistically it has been acquired by the parent, which holds all of the target's outstanding shares.

In either type of triangle, the parent has conducted an acquisition by merger, but has done so through a surrogate corporation without becoming a party to the merger. In form, the parent is a shareholder of a merger constituent—its subsidiary corporation. As such, the parent seems entitled to whatever shareholder rights are available in the merger, and its board will exercise such rights. Nothing in the Model Act specifically extends rights to the parent's shareholders.

The Model Act also does not provide rights for acquiror shareholders in the newest form of acquisition, the compulsory share exchange. This procedure, adopted in the Model Act in 1976, but not yet in widespread use, is intended as a simplified substitute for the reverse triangular merger. Under this form of acquisition, all shareholders (or shareholders of a particular class of shares) of the acquired company must transfer their shares to the acquiring corporation for the consideration set forth in the plan of exchange. Thus, assuming that the

11. Model Business Corp. Act. § 71(c) (1982);   .   .   .

exchange involves all classes of target shares, the target remains alive as a wholly owned subsidiary of the acquiror—precisely the result obtained by a reverse triangular merger. Although the Act requires approval of the plan by the boards of both corporations and grants voting and dissenters' rights to the shareholders of the target, it provides no rights for the acquiror's shareholders. This omission caps off the pattern in the Act whereby the rights granted to shareholders of merger survivors apparently may be avoided by selecting any form of acquisition other than a two-party merger. There is nothing extraordinary in this aspect of the Model Act. Most of the corporate acts display this pattern of explicitly granting rights to shareholders of an acquiror only when they are shareholders of a merger survivor.[15]

15. There are a few significant exceptions. California, for example, triggers voting and appraisal rights for shareholders of an acquiror in a merger or acquisition of substantially all the assets or the majority of shares of another corporation, whether the transaction is conducted directly or in triangular form. To assure that rights are not granted in acquisitions that do not significantly affect the acquiror's shareholders' interest in the corporation, they are withheld if, after the reorganization, the acquiror's shareholders will own more than 5/6 of the acquiror's total voting power. Cal. Corp. Code §§ 181, 1200-01, 1300 (West 1977 & Supp. 1982).

The New Jersey act affords rights to the shareholders of merger survivors when more than 20% of previously outstanding common shares are issued. N.J. Stat. Ann. §§ 14A:10-3, 14A:11-1 (West Supp. 1982–83). Further, if the transaction involves the issuance of more than 40% of previously outstanding common shares,

> shareholders of the corporation which proposes to acquire, directly or through a subsidiary, in exchange for its shares, obligations or other securities, some or all of the outstanding shares of another corporation, or some or all of the assets of a corporation, a business trust, a business proprietorship or a business partnership, shall have the same rights, if any, as they would if they were shareholders of a surviving corporation in a merger.

Id. § 14A:10-12. The section is clearly intended to award rights to the shareholders of acquirors other than merger survivors in acquisitions of anything from anyone in any type of transaction so long as the requisite consideration is issued.

Another significant exception to the Model Act pattern is found not in a corporate act, but in the requirements of the New York Stock Exchange, which provide:

> Stockholder approval is a prerequisite to listing securities to be issued for or in connection with the following: .   .   .
>
> 3. The acquisition, direct or indirect, of a business, a company, tangible or intangible assets or property or securities representing any such interests: .   .   .
>
> > (b) Where the present or potential issuance of common stock or securities convertible into common stock could result in an increase in outstanding common shares approximately 20%; or
> >
> > (c) Where the present or potential issuance of common stock and any other consideration has a combined fair value approximating 20% of the market value of the outstanding common shares.

New York Stock Exchange, Company Manual A-283, -284 (Jan. 25, 1978) (footnotes omitted). The circumstances in which the Exchange requires shareholder approval in acquisitions are about as broad as possible. As seen from the above excerpt, so long as the requisite amount of shares is issued, rights are triggered in any type of "direct or indirect" acquisition, presumably including triangular acquisitions conducted through subsidiaries. *See also* 2 Am. Stock Ex. Guide (CCH) ¶ 10,118–19 (June 1982). However, there is a peculiarity in the Exchange's formulation. Assuming a specified quorum exists, the Exchange's shareholder approval requirement is based not on a majority of outstanding shares but on a majority of votes cast. New York Stock Exchange, *supra*, at A-284. The New Jersey rules on shareholder approval also are based on votes cast. *See* N.J. Stat. Ann. § 14A:10-3(2) (West Supp. 1982–83). In contrast, under most corporate statutes, the standard for shareholder approval of acquisitions is based on a percentage of outstanding shares entitled to vote. *See, e.g.,* Cal. Corp. Code §§ 152, 1201(a) (West 1977 & Supp. 1982).

The Model Act is generally less form-oriented in its treatment of shareholders of an acquired corporation. If the target is a merger constituent, its shareholders obtain voting and dissenters' rights. When a corporation transfers all or substantially all of its assets outside the regular course of business, its shareholders are granted voting rights and, with some exceptions, dissenters' rights. If a corporation is acquired by the purchase of its shares in either a compulsory or voluntary share exchange, its shareholders still receive a fair measure of protection. In a compulsory share exchange, target shareholders receive both the right to vote and to dissent. In a voluntary share exchange the acquired corporation is not itself a party to the transaction. The acquiror offers to purchase the target's shares from its shareholders, each of whom decides whether he wishes to sell. There are no voting or dissenters' rights since no corporate action by the acquired corporation occurs and its shareholders are not compelled to exchange their shares. Shareholder protection rests on the individual right to sell or retain shares.

Although the above summary suggests that the Model Act's treatment of shareholders of an acquired corporation follows a sensible, nonformalistic pattern, at times the Act apparently places a premium on form in awarding rights to such shareholders. For example, the seller's shareholders do not obtain dissenters' rights when their corporation sells its assets for cash on terms requiring the distribution of the sale proceeds within one year.[20] Thus, shareholders cashed out as part of an asset sale cannot dissent and obtain payment for shares, although shareholders of a target acquired in a merger or compulsory share exchange retain dissenters' rights even if cash is the acquisition consideration. A comparable pattern is found in many jurisdictions. Even more dramatically, in Delaware and a few other states, while shareholders of a corporation acquired in a merger generally can exercise appraisal rights, the statute never grants appraisal to the shareholders of an asset seller.[23]

Before concluding this discussion of the rights of shareholders of an acquired corporation, we will note two cases where the Model Act, consistent with the vast majority of corporate statutes, seemingly denies any rights to those who in practical effect are shareholders of an acquired corporation. The first involves a venture structured in a parent-subsidiary configuration, with all or substantially all of the operating assets held by the subsidiary. If the subsidiary is acquired by merger or purchase of its assets, the transaction would not appear to generate

20. *Id.* § 80(a)(2) (1982). Unlike the current Model Act's language providing an exception to dissenters' rights when a sale of assets is "for cash on terms requiring that . . . the net proceeds . . . be distributed," the exception in the tentatively adopted revision of the Act refers to sales "pursuant to a plan" to distribute the net proceeds. *Id.* § 13.02(a)(3) (Exposure Draft 1983).

The failure of the Model Act to grant dissenters' rights in these cash sale transactions is by no means of academic interest only. Of course, since shareholders receive cash they do not need the remedy to avoid being locked into an investment that is drastically altered by a corporate fusion. Yet, sales for cash may be improvident or unfair and the right of dissent offers the opportunity for shareholders to obtain a higher price than that paid in the acquisition. *See* Buxbaum, *The Dissenter's Appraisal Remedy*, 23 U.C.L.A. L. Rev. 1229, 1249–51 (1976).

23. In Delaware, the appraisal right in mergers may be denied in certain instances in which shareholders hold actively traded shares. *See* Del. Code Ann. tit. 8, § 262(b)(1), (2) (Supp. 1982). However, under the statute, a corporation may provide in its certificate of incorporation that shareholders of merger constituents obtain appraisal in merger even if the right would otherwise be denied. This authority was expanded in 1981 to enable a corporation, in its certificate of incorporation, to grant its shareholders the appraisal right in other transactions, including sales of all or substantially all assets. *Id.* § 262(c).

rights for the parent's shareholders. As in the case of a triangular merger, the parent is not formally a party to the transaction but only the shareholder of a party. Thus, the parent's shareholders apparently receive no say in the acquisition despite the fact that all or substantially all of the venture's operating assets have been transferred.

The second case occurs when a smaller corporation acquires a larger and, in the process, effectively becomes the acquired corporation. To illustrate this upside-down acquisition, a corporation may purchase the assets of a larger venture and issue as payment a large block of stock constituting a majority of its outstanding shares. While the nominal acquiror effectively has been acquired, its formal role is that of an asset purchaser and under the literal language of the Model Act and other typical statutory formulations, the shareholders of the nominal acquiror are deprived of rights.

As written, the corporate statutes frequently seem to make form determinative in the award of shareholder rights. But did the drafters intend to base the award of significant rights on formalistic distinctions? To answer this question, the remainder of this article analyzes the corporate acts to determine if incongruities in their provisions are the result of such factors as incomplete drafting or oversight rather than conscious intent.

RIGHTS OF ACQUIROR SHAREHOLDERS

We will first examine the rights of shareholders of acquiring corporations. Most of the corporate acts—the traditional statutes as Professor Eisenberg describes them[24]—do not by their terms grant either voting or appraisal rights to the shareholders of acquirors other than merger survivors. Should these statutes be interpreted so that management cannot avoid rights for acquiror shareholders simply by conducting an acquisition in some form other than a two-party merger? (Here we focus only on the more common transaction in which a larger corporation acquires a smaller one. Upside-down acquisitions involve peculiar considerations and will be separately analyzed.) Should parents' shareholders in triangular mergers obtain the rights available to shareholders of merger survivors? In a three-party merger, the parent and not its subsidiary is providing the merger consideration and, in substance, is a merger constituent. Thus, the argument that the parent's shareholders should obtain "merger rights" has attracted strong support.

In *In re Penn Central Securities Litigation*,[26] involving a triangular merger, the federal district court stated: "It is especially appropriate to apply the *de facto* merger doctrine [to treat the transaction as a merger between the parent and the target] . . . where it is alleged . . . that the [parent's] shareholders were deprived of their rights of appraisal because of the form of the transaction."[27] Highly

24. M. Eisenberg, The Structure of the Corporation 217 (1976).

26. 367 F. Supp. 1158 (E.D. Pa. 1973).

27. · · ·

The issue of parents' shareholders' rights also has been litigated in Terry v. Penn Cent. Corp., 668 F.2d 188 (3d Cir. 1981). In that case, the court rejected plaintiffs' contention that the de facto merger doctrine should be applied to treat the parent as a merger constituent. However, the significance of the decision is limited. In 1959, amendments to the Pennsylvania corporations act limited the application of the de facto merger doctrine as it related to rights of dissenting shareholders. The court held that these amendments precluded a decision that the transaction could be deemed a de facto merger between the parent and the target. Thus, the court did not have to decide whether parents' shareholders have rights under a statute that contains no statement of hostility to the de facto merger doctrine.

respected commentators present similar views. Professors Cary and Eisenberg state: "[I]t can be argued that a triangular merger triggers voting and appraisal rights in [the parent's] shareholders on the theory that [the parent] should be deemed a constituent to the merger, or alternatively that such a result is necessary to prevent subversion of the merger statutes." Eisenberg, writing alone, is even more forceful, contending that the parent's shareholders should be awarded rights, "even without explicit provision, if the protections of the merger provisions are not to be subject to complete nullification." Although these views have an initial appeal, we believe there is cogent evidence that legislatures intended to deny rights to parents' shareholders in triangular mergers.

As seen earlier, the corporate statutes typically permit the use of shares of any corporation as merger consideration, thus openly inviting the conduct of three-party mergers in which *parent* shares are the merger consideration. Nearly all these provisions were adopted after it became clear that federal tax law sanctioned tax-free triangular mergers in which parent shares are the consideration.[30] Along with tax-free status, these mergers offer the convenience of merger (the assets and liabilities are transferred by operation of law) and permit the insulation of the target's liabilities in a subsidiary. Thus, the legislatures surely must have foreseen that the three-party merger, using parent shares, would enjoy widespread popularity, especially if it could be conducted free from whatever rights that would accrue to the parent's shareholders if the parent were the merger survivor. Indeed, it was predictable that triangular merger would become *the* form of tax-free acquisition, frequently to be used in transactions that involve the issuance of a substantial proportion of the parent's outstanding shares. Therefore, had the legislatures intended to award rights to parents' shareholders, it scarcely seems likely that they would have remained silent, relying on the courts to divine this intent. In view of the extraordinary significance of the matter and the ease with which legislatures explicitly could have provided rights for parents' shareholders, only a legislature in an extreme state of lassitude would have acted in this fashion. More plausibly, the traditional corporate acts mean what they say or, more precisely, what they do not say—parents' shareholders are not entitled to rights in triangular mergers.[32]

30. In 1967, the Internal Revenue Service, in the first published rulings on these mergers, concluded that a forward triangular merger may constitute a reorganization and therefore entitle the corporations and their shareholders to tax-free treatment if such merger meets the requirements of an assets-for-stock "C" reorganization, Rev. Rul. 67-326, 1967-2 C.B. 143, and a reverse triangular merger also may constitute a tax-free reorganization if it meets the requirements of a stock-for-stock "B" reorganization, Rev. Rul. 67-448, 1967-2 C.B. 144. Statutory amendments in 1968 and 1971 granted independent tax-free merger status to the forward and reverse triangular mergers. *See* I.R.C. § 368(a)(2)(D), (E) (1976 & Supp. IV 1980).   .   .   .

32.   .   .   .

It might be contended that a liquidation or short merger of the subsidiary into the parent that closely follows the triangular merger could lead a court to collapse the steps and treat the transaction as a two-party merger that would generate rights for the parent's shareholders. *See* Lowenstein, *New Form of "A" Reorganization Solves Many Corporate Acquisition Problems*, 44 L.A. Bar. Bull. 111, 133 (1969). Yet, this argument misses the point. If the legislatures intended to permit triangular mergers generally to occur without rights for a parent's shareholders, no policy concerns would be vindicated by awarding rights when the transaction is followed by an ordinary business decision not to retain the subsidiary's separate existence. *See also infra* notes 36–39 and accompanying text (discussing acquirors' shareholders' rights in nonmerger acquisitions).

The Model Act's treatment of acquiror shareholders under the recently created compulsory share exchange is fully consistent with and supports our view that parents' shareholders do not obtain rights in three-party mergers. As seen earlier, the Model Act adopted the compulsory share exchange as a simplified alternative to the more complex reverse triangular merger. Both techniques permit the acquiror to obtain all of the target's shares and retain the target as a wholly owned subsidiary. Thus, the acquiror in a compulsory share exchange occupies the same position as the parent in a reverse triangular merger. To conduct a compulsory share exchange, the Act explicitly requires approval of the transaction by the boards of both corporations, but awards voting and appraisal rights only to the shareholders of the acquired corporation. The decision to deny rights to acquirors' shareholders is unmistakable. ·

Our conclusions respecting acquiror shareholders' rights in these new forms of acquisition cast light upon a problem that was troublesome in the pretriangle era. (Note that the discussion in this section does not include the special case of the upside-down acquisition.) Before the advent of the triangles, there was significant litigation respecting the rights of acquirors' shareholders in transactions that formally were structured as asset purchases or voluntary share exchanges, but contained merger-like features. For example, in *Rath v. Rath Packing Co.*,[36] an asset purchase in exchange for the buyer's shares, coupled with the seller's dissolution and the buyer's assumption of the seller's liabilities, was deemed a de facto merger for purposes of awarding rights to the buyer's shareholders.[37] We will not discuss here the cases raising the de facto merger issue or conduct a reprise of the debate surrounding them.[38] The time has passed

36. 257 Iowa 1277, 136 N.W.2d 410 (1965).

37. Another leading case applying the de facto merger doctrine is Farris v. Glen Alden Corp., 393 Pa. 427, 143 A.2d 25 (1958). (*Farris* actually involved an upside-down acquisition and is discussed *infra* note 85.) *See also* Applestein v. United Bd. & Carton Corp., 60 N.J. Super. 333, 159 A.2d 146, *aff'd*, 33 N.J. 72, 161 A.2d 474 (1960) (share-for-share acquisition coupled with a short-merger of the acquired into the purchasing corporation was deemed a de facto merger). But see Heilbrunn v. Sun Chem. Corp., 38 Del. Ch. 321, 150 A.2d 755 (Sup. Ct. 1959), *aff'g* 37 Del. Ch. 552, 146 A.2d 757 (Ch. 1958), rejecting the de facto merger doctrine in a case involving rights of an acquiror's shareholders. Interestingly, after each of the above cited cases adopting the de facto merger doctrine was decided, the legislature of that state responded with legislation that in one fashion or another sought to remove the uncertainty created by the use of the doctrine. For example, in 1970, in an apparent effort to "overrule" *Rath,* the Iowa statute was amended to provide that "[t]he purchase by a corporation of all, or substantially all, of the assets of another corporation, domestic or foreign, followed by dissolution of the selling corporation, shall not, by itself, constitute a merger of such corporations." Iowa Code Ann. § 496A.68 (West Supp. 1982–83). *See also* N.J. Stat. Ann. § 14A:10–12 & commissioner's comment (West Supp. 1982–83); Pa. Stat. Ann. tit. 15, §§ 1311(F), 1908.B (Purdon Supp. 1982–83). Legislative disapproval of the de facto merger doctrine also is found in Va. Code § 13.1-77(d) (1978). In addition, Texas has an anti-de facto merger provision, but it appears to be a legislative effort to overturn a decision imposing liability upon an asset purchaser for obligations of the seller. *See* Tex. Stat. Ann. art. 5.10.B & bar committee comment 1957 to 1979 (1980); Western Resources Life Ins. Co. v. Gerhardt, 553 S.W.2d 783 (Tex. Civ. App. 1977), *application for writ of error refused, no reversible error.*

38. In analyzing asset transfers, Professor Eisenberg offers another theory that is somewhat different from the de facto merger doctrine. Eisenberg argues that merger is an ambiguous term, undefined in the corporate acts. He suggests that the legislatures, in using the term merger, contemplated a well-understood business transaction in which two corporations are fused, with the consideration normally consisting of the survivor's stock. Contending that the label the parties give to the transaction is not determinative, he concludes that certain stock-for-assets combinations, not

to debate the rights of acquiror shareholders in asset purchases or voluntary share exchanges. "Merger rights" should be extended to acquiror shareholders in these acquisitions only if such extension would further some policy in the merger sections. The standard is not met. If the legislatures permit even formal mergers to be conducted in three-party form, absent rights for the shareholders of the effective acquiror, what conceivable policy remains in the merger sections that could justify the award of rights to acquiror shareholders in asset purchases or voluntary share exchanges?[39]

We thus are drawn to the conclusion that the statutory patterns examined above deny rights to acquiror shareholders in any form of acquisition other than a two-party merger. The fact that such shareholders are the group normally less affected by the transaction presumably led the legislatures to devalue the importance of assuring them rights. The statutory retention of rights for shareholders of merger survivors is not an expression of legislative policy that properly can be extended to transactions deemed similar in substance. Therefore, any extension of rights for acquiror shareholders must be accomplished not by a result-oriented interpretation of the acts, but by the legislatures' reconsideration of their handiwork.

RIGHTS OF ACQUIRED SHAREHOLDERS IN MERGERS AND ASSET SALES

Although shareholders generally receive some statutory rights when their corporation is acquired in a transaction involving corporate action on its part, that is, when the target is acquired other than by a voluntary sale of shares by its shareholders, there may be differences in rights, depending upon the form of acquisition. Statutory provisions often reduce the rights of shareholders of an

formally mergers, could be deemed not de facto but de jure mergers within the meaning of the statutes. M. Eisenberg, *supra* note 24, at 224–31. We do not, however, consider the statutory term merger to be ambiguous and cannot concur that transactions structured as asset sales could be considered de jure mergers. Rather than representing some general concept of fusion, "merger," as used in the statutes, is a term of art, a shorthand designation for transactions conducted under a statutory procedure that terminates the existence of one constituent and transfers all of its assets and liabilities to the other. The peculiar statutory meaning of the term becomes clearer by recognizing that certain transactions not "well understood" as mergers may indeed be mergers. For example, if one corporation acquires a much smaller corporation for cash, in common usage the transaction would be characterized as a purchase; yet, if conducted through statutory merger procedures, it is undeniably a merger.

39. Indeed, the question largely may be of academic interest only. For example, if the de facto merger doctrine were still viable in purchase transactions a corporation that wanted to conduct a merger-like asset purchase without rights for its shareholders could do so in triangular form. Nothing in the corporate statutes precludes these transactions, and they could be conducted tax-free under the Internal Revenue Code. *See* I.R.C. § 368(a)(1)(C) (1976). Prior to the advent of the triangular merger, it is conceivable that a court would have granted "merger rights" to the parent's shareholders by analogizing the transaction to a two-party merger, the only kind of merger then in existence. Today, however, if a court did reconstruct the transaction it would have to analogize the triangular asset purchase to a triangular merger. In light of our conclusion that a triangular merger does not generate rights for the parent's shareholders, it follows that the reconstruction of a three-party asset purchase would not produce rights for the shareholders of the parent.

acquired corporation when asset sale rather than merger is the chosen form.[43] Disparities in rights most commonly involve appraisal, and our focus will be on that shareholder right.

In jurisdictions in which disparities in appraisal rights appear, an asset seller's shareholder may contend that whether or not the de facto merger doctrine applies for purposes of acquiror shareholder rights, when an asset sale is accompanied by factors indicative of a merger-like transaction, i.e., the assumption of the seller's liabilities and especially the seller's dissolution,[44] a court can apply the doctrine to grant the appraisal rights available in mergers to the acquired corporation's shareholders. In fact, it is most unlikely that shareholders of asset sellers will successfully invoke the de facto merger doctrine to obtain appraisal.

In the past, litigation could have been triggered in the many states that granted appraisal rights in mergers but categorically denied them in asset sales. Today, only a few states retain this statutory pattern and, of these, only Delaware is a significant corporate jurisdiction. In Delaware, there is nearly conclusive evidence that a court cannot apply the de facto merger doctrine to extend the appraisal rights available in mergers to asset sales. In *Hariton v. Arco Electronics, Inc.,*[46] the Delaware Supreme Court rejected the de facto merger approach when it denied appraisal to the seller's shareholders in an asset sale coupled with dissolution and the assumption of the seller's liabilities.[47] Since the legislature made no effort to overrule *Hariton* as part of the 1967 revision of its corporation act, it is safe to assume that the legislature was satisfied with this result.

At present, the Model Act is representative of the typical statutory pattern that varies appraisal rights between merger and asset sales. The Act generally grants appraisal to target shareholders in mergers and asset sales, but withholds appraisal when assets are sold for cash on terms requiring distribution of the sales proceeds. Thus, the Act specifically denies appraisal when an asset sale for cash closely resembles a merger (the proceeds are distributed and, in all

43. For simplicity, the textual discussion disregards the possibility that an act also may have a compulsory share-exchange procedure which grants the shareholders of the acquired the rights available in mergers. The existence of this procedure would not affect the textual analysis that follows. If an asset sale is not to be treated as a merger for purposes of awarding rights to the seller's shareholders, these rights surely could not become available by analogizing the transaction to a compulsory share exchange. Conversely, if the circumstances of the transaction are such that shareholders of an asset seller should receive the rights available in mergers, the existence of the share exchange procedure is irrelevant.

44. At an earlier time when cash generally was not permissible merger consideration, the use of shares rather than cash as payment in an asset sale might have been a critical factor in determining whether the sale could be considered of a merger-like nature. Today, with the broadened merger consideration provisions, mergers as well as asset sales may be conducted for any sort of consideration, and even cash sales carrying the appropriate baggage could be deemed to resemble mergers.

46. 41 Del. Ch. 74, 188 A.2d 123 (Sup. Ct. 1963).

47. In reaching its decision, the court relied upon the equal dignity approach and stated that "the sale-of-assets statute and the merger statute are independent of each other. They are, so to speak, of equal dignity, and the framers of a reorganization may resort to either type of corporate mechanics to achieve the desired end." *Id.* at 76, 188 A.2d at 125. *See also* Orzeck v. Englehart, 41 Del. Ch. 361, 365–66, 195 A.2d 375, 377–78 (Sup. Ct. 1963) (further developing the equal dignity theme).

likelihood, the corporation dissolves).[51] Therefore, it cannot be argued that by adding another merger attribute—the buyer's assumption of the transferor's liabilities —the de facto merger doctrine could be applied to reconstruct the cash asset sale-distribution transaction into a cash merger and thereby award appraisal rights to the seller's shareholders. Clearly, this result defies the language and intent of the cash asset sale-distribution exception to appraisal.

SHAREHOLDER RIGHTS IN SPECIAL ACQUISITION TRANSACTIONS

To this point we have seen that the judicious use of form may deeply affect rights for shareholders of acquiror and acquired corporations. The discussion concentrated on commonly-used acquisition techniques. Now we consider two special situations involving the rights of shareholders of an effectively-acquired corporation.

ACQUISITIONS OF SUBSIDIARIES BY MERGER OR ASSET TRANSFER

If all or substantially all of the assets of a venture are held by a subsidiary, should the acquisition of the subsidiary by merger with another company or the subsidiary's sale of its assets trigger rights for the parent's shareholders? Unless the transaction is governed by one of those few statutes that clearly grant rights for the parent's shareholders in such circumstances,[54] it would appear that the answer is no. The parent is simply a shareholder of a party to the acquisition, and the available shareholder rights presumably are exercisable by the parent's board but not by its shareholders.[55]

In discussing parent's shareholders' rights in these transactions, Eisenberg suggests that the right to vote the subsidiary's shares should pass through the parent to the parent's shareholders, each of whom would then vote the subsidiary's stock in that proportion which equals his proportionate holdings in the parent's stock. This pass-through doctrine also would afford appraisal rights, where appropriate, to the parent's shareholders by treating them as shareholders of the subsidiary.

51. Strictly speaking, the Model Act does not require the seller's dissolution as a condition to its denial of dissenters' rights in cash sales. Such rights are denied when the sale is "for cash on terms requiring that all or substantially all of the net proceeds of sale be distributed to the shareholders in accordance with their respective interests within one year after the date of sale . . . ." *Id.* § 80(a)(2) (1982). However, the Act obviously anticipates that the seller's dissolution normally will be a part of the transaction.

54. Only a few statutes contain provisions expressly addressing these transactions. *See* N.J. Stat. Ann. § 14A:10-11(3) (West Supp. 1982–83); Pa. Stat. Ann. tit. 15, § 1311.B (Purdon 1967); R.I. Gen. Laws § 7-1.1-72(e) (Supp. 1982). Although their phraseology varies, under all three an asset sale by a subsidiary which holds all or substantially all assets of the corporate complex will be treated as a sale of all or substantially all the assets of the parent. None of the acts expressly covers the acquisition by merger of such subsidiary, but presumably the intent of the statutes is to encompass such transactions.

55. On the other hand, it would seem that the parent's shareholders should obtain rights if the transaction took a formally different but substantively similar shape. Thus, if all or substantially all of the assets of the corporate complex are held in a subsidiary and the parent directly sells its shares in the subsidiary in a voluntary or compulsory share exchange, the parent's shareholders should receive rights under the asset-sale provisions because the parent is selling all or substantially all of its assets, i.e., its shares in the subsidiary.

The argument has force. In this instance there is evidence indicating that legislative policy would be furthered by awarding rights to the parent's shareholders.[58] As a practical matter, the parent has been acquired as surely as if it had directly held and transferred the venture's assets. A general policy of assuring at least some statutory protection to shareholders of corporations acquired in transactions requiring corporate action by the acquired appears on the face of the corporate acts. To be sure, many acts reduce appraisal rights for the shareholders of asset sellers to less than those provided in mergers. Yet, the statutes do not invite the use of form to eliminate all rights for shareholders who must sustain a change in their investment as a result of the acquisition of their corporation. For example, in Delaware voting rights for shareholders of acquired corporations are preserved in asset sales as well as mergers, although appraisal rights accrue only in mergers. Indeed, no jurisdiction generally denies voting rights to the shareholders of an asset seller.[59] Further evidence of legislative desire to preserve at least certain rights for target shareholders is found in the history of the Delaware small-scale merger provisions. As adopted in 1967, these provisions created a hiatus in investor protection. Under a literal reading of the original language, management could eliminate the voting rights of the shareholders of the acquired corporation in a reverse triangular merger. (Appraisal rights also could be eliminated in this fashion but undoubtedly that was never a matter of great concern in Delaware.) Soon after the problem was recognized, the statutory gap was plugged to assure that rights would accrue to the shareholders of the target in these mergers. Provisions similar to the corrected Delaware statute have been adopted elsewhere.

Presumably, the policy of protecting shareholders of a corporation acquired through corporate action is based on the fact that these shareholders, in all probability, will be compelled to accept a more drastic change of investment than will shareholders of the acquiror. Despite the failure of most legislatures explicitly to address the matter, we believe that this policy justifies the grant of rights for the parent's shareholders in acquisitions in which a subsidiary, holding all or substantially all the assets of the venture, sells its assets or is acquired by merger with another corporation. Corporations are not normally organized in this parent-holding-company–subsidiary configuration, and the

58. We do, however, suggest one problem with Eisenberg's approach. If the subsidiary is acquired by merger, Eisenberg apparently contends that the parent's shareholders should receive the rights available in merger. Yet, the parent is not formally a merger constituent and, as seen in the preceding section, the statutes frequently permit the use of form to reduce the rights of acquired shareholders to less than those provided in the merger sections. Under the approach we suggest in this subsection, the parent's shareholders will receive only those rights available to shareholders of asset sellers, a result we believe to be consonant with statutory policy. . . .

59. Occasionally, however, a statute denies even voting rights to the shareholders of an asset transferor when the sale is by a corporation in dissolution. See, e.g., Minn. Stat. Ann. § 302A.725.2 (West Special Pamphlet 1983); Pa. Stat. Ann. tit. 15, § 1311.A (Purdon 1967). Apparently, the rationale for this exception is the belief that the shareholders receive sufficient protection through their right to vote first on the dissolution before the board may conduct an asset sale on its own authority. If not satisfied with a proposed asset sale, shareholders can reject the dissolution and thereby prevent any transfer of assets. . . . However, even in jurisdictions with these provisions, if the sale is not pursuant to dissolution, the seller's shareholders retain the right to approve the sale. Indeed, even as far as dissenters' rights are concerned, although many statutes contain exceptions to the right in asset sales, only a few categorically deny it to the shareholders of the seller as well as the buyer. Most assure that, under at least some circumstances, the shareholders of the seller obtain the right. . . .

legislatures simply may have overlooked this kind of transaction. As Eisenberg notes, "[t]he megasubsidiary problem did not begin to take on major dimensions until the mid-1960s, prior to that time the pyramiding phenomenon of the Twenties and Thirties seemed to have all but disappeared, and even in the mid-1960s the corporate-law problems raised by megasubsidiaries had not really been identified."

It is particularly important to recognize that acquisitions of subsidiaries are not nearly as obvious a means of avoiding rights for shareholders on the acquired's side of the transaction as triangular mergers are in respect to the rights of those on the acquiror's side. A triangular merger may readily be conducted by any acquiring corporation simply by organizing a new subsidiary for use as a party to the merger. In contrast, parties customarily have not attempted to avoid rights for shareholders of an acquired by turning a single corporation into a parent-subsidiary configuration as the first step in a prearranged plan under which the subsidiary would hold the assets of the venture and, absent rights for the parent's shareholders, immediately be acquired by a third party. Indeed, even apart from the possibility that the acquisition of the subsidiary by the third party would trigger rights for the parent's shareholders, such a plan probably would not accomplish the desired avoidance of shareholder rights. Should the initial step involve placing all or substantially all of a corporation's assets into a newly created subsidiary, the transfer itself would probably constitute a sale of assets that would generate statutory rights for the transferor's shareholders.[66] Similarly, if a parent-subsidiary complex were developed by organizing a new corporation that would become the parent of a preexisting one by means of a triangular merger, the preexisting company would be the target in the transaction, thereby producing rights for its shareholders.[67] The vote required in either of these transactions would in effect be one on the intended acquisition of the subsidiary by a third party. The proxy rules would require that full disclosure of the planned acquisition be made prior to the vote that transforms the venture into parent-holding-company–subsidiary form. For these reasons, transfers by subsidiaries holding substantially all the assets of the venture are likely to be conducted only by corporations that are part of a previously standing parent-holding-company–subsidiary complex. Since this configuration remains somewhat unusual, these transfers raise shareholder rights' issues that do not thrust themselves upon the attention of a legislature.

In sum, the legislatures probably overlooked the problem of parents' shareholders' rights in acquisitions of subsidiaries. Nonetheless, it remains uncertain whether the courts will accept the argument that parents' shareholders are

---

66. *See* Campbell v. Vose, 515 F.2d 256, 259–60 (10th Cir. 1975).

67. As an illustration, a reverse triangular merger may be used. Under this procedure, the newly organized corporation (the parent-to-be) would in turn create its own subsidiary and fund it with its shares. The subsidiary then would be merged into the preexisting corporation. Upon completion of the merger, all of the shareholders of the preexisting corporation will have exchanged their shares for those of the newly organized corporation, which becomes the sole shareholder and parent of the preexisting one.

entitled to rights in subsidiary mergers and asset sales.[69] We suggest an approach that may make the parent's shareholders' case more appealing. Under this approach, it is not necessary to go beyond the terms of the statute in order to award them rights that are consonant with statutory policy. To be sure, most statutes do not directly address the matter at hand and in all probability the legislatures gave it no thought. Yet, though perhaps only fortuitously, in at least most transactions in which subsidiaries holding all or substantially all of the venture's assets are acquired by merger or asset transfer, the statutes may be read to grant parents' shareholders the rights available under the sale of assets provisions. The theory is that the subsidiary's merger or sale of its assets constitutes a sale by the parent of its shares in the subsidiary. Since the subsidiary's shares represent all or substantially all of the parent's assets, then a sale of all or substantially all of the parent's assets is occurring. Therefore, under the sale of assets provisions, the parent's shareholders must approve the transaction before the parent's board may consummate it by voting the subsidiary's shares in favor of the proposed merger or asset sale by the subsidiary. To the extent that the statute grants appraisal in a sale of all or substantially all assets, the parent's shareholders also would obtain such rights.[70]

But can this kind of transaction be deemed a sale of the subsidiary's shares and therefore a sale of the assets of the parent holding company?[71] When the subsidiary is acquired by merger or couples an asset sale with its dissolution, there is a strong argument that the transaction can be so characterized. Analogies are found in the context of federal securities law. Cases arising under rule 10b-5, promulgated under section 10(b) of the Securities Exchange Act of 1934, have found that a sale of shares by the shareholders of the acquired occurred in the course of a merger or an asset sale coupled with the seller's dissolution.

* * *

Most significantly, a commonsense understanding of the operation of mergers and asset sales coupled with dissolution supports the view that a sale of shares by the shareholders of the acquired may be a part of the transaction. A target

69. See Cross Properties, Inc. v. Brook Realty Co., 37 A.D.2d 193, 322 N.Y.S.2d 773 (App. Div. 1971), aff'd mem., 31 N.Y.2d 938, 293 N.E.2d 95, 340 N.Y.S.2d 928 (1972), rejecting the contention that a parent's shareholders were entitled to vote upon a subsidiary's asset sale. The court emphasized the absence of any indication of legislative intent to grant voting rights to the "beneficial" owners of a subsidiary, i.e., the parent's shareholders, when the subsidiary transfers its assets. For the reasons stated in the text, we consider the legislative failure specifically to address the matter to be neither surprising nor significant. Cross Properties is discussed at length in M. Eisenberg, supra note 24, at 294–99. As Eisenberg notes, the court's rejection of the argument that parents' shareholders are entitled to vote on a sale of assets by subsidiaries was dictum, since the transferred assets did not constitute substantially all of the assets of the corporate complex. Id. at 296. The dictum, however, is strong.   .   .   .   :

70. Under this approach, the transaction would be equated to one involving a direct sale of the subsidiary's shares in a voluntary or compulsory share exchange. See supra note 55.

71. While we use the term "sale," broader language is found in the corporate acts. For example, the Model Act's sale of assets provision includes not only "sale" but also "exchange or other disposition." Model Business Corp. Act § 79 (1982);   .   .   •

As Eisenberg notes, such terms "seem to be variants of the term 'sale,' in the sense that they contemplate a disposal of the corporation's assets for consideration. The apparent purpose of the added terms is to pick up dispositions for consideration other than cash, that is, barter-type transactions." See M. Eisenberg, supra note 24, at 229 n.15.

shareholder, in place of its share interest in the acquired corporation, has received the consideration paid in the acquisition. Thus, when a subsidiary holding all or substantially all the assets of a corporate complex is the acquired corporation, it is not difficult to characterize the transaction as a sale by the parent holding company of the shares it holds in the acquired subsidiary. As seen previously, since these shares constitute all or substantially all of the parent's assets, the parent's shareholders obtain rights under the sale of assets provisions.

In the case of an asset sale by a subsidiary that does not dissolve, the matter is cloudier. The securities law analogies discussed above do not apply to this situation. The fact that the parent retains its shares in a corporation which continues to possess the same value (albeit not the same kind of assets) makes it more difficult to deem the shares sold. It might be argued that, although the subsidiary is not dissolved, the nature of the parent's investment is so changed that the subsidiary's shares could rationally be deemed sold. Yet, it is far from clear that a court would interpret the transaction in this fashion. If it did not, then there would be no sale of shares by the parent and therefore the parent's shareholders would not obtain rights under the sale of assets provisions. In all events, this type of transaction will not take place with any frequency. A sale of all assets by a subsidiary that holds all or substantially all the assets of a venture is unlikely to occur without the subsidiary's dissolution. Typically, it is publicly held corporations that use the parent-holding-company–subsidiary configuration. It would be uncommon for these corporations to leave the proceeds of the subsidiary's asset sale in subsidiary solution. Thus, in at least most transactions in which subsidiaries holding all or substantially all the assets of a venture are acquired by merger or asset transfer, a court can award rights to parents' shareholders simply by applying the literal language of the statute.

UPSIDE-DOWN ACQUISITIONS

The final matter we consider is that of the rights available in acquisitions where the acquiror effectively is the acquired corporation. This upside-down acquisition may occur when a smaller corporation acquires a larger one and issues, directly or through a subsidiary, so substantial an amount of its shares that its shareholders, immediately prior to the acquisition, are left in a position normally associated with shareholders of an acquired corporation.

Assuming (as we do throughout this subsection) that the share-issuing corporation is not a merger survivor, the traditional statutes apparently do not grant voting or appraisal rights to its shareholders. In an earlier analysis of the rights of acquiror shareholders in acquisitions not structured in an upside-down fashion, we concluded that form governed these shareholders' rights. However, in turned-around transactions, the policy of protecting the shareholders of an acquired may justify the award to the shareholders of the share-issuing corporation of greater rights than the statutes apparently provide.[85] To be sure,

85. Indeed the courts, at times, have demonstrated a particular concern for the rights of shareholders of the "true" acquired in an upside-down acquisition. In Farris v. Glen Alden Corp., 393 Pa. 427, 143 A.2d 25 (1958), the de facto merger doctrine was applied to protect such shareholders. In *Farris*, the shareholders of an asset purchaser were left after the acquisition with only a minority interest in their corporation. A finding of de facto merger was premised in part on factors more indicative of an upside-down transaction than merger; for example, the court emphasized that the seller's directors were to receive a majority of the seats on the board of the purchaser, and the seller's shareholders were to wind up with the majority of the purchaser's stock. . . .

the legislatures' failure explicitly to award rights to shareholders of a corporation effectively acquired through the issuance of its shares could be deemed evidence of a legislative willingness to honor the form of an upside-down acquisition. But why would legislatures intend to permit management to circumvent rights provided for acquired corporations' shareholders simply by conducting the transaction in upside-down fashion? In most jurisdictions, there is no reason to believe that they had this intent.[86] It is not common for a corporation issuing its shares to constitute the effective acquired in an acquisition. Indeed, there often are disincentives to conducting a transaction in this fashion. For example, if an acquisition is structured as a triangular merger in which the smaller corporation adopts the role of a parent, its shareholders may be deprived of rights but rights will inure to the shareholders of the larger corporation that adopts the role of the acquired. As a result, there may be more shareholders whose votes have to be solicited and who may seek appraisal rights. Further, it would be unusual for a true acquiror to accept the status of a target corporation. Because it remains unusual to conduct acquisitions in upside-down fashion, it is probable that drafters have given only cursory attention to the shareholder-rights aspects of these acquisitions. Or they may have considered the possible avoidance of rights for the shareholders of the effectively acquired corporation a relatively minor problem of evasion of statutory policy that could be straightened out by the courts.

However, in this case, unlike that of acquisitions of subsidiaries, it is difficult to argue that the language of the statutes could be interpreted to grant rights to the shareholders of the "true" acquired. When acquisitions of subsidiaries were at issue, we contended that in at least most cases, appropriate rights could be awarded by deeming the parent an asset seller within the literal language of the statute. Because of the structure of an upside-down acquisition, it is doubtful that asset-seller status could be attributed to the share-issuing corporation. Its investment in its preacquisition assets remains unchanged in nature and amount. It simply is acquiring additional assets in exchange for its shares.[89] Yet,

---

See also Terry v. Penn Cent. Corp., 668 F.2d 188 (3d Cir. 1981), in which the court, having held that the parent in a triangular merger would not be deemed a constituent to the merger, stated in dicta, that "[a] different result might be reached if here, as in *Farris*, the acquiring corporation were significantly smaller than the acquired corporation such that the acquisition greatly transformed the nature of the successor corporation." *Id.* at 194 n.7.

86. If there is reason to believe that a legislature did consider the problem of the upside-down transaction and rejected the idea of awarding rights to the shareholders of the true acquired, its decision must be respected. For example, the Law Revision Commission commentary to the Michigan Act notes that Farris v. Glen Alden Corp., 393 Pa. 427, 143 A.2d 25 (1958), involved a reverse asset purchase and obviously disapproves of *Farris's* award of rights to the shareholders of the nominal purchaser. *See* 5 Michigan Law Revision Commission, *supra* note 42, at 216. Since the commentary was before the legislature during its deliberations on passage of the Act, this history suggests that a nominal acquiror in an upside-down acquisition should not be treated as an acquired for purposes of affording shareholder rights under the Michigan Act.

89. *But cf.* Farris v. Glen Alden Corp., 393 Pa. 427, 143 A.2d 25 (1958). In an alternate holding, the court found that the nominal purchaser in an upside-down asset acquisition was in reality the acquired corporation and therefore awarded its shareholders the rights of shareholders of an asset seller. It is not clear whether the court simply was applying statutory policy to grant rights to these shareholders or if it concluded that the nominal purchaser had literally sold its assets. If the latter is the case, the court seems to have placed considerable strain on language. In all events, it would be surprising if any court will treat a corporation issuing its shares as an asset seller within the meaning of the statute when the issuer is conducting a share acquisition or is the parent in a triangular merger.

although the statutes do not literally award rights to the shareholders of the corporation effectively acquired in these transactions, surely a court can extend the statutory terms to provide rights consonant with the legislative policy.[90] At times, a court can accomplish this result by resorting to the de facto merger doctrine.[91] Alternatively, without the use of legal handles, a court simply can apply policy to afford shareholders of a share-issuing corporation the rights that the legislature intended to assure to shareholders of an acquired corporation.

One final point remains. To provide guidance when an upside-down acquisition has occurred, we offer a more detailed test to determine when the share-issuing corporation should be deemed the acquired corporation. If, in any type of acquisition, whether conducted directly or through a subsidiary, a corporation issues, immediately or potentially, an amount of stock equalling more than 100% of either its previously outstanding voting shares (common or preferred) or its common shares, the issuer may be treated as an acquired. So dramatic a dilution either in the shareholders' voting power or in their proportionate residual equity interest should entitle them to the protection afforded shareholders of acquired corporations. We recognize that the courts may limit extension of rights in upside-down acquisitions to cases in which the nominal acquiror issues significantly more than the 100% figure mentioned above. However, prudent counsel should consider the possibility that rights will be awarded to the shareholders of the share-issuing corporation in any acquisition meeting the above test.

90. See M. Eisenberg, *supra* note 24, at 246–48. In determining what rights are to be granted to shareholders of the nominal acquiror in an upside-down acquisition, it is necessary to look to the policies underlying provisions granting rights to acquired corporation shareholders. We will restrict our discussion to statutes of the Model Act and Delaware variety. Generally, the Model Act assures voting and dissenters' rights to acquired corporation shareholders in all forms of acquisition involving corporate action by the acquired. The only significant exception is the denial of dissenters' rights in sales of all or substantially all assets for cash on terms requiring distribution of the net proceeds. *See supra* note 20 and accompanying text. In an upside-down acquisition, the nominal acquiror obviously is not receiving or distributing any sales proceeds. Consequently, it is clear that the general policy of providing dissenters' rights for the shareholders of an acquired corporation is applicable in an upside-down acquisition. Thus, in states following the Model Act pattern, shareholders of the nominal acquiror should receive both voting and dissenters' rights. In Delaware, shareholders of a corporation acquired in a merger are granted voting and appraisal rights, but shareholders of an asset seller receive only voting rights. As discussed earlier, the Delaware legislature has clearly sanctioned the use of form to avoid appraisal even for the shareholders of an acquired. Therefore, in an upside-down acquisition governed by Delaware law, the shareholders of the nominal acquiror, which is not formally a merger constituent, should at most obtain voting rights. As a practical matter, this normally would be the less important right. Since the nominal acquiror in an upside-down acquisition often would lack the requisite amount of authorized but unissued shares to conduct the transaction, an articles amendment authorizing additional shares would be necessary. The shareholder vote on the amendment would in effect constitute a referendum on the proposed acquisition.

91. For example, an upside-down triangular merger could be treated as a de facto merger between the parent and the target, producing "merger rights" for the parent's shareholders as shareholders of a merger survivor. Under the Model Act, this would afford them both voting and dissenters' rights, a result consonant with statutory policy. *See supra* note 90.

CONCLUSION

Throughout this article, we have attempted to interpret the corporate statutes with fidelity to their policies. At times, most significantly when rights of acquiror shareholders were at issue, there was no choice but to recognize a statutory policy permitting avoidance of rights by altering the form of the transaction. However, when dealing with the rights of the shareholders of a corporation which is effectively acquired in the two special acquisition patterns discussed above, our conclusions were quite different. Discerning a policy of affording protection to shareholders of an acquired, we have argued that this policy should be applied in these transactions. We have attempted, when possible, to make it easier to reach this result by culling shareholder rights from the literal terms of the statutes. In instances where this could not be accomplished, we have contended that the terms of a statute should be extended to provide rights consonant with its policy.

NOTE ON THE APPRAISAL REMEDY

Exclusivity of the Remedy. Once it is determined in what situations the appraisal remedy is available, there remain some important questions. Perhaps the most critical is whether appraisal is the dissenting shareholder's exclusive remedy when he objects to a transaction. When the statute is silent on the matter, courts have generally held that the availability of appraisal rights does not prevent a suit for an injunction or rescission based upon fraud, which probably includes a claim of unfair conduct by interested directors or controlling shareholders, although perhaps a more rigorous standard of unfairness would be imposed than if no appraisal remedy existed. See generally, Vorenberg, Esclusiveness of the Dissenting Stockholder's Appraisal Right, 77 Harv. L. Rev. 1189 (1964). Statutes like MBA §80 which expressly provide for exclusivity are obviously designed to reduce the opportunity for collateral attack, but the common exception for "fraudulent" conduct leaves ample room for judicial intervention, and the practical effect may simply be to raise the required standard of proof by the complaining party another notch or two.

Stock Valuation. Valuation of the stock in the appraisal proceeding has been a fertile area for litigation (and commentary). One recurring issue with respect to publicly-held stock has been how much weight to give to the market price when there is full, free and reasonably active market. For a time New York appeared to be a leader of the view that market price in such circumstance should be controlling, but that may have changed with the decision in Endicott Johnson Corp. v. Bade, 37 N.Y.2d 585, 338 N.E.2d 614 (1975), which upheld the appraiser's refusal to give any weight to market value; although the stock had recently been delisted, so that trading activity was substantially reduced, the court may have intended a broader scope for its comment that "market price is but an ingredient that must enter into the calculation for what it is worth, no more and no less".

Until very recently, Delaware, which has by far the greatest volume of the litigation in this area, had insisted upon consideration of an "asset value" factor and an investment value based upon capitalization of earnings, along with the market price if one existed, and some reasoned weighting of these elements in reaching the final figure; indeed, it was this Delaware approach which served as the model for the appraisal by the Maine Court in the Libby case, page 13 supra. For an illustration of the Delaware approach in action with respect to both the common and the preferred of a public corporation, see the Jacques Coe & Co. case, page 712 infra, which does not exactly inspire confidence in the process. However, in 1983 the Delaware Supreme Court, in Weinberger v. UOP, Inc., set out at page 684 infra, abandoned Delaware's traditional insistence upon a weighted average of assets, market price and earnings value, stating that the refusal to consider other generally accepted valuation techniques used in the financial community was "now clearly outmoded". The court observed that the discounted future cash flow method rejected by the Chancellor in judging the fairness of the price paid in the cash-out merger involved in Weinberger was in effect the basis on which the parent corporation determined the price at which to acquire the remaining stock of its subsidiary. The court added that since this more liberalized valuation approach would thereafter be applicable in appraisal proceedings, that should be the basic recourse of a minority stockholder seeking a financial remedy in a cash-out merger; however, the court preserved the possibility of direct judicial intervention in cases involving fraud, misrepresentation, self-dealing, or gross and palpable overreaching.

The Stock Market Exception. In 1967 Delaware adopted a so-called "stock market exception" which withholds the appraisal remedy when the stock is listed on a national securities exchange or is owned by at least 2000 shareholders of record. Del. Gen. Corp. Law §262(k). Many states have since enacted the listed stock exception, with a smaller number opting for the 2000 shareholder provision. In 1974 Delaware moved to confine these exceptions to cases where the shareholders either receive stock in the surviving entity or stock in another corporation which satisfies the the stock market exception. California's exception is subject to the condition that less than five percent of the shares seek appraisal.

The Model Act adopted the listed stock exception in 1969, but repealed it in 1978. The latter decision was explained as follows in a commentary prepared by Professor Conard for the ABA Committee responsible for the MBA, Amendments of Model Business Corporation Act Affecting Dissenters' Rights, 33 Bus. Law 2587, 2595-6 (1978):

> The . . . exception for shares listed on stock exchanges has been eliminated in the light of facts which have become more visible since the stock market exception was added to the Model Act in 1969. The 1970s have demonstrated again the possibility of a demoralized market in which fair prices are not available, and in which many companies publicly offer to buy their own shares because the market grossly undervalues them. Under these circumstances, access to market value is not a reasonable alternative for a dissenting shareholder. Moreover, a shareholder may be disqualified by state or federal securities laws from using the market because his shares are "restricted," because he is an "insider" who has acquired shares within six months, or because he possesses "inside information." Even if the dissenter is free to use the market, he may find it impractical to do so because his holdings are large and the market is thin. In any event, the market cannot reflect the value of the shares "excluding any appreciation or depreciation in anticipation" of the corporate change which gives rise to the dissenters' rights.

C. LIQUIDATION OF THE ACQUIRED CORPORATION

1. IN GENERAL

Unlike a merger, where the acquired corporation disappears by operation of law, when a combination transaction takes the form of either a stock acquisition or an asset acquisition the acquired corporation remains in existence, unless and until some further step is taken. Thus, in the case of a stock acquisition the acquired corporation becomes a controlled subsidiary of the acquiring corporation; and this parent-subsidiary format can be continued indefinitely if the parties so desire. If instead they prefer to end up with all the assets under a single corporate roof, as in a merger, it is necessary to take the additional step of liquidating the acquired corporation.

In an asset acquisition, of course, all of the assets have already been combined in the acquiring corporation; but the acquired corporation retains its separate existence and identity, as the owner of whatever stock and securities of the acquiring corporation it received in exchange for its assets. Once again, if the parties want to end up as in a merger, with only one corporation and with the former stockholders of the acquired corporation now owning stock of the acquiring corporation, the acquired corporation must be dissolved and its assets (i. e., the stock of the acquiring corporation) distributed to its stockholders in complete liquidation.

In either case, the elimination of the acquired corporation may be accomplished under the normal procedure for voluntary dissolution of a corporation. See generally, pages 565–567, supra. There must, of course, be due regard for the rights of creditors—and since typically there would be an assumption of the acquired corporation's liabilities by the acquiring corporation, either as an integral part of the acquisition transaction, in an asset acquisition, or in connection with the dissolution of the subsidiary pursuant to a stock acquisition, what that really means is facing up to the question of whether such assumption constitutes "adequate provision" within the meaning of the dissolution statutes. See pages 582–585, supra. Once the creditors are taken care of, the remaining assets of the corporation are to be distributed among the stockholders "according to their respective rights and interests". E. g., MBA § 87(b). The assets may be converted into cash to facilitate such a distribution; or, at least when there are no liquidation preferences (which not infrequently expressly require payment in cash), and no contrary stipulation in a "plan of liquidation" approved by the stockholders, the directors would seem to be free to distribute the property of the corporation in kind among the stockholders, except perhaps if a distribution in kind would subject stockholders to unreasonable difficulty and expense in administering property. See Shrage v. Bridgeport Oil Co., 31 Del.Ch. 305, 71 A.2d 882 (Ch.1950) (plan to distribute 1/267,200 interest in each of over 100 oil wells per share held unfairly burdensome to minority stockholders).

---

2. EFFECT OF LIQUIDATION PREFERENCES

Liquidation of the acquired corporation may be further complicated when it has stock with a liquidation preference outstanding, since if the liquidation preference exceeds the present market value of the stock the holders of the stock may be expected to insist that their preference be honored. This is particularly serious in the case of an asset acquisition, since as a practical matter the only alternative to liquidation is for the acquired corporation to carry on as a kind of holding company (of rather undiversified character), and there is no counterpart of the short merger statute to facilitate the elimination of the acquired corporation. Of course, it might be argued that since the overall transaction amounts in effect to the same thing as a merger, the participation of the preferred stock should be measured in the same way as it is in a merger, that is, by the present value of the stock, rather than by its liquidation preference. But in a merger the statute expressly authorizes the plan of merger to fix the conversion ratio and to provide for the issuance of stock of the acquiring corporation directly to the stockholders of the acquired corporation. On the other hand, as we have seen, a sale of assets does not carry with it any power to distribute the consideration received, much less to determine the basis upon which such consideration should be allocated among the various classes of stock of the acquired corporation. See pages 614–615, supra. Distribution of the assets of a corporation in liquidation can only be authorized pursuant to dissolution of the corporation, and in dissolution it seems clear that the distribution is governed by the contractual claim of each class, which would of course include any liquidation preference.

NEWMAN v. ARABOL MFG. CO.

New York Supreme Court, Special Term, 1963.
41 Misc.2d 184, 245 N.Y.S.2d 442.

Milton M. Wecht, Judge. The defendant Arabol Mfg. Co., a duly organized corporation, existing under the laws of the State of New York, had issued an outstanding 3630 shares of common stock, and 3720 shares of preferred stock, of which 150 shares of its preferred stock is in the hands of plaintiff, a testamentary Trustee. It then sold all of [its] assets and goodwill to the Borden Co., another defendant, and received therefor 49,600 shares of common stock of Borden.

The plaintiff at no time objected to this sale, nor to the transfer of Arabol's assets for 49,600 shares of Borden common. After this transfer, Arabol proceeded to ·buy back 3570 of its preferred shares for 10,710 shares of Borden stock, or 3 shares of Borden for each share of Arabol preferred. With respect to the remaining shares of Borden, or 38,890, Arabol intends to distribute these shares to the owners of its 3630 shares of common stock, or a bit over 10 shares of Borden for each share of Arabol common.

To this planned transfer, plaintiff, the holder of the outstanding 150 shares of Arabol preferred, objects, and argues that all the shareholders of Arabol, both the common and preferred, are entitled to equal distribution. As a matter of fact, to further emphasize his objection, he refused to accept the 450 shares of Borden transferred to his name or the dividend check from Borden, representing such shares which he received on the basis of the exchange of 3 for 1, hereinbefore mentioned, and started an action for an injunction and a declaratory judgment. . . .

*   *   *

The statutes . . . empowering a corporation to sell its property and to pay a dissenting stockholder the appraised value of his stock have no application to Arabol's plan. The attempt to distribute its assets in such a way as to give a holder of common stock a greater share of the corporate assets than a preferred stockholder is improper since there is nothing in the stock certificates or the charter authorizing such a differentiation. Plaintiff is not restricted to alternate courses of agreeing to the plan, or seeking appraisal, but can contest the planned distribution of assets in equity. . . .

* * *

It is clear that the difference in distribution between the 3 shares to the preferred stockholders and the 10 shares to the common stockholders does not constitute a dividend, it being the expressed intention of the corporation not to declare it a dividend now or in the future. Therefore, the preferred and common stock should share equally in the assets upon liquidation. . . .

Accordingly, . . . summary judgment in favor of plaintiff is granted.

---

3. ALTERATION OF PREFERRED STOCKHOLDERS' LIQUIDATION PREFERENCE

GOLDMAN v. POSTAL TELEGRAPH, INC. *

United States District Court, D. Delaware, 1943.
52 F.Supp. 763.

LEAHY, DISTRICT JUDGE. Diversity and the requisite amount establish jurisdiction.

The occasion has never arisen for the Delaware courts to determine where a certificate of incorporation provides a preference stock is to be paid $60 per share upon liquidation before any distribution is to be made to the common stockholders whether an amendment [of the certificate] . . . which attempts to provide that such preferred stockholder shall receive on dissolution less than the stated figure of $60 a share is valid. Absent a precise holding by the state court, a federal court must examine all the available data as to what the state tribunal would probably decide under such facts.

I. *The Plan.* Postal Telegraph, Inc., incorporated under the laws of Delaware in 1939 (herein called "Postal"), agreed to transfer to Western Union Telegraph Company (herein called "Western Union"), another Delaware corporation, all its assets. At the time

---

* Portions of the text and all the
court's footnotes omitted.

of the agreement plaintiff owned 500 shares of non-cumulative preferred stock of Postal which, by the terms of Postal's certificate of incorporation, entitled all preferred stockholders to a payment of $60 a share on liquidation before any distribution could be made to its common stockholders. On July 5, 1943, defendant Postal proposed three resolutions authorizing (1) the sale of all its assets to Western Union, conditioned upon the approval by Postal's stockholders of an amendment to its certificate of incorporation referred to in (2); (2) the amendment of Postal's certificate of incorporation so as to provide that the holders of defendant's non-cumulative preferred stock would receive in lieu of $60 per share on liquidation one share of Western Union B stock; and (3) formal dissolution of Postal. At the stockholders' meeting held on August 10, 1943, these resolutions were passed by a requisite vote over plaintiff's express objection. This suit followed.

The Postal-Western Union agreement provides that for the transfer of all the assets of Postal to Western Union, Postal will receive as part consideration 308,124 shares of Class B stock of Western Union. The entire amount of Class B stock to be received from Western Union will have a value substantially less than the aggregate liquidation preference of the preferred stock of Postal. Consequently, under its certificate of incorporation Postal's common stockholders—whose equity is deeply under water—would be entitled to receive nothing if ordinary liquidation occurred. Subject to various adjustments which do not have my immediate attention, Western Union will assume approximately $10,800,000 of Postal's liabilities. Postal's economic position is shown by its steady losses, aggregating over $13,500,000 from February 1, 1940, to May 31, 1943. . . .

In order to complete the proposed transfer of assets to Western Union, the vote of a majority of the outstanding stock of Postal was required under the Delaware law. . . . Postal's outstanding preferred was 256,769.9 and the number of shares of common was 1,027,-076.6. Hence, if all the preferred voted in favor of the plan, it would still be necessary to obtain the affirmative vote of approximately 400,000 shares of common. In order to obtain such vote, Postal's directors determined it advisable that the preferred's rights on liquidation be modified, so as to provide that out of the 308,124 shares of Class B stock of Western Union to be received by Postal, 256,770 shares would be distributed share for share for each of Postal's preferred and the balance of the Class B—51,354 shares—would be distributed to Postal's common stockholders, which was to be in the ratio of 1/20 of a share of Class B Western Union stock for each share of common stock of Postal.

As part of the plan, Western Union would also change its present 1,045,592 shares of capital stock into an equal number of shares of Class A stock without par value, which stock would be entitled to a non-cumulative dividend of $2 per share in each year before any dividends could be paid upon the Class B stock. After such dividend payment, the Class A and Class B stock are to participate on an equal basis in any dividends. . . .

Plaintiff here seeks, on behalf of himself and all other non-assenting shareholders, to enforce the liquidating rights which he contends are secured to him by the certificate of incorporation of Postal prior to the adoption of the resolution to amend it. . . .

Two issues are raised by the pleadings: (1) Whether the amendment to Postal's certificate of incorporation is authorized under Sec. 26 of the Delaware Corporation Law [the Delaware counterpart of MBA § 53, now Del. § 242], and (2) if Sec. 26 authorizes the present amendment whether the statute to this extent is constitutional.

II. *The Delaware Law.* The national and Delaware bars generally together with the legal literature especially have been unwilling to look directly at the radiations from the Delaware opinions which disclose what reclassification acts may be accomplished under Sec. 26 of the Delaware Corporation Law.

After much contemplation I concluded this is not the occasion to trace in limine the growth of the Delaware law in the field of corporate reclassification or rearrangement of stockholders' rights in order to show the development of a logical pattern of judicial thought on this and allied questions. Because the Delaware decisions are so crystalline in outline, I am mildly surprised there could be disagreement of interpretation as to just what may not be accomplished under the corporation statutes of that state.

Defendant's certificate of incorporation provides that, in the event of liquidation or dissolution, the holders of preferred stock are entitled to be paid $60 per share, plus all unpaid dividends (of which there are none), before any distribution is made to the holders of the common or junior stock. Sec. 26 provides that an amendment to a certificate of incorporation may alter or change "preferences" theretofore provided for a preferred stock, if the vote of a requisite majority is had. . . .

The right of preferred to priority in distribution of assets upon liquidation is clearly a preferential right within the meaning of the Delaware statutes. . . . I hold such right is subject to the amendment here involved under the particular language of Sec. 26. . . .

III. *The Constitutional Question.* Plaintiff's main contention is that if Sec. 26 authorizes the action taken by Postal it is unconstitutional, because such action will result in the destruction of what plaintiff calls his "vested" or "property" rights. Obviously, the determination of this question depends upon whether one accepts or rejects plaintiff's primary postulate of what is a "vested" or "property" right.

A person buying into a Delaware business corporation does so subject to the provisions of the particular charter and the Delaware Corporation Law. Delaware law assumes such person realizes Sec. 26 provides that *preferences* may be changed by a requisite majority vote. And preferred stockholders of a Delaware corporation when they buy into the particular enterprise accordingly consent in advance that whatever their preferences may be at the time they are subject to change by vote of the proper majority. . . . This is not a harsh rule. . . . It is one of the fundamental concepts of the Delaware law that protection is afforded against arbitrary action in the requirement that a majority of those affected by the amendment must vote in favor of it. This democratic principle, based, in reality, on a worldly or practical necessity, is that the voice of a majority must be accepted as an expression of what is best for the whole. Moreover, another concept established by the Delaware decisions is that, assuming a grant of power by statute, . . . exercise of such grant is always subject to the historical processes of the court of equity to gauge whether there has been an oppressive exercise of the power granted. . . . This is "fair and equitable" language. Where, as here, it is admitted there are no questions of unfairness involved, the only question remaining is one of classic constitutionality, involving only the contract clause and due process.

Plaintiff therefore contends that the rights of the preferred to priority of return of capital in distribution of assets upon liquidation are fixed, vested, or contractual rights and thus are constitutionally beyond reach of alteration by amendment under Sec. 26. Plaintiff presses the point that these preferential rights are analogous to the right of stockholders to accrued and unpaid dividends on preferred stock, and if it be said that Sec. 26 authorizes the alteration of such rights, then the statute is unconstitutional under the doctrine of Keller v. Wilson & Co. * . . .

* * *

It is clear on principle there can be no constitutional objections to the present amendment. Since the corporation is the creature of the state, and since the corporation law is a part of the corporate charter . . . it is self-evident the state has the right to reserve to itself, or a majority or more of the stockholders, the power to change the contract between the corporation and its stockholders or between its different classes of stockholders by an amendment to the charter after such contracts are made, even if a particular class of stockholders must suffer slightly. If a rationale is sought for this reservation of power, then a more cogent reason than that which exists in the case at bar would be difficult to find. Here, the public interest has a stake. We are concerned with two of the great communicating systems of this country. Duplicity of effort gone, an attendant increase in effi-

---

* [Ed. note] See text at note 11, page 668 infra.

ciency and decrease in waste will naturally make the public beneficiaries, in part, by the absorption of Postal by Western Union.
Viewed against the undoubted reservation of right by the state and
the public interest involved, changes in liquidating preferences seem
mild.

* * *

Plaintiff argues, however, that execution of the contract of sale
of assets by Postal and Western Union on May 13, 1943, gave to preferred a present right to payment of $60 per share, and that its right
to such payment on dissolution or liquidation then became a "fixed
and vested right". But the agreement of May 13, 1943, was not binding upon Postal, since by its terms it called for authorization by the
vote of its stockholders. . . . A sale of assets does not constitute
a dissolution or necessarily call for a liquidation. . . . Here,
Postal might have continued to hold the Class B shares of stock of
Western Union without distribution to its stockholders. In fact, such
a course was suggested in its proxy statement which it sent to all its
stockholders.

I conclude the execution of the May 13, 1943, contract for sale of
assets to Western Union did not accelerate the preferential right of
Postal's preferred stockholders to $60 a share on dissolution into a
"vested right" which could not thereafter be altered by amendment
under Sec. 26.

IV. *The Procedural Question.* At argument, plaintiff made his
last contention that defendant could not agree to sell its assets conditioned upon the power of the corporation to amend its certificate of
incorporation as a part of the transaction. There is no merit to this
view. . . . This court and the Delaware courts have recognized
the strategic position of common stock to hamper the desires of the
real owners of the equity of a corporation, and the tribute which common stock exacts for its vote under reclassification and reorganization. . . . [S]eparate meetings of Postal's stockholders could
have been called to (a) amend under Sec. 26 and (b) approve a sale
of assets under Sec. 65; for purposes of convenience and the saving of
expense, both steps were taken at one meeting. Nothing in the Delaware law forbids such a procedure. . . .

NOTE ON AMENDMENTS ALTERING THE RIGHTS
OF SHAREHOLDERS

NOTE: LIMITATIONS ON ALTERATION OF SHAREHOLDERS'
RIGHTS BY CHARTER AMENDMENT *

69 Harv.L.Rev. 538 (1956).

The general corporation laws in the principal states of incorporation
authorize majority interests to effect by charter amendment certain chang-

es in the rights of shareholders. The validity of such amendments depends on the scope of the authorizing statute, on whether the corporate charter was obtained before or after enactment of that statute, and on the judicial construction of the state's power to authorize changes in the contract of the shareholders *inter se*.[2]

Interpretation of the Authorizing Statute.—Statutory interpretation does not pose serious problems where, as in New York, the statute enumerates specifically those rights of investors which may be altered by charter amendment. However, corporation laws containing general authorizing language are common. An early Delaware statute allowed a majority of shareholders to make "any . . . change or alteration in . . . [the] Charter of incorporation that may be desired," with the proviso that if "preferences" were altered it must be done by a class vote. In a case where all the proposed amendments had been approved by a class vote, a Delaware court construed this statute to permit amendments changing voting rights and authorizing the issue of prior preferred stock, but to prohibit one canceling accrued dividends. The statute was subsequently amended to authorize changes in "preferences, or relative, participating, optional or other special rights of the shares." Although a federal court construed the statute as amended to permit cancellation of accrued dividends, in a subsequent case the Delaware court still refused to allow such an amendment.[11] The divergent results reached by these and other courts construing similar language indicate that the meaning given to general statutory authorizations is dictated not so much by the statutory language as by criteria similar to those which courts employ to determine whether the statute as applied is constitutional.

Limitations on Amendments Authorized by Statutes Enacted Subsequent to Incorporation.—The Supreme Court in Trustees of Dartmouth College v. Woodward [13] held that a corporate charter constitutes a contract between the state and the corporation and that the Constitution protects such contracts against alteration by the state. The state's power over the charter as a contract of the shareholders *inter se* was not involved in the Dartmouth College case, but it is likely that if, subsequent to incorporation, the state had sought to impose a change in the substantive rights of the shareholders, or had authorized a majority interest to impose such a change, this too would have been declared unconstitutional. Although the Court in the Dartmouth College case rested its decision on the impairment of contracts clause, the fourteenth amendment had not yet been adopted; having largely absorbed the contract clause, due process would be the more likely basis for constitutional attack today.

Mr. Justice Story stated by way of dictum in the Dartmouth College case that the state could, as a term of its contract with the corporation, reserve a power to amend the charter; and most states, either by statute or constitutional provision, have reserved such a power. However, it is doubtful, under modern conceptions, whether there is any such contract

2. The courts have come to regard the corporate charter as embodying three contracts: between the state and the corporation, the corporation and the shareholders, and the shareholders *inter se*. . . .

11. Keller v. Wilson & Co., 21 Del.Ch. 391, 190 A. 115 (Sup.Ct.1936). . . .

13. 17 U.S. (4 Wheat.) 518 (1819).

in which the right to amend is reserved since the relationship of the state to the corporation would seem regulatory rather than contractual. Corporations are no longer created by franchise and special legislative grant, as in the time of the Dartmouth College case. Instead they are authorized and controlled by general statutes applicable to all who adopt the corporate form of business organization. But even if the charter is a contract between the state and the corporation, a term permitting the state to amend its own contract would not seem to provide it with power over the shareholders' contract. Nevertheless, it might be argued that the reserved power, like all other terms of the corporation laws, becomes part of the charter by force of law,[23] and therefore part of the shareholders' contract *inter se*. Thus the shareholders would be deemed to have consented in advance to the exercise by the state of a power to amend the charter or to authorize the majority to do so. . . .

New Jersey[25] and several other states hold that the reserved power does not extend to the contract among the shareholders and that this contract can only be altered by the state in the "public interest." Some commentators have construed this position to preclude any change in the shareholders' contract. However, recent New Jersey cases, applying equitable principles to enjoin as unfair amendments authorized subsequent to incorporation, indicate that New Jersey may not fully subscribe to this position today. And within the limits of fairness, whether it be defined in terms of due process or the equitable power of courts, state power to authorize reasonable charter amendments would seem desirable in order to enable businesses incorporated under an earlier statute to adjust to a changing economy.

The Delaware courts have set constitutional limits to the state's power to authorize amendments by holding that it cannot authorize impairment of "vested" rights, such as the right to accrued dividends. However, since the shareholder cannot sue for such dividends unless they have been declared, and since on dissolution creditors have a prior claim on corporate assets, "vested" in this context does not seem to connote an assured right of enjoyment to the shareholder, and so is largely a fictional concept raised by the courts to protect the fruits of the shareholder's past investment. Although this seems to be a due process consideration of fairness, it has not been applied in other contexts, the Delaware courts having allowed the practical elimination of accrued dividends as a result of merger or the issue of prior preferred. Nevertheless, what is important to the shareholder is not the form of the alteration but its result.

It would seem preferable to examine whether such benefits as the corporation is likely to derive from a charter amendment are outweighed by the probable injury to the minority shareholders, rather than to base de-

---

25. Pronik v. Spirits Distributing Co., 58 N.J.Eq. 97, 42 A. 586 (Ch. 1899); Zabriskie v. Hackensack & N. Y. R. R., 18 N.J.Eq. 178 (Ch. 1867). [Ed. note: In the Zabriskie case, the chancellor expressed the view that while the reserved power changed the rule of the Dartmouth College case and thus made it possible for the legislature to make changes in a corporate charter for the benefit of the public, the reserved power could not justify giving "a power to one part of the incorporators as against the other, which they did not have before".]

23. Most state corporation laws provide that they shall be automatically included in the terms of the charter. . . .

cisions on such tests as a fictional "vested" rights theory. If an injury to the minority would result, the amendment can only be justified on the ground that it is necessary to enable the corporation to make adjustments essential to its continued existence. And it should appear, considering the alternatives that are available, that the amendment sought will be likely to produce financial stability. Furthermore, it is important that the minority receive a reasonable *quid pro quo* for the rights which it will lose under the amendment. Where the interests cannot be readily valued in monetary terms, as is the case with voting rights, it will be difficult to determine what is a fair exchange.

The problems inherent in applying a fairness test can be mitigated to some extent by placing the burden of going forward with the evidence upon the corporation once the minority shareholder has shown that the amendment works to his detriment. Since the corporation has presumably already examined the factors relevant to the proposed amendment, it will be in a better position than the shareholder to furnish proof on the issues of financial necessity, possible alternative plans, and the value of the rights of the different classes before and after the proposed amendments. This change from present practice, by relieving the shareholders of the expense and difficulty of obtaining information on these issues, will facilitate suit by those not able or willing to seek relief because of the smallness of their interests. Furthermore, if the majority knows that in case of suit it will have the burden of showing that the proposed plan is fair, greater attention may be given to fairness at the time the plan is formulated.

Limitations on Amendments Authorized by Statutes Enacted Prior to Incorporation.—Courts seem more reluctant to impose due process or equitable limitations on amendments authorized by statutes in existence at the time the corporate charter was obtained than on those where the statute was enacted after the date of incorporation. The reason for this greater judicial self-restraint might be that where the authorizing statute is in existence at the time of incorporation, shareholders are thought to be able to determine in advance how their interests could be modified by charter amendment. However, it is hardly feasible for a purchaser of corporate securities to examine the corporation laws in existence at the date of the charter for each state where a business in which he plans to invest is incorporated. Moreover, if the authorizing statute is not specific and has not been widely litigated, it will not apprise him of the extent of the power which may be available to the majority. Nevertheless, justification may be found for treating amendments differently where the statute was in existence at the date of the charter since the public interest may require that within a narrow limit, such as that imposed by the date of incorporation, there be a clear formulation of corporate power so as to enable corporations to amend their charters unhampered by repeated litigation. However, it would still seem desirable to apply fairness principles which will afford some protection to the interests of the investor.

Other Possible Safeguards.—In addition to any fairness limitations which may be imposed on charter amendments, other safeguards are available in some states. In a few jurisdictions, shareholders objecting to an amendment can obtain appraisal and purchase of their shares. To allow a shareholder whose rights are to be modified by the amendment the alternative of an appraisal or of an attack on the ground of unfairness provides an additional deterrent to adoption of unfair amendments by the majority, who presumably will want to avoid the expenditure of large sums in purchasing the stock of dissenters. However, if appraisal is made the exclusive remedy of the dissenting shareholder, so that he cannot seek an injunction on the ground of unfairness and so retain his investment and interest in future earnings, he may be forced to choose between accepting an unfair modification of his rights and selling his shares at the appraised price. Another safeguard available in many states is the requirement that a majority of each class adversely affected vote in favor of the amendment. However, this may not assure fairness to the dissenter, because a majority of his class may be induced to vote for a plan by the offer of a present cash payment, or because a majority may also own securities of another class which will benefit from the amendment. Furthermore despite SEC proxy rules, proxy returns continue to be relatively automatic, so that majority acceptance is no guarantee of a reasoned choice. On the other hand, a requirement of a high majority vote of each class may make class voting an effective device by forcing proponents of a charter amendment to offer generous terms in order to secure the vote necessary to the adoption of the plan.

Consideration of Fairness in the Context of Specific Charter Amendments.—Plans requiring charter amendments usually call for the alteration of numerous rights, so that in determining fairness it is necessary to consider the cumulative effect of all proposed changes.

(a) *Amendments to Eliminate Accrued Dividends and the Right to Future Accruals.*—Amendments to cancel accrued dividends are usually sought on the ground that the corporation must free earnings from the claims of the preferred before needed capital can be raised by a sale of additional common or of securities convertible into common. However, such a change not only reduces the present value of the preferred shareholder's stock, unless he is entitled to an appraisal which will take into account the accrued dividends, but also denies him the chance to recover the accruals through future dividends or asset priorities on dissolution. In addition, where the outlook for future earnings is favorable, other practical means of obtaining capital are likely to be available which will not prejudice the interests of any class; thus, long-term borrowing may be possible since the preferred's claim to accrued dividends will neither prevent‚the payment of interest nor impair creditors' rights on dissolution. And where the prospect of earnings is unfavorable the cancellation of accrued dividends will not hide a poor financial position from a careful investor.

An amendment to remove only the right to future accruals will not be nearly as effective in attracting new capital as one which cancels past accruals. But a loss of cumulative dividend rights may have as much impact on the value of a preferred shareholder's investment as a cancellation of past accruals, since the decreased certainty of return on the investment lowers the value of the preferred shares to prospective purchasers.

(b) *Amendments to Authorize an Issue of Prior Preferred.*—A change in the charter which authorizes an issue of new preferred with priority in dividends and assets for the purpose of raising new capital will generally not be unfair to existing classes. Although the dividend and dissolution rights of the prior preferred will be paramount, new capital and hence an opportunity for increased earnings will be available. The holders of common and of the present preferred, if the latter have the right to vote, presumably will not approve the change unless the additional resources appear likely to provide earnings at least sufficient to satisfy the claims of the new shares to dividends.

On the other hand, where the proposed issue is part of a plan to exchange prior preferred for the original preferred, there may be danger of unfairness, for the object is likely to be the elimination of accrued dividends rather than the acquisition of new capital. To induce acceptance of the plan, holders of the original preferred are frequently offered cash or other securities in addition to shares of the new issue. And they are given little practical alternative but to accept the proposed exchange. If a holder of the original preferred retains his shares,   . . . his claims to assets and dividends be subordinated to the claims of those who accept the exchange . . ..

* * *

(d) *Amendment of Provisions for Redemption* .   . . .—A reclassification of noncallable preferred shares as shares callable by the corporation at a certain price may be attempted when replacement capital can be obtained at a lower dividend rate, or when the corporation has cash or low yield securities which it could use in retiring preferred with a high dividend rate, thereby releasing more earnings for distribution to the common. Such a reclassification may also benefit the common by making it possible to retire preferred which has a right to participate in earnings in excess of its fixed dividend rate. However, the amendment providing for reclassification will be unfair unless the redemption price gives the preferred at least an amount which, when reinvested at the prevailing dividend rate of similar securities, will yield income equal to that received prior to redemption. Since the majority sets the call price, there is danger of unfairness unless the shareholder has the right to an appraisal which would take into account the possible loss of income to the preferred, or unless a high majority vote of each class is required.   .   .   .

* * *

(e) *Amendments of Liquidation Preferences.*—Especially when used in conjunction with a contemplated sale of assets, alteration of liquidation preferences may substantially injure the holders of the preferred. An amendment may be passed changing the terms of the preference to specify that the shareholder of the vendor corporation shall receive instead of cash certain securities of the proposed vendee corporation, the value of which is lower than that of the original liquidation preference. Although such plans seem unfair, courts have nevertheless upheld them.

(f) *Amendments of Voting and Pre-emptive Rights.*— . . . Where the common has voting control, complete withdrawal of the right to vote will in most instances only be sought against the preferred, since the common is unlikely to surrender its power. The contention that there is no injury to the preferred in removing its right to vote where the preferred cannot gain control ignores the possibility that holders of preferred, if joined by dissatisfied holders of common, may be able to prevent corporate action which will adversely affect their interests. An amendment providing for a transfer of the right to vote from the common to the preferred in the event of dividend arrearages on the preferred would not seem unfair to dissenting common, since the transfer of control would be the class with the most immediate financial interest. In such situations, by advancing its own interests the preferred will also bring the common nearer to participation in earnings. . . .

(g) *Merger and Consolidation as a Means of Avoiding Limitations on Charter Amendments.*—Those of the above rights which the courts have not allowed to be altered directly by amendment can nevertheless frequently be changed through merger or consolidation.[71] Even where the corporation creates a subsidiary solely for the purpose of effecting a merger and altering the rights of a class through an exchange of shares, the courts have generally refused to enjoin the plan unless there is a showing of fraud. Yet to preserve the effect of fairness limitations on charter amendments of certain rights, it would seem necessary also to apply a fairness test to other methods designed to alter these rights.

---

4. SPECIAL PROBLEMS IN THE LIQUIDATION OF A CONTROLLED SUBSIDIARY

a. STRAIGHT DISSOLUTION

If in a stock acquisition the acquiring corporation does not obtain all of the stock of the acquired corporation, a simple dissolution of the subsidiary (acquired corporation) accompanied by a liquidating distribution in kind may prove not to be a very effective way to get the subsidiary's business to the parent (acquiring corporation). For under that procedure the minority stockholders of the subsidiary would presumably end up as tenants in common with the parent in the subsidiary's assets, a situation likely to prove inconvenient for all concerned, to say the least. Can this problem be avoided by arranging a "plan of liquidation" of the subsidiary under which the parent would receive all of the operating assets of the subsidiary while the minority stockholders of the subsidiary would receive their pro rata share of the liquidation distribution in cash?

KELLOGG v. GEORGIA-PACIFIC PAPER CORP. *

United States District Court, W.D. Arkansas, 1964.   227 F.Supp. 719.

[Crossett Company was an Arkansas corporation engaged in the lumber business, with net assets of more than $100,000,000. A substantial majority of its stock was owned by three families, with the remainder held by the public, including the plaintiffs. During the spring of 1962 Georgia-Pacific began to acquire Crossett stock at $55 per share, starting with the majority stockholders, and by July had acquired 99.6% of the stock. The plaintiffs had an opportunity to sell their stock at $55 per share but refused. Thereafter, on July 30, 1962, at a meeting of the Crossett stockholders not attended by the plaintiffs, a plan of dissolution of Crossett was approved under which Georgia-Pacific was to take as its distributive share all of the assets and the business of Crossett, except for $54.85 per share in cash to be paid to the minority stockholders. The rate of $54.85 per share was apparently based upon the book value of the Crossett stock. The plaintiffs refused to accept the cash payment contemplated by the plan, and brought an action to have the plan declared invalid as a matter of law.]

HENLEY, DISTRICT JUDGE. . . .   It is the theory of the plaintiffs that Georgia-Pacific, as the majority stockholder of Crossett, owed plaintiffs, as minority stockholders, a fiduciary duty to manage the affairs and wind up the business of Crossett, including the liquidation of its assets, for the benefit and best interests of all of the stockholders, including the minority; that Georgia-Pacific and the Trustees had no right to adopt a plan of liquidation which would favor Georgia-Pacific at the expense of the plaintiffs; that plaintiffs and Georgia-Pacific were the beneficial owners of all of the assets of Crossett as tenants in common; that having dissolved the corporation Georgia-Pacific and the Trustees, after making provision for the payment of corporate debts (which appears to have been done), were required either to distribute the assets in kind among all of the stockholders in proportion to their stock ownership, or to sell all of the assets on the open market and divide the proceeds on a pro-rata basis. As indicated, plaintiffs contend that Georgia-Pacific had no right to take over the assets and affairs of Crossett as a going concern and require plaintiffs to accept a predetermined cash payment as compensation for their stock ownership.

In resisting the claim of plaintiffs the defendants contend that plaintiffs' interest in Crossett was too small to give them standing to contest the plan of liquidation; that they were dilatory in asserting their objections; that Georgia-Pacific and the Trustees have acted in the utmost good faith and with the utmost regard for the

---

* Statement of facts and footnotes by
the court omitted.

interests of plaintiffs; that the Trustees in working out a method of liquidation were faced with a number of alternatives, and selected the one which was most feasible and which was actually in the best interests of all concerned.

From its consideration of the facts of record in the light of what appear to be governing provisions and principles of law the Court is persuaded that while some of the contentions of the defendants may have some relevancy on the question of what relief is to be granted plaintiffs, none of them can be sustained as far as the legality of the plan of liquidation is concerned, and that plaintiffs are entitled at this time to a binding adjudication that the plan adopted was illegal.

The Arkansas statutes prescribe the method by which the affairs and assets of dissolved domestic corporations are to be liquidated. . . . Without stopping to abstract those statutory provisions in detail, they contemplate that the trustees in liquidation shall collect the corporate assets, pay or provide for the payment of corporate debts and liabilities, and distribute remaining assets in cash or in kind to the former stockholders in proportion to their stock ownership. Those statutes do not contemplate that the trustees in the absence of an agreement among the stockholders shall turn the corporate business and physical assets over to one stockholder or group of stockholders while requiring some other stockholder or stockholders to accept cash as his or their distributive share in liquidation.

As to the legality of the plan of liquidation, the case of Mason v. Pewabic Mining Company, 133 U.S. 50, 10 S.Ct. 224, 33 L.Ed. 524, decided in 1890, appears to be in point here. In that case the Pewabic Mining Company was in distressed financial condition; the majority stockholders of Pewabic were apparently not willing to put any more money into that corporation. Instead, they organized a new corporation which they controlled. It was decided that Pewabic would be dissolved; that Pewabic's assets would be turned over to the new corporation in satisfaction of the stock interest of the majority stockholders, and that the owners of the minority stock would be paid in cash for their stock on the basis of a valuation fixed by the majority. It was held that this method of winding up the affairs of Pewabic was illegal and was subject to injunction. The Court said (pp. 58–59 of 133 U.S., p. 228 of 10 S.Ct., 33 L.Ed. 524):

> "With regard to the main question, the power of the directors and of the majority of the corporation to sell all of the assets and property of the Pewabic Mining Company to the new corporation under the existing circumstances of this case, we concur with the circuit court. It is earnestly argued that the majority of the stockholders—such a relatively large majority in interest—have a right to control

in this matter, especially as the corporation exists for no other purpose but that of winding up its affairs, and that, therefore, the majority should control in determining what is for the interest of the whole, and as to the best manner of effecting this object. It is further said that in the present case the dissenting stockholders are not compelled to enter into a new corporation with a new set of corporators, but have their option, if they do not choose to do this, to receive the value of their stock in money.

"It seems to us that there are two insurmountable objections to this view of the subject. The first of these is that the estimate of the value of the property which is to be transferred to the new corporation and the new set of stockholders is an arbitrary estimate made by this majority, and without any power on the part of the dissenting stockholders to take part, or to exercise any influence, in making this estimate. They are therefore reduced to the proposition that they must go into this new company, however much they may be convinced that it is not likely to be successful, or whatever other objections they may have to becoming members of that corporation, or they must receive for the property which they have in the old company a sum which is fixed by those who are buying them out. The injustice of this needs no comment. If this be established as a principle to govern the winding up of dissolving corporations, it places any unhappy minority, as regards the interest which they have in such corporation, under the absolute control of a majority, who may themselves, as in this case, constitute the new company, and become purchasers of all the assets of the old company at their own valuation.

"The other objection is that there is no superior right in two or three men in the old company, who may hold a preponderance of the stock, to acquire an absolute control of the whole of it, in the way which may be to their interest, or which they may think to be for the interest of the whole. So far as any legal right is concerned, the minority of the stockholders has as much authority to say to the majority as the majority has to say to them: 'We have formed a new company to conduct the business of this old corporation and we have fixed the value of the shares of the old corporation. We propose to take the whole of it, and pay you for your shares at that valuation, unless you come into the new corporation, taking shares in it in payment of your shares in the old one.' When the proposition is thus presented, in the light of an offer made by a very small minority to a very large majority who object to it, the injustice of the proposition is readily seen; yet we know of no reason or authority why those holding a majority of the stock can place a value upon it at which a dissenting minority must sell or do something else which they think is against their interest, more than a minority can do. . . ."

* * *

The correctness of the Pewabic decision is manifest. To say that majority stockholders may dissolve a corporation and proceed to take over the business and principal assets for themselves while at the same time forcing the minority to take mere cash for their interests, the payments to be based on a valuation made by the majority, would be to confer upon the majority the power to confiscate the minority interest, thus depriving the minority shareholders of their interest in an existing business with its attendant possibilities of growth and appreciation in value, an interest which may be worth much more than the present cash value of the minority shares. Such should not be permitted.

In coming to the conclusion that the plan for the liquidation of Crossett which was adopted was illegal the Court does not mean to suggest that Georgia-Pacific or the Trustees have been guilty of any fraud or conscious oppression or conscious violation of any fiduciary duty. On the contrary, the Court assumes, and for summary judgment purposes must assume, that the defendants acted with subjective conscientiousness and fairness, and that the price offered for the minority stock was a fair price. But, those are not the questions before the Court at the moment.

While the interests of plaintiffs in Crossett were very small proportionately, those interests constituted property rights which plaintiffs are entitled to have declared and protected. When Georgia-Pacific decided to bring about the dissolution of Crossett rather than to continue its corporate existence and operations, it assumed the obligation to liquidate Crossett in accordance with law. It had a right to distribute the assets in kind or to put them on the block for sale and divide the proceeds, in either case treating all stockholders alike. It had no right to take over The Crossett Company as a going business and eliminate plaintiffs' interests in that company by cash payments.

To the argument that the method of liquidation selected was the only feasible one and was the alternative most beneficial to plaintiffs there is a conclusive answer. Georgia-Pacific was not required to dissolve and liquidate Crossett. Having chosen to dissolve and liquidate, it was required to do so lawfully. That a lawful liquidation might have produced less money or value to plaintiffs than the method selected is beside the point. Plaintiffs had the right to insist on a lawful liquidation, and they have done so.

The Court is going no further at this time than to declare and adjudicate that Georgia-Pacific's method of liquidating Crossett was not in accordance with law, and that plaintiffs are entitled to some relief. What specific relief should be awarded plaintiffs presents a serious problem which the Court is not now in a position to solve. Although plaintiffs are entitled to a protection of their rights, they have come into a court of equity, and the framing of an appropriate remedy rests to some extent in the discretion of the Court to be exercised within the framework of general principles of equity. The determination of the relief to be awarded plaintiffs may involve a balancing of the comparatively small interests of the plaintiffs, on the one hand, against the very large and significant interests involved on the other hand. Rights of innocent third parties may have intervened, which rights may have to be protected.

Without at all prejudging the matter, it may not be feasible to undo what has been done already. Or it may be that to divest Georgia-Pacific of its ownership of the Crossett properties might inflict undue hardship on Georgia-Pacific without any corresponding benefit to plaintiffs. It is possible that the plaintiffs may have to take money, and they may come out with less than Georgia-Pacific has offered. But, at the very least, they are entitled to the fair value of their stock, determined impartially, and are not required to accept a value fixed by the majority stockholders.

. . . The Court understands from counsel on both sides that in the past some settlement negotiations have been conducted. Those negotiations should be renewed in light of the Court's views herein set forth. If the negotiations are not fruitful, within about thirty days the Court will on short notice call a conference of counsel at which counsel should be prepared to discuss with the Court questions of further proceedings looking toward termination of the litigation by settlement or otherwise.

Accord, In Re San Joaquin Light & Power Corp., 52 Cal.App.2d 814, 127 P.2d 29 (1942) ("while [the statute] permits the distribution of assets other than money where this can be done fairly and ratably and in conformity with the articles, nothing herein in any way indicates an intention to permit a distribution in kind to some of the common stockholders while compelling others to turn in their stock for its present cash value"); Zimmermann v. Tide Water Associated Oil Co., 61 Cal.App.2d 585, 143 P.2d 409 (1943). On the other hand, as previously noted there may be circumstances where a liquidating corporation must offer a cash alternative to minority stockholders, if a straight distribution in kind would work a hardship upon them. See Shrage v. Bridgeport Oil Co., page 661 supra.

Can the problem posed by these cases be met by having the subsidiary sell its assets, at a fair price of course, to the parent corporation? As a practical matter, this would leave the minority stockholders of the subsidiary in the same position as under the approach rejected by the court in the Kellogg case—that is, with cash equivalent to their pro rata share of the value of the subsidiary's assets, as determined by the parent. But it would seem unreasonable to insist that the subsidiary's assets be put up for sale at public auction, thereby forcing the parent to risk losing the assets to a third party. And of course under the sale approach the minority stockholders would have the added protection of being entitled to close judicial scrutiny of the fairness of the price paid, since the parent would be subject to the normal rules applicable to a fiduciary purchasing property from itself. Compare Abelow v. Midstates Oil Corp., 189 A.2d 675 (Del.Sup.Ct.1963), discussed at page 698 infra, where such a sale procedure was sustained.

b. The "Short Merger" Procedure

The difficulties inherent in a straight-forward dissolution of a subsidiary may be avoided under so-called "short merger" statutes, such as MBA § 75A, which authorize a parent corporation owning a specified percentage of the stock of a subsidiary to merge the subsidiary into the parent without any vote or appraisal for the stockholders of the parent, and with only a cash payment to the minority stockholders of the subsidiary. Notice that merger can be a much more convenient way to get rid of a subsidiary than liquidation because a merger avoids any question as to the legal sufficiency of an assumption of liabilities and also eliminates all the paper work, such as deeds and the like, which would otherwise be required to transfer the subsidiary's property to the parent. In connection with the following analysis of short merger statutes, consider whether such provisions might better be viewed as a substitute for liquidation than as a type of merger, and whether that makes any difference.

GREENE, CORPORATE FREEZE–OUT MERGERS: A PROPOSED ANALYSIS
28 Stan.L.Rev. 487–490 (1976) *

Modern merger statutes allow the controlling shareholders of a corporation to acquire a new enterprise or to transfer its existing business to another corporation without the prior consent of the minority shareholders. In a complex industrial society where combinations of businesses are common, flexible means of acquisition and transfer must be available. A corporation seeking to acquire a going concern would be reluctant to purchase only the consenting shareholders' position in the acquired corporation if nonconsenting stockholders could not be eliminated—the potential for conflict would be too great. Combinations would be unlikely if consent of each stockholder of the acquiring company were required.

* * *

* Portions of the text and most footnotes omitted.

State legislatures have steadily amended corporation statutes to facilitate mergers.[7] As a result, cash, instruments of indebtedness, or securities (or any combination thereof) may be issued by the acquiring company to shareholders of the acquired company in the merger; furthermore, many jurisdictions no longer require that shareholders of the acquired corporation have a continuing equity interest in the combined enterprise. However, the appearance of a different type of merger has accompanied these liberalizations. The only purpose of this new merger, often called a freeze-out merger, is the elimination of the acquired corporation's minority stockholders.

Freeze-out mergers depart from the usual case in that the acquiring corporation (Y) is also the controlling stockholder of the acquired corporation (X). Therefore, Y can cause X to be merged into itself or its wholly owned subsidiary and eliminate the minority stockholders of X by providing in the plan of merger that each share of X is converted into cash. Since Y owns shares of X and is obligated as the surviving corporation to pay for X's shares, it will pay the minority stockholders cash for their shares but provide in the merger plan that each share of X that it owns will be cancelled in lieu of paying itself cash.[8]

7. Delaware is the foremost example of this trend. Not only is the required stockholder vote only a simple majority, see note 1 supra, but a short-form merger statute has been adopted allowing for merger of a 90%-owned subsidiary into its parent by resolution of the parent's Board. Del.Code Ann. tit. 8, § 253 (1974). In addition, the stockholders of the acquiring corporation no longer have the right to vote in certain cases. See E. Folk, supra note 1, at 324, 391.
The types of consideration that may be offered to the stockholders of the acquired corporation have been expanded to include cash and other property of the acquiring corporation. Before 1967, Delaware law required the shares of each constituent corporation to be convertible only into securities of the surviving corporation. Cash payments were permitted only for fractional shares. Del.Code Ann. tit. 8, § 251(b) (1953). A 1967 amendment permits cash or securities of another corporation to be issued for the shares of the constituent corporation. Id. § 251 (1968), and a 1969 amendment permits the use of "properties" including cash. Id. § 251 (1974). Such liberalizations enable Y to avoid severe dilution of its stock by allowing it to pay some or all of the purchase price in cash. . . .

8. Technically, a freeze-out involves either the total elimination of X's minority stockholders from the combined business resulting from the merger (i.e., cash is paid for the minority stockholders' shares of common stock) or a fundamental alteration of their equity interest (i.e., preferred stock is paid for the minority stockholders' shares of common stock). However, if Y issues shares of Y's common stock to X's minority stockholders, they continue to have an interest in the combined enterprise. There is still the question of whether the exchange ratio is fair, because Y controls both parties to the merger, and because Y forces X's minority shareholders to accept equity participations in what may be a substantially different enterprise. Thus, for the purposes of this Article, both situations are included when referring to the freeze-out of minority stockholders in a merger where Y controls both parties, since the minority stockholders in the latter are frozen out of the enterprise in which they invested. Y may be unwilling to issue its stock to X's minority stockholders because of the expense involved in registering the shares under the Securities Act of 1933, 15 U.S.C. §§ 77a-77bbbb (1970), or because of the dilutive effect on its outstanding shares.

Freeze-out mergers occur in a variety of contexts. Controlling stockholders may wish to eliminate a troublesome minority stockholder from their close corporation. Similarly, Y, a publicly held corporation, may have acquired the controlling shares of X by a tender offer, and subsequently wants to eliminate X's minority stockholders. Finally, the controlling stockholders may want X to go private—that is, to revert to a private corporation through a forced purchase of X's publicly held shares.[9]

Although each stockholder of X purportedly is treated the same in the merger, in reality the controlling stockholder continues its investment in X's business, while the minority stockholders must either accept the consideration offered or challenge its adequacy in an appraisal proceeding or litigation. Moreover, the minority stockholders not only run the substantial risk of receiving a low or unfair value for their shares by reason of the absence of bargaining, but also are forced to search for a subsequent investment equivalent to their investment in X. Finally, the minority stockholders may have to pay taxes as a result of the exchange. It is this unequal treatment and forced displacement in the absence of bargaining that distinguishes the freeze-out from the ordinary merger. Thus, even though the freeze-out merger may comply with the applicable statutes, it carries a potential for unfairness that does not exist when a combination of two unaffiliated companies is involved.[13]

* * *

9. Freeze-outs occurred long before merger statutes were liberalized. See note 7 supra. However, because cash alone was initially not permitted in mergers, they usually occurred (1) by way of a sale of assets to a shell corporation controlled by Y with a subsequent dissolution of X, see Theis v. Spokane Falls Gaslight Co., 34 Wash. 23, 74 P. 1004 (1904), (2) a dissolution of X forced by the controlling stockholders followed by a purchase of the business by the controlling stockholders who continued it in a new corporation, see Lebold v. Inland S.S. Co., 82 F.2d 351 (7th Cir. 1936), cert. denied, 316 U.S. 675 (1942), or (3) a merger in which X's minority stockholders were issued redeemable preferred stock, see Outwater v. Public Service Corp. of New Jersey, 103 N.J.Eq. 461, 143 A. 729 (1928). However, the revised merger statutes eliminated the restrictions on the types of consideration that could be issued in a merger or sale of assets transaction; therefore mergers became a safer way to effect a freeze-out. Not only does a modern merger involve only one step, but also the availability of appraisal helps to insulate the transaction from minority attack. In New York and Delaware, appraisal is not available in a sale of substantially all of a corporation's assets for cash. See Del.Code Ann. tit. 8, §§ 262, 271 (1974); N.Y.Bus.Corp. Law § 910(a)(1)(B) (McKinney Supp.1975). See also Hariton v. Arco Electronics, Inc., 40 Del.Ch. 326, 182 A.2d 22 (1962), aff'd, 41 Del.Ch. 74, 188 A.2d 123 (1963).

13. In the usual merger the price is negotiated at arm's length; there is little concern for protection of minority stockholders because they receive equal treatment. Thus, since the probability of unfairness to nonconsenting stockholders is so low and the probability of achieving overall business efficiencies through mergers so high, the foolproof protection of unanimous consent could be abrogated. Since any inroads the merger statutes made on the old

In [one type of] freeze-out, the acquiring corporation (Y) makes a tender offer for all of the outstanding shares of the acquired corporation (X). After acquiring control, Y promptly freezes-out the minority stockholders of X by voting its controlling interest in X in favor of a merger [15] with Y and by providing in the merger plan that shareholders of X be paid cash or other consideration. . . . [18] If Y acquires a specified minimum of X's shares, usually 90 to 95 percent, Y may utilize the short-form merger procedure available in many states. In a short-form merger, the Board of Directors of Y adopts a resolution merging X into Y. No meeting of the stockholders of X is required nor must prior notice of the merger be sent.[19]

common law rights would be subject to strong constitutional attack on the theory of impairment of contract rights, the corporation statutes had to strike a balance between corporation flexibility and minority rights. See Ballantine, Questions of Policy in Drafting a Modern Corporation Law, 19 Calif.L.Rev. 465 (1931). Indeed, appraisal may have served to strike the balance, thereby ensuring judicial toleration of the abrogation of common law minority rights. See id., at 482; Manning, supra note 3, at 246 n. 38. It follows that freeze-outs involving not a combination with a third party but an internal rearrangement of interests are not within the rationale advanced to remove the previously foolproof protection of minority stockholders. Corporate flexibility is not in all likelihood thought to require a right in the majority to expel the minority at will.

15. Once control is acquired by Y, the freeze-out may be accomplished by a merger, a sale of X's assets to a corporation wholly owned by Y followed by a liquidation of X, the simple liquidation of X, see . . . L. D. Kellog v. Georgia-Pacific Paper Corp., 227 F.Supp. 719 (W.D.Ark.1964), or a reverse stock split, see Teschner v. Chicago Title and Trust Co., 59 Ill.2d 452, 322 N.E.2d 54 (1974). The minority stockholders must be paid the fair value for their interests in any event. The analysis and proposals in the text apply to all freeze-outs however effected.

18. Even though Y may initially offer to purchase all shares for the same price, it is not required to offer the same price in the subsequent merger (although it is, of course, required to pay fair value). However, to the extent Y was willing to purchase all shares, and the freeze-out occurs promptly, cf. notes 69–70 infra and accompanying text, where "promptly" is defined as within 1 year, Y would probably have the burden of persuading an appraiser if it offered a lower price.

19. Under New York law a corporation that owns 95% or more of the stock of another may effectuate a merger by a resolution of its directors rather than a vote of the shareholders of X. N.Y.Bus.Corp. Law § 905 (McKinney Supp.1975). See also Del.Code Ann. tit. 8, § 253 (1975), requiring 90% ownership. Short-form merger statutes were initially adopted to facilitate a simplification of holding companies and operating utilities and to circumvent blocking or delaying tactics by minority stockholders; however, the procedure has since been made available to all corporations. It has significant freeze-out potential, especially when viewed as expressing a legislative determination that minority stockholders may be ejected under any circumstances. . . .

SECTION 2. FAIRNESS IN COMBINATION TRANSACTIONS

A. FAIRNESS BETWEEN THE CONSTITUENT CORPORATIONS

In the case of a combination involving unrelated corporations dealing at arm's length, it is most unlikely that a
minority shareholder could successfully attack the transaction on the ground of alleged unfairness of the terms. Even
if an available appraisal remedy is not the exclusive recourse in such circumstances, as it probably would be under
MBA §80, the courts have generally been very reluctant to
override the judgment of the managers of the constituent companies as to the comparative values of their respective contributions. Thus in Cole v. National Cash Credit Ass'n, 18
Del. Ch. 47, 156 A. 183, 188 (Ch. 1931), the court stated the
rule as follows:

> "The [disparity] must be so gross as to lead the
> court to conclude that it was due not to an honest
> error of judgment but rather to bad faith, or to a
> reckless indifference to the rights of others inter-
> ested. There is a presumption that the judgment of
> the governing body of a corporation, whether at the
> time it consists of directors or majority stockhold-
> ers, is formed in good faith and inspired by a bona
> fides of purpose."

The same test has been applied in cases involving an attack
on the price at which substantially all of a corporation's
assets were sold to a third party. E.g., Cottrell v. The
Pawcatuck Co., 36 Del.Ch. 169, 128 A.2d 225 (Sup. Ct. 1956)
("The plaintiff has failed to show any such gross inadequacy
of price as would justify an inference of reckless disregard
of the rights of the minority stockholders.")

This standard seems unexceptionable when the final bargain is the result of arm's length negotiations between the
constituent concerns, assuming there is also no indirect
self-dealing in the picture, such as a special side-deal for
the managers of a selling corporation in the form of lucrative long-term employment contracts or the like. Cf. Smith
v. Good Music Station, Inc., 36 Del. Ch. 262, 129 A.2d 242
(Ch. 1957), where a sale of assets was upheld despite a
generous employment contract extended to a 50% shareholder-
director by the purchaser; the court found that the amount he
was to receive was not out of line. Query whether the
existence of an improper side-deal should serve as a basis

for upsetting a completed transaction, rather than simply imposing a duty on the recipient of the special deal to share it with all his fellow stockholders.

However, the situation is very different when the directors or the controlling shareholders of one of the corporations have a significant interest in the other entity. A common illustration is the combination of a parent and a controlled subsidiary, where the parent is in position pretty much to dictate the terms of the transaction offered to the minority shareholders of the subsidiary:

WEINBERGER v. UOP, INC.*

Supreme Court of Delaware, 1983. 457 A.2d 701.

MOORE, Justice:

This post-trial appeal was reheard en banc from a decision of the Court of Chancery.[1] It was brought by the class action plaintiff below, a former shareholder of UOP, Inc., who challenged the elimination of UOP's minority shareholders by a cash-out merger between UOP and its majority owner, The Signal Companies, Inc.[2] Originally, the defendants in this action were Signal, UOP, certain officers and directors of those companies, and UOP's investment banker, Lehman Brothers Kuhn Loeb, Inc.[3] The present Chancellor held that the terms of the merger were fair to the plaintiff and the other minority shareholders of UOP. Accordingly, he entered judgment in favor of the defendants.

Numerous points were raised by the parties, but we address only the following questions presented by the trial court's opinion:

    1) The plaintiff's duty to plead sufficient facts demonstrating the unfairness of the challenged merger;

    2) The burden of proof upon the parties where the merger has been approved by the purportedly informed vote of a majority of the minority shareholders;

    3) The fairness of the merger in terms of adequacy of the defendants' disclosures to the minority shareholders;

    4) The fairness of the merger in terms of adequacy of the price paid for the minority shares and the remedy appropriate to that issue; and

    5) The continued force and effect of Singer v. Magnavox Co., Del.Supr., 380 A.2d 969, 980 (1977), and its progeny.

[1] In ruling for the defendants, the Chancellor re-stated his earlier conclusion that the plaintiff in a suit challenging a cash-out merger must allege specific acts of fraud, misrepresentation, or other items of misconduct to demonstrate the unfairness of the merger terms to the minority.[4] We approve this rule and affirm it.

[2, 3] The Chancellor also held that even though the ultimate burden of proof is on the majority shareholder to show by a preponderance of the evidence that the transaction is fair, it is first the burden of the plaintiff attacking the merger to demonstrate some basis for invoking the fairness obligation. We agree with that principle. However, where corporate action has been approved by an informed vote of a majority of the minority shareholders, we conclude that the burden entirely shifts to the plaintiff to show that the transaction was unfair to the minority. See, e.g., Michelson v. Duncan, Del.Supr., 407 A.2d 211, 224 (1979). But in all this, the burden clearly remains on those relying on the vote to show that they completely disclosed all material facts relevant to the transaction.

[4] Here, the record does not support a conclusion that the minority stockholder vote was an informed one. Material information, necessary to acquaint those shareholders with the bargaining positions of Signal and UOP, was withheld under circumstances amounting to a breach of fiduciary duty. We therefore conclude that this merger does not meet the test of fairness, at least as we address that concept, and no burden thus shifted to the plaintiff by reason of the minority shareholder vote. Accordingly, we reverse and remand for further proceedings consistent herewith.

[5] In considering the nature of the remedy available under our law to minority shareholders in a cash-out merger, we believe that it is, and hereafter should be, an appraisal under 8 · Del.C. § 262 as hereinafter construed. We therefore overrule Lynch v. Vickers Energy Corp., Del.Supr.,

---

1. Accordingly, this Court's February 9, 1982 opinion is withdrawn. [Ed. note: footnotes 2–4 omitted.]

429 A.2d 497 (1981) (*Lynch II*) to the extent that it purports to limit a stockholder's monetary relief to a specific damage formula. *See Lynch II*, 429 A.2d at 507–08 (McNeilly & Quillen, JJ., dissenting). But to give full effect to section 262 within the framework of the General Corporation Law we adopt a more liberal, less rigid and stylized, approach to the valuation process than has heretofore been permitted by our courts. While the present state of these proceedings does not admit the plaintiff to the appraisal remedy per se, the practical effect of the remedy we do grant him will be co-extensive with the liberalized valuation and appraisal methods we herein approve for cases coming after this decision.

Our treatment of these matters has necessarily led us to a reconsideration of the business purpose rule announced in the trilogy of *Singer v. Magnavox Co., supra; Tanzer v. International General Industries, Inc.*, Del.Supr., 379 A.2d 1121 (1977); and *Roland International Corp. v. Najjar*, Del.Supr., 407 A.2d 1032 (1979). For the reasons hereafter set forth we consider that the business purpose requirement of these cases is no longer the law of Delaware.

I.

The facts found by the trial court, pertinent to the issues before us, are supported by the record, and we draw from them as set out in the Chancellor's opinion.[5]

Signal is a diversified, technically based company operating through various subsidiaries. Its stock is publicly traded on the New York, Philadelphia and Pacific Stock Exchanges. UOP, formerly known as Universal Oil Products Company, was a diversified industrial company engaged in various lines of business, including petroleum and petro-chemical services and related products, construction, fabricated metal products, transportation equipment products, chemicals and plastics, and other products and services including land development, lumber products and waste disposal. Its stock was publicly held and listed on the New York Stock Exchange.

In 1974 Signal sold one of its wholly-owned subsidiaries for $420,000,000 in cash. *See Gimbel v. Signal Companies, Inc.*, Del. Ch., 316 A.2d 599, *aff'd*, Del.Supr., 316 A.2d 619 (1974). While looking to invest this cash surplus, Signal became interested in UOP as a possible acquisition. Friendly negotiations ensued, and Signal proposed to acquire a controlling interest in UOP at a price of $19 per share. UOP's representatives sought $25 per share. In the arm's length bargaining that followed, an understanding was reached whereby Signal agreed to purchase from UOP 1,500,000 shares of UOP's authorized but unissued stock at $21 per share.

This purchase was contingent upon Signal making a successful cash tender offer for 4,300,000 publicly held shares of UOP, also at a price of $21 per share. This combined method of acquisition permitted Signal to acquire 5,800,000 shares of stock, representing 50.5% of UOP's outstanding shares. The UOP board of directors advised the company's shareholders that it had no objection to Signal's tender offer at that price. Immediately before the announcement of the tender offer, UOP's common stock had been trading on the New York Stock Exchange at a fraction under $14 per share.

The negotiations between Signal and UOP occurred during April 1975, and the resulting tender offer was greatly oversubscribed. However, Signal limited its total purchase of the tendered shares so that, when coupled with the stock bought from UOP, it had achieved its goal of becoming a 50.5% shareholder of UOP.

Although UOP's board consisted of thirteen directors, Signal nominated and elected only six. Of these, five were either directors or employees of Signal. The sixth, a partner in the banking firm of Lazard Freres & Co., had been one of Signal's representatives in the negotiations and bargaining with UOP concerning the tender offer and purchase price of the UOP shares.

5. *Weinberger v. UOP, Inc.*, Del.Ch., 426 A.2d 1333, 1335–40 (1981).

However, the president and chief executive officer of UOP retired during 1975, and Signal caused him to be replaced by James V. Crawford, a long-time employee and senior executive vice president of one of Signal's wholly-owned subsidiaries. Crawford succeeded his predecessor on UOP's board of directors and also was made a director of Signal.

By the end of 1977 Signal basically was unsuccessful in finding other suitable investment candidates for its excess cash, and by February 1978 considered that it had no other realistic acquisitions available to it on a friendly basis. Once again its attention turned to UOP.

The trial court found that at the instigation of certain Signal management personnel, including William W. Walkup, its board chairman, and Forrest N. Shumway, its president, a feasibility study was made concerning the possible acquisition of the balance of UOP's outstanding shares. This study was performed by two Signal officers, Charles S. Arledge, vice president (director of planning), and Andrew J. Chitiea, senior vice president (chief financial officer). Messrs. Walkup, Shumway, Arledge and Chitiea were all directors of UOP in addition to their membership on the Signal board.

Arledge and Chitiea concluded that it would be a good investment for Signal to acquire the remaining 49.5% of UOP shares at any price up to $24 each. Their report was discussed between Walkup and Shumway who, along with Arledge, Chitiea and Brewster L. Arms, internal counsel for Signal, constituted Signal's senior management. In particular, they talked about the proper price to be paid if the acquisition was pursued, purportedly keeping in mind that as UOP's majority shareholder, Signal owed a fiduciary responsibility to both its own stockholders as well as to UOP's minority. It was ultimately agreed that a meeting of Signal's executive committee would be called to propose that Signal acquire the remaining outstanding stock of UOP through a cash-out merger in the range of $20 to $21 per share.

The executive committee meeting was set for February 28, 1978. As a courtesy, UOP's president, Crawford, was invited to attend, although he was not a member of Signal's executive committee. On his arrival, and prior to the meeting, Crawford was asked to meet privately with Walkup and Shumway. He was then told of Signal's plan to acquire full ownership of UOP and was asked for his reaction to the proposed price range of $20 to $21 per share. Crawford said he thought such a price would be "generous", and that it was certainly one which should be submitted to UOP's minority shareholders for their ultimate consideration. He stated, however, that Signal's 100% ownership could cause internal problems at UOP. He believed that employees would have to be given some assurance of their future place in a fully-owned Signal subsidiary. Otherwise, he feared the departure of essential personnel. Also, many of UOP's key employees had stock option incentive programs which would be wiped out by a merger. Crawford therefore urged that some adjustment would have to be made, such as providing a comparable incentive in Signal's shares, if after the merger he was to maintain his quality of personnel and efficiency at UOP.

Thus, Crawford voiced no objection to the $20 to $21 price range, nor did he suggest that Signal should consider paying more than $21 per share for the minority interests. Later, at the executive committee meeting the same factors were discussed, with Crawford repeating the position he earlier took with Walkup and Shumway. Also considered was the 1975 tender offer and the fact that it had been greatly oversubscribed at $21 per share. For many reasons, Signal's management concluded that the acquisition of UOP's minority shares provided the solution to a number of its business problems.

Thus, it was the consensus that a price of $20 to $21 per share would be fair to both Signal and the minority shareholders of UOP. Signal's executive committee authorized its management "to negotiate" with UOP "for a cash acquisition of the minority ownership in UOP, Inc., with the intention of presenting a proposal to [Signal's] board of directors . . . on March 6, 1978". Immediately after this February 28, 1978 meeting, Signal issued a press release stating:

The Signal Companies, Inc. and UOP, Inc. are conducting negotiations for the acquisition for cash by Signal of the 49.5 per cent of UOP which it does not presently own, announced Forrest N. Shumway, president and chief executive officer of Signal, and James V. Crawford, UOP president.

Price and other terms of the proposed transaction have not yet been finalized and would be subject to approval of the boards of directors of Signal and UOP, scheduled to meet early next week, the stockholders of UOP and certain federal agencies.

The announcement also referred to the fact that the closing price of UOP's common stock on that day was $14.50 per share.

Two days later, on March 2, 1978, Signal issued a second press release stating that its management would recommend a price in the range of $20 to $21 per share for UOP's 49.5% minority interest. This announcement referred to Signal's earlier statement that "negotiations" were being conducted for the acquisition of the minority shares.

Between Tuesday, February 28, 1978 and Monday, March 6, 1978, a total of four business days, Crawford spoke by telephone with all of UOP's non-Signal, i.e., outside, directors. Also during that period, Crawford retained Lehman Brothers to render a fairness opinion as to the price offered the minority for its stock. He gave two reasons for this choice. First, the time schedule between the announcement and the board meetings was short (by then only three business days) and since Lehman Brothers had been acting as UOP's investment banker for many years, Crawford felt that it would be in the best position to respond on such brief notice. Second, James W. Glanville, a long-time director of UOP and a partner in Lehman Brothers, had acted as a financial advisor to UOP for many years. Crawford believed that Glanville's familiarity with UOP, as a member of its board, would also be of assistance in enabling Lehman Brothers to render a fairness opinion within the existing time constraints.

Crawford telephoned Glanville, who gave his assurance that Lehman Brothers had no conflicts that would prevent it from accepting the task. Glanville's immediate personal reaction was that a price of $20 to $21 would certainly be fair, since it represented almost a 50% premium over UOP's market price. Glanville sought a $250,000 fee for Lehman Brothers' services, but Crawford thought this too much. After further discussions Glanville finally agreed that Lehman Brothers would render its fairness opinion for $150,000.

During this period Crawford also had several telephone contacts with Signal officials. In only one of them, however, was the price of the shares discussed. In a conversation with Walkup, Crawford advised that as a result of his communications with UOP's non-Signal directors, it was his feeling that the price would have to be the top of the proposed range, or $21 per share, if the approval of UOP's outside directors was to be obtained. But again, he did not seek any price higher than $21.

Glanville assembled a three-man Lehman Brothers team to do the work on the fairness opinion. These persons examined relevant documents and information concerning UOP, including its annual reports and its Securities and Exchange Commission filings from 1973 through 1976, as well as its audited financial statements for 1977, its interim reports to shareholders, and its recent and historical market prices and trading volumes. In addition, on Friday, March 3, 1978, two members of the Lehman Brothers team flew to UOP's headquarters in Des Plaines, Illinois, to perform a "due diligence" visit, during the course of which they interviewed Crawford as well as UOP's general counsel, its chief financial officer, and other key executives and personnel.

As a result, the Lehman Brothers team concluded that "the price of either $20 or $21 would be a fair price for the remaining shares of UOP". They telephoned this impression to Glanville, who was spending the weekend in Vermont.

On Monday morning, March 6, 1978, Glanville and the senior member of the Lehman Brothers team flew to Des Plaines to attend the scheduled UOP directors meeting. Glanville looked over the assembled information during the flight. The two had with them the draft of a "fairness opinion letter" in which the price had been left blank. Either during or immediately prior to the directors' meeting, the two-page "fairness opinion letter" was typed in final form and the price of $21 per share was inserted.

On March 6, 1978, both the Signal and UOP boards were convened to consider the proposed merger. Telephone communications were maintained between the two meetings. Walkup, Signal's board chairman, and also a UOP director, attended UOP's meeting with Crawford in order to present Signal's position and answer any questions that UOP's non-Signal directors might have. Arledge and Chitiea, along with Signal's other designees on UOP's board, participated by conference telephone. All of UOP's outside directors attended the meeting either in person or by conference telephone.

First, Signal's board unanimously adopted a resolution authorizing Signal to propose to UOP a cash merger of $21 per share as outlined in a certain merger agreement and other supporting documents. This proposal required that the merger be approved by a majority of UOP's outstanding minority shares voting at the stockholders meeting at which the merger would be considered, and that the minority shares voting in favor of the merger, when coupled with Signal's 50.5% interest would have to comprise at least two-thirds of all UOP shares. Otherwise the proposed merger would be deemed disapproved.

UOP's board then considered the proposal. Copies of the agreement were delivered to the directors in attendance, and other copies had been forwarded earlier to the directors participating by telephone. They also had before them UOP financial data for 1974–1977, UOP's most recent financial statements, market price information, and budget projections for 1978. In addition they had Lehman Brothers' hurriedly prepared fairness opinion letter finding the price of $21 to be fair. Glanville, the Lehman Brothers partner, and UOP director, commented on the information that had gone into preparation of the letter.

Signal also suggests that the Arledge-Chitiea feasibility study, indicating that a price of up to $24 per share would be a "good investment" for Signal, was discussed at the UOP directors' meeting. The Chancellor made no such finding, and our independent review of the record, detailed *infra*, satisfies us by a preponderance of the evidence that there was no discussion of this document at UOP's board meeting. Furthermore, it is clear beyond peradventure that nothing in that report was ever disclosed to UOP's minority shareholders prior to their approval of the merger.

After consideration of Signal's proposal, Walkup and Crawford left the meeting to permit a free and uninhibited exchange between UOP's non-Signal directors. Upon their return a resolution to accept Signal's offer was then proposed and adopted. While Signal's men on UOP's board participated in various aspects of the meeting, they abstained from voting. However, the minutes show that each of them "if voting would have voted yes".

On March 7, 1978, UOP sent a letter to its shareholders advising them of the action taken by UOP's board with respect to Signal's offer. This document pointed out, among other things, that on February 28, 1978 "both companies had announced negotiations were being conducted".

Despite the swift board action of the two companies, the merger was not submitted to UOP's shareholders until their annual meeting on May 26, 1978. In the notice of that meeting and proxy statement sent to shareholders in May, UOP's management and board urged that the merger be approved. The proxy statement also advised:

The price was determined after *discussions* between James V. Crawford, a director of Signal and Chief Executive Officer of UOP, and officers of Signal which took place during meetings on February 28, 1978, and in the course of several subsequent telephone conversations. (Emphasis added.)

In the original draft of the proxy statement the word "negotiations" had been used rather than "discussions". However, when the Securities and Exchange Commission sought details of the "negotiations" as part of its review of these materials, the term was deleted and the word "discussions" was substituted. The proxy statement indicated that the vote of UOP's board in approving the merger had been unanimous. It also advised the shareholders that Lehman Brothers had given its opinion that the merger price of $21 per share was fair to UOP's minority. However, it did not disclose the hurried method by which this conclusion was reached.

As of the record date of UOP's annual meeting, there were 11,488,302 shares of UOP common stock outstanding, 5,688,302 of which were owned by the minority. At the meeting only 56%, or 3,208,652, of the minority shares were voted. Of these, 2,953,812, or 51.9% of the total minority, voted for the merger, and 254,840 voted against it. When Signal's stock was added to the minority shares voting in favor, a total of 76.2% of UOP's outstanding shares approved the merger while only 2.2% opposed it.

By its terms the merger became effective on May 26, 1978, and each share of UOP's stock held by the minority was automatically converted into a right to receive $21 cash.

6. The parentheses indicate certain handwritten

II.

A.

A primary issue mandating reversal is the preparation by two UOP directors, Arledge and Chitiea, of their feasibility study for the exclusive use and benefit of Signal. This document was of obvious significance to both Signal and UOP. Using UOP data, it described the advantages to Signal of ousting the minority at a price range of $21–$24 per share. Mr. Arledge, one of the authors, outlined the benefits to Signal: [6]

Purpose Of The Merger

1) Provides an outstanding investment opportunity for Signal—(Better than any recent acquisition we have seen.)

2) Increases Signal's earnings.

3) Facilitates the flow of resources between Signal and its subsidiaries—(Big factor—works both ways.)

4) Provides cost savings potential for Signal and UOP.

5) Improves the percentage of Signal's 'operating earnings' as opposed to 'holding company earnings'.

6) Simplifies the understanding of Signal.

7) Facilitates technological exchange among Signal's subsidiaries.

8) Eliminates potential conflicts of interest.

Having written those words, solely for the use of Signal, it is clear from the record that neither Arledge nor Chitiea shared this report with their fellow directors of UOP. We are satisfied that no one else did either. This conduct hardly meets the fiduciary standards applicable to such a transaction. While Mr. Walkup, Signal's chairman of the board and a UOP director, attended the March 6, 1978 UOP board meeting and testified at trial that he had discussed the Arledge-Chitiea report with the UOP directors at this meeting, the record does not support this assertion. Perhaps it is the result of some confusion on Mr. Walkup's

comments of Mr. Arledge.

690

part. In any event Mr. Shumway, Signal's president, testified that he made sure the Signal outside directors had this report prior to the March 6, 1978 Signal board meeting, but he did not testify that the Arledge-Chitiea report was also sent to UOP's outside directors.

Mr. Crawford, UOP's president, could not recall that any documents, other than a draft of the merger agreement, were sent to UOP's directors before the March 6, 1978 UOP meeting. Mr. Chitiea, an author of the report, testified that it was made available to Signal's directors, but to his knowledge it was not circulated to the outside directors of UOP. He specifically testified that he "didn't share" that information with the outside directors of UOP with whom he served.

None of UOP's outside directors who testified stated that they had seen this document. The minutes of the UOP board meeting do not identify the Arledge-Chitiea report as having been delivered to UOP's outside directors. This is particularly significant since the minutes describe in considerable detail the materials that actually were distributed. While these minutes recite Mr. Walkup's presentation of the Signal offer, they do not mention the Arledge-Chitiea report or any disclosure that Signal considered a price of up to $24 to be a good investment. If Mr. Walkup had in fact provided such important information to UOP's outside directors, it is logical to assume that these carefully drafted minutes would disclose it. The post-trial briefs of Signal and UOP contain a thorough description of the documents purportedly available to their boards at the March 6, 1978, meetings. Although the Arledge-Chitiea report is specifically identified as being available to the Signal directors, there is no mention of it being among the documents submitted to the UOP board. Even when queried at a prior oral argument before this Court, counsel for Signal did not claim that the Ar-

ledge-Chitiea report had been disclosed to UOP's outside directors. Instead, he chose to belittle its contents. This was the same approach taken before us at the last oral argument.

Actually, it appears that a three-page summary of figures was given to all UOP directors. Its first page is identical to one page of the Arledge-Chitiea report, but this dealt with nothing more than a justification of the $21 price. Significantly, the contents of this three-page summary are what the minutes reflect Mr. Walkup told the UOP board. However, nothing contained in either the minutes or this three-page summary reflects Signal's study regarding the $24 price.

The Arledge-Chitiea report speaks for itself in supporting the Chancellor's finding that a price of up to $24 was a "good investment" for Signal. It shows that a return on the investment at $21 would be 15.7% versus 15.5% at $24 per share. This was a difference of only two-tenths of one percent, while it meant over $17,000,000 to the minority. Under such circumstances, paying UOP's minority shareholders $24 would have had relatively little long-term effect on Signal, and the Chancellor's findings concerning the benefit to Signal, even at a price of $24, were obviously correct. *Levitt v. Bouvier*, Del.Supr., 287 A.2d 671, 673 (1972).

[6] Certainly, this was a matter of material significance to UOP and its shareholders. Since the study was prepared by two UOP directors, using UOP information for the exclusive benefit of Signal, and nothing whatever was done to disclose it to the outside UOP directors or the minority shareholders, a question of breach of fiduciary duty arises. This problem occurs because there were common Signal-UOP directors participating, at least to some extent, in the UOP board's decision-making processes without full disclosure of the conflicts they faced.[7]

7. Although perfection is not possible, or expected, the result here could have been entirely different if UOP had appointed an independent negotiating committee of its outside directors to deal with Signal at arm's length. *See, e.g., Harriman v. E.I. duPont de Nemours & Co.*, 411

B.

[7] In assessing this situation, the Court of Chancery was required to:

examine what information defendants had and to measure it against what they gave to the minority stockholders, in a context in which 'complete candor' is required. In other words, the limited function of the Court was to determine whether defendants had disclosed all information in their possession germane to the transaction in issue. And by 'germane' we mean, for present purposes, information such as a reasonable shareholder would consider important in deciding whether to sell or retain stock.

* * * * * *

... Completeness, not adequacy, is both the norm and the mandate under present circumstances.

Lynch v. Vickers Energy Corp., Del.Supr., 383 A.2d 278, 281 (1977) (*Lynch I*). This is merely stating in another way the long-existing principle of Delaware law that these Signal designated directors on UOP's board still owed UOP and its shareholders an uncompromising duty of loyalty. The classic language of *Guth v. Loft, Inc.*, Del.Supr., 5 A.2d 503, 510 (1939), requires no embellishment:

A public policy, existing through the years, and derived from a profound knowledge of human characteristics and motives, has established a rule that demands of a corporate officer or director, peremptorily and inexorably, the most scrupulous observance of his duty, not only affirmatively to protect the interests of the corporation committed to his charge, but also to refrain from doing anything that would work injury to the corporation, or to deprive it of profit or advantage which his skill and ability

might properly bring to it, or to enable it to make in the reasonable and lawful exercise of its powers. The rule that requires an undivided and unselfish loyalty to the corporation demands that there shall be no conflict between duty and self-interest.

[8] Given the absence of any attempt to structure this transaction on an arm's length basis, Signal cannot escape the effects of the conflicts it faced, particularly when its designees on UOP's board did not totally abstain from participation in the matter. There is no "safe harbor" for such divided loyalties in Delaware. When directors of a Delaware corporation are on both sides of a transaction, they are required to demonstrate their utmost good faith and the most scrupulous inherent fairness of the bargain. *Gottlieb v. Heyden Chemical Corp.*, Del.Supr., 91 A.2d 57, 57–58 (1952). The requirement of fairness is unflinching in its demand that where one stands on both sides of a transaction, he has the burden of establishing its entire fairness, sufficient to pass the test of careful scrutiny by the courts. *Sterling v. Mayflower Hotel Corp.*, Del.Supr., 93 A.2d 107, 110 (1952); *Bastian v. Bourns, Inc.*, Del.Ch., 256 A.2d 680, 681 (1969), *aff'd*, Del.Supr., 278 A.2d 467 (1970); *David J. Greene & Co. v. Dunhill International Inc.*, Del.Ch., 249 A.2d 427, 431 (1968).

[9, 10] There is no dilution of this obligation where one holds dual or multiple directorships, as in a parent-subsidiary context. *Levien v. Sinclair Oil Corp.*, Del.Ch., 261 A.2d 911, 915 (1969). Thus, individuals who act in a dual capacity as directors of two corporations, one of whom is parent and the other subsidiary, owe the same duty of good management to both corporations, and in the absence of an independent nego-

---

F.Supp. 133 (D.Del.1975). Since fairness in this context can be equated to conduct by a theoretical, wholly independent, board of directors acting upon the matter before them, it is unfortunate that this course apparently was neither considered nor pursued. *Johnston v. Greene*, Del.Supr., 121 A.2d 919, 925 (1956). Particularly in a parent-subsidiary context, a

showing that the action taken was as though each of the contending parties had in fact exerted its bargaining power against the other at arm's length is strong evidence that the transaction meets the test of fairness. *Getty Oil Co. v. Skelly Oil Co.*, Del.Supr., 267 A.2d 883, 886 (1970); *Puma v. Marriott*, Del.Ch., 283 A.2d 693, 696 (1971).

tiating structure (see note 7, *supra*), or the directors' total abstention from any participation in the matter, this duty is to be exercised in light of what is best for both companies. *Warshaw v. Calhoun*, Del. Supr., 221 A.2d 487, 492 (1966). The record demonstrates that Signal has not met this obligation.

C.

The concept of fairness has two basic aspects: fair dealing and fair price. The former embraces questions of when the transaction was timed, how it was initiated, structured, negotiated, disclosed to the directors, and how the approvals of the directors and the stockholders were obtained. The latter aspect of fairness relates to the economic and financial considerations of the proposed merger, including all relevant factors: assets, market value, earnings, future prospects, and any other elements that affect the intrinsic or inherent value of a company's stock. Moore, *The "Interested" Director or Officer Transaction*, 4 Del.J. Corp.L. 674, 676 (1979); Nathan & Shapiro, *Legal Standard of Fairness of Merger Terms Under Delaware Law*, 2 Del.J. Corp.L. 44, 46–47 (1977). *See Tri-Continental Corp. v. Battye*, Del.Supr., 74 A.2d 71, 72 (1950); 8 *Del.C.* § 262(h). However, the test for fairness is not a bifurcated one as between fair dealing and price. All aspects of the issue must be examined as a whole since the question is one of entire fairness. However, in a non-fraudulent transaction we recognize that price may be the preponderant consideration outweighing other features of the merger. Here, we address the two basic aspects of fairness separately because we find reversible error as to both.

D.

[11] Part of fair dealing is the obvious duty of candor required by *Lynch I, supra*. Moreover, one possessing superior knowledge may not mislead any stockholder by use of corporate information to which the latter is not privy. *Lank v. Steiner*, Del. Supr., 224 A.2d 242, 244 (1966). Delaware

has long imposed this duty even upon persons who are not corporate officers or directors, but who nonetheless are privy to matters of interest or significance to their company. *Brophy v. Cities Service Co.*, Del. Ch., 70 A.2d 5, 7 (1949). With the well-established Delaware law on the subject, and the Court of Chancery's findings of fact here, it is inevitable that the obvious conflicts posed by Arledge and Chitiea's preparation of their "feasibility study", derived from UOP information, for the sole use and benefit of Signal, cannot pass muster.

The Arledge-Chitiea report is but one aspect of the element of fair dealing. How did this merger evolve? It is clear that it was entirely initiated by Signal. The serious time constraints under which the principals acted were all set by Signal. It had not found a suitable outlet for its excess cash and considered UOP a desirable investment, particularly since it was now in a position to acquire the whole company for itself. For whatever reasons, and they were only Signal's, the entire transaction was presented to and approved by UOP's board within four business days. Standing alone, this is not necessarily indicative of any lack of fairness by a majority shareholder. It was what occurred, or more properly, what did not occur, during this brief period that makes the time constraints imposed by Signal relevant to the issue of fairness.

The structure of the transaction, again, was Signal's doing. So far as negotiations were concerned, it is clear that they were modest at best. Crawford, Signal's man at UOP, never really talked price with Signal, except to accede to its management's statements on the subject, and to convey to Signal the UOP outside directors' view that as between the $20–$21 range under consideration, it would have to be $21. The latter is not a surprising outcome, but hardly arm's length negotiations. Only the protection of benefits for UOP's key employees and the issue of Lehman Brothers' fee approached any concept of bargaining.

As we have noted, the matter of disclosure to the UOP directors was wholly flawed by the conflicts of interest raised by the Arledge-Chitiea report. All of those conflicts were resolved by Signal in its own favor without divulging any aspect of them to UOP.

This cannot but undermine a conclusion that this merger meets any reasonable test of fairness. The outside UOP directors lacked one material piece of information generated by two of their colleagues, but shared only with Signal. True, the UOP board had the Lehman Brothers' fairness opinion, but that firm has been blamed by the plaintiff for the hurried task it performed, when more properly the responsibility for this lies with Signal. There was no disclosure of the circumstances surrounding the rather cursory preparation of the Lehman Brothers' fairness opinion. Instead, the impression was given UOP's minority that a careful study had been made, when in fact speed was the hallmark, and Mr. Glanville, Lehman's partner in charge of the matter, and also a UOP director, having spent the weekend in Vermont, brought a draft of the "fairness opinion letter" to the UOP directors' meeting on March 6, 1978 with the price left blank. We can only conclude from the record that the rush imposed on Lehman Brothers by Signal's timetable contributed to the difficulties under which this investment banking firm attempted to perform its responsibilities. Yet, none of this was disclosed to UOP's minority.

Finally, the minority stockholders were denied the critical information that Signal considered a price of $24 to be a good investment. Since this would have meant over $17,000,000 more to the minority, we cannot conclude that the shareholder vote was an informed one. Under the circumstances, an approval by a majority of the minority was meaningless. *Lynch I*, 383 A.2d at 279, 281; *Cahall v. Lofland*, Del.Ch., 114 A. 224 (1921).

Given these particulars and the Delaware law on the subject, the record does not establish that this transaction satisfies any reasonable concept of fair dealing, and the Chancellor's findings in that regard must be reversed.

E.

Turning to the matter of price, plaintiff also challenges its fairness. His evidence was that on the date the merger was approved the stock was worth at least $26 per share. In support, he offered the testimony of a chartered investment analyst who used two basic approaches to valuation: a comparative analysis of the premium paid over market in ten other tender offer-merger combinations, and a discounted cash flow analysis.

In this breach of fiduciary duty case, the Chancellor perceived that the approach to valuation was the same as that in an appraisal proceeding. Consistent with precedent, he rejected plaintiff's method of proof and accepted defendants' evidence of value as being in accord with practice under prior case law. This means that the so-called "Delaware block" or weighted average method was employed wherein the elements of value, i.e., assets, market price, earnings, etc., were assigned a particular weight and the resulting amounts added to determine the value per share. This procedure has been in use for decades. *See In re General Realty & Utilities Corp.*, Del.Ch., 52 A.2d 6, 14–15 (1947). However, to the extent it excludes other generally accepted techniques used in the financial community and the courts, it is now clearly outmoded. It is time we recognize this in appraisal and other stock valuation proceedings and bring our law current on the subject.

While the Chancellor rejected plaintiff's discounted cash flow method of valuing UOP's stock, as not corresponding with "either logic or the existing law" (426 A.2d at 1360), it is significant that this was essentially the focus, i.e., earnings potential of UOP, of Messrs. Arledge and Chitiea in their evaluation of the merger. Accordingly, the standard "Delaware block" or weighted average method of valuation, for-

694

merly employed in appraisal and other stock valuation cases, shall no longer exclusively control such proceedings. We believe that a more liberal approach must include proof of value by any techniques or methods which are generally considered acceptable in the financial community and otherwise admissible in court, subject only to our interpretation of 8 *Del.C.* § 262(h), *infra.* *See also* D.R.E. 702–05. This will obviate the very structured and mechanistic procedure that has heretofore governed such matters. *See Jacques Coe & Co. v. Minneapolis-Moline Co.,* Del.Ch., 75 A.2d 244, 247 (1950); *Tri-Continental Corp. v. Battye,* Del.Ch., 66 A.2d 910, 917–18 (1949); *In re General Realty and Utilities Corp., supra.*

Fair price obviously requires consideration of all relevant factors involving the value of a company. This has long been the law of Delaware as stated in *Tri-Continental Corp.,* 74 A.2d at 72:

The basic concept of value under the appraisal statute is that the stockholder is entitled to be paid for that which has been taken from him, viz., his proportionate interest in a going concern. By value of the stockholder's proportionate interest in the corporate enterprise is meant the true or intrinsic value of his stock which has been taken by the merger. In determining what figure represents this true or intrinsic value, the appraiser and the courts must take into consideration all factors and elements which reasonably might enter into the fixing of value. Thus, market value, asset value, dividends, earning prospects, the nature of the enterprise and any other facts which were known or which could be ascertained as of the date of merger and which throw any light on *future prospects* of the merged corporation are not only pertinent to an inquiry as to the value of the dissenting stockholders' interest, but *must be considered* by the agency fixing the value. (Emphasis added.)

This is not only in accord with the realities of present day affairs, but it is thoroughly

consonant with the purpose and intent of our statutory law. Under 8 *Del.C.* § 262(h), the Court of Chancery:

shall appraise the shares, determining their *fair* value exclusive of any element of value arising from the accomplishment or expectation of the merger, together with a fair rate of interest, if any, to be paid upon the amount determined to be the *fair* value. In determining such *fair* value, the Court shall take into account *all relevant factors* ... (Emphasis added)

See also Bell v. Kirby Lumber Corp., Del. Supr., 413 A.2d 137, 150–51 (1980) (Quillen, J., concurring).

It is significant that section 262 now mandates the determination of "fair" value based upon "all relevant factors". Only the speculative elements of value that may arise from the "accomplishment or expectation" of the merger are excluded. We take this to be a very narrow exception to the appraisal process, designed to eliminate use of *pro forma* data and projections of a speculative variety relating to the completion of a merger. But elements of future value, including the nature of the enterprise, which are known or susceptible of proof as of the date of the merger and not the product of speculation, may be considered. When the trial court deems it appropriate, fair value also includes any damages, resulting from the taking, which the stockholders sustain as a class. If that was not the case, then the obligation to consider "all relevant factors" in the valuation process would be eroded. We are supported in this view not only by *Tri-Continental Corp.,* 74 A.2d at 72, but also by the evolutionary amendments to section 262.

Prior to an amendment in 1976, the earlier relevant provision of section 262 stated:

(f) The appraiser shall determine the value of the stock of the stockholders ... The Court shall by its decree determine the value of the stock of the stockholders entitled to payment therefor ...

The first references to "fair" value occurred in a 1976 amendment to section 262(f), which provided:

(f) ... the Court shall appraise the shares, determining their fair value exclusively of any element of value arising from the accomplishment or expectation of the merger....

It was not until the 1981 amendment to section 262 that the reference to "fair value" was repeatedly emphasized and the statutory mandate that the Court "take into account all relevant factors" appeared [section 262(h)]. Clearly, there is a legislative intent to fully compensate shareholders for whatever their loss may be, subject only to the narrow limitation that one can not take speculative effects of the merger into account.

Although the Chancellor received the plaintiff's evidence, his opinion indicates that the use of it was precluded because of past Delaware practice. While we do not suggest a monetary result one way or the other, we do think the plaintiff's evidence should be part of the factual mix and weighed as such. Until the $21 price is measured on remand by the valuation standards mandated by Delaware law, there can be no finding at the present stage of these proceedings that the price is fair. Given the lack of any candid disclosure of the material facts surrounding establishment of the $21 price, the majority of the minority vote, approving the merger, is meaningless.

[12] The plaintiff has not sought an appraisal, but rescissory damages of the type contemplated by Lynch v. Vickers Energy Corp., Del.Supr., 429 A.2d 497, 505-06 (1981) (Lynch II). In view of the approach to valuation that we announce today, we see no basis in our law for Lynch II's exclusive monetary formula for relief. On remand the plaintiff will be permitted to test the fairness of the $21 price by the standards we herein establish, in conformity with the principle applicable to an appraisal—that fair value be determined by taking "into account all relevant factors" [see 8 Del.C. § 262(h), supra]. In our view this includes the elements of rescissory damages if the Chancellor considers them susceptible of proof and a remedy appropriate to all the

issues of fairness before him. To the extent that Lynch II, 429 A.2d at 505-06, purports to limit the Chancellor's discretion to a single remedial formula for monetary damages in a cash-out merger, it is overruled.

While a plaintiff's monetary remedy ordinarily should be confined to the more liberalized appraisal proceeding herein established, we do not intend any limitation on the historic powers of the Chancellor to grant such other relief as the facts of a particular case may dictate. The appraisal remedy we approve may not be adequate in certain cases, particularly where fraud, misrepresentation, self-dealing, deliberate waste of corporate assets, or gross and palpable overreaching are involved. Cole v. National Cash Credit Association, Del.Ch., 156 A. 183, 187 (1931). Under such circumstances, the Chancellor's powers are complete to fashion any form of equitable and monetary relief as may be appropriate, including rescissory damages. Since it is apparent that this long completed transaction is too involved to undo, and in view of the Chancellor's discretion, the award, if any, should be in the form of monetary damages based upon entire fairness standards, i.e., fair dealing and fair price.

[13] Obviously, there are other litigants, like the plaintiff, who abjured an appraisal and whose rights to challenge the element of fair value must be preserved.[8] Accordingly, the quasi-appraisal remedy we grant the plaintiff here will apply only to: (1) this case; (2) any case now pending on appeal to this Court; (3) any case now pending in the Court of Chancery which has not yet been appealed but which may be eligible for direct appeal to this Court; (4) any case challenging a cash-out merger, the effective date of which is on or before February 1, 1983; and (5) any proposed merger to be presented at a shareholders' meeting, the notification of which is mailed to the stockholders on or before February 23, 1983. Thereafter, the provisions of 8 Del.C. §262, as herein construed, respecting the scope of an appraisal and the means for perfecting the same, shall govern the financial remedy available to minority shareholders in a cash-

8. Under 8 Del.C. § 262(a), (d) & (e), a stockholder is required to act within certain time periods to perfect the right to an appraisal.

out merger. Thus, we return to the well established principles of *Stauffer v. Standard Brands, Inc.,* Del.Supr., 187 A.2d 78 (1962) and *David J. Greene & Co. v. Schenley Industries, Inc.,* Del.Ch., 281 A.2d 30 (1971), mandating a stockholder's recourse to the basic remedy of an appraisal.

III.

Finally, we address the matter of business purpose. The defendants contend that the purpose of this merger was not a proper subject of inquiry by the trial court. The plaintiff says that no valid purpose existed—the entire transaction was a mere subterfuge designed to eliminate the minority. The Chancellor ruled otherwise, but in so doing he clearly circumscribed the thrust and effect of *Singer. Weinberger v. UOP,* 426 A.2d at 1342–43, 1348–50. This has led to the thoroughly sound observation that the business purpose test "may be . . . virtually interpreted out of existence, as it was in *Weinberger*".[9]

The requirement of a business purpose is new to our law of mergers and was a departure from prior case law. *See Stauffer v. Standard Brands, Inc., supra; David J. Greene & Co. v. Schenley Industries, Inc., supra.*

9. Weiss, *The Law of Take Out Mergers: A Historical Perspective,* 56 N.Y.U.L.Rev. 624, 671, n. 300 (1981).

[14] In view of the fairness test which has long been applicable to parent-subsidiary mergers, *Sterling v. Mayflower Hotel Corp.,* Del.Supr., 93 A.2d 107, 109–10 (1952), the expanded appraisal remedy now available to shareholders, and the broad discretion of the Chancellor to fashion such relief as the facts of a given case may dictate, we do not believe that any additional meaningful protection is afforded minority shareholders by the business purpose requirement of the trilogy of *Singer, Tanzer,*[16] *Najjar,*[11] and their progeny. Accordingly, such requirement shall no longer be of any force or effect.

The judgment of the Court of Chancery, finding both the circumstances of the merger and the price paid the minority shareholders to be fair, is reversed. The matter is remanded for further proceedings consistent herewith. Upon remand the plaintiff's post-trial motion to enlarge the class should be granted.

•   •   •   •   •

REVERSED AND REMANDED.

10. *Tanzer v. International General Industries, Inc.,* Del.Supr., 379 A.2d 1121, 1124–25 (1977).

11. *Roland International Corp. v. Najjar,* Del. Supr., 407 A.2d 1032, 1036 (1979).

NOTE

The decision of the Delaware Supreme Court in the Sterling v. Mayflower Hotel Corp. case, cited in <u>Weinberger</u>, shows how far the court's thinking about values in combination transactions has come in the intervening years. In <u>Sterling</u>, Hilton Hotels Corp. had for a number of years owned more than 80% of the stock of Mayflower, and for some time had contemplated merging Mayflower into Hilton. An independent financial appraiser was retained to determine a fair exchange ratio, and on the basis of a comparison of earnings, dividends, book value and market price the appraiser concluded that Mayflower's shareholders should receive in the merger one share of Hilton stock for each share of Mayflower. Some months before the combination was undertaken Hilton made a tender offer for Mayflower shares at $19.10 per share. That price was somewhat higher than the market price of Hilton stock; it was also above the market price of Mayflower stock, even though it was clear that Hilton's policy of buying Mayflower stock at $19.10 per share had artificially raised the market. In any event, Hilton agreed in conjunction with the merter to pay $19.10 per share to any Mayflower minority shareholder who wished to sell rather than participate in the merger.

In support of their claim of unfairness the plaintiffs

introduced an appraisal of Mayflower's property at more than
$10,000,000, using reproduction cost less depreciation for the
hotel, whereas the share for share exchange rate in effect
valued the Mayflower property at less than $6,000,000. The
plaintiffs insisted that the exchange ratio should be set with
reference to the $10,000,000 figure, which would have entitled
them to approximately $27 per share, or around 1½ shares of
Hilton for each Mayflower share.

The court accepted the plaintiffs' contention that since
Hilton was on both sides of the transaction, the "burden of establishing its entire fairness" was on the defendants. However,
the court then failed to meet head-on the plaintiffs' charge of
gross disparity between their $10,000,000 reproduction figure
and the less than $6,000,000 value assumed in the one for one
exchange ratio. Instead, the court veered off on the rather
technical tack that the test of fairness in a merger was different than in a sale of assets, and that in a merger the $10,000,000
figure, referred to by the court as the "liquidating value," did
not have to be taken into account, at least so far as minority
stockholders having no power to compel a liquidation were concerned. Such an approach scarcely gives the impression that the
"entire fairness" of the transaction had been established.

Nevertheless, it is submitted that any seeming departure
from the court's fairness standard is more apparent than real.
For it is well recognized that the reproduction cost of an
asset is not necessarily a relevant measure of current value.
Certainly the term "liquidating value" used by the court was
a complete misnomer, since there was no evidence whatever that
such an amount could have been realized upon a liquidation of
Mayflower. Therefore, the short answer to the plaintiffs'
argument was that the $10,000,000 figure was not a significant
index to value, and hence there was no reason to take it into
account in testing the fairness of the exchange ratio adopted.
At a minimum, the court might have pointed out that if the
reproduction cost of the Mayflower property was entitled to
consideration, so was the reproduction cost of the Hilton
property underlying the stock transferred to Mayflower stockholders; and on that basis, as the defendants' evidence of reproduction cost confirmed, there was certainly no unfairness to
the Mayflower shareholders.

Unfortunately, however, the court instead seemed to accept
that premise that the $10,000,000 figure had some validity as
a measure of "liquidating value", as indicated by both the
court's use of that term and its stress upon the purported distinction between valuation for merger and valuation for a sale
of assets. That distinction seemed to imply that if Hilton had
chosen to eliminate Mayflower by purchasing its assets for stock

instead of by merger, the plaintiffs might have had a valid objection if the market value of Hilton's consideration did not approximate $10,000,000. But surely the fair market value of the Mayflower property could not vary by such an order of magnitude on the basis of the particular combination technique used. The reality is that this $10,000,000 figure was simply not a significant measure of value for any purpose.

A somewhat similar but much more troublesome question of valuation is presented by the decision in Abelow v. Midstates Oil Corp., 189 A. 2d 675 (Del.Sup.Ct.1963). There Midstates was an operating company; Middle Corporation was a holding company whose only significant asset was 96% of the stock of Midstates. The two companies, under their common management, decided that the operating assets should be sold. They obtained expressions of interest from a number of prospective buyers, embracing a variety of different approaches, including the acquisition of the assets directly from the operating company, the acquisition of the stock of the operating company from the holding company and the acquisition of the stock of the holding company from its stockholders. One of the two offers endorsed by the companies' investment bankers took the latter form, and a deal was ultimately worked out involving an exchange of 45 shares of the buyer's stock for each 100 shares of the holding company's stock. This ratio was based upon the comparative market values of the two stocks. On this basis, the total market value of the holding company's stock was about $30,500,000, which seemed to indicate that the operating company's stock, which was its only asset, was worth approximately $1450 per share. After acquiring about 95% of the stock of the holding company in this exchange, the buyer caused the holding company to buy the operating company's assets, preparatory to merging the holding company into the buyer, as had been contemplated from the outset. The price paid for the operating assets was approximately $25,000,000 plus assumption of liabilities, which produced a liquidating dividend of approximately $1125 per share of the operating company's stock.

Minority stockholders of the operating company attacked the transaction, contending that if the acquisition had taken a different form, such as a direct sale of the operating company's assets to the buyer, they would have received a figure closer to $1450 per share, corresponding to the valuation inherent in the exchange ratio used in the exchange of stock between the buyer and the stockholders of the holding company. But the court held that the management had no obligation either to adopt any particular form of transaction for the sale or to make sure that minority stockholders of the operating company were ultimately paid on a basis comparable to that afforded the stockholders of the holding company in the exchange transaction. In effect, the court agreed with the contention of the defendants that the only issue was the fairness of the price paid by the holding company for the operating company's assets, and accepted the evidence of the defendants' appraisal experts that the assets were worth no more than the price at which they were purchased. As to the plaintiffs' contention that the ratio upon which the buyer's stock was exchanged for stock of the holding company fixed the value of the operating company's stock, and indirectly its underlying assets, the court commented as follows:

Moreover, it is at least doubtful whether a comparison of a value based on market value of shares with asset value is of any assistance in this case. Cf. Sterling v. Mayflower Hotel Corporation, . . . (comparison of market value of stock and asset value in merger disapproved).

Citation of the Sterling case is somewhat ironic since in Sterling it was the appraised value which the court insisted upon ignoring (though for the wrong reasons), whereas in Abelow the court accepted appraised valuation and rejected the much more compelling evidence of the market value of stock actually paid to acquire (indirectly) the assets in question. Of course it may be that in some cases the total market value of the stock of a corporation can exceed the value of the underlying assets—in other words, the operation of the stock market may add some elements of value, as, for example, it seems to do in the case of stock dividends. Accordingly, it was presumably open to the defendants to show that there were elements of value in the stock of the holding company which were separate from and in addition to the value of the assets of the operating company. But mere appraisal evidence hardly seems a sufficient showing, particularly under the burden imposed by the Sterling case upon a parent corporation to establish the "entire fairness" of a purchase of assets from a controlled subsidiary.

B. FAIRNESS AMONG CLASSES OF STOCK OF THE SAME CORPORATION

1. IN GENERAL

Whenever a disappearing corporation in a merger has more than one class of stock, there may also be questions of fairness as between those classes. That is because the merger plan, in specifying the basis for conversion of the various classes of the disappearing corporation's stock into stock of the surviving corporation, fixes not only the total participation of the disappearing corporation but also the allocation thereof among its various classes of stock. (And the merger may also be used as an occasion to rearrange the interests of the various stock classes of the surviving corporation.)

Presumably the appropriate vehicle for objecting to the basis of allocation among the classes of one of the corporations would be an attack on the merger for unfairness, just as it is for complaining of the comparative treatment as between the constituent corporations. Here, however, the similarity between these two types of attack ends. For unlike the comparative treatment of the constituent corporations, the allocation among classes of stock of the same corporation is rarely the product of arm's-length negotiations of any kind. Obviously, the representatives of the other parties to the merger are concerned only with the total participation of each constituent; the allocation within each separate corporation plays no part in the bargaining process. So this allocation falls entirely to the management of the corporation, which is typically more closely identified with junior than with senior classes. And in some states, notably Delaware, there is not even the protection of the class vote which MBA §73 seems to afford in all such cases.

Despite this important difference between the two situations, the courts have generally drawn no distinction between the inter-corporate and the intra-corporate aspects of a merger so far as the applicable fairness standard is concerned. Thus in the Cole case, page 683 supra, no point was made of the fact that the complainant was a preferred stockholder in one of the constituents, although perhaps there the plaintiff was only concerned with the adequacy of the total participation accorded to his corporation and not with its allocation among the various classes. But in MacFarlane v. North American Cement Corp., 16 Del.Ch. 172, 157 A. 396 (Ch.1928), the plaintiff preferred stockholders expressly disclaimed any complaint about the total participation of their corporation, and instead levelled their attack directly on the comparative treatment of the preferred and common stockholders. Nevertheless, the court applied the same "grossly unfair" standard adopted in the Cole case, and refused to upset the proposed allocation between the two classes.

At first blush it looks as though the court in MacFarlane applied a totally unsuitable standard to the inter-class allocation. But it must be borne in mind that the plaintiffs in that case, like all stockholders in a merger, had the alternative of an appraisal remedy; and as noted earlier, that might justify limiting judicial review to cases of gross unfairness, despite the absence of arm's-length bargaining.

If it were decided that greater judicial scrutiny of the inter-class allocation in merger was called for, where would one look for the appropriate standard of fairness? Perhaps the closest analogy is to the recapitalization of a single corporation, where too the comparative treatment of two or more classes of stock may be drawn into question, particularly when the corporation is to end up with only common stock outstanding, which means that the former senior classes are to be "collapsed" into, i.e., exchanged for, common stock. In effect, in a merger the disappearing corporation is "recapitalized" in shares of the surviving corporation. But there is the rather important difference that in a merger there is almost invariably a right of appraisal (though not always a class vote), whereas in a "straight" recapitalization pursuant to an amendment of the certificate of incorporation there would only rarely be an appraisal right (although there would almost always be a class vote).

However, the fact is that in the recapitalization cases too the courts have exhibited considerable reluctance to review for fairness. Instead, particularly in Delaware, there has been a tendency to apply the same "gross unfairness" standard used in the merger cases. This is perhaps understandable when the recapitalization actually takes the form of a merger, as for example in Porges v. Vadsco Sales Corp., 27 Del.Ch. 127, 32 A.2d 148 (Ch.1943), where the merger of a parent corporation with its wholly-owned subsidiary was used as the vehicle for recapitalizing the parent. Such mergers have often been utilized as a substitute for a straightforward certificate amendment, in part because of a supposed greater latitude to change the rights of the stockholders, particularly with regard to arrearages on preferred stock.   And at least when the merger form is adopted appraisal rights for dissenting stockholders would normally be available, so it may do little harm to follow the merger precedents even though the transaction really amounts to a recapitalization of a single corporation.   But unfortunately, the courts have tended to apply the same "gross unfairness" standard in cases of "straight" recapitalization pursuant to certificate amendment, despite the absence of any appraisal remedy.   Indeed, in Barrett v. Denver Tramway Corp., 53 F.Supp. 198 (D.Del.1943), the court went so far as to sustain a plan of recapitalization even though it regarded the plan as unfair to the preferred stockholders.   The plan was one designed to eliminate cumulative dividend arrearages on preferred stock by inducing the preferred stockholders to exchange their existing stock for new prior preferred.   (See pages 671-672, supra.)   However, the new stock gave the preferred stockholders virtually nothing additional by way of annual dividends or liquidation preference to compensate them for the loss of their arrearages.   The court conceded that because of its voting control the common stock could exact some "tribute" from the preferred, but expressed doubt about a plan under which the "preferred receives nothing for what it is required to relinquish" while the common is not required to give up anything.

Nevertheless, the court concluded that since there was no "constructive fraud, bad faith, or gross unfairness," under the Delaware authorities the plan had to be upheld.   And even in New Jersey, where the courts have often been more sympathetic to complaints by preferred stockholders, e.g., Wessel v. Guantanamo Sugar Co., 134 N. J.Eq. 271, 35 A.2d 215 (Ch.1944), affirmed Murphy v. Guantanamo Sugar Co., 135 N.J.Eq. 506, 39 A.2d 431 (Ct.Err. & App.1944), one case has indicated that the fairness of a recapitalization need not be considered at all, so long as the certificate amendment is authorized by the statute and adopted by the required vote.   See Franzblau v. Capital Securities Co., Inc., 2 N.J.Super. 517, 64 A.2d 644 (1949).

This judicial reluctance to review the fairness of recapitalization plans has been the subject of considerable critical comment. See, e. g., Dodd, Fair and Equitable Recapitalizations, 55 Harv.L.Rev. 780 (1941); Walter, Fairness in State Court Recapitalization Plans— A Disappearing Doctrine, 29 B.U.L.Rev. 453 (1949).   Admittedly, judicial invalidation of a recapitalization plan for unfairness could lead to an impasse if the common stockholders thereafter refuse to approve a plan which gives the preferred stockholders enough to escape judicial condemnation.   But as a practical matter it is probably just as likely that judicial rejection of a plan would lead the parties to find some different accommodation of their respective interests which would be fair.   This was undoubtedly the premise of the Nebraska

Legislature in adopting a statute requiring the court to enjoin certificate amendments if the proponents do not "show that, to a reasonable probability, they are fair, just, and equitable to all shareholders affected thereby." Neb.Rev.Stat. § 21–1,162 (1954). See generally, Latty, Exploration of Legislative Remedy for Prejudicial Changes in Senior Shares, 19 U.Chi.L.Rev. 759 (1952).

Another type of case presenting valuation issues in a recapitalization setting has involved disputes between voting and non-voting classes of stock. Here again the Delaware courts have exhibited reluctance to upset transactions on account of unfairness. For example, Manacher v. Reynolds, 39 Del.Ch. 401, 165 A.2d 741 (Ch.1960), involved a holding company which had a closely-held class of voting stock, and 16 times as many shares of publicly-traded, non-voting, otherwise identical common. The holding company in turn owned a controlling block of the publicly-traded stock of a successful operating company. Since the non-voting stock of the holding company was selling at a price equivalent to only about two-thirds of the value of the equity they represented in the stock of the operating corporation, a minority holder bought an action to force the holding corporation to liquidate and distribute pro rata its shares of the operating corporation. The parties to the suit worked out a settlement under which, in contemplation of such a liquidation, the holding company was to be recapitalized by exchanging three shares of non-voting stock for each share of voting stock, which would give the holders of the voting stock about $40,000,000 more in stock of the operating company than they would have received in a pro rata distribution without any recapitalization. The plan was approved by a substantial majority of the disinterested holders of the non-voting stock. In sustaining the settlement against the objection that the plan of recapitalization was too generous to the holders of the voting stock, the court implied that a $40,000,000 premium was somewhat excessive, but upheld the transaction on the basis of the disinterested shareholder approval. See Case Comment, 109 U. of Pa. L.Rev. 887 (1961).

A somewhat similar situation was presented in Honigman v. Green Giant Co., 309 F.2d 667 (8th Cir.1962), where the corporation involved had 44 Class A voting shares and 429,000 Class B non-voting shares. The challenged recapitalization plan called for giving the Class B shares the right to vote, in consideration for allowing the Class A stock to be converted into Class B on the basis of 1000 to 1, the conversion to take place gradually over a period of ten years. The plan was approved by the overwhelming majority of Class B stockholders, as well as all the Class A stockholders. Minority Class B stockholders attacked the plan, but the District Court sustained it, and the Court of Appeals affirmed. The District Court expressly purported to review the fairness of the plan, but dwelt primarily upon the benefits which an increase in the number of voting shares might be expected to produce for the corporation, in connection with acquisitions or other equity financing. The court did not attempt to compare the value of the voting rights surrendered by the Class A stockholders with the amount of the premium which they received under the plan. And here, as in the Manacher case, the court obviously relied heavily upon the overwhelming approval by the holders of the Class B stock: "The court cannot ignore the persuasive fact that the holders of 92.3% of all outstanding Class B stock concluded that the plan was fair to them and likewise to the corporation. That fact speaks more persuasively than the arguments of those who attempt to theorize on unrealistic principles of so-called corporate democracy." 208 F.Supp. at 762. See Case Comment, 28 Mo.L.Rev. 512 (1963).

---

2. STANDARDS FOR TESTING INTER-CLASS FAIRNESS IN RECAPITALIZATIONS

a. THE ABSOLUTE PRIORITY APPROACH

If courts did undertake to review fairness as between senior and junior classes of stock in recapitalizations, what standards of fairness would be utilized? One possibility is the so-called "absolute priority" doctrine developed in reorganization proceedings under the Bankruptcy Act. Under that doctrine, the allocation of stock and securities of the reorganized company among the former creditors (and stockholders when the debtor is solvent) follows closely the pattern which would be used if the debtor corporation were forced to sell its assets and distribute the proceeds in liquidation. The first step is to value the enterprise, usually on the basis of capitalization of earnings, for the purpose of determining what classes are entitled to participate in the reorganization. Any class which would not receive anything if cash in the amount of the estimated enterprise value was distributed is excluded from the reorganization. Thus if a corporation being reorganized was valued at $5,000,000 and there were claims of creditors in excess of $5,000,000, no class of stock would be eligible to participate in the reorganization. On the other hand, if the claims of creditors amounted to only $3,000,000, at least the senior stock would be entitled to participate; the junior stock's right to participate would depend upon whether the total liquidation preference of the senior stock amounted to less than $2,000,000. In other words, under the absolute priority approach the corporation is treated "as if in liquidation", thus making the liquidation preference of senior stock (which of course normally includes any accrued but unpaid dividends) the measure of the claim of the senior stock; and junior stock is not entitled to participate in the plan at all unless the net enterprise value (in excess of claims of creditors) exceeds the total liquidation preference of the senior stock.

As between classes entitled to participate in the reorganization, the absolute priority doctrine requires that each senior class of claimants in turn receive full compensation for its claim before any junior class receives anything. This does not necessarily mean that each class must receive stock or securities having a present market value equal to the amount of its claim—as a practical matter, that would often not be possible, since the figure at which the market "values" the total of the new stock and securities of a reorganized company at the outset is generally less than the amount estimated as the enterprise value. But the plan must certainly aim at producing full compensation in the relatively near future if the reorganized company performs as is hoped. In addition, any class which is reduced in seniority must receive some compensation on that account. For example, if in a reorganization in which both preferred and common are entitled to participate, both classes are to receive new common stock so that the preferred are deprived of their former priority over the common, the preferred must receive compensation for such demotion in status as well as reasonable satisfaction of the amount of its liquidation preference. See generally Brudney, The Investment-Value Doctrine and Corporate Readjustments, 72 Harv. L.Rev. 645, 667–675 (1959).

While this absolute priority standard has the considerable advantage of providing a specific measure of the claim of senior stock, it seems clear that it would not constitute a feasible standard for fairness in voluntary recapitalization proceedings under state law. For one thing, a voluntary recapitalization, unlike a reorganization under the Bankruptcy Act, is not a substitute for liquidation, and hence the "as if in liquidation" measure of the competing claims seems out of place. Moreover, unlike a reorganization proceeding which under federal law does not require the approval of any junior class excluded from participation under the plan, a recapitalization under state law does need the approval of the necessary percentage of all stockholders entitled to vote; and there is no basis for excluding a class just because its "real" financial stake in the enterprise has dwindled or even disappeared. Accordingly, the consent of the junior stockholders, who typically have voting control, would be required for the adoption of any plan, and they could hardly be expected to approve a plan of recapitalization which provides for "as if in liquidation" treatment for the senior stockholders, particularly when that standard would call for total exclusion of the junior stock from participation in the plan. In this connection it is interesting to note the suggestion of the court in Barrett v. Denver Tramway Corp., page 763 supra, to the effect that new state legislation is needed to provide "for ascertainment of worthlessness of junior shares, after which, as a condition subsequent, the junior stocks' vote would not be necessary to effect an urgent reclassification plan."

b. THE INVESTMENT VALUE APPROACH

Perhaps a more apt test for fairness in recapitalization proceedings is represented by the so-called "investment value" approach which has been developed in connection with recapitalizations under the Public Utility Holding Company Act. In the simplification of corporate structures required by that Act, it was often necessary to determine whether and to what extent certain junior classes of stock might be entitled to participate in the revamped corporate structure. Here it was thought that the claims of the competing classes ought not to be measured on the "as if in liquidation" basis, regardless of the corporate technique actually used to achieve the simplification. Instead, it was held that the rights of the respective classes of stock should be determined on the basis of their "going-concern investment value"; and any class that was found to have some chance of ultimately receiving dividends was regarded as entitled to participate in the reorganized enterprise. Otis & Co. v. SEC, 323 U.S. 624, 65 S.Ct. 483, 89 L.Ed. 511 (1945).

BRUDNEY, THE INVESTMENT-VALUE DOCTRINE AND CORPORATE READJUSTMENTS*

72 Harv.L.Rev. 648–651, 657–660 (1959).

A. The Measure of the Surrendered Claim and Its Rationale

The claims of securities surrendered in corporate readjustments compelled by the simplification requirements of the Holding Company Act are determined, under the investment-value doctrine, by "the value of the securities on the basis of a going business and not as though a liquidation were taking place, except as it appears that liquidation could and would have taken place apart from the compulsion of [the Act]." This measure of claims is designed to make the readjustment a mechanism for transmuting the long-range going-concern value of the surrendered contract into equivalent value in another form, rather than a procedure for redistributing underlying values in satisfaction of the stated contractual commands of the security being surrendered. The "bundle of rights"—whether matured or unmatured—embodied in the surrendered security determines the scope or magnitude of its claim, not as it states obligations to be ful-

---

filled, but only to the extent that those obligations are in fact under-pinned by economic values in the enterprise. As a result, . . . the claim is measured neither by its *rights* on maturity nor by its *rights* in the going concern, but by its *value* on a going-concern basis. . . . In short, under the investment-value doctrine, "it is not the promise that a charter made to a stockholder but the current worth of that promise" that is the measure of the claim he is surrender-ing.

The doctrine was designed to meet the problem created by the disparity—often substantial—between the "value" of a security when it is assessed as a continuing claim on a going concern and the value of the corporation's available assets which the same security would, by its terms, be entitled to receive in a liquidation, recapitali-zation, merger, or other form of corporate readjustment compelled by . . . the Holding Company Act. To honor the contractual provision might be to entitle the security holder in any given case to more (or less) than the going-concern value of the security he is being forced to surrender. But except for the compulsion of [the Act], senior-security holders might not have the right to force, and junior-security holders might not have the desire to make, the proposed re-adjustment. The investment-value doctrine rests on the assumption that Congress did not intend enforcement of the overriding public policy of holding-company simplification to have "its effect visited on one class with a corresponding windfall to another class of security holders" or to result in shifting "investment values from one class of security holders to another." On that premise, both the Commis-sion and the Supreme Court, after some preliminary fumbling, con-cluded that the act (1) overrides the security contract—i. e., pre-cludes a corporate readjustment which it compels, from being a "ma-turing" event under the security contract merely by reason of such compulsion, even though the particular form of readjustment occur-ring was a contingency explicitly provided for in the contract; and (2) requires surrendering security holders to receive the long-term going-concern values which their securities have when the act com-pels their surrender—i.e., their claims are to be measured by their going-concern values rather than by the requirements of their con-tracts or by some other norm.

* * *

B. The Operation of the Investment-Value Doctrine . . .

Although the rationale on which the investment-value measure of claims is based has been made plain by the SEC and the courts, its operation in particular cases is not so plainly decipherable. Thus, initially, the Commission's inquiry was directed toward ascertaining whether at some future time—very often ten to twenty years later, and sometimes even longer—earnings could be expected, on concededly optimistic assumptions, to have paid off preferred-stock arrearages and to exceed preferred-dividend claims, so that at that time juniors might be expected to share in the earnings. If it so found, the Commission concluded that there was "some" value for the junior securities for which "some" participation in the reorganized enterprise was required to be allowed.[39] Later, the Commission developed a somewhat different technique in applying the investment-value concept. The assorted contractual rights of the surrendered senior security, both monetary and protective, were ascertained and the continuing economic values estimated to be available to satisfy those rights were examined; the results were either translated into dollar terms by capitalizing estimated future earnings or, as was most frequently the case, expressed descriptively in a comparison of the bundle of rights and long-term values surrendered with the bundle of rights and long-term values embodied in the new securities.

* * *

. . . [T]here is wide scope for the play of immeasurable judgment factors and, therefore, for a large range of equally correct results, in the determination of the "investment value" and the "equitable equivalent" of a surrendered security. The complexities and uncertainties intrinsic in valuing on an earnings basis and in determining equitable equivalence are not the only reasons for this. The dominant objective of transmuting continuing values in one form into the same values in another form results in the rejection of current market prices as the test of either the investment value of the old security or the equitable equivalence of the new security. . . .

———

As is indicated in note 39, supra, the standard for determining whether and to what extent a junior class is entitled to participate under the investment value doctrine is somewhat vague—and the early SEC authorities did not provide much guidance as to how the allocation was arrived at. For example, in *Federal Water Service Corpora-*

---

39. The permissible extent of such participation was determined by the Commission's "over-all judgment" which was "not susceptible of mathematical demonstration." . . . A finding of no value for a security (and therefore exclusion from participation) was made when estimated earnings would either not exceed the earnings claims of the securities prior in rank to that being valued or would not be sufficient to discharge such prior claims and arrearages on the prior securities within the "foreseeable" future. . . .

tion, 8 SEC 893, 10 SEC 194 (1941), a corporation with senior preferred, junior preferred, and common stock was being recapitalized into an all common stock structure. On the basis of estimated future earnings, the dividend arrearages on the senior preferred might have been cleared in about eleven years. The SEC concluded that the junior preferred had a "reasonable expectation of receiving earnings at some future time" and awarded them 5% of the new common, the other 95% of the new common having gone to the senior preferred. As to the old common, the SEC found that it had "no reasonable possibility of ever receiving anything", and it was excluded from participation.

In United Light and Power Co., 13 SEC 1 (1943), the corporation had preferred stock, with a total annual dividend requirement of $3,-600,000 and arrearages of $38,700,000, ahead of the common stock. The SEC estimated the future earnings of the company at $6,185,000, on which basis "it would take approximately fifteen years for the preferred dividend arrearages to be paid in full, if all consolidated net earnings were to be applied toward the payment of current and accumulated preferred dividends". In rejecting a proposal to give the old common stockholders 8.8% of the new common, the SEC said: "Under all the circumstances it is our view that a participation for the common of approximately 5%, while representing the maximum, would not exceed the permissible limits of fairness, and to secure our approval the plan must be modified to reduce the common stockholders' participation accordingly". Just how 5% was arrived at is not explained. However, a concurring opinion by Commissioner Burke did offer a clue in the suggestion that the present value of the earnings to which the old common would be entitled after fifteen years might be arrived at by capitalizing those earnings, using a fairly low multiplier because of the high risk, and then discounting the resulting figure to present worth to take account of the fifteen year delay.

This suggestion does afford a basis for computing the relative investment values of senior and junior classes by comparing their relative interests in the estimated future earnings of the enterprise. The interest of the preferred stock consists of a perpetual right to its fixed annual dividend plus the right to receive the excess of annual earnings over the fixed dividend requirement until its arrearages have been paid. The interest of the junior stock consists of the right to receive that excess in perpetuity, once the preferred arrearages have been paid.

Following the line suggested by Commissioner Burke, the value of these various rights in future earnings can be computed by capitalizing the relevant earnings. The total estimated earnings for the company may be divided into two layers, the first consisting of the preferred's fixed annual dividend, and the second consisting of the excess of the total estimated earnings over that amount. The first layer of the earnings stream, to which the preferred have a perpetual right, would be capitalized in the normal way, at an appropriate capitalization rate. As to the second layer of the earnings, which of course is the riskier portion and must be capitalized at a higher rate, the preferred's interest would constitute a terminable annuity for whatever period is required to pay off the preferred arrearages. Thereafter, that second layer of the earnings stream would belong to the common stock in perpetuity; and this right can be valued, as Commissioner Burke suggested, in the normal fashion for a perpetual annuity, provided that the resulting figure is then "discounted" to present value to reflect the fact that the interest of junior stock does not vest until the preferred arrearages have been paid off.

One of the few concrete illustrations of this approach appeared in Appendix A to the Answering Brief of Securities and Exchange Commission, dated April 1950, in Matter of Eastern Gas and Fuel Associates, in the United States District Court for the District of Massachusetts, Civil Action, No. 50–168, in which an order was made approving and enforcing a Plan filed by Eastern with the SEC under § 11(e) of the Holding Company Act of 1935, as described in 30 SEC 834 (1950). In that recapitalization junior preferred, with dividend arrearages, and common were changed into a single class of new common. The plan, as approved by the SEC and the court, allocated 87% of the new common to the old junior preferred and 13% of the new common to the old common.

The figures used in the illustration, which follows, are hypothetical, although the indicated allocation works out to approximately the same as the allocation under the approved plan.

APPENDIX A

The following example illustrates the application of the two-discount technique as a check on the exercise of overall judgment. It assumes that the reasonably foreseeable income of a corporation is $2,000,000, that the corporation has outstanding 200,000 shares of $5 preferred stock with an annual dividend preference of $1,000,000, and that there are dividend arrearages on such stock aggregating $5,000,000. It further assumes that rates of 10% and 20% appropriately measure the risk factors attaching to the preferred and common stocks, respectively. The calculation of the relative present worths

of the preferred and common stocks would then be made as
follows:

Annual earnings	$2,000,000
Preferred dividend requirements	1,000,000
Balance applicable to arrears and common stock	$1,000,000

Number of years required to satisfy the preferred dividend
arrearages of $5,000,000 on the assumption that all earnings
would be applied in satisfaction of dividend arrearages—
5 years.

		Indicated allocation percentage
Preferred Stock:		
Present worth of $1,000,000 a year in perpetuity, discounted * at 10%	$10,000,000	
Present worth of $1,000,000 a year for 5 years, discounted at 20% ($1 per year for 5 years at 20% has a present worth of $2.99)	2,990,000	
Total Present Worth of Preferred Stock	$12,990,000	86.6%
Common Stock:		
Present worth of $1,000,000 a year in perpetuity, beginning after 5 years, discounted at 20% ($1 per year in perpetuity beginning after 5 years, has a present worth of $2.01)		
Total Present Worth of Common Stock	2,010,000	13.4%
Total Preferred and Common Stock	$15,000,000	100.0%

This approach to the relative valuation of senior and junior classes is sometimes referred to as the "double discount method", presumably a reference to the fact that the interest of the junior stock in the
second layer of earnings is "discounted" twice, once in perpetuity, in
a traditional capitalization of earnings, and again in discounting the
figure arrived at back to present value. There are several items
worth noting in this connection. First, the capitalization rate selected
for the second layer of the earnings stream, here 20%, has a double
impact on the participation of the junior stock. Of course, it determines the total value of the second layer of the earnings stream, in
which alone the junior stock has any interest. But in addition the
capitalization rate determines how large a portion of the total value
of a particular earnings stream is attributable to the first few years

* [Ed. note] The word "discounted" as used here means the same as "cap-italized", and the rate specified is, as the capitalization rate always is, the reciprocal of the multiplier.

of the stream. As you might expect, the greater the risk attaching
to a particular layer of earnings, the greater the uncertainty about
what the years beyond the immediate future will bring, and hence the
greater the proportion of the total value of the earnings layer which is
attributable to the first few years. For example, as the Appendix A
illustration indicates, at a capitalization rate of 20%, approximately
⅗ of the total value of the earnings stream is attributable to the
first five years. At a capitalization rate of only 15%, on the other
hand, not only would the total value of the second layer of the earnings stream be greater (i. e., $6,667,000 instead of $5,000,000), but
also the portion attributable to the first five years would only be
approximately ½. Thus if a capitalization rate of 15% had been
used for the second layer of earnings in Appendix A, the interest of
the common stock would have amounted to approximately $3,333,500
(½ × $6,667,000) out of a total of $16,667,000 ($10,000,000 plus
$6,667,000), or approximately 20%.

A second observation about the Appendix A illustration relates
to the question of whether a terminable annuity for five years fully
reflects the interest of the preferred stock in the second layer of earnings. Actually, the preferred's rights in that second layer continue
until it has received its $5,000,000 in dividend arrearages, whether
that takes five years or fifty. And the important corollary of this
is that the interest of the junior stock does not necessarily start after
five years, but rather only after the second earnings layer has totaled
$5,000,000 (and it has been paid to the preferred). In effect then,
the preferred's interest in the second earnings layer is substantially
less risky than the common's interest in the same layer, and this suggests the need for using different capitalization rates for the two
interests.

See Generally, Masson, New Shares for Old (1958) 288–301.

---

c. THE APPRAISED VALUATION APPROACH

Whatever the merits of the investment value approach, it is
primarily useful only where a single type of consideration is being
allocated between the senior and junior stock, and all that is needed
is to determine the relative values of the respective classes. Where
a recapitalization calls for the distribution of different types of consideration to the two classes, as where the old preferred are to receive
a new class of preferred, while the old common retain common, in
order to test fairness it may be necessary to value in absolute terms
both the interest of each participating class and the consideration
offered in satisfaction of that interest under the plan. Here the closest analogy is to appraisal of the stock of dissenting stockholders,
where too the objective is to translate either preferred or common
stock into absolute dollar terms. In the case of a simple one-class

corporation, this may be simply a variant of enterprise valuation. But the treatment of senior stock under this approach may give rise to some additional problems, as the following case suggests:

JACQUES COE & CO. v. MINNEAPOLIS-MOLINE CO.

Court of Chancery of Delaware, 1950.
31 Del.Ch. 368, 75 A.2d 244.

SEITZ, VICE CHANCELLOR. An appraiser . . . appraised the preferred and common stock of stockholders who chose not to accept the terms of a merger. This is the decision on exceptions to the appraiser's report.

The defendant corporation's preferred stock contract provided for a liquidation price of $110 per share plus accrued dividends. They amounted to $29.60 as of February 21, 1949. The call price was of an equal aggregate amount. The contract had certain provisions for retiring the preferred stock, but the corporation was in substantial default thereon. So long as the dividend arrearages exceeded $6.50 per share, the preferred stockholders had exclusive voting power.

In determining net asset value for the preferred, the appraiser decided that in no event should it exceed $139.60—the liquidation value plus accrued dividends. The appraiser determined the net asset value of the common stock to be $32.54. This amount was based on the acceptance of an expert witness' net asset evaluation of $26.80 per share less $1.12 per share which represented an amortization item which the appraiser concluded the expert witness had improperly excluded. The appraiser then added $6.86 per share representing good will.

The appraiser decided that net asset value should be weighted at 40% for the preferred stock and 20% for the common. In stating his reasoning in connection with the weighting factor, the appraiser stated that the preferred had been weighted much more heavily than the common because of the substantial advantages which the preferred possessed over the common under the charter provision.

The appraiser decided that a fair market value, uninfluenced by the merger, existed on February 21, 1949—the date of merger. I find no error in this conclusion. The market price for the preferred on that date was $113 per share, while the common was $12.13 per share.

The appraiser weighted the market value of the preferred stock at 30% and the common at 45%. In explaining the weight given to the market price the appraiser stated that the common was entitled to more weight than the preferred because of the greater market activity of the common stock. He also pointed out that substantial weight was given the market value of the common because that price represented the considered judgment of numerous investors and speculators—backed up by their own savings. This is, of course, certainly true to a degree.

Finally, the appraiser capitalized the earnings and dividends by taking the average earnings for the preferred and common for a 5-year period.* Multiplying these yearly earnings by the factor of 5, the appraiser arrived at a figure of $149 per share as the earnings-dividends value for the preferred. The appraiser pointed out that arrearages were not included under this element because he had already taken them into account under net asset value. Capitalized for the same period, the per share value of the common stock based on earnings and dividends amounted to $16.90.

The appraiser weighted earnings and dividends at 30% on the preferred and 35% on the common. The appraiser stated that this element was not weighted more heavily as to the common stock because of the failure to pay dividends thereon. The earning prospects of the company did appear to be good.

In order to resolve some of the questions posed by the various exceptions, it is necessary to consider, in a general way, the appraiser's approach to his duties under the statute.

Conceivably, an appraiser in weighting various elements of value and arriving at an appraised value might not articulate his mental processes. However, I believe an appraiser should state the monetary value which he has ascribed to the more substantial elements of value considered and the weight he has given each such element in arriving at his appraised value. I shall not pause to discuss the many infirmities involved in any evaluation process. The important thing is that the appraiser must, under the statute, arrive at a dollar and cents' appraisal. Consequently, the appraiser should state the value of the elements given independent weight and the weight given to each in arriving at the appraised value. This procedure will render the valuation process a little less arbitrary and will permit a review at least on a degree basis.

The present appraiser first determined asset value, market value and value derived from earnings and dividends. He then weighted

---

* [Ed. note] The "average earnings for the preferred" used in this computation were computed by simply dividing the net income of the corporation each year by the number of preferred shares outstanding. For the five years 1944–1948 these figures were approximately $13 per share, $10, $17, $46, and $63, producing an average of $29.80. Of course, the preferred could not in fact receive these amounts; they were limited to their fixed annual dividend of $6.50 per share, plus any payments made on the accumulated arrearages (which payments averaged $1.50 per year during 1944–1948).

The average earnings for the common were derived by deducting the fixed annual preferred dividend from net income and dividing the remainder by the number of common shares outstanding. The average for the period 1944–1948 of approximately $3.40 included earnings per share for 1948 of $8 per share.

these elements and arrived at his appraised value. Counsel for the defendant corporation contends that the appraiser committed error in so doing because he contends that the Supreme Court in Tri-Continental v. Battye, Del.Ch., 74 A.2d 71, 72, held that where an active market exists, and is uninfluenced by "artificial" factors, such market price is controlling in fixing value under the appraisal statute. I do not so construe the Supreme Court's decision, despite certain features of that opinion, because the Supreme Court there said: "In determining what figure represents this true or intrinsic value, the appraiser and the courts must take into consideration all factors and elements which reasonably might enter into the fixing of value. Thus, market value, asset value, dividends, earning prospects, the nature of the enterprise and any other facts which were known or which could be ascertained as of the date of merger and which throw any light on future prospects of the merged corporation are not only pertinent· to an inquiry as to the value of the dissenting stockholders' interest, but must be considered by the agency fixing the value."

I conclude that the appraiser properly considered elements other than market value in arriving at his evaluation. This consideration took the form of giving independent weight to some of them, and correctly so, in my opinion.

The preferred stockholders contend that the protective features of their stock were so great that they should have been considered by the appraiser as an independent element of value and weighted accordingly. Did the appraiser commit error in failing to treat the protective features of the preferred stock as an element of value to be weighted separately? I think not. It is apparent that, to a degree, many of the so-called "substantial" elements of value may and often do encompass each other. For example, market value may well reflect earnings and dividend prospects. However, in order to effectuate the object of the appraisal statute as construed by our Supreme Court, it is necessary that various factors be considered and, where appropriate, some of them given independent weight. It seems to me that in order to make the appraisal procedure work realistically the court should not disturb the appraiser's determination that a particular factor should not be given independent weight unless that determination is arbitrary or unreasonable in the premises. I say so because, as previously stated, a value factor may well be fairly reflected in an element of value given independent weight—as the appraiser here recognized. It seems to me that the value factor based on the protective features of the preferred stock is fairly reflected in varying degrees in the elements of value actually given independent weight by the appraiser.

The preferred stockholders contend that it was error to limit net asset value to the call or liquidation price when the asset value was more than twice that amount. They concede that the final appraised value should not have exceeded the call or liquidation price, but they urge that such a limitation should not have been placed on net asset value which constituted but one element of the appraised value. Obviously the more assets there are, the more the preferred is protected but this should not increase the amount of net assets attributable to the preferred. The appraiser properly limited net asset value to the call or liquidation price where the net assets were substantially in excess of such prices because he was seeking value at a particular time. The stockholders' contention, if here adopted, would result in a distortion of the ultimate value of the preferred stock.

* * *

Both the stockholders and the corporation have excepted to the weight which the appraiser gave net asset value in computing the appraised value of both the preferred and common stock. I have examined the arguments of counsel and the appraiser's report and I find nothing which would justify the conclusion that the weights assigned by the appraiser to this element were arbitrary or unreasonable. The appraiser committed no error.

The preferred stockholders took two exceptions to the appraiser's calculation of the earnings-dividends element of value. They say the appraiser should have included the $29.60 per share accrued dividends and should have multiplied the average earnings by a factor larger than 5.

The appraiser included accrued dividends in determining net asset value. The preferred stockholders urge that it should also have been included under earnings and dividends because the earnings were adequate to pay such arrearages. I find no error in refusing to consider this item under two elements of value. It is argued that by incorporating it under one item which was weighted 40%, the appraiser has necessarily weighted it only 40%. If other elements of value are weighted, then the same must be true of dividends arrearages. We are not dealing with a dissolution or liquidation.

In calculating the earnings-dividends value the appraiser multiplied average earnings by the factor of 5. The preferred think this factor was too small. The factor employed by the appraiser is within the range of reason and will not be disturbed. Substantially the same exceptions as to this element are taken by the common stock and my conclusion as to the preferred also applies to the common.

* * *

I find the per share value of the preferred to be $131.74 and the common $17.88.

NOTE ON VALUATION IN DELAWARE APPRAISAL PROCEEDINGS

Delaware has led the way in refusing to treat market value as controlling even where there is a full, free and active market, uninfluenced by the proposed transaction which gives rise to the right of appraisal. The leading case is Chicago Corp. v. Munds, 20 Del.Ch. 142, 172 A. 452 (1934), where the Chancellor said:

> The experience of recent years is enough to convince the most casual observer that the market in its appraisal of values must have been woefully wrong in its estimates at one time or another within the interval of a space of time so brief that fundamental conditions could not possibly have become so altered as to affect true worth. Markets are known to gyrate in a single day. The numerous causes that contribute to their nervous leaps from dejected melancholy to exhilarated enthusiasm and then back again from joy to grief, need not be reviewed. It would be most unfortunate indeed either for the consolidated corporation or for the objecting stockholder if, on the particular date named by the statute for the valuation of the dissenter's stock, viz., the date of the consolidation, the market should be in one of its extreme moods and the stock had to be paid for at the price fixed by the quotations of that day. Even when conditions are normal and no economic forces are at work unduly to exalt or depress the financial hopes of man, market quotations are not safe to accept as unerring expressions of value. The relation of supply to demand on a given day as truly affects the market value of a stock as it does of a commodity; and temporary supply and demand are in turn affected by numerous circumstances which are wholly disconnected from considerations having to do with the stock's inherent worth.

As previously noted, prior to the decision in the Weinberger case, page 684 supra, the Delaware courts insisted upon taking into account at least two other elements, an earnings factor and an asset factor. However, both of these elements presented some troublesome questions. For example, the earnings factor, which in practice amounts pretty much to a traditional capitalization of earnings, depends upon selecting an appropriate capitalization rate; and for this purpose resort is usually made to comparable price-earnings ratios in the market. But why should the market's price-earnings ratio for other stocks be relied upon, when its valuation of the stock being appraised is rejected as untrustworthy?

As to the asset value factor, among the questions which arise are whether book value or "current" value should be used as the measure, and whether intangible assets are included. The difficulties with these issues are well illustrated in the Libby case, page 13 supra. When the asset value factor was originally injected into the picture in the Chicago Corporation case, supra, it was with relation to an investment corporation, whose assets consisted in large measure of marketable stocks and debt securities with a readily ascertainable value; the same was true in the

Tri-Continental case (cited in Jacques Coe), which stressed the fact that the stock of an investment company often sells at a discount from its underlying asset values. This is a far cry from the industrial area, into which this factor has been imported, where computation of asset value is no less complicated than making the overall determination of enterprise value itself.

As a postscript to the relationship between valuation for the purpose of appraising a dissenting stockholder's stock and valuation for the purpose of testing fairness in a recapitalization, note should be taken of the recapitalization of York Ice Machine Corporation which ultimately produced a proceeding of each type. At the time of the recapitalization in early 1941, York had outstanding 56,731 shares of 7%, $100 par, cumulative preferred stock with dividend arrearages of $88.25 per share, and 161,481 shares of common stock. The income of the company for its most recent five fiscal years, 1936–1940, had varied rather sharply, being respectively a profit of $165,000, a profit of $975,000, a loss of $119,000, a loss of $185,000 and a profit of $483,000. The plan called for a merger of the company into a wholly-owned subsidiary created expressly for that purpose, with an exchange ratio of 15 shares of new common for each share of old preferred, and one share of new common for each old common share. Thus the preferred received 83.2% of the new common, and the old common got 16.8%.

Objecting preferred stockholders brought an action in the federal district court attacking the plan, primarily on the ground that a Delaware corporation had no power to eliminate preferred stock arrearages in this fashion. However, the District Court sustained the recapitalization, so far as corporate power was concerned, and the Court of Appeals for the Third Circuit affirmed. Hottenstein v. York Ice Machinery Corp., 136 F.2d 944 (3d Cir. 1943).

The objecting stockholders also attacked the plan of recapitalization as unfair to the preferred stockholders. In dealing with this issue, the District Court first distinguished review of a plan of reorganization under the Bankruptcy Act, where court approval is affirmatively required; as to review of a merger under state law, the court held that an injunction could be granted only if "the plan is so unfair as to shock the conscience of the court and to amount to fraud", citing the MacFarlane case, page 700 supra. Nevertheless, the court then seemed to talk in "absolute priority" terms when it continued as follows:

> The value of the preferred stock, if the common stock has any value, is approximately $10,000,000, including accumulated dividends. Therefore, if the value of the interest which the preferred stockholders receive under the plan of merger is as much or more than $10,000,000, it certainly is not so grossly unfair as to shock the conscience of the court.

And insofar as the interest given to the preferred stockholders has less than that value, the plan approaches the point at which it must be deemed so unfair that the merger should be enjoined. [45 F.Supp. at 438.]

The reference to "$10,000,000," though never explained by the court, must surely have come from the liquidation preference of the preferred, which did amount to almost $10,000,000. Certainly, the figure had no relation to the market value of the stock, which at the time of the recapitalization was about $45 per share, for a total of less than $2,500,000.

In any event, the District Court concluded that, on the evidence submitted as to the total value of the enterprise, the value of the new common stock allocated to the preferred stockholders was not substantially less than $10,000,000. Looking first at the asset value factor, the court noted that while book value was substantially below $10,000,000, this figure was the product of an arbitrary writedown of asset values at a time long before the plan of recapitalization was contemplated. On the other hand, replacement cost (less depreciation) was apparently almost $15,000,000, although it was conceded that this was much higher than the fair value of the assets. The court observed that splitting the difference between book value and replacement cost produced a figure in excess of $10,000,000; and this seemed to satisfy the court that the asset value factor supported an overall enterprise value in excess of $10,000,000.

Turning to the earnings value factor, the lower court noted the difficulty of predicting future earnings for a corporation which had had such wide fluctuations in earnings in the past. However, the court observed that net income for the year 1941, in which the recapitalization occurred, had been at least $800,000, of which the 83% interest awarded to the preferred stockholders would have been entitled to approximately $665,000; in the court's view this confirmed that the stock received by the preferred was not worth substantially less than $10,000,000. (Notice that in effect the court applied a multiplier of about 15 times earnings.)

The District Court's decision on fairness was also affirmed. In a much briefer analysis of the issue, the Court of Appeals, while conceding that the book value of the corporation's assets was less than the liquidation preference of the preferred, stressed the facts that the earnings had increased substantially, that the recapitalization gave the preferred stockholders voting control, and that when the plan became public the preferred stock nearly doubled in price. The court concluded that "it is not unjust under all the circumstances of the case at bar to treat the equity of the common stockholders as being worth approximately 17% of the stock of the surviving corporation".

The objecting preferred stockholders then commenced a proceeding for the appraisal of their stock under the provisions of the Delaware statute. A majority of the appraisers fixed the value of the stock at $90 per share (approximately twice the market price of $45); the third appraiser fixed the value at $197.50, (apparently on the basis of the redemption price of the preferred, which included par of $100, a premium of $7.50, and accrued dividends of about $90). While the report of the appraisers was awaiting review by the Delaware Chancellor, the objecting stockholders filed a special bill with the Court of Appeals for the Third Circuit protesting the fact that in the earlier federal court proceeding the corporation had contended that its assets were worth more than $10,000,000, whereas in the state court appraisal proceeding the corporation had presented evidence that the assets were worth very much less. Hottenstein v. York Ice Machinery Corp., 146 F.2d 835 (3d Cir. 1944). The Court of Appeals commented as follows:

> Obviously, if the assets of York Ice Machinery Corporation were worth only $5,000,000 at the time of the merger, common stockholders should have received far less, if any, recognition. If the value found for the preferred stock by the appraisers is correct it seems probable that the value suggested for the assets . . . [during the earlier proceedings] was far too high. Conceding that the value of the assets is not invariably, or even necessarily, reflected in stock values, the . . . comparatively low value attributed to the stock by the appraisers does not coincide with the asset picture seemingly presented by the defendant to the District Court of Delaware.

However, the court reluctantly denied leave to file the bill of review on the ground that under state law commencement of appraisal proceedings terminated the petitioners' status as stockholders.

Subsequently, the report of the appraisers came on for review before the Chancellor. Root v. York Corp., 29 Del.Ch. 351, 50 A.2d 52 (1946). The Chancellor noted that "based on evidence of asset value, it is . . . evident that the corporation did claim in the injunction suit that the common stock of York Ice Machinery Corporation had some equity, while before the appraisers it claimed that the value of the preferred stock was worth less than par and the accumulated dividends thereon." However, the Chancellor was not unduly concerned about this apparent inconsistency. He observed that in the appraisal proceeding only the value of the preferred stock was pertinent, and that in valuing the stock, asset value was not the sole controlling factor. Instead, all relevant factors were to be taken into account; and since the appraisers had done that, their valuation was sustained.

SECTION 3. FINANCIAL ASPECTS OF CORPORATE COMBINATIONS

A. INTRODUCTION

One of the important questions in every corporate combination is how to account for the acquired assets on the books of the acquiring corporation. A related question is the effect of the combination transaction on the proprietary accounts of the acquiring corporation. To illuminate these issues, let us start with the simple case of a corporation which purchases a new asset, say a building, from an individual for cash. Obviously the building should be recorded on the books of the acquiring corporation at its cost, and thereafter treated in accordance with the corporation's normal practice for depreciable assets. The same would be true if the corporation acquired the building in exchange for its stock, except that, as we have seen before, there is no longer quite as ready a measure of the cost of the building. Ordinarily, the "cost" of property acquired for stock is the fair market value of the stock exchanged for it, which in turn, at least in an arm's-length transaction, is normally equal to the fair market value of the property at the date of acquisition. In other words, the end result is the same as if the stock had been issued for cash which was then used to acquire the assets. And just as in the case of an issuance of stock for cash, so when stock is issued for property any excess of the consideration received over the stated capital attributable to the stock is credited to capital surplus.

Should the transaction be treated differently if the building is acquired from a corporation rather than an individual? The answer seems clearly "no", if the acquiring corporation is simply obtaining an additional facility for the conduct of its operations. And it should make no difference whether the acquisition is for cash or for stock, or whether the building represents all or only a portion of the assets of the selling corporation. Accordingly, the figure at which the building was carried on the books of the selling corporation, and *a fortiori* that corporation's earned surplus or deficit, would be of no concern to the acquiring corporation.

However, suppose that the acquiring corporation, X, is a real estate corporation owning only one piece of property—and that X is acquiring from Y corporation the latter's only piece of property. Now the transaction begins to look more like a combination of two separate businesses into a single unified enterprise than a mere "purchase" of property. Assuming that the two pieces of property are of equal value, the old Y stockholders should end up owning one half of the stock of the combined enterprise (hereinafter referred to as "X–Y"). Such a combination transaction seems analogous to the formation of a partnership, although of course the enterprise is to be carried on in corporate form; in essence, the two groups of shareholders are "pooling their interests" for the future.

In such circumstances, there is much to be said for accounting for the transaction by simply combining the accounts of the two corporations (of course after eliminating any inter-corporate items which might exist.) This would treat the combination as nearly as possible as though the two enterprises had been carried on together from the outset. Thus the opening balance sheet for the combined enterprise would be derived by pooling the assets and liabilities of the two corporations, at the figures at which they appear on the books of the respective companies. Similarly, the net worth accounts, i. e., stated capital and the various types of surplus, for the combined enterprise might be derived by pooling the respective balances in such accounts on the books of the separate corporations. Here, however, some departure from a strict "pooling" approach would become necessary since the stated capital for the acquiring corporation after a combination transaction, like that of any other corporation, must be determined in accordance with the governing statute, and the figure called for might well be different from the arithmetic sum of the stated capital accounts of the constituent corporations. For example, if the acquiring corporation issued par stock in making the acquisition, the increase in its stated capital would be measured, under a typical statute like MBA § 21, by par times the additional number of shares issued; and it would be the sheerest coincidence if that figure was precisely equal to the stated capital of the acquired corporation.

To make our illustration more concrete, assume that the balance sheets for the two corporations being combined are as follows:

X

Cash	$200,000	Stat. Cap. (10,000 shares of $40 par)	$400,000
		Cap. Surp.	300,000
Building (net)	900,000	Earn. Surp.	400,000

Y

| Building (net) | $1,100,000 | Stat. Cap. (10,000 shares of $100 par) | $1,000,000 |
| | | Earn. Surp. | 100,000 |

Assume further that Y is to be merged into X, with the Y shareholders exchanging their stock for X stock on a share for share basis. Under MBA § 21 X's stated capital after the merger would be $800,-000 (20,000 shares of $40 par stock), absent some additional step affecting stated capital such as a transfer to that account from surplus under § 21. If all the other accounts of X and Y were pooled while the stated capital for the combination was fixed at $800,000, the balance sheet for the new X–Y corporation would not balance. This should not be surprising, since so far no account has been taken of the fact that in the course of the merger there was a reduction of the stated capital attributable to Y from its original $1,000,000 to the $400,000 figure corresponding to the X stock issued in exchange for the Y stock.

It is easy enough to see what adjustment should be made. If Y had reduced its capital from $1,000,000 to $400,000 prior to the merger, it would have produced $600,000 in capital surplus, which presumably would have been pooled with X's capital surplus on the books of X–Y. There is no reason to treat a reduction of capital in the course of the merger any differently, and accordingly, the decline in total stated capital should be offset by an equivalent increase in capital surplus:

		X–Y	
Cash	$200,000	Stat. Cap. (20,000 shares of $40 par)	$800,000
		Cap. Surp.	900,000
Buildings (net)	2,000,000	Earn. Surp.	500,000

Similarly, a combination transaction may result in an increase in total stated capital, if the par or stated value of the stock of the acquiring corporation issued to the acquired corporation's shareholders exceeds the stated capital of the acquired corporation. In that event there will be a corresponding decrease in the overall surplus of the combination—in effect there has been a capitalization (i. e., a transfer to capital) of some of the acquired corporation's surplus. In the absence of some statutory guidance, it would appear that the management is free to decide which type of surplus should be reduced, capital or earned.

The foregoing illustration of the pooling approach was simplified by assuming that the two corporations were equal both in actual value and in book value, and that a share for share exchange ratio was appropriate. However, the pooling approach may also be applied to more complicated transactions. For example, assume that in the previous illustration, on the basis of earnings, reproduction cost and any other relevant elements of value, X is regarded as worth $1,200,-000, or $120 a share, while Y is valued at $2,400,000 or $240 per share. Presumably, under these circumstances Y's stockholders would insist upon receiving two-thirds of the total stock in the event of a combination with X, so that if X were to be the surviving entity, the Y stockholders would get 20,000 shares of X stock. The only difference that this would make in the application of the pooling approach is that now Y would be treated as having reduced its capital from $1,000,000 only down to $800,000 (20,000 shares of X's $40 par stock) instead of to $400,000, so that X-Y's stated capital would be $400,000 more than before, and its capital surplus would be $400,000 less. All other accounts for the combination would remain just as they were before. This is quite a small change in appearance for what is really quite a large difference in substance between the two transactions. The reason for this is that the pooling approach, consistent with its theory of reflecting the combination as though the separate corporations had been operated together from the outset, takes no direct account of the current value of either of the two enterprises.

Let us now consider how this transaction would look if it were treated as a "straight" purchase of Y's assets by X in exchange for its stock. As in any purchase, X would record the assets acquired from Y at their cost, measured by the sum of the value of the stock issued to acquire the property plus the amount of any liabilities assumed. Where the stock of the acquiring corporation is traded in a full, fair and free market, and there is no reason to believe the proposed acquisition will have a substantial impact on the market value of the stock, the quoted market price will commonly be used as the measure of the "cost" of the assets acquired. Where there is no such dependable quoted market figure for the stock of the acquiring corporation, or where the proposed issue is so large with relation to the amount of stock already outstanding that the quoted market price of the latter may no longer be significant, then as noted earlier the fair market value of the assets acquired may provide the best measure of the "cost" of those assets to the acquiring corporation.

Assuming a "cost" of $2,400,000 for Y's property here, it would be recorded at that figure on X-Y's balance sheet. In the typical case where the acquired corporation has a number of different assets, rather than a single item of property as in our illustration, it would be necessary to determine the value of the various assets in order to properly allocate this "cost" among them. And in many cases the total amount paid by the acquiring corporation will exceed the highest defensible value for the listed assets of the acquired corporation, which means that part of the price is being paid for the goodwill of the acquired corporation. The emergence of such a goodwill asset in a combination transaction is one of the most ticklish aspects in the whole combination area, in part because of the great uncertainty which presently exists as to the extent, if any, to which such goodwill should thereafter be amortized on the books of the acquiring corporation. See page 792 infra.

As to the effect viewing the transaction as a "purchase" has on the right-hand side of the acquiring corporation's balance sheet, of course stated capital is still increased by the total par value of the stock issued to acquire the assets, here $800,000. However, there is no longer any carryover of the earned surplus of the acquired corporation, and instead the entire excess of the value of the assets acquired over the increase in stated capital (plus any liabilities assumed), here $1,600,000, would be credited to capital surplus.

The differences between the pooling and the purchase approaches may thus be summarized as follows. Under the purchase approach, full recognition is given to the current value of the assets acquired, as measured by the bargain between the parties; but there is no carryover of any of the surplus accounts of the disappearing enterprise. Under the pooling approach, the surplus accounts of the constituent corporations, after adjustment for any change in the stated capital attributable to the acquired corporation, are carried over onto the books of the acquiring corporation; but no account is taken of the present value of the assets of any of the constituent corporations.

It should not be thought, however, that under the pooling approach the value of the assets of the acquired corporation can be ignored entirely. For example, in determining the total amount of par value stock which the acquiring corporation may issue in exchange for the acquired corporation's property under typical corporation statutes like MBA §§ 18 and 19, it is the actual value of the assets acquired which controls, not the book value, regardless of whether the transaction is accounted for under the pooling of interests approach. This means that if the acquiring corporation issues stock with a total par value in excess of the value of the net assets of the acquired corporation, such stock would be watered, even though that total par value did not exceed the book value of the net assets of the acquired corporation. Conversely, if the acquired corporation's assets have substantially appreciated in value, the acquiring corporation may issue stock having a total par value equivalent to the current value of the acquired corporation's assets without running afoul of the watered stock provisions; however, under the pooling of interests approach a deficit would emerge because the book value of the acquired corporation's assets carried over to the books of the acquiring corporation would not balance the par value of the stock issued.

It should be noted that the revaluation of the acquired corporation's assets under the purchase approach is regarded in some quarters as an important advantage of that approach. Remember that many people would like to see assets revalued generally because it results in a clearer picture of the "amount" of invested capital actually at work in the enterprise, and puts annual depreciation on a current price-level basis. And a primary obstacle to such general revaluation—the lack of objective criteria of value—is often thought to be overcome in cases where unrelated corporations are combined, since the terms of the combination transaction will provide a measure of the value of the assets of the acquired corporation. Accordingly, it has sometimes been urged that any combination transaction should be seized as an opportunity to put the assets of the acquired corporation on a current value basis. E. g., May, Business Combinations: An Alternative View, 103 J. Accountancy (April, 1957) 33.

There are, however, some difficulties with this view. For one thing, the terms of the combination transaction do not necessarily determine *absolute* values for either of the constituent corporations, since it is sufficient for combination purposes merely to determine the *relative* values of the contributions being made by the respective concerns. And so far as relative values are concerned, the terms of the combination transaction provide as much guide to the value of the assets of the acquiring corporation as for the acquired corporation. Therefore, there seems little reason to distinguish between the two corporations so far as using a combination transaction to put assets on a current value basis is concerned. This is all the more true when it is recalled that any distinction between acquired and acquiring corporations in this regard will raise the same type of issue— as to which is "really" which—as is presented in the *de facto* merger cases.

To be sure, where there are dependable market quotations for the stock of either or both of the constituent corporations, they would seem to afford a guide to *absolute* values. But here the point may prove too much. If, for example, the market price of the acquiring corporation's stock is used to measure the value of the assets of the acquired corporation, would it not *a fortiori* establish the value of the acquiring corporation's assets, since that is after all what the market value of the stock represents? On the other hand, if that is so, what turns on there being a combination transaction? Why shouldn't the market price of a corporation's own stock be used as a basis for re-valuation of its assets from time to time whether or not any combination transaction is involved?

Fiflis, Accounting for Mergers, Acquisitions and Investments, in a Nutshell . . ., 37 Bus. Law. 89, 94–106, contains the following excellent analysis of the purchase-pooling dichotomy:*

I. ACCOUNTING FOR ASSETS ACQUISITIONS: *I.E.*, ACQUISITIONS RESULTING IN ONE SURVIVING CORPORATION

The simplest situation, and one for which the accounting is familiar to most business lawyers, is that in which an entity acquires substantially all the assets and liabilities of a second business entity, by merger, consolidation or purchase of assets, and remains as the sole survivor in the economic unit—the so-called assets acquisition. The question in this case is: should the acquisition be accounted for as a "purchase," or as a "pooling of interests"?

Before examining these two alternatives, we should make certain that the accounting for purchase of an isolated asset and assumption of a liability is clearly in mind.

---

*Portions of the text and all but two of the footnotes omitted.

A. Accounting for the Purchase of Isolated Assets Not a Going Concern

If *A* Corp. were to buy land from *B* Corp. (carried by *B* Corp. on its books at $35,000) at a price of $20,000 in cash plus assumption of an $80,000 note bearing interest at the current market rate, that purchase would be accounted for in *A*'s journal as follows:

Land	$100,000	
Cash		$20,000
Note Payable		$80,000[9]

The important result to notice here is that the acquired asset is shown at its $100,000 cost to *A*, regardless of the $35,000 book carrying value of the seller, *B*.

If several individual assets were to be acquired from *B* for a lump sum in what is often referred to as a "basket purchase," they also would be carried by *A* at their cost to *A*, although a problem would arise concerning allocation of the lump sum among the several items. In this situation, generally accepted accounting principles ("GAAP") provide that the total price should be allocated among the assets proportionately to their individual fair values. In subsequent income statements, those assets which are depreciable or amortizable will be charged to expense as the assets are used up.

B. "Purchase" Accounting for an Assets Acquisition of a Going Concern

What should be the method of accounting when, instead of the purchase of isolated assets, control is acquired over an entire business as a going concern?

1. MEASUREMENT AT CURRENT COST TO ACQUIRING COMPANY

By our hypothesis, control is acquired by *A* Corp., *B* Corp. disappears from the economic entity, and *B* or *B*'s shareholders receive either *A* Corp. stock or other property. This will result in a "business combination" which, to accountants, means *A* Corp.'s acquisition of control, in any form, over the business of *B* Corp.

Assuming for the moment that the acquisition will be accounted for as a "purchase," this means that the acquired assets will be entered on the acquirer's books at their current cost to it and liabilities will be credited at their current values; *i.e.*, the total purchase price will be allocated among the individual assets and liabilities acquired to the extent of their fair market values. This is one of the two most important consequences of accounting for the combination as a purchase, for it means that, in the usual case, where current cost is higher than the seller's book carrying value, the buyer's future income statements will be charged with greater expenses than the seller's statements would have shown as these assets are depreciated or amortized. The result is that the increment in the buyer's income resulting from the acquisition usually will be less than the seller's income would have been without the combination.

2. GOODWILL ARISING ON A PURCHASE

If the combination is to be accounted for as a purchase, there may be a second important impact on accounting income after the combination. When the purchase is of a going business enterprise rather than of merely isolated assets, the parties typically will have determined a total price not based on values of individual assets but on the going-concern value, which frequently will be in excess of the fair values attributable to the isolated assets net of liabilities. In these circumstances, instead of allocating the full purchase price among only the assets appearing on B's books, accountants recognize that intangible assets, usually called "goodwill," should appear on the books of A Corp.

Here again a problem arises concerning allocation of the lump sum purchase price among the acquired assets, including the goodwill, but it is resolved by a two-step process different from the one-step technique described for the basket purchase of isolated assets. First the purchase price is allocated among the tangible and identifiable intangible (*e.g.*, patents) assets acquired according to their fair value; then any residue is debited to the new intangible asset account, goodwill.

To illustrate, assume balance sheets in columnar form for corporations A and B prior to A's acquisition of B, as below:

Balance Sheets (000's omitted)

	A Corp.	B Corp.
Assets:		
Cash	$ 50,000	$ 0
Inventory	20,000	10,000
Plant	70,000	15,000
Land		5,000
Totals	$140,000	$30,000
Liabilities and Equity:		
Accounts payable	$ 24,000	$15,000
Equity:		
Capital stock	$ 30,000	$ 6,000
Capital surplus	39,000	4,200
Earned surplus	47,000	4,800
Totals	$140,000	$30,000

Further, assume that A Corp. buys the assets and assumes the liabilities of B for cash paid to B in the amount of $30,000,000 and that no new identifiable assets appear. The form of journal entry for A, omitting all but one of the figures, will be (000's omitted):

Inventory	a	
Plant	b	
Land	c	
Goodwill	d	
Accounts payable		e
Cash		$30,000

The values, a, b and c, to be attributed to the three identifiable assets will be determined as the fair market value of each. Then the accounts payable will be valued at $15,000,000 if there is no reason to decrease or increase them. Any excess of credits over debits will be balanced by a debit to goodwill. Thus, if the inventory has a fair market value of $12,000,000, plant, $18,000,000, and land, $10,000,000, goodwill will be debited in the amount of $5,000,000, assuming accounts payable are valued at $15,000,000.

* * *

Manifestly, future periods' income for A will then be chargeable for the aggregate cost of goods sold in the amount debited to inventory and for depreciation of the fair market value of the former B Corp. plant. An accounting rule also requires the amortization of the goodwill account over not more than forty years by periodic charges to expense. Notice that this amortized goodwill has a greater impact on reported net income than do most other expense charges; since amortization of goodwill is not tax deductible, there is no partially offsetting reduction in tax expense on the income statement.

* * *

4. FORM OF PURCHASE

Returning to our illustration, and still assuming purchase accounting, even if the consideration given by A Corp. is other than cash, the acquired assets and liabilities will be entered on A's books at their cost to A, although the consideration paid will be credited to some account other than the cash account. For example, if $10,000,000 par value of A's preferred stock having a current value of $30,000,000, were the consideration in the above illustration, the credit, instead of being to cash account, would be to a capital stock account in the amount of $10,000,000, plus some capital surplus account for $20,000,000, aggregating the net cost of the acquisition. (Of course, the assumption of the $15,000,000 liability is also part of the price paid and will be credited, as well.) The journal entry would be (000's omitted):

Inventory	$12,000	
Plant	18,000	
Land	10,000	
Goodwill	5,000	
Accounts payable		15,000
Capital stock—$10 par preferred stock		10,000
Capital surplus		20,000

This treatment applies to any acquisition by A Corp. if it is to be accounted for as a purchase, whether the transaction is a merger, consolidation, or purchase of assets and an assumption of liabilities on the one hand, or, on the other hand, is an acquisition of B Corp.'s shares followed by: a statutory merger of A and B; a liquidating dividend by B; or any other set of transactions which would result in A holding the assets and liabilities of B and B disappearing as a separate entity.

C. "Pooling of Interests" for an Assets Acquisition of a Going Concern

1. POOLING ACCOUNTING

Accountants purport to find a fundamental difference between a "purchase" of a business by another entity and a combination whereby the shareholders of the acquired business continue in interest by receiving voting common stock in the surviving entity—a "pooling of interests." "In accounting theory, a 'pooling' is conceptualized as a flowing together of two continuing separate entities, with a substantial continuity of ownership, properties and management, whereas a 'purchase' of one by the other is thought of as more closely akin to a termination of one enterprise and the acquisition of its component parts by another."[30] A classic case for "pooling" would be the statutory merger of two corporations of similar size with the common shareholders of each holding common stock in similar amounts in the surviving entity.

The accounting for such a pooling of interests is radically different from purchase accounting and rests on the notion that when two entities come together, with the interests in rights and rewards of the owners of each continuing, the old basis of accounting for each should continue. This means that the book carrying values of the assets and liabilities of each entity are continued on the books of the new or surviving entity and the earned surpluses of the two are combined. Subsequent income statements, of course, are charged with depreciation and amortization expenses based on the old recorded amounts. Further, accounting for income under pooling is different from purchase accounting in that, irrespective of when the combination occurs during the year, the income of the two entities for the year of the combination is combined on the income statement of the new or surviving entity. Finally, if any prior years' income statements of A are restated, the incomes of A and B will be combined retroactively on those restated income statements although the two entities were independent at that time.

30.
  CCH, Financial Accounting Standards Board, Accounting Principles Board and Committee on Accounting Procedure Financial Accounting Standards 245 (1977), describes poolings and purchases as follows:

Pooling of Interests Method

  The pooling of interests method accounts for a business combination as the uniting of the ownership interests of two or more companies by exchange of equity securities. No acquisition is recognized because the combination is accomplished without disbursing resources of the constituents. Ownership interests continue and the former bases of accounting are retained. The recorded assets and liabilities of the constitutents are carried forward to the combined corporation at their recorded amounts. Income of the combined corporation includes income of the constituents for the entire fiscal period in which the combination occurs. The reported income of the constituents for prior periods is combined and restated as income of the combined corporation.

Purchase Method

  The purchase method accounts for a business combination as the acquisition of one company by another. The acquiring corporation records at its cost the acquired assets less liabilities assumed. A difference between the cost of an acquired company and the sum of the fair values of tangible and identifiable intangible assets less liabilities is recorded as goodwill. The reported income of an acquiring corporation includes the operation of the acquired company after acquisition, based on the cost to the acquiring corporation.

To illustrate, assume the same data for A and B as before, but that this time, instead of A purchasing B's assets for cash and assumption of the liability, it acquires them for 1,000,000 shares of $10 par value common stock, valued at $30,000,000, plus assumption of the liability. The journal entry, on a pooling basis, on A's books at the time of the acquisition of B's net assets will be (000's omitted):

Inventory	$10,000	
Plant	15,000	
Land	5,000	
Accounts payable		$15,000
Capital stock		10,000
Earned surplus		4,800
Capital surplus		200

Note that B's assets, liabilities and earned surplus are simply transferred at the same carrying value as on B's books—as called for by the pooling concept that this is a marriage of two entities with neither one acquiring the other; just as A's old carrying values and earned surplus continue, so do B's. The credit to capital stock is to evidence the issuance of the A shares and is in the amount of the aggregate par (or stated) value of the shares issued. The capital surplus credit is in the amount necessary to balance the other credits with the debits. Also note that if the net assets acquired in excess of capital stock issued were *less* than B's earned surplus, only an amount of earned surplus equal to that excess would have been credited on A's books.[37]

* * *

As already noted, under pooling a unique accounting for income also appears: for the period in which the combination occurs, the income of B is added to the surviving corporation's income statement and on restatement of any prior period's income, the combined income of both corporations must be set forth. Finally, of course, as a consequence of B's assets being carried at the old book carrying value of B, which is typically lower than the value paid by A, A's future income statements typically will show lesser amounts for costs of goods sold, depreciation, and other deferred costs than they would under purchase accounting—and no expense whatsoever for amortization of goodwill, since none arises. Put another way, the increment to A's income on a pooling tends toward being equal to what B's individual income is or would have been for that same period.

---

37. This could be viewed as the result of the mechanics of double-entry bookkeeping. Many would quarrel, however, with the assertion that these results are mechanically dictated by double-entry bookkeeping requirements. *See* APB Op. No. 16 ¶ 53 (1970) which describes a principled basis for the bookkeeping. It states that the capital (*i.e.*, stated value or par value plus capital surplus) of A and B are added together as are the earned surplus amounts on the combined corporations' balance sheet; if the new combined capital stock exceeds that of A and B together, the excess first reduces combined capital surplus and then reduces combined earned surplus. Implicit is the rationale that this is the equivalent of capitalizing B's surplus, first the capital surplus and then the earned surplus to the extent necessary to cover the par or stated value.

2. REASONS FOR POOLING

These accounting results are believed by many to be the major motivation for the invention of pooling and the reason for its continued existence. Thus, many corporate acquirers desire, and perhaps could not succeed without, accounting for acquisitions which result in (a) lower reported depreciation and amortization expenses than would be shown under purchase accounting with the consequential higher income and rate of return, (b) carryover of the acquired firm's earned surplus, and (c) combination of earnings in the income statements for the year of acquisition and for restatements of prior years' earnings.

It should be noted that if pooling were not an available accounting choice, acquirers would make decisions about acquisitions independently of the choice of accounting treatment, and presumably would structure some acquisitions to minimize the actual costs—something which is not always done now because of the corrupting influence of pooling accounting. Perhaps for that reason, resources are being inefficiently allocated today.

One asserted ground for legitimization of pooling treatment has been the tax-free reorganization rules under the Internal Revenue Code. Under the code, many statutory mergers and consolidations, exchanges of shares and sales of assets for shares have been defined as reorganizations which are "tax-free" to investors and the corporations involved. Consistent with the tax-free treatment for the corporate constituents, however, the corporations' tax bases for assets remain and are carried over to the reorganized company, as is the tax area's near-kin to earned surplus, "earnings and profits." Proponents of pooling have urged that this is similar to pooling's treatment of the assets and surplus of both constituents—which retain their old book carrying values. They urge in effect that what is good for Uncle Sam is good for corporate accounting, but the logic of this assertion is not apparent—especially since pooling accounting is not limited to tax-free reorganizations and purchase accounting is not limited to taxable ones.

Other theoretical underpinnings may exist for pooling accounting, especially when in fact A and B are equally matched; in this situation, it would require some deviation from the historical cost convention to require either or both A and B to reflect new values in their accounts. The battle over pooling rages unabated in the literature.

3. CRITERIA FOR POOLING

The questionable legitimacy of pooling, based as it is, largely in the attractiveness to managers of its financial statement results and the illogical implication that imperfect parallelism with the Internal Revenue Code is desirable, indicates a weak-principled basis for distinguishing situations where either pooling or purchase accounting should be prescribed.

* * *

B. STANDARDS FOR DECIDING WHETHER A TRANSACTION IS A POOLING OR A PURCHASE

The criteria for deciding between purchase and pooling accounting are set out in Opinion No. 16 of the Accounting Principles Board, promulgated in 1970 along with Opinion No. 17 dealing with goodwill. Those two opinions are summarized as follows in 130 J. Accountancy (Sept. 1970) 9-10:

Opinion No. 16, "Business Combinations," provides that the purchase method and the pooling-of-interests method are both acceptable in accounting for business combinations, but not as optional alternatives for a given merger. A business combination which meets all of certain specified conditions would be treated as a pooling of interests. All other business combinations would be accounted for as a purchase of one or more companies by another company.

The following conditions must be met if pooling-of-interests accounting is to be used:

Each of the combining companies is autonomous and independent and has not been a subsidiary or division of another corporation within two years before the plan of combination is initiated.

The combination is effected in a single transaction or is completed according to a specific plan within one year.

A corporation issues only common stock with rights identical to those of the majority of its outstanding voting common stock in exchange for substantially all of the voting common stock interest of another company.

Each of the combining companies maintains substantially the same voting common stock interest, with no exchanges, retirements, or distributions to stockholders in contemplation of effecting the combination.

Each of the combining companies reacquires shares of voting common stock only for purposes other than business combinations, and no company reacquires more than a normal number of shares after the date the plan of combination is initiated.

The ratio of interest of an individual common stockholder to those of other common stockholders in a combining company remains the same as a result of the exchange of stock to effect the combination.

The voting rights to which the common stock ownership interests in the resulting combined corporation are entitled are exercisable by the stockholders; the stockholders are neither deprived of nor restricted in exercising those rights.

The combination is resolved at the date the plan is consummated and no provisions of the plan relating to the issue of securities or other consideration are pending.

The combined corporation does not agree directly or indirectly to retire or reacquire all or part of the common stock issued to effect the combination.

The combined corporation does not enter into other financial arrangements for the benefit of the former stockholders of a combining company, such as a guaranty of loans secured by stock issued in the combination, which in effect negates the exchange of equity securities.

The combined corporation does not intend or plan to dispose of a significant part of the assets of the combining companies within two years after the combination except to eliminate duplicate facilities or excess capacity and those assets that would have been disposed of in the ordinary course of business of the separate company.

Opinion No. 17, "Intangible Assets," provides that companies should record as assets the costs of intangible assets acquired from others, including goodwill acquired in business combinations accounted for as purchases. A company may also record as assets the costs of developing identifiable intangible assets but should record as expenses the cost of developing intangible assets which are not specifically identifiable, such as goodwill.

The cost of each type of intangible asset should be amortized from date of acquisition by systematic charges to income over its estimated useful life, but not longer than 40 years. If the life of the intangible asset is estimated to exceed 40 years, the period of amortization should be exactly 40 years, not an arbitrary shorter period.

C. PURCHASE AND POOLING UNDER THE CORPORATION STATUTES

Until quite recently, there had been little attention paid to the purchase-pooling dichotomy in the corporation statutes. Indeed, as we have already seen, only in the case of statutory merger or consolidation did the statutes even take special note of combination transactions. Thus where a combination took the form of an acquisition of assets (or stock), it was treated just like any other purchase of property for stock, with the acquired property presumably recorded at its fair market value at the date of acquisition. And while there was perhaps no absolute mandate against carrying forward the acquired corporation's property at book value, there was certainly no warrant for any carry-over of the earned surplus of the acquired corporation.

However, in the case of merger or consolidation a few of the statutes did expressly contemplate carry-forward of the earned surplus of the acquired corporation (without, however, any corresponding dictate as to property valuation). A typical provision of this kind was former

§76 **(g)** of the Model Act (which was dropped in the 1962 amendments, in conjunction with the addition of the last sentence of § 2(*l*) and the third paragraph of §21, neither of which had any counterpart in the Act prior to 1962.)   Prior to its elimination in 1962, §76 **(g)** read as follows:

> The net surplus of the merging or consolidating corporations which was available for the payment of dividends immediately prior to such merger or consolidation, to the extent that such surplus is not transferred to stated capital or capital surplus by the issuance of shares or otherwise, shall continue to be available for the payment of dividends by such surviving or new corporation.

As in the case of so many of the Model Act provisions, § 76(g) had come from the Illinois statute, where the counterpart provision is section 69(g). The following commentary on this provision appears in 1 Ill.Bus.Corp.Act Ann. (1947) 281:

> *Dividends after merger or consolidation.* Paragraph **(g)** of section 69 was inserted in order to negative any intention that a merger or consolidation should of itself effect a capitalization or "freezing" of the earned surplus of the corporations losing their separate existence. Without this provision such a result might have been supposed to follow from the application of the definition of stated capital in § 2(k) [the counterpart of MBA § 2(j)]. Thus in the absence of special provision in the plan of merger or consolidation the stated capital and paid-in surplus, if any, applicable to the respective shares of the constituent corporations would determine the stated capital and paid-in surplus applicable to the shares of the surviving or new corporation into which they were transformed. Any alteration in such amounts should be provided for as part of the plan. . . .
>
> If one of the constituent corporations had a deficit prior to the merger or consolidation and another had a surplus available for dividends, only the net surplus, if any, remains available for dividends under paragraph **(g)**.

As an aid to understanding the reasons for the aforementioned 1962 amendments to the Model Act, deleting § 76(g) and adding the last sentence of § 2(*l*) and the third paragraph of § 21 the following background items may be instructive. First, it appears that in 1961 the Committee on Corporate Laws of the American Bar Association, which prepared the Model Act and has responsibility for any amendments, received a letter calling attention to problems raised by § 76 **(g)** in the following terms:

> 1. The use of the term "net surplus . . . available for the payment of dividends" is puzzling, since it raises the

question of why the terms defined in section 2, such as "earned surplus" or "capital surplus" were not employed. Prior to the amendment of section 76 (g) [in 1957] to include the words "or capital surplus" after the words "stated capital", it seemed likely that the phrase was not limited to "earned surplus", not only because it would have been simple to say "earned surplus", but also because capital surplus is "available", at least for stock dividends. With the amendment to 69(g) to insert the words "or capital surplus" after the words "stated capital", it becomes much harder to construe the phrase "surplus . . . available for the payment of dividends" to include capital surplus, though it is far from clear that any change in coverage was intended by the aforementioned amendment. Perhaps this peculiar phrase is primarily attributable to the somewhat similar language used in the Illinois statute; but it may be noted that the phrase is just as troublesome there as in the Model Act.

2. Section 76(g) seems to eliminate the emerging distinction between a "pooling of interests" and a "purchase" by treating all mergers or consolidations pursuant to the Model Act as poolings, at least for the purpose of handling the surplus accounts. In view of the very sensible reliance upon accounting developments in other sections of the Act, it seems unfortunate to preclude correlation between established accounting principles and the Model Act in this area.

3. The difficulty referred to in paragraph 2 is heightened by the treatment accorded by the Model Act to acquisition transactions which take the form of a purchase of assets. There it appears that netting of earned surplus is not permitted, whether or not the transaction meets the accounting tests for a pooling of interests, since there is no counterpart of section 76(g) which is applicable in connection with purchase transactions. The result is that under the Model Act the form of the transaction becomes conclusive on the issue of whether the surplus accounts of the combining enterprises should be netted. Is it not sounder to attempt to minimize the differences between merger and purchase of assets, as the tax and accounting approaches do?

4. Finally, the addition of the words "or capital surplus" after the words "stated capital" in section 76(g) introduces another element of confusion. In the normal "pooling of interests" situation, which section 76 (g) seems to contemplate, there is no occasion for a transfer of earned surplus (and *a fortiori* existing capital surplus), to capital surplus, whether on account of issuance of shares or for any other reason. It is true that if the par value of the new shares being issued by the surviving entity in a merger exceeds the par value of the

shares which are being replaced, a transfer to stated capital may be required. Otherwise, however, the process seems to be simply one of netting the respective surplus accounts, and there is no basis for the creation of any additional capital surplus.

Quite the reverse is true in the "purchase of assets" situation. There of course no netting of surplus accounts at all occurs; and the excess of the value of the net assets acquired over the par value of the new stock issued to acquire those assets does augment capital surplus. But since as already noted the whole pattern of section 76 (g) seems to preclude the "purchase of assets" approach in a merger or consolidation, it is hard to see just what the significance of the addition of those words "or capital surplus" was intended to be.

In addition to this and perhaps other correspondence, the Committee had before it the example in Pennsylvania which in 1959 had taken the lead in amending its corporation statute to allow greater flexibility in accounting for combination transactions. Pa.B.C.L. § 704F; see Hackney, Financial Accounting For Parents and Subsidiaries—A New Approach to Consolidated Statements, 25 Pitt.L.Rev. 8, 15–18 (1963).

The 1962 amendments are analyzed in the following terms by the chairman of the committee which prepared them, in Gibson, Surplus, So What? — The Model Act Modernized, 17 Bus.Law. 476, 481–483 (1962):

> While the pooling of interests concept is defined in [the predecessor of APB Op.No.16]in terms realistic enough for accounting purposes, they lack the specificity of legal rules. Thus the new doctrine is said to apply whenever two or more corporations are "brought together" or "combined" for the purpose of carrying on the previously conducted businesses. The concept of being "brought together" sounds more like the law of domestic relations than corporation law, even suggesting problems of compatibility. "Combined" falls equally short of any known word of art in corporate practice. Were we to make the result depend on subjective inquiry into "purpose", we should depart altogether from the traditional technique of corporate law that, in the absence of fraud, everyone may rely on the form of the transaction.
>
> In addition to these dissimilarities of idiom, the accounting standards that operate in the pooling of interests doctrine are also remote from accepted corporate law requirements. For example, it is required that there be a continuity of ownership by "substantially all the ownership interests", that there be no material alteration of "relative voting rights"

and above all that there be a "continuity" of managerial personnel. It is quite apparent that no statute of familiar corporate form could be written in such terms and an effort to employ them would leave the availability of the statute, and the limits of its operation, open to serious doubt. It would be still less satisfactory to enact that earned surplus might be carried forward in any transaction where permitted by sound accounting practice, since this would in effect abdicate control by law and leave the whole matter to accounting rules as they might from time to time be administered. It is known, moreover, that judgments sometimes differ as to their effect. In short, unless definite standards were to be adopted in the Act, businessmen would never know in advance the legal consequences that might follow from an attempt to effect a "pooling of interests".

The real remedy, in the judgment of the Committee on Corporate Laws, was to look directly to the end sought—the carry forward of earned surplus. There appears to be no compelling reason of public policy or business necessity for not providing that in all transactions of merger or consolidation or acquisition of assets, or even in a mere acquisition of control, the earned surplus of both participating corporations may properly be considered as earned surplus, rather than capital surplus, of the resulting enterprise. The significance of earned surplus to the investment world is more important than any artistic incidents of legal technique, such, for example, as the theory of survival of corporate personality that might possibly have prompted the exception in the merger law. As in the case of the law merchant, the law should follow business rather than obstruct it unless some public policy requires otherwise.

On this premise, there is no reason from the point of view of corporate law why the continuation of earned surplus should not be permitted in every transaction of this general nature, so far as the policies of corporate law alone are concerned, even if the permission accorded by accounting practice is more limited in its effect. All that means is that, so far as the law is concerned, the privilege is unmistakably accorded in each such instance, though in some instances the accountants will not permit its utilization in full. So far from this being an objection, it is indeed a recommendation. The mere circumstance that accounting practice has recently changed and now necessitates an amendment of the Model Act shows that further changes, with consequential amendments, may be needed in the future. Room for further learning by accountants should be left. Moreover, corporate law has tended more and more in the direction of a simple set of workable ground rules for the corporate enterprise, leaving regulation either to the equitable jurisdiction of the courts or to regulation through statutes of a policing nature or through the informed judgment of administrative agencies. In short, corporate law should not attempt to particularize all foreseeable situations of the future, since they will look very different when the future comes. . . .

In analyzing the present posture of the Model Act, be sure to differentiate between the question of whether the earned surplus or deficit of the acquired corporation may (or must) be carried over, a subject with which the new provisions expressly deal, and the question of the basis on which the assets of the acquired corporation should be recorded on the books of the acquiring corporation, a subject that is not even alluded to in the statute (as it was not in the pre-1962 provisions either). To the accountants, it is assumed that these two issues are always linked: carryover of the assets at book value goes with carryover of earned surplus (under the pooling approach); recording the assets at cost goes with no carryover of earned surplus (under the purchase approach). Consider whether the Model Act preserves this symmetry, and indeed whether the Act contemplates the carryover of asset book values under any circumstances. Cf. MBA §§ 19, 21.

The latest word on the relationship between accounting principles and the corporation statute comes from Professor Fiflis' article, page 725 supra, at 108-109:

D. A Note on Accounting Fixed by Law

Without attempting a full-scale analysis of the relationship of law to accounting, it should be noted at this point that corporation code provisions regulating dividends (including the effect of corporate combinations on capital and surplus) may alter, in the view of a small minority of accountants, the above-described presentation of accounting data on financial statements.

For example, the governing corporation statute may prescribe that on a merger, the earned surplus of the merging corporation shall be available to the survivor for dividend purposes. Some accountants may believe that under such a statute, even if the merger would not be considered a pooling for any reason, the earned surplus required to be available for dividends should be presented on the audited balance sheet as part of the survivor's earned surplus. Other accountants disagree.

Notwithstanding, it would seem that dividend law, once a more powerful influence on accounting presentation, now has merely a vestigial effect.[52] At

---

52. Hackney, *Accounting Principles in Corporation Law*, 30 Law and Contemp. Prob. 795 n.13 (1965) stated as early as 1965:

> In prior years, the law was considered one of the essential sources dictating in part the development of good accounting practice. Dicksee's pioneering work entitled *Goodwill*

the present time lawyers must follow accounting for the most part in ascertaining dividend limitations.

Indeed, the movement in corporation law is away from tying law to GAAP. If the latest revisions of the MBCA's financial provisions become widely adopted, both accounting and dividend law will be divorced and thereby be vastly improved.

That being so, this paper informs lawyers of accounting practices rather than informing accountants as to dividend law. In any event, to the extent that dividend law may continue to affect balance sheet presentations of corporate equity, lawyers are equipped to explain that law to accountants and need no further aid here.

(1900) commenced with an introductory chapter consisting of an "outline of the law relating to good will." Hatfield's and May's writings are sprinkled with case citations and quotations from opinions. Dean spoke in 1949 of the circuitry of reference when a lawyer, "asked to pass upon a legal concept deriving its meaning, in whole or part, from accounting concepts, in the absence of statutory authority or case law, turns to the accountant for help in determining ['g.a.a.p.']," while he in turn is met with a request from the accountant for advice as to "the applicable legal principles to be followed" in the same determination. Arthur H. Dean, An Inquiry into the Nature of Business Income Under Present Price Levels 49 (1949). The current view is that

"broad [accounting] principles must transcend the historical limitations of profits 'available for dividends' or 'subject to income tax.' This is not to say that the effects of dividends and of taxes should be ignored; to do so would ignore a significant part of the environment in which accounting operates. Rather the task is to formulate those principles which will enable us to measure the resources held by specific entities and the related changes *before* consideration of taxes and dividends. The measurements should be independent of the dividend and the tax questions but, at the same time, should facilitate the solution of those questions. . . ."

Robert T. Sprouse & Maurice Moonitz, A Tentative Set of Broad Accounting Principles for Business Enterprises 10 (AICPA Accounting Research Study No. 3, 1962).

SECTION 4. TAX INCIDENTS OF COMBINATION TRANSACTIONS

A. GENERAL BACKGROUND

Absent some special statutory provisions, the various exchange transactions which are inherent in corporate combinations, both those between corporations and those between corporations and stockholders, would presumably constitute taxable transactions under the basic exchange provisions of §§ 1001 and 1002. However, as we have already seen in connection with recapitalizations, a very important exception to ordinary exchange treatment is provided by the reorganization provisions of the Code, and the various modes of corporate combinations represent the most important, and complex, types of reorganization. Accordingly, a detailed analysis of the reorganization pattern applicable to combination transactions is in order at this point.

There are two important consequences which flow from qualification as a reorganization. One is of course complete or partial nonrecognition of gain, which is provided by §§ 354 and 361. The other is that usual corollary of non-recognition, the carryover of basis, which means that the basis of property in the hands of the new owner is either the same as it was in the prior owner's hands or the same as the new owner's basis in the property exchanged by him. It may be helpful to divide our analysis into two parts, looking first at the tax incidents to the corporations being combined, and then at the tax incidents to the stockholders (and security holders).

Before doing so, however, we should briefly review the types of combination transactions which can qualify as a reorganization. For this purpose, it is important to note that unless a transaction fits one of the specific definitions in §368(a)(1), reorganization treatment will not be available; the introductory language in §368(a)(1) specifies that the term "reorganization" means, rather than includes, the transactions thereafter specified.

We have already seen in the Darrell article at the beginning of this chapter a description of the three most traditional forms of combination transaction: a statutory merger or consolidation (usually referred to as an "A reorganization"); a stock acquisition in which the acquiring corporation obtains stock from the shareholders of the acquired corporation in exchange solely for its own voting stock (or that of its parent) and ends up with at least 80% control of the acquired corporation (a "B reorganization"); and an asset acquisition, in which the acquiring corporation exchanges solely its own voting stock or that of its parent (with limited exceptions to be discussed later) for substantially all of the assets of another corporation (a "C reorganization").

As indicated in the article by Professors Schulman and Schenk, at page 641 supra, these traditional statutory modes of combination have been augmented by so-called "triangular mergers". The introduction of these combination forms will be reviewed in more detail at pages 753-754, infra. Suffice it to say here that §368(a)(2)(D) extends qualification as an A reorganization treatment to acquisition of a corporation by merging it into a subsidiary in exchange for the parent corporation's stock (a "triangular merger"); and §368(a)(2)(E) allows A reorganization treatment for the merger of a controlled subsidiary into the outside corporation being acquired, in exchange for stock of the parent corporation (a "reverse triangular merger").

1. NON-RECOGNITION AND BASIS FOR CORPORATE TRANSFERORS AND TRANSFEREES

Here the basic non-recognition section is § 361. Section 361(a) provides that no gain shall be recognized to a corporation which transfers its assets in a transaction constituting a reorganization under § 368. This would include the transfer of all or substantially all of its assets by the acquired corporation in an assets acquisition (hereinafter "C reorganization"); and it would also apply to a statutory merger or consolidation (hereinafter "A reorganization") if such transactions are regarded as including a transfer of property from the disappearing corporation to the surviving corporation, instead of being more in the nature of a "coalescence" of the two corporations. Section 361(a) is applicable only if the exchange is solely for stock or securities (plus assumption of liabilities, by virtue of §§ 368(a)(1)(C) and 357). If some other consideration passes to the acquired corporation in a C reorganization, as it may to a limited extent by virtue of § 368(a)(2)(B), § 361(a) becomes inapplicable. However, § 361 (b)(1) will then apply, either to prevent recognition of gain to the corporation if the "boot" (i.e., the consideration other than stock, securities and assumption of liabilities) is distributed to shareholders of the acquired corporation *pursuant to the plan of reorganization*, or to limit recognition to the amount of the boot if it is not so distributed. Whether or not boot is present, § 361(b)(2) prohibits the recognition of loss by the acquired corporation.

Section 358 prescribes the basis of the acquired corporation in the non-recognition property received; as in the case of § 351 transactions, the basis is the same as the basis of the assets transferred, increased by the amount of any gain recognized, and decreased by the amount of any cash and the fair market value of any other boot received, plus the amount of any liabilities assumed or to which the transferred property was subject.

The basis of the acquiring corporation in the assets it receives is determined under § 362(b), which operates in the same manner as

§ 362(a) (1) in the case of the transferee corporation under § 351. That is, the acquiring corporation takes the assets at their basis in the hands of the acquired corporation, increased by the amount of any gain recognized by the acquired corporation. Thus both the acquiring corporation and the acquired corporation end up with a basis determined with reference to the original basis of the acquired corporation's property (aside from adjustments for boot or liabilities), so that the possibility of two gains or two losses exist.

2. NON-RECOGNITION AND BASIS FOR SHAREHOLDERS AND SECURITY HOLDERS

Here, as we have already seen in connection with recapitalizations, the basic non-recognition section is § 354, which provides that "no gain or loss shall be recognized if stock or securities in a corporation a party to a reorganization are, in pursuance of the plan of reorganization, exchanged solely for stock or securities in such corporation or in another corporation a party to the reorganization". Under this section the exchange by the acquired corporation's shareholders of their stock for stock of the acquiring corporation in an A reorganization or in a stock acquisition (hereinafter "B reorganization") would be tax-free.

In a C reorganization, unless the acquired corporation is liquidated there will be no tax incidents to its shareholders, since they will merely continue as shareholders of the acquired corporation. However, where the acquired corporation liquidates and distributes the stock of the acquiring corporation, in effect the shareholders of the acquired corporation exchange their stock for stock of the acquiring corporation; if the liquidation is "pursuant to the plan of reorganization", the transaction will be covered by § 354(a).

As noted in the analysis of recapitalization transactions, § 354 (a) applies only to an exchange which is solely for stock (and/or securities in a principal amount not exceeding the principal amount of any securities surrendered) ; the presence of any boot, (i.e., money, property, or principal amount of securities in excess of the principal amount of securities surrendered) prevents the application of § 354. In that event, § 356(a) would come into play and tax the gain on the transaction to the extent of the boot. And if the transaction has the "effect of the distribution of a dividend" within the meaning of § 356(a) (2), the boot, to the extent it does not exceed the amount of the gain on the transaction, would be taxed as a dividend. Whether or not boot is involved, §§ 354(a) and 356(c) prevent the recognition of any loss.

The basis of property received in exchanges governed by §§ 354 or 356 is prescribed by § 358(a). Under that section, the basis of any non-recognition property received is equal to the basis of any property given up, increased in the amount of any gain recognized and decreased by the amount of any cash or the fair market value of any other boot received in the transaction.

B. JUDICIAL LIMITATIONS ON QUALIFICATION AS A REORGANIZATION

1. IN GENERAL

Even though, as previously noted, a transaction can not qualify for reorganization treatment unless it fits one of the specific definitions in §368(a), the converse is not true—that is, not every transaction which literally complies with one of the specified definitions of reorganization in § 368 (a)(1) will qualify for the favorable reorganization treatment. Because taxpayers have often sought to cast in the reorganization mold transactions which really do not belong there, the courts have found it necessary to go beyond the bare words of the statute and try to determine whether the particular transaction comes within the spirit of the tax-free reorganization provisions. We have already seen one illustration in the recapitalization area, in the Bazley case, at page 331 supra, where the Supreme Court held that a transaction which concededly constituted a recapitalization under state law nevertheless did not qualify as a reorganization for tax purposes.

A number of the extra-statutory standards developed by the courts for testing purported reorganization transactions have crystallized into general principles. Foremost among these is the "business purpose" doctrine, which stems from the landmark case of Gregory v. Helvering, 293 U.S. 465, 55 S.Ct. 266, 79 L.Ed. 596, 97 A.L.R. 1355 (1935). There the Supreme Court held that a transaction which complied literally with the then-existing divisive reorganization provisions nevertheless did not qualify for tax-free treatment because the entire arrangement had no business purpose and was designed solely to accomplish what in effect was a dividend to the stockholder. The business purpose doctrine is now expressly incorporated in the reorganization regulations, Reg. § 1.368–1(b); and it has of course spread far beyond the reorganization area to become one of the basic principles in the tax field.

Another doctrine of general importance which has had a special impact in the reorganization area is the "step transaction" doctrine. Under this principle, purportedly separate transactions will be amalgamated into a single transaction when it appears that they were really component steps intended from the outset to be taken for the purpose of reaching the ultimate result. For example, in Heller v.

Commissioner, 2 T.C. 371 (1943), affirmed, 147 F.2d 376 (9th Cir. 1945), the stockholders of a Delaware corporation wanted to reincorporate under California law, which is a classic type of tax-free transaction. However, the stockholders wanted to recognize the unrealized loss they had on their stock in the Delaware corporation. Accordingly, they organized a California corporation and purchased its stock with cash borrowed from a bank which was also a creditor of the Delaware corporation. The California corporation then purchased the assets of the Delaware corporation for cash, augmented by a loan from the same bank. The Delaware corporation used the cash it received to pay off its bank loan, and then dissolved, distributing the balance of the cash in liquidation to its stockholders. Presumably, the stockholders then repaid their own bank loans. *Held*, the transaction constituted a reorganization so that no loss could be recognized by the stockholders upon the liquidation: "The effect of all the steps taken was that petitioner made an exchange of stock of one corporation for stock of another pursuant to a plan of reorganization."

2. CONTINUITY OF INTEREST

Perhaps the most important judicial doctrine in the reorganization area has been "continuity of interest", which is not only firmly embedded in the regulations, Reg. § 1.368–1(b), but has also played an important part in the development of the statutory definition of B and C reorganizations. The continuity of interest doctrine seems to stem from Cortland Specialty Co. v. Commissioner, 60 F.2d 937 (2d Cir. 1932), involving an earlier rudimentary definition of reorganization which included any acquisition by one corporation of substantially all the properties of another corporation. In the Cortland case, substantially all of the property of one corporation had indeed been acquired by another corporation, in exchange for cash and short-term promissory notes, but the court held that the transaction did not qualify as a reorganization for tax purposes since that term presupposes a "continuance of interest on the part of the transferor in the properties transferred." In effect, then, the continuity of interest doctrine constituted the instrument for preventing what was essentially a sale transaction from obtaining reorganization treatment.

Only one year later, in Pinellas Ice & Cold Storage Co. v. Commissioner, 287 U.S. 462, 53 S.Ct. 257, 77 L.Ed. 428 (1933), this question came before the Supreme Court, which held that to qualify as a reorganization "the seller must acquire an interest in the affairs of the purchasing company more definite than that incident to ownership of its short-term purchase-money notes." Two years later came Helvering v. Minnesota Tea Co., 296 U.S. 378, 56 S.Ct. 269, 80 L.Ed. 284 (1935), where a transfer of assets for common stock worth approximately $700,000 (and amounting to about 7% of the acquiring corporation's outstanding stock) plus cash of approximately $425,000 was sustained as reorganization. After referring to the statement in the Pinellas case that an "interest" must be acquired in the transferee, the Court said:

> And we now add that this interest must be definite and material; it must represent a substantial part of the value of the thing transferred. This much is necessary in order that the result accomplished may genuinely partake of the nature of merger or consolidation. . . .

> The transaction here was no sale, but partook of the nature of a reorganization, in that the seller acquired a definite and substantial interest in the purchaser.

> True it is that the relationship of the taxpayer to the assets conveyed was substantially changed, but this is not inhibited by the statute. Also, a large part of the consideration was cash. This, we think, is permissible so long as the taxpayer received an interest in the affairs of the transferee which represented a material part of the value of the transferred assets.

In the same year, in John A. Nelson Co. v. Helvering, 296 U.S. 374, 56 S.Ct. 273, 80 L.Ed. 281 (1935), the Court found the requisite continuity of interest where assets were transferred for preferred stock and cash. The preferred stock was non-voting except upon default in dividends. The Court commented as follows:

> The owner of preferred stock is not without substantial interest in the affairs of the issuing corporation, although denied voting rights. The statute does not require participation in the management of the purchaser.

The line between debt and equity never glowed more brightly than after the last of the important Supreme Court decisions in the continuity of interest field, Le Tulle v. Scofield, 308 U.S. 415, 60 S.Ct. 313, 84 L.Ed. 355 (1940), where the court held that bonds did not satisfy the requisite continuity, so that a transfer of assets for cash and ten-year bonds secured by a mortgage did not qualify as a reorganization. The Court said:

> In applying our decision in the Pinellas [case, supra], the courts have generally held that receipt of long-term bonds as distinguished from short-term notes constitutes the retention of an interest in the purchasing corporation. There has naturally been some difficulty in classifying the securities involved in various cases.

> We are of opinion that the term of the obligations is not material. Where the consideration is wholly in the transferee's bonds, or part cash and part such bonds, we think it cannot be said that the transferor retains a proprietary

interest in the enterprise. On the contrary, he becomes a creditor of the transferee; and we do not think that the fact referred to by the Circuit Court of Appeals, that the bonds were secured solely by the assets transferred and that, upon default, the bondholder would retake only the property sold, changes his status from that of a creditor to one having a proprietary stake, within the purview of the statute.

However, Congress had already decided not to leave the development of the continuity of interest doctrine entirely to the courts. Because of the multiplying efforts to fit what were essentially sale transactions within the protective reorganization cloak, Congress had acted in 1934 to substantially restrict the scope of the reorganization provisions. In effect, a rather extreme continuity of interest limitation was built directly into the statutory definition of the B and C reorganizations by the requirement that the acquisition must be *solely for voting stock*. (The exception for assumption of liabilities in C reorganizations came into the statute in 1939; the 20% leeway from the solely voting stock requirement for C reorganizations under § 368(a)(2)(B) came in 1954.) However, the definition of an A reorganization simply in terms of "a statutory merger or consolidation" was left unchanged.

Since Congress was clearly concerned with the continuity of interest concept at the time of the 1934 amendments, the absence of any reference to the matter in connection with A reorganizations might have led to the view that continuity of interest was not required for an A reorganization. Nevertheless, in Roebling v. Commissioner, 143 F.2d 810 (3d Cir. 1944), the court held that the continuity of interest requirement was applicable to an A reorganization, and hence rejected reorganization treatment for a merger when the stockholders of the acquired corporation received only bonds of the acquiring corporation. In Southwest Natural Gas Co. v. Commissioner, 189 F.2d 332 (5th Cir. 1951), continuity of interest was found lacking in a statutory merger despite the fact that the consideration received by the stockholders of the acquired corporation included 16% of the outstanding common stock of the acquiring corporation. However, the value of this 16% stock interest was only about $5500, out of a total consideration in cash, bonds, and stock of almost $600,000; moreover, some 41% of the acquired corporation's stockholders had elected to forego any continued participation in the combined enterprise in favor of receiving only cash. On the other hand, as the dissenting opinion pointed out, there was in fact a greater continuity of interest than there appeared to be, since a group owning 35% of the acquired corporation's stock before the merger also owned 85% of the acquiring corporation's stock, and they ended up with an 88% equity interest in the combination.

The Southwest Natural Gas opinion phrased the continuity of interest test as follows:

> While no precise formula has been expressed for determining whether there has been retention of the requisite interest, it seems clear that the requirement of continuity of interest consistent with the statutory intent is not fulfilled in the absence of a showing: (1) that the transferor corporation or its shareholders retained a substantial proprietary stake in the enterprise represented by a material interest in the affairs of the transferee corporation, and, (2) that such retained interest represents a substantial part of the value of the property transferred.

Taken literally, the first of these requirements would normally depend in the first instance on the relative size of the two corporations. Where the acquired corporation is very much smaller than the acquiring corporation, the stockholders of the acquired corporation might not have a "substantial" or "material" interest in the acquiring corporation even if the consideration they received consisted solely of voting common stock. However, this *quantitative* aspect has not been stressed in the cases, and it does not presently appear to be a significant factor in Service policy.

The second requirement seems to look to the ratio of that part of the consideration received by the acquired corporation's shareholders which constitutes a continuing proprietary interest to the total consideration received. It is this *qualitative* aspect of the continuity of interest doctrine that was stressed in the Minnesota Tea case, supra, and of course the Southwest Natural Gas case itself turned primarily on this factor. Certain subsidiary questions arise here which are easier to state than answer: (1) Will a higher ratio of consideration providing a proprietary interest be required when the acquired corporation is substantially smaller than the acquiring corporation, so that the continuing interest of the stockholders of the former would be relatively small in any event? (2) Does the required ratio turn at all upon the type of proprietary interest consideration involved, so that a lower ratio might be permitted if voting common of the acquiring corporation is used than, say, if non-voting preferred is used?

To some extent the importance of the qualitative aspect of the continuity of interest doctrine has been somewhat lessened by the addition of §§ 354(a)(2) and 356(d) in the 1954 Code, treating as boot any excess in principal amount of securities received over the principal amount of securities surrendered. And of course if only securities are received and none is surrendered, the transaction does not come under §§ 354 or 356 at all, but reverts to §§ 331, 346 or 302. These provisions, however, only relate to the tax consequences to the acquired corporation's stockholders. The basis to the acquiring corporation of the assets acquired in the merger still depends upon whether there has been a "reorganization". In addition, the question of whether boot might be taxable as a dividend under §§ 356(a)(2), rather than simply as part of the consideration in an exchange transaction, may turn on the presence of a reorganization.

There is one other aspect of the continuity of interest doctrine which was actually presented in the Southwest Natural Gas case but was not expressly referred to in the court's formulation of the test. Might the necessary continuity of interest be found lacking if a substantial number of shareholders, of either the acquired corporation or the acquiring corporation, refuse to participate in the merger and pursue the statutory appraisal remedy to obtain cash? In the Southwest Natural Gas case, the plan of merger itself afforded the stockholders of the acquired corporation the option of taking cash, and some 41% of the stockholder elected that alternative. Thus, even if all the other stockholders had received nothing but voting stock, the failure of almost half of the stockholders of the acquired corporation to continue any participation in the enterprise might have raised serious doubts as to the necessary continuity of interest. Of course in the absence of a cash alternative under the merger plan, the percentage of non-participating stockholders would normally be substantially lower, since typically the merger statutes require the approval of at least two-thirds of the stockholders; and in many situations even an approved merger could not be consummated in the face of any substantial body of dissenting shareholders, because of the lack of necessary cash.

Most of the questions as to how to measure the amount of continuity of interest needed to qualify for an A reorganization have now been answered by the concrete guideline continued in Section 3.02 of Rev. Proc. 77-27, set out on page 158 supra: the continuity of interest requirement will be satisfied if the shareholders of the acquired corporation receive stock in the acquiring corporation which is equal in value to at least 50 percent of the total value of the outstanding stock of the acquired corporation just before the merger. It is not necessary that each shareholder receive stock equal in value to 50 percent of his stock interest in the acquired corporation, as long as one or more of the stockholders end up with stock which in the aggregate has a value equal to 50 percent of the value of all the previously outstanding stock of the acquired corporation.

Questions of what qualifies as "stock" may arise in connection with A reorganizations both as a matter of determining whether the necessary continuity of interest is present, and, assuming that hurdle is cleared, in determining whether there is "boot" which would require the recognition of gain under § 356. Thus, the question may be asked whether redeemable preferred stock provides the requisite continuity of interest, since if the stockholders of an acquired corporation received only redeemable preferred they would be subject to being ousted from the surviving corporation at any time. While there does not appear to be any authority dealing expressly with this question, it should be noted that according to the opinion of the Board of Tax Appeals, the preferred stock approved as providing the necessary continuity of interest in the John A. Nelson Co. case, page 742 supra, was in fact subject to redemption in accordance with an unspecified schedule. See 28 B.T.A. 529, 542 (1933). Moreover, in Atlantic City Electric Co. v. Commissioner, 288 U.S. 152, 53 S.Ct. 383, 77 L.Ed. 667 (1932), involving the question whether redeemable, voting preferred stock should be taken into account in measuring the extent of a parent corporation's control over a subsidiary for the purpose of applying an early version of the consolidated return regulations, the court stated that the owners of the redeemable preferred stock "were not in the position of creditors, but were stockholders with a proprietary interest in the corporate undertaking". On the other hand, if only redeemable preferred was issued and the stock was actually redeemed shortly thereafter, it seems likely that a serious question as to continuity of interest would arise; and this would certainly be true if it were shown that an early redemption had been contemplated from the outset.

As to stock options and warrants, according to Reg. § 1.354–1(e) they "are not included in the term 'stock or securities' ", which means that they not only do not contribute to the continuity of interest but in fact represent taxable boot. Bateman v. Commissioner, 40 T.C. 408 (1963). The Bateman case goes on to hold that although warrants received along with stock in a statutory merger do constitute boot, they cannot be taxed as a dividend under § 356(a) (2) because § 316 only taxes distributions of "property" as a dividend, and § 317 specifically excludes warrants from the definition of "property".

Questions may also arise in connection with such mechanical adjuncts to combination transactions as fractional shares and contingent interests in shares. As to the latter, Mr. Darrell noted, at page 632 supra, that such contingent interests may stem from an arrangement under which some of the stock to be issued to stockholders of the acquired corporation is temporarily withheld as security against the possibility of unknown or contingent liabilities. Alternatively, the acquired corporation's shareholders may be entitled to receive additional voting shares in the future upon the fulfillment of a specified condition, such as the acquired corporation achieving a particular level of earnings.

Sometimes the contingent right to more shares is evidenced by a certificate, which may itself be negotiable. In Carlberg v. United States, 281 F.2d 507 (8th Cir. 1960), such certificates were held to constitute "stock" rather than boot under §354, thereby qualifying for non-recogni-

tion of gain under §354. (A more troublesome question
is whether contingent stock rights can satisfy the
voting stock requirement applicable to B and C reorganizations; the current Service guidelines on the status
of contingent stock are set out in Rev. Proc. 77-37,
1977-2 Cum. Bull. 568, page 156 supra, Sections 3.03
and 3.06, which are discussed at page 780 infra.)

Fractional shares pose an even more important practical problem, since they will be present in virtually every
combination transaction, except where the exchange ratio
calls for an even multiple of the acquiring corporation's
stock for each share of the acquired corporation. However,
it is generally accepted that fractional shares represent
"stock" rather than boot for the purpose of non-recognition of gain under §354; and this result is not affected
by the common practice of acquiring corporations to make
arrangements for the recipient stockholders either to purchase an additional fractional interest sufficient to make
a full share or to sell their fractional shares. Of course
upon a sale of a fractional interest, the stockholder
would realize gain or loss measured by the difference between the amount of cash received and the allocated basis
of the fractional interest sold. On the other hand, if the
plan of reorganization called for a direct payment of cash
in lieu of fractional shares to all shareholders, the cash
might then be regarded as boot, and hence subject to taxation as a dividend under §356(a)(2). (The harder question
of whether fractional shares may violate the "solely for
voting stock" requirement in B and C reorganizations will
be discussed at page 779 infra.)

3. CONTINUITY OF BUSINESS ENTERPRISE

Reg. §1.368-1(b) states that one of the requisites for
a valid reorganization is "a continuity of the business
enterprise under the modified corporate forum". For a time
this was regarded as imposing a variant of the continuity of
interest test, in effect requiring that the business activities conducted by the constituent corporations be continued
by the combined entity, so that the former stockholders would
retain their interest in those business. E.g., Rev. Rul.
56-330, 1956-2 Cum. Bull. 204 (no reorganization when real
estate corporations transferred all of their assets to a
newly-formed insurance company solely for its voting stock,
but the real estate business was not continued). Under this
view the continuity of business enterprise factor closely
paralled the requirement for a pooling of interest under
APB Op. No. 16, page 732 supra, that there be no planned disposition of any substantial portion of the assets of the
combining companies.

However, in Bentsen v. Phinney, 199 F.Supp. 363 (S.D.Tex.1961), which apparently involved the very transaction to which Rev.Rul. 56–330 had been addressed, the court held that if the continuity of business enterprise test in the regulations required that the acquiring corporation engage in the same type of business as the acquired corporation, or a similar business, it went beyond the statute and was invalid. In the court's view, all that was required was a continuation of some business activity.

The Service has since renounced its earlier position and adopted the view expressed in the Bentsen case. In Rev.Rul. 63–29, 63–1 Cum. Bull. 77, a corporation formerly engaged in the manufacture of children's toys had sold practically all of its operating assets to third parties for cash and notes. Thereafter it acquired, solely for voting stock, all of the property of a corporation engaged in the distribution of steel products, and it used the proceeds of the sale of its toy business to expand its newly acquired steel products business. The ruling states that the continuity of business enterprise test is satisfied so long as "the surviving corporation was organized to engage in a business enterprise", and holds that "the surviving corporation need not continue the activities conducted by its predecessors". Notwithstanding the possible distinction between the instant situation, where at least a business enterprise previously carried on by one of the constituents was continued by the surviving entity, and Rev.Rul. 56–330, where the acquiring corporation was formed to carry on an entirely new and distinct activity, Rev.Rul. 63–29 went on to revoke Rev.Rul. 56–330, stating that the conclusions reached in the present ruling were equally applicable to the question involved in the earlier one.

4. USE OF A SUBSIDIARY IN REORGANIZATION ACQUISITIONS

One of the early judge-made limitations on qualification as a reorganization, with roots in the continuity of interest doctrine as well as the "party to a reorganization" requirement of § 354, precluded reorganization treatment where a subsidiary corporation effected an acquisition in exchange for stock of its parent. The same was true where a parent corporation acquired the assets or stock of a corporation for its own stock but promptly transferred what it acquired to a subsidiary in pursuance of the plan of reorganization. E. g., Groman v. Commissioner, 302 U.S. 82, 58 S.Ct. 108, 82 L.Ed. 63 (1937). However, in the 1954 Code these limitations were virtually eliminated so far as C reorganizations were concerned. Under § 368 (a) (1) (C), an asset acquisition by a subsidiary corporation qualifies as a C reorganization if the consideration given for the assets consists solely of voting stock of a corporation in control of the acquiring corporation. And the parent corporation would be a "party to the reorganization" under the language of § 368(b), second sentence. However, it should be noted that the subsidiary may not use both its own stock and its parent's stock in the same transaction. Reg. § 1.368–2(d)(1).

If the parent first acquires the assets of the acquired corporation itself but then transfers them to a subsidiary, the transaction still qualifies as a C reorganization by virtue of § 368(a)(2)(C); and again the parent corporation is a party to the reorganization under § 368(b), last sentence. Section 368(a)(2)(C) also permits the acquiring corporation in an A reorganization to place the acquired assets in a controlled subsidiary without disqualifying the transaction as a reorganization.

In 1964 §368 was amended to conform the treatment of B reorganizations to that afforded C reorganizations so far as use of a subsidiary is concerned. §368(a)(1)(B), (a)(2)(C), and (b).

These developments left A reorganizations at a disadvantage, since there was still no statutory authorization for acquiring a corporation by merging it into a subsidiary, using the parent's stock. This deficiency was cured in 1968 with the addition of §368(a)(2)(D), which expressly allows A reorganization treatment for such a statutory merger so long as only the parent corporation's stock is used, and none of the subsidiary's; as a corollary, §368(b) was amended to make the parent corporation a party to the reorganization in such circumstances, so that its stock can be received tax–free under §354.

Because § 368(a)(2)(D) speaks in terms of acquiring substantially all of the properties of the acquired corporation in exchange for stock of the acquiring corporation's parent, it might have been argued that in this type of merger, unlike the normal statutory merger under § 368(a)(1)(A), only stock could be used as consideration, or at least that substantially all the assets had to be acquired for stock. This would have imposed on such mergers a much tighter continuity of interest test than the one applicable to ordinary mergers, though still not as stringent as the solely for *voting* stock test applicable to B and C reorganizations (subject to the 20% leeway for C reorganizations). However, both the legislative history of § 368(a)(2)(D) and present Service ruling policy appear to confirm that mergers under the new provision need meet only the same continuity of interest test, permitting the use of substantial "boot", as is applicable to ordinary non-subsidiary mergers under § 368(a)(1)(A).

In 1971 the scope of permissible "subsidiary merger" techniques was further broadened by the addition of § 368(a)(2)(E), which allows qualification as an A reorganization for a merger of a controlled subsidiary *into* the outside corporation being acquired, with the former stockholders of the acquired corporation receiving stock of the parent from the controlled subsidiary, which in turn receives the properties of the acquired corporation. Notice, however, that in this reverse triangular technique the former stockholders of the acquired corporation must receive voting stock of the parent in exchange for stock amounting to control of the acquired corporation.

These were changes of considerable practical importance because it may make it possible to obtain the tax advantage of statutory merger, consisting of greater flexibility as to the form of consideration permitted, together with the non-tax advantages of automatic transfer of property and assumption of liabilities by operation of law which flow from a statutory merger, while avoiding the substantial corporate disadvantages which normally inhere in such a merger, i. e., granting voting rights and appraisal remedies to the stockholders of both corporations. To illustrate, if corporation X wishes to acquire corporation Y, X can transfer the necessary amount of its own stock (and any other consideration that may be desired) to a newly-formed subsidiary and then merge Y into that subsidiary in exchange for the X stock (plus any other consideration, as long as it does not include any of the subsidiary's stock). In form, at least, X would not be a party to the merger under corporate law, and according to the Schulman and Schenk piece, page 641 supra, the de facto merger doctrine would not be applicable to give X's stockholders either voting or appraisal remedies.

The following excerpts from the Senate Finance Committee Report accompanying the 1971 authorization of reverse triangular mergers provide an excellent account of the reasoning behind that provision, as well as the earlier approval of direct triangular mergers:

SENATE FINANCE COMMITTEE REPORT, PUBLIC LAW 91–693

S. Rep. No. 91–1533, 91st Cong., 2d Sess. 622–23 (1971).

[H.R. 19562] amends the tax law to permit a tax-free statutory merger when stock of a parent corporation is used in a merger between a controlled subsidiary of the parent and another corporation, and the other corporation survives—here called a "reverse merger."

* * *

In 1968 Congress added a provision to the tax laws permitting statutory mergers where the stock of the parent of the corporation making the acquisition was used in the acquisition (sec. 368(a)(2)(D)). At the time that statute was enacted, the use of stock of a parent corporation was permitted in the type of reorganization involving the acquisition of stock (subparagraph (B)) and in the type of reorganization involving the acquisition of assets (subparagraph (C)) but was not permited in the case of a statutory merger of a subsidiary. After noting this fact, the House committee report went on to explain the reasons for the amendment as follows:

> Apparently the use of a parent's stock in statutory mergers was not initially provided for because there was no special concern with the problem at the time of the adoption of the 1954 code. However, this is no longer true. A case has been called to the attention of your committee in which it is desired to have an operating company merged into an operating subsidiary in exchange for the stock of the parent holding company. Your committee sees no reason why tax-free treatment should be denied in cases of this type where for any reason the parent cannot or, for business or legal reasons, does not want to acquire the assets (even temporarily) through a merger.

> For the reasons set forth above your committee concluded that it was desirable to permit the use of the stock of the parent corporation in a statutory merger in acquiring a corporation in essentially the same manner as presently is available in the case of other tax-free acquisitions. (House report on H.R. 18942 (90th Cong.).)

Thus, under existing law, corporation X (an unrelated corporation) may be merged into corporation S (a subsidiary) in exchange for the stock in corporation P (the parent of S) in a tax-free statutory merger. However, if for business and legal reasons (wholly unrelated to Federal income taxation) it is considered more desirable to merge S into X (rather than merging X into S), so that X is the surviving corporation—a "reverse merger"—the transaction is not a tax-free statutory merger.

Although the reverse merger does not qualify as a tax-free statutory merger, it may, in appropriate circumstances, be treated as tax-free as a stock-for-stock reorganization (subparagraph (B)). However, in order to qualify as a tax-free stock-for-stock reorganization it is necessary that the acquisition be *solely* for voting stock and that no stock be acquired for cash or other consideration. Thus, if a small amount of the stock of X (the unrelated corporation) is acquired for cash before the merger of S into X, there often may be doubt as to whether or not the transaction will meet the statutory requirements of a stock-for-stock reorganization.

The committee agrees with the House, that there is no reason why a merger in one direction (S into X in the above example) should be taxable, when the merger in the other direction (X into S), under identical circumstances, is tax-free. Moreover, it sees no reason why in cases of this type the acquisition needs to be made solely for stock. For these reasons the amendment makes statutory mergers tax-free in the circumstances described above.   *   *   *

C. SPECIAL PROBLEMS IN B REORGANIZATIONS

CHAPMAN v. COMMISSIONER *

United States Court of Appeals, First Circuit, 1980.

618 F.2d 856.

CAMPBELL, Circuit Judge. . . . We must decide whether the requirement of Section 368(a)(1)(B) ** that the acquisition of stock in one corporation by another be solely in exchange for voting stock of the acquiring corporation is met where, in related transactions, the acquiring corporation first acquires 8 percent of the acquiree's stock for cash and then acquires more than 80 percent of the acquiree in an exchange of stock for voting stock. The Tax Court agreed with the taxpayers that the latter exchange constituted a valid tax-free reorganization. Reeves v. Commissioner, 71 T.C. 727 (1979).

The Facts. Appellees were among the more than 17,000 shareholders of the Hartford Fire Insurance Company who exchanged their Hartford stock for shares of the voting stock of International Telephone and Telegraph Corporation pursuant to a formal exchange offer from ITT dated May 26, 1970. On their 1970 tax returns, appellees did not report any gain or loss from these exchanges. Subsequently, the Internal Revenue Service assessed deficiencies . . .. Appellees petitioned the Tax Court for redetermination of these deficiencies, and their cases were consolidated with those of twelve other former Hartford shareholders. The Tax Court, with five judges dissenting,[3] granted appellees' motion for summary judgment, and the Commissioner of Internal Revenue filed this appeal.

The events giving rise to this dispute began in 1968, when the management of ITT, a large multinational corporation, became interested in acquiring Hartford as part of a program of diversification. In October 1968, ITT executives approached Hartford about the possibility of merging the two corporations. This proposal was spurned by Hartford, which at the time was considering acquisitions of its own. In November 1968, ITT learned that approximately 1.3 million shares of Hartford, representing some 6 percent of Hartford's voting

---

* Portions of the opinion and many of the footnotes omitted.

** [Ed. note: "(B) the acquisition by one corporation, in exchange solely for all or a part of its voting stock . . ., of stock of another corporation if, immediately after the acquisition, the acquiring corporation has control of such other corporation (whether or not such acquiring corporation had control immediately before the acquisition);]

3. Judge Tannenwald wrote the opinion for a plurality of the Tax Court, two judges concurred only in the result, and five dissented. Four judges did not participate and one vacancy existed at the time. We are informed by counsel for the Commissioner that this necessarily indicates the majority, including concurrences, consisted of six members of the court.

stock, were available for purchase from a mutual fund. After assuring Hartford's directors that ITT would not attempt to acquire Hartford against its will, ITT consummated the $63.7 million purchase from the mutual fund with Hartford's blessing. From November 13, 1968 to January 10, 1969, ITT also made a series of purchases on the open market totalling 458,000 shares which it acquired for approximately $24.4 million. A further purchase of 400 shares from an ITT subsidiary in March 1969 brought ITT's holdings to about 8 percent of Hartford's outstanding stock, all of which had been bought for cash.

In the midst of this flurry of stockbuying, ITT submitted a written proposal to the Hartford Board of Directors for the merger of Hartford into an ITT subsidiary, based on an exchange of Hartford stock for ITT's $2 cumulative convertible voting preferred stock. Received by Hartford in December of 1968, the proposal was rejected in February of 1969. A counter-proposal by Hartford's directors led to further negotiations, and on April 9, 1969 a provisional plan and agreement of merger was executed by the two corporations. While not unlike the proposal Hartford had earlier rejected, this plan was somewhat more favorable to Hartford's stockholders.[4] The merger agreement was conditioned upon approval, as required under state law, by the shareholders of the two corporations and by the Connecticut Insurance Commissioner. . . . .

Meanwhile, on April 15, 1969, attorneys for the parties sought a ruling from the IRS that the proposed transaction would constitute a reorganization under Section 368(a)(1)(B) of the Internal Revenue Code of 1954, so that, among other things, gain realized on the exchange by Hartford shareholders would not be recognized, see 26 U.S.C. § 354(a)(1). By private letter ruling, the Service notified the parties on October 13, 1969 that the proposed merger would constitute a nontaxable reorganization, provided ITT unconditionally sold its 8 percent interest in Hartford to a third party before Hartford's shareholders voted to approve or disapprove the proposal. On October 21, the Service ruled that a proposed sale of the stock to Mediobanca, an Italian bank, would satisfy this condition, and such a sale was made on November 9.

On November 10, 1969, the shareholders of Hartford approved the merger, which had already won the support of ITT's shareholders in June. On December 13, 1969, however, the merger plan ground to a halt, as the Connecticut Insurance Commissioner refused to endorse the arrangement. ITT then proposed to proceed with a voluntary

---

4. In particular, the annual dividend on the preferred shares was to be $2.25 rather than $2.00, and the conversion ratio was set at a rate more favorable to Hartford shareholders.

exchange offer to the shareholders of Hartford on essentially the same terms they would have obtained under the merger plan. After public hearings and the imposition of certain requirements on the post-acquisition operation of Hartford, the insurance commissioner approved the exchange offer on May 23, 1970, and three days later ITT submitted the exchange offer to all Hartford shareholders. More than 95 percent of Hartford's outstanding stock was exchanged for shares of ITT's $2.25 cumulative convertible voting preferred stock. The Italian bank to which ITT had conveyed its original 8 percent interest was among those tendering shares, as were the taxpayers in this case.

In March 1974, the Internal Revenue Service retroactively revoked its ruling approving the sale of Hartford stock to Mediobanca, on the ground that the request on which the ruling was based had misrepresented the nature of the proposed sale. Concluding that the entire transaction no longer constituted a nontaxable reorganization, the Service assessed tax deficiencies against a number of former Hartford shareholders who had accepted the exchange offer. Appellees, along with other taxpayers, contested this action in the Tax Court, where the case was decided on appellees' motion for summary judgment. For purposes of this motion, the taxpayers conceded that questions of the merits of the revocation of the IRS rulings were not to be considered; the facts were to be viewed as though ITT had not sold the shares previously acquired for cash to Mediobanca. The taxpayers also conceded, solely for purposes of their motion for summary judgment, that the initial cash purchases of Hartford stock had been made for the purpose of furthering ITT's efforts to acquire Hartford.

The Issue. Taxpayers advanced two arguments in support of their motion for summary judgment. Their first argument related to the severability of the cash purchases from the 1970 exchange offer. Because 14 months had elapsed between the last of the cash purchases and the effective date of the exchange offer, and because the cash purchases were not part of the formal plan of reorganization entered into by ITT and Hartford, the taxpayers argued that the 1970 exchange offer should be examined in isolation to determine whether it satisfied the terms of Section 368(a)(1)(B) of the 1954 Code. The Service countered that the two sets of transactions—the cash purchases and the exchange offer—were linked by a common acquisitive purpose, and that they should be considered together for the purpose of determining whether the arrangement met the statutory requirement that the stock of the acquired corporation be exchanged "solely for . . . voting stock" of the acquiring corporation. The Tax Court did not reach this argument; in granting summary judgment it relied entirely on the taxpayers' second argument.

For purposes of the second argument, the taxpayers conceded *arguendo* that the 1968 and 1969 cash purchases should be considered "parts of the 1970 exchange offer reorganization." Even so, they insisted upon a right to judgment on the basis that the 1970 exchange of stock for stock satisfied the statutory requirements for a reorganization without regard to the presence of related cash purchases. The Tax Court agreed with the taxpayers, holding that the 1970 exchange in which ITT acquired more than 80 percent of Hartford's single class of stock for ITT voting stock satisfied the requirements of Section 368(a)(1)(B), so that no gain or loss need be recognized on the exchange under Section 354(a)(1). The sole issue on appeal is whether the Tax Court was correct in so holding.

I.

We turn first to the statutory scheme under which this case arose. . . . [Section 354(a)(1)(B)] establishes two basic requirements for a valid, tax-free stock-for-stock reorganization. First, "the acquisition" of another's stock must be "solely for . . . voting stock." Second, the acquiring corporation must have control over the other corporation immediately after the acquisition.

The single issue raised on this appeal is whether "the acquisition" in this case complied with the requirement that it be "solely for . . . voting stock." It is well settled that the "solely" requirement is mandatory; if any part of "the acquisition" includes a form of consideration other than voting stock, the transaction will not qualify as a (B) reorganization. See Helvering v. Southwest Consolidated Corp., 315 U.S. 194, 198, 62 S.Ct. 546, 550, 86 L.Ed. 789 (1942) (" 'Solely' leaves no leeway. Voting stock plus some other consideration does not meet the statutory requirement"). The precise issue before us is thus how broadly to read the term "acquisition." The Internal Revenue Service argues that "the acquisition . . . of stock of another corporation" must be understood to encompass the 1968–69 cash purchases as well as the 1970 exchange offer. If the IRS is correct, "the acquisition" here fails as a (B) reorganization. The taxpayers, on the other hand, would limit "the acquisition" to the part of a sequential transaction of this nature which meets the requirements of subsection (B). They argue that the 1970 exchange of stock for stock was itself an "acquisition" by ITT of stock in Hartford solely in exchange for ITT's voting stock, such that after the exchange took place ITT controlled Hartford. Taxpayers contend that the earlier cash purchases of 8 percent, even if conceded to be part of the same acquisitive plan, are essentially irrelevant to the tax-free reorganization otherwise effected.

The Tax Court accepted the taxpayers' reading of the statute . . . . . The plurality opinion stated its "narrow" holding as follows:

> "We hold that where, as is the case herein, 80 per cent or more of the stock of a corporation is acquired in one transaction, in exchange for which only voting stock is furnished as consideration, the 'solely for voting stock' requirement of section 368 (a)(1)(B) is satisfied."

71 T.C. at 741. The plurality treated as "irrelevant" the 8 percent of Hartford's stock purchased for cash, although the opinion left somewhat ambiguous the question whether the 8 percent was irrelevant because of the 14-month time interval separating the transactions or because the statute was not concerned with transactions over and above those mathematically necessary to the acquiring corporation's attainment of control.

II.

For reasons set forth extensively in section III of this opinion, we do not accept the position adopted by the Tax Court.[16] Instead we side with the Commissioner on the narrow issue presented in this appeal, that is, the correctness of taxpayers' so-called "second" argument premised on an assumed relationship between the cash and stock transactions. As explained below, we find a strong implication in the language of the statute, in the legislative history, in the regulations, and in the decisions of other courts that cash purchases which are concededly "parts of" a stock-for-stock exchange must be considered constituent elements of the "acquisition" for purposes of applying the "solely for . . . voting stock" requirement of Section 368(a)(1)(B). We believe the presence of nonstock consideration in such an acquisition, regardless of whether such consideration is necessary to the gaining of control, is inconsistent with treatment of the acquisition as a nontaxable reorganization. It follows for purposes of taxpayers' second argument—which was premised on the assumption that the cash transactions were part of the 1970 exchange offer reorganization—that the stock transfers in question would not qualify for nonrecognition of gain or loss.

16. Taxpayers in this case have also argued that we should adopt the reasoning of the district court in Pierson v. United States, 472 F.Supp. 957 (D.Del.1979), another case arising on these same facts. The plaintiff in Pierson paid the tax assessed by the IRS after it revoked its private letter ruling, and then sued in district court for a refund, advancing substantially the same arguments presented to the Tax Court. The Pierson court reached a result similar to the Tax Court's . . . . We are given to understand by the parties to this appeal that the Pierson case is being appealed in the Third Circuit. [Ed. note: The case has since been decided the Court of Appeals for the Third Circuit, sub nom. Heverly v. Commissioner, — F.2d — (1980), in favor of the Government, on grounds paralleling those adopted by the Court of Appeals for the First Circuit in the instant case.]

Our decision will not, unfortunately, end this case. The Tax Court has yet to rule on taxpayers' "first" argument. . . . The question of what factors should determine, for purposes of Section 368(a)(1)(B), whether a given cash purchase is truly "related" to a later exchange of stock requires further consideration by the Tax Court, as does the question of the application of those factors in the present case. We therefore will remand this case to the Tax Court for further proceedings on the question raised by the taxpayers' first argument in support of their motion for summary judgment.

We view the Tax Court's options on remand as threefold. It can hold that the cash and stock transactions here in question are related as a matter of law—the position urged by the Commissioner—in which case, under our present holding, there would not be a valid (B) reorganization. On the other hand, the Tax Court may find that the transactions are as a matter of law unrelated, so that the 1970 exchange offer was simply the final, nontaxable step in a permissible creeping acquisition. Finally, the court may decide that, under the legal standard it adopts, material factual issues remain to be decided, so that a grant of summary judgment would be inappropriate at this time.[17]

17. We do not intend to dictate to the Tax Court what legal standard it should apply in determining whether these transactions are related. We would suggest, however, that the possibilities should include at least the following; perhaps others may be developed by counsel or by the Tax Court itself.

One possibility—advanced by the taxpayers—is that the only transactions which should be considered related, and so parts of "the acquisition," are those which are included in the formal plan of reorganization adopted by the two corporations. The virtues of this approach—simplicity and clarity—may be outweighed by the considerable scope it would grant the parties to a reorganization to control the tax treatment of their formal plan of reorganization by arbitrarily including or excluding certain transactions. A second possibility—urged by the Commissioner—is that all transactions sharing a single acquisitive purpose should be considered related for purposes of Section 368(a)(1)(B). Relying on an example given in the legislative history, see S.Rep.No. 1622, 83rd Cong., 2d Sess. 273, reprinted in [1954] U.S.Code Cong. & Admin.News, pp. 4621, 4911 [herein-after cited as 1954 Senate Report], the Commissioner would require a complete and thoroughgoing separation, both in time and purpose, between cash and stock acquisitions before the latter would qualify for reorganization treatment under subsection (B).

A third possible approach, lying somewhere between the other two, would be to focus on the mutual knowledge and intent of the corporate parties, so that one party could not suffer adverse tax consequences from unilateral activities of the other of which the former had no notice. . . . Such a rule would prevent, for example, the situation where the acquiree's shareholders expect to receive favorable tax treatment on an exchange offer, only to learn later that an apparently valid (B) reorganization has been nullified by anonymous cash purchases on the part of the acquiring corporation. . . .

Difficulties suggest themselves with each of these rules, and without benefit of thorough briefing and argument, as well as an informed decision by the lower court, we are reluctant to proceed further in exploring this issue. We leave to the Tax Court the task of breaking ground here.

III.

A. Having summarized in advance our holding, and its intended scope, we shall now revert to the beginning of our analysis, and, in the remainder of this opinion, describe the thinking by which we reached the result just announced. We begin with the words of the statute itself. The reorganization definitions contained in Section 368(a)(1) are precise, technical, and comprehensive. They were intended to define the exclusive means by which nontaxable corporate reorganizations could be effected. . . . In examining the language of the (B) provision, we discern two possible meanings. On the one hand, the statute could be read to say that a successful reorganization occurs whenever Corporation X exchanges its own voting stock for stock in Corporation Y, and, immediately after the transaction, Corporation X controls more than 80 percent of Y's stock. On this reading, purchases of shares for which any part of the consideration takes the form of "boot" should be ignored, since the definition is only concerned with transactions which meet the statutory requirements as to consideration and control. To take an example, if Corporation X bought 50 percent of the shares of Y, and then almost immediately exchanged part of its voting stock for the remaining 50 percent of Y's stock, the question would arise whether the second transaction was a (B) reorganization. Arguably, the statute can be read to support such a finding. In the second transaction, X exchanged only stock for stock (meeting the "solely" requirement), and after the transaction was completed X owned Y (meeting the "control" requirement).

The alternative reading of the statute—the one which we are persuaded to adopt—treats the (B) definition as prescriptive, rather than merely descriptive. We read the statute to mean that the entire transaction which constitutes "the acquisition" must not contain any nonstock consideration if the transaction is to qualify as a (B) reorganization. In the example given above, where X acquired 100 percent of Y's stock, half for cash and half for voting stock, we would interpret "the acquisition" as referring to the entire transaction, so that the "solely for . . . voting stock" requirement would not be met. We believe if Congress had intended the statute to be read as merely descriptive, this intent would have been more clearly spelled out in the statutory language.[18]

---

18. For example, Congress could have used the word "any" rather than the word "the" before "acquisition" in the first line of the (B) definition. This would have tended to negate the implication that this definition prescribes the conditions a transaction *must* meet to qualify, rather than simply describing that part of a transaction which is entitled to the statutory tax deferral.

We recognize that the Tax Court adopted neither of these two readings. For reasons to be discussed in connection with the legislative history which follows, the Tax Court purported to limit its holding to cases, such as this one, where more than 80 percent of the stock of Corporation Y passes to Corporation X in exchange solely for voting stock. The Tax Court presumably would assert that the 50/50 hypothetical posited above can be distinguished from this case, and that its holding implies no view as to the hypothetical. See 71 T.C. at 742. The plurality opinion recognized that the position it adopted creates no small problem with respect to the proper reading of "the acquisition" in the statutory definition. See 71 T.C. at 739, 741. In order to distinguish the 80 percent case from the 50 percent case, it is necessary to read "the acquisition" as referring to at least the amount of stock constituting "control" (80 percent) where related cash purchases are present. Yet the Tax Court recognized that "the acquisition" cannot always refer to the conveyance of an 80 percent bloc of stock in one transaction, since to do so would frustrate the intent of the 1954 amendments to permit so-called "creeping acquisitions." [19]

The Tax Court's interpretation of the statute suffers from a more fundamental defect, as well. In order to justify the limitation of its holding to transactions involving 80 percent or more of the acquiree's stock, the Tax Court focused on the *passage* of control as the primary requirement of the (B) provision. This focus is misplaced. Under the present version of the statute, the *passage* of control is entirely irrelevant; the only material requirement is that the acquiring corporation *have* control immediately after the acquisition. As the statute explicitly states, it does not matter if the acquiring corporation already has control before the transaction begins, so long as such control exists at the completion of the reorganization. Whatever talismanic quality may have attached to the *acquisition* of control under previous versions of the Code, see Part III B infra, is altogether absent from the version we must apply to this case. In our view, the statute should be read to mean that the related transactions that constitute "the acquisition," whatever percentage of stock they may represent, must meet both the "solely for voting stock" and the "control immediately after" requirements of Section 368(a)(1)(B). Neither the reading given the statute by the Tax Court, nor that proposed as the first alternative above, adequately corresponds to the careful language Congress employed in this section of the Code.

B. The 1924 Code defined reorganization, in part, as "a merger or consolidation (including the acquisition by one corporation of at

---

19. For a more complete discussion of "creeping acquisitions," see Part III B infra. . . .

least a majority of the voting stock and at least a majority of the total number of shares of all other classes of stock of another corporation, or substantially all the properties of another corporation)." Pub.L. No. 68–176, c. 234, § 203(h)(1), 43 Stat. 257. Although the statute did not specifically limit the consideration that could be given in exchange for stock or assets, courts eventually developed the so-called "continuity of interest" doctrine, which held that exchanges that did not include some quantum of stock as consideration were ineligible for reorganization treatment for lack of a continuing property interest on the part of the acquiree's shareholders. . . .

Despite this judicial development, sentiment was widespread in Congress that the reorganization provisions lent themselves to abuse, particularly in the form of so-called "disguised sales." . . . In 1934, the House Ways and Means Committee proposed abolition of the stock-acquisition and asset-acquisition reorganizations which had appeared in the parenthetical section of the 1924 Act quoted above. . . . The Senate Finance Committee countered with a proposal to retain these provisions, but with "restrictions designed to prevent tax avoidance." . . . One of these restrictions was the requirement that the acquiring corporation obtain at least 80 percent, rather than a bare majority, of the stock of the acquiree. The second requirement was stated in the Senate Report as follows: "the acquisition, whether of stock or of substantially all the properties, must be in exchange solely for the voting stock of the acquiring corporation." Id. at 17. The Senate amendments were enacted as Section 112(g)(1) of the Revenue Act of 1934, 48 Stat. 680, which provided in pertinent part:

"(1) The term 'reorganization' means (A) a statutory merger or consolidation, or (B) the acquisition by one corporation in exchange solely for all or a part of its voting stock: of at least 80 per centum of the voting stock and at least 80 per centum of the total number of shares of all other classes of stock of another corporation; or of substantially all the properties of another corporation. . . ."

Congress revised this definition in 1939 in response to the Supreme Court's decision in United States v. Hendler, 303 U.S. 564, 58 S.Ct. 655, 82 L.Ed. 1018 (1938), which held that an acquiring corporation's assumption of the acquiree's liabilities in an asset acquisition was equivalent to the receipt of "boot" by the acquiree. Since virtually all asset-acquisition reorganizations necessarily involve the assumption of the acquiree's liabilities, a literal application of the "solely for . . . voting stock" requirement would have effectively abolished this form of tax-free reorganization. In the Revenue Act of 1939, Congress separated the stock-acquisition and asset-acquisition provisions in order to exempt the assumption of liabilities in the latter category of cases from the "solely for . . . voting stock" requirement. Section 112(g)(1) of the revised statute then read, in pertinent part, as follows:

> "(1) the term 'reorganization' means (A) a statutory merger or consolidation, or (B) the acquisition by one corporation, in exchange solely for all or a part of its voting stock, of at least 80 per centum of the voting stock and at least 80 per centum of the total number of shares of all other classes of stock of another corporation, or (C) the acquisition by one corporation, in exchange solely for all or a part of its voting stock, of substantially all the properties of another corporation, but in determining whether the exchange is solely for voting stock the assumption by the acquiring corporation of a liability of the other, or the fact that property acquired is subject to liability, shall be disregarded. . . . "

The next major change in this provision occurred in 1954. In that year, the House Bill, H.R. 8300, would have drastically altered the corporate reorganization sections of the Tax Code, permitting, for example, both stock and "boot" as consideration in a corporate acquisition, with gain recognized only to the extent of the "boot." . . . The Senate Finance Committee, in order to preserve the familiar terminology and structure of the 1939 Code, proposed a new version of Section 112(g)(1), which would retain the "solely for . . . voting stock" requirement, but alter the existing control requirement to permit so-called "creeping acquisitions." Under the Senate Bill, it would no longer be necessary for the acquiring corporation to obtain 80 percent or more of the acquiree's stock in one "reorganization." The Senate's proposal permitted an acquisition to occur in stages; a bloc of shares representing less than 80 percent could be added to earlier acquisitions, regardless of the consideration given earlier, to meet the control requirement. The Report of the Senate Finance Committee gave this example of the operation of the creeping acquisition amendment:

> "[C]orporation A purchased 30 percent of the common stock of corporation W (the only class of stock outstanding) for cash in 1939. On March 1, 1955, corporation A offers to exchange its own voting stock for all the stock of corporation W tendered within 6 months from the date of the offer. Within the 6 months period corporation A acquires an additional 60 percent of the stock of W for its own voting stock. As a result of the 1955 transactions, corporation A will own 90 percent of all of corporation W's stock. No gain or loss is recognized with respect to the exchanges of the A stock for the W stock."

1954 Senate Report, supra note 17, at 273. See also Treas.Reg. § 1.368–2(c) (1960).

At the same time the Senate was revising the (B) provision, (while leaving intact the "solely for . . . voting stock" requirement), it was also rewriting the (C) provision to explicitly permit up to 20 percent of the consideration in an asset acquisition to take the form of money or other nonstock property. See 26 U.S.C. § 368 (a)(2)(B). The Senate revisions of subsections (B) and (C) were ultimately passed, and have remained largely unchanged since 1954. (See footnote 1 for present text.) Proposals for altering the (B) provision to allow "boot" as consideration have been made, but none has been enacted.[22]

As this history shows, Congress has had conflicting aims in this complex and difficult area. On the one hand, the 1934 Act evidences a strong intention to limit the reorganization provisions to prevent forms of tax avoidance that had proliferated under the earlier revenue acts. This intention arguably has been carried forward in the current versions through retention of the "solely for . . . voting stock" requirement in (B), even while the (C) provision was being loosened. On the other hand, both the 1939 and 1954 revisions represented attempts to make the reorganization procedures more accessible and practical in both the (B) and (C) areas. In light of the conflicting purposes, we can discern no clear Congressional mandate in the present structure of the (B) provision, either in terms of the abuses sought to be remedied or the beneficial transactions sought to be facilitated. At best, we think Congress has drawn somewhat arbitrary lines separating those transactions that resemble mere changes in form of ownership and those that contain elements of a sale or purchase arrangement. In such circumstances we believe it is more appropriate to examine the specific rules and requirements Congress enacted, rather than some questionably delineated "purpose" or "policy," to determine whether a particular transaction qualifies for favorable tax treatment.

To the extent there is any indication in the legislative history of Congress' intent with respect to the meaning of "acquisition" in the (B) provision, we believe the intent plainly was to apply the

22. See, e. g., H.R.Rep.No. 4459, 86th Cong., 1st Sess. § 26 (1959). See also *Columbia Comment*, supra note 19, at 798 & n. 169. Furthermore, the legislative report accompanying a later revision of Section 368(a)(1) explicitly stated that cash is not permitted in a (B) reorganization:

"[I]n order to qualify as a tax-free stock-for-stock [B] reorganization it is necessary that the acquisition be *solely* for voting stock and that no stock be acquired for cash or other consideration." (Emphasis in original.)

S.Rep.No. 1533, 91st Cong., 2d Sess. 2–3, reprinted in [1970] U.S.Code Cong. & Admin.News, pp. 6123, 6123–24. . .

"solely" requirement to all related transactions. In those statutes where Congress intended to permit cash or other property to be used as consideration, it made explicit provision therefor. See, e. g., 26 U.S.C. § 368(a)(2)(B). It is argued that in a (B) reorganization the statute can be satisfied where only 80 percent of the acquiree's stock is obtained solely for voting stock, so that additional acquisitions are irrelevant and need not be considered. In light of Congress' repeated, and increasingly sophisticated, enactments in this area, we are unpersuaded that such an important question would have been left unaddressed had Congress intended to leave open such a possibility. We are not prepared to believe that Congress intended—either when it enacted the 1934, the 1939, or the 1954 statutes—to permit a corporation to exchange stock tax-free for 80 percent of the stock of another and in a related transaction to purchase the remaining 20 percent for cash. The only question we see clearly left open by the legislative history is the degree of separation required between the two transactions before they can qualify as a creeping acquisition under the 1954 amendments. This is precisely the issue the Tax Court chose not to address, and it is the issue we now remand to the Tax Court for consideration.

C.   Besides finding support for the IRS position both in the design of the statute and in the legislative history, we find support in the regulations adopted by the Treasury Department construing these statutory provisions. We of course give weight to the statutory construction contemporaneously developed by the agency entrusted by Congress with the task of applying these laws. . . .   The views of the Treasury on tax matters, while by no means definitive, undoubtedly reflect a familiarity with the intricacies of the tax code that surpasses our own.

* * *

When we turn to the regulations under the 1954 Act, the implication that the entire transaction must be judged under the "solely" test is stronger still.

> "In order to qualify as a 'reorganization' under section 368(a) (1)(B), the *acquisition* by the acquiring corporation of stock of another corporation must be in exchange solely for all or a part of the voting stock of the acquiring corporation . . .   and the acquiring corporation must be in control of the other corporation immediately after *the transaction*. If, for example, Corporation X in one transaction exchanges nonvoting preferred stock or bonds *in addition to* all or a part of its voting stock in the acquisition of stock of Corporation Y, the transaction is not a reorganization under section 368(a)(1)(B)." (Emphasis supplied.)

Treas.Reg. § 1.368–2(c) (1960). The equation of "transaction" and "acquisition" in the above-quoted passage is particularly significant, since it seems to imply a functional test of what constitutes "the acquisition" as opposed to a view of "the acquisition" as simply that part of a transaction which otherwise satisfies the statutory requisites. The regulation also goes on to say, in explaining the treatment of creeping acquisitions:

> "The acquisition of stock of another corporation by the acquiring corporation solely for its voting stock . . . is permitted tax-free even though the acquiring corporation already owns some of the stock of the other corporation. Such an acquisition is permitted tax-free in a single transaction or in a series of transactions taking place over a relatively short period of time such as 12 months."

Treas.Reg. § 1.368–2(c). This regulation spells out the treatment afforded related acquisitions, some of which occur before and some after the acquiring corporation obtains the necessary 80 percent of stock in the acquiree. It would be incongruous, to say the least, if a series of stock-for-stock transactions could be combined so that the tax-free treatment of later acquisitions applied to earlier ones as well, yet a related cash purchase would be ignored as irrelevant. This section reinforces our view that all related transactions must be considered part of "the acquisition" for purposes of applying the statute.

D. Finally, we turn to the body of case law that has developed concerning (B) reorganizations to determine how previous courts have dealt with this question. Of the seven prior cases in this area, all to a greater or lesser degree support the result we have reached, and none supports the result reached by the Tax Court. We recognize that the Tax Court purported to distinguish these precedents from the case before it, and that reasonable persons may differ on the extent to which some of these cases directly control the question raised here. Nevertheless, after carefully reviewing the precedents, we are satisfied that the decision of the Tax Court represents a sharp break with the previous judicial constructions of this statute, and a departure from the usual rule of stare decisis, which applies with special force in the tax field where uncertainty and variety are ordinarily to be avoided.

Of the seven precedents, the most significant would seem to be Howard v. Commissioner, 238 F.2d 943 (7th Cir. 1956), rev'g, 24 T.C. 792 (1955), which stands out as the one case prior to *Reeves* that specifically addressed the issue raised herein. In *Howard*, the Truax-Traer Coal Company acquired 80.19 percent of the outstanding stock of Binkley Coal Company solely in exchange for Truax-Traer voting stock. At the same time and as part of the same plan of acquisition,

Truax-Traer purchased the other 19.81 percent of Binkley's stock for cash. The taxpayers, former shareholders of Binkley who had exchanged their shares solely for voting stock, sold some of the Truax-Traer stock they had received in August 1950, the same year as the exchange. The Commissioner, treating the exchange as a taxable event and not a reorganization, employed a new holding period, beginning with the effective date of the exchange, and treated the taxpayers' gain on their sale of the Truax-Traer stock as a short-term capital gain. The Tax Court sustained the Commissioner, concluding the exchange had not been made "solely for . . . voting stock," as required by the 1939 Act, even though the cash purchases were not essential to Truax-Traer's acquisition of control. 24 T.C. at 804.

The Seventh Circuit, after reviewing the legislative history of Section 112(g)(1)(B) of the 1939 Code, agreed with the Tax Court's conclusion that the presence of cash purchases prevented the transaction from meeting the "solely" requirement of the statute. Like the Tax Court, the court of appeals relied heavily on two prior decisions arising in slightly different contexts. The principal linchpin of the Seventh Circuit's decision was Helvering v. Southwest Consolidated Corp., 315 U.S. 194, 62 S.Ct. 546, 86 L.Ed. 789 (1942), in which the Supreme Court denied tax-free treatment to an asset acquisition under the 1934 Act because a substantial amount of the consideration was given in the form of stock warrants and cash. The Court first noted that under the law existing before 1934, this transaction would have been a perfectly valid tax-free reorganization. The revised statute, see . . . supra, had made the continuity of interest test much stricter, however:

> "Congress has provided that the assets of the transferor corporation must be acquired in exchange 'solely' for 'voting stock' of the transferee. 'Solely' leaves no leeway. Voting stock plus some other consideration does not meet the stautory requirement."

315 U.S. at 198, 62 S.Ct. at 550. The Seventh Circuit noted that in the 1934 Act the asset and stock acquisition reorganizations were dealt with in the same clause both in the statutory language and in the legislative history. It therefore seemed reasonable to the Seventh Circuit to conclude that the Supreme Court's "no leeway" rule for asset acquisitions applied with equal force to stock acquisitions.

Appellees argue that *Southwest Consolidated* is distinguishable from the present facts, and, implicitly, that it should not have been relied on by the *Howard* court. This argument rests, in our view, on a strained reading of *Southwest Consolidated*. The taxpayers point out that the nonstock consideration in that case amounted to 37 percent of the total consideration, by the Tax Court's reckoning. Further, they say that the stock and nonstock consideration could not be separated where one bundle of assets was exchanged for one bundle of consideration, so that *Southwest Consolidated* was essentially a mixed consideration case. We disagree. Had the Supreme Court chosen to decide the issue of whether "substantially all" the assets of one corporation were obtained solely for voting stock, it could have allocated the consideration on a proportional basis, much as the Tax Court did in making its calculations. The Supreme Court did not consider, however, whether the voting stock consideration was sufficient to cover "substantially all" the assets, so that Section 112(g)(1)(B) would be satisfied. The Court determined rather that the presence of *any* nonstock consideration in the acquisition negated the possibility of a valid tax-free reorganization. While the facts were such that the Court could have reached the same result on another rationale, this does not detract from the weight of its words. The Seventh Circuit was, in our opinion, justified in resting its holding by analogy on the decision in *Southwest Consolidated.*

The other case principally relied on by the *Howard* court was Commissioner v. Air Reduction Co., 130 F.2d 145 (2d Cir.), cert. denied, 317 U.S. 681, 63 S.Ct. 201, 87 L.Ed. 546 (1942). On January 1, 1935, Air Reduction Co. already owned 95,181 shares of stock in the Pure Carbonic Company, of which 87,275 had been acquired in exchange for Air Reduction stock and 7,906 had been bought for cash. During 1935, Air Reduction acquired 100 percent ownership of Carbonic by purchasing 14,771 shares for cash and exchanging 5,258 shares of its own treasury stock for the remaining 22,347 shares of Carbonic stock. Altogether, about 82 percent of Carbonic's stock was acquired solely for shares of Air Reduction stock. Air Reduction principally argued that it could not have recognized gain on trading in its own treasury stock, an argument the court rejected. In a separate argument, raised for the first time on appeal, the company asserted that the stock acquisition constituted a nontaxable reorganization. The Second Circuit rejected this argument as well:

> "[T]his theory is not tenable because the definition of reorganization in § 112(g)(1)(B) of the 1934 Act . . . contemplates only situations where the exchange is made 'solely' for voting stock. Here over 17% of the Pure Carbonic stock was purchased for cash. Cf. Helvering v. Southwest Consolidated Corp. . . . ."

130 F.2d at 148. The Second Circuit, from its language, evidently would not have approved a transaction where, as here, more than 8 percent of the acquiree's stock was purchased for cash. The fact that more than 80 percent of Pure Carbonic's stock, a sufficient

amount for control, was acquired solely for stock was not considered determinative.

The Tax Court, in addition to casting aspersions on the Second Circuit's judicial craftsmanship ("the question was a subsidiary one and may not have attracted much attention" 71 T.C. at 738 n. 15), asserted that *Air Reduction* was factually distinguishable because it did not involve a single, readily identifiable transaction in which control was passed solely for allowable consideration. In the Tax Court's words, it was necessary to "pick and choose" which transactions to consider as leading to control in order to establish that control was acquired solely for voting stock. The Second Circuit made no mention of this aspect of the case, however, nor did it discuss the related issue of whether a reorganization under the 1934 Act could be conducted in stages at all. As the citation to *Southwest Consolidated* makes clear, the Second Circuit took it as settled that *any* appreciable nonstock consideration in a (B) acquisition precludes treatment as a reorganization.

Besides questioning its lineage, the Tax Court plurality made three attempts to distinguish the *Howard* case or undercut its holding. First, the Tax Court argued that *Howard* was a case in which "some stockholders involved in the one exchange transaction . . . received cash." 71 T.C. at 737. The impact of this distinction is less than clear. There was no finding in *Howard* that any stockholder received both cash and stock for the *same* shares. In both *Howard* and this case, more than 80 percent of the shares were exchanged for stock only, and additional shares were purchased for cash. The only possible meaning of the Tax Court's statement is that it did not consider the 1968–69 cash purchases and the 1970 exchange offer part of "one exchange transaction." Yet, the taxpayers' specific concession on motion for summary judgment was that the two events should be assumed to constitute "parts of the 1970 exchange offer reorganization." . . .

The Tax Court's second attack on *Howard*, contained in footnote 12, is equally unpersuasive. The fact that one shareholder of Binkley (the acquiree) received voting stock for some of its shares and cash for other shares, so that the 80 percent necessary for control was not acquired from shareholders receiving only stock, was not relied on by the Seventh Circuit. Furthermore, the focus of the statute is on the consideration furnished in the exchange, not on the consideration received by a particular shareholder. Any rule premised on the consideration each shareholder received would quickly founder on the realities of the stock market. Corporations could rarely assure themselves that an exchange for more than 80 percent of one corporation's stock would not be tainted by some stockholder's withholding of shares to sell to the acquiring corporation through the relative anonymity of market transactions. Indeed, in this case there is no proof that some of ITT's earlier market purchases were not made from shareholders of Hartford who later exchanged other shares for ITT's voting stock. . . . The Tax Court's rule could only practically provide nontaxable treatment to transactions in which more than 80 percent of *shares* were exchanged for voting stock; a rule that limited the consideration going to *shareholders* would be unenforceable.

The third line of assault on *Howard* is the assertion that the *Howard* decision was cast in doubt by Turnbow v. Commissioner, 368 U.S. 337, 82 S.Ct. 353, 7 L.Ed.2d 326 (1961), aff'g, 286 F.2d 669 (9th Cir. 1960). To go back for a moment, in *Howard* the Seventh Circuit affirmed the Tax Court's holding that cash consideration precluded a (B) reorganization, but then went on to hold that the taxpayer was nevertheless entitled to nonrecognition of gain on the exchange under Section 112(c)(1) of the 1939 Code (the predecessor of current section 356(a)(1)). . . . .

The argument that *Turnbow* undercuts *Howard's* first holding, even though that holding was not an issue in *Turnbow*, rests on two grounds. First, the Tax Court quoted at length from the government's Supreme Court brief in *Turnbow* [34] where the government, for tactical reasons, argued that some cash might be allowable in a (B) reorganization. The brief also questioned whether the *Howard* decision would survive. Consequently, the Tax Court said, the Supreme Court left open the question decided in *Howard* by limiting its holding to the facts of *Turnbow*, where 70 percent of the consideration was cash. Support for this position is sought in the Supreme Court's statement that "[t]hat holding [70 percent cash is not a valid (B) reorganization] determines this case and is all we decide," 368 U.S. at 344, 82 S.Ct. at 357, and the later statement that "we have no need or occasion to follow the parties into, or to decide, collateral questions." Id.

34. "It cannot be said with certainty, for that matter, that there could not be 'other property' in a transaction qualifying as a 'B' or 'C' reorganization. While those definitions do literally require that 'solely . . . voting stock' be given, that requirement raises questions of interpretation (not involved in this case) that have not yet been finally resolved. For example, since sec. 112(g)(1)(B) requires only that 80% of the stock of another corporation be acquired, it is arguable that the definition is met if the consideration allocable to at least 80% of the stock consists of voting stock, notwithstanding that the acquiring corporation also acquires additional shares (e. g., from dissenting stockholders) for money or other property. That was in fact the situation in the *Howard* case, in which the acquiring corporation gave solely voting stock for 81% of the shares but gave cash to a dissenting minority for the remaining 19%. While the Seventh Circuit held that the cash given the minority precluded a 'B' reorganization, the question is a debatable one and there is no assurance that other courts would follow that decision [Brief for Government n. 7 at 21.]" 71 T.C. at 737 n. 13.

We find the contrary conclusion more persuasive. Although the government had questioned *Howard's* first holding, the Supreme Court indicated no hesitance or doubt with respect to it. Indeed, the Court stated near the outset of its opinion:

> "There is no dispute between the parties about the fact that the transaction involved was not a 'reorganization' as defined in § 112(g)(1)(B), because 'the acquisition by' Foremost was not 'in exchange *solely* for   .   .   . its voting stock', but was partly for such stock and partly for cash. Helvering v. Southwest Consolidated Corp., 315 U.S. 194 [62 S.Ct. 546, 88 L.Ed. 789.]" (Emphasis in original.)

368 U.S. at 341. We read no implication here, or anywhere else in the opinion, that the Court felt *Howard* to be an inaccurate statement of the law or that some specific issue was being reserved for later decision. If anything, the citation of *Southwest Consolidated* in connection with the "solely" requirement of subsection (B) would seem to imply that the strict reading of the statute continued to apply to (B) reorganizations even after (B) and (C) were separated in the statute (1939) and after cash of up to 20 percent was permitted in (C) reorganizations (1954).

In short, we find *Howard* factually and legally indistinguishable from *Reeves*, and see no reason to question its continuing vitality. Even were we doubtful as to the correctness of the result reached in *Howard* (and we are not), we would nonetheless be reluctant to see a rule of tax law which has stood virtually unchallenged by courts for 25 years discarded so unceremoniously. As the dissenting judges of the Tax Court noted, much tax planning must proceed on the basis of settled rules. Avoidance of risk and uncertainty are often the keys to a successful transaction. Transactions may have been structured on the basis of *Howard*, with cash intentionally introduced to prevent reorganization treatment. Where a long standing tax rule of this sort is not clearly contrary to Congressional intent or markedly inconsistent with some generally accepted understanding of correct doctrine, we think the proper body to make changes aimed at improving the law is Congress, and not the courts. The complex and delicate judgments as to proper tax policy, and the balancing of interests between corporations, their shareholders, and the public, required to formulate appropriate rules in this area are not the proper province of courts. Our role is to interpret the mandate of Congress as best we can, and to adhere to the reasonable standards supplied by our predecessors where possible. Our role is emphatically not to read into the tax law our own notions of "well-ordered universe."   .   .   .

Our reading of the statute is reinforced by another more recent circuit decision as well. In Mills v. Commissioner, 331 F.2d 321 (5th

Cir. 1964), rev'g, 39 T.C. 393 (1962), the issue was whether cash payments for fractional shares in an exchange prevented a nontaxable reorganization. General Gas Corporation, the acquiror, offered the three taxpayers, sole stockholders in three small gas corporations, shares of General common stock in exchange for all of their stock. The number of General shares to be exchanged—at a value of $14 per share—was to be determined by measuring the net book value of the three small corporations. In the event the purchase price was not evenly divisible by 14, cash was to be paid in lieu of fractional shares. As a result, each taxpayer received 1,595 shares of General stock and $27.36 in cash. The Tax Court held this transaction invalid as a tax-free reorganization, declining to adopt a *de minimis* rule. 39 T.C. at 400. The Fifth Circuit agreed that cash could not form any part of the consideration in a (B) reorganization, but concluded in reversing the Tax Court that the fractional-share arrangement was merely a bookkeeping convenience and not an independent part of the consideration. 331 F.2d at 324–25.

Taxpayers, and the Tax Court argued that *Mills* was distinguishable, despite its sweeping language, because each shareholder of the acquired corporations received both stock and cash in the exchange. We have discussed earlier our reasons for rejecting any rule premised on the consideration received by the acquiree's shareholders. If *Mills* were distinguishable at all, it would be only because the consideration for some of the *shares* in *Mills* consisted of both stock and cash. But even this distinction evaporates when one notes that the one share in each exchange for which a fractional share would have been necessary never constituted more than 20 percent of the stock of any one of the acquiree corporations (since each shareholder held at least six shares in each corporation). In every exchange it was theoretically possible to identify a bloc of more than 80 percent of the stock of the acquiree which was exchanged solely for the voting stock of the acquiring corporation. Thus, in the only case raising the issue now before us under the 1954 Code, the Tax Court accepted as a premise that no cash was permissible as consideration in a (B) reorganization, even where the facts showed that control had passed solely for voting stock.

IV.

We have stated our ruling, and the reasons that support it. In conclusion, we would like to respond briefly to the arguments raised by the Tax Court, the District Court of Delaware, and the taxpayers in this case against the rule we have reaffirmed today. The principal argument, repeated again and again, concerns the supposed lack of policy behind the rule forbidding cash in a (B) reorganization where the control requirement is met solely for voting stock. It is true that the Service has not pointed to tax loopholes that would be opened were the rule to be relaxed as appellees request. We also recognize, as the Tax Court and others have highlighted, that the rule may produce results which some would view as anomalous. For example, if Corporation X acquires 80 percent of Corporation Y's stock solely for voting stock, and is content to have the remaining 20 percent outstanding, no one would question that a valid (B) reorganization has taken place. If Corporation X then decides to purchase stock from the remaining shareholders, the *Howard* rule might result in loss of nontaxable treatment for the stock acquisition if the two transactions were found to be related. See 71 T.C. at 740–41. The Tax Court asserted that there is no conceivable Congressional policy that would justify such a result. Further, it argued, Congress could not have felt that prior cash purchases would forever ban a later successful (B) reorganization since the 1954 amendments, as the legislative history makes clear, specifically provided that prior cash purchases would not prevent a creeping acquisition.

While not without force, this line of argument does not in the end persuade us. First of all, as already discussed, the language of the statute, and the longstanding interpretation given it by the courts, are persuasive reasons for our holding even in the absence of any clear policy behind Congress' expression of its will. Furthermore, we perceive statutory anomalies of another sort which the Tax Court's rule would only magnify. It is clear from the regulations, for example, that a corporation which already owned as much as 80 percent of another's stock, acquired solely for cash, could in some circumstances acquire all or a part of the remainder solely for voting stock as a valid (B) reorganization. Why, then, could not as little as 10 percent of an acquisition constitute a (B) reorganization, if made solely for voting stock, even though the remaining transactions—totaling more than 80 percent—were made for nonstock consideration? If it is true that Congress did not view related cash transactions as tainting a stock-acquisition reorganization, why would it enact a "solely for . . . voting stock" requirement at all, except to the extent necessary to prevent mixed consideration of the sort employed in the "disguised sales" of the twenties?

Possibly, Congress' insertion of the "solely for . . . voting stock" requirement into the 1934 Act was, as one commentator has suggested, an overreaction to a problem which could have been dealt with through more precise and discriminating measures. But we do not think it appropriate for a court to tell Congress how to do its job in an area such as this. If a more refined statutory scheme would be appropriate, such changes should be sought from the body empowered to make them. While we adhere to the general practice of construing statutes so as to further their demonstrated policies, we have no license to rework whole statutory schemes in pursuit of policy goals which Congress has nowhere articulated. Appellees have not shown us any reason to believe that reaffirmation of the settled rule in this area will frustrate the Congressional purpose of making the (B) reorganization provision generally available to those who comply with the statutory requirements.

A second major argument, advanced primarily by the district court in *Pierson*, is that the previous cases construing this statute are suspect because they did not give proper weight to the changes wrought by the 1954 amendments. In particular, the court argued the liberalization of the "boot" allowance in (C) reorganizations and the allowance of creeping (B) acquisitions showed that Congress had no intent or desire to forbid "boot" of up to 20 percent in a (B) reorganization. As we have discussed earlier, we draw the opposite conclusion from the legislative history. Liberalization of the (C) provision shows only that Congress, when it wished to do so, could grant explicit leeway in the reorganization rules.* Nor do the creeping acquisition rules mark such a departure from a strict reading of the "solely" requirement as to persuade us that Congress intended to weaken it with respect to related transactions. One has only to look at the illustration given in the legislative history, with its separation of 16 years between the cash and stock transactions, to see that Congress did not indicate positive approval of the type of acquisition covered by the district court's holding.

A third argument asserts that reliance on the literal language of the 1954 Code, and in particular a focus on the interpretation of

* [Ed. note] In Heverly v. Commissioner, the decision by the Court of Appeals for the Third Circuit on companion appeals to that circuit, see ed. note addition to footnote 16, supra, the court rationalized the permission to use some boot in (C) reorganizations as follows:

The provision allowing cash or other property in a clause C transaction was added in 1954. . . . Contrary to what taxpayers argue, this provision, § 368(a)(2)(B), does not allow substantially more flexibility in clause C transactions than in clause B transactions. If cash or other property is given, the liabilities assumed by the acquiring corporation must be included in the total twenty percent allowable nonstock consideration, whereas the assumption of liabilities need not be counted against the solely for voting stock requirement if no nonstock consideration is exchanged. Thus, since provision must be made for creditors, and since rarely will the transferor corporation have less than twenty percent of its asset value encumbered by liabilities, the apparent permissibility of cash or other property under clause C is almost inevitably illusory. We believe Congress was fully aware of, and probably intended, this limitation on nonstock consideration under clause C. . .

The negative relationship of liabilities assumed to cash or other property in an assets acquisition strongly indicates that the allowance of cash or other property under clause C was also intended to allow accommodation of creditors, just as was the provision for assumption of liabilities. But because provision for creditors is of minimal concern in a stock acquisition, this rationale has no relevance to clause B.

"acquisition," is unjustified because the 1954 Code was not intended to alter the status of (B) reorganizations under the 1934 and 1939 Codes. According to this argument, the acquisition of at least 80 percent of the acquiree's stock solely for voting stock was allowed under the pre-1954 version, and must still be allowed even though the present statute refers only to "the acquisition . . . of stock" with no percentage specified. This argument assumes the answer to the question that is asked. As *Howard* and *Southwest Consolidated* illustrate, it has been the undeviating understanding of courts, until now, that the pre-1954 statutes did *not* allow cash or other "boot" in a (B) reorganization. It cannot be inferred that Congress left intact a rule which never existed by enacting language inconsistent with such a rule.

Finally, we see no merit at all in the suggestion that we should permit "boot" in a (B) reorganization simply because "boot" is permitted in some instances in (A) and (C) reorganizations. Congress has never indicated that these three distinct categories of transactions are to be interpreted *in pari materia.* In fact, striking differences in the treatment of the three subsections have been evident in the history of the reorganization statutes.[42] We see no reason to believe a difference in the treatment of "boot" in these transactions is impermissible or irrational.

Accordingly, we vacate the judgment of the Tax Court insofar as it rests on a holding that taxpayers were entitled to summary judgment irrespective of whether the cash purchases in this case were related by purpose or timing to the stock exchange offer of 1970. The case will be remanded to the Tax Court for further proceedings consistent with this opinion.

Vacated and remanded.

---

42. For example, under the 1954 version of the (C) reorganization, voting stock of a parent corporation could be used to acquire assets for a subsidiary. A similar provision was not added to the (B) section until 1964. Revenue Act of 1964, Pub.L.No.88–272, § 218(a), 78 Stat. 57.

1. NOTE ON B REORGANIZATIONS

a.   Integration of Acquisitions

Under the decision in <u>Chapman</u>, the question of qualification as a reorganization will turn on whether the earlier cash deal is integrated with the later stock trans-action to constitute a single "acquisition" within the meaning of §368(a)(1)(B). Some indication as to what the Service may regard as necessary to avoid integration is afforded by Reg. 1.368-(2)(c): in illustrating the operation of so-called "creeping control" in a B reorganization, the regulation puts the case of a cash purchase of 30% of the stock of the acquired corporation, followed by an acquisition of 60% of the stock solely for voting stock of the acquiring corporation sixteen years later! No doubt something less will do, but bearing in mind the inherent relationship between successive acquisitions of stock of the same corpor-ation, it seems clear that taxpayers will confront a heavy burden in trying to establish that an earlier stock purchase for cash was not part of an overall plan to obtain control of the acquired corporation.

On the other side of the coin, suppose a corporation, using nothing but its voting stock, acquires stock of another corporation from time to time over a period of years; if and when the acquiring corporation finally reaches a position of 80% ownership, would reorganization treatment be available for all of the acquisitions, even the earliest ones? If so, how should they be treated in the meantime, before it is clear that control will be achieved? After all, the statute does call for the existence of the 80% control "immediately after the acquisition." The integration approach of <u>Chapman</u> is not a very satisfactory test in this situation, since the most reasonable inference is likely to be that the acquiring corporation had a general hope, perhaps even a plan, of obtaining control if possible, although it was not suffi-ciently bent upon that objective to undertake a broadscale tender offer. Reg. §1.368-2(c) suggests a guideline, by referring to an acquisition "in a single acquisition or in a series of acquisitions taking place over a relatively short period of time such as 12 months." That probably rules out acquisitions several years earlier; but does it afford tax-free treatment to all acquisitions within twelve months of obtaining control? And is the 12-month period to be viewed as a general guide or a precise standard?

In American Potash & Chemical Corp. v. United States, 402 F.2d 1000 (Ct.Cl. 1968), P made two separate offers to acquire all of the stock of W; the first in August 1954, at the rate of one P share for 6.5 W shares, which expired on November 18, 1954, and was accepted by 48% of the W shareholders; the second in November, 1955, after the market price of P's shares had risen substantially, at the rate of one P share for seven W shares, and all the remaining W shareholders accepted by December, 1955. Here it was to the Government's advantage to show that the overall acquisition qualified as a B reorganization (since that would prevent a step-up in the basis of W's assets upon its liquidation into P corporation). However, the Government had not originally pressed the reorganization point, and in a prior opinion the Court of Claims had simply observed that the overall transaction could not qualify as a B reorganization because it took place over a period of 14 months, rather than the twelve month period referred to in the regulations. 399 F.2d 194 (Ct. Cl. 1968).

Upon rehearing, the Government specifically argued for B reorganization treatment, along the lines indicated in the following response by the court:

> Defendant submits, for the first time in this case, the argument that the 12-month rule of Treasury Regulation 1.368-2(c) is merely a guideline to determine which exchanges of a series of exchanges of stock for stock qualify as tax-free under the B reorganization provisions. In our view, all of the individual acquisitions which form a series of stock for stock acquisitions over a period in excess of 12 months (which result in control) do not qualify as tax-free under the reorganization provisions unless the entire series is proved to have been part of a continuing offer to purchase. Defendant argues that plaintiff's admitted intent to acquire Wecco's assets reveals that there was a clear connection between all of the acquisitions and that therefore a continuing offer existed. Plaintiff's response is that two offers to purchase all of the stock are involved (which cannot be deemed a continuing offer) and, therefore, not having obtained control within 12 months, a B reorganization did not occur.

Alternatively, defendant argues that the final acquisition of 52% of the Wecco stock (whereby control was obtained) itself qualifies as a tax-free exchange within the definition of a B reorganization and, therefore, a carryover basis for depreciation is appropriate for all of the assets later acquired by liquidation. This assumes that several separate exchanges were made and that the last acquisition was not part of a continuing offer to acquire stock.

The facts surrounding the relationship between the two offers and the several exchanges, inter se, and their relationship to the later liquidation revolve around unsettled questions of fact. . . . [402 F.2d at 1001; footnotes omitted.]

Accordingly, the court added the question of qualification as a B reorganization to the remand that had previously been ordered, but no further proceedings in the matter have been reported.

b.   The "Voting Stock" Requirement

Needless to say, some difficult questions arise as to what constitutes "voting stock" for the purpose of qualifying as a B (or C) reorganization. Of course, for openers the instruments must represent "stock," which brings into play the issues discussed above in connection with continuity of interest. And to satisfy the "voting" requirement, the stock must have power to vote for at least some of the directors.

One particular problem area alluded to earlier involves contingent rights to stock, which generally fall into one of two categories: a right to additional stock in the future if a specified condition is satisfied, such as achievement of a certain earnings level, or a portion of the total stock in escrow, to be returned to the acquiring corporation in case of an adverse development, such as the appearance of an unforeseen liability. Literally, a contingent stock interest, particularly one yet to be earned, does not at that point represent voting stock as such. Nevertheless, Rev. Rul. 66-112, 1966-1 Cum. Bull. 68, ruled that the "solely for voting stock" test was not violated by a contingent right to additional voting shares so long as that interest was not

assignable prior to ripening into the receipt of the shares.
Detailed guidelines for a favorable ruling on contingent
rights to stock are now incorporated in Rev. Proc. 77-37,
1977-2 Cum. Bull. 568, page 156 supra. As to contingent
stock which may be "earned" later by achieving certain
performance standards, Section 3.03 limits the payout time
to five years, precludes assignability of the contingent
interest, and requires the maximum number of shares involved
to be specified. Incidentally, when and if the contingent
stock is received in these circumstances, the delay in
payment will result in some interest being focused and taxed
as such under §483. See Reg. §1.483-1(b)(6), Ex. 7.

As to stock put in escrow for possible return to the
acquiring corporation, Section 3.06 requires that the escrowed
stock be actually issued and outstanding, and amount to no
more than 50% of the total shares involved in the transaction;
that the escrow not last more than five years; and that
during the interim the former shareholders of the acquired
corporation be entitled to all voting rights and dividends
on the escrowed shares.

The use of fractional shares does not in and of itself
violate the "voting stock" requirement, and the fractions
represent stock rather than boot so far as non-recognition
of gain is concerned. Rev. Rul. 55-59, 1955-1 Cum. Bull.
35. Moreover, arrangements to allow the recipients of
fractional shares to either round up to a full share or sell
their fractional shares do not run afoul of the solely for
voting stock test. This seems to have been conceded by the
Government in Mills v. Commissioner (a case involving the
effect of actually distributing cash to the stockholders in
lieu of fractional shares, as described in the Chapman
opinion at page 773 supra), where the court observed:

> Counsel for the Commissioner suggested in
> argument that the parties might have followed
> another course. He stated that the Internal
> Revenue Service has recognized procedures under
> which fractional shares may be handled in a quali-
> fying reorganization. Thus he says that it would
> be proper for the corporation, at the direction of
> the person entitled to a fractional share, to buy
> an additional fraction to make a whole share for
> him or to sell the fractional share for his account
> to another shareholder or on the open market; or

for the corporation to appoint an independent
agent to carry out this task. And, since the
Service recognizes that in a reorganization the
acquiring corporation is responsible for distributing its stock in an appropriate number of shares,
including fractions, to each exchanging shareholder,
it has taken the position that such an agent's
expenses may be paid by the acquiring corporation.

As to the question actually present in Mills, it seems
clear enough that direct cash payments to stockholders on
account of fractional shares do literally violate the solely
for voting stock standard, and the Tax Court in Mills so
held. But, as indicated in the Chapman opinion, the Court
of Appeals in Mills rejected a strict construction of the
statute and held that cash paid in lieu of fractional shares
did not constitute "additional independent consideration";
rather it represented merely a mechanical adjunct to what
was desired and intended to be consideration composed exclusively of voting stock. The Service has acceded to this
view, so long as the cash is not "separately bargained-for
consideration." Rev. Rul. 66-365, 1966-2 Cum. Bull. 116.

The solely for voting stock test has been relaxed in
another important practical context by Rev. Rul. 73-54,
1973-1 Cum. Bull. 187, set out at page 804 infra. That
ruling allows the acquiring corporation in either a B or a C
reorganization to pay or assume expenses of the acquired
corporation or its shareholders which are solely and directly
related to the reorganization transaction, such as legal and
accounting fees, printing and clerical costs, underwriting
and SEC registration fees, and transfer agents' expenses.
However, the ruling warns that any transfer of cash or other
property to the acquired corporation or its shareholders
continues to be a disqualification, even though the cash or
property is to be used to pay expenses of the reorganization.
In addition, the ruling specifically precludes payment or
assumption of expenses not directly related to the reorganization, giving as examples fees for investment or estate
planning advice, or costs incurred by shareholders for
legal, accounting or investment advice pertaining to participation in the reorganization.

c.   Basis Aspects

In a B reorganization, the assets of the acquired corporation are not affected by the reorganization exchange between its stockholders and the acquiring corporation. The latter's basis in the stock obtained from the acquired corporation's stockholders is a carryover basis from the transferring stockholders, under §362(b).

Obviously, it may prove rather inconvenient for the acquiring corporation to have to ascertain its basis from the stockholders of the acquired corporation. Fortunately, however, this carryover basis becomes relevant only if the acquiring corporation subsequently disposes of the stock in a taxable transaction; in the more likely event of a liquidation of the acquired corporation (as in the American Potash case, page 778 supra), the acquiring corporation's basis in the acquired corporation's stock drops out of the picture, as will be discussed in subsection 2 below.

d.   Redemption by the Acquired Corporation

Suppose the acquired corporation redeems some of its stock in contemplation of a stock acquisition, in order to reduce the number of shares outstanding and thereby make it easier for the acquiring corporation to obtain the required 80% control in exchange for its voting stock. Literally, such a redemption transaction does not conflict with the solely for voting stock test, which is a restriction on the acquiring corporation. But if the acquiring corporation directly or indirectly supplies the cash needed to finance the redemption by the acquired corporation, disqualification will result, e.g., Rev. Rul. 75-360, 1975-2 Cum. Bull. 110; and there is not much difference as a practical matter between the acquiring corporation supplying the necessary cash, and obtaining the acquired corporation drained of its own cash and therefore in need of a cash infusion from the acquiring corporation.

There is also the question whether the redemption will succeed in establishing a new base for the purpose of applying the 80 percent control test. Some clue as to how the Service may view this issue is afforded by the warning contained in Section 3.02 of Rev. Proc. 77-37, page 157 supra, which is operative in the somewhat analogous context of determining whether the amount of continuity of interest required for an

A reorganization is present. Section 3.02 provides that in testing for the required 50% continuity of interest, described at page 749 supra, "sales, redemptions, and other dispositions of stock occurring prior or subsequent to the exchange which are part of the plan of reorganization will be considered in determining whether there is a 50% continuing interest through stock ownership as of the effective date of the reorganization."

What is the impact of the following ruling on this question of the effect of a redemption of stock by the acquired corporation on qualification as a B reorganization?

REVENUE RULING 68–285

1968–1 Cum.Bull. 147.

Advice has been requested whether there can be a reorganization under section 368(a)(1)(B) of the Internal Revenue Code of 1954 if the corporation to be acquired established an escrow account from its own funds to pay dissenting shareholders who elect to accept cash for their stock in the acquired corporation according to the provisions of a state banking law, rather than exchange their stock for stock in the acquiring corporation.

Corporation X and corporation Y are banking corporations. X wanted to acquire all of the outstanding stock of Y in exchange for voting stock of X. In order to be assured 100 percent control of Y. X elected, pursuant to a plan, to acquire the Y stock in accordance with the state's banking law.

The state banking law allows dissenting shareholders of the acquired corporation to register their dissent and elect to be paid cash for their shares in the acquired corporation. Under the provisions of the state banking law, any shareholder of the acquired corporation who elects not to participate in the exchange must completely terminate his stock ownership in the acquired corporation. Shareholders of Y owning 25 percent of the outstanding stock of Y elected not to participate in the exchange and they all perfected their election to dissent under the state banking law.

Y established an escrow account and transferred from its funds to this account sufficient cash to pay all of the Y shareholders who desired to perfect their rights under the state banking law. All payments were made from the escrow account and no cash payments were made by X either to Y, the dissenting shareholders of Y, or to the escrow account. The balance remaining in the escrow account after the dissenting shareholders were paid was returned to Y. These payments were made both before and after the exchange of X stock for Y stock.

Section 368(a) (1) (B) of the Code defines as a reorganization the acquisition by one corporation, in exchange solely for all or a part of its voting stock (or in exchange solely for all or part of the voting stock of a corporation that is in control of the acquiring corporation), of stock of another corporation if, immediately after the acquisition, the acquiring corporation has control of such other corporation (whether or not the acquiring corporation had control immediately before the acquisition).

Establishment by Y of an escrow account to pay dissenting shareholders under the circumstances described above will not preclude a reorganization under section 368(a) (1) (B) of the Code. This is true even though Y had not redeemed all the dissenting shareholders' stock prior to the effective date of the exchange. Under the state banking law, each dissenting shareholder of Y ceased to have any shareholder rights except the right to demand payment for the fair market value of his shares. Therefore, immediately after the exchange, X owned all the outstanding Y stock.

Revenue Ruling 55–440, C.B. 1955–2, 226, involved the question of whether preferred shares that had been called for redemption but not yet surrendered at the time of the exchange should be counted as "stock" under section 368(c) of the Code for the purpose of determining whether the 80 percent control requirement of section 368(a) (1) (B) of the Code had been satisfied. Revenue Ruling 55–440 held that the rights of the owners of the preferred stock *as stockholders* had terminated upon the call of the preferred shares and they thereafter possessed only the right to demand the call price upon the presentation of such shares for redemption. Based on this determination, Revenue Ruling 55–440 concluded that the transaction is a reorganization within the meaning of section 368(a) (1) (B) of the Code, regardless of the number of shares of preferred stock of the acquired company that at the time of the consummation of the stock for stock exchange had not been presented for redemption.

Similarly, the acquisition of the outstanding stock of Y in exchange for voting stock of X is a reorganization under section 368(a) (1) (B) of the Code even though, in accordance with state banking law, an escrow account was established in order to pay dissenting shareholders for their stock and even though the stock of some dissenting shareholders was not redeemed until after the consummation of the exchange. Thus, no gain or loss will be recognized to the shareholders of Y who exchanged their stock in Y solely for X voting stock, under section 354(a) of the Code.

However, it should be noted that section 368(a) (1) (B) of the Code does not treat as a reorganization any transaction in which the acquiring corporation pays the dissenting shareholders or reimburses the acquired corporation for its payment to the dissenting shareholders.

In the analogous setting of determining whether a
parent corporation owns 80 percent of the stock of a subsidiary in order to be eligible for a tax-free liquidation
under §332 (to be discussed in the subsection which immediately follows), the authorities have been somewhat conflicting. In Rev. Rul. 70-106, 1970-1 Cum. Bull. 70, Y
corporation owned 75 percent of the stock of X corporation
and wished to liquidate X under §332. The minority stockholders agreed to have their 25 percent of the outstanding
stock redeemed by X, which was then liquidated. The ruling
held that Y did not meet the 80 percent ownership test for a
§332 liquidation, because "the plan of liquidation was
adopted at the time Y reached the agreement with the minority shareholders and, at such time, Y owned seventy-five
percent of the stock of X."

It is not clear whether Rev. Rul. 70-106 was making a
factual finding as to the time of the adoption of the plan
of liquidation, or drawing an inference as a matter of law
(on the basis that the obvious purpose of the redemption was
to bring the liquidation under §332). But in George L.
Riggs, Inc. v. Commissioner, 64 T.C. 474 (1975), involving a
situation much like that in Rev. Rul. 70-106, the court made
a careful examination of the actions taken by the parent
corporation during the period prior to the increase in the
parent's stock interest in the subsidiary to 80 percent by
way of the redemption, and concluded that although an intention to liquidate the subsidiary was evidenced by some of
the steps, particularly the vote to sell all of its assets,
that was not equivalent to the actual adoption of a plan of
liquidation. Then the redemption of stock intervened, and
by the time the plan of liquidation was adopted the parent
corporation had obtained 80 percent ownership of the
subsidary.

It might also be noted that if in Rev. Rul. 70-106 Y
had itself purchased the stock from the X minority stockholders, §332 would apparently have been available. See
Rev. Rul. 75-521, 1975-2 Cum. Bull. 120, which distinguished
Rev. Rul. 70-106 on the ground that there the redemption
distribution was in effect part of the overall distribution
in liquidation, whereas a purchase of stock by the parent is
not part of a liquidating distribution and does not constitute the adoption of a plan of liquidation. (In the same
vein, a parent corporation which desires to stay out of
§332, for example, to recognize a loss, may do so by selling

enough of its stock in the subsidiary to reduce its holdings below the 80 percent line. Commissioner v. Day & Zimmerman, Inc., 151 F.2d 517 (3d Cir. 1945) (sale at public auction to corporation's treasurer who purchased the stock with his own funds).)

2. LIQUIDATION OF A SUBSIDIARY ACQUIRED IN A B REORGANIZATION

a. RECOGNITION OF GAIN OR LOSS

Although of course ordinarily the liquidation of a corporation is a taxable transaction to the stockholders, under § 332 a parent corporation may liquidate a subsidiary without recognition of gain or loss if the parent owns "at least 80 percent of the total combined voting power of all classes of stock entitled to vote and . . . at least 80% of the total number of shares of all other classes of stock (except nonvoting stock which is limited and preferred as to dividends)". It is to be noted that the stock ownership requirement of § 332 is almost identical to the control test of § 368(c) except that under § 332 non-voting preferred stock of the subsidiary may be ignored. Accordingly, if a subsidiary was acquired in a transaction which qualified as a B reorganization, it would presumably be eligible for liquidation under § 332.

However, § 332 reaches well beyond reorganization acquisitions, since under that section it makes no difference how or for what consideration the necessary stock ownership was acquired — a subsidiary acquired for cash is just as eligible for liquidation under § 332 as one acquired solely for voting stock. All that is required is that the necessary stock ownership exist on the date of the adoption of the plan of liquidation (and continue until the property has been received in liquidation). And the difference in the stock ownership requirement between § 332 and § 368(c), i. e., that non-voting preferred does not count under § 332 but does under § 368(c), affords another illustration of a transaction which may qualify for a tax-free liquidation under § 332 although the acquisition did not qualify as a tax-free reorganization under § 368(a)(1)(B).

Upon the liquidation of a subsidiary, as in any other complete liquidation, §336 operates to prevent recognition of gain or loss except in connection with installment obligations owned by the subsidiary. The other exception in §336, for lifo inventory, by its terms does not apply to a liquidation under §332 so long as the parent corporation takes a carryover basis in the assets received from the subsidiary (a subject discussed in the next subsection). In addition, §§1245 and 1250, which normally override §336 to tax depreciation recapture, do not apply to the liquidation of a subsidiary under §332 if it results in a carry-over basis for the subsidiary's assets.

The relationship of §337 to liquidations under §332 is somewhat more complex. If the subsidiary sells assets at a gain in the course of a complete liquidation, the application of both §337 and §332 would allow the overall enterprise to convert appreciated assets into cash in the hands of the parent without any tax on the gain. To prevent this result §337(c)(2) provides that non-recognition under §337 is not available in the case of a liquidation to which §332 applies. Hence if the parent corporation resorts to a purchase of the subsidiary's assets in conjunction with the liquidation (perhaps in an effort to avoid state law problems that might arise with minority stockholders of the subsidiary if that corporation were simply liquidated, see pages 674-682, supra), the subsidiary will have to recognize gain on the transaction (including any depreciation recapture as ordinary income), although this will be offset by a cost, rather than carryover, basis for the parent in the purchased assets.

There has been a problem with the application of §332 to the liquidation of a subsidiary when the parent itself thereafter promptly liquidates. If §332 applies to allow tax-free liquidation of the subsidiary and then §337 prevents recognition of gain upon the sale of the assets by the parent, all recognition of gain would be avoided at the corporate level; yet, as noted above, the subsidiary could not have sold its own assets under the protection of §337, by virtue of §337(c)(2). Fairfield S.S. Corp. v. Commissioner, 157 F.2d 321 (2d Cir. 1946), indicated that the predecessor of §332 was limited to unifying a continuing enterprise under one corporate roof, and hence was not available if the parent also liquidated. However, Rev. Rul. 69-172, 1969-1 Cum. Bull. 99, appears to assume that §332 applies even though the parent is also liquidated. In any event, it seems that the parent could be liquidated first, and then a sale of the former subsidiary's assets would be protected by §337; although the parent corporation's shareholders would be taxed upon the liquidation of the parent, there would be little or no further tax upon the subsequent liquidation of the subsidiary because the shareholders would have a basis in the shares of the subsidiary equal to fair market value, as a result of the taxable liquidation of the parent, per §334(a).

b. Basis of the Subsidiary's Assets

The general basis provision applicable in connection
with the tax-free liquidation of a subsidiary is §334(b)(1),
which provides for a carryover to the parent of the subsidiary's basis in its assets. Notice that, by virtue of this
provision, a B reorganization acquisition of stock followed
by a liquidation of the subsidiary leaves all the parties in
exactly the same tax position as in a merger, since the
acquired corporation's stockholders will have a carryover
basis in their stock of the acquiring corporation, pursuant
to §358, and the acquiring corporation gets a carryover
basis in the assets of the subsidiary under §334(b)(1). As
previously noted, upon liquidation of the subsidiary the
parent's carryover basis in the stock of the acquired corporation derived from the latter's former stockholders drops
out of the picture. Prima facie, §334(b)(1) would lead to
the same result if the parent acquired the stock of the
acquired corporation in a taxable transaction, and therefore
had a cost basis in that stock, reflecting the parent's
actual economic investment: upon a liquidation of the
acquired corporation to which §332 applies the parent's cost
basis in the stock would disappear, and the parent would
again receive a carryover basis in the subsidiary's assets
under §334(b)(1). However, prior to the 1954 Code, courts
had been treating a non-reorganization acquisition of 80
percent or more of the stock of a corporation followed
promptly by its liquidation as akin to a direct purchase of
the assets, entitling the parent to a basis in the acquired
corporation's assets measured by the parent's cost of the
stock (which of course also represented the parent's economic
investment in the assets). This so-called Kimbell-Diamond
doctrine was not applicable when the parent's acquisition of
the stock constituted a B reorganization, since that would
have prevented using a B reorganization plus a liquidation
of the acquired corporation to reach the same end point as
in a statutory merger. The notion of a cost basis for the
assets of an acquired corporation obtained through a stock
acquisition followed by liquidation has had a very checkered
career over the intervening years, which is succintly re-
counted, right up through the revolutionary change wrought
by the Tax Equity and Fiscal Responsibility Act of 1982
("TEFRA"), in the following paragraphs (without the footnotes)
from Ward, the TEFRA Amendments to Subchapter C: Corporate
Distributions and Acquisitions," 8 Journ. Corp. Law 277,
308-310 (1983), followed by excerpts from the explanation of

the 1982 amendments from the report by the staff of the Joint Committee:

II. STATUTORY KIMBELL-DIAMOND TRANSACTIONS AND NEW CODE SECTION 338

A. Background

Under the 1939 Code predecessor of section 332, a parent corporation generally recognized no gain or loss on a liquidation of an eighty-percent-owned subsidiary. In addition, under the 1939 Code predecessor of section 334(b)(1), the parent generally assumed the subsidiary's basis in property acquired in the liquidation. The 1939 Code did not explicitly address the proper basis for assets acquired by a parent corporation when it purchased the stock of a subsidiary and then promptly liquidated the subsidiary to acquire the subsidiary's assets. In the 1951 *Kimbell-Diamond Milling Co.* case, the Internal Revenue Service successfully argued that the parent's acquisition and liquidation of the subsidiary were interdependent steps in a plan to acquire the subsidiary's assets, and thus, the parent's basis in the assets should be the price paid for the stock rather than a transferred basis. *Kimbell-Diamond* was later used by taxpayers to obtain a stepped-up basis for the assets acquired from a target corporation.

The application of *Kimbell-Diamond* was uncertain, however, as it depended upon the intention cf the acquiring corporation's management and the target's liquidation within a reasonable time after the stock purchase. Congress sought to eliminate that uncertainty by enacting section 334(b)(2) in the 1954 Code. That section provided that the acquiring corporation's basis for the assets acquired in the liquidation of its subsidiary was the adjusted basis of the acquiring corporation's stock in the subsidiary. Whenever the transaction was treated as an asset purchase under section 334(b)(2), the tax attributes, including loss carryovers, of the liquidated subsidiary were terminated. Section 334(b)(2) was applicable, however, only if the parent corporation purchased at least eighty percent of the subsidiary's stock during a twelve-month period and adopted a plan of liquidation not more than two years after acquiring the requisite eighty-percent control. If these requirements were not satisfied, the parent generally assumed the subsidiary's basis under section 334(b)(1) and assumed its other tax attributes under section 381.

Although section 334(b)(2) asset-purchase treatment was ostensibly mandatory whenever the formal requirements of the section were satisfied, section 334(b)(2) had effectively become an elective provision, at least for those acquiring corporations that had the benefit of sophisticated tax counsel. The purchasing corporation could elect between asset-purchase and stock-purchase treatment by its choice of the formal corporate procedures to be followed after the acquisition. Frequently the choice of corporate procedure involved no substantive nontax considerations. For example, suppose the acquiring corporation wanted to obtain a cost basis for the acquired corporation's assets, but also wanted to continue to operate the acquired corporation as a separate subsidiary. The acquiring corporation (P Corp.) might organize a new subsidiary (New T Corp.) and transfer to it sufficient cash to purchase all of the stock of a target corporation (Old T Corp.). New T Corp. would then purchase the stock of Old T Corp., liquidate Old T Corp. in a transaction qualifying under section 334(b)(2), and change its name to Old T Corp. P Corp. would then own a corporation called Old T Corp. as a first-tier subsidiary, and Old T Corp. would have a cost basis for its assets. Although a tax would be imposed on the sellers of the Old T Corp. stock, no corporate-level tax generally would be paid by Old T Corp. since its liquidating distribution would qualify for nonrecognition under section 336.

If P Corp. haa preferred to maintain Old T Corp.'s adjusted basis or other tax attributes, however, it could have purchased the Old T Corp. stock and operated Old T Corp. as a first-tier subsidiary. In that case, Old T Corp.'s asset basis and other tax attributes were unaffected. If P Corp. preferred to own the Old T Corp. assets directly, it could merge into Old T Corp. and change Old T Corp.'s name to P Corp. Still the asset basis and the tax attributes of the two corporations were preserved. In effect, P Corp. could choose whether to continue or terminate the tax attributes of Old T Corp., depending upon how it structured the transaction. Frequently, the decision whether to liquidate Old *T* Corp. could be based almost entirely on tax considerations because the liquidation usually would have little economic significance, particularly if Old *T* Corp. were liquidated into a subsidiary of *P* Corp. Thus, significant differences in tax treatment had come to depend upon largely formalistic differences in the structure of the transaction.

By making selected purchases of the target corporation's assets before purchasing its stock, an acquiring corporation might obtain a cost basis for the target's low basis assets and a transferred basis for the acquired corporation's high basis assets if the acquired corporation were not liquidated.

* * *

It was also uncertain whether the common law *Kimbell-Diamond* rule survived the enactment of section 334(b)(2). The Court of Claims held in *American Potash & Chemical Corp. v. United States* that the enactment of section 334(b)(2) had not preempted the common law rule. Other courts, however, refused to follow the holding in *American Potash*, and the status of the common law *Kimbell-Diamond* rule remained unclear.

B. General Scope of New Section 338

TEFRA supplants former Code section 334(b)(2) with new Code section 338, which also supercedes the common law *Kimbell-Diamond* rule. Under the new provision, a corporation (the purchasing corporation) that purchases eighty-percent control of another corporation (the target corporation) within a twelve-month period may elect to treat the acquisition of the target corporation's stock as an asset purchase, regardless of whether the target is liquidated. If the purchasing corporation makes (or is deemed to have made) a section 338 election, the target corporation is treated as having sold all of its assets in a single transaction to which section 337 applies, and the target corporation is thereafter treated as a new corporation that purchased the assets. The statute prescribes criteria for determining the hypothetical sale price and the date on which the hypothetical sale is deemed to have occurred. The new measure thus permits the purchasing corporation, at its election, to obtain a cost basis for the target's assets without completely liquidating the target.

* * *

To preclude the purchasing corporation from obtaining a stepped-up basis for selected assets while preserving the target's basis for the remaining assets, new section 338 requires consistent treatment of all the assets of the target and its affiliated corporations. Under the consistency requirement, a purchasing corporation generally is deemed to have elected asset-purchase treatment if, within a statutorily prescribed consistency period, it acquires any assets from the target corporation or its affiliates. The consistency requirement eliminates one of the most objectionable features of the prior law, which permitted the purchasing corporation to obtain the benefits of both asset-purchase and stock-purchase treatment in a single acquisition. By integrating the various steps that may precede or follow a stock acquisition, new section 338 treats the entire transaction as either a stock purchase or an asset purchase.

GENERAL EXPLANATION, TAX EQUITY AND FISCAL RESPONSIBILITY ACT OF 1982

Staff of Joint Committee on Taxation (Dec. 31, 1982) at 131–139.

[Pre-TEFRA] Law

Upon the complete liquidation of a subsidiary corporation, 80 percent of the voting power and 80 percent of the total number of shares of all other classes of stock (other than nonvoting preferred stock) of which is owned by the parent corporation, gain or loss is generally not recognized and the basis of the subsidiary's assets and its other tax attributes are carried over (secs. 332, 334(b)(1), and 381(a)).

Under [pre-TEFRA] law, however, if the controlling stock interest was acquired by purchase within a 12-month period and the subsidiary was liquidated pursuant to a plan of liquidation adopted within 2 years after the qualifying stock purchase was completed, the transaction was treated as in substance a purchase of the subsidiary's assets (sec. 334(b)(2)). The acquiring corporation's basis in the "purchased" assets was the cost of the stock purchased as adjusted for items such as liabilities assumed, certain cash or dividend distributions to the acquiring corporation, and postacquisition earnings and profits of the subsidiary. The liquidating distributions could be made over a 3-year period beginning with the close of the taxable year during which the first of a series of distributions occurs (sec. 332(b)(3)). Thus, this treatment applied even though the liquidation could extend over a 5-year period after control had been acquired.

In these cases, when the assets were treated as purchased by the acquiring corporation, recapture income was taxed to the liquidating corporation, the investment tax credit recapture provisions were applicable, and tax attributes, including carryovers, of the liquidated corporation were terminated.

Cases interpreting the law applicable before the rules in section 334(b)(2) were adopted, treated the purchase of stock and prompt liquidation in some cases as a purchase of assets (Kimbell-Diamond Milling Co. v. Commissioner, 14 T.C. 74, aff'd per curiam, 187 F.2d 718 (5th Cir.), cert. denied, 342 US 827 (1951)). It is not clear whether such treatment still applied after the enactment of section 334(b)(2) in cases where the requirements of that provision were not met.

A stock purchase and liquidation was treated as a purchase of all the assets of the acquired corporation under [pre-TEFRA] law if section 334(b)(2) applied. Revision of the special treatment of partial liquidations under [TEFRA] restricts the options of a corporate purchaser seeking to treat a purchase of a corporation as a purchase of assets in part combined with a continuation of the tax attributes of the acquired entity. Neither [pre-TEFRA] law nor [TEFRA's] revision of the treatment of partial liquidations restrict a corporate purchaser from achieving such selectivity by purchasing assets directly from a corporation while concurrently purchasing the corporation's stock. Selectivity could also be achieved if an acquired corporation, prior to the acquisition, dispersed its assets in tax-free transactions among several corporations which could be separately purchased. The corporate purchaser then through selective qualifying liquidations could obtain asset purchase treatment for one or more acquired corporations while preserving the tax attributes of one or more other corporations.

Reasons for Change

While section 334(b)(2) did not permit selectivity within the context of a single corporation in that the transaction was treated as wholly an asset purchase or wholly a stock purchase, inconsistency was inherent in permitting a continuation of the acquired corporation's tax attributes for up to 5 years after a stock purchase while also treating the transaction as though assets had been purchased.

* * *

[T]he extended period that could elapse between stock purchase and liquidation required complex adjustments for earnings or deficits of the acquired corporation during the intervening period as well as for sales of assets and other items during such period in order to properly allocate the cost of the stock to the assets upon their ultimate distribution. Existing case law permitted a stepped-up basis for assets distributed in liquidation that in some cases exceeded the cost basis that would be applicable if the assets were purchased directly by the controlling corporation. See, R. M. Smith, Inc., 69 T.C. 317 (1977).

[Pre-TEFRA] law also provided unwarranted tax motivations for structuring a corporate acquisition as in part a purchase of assets and in part a purchase of stock or as a purchase of several corporations historically operated as a unit in order to preserve selectivity of tax treatment. These motivations included the ability to achieve a stepped-up basis for some assets while avoiding recapture tax and other unfavorable tax attributes with respect to other assets.

Explanation of Provisions

General treatment of stock purchase as asset purchase

[TEFRA] repeals the provision of prior law (sec. 334(b)(2)) that treated a purchase and liquidation of a subsidiary as an asset purchase. The amendments made by the Act were also intended to replace any nonstatutory treatment of a stock purchase as an asset purchase under the *Kimbell-Diamond* doctrine. Instead, an acquiring corporation, within 75 days after a qualified stock purchase, except as regulations may provide for a later election, may elect to treat an acquired subsidiary (target corporation) as if it sold all its assets pursuant to a plan of complete liquidation at the close of the stock acquisition date. The target corporation will be treated as a new corporation that purchased the assets on the day following such date. Gain or loss will not be recognized to the target corporation, except for gain or loss attributable to stock held by minority shareholders as described below, to the same extent gain or loss is not recognized (sec. 337) when a corporation sells all its assets in the course of a complete liquidation. This provision was intended to provide nonrecognition of gain or loss to the same extent that gain or loss would not be recognized under section 336 if there were an actual liquidation of the target corporation on the acquisition date to which prior law section 334(b)(2) applied.

* * *

A qualified stock purchase occurs if 80 percent or more of the voting power and 80 percent of the total number of shares of other classes of stock (except nonvoting, preferred stock) is acquired by purchase during a 12-month period (the acquisition period). The acquisition date is the date within such acquisition period on which the 80-percent purchase requirement (the qualified stock purchase) is satisfied. Generally, the 80-percent purchase requirement may be satisfied through the combination of stock purchases and redemptions. However, it is expected that the regulations will provide rules to prevent selective asset distributions.

The election is to be made in the manner prescribed by regulations and, once made, will be irrevocable.

Treatment of target corporation as new corporation

The assets of the target corporation will be treated as sold (and purchased) for an amount equal to the grossed up basis of the acquiring corporation in the stock of the target corporation on the acquisition date. The amount is to be adjusted under regulations for liabilities of the target corporation and other relevant items. It was anticipated that recapture tax liability of the target corporation attributable to the deemed sale of its assets is an item which may result in an adjustment under the regulations.

Under the gross-up formula, if the acquiring corporation owns less than 100 percent by value of the target corporation's stock on the acquisition date, the deemed purchase price is grossed up to equal 100-percent ownership by the acquiring corporation. It was not intended that minority shareholders in the target corporation be treated as having exchanged their shares for stock in the new corporation. However, nonrecognition of gain or loss to the target corporation is limited, unless the target corporation is liquidated within one year after the acquisition date, to the highest actual percentage by value of target corporation stock held by the acquiring corporation during the one-year period beginning on the acquisition date.

If, in connection with a qualified stock purchase with respect to which an election is made, the target corporation makes a distribution in complete redemption of all the stock of a shareholder (other than the acquiring corporation), section 336 of the Code will apply to the distribution as if it were made in a complete liquidation. This will preclude gain from being recognized to the target corporation under the provisions relating to stock redemptions by a continuing corporation.

The Act provides that the deemed sale (and purchase) of all its assets by the target corporation applies for purposes of subtitle A of the Internal Revenue Code and is deemed to occur at the close of the acquisition date in a single transaction. Under these rules, the provisions of subtitle F of the Code relating to assessment, collection, refunds, statutes of limitations, and other procedural matters apply without regard to the status of the target corporation as a new corporation. The target corporation thus remains liable for any tax liabilities incurred by it for any period prior to the election. The target corporation is required to file an income tax return for its taxable year ending as of the close of the acquisition date.

* * *

Definition of purchase

The term "purchase" is defined as it was under [pre-TEFRA] law (sec. 334(b)(3)) to exclude acquisitions of stock with a carryover basis or from a decedent, acquisitions in an exchange to which section 351 applies, and acquisitions from a person whose ownership is attributed to the acquiring person under section 318(a). Attribution under section 318(a)(4) relating to options will be disregarded for this purpose. However, if, as a result of a stock purchase, the purchasing corporation is treated under section 318(a) as owning stock in a third corporation, the purchasing corporation will be treated as having purchased stock in such third corporation but not until the first day on which ownership of such stock is considered as owned by the purchasing corporation under section 318(a). . . .

Consistency requirement

The rules require consistency where the purchasing corporation makes qualified stock purchases of two or more corporations that are members of the same affiliated group. For this purpose, purchases by a member of the purchasing corporation's affiliated group, except as regulations provide otherwise, are treated as purchases by the purchasing corporation. The consistency requirement applies as well to a combination of a direct asset acquisition and qualified stock purchase.

The consistency requirement applies with respect to purchases over a defined "consistency period" determined by reference to the acquisition date applicable to the target corporation. The "consistency period" is the one-year period preceding the target corporation acquisition period plus the portion of the acquisition period up to and including the acquisition date, and the one-year period following the acquisition date. Thus, if all the target corporation's stock is purchased on the same day by the purchasing corporation, the one-year period immediately preceding and the one-year period immediately following such date are included in the consistency period. If, within such period, there is a direct purchase of assets from the target corporation or a target affiliate by the purchasing corporation, the rules require that the acquisition of the target corporation be treated as an asset purchase.

The consistency period may be expanded in appropriate cases by the Secretary where there is in effect a plan to make several qualified stock purchases or any such purchase and asset acquisition with respect to a target corporation and its target affiliates.

* * *

An acquisition of assets from the target corporation or a target affiliate during the consistency period applicable to the target corporation will require the qualified stock purchase of the target corporation to be treated as a purchase of assets. In applying these rules, stock in a target affiliate is not to be treated as an asset of any other target affiliate or of the target corporation.

In applying these rules, acquisitions of assets pursuant to sales by the target corporation or a target affiliate in the ordinary course of its trade or business and acquisitions in which the basis of assets is carried over will not cause the consistency requirement to apply. The sale by a target corporation will be considered as a sale in the ordinary course of business for this purpose even though it is not customary in the course of the selling corporation's business provided it is a transaction that is a normal incident to the conduct of a trade or business, such as a sale of used machinery that was employed in the seller's trade or business.

Where there are, within a consistency period, only qualified stock purchases of the target corporation and one or more target affiliates by the purchasing corporation, an election with respect to the first purchase will apply to the later purchases. A failure to make the election for the first purchase will preclude any election for later purchases.

To prevent avoidance of the consistency requirements, the Act authorizes the Secretary to treat stock acquisitions which are pursuant to a plan and which satisfy the 80-percent requirement to be treated as qualified stock purchases even though they are not otherwise so defined. For example, an acquiring corporation may acquire 79 percent of the stock of a target corporation and, within a year, purchase assets from such corporation or a target affiliate planning to purchase the remaining target corporation stock more than one year after the original stock purchase. The Secretary may under these circumstances treat the purchase of the target corporation's stock as a deemed sale of its assets by the target corporation. [Section 338(i)] also authorizes such regulations as may be necessary to ensure that the requirements of consistency of treatment of stock and asset purchases with respect to a target corporation and its target affiliates are not circumvented through the use of other provisions of the law or regulations, including the consolidated return regulations.

* * *

The Act provides regulatory authority pursuant to which the Secretary may determine that the deemed election will not apply as the result of a *de minimis* acquisition of assets and may also preclude the application of the deemed election rule if it is determined that the taxpayer has acquired assets in order to avoid the 75-day limit on the period after the acquisition date within which the election must be made.

The application of the consistency requirements is illustrated in the following examples. * * *

Example 1

The acquiring corporation makes a qualified stock purchase of T's stock and within a one-year period purchases assets from T or a target affiliate of T. The acquiring corporation is deemed to have made an election with respect to T as of the acquisition date applicable to T.

Example 2

The acquiring corporation makes a qualified stock purchase of T's stock and makes the election within 75 days of the acquisition date. The acquiring corporation is treated as having acquired by purchase the stock of any other corporation owned by T actually or constructively which is attributed to the acquiring corporation under section 318(a) (other than sec. 318(a)(4)). To the extent that such treatment results in qualified stock purchases by the acquiring corporation of other corporations actually or constructively owned by T, the election with respect to T applies to all such corporations. Each such corporation will be treated as having sold (and as having purchased as a "new" corporation) its assets on the acquisition date with respect to T. Gain or loss will not be recognized to the extent gain or loss is not recognized under section 337. The deemed sale price of the assets will be determined by reference to the grossed-up amount allocated to the stock of each selling corporation as a result of the qualified stock purchase and election with respect to T.

Example 3

P, an acquiring corporation, makes a qualified stock purchase of all the stock of corporation T on February 1, 1983. No election is made. On December 1, 1983, P makes a qualified stock purchase of all the stock of corporation U, a target affiliate of corporation T. No election may be made with respect to corporation U.

D. SPECIAL PROBLEMS IN C REORGANIZATIONS

---

1. EXCEPTIONS TO THE "SOLELY FOR VOTING STOCK" REQUIREMENT

As previously noted, two important exceptions have been engrafted onto the "solely for voting stock" requirement for C reorganizations. The first, which is embodied in the definition itself in § 368(a)(1)(C), provides that in applying the "solely for voting stock" test the fact that the acquiring corporation assumes the liabilities of the acquired corporation, or takes its property subject to liabilities, may be disregarded. This exception responds to the needs of business practice, as the acquiring corporation in a combination transaction normally must take over the liabilities of the acquired corporation one way or another. Since this does not disqualify an A reorganization (or the tax-free liquidation of a subsidiary after a B reorganization), there seems little reason why it should preclude the C form.

Under this exception, it appears that the acquiring corporation may issue its own securities in place of the securities of the acquired corporation. See Southland Ice Co. v. Commissioner, 5 T.C. 842, 850 (1945). However, the terms of the new securities should not vary too much from the old, lest the transaction be regarded as the issuance of new securities constituting boot rather than a mere assumption of the old securities.

The second exception to the "solely for voting stock" requirement is the provision in § 368(a)(2)(B), added in 1954, which permits some leeway for consideration other than voting stock so long as at least 80% of the *fair market value* of *all* of the property of the acquired corporation is obtained solely for voting stock. This 20% leeway is directly related to the assumption of liabilities provision, since any liabilities assumed by the acquiring corporation (or to which property of the acquired corporation is subject) must be counted as consideration other than voting stock for the purpose of measuring the 20%. Thus when the total of the liabilities assumed by the acquiring corporation (or to which property of the acquired corporation is subject) exceeds 20% of the fair market value of all the property of the acquired corporation, the 20% provision provides no additional leeway at all. Because of this, as well as the difficulty of ascertaining the value of the corporation's assets with certainty, this 20% provision seems destined to be of rather limited practical importance.

The 20% provision has no counterpart in B reorganizations. On the other hand, it still leaves C reorganizations well behind A reorganizations, which are not subject to the "solely for voting stock" requirement at all. Technical differences of this kind among the various types of reorganization transactions seems to be simply statutory aberrations, and there have been many calls, both inside and outside of Congress, for their elimination. But so long as these differences continue, they must be kept constantly in mind when selecting the form of reorganization in any particular case.

There are of course the same questions of what constitutes "voting stock" as were encountered in connection with B reorganizations, but with one possible difference so far as the problem of fractional shares is concerned. Theoretically, the acquiring corporation in a C reorganization is not directly involved with fractional shares since it simply issues the specified total number of shares to the acquired corporation in exchange for the latter's assets. The need for fractional shares arises when the acquired corporation is liquidated and the shares of the acquiring corporation are distributed to the stockholders of the acquired corporation in exchange for their stock, and·

the acquiring corporation could remain aloof from this aspect of the transaction. But as a practical matter the acquiring corporation must assist the acquired corporation in dealing with this problem, presumably by making fractional shares or scrip available to the acquired corporation. However, as in the analogous B reorganization case, it is not a violation of the "solely for voting stock" requirement for the acquiring corporation to include scrip or fractional shares in the consideration transferred to the acquired corporation, or to help in arranging for the sale or purchase of fractional interests, so long as the acquiring corporation does not itself, directly or indirectly, supply any cash in the transaction.

For a comprehensive analysis of the various problems involved in C reorganizations, including both the foregoing and those discussed below, see Goldman, The C Reorganization, 19 Tax L.Rev. 31 (1963).

---

2. ACQUISITION OF "SUBSTANTIALLY ALL" OF THE ACQUIRED CORPORATION'S PROPERTY

REVENUE RULING 57–518

1957–2 Cum.Bull. 253.

Advice has been requested as to the Federal income tax consequences of a reorganization between two corporations under the circumstances described below.

The M and N corporations were engaged in the fabrication and sale of various items of steel products. For sound and legitimate business reasons, N corporation acquired most of M corporation's business and operating assets. Under a plan of reorganization, M corporation transferred to N corporation (1) all of its fixed assets (plant and equipment) at net book values, (2) 97 percent of all its inventories at book values, and (3) insurance policies, and other properties pertaining to the business. In exchange therefor, N corporation issued shares of its voting common stock to M corporation.

The properties retained by M corporation include cash, accounts receivable, notes, and three percent of its total inventory. The fair market value of the assets retained by M was roughly equivalent to the amount of its liabilities. M corporation proceeded to liquidate its retained properties as expeditiously as possible and applied the proceeds to its outstanding debts. The property remaining after the discharge of all its liabilities was turned over to N corporation, and M corporation was liquidated.

* * *

The specific question presented is what constitutes "substantially all of the properties" as defined in [§ 368(a) (1) (C)] of the Code. The answer will depend upon the facts and circumstances in each case rather than upon any particular percentage. Among the elements of importance that are to be considered in arriving at the conclusion are the nature of the properties retained by the transferor, the purpose of the retention, and the amount thereof. In Milton Smith, et al. v. Commissioner, 34 B.T.A. 702 . . . (1936), a corporation transferred 71 percent of its gross assets. It retained assets having a value of $52,000, the major portion of which was in cash and accounts receivable. It was stated that the assets were retained in order to liquidate liabilities of approximately $46,000. Thus, after discharging its liabilities, the outside figure of assets remaining with the petitioner would have been $6,000, which the court stated was not an excessive margin to allow for the collection of receivables with which to meet its liabilities. No assets were retained for the purpose of engaging in any business or for distribution to stockholders. In those circumstances, the court held that there had been a transfer of "substantially all of the assets" of the corporation. The court very definitely indicated that a different conclusion would probably have been reached if the amount retained was clearly in excess of a reasonable amount necessary to liquidate liabilities. Furthermore, the court intimated that transfer of all of the net assets of a corporation would not qualify if the percentage of gross assets transferred was too low. Thus, it stated that, if a corporation having gross assets of $1,000,000 and liabilities of $900,000 transferred only the net assets of $100,000, the result would probably not come within the intent of Congress in its use of the words "substantially all."

The instant case, of the assets not transferred to the corporation, no portion was retained by M corporation for its own continued use inasmuch as the plan of reorganization contemplated M's liquidation. Furthermore, the assets retained were for the purpose of meeting liabilities, and these assets at fair market values, approximately equaled the amount of such liabilities. Thus, the facts in this case meet the requirements established in the case of Milton Smith, supra.

The instant case is not in conflict with I. T. 2373, C. B. VI–2 19 (1927), which holds that, where one corporation transferred approximately three-fourths of its properties to another corporation for a consideration of bonds and cash, it did not dispose of "substantially all the properties" owned by it at the time and, therefore, no corporate reorganization took place, so that the transaction constituted an exchange of property resulting in a gain or loss to the transferor for income tax purposes. I. T. 2373, supra, is obsolete to the extent that it implies that a corporate reorganization could have occurred where there was no continuity of interest. However, that ruling is still valid with regard to its discussion of the question of what constitutes "substantially all of the properties." From the facts as stated in that case, it appears that a major part of the 25 percent of the assets retained were operating assets, and it does not appear that they were retained for the purpose of liquidating the liabilities of the corporation. On the contrary, it seems likely that the corporation may have contemplated continuation of its business or the sale of the remainder of its operating assets to another purchaser. As a result, I. T. 2373, supra, is clearly distinguishable from the instant case.

Accordingly, since the assets transferred by M to N constitute "substantially all" of the assets of the transferor corporation within the meaning of that statutory phrase, the acquisition by N corporation, in exchange solely for part of its voting common stock, of the properties of M corporation pursuant to the plan will constitute a reorganization within the purview of section 368(a) (1) (C) of the Code. No gain or loss is recognized to the transferor as a result of the exchange of its property for common stock of the transferee under section 361 of the Code; and no gain or loss is recognized to the shareholders of M corporation, under section 354(a) (1) of such Code, as the result of their receipt of N common stock.

According to the specific guidelines now contained in Rev. Proc. 77-37, Section 3.01, page 157 supra, the "substantially all" requirement in §368(a)(1)(C) will be regarded as satisfied if the transfer of assets by the acquired corporation represents at least 90 percent of the fair market value of the gross assets and at least 70 percent of the net assets immediately prior to the transfer. The guideline adds that any payments to dissenters, or redemptions, or unusual distributions made by the acquired corporation immediately before the transfer and which are part of the plan **of** reorganization will be included in the assets of the corporation immediately prior to the transfer.

3. LIQUIDATION OF THE ACQUIRED CORPORATION

It is to be noted that the definition of a C reorganization does not include the liquidation of the acquired corporation (just as is true in connection with a B reorganization), and it is clear that qualification as a reorganization does not depend upon there being such a liquidation. E. g., Helvering v. Minnesota Tea Co., 296 U.S. 378, 56 S.Ct. 269, 80 L.Ed. 284 (1935). However, the liquidation of the acquired corporation can be included within the "plan of reorganization" (notwithstanding Reg. § 1.368–2(g) which purports to limit the plan "to such exchanges or distributions as are directly a part of the transaction specifically described as a reorganization" in § 368), thereby making § 354 applicable to the receipt of the acquiring corporation's stock by the stockholders of the acquired corporation upon the liquidation of the acquired corporation. E. g., Rev.Rul. 57–518, set out just above. Were this not so, it would not be possible to use the C reorganization route to get the stock of the acquiring corporation to the stockholders of the acquired corporation tax-free, since there is no counterpart of § 332 to provide non-recognition treatment for the liquidation of the acquired corporation in such circumstances.

The harder question is whether the parties are free *not* to include the liquidation of the acquired corporation in the plan of reorganization if they prefer. If so, it would mean that in a C reorganization the recognition of gain or loss by the stockholders of the acquired corporation would become elective, depending upon whether the liquidation was included within the plan. But it seems more likely that whenever liquidation of the acquired corporation is contemplated from the outset, it will be regarded as a part of the plan of reorganization whether or not the liquidation is expressly included in the plan and even if it does not occur until a substantial time after the acquisition transaction. See Wilson v. Commissioner, 20 T.C.M. 676 (1961) (liquidation of the acquired corporation three years after the transfer of assets held, at the urging of the taxpayer, to be pursuant to the plan of reorganization). See generally, Manning, "In Pursuance of the Plan of Reorganization": The Scope of the Reorganization Provisions of the Internal Revenue Code, 72 Harv.L.Rev. 881, 885–890, 910–917 (1959).

---

4. EFFECT OF THE ACQUIRING CORPORATION'S OWNERSHIP OF STOCK IN THE ACQUIRED CORPORATION

There has been a problem where the acquiring corporation in a C reorganization owns stock in the acquired corporation, a situation sometimes referred to as a "creeping acquisition" because the acquiring corporation has already moved partway down the path (though admittedly a different one) toward acquisition of the acquired corporation. In such cases, when the acquired corporation is liquidated the acquiring corporation (in its capacity as a stockholder of the acquired corporation) will receive back some of the stock it transferred in exchange for the acquired corporation's assets; accordingly, it might be argued that the acquiring corporation has in effect received some of the assets of the acquired corporation on account of the stock it owned in the acquired corporation rather than in exchange for its own stock. Bausch & Lomb Optical Co. v. Commissioner, 267 F.2d 75 (2d Cir. 1959), adopts this view, denying C reorganization treatment under the 1939 Code where corporation P, which earlier had acquired 79% of the stock of corporation S for cash, issued its stock for the assets of corporation S and then liquidated S, with P thus receiving

back 79% of the stock it had issued.   Accord, Rev.Rul. 54–396, 54–2
Cum.Bull. 147 (ruling on the Bausch & Lomb transaction).   See gen-
erally, Seplow, Acquisition of Assets of a Subsidiary: Liquidation or
Reorganization, 73 Harv.L.Rev. 484 (1960).

   This is another of those very troublesome variations among the
types of reorganization which often amount to a trap for the unwary.
As we have seen, creeping control is now permitted for B reorganizations; and in A reorganizations, which are even more closely analogous
to asset acquisitions, ownership of stock by the acquiring corporation
in the corporation to be acquired does not seem to present any problem.
Cf. Helvering v. Winston Bros. Co., 76 F.2d 381 (8th Cir. 1935).   It
is also possible to avoid the Bausch & Lomb result while still pursuing
the C reorganization route.   First, it appears that reorganization
qualification can be achieved by not liquidating the acquired corporation, even if all of the stockholders other than the acquiring corporation turn in their acquired corporation stock and receive stock of the
acquiring corporation in exchange.   See Rev.Rul. 57–278, 1957–1
Cum.Bull. 124.   Second, apparently the two corporations can safely
combine in a C reorganization by both transferring their assets to a
new corporation, and then liquidating.   George v. Commissioner, 26
T.C. 396 (1956).

---

5.   CLAIMS OF DISSENTING STOCKHOLDERS AND REORGANIZATION
            EXPENSES OF THE ACQUIRED CORPORATION

   While in a merger the appraisal claims of the dissenting stockholders of both corporations are usually lodged against the surviving,
acquiring corporation, e. g., MBA § 74, in an asset acquisition if the
stockholders of the acquired corporation who object to the sale of assets have any right to appraisal at all their claims must usually be
filed against the acquired corporation.   Ibid.   This can lead to some
significant tax complications.   It is clear that if the acquiring corporation attempted to supply the acquired corporation with the cash to pay
the dissenting stockholders' claims it would represent boot which could
disqualify the transaction as a C reorganization if the amount of the
cash (together with any liabilities assumed) exceeded 20% of the
fair market value of the acquired corporation's property.   However, as
a practical matter this is not a matter of any real concern since the
amount to which the dissenting shareholders are entitled would rarely
have been determined in time to have the acquiring corporation supply
the cash anyway.   Normally, it would be more feasible to simply have
the acquiring corporation assume the acquired corporation's liability
to dissenting stockholders, which would make the situation closely
comparable to what occurs in a merger.   But this approach runs head
on into the decision in Helvering v. Southwest Consolidated Corp., 315
U.S. 194, 62 S.Ct. 546, 86 L.Ed. 789 (1942), which held that since the
liability to dissenters arose out of the reorganization plan itself it did

not constitute "a liability of the other" corporation within the meaning of § 368(a)(1)(C) and therefore its assumption constituted boot. In Southwest Consolidated the liability assumed was actually one to a bank for funds borrowed to pay the dissenting stockholders, but it could hardly be doubted that the result would have been the same if the acquiring corporation had assumed the liability to the dissenters directly.

The other obvious alternative for dealing with dissenters is to have the acquired corporation use its own assets to pay their claims. This approach seemed to be approved in Southland Ice Co. v. Commissioner, 5 T.C. 842 (1945), since the court sustained reorganization treatment where dissenters were paid with cash obtained by the acquired corporation from its operations during the reorganization period. To be sure, this means that the acquiring corporation would not be acquiring *all* of the acquired corporation's assets. But as the court in the Southland Ice case noted the statute only requires the acquisition of "substantially all" the assets; and the court was satisfied that this requirement was sufficient to police the acquired corporation's use of its own assets to pay dissenters.

Often the amount due to dissenters can not be determined by the time when the transfer of the acquired corporation's assets to the acquiring corporation is called for. In that event the acquired corporation can simply exclude from the property sold to the acquiring corporation enough of its liquid assets to meet the dissenters' claims. See Roosevelt Hotel Co. v. Commissioner, 13 T.C. 399 (1949). Presumably, this could be coupled with an arrangement to transfer any excess of the liquid assets retained over the amount ultimately required to meet the dissenters' claims to the acquiring corporation for additional stock, in accordance with some predetermined formula. Alternatively, the acquired corporation could transfer all of its assets to the acquiring corporation and then sell enough of the stock received from the acquiring corporation to obtain the amount needed to pay dissenters (subject to some possible SEC problems, to say nothing of the depressed market which might result from such an immediate, quasi-forced sale of stock). However, these approaches present some practical difficulties when, as is typically the case, it is contemplated that the acquired corporation will be liquidated promptly and the stock of the acquiring corporation will be distributed to the stockholders of the acquired corporation in exchange for their stock. Normally in such cases the plan submitted to the stockholders of the acquired corporation would be expected to specify the ratio upon which the stock of the acquired corporation would be exchanged for stock of the acquiring corporation in the liquidation, just as a plan of merger specifies the exchange ratio when the merger route is followed. But if the value determined for the dissenters' stock in the appraisal proceeding should turn out to be significantly greater than the amount allocated to them under the plan (and of course the dissenters are "betting" that they can show a substantially higher value for their stock), the amount available for distribution to non-dissenting stockholders upon the liqui-dation of the acquired corporation would be proportionately reduced, and the exchange ratio would be thrown askew. Indeed, what this means is that it may not be possible to fix an exchange ratio in ad-vance. And if the acquired corporation can not tell its stockholders at the outset what they can expect to receive under the plan, it may be difficult to secure the necessary stockholder approval.

These uncertainties are inherent in any procedure which throws on the acquired corporation, rather than the acquiring corporation, the risk that dissenters will be awarded substantially more in the ap-praisal proceeding than they were to receive under the plan. Con-versely, these difficulties evaporate under any plan which shifts that risk on to the acquiring corporation, where it is in a merger. For ex-ample, the plan might provide that as soon as the number of dissenting shares is known the acquiring corporation will transfer sufficient stock to take care of all the non-dissenting stockholders of the acquired cor-poration in accordance with the agreed-upon exchange ratio; but the acquired corporation would be permitted to retain enough cash to pro-vide a safety margin in the event of a generous appraisal award, with any excess over the actual appraisal award to be remitted to the acquir-ing corporation. But the trouble with this approach, or any other one which shifts the risk of the appraisal award to the acquiring corpora-tion, is that it is not really distinguishable from a direct assumption of the appraisal liability by the acquiring corporation and therefore runs a serious risk of disqualifying the reorganization under the Southwest Consolidated case.

An analogous problem arises in connection with the reorganiza-tion expenses of the acquired corporation, which would also seem to produce a liability arising out of the reorganization plan itself within the meaning of the Southwest Consolidated case. But the Tax Court, in the Roosevelt Hotel case, supra, confined Southwest Consolidated to the assumption of the liability to dissenters and held that the acquiring corporation's assumption of the liability for other expenses of the acquired corporation did not constitute boot. This view has now been expressly adopted by the Service in the following ruling:

REVENUE RULING 73–54

1973–1 Cum.Bull. 187.

Advice has been requested whether the payment or assumption by the acquiring corporation of valid reorganization expenses of the ac-quired corporation or its shareholders violates the "solely for voting stock" requirement of section 368(a)(1)(C) of the Internal Revenue Code of 1954.

Pursuant to a plan of reorganization, X corporation proposes to transfer substantially all of its properties to Y corporation in exchange for shares of voting stock of Y followed by the distribution of the Y stock to the shareholders of X in the dissolution of X. As part of the plan of reorganization Y agrees to pay or assume certain expenses. These expenses are legal and accounting expenses; appraisal fees; administrative costs of the acquired corporation directly related to the reorganization such as those incurred for printing, clerical work, telephone and telegraph; security underwriting and registration fees and expenses; transfer taxes, and transfer agents' fees and expenses. These expenses are solely and directly related to the reorganization.

In order to satisfy the definition of a reorganization under section 368(a)(1)(C) of the Code, the consideration to be transferred by the acquiring corporation must consist solely of all or a part of its voting stock (or voting stock of a corporation which is in control of it). Thus, an acquisition of property for all or a part of the acquiring corporation's voting stock and other property cannot qualify under section 368(a)(1)(C) unless section 368(a)(2)(B) applies. As the Supreme Court of the United States stated in Helvering v. Southwest Consolidated Corp., 315 U.S. 194 (1942), Ct.D. 1544, C.B. 1942-1, 215:

" 'Solely' leaves no leeway. Voting stock plus some other consideration does not meet the statutory requirement."

In *Southwest Consolidated Corp.*, the Court held that the "solely for voting stock" requirement is violated where the acquiring corporation directly or indirectly transfers to the acquired corporation or its shareholders property other than voting stock in exchange for the equity interest being acquired.

However, in several court decisions, payments by the acquiring corporation of expenses arising in a reorganization have been held not to represent additional consideration [citing the Roosevelt Hotel case].

Although the acquired corporation and its shareholders are relieved of the reorganization expenses otherwise attributable to them nevertheless, they will be receiving solely voting stock of the acquiring corporation. They will receive no other consideration from the transferee in exchange for the transferor's property.

Accordingly, it is held that the payment or assumption by the acquiring corporation of the valid reorganization expenses in the instant case will not prevent the plan from satisfying the definition of a reorganization under the above provision of the Code. Pursuant to the provisions of section 361(a) and section 354(a)(1) of the Code no gain or loss will be recognized to the acquired corporation or its shareholders, respectively. The principles of this Revenue Ruling are equally applicable to such valid reorganization expenses that are paid or assumed by an acquiring corporation in a reorganization described in section 368(a)(1)(B) of the Code. Valid reorganization expenses which may be paid or assumed by an acquiring corporation without violating the solely for voting stock requirement of section 368(a)(1)(B) or (C) of the Code are not necessarily limited to those involved in the instant case.

Expenses that are not solely and directly related to the reorganization, the transfer of the property of the acquired corporation for stock of the acquiring corporation, or the exchange of the equity interests of the shareholders of the acquired corporation for stock of the acquiring corporation, are other property if paid or assumed by the acquiring corporation and will prevent the transaction from satisfying the solely for voting stock requirement of section 368(a)(1)(B) or (C) of the Code. Examples of such expenses are fees incurred for investment or estate planning advice and those incurred by an individual shareholder, or group of shareholders, for legal, accounting or investment advice or counsel pertaining to participation in, or action with respect to, the reorganization. In addition, where the obligation to pay an applicable state transfer tax is solely that of a shareholder, payment or assumption of such tax by the acquiring corporation will violate the solely for voting stock requirement of section 368(a)(1)(B) or (C) of the Code.

Further, this ruling is not applicable and the transaction will not qualify under section 368(a)(1)(B) or (C) of the Code to situations in which there is a transfer by the acquiring corporation of cash or property other than voting stock to the acquired corporation or its shareholders with the intention that the acquired corporation or its shareholders will pay the expenses of the acquired corporation or its shareholders even though they are solely and directly related to the reorganization.

However, the Service is still not prepared to reject the actual holding in Southwest Consolidated: hence if the acquiring corporation assumes the obligation of the acquired corporation for the claims of its dissenting shareholders, that will violate the solely for voting stock test, and thereby preclude qualification as a C reorganization (unless the amount involved fits within the 20 percent leeway). Rev. Rul. 73-102, 73-102, 1973-1 Cum. Bull. 186.

SECTION 5. CARRYOVER OF TAX ATTRIBUTES IN COMBINATION TRANSACTIONS

A. IN GENERAL

One of the most important tax questions in connection with combination transactions is to what extent the acquiring corporation succeeds to the characteristics, benefits, and obligations of the acquired corporation pursuant to a tax-free combination. Prior to 1954 what few rules there were in this area came mainly from the courts. There was no consistent judicial pattern, and the result seemed to depend primarily on the nature of the particular tax item involved. Most of the cases related to either earnings and profits or net operating losses, both of which will be considered in more detail below. However, it may be useful to illustrate the general problem with an example from outside those two areas. In Mendham Corporation v. Commissioner, 9 T.C. 320 (1947), the acquiring corporation in a combination transaction had received from the acquired corporation property subject to a mortgage which had been placed by the acquired corporation. Subsequently, the mortgagee foreclosed the mortgage and took over the property, but did not assert any deficiency. If this foreclosure had occurred while the acquired corporation still held the property, the transaction would have been viewed as a transfer of the property in satisfaction of the mortgage debt, giving rise to recognized gain in the amount of the difference between the mortgage debt and the depreciated basis of the property. Here, however, while the acquired corporation had obtained the money on the mortgage, it was the acquiring corporation which was yielding the property to satisfy the debt. Nevertheless, the Tax Court upheld the Commissioner's contention that the acquiring corporation should recognize the gain, on the ground that in a tax-free combination the acquiring corporation stepped completely into the shoes of the acquired corporation.

The 1954 Code in § 381 introduced the first statutory effort to deal comprehensively with the carryover of items from the acquired corporation to the acquiring corporation in a corporate combination. The transactions subject to § 381 are: A, C, and F reorganizations; D reorganizations which do not involve any corporate division; and tax-free liquidations of a subsidiary in which the parent takes the basis of the subsidiary's assets. In other words, the section applies generally where the acquiring corporation in effect absorbs the acquired corporation.

---

*All of Section 5 is taken from the prior edition without revision.

It is not clear whether in a C reorganization it is necessary that the acquired corporation be liquidated for § 381 to apply. If not, the section may lead to the rather anomalous result that the various attributes of the acquired corporation go over to the acquiring corporation even though the acquired corporation remains in existence.

The tax items covered by § 381 are specifically enumerated in subsection (c) and include such important attributes as net operating loss carryovers, earnings and profits, methods of accounting, and various elections. Although the statutory list is not exhaustive, there is no catch-all clause. However, the section is not intended to be exclusive, and the Senate Finance Committee Report, S.Rep.No. 1622, 83rd Cong., 2d Sess. 277 (1954), states that the section is "not intended to affect the carryover treatment of an item or tax attribute not specified in the section or the carryover treatment of items or tax attributes in corporate transactions not described in subsection (a)." Thus it would seem that such rules as that of the Mendham case, supra, which are not dealt with in the section, would continue to be applicable.

See generally, Reese, Reorganization Transfers and Survival of Tax Attributes, 16 Tax.L.Rev. 207 (1961).

B. CARRYOVER OF EARNINGS AND PROFITS

The pre-1954 judicial authorities relating to the carryover of earnings and profits, and the pattern adopted by § 381(c)(2), are well summarized in the following:

NESSON, EARNINGS AND PROFITS DISCONTINUITIES UNDER THE 1954 CODE*

77 Harv.L.Rev. 452–456 (1964).

A. Sansome, Phipps, and Frelbro

Commissioner v. Sansome,[8] uniformly recognized as the "leading case," posed the problem of the disappearing earnings account in its starkest form. In a tax-free reorganization, corporation N, with substantial earnings and profits, transferred all its assets to corporation

---

8. 60 F.2d 931 (2d Cir. 1932).

M in return for all M's stock and then liquidated. The same share-holders thus owned the same business under a new name. Noting that a corporate distribution to be taxable as a dividend must be "out of its earnings or profits," and noting further that the new corporation had no earnings and profits of its own, the shareholders of M argued that since distributions made subsequent to the reorganization were not out of "its" — M's — earnings and profits, they were capital distributions. Judge Hand, however, refused to place so much weight on the statutory "its"; he reasoned that Congress could not have intended that by a nontaxable change in corporate form, earnings and profits — and thus dividend taxation — could so easily be eliminated. From this simple beginning great confusion developed. When corporate structure was more substantially changed by reorganization, as when new capital was introduced, or a corporation merged with another operating corporation, there was some judicial resistance to the survival of earnings after the transaction. On the other hand, some courts seem to have developed the notion that earnings and profits represent an obligation to the Government and that no tax-free transaction should impair that obligation. In Robinette,[13] Sansome was extended to apply to tax-free liquidations of subsidiaries; it was held that earnings and profits of the liquidated subsidiary should carry over to the parent. Then in Phipps [14] it was argued that earnings should be reduced when a parent corporation with substantial earnings and profits liquidated wholly owned subsidiaries having substantial deficits. Mr. Justice Murphy, fearful of tax avoidance, spoke for a unanimous Supreme Court in holding that the subsidiaries' deficits could not be allowed to offset the parent's earnings, and thus should be totally disregarded. It was evidently of no moment in the Court's view whether the parent had actually sought out and purchased deficit corporations intending to reduce the parent's earnings and profits, or whether the parent had purchased or formed the subsidiaries long before to carry on business enterprises which had subsequently soured. Rather, the controlling consideration was that, absent the tax-free unification, the parent could not have used its subsidiaries' deficits to reduce its earnings. The Court distinguished the converse situation in Harter,[15] in which a liquidated subsidiary's earnings were apparently allowed to offset the parent's deficit. Justice Murphy reasoned that since the Harter parent, without liquidation, could have made use of its deficit by having its subsidiary pay dividends to the extent of the parent's deficit, the deficit should be permitted to offset earnings on liquidation. The Phipps-Harter result seems to make the use or loss of a deficit depend on which corpora-

13. Robinette v. Commissioner, 148 F.2d 513 (9th Cir. 1945).

14. Commissioner v. Phipps, 336 U.S. 410 (1949).

15. Harter v. Helvering, 79 F.2d 12 (2d Cir. 1935). That a deficit was permitted to offset earnings is deducible only from the figures used in the opinion, not from the text of the opinion itself.

tion was the parent. Where the parent-subsidiary relationship has already been established, as will be the case when the parent acquired the subsidiary to carry on a business enterprise and thought of the benefits of liquidation only at a later time, the flexibility necessary to avoid Phipps has already been lost. But when a corporation with earnings begins with the more questionable motive of earnings reduction, it can structure the acquisition transaction so that the deficit corporation becomes the parent and survives. The simplest method would have a deficit corporation acquire the stock of a profitable corporation in a (B) reorganization and then liquidate the profitable corporation.

It would seem, then, that the reasoning of Phipps is weak and that its result — total elimination of a liquidated subsidiary's deficit when the parent has earnings — is extremely harsh. Nonetheless, as recently as 1961, the Tax Court extended the reach of Phipps to the point of absurdity. The Frelbro [17] case, arising under the 1939 Code, involved a merger of two deficit corporations. Clearly in such a case earnings reduction could not have motivated the consolidation since neither corporation had any earnings to reduce. Nevertheless the court refused to allow the deficits of the two corporations to cumulate. Its reasoning is, to say the least, questionable:

> Following petitioner's position to its logical conclusion would result in an inconsistency demonstrated by the following hypotheticals:
>
> 1. E corporation has a $1 credit balance and D has a $1 million debit balance in their respective earnings and profits accounts. In a tax-free reorganization the two are consolidated to form F and (under the Phipps doctrine) F acquires a $1 credit balance in its earnings and profits.
>
> 2. Same facts except that E has a $1 deficit in earnings and profits. F acquires $1,000,001 debit in its earnings and profits.
>
> What petitioner overlooks is that the evil which the Court was meeting in the Phipps case is still present if corporations are permitted to "pool" deficits and use them interchangeably.

The immediate "evil" in Phipps was that a parent corporation might wipe out its existing earnings and profits by liquidating its subsidiaries, and this without reference to any comparison between the parent's investment in a subsidiary's stock and the basis of the assets received on liquidation. This immediate "evil" certainly did not exist in Frelbro. If the court was worried about the "pooled" deficit offsetting future earnings, the opinion could not have been

17. Frelbro Corp., 36 T.C. 864 (1961), rev'd on other grounds, 315 F.2d 784 (2d Cir. 1963).

regarded as within Phipps. The court clearly recognized the harshness of Phipps as indicated by hypothetical (1) ; nonetheless, its decision goes a step beyond.

B.   The 1954 Code

A further surprising aspect of the Frelbro opinion is its failure to make mention of the 1954 Code. Section 381 would have applied to the facts of Frelbro had they arisen after 1954, and it is clear that in section 381(c)(2) Congress substantially qualified Phipps, retaining the immediate results of Phipps but clearly rejecting the Frelbro implications. In all liquidations or reorganizations in which the acquiring corporation takes substantially all the assets of the acquired corporation with continuity of basis the new Code provides that earnings cumulate where both corporations have earnings and that deficits cumulate where both corporations have deficits. Where one corporation has earnings and the other a deficit, both the earnings account and the deficit account carry over but do not offset each other; rather the two accounts must be separately maintained, and any earnings of the resulting corporation subsequent to the unification must first exhaust the deficit account before accumulated earnings are increased. In this compromise both the harshness of Phipps and the upstream-downstream Harter-Phipps distinction are eliminated.

The section 381 compromise is by and large a good resolution of a difficult problem. However, its treatment of deficits is not totally beyond criticism. To the shareholders of a corporation with a sure earnings future it may make very little difference in the long run whether an acquired deficit offsets future rather than accumulated earnings; however, it should be kept in mind that the accumulated earnings account must be completely exhausted before shareholders benefit from a deficit. The section 381 compromise does prevent deficits from being directly subtracted from earnings, but if the earnings and profits of the acquiring corporation were low enough to begin with so that ordinary dividend distributions sufficient to exhaust them would not be prohibitively expensive to the shareholders, then future earnings of the corporation would be distributable as capital to the extent of the deficit. Arguments may be made to undercut this criticism. First, since regardless of deficits distributions are dividends to the extent of current earnings, the picture of the prosperous corporation distributing its earnings as capital is clearly exaggerated. Nonetheless, distributions in excess of current earnings will not be treated as dividends. Second, it may be argued that a corporation with low or nonexistent accumulated earnings is not likely to have enough assurance of future earnings to make a deficit acquisition worthwhile. However, this observation would not apply to a corporation formed to carry on a new enterprise, or to an existing corporation that develops new prospects. Third, it may be argued that the abuse possible under section 381 will be curbed by section 269. It is unclear, however, that the present section 269 would have such application.

C. NET OPERATING LOSSES

---

1. MECHANICS OF THE OPERATING LOSS CARRYOVER PROVISIONS

Before attempting to analyze the impact of combination transactions on operating loss carryovers, it would be well to examine the provisions governing the carryover of losses generally.

HAWKINS, MECHANICS OF CARRYING LOSSES TO OTHER YEARS*

14 West.Res.L.Rev. 241, 242–251 (1963).

GENERAL EXPLANATION

The basic rule is that a net operating loss can be carried back three years and forward five years,[2] being "used up" against the income of these years taken in chronological order. Thus, a loss incurred in 1959 is carried first to the third preceding year, 1956. If the 1956 income was not sufficient to completely use up the loss, the balance is then carried to the second preceding year, 1957. The remainder, not used up in that year, is then carried to 1958, and the then balance, if any, is carried to 1960, the first year following the loss, and so forth.

The chronological rule applies in carrying losses *to* a year as well as *from* a year. If 1960 is assumed to be a profitable year, the total amount which can be deducted from its profits on account of net operating losses carried over from all eight years (the five preceding years plus the three following years) is known as the net operating loss *deduction* for 1960. However, in determining which losses were actually used up in eliminating the 1960 profits, one begins with the losses from the earliest of the eight years, in this case 1955. If no operating loss was incurred in 1955, or if it was incurred but was used up against the income of the years before 1960 to which it could be carried, or if the balance not used up was insufficient to wipe out all

---

* Reprinted by permission of the Western Reserve Law Review. Portions of
   the text and footnotes omitted.

2. The Code refers to "taxable years."
    Thus, a short fiscal year counts as a
    full year for carrying purposes. Treas.
    Reg. § 1.172–4(a) (2). . . .

the 1960 profits, one proceeds to the losses, if any, from the next year, 1956, and then to the losses of 1957, and so forth.

A complication in the carryover procedure lies in determining how much of the loss from 1959 was "used up" in 1956, in order to know how much of the loss remains to be carried to 1957. The "used up" portion is not simply the 1956 taxable income, but the 1956 taxable income subject to a series of modifications.[4] These modifications include some, but not all, of the modifications made in computing a net operating loss in the first place.* In particular, the net operating loss deduction is allowed but only to the extent of losses carried to the year in question, 1956, from years preceding the loss year in question, 1959.

. . .

A final basic point is the procedure involved. In preparing almost any timely income tax return, it will be possible to compute the net operating loss deduction only to the extent that this consists of loss carryovers from the five preceding years. If the succeeding three years give rise to losses the carryback of which reduces the tax due for the year in question, it is necessary to obtain a refund. This can be done either by an ordinary claim for refund or by means of a "tentative carryback adjustment." This adjustment is governed by section 6411, which provides that if the taxpayer applies for the adjustment on the proper form within twelve months of the end of the loss year, the Commissioner shall normally grant the refund within ninety days. The Commissioner need not allow the application, however, if he finds errors which he is unable or unwilling to correct within the ninety days. (The errors in question are those made in relation to the carryback: disagreement as to the merits of the return originally filed for the profitable year is not a proper gound for disallowing the application). In any event, proper or improper, the disallowance of the application for a tentative carryback adjustment is not an adequate foundation for a suit for refund. If the application procedure under section 6411 is not successful, the taxpayer must revert to a regular claim for refund.

* * *

SPECIAL PROBLEMS IN CARRYING LOSSES

Statute of Limitations

The general rule is that the statute of limitations is open for carrying back losses to earlier years as long as it is open for filing claims for

---

4. Code § 172(b) (2). . . .

* [Ed. note] In using this modified taxable income test both for computing the operating loss for a particular year and for measuring the amount of the operating loss carryover which is "used up" by the various years to which it may be carried, the 1954 Code is substantially more favorable to taxpayers than the pre-1954 "economic income" standard, which included such adjustments as adding back the 85% dividends received deduction. See United States v. Whitney Land Co., 324 F.2d 33 (8th Cir. 1963).

refund for the year in which the loss was incurred. The same rule applies in determining the limitations period for assessing deficiencies "attributable to the application to the taxpayer of a net operating loss carryback" (including a tentative carryback adjustment).

The extent to which the statute is opened up is uncertain. Under the statute governing deficiencies, assessments are limited to items "attributable to the carryback." The same test governs the Commissioner's review of an application for a tentative carryover adjustment. Both the Tax Court and the Commissioner agree that under this test, the merits of the return for the year to which the loss is carried are not opened up for re-examination: the only issue is whether the amount of the net operating loss deduction attributable to the carryback in question is correct. The Court of Appeals for the Second Circuit holds, however, that if a claim for refund is filed based on a loss carryback, the Commissioner can offset against the claim deficiencies arising from any other item for the year to which the loss is carried, even though the ordinary period of limitations on assessments for that year has expired.[20] It argues that otherwise, a taxpayer carrying back a loss is in a better position than a taxpayer actually incurring the loss in the earlier year.[21] The effect of its rule is to put taxpayers [who get a so-called "quickie" refund under the tentative carryback adjustment procedure] in a better position than taxpayers who have chosen [the regular refund approach].

* * *

Choice of Law

The loss year, the three preceding years, and the five following years, add up to a nine-year period which may be involved in a carryover problem. Since the fateful year 1913, our tax law has never survived any period of anything like this length without undergoing extensive changes. Accordingly, it is necessary to choose which of the tax laws shall prevail of those which obtained at different times during the carryover period.

While the authorities are not complete enough to permit absolute certainty, the "better view" would seem to be summed up by the following rules.

(1) The years to which a loss may be carried is determined by the law in effect in the year the loss was incurred.

---

20. Commissioner v. Van Bergh, 209 F. 2d 23 (2d Cir. 1954).

21. Id. at 24. This is probably not true. Under the Van Bergh rule, the Commissioner has a second chance to audit the earlier return, which he would not have had if the loss had been incurred in the earlier year. If the loss had been then incurred, there is no reason to suppose it would have *increased* the chance the first audit would have uncovered a different unrelated issue; it is more likely in practice that the reduction of reported taxable income would have *decreased* the revenue agent's interest. . . .

(2) All computations shall be made according to the law governing the year to which the computation primarily relates. By "computation" is meant the calculations relating to any one year, to wit, the calculation of the amount of the loss in the loss year, the calculation of the amount of the loss "used up" in an intervening year, and the calculation of the net operating loss deduction for the profitable year in question, but excluding any part of such calculation which relates primarily to another year.

(3) The statute of limitations applicable to the year of the loss determines the period for filing a refund claim based on carryback of the loss.

*   *   *

Carryover Destroyed by Capital Gain

If a corporation has a net operating loss deduction greater than its income apart from long term capital gain, the deduction may be "used up" in that year without producing any tax saving whatever.

Assume a long term capital gain of $100,000 and a net operating loss deduction which exceeds the corporation's ordinary taxable income (computed before such deduction) by $40,000. The corporation will use the "alternative tax" under which it must pay twenty-five per cent of its long term capital gain *unreduced by the net operating loss deduction*.[45] This tax would be $25,000. If the alternative tax were not used, the capital gain would be taxed as ordinary income,[46] *after* deduction of the net operating loss deduction, which would produce a tax of $25,700.

The alternative tax would be no greater and no less than if the corporation had not had a net operating loss deduction at all. Nevertheless, in computing the amount of the loss carried to the following year, the full capital gain is deducted from the loss even though the alternative tax was used.[47] On the assumed figures, accordingly, the loss would be completely wiped out in a year in which it did no good.

The same rules apply in determining whether in the year of the capital gain an excess of ordinary deductions over ordinary income gives rise to a net operating loss.[48]

NOTE ON OPERATING LOSS CARRYOVERS

A concrete example may help to illuminate the operation of the net operating loss carryover provisions. Suppose that X corporation incurred an

45. Code § 1201(a); Rev.Rul. 56–247, 1956–1 Cum.Bull. 383; Weil v. Commissioner, 229 F.2d 593 (6th Cir. 1956).

46. If an individual does not use the alternative tax he nevertheless includes only fifty per cent of the long term capital gain in ordinary income, Code § 1202, but this section does not apply to corporations. . . .

47. Code § 172(b) (2).

48. Code § 172(c).

operating loss of $20,000 in 1958. As noted above, the loss would first be carried to the earliest year to which it could apply, here 1955. Regardless of whether the year 1955 would be closed under the normal statute of limitations, it would be open for a claim for refund on account of the loss carryback from 1958 for as long as the year 1958 itself remained open for claims for refund. On the other hand, under the Van Bergh case, supra, even if 1955 were closed so far as assessment of a deficiency is concerned, the Commissioner would nevertheless be free to show that X's taxable income for that year was actually higher than the amount reported, and to use any such deficiency to offset the operating loss carryback and thereby reduce or eliminate any claim for refund.

Now suppose that X's reported taxable income for the year 1955 was exactly $0. In that event, *prima facie* none of the 1958 operating loss would be "used up" in 1955 and the entire $20,000 of loss would then be carried to 1956. Of course again in 1956 it would be open to the Commissioner to recompute X's taxable income and use any deficiency so determined to offset the loss carryback. Would it also be open to the Commissioner to recompute taxable income for 1955 for the purpose of offsetting the net operating loss carryback from 1958 by "using it up" in 1955 (although without any tax benefit to X), thereby reducing or eliminating the amount of the loss to be carried to 1956? Just this approach was sustained in Phoenix Coal Co. v. Commissioner, 231 F.2d 420 (2d Cir. 1956), where the court regarded it as a logical extension of the Van Bergh doctrine. The Phoenix Coal case was recently followed in Springfield Street Railway Co. v. United States, 160 Ct.Cl. 111, 312 F.2d 754 (1963), with a rather interesting reverse twist: the taxpayer was allowed to show that its actual taxable income for an earlier, barred year was in fact less than the amount reported, in order to reduce the amount of operating loss carryback "used up" in that year and thus increase the amount which could be carried to later, open years. Accord, Rev.Rul. 65–96, 1965–1 Cum.Bull. 126.

These same rules are operative in connection with loss carryforwards. Thus if X was seeking to carry forward the 1958 loss to subsequent years, the fact that 1958 itself had become closed under the statute of limitations would not prevent the Commissioner from recomputing the alleged loss in 1958 for the purpose of reducing or eliminating the loss carryover to later years. The State Farming Co., Inc. v. Commissioner, 40 T.C. 774 (1963); Phoenix Electronics, Inc. v. United States, 164 F.Supp. 614 (D.Mass.1958); Rev.Rul. 56–285, 1956–1 Cum.Bull. 134. Presumably the Phoenix Coal rule would be applicable to any year intervening between the loss year and the year to which the loss is being carried forward, so that even if such intervening year is itself closed the Commissioner is free to recompute taxable income for the purpose of "using up" the operating loss and reducing or eliminating the amount remaining to be carried forward to later years.

Returning now to our previous example, suppose that while there was no error in X's reported taxable income for either 1955 or 1956, X had had an operating loss in 1954 which could have been utilized as a carryforward to 1956 but was in fact never used by X at all. Assuming that it is now too late to use the 1954 loss as the basis for a refund for 1956, could the Commissioner nevertheless maintain that the 1956 taxable income had been "constructively" used up by the 1954 operating loss, so that there was no longer any 1956 income against which to apply the 1958 loss? While the Service has expressly ruled in the affirmative on this question, Rev.Rul. 218, 1953–2 Cum.Bull. 176, its position has recently been rejected in what appears to be the only litigated case on this issue. Brandon v. United States, 204 F.Supp. 912 (N.D.Ga.1962).

The Brandon opinion is rather disappointing in that it does not even mention Rev.Rul. 218, and indeed does little more than state the facts and hold for the taxpayer. But this much is clear — the Brandon case does not represent any basic departure from the general rule requiring an operating loss to be carried to other years in chronological order. For in the Brandon case the later operating loss which was the basis for the claim for refund was in fact being carried to earlier years in perfect chronological order. And the chronological requirement has been reaffirmed at least twice since Brandon (without any reference to that decision). Romer v. United States, 216 F. Supp. 832 (S.D.N.Y.1963); Eisenberg v. Commissioner, 22 T.C.M. 333 (1963).

What the Brandon decision seems to stand for is the proposition that a taxpayer may elect to waive a particular operating loss and not use it at all. At first blush, this certainly seems perfectly sensible. As Mr. Hawkins points out in a portion of his article not included in the foregoing excerpts, 14 West.Res.L.Rev. at 247, it would seem that the Commissioner could not defeat a refund claim for 1956 by showing that in that year the taxpayer overlooked some ordinary deduction, such as interest, which would have wiped out the taxable income for the year. If so, why should the result be any different where the overlooked deduction is an operating loss carryforward from 1954?

In addition, a rule contrary to Brandon could lead to an enormous proliferation of efforts to redetermine the income of barred years under the Phoenix Coal doctrine. Any time the taxpayer sought to carry a loss back to a prior year, the Commissioner could try to show that there had actually been a loss in some earlier year which could (and under a contra-Brandon view, *should*) have been carried to the year for which a refund was sought, thus "wiping out" the income of that year. Presumably, taxpayers would respond by attempting to establish that the income of some intervening year was actually higher than the amount reported, in order to absorb the loss established by the Commissioner before it could be carried to the refund year. Notice that among other things the parties' normal roles in tax litigation would be reversed, with the Commissioner trying to show that the taxpayer had a loss in some year and the taxpayer trying to show that for some other year his income was actually higher than reported.

On the other hand, the Brandon result presents the spectre of allowing a taxpayer to use the same operating loss twice. To illustrate in terms of the above example, assume that under the Brandon decision X was able to secure a refund for 1956 on the basis of the 1958 loss despite the unused 1954 loss. However, in determining whether any of the 1958 loss remained to be carried forward to 1957 and later years, X might be able to argue that none of that loss was used up in 1956, because the 1956 income was "wiped out" by the earlier 1954 loss. Such an argument is quite analogous to the one which the taxpayer successfully advanced in the Springfield Street Railway Co. case, supra. Moreover, the express language of § 172(b)(2) seems to support the argument. After providing that the "portion of [a] loss which shall be carried to each of the other 7 taxable years shall be the excess, if any, of the amount of such loss over the sum of the taxable income for each of the prior taxable years to which such loss may be carried", the statute goes on to provide that the "taxable income for any such prior taxable year" shall be adjusted to take account of the net operating loss deduction for any year prior to the loss year in question. In terms this would seem to mean that in our example the amount of the 1958 loss used up in 1956 would be no more that the 1956 income *less* the 1954 operating loss.

Hawkins, op. cit. supra, at 247–248, reached the conclusion that the same operating loss could be used twice under the Brandon rule. He did not regard this as objectionable because it would merely put the taxpayer where he would have been if he had in fact taken advantage of the earlier loss. Nevertheless, it is hard to believe that such a double use of an operating loss would be permitted. See Sanden, Techniques and Computations of the Net Operating Loss Deduction, 21 N.Y.U. Inst.Fed.Tax. 1227, 1231 (1963). It seems more likely that if the Brandon approach is to be followed, the earlier operating loss would be regarded as waived for all purposes, and therefore not be taken into account in the computation under § 172(b)(2). The same result would be reached by adopting the view that the actual use of a net operating loss carryover to secure a refund for a particular year necessarily "uses up" the loss to that extent, thereby reducing or eliminating the amount left to be carried to later years.

———

2. CARRYOVER OF OPERATING LOSSES IN CORPORATE COMBINATIONS

The question of the impact of a combination transaction on the operating loss carryovers of the constituent corporations is really but one aspect of the broader question as to how changes in the stockholders and/or business of a corporation affect its operating loss carryovers. Thus, for example, the merger of a profitable corporation into a loss corporation is in the first instance no more than a particular illustration of the acquisition of a new business by a loss corporation plus a significant change in its stockholders. Nevertheless, it is worth singling out tax-free combinations for special attention at the outset because so much of the early development concerning operating loss carryovers involved cases of this kind.

———

a. Survival of Operating Losses under Prior Law

Originally, the only statutory standard for judging whether a particular corporate transformation affected an existing loss carryover came from the words of the predecessor of § 172 allowing "the taxpayer" to utilize its operating losses. In the case of a corporation it was generally assumed that the corporate entity, rather than its owners, constituted "the taxpayer". Thus when a new corporation was organized to take over another corporation's business, the successor could not carry forward the operating loss of its predecessor even though the creditors and stockholders remained identical, because the successor was not "the taxpayer" which had sustained the loss. New Colonial Ice Co. v. Helvering, 292 U.S. 435, 54 S.Ct. 788, 78 L.Ed. 1348 (1934). The corollary of this strict entity approach seemed to be that so long as the corporation which suffered the loss did remain intact, its operating losses could be carried forward even though there had been a complete change in its stockholders and its business. Alprosa Watch Corp. v. Commissioner, 11 T.C. 240 (1948).

An important departure from this strict entity concept came in Stanton Brewery, Inc. v. Commissioner, 176 F.2d 573 (2d Cir. 1949), which held that upon the merger of a wholly-owned subsidiary into its parent, the parent was the same "taxpayer" as the subsidiary and was therefore entitled to carry forward the subsidiary's operating losses. Since the New Colonial Ice case was distinguished on the ground that no statutory merger had been involved, Stanton seemed to mean that a statutory merger (or consolidation) could be relied on to preserve the loss carryovers of each of the constituents. But in 1957 the Supreme Court laid this notion to rest in Libson Shops Inc. v. Koehler, 353 U.S. 382, 77 S.Ct. 990, 1 L.Ed.2d 924 (1957), which involved a statutory merger of sixteen separate corporations, each operating a single retail store, into the taxpayer, which performed management services for the others. All seventeen corporations were owned by the same stockholders in the same proportions. Three of the 16 retail corporations had operating loss carryovers which the taxpayer sought to carry forward against the post-merger profits of the combination. The three loss stores continued to lose money. In disallowing the carryovers, the Court rejected the view that the surviving corporation in a merger was automatically the same "taxpayer" as each of the constituents and thereby entitled to carry forward their operating losses. Instead, the Court adopted the contention of the Government that pre-merger loss carryovers could be offset against post-merger income "only to the extent that this income is derived from the operation of substantially the same business which produced the loss." Thus was born the "same business" test, which has plagued the operating loss carryover area ever since.

However, so far as tax-free combinations were concerned, the Libson Shops approach was in effect still-born, since some three years earlier the 1954 Code had already adopted a specific solution to the New Colonial Ice-Stanton hassle about the "same taxpayer" in such cases.

---

b. THE 1954 CODE TREATMENT

As previously noted, § 381 of the 1954 Code provides for a carryover of certain tax attributes of a corporation whose assets are acquired in a tax-free liquidation or reorganization, and net operating losses are expressly included, under § 381(c)(1). As we have just seen, in 1954 when the new Code provisions were adopted there had as yet been little judicial development of the rules under the 1939 Code, and in particular the Libson Shops decision was still three years away. Thus the new provisions were probably directed primarily at the conflict over corporate entity, and the major thrust was to make it clear that in the transactions covered by § 381 the operating loss carryovers of the constituent corporations could be preserved regardless of which was the surviving entity. (However, as we shall see there may still be some differences in result depending upon which corporation survives.)

Turning to the operation of § 381(c)(1), it should first be noted that the statute is not needed when the loss corporation is the surviving entity. The loss corporation can simply continue to carry forward its own operating losses against "its own" income, although of course that income is now augmented by the earnings produced by the assets obtained from the acquired profit corporation. The only special provision of note here is § 381(b)(3) which prohibits carrying back pre- or post-combination losses of the acquiring corporation against the pre-combination profits of the acquired corporation.

It is when the loss corporation is the one acquired that § 381(c) (1) is called into play. The mechanics of § 381(c)(1) are somewhat complex (although happily not as much so as they look, except where more than one of the constituents has losses to carry forward) primarily because the acquired corporation's losses may be carried forward only against the post-combination income of the acquiring corporation, and cannot be applied to any income of the acquiring corporation accrued prior to the combination date. Accordingly, unless the combination occurs on the last day of the acquiring corporation's fiscal year, it is necessary to allocate the acquiring corporation's income for that year between the pre-combination period and the post-combination period. Instead of leaving this to an actual accounting determination, the statute calls for dividing the acquiring corporation's fiscal year into two parts, referred to as the "pre-acquisition part year" and the "post-acquisition part year", and allocating the total income of the acquired corporation for the year (which would include the post-combination income or loss from the assets obtained from the acquired corporation) in proportion to the number of days in each part. The post-acquisition part year (running from the day after the acquisition to the end of the fiscal year of the acquiring corporation) then becomes the first year of the acquiring corporation to which operating losses of the acquired corporation can be carried.

As already suggested, § 381(c)(1) does not make it entirely immaterial which corporation is the surviving entity. For one thing, it will make a difference if the acquiring corporation suffers post-combination losses. Since such losses can only be carried back against the acquiring corporation's pre-combination profits, and not those of the acquired corporation, there is a distinct advantage in making the profitable corporation the surviving entity.

On the other hand, making the profitable company the acquiring corporation may result in a significant disadvantage in connection with the period for which the corporation's losses can be carried forward. That is because by virtue of § 381(b)(1) the taxable year of the acquired corporation ends on the date of the acquisition, which means that unless the acquisition takes place on the last day of the acquired corporation's year, a short taxable year for the acquired corporation will result. But that short taxable year still counts as one of the five years for which an operating loss may be carried forward under § 172(b)(1), see Reg. § 1.381(c)(1)–1(e)(3); and the post-acquisition part year of the acquiring corporation to which the loss carryover of the acquired corporation is first carried also counts as one of the years in the § 172(b)(1) computation. Accordingly, whenever the loss company is the acquired corporation and the acquisition does not occur at the end of that company's fiscal year, the result will be some reduction in the permissible carryover period; and in the common case where the two corporations are both on a calendar year (or otherwise have the same fiscal year), the carryover period will be reduced by a full year, from five years to four. To illustrate, if two calendar year taxpayers were combined on June 30, 1964, the acquired loss corporation's short taxable year 1/1/64–6/30/64 would count as one of the five years under § 172(b)(1), and the post-acquisition part year of the acquiring corporation, 7/1/64–12/31/64, would also count as a year. If instead the loss corporation were the surviving entity, all of 1964 would only count as one year in the computation of the five year carryover period.

It may help to illustrate the operation of § 381(c)(1) with a concrete example. Suppose that X corporation's operating history for the five years prior to 1964 was as follows:

Year	(Net Loss)
1963	0
1962	($30,000)
1961	(60,000)
1960	(50,000)
1959	(35,000)

Suppose further than on November 1, 1964, at which time X's net income before taxes for the year to date amounts to $30,000, X is merged into Y corporation in a transaction to which § 381 applies. Y's total income before taxes for the calendar year 1964 (including the contribution made by X's assets during the last one-sixth of the year, November 1 to December 31) turns out to be $408,000.

In computing the loss carryover from X to Y, it should first be noted that none of the 1959 loss of $35,000 can be included. That loss expired in X's short taxable year ending October 31, 1964, which constituted the fifth year after the year of the loss. Of course $30,000 of that $35,000 loss served to offset the income earned by X during its short taxable year ending October 31, 1964; but the remaining $5,000 of loss would expire without producing any tax advantage. If the amount of carryover wasted in this way was more substantial, consideration would have to be given to making the loss corporation the acquiring corporation, which as noted above would eliminate the short taxable year for the loss corporation and allow the remainder of the 1959 loss to be applied against the earnings of the combined enterprise for the period November 1 to December 31, 1964. Alternatively, where, as here, the loss corporation is currently producing earnings, the waste of loss carryover could be avoided (or at least reduced) by postponing the combination transaction until December 31, 1964, thereby again eliminating the short taxable year for X and making it possible to at least apply the remaining balance of the 1959 loss against X's own earnings for the rest of the year 1964.

Assuming, however, that the merger of X into Y on November 1, 1964 took place as assumed, the loss carryover from X to Y would total $140,000; and the first year to which that amount could be carried would be Y's post-acquisition part year, running from November 1, 1964 to December 31, 1964. Y's income before taxes for that post-acquisition part year would be computed by determining the amount which bears the same ratio to Y's total income before taxes for 1964 ($408,000) as the number of days in the post-acquisition part year (61) bears to the total number of days in the year (366), or one-sixth of $408,000. The resulting figure, $68,000, would represent the amount of Y's 1964 income which could be offset by X's loss carryover. (Notice that if this figure had been less than $50,000, so that less than $50,000 of X's loss carryover could be used in 1964, the difference between the amount actually so used and $50,000 would be wasted, since X's 1960 loss of $50,000 would have expired in any event in Y's post-acquisition part year, that being the 5th year after the year in which the $50,000 loss was incurred.) The remaining $72,000 of X's loss carryover would be available to be carried forward against Y's income for 1965 and subsequent years.

---

3.   LIMITATIONS ON LOSS CARRYOVERS IN COMBINATION TRANSACTIONS

a.   SECTION 382(b)

After granting broad authority to carry over operating losses in combination transactions in § 381, the 1954 Code expressly limits this privilege by providing in § 382(b) for a reduction in the loss carryovers unless the stockholders of the loss corporation end up with at least 20% of the fair market value of the outstanding stock of the combined enterprise. An excellent analysis of § 382(b) appears in the following:

COMMENT, NET OPERATING LOSS CARRYOVERS AND CORPORATE ADJUSTMENTS: RETAINING AN ADVANTAGEOUS TAX HISTORY UNDER LIBSON SHOPS AND SECTIONS 269, 381, AND 382 [13]

69 Yale L.J. 1249–1257 (1960).

For example, where X, a loss corporation, was merged into Y Corporation in an (A) reorganization, Y Corporation — the survivor — will inherit X's carryover without limitation by section 382(b) only if X's former shareholders receive at least a 20 per cent interest in Y. Section 382(b) also affects transactions not governed by section 381(a) since carryforwards of the acquiring corporation are expressly made subject to its provisions; section 381(a) deals only with the tax attributes of the transferor corporation.

Thus, if Y Corporation merged into X Corporation, a loss corporation, in an (A) reorganization, . . . unless X's former shareholders retain a 20 per cent interest in X, section 382(b) would limit X's own carryover. Stated differently, if Y's former shareholders receive more than 80 per cent interest in X pursuant to the plan of reorganization, X's carryover will be reduced. Section 382(b) does not apply to tax-free liquidations of subsidiaries (although they are included within 381(a) (1)), taxfree transactions other than those described in section 381(a) (2),* or any taxable transaction. Additionally, section 382(b) has no applicability to carrybacks.

Underlying section 382(b) is an apparent belief that certain shifts in ownership indicate abuse of the corporate carryover privilege. Congress did not want a totally new group of shareholders to reap the benefit of a loss incurred by a corporation under different ownership even though the loss corporation's shareholders have benefited by receiving a premium as a result of the carryover. Thus, the statute attempts to ensure that the corporation which ultimately utilizes the carryover be at least one-fifth owned by persons on whom the loss "really" fell. Congress might have left prevention of manipulation of losses to section 269. But the difficulties of proving a principal tax avoidance purpose highlighted the need for an "objective" test

---

13. Copyright, Yale Law Journal, 1960. Reprinted by permission. Portions of the text and most of the footnotes omitted.

* [Ed. note] Thus a transaction consisting of a stock acquisition qualifying under § 368(a) (1) (B) followed by a liquidation qualifying under § 332 would literally be free of § 382(b). However, the regulations warn that such a two-step acquisition may well be viewed as a § 368(a) (1) (C) reorganization "for purposes of § 382 (b)." Reg. § 1.382(b)–1(c).

which could be used to disallow carryovers. Perhaps the search for objectivity also prompted the failure to adopt any type of "same business" test. Whatever the rationale, many problems of construction arise under section 382(b) which may diminish its value as an objective supplement to section 269.

The first hurdle in determining whether the stockholders of the loss corporation own less than a 20 per cent interest of the acquiring corporation is ascertainment of the "stockholders" of the loss corporation. Section 382(b) might be interpreted to require that every shareholder of the loss corporation receive stock in the acquiring corporation. But under the usual "continuity of interest" test applied in reorganizations only the group as a whole is considered. Thus if any shareholder of the loss corporation, or any group of shareholders, own the requisite 20 per cent, section 382(b) will probably be satisfied. .   .   .

The continuity of interest might be rendered nugatory unless section 382(b)'s reference to "immediately after the reorganization" is given an expansive meaning. .   .   .   To prevent avoidance of section 382(b), "immediately after the reorganization" should be interpreted in the same manner as those words are read under section 351. Under this reading, a sale of stock shortly after the reorganization which is deemed an integral part of the transaction will disqualify the shares sold from being counted toward the 20 per cent since "momentary control" would not be sufficient. .   .   .

In one situation, the requirement that the loss corporation's *shareholders* own stock in the acquiring corporation "immediately after" the reorganization may make the allowance of a carryforward under section 381(a) illusory. .   .   .   If the transferor-loss corporation retains the stock, its stockholders would not "own" the stock of the acquiring corporation "immediately after" the transaction and the 20 per cent continuity of interest requirement would not be satisfied. .   .   .   This problem may be avoided if the transaction is cast so that the loss corporation is the acquiring corporation in the (C) reorganization. The loss corporation's shareholders would continue to "own" the same stock which they had previously owned; whether the transferor remained in existence would be unimportant since ownership of stock by the nonloss corporation's shareholders is irrelevant under section 382(b).

*   *   *

If no problems of ownership arise, owners of the loss corporation will still have to demonstrate that their interest in the acquiring corporation qualifies as "stock." For purposes of section 382 "stock" is defined, in section 382(c), as "all shares except nonvoting stock which is limited and preferred as to dividends." Thus either voting or financial equity in the acquiring corporation will suffice. The theory underlying section 382(b) was apparently that the loss corporation's shareholders must retain a significant economic stake in the acquiring corporation so that "too much" of the carryover's benefit does not accrue to outsiders. The right to vote, however, does not seem sufficiently related to enjoyment of the carryover. Additionally, the statute does not give specific content to the phrase "nonvoting stock" and it could be interpreted narrowly so that any stock with a contingent right to vote would qualify as "stock." On the other hand, if the construction of a similar phrase in section 1504 which defines the type of stock ownership required for consolidated returns "affiliation" will be applicable to section 382(c), stock possessing the right to vote only when dividend arrearages or other contingencies occur will probably not qualify. In any event, use of voting preferred stock to acquire a carryover is limited by section 382(b)'s requirement that the stock represent 20 per cent of the fair market value of the acquiring corporation's "stock." When a profitable corporation acquires a loss corporation's assets many shares of such nonparticipating stock will probably have to be issued for the value to equal 20 per cent of all outstanding "stock."

Owning stock in the acquiring corporation will not satisfy section 382(b), however, unless persons holding such stock acquired it "as a result of owning stock of the loss corporation." Apparently section 382(c)'s definition of "stock" applies to the stock previously owned as well as to that acquired, so that the new shareholders of the acquiring corporation must have held either voting stock in the loss corporation or stock which was not limited and preferred as to dividends. This requirement creates a strict continuity-of-interest test, since only the interest of persons with voting or financial equity in both the loss corporation and the acquiring corporation will be counted toward the requisite 20 per cent. Curiously, however, a person with a financial equity in the loss corporation and only voting equity in the acquiring corporation will, under the statutory language, be counted, even though his interest has been drastically altered. The Senate Committee Report on section 382(b) indicated that the section was designed only to force the acquiring corporation to give up a 20 per cent share. This result could have been achieved by focusing solely on the stock given up, without regard to the prior interest of the new owners. But even if the statutory definition of "stock" is applied to the interest given up by the loss corporation's shareholders, the restriction may be circumvented. Knowing that a merger is imminent, the shareholders of the loss corporation can agree to a recapitalization which will give the preferred stock voting rights. Stock subsequently obtained by the preferred holders will thus be counted toward the 20 per cent requirement. The extent to which the Service must recognize this transaction is speculative.

Section 382(b) (6) may provide another method of avoiding the requirement that the 20 per cent be held by former holders of the loss corporation's "stock." This subsection was designed to mesh the general 20 per cent requirement with three party transactions qualifying as (C) reorganizations. . . . In contrast to section 382(b) (1) (B) which applies to two party transactions, section 382(b) (6) only refers to a 20 per cent interest obtained "as a result of the reorganization" and not "as a result of owning stock in the loss corporation." Thus section 382(b) (6) seems to ignore the quality of stock given up by the loss corporation's stockholders. Under this construction, the limitations of section 382(b) (1) (B) on the type of stock which must be surrendered by the loss corporation's shareholders could be evaded by recasting an ordinary two-party (C) reorganization as a three-party transaction. . . . This evasion can be frustrated, however, if "stockholders" in section 382(b) (6) is construed to incorporate section 382(c)'s definition of "stock." The difference in language between section 382(b) (6) and section 382(b) (1) (B) was probably inadvertent and no difference in outcome was intended.

The entire 20 per cent problem is moot if the reorganization involves two corporations owned by the same economic group. Under section 382(b) (3) the limitation of the carryforward "shall not apply if the transferor corporation and the acquiring corporation are owned substantially by the same persons in the same proportion."[248] Congress must have assumed that such transactions do not involve tax avoidance, because the people whose corporation sustained the loss are the persons who will ultimately benefit from the carryforward. In any event, section 382(b) (3) may have little significance in the light of section 382(b) (1) (B). Assume that individuals A and B each own 50 per cent of loss corporation X and profitable corporation Y. If X is merged into Y in a (C) reorganization so that A and B surrender their stock in X for stock in Y, section 382(b) (1) (B) is satisfied if the new stock they receive in Y is equivalent to 20 per cent of the value of Y's outstanding stock. This requirement presents no difficulty since A and B's equity interests will be unaffected if Y Corporation prints new stock certificates to satisfy the 20 per cent requirement. Therefore, while section 382(b) (3) eliminates the need to issue new stock in this situation, it is not needed to transfer the carryover.[250] Even for this limited purpose section 382(b) (3) may

---

248. This language seems to have meant "owned by *substantially* the same persons in *substantially* the same proportions." In the statute as written it is arguable that "substantially" (an adverb) modifies "owned"; therefore "same persons in the same proportion" means exactly the same. [Ed. note: The regulations contain examples indicating that where two persons each own 50% of the stock of one corporation, ownership of 48% and 52% respectively of the second corporation's would qualify under § 382(b) (3), but ownership of 60%, and 40% would not. Reg. § 1.382(b)–1(d) (2), Ex. 1 and 2.]

250. If X Corporation is worth substantially less than Y Corporation, however, the Commissioner could argue, in the absence of § 382(b) (3), that the 20% interest was not acquired as a result of the surrender of X stock but only to meet the statutory requirement. Such an argument would be based on the origin of the 20% requirement. The original House bill denied nonrecognition treatment to reorganizations of closely held companies where, in general, one of the two combining corporations was worth more than four times as much as the other. Hence, the 20% test of § 382

be difficult to apply because no content is given to the word "own." Suppose that an individual owns stock in the acquiring corporation and bonds in the transferor. In some circumstances a bondholder may be viewed as an owner, but section 382(b) (3) does not indicate whether "ownership" includes ownership of stock or securities other than those defined in 382(c). Additionally, there is no indication whether ownership in "substantially . . . the same proportion" is to be measured by financial equity or by voting equity. Since voting equity is sufficient for other parts of section 382(b), a substantially similar share of voting power in both corporations may satisfy section 382(b) (3) although financial interests are disparate. Or, perhaps only financial interests are to be considered, irrespective of voting rights.* Once the measuring factors are ascertained, what is "substantially . . . in the same proportion" will still have to be determined.

If section 382(b) (3) is inapplicable and the 20 per cent requirement of section 382(b) (1) (B) is not satisfied, section 382(b) (2) provides for a proportional reduction of the amount of the available carryforward. The carryforward will be reduced 5 per cent for every one per cent less than 20 which the loss corporation's shareholders obtain or retain in the acquiring corporation. For example, if these shareholders obtain twelve per cent, the acquiring corporation will inherit $^{12}/_{20}$ (60 per cent) of the carryover. . . .

NOTE ON MECHANICS OF § 382(b)

The mechanics of reducing an operating loss carryover pursuant to § 382 (b) are somewhat complicated by the need for integrating the reduction into the general carryforward process, under which the operating loss of each prior year is applied in chronological order and expires after a period of five years. One way of handling this would be simply to reduce the operating loss of each prior year by the percentage called for under § 382(b) and then just follow the normal procedure for "using up" the balance of each such loss. To illustrate, suppose that at the time of its acquisition on November 1, 1964, X had a total operating loss carryover of $140,000, consisting of $120,000 which was incurred in 1960 and was due to expire in the post-acquisition part year of 1964 of the acquiring corporation, Y, and $20,000 incurred in 1961 and therefore not due to expire until Y's year 1965. Suppose further that the stockholders of X received 13.4% of the stock of Y, which would make the § 382(b) reduction 33%. If this reduction percentage was simply applied to each year's losses, the carryovers from X would become $80,400 due to expire in Y's 1964 post-acquisition part year, and $13,400 due to expire in 1965, making a total carryover of $93,800. These losses would first be carried to Y's post-acquisition part year, in which, let us assume, the income before

<hr>

(b). The Government could, on this theory, argue that "as a result of owning stock in the loss corporation" requires a comparison of the values of the transferor and acquiring corporations. . . .

* [Ed. note] The regulation examples indicate that "fair market value", which is expressly the factor to which the basic 20% test is applied, will also be used in applying the § 382(b) (3) test. Reg. § 1.382(b)–1(d) (2).

taxes (computed in accordance with § 381(c) (1)) amounted to $68,000. In that event, only $68,000 of the loss carryover would be effectively "used" in Y's post-acquisition part year; but the entire $80,400 from the 1960 loss would be gone, having expired by the passage of time, and only the $13,400 from the 1961 loss would be available as a carryforward to 1965.

While the foregoing would seem to be an entirely appropriate method for handling the § 382(b) reduction, the statute in fact calls for a different procedure. Under § 382(b)(1) the reduction is applied in gross to "the total net operating loss carryover from prior taxable years of the loss corporation to the first taxable year of the acquiring corporation ending after the date of transfer". However, as a corollary to this approach § 382(b)(4) provides that in computing the loss carryovers to subsequent taxable years, the income for that first taxable year of the combined enterprise must be constructively increased by the total amount of the § 382(b) reduction.

Applying this procedure to the foregoing example, the total loss carryover from X to Y's post-acquisition part year would be reduced to $93,800, just as before; and again $68,000 of that amount would be offset against Y's net income for that period. The difference comes in computing the amount of loss carryover which can be carried forward to 1965. Here the § 382(b) reduction is ignored, and the computation is made upon the basis of the original, unreduced amount of the loss carryovers; but in determining how much of the loss carryovers was "used up" in Y's post-acquisition part year the income of that period is treated as though it was actually larger by the amount of the § 382(b) reduction. Thus the amount of X's loss carryover used up in Y's post-acquisition part year would amount to $114,200 (actual net income of $68,000 plus constructive increase of $46,200), thereby apparently leaving $25,800 of loss to be carried forward to 1965. Actually, of course the full $25,800 could not be carried to 1965, since the entire $120,000 loss from 1960 would have expired by the passage of time, regardless of how much of it had been "used up" in Y's post-acquisition part year, and only the $20,000 loss from 1961 would remain eligible for carryforward. But the important point is that since under the statutory procedure the § 382(b) reduction is only applicable as such in the first year of Y to which X's losses are carried, and not to any subsequent years, the entire $20,000 loss from 1961 could be carried to 1965, whereas under the previous approach the carryforward to 1965 was limited to $13,400.

What this means is that the mechanics adopted by the statute throw the major brunt of a § 382(b) reduction upon the losses of the earliest years, instead of spreading it pro rata among all of the losses of prior years. This approach is quite favorable to taxpayers, since it does not seem that it could ever produce any disadvantage, and it may often materially benefit the taxpayer, as it does in the foregoing case where all of the § 382(b) reduction is offset against losses which would have expired by the passage of time anyway.

---

b.   SECTION 382(a)

Section 382(a) represents an effort to establish objective criteria for limiting a corporation's carryover of its own operating losses where there has been a substantial change in the stock ownership of the corporation *and* it has not continued to carry on substantially the same business conducted before the change in stock ownership. This of course is the classic case of "trafficking in loss corporations", with which Congress was particularly concerned in 1954. See S.Rep.No. 1622, 83d Cong., 2d Sess. 53 (1954). However, § 382(a) has no application to tax-free combination transactions even if the loss corporation remains in existence (as where it is the acquiring corporation, or where it is the acquired corporation in a B reorganization and is not liquidated), since § 382(a) (4) expressly confines this provision to cases when the change in stock ownership does not involve any carry-over basis; in a tax-free combination, of course, the change in the loss corporation's stock ownership would involve a carryover basis. Accordingly, further consideration of § 382(a) will be postponed until the discussion of operating loss carryovers in non-reorganization transactions, in paragraph 4 below.

c. THE LIBSON SHOPS DOCTRINE

Although the Libson Shops case, page 848 supra, was decided under the 1939 Code, the Service has insisted that the "same business" test announced there may also be applicable under the 1954 Code. However, as the following excerpt indicates, the Service has not sought to import this doctrine into the tax-free combination area, so here again further discussion of the issue will be postponed until paragraph 4 below.

REVENUE RULING 58–603

1958–2 Cum.Bull. 147.

In Libson Shops, Inc., v. Koehler, . . . the Supreme Court of the United States announced the principle that, under the Internal Revenue Code of 1939, a surviving corporation in a merger may not carry over and deduct pre-merger net operating losses of one business against post-merger income of another business which was operated and taxed separately before the merger. The principle announced in that case will not be relied upon by the Internal Revenue Service under the Internal Revenue Code of 1954 as to a merger or any other transaction described in section 381(a) of the 1954 Code. However, see sections 382(b) and 269 of the 1954 Code for the possible disallow-ance of net operating loss carryovers in such transactions . . .

------

d. SECTION 269

An analysis of the development of § 269 as an anti-avoidance tool appears at pages 168–169, supra, and should be reviewed at this point. In recent years the Service has had a good deal of success in relying upon § 269 in the area of loss carryovers. See generally, Feder, The

Application of Section 269 to Corporations Having Net Operating Loss Carryovers and Potential Losses, 21 N.Y.U.Inst.Fed.Tax 1277 (1963). Moreover, in 1962 the final regulations under § 269 finally appeared, and they clearly confirm the Service's intention to apply this section quite broadly to limit "trafficking" in loss carryovers. Needless to say, however, there remain a number of unanswered problems in connection with § 269, quite apart from the always troublesome questions associated with determining purpose.

The potential impact of § 269 on combination transactions can best be illustrated by a series of examples. Consider first the typical case in which a loss corporation is acquired in a merger (or assets acquisition) to which § 381 applies. Such a transaction would obviously be subject to § 269(a)(2), since the acquiring profit corporation would take the acquired loss corporation's property at the latter's basis. Would it make any difference if the loss carryovers had already been reduced to some extent (but not eliminated) under § 382 (b)? The Senate Finance Committee Report, S.Rep.No.1622, 83d Cong., 2d Session 284 (1954), contains an implication that once § 382 (b) applies to limit a carryover, § 269 "shall not also be applied". But this would mean that by planning for a small reduction under § 382(b), complete immunity from § 269 could be obtained. Reg. § 1.269–6 flatly rejects this position and requires that to whatever extent a carryover survives § 382(b) it must also pass the screen of § 269.

Suppose that the combination takes the form of the loss corporation acquiring the profitable one. Assuming that the former stockholders of the profit corporation end up with at least 50% of the stock of the loss corporation, the transaction would be subject to § 269(a) (1) — unlike § 382(a), § 269(a).(1) is equally applicable to tax-free acquisitions of control. Presumably, § 269(a)(2) could also be applicable, since the loss corporation has acquired the profit corporation's property and holds it at a carryover basis. To be sure, that acquisition of property from the profit corporation did not itself produce or increase any loss carryover, but it does enable the loss corporation to enjoy the benefit of its already-existing loss carryover, and under the Coastal Oil approach to § 269(a)(2), see page 169 supra, that may be enough to bring this section into play.

However, this example serves as another illustration of the flaw in the Coastal Oil interpretation of § 269(a)(2). If the loss corporation acquires profit-making assets in a taxable transaction, § 269(a) (2) would clearly be inapplicable even though the tax benefit would be exactly the same. In other words, in this situation the carryover of asset basis, despite being the operative condition for the application of § 269(a)(2), is actually irrelevant to the tax benefit achieved. It may make more sense to confine § 269(a)(2) to cases where the tax benefit in question is related to the carryover of asset basis, either directly, as in the case of high basis, low value assets, or collaterally, as in the case of a corresponding carryover of losses. See Feder, op. cit. supra, at 1297–98.

Curiously, the regulations contain no example of a combination transaction involving the acquisition of a profit corporation by a loss corporation. But this much seems clear: one way or another, § 269 should be no less applicable when the combination transaction proceeds in this direction as when the profit corporation acquires the loss corporation.

Suppose that the combination takes the form of an acquisition of the stock of the loss corporation by the profit corporation. What alternatives are available for offsetting the loss carryovers against the profits of the acquiring corporation (apart from using consolidated returns, which will be discussed in the next section)? One possibility is to liquidate the subsidiary loss corporation and try to transfer the loss carryovers to the parent profit corporation under § 381(c)(1). But that is possible, per § 381(a)(1), only if the parent takes the assets from the subsidiary at the latter's basis under § 334(b)(1) (rather than at the parent's cost of the stock under § 334(b)(2)) — and in that event, § 269(a)(2) would be operative, just as it would in the case of a direct asset acquisition in an A or C reorganization. To be sure, the exception for common control in § 269(a)(2) would be literally applicable, but the fleeting control involved in these circumstances would probably be ignored under the step transaction doctrine.

Another possibility would be for the parent corporation to transfer some of its own profit-making assets to its newly-acquired subsidiary. Under the Coastal Oil interpretation, § 269(a)(2) would seem to be applicable: the transfer of assets would enable the loss corporation to "enjoy" its existing carryovers. And the exception for common control would not apply since neither the transferee (subsidiary) corporation nor its stockholders would have been in control of the transferor (parent) corporation immediately before the transfer. The regulations, § 1.269–6, Ex. 3, expressly provide that this type of case is subject to § 269(a)(2), thus confirming the Coastal Oil approach. However, it should be noted that the regulation example specifies that it is dealing with a case in which if the loss subsidiary was liquidated its assets would be taken by the parent at the latter's stock cost under § 334(b)(2), and the operating losses would not carryover under § 381(c)(1). This seems to be an effort to make it clear that acquisition of the stock of the loss corporation did not qualify as a B reorganization (since a reorganization acquisition would not constitute a "purchase" under § 334(b)(3) and hence a § 334(b)(2) basis would not be possible); but the example gives no clue as to what difference it would make, if any, if the circumstances were otherwise so that the losses would carryover in a liquidation.

Presumably § 269(a)(1) could also apply to this type of case, under a kind of step transaction approach, if the purpose of the profit corporation's acquisition of control of the loss corporation was to obtain the benefit of the latter's loss carryovers by transferring profit-making assets to it.

What is the role of § 269(c) in combination transactions? As is true of the rest of § 269, subsection (c) applies equally to tax-free acquisitions. But it is difficult to fathom just what this provision was designed to accomplish. Reg. § 1.269–5 indicates that "substantially disproportionate to" is intended to mean "substantially less than". Applying this interpretation to a purchase of high basis, low value assets, it would appear that the presumption arises if the purchase price is based primarily on value, and does not include any additional element for the attractive tax attributes. In other words, the section seems to treat the beneficial tax attributes as property which the purchaser *should pay for*, although the general theme of § 269 would seem to cut the other way, i. e., that the purchaser should not be buying the tax attributes as such. This curious inconsistency has been noted by the Tax Court on several occasions. See H. F. Ramsey Co. Inc. v. Commissioner, 43 T.C. 500, 517 (1965); The Wallace Corporation v. Commissioner, 23 T.C.M. 39, 53, note 6 (1964). In any event, it seems likely that a purchaser who is not swayed by tax factors and sticks to asset value will not run afoul of § 269, no matter how "disproportionate" the price within the meaning of § 269(c). This means that the onus of § 269(c) may fall most heavily upon the purchaser who does pay something extra on account of the tax attributes, so that he can not deny that the potential tax advantages were in the picture, but does not pay enough extra to escape the "substantially disproportionate" price test. And what standards are available for determining how much is "enough" in this context, bearing in mind the uncertainty of the value of the prospective tax benefits in view of their dependence on the purchaser's future income?

---

e.   CONSOLIDATED RETURNS

The following case serves as both a postscript to the preceding material on § 269 and an introduction to the subject of consolidated returns.

ZANESVILLE INVESTMENT CO. v. COMMISSIONER [14]

United States Courts of Appeals, Sixth Circuit, 1964.   335 F.2d 507.

LEVIN, DISTRICT JUDGE. The question presented for decision is whether Section 269 of the Internal Revenue Code of 1954 or some judicially enunciated principle of law prevents the offsetting in a consolidated return of cash operating losses and losses realized on

14. Portions of the opinion and all of
the footnotes omitted.

the sale of physical assets sustained after affiliation by one corporate member of an affiliated group with the post-affiliation profits of another corporate member thereof, where it could be anticipated that such operating losses would be incurred.

The cases principally relied on by the Government are not apposite, as they all concern situations where a taxpayer was attempting to utilize built-in tax losses (i. e., losses which had economically accrued prior to the affiliation but which had not as yet been realized in a tax sense), whereas the taxpayer in this case is attempting to offset actual cash losses incurred both economically and taxwise after the affiliation.

Since the Government cites no authority in point and independent research discloses none, it will be necessary to review the history of Section 269 and the consolidated returns provisions to determine whether the interpretation sought by the Commissioner is correct. The facts of this case are as follows:

During the period 1951 through August 31, 1955, a coal mine corporation (Muskingum Coal Company), which in prior years had been highly profitable (almost four million dollars of net income in the period 1945 to 1950), sustained operating losses of about $730,000 in an attempt to develop a new mine opening to replace the prior mine opening which had been exhausted. These losses had been financed in part by loans from the taxpayer and its wholly-owned subsidiary, Earl J. Jones Enterprises, Inc., totaling $320,268.68, during the period from September 1953 to August 1955, of which $42,930.79 was repaid. Enterprises was profitably engaged in operating a newspaper.

In September 1955, Muskingum was in the process of attempting to solve its problems through a new type of mechanization, but encountered continuing difficulty. Muskingum did not have adequate funds either to finance the purchase of such equipment or absorb the operating losses that almost certainly would continue to be sustained before profitable operations might be expected.

At this juncture, on September 1, 1955, Earl J. Jones, the sole stockholder of Muskingum since 1945, transferred all the stock thereof to the taxpayer (of which, since 1948, he was also the sole stockholder).

The Tax Court found (38 T.C. at p. 414) that the principal purpose of the transfer to the taxpayer of the stock of Muskingum (the losing coal mine business) was to utilize Muskingum's "anticipated" losses on a consolidated return to be filed with the other members of the affiliated group, including the profitable newspaper publisher (Enterprises) and that this was interdicted under the provisions of Section 269 . . .

The taxpayer, Enterprises, and Muskingum filed consolidated returns for 1955 and 1956. Muskingum sustained an operating loss of $176,806 during the period September 1 to December 31, 1955, and an operating loss of $369,950 during the period January 1 to July 10, 1956. In July 1956 Muskingum sold its mine properties at a net loss of about $480,000 and later filed a petition in bankruptcy. Enterprises' taxable income in 1955 was $175,283.61 and during the first seven months of 1956 was $102,496.46. Enterprises operated profitably also in subsequent periods.

Both prior and subsequent to affiliation, Muskingum's operations were extensive, its sales were at an annual rate in excess of two million dollars, and it employed several hundred persons throughout the period in question. Muskingum attempted to sell its properties between October 1955 and June 1956, and various transactions were discussed, negotiated, and, in two cases, documented; but none was consummated. Had any been consummated, Muskingum's properties would have been disposed of at a tax gain rather than a loss.

It is not disputed that Muskingum and the other members of the affiliated group that were financing it were engaged in a good faith but unsuccessful attempt to overcome the engineering problems and thereby render operations at the second mine opening economically profitable. In this connection, the taxpayer and Enterprises made further advances of $161,359.28 to Muskingum in the post-affiliation period, of which $44,966.59 was repaid. The total investment in physical assets, in an attempt to bring in the second mine opening, was $1,026,610.30, of which $247,309.01 was spent in the post-affiliation period. It would thus appear that approximately $247,000 of the $480,000 net loss realized on the sale of Muskingum's properties was paid for in cash after affiliation. The Government has not contended that such loss was incurred in an economic sense prior to affiliation.

Section 129 of the Internal Revenue Code of 1939, now Section 269 of the I.R.C. of 1954, was added in early 1944 to prevent the distortion through tax avoidance of the deduction, credit, and allowance provisions of the Code and, particularly, the then recently developed practice of corporations with large incomes acquiring corporations with built-in losses, credits, or allowances . . . . Most of the cases that have arisen under Section 269 and its predecessor, Section 129, have dealt with the sale by one control group to another of a corporation with, typically, a net-operating loss carryover, and the efforts of the new control group to utilize this carryover by funneling otherwise taxable income to a point of alleged confluence with the carryover.

Until this case, the Commissioner made no attempt in the approximately twenty years since enactment of Section 129 (now Section 269), so far as the reported cases indicate, to deny a taxpayer the right to offset an out-of-pocket dollar loss incurred after affiliation with post-affiliation income. We do not believe that Section 269 requires such a result.

An examination of the Senate Finance Committee report accompanying the Revenue Act of 1943, which enacted Section 129 of the I.R.C. of 1939, reveals that the statutory language cannot be mechanically interpreted and that all acquisitions that result in tax saving are not prohibited. The test, according to the Senate Finance Committee, is:

". . . whether the transaction or a particular factor thereof 'distorts the liability of the particular taxpayer' when the 'essential nature' of the transaction or factor is examined in the light of the *'legislative plan'* which the deduction or credit is intended to effectuate." 1944 Cum.Bull., p. 1017. (Emphasis added.)

* * *

In deciding whether the essential nature of the transaction before this court violates the "legislative plan," the fact that the Tax Court's decision is the first in the heavily litigated tax field where a court was asked to deny a taxpayer the right to use real post-affiliation losses, incurred and paid in cash after affiliation, against post-affiliation income suggests that the legislative plan may not be violated by allowing the deduction.

Individuals, partnerships, and corporations have long been permitted to offset the losses incurred in one business of the taxpayer against profits realized by another business of the same taxpayer. Thus, there is no "legislative plan" that prohibits such offsetting. In fact, the Internal Revenue Code permits an individual, partnership, or corporate taxpayer to do just that.

But here, the loss was incurred by one entity, and the profit was realized by another. What is the legislative plan in this regard?

Congress first required and now permits certain affiliated corporations to file consolidated returns and to offset the losses of one against the profits of another. The consolidated return regulations forbid the use of pre-affiliation losses of one entity against pre- or post-affiliation consolidated income (Reg. 1.1502–31(b) (3)) but have never suggested that post-affiliation losses may not be utilized against post-affiliation consolidated income. In fact, these regulations specifically permit the use of post-affiliation losses against post-affiliation consolidated income. (Reg. 1.1502–31(b)).

All the cases cited by the Government where consolidation was denied involved situations where the taxpayer sought to take advantage of the realization after affiliation of losses which in an economic sense had occurred prior to the affiliation. In J. D. & A. B. Spreckels Company, 41 B.T.A. 370 (1940), after the loss corporation had contracted to sell its remaining asset at a tax loss of $192,000, its sole stockholder transferred all its capital stock to the taxpayer there before the court. The sale was consummated, and the economic loss of $192,000 incurred prior to the affiliation was realized in a tax sense.

The Tax Court (then the Board of Tax Appeals) refused to permit such loss (which, to repeat, had accrued prior to the affiliation) to be utilized against the income of other members of the new affiliated group.

In Elko Realty Company, 29 T.C. 1012 (1958), affirmed in Elko Realty Company v. Commissioner, 260 F.2d 949 (3rd Cir. 1958), the taxpayer corporation acquired for a nominal consideration the stock of two separate corporations each owning apartment houses which were subject to FHA insured mortgages in excess of their cost, and an attempt was made to utilize the large depreciation losses against consolidated income. It was found that there was no intent that the apartment house corporations could ever be made to operate profitably. There was no showing that the value of the apartment houses at the time of the acquisition equalled the bases for depreciation. Compare Regulation 1.1502–31(b) excluding in the determination of the consolidated income deductions with respect to the sale or exchange of capital assets to the extent that such deductions are attributable to events preceding the affiliation.

R. P. Collins & Co., Inc. v. United States, 303 F.2d 142 (1st Cir. 1962), was concerned with an acquisition by one control group from another of stock of a corporation owning property with a built-in tax loss. A deduction for the tax loss was claimed on the subsequent sale of the property and realization of the economic loss incurred prior to affiliation. Post-affiliation operating losses were also suffered and a majority of the court thought that their utilization should also be denied because once it was determined that the acquisition was within the coverage of Section 269 all losses, including post-affiliation economic losses, must be denied. The dissenting judge would have allowed the post-affiliation operating loss. Collins, however, is not authority for the proposition here advanced by the Government because even the majority would not have disallowed the post-affiliation operating loss if it stood by itself, as it does in this case, and only denied the post-affiliation operating loss because it was thought to be tainted as in respect to the built-in loss the use of which, as we have seen, Section 269 was designed to prevent. The fact that the dissenting judge in Collins would have allowed the post-affiliation operating loss and the two majority judges denied it only because it was tainted ("They are tarred by the same brush," 303 F.2d at p. 146), as incidental to the built-in loss, tends to support the taxpayer's view that post-affiliation operating losses standing by themselves are not within the coverage of Section 269.

An individual or corporate member of a partnership is entitled to offset the losses of the partnership (except to the extent they exceed the basis of the member's interest in the partnership) against income derived by such member from other sources, including from other partnerships. . . . An individual stockholder of a tax option

(Sub-Chapter S) corporation is permitted, to the extent of his investment, to utilize the losses of such a corporation against other income.

. . .

Similarly, had Earl Jones dissolved all three corporations he could have utilized the Muskingum losses against the publishing company's profits; or if he had dissolved Muskingum and contributed its property to the taxpayer or to Enterprises he could have accomplished a similar result.

In Revenue Ruling 63–40, 1963–1 Cum.Bull. 46, the Internal Revenue Service stated its view that where there is no change in the control group, Section 269 was not applicable to the addition of a new profitable business to a loss corporation, which had discontinued the money losing business, even if the means by which this was accomplished was the purchase by the loss corporation of the stock of the money-making business and the transfer of its assets in liquidation to its new stockholder. Compare Kolker Brothers, Inc., 35 T.C. 299 (1960).

Section 382 of the Internal Revenue Code of 1954 expressly permits the use of historical losses against the income of other businesses where either there has not been a change in the control group (as defined therein) or there has not been a substantial change in the trade or business conducted before the change in control. One would think that if the same control group could, after the loss, add new income (Revenue Ruling 63–40, supra), there would be no objection to the offsetting of a future loss against future income. The latter case, which is the case before this court, would appear to be a stronger one for the taxpayer.

Although the Government is correct in stating that the transaction must be viewed in the light of what was done, rather than on the basis of what might have been done, one is left with the definite impression that there is no legislative plan to deny the utilization of post-affiliation losses against post-affiliation income and one suspects that one of the basic reasons why taxpayers consolidated corporations and paid the two per cent penalty that prior to the enactment of the Revenue Act of 1964 was payable on consolidated taxable income, was to be able to offset the losses of one corporation against the profits of another. Inherent in the concept of consolidation is the offsetting of loss against income.

The legislative plan is perhaps best revealed by the following excerpts from the Senate Finance Committee report accompanying the Revenue Act of 1928:

> "The permission to file consolidated returns by affiliated corporations merely recognizes the business entity as distinguished from the legal corporate entity of the business enterprise. Unless the affiliated group as a whole in the conduct of its business enterprise shows net profits, the individuals

conducting the business have realized no gain. The failure to recognize the entire business enterprise means drawing technical legal distinctions, as contrasted with the recognition of actual facts. The mere fact that by legal fiction several corporations owned by the same stockholders are separate entities should not obscure the fact that they are in reality one and the same business owned by the same individuals and operated as a unit. To refuse to recognize this situation and to require for tax purposes the breaking up of a single business into its constituent parts is just as unreasonable as to require a single corporation to report separately for tax purposes the gains from its sales department, from its manufacturing activities, from its investments, and from each and every one of its agencies. It would be just as unreasonable to demand that an individual engaged in two or more businesses treat each business separately for tax purposes. . . ."

The Regulations promulgated pursuant to such authority have, as appears above, only prohibited the association of pre-affiliation losses with pre- or post-affiliation consolidated income, and have never prevented the offsetting of post-affiliation consolidated income with post-affiliation losses. The legislative plan has clearly been to encourage the filing of consolidated returns . . .

This legislative attitude also finds expression in the House and Senate reports accompanying the Revenue Act of 1964, both of which contain the following statement:

"General reasons for provision.—The bill removes the special 2-percent penalty tax on the privilege of filing a consolidated return, in part because the return of commonly controlled corporations as a single economic unit for tax purposes is in accord with the reality of the situation. Moreover, there appears to be no reason why, where a group of commonly controlled corporations are willing to have their operations consolidated for tax purposes, the mere presence of more than one corporate organization in the group should result in any penalty tax. No such penalty, for example, is exacted in the case of other corporate organizations operating through divisions rather than separate corporations."

We have seen that the principal purpose of Section 269 was to deny those losses, credits, deductions, etc., which could only be obtained by acquiring (generally, by buying) a corporation which, because of its own history, had obtained such benefits and which benefits the acquiring person could not otherwise obtain.

* * *

It is noteworthy that the cases construing Section 269 to date have all involved situations where the loss sought to be utilized flowed from the corporation's individual past history or from the fact that the corporate rather than some other form of business organization was involved and was otherwise unobtainable under any other provision of the Code. But, as we have seen, that is not the case here, as Muskingum's losses could have been realized and offset against other income if the several businesses had been conducted in non-corporate forms or if Muskingum's assets had been dissolved into the taxpayer.

In this case, it may well be, as the Tax Court found, that the taxpayer desired to offset anticipated losses against income; but there is no evidence that such objective is violative of the legislative plan which permits just that in an effort to counter-balance profits with losses. The over-all purpose of Section 269 was to prevent distortion of a taxpayer's income resulting from the utilization of *someone else's loss* or a *built-in but unrealized loss* . . .; but there is no indication that Section 269 was designed to prohibit the utilization of future losses against future income merely because a corporate rather than a partnership or individual proprietorship form of business enterprise was involved. We believe that it would be a distortion to deny the utilization of these losses which were incurred in good faith to save a business and that Section 269 does not require any such result.

In a recent decision, Naeter Brothers Publishing Co., 42 T.C. 1, decided April 2, 1964, the Tax Court, in an almost identical fact situation held that consolidation would be permitted. The following appears in the court's opinion:

"We think the anticipated consequences were Missourian's continued operating losses for a short time to be followed by profitable operation. It can hardly be said this was not realistic for it is exactly what did happen."

Actually, the portion of the business that caused the losses in the cited case never did become profitable. ". . . Missourian, apparently despairing of any profitable operations in the printing division, sold the . . ." same. The portion of the loss corporation's business that was profitable after said disposition was profitable before it. In any event, there is no basis for reaching different results based on whether the hoped-for ultimate profitable operation is in fact realized. Hindsight is always better than foresight, but should not be elevated to a standard for determining those consolidations that will be permitted and those that will be denied.

In view of this court's decision, it is unnecessary to consider taxpayer's alternative arguments that there was no acquisition because Earl J. Jones (the underlying controlling person) owned the stock of Muskingum many years before the prohibited purpose could come to mind, or that a loss deduction should be allowed alternatively at least to the extent of the loss realized on the sale of the physical assets in July 1956; the Government does not contend that this is a built-in loss (Regulation 1.1502–31(b) (9)). . . .

This case is remanded to the Tax Court for the entry of a judgment not inconsistent with this opinion.

Reversed.

NOTE ON CONSOLIDATED RETURNS

As the Zanesville case illustrates, consolidated returns may make it possible to offset the losses of one corporation against the profits of another even though the two corporations remain in existence and maintain their separate identities. Thus in the combination area consolidated returns could come into play when the combination takes the form of a B reorganization, and the acquired corporation is not liquidated. However, quite apart from § 269, there are some limitations on the use of consolidated returns to achieve tax advantages, particularly in connection with net operating loss carryovers; accordingly, a brief review of the rules governing consolidated returns is appropriate at this point.

While the primary source of authority for the use of consolidated returns is the statute, §§ 1501–1504, most of the rules governing the operation of consolidated returns are to be found in the regulations, which have a kind of semi-legislative status since the statute specifically delegates such rule-making power to the Secretary in this area. During 1964–1965 these regulations were the subject of a lengthy study by the Treasury and late in 1965 the Treasury promulgated proposed new regulations which represented a substantial revision. See generally, Cohen, The New Consolidated Return Regs: A Bird's-Eye View of the Extensive Changes, 24 Journ. of Tax. 82 (1966). Since there is little reason to expect that the final regulations will differ much from these proposed regulations, this analysis will focus principally on the proposed regulations.

As a starting point, it should be noted that consolidated returns may be filed by any "affiliated" group of corporations, which means any group of corporations connected through stock ownership with a common parent corporation if at least 80% of the voting stock and 80% of the non-voting common stock of each subsidiary is owned by one or more members of the group, and the common parent corporation owns that percentage of the stock of at least one other member of the group. When an affiliated group has remained the same throughout the taxable years involved, it is treated taxwise much the same as a single corporation, and any operating loss incurred by the group can be carried backwards and forwards in the same manner as for a single corporation. But when a group is newly formed (as in an acquisition transaction), or a corporation is added to (or dropped from) an existing consolidated group, the regulations impose certain limitations on carrying losses to or from a separate return year. Under Prop.Reg. § 1.1502–21 (as well as under the prior regulations), losses sustained by a corporation prior to the time of joining in a consolidated return (unless the corporation was a member of the affiliated group on every day of the year in which the loss occurred, even though it did not join in a consolidated return for that year) can only be carried forward against income produced by the loss corporation after consolidation, and cannot be applied against the income of other corporations in the group. Thus, for example, in the straightforward case of a profitable corporation acquiring the stock of a corporation with operating loss carryovers in a B reorganization (or in a taxable transaction, for that matter), the loss corporation's carryovers can only be applied against the future income of the loss corporation; and the same would be true if the transaction took the form of the loss corporation acquiring the stock of the profitable corporation.

However, there is still some room for maneuver. For example, after acquiring the stock of the loss corporation the profitable corporation might transfer some of its own profit-making assets to the loss corporation, thus assuring the loss corporation of income against which to apply its existing loss carryovers. In a sense, permitting this would seem to be inconsistent with the bar in the regulations against using pre-consolidation losses of one corporation against the post-consolidation income of the other. On the other hand, that bar is itself inconsistent with the fact that under § 381(c) (1) such losses and profits can be offset against each other if the two enterprises are combined into a single corporation, either pursuant to an A or C reorganization, or upon the liquidation of the acquired corporation after a B reorganization. Even more important, acquiring a loss corporation and injecting profit-making assets into it is not really a consolidated return problem anyway, since that can occur just as well if the corporations are filing separate returns. In other words, this is actually a variation of the single corporation case, where the question is to what extent the corporation's own loss carryovers survive a significant change in stock ownership and/or business operations. Assuming the acquisition took the form of a B reorganization, so that the change in stock ownership occurred in a non-taxable transaction, § 382(a) would not apply; but as we saw above, § 269 could be applicable, and, if it is still alive under the 1954 Code, so could the Libson Shops doctrine, discussed below, which was applied under the 1939 Code in just this type of situation. Commissioner v. Virginia Metal Products, Inc., 290 F.2d 675 (3d Cir. 1961).

Suppose the parent corporation of an affiliated group with existing loss carryovers acquires the stock of a profitable corporation. Literally, the limitation in the regulations on carrying forward pre-consolidation losses would not bar the utilization of this *consolidated loss*. But Prop.Reg. § 1.1502–21 (d) provides in effect that where there has been a 50% change in the stock ownership of a consolidated group with loss carryovers (whether by purchase or tax-free reorganization), those losses may be carried forward only against the income of the old members of the group. This provision will normally operate to prevent offsetting existing loss carryovers against the profits of a new member of the group since the acquisition of a profitable corporation will generally result in its stockholders owning more than 50% of the acquiring loss parent's stock.

Under the prior regulations there were some special problems with regard to the operation of the loss carryover provisions in cases where the subsidiary had been created by the parent rather than acquired by it. Thus in Ruppert Plumbing & Heating Co. v. Commissioner, 39 T.C. 284 (1962), the question was whether the bar in the regulations against applying the pre-consolidation losses of one corporation against post-consolidation profits of a different corporation meant that a loss corporation which had transferred some of its assets to a newly-formed subsidiary could not carry forward its losses against the profits subsequently earned by the subsidiary. The Tax Court held that the regulation applied; but this decision has been overruled by Prop.Reg. § 1.1502–1(f), which provides, in effect, that losses of the common parent of an affiliated group may be carried forward without limitation against consolidated income, even though the parent's losses were incurred before the consolidated return period, subject of course to the 50% change of ownership limitation described above.

As to loss carrybacks, the general rule is that losses suffered during the consolidation period by a corporation which filed separate returns in prior years can only be carried back against the separate income of the loss corporation. However, if the loss corporation was not in existence in the prior years, then the loss incurred in the consolidation period can be included in the amount carried back against the consolidated income of the group in those prior years. Prop.Reg. § 1.1502–79(a)(2).

As the Zanesville opinion indicates, the consolidated return regulations have also sought to limit the use of consolidated returns to take advantage of so-called "built-in" losses, that is, losses which have already been economically incurred but have not yet been recognized for tax purposes. The classic "built-in" case is the corporation with high basis, low value assets whose stock is acquired by a profitable corporation which then files consolidated returns in an effort to utilize this built-in loss as it is recognized by the subsidiary either by sale of the assets or through the deduction for depreciation. Under Prop.Reg. § 1.1502–15 such built-in losses are not automatically disallowed, but are treated as if they were in fact recognized before the acquisition or affiliation date, and are then subjected to the limitations applicable to the carryover of net operating losses from pre-consolidation years. However, this limitation is not applicable (1) if the corporation with the built-in loss has been a member of the affiliated group for more than ten years at the start of the year in which the loss in question is actually recognized for tax purposes, or (2) if immediately before the date the corporation became a member of the group "the aggregate of the adjusted basis of all the assets (other than cash and good will) of such corporation did not exceed the fair market value of such assets by more than 15%".

When a loss subsidiary is liquidated, problems may arise with regard to the relationship between (1) the parent's utilization of the subsidiary's operating loss carryovers, and (2) any loss suffered by the parent in its investment in the subsidiary. Particularly in the case where the parent corporation itself organized the subsidiary and was the sole stockholder, there would often be a close economic relationship between the amount of the subsidiary's operating losses and the amount of the parent's investment loss. Normally, a corporation is entitled to an ordinary loss deduction for any advances made to its subsidiary; and by virtue of § 165(g)(3) a parent corporation which owns 95% of the stock of a subsidiary may also obtain an ordinary loss deduction for losses sustained on its investment in the stock or securities of the subsidiary. But in Charles Ilfeld Co. v. Hernandez, 292 U.S. 62, 54 S.Ct. 596, 78 L.Ed. 1127 (1934), a parent corporation which had offset the operating losses of its subsidiaries against its own income through the use of consolidated returns was not permitted to later deduct its investment losses in the subsidiaries, the Court stating that the parent should not be allowed to deduct twice what was in effect the same loss.

In a similar vein, suppose there are no consolidated returns in the picture, so that upon the liquidation of a loss subsidiary the parent is entitled to deduct its losses upon its advances to or investments in the subsidiary;

but the parent also seeks to carry over the subsidiary's operating losses, in accordance with § 381. Although nothing in § 381 limits the carryover in such circumstances, Marwais Steel Co. v. Commissioner, 354 F.2d 997 (9th Cir. 1965), refused to permit the carryover because it would result in a double deduction, the court relying principally on the Ilfeld case.

---

4. LIMITATIONS ON LOSS CARRYOVERS IN NON-REORGANIZATION TRANSACTIONS

It is in connection with non-reorganization acquisitions that most of the current furor relating to operating loss carryovers has arisen, particularly with regard to the question of the continued vitality of the Libson Shops doctrine under the 1954 Code:

REVENUE RULING 63–40

1963–1 Cum.Bull. 46.

Advice has been requested whether either the rationale of the decision in Libson Shops, Inc. v. Koehler, . . . or the provisions of section 269 of the Internal Revenue Code of 1954 prevent the use of a net operating loss carryover under the circumstances described below.

1. The M corporation was organized in 1947 by three individuals who owned an equal number of shares of its authorized and outstanding stock. From the date of its incorporation until the early part of 1958 it was engaged in the fabrication and sale, through distributors, of household light steel products. The business was successful during its early years of operation. However, commencing in 1953 it sustained losses in each of its taxable years and over the period ending December 31, 1957, had accumulated substantial net operating losses.

In 1958 M corporation purchased for cash, at fair market value, all of the assets of N corporation, which had a history of successful operation of drive-in restaurants. M and N were unrelated corporations and none of the shareholders of M corporation owned, directly or indirectly, any stock of N corporation. The funds for the cash purchase were derived in part from M corporation's own business assets and in part from an equal contribution to its capital of cash by its three stockholders. Shortly thereafter, M corporation discontinued its former business activity, sold the assets connected therewith, and engaged exclusively in the business of operating the chain of drive-in restaurants formerly operated by the N corporation.

Under the facts presented, neither section 269 nor section 382 of the Code is applicable and the sole question raised is whether the rationale of the Libson Shops decision bars the allowance of the net operating loss deduction attributable to losses incurred prior to the acquisition of the new business activity for M corporation's taxable year ended December 31, 1958.

In cases, like the one discussed above, arising under section 122 of the Internal Revenue Code of 1939 or section 172 of the 1954 Code in which losses have been incurred by a single corporation and there has been little or no change in the stock ownership of the corporation during or after the period in which the losses were incurred, the Internal Revenue Service will not rely on the rationale of the Libson Shops decision to bar the corporation from using losses previously incurred by it solely because such losses are attributable to a discontinued corporate activity. Accordingly, since there was no change in stock ownership in M corporation either before the discontinuance of its former business activity or after the commencement of its new business activity, a net operating loss deduction is allowable for its taxable year ended December 31, 1958.

However, if there is more than a minor change in stock ownership of a loss corporation which acquires a new business enterprise, the Service may continue to contest the deductibility of the carryover of the corporation's prior losses against income of the new business enterprise. . . .

2. Advice has also been requested whether the Service would apply different treatment to a case involving the same facts as are set out in the foregoing except for a difference in the method of acquisition by M corporation of the assets of N corporation. In this second case M corporation first attempted in extended negotiations to purchase the assets of N corporation, but the shareholders of N corporation were unwilling to consummate the transaction except by way of the sale of their stock to M corporation. M corporation purchased the stock of N corporation for cash, at fair market value, solely for the purpose of acquiring its assets to earn a profit with those assets and *immediately* liquidated that corporation under such circumstances that the basis of the assets to M corporation will be determined by the amount it paid for the stock of N corporation.

Under the facts of this second case, the Service will not contend that the acquisition of control of N corporation has as its principal purpose the evasion or avoidance of Federal income tax for purposes of section 269(a) of the Code. Accordingly, section 269 of the Code will not, under these facts, bar the M corporation from carrying over its prior losses and the conclusion reached with respect to the first case is equally applicable here.

No opinion is expressed as to other cases where the facts show that the purchase price is payable over a substantial period of time (whether or not specifically payable only out of earnings of the business) or exceeds fair market value or where other circumstances may justify the application of section 269 of the Code. . . .

847

Corporate aspects, see Corporate Combinations.
Merger, 743-755.
   Continuity of interest doctrine, 744-750.
Non-recognition,
   Corporations, 741-742.
   Shareholders, 742-743.
Recapitalization,
   Definition, 320-322.
   Having the effect of a dividend, 322-324.
   Preferred stock, 326-329.
   Relation to stock dividend, 291-294, 325.
   Securities, 329-331.
Stock acquisition, 755-786.
   Effect of related redemption, 782-786.
   Expenses of the acquired corporation's stockholders,
      781-782.
   Liquidation of subsidiary acquired corporation,
      see Liquidation.
   "Solely for voting stock" requirement, 820-822.

REPURCHASE OF STOCK
Accounting for treasury stock, 340-342.
   Cancellation of treasury stock, 341-342.
Fund available, 332-338.
   Test for installment repurchase, 342-357.
Ousting troublesome stockholders, 357-387.
   Role of overcapitalization, 383-386.
Preserving control, 357-387.
   Liability of directors, 386-387.
Pro rata offer to all stockholders, 378-383.
Securities law aspects, 388-392.
Tax treatment, see Redemption.

SALE OF ASSETS
Distinguished from dissolution, 565-567.
Pursuant to dissolution, see Liquidation.
Requirement of stockholder approval, 567-580.

SECTION 306 STOCK, 297-311.

SECTION 1244 STOCK, 180-183.

SECURITIES
Characteristics of debt securities, 74-79.
Tax law,
   Effect on tax-free incorporation,
      see Incorporation.

*

Appendix A

BUSINESS PLANNING PROBLEM NO. I

HER-BELT, INC.

A. Business History and Background

For the last five years, Mr. Joseph Propp has been engaged
as a sole proprietor in the business of manufacturing and selling
women's belts and handbags, under the name "Her-Belt Company".
Prior to that, Mr. Propp ran a ladies' clothing shop, in a small
one-store building he inherited from his uncle. About six years
ago he began designing and making belts and handbags as a hobby
and selling them in his shop. His efforts were so well received
by his customers that within a year he had decided to devote
himself exclusively to manufacturing. He converted the store
into ground-floor manufacturing premises and picked up the necessary machinery, mostly second-hand. Although from the outset the
business has been both inadequately capitalized and under-staffed,
with Mr. Propp attempting to personally supervise all three major
phases of the business, designing, sales, and production, the
business has shown a steady growth.

A little over a year ago, Mr. Propp decided that the selling
end of the business, which he already had found to be burdensome,
needed substantially more time and attention. He felt the need
for both better relations with customers and closer supervision
of the six salesmen who carry the Her-Belt lines (along with
non-competitive products of other manufacturers) on a commission
basis in the sales territories. Accordingly, Mr. Propp approached
Mr. Survant, his best salesman, and asked him to take over the
job of sales manager at a salary of $29,000 per year, plus com-
missions of 5% on sales in excess of $400,000. Survant was
attracted by this idea, but he indicated that he was interested
in becoming more than a mere employee of the business. Propp was
not willing to offer Survant any ownership interest in the enterprise at this point, since he was untried as a sales manager; in
addition, it did not seem that Survant could contribute any
capital, which the business greatly needed. There was also the
fact that Propp had been giving some thought to incorporating his
business and was reluctant to make any major changes before
resolving that issue. The parties reached an arrangement by
which Survant would take the job as sales manager for a year. If
he made a success of it and wanted to continue, he was to receive
a "one-fifth share of the business".

Survant started his new job at the beginning of the most
recent fiscal year, and soon had the sales operation functioning
smoothly. In the course of supervising the activities of the
salesmen, he went on the road himself for a couple of months,
opening up new territories and talking to the customers. He also
introduced some innovations, such as renting a New York showroom
for two weeks at the beginning of both the spring and fall seasons
to display the new lines. Survant has also taken over general
supervision of the office work, including correspondence with
customers and bookkeeping.

The production phases of the business have remained under
Mr. Propp's personal supervision, although a production foreman
is now in immediate charge of the day-to-day operations in the
plant. The production force includes about 40 semi-skilled
operators working on the various machines, with a few more people
engaged in receiving and shipping. The production operations
consist principally of cutting, stamping, and punching the leather
or fabric with semi-automatic machines, plus stitching and fin-
ishing operations.

Mr. Propp still designs all of the belts and bags himself.
When considering a design for the line, he consults with the
production foreman to estimate the direct costs of making the
item. He then confers with Mr. Survant to estimate the price for
which the item can probably be sold. If the spread is sufficient
to cover the normal mark-up, the item is included in the line.

Mr. Propp also does all the buying for the business. Leather
and fabrics are bought at market prices in varying quantities,
mostly locally. The buckles and the other ornamentation, which
are an important element in the styling of the belts and bags,
are obtained from a number of different specialty houses, principally in New York, with Mr. Propp making his selections pretty
much as the fancy strikes him.

The most recent fiscal year, which ended about a month ago,
was a banner year for the business. Net sales went up almost
$200,000, to over $590,000, and Propp is enthusiastic about
Survant's work. Although the increase in net profit was less
than might have been expected for such a substantial increase in
volume, both men are optimistic about the future prospects for
the business.

B.   Present Problems of the Business

Both Propp and Survant recognize that the business needs
more capital, if it is to realize its potential. Survant thinks
it needs tighter management as well.

Survant's father-in-law, Mr. Capal, is a retired stockbroker
of some means, with most of his capital invested in securities.
Partly to help Survant get established, and partly because he is
impressed with the prospects of the business, he is prepared to
put from $50,000 to $60,000 into it, provided Survant is given
authority to exercise general supervision of financial matters.
Since such funds would have to be raised by liquidating other
investments, Capal would want some income to replace what he
would be giving up; but of course he also wants to be able to
share in any future growth of the company.

Survant and Propp have talked about possible uses for additional funds in the business. They agree that $50,000 to $60,000
could be a terrific shot in the arm, particularly for the following
purposes:

a. Conversion of the unfinished second floor of the build-
    ing into additional manufacturing and office space, to
    permit expanded and more efficient operations.

b. Establishment of a New York showroom.

c. Advertising.

d. Travel by Survant to the southwest and the west coast
    to open up potential markets which are not as yet being
    reached by the Her-Belt line.

e. Working capital.

The parties have also discussed briefly the subject of
management control. Survant wants a free hand on the selling
end. Propp is interested primarily in retaining final authority
over design and producton of the company's lines.

C. Personal Information About the Parties

Mr. Propp is 42 years old, married and has two children -- a
son, 17, who will be starting college next fall, and a daughter,
10. He lives in a $60,000 house in which his equity is about
$27,000. In addition, he has about $8,000 in savings and investments.

Mr. Survant is 36 years old, married and has an 8 year old
son. He has $10,000 equity in his modest home, plus a very
modest bank account.

Mr. Capal is 65 years old, and lives with Mrs. Capal in an
apartment. They have two children, Mrs. Survant, and a married
son who is a doctor in California. Aside from personal effects,
Mr. Capal has investments which produce an annual income of over
$75,000.

D. Proposed Plans

Before any of the parties consulted a lawyer, they did a
good deal of talking among themselves. They think there ought to
be a corporation, to be called Her-Belt, Inc.

Survant thought it might be a good idea for Capal to lend
the money to the business and take back notes, with the opportunity of turning them in for stock after, say, five or ten years.
The question of who was to have the say about what was to be tied
down in writing, so that there would be no argument later on.
Survant also wants a long-term contract as sales manager.

When Propp mentioned this plan to his accountant, the latter
suggested that Propp, too, could "lend" part of his contribution
to the company. Then each of the three men could take some
stock, and share in the growth that way. As for fixing up the
officerships and who does what in the business, the accountant
said that the lawyers would take care of that.

The accountant also reminded Propp that the current value of some of his assets was substantially in excess of the book value. They estimate that it would cost at least $40,000 to replace the machinery and equipment in their present condition. The present value of the land and building is approximately $42,000. When Propp inherited this property it was subject to a mortgage of $40,000 with 10 years to run, and the equity was valued at $10,000. About eighteen months ago, Propp gave a second mortgage on the property to secure a loan of $20,500, to be amortized over an eight year period.

A capsule memo to the file by the lawyer consulted by these parties, or any of them, might read as follows:

"1. Capal and Survant apparently want to get, between them, a half interest in the new corporation, in return for what they are putting in. This will have to be checked out.

"2. Setting up the capital structure will take some thought. Too much in notes looks risky to me. Also, if we're ever going to want any preferred stock in this set-up, we should put it in at the beginning.

"3. We will want to incorporate here, under the MBCA. The control problems can probably be worked out with by-laws defining officers' powers, such as: 'The president shall have general authority over the design and production of belts and handbags.'

"4. I think we should work toward a 50-50 split on the board of directors. Depending on the capital structure we decide on, cumulative voting may do the job. Maybe we should use separate classes of common, each to elect a specified number of directors.

"5. What are the tax elements in the picture? We want to be sure to keep them in mind in working out the deal.

"6. Is there anything to be gained by setting up more than one company?"

The following are financial statements for the business on the accrual basis for the last three fiscal years:

JOSEPH PROPP dba HER-BELT COMPANY

Comparative Balance Sheets (in 000's)

Assets

	Three Years Ago	Two Years Ago	Last Year
Cash	10.0	15.4	20.0
Acc. Rec. (net)	26.3	40.2	75.8
Materials Inventory	13.9	19.7	37.2
Work in Process and Finished Goods	16.2	23.2	41.5
Prepaid Expenses	1.0	1.0	.3
Land and Building (net)	35.0	32.5	30.0
Mach. and Equip. (net)	14.0	33.2	31.4
Automobiles (net)	3.0	8.7	6.0
Furn. and Fixt. (net)	6.6	5.1	4.8
TOTAL ASSETS	126.0	179.0	247.0

Liabilities and Proprietorship

	Three Years Ago	Two Years Ago	Last Year
Notes Payable	8.5	8.7	7.1
Accounts Payable	57.7	79.1	124.4
Expenses Payable	7.8	9.2	11.5
First Mortgage Loan	22.0	18.0	13.0
Second Mortgage Loan	---	20.0	19.0
TOTAL LIABILITIES	96.0	135.0	175.0
Proprietorship			
Opening Balance	24.0	30.0	44.0
Net Profit for Year	42.0	52.0	68.0
Less Proprietor's Withdrawals	(36.0)	(38.0)	(40.0)
Final Proprietorship	30.0	44.0	72.0
TOTAL LIAB. AND PROPR.	126.0	179.0	247.0

A6

JOSEPH PROPP dba HER-BELT COMPANY

Comparative Income Statements (in 000's)

	Three Years Ago	Two Years Ago	Last Year
Net Sales	310.9	400.0	592.7
Less: Production Costs	211.4	268.2	401.3
Gross Profit	99.5	131.8	191.4
Expenses:			
Selling	38.8	56.7	90.4
Overhead	18.7	23.1	33.0
Total	57.5	79.8	123.4
NET PROFIT	42.0	52.0	68.0

OUTLINE OF TOPICS TO BE CONSIDERED, WITH PAGE
REFERENCES TO RELEVANT MATERIAL*

I. For general background, read casebook, pages 95–105.

II. Valuation of an enterprise: see generally, pages 1–6.
    A. Valuing a small enterprise:
        1. Valuation methods: 7–12.
        2. The role of asset valuation: 12–13.
        3. As background, valuation of a large public
           enterprise: 13–30.
        4. Capitalization of earnings:
           a. The earnings estimate: 30–34, 44–45.
           b. The capitalization rate: 34–44, 45–47.
        5. Additional reflections on value: 47–57.
    B. What is the lawyer's role in valuation?

III. Allocation of managerial control among the parties
    A. Allocating control of the board of directors:
        58–68, 100 (at 7)–101, 102 (1st full ¶); Table
        1, following this outline. See also MBA §§34,
        39, 59(c), 60, and 143.
        1. Consider the use of stock having voting rights
           but no financial interest to give a partic-
           ipant more voting power.

---

* Ordinarily, no separate reference will be made to the relevant sections of the Model Business Corporation Act (MBA) or the Internal Revenue Code (IRC) when such sections are referred to in the cited casebook material.

TABLE 1

Alternative Allocations of 1000 Shares of Common Stock Representing the Entire Financial Interest in the Enterprise *

	(1) All One Class	(2) Using Non-Voting Stock		(3) Using Non-Equity Stock		(4) Classification of Directors		
		Voting	No-Vote	Equity	No-Equity	Class A (2 Directors)	Class B (1 Dir.)	Class C (1 Dir.)
Propp	500	250	250	500	—	500		
Capal	375	125	250	375	—		375	
Survant	125	125	—	125	100			125

* Assuming (for illustrative purposes only) that S had become the owner of a full one-fifth of P's business, so that C need put up only an amount equal to three-fifths of the value of P's business to entitle C and S between them to a 50% interest in the joint enterprise.

TABLE 2

TAX IMPACT OF §351*

	If §351 applies	If §351 does not apply
Gain to P:	0	$34,000 - the excess of the amount realized (the value of the stock and seniors received, $100,500, plus liabilities assumed of $175,000) over P's basis of $241,500 (after eliminating the autos and adding the new $500 in cash)
Basis to Corp. of P's assets:	$241,500 (per §362, carry-over from P's books (less autos) plus $500 for common)	$275,500 (cost, the sum of $100,500 in value of stock and securities given up plus $175,000 in liabilities assumed)
Basis to P of what he gets:	$66,500 (per §358, carry-over from basis of what he transferred, $241,500, less liabilities assumed of $175,000)	$100,500 (cost, equal to the value of the business he surrendered, $100,000, plus the additional cash of $500 he paid)

*Assuming that P transfers his business, valued at $100,000 (after elimination of the autos as not needed in the business), for seniors, and pays $500 in cash for the common, and that the "package" of seniors and common P gets has a value of $100,500.

TABLE 3

An Alternative Approach to the Incorporation Transaction

P

$9,000 - to S, in satisfaction of prior "arrangement"

$5,000 - for 500 shares of common

94,500 - for senior securities

101,500

(1,000)- from tax saving on payment to S

$100,500 Total outlay

C

$1,000 - gift to S

2,500 - for 250 shares of common

56,750 - for seniors

$60,250 - Total outlay

S

$2,500 - for 250 shares of common

750 - taxes on payment from P

$3,250

Less: $3,000 - received from P and C

$ 250 Total outlay

Note 1. Total received by corporation from P, C and S equals 161,000.

Note 2. "Discount" on seniors: for P, $5,500 on $100,000 = 5.5%
                               for C, $3,250 on $60,000 = 5.4%

Note 3. If $351 applies, P's carryover basis of $65,500 ($66,500, per Table 2, less the $1,000 net after-tax cost of payment to S) would be allocated between common and seniors as follows:

Common: 5,000/99,500 x $65,500 = $3,290

Seniors: 94,500/99,500 x $65,500 = $62,210

TABLE 4

Application of Control Test under § 351 to Classification of Stock
(per I.T. 3896, page 153)

	Alternative 1				**Alternative 2**		
	Class A (2 D's)	Class B (1 D)	Class C (1 D)		Class A (2 D's)	Class B (1 D)	Class C (1 D)
P	500			P	400		100
C		250		C		250	
S			250	S			250

Computation of Voting Power of Transferor Group (P and C):

Alternative 1		**Alternative 2**	
$100\% \times 50\%$ of Class A = 50%		$100\% \times 50\%$ of Class A = 50%	
$100\% \times 25\%$ of Class B = 25%		$100\% \times 25\%$ of Class B = 25%	
$0 \times 25\%$ of Class C = 0		$2/7 \times 25\%$ of Class C = 7%	
Total	75%	Total	82%

TABLE 5

Alternative Allocations of $160,000 of Senior Securities
Between Debt and Preferred Stock (000 omitted)

	Common	1 Bonds	Pfd	2 Bonds	Pfd	3 Bonds	Pfd	4 Bonds	Pfd
Propp	50%	$75	$25	$50	$50	$37.5	$62.5	$ 0	$100
Capal	25%	45	15	30	30	22.5	37.5	60	0
Survant	25%	0	0	0	0	0	0	0	0
	100%	$120	$40	$80	$80	$60.0	$60.0	$60	$100

[Note: there is NO Problem II]

Problem No. III

NATIONAL STEEL FOUNDRIES, INC.

National Steel Foundries, Inc. is a corporation organized under the Model Business Corporation Act. Its principal business is the manufacture of steel castings.

National is the successor to a partnership composed of the Statler and Moss families, each of whom had a 50% interest. The Statler family consists of Harold F. Statler, his sister, Margaret Statler Nellis, and two nephews, Mark E. Statler and Robert F. Nellis. The Moss family originally consisted of Ben Moss and his wife Edna. Ben Moss died about four years ago, and his two daughters, Jacqueline M. Carter and Jane S. Moss, succeeded to his interest in the partnership.

Three years ago, the business was incorporated under the name of National Steel Foundries, Inc. In exchange for the partnership assets, the corporation assumed the liabilities and issued 3,000 shares of $100 par value common stock. The following table shows the number of shares owned by each shareholder, together with any corporate office held:

Name	Office	Shares
Harold F. Statler	President; Director	375
Margaret S. Nellis	Sec.-Treas.; Director	375
Mark E. Statler	Vice-president	375
Robert F. Nellis	2nd Vice-president	375
Edna W. Moss	Director	750
Jacqueline M. Carter	-	375
Jane S. Moss	-	375

The basis of the stock for tax purposes is $80 per share for each of the shareholders except Jacqueline Carter and Jane Moss, whose basis is $100 per share.

The board of directors since the time of incorporation has consisted of Harold F. Statler, Margaret S. Nellis, and Edna W. Moss. Other than serving as a director, Edna Moss has taken no active part in the business. Her daughters hold no positions with the company. All four members of the Statler family are salaried executives who devote substantially full time to managing the company's business.

The after-tax earnings of the company for the last three years have been $150,000, $160,000 and $170,000. During this period, dividends of $40,000 a year have been declared and paid, resulting in income of $10,000 per year to Edna Moss and $5,000 per year to each of her two daughters.

Edna and her two daughters have been dissatisfied for some time with the amount of income they have been receiving from their stockholdings in the company. They are also concerned about having the amount of their income wholly dependent upon the decision of the Statler family as to how large a dividend should be paid each year.

On the other hand, the Statlers prefer not to increase the amount of the dividends. They hope that after the company finishes paying off its existing notes it may be able to embark upon an expansion program, which they would prefer to finance primarily out of accumulated earnings. In addition, since the members of the Statler family receive reasonably good salaries they do not particularly need any additional dividend income.

About a year ago, Edna Moss held some conferences with Harold Statler about selling either the business or the stock. Shortly thereafter, Harold Statler advised a broker that the business might be acquired for $500 per share. A few parties showed some interest in the business, but none of them were willing to consider it at that price. One group offered to pay $1,000,000 for the plant, but Mr. Statler told them that the assets were not available on a piece-meal basis. In addition, Mr. Statler had obtained an informal opinion from an appraiser that it might cost as much as $1,500,000 to reproduce the company's plant today.

Early this year, Edna Moss discussed with George Knight, an accountant who was a friend of both families, the possibility of rearranging the stockholdings of the Moss family in some way which would increase their annual return and also make it less subject to the discretion of the Statlers. Mr. Knight has taken care of the tax returns of both the corporation and the individual stockholders, and is familiar with the general situation and the interests of the various parties. With Edna's encouragement, Knight discussed the matter with the Statler family, who indicated that they were willing to have him pursue the matter and attempt to work out some type of plan.

After considerable discussion with the parties, Knight has come up with a tentative plan. The corporation would authorize a new issue of 6,000 shares of $100 preferred stock. This preferred stock would carry a cumulative dividend rate of $10 per share, and payment of the dividend would be mandatory in any year in which it was earned. The preferred would also have a liquidation preference of par plus unpaid dividends, and would be redeemable after 10 years from the date of issue at $115 per share plus any unpaid dividends.

The new preferred would be issued as a stock dividend on the present common stock, on the basis of two shares of the new preferred on each share of common. After this distribution, the Moss family would exchange the 1,500 shares of common stock which they own for the 3,000 shares of preferred stock received by the Statler family, so that the Moss family would end up owning all 6,000 shares of the new preferred stock and the Statler family would own all 3,000 shares of the common stock.

Mr. Knight is also giving consideration to making the preferred convertible into common, primarily to provide the Mosses some protection against a sharp increase in the value of the enterprise. His current notion is a conversion ratio of one share of common for four shares of preferred, for a period of perhaps five years.

The balance sheet for National as of the close of its most recent fiscal year was as follows:

Cash	$135,000	Accounts Payable	$340,000
Acc. Rec.(less Allow.)	225,000	Notes Payable	250,000
Inventory	260,000	Stat. Cap. (3000	
Plant (less Deprec.)	620,000	shares of $100 par)	300,000
Deferred Expenses	10,000	Earned Surplus	360,000
	$1,250,000		$1,250,000

At Mr. Knight's suggestion, the parties have asked for our advice as to how to effect this transaction under the corporation statute, and what the tax consequences would be.

OUTLINE OF TOPICS, WITH REFERENCES TO RELEVANT MATERIAL

I. Corporate aspects.

A. Creation of the new preferred stock.

  1. Authorization: 94.

  2. Fixing the terms: 74-94.

B. Distribution of the proposed stock dividend.

  1. Legal sources of dividends in general: 217, 226-229; MBA §§2, 45, 46 (plus related Comments).

  2. Special aspects of stock dividends: 245-253.

    a. Liabilities for violation of the statute: MBA §§19, 25 and 48 (plus related Comments).

C. Techniques for enlarging the corporation's capacity to issue stock dividends:

  1. Use of low par or no-par stock: 217-225.

    a. Is there any required minimum amount of consideration which must be received upon the issuance of stock with a liquidation preference? See particularly, Ill. OAG No. 473, 223.

    b. Is there any required minimum amount of stated capital which must be assigned to stock with a liquidation preference upon its issuance? See particularly, Ill. OAG No. 727, in note on 225; cf. MBA §§21 (2d ¶), 46(d) and 69 (last ¶).

  2. Revaluation of assets : 230-244, 253-254, 332-336; Comments to MBA §§2, 45, and 48.

  3. Reduction of capital to create reduction surplus: 254 - top of 264; Comments to MBA §§2 and 69.

    a. Does an amendment of the certificate which decreases the par value of the outstanding shares automatically reduce capital? If not, what else must be done?

    b. Does an amendment which changes the outstanding shares from par to no-par automatically reduce capital? If not, what else must be done?

    c. Can capital be reduced by decreasing the number of shares outstanding? If so, does this route require an amendment of the certificate?

    d. Is it permissible and/or desirable to reduce the common capital in the instant problem by more than $240,000? MBA §§70 (3d¶) and 46 last ¶); 264-266; cf. 266-270.

D. Fairness of the deal. (For the purpose of any computations, assume that the enterprise value of National Steel is $1,200,000.)

    1. Compare the value of what the Mosses would receive with the value of what they give up, and also with the value of what the Statlers end up owning. Tables 1–3, infra; 294–297. Does MBA §97(a) have a role here?

    2. Effect of the convertibility alternative: Table 4, infra; 85–88.

II. Tax aspects.

A. Tax incidents of the stock dividend; historical background, 279–284; current law, 284–291; special §305(c) aspects, 291–294.

B. Tax incidents of the exchange among the shareholders.

    1. Taxability of exchanges generally: IRC §§1001, 1002.

       a. Any chance for non-recognition? IRC §§ 354, 1031, 1032, 1036.

    2. Computation of gain or loss.

       a. Amount realized: IRC §1001(b); Reg. §1.1001-1(a).

       b. Basis of stock given up: IRC §307; Reg. §1.307-1.

       c. For the purpose of any computations, assume that the total value of National Steel is $1,200,000.

    3. Special tax treatment of "section 306 stock": 297–304 (plus 304–311 as background); 271–273; Rev. Proc. 77-37, section 5, page 160; Tables 5 and 6, infra.

       a. Earnings and profits: 238–239, 273–274. (For computation purposes, assume that National Steel has earnings and profits of $360,000.)

C. Tax status of the parties after the exchange.

    1. Basis: IRC §§307, 1011, 1012, 1016.

    2. Does any "taint" under §306 remain?

TABLE 1

As a possible aid in evaluating the preferred stock deal for the Mosses, compare the following:

What the Mosses Have Now	What the Mosses Get	What the Statlers Get
The right to an undivided one-half of an earnings stream estimated at, say, $170,000 (but the amount paid out each year is controlled by the other 50% owner).	The first $60,000 from an earnings stream estimated at, say, $170,000 (and the $60,000 must be paid out if earned).	Everything after the first $60,000, from an earnings stream estimated at, say, $170,000.

TABLE 2

The significance of the <u>first</u> $60,000 of the earnings stream may be suggested by the following chart, which illustrates the so-called "segmented" approach to capitalization of earnings, an effort to refine the selection of a multiplier by using different multipliers for various portions of the earnings stream (which is assumed to total $170,000), to different levels of riskiness:

```
(Approx. 8.3%) 12  x the first $34,000 of earnings = 408,000
(   "   10.5%) 9.5 x the second  "    "       "    = 323,000
(   "   14.3%)  7  x the third   "    "       "    = 238,000
(   "   22.2%) 4.5 x the fourth  "    "       "    = 153,000
(   "     50%)  2  x the fifth    "    "       "    =  68,000
             Total (the same as 7 x $170,000) $1,190,000
```

But consider whether this segmented approach takes sufficient account of the possibility of growth - i.e., perhaps the segments should be in terms of the first, second, etc. $34,000, <u>or</u> one-fifth of the total earnings stream, whichever is larger.

TABLE 3

Another way of looking at the same phenomenon is to take a $1,000,000 earnings stream, (which, it may be assumed, might be appropriately capitalized overall at 10%, a multiplier of 10), and dividing it into three segments, roughly paralleling the return on bonds, preferred stock, and common:

<u>Thirty years ago it might have looked like this:</u>

```
(Approx. 6%)      16.5 x first $300,000 = $4,950,000
(   "    8%)      12.5 x next   200,000 =  2,500,000
(   "   20%)       5.1 x final  500,000 =  2,550,000
```

<u>Fifteen years ago it might have looked more like this:</u>

```
(Approx. 7.5%)    13   x first $300,000 = 3,900,000
(   "    9.5%)    10.5 x next   200,000 = 2,100,000
(   "   12.5%)     8   x final  500,000 = 4,000,000
```

<u>Today, we face something of this order:</u>

```
(Approx. 11%)      9   x first  300,000 = 2,700,000
(   "    13%)      7.5 x next    200,000 = 1,500,000
(   "    8.5%)    11.6 x final   500,000 = 5,800,000
```

TABLE 4

Effect of various convertibility ratios for 6000 shares of preferred (assuming 3000 shares of common outstanding before conversion):

Ratio (Common for Preferred)	Total Common After Conversion	Amount Owned by Mosses	Percentage
1 for 4	4500	1500	33 1/3%
1 for 3	5000	2000	40 %
5 for 12	5500	2500	45.5 %
1 for 2	6000	3000	50 %

TABLE 5

(Assumes that (1) the enterprise value is $1,200,000; (2) the Mosses' 50% common stock interest is worth one-half of total common stock value; and (3) the new preferred is worth $600,000, reducing the total common value to $600,000)

	Original Common	Basis	Dividend of Preferred	Preferred Basis (§307)	Common Basis	Amount Realized	Gain
Mrs. Moss	750	$60,000	1500 shs.	$30,000	$30,000	$150,000	$120,000
Each Daughter	375	37,500	750 shs.	18,750	18,750	75,000	56,250
Statler Group	1500	120,000	3000 shs.	60,000	60,000	300,000	See Note

TABLE 6

(Assumes that (1) the enterprise value is $1,200,000; (2) the Mosses' 50% common stock interest is subject to a 20% discount for lack of control, making it worth $480,000; (3) the Statlers' 50% common stock interest, which currently is in control, should reflect a premium of 20%, making it worth $720,000; and (4) the new preferred is worth $720,000, reducing the total common value to $720,000)

	Original Common	Basis	Dividend of Preferred	Preferred Basis (§307)	Common Basis	Amount Realized	Gain
Mrs. Moss	750	$ 60,000	1500 shs.	$30,000	$30,000	$120,000	$90,000
Each Daughter	375	37,500	750 shs.	18,750	18,750	60,000	41,250
Statler Group	1500	$120,000	3000 shs.	$40,000	$80,000	$240,000	See Note

Note

The amount realized by the Statlers is subject to §306. Treating the Statlers as a group (though of course they are actually taxed as individuals), the §306 computation is as follows:

```
Amount Realized ..............$300,000 or $240,000
Ratable share of earnings and profits
  attributable to Statlers' preferred
  (one-half of assumed $360,000) .......  180,000     180,000
  Balance remaining                     $120,000    $ 60,000
Less: Basis of Statlers' preferred ......  60,000      40,000
  Capital gain (or loss) ......         $ 60,000    $ 20,000
```

Herwitz–Bus.Planning Tem. 2nd Ed.—29

Problem No. III

NATIONAL STEEL FOUNDRIES, INC.

Unit 2

After further consideration of the situation, the following amended plan has been advanced as less likely to encounter unfavorable tax consequences. Instead of distributing the preferred stock described in Unit I as a stock dividend, National would offer to exchange such preferred for its common stock, on the basis of six shares of preferred stock for each share of common surrendered. The Moss family would accept this offer and exchange all of its common stock, thus receiving 6000 shares of the new preferred stock. The Statler family would decline the offer, which would leave them with all of the outstanding common stock and none of the preferred. The attorney has been requested to consider the tax incidents of this new plan, and the steps necessary to accomplish it under the corporate statute.

OUTLINE OF TOPICS, WITH REFERENCES TO RELEVANT MATERIAL

I. Tax incidents of the proposed plan.
   A. Qualification as a recapitalization: 320-329.
      1. Impact of IRC § 306; page 325.

      2. Effect of failure to qualify as a recapitalization: cf. §§ 302 and 305.
   B. Treatment of the exchanges among the stockholders under Unit I as "pursuant to" a recapitalization under § 354: Reg. § 1.368-2(g).
II. Effecting the proposed transaction under the corporate statute.
   A. Recapitalization route: 311-314; cf. MBA §§58(f), 60(d).
      1. Special problem of an "uphill" exchange: MBA §§ 66-68,15(e); 85-87.
      2. "Backing" the new shares: MBA §18 (last para.); cf. § 15(e).
   B. Repurchase route: MBA § 6

Problem No. III   Unit 3

NATIONAL STEEL FOUNDRIES, INC.

After further consideration of the situation, Mrs. Moss and
her daughters have decided that they would prefer to sell out
their National Steel stock. While there are no prospective outside buyers, and the Statler family has no interest in buying the
Moss stock personally, they are willing to have the corporation
make the purchase, provided that the payments can be spread over
a substantial number of years. The Mosses are prepared to accept
an installment payment arrangement, as long as there is a significant amount of cash at the outset, something in the order of fifteen
percent of the total price, and the deferred payments carry a
reasonable rate of interest. The tentative plan now being considered
by the parties calls for National Steel to purchase the 1,500 shares
of stock owned by the Moss family for $600,000, payable on the
following terms:

> To Mrs. Moss for her 750 shares, $50,000 in cash, and
> a note for $250,000, with interest at 8%; payments covering
> both interest and amortization of principal to be made at
> the rate of $12,630 every six months for 20 years (40 install-
> ments), the first payment to be due six months after the last
> day of the month in which the note is executed.

> To each daughter for her 375 shares, $20,000 in cash,
> and a note for $130,000, with interest at 8%; payments
> covering both interest and amortization of principal to be
> made at the rate of $5,750 every six months for 30 years
> (60 installments).

> The specified notes would be secured by the stock
> acquired, and would include some reasonable limitation on
> salaries and dividends, plus an acceleration clause upon
> default at any time after 5 years. The total interest
> liability on the note to Mrs. Moss amounts to $255,200.

OUTLINE OF TOPICS, WITH REFERENCES TO
RELEVANT MATERIAL

I. Corporate aspects.
   A. Recapitalization: 315-320.
   B. Repurchase.
      1. Power to repurchase: 332-338.
      2. Accounting for treasury shares: 340-342.
         a. If the corporation repurchased 900 shares
             from the Mosses for $360,000, how many
             more shares could the corporation re-
             purchase at $400 per share without any
             vote of the stockholders?
      3. Special aspects of an installment repurchase
          transaction: 342-357.
   C. Protective provisions for the proposed notes:
       92-94.

1. The special problem of giving noteholders
   control in the event of default.
   a. Voting rights for noteholders: 83–85;
      see comment to MBA §33
   b. Pledge of stock as security for the
      notes, using the repurchased stock,
      and/or some of the Statlers' stock,
      and/or authorized but unissued stock.
   c. Voting trust.

II. Tax incidents of the proposed transaction.
   A. Recapitalization: 320–322, 329–331.
      1. Consider a possible compromise solution
         under which Mrs. Moss (and her daugh-
         ters) would receive half in cash and notes
         (for Mrs. Moss, $15,000 in cash and a
         note in the face amount of $125,000),
         and half in preferred stock (for Mrs.
         Moss, 1500 shares): 322–324.
   B. Repurchase of stock.
      1. Impact on the remaining stockholders:
         424–429.
      2. Recognition of gain or loss by the cor-
         poration: 419–top of 421.
      3. Impact on the withdrawing stockholders:
         IRC §302(b)(3); 421(at f)–422 (at 2).
   C. Time and method of reporting gain on the
      transaction: 430–436.
      1. Consider how Mrs. Moss should report this
         transaction for tax purposes for the
         year in which it takes place, assuming that
         she receives the down-payment of $50,000 and
         the first $12,630 installment in that year,
         and that the "real" principal amount of the
         note for $250,000, computed by discounting
         it on the basis of an interest rate of 10%
         (as now required by IRC §483), is $216,800:
         Tables 1, 2 and 3 following this Outline.
         a. Installment method: 436–438.
         b. Open transaction method: 439–448.
         c. Closed transaction method: 448–450.
         d. The role of discount: 450–454.
         e. Accounting for interest: 454–466.
         f. The impact of §483: 466–473.

Problem III, Unit 3

TABLE 1

Tax Treatment of Mrs. Moss under Closed Transaction Approach

(a) Sale of Stock:

Cash Received . . . . $ 50,000
Note for $250,000, valued at 216,800*
   Total Amount Realized 266,800
Less: Basis of Mrs. Moss Stock 60,000
   Taxable Gain $206,800

(b) Receipt of Payments on the Note:

Total Principal Received (assuming payment
  in full) 216,800*
Less: Basis of the Note (equal to value taxed
  upon receipt). 216,800
   Taxable Gain 0

*The "true principal" of the note, computed by discounting it at 10% under §483,
which is assumed for the moment to be the fair market value. (The Tables in the
Regulations under §483 suggest that the total interest on the note, at 8% compounded semi-annually, may be more than the interest would be under the de minimis
rate of 9%, compounded annually, in which event §483 would not come into play,
but for the purposes of this illustration it is assumed that §483 is in operation.)

TABLE 2

(a) Amount of interest and principal in each installment received by
Mrs. Moss, assuming straight-line allocation of both the express
interest of 8% and the additional unstated interest imputed under §483
(to bring the rate up to 10%):

Express Interest	Unstated Interest	Principal	Total
$6,380	$830	$5,420	$12,630

(b) Amount of interest and principal in each of the first three
installments, assuming that the express interest of 8% is reflected
on the declining-balance basis, while continuing with straight-line
allocation of the unstated interest (pursuant to the dictates of §483):

	Express Interest	Unstated Interest	Principal	Total
First Installment	$10,000	$830	$1,800	$12,630
Second Installment	$ 9,895	$830	$1,905	$12,630
Third Installment	$ 9,785	$830	$2,015	$12,630

TABLE 3

Application of Installment Method

Cash down-payment . . . . $ 50,000
Sum of installment payments of principal . . . 216,800
  Total Contract Price 266,800
Less: Basis of stock of Mrs. Moss 60,000
  Gross Profit $206,800

$$\frac{\text{Gross Profit}}{\text{Total Contract Price}} = \frac{\$206,800}{\$266,800} = 77.5\%$$

Computation of Taxable Income in First Year*

77.5% x $50,000 down-payment $38,750
77.5% x portion of first installment
       representing principal ($1,800) . . . 1,395
             Total capital gain $40,145

If include 40% in ordinary income, ... 16,060
Add: Interest in first installment 10,830
Total included in ordinary income in first year $26,890

---

* Assuming that in addition to the down-payment one
  installment is received that year, with express interest
  allocated on the declining-balance basis, while unstated
  interest under §483 is reflected on the straight-line
  basis.

Problem No. IV

CARGILL COMPANY, INC.

The Background of the Problem.

Cargill Company, a corporation subject to the Model Business Corporation Act, owns and operates a large department store in a mid-western city. Cargill has outstanding only one class of common stock, over half of which has been owned by members of the Jenkins family for many years. The remainder of the stock is publicly held. The interest of the Jenkins family in the Cargill store began with the investment by the four Jenkins brothers at the time of the company's capital readjustment in the 1960's at which time Herbert Jenkins became president. The store grew rapidly under the Jenkins management, and within fifteen years the number of departments had increased from seventeen to forty-six, and net worth had more than quadrupled. Mr. Jenkins followed a consistent policy of attracting customers from low income groups. A variety of credit plans were installed, and approximately two-thirds of total sales were made on a credit basis.

In more recent years the costs of extending credit to retail customers have risen substantially, as a result of administrative expenses and bad debt losses. This has cut into Cargill's profit margins, particularly in comparison with those competitors who have not relied upon credit sales as much as Cargill. For the last decade some members of the Jenkins family have been urging that the company put less emphasis on credit sales, but Mr. Herbert Jenkins, who was by far the largest single stockholder as well as the president of the company, always resisted any change in this regard.

Mr. Herbert Jenkins' health began to fail about four years ago, and a year later he retired from the active management of the store, although he continued as chairman of the board of directors. His only son, James, who had already been in practical charge for more than a year, succeeded him as president. Herbert's brother, Kent Jenkins, who owns the second largest stock interest in Cargill, is still active in the management. The other two members of the board of directors are the company's retired former accountant, and a cousin of James Jenkins who holds no other position in the store.

Since succeeding his father as chief executive officer, James has tried to lessen the store's dependency upon credit sales. A number of the company's credit plans have been eliminated. Although sales fell off two years ago, the most recent fiscal year (which ended just a couple of months ago) proved more successful, and the management is hopeful that it will not have to return to the former high percentage of credit sales. (Financial statements are set out at the end of the problem.)

Mr. Herbert Jenkins died six months ago. Some years before, in connection with his personal financial operations, Mr. Herbert Jenkins had borrowed $600,000 against the security of his 45,880 shares of Cargill common stock and other collateral. Shortly after the loan had been incurred the market value of the company's stock declined, and except for brief periods the loan remained "under water" continuously until Mr. Jenkins' death. While the bank had renewed the loan from year to year despite the decreased market value of the collateral, it was now pressing the estate for settlement.

Under Herbert Jenkins' will, James Jenkins was named sole executor and was also the sole residuary beneficiary. The only other beneficial interest under the will was that of Kent Jenkins, who received a specific legacy of $25,000. However, at present the estate of Herbert Jenkins appears to be insolvent. The assets include the pledged Cargill stock, which at present market has a value of approximately $458,800, life insurance of $60,000, and other property worth about $76,000, totaling approximately $595,000. The liabilities consist of the bank loan against which the Cargill stock is pledged, amounting to $580,000, and other liabilities of approximately $45,000, totaling $625,000.

The present distribution of the Cargill common stock is as follows:

Estate of Herbert Jenkins	45,880 shares (pledged)
Kent Jenkins	15,600
James Jenkins	9,200
Mrs. James Jenkins	4,000
Other relatives and store executives	6,000
Total	80,680
Outside holders	58,126
Total Outstanding Stock	138,806

Although a majority of the company's stock is closely held by the Jenkins family, the issue is traded in the over-the-counter market, and is currently quoted at 9½ bid, 10½ asked. The management of Cargill Company has been aware for some time that an investor in another city, Fred Danton, had accumulated a considerable block of the stock, partly on the market and partly from one of the cousins of James Jenkins. In addition, trading activity in the stock has stepped up considerably since the death of Herbert Jenkins. Mr. Danton has asked to be added to the Cargill directorate, but his request was not granted because the management was in doubt as to his motives. A few months ago Mr. Danton offered to buy the stock held as collateral by the bank at a price substantially higher than the then existing quoted range of 8½ bid, 9½ asked. This situation forced James Jenkins to try to reach some decision on the method of satisfying the bank's claim against the estate.

Alternative Plans Studied by James Jenkins

Although James Jenkins was not able personally to take over the pledged stock and pay off the note, he thought he could probably settle the estate without undue financial sacrifice if the bank elected to liquidate the collateral gradually at the present market price of about $10 per share. This procedure, however, would threaten his control of the store. This threat was all the more serious because, as a result of some recent differences of opinion, he was no longer sure that he could count on all-out support from Kent Jenkins.

The bank officers had showed their appreciation of the executor's problem by telling Mr. Danton that they felt obliged to respect the wishes of the executor of the estate as to disposition of the collateral. However, Mr. Arthur, the vice-president of the bank, which has also handled most of Cargill's financing, did express the hope that Mr. Jenkins would soon decide on a plan to clear the loan before the bank was "placed in the embarrassing position" of receiving definite offers that it would be obliged to consider and expect Mr. Jenkins to match.

This pressure by the bank forced Mr. Jenkins to give attention to Mr. Danton's offer. Accordingly, he arranged a conference with Mr. Danton, who disclosed that he already owned or directly controlled nearly 7,000 shares and claimed to speak for approximately 11,000 additional shares. At this conference Mr. Danton named a tentative price of 14½ at which he offered to buy the estate stock or a major portion of it. As evidence that he was willing to cooperate in any program to avoid a struggle for control, he also offered "to go either way", that is, to sell his own stock back to the Jenkins interests at the same price he offered to pay for the pledged stock. Mr. Jenkins' advisors believe that Mr. Danton would pay as high as 15 for the estate stock—a price that would leave Mr. Jenkins, after the specific legacy of $25,000 to Kent Jenkins, a net inheritance of approximately $175,000. Although Mr. Jenkins believes that the market has consistently undervalued the Cargill stock, the prospect of a price $5 in excess of the current market figure of approximately $10 per share can scarcely be ignored, particularly since the stock was as low as $6 per share only a couple of years ago, and the current price might well have been influenced by Mr. Danton's buying activities. Mr. Arthur suggested that Mr. Jenkins carefully consider this offer, advising him that he might not be unwise to accept such a settlement and take his chances on the management set-up.

However, if he was obliged to sell the estate stock Mr. Jenkins would naturally prefer to surrender it into friendly hands, or at least neutral hands, rather than to Danton. A group of Mr. Jenkins' friends and store executives offered to assist him in maintaining control by investing as much as $72,000 in the estate stock, but Mr. Jenkins was hesitant to allow them to pay more than the current market price.

Several proposed compromise plans, which would maintain the existing proportions of control, proved unsatisfactory either to Mr. Jenkins or to Mr. Danton. At a second conference, however, Mr. Danton exhibited greater willingness to liquidate his group's holdings in Cargill Company, and he repeated his previous offer to sell out to the Jenkins interests, even intimating that he might reduce his earlier price of 14½ by as much as a full point.

Mr. Jenkins saw possibilities in this turn of the negotiations, and undertook a survey of the total resources he might be able to command in order to acquire control of both the estate stock and the Danton stock. He estimated that he would be able to raise a maximum of $180,000 from his own personal resources. There was also the offer of friends and company executives to spend as much as $72,000 for the purchase of stock to support the Jenkins management. Mr. Jenkins thought he might be able to borrow an additional $250,-000 on his own credit, pledging the stock to be purchased as collateral; however, he hesitated to incur a personal debt for this purpose as it threatened merely to perpetuate the present situation. In any case, the sums from all these sources would not have enabled him to both settle with the bank and buy out Mr. Danton.

Accordingly, Mr. Jenkins turned to the possibility of using the resources of Cargill Company in financing this broader stock acquisition program. As the store was in excellent financial condition, with a favorable net current asset position, it seemed clear that Cargill could finance the entire transaction without difficulty (although of course there was still the possibility that it would turn out to be desirable to return to the heavy emphasis on credit sales, which would increase the store's working capital needs). Alternatively, the company could undoubtedly borrow the amount needed on reasonable terms.

The Questions Raised by the Proposed Plan

In pursuing the possibility of arranging for repurchase by the company, Mr. Jenkins engaged two investment counsel firms to prepare independent appraisals of the Cargill stock. Both of these organizations came out with a value very close to $12.50 per share. If satisfactory arrangements for the repurchase of the estate stock by Cargill Company could be made, Mr. Jenkins intended to purchase the

Danton stock, which had been offered only at a higher price, for his personal account.

In the course of conversation between Mr. Jenkins and the bank officers, Mr. Arthur raised the question of whether the proposed price of $12.50 per share to be paid to the estate for its stock might not lead many of the public stockholders to ask for the opportunity to sell their stock back to the company at the same price. If all of the public shareholders were given this option, the company might be obliged to repurchase as many as 104,000 shares, which would require $1,300,000. Such an amount was regarded as beyond Cargill's financial capacity on its own. In fact, Mr. Arthur had suggested that, from the bank's point of view, net current assets should not be reduced much below $1,800,000 in carrying out any repurchase program, which meant that the company should limit its expenditure to about $900,000. However, Mr. Jenkins and his advisers think that even if a repurchase offer were made to all stockholders at $12.50 a share, it might well turn out that no more than 25,000 of the publicly-owned shares would be offered, in which event less than $900,000 would be required to finance the corporation's whole repurchase program. In addition, Mr. Arthur indicated that if it were needed the bank would be willing to consider a term loan of $500,000, repayable over a five-year period.

Prior to putting the repurchase proposal before the board of directors, Mr. Jenkins has asked counsel to study the matter and to advise him of any corporate, tax, or other problems which might be encountered.

Financial statements, on the accrual basis, for the last three years follow:

CARGILL COMPANY

Comparative Balance Sheets (in thousands of dollars)

Assets	Last Year	Two Years Ago	Three Years Ago
Cash and Demand Deposits	1,043	678	430
U.S. Government Securities (at Cost)	400	200	-
Accounts Receivable (less Reserve)	1,179	1,410	1,922
Inventories (Fifo)	1,069	992	990
Cash Surrender Value of Life Insurance	-	208	196
Total Current Assets	3,691	3,488	3,538
Miscellaneous Investments - at Cost	54	41	24
Improvements to Leased Property (after Depreciation)	393	439	455
Deferred Charges	68	91	90
Total Assets	4,206	4,059	4,107

Liabilities and Net Worth	Last Year	Two Years Ago	Three Years Ago
Notes Payable to Banks	340	580	820
Accounts Payable	362	364	371
Accrued Liabilities	157	134	114
Federal Income Taxes Payable	60	43	69
Social Security Taxes Payable	64	34	53
Dividends Payable	35	35	35
Total Current Liabilities	1,018	1,190	1,462
Reserve for Contingencies	77	63	-
Common Stock (138,806 no-par shares)	666	666	666
Earned Surplus	2,445	2,140	1,979
Total Liabilities and Net Worth	4,206	4,059	4,107

CARGILL COMPANY

Comparative Statements of Income and Surplus
(in thousands of dollars)

	Last Year	Two Years Ago	Three Years Ago
Gross revenues (incl. interest income)	12,305	11,942	12,784
Less returns, allowances and discounts	1,283	1,148	1,588
Net sales	11,022	10,794	11,196
Less: Cost of goods sold	7,237	6,980	7,251
Operating expenses	3,536	3,621	3,631
Profit	249	193	314
Less: Income taxes	98	87	150
Net income for year	151	106	164
Net income per share	1.11	.76	1.18
Add: Surplus at beginning of year	2,140	1,979	1,850
Restorations to surplus	189 [1]	90 [2]	—
Total income and surplus	2,480	2,175	2,014
Less: Charges against surplus Dividends	35	35	35
Surplus at end of year	2,445	2,140	1,979

1. Excess of proceeds of insurance on life of late chairman of board over cash surrender value.
2. Portion of reserve for doubtful accounts restored to surplus.

OUTLINE OF TOPICS, WITH REFERENCES TO RELEVANT MATERIAL

I. Corporate aspects.

    A. The problem of "interested" directors: MBA § 41.

        1. Authorization of the proposed transaction.

        2. Fairness.

        3. What effect would ratification by the shareholders have?

    B. Special problems in the repurchase of stock: 357–378 (at 2).

        1. Is a pro rata repurchase offer necessary or desirable? 378–383.

        2. Is "overcapitalization" a relevant element in this situation? 383–386; Table 1, infra.

II. Tax aspects—continued

    C. The accumulated earnings tax —continued

        4. The special problem of accumulation of earnings to finance a redemption: Part III of Mountain <u>State</u> case, 338–340; 540–564.

TABLE 1

Comparison of effect on other shareholders of using $573,000 to pay a special dividend instead of redeeming the stock owned by the estate:

Special Dividend of $573,000

Distribution of $573,000 on 138,806 shares means dividend per
    share of .... $ 4.10
Total dividend received by owner of five shares 20.50
Less ordinary income tax (assuming approx. 40% rate) 8.20
                    After tax net 12.30
Market value of five shares (assuming per share value remains
    at $10) 50.00
                Total $62.30

Redemption of Estate Stock

If instead the $573,000 is used to redeem the 45,880 shares from the estate, the total shares outstanding will decline to 92,926; assuming that net income remains at about last year's $151,000, earnings per share will rise to $151,000 ÷ 92,926 .... $ 1.62

The current multiplier is $10 ÷ $1.11 (current market price divided by last year's earnings per share) 9

Assuming the multiplier remains the same, the market value per share will rise to 9 × $1.62, approximately $14.50

    Total value of five shares $72.50

If owner of five shares wants some cash in hand, one share could be sold for $14.50; assuming a basis of $10 per share, the capital gains tax on gain of $4.50 might amount to approximately 75¢, leaving the shareholder with cash in hand of $13.75

Market value of four remaining shares (ignoring the potential capital gains tax on $18 of gain on the four shares) $58.00
              Total $71.75

TABLE 2

Cargill Stock Owned by the Estate

Directly owned	45,880
Attributed from Kent	15,600
Attributed from James	9,200
Attributed from James's wife (via James)	4,000
Total	74,680

Percentage owned by estate $= \dfrac{74,680}{138,806}$ = 53.8%

80% of 53.8% [§302(b)(2)] = 43.04%

Percentage owned by the estate after
   redemption of its 45,880 $= \dfrac{28,800}{92,926}$ = 31%

Percentage owned by the estate after
   redemption of both its 45,800 and
   26,120 from the public (a total re-
   demption cost of $900,000) $= \dfrac{28,800}{66,806}$ = 43.11%

If James has an option on stock of
   Danton group, the total owned by the
   estate directly and constructively
   would be 92,680 (74,680 plus
   18,000), and the estate's percentage
   ownership would be $\dfrac{92,680}{138,806}$ = 66.8%

80% of 66.8% = 53.4%

Percentage owned by the estate
   after redemption of its 45,880
   (but none from the public) $= \dfrac{46,800}{92,926}$ = 50.3%

Problem No. IV

CARGILL COMPANY, INC.

Assume that the board of directors of Cargill Company has decided that the best course of action for all concerned is the liquidation of the enterprise. The board is now considering the following three alternatives, and has asked counsel to analyze the tax and corporate issues posed and to recommend a course of action.

Plan A: Bulk Sale

The first is the sale of the enterprise to another department store company, United Stores, Inc., which is actively interested in taking over the Cargill business. After a number of meetings with Cargill, United has offered to pay $2,400,000 to acquire all of Cargill's assets except the cash and government securities. While the parties have carefully refrained from any allocation of specific dollar amounts to particular assets, in order to preserve maximum flexibility for tax purposes on both sides, there are some clear indications as to United's views about the value of the various items. Most of the contention between the parties about price has related to Cargill's inventory, which is carried at lower of cost or market under FIFO. About half of the inventory consists of appliances of various kinds, on which Cargill has long had a strong position in the market because the company's excellent sources have enabled it to acquire these goods at very attractive prices. United expects to do well with this portion of the inventory, and is also quite anxious to preserve the relationship with Cargill's sources. The rest of the inventory, consisting of standard department store fare such as clothing and accessories, is a small factor in United's operations; United has little interest in these items and plans to close them out as quickly as possible if the deal goes through. Accordingly, while United has talked in terms of an approximately 20% discount from book value for the whole inventory, its thinking is really more in terms of pretty close to full book value for the hardware, and a 40% discount for the other half of the inventory. As to the accounts receivable, which have a gross face amount of $1,265,000, United regards the allowance for bad debts of $86,000 as sufficient on the basis of Cargill's experience, but believes that a discount of about 5% from the net figure is in order because collection often becomes more difficult when a business changes hands. Similar considerations lead to a 20% discount for the deferred charges. With respect to the "Improvements to Leased Property" (the store furnishings and fixtures), United is reluctant to allow more than 50% of the book value because of a contemplated substantial program of renovation and refurbishing. ·

The "Miscellaneous Investments" account on Cargill's balance sheet represents a series of stock purchases, which now amounts to a 20% interest, in a small but growing clothing manufacturer which has become an increasingly important Cargill supplier; Cargill believes that its holdings in this company are presently worth at least $120,000, and United, which has made no secret of its interest in this investment, has pretty much accepted that valuation. The rest of the $2,400,000 figure is attributable to Cargill's intangibles, such as its name, its location, and the going-concern value of the business.

If the deal with United works out, Cargill would sell its government securities, and then the total cash from all sources remaining after the payment of liabilities plus the expenses of the liquidation would be distributed pro rata to the stockholders.

Plan B: Piece-Meal Sale of Assets

Another course being weighed by the Cargill management is a piece-meal sale of the company's property. The management is optimistic that it could sell its existing inventory for cash in a going-out-of-business sale and realize close to the present book value (after the expenses of conducting the sale). The thought is that such a sale could be carried out with a skeleton staff, so that even at bargain prices the hardware inventory could produce a net profit of $100,000, while the loss on the rest of the inventory should be held to the same figure. The management believes that the company could also realize as much as $10,000 for the company's name and customers' list, and perhaps $100,000 on the improvements (maybe more, if whoever takes over the premises turns out to be interested in retaining these fixtures). As to the accounts receivable, management is confident that it can collect within $20,000 of the net book value; they also feel that at least 80% of the deferred charges can be recovered. They do not anticipate any difficulty in realizing the estimated value of the miscellaneous investment in the amount of $120,000. On these assumptions, this approach might be expected to yield proceeds of approximately $2,512,000, some $112,000 more than under Plan A.

Plan C: Distribution in Kind to the Shareholders

A quite different approach has been suggested by one of the directors, under which the corporation would promptly pay off its liabilities and be dissolved, with all its remaining assets distributed in kind to the shareholders as tenants in common. Thereafter, representatives of the shareholders would arrange for the disposition of the various assets along the same lines envisioned in Plan B. The net proceeds from the sale of the various assets, plus the funds collected on the accounts receivable, and the cash received in the liquidation of the corporation would be divided among the stockholders in accordance with their former stock-holdings.

OUTLINE OF TOPICS, WITH REFERENCES TO RELEVANT MATERIAL

I. Corporate aspects.

    A. Dissolution of the corporation: 565–567.

       1. Rights of creditors: 580–585. .

    B. Sale of substantially all of the corporate assets: 567–578; 651–654.

       1. Can any of the three Plans be carried out under MBA § 77 without having to also proceed under § 79?

       2. Can either Plan A or Plan B be carried out without resorting to MBA § 84, as by proceeding under § 79 and then relying on reduction of capital to make it possible to distribute the net assets to the stockholders? If so, would it then be possible to avoid appraisal rights for dissenting stockholders under § 80? Table 1, infra.

II. Tax aspects.

    A. Tax incidents to the corporation under Plans A and B.

       1. **Applicability of § 337: 586–593, 594–602.**

       2. **Recognition of income despite § 337: 593–594. 603–613.**

       3. Analyze Plans A and B, making the following assumptions: (1) the management would like to avoid appraisal rights for shareholders under MBA §80(b), whether or not a shareholders' vote under MBA § 79 is required; (2) the corporate book value of each asset is the same as its tax basis; (3) the amount paid for each of the various items is as indicated in the description of the two plans; and (4) gain on any item disposed of under the plans, except inventory or accounts receivable, would be capital, while loss on any item except the Miscellaneous Investment would be ordinary (obviously, as to inventory or accounts receivable, and pursuant to $1231 with respect to the other assets), which could produce a loss carryback, leading to a refund of prior years' taxes. Consider ways of maximizing the tax benefits under each plan and decide what approach you would recommend. See Tables 1 and 2, on the following page.

    B. Compare the tax incidents to the corporation under Plan C.

       1. Effect of a distribution in kind: § 336; 603–613; cf. 274–278.

       2. Effect of later sale of the property received by the shareholders: first ed. note, 586; 614–622; Rev. Proc. 84–22, section 3.01(21), on 613.

    C. Tax incidents to the shareholders of the proposed liquidation transactions: §§ 331, 333; second ed. note, 586.

TABLE 1

Computation of Loss under Plan A

	Present Net Book Value	Estimated Portion of Price Allocable	Gain or (Loss)
Accounts Receivable	$1,179,000	$1,120,000	($59,000)
Inventory	1,069,000	855,000	(214,000)
Improvements	393,000	197,000	(196,000)
Deferred Charges	68,000	54,000	(14,000)
Miscellaneous Investments	54,000	120,000	66,000
Intangibles	0	54,000	54,000
	$2,763,000	$2,400,000	($363,000)

TABLE 2

Comparison of Tax Effects of the Various Plans

	Proceeds	Tax Loss (Assuming Tax Basis Equals Book Value)	Tax Refund (or Other Tax Saving to the Corporation)	Amount Available to Stockholders in Excess of $2,400,000
Plan A	$2,400,000	$363,000	say, $150,000	$150,000
Plan B	2,512,000	250,000	say, 98,000	210,000
Plan A Straddle	2,400,000	483,000	say, 200,000	200,000
Plan B Straddle	2,512,000	326,000	say, 133,000	245,000
Plan B-C*	2,512,000	426,000	say, 173,000	285,000

*Corporation sells loss assets itself (in a transaction not qualifying under §337), while distributing its gain assets (including the hardware half of the inventory) to the shareholders for sale by them.

Problem No. V

ADAMS-WOOD CORPORATION

Adams Corporation is an Ames corporation engaged in the business of making and selling electrical appliances. The Adams family owns about 50% of the 400,000 shares of common stock outstanding, and the remaining shares are held by the public.

Wood Corporation is an Ames corporation engaged in the business of making and selling insulating material and specialty chemicals. The Wood family owns 40% of the 100,000 shares of common stock outstanding, and has been in control of the corporation for many years. The remaining 60,000 shares of common are held by the public. Wood also has outstanding 6,000 shares of $40 par, cumulative preferred stock with a dividend rate of $4 per year. The preferred stock is non-voting, has a liquidation preference of par plus accrued but unpaid dividends, and is callable at $45 per share plus any unpaid dividends. The Wood family owns about 5% of the preferred stock.

These two corporations have long dealt with each other. They are now considering combining their operations into a single enterprise, in order to achieve greater stability and efficiency. The following are the balance sheets for the two corporations as of the close of their most recent years.

ADAMS CORPORATION

Assets		Liabilities	
Cash	$ 75,000	Current Liabilities	$300,000
U. S. Government Bonds	150,000	Mortg. Note Payable	200,000
Accounts Receivable			
(after reserve)	175,000	Capital Stock (400,000	
Inventory	250,000	shs. $1 par common)	400,000
Plant (net after reserve)	850,000	Earned Surplus	600,000
	$1,500,000		$1,500,000

WOOD CORPORATION

Assets		Liabilities	
Cash	$ 50,000	Current Liabilities	$260,000
Accounts Receivable		Notes Payable	300,000
(after reserve)	170,000	Preferred Stock (6000	
		shs. $40 par)	240,000
Inventory	200,000	Common stock (100,000	
		shs. $5 par)	500,000
Plant (net after reserve)	780,000	Earnings (Deficit)	(100,000)
	$1,200,000		$1,200,000

The average earnings of Adams Corporation for the past five years have been $250,000 per year after taxes. The price of the common stock in the over-the-counter market has ranged during that period from a low of 3½ to a high of 6, and the stock is currently quoted at 4½ bid, 5½ asked.

Wood Corporation had been fairly successful until the beginning of the current decade, and its net income averaged approximately $100,000 for a number of years. Since Wood's business was relatively stable during that period, there was no need to accumulate substantial amounts of earnings, and the company had therefore pursued a quite liberal dividend policy on its common stock. However, just about ten years ago, the original founder of the Wood business died, and during the next few years Wood Corporation experienced increasing difficulty as a result of ineffective management and more intense competition. For several years Wood just managed to break even; then, six years ago, Wood showed a loss for the first time in its history, in the amount of $20,000. The next three years saw a succession of further losses, amounting to $40,000, $50,000, and $60,000 successively, which resulted in wiping out the company's previously accumulated earnings and producing a deficit of $95,000.

Two years ago, Frank Wood, a nephew of the original founder, became the chief executive officer of the corporation. Under his direction the company substantially overhauled its operations, and by the end of that year the company appeared to have "turned the corner", having succeeded in holdings its loss for the year to $30,000 (which increased the total deficit to $125,000.) For its most recent fiscal year, which ended a few months ago, the company was in the black to the tune of $25,000 before taxes (no taxes being due because of the prior losses); the best estimate of net income before taxes for the current year is approximately $36,000. The managements of both companies are hopeful that the proposed combination will speed up the restoration of the earning power of the Wood business.

No dividends have been paid on the Wood preferred stock for five years, so the dividend arrearage on the stock at the close of the most recent fiscal year amounted to $20 per share, a total of $120,000. The price of the preferred in the over-the-counter market during the last five years has ranged from a low of $19 to a high of $32, and the stock is currently quoted at $30 bid, $32 asked. The price of the Wood common stock in the over-the-counter market during the same period has ranged from a low of 1/4 to a high of 1 and 1/4, and the stock is currently quoted at 3/4 bid, 1 asked.

The following plans have been proposed for combining the two corporations into a single enterprise:

Plan A

Wood Corporation would be merged into Adams, which would be the surviving entity. Preferred stockholders of Wood would receive seven shares of Adams stock for each share of Wood preferred. Common stockholders of Wood would receive one share of Adams common for each five shares of Wood common stock.

Plan B

Adams would make a general offer to Wood shareholders to exchange their Wood stock for Adams stock on the basis of one share of Adams common stock for each five shares of Wood common, and seven shares of Adams common for each share of Wood preferred. The offer would be open for six months, and would be contingent upon acceptance by the holders of at least enough shares of Wood common and preferred to give Adams absolute control of Wood, including the power to liquidate Wood, to merge it into Adams, or to sell all the assets of Wood. A group owning 15% of the Wood common has indicated that they would not accept Adams stock, but would be willing to sell to Adams for cash. If a price can be agreed upon, it is contemplated that Adams would purchase these shares, which would leave a smaller balance of Wood common shares to be acquired under the exchange offer.

An alternative plan being considered by the parties calls for Wood to acquire the stock of Adams, by offering to exchange five shares of Wood common for each share of Adams common.

Plan C

Wood would transfer all of its assets to Adams in exchange for 62,000 shares of Adam's common stock and the assumption of all of Wood's liabilities. Wood would then dissolve and distribute the Adams common stock to the Wood shareholders on the basis of 7 shares of Adams common for each share of Wood preferred and one share of Adams common for each five shares of Wood common.

The parties are also considering having Wood acquire all the assets of Adams, in exchange for 2,000,000 shares of Wood common stock and the assumption of all of Adams' liabilities. At the same time Wood would eliminate its preferred stock, by exchanging 35 shares of Wood common for each share of preferred. Adams would dissolve, with the Adams shareholders receiving 5 shares of Wood common for each share of Adams.

In another variant, Wood would transfer its assets to Adams in exchange for 8857 shares of a new class of $40 par, $4.50 cumulative preferred stock of Adams, with a liquidation preference and call price equal to par plus accrued dividends, and a right to vote, share for share with the common. Upon dissolution, Wood would distribute the

Adams preferred stock to its shareholders on the basis of one share of the new Adams preferred for each share of Wood preferred, and one share of the Adams preferred for each 35 shares of Wood common.

The lawyers for the two corporations have been asked to analyze the various legal aspects of these alternative combination plans, and to recommend a course of action to their respective clients.

OUTLINE OF TOPICS, WITH REFERENCES TO RELEVANT MATERIAL

I. Corporate aspects of combination transactions.
   A. Corporate mechanics: see generally, 623-634, 635-641.
      1. Statutory merger.
         a. Action by the board of directors.
         b. Notice to the shareholders.
            i. Which of the two alternatives under MBA §73, a copy of the plan of merger or a summary, would you choose?
            ii. What if the notice to shareholders under §73 fails to inform them of their right to dissent and seek appraisal?: MBA §81(b); 634-635.
         c. Vote of the shareholders.
            i. If no class vote were required, how many shares of Wood common and preferred would have to be voted in favor of the merger for it to be approved? See MBA §§ 32 and 73 (plus Comment); cf. 637.
            ii. Is the Wood preferred entitled to a class vote?
            iii. Assuming that 5,000 shares of Wood preferred are voted in favor of the merger, how many shares of Wood common would have to be voted in favor of the merger for it to be approved? See Comment to MBA §60.
         d. Amendment of the certificate of incorporation.

2. As between different classes of stock of the
    same corporation.
    a. Availability of judicial review: 699-703.
    b. Standards for testing fairness: Determine
        the relative values of the Wood pre-
        ferred and common under each of the
        following methods (assuming, for this
        purpose, that the best estimate of
        Wood's future earning power is $48,000
        per year).
        i.   The absolute priority approach:
                703-704.
        ii.   The investment value approach:
                705-711.
        iii.   The appraised valuation approach:
                711-719; 693 (at E)-696 (at III).

C. Financial aspects of corporate combinations: see
    generally, 720-731.
    1. For each of the three basic plans, consider:
        a. Whether it constitutes a pooling or a
            purchase: 732-733.
        b. How to account for the transaction:
            Table 1, infra.
        c. The impact of the corporation statute;
            733-739.
            i.   Could there be a watered stock
                    problem in connection with the
                    stock issued to the acquired
                    corporation or its stockholders?
    2. Suppose that Adams Corporation is acquired
        in a statutory merger by X, a listed
        corporation with 900,000 shares of $1
        par common stock outstanding, earning $1
        per share and selling at $20 per share,
        in exchange for 100,000 new shares of
        common. See Table 2, infra.
II. Tax aspects of the proposed combination
    transactions.
    A. In general: 739-740; Table 3, infra.
        1. Tax incidents of a corporate
            reorganization.
            a. To the corporations: 741-742.
            b. To the shareholders: 742-743.
        2. Qualification as a reorganization.
            a. In general: 743-744.

b. Business purpose: 743.
c. Continuity of business enterprise: 750-751.
d. Use of a subsidiary: 751-754.
B. Special problem of continuity of interest in a merger.
  1. Quality and quantity of consideration received by shareholders of the acquired corporation: 744-750.
  2. Effect of dissenters' appraisal rights: 748.
C. Special problems in a B reorganization.
  1. The "solely for voting stock:"requirement: 755-782 (up to d).
    a. If the Adams exchange offer was not expected to bring in more than 70% of the Wood Common, could the 15% available for cash be used to help achieve a B reorganization? 782-786.
  2. Liquidation of the subsidary acquired corporation.
    a. Non-recognition of gain or loss: 788-796.
    b. Basis aspects: 788-796.
D. Special problems in a C reorganization:
  1. The "solely for voting stock:" requirement.
    a. Assumption of liabilities: 796-797.
    b. The 20% leeway: 797-798.
    c. The use of preferred stock, under alternative Plan C: 630 (1st full ¶); bottom of 748-749.
    d. Dissenters' appraisal rights: 802-806.
  2. The requirement that "substantially all" the assets be acquired: 798-800.
  3. Liquidation of the acquired corporation: 800-801.
E. Is it possible under either Plan B or Plan C to achieve both recognition of loss for the Wood stockholders and preservation of the existing basis of Wood's assets?
F. Carryover of tax attributes: see generally 807-808.
  1. Carryover of earnings and profits: 808-812.
  2. Carryover of net operating losses.
    a. Mechanics of loss carryovers: 812-818.
    b. Preservation of loss carryovers in combination transactions: 818-822.

A44

3. Assume that (1) Wood is to be merged into Adams
next November 1; (2) Wood and Adams are both
on a calendar year; (3) at that time Wood's
income before taxes for the year to date will
amount to $30,000; and (4) Adams' total
income before taxes for the full calendar
year will be $450,000 (including the post-
merger contribution from Wood's assets).
Compute the amount of Wood's operating loss
carryover available to Adams for that year
and the following year (without regard to
§382(b).)

4. Limitations on loss carryovers.
   a. Section 382(b); 822-828.
   b. The Libson Shops doctrine: 829.
   c. Section 269: 829-832.
   d. Consolidated return obstacles: 832-841.

Table 1

ADAMS CORP.'s BALANCE SHEET AFTER ACQUISITION OF WOOD CORP.

	Pooling	Purchase	Model Act
Assets (from Adams)	$1,500,000	1,500,000	$1,500,000
Assets (from Wood)	1,200,000	870,000[4]	?[6]
Liabilities (from Adams)	500,000	500,000	500,000
Liabilities (from Wood)	560,000	560,000	560,000
Stated Capital	462,000[1]	462,000[1]	462,000[1]
Capital Surplus	678,000[2]	248,000[5]	?[6]
Earned Surplus	500,000[3]	600,000	?[7]

Notes

1. Adams' present stated capital of $400,000 plus 62,000 new shares of $1 par issued to Wood's shareholders.

2. The difference between Wood's stated capital of $740,000 and the $62,000 increase in Adams' stated capital.

3. The sum of Adams' $600,000 and Wood's deficit of $100,000.

4. The total cost of Wood's assets, equal to the sum of $560,000 of Wood's liabilities assumed plus the $310,000 fair market value of the Adams common issued to Wood's shareholders (62,000 shares valued at $5 per share).

5. The difference between the $310,000 of consideration received for the 62,000 shares of Adams common and the $62,000 allocated to state capital.

6. See MBA §§17, 18 and 19.

7. See MBA §§2(1) and 19 (3rd paragraph).

Table 2

RECORDING THE ACQUISITION OF ADAMS CORP. ON X CORP.'s BALANCE SHEET

	Pooling	Purchase	Model Act
Current Assets (from Adams)	$850,000	$850,000	$850,000
Fixed Assets (from Adams)	650,000	1,050,000[4]	?[6]
Intangible Assets	0	600,000[4]	?[6]
Liabilities (from Adams)	500,000	500,000	500,000
Increase in Stated Capital	100,000[1]	100,000[1]	100,000[1]
Increase in Capital Surplus	300,000[2]	1,900,000[5]	?[6]
Increase in Earned Surplus	600,000[3]	-	?[7]

Notes

1. 100,000 shares of X's $1 par common stock issued to Adams' shareholders.

2. The difference between Adams' stated capital of $400,000 and the $100,000 increase in X's stated capital.

3. Carryover of Adams' earned surplus.

4. The total cost of the Adams assets is $2,500,000, consisting of $500,000 in in liabilities assumed plus the $2,000,000 fair market value of the X common issued to the Adams shareholders (100,000 shares valued at $20 per share); of the $1,000,000 excess over Adams' present book value, it is assumed that $400,000 is allocable to the fixed assets and $600,000 to intangibles.

5. The difference between the $2,000,000 of consideration received for the 100,000 shares of X common and the $100,000 allocated to stated capital.

6. See MBA §§17, 18 and 19.

7. See MBA §§2(1) and 19 (3rd paragraph).

Table 3

TAX IMPACT OF STATUTORY MERGER

	Reorganization	Non-Reorganization
Loss to Wood common stockholders (assuming an average basis of $4 per share, a total basis of $400,000):	None recognized	$300,000, $3 per share (equal to total basis of $400,000 minus amount realized of $100,000)
Gain to Wood preferred stockholders (assuming average basis of $34 per share, a total basis of $204,000):	None recognized	$6,000, $1 per share (equal to amount realized consisting of 42,000 shares of Adams common valued at $5 per share, a total of $210,000, less total basis of $204,000)
Basis to W common stockholders of the 20,000 shares of Adams common they receive:	$400,000, $20 per A share (carryover under §358 of assumed average basis of $4 per W common share)	$100,000, $5 per A share (cost, measured by the value of the W shares surrendered, which presumably equals the value of the A shares received)
Basis to Adams Corp. of W assets acquired:	$1,200,000 (carryover under §362(b) from W's books)	$870,000 (cost, equal to the sum of $310,000, the value of the total A stock transferred, and $560,000, the W liabilities assumed)

Appendix B

MODEL BUSINESS CORPORATION ACT*

TABLE OF SECTIONS

*See note on page B4

MODEL BUSINESS CORPORATION ACT*

§ 1. SHORT TITLE

* * *

§ 2. DEFINITIONS

As used in this Act, unless the context otherwise requires, the term:

(a) "Corporation" or "domestic corporation" means a corporation for profit subject to the provisions of this Act, except a foreign corporation.

(b) "Foreign corporation" . . . .

(c) "Articles of incorporation" means the original or restated articles of incorporation or articles of consolidation and all amendments thereto including articles of merger.

(d) "Shares" means the units into which the proprietary interests in a corporation are divided.

(e) "Subscriber" means one who subscribes for shares in a corporation, whether before or after incorporation.

(f) "Shareholder" means one who is a holder of record of shares in a corporation. If the articles of incorporation or the by-laws so provide, the board of directors may adopt by resolution a procedure whereby a shareholder of the corporation may certify in writing to the corporation that all or a portion of the shares registered in the name of such shareholder are held for the account of a specified person or persons. The resolution shall set forth (1) the classification of shareholder who may certify, (2) the purpose or purposes for which the certification may be made, (3) the form of certification and information to be contained therein, (4) if the certification is with respect to a record date or closing of the stock transfer books within which the certification must be received by the corporation and (5) such other provisions with respect to the procedure as are deemed neces-

---

*[Ed. note] The Model Business Corporation Act was prepared by the Committee on Corporate Laws of the American Bar Association's Section of Corporation, Banking and Business Law, and was originally published in 1950. Since that time the Act has been adopted substantially in whole or at least in large part by well over half of the states. In the meantime the Committee has continued to supervise the development of the Act, and numerous amendments have been made, including a significant revision in 1969. The version of the Act set out here includes virtually all of the changes to date, except for some major amendments to the financial provisions adopted in 1980, which have not yet been incorporated by most of the Model Act progeny (but a description of these changes is set out following the text of the Act).

sary or desirable. Upon receipt by the corporation of a certification complying with the procedure, the persons specified in the certification shall be deemed, for the purpose or purposes set forth in the certification, to be the holders of record of the number of shares specified in place of the shareholder making the certification.

(g) "Authorized shares" means the shares of all classes which the corporation is authorized to issue.

(h) "Treasury shares" means shares of a corporation which have been issued, have been subsequently acquired by and belong to the corporation, and have not, either by reason of the acquisition or thereafter, been cancelled or restored to the status of authorized but unissued shares. Treasury shares shall be deemed to be "issued" shares, but not "outstanding" shares.

(i) "Net assets" means the amount by which the total assets of a corporation exceed the total debts of the corporation.

(j) "Stated capital" means, at any particular time, the sum of (1) the par value of all shares of the corporation having a par value that have been issued, (2) the amount of the consideration received by the corporation for all shares of the corporation without par value that have been issued, except such part of the consideration therefor as may have been allocated to capital surplus in a manner permitted by law, and (3) such amounts not included in clauses (1) and (2) of this paragraph as have been transferred to stated capital of the corporation, whether upon the issue of shares as a share dividend or otherwise, minus all reductions from such sum as have been effected in a manner permitted by law. . . .

(k) "Surplus" means the excess of the net assets of a corporation over its stated capital.

(l) "Earned surplus" means the portion of the surplus of a corporation equal to the balance of its net profits, income, gains and losses from the date of incorporation, or from the latest date when a deficit was eliminated by an application of its capital surplus or stated capital or otherwise, after deducting subsequent distributions to shareholders and transfers to stated capital and capital surplus to the extent such distributions and transfers are made out of earned surplus. Earned surplus shall include also any portion of surplus allocated to earned surplus in mergers, consolidations or acquisitions of all or substantially all of the outstanding shares or of the property and assets of another corporation, domestic or foreign.

(m) "Capital surplus" means the entire surplus of a corporation other than its earned surplus.

(n) "Insolvent" means inability of a corporation to pay its debts as they become due in the usual course of its business.

(o) "Employee" includes officers but not directors. A director may accept duties which make him also an employee.

COMMENT *

The starting point in these definitions (section 2(i) through (m)) is the definition of "net assets." The Model Act makes no attempt to prescribe how assets are to be valued or how the exact amount of corporate obligations is to be determined. These decisions are left to the directors who may be personally liable for error, as stated in section 48.

By general accounting practice assets are recorded as having a value equal to their cost less depreciation, except in the case of certain readily marketable assets where current transactions afford a dependable guide. The common starting point in all cases is cost. The Model Act, therefore, authorizes the directors to consider assets as having a value equal to their book value, if they do so in good faith.** (See section 48.) It is implicit that values are constantly changing, and if they become so seriously impaired that a director cannot be shown to be acting in good faith if he continues to regard them as still having a value equal to their book value, he may be liable if he does so. In such cases current fair or sound value for the purposes of the business becomes the governing limit. . . .

. . . The concept of "stated capital" is simple, i.e., the par value of issued shares and all or some designated part of the consideration received on the issue of shares without par value. However, since the Model Act permits considerable flexibility in the treatment of capital accounts, like most corporate statutes today, the concept cannot be fully understood without reference to other sections of the Act. Thus, section 21 describes how "stated capital" is to be determined in certain circumstances and how additions may be made to it from surplus, and sections 67, 68 and 69 describe steps that in each case will result in a reduction of stated capital.

---

*[Ed. note] The Model Business Corporation Act Annotated (2d ed. 1971) contains comments on each of the sections of the Act, designed to aid both practitioners and courts in interpreting the provisions. Excerpts from these comments which may be particularly helpful are set out following the related provisions.

**[Ed. note] The provision here referred to was deleted as unnecessary in 1974. See last paragraph of comment on § 48, and ed. note thereto.

Having defined "net assets" and "stated capital," the excess of the former over the latter is "surplus," and that is precisely how the Model Act defines it. But "surplus" may arise in several ways, which are basically two. It may arise from the operations of the business, representing the total net profits, income, gains and losses, to the extent not distributed, and is often referred to in contemporary accounting practice as "retained earnings". Quite a different type of surplus arises from certain capital transactions, like a subscription to stock having par value at a price above par value. The excess has the attributes of capital, but does not come within the definition of stated capital. It is therefore defined as capital surplus. This differentiation makes it possible to protect the classic concept that current earnings are available for distribution to shareholders while capital should be maintained intact until the shareholders take some action to authorize a different course. But it should be remembered that however large retained earnings may be, "surplus," including "earned surplus," is still subject to the asset test mentioned above by which the recorded surplus is reduced by a decline in the value of the assets when the decline becomes so marked that a director may not in good faith continue to regard the assets as still having a current fair or sound value for the purposes of the business equal to their book value. Where directors revalue assets upward, the corresponding credit is to capital surplus.

Assets enhance in value and this unquestionably improves the corporation's financial strength, but is this enhancement "profits" that may be distributed to shareholders? If not, does the enhancement become a profit when the asset has been sold at the higher price? Statutes have attempted to cope with these problems with a multitude of defined terms but invariably with the purpose of differentiating between the concepts that have been defined in the Model Act as "earned surplus" and "capital surplus." Briefly, all profits from the enterprise and all gains and losses, whether from operations or from transactions involving capital assets, are treated in the Model Act as earned surplus and all else is capital surplus. Unlike some statutes, the Model Act has no provision specifically related to revaluation of assets or to the utilization of values not yet realized.

"Earned surplus" is the cumulative result of profits, gains and losses from a given starting point. . . .

Capital surplus may arise from the sale of par value shares for more than par or from an allocation thereto by the board of any portion of the consideration received for

no par shares (section 21). It may result from a conversion
of shares (section 18), or from a reduction of stated capital
or a transfer from earned surplus (sections 69 and 70). It
may be decreased by a conversion of shares (section 18) and
by a distribution in partial liquidation to shareholders
(section 46). It may be used as a measure of the power of
the corporation to purchase its own shares, if authorized by
the articles or if approved by a majority of the outstanding
shares entitled to vote (section 6), and to decrease or
eliminate a deficit (section 70).

*　　*　　*

The only comment pertinent to subsection (n), "insolvent," is that the term is used in an equity sense and not
in a bankruptcy sense.

§ 3. PURPOSES

Corporations may be organized under this Act for any lawful purpose or purposes, except for the purpose of banking or insurance.

§ 4. GENERAL PURPOSES

Each corporation shall have power:

(a) To have perpetual succession by its corporate name unless a
limited period of duration is stated in its articles of incorporation.

(b) To sue and be sued, complain and defend, in its corporate
name.

(c) To have a corporate seal which may be altered at pleasure,
and to use the same by causing it, or a facsimile thereof, to be impressed or affixed or in any other manner reproduced.

(d) To purchase, take, receive, lease, or otherwise acquire, own,
hold, improve, use and otherwise deal in and with, real or personal
property, or any interest therein, wherever situated.

(e) To sell, convey, mortgage, pledge, lease, exchange, transfer
and otherwise dispose of all or any part of its property and assets.

(f) To lend money to its employees other than its officers and directors, and otherwise assist its employees, officers and directors.

(g) To purchase, take, receive, subscribe for, otherwise acquire,
own, hold, vote, use, employ, sell, mortgage, lend, pledge, or otherwise
dispose of, and otherwise use and deal in and with, shares or other interests in, or obligations of, other domestic or foreign corporations,
associations, partnerships or individuals, or direct or indirect obligations of the United States or of any other government, state, territory,
governmental district or municipality or of any instrumentality thereof.

(h) To make contracts and guarantees and incur liabilities, borrow money at such rates of interest as the corporation may determine, issue its notes, bonds, and other obligations, and secure any of its obligations by mortgage or pledge of all or any of its property, franchises and income.

(i) To lend money for its corporate purposes, invest and reinvest its funds and take and hold real and personal property as security for the payment of funds so loaned or invested.

(j) To conduct its business, carry on its operations, and have offices and exercise the powers granted by this Act in any state, territory, district, or possession of the United States, or in any foreign country.

(k) To elect or appoint officers and agents of the corporation, and define their duties and fix their compensation.

(l) To make and alter by-laws, not inconsistent with its articles of incorporation or with the laws of this State, for the administration and regulation of the affairs of the corporation.

(m) To make donations for the public welfare or for charitable, scientific or educational purposes; and in time of war to make donations in aid of war activities.

(n) In time of war to transact any lawful business in aid of the United States in the prosecution of the war.

(o) To pay pensions and establish pension plans, pension trusts, profit-sharing plans, stock bonus plans, stock option plans and other incentive plans for any or all of its directors, officers and employees.

(p) To cease its corporate activities and surrender its corporate franchise.

(q) To have and exercise all powers necessary or convenient to effect any or all of the purposes for which the corporation is organized.

§5. INDEMNIFICATION OF OFFICERS, DIRECTORS EMPLOYEES AND AGENTS [Omitted]

§ 6. RIGHT OF CORPORATION TO ACQUIRE AND DISPOSE OF ITS OWN SHARES

A corporation shall have the right to purchase, take, receive or otherwise acquire, hold, own, pledge, transfer or otherwise dispose of its own shares, but purchases of its own shares, whether direct or indirect, shall be made only to the extent of unreserved and unrestricted earned surplus available therefor, and, if the articles of incorporation so permit or with the affirmative vote of the holders of at least two-thirds of all shares entitled to vote thereon, to the extent of unreserved and unrestricted capital surplus available therefor.

To the extent that earned surplus or capital surplus is used as the measure of the corporation's right to purchase its own shares, such surplus shall be restricted so long as such shares are held as treasury shares, and upon the disposition or cancellation of any such shares the restriction shall be removed pro tanto.

Notwithstanding the foregoing limitation, a corporation may purchase or otherwise acquire its own shares for the purpose of:

(a) Eliminating fractional shares.

(b) Collecting or compromising indebtedness to the corporation.

(c) Paying dissenting shareholders entitled to payment for their shares under the provisions of this Act.

(d) Effecting, subject to the other provisions of this Act, the retirement of its redeemable shares by redemption or by purchase at not to exceed the redemption price.

No purchase of or payment for its own shares shall be made at a time when the corporation is insolvent or when such purchase or payment would make it insolvent.

COMMENT

The law in the United States has changed completely on the right of a corporation to acquire its own shares. Formerly it was not permitted for a variety of reasons. In part it was thought that this was beyond the purposes of the corporation, in part that it would accomplish a reduction of capital without following the prescribed procedure. . . . Today, however, the power of a corporation to acquire its own shares is recognized in all jurisdictions either by express statutory provision, as in the Model Act, or by implication or decision. England still adheres to the earlier rule.

The most fundamental restriction is inherent in the corporate form itself, that is, that the owner may not prefer himself to the disadvantage of his creditor. No matter what the books may show as to the cost of assets, the amounts of current assets and of liabilities and the amount of earned surplus, any acquisition of shares for value involves a distribution of assets to one or more of the owners of the business. Thus the Model Act forbids any such acquisition when the corporation is insolvent or when the transaction would make it so, that is, unable "to pay its debts as they become due in the usual course of its business" (section 2(n)). This limitation is factual and current, not formal or historical. It is pervasive and absolute. Directors are personally liable for its violation (section 48(b)) and shareholders receiving such payments may be compelled by creditors to repay.

But assuming that the financial position raises no
problem of protection of creditors, they have no legal
interest in the disposition of earned surplus. The corporation is free to distribute all or any part of earned surplus
pro rata among all shareholders as a dividend. Creditors
are no more adversely affected if this surplus is paid out
to particular shareholders in acquisition of their shares.
It is only the non-receiving shareholders who might be
adversely affected, as where the payment consummates some
fraudulent or inequitable plan to confer an unfair advantage
on the selling shareholders, especially if they are members
of the management group. But where a proper corporate
purpose will be served, the Model Act unconditionally confers
the power to acquire shares out of earned surplus. . . .

*   *   *

It has been argued that any acquisition of shares,
involving, as it does, the disposition of cash or the equivalent, should immediately reduce earned surplus in like
amount. But the Model Act regards treasury shares as in a
transitional state. They are not assets, since they add
nothing to the assets of the corporation, which already owns
all of its assets. They are acquired with the ultimate view
of either cancellation or resale. In the former event, the
requisite proceedings for the reduction of stated capital
being had, clearly it is capital that is reduced, leaving
earned surplus unaffected [except of course to the extent
the cost of the treasury shares exceeds the amount of the
reduction of stated capital]. But if the shares are resold
at the same price, this restores the original situation, by
which earned surplus again remains unaffected. (If the
shares are resold at a greater or less price, the difference
is reflected in credits or charges to capital surplus, if
available.) But pending either of these ultimate steps, it
remains true that cash has been disposed of for the acquisition of shares, producing the same financial situation as if
it had never been earned. So there is at least a potential
reduction of earned surplus in that amount. To reflect this
contingency, the Model Act requires that each disposition of
cash or the equivalent for the acquisition of shares shall
be reflected by a corresponding restriction on earned surplus, which restriction will remain on the books until the
shares are cancelled or resold. This not only protects the
principles of the Model Act but also reflects sound accounting
opinion.

§§ 7-14. [For subject matter, see Table of Sections.]

§ 15. **AUTHORIZED SHARES**

Each corporation shall have power to create and issue the number of shares stated in its articles of incorporation. Such shares may be divided into one or more classes, any or all of which classes may consist of shares with par value or shares without par value, with such designations, preferences, limitations, and relative rights as shall be stated in the articles of incorporation. The articles of incorporation may limit or deny the voting rights of or provide special voting rights for the shares of any class to the extent not inconsistent with the provisions of this Act.

Without limiting the authority herein contained, a corporation, when so provided in its articles of incorporation, may issue shares of preferred or special classes:

(a) Subject to the right of the corporation to redeem any of such shares at the price fixed by the articles of incorporation for the redemption thereof.

(b) Entitling the holders thereof to cumulative, noncumulative or partially cumulative dividends.

(c) Having preference over any other class or classes of shares as to the payment of dividends.

(d) Having preference in the assets of the corporation over any other class or classes of shares upon the voluntary or involuntary liquidation of the corporation.

(e) Convertible into shares of any other class or into shares of any series of the same or any other class, except a class having prior or superior rights and preferences as to dividends or distribution of assets upon liquidation, but shares without par value shall not be converted into shares with par value unless that part of the stated capital of the corporation represented by such shares without par value is, at the time of conversion, at least equal to the aggregate par value of the shares into which the shares without par value are to be converted or the amount of such deficiency is transferred from surplus to stated capital.

§ 16. **ISSUANCE OF SHARES OF PREFERRED OR SPECIAL CLASSES IN SERIES**

If the articles of incorporation so provide, the shares of any preferred or special class may be divided into and issued in series. If the shares of any such class are to be issued in series, then each series shall be so designated as to distinguish the shares thereof from the shares of all other series and classes. Any or all of the series of any such class and the variations in the relative rights and preferences as between different series may be fixed and determined by the articles of incorporation, but all shares of the same class shall be identical except as to the following relative rights and preferences, as to which there may be variations between different series:

(A) The rate of dividend.

(B) Whether shares may be redeemed and, if so, the redemption price and the terms and conditions of redemption.

(C) The amount payable upon shares in event of voluntary and involuntary liquidation.

(D) Sinking fund provisions, if any, for the redemption or purchase of shares.

(E) The terms and conditions, if any, on which shares may be converted.

(F) Voting rights, if any.

If the articles of incorporation shall expressly vest authority in the board of directors, then, to the extent that the articles of incorporation shall not have established series and fixed and determined the variations in the relative rights and preferences as between series, the board of directors shall have authority to divide any or all of such classes into series and, within the limitations set forth in this section and in the articles of incorporation, fix and determine the relative rights and preferences of the shares of any series so established.

In order for the board of directors to establish a series, where authority so to do is contained in the articles of incorporation, the board of directors shall adopt a resolution setting forth the designation of the series and fixing and determining the relative rights and preferences thereof, or so much thereof as shall not be fixed and determined by the articles of incorporation.

Prior to the issue of any shares of a series established by resolution adopted by the board of directors, the corporation shall file in the office of the Secretary of State a statement setting forth:

(a) The name of the corporation.

(b) A copy of the resolution establishing and designating the series, and fixing and determining the relative rights and preferences thereof.

(c) The date of adoption of such resolution.

(d) That such resolution was duly adopted by the board of directors.

Such statement shall be executed in duplicate by the corporation by its president or a vice president and by its secretary or an assistant secretary, and verified by one of the officers signing such statement, and shall be delivered to the Secretary of State. . . .

Upon the filing of such statement by the Secretary of State, the resolution establishing and designating the series and fixing and determining the relative rights and preferences thereof shall become effective and shall constitute an amendment of the articles of incorporation.

§ 17. SUBSCRIPTIONS FOR SHARES

A subscription for shares of a corporation to be organized shall be irrevocable for a period of six months, unless otherwise provided by the terms of the subscription agreement or unless all the subscribers consent to the revocation of such subscription.

Unless otherwise, provided in the subscription agreement, subscriptions for shares, whether made before or after the organization of a corporation, shall be paid in full at such time, or in such installments and at such times, as shall be determined by the board of directors. Any call made by the board of directors for payment on subscriptions shall be uniform as to all shares of the same class or as to all shares of the same series, as the case may be. In case of default in the payment of any installment or call when such payment is due, the corporation may proceed to collect the amount due in the same manner as any debt due the corporation. The by-laws may prescribe other penalties for failure to pay installments or calls that may become due, but no penalty working a forfeiture of a subscription, or of the amounts paid thereon, shall be declared as against any subscriber unless the amount due thereon shall remain unpaid for a period of twenty days after written demand has been made therefor. . . . In the event of the sale of any shares by reason of any forfeiture, the excess of proceeds realized over the amount due and unpaid on such shares shall be paid to the delinquent subscriber or to his legal representative.

§ 18. CONSIDERATION FOR SHARES

Shares having a par value may be issued for such consideration expressed in dollars, not less than the par value thereof, as shall be fixed from time to time by the board of directors.

Shares without par value may be issued for such consideration expressed in dollars as may be fixed from time to time by the board of directors unless the articles of incorporation reserve to the shareholders the right to fix the consideration. In the event that such right be reserved as to any shares, the shareholders shall, prior to the issuance of such shares, fix the consideration to be received for such shares, by a vote of the holders of a majority of all shares entitled to vote thereon.

Treasury shares may be disposed of by the corporation for such consideration expressed in dollars as may be fixed from time to time by the board of directors.

That part of the surplus of a corporation which is transferred to stated capital upon the issuance of shares as a share dividend shall be deemed to be the consideration for the issuance of such shares.

In the event of the issuance of shares upon the conversion or exchange of indebtedness or shares, the consideration for the shares so issued shall be (1) the principal sum of, and accrued interest on, the indebtedness so exchanged or converted, or the stated capital then represented by the shares so exchanged or converted, and (2)

that part of surplus, if any, transferred to stated capital upon the issuance of shares for the shares so exchanged or converted, and (3)
any additional consideration paid to the corporation upon the issuance
of shares for the indebtedness or shares so exchanged or converted.

COMMENT

The forerunners of what the Model Act now defines as
"stated capital" (see sections 2(j) and 21) were phrased in
terms of the currency received on the issuance of shares.
When property became an acceptable substitute for currency
as consideration, a requirement that consideration be expressed
in dollars was necessary so that such consideration could be
represented on the balance sheet.

The Model Act prescribes only the minimum that must be
transferred from surplus to stated capital in the event of a
share dividend, conversion or exchange of shares. A practi-
tioner considering a share dividend or a stock split should
seek accounting advice, for currently accepted accounting
principles require, under certain circumstances, the transfer
from earned surplus to stated capital or capital surplus of
a greater number of dollars than the minimum required in the
Model Act . . ..

§ 19. PAYMENT FOR SHARES

The consideration for the issuance of shares may be paid, in whole
or in part, in money, in other property, tangible or intangible, or in
labor or services actually performed for the corporation. When payment of the consideration for which shares are to be issued shall have
been received by the corporation, such shares shall be deemed to be
fully paid and non-assessable.

Neither promissory notes nor future services shall constitute payment or part payment for the issuance of shares of a corporation.

In the absence of fraud in the transaction, the judgment of the
board of directors or the shareholders, as the case may be, as to the
value of the consideration received for shares shall be conclusive.

COMMENT

Every item of consideration, except that part, if any,
received in dollars, must be translated into dollars for
balance sheet purposes. For this reason, the valuation of
property and services is of importance to those potential
creditors who do not have the time or the means to look
behind the balance sheet and must rely on published figures.

Creditors were the chief complainants in the so-called "watered stock" cases that arose in the late 19th and early 20th centuries. Creditor grievances are not numerous today, primarily because of the prophylactic effect of regulations of public service commissions, "blue sky" laws adopted in many states, and the Securities Act of 1933.

The valuation of property and services has always been and is today of importance also to existing shareholders vis-à-vis new shareholders, for overvalued consideration unfairly dilutes the interests of existing shareholders.

§ 20. STOCK RIGHTS AND OPTIONS

Subject to any provisions in respect thereof set forth in its articles of incorporation, a corporation may create and issue, whether or not in connection with the issuance and sale of any of its shares or other securities, rights or options entitling the holders thereof to purchase from the corporation shares of any class or classes. Such rights or options shall be evidenced in such manner as the board of directors shall approve and, subject to the provisions of the articles of incorporation, shall set forth the terms upon which, the time or times within which and the price or prices at which such shares may be purchased from the corporation upon the exercise of any such right or option. If such rights or options are to be issued to directors, officers or employees as such of the corporation or of any subsidiary thereof, and not to the shareholders generally, their issuance shall be approved by the affirmative vote of the holders of a majority of the shares entitled to vote thereon or shall be authorized by and consistent with a plan theretofore approved by such a vote of shareholders and set forth or incorporated by reference in the instrument evidencing each such right or option. In the absence of fraud in the transaction, the judgment of the board of directors as to the adequacy of the consideration received for such rights or options shall be conclusive. The price or prices to be received for any shares having a par value, other than treasury shares to be issued upon the exercise of such rights or options, shall not be less than the par value thereof.

§ 21. DETERMINATION OF AMOUNT OF STATED CAPITAL

In case of the issuance by a corporation of shares having a par value, the consideration received therefor shall constitute stated capital to the extent of the par value of such shares, and the excess, if any, of such consideration shall constitute capital surplus.

In case of the issuance by a corporation of shares without par value, the entire consideration received therefor shall constitute stated capital unless the corporation shall determine as provided in this section that only a part thereof shall be stated capital. Within a period of sixty days after the issuance of any shares without par value, the board of directors may allocate to capital surplus any portion of the consideration received for the issuance of such shares. No such allocation shall be made of any portion of the consideration received for shares without par value having a preference in the assets of the corporation in the event of involuntary liquidation except the amount, if any, of such consideration in excess of such preference.

If shares have been or shall be issued by a corporation in merger or consolidation or in acquisition of all or substantially all of the outstanding shares or of the property and assets of another corporation, whether domestic or foreign, any amount that would otherwise constitute capital surplus under the foregoing provisions of this section may instead be allocated to earned surplus by the board of directors of the issuing corporation except that its aggregate earned surplus shall not exceed the sum of the earned surpluses as defined in this Act of the issuing corporation and of all other corporations, domestic or foreign, that were merged or consolidated or of which the shares or assets were acquired.

The stated capital of a corporation may be increased from time to time by resolution of the board of directors directing that all or a part of the surplus of the corporation be transferred to stated capital. The board of directors may direct that the amount of the surplus so transferred shall be deemed to be stated capital in respect of any designated class of shares.

§ 22. EXPENSES OF ORGANIZATION, REORGANIZATION AND FINANCING

The reasonable charges and expenses of organization or reorganization of a corporation, and the reasonable expenses of and compensation for the sale or underwriting of its shares, may be paid or allowed by such corporation out of the consideration received by it in payment for its shares without thereby rendering such shares not fully paid or assessable.

§ 23. CERTIFICATES REPRESENTING SHARES

The shares of a corporation shall be represented by certificates signed by the president or a vice president and the secretary or an assistant secretary of the corporation, and may be sealed with the seal of the corporation or a facsimile thereof. The signatures of the president or vice president and the secretary or assistant secretary upon a certificate may be facsimiles if the certificate is countersigned by a transfer agent, or registered by a registrar, other than the corporation itself or an employee of the corporation. In case any officer who has signed or whose facsimile signature has been placed upon such certificate shall have ceased to be such officer before such certificate is issued, it may be issued by the corporation with the same effect as if he were such officer at the date of its issue.

Every certificate representing shares issued by a corporation which is authorized to issue shares of more than one class shall set forth upon the face or back of the certificate, or shall state that the corporation will furnish to any shareholder upon request and without charge, a full statement of the designations, preferences, limitations, and relative rights of the shares of each class authorized to be issued and, if the corporation is authorized to issue any preferred or special class in series, the variations in the relative rights and preferences between the shares of each such series so far as the same have been fixed and determined and the authority of the board of directors to fix and determine the relative rights and preferences of subsequent series.

Each certificate representing shares shall state upon the face thereof:

(a) That the corporation is organized under the laws of this State.

(b) The name of the person to whom issued.

(c) The number and class of shares, and the designation of the series, if any, which such certificate represents.

(d) The par value of each share represented by such certificate, or a statement that the shares are without par value.

No certificate shall be issued for any share until such share is fully paid.

§ 24. FRACTIONAL SHARES

A corporation may (1) issue fractions of a share, (2) arrange for disposition of fractional interests by those entitled thereto, (3) pay in cash the fair value of fractions of a share as of the time when those entitled to receive such fractions are determined, or (4) issue scrip in registered or bearer form which shall entitle the holder to receive a certificate for a full share upon the surrender of such scrip aggregating a full share. A certificate for a fractional share shall, but scrip shall not unless otherwise provided therein, entitle the holder to exercise voting rights, to receive dividends thereon, and to participate in any of the assets of the corporation in the event of liquidation. The board of directors may cause such scrip to be issued subject to the condition that it shall become void if not exchanged for certificates representing full shares before a specified date, or subject to the condition that the shares for which such scrip is exchangeable may be sold by the corporation and the proceeds thereof distributed to the holders of such scrip, or subject to any other conditions which the board of directors may deem advisable.

§ 25. LIABILITY OF SUBSCRIBERS AND SHAREHOLDERS

A holder of or subscriber to shares of a corporation shall be under no obligation to the corporation or its creditors with respect to such shares other than the obligation to pay to the corporation the full consideration for which such shares were issued or to be issued.

Any person becoming an assignee or transferee of shares or of a subscription for shares in good faith and without knowledge or notice that the full consideration therefor has not been paid shall not be personally liable to the corporation or its creditors for any unpaid portion of such consideration.

An executor, administrator, conservator, guardian, trustee, assignee for the benefit of creditors, or receiver shall not be personally liable to the corporation as a holder of or subscriber to shares of a corporation but the estate and funds in his hands shall be so liable.

No pledgee or other holder of shares as collateral security shall be personally liable as a shareholder.

§ 26. SHAREHOLDERS' PREEMPTIVE RIGHTS *

The shareholders of a corporation shall have no preemptive right to acquire unissued or treasury shares of the corporation, or securities of the corporation convertible into or carrying a right to subscribe to or acquire shares, except to the extent, if any, that such right is provided in the articles of incorporation.

§ 27. BY-LAWS

The initial by-laws of a corporation shall be adopted by its board of directors. The power to alter, amend or repeal the by-laws or adopt new by-laws shall be vested in the board of directors unless reserved to the shareholders by the articles of incorporation. The by-laws may contain any provisions for the regulation and management of the affairs of the corporation not inconsistent with law or the articles of incorporation.

§ 27A (OPTIONAL) BY-LAWS AND OTHER POWERS IN EMERGENCY

* * *

§ 28. MEETINGS OF SHAREHOLDERS

Meetings of shareholders may be held at such place, either within or without this State, as may be stated in or fixed in accordance with the by-laws. If no other place is stated or so fixed, meetings shall be held at the registered office of the corporation.

An annual meeting of the shareholders shall be held at such time as may be stated in or fixed in accordance with the by-laws. If the annual meeting is not held within any thirteen-month period the Court [designated] may, on the application of any shareholder, summarily order a meeting to be held.

Special meetings of the shareholders may be called by the president, the board of directors, the holders of not less than one-tenth of all the shares entitled to vote at the meeting, or such other persons as may be authorized in the articles of incorporation or the by-laws.

---

*An alternative to this section, §26A, would grant preemptive rights unless otherwise provided in the articles, but with several exceptions, such as for shares issued to officers and employees with the approval of the shareholders, shares issued otherwise than for cash, and, with respect to holders of non-voting shares, for shares with voting power.

§ 29. NOTICE OF SHAREHOLDERS' MEETINGS

Written notice stating the place, day and hour of the meeting and, in case of a special meeting, the purpose or purposes for which the meeting is called, shall be delivered not less than ten nor more than fifty days before the date of the meeting, either personally or by mail, by or at the direction of the president, the secretary, or the officer or persons calling the meeting, to each shareholder of record entitled to vote at such meeting. If mailed, such notice shall be deemed to be delivered when deposited in the United States mail addressed to the shareholder at his address as it appears on the stock transfer books of the corporation, with postage thereon prepaid.

§ 30. CLOSING OF TRANSFER BOOKS AND FIXING REC-ORD DATE

* * *

§ 31. VOTING RECORD

* * *

§ 32. QUORUM OF SHAREHOLDERS

Unless otherwise provided in the articles of incorporation, a majority of the shares entitled to vote, represented in person or by proxy, shall constitute a quorum at a meeting of shareholders, but in no event shall a quorum consist of less than one-third of the shares entitled to vote at the meeting. If a quorum is present, the affirmative vote of the majority of the shares represented at the meeting and entitled to vote on the subject matter shall be the act of the shareholders, unless the vote of a greater number or voting by classes is required by this Act or the articles of incorporation or by-laws.

COMMENT

The Model Act, as do corporation statutes generally, specifies in various sections the percentage of outstanding shares which must be voted affirmatively for certain corporate actions to be effected. Under the Model Act all other matters coming before meetings of shareholders are, in the absence of a provision to the contrary in the Act itself or the articles or the by-laws, to be decided by a majority vote, and the second sentence of section 32 makes it clear that the majority in question is a majority of the voting shares represented at the meeting if a quorum is present, rather than a majority of the voting shares outstanding.

The Model Act, as do the statutes in many jurisdictions, provides that the articles or the by-laws may require more than a majority vote (section 143), and permits (sections 15 and 33) the articles to limit or deny the voting rights of shares except as to those changes of substantive rights with

respect to which a class vote is required by section 60,
provided that full voting rights must exist either in one
class or collectively in several classes. In 1969 section
33 was amended to permit the articles to provide that shares
may have more or less than one vote.

The matters as to which the Model Act requires the
affirmative vote of a percentage of shares (decreased from
two-thirds to a majority by amendment of the Model Act
adopted in 1967) based on outstanding shares rather than
shares represented at a meeting, together with a like vote
of the outstanding shares of each class entitled to vote
thereon as a class, [include] amendments to the articles
(section 59), mergers or consolidations (section 73), sales
or mortgages of assets not in the regular course of business
(section 79), [and] voluntary dissolution (section 84).

§ 33. VOTING OF SHARES

Each outstanding share, regardless of class, shall be entitled
to one vote on each matter submitted to a vote at a meeting of shareholders, except as may be otherwise provided in the articles of incorporation. If the articles of incorporation provide for more or less than
one vote for any share, on any matter, every reference in this Act to
a majority or other proportion of shares shall refer to such a majority
or other proportion of votes entitled to be cast.

Neither treasury shares, nor shares held by another corporation
if a majority of the shares entitled to vote for the election of directors
of such other corporation is held by the corporation, shall be voted at
any meeting or counted in determining the total number of outstanding shares at any given time.

A shareholder may vote either in person or by proxy executed in
writing by the shareholder or by his duly authorized attorney-in-fact.
No proxy shall be valid after eleven months from the date of its execution, unless otherwise provided in the proxy.

(Either of the following prefatory phrases may be inserted here:
"The articles of incorporation may provide that" or "Unless the articles of incorporation otherwise provide") . . . at each election
for directors every shareholder entitled to vote at such election shall
have the right to vote, in person or by proxy, the number of shares
owned by him for as many persons as there are directors to be elected
and for whose election he has a right to vote, or to cumulate his votes
by giving one candidate as many votes as the number of such directors
multiplied by the number of his shares shall equal, or by distributing
such votes on the same principle among any number of such candidates.

Shares standing in the name of another corporation, domestic
or foreign, may be voted by such officer, agent or proxy as the by-
laws of such corporation may prescribe, or, in the absence of such
provision, as the board of directors of such corporation may determine.

Shares held by an administrator, executor, guardian or conservator may be voted by him, either in person or by proxy, without a transfer of such shares into his name. Shares standing in the name of a trustee may be voted by him, either in person or by proxy, but no trustee shall be entitled to vote shares held by him without a transfer of such shares into his name.

Shares standing in the name of a receiver may be voted by such receiver, and shares held by or under the control of a receiver may be voted by such receiver without the transfer thereof into his name if authority so to do be contained in an appropriate order of the court by which such receiver was appointed.

A shareholder whose shares are pledged shall be entitled to vote such shares until the shares have been transferred into the name of the pledgee, and thereafter the pledgee shall be entitled to vote the shares so transferred.

On and after the date on which written notice of redemption of redeemable shares has been mailed to the holders thereof and a sum sufficient to redeem such shares has been deposited with a bank or trust company with irrevocable instruction and authority to pay the redemption price to the holders thereof upon surrender of certificates therefor, such shares shall not be entitled to vote on any matter and shall not be deemed to be outstanding shares.

COMMENT

The purpose of providing, as some statutes do, for the granting of voting rights to holders of debt is to give them a voice in management. Provisions granting such rights may promote avoidance of the disruption, expense and delay of foreclosure or bankruptcy proceedings. The same ends may be achieved by pledging shares of the corporation and making appropriate provision as to the exercise of voting rights by the pledgee, or by the creation of a voting trust.

§ 34. VOTING TRUSTS AND AGREEMENTS AMONG SHAREHOLDERS

Any number of shareholders of a corporation may create a voting trust for the purpose of conferring upon a trustee or trustees the right to vote or otherwise represent their shares, for a period of not to exceed ten years, by entering into a written voting trust agreement specifying the terms and conditions of the voting trust, by depositing a counterpart of the agreement with the corporation at its registered office, and by transferring their shares to such trustee or trustees for the purposes of the agreement. Such trustee or trustees shall keep a record of the holders of voting trust certificates evidencing a beneficial interest in the voting trust, giving the names and addresses of all such holders and the number and class of the shares in respect of which the voting trust certificates held by each are issued, and shall deposit a copy of such record with the corporation at its registered office. The counterpart of the voting trust agreement and the copy of such record so deposited with the corporation shall be subject to the same right of examination by a shareholder of the corporation, in person or by agent or attorney, as are the books and records of the corporation, and such counterpart and such record shall be subject to examination by any holder of record of voting trust certificates, either in person or by agent or attorney, at any reasonable time for any proper purpose.

Agreements among shareholders regarding the voting of their shares shall be valid and enforceable in accordance with their terms. Such agreements shall not be subject to the provisions of this section regarding voting trusts.

§ 35. BOARD OF DIRECTORS

All corporate powers shall be exercised by or under authority of, and the business and affairs of a corporation shall be managed under the direction of, a board of directors except as may be otherwise provided in this Act or the articles of incorporation. If any such provision is made in the articles of incorporation, the powers and duties conferred or imposed upon the board of directors by this Act shall be exercised or performed to such extent and by such person or persons as shall be provided in the articles of incorporation. Directors need not be residents of this State or shareholders of the corporation unless the articles of incorporation or by-laws so require. The articles of incorporation or by-laws may prescribe other qualifications for directors. The board of directors shall have authority to fix the compensation of directors unless otherwise provided in the articles of incorporation.

A director shall perform his duties as a director, including his duties as a member of any committee of the board upon which he may serve, in good faith, in a manner he reasonably believes to be in the best interests of the corporation, and with such care as an ordinarily prudent person in a like position would use under similar circumstances. In performing his duties, a director shall be entitled to rely on information, opinions, reports or statements, including financial statements and other financial data, in each case prepared or presented by:

(a) one or more officers or employees of the corporation whom the director reasonably believes to be reliable and competent in the matters presented,

(b) counsel, public accountants or other persons as to matters which the director reasonably believes to be within such person's professional or expert competence, or

(c) a committee of the board upon which he does not serve, duly

designated in accordance with a provision of the articles of incorporation or the by-laws, as to matters within its designated authority,
which committee the director reasonably believes to merit confidence,
but he shall not be considered to be acting in good faith if he has
knowledge concerning the matter in question that would cause such
reliance to be unwarranted. A person who so performs his duties
shall have no liability by reason of being or having been a director
of the corporation.

A director of a corporation who is present at a meeting of its
board of directors at which action on any corporate matter is taken
shall be presumed to have assented to the action taken unless his dissent shall be entered in the minutes of the meeting or unless he shall
file his written dissent to such action with the secretary of the meeting before the adjournment thereof or shall forward such dissent by
registered mail to the secretary of the corporation immediately after
the adjournment of the meeting. Such right to dissent shall not apply
to a director who voted in favor of such action.

COMMENT

[See Comment to Section 48]

§ 36. NUMBER AND ELECTION OF DIRECTORS

The board of directors of a corporation shall consist of one or
more members. The number of directors shall be fixed by, or in the
manner provided in, the articles of incorporation or the by-laws, except
as to the number constituting the initial board of directors, which number shall be fixed by the articles of incorporation. The number of directors may be increased or decreased from time to time by amendment
to, or in the manner provided in, the articles of incorporation or the
by-laws, but no decrease shall have the effect of shortening the term
of any incumbent director. In the absence of a by-law providing for
the number of directors, the number shall be the same as that provided
for in the articles of incorporation. The names and addresses of the
members of the first board of directors shall be stated in the articles of
incorporation. Such persons shall hold office until the first annual
meeting of shareholders, and until their successors shall have been
elected and qualified. At the first annual meeting of shareholders and
at each annual meeting thereafter the shareholders shall elect directors
to hold office until the next succeeding annual meeting, except in case
of the classification of directors as permitted by this Act. Each director shall hold office for the term for which he is elected and until his
successor shall have been elected and qualified.

§ 37. CLASSIFICATION OF DIRECTORS

When the board of directors shall consist of nine or more members, in lieu of electing the whole number of directors annually, the
articles of incorporation may provide that the directors be divided into

either two or three classes, each class to be as nearly equal in number as possible, the term of office of directors of the first class to expire at the first annual meeting of shareholders after their election, that of the second class to expire at the second annual meeting after their election, and that of the third class, if any, to expire at the third annual meeting after their election. At each annual meeting after such classification the number of directors equal to the number of the class whose term expires at the time of such meeting shall be elected to hold office until the second succeeding annual meeting, if there be two classes, or until the third succeeding annual meeting, if there be three classes. No classification of directors shall be effective prior to the first annual meeting of shareholders.

§ 38. VACANCIES

Any vacancy occurring in the board of directors may be filled by the affirmative vote of a majority of the remaining directors though less than a quorum of the board of directors. A director elected to fill a vacancy shall be elected for the unexpired term of his predecessor in office. Any directorship to be filled by reason of an increase in the number of directors may be filled by the board of directors for a term of office continuing only until the next election of directors by the shareholders.

§ 39. REMOVAL OF DIRECTORS

At a meeting of shareholders called expressly for that purpose, directors may be removed in the manner provided in this section. Any director or the entire board of directors may be removed, with or without cause, by a vote of the holders of a majority of the shares then entitled to vote at an election of directors.

In the case of a corporation having cumulative voting, if less than the entire board is to be removed, no one of the directors may be removed if the votes cast against his removal would be sufficient to elect him if then cumulatively voted at an election of the entire board of directors, or, if there be classes of directors, at an election of the class of directors of which he is a part.

Whenever the holders of the shares of any class are entitled to elect one or more directors by the provisions of the articles of incorporation, the provisions of this section shall apply, in respect to the removal of a director or directors so elected, to the vote of the holders of the outstanding shares of that class and not to the vote of the outstanding shares as a whole.

§ 40. QUORUM OF DIRECTORS

A majority of the number of directors fixed by or in the manner provided in the by-laws, or in the absence of a by-law fixing or providing for the number of directors, then of the number stated in the articles of incorporation, shall constitute a quorum for the transaction of business unless a greater number is required by the articles of incorporation or the by-laws. The act of the majority of the directors present at a meeting at which a quorum is present shall be the act of the board of directors, unless the act of a greater number is required by the articles of incorporation or the by-laws.

§ 41. DIRECTOR CONFLICTS OF INTEREST

No contract or other transaction between a corporation and one or more of its directors or any other corporation, firm, association or entity in which one or more of its directors are directors or officers or are financially interested, shall be either void or voidable because of such relationship or interest or because such director or directors are present at the meeting of the board of directors or a committee thereof which authorizes, approves or ratifies such contract or transaction or because his or their votes are counted for such purpose, if:

(a) the fact of such relationship or interest is disclosed or known to the board of directors or committee which authorizes, approves, or ratifies the contract or transaction by a vote or consent sufficient for the purpose without counting the votes or consents of such interested directors; or

(b) the fact of such relationship or interest is disclosed or known to the shareholders entitled to vote and they authorize, approve or ratify such contract or transaction by vote or written consent; or

(c) the contract or transaction is fair and reasonable to the corporation.

Common or interested directors may be counted in determining the presence of a quorum at a meeting of the board of directors or a committee thereof which authorizes, approves or ratifies such contract or transaction.

COMMENT

[Section 41 provides] that contracts or transactions involving an interested director will not be void or voidable solely because of the director's interest if certain conditions are met. In all other respects equitable principles will continue to be applicable. The function of section 41 is not to provide a basis for validating for all purposes a contract or transaction between an interested director and his corporation, but simply to establish that such contract or transaction is not automatically void or voidable solely by reason of the director's interest. The New Jersey Corporation Law Revision Commission, in explaining its new statute, stated that the existing rules operated harshly in many respects, and that its revision would eliminate the inequities and uncertainties caused by the existing rules, leaving undisturbed the power of the courts to deal with such matters under general equitable principles.

Section 41 incorporates in substance the general tests established in most of the recent statutes, particularly the current provisions in California, New York, Delaware and New Jersey. It disposes of the case law rules related to quorum and voting problems if the director's personal interest is disclosed or known to the directors whose authorization is sufficient without counting the vote of the interested director, or if such interest is disclosed or known to the shareholders who approve or ratify the contract or transaction, or if the contract or transaction is fair and reasonable to the corporation.

§ 42. EXECUTIVE AND OTHER COMMITTEES

If the articles of incorporation or the by-laws so provide, the board of directors, by resolution adopted by a majority of the full board of directors, may designate from among its members an executive committee and one or more other committees each of which, to the extent provided in such resolution or in the articles of incorporation or the by-laws of the corporation, shall have and may exercise all the authority of the board of directors, except that no such committee shall have authority to (i) declare dividends or distributions, (ii) approve or recommend to shareholders actions or proposals required by this Act to be approved by shareholders, (iii) designate candidates for the office of director, for purposes of proxy solicitation or otherwise, or fill vacancies on the board of directors or any committee thereof, (iv) amend the by-laws, (v) approve a plan of merger not requiring shareholder approval, (vi) reduce earned or capital surplus, (vii) authorize or approve the reacquisition of shares unless pursuant to a general formula or method specified by the board of directors, or (viii) authorize or approve the issuance or sale of, or any contract to issue or sell, shares or designate the terms of a series of a class of shares, provided that the board of directors, having acted regarding general authorization for the issuance or sale of shares, or any contract therefor, and, in the case of a series, the designation thereof, may, pursuant to a general formula or method specified by the board by resolution or by adoption of a stock option or other plan, authorize a committee to fix the terms of any contract for the sale of the shares and to fix the terms upon which such shares may be issued or sold, including, without limitation, the price, the dividend rate, provisions for redemption, sinking fund, conversion, voting or preferential rights, and provisions for other features of a class of shares, or a series of a class of shares, with full power in such committee to adopt any final resolution setting forth all the terms thereof and to authorize the statement of the terms of a series for filing with the Secretary of State under this Act.

Neither the designation of any such committee, the delegation thereto of authority, nor action by such committee pursuant to such authority shall alone constitute compliance by any member of the board of directors, not a member of the committee in question, with his responsibility to act in good faith, in a manner he reasonably believes to be in the best interests of the corporation, and with such care as an ordinarily prudent person in a like position would use under similar circumstances.

§ 43. PLACE AND NOTICE OF DIRECTORS' MEETINGS; COMMITTEE MEETINGS

Meetings of the board of directors, regular or special, may be held either within or without this State.

Regular meetings of the board of directors or any committee designated thereby may be held with or without notice as prescribed in the by-laws. Special meetings of the board of directors or any committee designated thereby shall be held upon such notice as is prescribed in the by-laws. Attendance of a director at a meeting shall constitute a waiver of notice of such meeting, except where a director attends a meeting for the express purpose of objecting to the transaction of any business because the meeting is not lawfully called or convened. Neither the business to be transacted at, nor the purpose of, any regular or special meeting of the board of directors or any committee designated thereby need be specified in the notice or waiver of notice of such meeting unless required by the by-laws.

Except as may be otherwise restricted by the articles of incorporation or by-laws, members of the board of directors or any committee designated thereby may participate in a meeting of such board or committee by means of a conference telephone or similar communications equipment by means of which all persons participating in the meeting can hear each other at the same time and participation by such means shall constitute presence in person at a meeting.

§ 44. ACTION BY DIRECTORS WITHOUT A MEETING

Unless otherwise provided by the articles of incorporation or by-laws, any action required by this Act to be taken at a meeting of the directors of a corporation, or any action which may be taken at a meeting of the directors or of a committee, may be taken without a meeting if a consent in writing, setting forth the action so to be taken, shall be signed before such action by all of the directors, or all of the members of the committee, as the case may be. Such consent shall have the same effect as a unanimous vote.

§ 45. DIVIDENDS

The board of directors of a corporation may, from time to time, declare and the corporation may pay dividends in cash, property, or its own shares, except when the corporation is insolvent or when the payment thereof would render the corporation insolvent or when the declaration or payment thereof would be contrary to any restriction contained in the articles of incorporation, subject to the following provisions:

(a) Dividends may be declared and paid in cash or property only out of the unreserved and unrestricted earned surplus of the corporation, except as otherwise provided in this section.

[Alternative] (a) Dividends may be declared and paid in cash or property only out of the unreserved and unrestricted earned surplus of the corporation, or out of the unreserved and unrestricted net earnings of the current fiscal year and the next preceding fiscal year taken as a single period, except as otherwise provided in this section.

(b) If the articles of incorporation of a corporation engaged in the business of exploiting natural resources so provide, dividends may be declared and paid in cash out of the depletion reserves, but each such dividend shall be identified as a distribution of such reserves and the amount per share paid from such reserves shall be disclosed to the shareholders receiving the same concurrently with the distribution thereof.

(c) Dividends may be declared and paid in its own treasury shares.

(d) Dividends may be declared and paid in its own authorized but unissued shares out of any unreserved and unrestricted surplus of the corporation upon the following conditions:

(1) If a dividend is payable in its own shares having a par value, such shares shall be issued at not less than the par value thereof and there shall be transferred to stated capital at the time such dividend is paid an amount of surplus at least equal to the aggregate par value of the shares to be issued as a dividend.

(2) If a dividend is payable in its own shares without par value, such shares shall be issued at such stated value as shall be fixed by the board of directors by resolution adopted at the time such dividend is declared, and there shall be transferred to stated capital at the time such dividend is paid an amount of surplus equal to the aggregate stated value so fixed in respect of such shares; and the amount per share so transferred to stated capital shall be disclosed to the shareholders receiving such dividend concurrently with the payment thereof.

(e) No dividend payable in shares of any class shall be paid to the holders of shares of any other class unless the articles of incorporation so provide or such payment is authorized by the affirmative vote or the written consent of the holders of at least a majority of the outstanding shares of the class in which the payment is to be made.

A split-up or division of the issued shares of any class into a greater number of shares of the same class without increasing the stated capital of the corporation shall not be construed to be a share dividend within the meaning of this section.

COMMENT

. . . . Every state has statutory limits which the directors may not exceed in the amount of dividends which they pay. In the Model Act, section 45 states the maximum limitations.

Legal maximum limits on dividends should be distinguished from the limits of business advisability. Ordinarily direc-

tors base their dividend policy on profits, and they distribute
only a portion of profits to shareholders.

The Model Act permits distributions other than dividends.
See section 46 and the comment concerning sections 2(i)-2(m).

*   *   *

Historically, dividends were payable out of profits,
and the word "dividend" implies a division of profits.
Furthermore, the theory developed that a corporation should
protect its capital for the benefit of third parties who
deal with it. One way of defining the protection of capital
is to prohibit dividends which exceed the surplus of the
corporation since surplus is the excess of net assets over
capital. That is the limitation which is in effect in most
of the states. However, the Model Act and some states which
have followed it limit dividends to the portion of surplus
resulting from accumulated profits, which is earned surplus. . . .

The directors may create reserves out of earned surplus.
See section 70. Subsection (a) of this section 45 contemplates
also that earned surplus may be restricted. Restrictions
may be agreed upon with creditors, for instance, in an
indenture or in a bank loan agreement. Typically such a
restriction might limit dividends to earned surplus in
excess of a specified amount. . . . Another type of restriction is imposed by law, as in section 6, which provides that
if earned surplus is used to purchase the corporation's own
shares, the amount of surplus so used is restricted so long
as the purchased shares are held in the treasury. The net
amount of earned surplus available for dividends must be
exclusive of all portions reserved or restricted.

*   *   *

In some states the existence of surplus does not depend
solely upon historical values but may depend upon the current
value of the corporation's assets, which does not necessarily
stay at book value but may go up or down. Earned surplus,
on the other hand, depends not on the value of the corporation's assets (unless there has been a substantial loss in
value), but upon the cumulative results of its operations.
Accounting practice and concepts necessarily are involved in
determining both surplus and earned surplus. They change
from time to time, in large degree independently of the law.

*   *   *

The basic difference between a stock dividend and a
stock split is that a dividend purports to distribute earnings
while a stock split does not; but stock splits are often
effected by declaration of stock dividends. This course of
action is feasible if the corporation has sufficient authorized and unissued shares. Often a stock split also involves
some change in the par or stated value of the shares which

are split and requires a meeting of shareholders. Thus a
true stock split of 100,000 $5 par value shares would create
200,000 $2.50 par value shares. But a distribution of one
share for every two held, although a dividend in form and
requiring a transfer to stated capital of earned surplus in
amount equal to the par or stated value of the dividend
shares, is usually considered a "split" rather than a dividend.

§ 46. DISTRIBUTIONS FROM CAPITAL SURPLUS

The board of directors of a corporation may, from time to time,
distribute to its shareholders out of capital surplus of the corporation
a portion of its assets, in cash or property, subject to the following
provisions:

(a) No such distribution shall be made at a time when the corporation is insolvent or when such distribution would render the
corporation insolvent.

(b) No such distribution shall be made unless the articles of incorporation so provide or such distribution is authorized by the affirmative vote of the holders of a majority of the outstanding shares of
each class whether or not entitled to vote thereon by the provisions
of the articles of incorporation of the corporation.

(c) No such distribution shall be made to the holders of any
class of shares unless all cumulative dividends accrued on all preferred
or special classes of shares entitled to preferential dividends shall
have been fully paid.

(d) No such distribution shall be made to the holders of any
class of shares which would reduce the remaining net assets of the
corporation below the aggregate preferential amount payable in event
of involuntary liquidation to the holders of shares having preferential
rights to the assets of the corporation in the event of liquidation.

(e) Each such distribution, when made, shall be identified as
a distribution from capital surplus and the amount per share disclosed
to the shareholders receiving the same concurrently with the distribution thereof.

The board of directors of a corporation may also, from time to
time, distribute to the holders of its outstanding shares having a
cumulative preferential right to receive dividends, in discharge of
their cumulative dividend rights, dividends payable in cash out of the
capital surplus of the corporation, if at the time the corporation has
no earned surplus and is not insolvent and would not thereby be rendered insolvent. Each such distribution, when made, shall be identified as a payment of cumulative dividends out of capital surplus.

§ 47. LOANS TO EMPLOYEES AND DIRECTORS

A corporation shall not lend money to or use its credit to assist
its directors without authorization in the particular case by its shareholders, but may lend money to and use its credit to assist any employee of the corporation or of a subsidiary, including any such em-

ployee who is a director of the corporation, if the board of directors decides that such loan or assistance may benefit the corporation.

§ 48.   LIABILITIES OF DIRECTORS IN CERTAIN CASES

In addition to any other liabilities, a director shall be liable in the following circumstances unless he complies with the standard provided in this Act for the performance of the duties of directors:

(a) A director who votes for or assents to the declaration of any dividend or other distribution of the assets of a corporation to its shareholders contrary to the provisions of this Act or contrary to any restrictions contained in the articles of incorporation, shall be liable to the corporation, jointly and severally with all other directors so voting or assenting, for the amount of such dividend which is paid or the value of such assets which are distributed in excess of the amount of such dividend or distribution which could have been paid or distributed without a violation of the provisions of this Act or the restrictions in the articles of incorporation.

(b) A director who votes for or assents to the purchase of the corporation's own shares contrary to the provisions of this Act shall be liable to the corporation, jointly and severally with all other directors so voting or assenting, for the amount of consideration paid for such shares which is in excess of the maximum amount which could have been paid therefor without a violation of the provisions of this Act.

(c) A director who votes for or assents to any distribution of assets of a corporation to its shareholders during the liquidation of the corporation without the payment and discharge of, or making adequate provision for, all known debts, obligations, and liabilities of the corporation shall be liable to the corporation, jointly and severally with all other directors so voting or assenting, for the value of such assets which are distributed, to the extent that such debts, obligations and liabilities of the corporation are not thereafter paid and discharged.

Any director against whom a claim shall be asserted under or pursuant to this section for the payment of a dividend or other distribution of assets of a corporation and who shall be held liable thereon, shall be entitled to contribution from the shareholders who accepted or received any such dividend or assets, knowing such dividend or distribution to have been made in violation of this Act, in proportion to the amounts received by them.

Any director against whom a claim shall be asserted under or pursuant to this section shall be entitled to contribution from the other directors who voted for or assented to the action upon which the claim is asserted.

COMMENT

In recent years, a growing number of jurisdictions have introduced, in their business corporation acts, an affirmative statement of a standard of care for directors and, in many instances, officers. Recognizing this trend, it has been determined desirable to provide a standard in the Model Act which would promote uniformity in the development by statute of the basis on which a director's performance shall be judged. The standard provided in Section 35, as revised [in 1974], sets forth the duty of care applicable to directors (including a director's right to rely on others), reflects the good faith concept embodied in the so-called "business judgment rule," which has been viewed by the courts as a fundamental precept for many decades, and to the extent possible parallels the Act's indemnification provisions.

By combining the requirement of good faith with the statement that a director must act "with such care as an ordinarily prudent person in a like position would use under similar circumstances," Section 35 incorporates the familiar concept that, these criteria being satisfied, a director should not be liable for an honest mistake of business judgment. A director attempting to create profits for his corporation will frequently make decisions involving risk for the enterprise. No personal liability should be imposed upon him in the event his good faith decision, in the exercise of business judgment, later seems to have been erroneous.

As a concomitant to the formulation of a standard of care, the Act has been modified to broaden both (i) the range of situations (presently limited in Section 48 to dividends, acquisitions by a corporation of its stock and distributions to stockholders) in which directors will have available to them, by force of statute, the right to rely on others and (ii) the range of materials on which directors will have the right to rely. In view of the persistent increase over the years in the complexity of corporate affairs, and hence in the number and complexity of the matters which directors must consider, retention of any limitation upon the right of reliance to specified categories of director actions is felt no longer warranted. . . .

A director complying with the standards expressed in the first sentence of the second paragraph of Section 35 will be entitled to rely upon information, opinions, reports or statements, including financial statements and other financial data, in [the circumstances there described]. Inherent in the good faith standard is the requirement that, in order to be entitled to rely on such reports, statements, opinions and other matters, the director must have read, or been present at the meeting at which is orally presented, the report or statement in question and must not have any pertinent knowledge which would cause him to conclude that he should not rely thereon. In making a judgment as to the reliability and competence of the source of information upon which a director proposes to rely, he must comply with the standard of care discussed above.

As for reliance upon outside advisors, it is intended that there be included not only the professional disciplines customarily supervised by state authorities, such as lawyers, accountants and engineers, but also other fields involving special experience and skills, such as geologists, management consultants and real estate appraisers. . . .

By reason of the changes treated in the previous paragraphs, the Committee determined that the provision included in Section 48 with regard to reliance on the corporation's assets being of their book value could be eliminated, for the reason that other provisions contained in the amendment deal more appropriately with the circumstances in which this provision might have applied.*

---

*[Ed. note] The provision eliminated in the 1974 amendments had precluded director liability under subparagraphs (a), (b) or (c) of §48 if he relied in good faith upon financial statements presented by the appropriate corporate officer or the outside accountants, or "if in good faith in determining the amount available for any such dividend or distribution he considered the assets to be at their book value".

§ 49. PROVISIONS RELATING TO ACTIONS BY SHAREHOLDERS

* * *

§ 50. OFFICERS

The officers of a corporation shall consist of a president, one or more vice presidents as may be prescribed by the by-laws, a secretary, and a treasurer, each of whom shall be elected by the board of directors at such time and in such manner as may be prescribed by the by-laws. Such other officers and assistant officers and agents as may be deemed necessary may be elected or appointed by the board of directors or chosen in such other manner as may be prescribed by the by-laws. Any two or more offices may be held by the same person, except the offices of president and secretary.

All officers and agents of the corporation, as between themselves and the corporation, shall have such authority and perform such duties in the management of the corporation as may be provided in the by-laws, or as may be determined by resolution of the board of directors not inconsistent with the by-laws.

§ 51. REMOVAL OF OFFICERS

Any officer or agent may be removed by the board of directors whenever in its judgment the best interests of the corporation will be served thereby, but such removal shall be without prejudice to the contract rights, if any, of the person so removed. Election or appointment of an officer or agent shall not of itself create contract rights.

§ 52. BOOKS AND RECORDS

Each corporation shall keep correct and complete books and records of account and shall keep minutes of the proceedings of its shareholders and board of directors and shall keep . . . a record of its shareholders, giving the names and addresses of all shareholders and the number and class of the shares held by each. . . .

Upon the written request of any shareholder or holder of voting trust certificates for shares of a corporation, the corporation shall mail to such shareholder or holder of voting trust certificates its most recent financial statements showing in reasonable detail its assets and liabilities and the results of its operations.

§ 53. INCORPORATORS

One or more persons, or a domestic or foreign corporation, may act as incorporator or incorporators of a corporation by signing and delivering in duplicate to the Secretary of State articles of incorporation for such corporation.

§ 54. ARTICLES OF INCORPORATION

The articles of incorporation shall set forth:

(a). The name of the corporation.

(b) The period of duration, which may be perpetual.

(c) The purpose or purposes for which the corporation is organized which may be stated to be, or to include, the transaction of any or all lawful business for which corporations may be incorporated under this act.

(d) The aggregate number of shares which the corporation shall have authority to issue; if such shares are to consist of one class only, the par value of each of such shares, or a statement that all of such shares are without par value; or, if such shares are to be divided into classes, the number of shares of each class, and a statement of the par value of the shares of each such class or that such shares are to be without par value.

(e) If the shares are to be divided into classes, the designation of each class and a statement of the preferences, limitations and relative rights in respect of the shares of each class.

(f) If the corporation is to issue the shares of any preferred or special class in series, then the designation of each series and a statement of the variations in the relative rights and preferences as between series in so far as the same are to be fixed in the articles of incorporation, and a statement of any authority to be vested in the board of directors to establish series and fix and determine the variations in the relative rights and preferences as between series.

(g) If any preemptive right is to be granted to shareholders, the provisions therefor.

(h) Any provision, not inconsistent with law, which the incorporators elect to set forth in the articles of incorporation for the regulation of the internal affairs of the corporation, including any provision restricting the transfer of shares and any provision which under this Act is required or permitted to be set forth in the by-laws.

(i) The address of its initial registered office, and the name of its initial registered agent at such address.

(j) The number of directors constituting the initial board of directors and the names and addresses of the persons who are to serve as directors until the first annual meeting of shareholders or until their successors be elected and qualify.

(k) The name and address of each incorporator.

It shall not be necessary to set forth in the articles of incorporation any of the corporate powers enumerated in this Act.

§ 55. FILING OF ARTICLES OF INCORPORATION
* * *

§ 56. EFFECT OF ISSUANCE OF CERTIFICATE OF INCORPORATION

Upon the issuance of the certificate of incorporation, the corporate existence shall begin, and such certificate of incorporation shall be conclusive evidence that all conditions precedent required to be performed by the incorporators have been complied with and that the corporation has been incorporated under this Act, except as against this State in a proceeding to cancel or revoke the certificate of incorporation or for involuntary dissolution of the corporation.

§ 57. ORGANIZATION MEETING OF DIRECTORS
* * *

§ 58. RIGHT TO AMEND ARTICLES OF INCORPORATION

A corporation may amend its articles of incorporation, from time to time, in any and as many respects as may be desired, so long as its articles of incorporation as amended contain only such provisions as might be lawfully contained in original articles of incorporation at the time of making such amendment, and, if a change in shares or the rights of shareholders, or an exchange, reclassification or cancellation of shares or rights of shareholders is to be made, such provisions as may be necessary to effect such change, exchange, reclassification or cancellation.

In particular, and without limitation upon such general power of amendment, a corporation may amend its articles of incorporation, from time to time, so as to:

(a) To change its corporate name.

(b) To change its period of duration.

(c) To change, enlarge or diminish its corporate purposes.

(d) To increase or decrease the aggregate number of shares, or shares of any class, which the corporation has authority to issue.

(e) To increase or decrease the par value of the authorized shares of any class having a par value, whether issued or unissued.

(f) To exchange, classify, reclassify or cancel all or any part of its shares, whether issued or unissued.

(g) To change the designation of all or any part of its shares, whether issued or unissued, and to change the preferences, limitations, and the relative rights in respect of all or any part of its shares, whether issued or unissued.

(h) To change shares having a par value, whether issued or unissued, into the same or a different number of shares without par value, and to change shares without par value, whether issued or unissued, into the same or a different number of shares having a par value.

(i) To change the shares of any class, whether issued or unissued, and whether with or without par value, into a different number of shares of the same class or into the same or a different number of shares, either with or without par value, of other classes.

(j) To create new classes of shares having rights and preferences either prior and superior or subordinate and inferior to the shares of any class then authorized, whether issued or unissued.

(k) To cancel or otherwise affect the right of the holders of the shares of any class to receive dividends which have accrued but have not been declared.

(l) To divide any preferred or special class of shares, whether issued or unissued, into series and fix and determine the designations of such series and the variations in the relative rights and preferences as between the shares of such series.

(m) To authorize the board of directors to establish, out of authorized but unissued shares, series of any preferred or special class of shares and fix and determine the relative rights and preferences of the shares of any series so established.

(n) To authorize the board of directors to fix and determine the relative rights and preferences of the authorized but unissued shares of series theretofore established in respect of which either the relative rights and preferences have not been fixed and determined or the relative rights and preferences theretofore fixed and determined are to be changed.

(o) To revoke, diminish, or enlarge the authority of the board of directors to establish series out of authorized but unissued shares of any preferred or special class and fix and determine the relative rights and preferences of the shares of any series so established.

(p) To limit, deny or grant to shareholders of any class the preemptive right to acquire additional or treasury shares of the corporation, whether then or thereafter authorized.

COMMENT

The broad power to amend conferred by the Model Act is intended to lay at rest the "vested rights" doctrine which originated with the United States Supreme Court decision in the Dartmouth College case (1819). · · ·
Although most of the states adopted constitutional provisions reserving the power to amend in an attempt to override the Dartmouth College decision, courts in certain jurisdictions developed the doctrine of "vested rights," holding that particular rights were immune from change in the absence of unanimous consent.

One of the major purposes of the Model Act was to sweep aside the complexities of judicial decisions on vested rights which were increasingly handicapping the conduct of business through the corporate form. Accordingly the amendment power under section 58 is both general and specific. The general power of amendment is broadly worded to permit any amendment if the new provision might lawfully be contained in original articles at the time of making the amendment. The specific powers to amend relate to those matters which either have been held in the past or, because of their importance, might otherwise be held to be "vested rights." Perhaps the area of greatest controversy has been the power to eliminate accrued dividend arrearages on cumulative preferred stock. Section 58(k) now specifically permits an amendment to cancel or otherwise affect the right of the holders of the shares of any class to receive dividends which have accrued but have not been declared.

In the "vested rights" cases the courts were construing a general statutory power to amend a charter as not applying to particular rights conferred on shareholders in the original articles. There is no occasion for such statutory construction under the Model Act. The specification of matters that may be amended necessarily takes them out of the category of "vested rights." The general language of the first sentence of section 58 is intended to have universal application and is not narrowed by the succeeding enumeration. The latter is included solely to rebut any presumption of "vested rights."

§ 59. PROCEDURE TO AMEND ARTICLES OF INCORPORATION

Amendments to the articles of incorporation shall be made in the following manner:

(a) The board of directors shall adopt a resolution setting forth the proposed amendment and, if shares have been issued, directing that it be submitted to a vote at a meeting of shareholders, which may be either the annual or a special meeting. . . .

(b) Written notice setting forth the proposed amendment or a summary of the changes to be affected thereby shall be given to each shareholder of record entitled to vote thereon within the time and in the manner provided in this Act for the giving of notice of meetings of shareholders. If the meeting be an annual meeting, the proposed amendment or such summary may be included in the notice of such annual meeting.

(c) At such meeting a vote of the shareholders entitled to vote thereon shall be taken on the proposed amendment. The proposed amendment shall be adopted upon receiving the affirmative vote of the holders of a majority of the shares entitled to vote thereon, unless any class of shares is entitled to vote thereon as a class, in which event the proposed amendments shall be adopted upon receiving the affirmative vote of the holders of a majority of the shares of each class of shares entitled to vote thereon as a class and of the total shares entitled to vote thereon.

Any number of amendments may be submitted to the shareholders, and voted upon by them, at one meeting.

§ 60. CLASS VOTING ON AMENDMENTS

The holders of the outstanding shares of a class shall be entitled to vote as a class upon a proposed amendment, whether or not entitled to vote thereon by the provisions of the articles of incorporation, if the amendment would:

(a) Increase or decrease the aggregate number of authorized shares of such class.

(b) Increase or decrease the par value of the shares of such class.

(c) Effect an exchange, reclassification or cancellation of all or part of the shares of such class.

(d) Effect an exchange, or create a right of exchange, of all or any part of the shares of another class into the shares of such class.

(e) Change the designations, preferences, limitations or relative rights of the shares of such class.

(f) Change the shares of such class, whether with or without par value, into the same or a different number of shares, either with or without par value, of the same class or another class or classes.

COMMENT

Section 60 must be read in conjunction with section 59. An otherwise non-voting class cannot by its own favorable vote under section 60 adopt an amendment if the amendment fails to win a majority of all shares entitled to vote thereon. Section 60 does not preclude additional provisions for class voting to be set forth in the articles but, of course, the articles cannot deprive any class of the voting rights granted to a class under section 60.

(g) Create a new class of shares having rights and preferences prior and superior to the shares of such class, or increase the rights and preferences or the number of authorized shares of any class having rights and preferences prior or superior to the shares of such class.

(h) In the case of a preferred or special class of shares, divide the shares of such class into series and fix and determine the designation of such series and the variations in the relative rights and preferences between the shares of such series, or authorize the board of directors to do so.

(i) Limit or deny any existing preemptive rights of the shares of such class.

(j) Cancel or otherwise affect dividends on the shares of such class which have accrued but have not been declared.

§ 61. ARTICLES OF AMENDMENT

The articles of amendment shall be executed in duplicate by the corporation by its president or a vice president and by its secretary or an assistant secretary, and verified by one of the officers signing such articles, and shall set forth:

(a) The name of the corporation.

(b) The amendments so adopted.

(c) The date of the adoption of the amendment by the shareholders, or by the board of directors where no shares have been issued.

(d) The number of shares outstanding, and the number of shares entitled to vote thereon, and if the shares of any class are entitled to vote thereon as a class, the designation and number of outstanding shares entitled to vote thereon of each such class.

(e) The number of shares voted for and against such amendment, respectively, and, if the shares of any class are entitled to vote thereon as a class, the number of shares of each such class voted for and against such amendment, respectively.

(f) If such amendment provides for an exchange, reclassification or cancellation of issued shares, and if the manner in which the same shall be effected is not set forth in the amendment, then a statement of the manner in which the same shall be effected.

(g) If such amendment effects a change in the amount of stated capital, then a statement of the manner in which the same is effected and a statement, expressed in dollars, of the amount of stated capital as changed by such amendment.

§ 62. FILING OF ARTICLES OF AMENDMENT

Duplicate originals of the articles of amendment shall be delivered to the Secretary of State. If the Secretary of State finds that the articles of amendment conform to law, he shall, when all fees and franchise taxes have been paid as in this Act prescribed:

(1) Endorse on each of such duplicate originals the word "Filed," and the month, day and year of the filing thereof.

(2) File one of such duplicate originals in his office.

(3) Issue a certificate of amendment to which he shall affix the other duplicate original.

The certificate of amendment, together with the duplicate original of the articles of amendment affixed thereto by the Secretary of State, shall be returned to the corporation or its representative.

§ 63. EFFECT OF CERTIFICATE OF AMENDMENT

The amendment shall become effective upon the issuance of the certificate of amendment by the Secretary of State, or on such later date, not more than thirty days subsequent to the filing thereof with the Secretary of State, as shall be provided for in the articles of incorporation.

No amendment shall affect any existing cause of action in favor of or against such corporation, or any pending suit to which such corporation shall be a party, or the existing rights of persons other than shareholders; and, in the event the corporate name shall be changed by amendment, no suit brought by or against such corporation under its former name shall abate for that reason.

§ 64. RESTATED ARTICLES OF INCORPORATION

* * *

§ 65. AMENDMENT OF ARTICLES OF INCORPORATION IN REORGANIZATION PROCEEDINGS

* * *

§ 66. RESTRICTION ON REDEMPTION OR PURCHASE OF REDEEMABLE SHARES

No redemption or purchase of redeemable shares shall be made by a corporation when it is insolvent or when such redemption or purchase would render it insolvent, or which would reduce the net assets below the aggregate amount payable to the holders of shares having prior or equal rights to the assets of the corporation upon involuntary dissolution.

§ 67. CANCELLATION OF REDEEMABLE SHARES BY REDEMPTION OR PURCHASE

When redeemable shares of a corporation are redeemed or purchased by the corporation, the redemption or purchase shall effect a cancellation of such shares, and a statement of cancellation shall be filed as provided in this section. Thereupon such shares shall be restored to the status of authorized but unissued shares, unless the articles of incorporation provide that such shares when redeemed or purchased shall not be reissued, in which case the filing of the statement of cancellation shall constitute an amendment to the articles of incorporation and shall reduce the number of shares of the class so cancelled which the corporation is authorized to issue by the number of shares so cancelled.

The statement of cancellation shall be executed in duplicate by the corporation by its president or a vice president and by its secretary or an assistant secretary, and verified by one of the officers signing such statement, and shall set forth:

(a) The name of the corporation.

(b) The number of redeemable shares cancelled through redemption or purchase, itemized by classes and series.

(c) The aggregate number of issued shares, itemized by classes and series, after giving effect to such cancellation.

(d) The amount, expressed in dollars, of the stated capital of the corporation after giving effect to such cancellation.

(e) If the articles of incorporation provide that the cancelled shares shall not be reissued, then the number of shares which the corporation has authority to issue, itemized by classes and series, after giving effect to such cancellation.

Duplicate originals of such statement shall be delivered to the Secretary of State. If the Secretary of State finds that such statement conforms to law, he shall, when all fees and franchise taxes have been paid as in this Act prescribed:

(1) Endorse on each of such duplicate originals the word "Filed," and the month, day and year of the filing thereof.

(2) File one of such duplicate originals in his office.

(3) Return the other duplicate original to the corporation or its representative.

Upon the filing of such statement of cancellation, the stated capital of the corporation shall be deemed to be reduced by that part of the stated capital which was, at the time of such cancellation, represented by the shares so cancelled.

Nothing contained in this section shall be construed to forbid a cancellation of shares or a reduction of stated capital in any other manner permitted by this Act.

§ 68. CANCELLATION OF OTHER REACQUIRED SHARES

A corporation may at any time, by resolution of its board of directors, cancel all or any part of the shares of the corporation of any class reacquired by it, other than redeemable shares redeemed or purchased, and in such event a statement of cancellation shall be filed as provided in this section.

The statement of cancellation shall be executed in duplicate by the corporation by its president or a vice president and by its secretary or an assistant secretary, and verified by one of the officers signing such statement, and shall set forth:

(a) The name of the corporation.

(b) The number of reacquired shares cancelled by resolution

duly adopted by the board of directors, itemized by classes and series, and the date of its adoption.

(c) The aggregate number of issued shares, itemized by classes and series, after giving effect to such cancellation.

(d) The amount, expressed in dollars, of the stated capital of the corporation after giving effect to such cancellation.

Duplicate originals of such statement shall be delivered to the Secretary of State. If the Secretary of State finds that such statement conforms to law, he shall, when all fees and franchise taxes have been paid as in this Act prescribed:

(1) Endorse on each of such duplicate originals the word "Filed," and the month, day and year of the filing thereof.

(2) File one of such duplicate originals in his office.

(3) Return the other duplicate original to the corporation or its representative.

Upon the filing of such statement of cancellation, the stated capital of the corporation shall be deemed to be reduced by that part of the stated capital which was, at the time of such cancellation, represented by the shares so cancelled, and the shares so cancelled shall be restored to the status of authorized but unissued shares.

Nothing contained in this section shall be construed to forbid a cancellation of shares or a reduction of stated capital in any other manner permitted by this Act.

§ 69. REDUCTION OF STATED CAPITAL IN CERTAIN CASES

A reduction of the stated capital of a corporation, where such reduction is not accompanied by any action requiring an amendment of the articles of incorporation and not accompanied by a cancellation of shares, may be made in the following manner:

(A) The board of directors shall adopt a resolution setting forth the amount of the proposed reduction and the manner in which the reduction shall be effected, and directing that the question of such reduction be submitted to a vote at a meeting of shareholders, which may be either an annual or a special meeting.

(B) Written notice, stating that the purpose or one of the purposes of such meeting is to consider the question of reducing the stated capital of the corporation in the amount and manner proposed by the board of directors, shall be given to each shareholder of record entitled to vote thereon within the time and in the manner provided in this Act for the giving of notice of meetings of shareholders.

(C) At such meeting a vote of the shareholders entitled to vote thereon shall be taken on the question of approving the proposed reduction of stated capital, which shall require for its adoption the affirmative vote of the holders of a majority of the shares entitled to vote thereon.

When a reduction of the stated capital of a corporation has been approved as provided in this section, a statement shall be executed in duplicate by the corporation by its president or a vice president and by its secretary or an assistant secretary, and verified by one of the officers signing such statement, and shall set forth:

(a) The name of the corporation.

(b) A copy of the resolution of the shareholders approving such reduction, and the date of its adoption.

(c) The number of shares outstanding, and the number of shares entitled to vote thereon.

(d) The number of shares voted for and against such reduction, respectively.

(e) A statement of the manner in which such reduction is effected, and a statement, expressed in dollars, of the amount of stated capital of the corporation after giving effect to such reduction.

Duplicate originals of such statement shall be delivered to the Secretary of State. If the Secretary of State finds that such statement conforms to law, he shall, when all fees and franchise taxes have been paid as in this Act prescribed:

(1) Endorse on each of such duplicate originals the word "Filed," and the month, day and year of the filing thereof.

(2) File one of such duplicate originals in his office.

(3) Return the other duplicate original to the corporation or its representative.

Upon the filing of such statement, the stated capital of the corporation shall be reduced as therein set forth.

No reduction of stated capital shall be made under the provisions of this section which would reduce the amount of the aggregate stated capital of the corporation to an amount equal to or less than the aggregate preferential amounts payable upon all issued shares having a preferential right in the assets of the corporation in the event of involuntary liquidation, plus the aggregate par value of all issued shares having a par value but no preferential right in the assets of the corporation in the event of involuntary liquidation.

COMMENT

A reduction of stated capital . . . creates a corresponding capital surplus (section 70), which may be distributed to shareholders in the manner prescribed in section 46, or be applied against an existing deficit [in surplus]. . . . [An earlier version on this Comment added the following: "This Section is applicable to action involving nothing more than a reduction of the stated capital represented by issued shares of no par value or, in the case of shares with par value where the stated capital represented thereby has been increased to an amount above par value, a reduction of such stated capital to an amount not less than the par value."]

§ 70. SPECIAL PROVISIONS RELATING TO SURPLUS AND RESERVES

The surplus, if any, created by or arising out of a reduction of the stated capital of a corporation shall be capital surplus.

The capital surplus of a corporation may be increased from time to time by resolution of the board of directors directing that all or a part of the earned surplus of the corporation be transferred to capital surplus.

A corporation may, by resolution of its board of directors, apply any part or all of its capital surplus to the reduction or elimination of any deficit arising from losses, however incurred, but only after first eliminating the earned surplus, if any, of the corporation by applying such losses against earned surplus and only to the extent that such losses exceed the earned surplus, if any. Each such application of capital surplus shall, to the extent thereof, effect a reduction of capital surplus.

A corporation may, by resolution of its board of directors, create a reserve or reserves out of its earned surplus for any proper purpose or purposes, and may abolish any such reserve in the same manner. Earned surplus of the corporation to the extent so reserved shall not be available for the payment of dividends or other distributions by the corporation except as expressly permitted by this Act.

§ 71. PROCEDURE FOR MERGER

Any two or more domestic corporations may merge into one of such corporations pursuant to a plan of merger approved in the manner provided in this Act.

The board of directors of each corporation shall, by resolution adopted by each such board, approve a plan of merger setting forth:

(a) The names of the corporations proposing to merge, and the name of the corporation into which they propose to merge, which is hereinafter designated as the surviving corporation.

(b) The terms and conditions of the proposed merger.

(c) The manner and basis of converting the shares of each corporation into shares, obligations or other securities of the surviving corporation or of any other corporation or, in whole or in part, into cash or other property.

(d) A statement of any changes in the articles of incorporation of the surviving corporation to be effected by such merger.

(e) Such other provisions with respect to the proposed merger as are deemed necessary or desirable.

§ 72. PROCEDURE FOR CONSOLIDATION

Any two or more domestic corporations may consolidate into a new corporation pursuant to a plan of consolidation approved in the manner provided in this Act.

The board of directors of each corporation shall, by a resolution adopted by each such board, approve a plan of consolidation setting forth:

(a) The names of the corporations proposing to consolidate, and the name of the new corporation into which they propose to consolidate, which is hereinafter designated as the new corporation.

(b) The terms and conditions of the proposed consolidation.

(c) The manner and basis of converting the shares of each corporation into shares, obligations or other securities of the new corporation or of any other corporation or, in whole or in part, into cash or other property.

(d) With respect to the new corporation, all of the statements required to be set forth in articles of incorporation for corporations organized under this Act.

(e) Such other provisions with respect to the proposed consolidation as are deemed necessary or desirable.

§ 72A. PROCEDURE FOR SHARE EXCHANGE

All the issued or all the outstanding shares of one or more classes of any domestic corporation may be acquired through the exchange of all such shares of such class or classes by another domestic or foreign corporation pursuant to a plan of exchange approved in the manner provided in this Act.

The board of directors of each corporation shall, by resolution adopted by each such board, approve a plan of exchange setting forth:

(a) The name of the corporation the shares of which are proposed to be acquired by exchange and the name of the corporation to acquire the shares of such corporation in the exchange, which is hereinafter designated as the acquiring corporation.

(b) The terms and conditions of the proposed exchange.

(c) The manner and basis of exchanging the shares to be acquired for shares, obligations or other securities of the acquiring corporation or any other corporation, or, in whole or in part, for cash or other property.

(d) Such other provisions with respect to the proposed exchange as are deemed necessary or desirable.

The procedure authorized by this Section shall not be deemed to limit the power of a corporation to acquire all or part of the shares of any class or classes of a corporation through a voluntary exchange or otherwise by agreement with the shareholders.

COMMENT

[Section 72A was added in 1974 to] establish a procedure by which direct exchanges of shares in corporate combinations

may be effected utilizing the same safeguards, notice requirements and shareholder voting rights required for comparable
mergers and similar transactions and resulting in the same
binding effect upon shareholders.

It is often desirable to effect a reorganization or
combination in such a way that the corporation to be acquired
does not go out of existence, and after the transaction
becomes a subsidiary of the acquiring corporation or holding
company, the securities of which are issued in the transaction.

Under the Model Act [apart from §72A], the same end
result may be obtained by the formation of a new subsidiary
of the acquiring or holding company, followed by a merger of
that new subsidiary into the corporation to be acquired in
which securities of the new subsidiary's parent are exchanged
for securities of the corporation to be acquired. This may
be done under the authority of Section 71(c) of the Model
Act . . . . This procedure is often cumbersome and requires
the utilization of a number of extraneous technical steps
that have no real substance.

[Section 72A provides] a direct, straight-forward
procedure for a corporate transaction while preserving the
same safeguards and procedures that now apply generally to
mergers and similar transactions.

Under Section 72A, all shares of a particular class of
shares must be included in the plan on the same basis but
treasury shares may be included or excluded. Shares of one
or more classes may be excluded from the plan. The procedure
calls for directors' action by both corporations, but does
not require shareholder action by the acquiring corporation
unless that is required for some additional reason (such as
provisions of the Articles of Incorporation, the necessity
for increasing authorized shares, or the requirements of
foreign law). In addition, it is not necessary for the
jurisdiction of incorporation of an acquiring foreign corporation to have any similar or special legislation in order
for the acquiring foreign corporation to participate in the
exchange, even though the share exchange procedure cannot be
utilized under the Model Act with respect to the acquired
corporation without the adoption of the amendments to the
law of the jurisdiction of its incorporation. The Section
contemplates a plan of exchange embodying the same basic
elements found in a plan of merger or consolidation. As
provided in the last sentence of Section 72A, the introduction
of this procedure does not limit any procedures now available
for exchanges of shares.

Changes in Section 73 are made to conform the provisions to the requirements of new Section 72A. All voting rights are made comparable to the analogous merger situation.

§ 73. APPROVAL BY SHAREHOLDERS

(a) The board of directors of each corporation in the case of a merger or consolidation, and the board of directors of the corporation the shares of which are to be acquired in the case of an exchange, upon approving such plan of merger, consolidation or exchange, shall, by resolution, direct that the plan be submitted to a vote at a meeting of its shareholders, which may be either an annual or a special meeting. Written notice shall be given to each shareholder of record, whether or not entitled to vote at such meeting, not less than twenty days before such meeting, in the manner provided in this Act for the giving of notice of meetings of shareholders, and, whether the meeting be an annual or a special meeting, shall state that the purpose or one of the purposes is to consider the proposed plan of merger, consolidation or exchange. A copy or a summary of the plan of merger, consolidation or exchange, as the case may be, shall be included in or enclosed with such notice.

(b) At each such meeting, a vote of the shareholders shall be taken on the proposed plan. The plan shall be approved upon receiving the affirmative vote of the holders of a majority of the shares entitled to vote thereon of each such corporation, unless any class of shares of any such corporation is entitled to vote thereon as a class, in which event, as to such corporation, the plan shall be approved upon receiving the affirmative vote of the holders of a majority of the shares of each class of shares entitled to vote thereon as a class and of the total shares entitled to vote thereon. Any class of shares of any such corporation shall be entitled to vote as a class if any such plan contains any provision which, if contained in a proposed amendment to articles of incorporation, would entitle such class of shares to vote as a class and, in the case of an exchange, if the class is included in the exchange.

(c) After such approval by a vote of the shareholders of each such corporation, and at any time prior to the filing of the articles of merger, consolidation or exchange, the merger, consolidation or exchange may be abandoned pursuant to provisions therefor, if any, set forth in the plan.

(d)(1) Notwithstanding the provisions of subsections (a) and (b), submission of a plan of merger to a vote at a meeting of shareholders of a surviving corporation shall not be required if:

(i) the articles of incorporation of the surviving corporation do not differ except in name from those of the corporation before the merger,

(ii) each holder of shares of the surviving corporation which were outstanding immediately before the effective date of the merger is to hold the same number of shares with identical rights immediately after,

(iii) the number of voting shares outstanding immediately after the merger, plus the number of voting shares issuable on conversion of other securities issued by virtue of the terms of the merger and on exercise of rights and warrants so issued, will not exceed by more than 20 percent the number of voting shares outstanding immediately before the merger, and

(iv) the number of participating shares outstanding immediately after the merger, plus the number of participating shares issuable on conversion of other securities issued by virtue of the terms of the merger and on exercise of rights and warrants so issued, will not exceed by more than 20 percent the number of participating shares outstanding immediately before the merger.

(2) As used in this subsection:

(i) "voting shares" means shares which entitle their holders to vote unconditionally in elections of directors;

(ii) "participating shares" means shares which entitle their holders to participate without limitation in distribution of earnings or surplus.

COMMENT

Because of the fundamental change in corporate existence that may result from a merger or consolidation, it was [earlier] thought that sound reasons exist for requiring more than a bare majority of voting shares for the imposition of such an alteration on the minority. The extent to which the margin may be increased above that point involves a balancing with the need to prevent a small minority from arbitrarily blocking the wishes of a substantial majority. Accordingly, the Model Act originally adopted two-thirds as a point for attaining reasonable balance. However, in 1969 an amendment reduced the required vote from two-thirds to a majority in recognition of the generally prevailing view that, unless otherwise provided in the articles, a minority should not be permitted to block the wishes of the majority. This is in keeping with similar amendments applicable to several other sections where a two-thirds vote was formerly required.

The Model Act as originally drafted provided that each share carried the right to vote on a proposed plan of merger or consolidation, whether or not entitled to vote under the articles of incorporation. In 1962 an amendment eliminated this provision on the ground that shareholders who had waived the right to vote on all other fundamental issues deserved no inalienable right to vote on mergers and consolidations, and voting on a proposed plan of merger or consolidation was made conditional upon receiving only the affirmative vote of holders of a majority of the shares entitled to vote thereon. Class voting is required if the plan of merger or consolidation contains any provision which, if contained in a proposed amendment to the articles, would entitle such class of shares to vote as a class.

§ 74. ARTICLES OF MERGER, CONSOLIDATION OR EXCHANGE

(a) Upon receiving the approvals required by sections 71, 72 and 73, articles of merger or articles of consolidation shall be executed in duplicate by each corporation by its president or a vice president and by its secretary or an assistant secretary, and verified by one of the officers of each corporation signing such articles, and shall set forth:

(1) The plan of merger or the plan of consolidation;

(2) As to each corporation, either (i) the number of shares outstanding, and, if the shares of any class are entitled to vote as a class, the designation and number of outstanding shares of each such class, or (ii) a statement that the vote of shareholders is not required by virtue of subsection 73(d);

(3) As to each corporation the approval of whose shareholders is required, the number of shares voted for and against such plan, respectively, and, if the shares of any class are entitled to vote as a class, the number of shares of each such class voted for and against such plan, respectively.

(b) Duplicate originals of the articles of merger, consolidation or exchange shall be delivered to the Secretary of State. If the Secretary of State finds that such articles conform to law, he shall, when all fees and franchise taxes have been paid as in this Act prescribed:

(1) Endorse on each of such duplicate originals the word "Filed," and the month, day and year of the filing thereof.

(2) File one of such duplicate originals in his office.

(3) Issue a certificate of merger, consolidation or exchange to which he shall affix the other duplicate original.

(c) The certificate of merger, consolidation or exchange together with the duplicate original of the articles affixed thereto by the Secretary of State, shall be returned to the surviving, new or acquiring corporation, as the case may be, or its representative.

§ 75. MERGER OF SUBSIDIARY CORPORATION

Any corporation owning at least ninety per cent of the outstanding shares of each class of another corporation may merge such other corporation into itself without approval by a vote of the shareholders of either corporation. Its board of directors shall, by resolution, approve a plan of merger setting forth:

(a) The name of the subsidiary corporation and the name of the corporation owning at least ninety per cent of its shares, which is hereinafter designated as the surviving corporation.

(b) The manner and basis of converting the shares of the subsidiary corporation into shares, obligations or other securities of the surviving corporation or of any other corporation or, in whole or in part, into cash or other property.

A copy of such plan of merger shall be mailed to each shareholder of record of the subsidiary corporation.

Articles of merger shall be executed in duplicate by the surviving corporation by its president or a vice president and by its secretary or an assistant secretary, and verified by one of its officers signing such articles, and shall set forth:

(a) The plan of merger;

(b) The number of outstanding shares of each class of the subsidiary corporation and the number of such shares of each class owned by the surviving corporation; and

(c) The date of the mailing to shareholders of the subsidiary corporation of a copy of the plan of merger.

On and after the thirtieth day after the mailing of a copy of the plan of merger to shareholders of the subsidiary corporation or upon the waiver thereof by the holders of all outstanding shares duplicate originals of the articles of merger shall be delivered to the Secretary of State. If the Secretary of State finds that such articles conform to law, he shall, when all fees and franchise taxes have been paid as in this Act prescribed:

(1) Endorse on each of such duplicate originals the word "Filed," and the month, day and year of the filing thereof;

(2) File one of such duplicate originals in his office; and

(3) Issue a certificate of merger to which he shall affix the other duplicate original.

The certificate of merger, together with the duplicate original of the articles of merger affixed thereto by the Secretary of State, shall be returned to the surviving corporation or its representative.

§ 76. EFFECT OF MERGER, CONSOLIDATION OR EXCHANGE

A merger, consolidation or exchange shall become effective upon the issuance of a certificate of merger, consolidation or exchange by the Secretary of State, or on such later date, not more than thirty days subsequent to the filing thereof with the Secretary of State, as shall be provided for in the plan.

When a merger or consolidation has become effective:

(a) The several corporations parties to the plan of merger or consolidation shall be a single corporation, which, in the case of a merger, shall be that corporation designated in the plan of merger as the surviving corporation, and, in the case of a consolidation, shall be the new corporation provided for in the plan of consolidation.

(b) The separate existence of all corporations parties to the plan of merger or consolidation, except the surviving or new corporation, shall cease.

(c) Such surviving or new corporation shall have all the rights, privileges, immunities and powers and shall be subject to all the duties and liabilities of a corporation organized under this Act.

(d) Such surviving or new corporation shall thereupon and thereafter possess all the rights, privileges, immunities, and franchises, of a public as well as of a private nature, of each of the merging or consolidating corporations; and all property, real, personal and mixed, and all debts due on whatever account, including subscriptions to shares, and all other choses in action, and all and every other interest of or belonging to or due to each of the corporations so merged or consolidated, shall be taken and deemed to be transferred to and vested in such single corporation without further act or deed; and the title to any real estate, or any interest therein, vested in any of such corporations shall not revert or be in any way impaired by reason of such merger or consolidation.

(e) Such surviving or new corporation shall thenceforth be responsible and liable for all the liabilities and obligations of each of the corporations so merged or consolidated; and any claim existing or action or proceeding pending by or against any of such corporations may be prosecuted as if such merger or consolidation had not taken place, or such surviving or new corporation may be substituted in its place. Neither the rights of creditors nor any liens upon the property of any such corporation shall be impaired by such merger or consolidation.

(f) In the case of a merger, the articles of incorporation of the surviving corporation shall be deemed to be amended to the extent, if any, that changes in its articles of incorporation are stated in the plan of merger; and, in the case of a consolidation, the statements set forth in the articles of consolidation and which are required or permitted to be set forth in the articles of incorporation of corporations organized under this Act shall be deemed to be the original articles of incorporation of the new corporation.

When a merger, consolidation or exchange has become effective, the shares of the corporation or corporations party to the plan that are, under the terms of the plan, to be converted or exchanged, shall cease to exist, in the case of a merger or consolidation, or be deemed to be exchanged in the case of an exchange, and the holders of such shares shall thereafter be entitled only to the shares, obligations, other securities, cash or other property into which they shall have been converted or for which they shall have been exchanged, in accordance with the plan, subject to any rights under Section 80 of this Act.

§ 77. MERGER, CONSOLIDATION OR EXCHANGE OF SHARES BETWEEN DOMESTIC AND FOREIGN CORPORATIONS

One or more foreign corporations and one or more domestic corporations may be merged or consolidated, or participate in an exchange, in the following manner, if such merger, consolidation or exchange is permitted by the laws of the state under which each such foreign corporation is organized:

(a) Each domestic corporation shall comply with the provisions of this Act with respect to the merger, consolidation or exchange, as the case may be, of domestic corporations and each foreign corporation shall comply with the applicable provisions of the laws of the state under which it is organized.

(b) If the surviving or new corporation in a merger or consolidation is to be governed by the laws of any state other than this State, it shall comply with the provisions of this Act with respect to foreign corporations if it is to transact business in this State, and in every case it shall file with the Secretary of State of this State:

(1) An agreement that it may be served with process in this State in any proceeding for the enforcement of any obligation of any domestic corporation which is a party to such merger or consolidation and in any proceeding for the enforcement of the rights of a dissenting shareholder of any such domestic corporation against the surviving or new corporation;

(2) An irrevocable appointment of the Secretary of State of this State as its agent to accept service of process in any such proceeding; and

(3) An agreement that it will promptly pay to the dissenting shareholders of any such domestic corporation, the amount, if any, to which they shall be entitled under provisions of this Act with respect to the rights of dissenting shareholders.

§ 78. SALE OF ASSETS IN REGULAR COURSE OF BUSINESS AND MORTGAGE OR PLEDGE OF ASSETS

The sale, lease, exchange, or other disposition of all, or substantially all, the property and assets of a corporation in the usual and regular course of its business and the mortgage or pledge of any or all property and assets of a corporation whether or not in the usual and regular course of business may be made upon such terms and conditions and for such consideration, which may consist in whole or in part of money or property, real or personal, including shares of any other corporation, domestic or foreign, as shall be authorized by its board of directors; and in any such case no authorization or consent of the shareholders shall be required.

§ 79. SALE OF ASSETS OTHER THAN IN REGULAR COURSE OF BUSINESS

A sale, lease, exchange, or other disposition of all, or substantially all, the property and assets, with or without the good will, of a corporation, if not in the usual and regular course of its business, may be made upon such terms and conditions and for such consideration, which may consist in whole or in part of cash or other property, including shares, obligations or other securities of any other corporation, domestic or foreign, as may be authorized in the following manner:

(a) The board of directors shall adopt a resolution recommending such sale, lease, exchange, or other disposition and directing the submission thereof to a vote at a meeting of shareholders, which may be either an annual or a special meeting.

(b) Written notice shall be given to each shareholder of record, whether or not entitled to vote at such meeting, not less than twenty days before such meeting, in the manner provided in this Act for the giving of notice of meetings of shareholders, and, whether the meeting be an annual or a special meeting, shall state that the purpose, or one of the purposes is to consider the proposed sale, lease, exchange, or other disposition.

(c) At such meeting the shareholders may authorize such sale, lease, exchange, or other disposition and may fix, or may authorize the board of directors to fix, any or all of the terms and conditions thereof and the consideration to be received by the corporation therefor. Such authorization shall require the affirmative vote of the holders of a majority of the shares of the corporation entitled to vote thereon, unless any class of shares is entitled to vote thereon as a class, in which event such authorization shall require the affirmative vote of the holders of a majority of the shares of each class of shares entitled to vote as a class thereon and of the total shares entitled to vote thereon.

(d) After such authorization by a vote of shareholders, the board of directors nevertheless, in its discretion, may abandon such sale, lease, exchange, or other disposition of assets, subject to the rights of third parties under any contracts relating thereto, without further action or approval by shareholders.

The vote of shareholders required to authorize a transaction within the scope of section 79 is a majority of the voting shares, a majority of the shares of any class which has been given a class vote on such a transaction by the articles and a majority of the total shares entitled to vote thereon.

§ 80. RIGHT OF SHAREHOLDERS TO DISSENT AND OBTAIN PAYMENT FOR SHARES

(a) Any shareholder of a corporation shall have the right to dissent from, and to obtain payment for his shares in the event of, any of the following corporate actions:

(1) Any plan of merger or consolidation to which the corporation is a party, except as provided in subsection (c) ;

(2) Any sale or exchange of all or substantially all of the property and assets of the corporation not made in the usual or regular course of its business, including a sale in dissolution, but not including a sale pursuant to an order of a court having jurisdiction in the premises or a sale for cash on terms requiring that all or substantially all of the net proceeds of sale be distributed to the shareholders in accordance with their respective interests within one year after the date of sale;

(3) Any plan of exchange to which the corporation is a party as the corporation the shares of which are to be acquired;

(4) Any amendment of the articles of incorporation which materially and adversely affects the rights appurtenant to the shares of the dissenting shareholder in that it:

(i) alters or abolishes a preferential right of such shares;

(ii) creates, alters or abolishes a right in respect of the redemption of such shares, including a provision respecting a sinking fund for the redemption or repurchase of such shares;

(iii) alters or abolishes a preemptive right of the holder of such shares to acquire shares or other securities;

(iv) excludes or limits the right of the holder of such shares to vote on any matter, or to cumulate his votes, except as such right may be limited by dilution through the issuance of shares or other securities with similar voting rights; or

(5) Any other corporate action taken pursuant to a shareholder vote with respect to which the articles of incorporation, the bylaws, or a resolution of the board of directors directs that dissenting shareholders shall have a right to obtain payment for their shares.

(b) (1) A record holder of shares may assert dissenters' rights as to less than all of the shares registered in his name only if he dissents with respect to all the shares beneficially owned by any one person, and discloses the name and address of the person or persons on whose behalf he dissents. In that event, his rights shall be determined as if the shares as to which he has dissented and his other shares were registered in the names of different shareholders.

(2) A beneficial owner of shares who is not the record holder may assert dissenters' rights with respect to shares held on his behalf, and shall be treated as a dissenting shareholder under the terms of this section and section 31 if he submits to the corporation at the time of or before the assertion of these rights a written consent of the record holder.

(c) The right to obtain payment under this section shall not apply to the shareholders of the surviving corporation in a merger if a vote of the shareholders of such corporation is not necessary to authorize such merger.

(d) A shareholder of a corporation who has a right under this section to obtain payment for his shares shall have no right at law or in equity to attack the validity of the corporate action that gives rise to his right to obtain payment, nor to have the action set aside or rescinded, except when the corporate action is unlawful or fraudulent with regard to the complaining shareholder or to the corporation.

§ 81. PROCEDURES FOR PROTECTION OF DISSENTERS' RIGHTS

(a) As used in this section:

(1) "Dissenter" means a shareholder or beneficial owner who is entitled to and does assert dissenters' rights under section 80, and who has performed every act required up to the time involved for the assertion of such rights.

(2) "Corporation" means the issuer of the shares held by the dissenter before the corporate action, or the successor by merger or consolidation of that issuer.

(3) "Fair value" of shares means their value immediately before the effectuation of the corporate action to which the dissenter objects, excluding any appreciation or depreciation in anticipation of such corporate action unless such exclusion would be inequitable.

(4) "Interest" means interest from the effective date of the corporate action until the date of payment, at the average rate currently paid by the corporation on its principal bank loans, or, if none, at such rate as is fair and equitable under all the circumstances.

(b) If a proposed corporate action which would give rise to dissenters' rights under section 80(a) is submitted to a vote at a meeting of shareholders, the notice of meeting shall notify all shareholders that they have or may have a right to dissent and obtain payment for their shares by complying with the terms of this section, and shall be accompanied by a copy of sections 80 and 81 of this Act.

(c) If the proposed corporate action is submitted to a vote at a meeting of shareholders, any shareholder who wishes to dissent and obtain payment for his shares must file with the corporation, prior to the vote, a written notice of intention to demand that he be paid fair compensation for his shares if the proposed action is effectuated, and shall refrain from voting his shares in approval of such action. A shareholder who fails in either respect shall acquire no right to payment for his shares under this section or section 80.

(d) If the proposed corporate action is approved by the required vote at a meeting of shareholders, the corporation shall mail a further notice to all shareholders who gave due notice of intention to demand payment and who refrained from voting in favor of the proposed action. If the proposed corporate action is to be taken without a vote of shareholders, the corporation shall send to all shareholders who are entitled to dissent and demand payment for their shares a notice of the adoption of the plan of corporate action. The notice shall (1) state where and when a demand for payment must be sent and certificates of certificated shares must be deposited in order to obtain payment, (2) inform holders of uncertificated shares to what extent transfer of shares will be restricted from the time that demand for payment is received, (3) supply a form for demanding payment which includes a request for certification of the date on which the shareholder, or the person on whose behalf the shareholder dissents, acquired beneficial ownership of the shares, and (4) be accompanied by a copy of sections 80 and 81 of this Act. The time set for the demand and deposit shall be not less than 30 days from the mailing of the notice.

(e) A shareholder who fails to demand payment, or fails (in the case of certificated shares) to deposit certificates, as required by a notice pursuant to subsection (d) shall have no right under this section or section 80 to receive payment for his shares. If the shares are not represented by certificates, the corporation may restrict their transfer from the time of receipt of demand for payment until effectuation of the proposed corporate action, or the release of restrictions under the terms of subsection (f). The dissenter shall retain all other rights of a shareholder until these rights are modified by effectuation of the proposed corporate action.

(f)(1) Within 60 days after the date set for demanding payment and depositing certificates, if the corporation has not effectuated the proposed corporate action and remitted payment for shares pursuant to paragraph (3), it shall return any certificates that have been deposited, and release uncertificated shares from any transfer restrictions imposed by reason of the demand for payment.

(2) When uncertificated shares have been released from transfer restrictions, and deposited certificates have been returned, the corporation may at any later time send a new notice conforming to the requirements of subsection (d), with like effect.

(3) Immediately upon effectuation of the proposed corporate action, or upon receipt of demand for payment if the corporate action has already been effectuated, the corporation shall remit to dissenters who have made demand and (if their shares are certificated) have deposited their certificates the amount which the corporation estimates to be the fair value of the shares, with interest if any has accrued. The remittance shall be accompanied by:

(i) the corporation's closing balance sheet and statement of income for a fiscal year ending not more than 16 months before the date of remittance, together with the latest available interim financial statements;

(ii) a statement of the corporation's estimate of fair value of the shares; and

(iii) a notice of the dissenter's right to demand supplemental payment, accompanied by a copy of sections 80 and 81 of this Act.

(g)(1) If the corporation fails to remit as required by subsection (f), or if the dissenter believes that the amount remitted is less than the fair value of his shares, or that the interest is not correctly determined, he may send the corporation his own estimate of the value of the shares or of the interest, and demand payment of the deficiency.

(2) If the dissenter does not file such an estimate within 30 days after the corporation's mailing of its remittance, he shall be entitled to no more than the amount remitted.

(h)(1) Within 60 days after receiving a demand for payment pursuant to subsection (g), if any such demands for payment remain unsettled, the corporation shall file in an appropriate court a petition requesting that the fair value of the shares and interest thereon be determined by the court.

(2) An appropriate court shall be a court of competent jurisdiction in the county of this state where the registered office of the corporation is located. If, in the case of a merger or consolidation or exchange of shares, the corporation is a foreign corporation without a registered office in this state, the petition shall be filed in the

county where the registered office of the domestic corporation was last located.

(3) All dissenters, wherever residing, whose demands have not been settled shall be made parties to the proceeding as in an action against their shares. A copy of the petition shall be served on each such dissenter; if a dissenter is a nonresident, the copy may be served on him by registered or certified mail or by publication as provided by law.

(4) The jurisdiction of the court shall be plenary and exclusive. The court may appoint one or more persons as appraisers to receive evidence and recommend a decision on the question of fair value. The appraisers shall have such power and authority as shall be specified in the order of their appointment or in any amendment thereof. The dissenters shall be entitled to discovery in the same manner as parties in other civil suits.

(5) All dissenters who are made parties shall be entitled to judgment for the amount by which the fair value of their shares is found to exceed the amount previously remitted, with interest.

(6) If the corporation fails to file a petition as provided in paragraph (1) of this subsection, each dissenter who made a demand and who has not already settled his claim against the corporation shall be paid by the corporation the amount demanded by him, with interest, and may sue therefor in an appropriate court.

(i)(1) The costs and expenses of any proceeding under subsection (h), including the reasonable compensation and expenses of appraisers appointed by the court, shall be determined by the court and assessed against the corporation, except that any part of the costs and expenses may be apportioned and assessed as the court may deem equitable against all or some of the dissenters who are parties and whose action in demanding supplemental payment the court finds to be arbitrary, vexatious, or not in good faith.

(2) Fees and expenses of counsel and of experts for the respective parties may be assessed as the court may deem equitable against the corporation and in favor of any or all dissenters if the corporation failed to comply substantially with the requirements of this section, and may be assessed against either the corporation or a dissenter, in favor of any other party, if the court finds that the party against whom the fees and expenses are assessed acted arbitrarily, vexatiously, or not in good faith in respect to the rights provided by this section and section 80.

(3) If the court finds that the services of counsel for any dissenter were of substantial benefit to other dissenters similarly situated, and should not be assessed against the corporation, it may award to these counsel reasonable fees to be paid out of the amounts awarded to the dissenters who were benefitted.

(j)(1) Notwithstanding the foregoing provisions of this section, the corporation may elect to withhold the remittance required by subsection (f) from any dissenter with respect to shares of which the dissenter (or the person on whose behalf the dissenter acts) was not the beneficial owner on the date of the first announcement to news media or to shareholders of the terms of the proposed corporate action. With respect to such shares, the corporation shall, upon effectuating the corporate action, state to each dissenter its estimate of the fair value of the shares, state the rate of interest to be used (explaining the basis thereof), and offer to pay the resulting amounts on receiving the dissenter's agreement to accept them in full satisfaction.

(2) If the dissenter believes that the amount offered is less than the fair value of the shares and interest determined according to this section, he may within 30 days after the date of mailing of the corporation's offer, mail the corporation his own estimate of fair value and interest, and demand their payment. If the dissenter fails to do so, he shall be entitled to no more than the corporation's offer.

(3) If the dissenter makes a demand as provided in paragraph (2), the provisions of subsections (h) and (i) shall apply to further proceedings on the dissenter's demand.

§82 VOLUNTARY DISSOLUTION BY INCORPORATORS

A corporation which has not commenced business and which has not issued any shares may be voluntarily dissolved by its incorporators at any time . . . .

§83 VOLUNTARY DISSOLUTION BY CONSENT OF SHAREHOLDERS

A corporation may be voluntarily dissolved by the written consent of all of its shareholders.

Upon the execution of such written consent, a statement or intent to dissolve shall be executed in duplicate by the corporation by its president or a vice president and by its secretary or an assistant secretary, and verified by one of the officers signing such statement, which statement shall set forth:

(a) The name of the corporation.

(b) The names and respective addresses of its officers.

(c) The names and respective addresses of its directors.

(d) A copy of the written consent signed by all shareholders of the corporation.

(e) A statement that such written consent has been signed by all shareholders of the corporation or signed in their names by their attorneys thereunto duly authorized.

§84   VOLUNTARY DISSOLUTION BY ACT OF CORPORATION

A corporation may be dissolved by the act of the corporation, when authorized in the following manner:

(a) The board of directors shall adopt a resolution recommending that the corporation be dissolved, and directing that the question of such dissolution be submitted to a vote at a meeting of shareholders, which may be either an annual or a special meeting.

(b) Written notice shall be given to each shareholder of record entitled to vote at such meeting within the time and in the manner provided in this Act for the giving of notice of meetings of shareholders, and, whether the meeting be an annual or special meeting, shall state that the purpose, or one of the purposes, of such meeting is to consider the advisability of dissolving the corporation.

(c) At such meeting a vote of shareholders entitled to vote there at shall be taken on a resolution to dissolve the corporation. Such resolution shall be adopted upon receiving the affirmative vote of the holders of a majority of the shares of the corporation entitled to vote thereon, unless any class of shares is entitled to vote thereon as a class, in which event the resolution shall be adopted upon receiving the affirmative vote of the holders of a majority of the shares of each class of shares entitled to vote thereon as a class and of the total shares entitled to vote thereon.

(d) Upon the adoption of such resolution, a statement of intent to dissolve shall be executed in duplicate by the corporation by its president or a vice president and by its secretary or an assistant secretary, and verified by one of the officers signing such statement, which statement shall set forth:

(1) The name of the corporation.

(2) The names and respective addresses of its officers.

(3) The names and respective addresses of its directors.

(4) A copy of the resolution adopted by the shareholders authorizing the dissolution of the corporation.

(5) The number of shares outstanding, and, if the shares of any class are entitled to vote as a class, the designation and number of outstanding shares of each such class.

(6) The number of shares voted for and against the resolution, respectively, and, if the shares of any class are entitled to vote as a class, the number of shares of each such class voted for and against the resolution, respectively.

§85   FILING OF STATEMENT OF INTENT TO DISSOLVE

Duplicate originals of the statement of intent to dissolve, whether by consent of shareholders or by act of the corporation, shall be delivered to the Secretary of State. If the Secretary of State finds that such statement conforms to law, he shall, when all fees and franchise taxes have been paid as in this Act prescribed:

(a) Endorse on each of such duplicate originals the word "Filed," and the month, day and year of the filing thereof.

(b) File one of such duplicate originals in his office.

(c) Return the other duplicate original to the corporation or its representative.

§86   EFFECT OF STATEMENT OF INTENT TO DISSOLVE

Upon the filing by the Secretary of State of a statement of intent to dissolve, whether by consent of shareholders or by act of the corporation, the corporation shall cease to carry on its business, except in so far as may be necessary for the winding up thereof, but its corporate existence shall continue until a certificate of dissolution has been issued by the Secretary of State or until a decree dissolving the corporation has been entered by a court of competent jurisdiction as in this Act provided.

§87   PROCEDURE AFTER FILING OF STATEMENT OF INTENT TO DISSOLVE

After the filing by the Secretary of State of a statement of intent to dissolve:

(a) The corporation shall immediately cause notice thereof to be mailed to each known creditor of the corporation.

(b) The corporation shall proceed to collect its assets, convey and dispose of such of its properties as are not to be distributed in kind to its shareholders, pay, satisfy and discharge its liabilities and obligations and do all other acts required to liquidate its business and affairs, and, after paying or adequately providing for the payment of all its obligations, distribute the remainder of its assets, either in cash or in kind, among its shareholders according to their respective rights and interests.

(c) The corporation, at any time during the liquidation of its business and affairs, may make application to a court of competent jurisdiction within the state and judicial subdivision in which the registered office or principal place of business of the corporation is situated, to have the liquidation continued under the supervision of the court as provided in this Act.

§88   **REVOCATION OF VOLUNTARY DISSOLUTION PROCEEDINGS BY CONSENT OF SHAREHOLDERS**

By the written consent of all of its shareholders, a corporation may, at any time prior to the issuance of a certificate of dissolution by the Secretary of State, revoke voluntary dissolution proceedings theretofore taken, in the following manner:

Upon the execution of such written consent, a statement of revocation of voluntary dissolution proceedings shall be executed in duplicate by the corporation by its president or a vice president and by its secretary or an assistant secretary, and verified by one of the officers signing such statement, which statement shall set forth:

(a) The name of the corporation.

(b) The names and respective addresses of its officers.

(c) The names and respective addresses of its directors.

(d) A copy of the written consent signed by all shareholders of the corporation revoking such voluntary dissolution proceedings.

(e) That such written consent has been signed by all shareholders of the corporation or signed in their names by their attorneys thereunto duly authorized.

§89   **REVOCATION OF VOLUNTARY DISSOLUTION PROCEEDINGS BY ACT OF CORPORATION**

By the act of the corporation, a corporation may, at any time prior to the issuance of a certificate of dissolution by the Secretary of State, revoke voluntary dissolution proceedings theretofore taken, in the following manner:

(a) The board of directors shall adopt a resolution recommending that the voluntary dissolution proceedings be revoked, and directing that the question of such revocation be submitted to a vote at a special meeting of shareholders.

(b) Written notice, stating that the purpose or one of the purposes of such meeting is to consider the advisability of revoking the voluntary dissolution proceedings, shall be given to each shareholder of record entitled to vote at such meeting within the time and in the manner provided in this Act for the giving of notice of special meetings of shareholders.

(c) At such meeting a vote of the shareholders entitled to vote thereat shall be taken on a resolution to revoke the voluntary dissolution proceedings, which shall require for its adoption the affirmative vote of the holders of a majority of the shares entitled to vote thereon.

(d) Upon the adoption of such resolution, a statement of revocation of voluntary dissolution proceedings shall be executed in duplicate by the corporation by its president or a vice president and by its secretary or an assistant secretary, and verified by one of the officers signing such statement, which statement shall set forth:

(1) The name of the corporation.

(2) The names and respective addresses of its officers.

(3) The names and respective addresses of its directors.

(4) A copy of the resolution adopted by the shareholders revoking the voluntary dissolution proceedings.

(5) The number of shares outstanding.

(f) The number of shares voted for and against the resolution, respectively.

§90   FILING OF STATEMENT OF REVOCATION OF VOLUNTARY DISSOLUTION PROCEEDINGS

* * *

§91   EFFECT OF STATEMENT OF REVOCATION OF VOLUNTARY DISSOLUTION PROCEEDINGS

* * *

§92   ARTICLES OF DISSOLUTION

If voluntary dissolution proceedings have not been revoked then when all debts, liabilities and obligations of the corporation have been paid and discharged, or adequate provision has been made therefor, and all of the remaining property and assets of the corporation have been distributed to its shareholders, articles of dissolution shall be executed in duplicate by the corporation by its president or a vice president and by its secretary or an assistant secretary, and verified by one of the officers signing such statement, which statement shall set forth:

(a) The name of the corporation.

(b) That the Secretary of State has theretofore filed a statement of intent to dissolve the corporation, and the date on which such statement was filed.

(c) That all debts, obligations and liabilities of the corporation have been paid and discharged or that adequate provision has been made therefor.

(d) That all the remaining property and assets of the corporation have been distributed among its shareholders in accordance with their respective rights and interests.

(e) That there are no suits pending against the corporation in any court, or that adequate provision has been made for the satisfaction of any judgment, order or decree which may be entered against it in any pending suit.

§93 FILING OF ARTICLES OF DISSOLUTION

Duplicate originals of such articles of dissolution shall be delivered to the Secretary of State. If the Secretary of State finds that such articles of dissolution conform to law, he shall, when all fees and franchise taxes have been paid as in this Act prescribed:

(1) Endorse on each of such duplicate originals the word "Filed," and the month, day and year of the filing thereof.

(2) File one of such duplicate originals in his office.

(3) Issue a certificate of dissolution to which he shall affix the other duplicate original.

The certificate of dissolution, together with the duplicate original of the articles of dissolution affixed thereto by the Secretary of State shall be returned to the representative of the dissolved corporation. Upon the issuance of such certificate of dissolution the existence of the corporation shall cease, except for the purpose of suits, other proceedings and appropriate corporate action by shareholders, directors and officers as provided in this Act.

§94 INVOLUNTARY DISSOLUTION

A corporation may be dissolved involuntarily by a decree of the [designated] court in an action filed by the Attorney General when it is established that:

(a) The corporation has failed to file its annual report within the time required by this Act, or has failed to pay its franchise tax on or before the first day of August of the year in which such franchise tax becomes due and payable; or

(b) The corporation procured its articles of incorporation through fraud; or

(c) The corporation has continued to exceed or abuse the authority conferred upon it by law; or

(d) The corporation has failed for thirty days to appoint and maintain a registered agent in this State; or

(e) The corporation has failed for thirty days after change of its registered office or registered agent to file in the office of the Secretary of State a statement of such change.

§95   NOTIFICATION TO ATTORNEY GENERAL

* * *

§96   VENUE AND PROCESS

* * *

§97   JURISDICTION OF COURT TO LIQUIDATE ASSETS AND BUSINESS OF CORPORATION

The [designated] courts shall have full power to liquidate the assets and business of a corporation:

(a) In an action by a shareholder when it is established:

(1) That the directors are deadlocked in the management of the corporate affairs and the shareholders are unable to break the deadlock, and that irreparable injury to the corporation is being suffered or is threatened by reason thereof; or

(2) That the acts of the directors or those in control of the corporation are illegal, oppressive or fraudulent; or

(3) That the shareholders are deadlocked in voting power, and have failed, for a period which includes at least two consecutive annual meeting dates, to elect successors to directors whose terms have expired or would have expired upon the election of their successors; or

(4) That the corporate assets are being misapplied or wasted.

(b) In an action by a creditor:

(1) When the claim of the creditor has been reduced to judgment and an execution thereon returned unsatisfied and it is established that the corporation is insolvent; or

(2) When the corporation has admitted in writing that the claim of the creditor is due and owing and it is established that the corporation is insolvent.

(c) Upon application by a corporation which has filed a statement of intent to dissolve, as provided in this Act, to have its liquidation continued under the supervision of the court.

(d) When an action has been filed by the Attorney General to dissolve a corporation and it is established that liquidation of its business and affairs should precede the entry of a decree of dissolution.

Proceedings under clause (a), (b) or (c) of this section shall be brought in the county in which the registered office or the principal office of the corporation is situated.

It shall not be necessary to make shareholders parties to any such action or proceeding unless relief is sought against them personally.

§98   **PROCEDURE IN LIQUIDATION OF CORPORATION BY COURT**

In proceedings to liquidate the assets and business of a corporation the court shall have power to issue injunctions, to appoint a receiver or receivers pendente lite, with such powers and duties as the court, from time to time, may direct, and to take such other proceedings as may be requisite to preserve the corporate assets wherever situated, and carry on the business of the corporation until a full hearing can be had.

After a hearing had upon such notice as the court may direct to be given to all parties to the proceedings and to any other parties in interest designated by the court, the court may appoint a liquidating receiver or receivers with authority to collect the assets of the corporation, including all amounts owing to the corporation by shareholders on account of any unpaid portion of the consideration for the issuance of shares. Such liquidating receiver or receivers shall have authority, subject to the order of the court, to sell, convey and dispose of all or any part of the assets of the corporation wherever situated, either at public or private sale. The assets of the corporation or the proceeds resulting from a sale, conveyance or other disposition thereof shall be applied to the expenses of such liquidation and to the payment of the liabilities and obligations of the corporation, and any remaining assets or proceeds shall be distributed among its shareholders according to their respective rights and interests. The order appointing such liquidating receiver or receivers shall state their powers and duties. Such powers and duties may be increased or diminished at any time during the proceedings.

The court shall have power to allow from time to time as expenses of the liquidation compensation to the receiver or receivers and to attorneys in the proceeding, and to direct the payment thereof out of the assets of the corporation or the proceeds of any sale or disposition of such assets.

A receiver of a corporation appointed under the provisions of this section shall have authority to sue and defend in all courts in his own name as receiver of such corporation. The court appointing such receiver shall have exclusive jurisdiction of the corporation and its property, wherever situated.

§99   QUALIFICATIONS OF RECEIVERS

A receiver shall in all cases be a natural person or a corporation authorized to act as receiver, which corporation may be a domestic corporation or a foreign corporation authorized to transact business in this State, and shall in all cases give such bond as the court may direct with such sureties as the court may require.

§100   FILING OF CLAIMS IN LIQUIDATION PROCEEDINGS

In proceedings to liquidate the assets and business of a corporation the court may require all creditors of the corporation to file with the clerk of the court or with the receiver, in such form as the court may prescribe, proofs under oath of their respective claims. If the court requires the filing of claims it shall fix a date, which shall be not less than four months from the date of the order, as the last day for the filing of claims, and shall prescribe the notice that shall be given to creditors and claimants of the date so fixed. Prior to the date so fixed, the court may extend the time for the filing of claims. Creditors and claimants failing to file proofs of claim on or before the date so fixed may be barred, by order of court, from participating in the distribution of the assets of the corporation.

§101   DISCONTINUANCE OF LIQUIDATION PROCEEDINGS

The liquidation of the assets and business of a corporation may be discontinued at any time during the liquidation proceedings when it is established that cause for liquidation no longer exists. In such event the court shall dismiss the proceedings and direct the receiver to redeliver to the corporation all its remaining property and assets.

§102   DECREE OF INVOLUNTARY DISSOLUTION

In proceedings to liquidate the assets and business of a corporation, when the costs and expenses of such proceedings and all debts, obligations and liabilities of the corporation shall have been paid and discharged and all of its remaining property and assets distributed to its shareholders, or in case its property and assets are not sufficient to satisfy and discharge such costs, expenses, debts and obligations, all the property and assets have been applied so far as they will go to their payment, the court shall enter a decree dissolving the corporation, whereupon the existence of the corporation shall cease.

§103   FILING OF DECREE OF DISSOLUTION

In case the court shall enter a decree dissolving a corporation, it shall be the duty of the clerk of such court to cause a certified copy of the decree to be filed with the Secretary of State. No fee shall be charged by the Secretary of State for the filing thereof.

§104   DEPOSIT WITH STATE TREASURER OF AMOUNT DUE CERTAIN SHAREHOLDERS

Upon the voluntary or involuntary dissolution of a corporation, the portion of the assets distributable to a creditor or shareholder who is unknown or cannot be found or who is under disability and there is no person legally competent to receive such distributive portion, shall be reduced to cash and deposited with the State Treasurer and shall be paid over to such creditor or shareholder or to his legal representative upon proof satisfactory to the State Treasurer of his right thereto.

§105   SURVIVAL OF REMEDY AFTER DISSOLUTION

The dissolution of a corporation either (1) by the issuance of a certificate of dissolution by the Secretary of State, or (2) by a decree of court when the court has not liquidated the assets and business of the corporation as provided in this Act, or (3) by expiration of its period of duration, shall not take away or impair any remedy available to or against such corporation, its directors, officers, or shareholders, for any right or claim existing, or any liability incurred, prior to such dissolution if action or other proceeding thereon is commenced within two years after the date of such dissolution. Any such action or proceeding by or against the corporation may be prosecuted or defended by the corporation in its corporate name. The shareholders, directors and officers shall have power to take such corporate or other action as shall be appropriate to protect such remedy, right or claim. If such corporation was dissolved by the expiration of its period of duration, such corporation may amend its articles of incorporation at any time during such period of two years so as to extend its period of duration.

(§§106–142 OMITTED)*

§143   GREATER VOTING REQUIREMENTS

Whenever, with respect to any action to be taken by the shareholders of a corporation, the articles of incorporation require the vote or concurrence of the holders of a greater proportion of the shares, or of any class or series thereof, than required by this Act with respect to such action, the provisions of the articles of incorporation shall control.

§144   WAIVER OF NOTICE

Whenever any notice is required to be given to any shareholder or director of a corporation under the provisions of this Act or under the provisions of the articles of incorporation or by-laws of the corporation, a waiver thereof in writing signed by the person or persons en-

---

* These sections relate to foreign corporations, annual reports, fees and franchise taxes, penalties, and certain miscellaneous provisions.

titled to such notice, whether before or after the time stated therein, shall be equivalent to the giving of such notice.

§145 **ACTION BY SHAREHOLDERS WITHOUT A MEETING**

Any action required by this Act to be taken at a meeting of the shareholders of a corporation, or any action which may be taken at a meeting of the shareholders, may be taken without a meeting if a consent in writing, setting forth the action so taken, shall be signed by all of the shareholders entitled to vote with respect to the subject matter thereof.

Such consent shall have the same force and effect as a unanimous vote of shareholders, and may be stated as such in any articles or document filed with the Secretary of State under this Act.

§146 **UNAUTHORIZED ASSUMPTION OF CORPORATE POWERS**

All persons who assume to act as a corporation without authority to do so shall be jointly and severally liable for all debts and liabilities incurred or arising as a result thereof.

§147 **APPLICATION TO EXISTING CORPORATIONS**

The provisions of this Act shall apply to all existing corporations organized under any general act of this State providing for the organization of corporations for a purpose or purposes for which a corporation might be organized under this Act, where the power has been reserved to amend, repeal or modify the act under which such corporation was organized and where such act is repealed by this Act.

§148 **APPLICATION TO FOREIGN AND INTERSTATE COMMERCE**

* * *

§149 **RESERVATION OF POWER**

The [legislature] shall at all times have power to prescribe such regulations, provisions and limitations as it may deem advisable, which regulations, provisions and limitations shall be binding upon any and all corporations subject to the provisions of this Act, and the [legislature] shall have power to amend, repeal or modify this Act at pleasure.

(§§150–152 OMITTED)

PROPOSED REVISIONS IN THE MODEL BUSINESS CORPORATION ACT

CHANGES IN THE MODEL BUSINESS CORPORATION ACT— AMENDMENTS TO FINANCIAL PROVISIONS *

34 Bus.Law. 1867 (1979).

A REPORT OF COMMITTEE ON CORPORATE LAWS

* * *

I. General Comment

The amendments to the financial provisions of the Model Business Corporation Act (the "Model Act") reflect a complete modernization of all provisions of the Model Act concerning financial matters, including(a) the elimination of the outmoded concepts of stated capital and par value, (b) the definition of "distribution" as a broad term governing dividends, share repurchases and similar actions that should be governed by the same standard, (c) the reformulation of the statutory standards governing the making of distributions, (d) the elimination of the concept of treasury stock, and (e) the making of a number of technical and conforming changes which are necessary or advisable in connection with the basic revisions.

It has long been recognized by practitioners and legal scholars that the pervasive statutory structure in which "par value" and "stated capital" are basic to the state corporation statutes does not today serve the original purpose of protecting creditors and senior security holders from payments to junior security holders, and may, to the extent security holders are led to believe that it provides some protection, tend to be misleading. In light of this recognized fact, the Committee on Corporate Laws has, as part of a fundamental revision of the financial provisions of the Model Act, deleted the mandatory concepts of stated capital and par value. In the Model Act as in effect prior to the amendments, dividends and stock repurchases could not lawfully be made by a corporation if, after giving effect thereto, the corporation would be insolvent in the equity sense, *i. e.,* unable to pay its obligations as they become due in the ordinary course of business. The Committee concluded that this is the fundamentally important test and should be retained without change. For ease of reference, the substantive test is now contained in new section 45 rather than being continued as a definition in former section 2(n).

Upon the elimination of par value and stated capital, the Committee considered at length the question of what, if any, new or different standards should control dividends and share repurchases in addition to the equity-insolvency test. The Committee concluded that the Model Act should also contain a balance sheet test, which is also included in section 45. In a departure from existing statutory provisions, the balance sheet test is explicitly authorized to be determined on the basis of either financial statements prepared under accounting practices and principles that are reasonable in the circumstances, or, in the alternative, a fair valuation or other method that is reasonable in the circumstances. Subject to the test of reasonableness in the circumstances and the standard of care stated in section 35, the board of directors is entitled to exercise its business judgment in arriving at a determination under either method.

In reformulating the Model Act financial provisions, the Committee faced and drafted provisions for several more technical issues. First, a definition of "distribution", which is designed to include dividends, stock redemptions and all other similar payments in respect of a corporation's own stock, has been added, on the generally recognized ground that the same fundamental tests should apply to all (new section 2(k)). In addition, new section 45, the heart of the revisions, deals with the following:

(a) *Timing of the measurement of the validity of the distribution.* (Normal dividends are measured when authorized, i. e., declared; otherwise a distribution is tested at the time of incurrence of indebtedness or transfer of property.)

(b) *Redemption related debt.* (The validity of its issuance, which will be a "distribution", is to be tested at the time of incurrence of debt; such debt is not to be automatically subordinated to past or future creditors.

(c) *Indirect distributions*, e. g., purchases of parent company stock by a subsidiary whose actions are controlled by the parent. (These are "distributions" by the parent and are covered by the general term "indirect".)

(d) *Stock dividends and splits.* (These transactions, which do not remove assets from the corporation, are excluded from the definition of distribution.)

(e) *Distribution of the corporation's own debt.* (If a corporation distributes its own promissory obligations as a dividend and receives nothing in return, the transaction is a distribution.)

The Committee also concluded that the concept of treasury stock should be eliminated, and that reacquired shares should automatically be restored to the status of authorized but unissued stock, unless the articles prohibit reissuance. This is based upon the judgme. that treasury stock should have no meaningful or valid status of an substance, particularly in view of the elimination of par value, and stated capital, and of surplus as a measuring limitation (nor any advantage except perhaps to permit listed companies to save modestly on stock exchange listing fees in some cases).

In addition to these basic revisions, numerous miscellaneous and conforming changes have been made in the amendments.

II. Amendments to Financial Provisions of the Model Business Corporation Act *

1. Revise section 2 ** by deleting the definitions contained in 2(h), 2(i), 2(j), 2(k), 2(l), 2(m), 2(n), relettering 2(o) as 2(h) and adding a new paragraph 2(i) as follows:

> (i) "Distribution" means a direct or indirect transfer of money or other property (except its own shares) or incurrence of indebtedness, by a corporation to or for the benefit of any of its shareholders in respect of any of its shares, whether by dividend or by purchase, redemption or other acquisition of its shares, or otherwise.

2. Delete the second, third and fourth paragraphs of section 6 and revise the section to read as follows:

§ 6. [Right] Power of Corporation to Acquire [and Dispose of] Its Own Shares

> A corporation shall have the [right] power to [purchase, take, receive or otherwise] acquire[, hold, own, pledge, transfer or otherwise dispose of] its own shares. All of its own shares acquired by a corporation shall, upon acquisition, constitute authorized but unissued shares, unless the articles of incorporation provide that they shall not be reissued, in which case the authorized shares shall be reduced by the number of shares acquired. [but purchases of its own shares, whether direct or indirect, shall be made only to the extent of unreserved and unrestricted earned surplus available therefor, and, if the articles of incorporation so permit or with the affirmative vote of the holders of a majority of all shares entitled to vote thereon, to the extent of unreserved and unrestricted capital surplus available therefor.]

> If the number of authorized shares is reduced by an acquisition, the corporation shall, not later than the time it files its next annual report under this Act with the Secretary of State, file a statement of cancellation showing the reduction in the authorized shares. The statement of cancellation shall be executed in duplicate by the corporation by its president or a

* [Note by the Committee] Where appropriate, [brackets] indicate deletions: underlining indicates additions.

** [Ed. note] References to the sections proposed for amendment in this Report are to the current section numbers adopted in 1969, which are shown in brackets in the reprint of the Act at pages 64–120, supra. See footnote 1, page 60, supra.

vice president and by its secretary or an assistant secretary, and verified by one of the officers signing such statement, and shall set forth:

(a) The name of the corporation.

(b) The number of acquired shares cancelled, itemized by classes and series.

(c) The aggregate number of authorized shares, itemized by classes and series, after giving effect to such cancellation.

Duplicate originals of such statement shall be delivered to the Secretary of State. If the Secretary of State finds that such statement conforms to law, he shall, when all fees and franchise taxes have been paid as in this Act prescribed:

(1) Endorse on each of such duplicate originals the word "Filed", and the month, day and year of the filing thereof.

(2) File one of such duplicate originals in his office.

(3) Return the other duplicate original to the corporation or its representative.

3. Revise the second sentence of the first paragraph of section 15 as follows:

Such shares may be divided into one or more classes [, any or all of which classes may consist of shares with par value or shares without par value,] with such designations, preferences, limitations, and relative rights as shall be stated in the articles of incorporation.

4. Revise the second paragraph of section 15 by amending subparagraph (e) as follows:

(e) Convertible into shares of any other class or into shares of any series of the same or any other class, except a class having prior or superior rights and preferences as to dividends or distribution of assets upon liquidation [, but shares without par value shall not be converted into shares with par value unless that part of the stated capital of the corporation represented by such shares without par value is, at the time of conversion, at least equal to the aggregate par value of the shares into which the shares without par value are to be converted or the amount of any such deficiency is transferred from surplus to stated capital].

5. Recaption section 18 as "Issuance of Shares", delete the first, third, fourth and fifth paragraphs of section 18 and revise the second paragraph as follows:

Subject to any restrictions in the articles of incorporation:

(a) Shares [without par value] may be issued for such consideration [expressed in dollars as may be fixed from time to time by the board of directors] as shall be authorized by the board of directors establishing a price (in money or other consideration) or a minimum price or general formula or method by which the price will be determined; and [unless the articles of incorporation reserve to the shareholders the right to fix the consideration. In the event that such right be reserved as to any shares, the shareholders shall, prior to the issuance of such shares, fix the consideration to be received for such shares by a vote of the holders of a majority of all shares entitled to vote thereon.]

(b) Upon authorization by the board of directors, the corporation may issue its own shares in exchange for or in conversion of its outstanding shares, or distribute its own shares, pro rata to its shareholders or the shareholders of one or more classes or series, to effectuate stock dividends or splits, and any such transaction shall not require consideration; provided, that no such issuance of shares of any class or series shall be made to the holders of shares of any other class or series unless it is either expressly provided for in the articles of incorporation, or is authorized by an affirmative vote or the written consent of the holders of at least a majority of the outstanding shares of the class or series in which the distribution is to be made.

6. Revise section 19 by replacing "cash" in line 2 of the first paragraph with "money", by deleting "deemed to be fully paid and" in the penultimate line of the first paragraph.

7. Revise section 20 by deleting the last sentence of the Section.

8. Delete in its entirety present section 21, "Determination of Amount of Stated Capital".

9. Delete "fully paid or" and replace "not" with "non-" in section 22.

10. Revise section 23 by (a) deleting subsection (d) ("The par value of each share represented by such certificate, or a statement that the shares are without par value,"); and (b) by deleting the next to the last paragraph thereof ("No certificate shall be issued for any share until such share is fully paid") and substituting therefor "No certificate shall be issued for any share until the consideration established for its issuance shall have been paid."

11. Revise section 24 by changing "cash" to "money".

12. Revise section 26 by deleting "or treasury" in the second line.

13. Revise section 26A [Alternative section 26] by deleting "or treasury" in the second line and changing "cash" to "money" in subparagraph (a)(2).

14. Revise the second paragraph of section 33 by deleting the words, "Neither treasury shares, nor", and inserting "not" after "shall".

15. Revise section 42 by replacing "declare dividends or" in line 17 with "authorize", and by eliminating clause (vi) of the first paragraph thereof and renumbering following clauses appropriately.

16. Delete in its entirety section 45 and add a new Section 45 as follows:

§ 45. Distributions to Shareholders

Subject to any restrictions in the articles of incorporation, the board of directors may authorize and the corporation may make distributions, except that no distribution may be made if, after giving effect thereto, either:

(a) the corporation would be unable to pay its debts as they become due in the usual course of its business; or

(b) the corporation's total assets would be less than the sum of its total liabilities and (unless the articles of incorporation otherwise permit) the maximum amount that then would be payable, in any liquidation, in respect of all outstanding shares having preferential rights in liquidation.

Determinations under subparagraph (b) may be based upon (i) financial statements prepared on the basis of accounting practices and principles that are reasonable in the circumstances, or (ii) a fair valuation or other method that is reasonable in the circumstances.

In the case of a purchase, redemption or other acquisition of a corporation's shares, the effect of a distribution shall be measured as of the date money or other property is transferred or debt is incurred by the corporation, or as of the date the shareholder ceases to be a shareholder of the corporation with respect to such shares, whichever is earlier. In all other cases, the effect of a distribution shall be measured as of the date of its authorization if payment occurs 120 days or less following the date of authorization, or as of the date of payment if payment occurs more than 120 days following the date of authorization.

Indebtedness of a corporation incurred or issued to a shareholder in a distribution in accordance with this Section shall be on a parity with the indebtedness of the corporation to its general unsecured creditors except to the extent subordinated by agreement.

17. Delete in its entirety section 46.

18. Revise section 48 by deleting subparagraphs (b) and (c) of the first paragraph and revising the remainder of the first paragraph and the second and third paragraphs as follows:

In addition to any other liabilities, a director [shall be liable in the following circumstances unless he complies with the standard provided in this Act for the performance of the duties of directors: (a) A director] who votes for or assents to [the declaration of any dividend or other] any distribution [of the assets of a corporation to its shareholders] contrary to the provisions of this Act or contrary to any restrictions contained in the articles of incorporation, shall, unless he complies with the standard provided in this Act for the performance of the duties of directors, be liable to the corporation, jointly and severally with all other directors so voting or assenting, for the amount of such dividend which is paid or the value of such [assets which are distributed] distribution in excess of the amount of such [dividend or] distribution which could have been made [paid or distributed] without a violation of the provisions of this Act or the restrictions in the articles of incorporation.

Any director against whom a claim shall be asserted under or pursuant to this section for the making [payment] of a [dividend or other] distribution [of assets of a corporation] and who shall be held liable thereon, shall be entitled to contribution from the shareholders who accepted or received any such distribution [dividend or assets], knowing such [dividend or] distribution to have been made in violation of this Act, in proportion to the amounts received by them.

Any director against whom a claim shall be asserted under or pursuant to this section shall be entitled to contribution from any [the] other director[s] who voted for or assented to the action upon which the claim is asserted and who did not comply with the standard provided in this Act for the performance of the duties of directors.

19. Revise subparagraph (d) of the first paragraph of section 54 as follows:

(d) The aggregate number of shares which the corporation shall have authority to issue[; if such shares are to consist of one class only, the par value of each of such shares, or a statement that all the shares are without par value;] and [or], if such shares are to be divided into classes, the number of shares of each class[, and a statement of the par value of the shares of each such class or that such shares are to be without par value.]

20. Further revise section 54 by deleting subparagraph (h) of the first paragraph, relettering the remaining subparagraphs (i) through (k) as (h) through (j) and adding the following paragraph immediately after subparagraph (j):

In addition to provisions required therein, the articles of incorporation may also contain provisions not inconsistent with law regarding:

(1) the direction of the management of the business and the regulation of the affairs of the corporation;

(2) the definition, limitation and regulation of the powers of the corporation, the directors, and the shareholders, or any class of the shareholders, including restrictions

on the transfer of shares;

(3) the par value of any authorized shares or class of shares;

(4) any provision which under this Act is required or permitted to be set forth in the by-laws.

21. Revise section 58 by deleting subparagraph (h) of the second paragraph, relettering the remaining subparagraphs of the second paragraph, and revising relettered subparagraphs (e), (h) and (o) to read as follows:

(e) To provide, change or eliminate any provision with respect to the par value of any shares or class of shares [increase or decrease the par value of the authorized shares of any class having a par value, whether issued or unissued].

[(i)](h) To change the shares of any class, whether issued or unissued [and whether with or without par value,] into a different number of shares of the same class or into the same or a different number of shares [, either with or without par value,] of other classes.

[(p)](o) To limit, deny or grant to shareholders of any class the preemptive right to acquire additional [or treasury] shares of the corporation, whether then or thereafter authorized.

22. Revise subparagraph (a) of section 59 by inserting the following sentence between the present second and third sentences thereof.

If the corporation has only one class of shares outstanding, an amendment solely to change the number of authorized shares to effectuate a split of, or stock dividend in, the corporation's own shares, or solely to do so and to change the number of authorized shares in proportion thereto, may be adopted by the board of directors; and the provisions for adoption by shareholders shall not apply, unless otherwise provided by the articles of incorporation.

23. Revise section 60(a) by deleting subparagraph (b) and relettering the remaining subparagraphs, and (b) by amending subparagraph (e) (old subparagraph (f) as follows:

(e) Change the shares of such class [, whether with or without par value,] into the same or a different number of shares [, either with or without par value,] of the same class or another class or classes.

24. Revise section 61 by deleting subparagraph (g).

25. Delete in their entirety old sections 66, 67, 68, 69 and 70.

* * *

†